CALIFORNIA Trial Objections
TENTH EDITION

Authors
Edwin A. Heafey, Jr.
Stephen G. Blitch

Project Manager
Norma Piatt
CEB Attorney

CONTINUING EDUCATION OF THE BAR ▪ CALIFORNIA
Oakland, California
For update information call 1-800-232-3444
Website: ceb.com

Library of Congress Catalog Card No. 95-69537

©1995, 1996, 1997, 1998, 1999, 2000, 2002, 2004 by The Regents of the University of California
Printed in the United States of America
ISBN 0-7626-0817-X

CP-32557

CONTINUING EDUCATION OF THE BAR • CALIFORNIA

By agreement between the Board of Governors of the State Bar of California and The Regents of the University of California, Continuing Education of the Bar—California (CEB) offers an educational program for the benefit of practicing lawyers. This program is administered by a Governing Committee whose members include representatives of the State Bar and the University of California.

Practice books are published as part of this program. Authors are given full opportunity to express their individual legal interpretations and opinions; these opinions are not intended to reflect the position of the State Bar of California or of the University of California. Materials written by employees of state or federal agencies are not to be considered statements of governmental policies.

CEB is self-supporting. CEB receives no subsidy from State Bar dues or from any other source. CEB's only financial support comes from the sale of CEB publications, programs, and other products. CEB's publications and programs are intended to provide current and accurate information and are designed to help attorneys maintain their professional competence. Publications are distributed and oral programs presented with the understanding that CEB does not render any legal, accounting, or other professional service. Attorneys using CEB publications or orally conveyed information in dealing with a specific legal matter should also research original sources of authority. CEB's publications and programs are not intended to describe the standard of care for attorneys in any community, but rather to be of assistance to attorneys in providing high quality service to their clients and in protecting their own interests.

CEB considers the publication of any CEB practice book the beginning of a dialogue with our readers. The periodic updates to this book will give us the opportunity to make corrections or additions you suggest. If you are aware of an omission or error in this book, please share your knowledge with other California lawyers. Send your comments to:

Update Editor
Continuing Education of the Bar—California
300 Frank H. Ogawa Plaza, Suite 410
Oakland, CA 94612-2001
customer_service@ceb.ucop.edu

CEB Governing Committee

M.R.C. Greenwood, Oakland, Chairperson
James E. Towery, San Jose, Vice-Chairperson
Marilyn D. Anticouni, Santa Barbara
The Honorable David B. Flinn, Martinez
Sidney K. Kanazawa, Santa Monica
Dean Mary Kay Kane, San Francisco
John Plotts, Oakland
Victor C. Rowley, San Francisco
Julius M. Zelmanowitz, Oakland

Contents

Preface xi
Foreword to the Tenth Edition xiii
Foreword to the Ninth Edition xv
About the Authors xvii
Consultants xix
Cutoff Dates xxi

Part I: Basic Considerations

1   Right to Present Relevant Evidence 1

2   Motions in Limine 13

3   Order of Proof 31

4   Objecting to Evidence 39

5   Responding to Objections 53

Part II: Objections to Jury Voir Dire

6   Objections to Jury Voir Dire 63

Part III: Objections to Form of Question

7   Question Is Ambiguous or Unintelligible 121

8   Question Is Compound 123

9   Question Is Too General 125

10   Question Calls for Narrative Answer 127

11   Question Has Been Asked and Answered 129

12   Question Misquotes Witness 133

13	Question Is Leading	135
14	Question Is Argumentative	143
15	Question Assumes Fact in Dispute or Not in Evidence	145
16	Question Calls for Speculation	151

Part IV: Objections to Offered Evidence

17	Irrelevant Evidence	155
18	Incompetent Witness	161
19	Hearsay	175
20	Inadmissible Opinion	211
21	Insufficient Foundation	239
22	Improper Impeachment	251
23	Improper Rehabilitation	263
24	Excluding Secondary Evidence	267
25	Inadmissible Parol Evidence	271
26	Cross-Examination Exceeds Scope of Direct Examination	279
27	Corpus Delicti Not Proved	289
28	Illegally Obtained Evidence	297
29	Objecting to Misconduct	307
30	Unduly Inflammatory	349
31	Excluding Relevant Evidence Under Evid C §352	355

32	Other Policy Exclusions of Evidence	369

Part V: Privileges

33	Privileges: General Rules and Considerations	379
34	Attorney-Client Privilege	407
35	Work Product Doctrine	431
36	Physician-Patient Privilege	441
37	Psychotherapist-Patient Privilege	457
38	Counselor-Sexual Assault Victim Privilege	477
39	Counselor-Domestic Violence Victim Privilege	487
40	Privilege for Confidential Marital Communications	497
41	Privilege Not to Testify Against Spouse	507
42	Privilege Not To Be Called as Witness Against Spouse	523
43	Privilege for Official Information	533
44	Privilege for Identity of Informer	549
45	Trade Secrets Privilege	559
46	Privilege Against Self-Incrimination	565
47	Privilege of Defendant in Criminal Case Not To Be Called and Not To Testify	587
48	Journalist's Immunity From Contempt	597
49	Voter's Privilege	611
50	Penitent's Privilege	615

51 Cleric's Privilege 621

Part VI: Additional Remedies

52 Motion to Strike 627

53 Jury Admonitions 637

54 Motion for Continuance 643

55 Extraordinary Writs 655

56 Motion for Mistrial 659

57 Contempt 667

Table of Statutes, Regulations, and Rules 679
Table of Cases 697
Table of References 733
Table of Forms 735
Index 737

Preface

CEB and California attorneys and judges owe a great debt to the late Edwin A. Heafey, Jr., who took many months from his trial schedule to write, revise, and update his classic California Trial Objections, originally published by CEB in 1967. The late Mr. Heafey's firm, Crosby, Heafey, Roach & May, allowed Mr. Heafey as much time as was necessary to complete work on the first nine editions of this book.

Trial attorneys with varying levels of experience have found California Trial Objections to be an invaluable resource. Several California trial judges place a copy of the book at each counsel's table at the beginning of every trial and require counsel to stay within the objections identified in the book.

CEB gratefully acknowledges the assistance of the attorneys and judges who contributed their comments to chapter manuscripts in previous editions. For a list of these consultants, see p xvii.

Robert W. Burke, Jr., prepared the index. Copy editing and production were handled by CEB staff.

The book was designed by Grier Thornburg. Composition was performed by CEB's Electronic Publishing Staff.

CEB plans to update this book on a regular basis. We solicit your suggestions and comments to help us keep it accurate and up to date.

Tenth Edition. The author of the tenth edition is Stephen G. Blitch, a former student of Professor Heafey's at the University of California School of Law (Boalt Hall) and, for more than 25 years, a friend and colleague of Mr. Heafey's at the law firm of Crosby, Heafey, Roach & May. Mr. Blitch, who continues his litigation and trial practice in Oakland at Reed Smith LLP, the successor law firm to Crosby, Heafey, Roach & May, worked with CEB to update and revise Mr. Heafey's book. The project supervisor of this book was CEB attorney Norma Piatt. Legal editing was performed by Enrique De Anda and Norma Piatt. Legal research analysis was provided by Andy Rosner, Yvette Davis, Julie Hansen, and Sally St. Lawrence. Paul Green handled copyediting and production. Jenny A. Jones updated the index. Composition was performed by CEB's Electronic Publishing staff.

Pamela J. Jester
Director

Foreword to the Tenth Edition

I first met Ed Heafey in the early 1970s, when he was already (in his early forties) a veteran of well over 100 jury trials to verdict. Like many civil trial lawyers of that time, he was called to trial 15 or 20 times a year. By contrast, in today's legal world many accomplished and respected civil litigators will see fewer trials in a lifetime than Mr. Heafey saw in an average year of practice.

Even if you do not try many cases, the need for you to know and understand the rules of evidence is undiminished. As an advocate for your clients before a judge or in a settlement setting, you must still know how to distinguish the admissible from the inadmissible evidence (or, at least, how to argue the distinctions). And you must still be prepared for those occasions, however rare, when the matter in litigation cannot be settled and you must take your case to the jury. It is in jury trials that this volume will be most useful to you, as it provides up-to-date analysis, citations to cases, and practical observations for each evidentiary objection that might arise.

In the first edition of this book, published in 1967, the inside front and back covers listed all of the available objections to evidence, along with the corresponding chapter number of the book. It was easy to make an 8½ by 11 copy of the entire list of objections to include in the trial binder. In recent versions of the book, including this one, the full list of objections is found in two places: on the outside back cover, and on a separate plasticized insert included with the book. This quick and easy reference will help you to organize your thoughts in the heat of trial, and will help you make the most of your trial objections.

Stephen G. Blitch

Foreword to the Ninth Edition

Over the last 15 years, there have been dramatic changes taking place in our courts and with the judges and trial lawyers who work in these courts. It is worth beginning with this subject and listing the more important changes, since they directly affect the continued relevance of a text like California Trial Objections.

From the trial lawyer's standpoint, major developments have occurred in the way the trial itself, whether civil or criminal, proceeds. The increasing use of "time limits" requires new skills for trial lawyers and creates even more pressure for them to understand court rules, evidence rules, and the art of advocacy. Time limits on jury selection, opening statements and closing arguments, hours per side, the number of witnesses, and methods of document production require that trial lawyers be even more knowledgeable than before in "managing" the trial itself.

From the judge's standpoint, there is a major effort, both legislatively and in the California Rules of Court, to streamline trial proceedings so that the administration of justice is more efficient, while at the same time affording the parties due process and a fair trial. The workload of judges, federal and state, is enormous (and the compensation minimal), which itself leads to greater demands by judges that lawyers know what is required of them.

On the civil side, all the above is occurring at a time when fewer lawyers have trial experience; most trial lawyers today probably have fewer than 20 jury trials to verdict. This lack of stand-up experience is frustrating—not only for the lawyer, but for the trial judge and the watching clients as well. On the criminal side, there are ample jury trials, but often they are tried by young lawyers getting experience. As a result, there is a greater need for lawyers to read as much as they can about trials, procedures, and court rules.

It is also useful to discuss the history of this book. For 17 years, I taught a course in trial practice at Boalt Hall at the University of California (Berkeley). The first edition of this book began there. It was clear that if law students wanted to become trial lawyers, they needed more than an evidence course that was a moon-shot away from the dynamics of controlling evidence and conduct in a courtroom. Additionally, numerous other subjects and skills that must be second nature to a trial attorney are not taught in law school. Motions in limine, rules governing jury selection, how to use and phrase multiple objections and responses, and the various tactics, strategies, and alternatives to objecting were never encountered in a classroom. This book followed.

After the first edition was published, it became clear that the book had far greater application to practicing attorneys than to law students. This should not have been a surprise. In the late 1980s, judges, from the Chief Justice of the United States Supreme Court on down, were bitterly complaining that the quality of advocacy they were witnessing day after day was "appalling." One well-known federal judge estimated that 85 percent of the trial attorneys that appeared in his courtroom failed to understand the basic principles and strategies involved in controlling courtroom evidence. As a result, both the client and the jury system suffered. The book therefore found an eager audience, unprepared by their formal education and castigated for their inexperience by the very judges they needed to impress.

This book has received regular updates that include comments on changes in the trial process. Among recent developments that we continue to address is the unfortunate and unnecessary decline in civility during discovery and trial. So-called "Rambo" tactics and "scorched-earth mentality" have reached unacceptable levels and become the subject of continuing and numerous articles and lectures. Taking this into account, we make practical suggestions to judges throughout the book on how to stop abusive conduct and, where applicable, how to use several new statutes dealing with punishment of attorneys by fine, assessment of attorney fees and costs, and procedurally striking pleadings or excluding evidence. Recent statutes expand the courts' sanction remedies, as does Cal Rules of Ct 227. Hopefully, this book will help inform attorneys of the multiple sanctions now available to courts, which should translate into trial attorneys being more professional and no less effective.

From my perspective, this book has become even more necessary for the lawyer who is called to trial.

Looking to the future, lawyers should expect civil jury trials to remain under attack, as challenges to the necessity of a jury trial remain vigorously debated and questions continue as to whether juries are "up to the task," are too expensive, cause unnecessary delay, and "just don't understand." One effect of this debate is seen in the growth of the "rent-a-judge" business, which many have substituted, in a peremptory fashion, for courts entirely. Future analysis of private arbitration in turn will raise questions regarding the fundamental right to a public trial, secret arbitration hearings, arguments that private arbitration is a venue for the rich alone, that it lacks any meaningful appellate review, and that this private resolution proceeding is often the result of adhesion contracts compelling unwilling participation. In the future, this subject should keep our courts and legislators busy as major public policy issues are recognized.

Finally, my special thanks to the experts listed on the consultants page: They have helped with this effort enormously. To my partners at Crosby, Heafey, Roach & May, who gave me the time to work on this because they understand the old saying, "First things first." Thank you.

Edwin A. Heafey, Jr.
June 2002

About the Authors

Edwin A. Heafey, Jr. was a Director in the California firm of Crosby, Heafey, Roach & May, with offices in Oakland, San Francisco, and Los Angeles, where he specialized in civil litigation in both state and federal courts. He was a graduate of Stanford Law School. Mr. Heafey was a member of the American College of Trial Lawyers, a member and past president of the American Board of Trial Advocates, and a member of the International Society of Barristers. He taught trial practice at Boalt Hall, University of California (Berkeley), for 17 years. Mr. Heafey had been listed in The Best Lawyers in America (Woodward/White, 1987-2000).

Stephen G. Blitch is a partner in the firm of Reed Smith, the successor firm to Crosby, Heafey, Roach & May, where he has practiced in combination for more than 25 years. He specializes in trial practice with an emphasis on business litigation, including business torts, product liability, class actions, construction, real estate, financial services, and environmental litigation in both federal and state courts. He lectures frequently on the subjects of trial evidence and trial practice, and has taught for the National Institute for Trial Advocacy (NITA). He is a graduate of the University of California, Berkeley, College of Environmental Design (Architecture) and School of Law (Boalt Hall). He is a member of the Board of Governors of the Association of Business Trial Lawyers, a member and past Director of the Alameda County Bar Association and past chair of its Trial Practice Section, a member of the Litigation Section of the California State Bar Association, and a member of the Bar Association of San Francisco.

Consultants

CEB is grateful to each of the following attorneys and judges, who served as consultants on previous editions of this book by reviewing and commenting on chapter manuscripts. Their valuable insights and suggestions have made the book more accurate, more practical, and more reflective of California practice.

Wylie Aitken
  Aitken, Aitken & Cohn, Santa Ana

Cristina Arguedas
  Cooper, Arguedas & Cassman, Emeryville

Edward Imwinkelried
  University of California, School of Law (Davis)

Joel Kleinberg
  Los Angeles

Michael J. Lightfoot
  Lightfoot, Vandevelde, Sadowsky & Medvene, Los Angeles

Ephraim Margolin
  San Francisco

The Honorable William A. McKinstry
  Judge of the Superior Court, Alameda County

Cutoff Dates

We completed legal editing of this book at the end of May 2004. We reviewed case citations through these cutoffs:

- Shepard's California Citations at 31 C4th 990, 113 CA4th 242, 157 L Ed 2d 332, 347 F3d 214, 282 F Supp 2d 1372.

- Shepard's United States Citations at 157 L Ed 2d 262, 346 F3d 1359, 280 F Supp 2d 1381.

- Shepard's Federal Citations at 157 L Ed 2d 327, 347 F3d 17, 281 F Supp 2d 1356.

We reviewed California and federal statute citations for amendments and repeals through these cutoffs:

- Stats 2004, ch 36.

- 117 Stat 1391.

We try to add significant statutory and judicial developments, subsequent histories of cases, and other matters such as new forms and regulations after legal editing is completed, but you should not assume that all developments after the listed cutoff dates have been included.

1
Right to Present Relevant Evidence

I. INTRODUCTION
    A. Using This Book to Object and Respond to Objections   §1.1
    B. Organization and Scope of Book   §1.2

II. "EVIDENCE" DEFINED   §1.3

III. WHAT CONSTITUTES RELEVANT EVIDENCE
    A. Civil Cases   §1.4
    B. Criminal Cases   §1.5
        1. Proposition 8   §1.6
        2. Proposition 115   §1.7

IV. APPLICATION OF EVIDENCE CODE
    A. Civil Cases   §1.8
    B. Criminal Cases   §1.9
        1. Provisions That Differ in Criminal Trials   §1.10
        2. Provisions That Do Not Apply in Criminal Trials   §1.11

V. APPLICATION OF CONSTITUTION AND CASE LAW TO CRIMINAL CASES   §1.12

VI. CHECKLIST: OBJECTING TO EVIDENCE §1.13

I. INTRODUCTION

§1.1   A. Using This Book to Object and Respond to Objections

As attorneys who have tried cases know, counsel must be prepared to object and to respond to objections during trial. Because the evidence presented to jurors forms the basis for their verdict, seasoned trial attorneys find ways to present the evidence favorable to their client's case while successfully limiting the evidence opposing counsel seeks to introduce. This book focuses primarily on the attorney making the objection, but the author's commentary and strategies will be equally useful to attorneys responding to objections.

Most objections can be identified before trial. By reviewing the evidence in the case, counsel will be able to determine the significant objections that counsel should make and those that opposing counsel is likely to make. Counsel can use this book before trial to identify and research appropriate objections and prepare any notes that will be needed during trial.

Despite counsel's best preparation, the need to object to unanticipated questions, answers, or evidence and to respond to unexpected objections will almost certainly arise during trial. The laminated chart accompanying this book can be placed in counsel's trial notebook. It provides easily accessed lists of objections for use during trial. In addition, counsel can use the checklist in §1.13 to help in quickly analyzing evidence or a question to determine which objections might apply.

This book has been published in a softcover format to make it more user friendly so that counsel can easily bring it to court for use during recesses and in chambers conferences. To quickly find appropriate information in the book, counsel should consult:

- The inside cover at the front of the book, which contains a list of each major objection discussed in the book;
- The inside cover at the back of the book, which contains a list of responses to objections and judicial sanctions;
- The table of contents at the beginning of the book, which contains the title and beginning page number of each chapter;
- The chapter outlines at the beginning of each chapter, which contain each topic covered in the chapter;
- The tables of statutes and cases;
- The table of references; and
- The index.

To eliminate the need to refer to an additional book, significant Evidence Code provisions are quoted in full in the chapters in which these statutes are discussed.

§1.2 B. Organization and Scope of Book

This book is organized in six main parts, each containing a number of chapters. There is a separate chapter for each objection. The actual statement of each objection is at the end of the chapter that discusses the objection.

- *Part I: Basic Considerations.* Chapters 1–5 review the basic considerations relating to the presentation of evidence. Here we stand back from the trial and see the interrelationship between the basic right of a litigant to present evidence and the procedures for objecting to evidence and responding to objections. Because most trials begin in the judge's chambers, chap 2 includes a new discussion of motions in limine and informal discussions with the judge and opposing counsel that establish the ground rules for the trial and make unnecessary many of the objections and claims of privilege that would otherwise be made in the jury's presence.

- *Part II: Objections to Jury Voir Dire.* Chapter 6 considers the special field of objections during jury selection. It discusses the major differences between civil trials and criminal trials.

- *Part III: Objections to Form of Question; Part IV: Objections to Offered Evidence.* The objections in chaps 7-16 relate to the form of the question asked of a witness. The objections in chaps 17-32 relate to the substance of the evidence being offered. Considerable emphasis is placed throughout on trial strategies in determining when to raise objections, when not to raise objections, and how to avoid objections by using alternative strategies and remedies. Responses available to the proponent of the evidence are reviewed in detail.

- *Part V: Privileges.* Chapters 33-51 describe the complex world of privileges, which is included in this book because the act of invoking a privilege, like that of making an objection, is a method of excluding offered evidence. The reader is warned that, in dealing with privileges, the Evidence Code uses a nomenclature all its own that may seem confusing at first glance. To minimize this confusion, it is suggested that the reader study chap 33 on general rules and considerations before tackling the rest of Part V. Each privilege is analyzed from the standpoint of its nature and purpose, when it is applicable, how it is invoked, and how it is terminated. Although the discussion in Part V focuses on the assertion of privileges during trial, it should also prove useful within the context of discovery.

- *Part VI: Additional Remedies.* Chapters 52-57 present methods for attacking improper evidence other than objections and claims of privilege. These alternatives include motions to strike, jury admonitions, requests for continuances when the admission of evidence would take the party by surprise, extraordinary writs, motions for mistrial, and the trial judge's contempt powers. All are examined from the point of view of an attorney's needs during trial.

Attorneys trying their first case may want to begin by reading chap 3 on the order of proof, which describes the order in which the trial will proceed; chap 4 on objecting to evidence, which covers reasons for objecting or not objecting, how to make objections, and alternatives to objecting; and chap 5 on responding to objections, which analyzes various ways of responding to objections and explains what to do when opposing counsel's objection is sustained.

The admissibility of evidence in judicial proceedings is determined by evidence rules based on public policy, decisional law, or statute. Discussion of appropriate objections and responses in these special proceedings is beyond the scope of this book. The following are examples of proceedings governed by different evidentiary rules: arbitration proceedings (see CCP §§1280–1298.8; see generally Practicing California Judicial Arbitration (Cal CEB 1983)); state administrative proceedings under the Administrative Procedure Act (Govt C §§11500–11530; see generally California Administrative Hearing Practice (2d ed Cal CEB 1997)); and grand jury proceedings (Evid C §300; see generally California Criminal Law Procedure and Practice (7th ed Cal CEB 2004).

§1.3 II. "EVIDENCE" DEFINED

"Evidence" means testimony, writings, material objects, or other things presented to the senses that are offered to prove the existence or nonexistence of a fact. Evid C §140. This definition includes anything offered in evidence whether or not it is ruled admissible. See Evid C §140. "Proof" is the establishment by evidence of a requisite degree of belief concerning a fact in the mind of the trier of fact. Evid C §190. Proof need not be direct; it may arise from a presumption or an inference.

A "presumption" is an assumption required by law to be made when a fact or group of facts is found or otherwise established in the action. Presumptions, which are either conclusive or rebuttable, are not evidence. Evid C §600(a). Every rebuttable presumption affects either the burden of producing evidence or the burden of proof. Evid C §601. In a criminal action, for example, the presumption of innocence may be overcome by facts showing guilt beyond a reasonable doubt. Thus, the effect of a presumption affecting the burden of proof imposes on the party against whom it operates the burden of proof on the nonexistence of the presumed fact. Evid C §606.

An "inference" is different from a presumption because the particular conclusion is not required by law. Rather, an inference is a deduction that may logically and reasonably be drawn from a fact or group of facts found or otherwise established in the action. Evid C §600(b).

"Physical evidence" is "real" or "demonstrative." "Demonstrative evidence" is a physical object created for presentation at trial to explain, clarify, or dramatize a party's position. See 2 Witkin, California Evidence, *Demonstrative Evidence* §1 (4th ed 2000). See also *People v Rodrigues* (1994) 8 C4th 1060, 36 CR2d 235. Expert witnesses commonly use demonstrative evidence such as computer simulations or other visual aids to help explain their testimony.

III. WHAT CONSTITUTES RELEVANT EVIDENCE

§1.4 A. Civil Cases

Whether a judge considers evidence to be weak or strong, it is relevant and admissible if it has "any tendency in reason to prove or disprove any disputed fact that is of consequence to the determination of the action." Evid C §210. The "weight" to be given evidence is within the discretion of the trier of fact and has no bearing on admissibility. *People v Yu* (1983) 143

CA3d 358, 376, 191 CR 859; *People v Cordova* (1979) 97 CA3d 665, 669, 158 CR 852.

§1.5   B. Criminal Cases

The application of the concept of "relevant evidence" in criminal cases is somewhat different from its application in civil cases, based primarily on passage in 1982 of Proposition 8, The Victim's Bill of Rights (see Cal Const art I, §28), and Proposition 115, the Crime Victims Justice Reform Act (Cal Const art I, §§14.1, 20, 24, 29). See §§1.6–1.7.

§1.6   1. Proposition 8

In reaction to the public perception that the court system had become too lenient with criminals, Proposition 8 sought to level the playing field between victim and accused by easing restrictions on the admissibility of evidence in certain areas. One portion of Proposition 8 expanded the concept of what is relevant in criminal cases (Cal Const art I, §28(d)):

> Right to Truth-in-Evidence. Except as provided by statute hereafter enacted by a two-thirds vote of the membership in each house of the Legislature, relevant evidence shall not be excluded in any criminal proceeding, including pretrial and post conviction motions and hearings, or in any trial or hearing of a juvenile for a criminal offense, whether heard in juvenile or adult court. Nothing in this section shall affect any existing statutory rule of evidence relating to privilege or hearsay, or Evidence Code, Sections 352, 782, or 1103. Nothing in this section shall affect any existing or constitutional right of the press.

Section 28(d) has been applied in criminal cases to broaden the concept of relevance in a number of areas. See, *e.g., People v Wheeler* (1992) 4 C4th 284, 14 CR2d 418; *People v Lankford* (1989) 210 CA3d 227, 240, 258 CR 322; *People v Harris* (1989) 47 C3d 1047, 255 CR 352. See also *Resurrecting California's Old Law on Character Evidence*, 23 Pac LJ 1005, 1020 (1992). Proposition 8 specifically retained, however, the trial courts' discretionary power to exclude evidence under Evid C §352. See Cal Const art I, §28(d); *People v Castro* (1985) 38 C3d 301, 211 CR 719.

In addition to expanding the concept of relevance in criminal cases, Proposition 8 prohibits plea bargaining in certain types of cases (see Pen C §1192.7), abolished the diminished capacity defense (see Pen C §25(a)), changed the insanity standard (see Pen C §25(b)), and changed or modified previous California case law interpreting search and seizure issues (see Cal Const art I, §28).

§1.7   2. Proposition 115

"Relevant evidence" in criminal cases was expanded again in 1990 by the passage of Proposition 115, the Crime Victims Justice Reform Act (Cal Const art I, §§14.1, 20, 24, 29). Another reaction to the public perception that the courts and legislature often ignore the rights of crime victims, this initiative sought to ease the restrictions on the admissibility of evidence even further. In part, Proposition 115:

- Allows certain hearsay statements if offered at a preliminary hearing, as provided in Pen C §872 (Evid C §1203.1; see *Whitman v Superior Court* (1991) 54 C3d 1063, 2 CR2d 160);

- Prohibits post-indictment preliminary hearings (Cal Const art I, §14.1; see *Bowens v Superior Court* (1991) 1 C4th 36, 2 CR2d 376);

- Establishes the People's right to a speedy, public trial (Cal Const art I, §29); but see *Miller v Superior Court* (1999) 21 C4th 883, 89 CR2d 834 (right to a speedy trial does not mean a right of access to evidence in contravention of previously existing evidentiary privileges and immunities including those under Cal Const art I, §2(b) media shield law);

- Provides for reciprocal discovery (see Pen C §§1054-1054.7; *Izazaga v Superior Court* (1991) 54 C3d 356, 285 CR 231); and

- Formerly required the court to conduct jury examination (see CCP §223 (prior to amendment by Stats 2000, ch 192, which provides that, beginning January 1, 2001, counsel may conduct voir dire after court's initial examination); see ch 6).

One major part of Proposition 115, the attempt to amend Cal Const art I, §24, was found unconstitutional in *Raven v Deukmejian* (1990) 52 C3d 336, 276 CR 326. That amendment stated that the California Constitution could provide no greater protection than the federal constitution with regard to the following rights: to equal protection, due process, and the assistance of counsel; to be personally present with counsel; to a speedy and public trial; to compel the attendance of witnesses; to confront the witness against the defendant; to be free from unreasonable searches and seizures; to privacy; to not be compelled to be a witness against himself or herself; to not be placed twice in jeopardy for the same offense; and not to suffer the imposition of cruel or unusual punishment. Invalidating Proposition 115's amendment of art I, §24, the supreme court held that "Proposition 115 not only unduly restricts judicial power, but it does it in a way that severely limits the independent force and effect of the California Constitution." 52 C3d at 353. The court found the amendment severable and allowed the remaining provisions of the initiative to take effect.

For more detailed discussion of criminal procedure, see generally California Criminal Law Procedure and Practice (7th ed Cal CEB 2004).

IV. APPLICATION OF EVIDENCE CODE

§1.8   A. Civil Cases

The Evidence Code applies "in every action before the Supreme Court or a court of appeal, or superior court, including proceedings in such actions conducted by a referee, court commissioner, or similar officer," except as otherwise provided by statute. Evid C §300.

The right to present evidence is generally the same in both civil and criminal cases. Evid C §§12(a), 105, 300; Pen C §1102. The primary evidentiary issues that differ in criminal cases are discussed in §§1.10–1.11.

§1.9   B. Criminal Cases

The right to present evidence is generally the same in both civil and criminal cases. Evid C §§12(a), 105, 300; Pen C §1102. See §1.8. In several areas of evidentiary law, however, criminal cases differ from civil ones. See §1.10–1.11.

§1.10   1. Provisions That Differ in Criminal Trials

The following Evidence Code provisions differ in criminal trials or are more commonly used in criminal trials:

- 351.1 (polygraph evidence);
- 352.1 (sexual abuse victim's address and telephone number);
- 402(b) (hearing of confessions outside of jury's presence);
- 501 (burden of proof subject to Pen C §1096);
- 520 (burden of proof when crime involved);
- 522 (burden of proof on insanity);
- 607 (presumption affecting burden of proof);
- 731 (payment of experts);
- 754(j) (interpreters for deaf or hearing impaired);
- 782 (evidence of sexual conduct offered to attack credibility of complaining witness);
- 795 (previous hypnosis of witness);
- 915 (portions of statute concern identification of informer);
- 930 (defendant in criminal case has privilege not to be called as witness and not to testify);
- 985 (no privilege for confidential marital communications under specified conditions);

- 986 (no privilege for confidential marital communications in juvenile delinquency and dependency cases);
- 987 (no privilege for confidential marital communications in criminal proceeding when offered by defendant who is one of spouses);
- 998 (no physician-patient privilege in criminal proceedings);
- 1004–1005 (no physician-patient privilege in certain proceedings to establish incompetence or to commit patient);
- 1017 (no psychotherapist-patient privilege if court appoints psychotherapist to examine patient);
- 1023 (no psychotherapist-patient privilege in certain sanity proceedings);
- 1025 (no psychotherapist-patient privilege in certain competence proceedings);
- 1035.4 (portion of statute excepts counselor-sexual assault victim privilege in certain criminal proceedings);
- 1037.2 (portion of statute excepts counselor-domestic violence victim privilege in certain criminal proceedings);
- 1041 (identity of informer);
- 1043, 1045 (discovery of police personnel records);
- 1046 (excessive force by police);
- 1047 (personnel records of police officers; exemption from disclosure);
- 1061–1063 (portion concerns trade secrets in criminal proceedings);
- 1101–1103 (character evidence);
- 1107 (battered women's syndrome);
- 1108 (commission of another sexual offense as evidence);
- 1153 (guilty plea as evidence in proceeding);
- 1156 (hospital mortality studies);
- 1157 (professional review committees);
- 1203.1 (hearsay statements at preliminary hearings);
- 1204 (hearsay in criminal actions that is inadmissible under federal or state constitutions);
- 1223 (conspirators' statements);
- 1228 (statements by minors under age 12 in cases involving certain sexual crimes);
- 1238 (statement concerning prior identification);

- 1293 (testimony of child victim at preliminary hearing);
- 1350 (statements of unavailable witnesses in serious felony cases); and
- 1410.5 (graffiti).

§1.11   2. Provisions That Do Not Apply in Criminal Trials

Some Evidence Code sections do not apply in criminal cases, including the following common ones:

- 776 (calling adverse witness as witness in counsel's own case). The statute does not apply to criminal cases; it refers only to calling a "party to the record of any civil action." In criminal cases, however, the same result achieved in civil cases under Evid C §776 may be reached through other means, with one exception: A defendant may not be called as a witness by the prosecution (Evid C §930). Otherwise, both sides in a criminal case have the ability to subpoena any witness they wish to testify (subject to objection by opposing counsel under, e.g., Evid C §352). Leading questions are permissible "under special circumstances where the interests of justice otherwise require." Evid C §767(a). The §767(a) exception is commonly applied to witnesses who are adverse to the party calling the witness. Comment to Evid C §767. See also Evid C §765(a), which gives the court the right to control the mode of interrogation of a witness.

- 786 (evidence of character traits other than honesty or veracity). See *People v Harris* (1989) 47 C3d 1047, 255 CR 352 (§786 does not apply, based on Cal Const art I, §28(d)).

- 787 (specific instances of conduct to prove character trait). See *People v Wheeler* (1992) 4 C4th 284, 14 CR2d 418; *People v Harris, supra*; *People v Lankford* (1989) 210 CA3d 227, 258 CR 322 (§787 does not apply, based on Cal Const art I, §28(d)).

- 788 (does not prevent introduction of relevant misdemeanor misconduct for impeachment). See *People v Wheeler, supra*, based on Cal Const art I, §28(d). Misdemeanor conviction may not be introduced, however, because it is inadmissible hearsay.

- 790 (good character). See *People v Taylor* (1986) 180 CA3d 622, 225 CR 733 (§790 does not apply, based on Cal Const art I, §28(d)).

- 1152 (evidence of offer to compromise). *People v Muniz* (1989) 213 CA3d 1508, 262 CR 743 (§1152 does not apply in criminal cases).

§1.12   V. APPLICATION OF CONSTITUTION AND CASE LAW TO CRIMINAL CASES

A number of evidentiary issues that are unique to criminal cases or that are treated differently have also been established by the California Constitution or by case law. The more common issues concerning the admissibility of evidence in criminal law that differ from civil law follow:

- Failed plea bargain. Compare Evid C §§1153-1153.5 and Pen C §1192.4 (not admissible) with Cal Const art I, §28(d) and *People v Pacchioli* (1992) 9 CA4th 1331, 12 CR2d 156 (admissible). See also *People v Crow* (1994) 28 CA4th 440, 33 CR2d 624 (statement of defendant in plea negotiations not admissible against defendant in case-in-chief but may be used to impeach if defendant takes stand).

- Illegally seized evidence. See Pen C §1538.5.

- Admission of testimony from preliminary hearing. Evid C §1235. See *Crawford v Washington* (2004) ___ US ___, 158 L Ed 2d 177, 124 S Ct 1354 (testimonial evidence admissible without Sixth Amendment confrontation clause violation only if witness is unavailable and defendant had prior opportunity to cross-examine), disapproving *Ohio v Roberts* (1980) 448 US 56, 65, 65 L Ed 2d 597, 100 S Ct 2531.

- Immunized testimony. Pen C §§1324-1324.1, 4001.1; Health & S C §11367.

- Confessions and admissions. See California Criminal Law Procedure and Practice, chap 30 (7th ed Cal CEB 2004).

- Felony convictions and misdemeanor facts to impeach. See Crim Law §§35.45-35.51.

- Bad acts to prove issue in case. See Crim Law §§35.52-35.55.

- Failure to prove corpus delicti. See *People v Diaz* (1992) 3 C4th 495, 528, 11 CR2d 353.

- Proof of prior convictions that are charged in charging document. See Crim Law §§31.25, 35.25.

- Witnesses who may need separate representation because of self-incrimination problems. See Crim Law, chap 49.

- Mental competence and mental defenses. See Crim Law, chap 54.

- Evidence that someone other than defendant committed crime charged. See *People v Hall* (1986) 41 C3d 826, 833, 226 CR 112.

- Evidence of defendant's character for violence may be introduced if similar evidence is admitted against victim, based on Evid C §1103. See *People v Blanco* (1992) 10 CA4th 1167, 13 CR2d 176.

§1.13   VI. CHECKLIST: OBJECTING TO EVIDENCE

The following system is a way of quickly reviewing possible objections both before and during trial. Counsel should be able to easily recall the key words during the heat of battle. Objections should not be limited to one ground if several grounds are warranted.

- *Incompetent.* Is the witness competent to testify at all? Is the witness competent to testify on a particular issue? For example, does the question ask a lay witness for expert testimony, or does the witness lack personal knowledge of the facts? See chap 18.

- *Irrelevant.* Does the question call for irrelevant evidence? Evidence must be relevant to be admissible. Evid C §350. See chap 17.

- *Hearsay.* Does the question ask for hearsay? See chap 19.

- *No foundation.* Is the foundation incomplete or missing? The most common foundational issues involve authenticating writings, establishing identity, showing personal knowledge, the various requirements for introducing opinion evidence, and relevance. See chap 21.

- *Privileged.* Does the question ask for privileged information? See chaps 34–50.

- *Form of question incorrect.* Is the form of the question incorrect? The question may, *e.g.,* be compound, call for a narrative answer, or call for speculation. See chaps 7–16.

- *Evid C §352.* Does the question call for evidence that should be excluded under the broad exclusionary rules of Evid C §352? See chap 32.

- *Other objections.* Is there some other reason for objecting that does not fall in the categories above, *e.g.,* improper impeachment, improper rehabilitation, not the best evidence? See generally chaps 22–33.

Scanning the laminated card that accompanies this book may also help counsel quickly identify the appropriate objection or objections during trial.

2
Motions in Limine

I. HISTORY §2.1

II. DEFINITION §2.2

III. USES OF MOTION IN LIMINE
   A. To Exclude Evidence §2.3
   B. To Seek Limiting Instructions §2.4
   C. To Prevent Undue Prejudice §2.5
   D. To Prohibit Use of Evidence as Sanction for Abuse of Discovery §2.6
   E. To Seek Admission of Evidence §2.7

IV. BENEFITS AND RISKS OF MAKING MOTION
   A. Benefits §2.8
   B. Risks §2.9
   C. Judge's View §2.10

V. PROCEDURES
   A. Timing of Motion §2.10A
   B. Format and Notice Requirements
      1. Written Motions in Limine §2.11
      2. Oral Motions in Limine §2.12

VI. IN LIMINE ORDERS
   A. Preliminary or Conditional Rulings §2.13
   B. Final Rulings §2.14

VII. RENEWING MOTION DURING TRIAL TO PRESERVE GROUND FOR APPEAL
   A. Reiteration Rule §2.15
   B. Making a Record §2.16

VIII. VIOLATIONS OF IN LIMINE ORDERS §2.17

IX. PRESERVING RECORD ON APPEAL §2.18

X. FORMS
   A. Form: Motion in Limine §2.19
   B. Form: Order in Limine §2.20

§2.1 I. HISTORY

The motion in limine is now a dominant procedure for obtaining rulings on evidentiary matters, attorney conduct issues, and trial management in advance of trial or, if made during trial, before the problem arises with the jury present. The motion in limine is used nationwide in federal and state courts, in civil and criminal cases.

NOTE▶ The in limine motion is misused when the trial judge is asked to assume facts without context or in advance of orders of proof. The motion is always heard outside the presence of the jury.

Although still a statutory orphan in both state and federal courts, the motion in limine is so well established in trial practice, case law, and local rules of court that to trace its lineage would serve no purpose. Implicit statutory support for the motion can be found in the court's authority to provide for the orderly conduct of proceedings in CCP §128(a)(3) and to admit relevant evidence (Evid C §350), exclude prejudicial evidence (Evid C §352), and determine the admissibility of evidence out of the presence and hearing of the jury. Evid C §402(b). For examples of recognition of the motion in case law, see *People v Brown* (2003) 31 C4th 518, 547, 3 CR3d 145; *Edwards v Centrex Real Estate Corp.* (1997) 53 CA4th 15, 27, 61 CR2d 518.

For a general discussion of motions in limine, see *People v Morris* (1991) 53 C3d 152, 188, 279 CR 720; *Kelly v New West Fed. Savings* (1996) 49 CA4th 659, 56 CR2d 803; *Peat, Marwick, Mitchell & Co. v Superior Court* (1988) 200 CA3d 272, 288, 245 CR 873; California Trial Practice: Civil Procedure During Trial, chap 7 (3d ed Cal CEB 1995); Brosnahan, *Motions in Limine in Federal Civil Trials*, SE 99 ALI-ABA 221 (2000); Colbert, *The Motion in Limine in Politically Sensitive Cases—Silencing the Defendant at Trial*, 29 Stan L Rev 1271 (1987).

§2.2 II. DEFINITION

"In limine" is Latin for "at the threshold" or "outset" or "preliminarily." The Latinism is so embedded in the jargon of trial practice that it is not likely to be displaced. Garner, A Dictionary of Modern Legal Usage (2d ed) 1995, Oxford University Press. Although motions in limine may be filed after the trial begins, they are usually filed for hearing at the final pretrial conference. See *People v Morris* (1991) 53 C3d 152, 188, 279 CR 720. These motions play a major role in trial strategies. Without reservation, it can be said that experienced trial counsel universally use these motions to advance the cause of their client.

Although customarily in writing, oral motions in limine are allowed by most judges (see, *e.g., Pierce v J.C. Penney Co.* (1959) 167 CA2d 3, 13, 334 P2d 117), and counsel should ensure that an oral motion is made on the record. See §2.12. A motion in limine should also be made after evidence is proffered and its undue prejudice becomes apparent. See *Hyatt v Sierra Boat Co.* (1978) 79 CA3d 325, 327, 145 CR 47.

III. USES OF MOTION IN LIMINE

§2.3   A. To Exclude Evidence

As a litigation strategy, the motion in limine's potential is as broad as the trial attorney's scholarship, legal skills, and imagination. Its most common application is to exclude:

- Evidence that consumes unnecessary time (*e.g.,* cumulative evidence), creates a substantial danger of undue prejudice, confuses the issues, or is misleading when weighed against the probative value of the challenged evidence. Evid C §352; Fed R Evid 403. See, *e.g., McClain v Great Am. Ins. Cos.* (1989) 208 CA3d 1476, 1487, 256 CR 863 (excluding evidence of employee's sexual preferences and conduct in wrongful termination action when there was no evidence that sexual behavior contributed to discharge); *People v Smith* (1973) 33 CA3d 51, 69, 108 CR 698, overruled on other grounds in 22 C3d at 327 n7 (gory photographs). See chap 31 for a detailed discussion of circumstances in which counsel may ask a judge to invoke Evid C §352 to exclude evidence.

- Evidence that lacks foundation (Evid C §401), including demonstrative evidence for which no foundation is possible and experimental evidence revealed during discovery to lack foundation (see Evid C §§400–406; *Culpepper v Volkswagen of Am., Inc.* (1973) 33 CA3d 510, 52, 109 CR 110).

- An expert witness or specific expert testimony. CCP §2034(j); *Zellerino v Brown* (1991) 235 CA3d 1097, 1117, 1 CR2d 222 (exclusion of expert testimony for unreasonably failing to comply with exchange); *Hyatt v Sierra Boat Co.* (1978) 79 CA3d 325, 337, 145 CR 47 (speculative expert testimony excluded).

- A lay witness's opinion on specific subject matter. See Evid C §800. See also *Jambazian v Borden* (1994) 25 CA4th 836, 848, 30 CR2d 768.

- Inadmissible parol evidence. See chap 25.

- Hearsay if a crucial issue is involved. See chap 19.

- Polygraph evidence in criminal actions. Evid C §351.1.

- Secondary evidence of the content of a writing. See Evid C §1521(a) (grounds for exclusion).

- Inadmissible evidence in business records or other "writings" relied on by witnesses. Evid C §§250, 356, 1201. See *Barr v Scott* (1955) 134 CA2d 823, 286 P2d 552.

- Evidence that, if admitted, would violate someone's rights. See *U.S. v Rosenberg* (3d Cir 1986) 806 F2d 1169.
- Privileged statements. See chaps 33–51.
- Evidence supporting specific defenses.
- Evidence of subsequent remedial measures. Evid C §1151.
- Evidence of settlement discussions. Evid C §1152.
- Evidence or admissions made in the course of mediation consultations. Evid C §1152.5.
- Evidence of insurance. Evid C §1155.
- Evidence of specific instances of conduct offered to prove trait of character. See Evid C §787.
- Evidence of prior felony convictions. See Evid C §788; §§22.8, 31.3.

§2.4   B. To Seek Limiting Instructions

Evidence is often relevant only with respect to specific parties, issues, or causes of action. See Evid C §355. Therefore, a motion in limine may be made to request limiting instructions to explain to the jury the limited consideration they should give certain evidence. Evid C §355. See, *e.g.*, CACI 206 (evidence admitted for limited purpose), 207 (evidence applicable to only one party).

§2.5   C. To Prevent Undue Prejudice

Motions in limine are an effective means of controlling prejudicial misconduct of opposing counsel during trial. Potential conduct problems at trial may be forecast by your opponent's discovery product, pretrial arguments, the content of documents, or what is revealed by pretrial discovery. Anticipated "loaded" words or phrases that may cause undue prejudice at trial are properly curtailed by rulings in limine. See *Zal v Steppe* (9th Cir 1992) 968 F2d 924. A motion may also seek to prohibit an attorney or a party from wearing specific dress or symbols. See Colbert, *The Motion in Limine in Politically Sensitive Cases: Silencing the Defendant at Trial*, 39 Stan L Rev 1271 (1987); Note, *Zal v Steppe: Ninth Circuit Approval of an In Limine Ban of Specific Words*, 23 Golden Gate U L Rev 35 (1993). See also 2 Hunter, Federal Trial Handbook §6.4 (3d ed 1993).

When improper conduct by trial counsel is predictable (*e.g.*, improper subjects or questions during voir dire, mentioning or displaying improper matter in opening statement), these matters are consistently raised in limine before trial begins. See *People v Williams* (1981) 29 C3d 392, 408, 174 CR 317; *Smith v Covell* (1980) 100 CA3d 947, 161 CR 377; *Rousseau v West Coast House Movers* (1967) 256 CA2d 878, 882, 64 CR 655.

§2.6 D. To Prohibit Use of Evidence as Sanction for Abuse of Discovery

A motion in limine seeking to prohibit the use of evidence may be granted as a sanction for the abuse of discovery. In *Peat, Marwick, Mitchell & Co. v Superior Court* (1988) 200 CA3d 272, 287, 245 CR 873, the defendant unsuccessfully argued that the sanction for discovery abuse is governed by statute and that it is not up to the courts to control and prevent abuses in the trial process. The court found that an in limine motion was the proper procedure for excluding evidence as a sanction for discovery abuse. See CCP §2023. See also *Zellerino v Brown* (1991) 235 CA3d 1097, 1 CR2d 222 (in limine motion granted after defense counsel unreasonably failed to comply with order compelling exchange of expert witness information). See CCP §2034(e) for other expert witness sanctions. See also *People v Coleman* (1985) 38 C3d 69, 211 CR 102; *Grimshaw v Ford Motor Co.* (1981) 119 CA3d 757, 174 CR 348.

Other possible sanctions against engaging in conduct that is an abuse of the discovery process include (CCP §2023(b)):

- Evidence sanctions;
- Terminating sanctions;
- Pleading sanctions; and
- Monetary sanctions, including the payment of reasonable expenses and attorney fees.

§2.7 E. To Seek Admission of Evidence

Motions in limine may be used to obtain rulings before trial that certain evidence is admissible. See, *e.g., People v Jennings* (1988) 46 C3d 963, 975, 251 CR 278; *Pugh v See's Candies, Inc.* (1988) 203 CA3d 743, 757, 250 CR 195. Although this trial tactic may be beneficial in a small number of cases, the proponent of evidence is not required to establish admissibility of evidence. See *Abbett Elec. Corp v Sullwold* (1987) 193 CA3d 708, 238 CR 496.

For example, motions in limine to rule evidence admissible are proper when counsel desires to present crucial evidence but opposing counsel is likely to object repeatedly to its admission during trial. Motions in limine to admit evidence can be helpful before trial to request a site visit during trial; to admit specific photographs, demonstrative evidence, or scientific experiments; or to admit subject- or issue-related "writings" in complex litigation or multidocument litigation. Trial judges, however, at times express dismay at the overuse of motions in limine.

IV. BENEFITS AND RISKS OF MAKING MOTION

§2.8 A. Benefits

Making in limine motions is a productive strategy that allows both the court and counsel to gain better control over a trial by:

- *Avoiding mistrial or the need for curative instructions.* Once jurors have been exposed to evidence that causes undue prejudice, it is difficult to "unscramble the egg" by curative instructions to the jury (*i.e.*, admonitions) or motions to strike. *Hyatt v Sierra Boat Co.* (1978) 79 CA3d 325, 327, 145 CR 47. As some lawyers say, motions in limine keep the "cat in the bag."

- *Limiting issues.* A motion in limine not only pares down the evidence, it narrows the issues in a similar way as a motion for summary judgment, a judgment on the pleadings, or a motion to suppress. If the evidence supporting a claim or defense is excluded, so is the claim or defense. See, *e.g.*, *Newman v Emerson Radio Corp.* (1989) 48 C3d 973, 977, 258 CR 592 (court granted defendant's motion in limine to exclude plaintiff's evidence on ground that plaintiff's actions based on oral contracts were barred by statute of frauds); *Ladas v California State Auto. Ass'n* (1993) 19 CA4th 761, 769, 23 CR2d 810 (after court granted defendant's in limine motion to exclude, based on parol evidence rule, all evidence offered by plaintiffs to prove their claims, judgment entered in defendant's favor).

- *Saving time.* When a motion in limine is granted, trial time may be saved because certain witnesses need not be called or prepared, particular exhibits need not be compiled, potential foundations need not be considered, and specific legal issues can be resolved or narrowed before trial.

- *Maintaining jurors' attention and respect.* When an issue has already been resolved through a motion in limine, the jury is spared the spectacle and profound frustration of sidebar conferences, demands that the jurors be excused while attorneys argue, or the tedium of sitting in the jury box while the participants retreat to the judge's chambers. Further, attorneys are spared the spectacle of having to object repeatedly, as if, from the jurors' perspective, they are trying to hide the facts by using technicality and legalspeak.

- *Eliminating improper argument in front of jury.* When the relevant subjects for trial are clear to all counsel and "don't mention or display" orders are obtained in limine, a fair trial becomes much easier to obtain for all involved and the risk of a possible mistrial is avoided.

- *Improving quality of advocacy.* A motion in limine may improve the quality of counsel's advocacy. Rather than standing to object in the heat of trial, counsel can develop a reasoned argument based on careful research and advanced thinking. The judge benefits from a full hearing outside the presence of the jury and is better able to respond with an informed ruling.

§2.9 B. Risks

Although motions in limine enable attorneys to influence the course of the trial and may save everyone trial time, counsel should be aware of the following risks in making such motions:

- *"Showing your hand."* A motion in limine may call attention to evidence that counsel's opponent might not have anticipated. "Trial by ambush" may be an anachronism in this day and age, but seasoned attorneys still know how to take advantage of surprise or, more importantly, lack of preparation by their opponents.

- *Prejudice to the party opposing the motion.* When opposing the motion, trial counsel should not have to present evidence to oppose hypothetical, theoretical, or speculative matters that would only result in forcing a premature disclosure of evidence.

- *Taking issues out of context.* This is the basic reason why in limine rulings are made conditional until the judge is actually able to determine during trial the context in which the evidence is offered. In limine motions may, in effect, ask the judge to rule in a vacuum rather than allowing the court to wait and hear the evidence as it is actually presented. The judge, of course, can order that the proffered evidence be presented outside the presence of the jury. In chambers, the judge will admonish counsel not to refer to this evidence during opening statements or at any time before a ruling is secured. Counsel should warn witnesses about these conditional rulings. Both counsel and witnesses should avoid mentioning the challenged areas until a final ruling is obtained. See §2.13.

- *Cost of preparing motion.* Counsel considering a motion in limine should weigh the costs of researching and briefing the motion against the potential prejudice that the motion seeks to avoid. It may be a better and more cost-effective strategy to wait and object to the evidence when the proponent offers it at trial.

§2.10 C. Judge's View

Case law, local rules, and the "local-local rules" of particular judges (*i.e.,* the trial judges' own rules) clearly indicate that California trial judges favor the use of motions in limine to resolve issues early in the trial process. Judges recognize that in some cases the benefits of such motions usually outweigh the risks and time consumed:

- *Less risk of error.* Judges recognize that the time and expense caused by mistrial can often be avoided by considering questions involving conduct, testimony, and exhibits before trial in response to in limine motions.

- *Less tedium and delay.* Judges resent the tedium and delay of numerous sidebar conferences, in chambers conferences, and jury-recessed conferences while subjects are analyzed out of the hearing of the jury.

V. PROCEDURES

§2.10A   A. Timing of Motion

A motion in limine can be made before trial, at its outset, or at any point during the trial but before the admission or use of the evidence that is the subject of the motion. The motion is most effective when made before trial to prevent the proponent of the evidence from referring to the evidence during voir dire or in opening statement.

The timing of the motion may also be affected by the local rules of the court in which the action is pending and may depend on whether that court has adopted a single-assignment system or a master calendar system. See California Trial Practice: Civil Procedure During Trial §7.15 (3d ed Cal CEB 1995). It is always good practice to consult with the clerk of the trial judge to ascertain how the judge handles motions in limine.

B. Format and Notice Requirements

§2.11   1. Written Motions in Limine

Many local rules require that motions in limine be made in writing. A written motion also provides a record of each party's position on appeal. A written motion in limine must comply with the format requirements of Cal Rules of Ct 201 and other applicable local court rules and specific courtroom rules. For example, Los Angeles Superior Court Rule 8.92 provides in part:

(a) Motions made for the purpose of precluding the mention or display of inadmissible and prejudicial matter in the presence of the jury shall be accompanied by a declaration that includes the following:

(1) A clear identification of the specific matter alleged to be inadmissible and prejudicial;

(2) A representation to the court that the subject of the motion has been discussed with opposing counsel and that opposing counsel has either indicated that such matter will be mentioned or displayed in the presence of the jury before it is admitted in evidence or that counsel has refused to stipulate that such matter will not be mentioned or displayed in the presence of the jury unless and until it is admitted in evidence;

(3) A statement of the specific prejudice that will be suffered by the moving party if the motion is not granted;

(4) If the motion seeks to make binding an answer given in response to discovery, the declaration must set forth the question and the answer and state why the use of the answer for impeachment will not adequately

protect the moving party against prejudice in the event that evidence inconsistent with the answer is offered.

No notice of motion or hearing is required for a motion in limine filed before or during trial. Cal Rules of Ct 312(d). The motion must meet the same requirements as other motions (*i.e.*, Cal Rules of Ct 313, 315, and 316) by including the following:

- Applicable declarations, exhibits, demonstrative evidence, deposition testimony, and the like;
- Points and authorities (Cal Rules of Ct 313); and
- Proposed written order that specifically references the evidence to be excluded or admitted (to eliminate misunderstandings about the ruling sought and to facilitate enforcement of the order).

Although written motions in limine may be filed after the trial begins, this practice is not common. See *People v Morris* (1991) 53 C3d 152, 188, 279 CR 720. Typically, motions in limine are made in writing before trial. See §2.19 for form of motion and §2.20 for form of proposed order.

§2.12   2. Oral Motions in Limine

Even when local rules require written motions, most courts will permit oral motions in limine to be made during the course of trial, especially when the need for the motion was not apparent before trial. Oral motions in limine are also allowed by some judges. See *Pierce v J.C. Penney Co.* (1959) 167 CA2d 3, 5 n1, 334 P2d 117.

Oral in limine motions are made outside the presence of the jury. See Evid C §402(b). To prevent misunderstandings and to protect appellate review, an oral motion in limine should be made on the record.

VI. IN LIMINE ORDERS

§2.13   A. Preliminary or Conditional Rulings

When appropriate, judges will issue preliminary or conditional rulings at trial until the context in which the evidence is offered becomes clear. Before trial, judges are likely to make their rulings on in limine motions final only when the subject of the motion is clear and ripe for disposition.

Although a judge may be grateful that troublesome issues are presented through a motion in limine, the judge may not feel that a final order is appropriate at that time. Instead, the judge may rule conditionally, or not at all, subject to the motion's being renewed at a later time. The judge may want to hear how the evidence is presented, understand the context in which the evidence is presented, and evaluate the effect of other evidence on the subject matter of the motion. For example, the judge may decide that it is too early to foreclose evidence and that the attorneys should have an opportunity to present their best case. Judges recognize that witnesses may not appear, that foundations may fail, and that evidence may be too tenuous for early disposition.

If the judge makes a conditional ruling, the parties may be ordered to consult with the judge outside the presence of the jury before mentioning the area challenged by the motion in limine. A judge who makes a conditional ruling usually says in effect: "I don't want you going into this area in the presence of the jury without first obtaining a final ruling on this motion."

§2.14   B. Final Rulings

The following is an example of a final ruling that might be made in a civil case: "It is my ruling that neither defense counsel nor any witness may present evidence that the deceased 12-year-old son had a terminal illness." The following final ruling might be made in a criminal case: "It is my ruling that photographs 101, 102, and 103 are simply too gruesome, and unduly prejudicial, when weighed against their probative value under Evidence Code section 352. I therefore order that no party use or refer to or display these photographs."

VII. RENEWING MOTION DURING TRIAL TO PRESERVE GROUND FOR APPEAL

§2.15   A. Reiteration Rule

Unless the court declares them to be final, rulings on motions in limine are considered interlocutory. Thus, a motion that is denied may be renewed during trial. If the judge grants a motion in limine, counsel should renew the motion during trial when the judge has a more complete record. See *In re Charbonneau* (1974) 42 CA3d 505, 514, 116 CR 153.

When the court's ruling is based on deficiencies in the motion itself, motions to augment or to reconsider are proper. When making a motion to reconsider, counsel should seek an interim order that opposing counsel not offer the challenged evidence until a further hearing is held.

Just as the party whose motion is denied may renew the motion, the party against whom a motion in limine is granted may seek reconsideration as well. See, *e.g., County Sanitation Dist. v Watson Land Co.* (1993) 17 CA4th 1268, 1283, 22 CR2d 117 (motion for continuance to augment expert list).

At trial, an offer of proof may be used to show that an exclusionary ruling should be reversed and also to preserve the issue for appeal. See *U.S. v Palmer* (9th Cir 1993) 3 F3d 300, 304. The ground is also preserved for appeal by (a) a renewed objection at trial made before the evidence is admitted and (b) a motion to strike made after the evidence is admitted.

Even if the court reaffirms an in limine ruling, the skilled attorney will listen carefully during trial for opportunities to claim that:

- Opposing counsel has "opened the door" to the admissible but excluded evidence or has waived the point because of certain testimony or conduct;
- The same evidence may be admissible under a different legal theory; or
- Additional witnesses may solve the admissibility problem.

§2.16   B. Making a Record

A serious violation of court orders in limine requires counsel, usually outside the presence of the jury, to make a timely objection and make a record of what occurred, the degree of damage caused, and the sanction being sought. Thus, a trial attorney must be ever vigilant as the trial proceeds to ensure that all court orders are obeyed by opposing counsel.

§2.17   VIII. VIOLATIONS OF IN LIMINE ORDERS

A court has inherent power to control proceedings before it to ensure the orderly administration of justice and to maintain the court's dignity and authority. These powers are enumerated in CCP §128(a), which provides in part:

> Every court shall have the power to do all of the following:
>
> . . . .
>
> (3) To provide for the orderly conduct of proceedings before it, or its officers.
>
> (4) To compel obedience to its judgments, orders, and process, and to the orders of a judge out of court, in an action or proceeding pending therein.
>
> . . . .
>
> (8) To amend and control its process and orders so as to make them conform to law and justice.

As with the violation of any court order, the judge has various options with respect to punishment for a violation of an in limine order. The judge should first determine whether the violation is deliberate or inadvertent and, if deliberate, the degree of prejudice caused or the degree of disobedience involved. The judge should assess the damage that the violation causes to the other side's case. Depending on the type of sanction being considered, the violating attorney may have a right to counsel. See chap 57.

The sanction imposed is discretionary based on the circumstances. The sanction may range from a stern admonishment in front of the jury; a finding of misconduct of counsel and an instruction to the jury to disregard the evidence or conduct; a further order barring related evidence, witnesses, or exhibits; or allowing the other side to reopen its case and present rebuttal evidence. Serious willful violations and disobedience may result in findings of contempt and appropriate penalties based on such a finding. In egregious situations, the judge may also grant a mistrial and assess costs and attorney fees against a willfully disobedient attorney. See CCP §§128, 575.2; Pen C §166; Cal Rules of Ct 227. On objecting to misconduct, see chap 29. See also *Sabella v Southern Pac. Co.* (1969) 70 C2d 311, 320, 74 CR 534; *Simmons v Southern Pac. Transp. Co.* (1976) 62 CA3d 341, 133 CR 42 (professional misconduct); *Hawk v Superior Court* (1974) 42 CA3d 108, 116 CR 713 (contempt); *In re Charbonneau* (1974) 42 CA3d 505, 513, 116 CR 153 (contempt). The trial judge's primary concern should be the degree of damage and prejudice caused by the violation. If the prejudicial misconduct cannot be cured, then a mistrial may be necessary.

Code of Civil Procedure §1209 lists various acts and omissions constituting contempt, which may apply to flagrant attempts to present evidence in the face of a contrary in limine order. The Rules of Professional Conduct also apply to counsel who violate court orders. See Cal Rules of Prof Cond 5-200. See also Bus & P C §§6076-6077. Major types of contempt are classified in CCP §1209 and Pen C §166. See chap 57 on contempt.

The failure to comply with the California Rules of Court, local rules, or orders of the trial court may lead to sanctions including paying the opposing party's expenses, attorney fees, and "any other sanctions permitted by law." Cal Rules of Ct 227(b).

In addition, local rules are likely to provide for sanctions for violation of its orders. For instance, Los Angeles Super Ct R 8.0 states:

> The court may impose appropriate sanctions for the failure or refusal to comply with the Rules, including possible dismissal, striking of pleadings, vacation of trial date and/or monetary sanctions against the party in violation in the amount of costs and actual expenses, including attorneys fees incurred by any and all other parties. Monetary sanctions also may be imposed for such violation against any party, party's attorney or witness payable to the County of Los Angeles. In the discretion of the trial judge, upon application in a particular case these rules herein may be applied differently or not at all.

The trial judge may enforce court orders sua sponte or on the request of opposing counsel.

Trial counsel responding to violations of in limine orders must weigh the benefits of proceeding against the harm that has been done and the type of sanction required. For example, counsel may not wish to move for a mistrial if the trial is going favorably.

§2.18 IX. PRESERVING RECORD ON APPEAL

Failure to make a timely objection before or when objectionable matters are mentioned or introduced may prevent counsel from raising the issue on appeal. In *Estelle v Williams* (1976) 425 US 501, 48 L Ed 2d 126, 96 S Ct 1691, for example, the United States Supreme Court found no error in trying the defendant while he wore prison garb because there was no objection on the record. See Evid C §353, which requires a timely objection and a statement of the specific ground for the objection before a finding can be set aside or a judgment reversed. See also California Civil Appellate Practice §5.45 (3d ed Cal CEB 1996).

For purposes of appellate review, counsel must ensure that a proper record is made of an adverse ruling to a motion in limine. What is necessary to preserve the ground for appeal depends on the type of ruling:

- *Did the motion seek to exclude evidence?* If a motion to exclude evidence is denied, counsel should renew the objection during trial before the evidence is admitted unless there is a stipulation that the objection be deemed "continuing." See *People v Jennings* (1988) 46 C3d 963, 975, 251 CR 278. This rule is sometimes called the "reiteration requirement."

- *Did the motion seek to admit evidence?* If evidence is ruled admissible, counsel should renew the objection during trial before the evidence is proffered. This step allows the judge to consider the court's ruling in context.

- *Was the ruling preliminary or conditional?* If so, the issue must be raised again during trial by objection.

- *Was the ruling final or absolute?* If so, the record is clear, and counsel need not raise the issue again. Trial attorneys often continue to raise such issues, however, either directly or by using other witnesses or documents. The judge may cut off this line of pursuit by reminding counsel that a ruling on this issue has already been made.

Although it is wise to make a formal motion in limine before objectionable evidence is mentioned or introduced, merely raising the issue and discussing it at a pretrial hearing conference has been considered sufficient in one case to save the party's chances of preserving the ground for appeal. But see *Pierce v J.C. Penney Co.* (1959) 167 CA2d 3, 334 P2d 117, judgment for the plaintiff in a slip-and-fall case was reversed because evidence of subsequent safety measures had been erroneously admitted. Noting that the issue of law and the applicable authorities on the admissibility of this evidence had been fully discussed in chambers before the trial (167 CA2d at 5 n1), the appellate court held that this preliminary discussion had cured any insufficiency in the form of the defendant's objection and had preserved the question for appeal (167 CA2d at 13).

A successful motion serves the same purpose as an unsuccessful objection in preserving the record for appeal. See, *e.g., Sacramento & San Joaquin Drainage Dist. v Reed* (1963) 215 CA2d 60, 29 CR 847, modified on other grounds at 217 CA2d 611, 31 CR 754. The motion must, however, be sufficiently clear and specific to allow the appellate court to determine whether it would have been redundant to have also objected at the time the evidence was going to be introduced. In *Sacramento,* the plaintiff unsuccessfully moved at the outset of trial to have certain evidence of damages excluded for all purposes. The trial court allowed limited admissibility of the evidence. In discussing the effect of the plaintiff's not having moved to strike certain portions of the damaging testimony during trial, the appellate court stated (215 CA2d at 68):

> The motion in this case was precisely directed at a well-defined issue. It was an entirely proper mode of objection. Once the trial court ruled on it, no further objections or motions were necessary to preserve the point for appeal purposes.

Regardless of whether the trial court's reasons for granting the motion in limine are valid, the order will be upheld on appeal if the trial court's decision is proper under any other applicable legal theory. *Lemer v Boise Cascade, Inc.* (1980) 107 CA3d 1, 10, 165 CR 555.

If an issue on appeal is attorney misconduct in anticipation of which a motion in limine had been granted, the appellate court must determine whether the misconduct was sufficiently prejudicial to warrant a reversal. The court will consider the seriousness of the misconduct, the general atmosphere of the trial (including the judge's control), the likelihood of undue prejudice, and the effect of objections or admonitions under all the circumstances. See *Cucamonga County Water Dist. v Southwest Water Co.* (1971) 22 CA3d 245, 264, 99 CR 557. The trial court's evaluation of the prejudicial effect of the misconduct was accorded great weight by the appellate court in *Vogt v McLaughlin* (1959) 172 CA2d 498, 342 P2d 481.

X. FORMS

§2.19 A. Form: Motion in Limine

_ _[Name of attorney; State Bar number]_ _
_ _[Address]_ _
_ _[Telephone and fax number]_ _
_ _[E-mail address]_ _
Attorney for _ _[e.g., plaintiff]_ _, _ _[name]_ _

Superior Court, County of _ _ _ _ _ _

[Limited Civil Case]

_ _[Name(s)]_ _ Plaintiff(s) vs _ _[Name(s)]_ _ Defendant(s)	))))))))	No. _ _ _ _ _ _ MOTION IN LIMINE TO _ _[specify]_ _; POINTS AND AUTHORITIES; PROPOSED ORDER Hearing: _ _[date; time]_ _ Department: _ _ _ _ _ _ _ _ Trial Date: _ _[date]_ _

[If appropriate, add]

Amount demanded _ _[exceeds/does not exceed]_ _ $10,000.

[Continue]

_ _[Plaintiff/Defendant]_ _, _ _[name]_ _, **moves this Court for an order instructing** _ _[defendant/plaintiff]_ _, _ _[name]_ _, **and** _ _[his/her]_ _ **attorney and witnesses regarding the following matters:**

1. It is irrelevant to this case _ _[e.g., that plaintiff received collateral benefits for the injuries suffered as a result of the accident that is the subject of this action/that plaintiff was remarried after the wrongful death of _ _[his/her]_ _ spouse/to admit evidence of other accidents that happened at _ _[location]_ _ that are not similar and not related to this accident/to admit tests of a simulated accident that are not substantially similar to the facts in this case]_ _.

2. Any comment on or attempted display of the above evidence will be improper and highly prejudicial to _ _[plaintiff/defendant]_ _. Even if the Court sustained an objection to the evidence at trial and instructed

the jury to disregard it, the evidence would be so prejudicial that _ _[plaintiff/defendant]_ _ could not receive a fair trial.

3. Accordingly, _ _[plaintiff/defendant]_ _ asks this Court for an order _ _[e.g., admonishing _ _[defendant/plaintiff]_ _, _ _[his/her/its]_ _ counsel, and _ _[his/her/its]_ _ witnesses not to attempt to introduce or display such evidence in any form and not to suggest, comment directly or indirectly on, or refer to the evidence in any way before the jury without first obtaining the Court's permission]_ _.

4. **The Court is further requested to direct** _ _[e.g., _ _[defendant/plaintiff]_ _'s counsel to caution, warn, and instruct _ _[defendant/plaintiff]_ _'s witnesses not to make any reference to such evidence and to follow the same order]_ _.

This motion is based on all pleadings, papers, and records in this action; the evidence presented at the hearing of this matter; the attached memorandum of points and authorities; and any evidence received at the hearing.

Date: _ _ _ _ _ _

_ _[Signature]_ _
_ _[Typed name]_ _
Attorney for _ _[name]_ _

Copies: Original (file with court clerk with proof of service); copies for service (one for each attorney of record and unrepresented party); office copies.

Comment: The form of papers presented for filing is set forth in Cal Rules of Ct 201. A memorandum of points and authorities must accompany the motion. See Cal Rules of Ct 313. A proposed order that specifically refers to the evidence to be excluded should also be attached; see §2.20. Check local rules for additional requirements. See §2.11.

§2.20   B. Form: Order in Limine

Superior Court, County of _ _ _ _ _ _

[Limited Civil Case]

_ _[Name(s)]_ _	)	No. _ _ _ _ _ _
Plaintiff(s)	)	
	)	**ORDER IN LIMINE**
vs	)	
	)	**Hearing:** _ _[date; time]_ _
_ _[Name(s)]_ _	)	**Department:** _ _ _ _ _ _ _ _
Defendant(s)	)	**Trial Date:** _ _[date]_ _
_____	)	

[If appropriate, add]

Amount demanded _ _[exceeds/does not exceed]_ _ $10,000.

[Continue]

The motion of _ _[plaintiff/defendant]_ _, _ _[name]_ _, **for an order instructing** _ _[defendant/plaintiff]_ _, _ _[name]_ _, **and** _ _[his/her]_ _ **attorney and witnesses regarding certain matters in limine was heard by the Court on** _ _[date]_ _. **Plaintiff appeared as represented by** _ _[name of plaintiff's attorney]_ _ **and defendant appeared as represented by** _ _[name of defendant's attorney]_ _.

The Court, having considered the pleadings and others papers submitted and heard the arguments of counsel, finds as follows on the matters contained in the motion:

1. It is irrelevant to this case _ _[e.g., that plaintiff received collateral benefits for the injuries suffered as a result of the accident that is the subject of this action/that plaintiff was remarried after the wrongful death of _ _[his/her]_ _ spouse/to admit evidence of other accidents that happened at _ _[location]_ _ that are not similar and not related to this accident/to admit tests of a simulated accident that are not substantially similar to the facts in this case]_ _.

2. Any comment on or attempted display of the above evidence is improper and highly prejudicial to _ _[plaintiff/defendant]_ _.

IT IS ORDERED that the motion is _ _[specify whether the motion is granted, denied, or granted in part and denied in part, and describe with as much specificity as possible the limits on introducing or mentioning the evidence in question]_ _.

Date: _ _ _ _ _ _   _ _[Signature]_ _
                           Judge of the _ _[title of court]_ _

Copies: Original (file with court clerk with proof of service); copies for service (one for each attorney of record and unrepresented party); office copies.

Comment: The form is a proposed order for submission to the trial judge in conjunction with the written motion in limine. Check local rules for additional requirements. See §2.11.

3
Order of Proof

I. TRIAL COURT'S POWER TO REGULATE §3.1

II. USUAL ORDER OF PROCEEDINGS §3.2
   A. Civil Trials §3.3
   B. Criminal Trials §3.4

III. ORDER OF EXAMINING WITNESS
   A. Usual Order §3.5
   B. Conditional Admission of Testimony §3.6

IV. ORDER OF DETERMINING ISSUES
   A. Civil Trials §3.7
   B. Criminal Trials §3.8

V. RULING ON ORDER OF PROOF IS NOT RULING ON ADMISSIBILITY §3.9

§3.1 I. TRIAL COURT'S POWER TO REGULATE

The trial judge controls the order in which proof is presented. Evid C §320. Judicial discretion in this area is extremely broad. The court may also delay ruling on the order of proof. *County of San Luis Obispo v Bailey* (1971) 4 C3d 518, 527, 93 CR 859 (county unsuccessfully claimed that trial court's delay in ruling permitted condemnees to present to jury substantial amount of evidence relating to prescriptive easement later determined not to have been acquired). In addition to controlling the order of proof presented by the parties, the court, on its own motion, may call and interrogate witnesses (Evid C §775; see *People v Carlucci* (1979) 23 C3d 249, 255, 152 CR 439), appoint experts (Evid C §§730-732), and provide for interpreters and translators (Evid C §§752-754).

A ruling determining the order of proof will not be disturbed on appeal unless there has been an abuse of discretion resulting in prejudicial error (see *County of San Luis Obispo v Bailey, supra*; *Gherman v Colburn* (1977) 72 CA3d 544, 584, 140 CR 330) or, in criminal matters, unless the order of proof affects the outcome of the trial (see *People v Enos* (1973) 34 CA3d 25, 41, 109 CR 876; see also Pen C §§1093-1094). As indicated by the phrase in Evid C §320, "except as otherwise provided by law," under certain circumstances a trial judge may not exercise discretion in ruling on the order of proof. See CCP §§597.5-598.

The trial court's power to control the order of proof under Evid C §320 should not be confused with the related power of the trial court to control the mode of interrogation. See Evid C §765. See also chap 13.

§3.2   II. USUAL ORDER OF PROCEEDINGS

As indicated in the Comment to Evid C §320, the order of proof "ordinarily" should be as prescribed in CCP §607 or §631.7 or in Pen C §§1093-1094. These provisions describe the usual order of proceedings, reserving to the trial judge the power to direct that a different order be followed.

§3.3   A. Civil Trials

Under CCP §607, after the jury has been sworn, the trial must proceed in the following order unless the court directs otherwise for special reasons:

   1. The plaintiff may state the issue and his case;

   2. The defendant may then state his defense, if he so wishes, or wait until after plaintiff has produced his evidence;

   3. The plaintiff must then produce the evidence on his part;

   4. The defendant may then open his defense, if he has not done so previously;

   5. The defendant may then produce the evidence on his part;

   6. The parties may then respectively offer rebutting evidence only, unless the court, for good reason, in furtherance of justice, permit[s] them to offer evidence upon their original case;

   7. When the evidence is concluded, unless the case is submitted to the jury on either side or on both sides without argument, the plaintiff must commence and may conclude the argument;

   8. If several defendants having separate defenses, appear by different counsel, the court must determine their relative order in the evidence and argument;

   9. The court may then charge the jury.

The same order of proceedings applies to civil cases tried without a jury. CCP §631.7.

§3.4   B. Criminal Trials

Under Pen C §1093, after the jury has been sworn (unless a jury trial has been waived), the trial must proceed in the following order unless the court directs otherwise:

   (a) If the accusatory pleading be for a felony, the clerk shall read it, and state the plea of the defendant to the jury, and in cases where it charges a previous conviction, and the defendant has confessed the same, the clerk in reading it shall omit therefrom all that relates to such previous conviction. In all other cases this formality may be dispensed with.

(b) The district attorney, or other counsel for the people, may make an opening statement in support of the charge. Whether or not the district attorney, or other counsel for the people, makes an opening statement, the defendant or his or her counsel may then make an opening statement, or may reserve the making of an opening statement until after introduction of the evidence in support of the charge.

(c) The district attorney, or other counsel for the people shall then offer the evidence in support of the charge. The defendant or his or her counsel may then offer evidence in support of the defense.

(d) The parties may then respectively offer rebutting testimony only, unless the court, for good reason, in furtherance of justice, permit them to offer evidence upon their original case.

(e) When the evidence is concluded, unless the case is submitted on either side, or on both sides, without argument, the district attorney, or other counsel for the people, and counsel for the defendant, may argue the case to the court and jury; the district attorney, or other counsel for the people, opening the argument and having the right to close.

(f) The judge may then charge the jury, and shall do so on any points of law pertinent to the issue, if requested by either party; and the judge may state the testimony, and he or she may make such comment on the evidence and the testimony and credibility of any witness as in his or her opinion is necessary for the proper determination of the case and he or she may declare the law. At the beginning of the trial or from time to time during the trial, and without any request from either party, the trial judge may give the jury such instructions on the law applicable to the case as the judge may deem necessary for their guidance on hearing the case. Upon the jury retiring for deliberation, the court shall advise the jury of the availability of a written copy of the jury instructions. The court may, at its discretion, provide the jury with a copy of the written instructions given. However, if the jury requests the court to supply a copy of the written instructions, the court shall supply the jury with a copy.

Under Pen C §1094, the order of procedure prescribed in Pen C §1093 may be departed from if required by the state of the pleadings or for any other good reason in the court's sound discretion.

III. ORDER OF EXAMINING WITNESS

§3.5 A. Usual Order

Evidence Code §772 outlines the usual order for the various phases of examination of a witness:

(a) The examination of a witness shall proceed in the following phases: direct examination, cross-examination, redirect examination, recross-examination, and continuing thereafter by redirect and recross-examination.

(b) Unless for good cause the court otherwise directs, each phase of the examination of a witness must be concluded before the succeeding phase begins.

(c) Subject to subdivision (d), a party may, in the discretion of the court, interrupt his cross-examination, redirect examination, or recross-examination of a witness, in order to examine the witness upon a matter not within the scope of a previous examination of the witness.

(d) If the witness is the defendant in a criminal action, the witness may not, without his consent, be examined under direct examination by another party.

Direct, cross-examination, redirect examination, and recross-examination are defined in Evid C §§760, 761, 762, and 763, respectively. Special rules relating to witness examinations appear in Evid C §§765–778, *e.g.*, mode of interrogation (see Evid C §765), scope of cross-examination (see Evid C §773(a)), right to reexamine (see Evid C §774), exclusion of witnesses (see Evid C §777), and recall of witnesses (see Evid C §778). Most of these provisions empower the trial judge to permit exceptions in the interests of justice, as does Evid C §772, quoted above, which governs the order of examination. See Evid C §§760–763.

§3.6   B. Conditional Admission of Testimony

Proceeding in the usual order frequently raises a problem when the admissibility of proposed testimony depends on other, preliminary proof. For example, a statement may not be relevant unless some other fact is proved first. On rules for laying the foundation under Evid C §401.6, see chap 21.

The problem presented in such a situation is whether to interrupt the examination of the witness then on the stand to dispose of the foundational issue or to introduce the testimony conditionally, subject to proof of the preliminary fact being supplied later in the trial. The trial judge clearly has the power, under Evid C §403(b), to permit testimony to be introduced conditionally if the foundation concerns relevancy (Evid C §403(a)(1)), the authenticity of a writing (Evid C §403(a)(3)), or the identity of a declarant (Evid C §403(a)(4)). The court clearly lacks the power, however, to allow a witness to testify conditionally against an objection that there has not been a preliminary showing of the witness's personal knowledge of the subject matter. Evid C §§403(a)(2), 403(b), 702(a).

The Evidence Code is silent on the court's power to postpone the proof of other preliminary facts (*i.e.*, those governed by Evid C §405). That power may, however, be implied from the phrase "unless for good cause the court otherwise directs" in Evid C §772(b) or perhaps from the general authority granted to the trial judge by Evid C §320 to regulate the order of proof in the judge's discretion. See *County of San Luis Obispo v Bailey* (1971) 4 C3d 518, 527, 93 CR 859.

IV. ORDER OF DETERMINING ISSUES

§3.7   A. Civil Trials

On the motion of any party or on the court's own motion, the trial judge may order that special defenses constituting a bar to the action (*e.g.,* statute of limitations) or a ground for abatement (*e.g.,* prior judgment) be tried separately before any other issue is tried. CCP §597; *Donovan v Security-First Nat'l Bank* (1945) 67 CA2d 845, 852, 155 P2d 856, disapproved on other grounds in 57 C2d at 252 (validity of alleged release and agreement tried separately by order of court on own motion; construing former CCP §2042, now Evid C §320); *Booth v Bond* (1942) 56 CA2d 153, 132 P2d 520 (alleged release tried separately by order of court on own motion; construing first sentence of former CCP §2042, now Evid C §320). But see *Cook v Superior Court* (1971) 19 CA3d 832, 834, 97 CR 189, criticized in *Cohn v Bugas* (1974) 42 CA3d 381, 389 n7, 116 CR 810. For a suggested form for this motion, see California Civil Procedure Before Trial §63.16 (3d ed Cal CEB 1990); California Civil Litigation Forms Manual §40.4 (Cal CEB 1980).

When a statute of limitations defense is asserted in a malpractice action, the limitations question must be tried separately and before any other issue in the case if the issue is raised by any party by motion or by the court on its own motion. CCP §597.5; *County of Kern v Superior Court* (1978) 82 CA3d 396, 147 CR 248.

On the motion of any party or on the court's own motion, the trial of any issue or any part of an issue may be tried before any other issue or part of an issue. CCP §598. The statutory bases for counsel's motion are "the convenience of witnesses, the ends of justice, or the economy and efficiency of handling the litigation would be promoted thereby." CCP §598. An order bifurcating the trial of an issue or any part of an issue under CCP §598 must be made no later than the close of the pretrial conference or, in other cases, no later than 30 days before the trial date. These time limitations do not apply to the trial of special defenses under CCP §§597 and 597.5 or when the motion to bifurcate is made by the court.

It is customary for the trial judge to order that equitable issues be tried ahead of legal issues, inasmuch as disposition of the equitable issues may obviate the need to proceed further. See, *e.g., Peterson v Peterson* (1946) 74 CA2d 312, 321, 168 P2d 474; 3 Witkin, California Evidence, *Presentation at Trial* §45 (4th ed 2000). For the same reason, issues of law are often tried before issues of fact; the line between the two, however, is notoriously difficult to draw. See 3 Witkin, California Procedure, *Actions* §130 (4th ed 1997). In certain cases the issues of law must be disposed of by the judge before a jury may try the issues of fact, *e.g.,* actions for the recovery of specific real or personal property, actions for money alleged to be due under a contract, actions for damages for breach of contract, and actions for damages for injuries. CCP §592.

The discretion of the trial court is not without limitation. In *Cook v Superior*

Court, supra, the court held that a trial court is not authorized to bifurcate issues and order trial of part of the liability issue and then part of the damages issue before trial of another part of the liability issue. Although this case was decided under former CCP §598, the court's holding would be same under current CCP §598.

§3.8 B. Criminal Trials

As in civil cases, defenses constituting a bar to an action that may be decided by the court are usually tried separately before any other issue is tried. For example:

- The defense of once in jeopardy is tried by the court if, as a matter of law, the prior proceeding could not constitute double jeopardy. *People v Greer* (1947) 30 C2d 589, 595, 184 P2d 512. If the jury tries the issue, the order of presentation of evidence is as ordered by the court. See Pen C §1093.

- The defense of the statute of limitations, although usually raised before trial, is a jurisdictional issue that may be raised at any time before or after judgment. See *People v Morris* (1988) 46 C3d 1, 13 n4, 249 CR 119.

Defenses to be tried by the jury are tried in an order determined by the court (see Pen C §1093). Some issues must be tried in an order set by statute. For example:

- *Plea of not guilty by reason of insanity (NGI)* (see Pen C §1017). If the defendant enters both a plea of guilty and a plea of NGI, evidence concerning guilt or innocence is presented first, and a verdict returned, before trial of the NGI plea occurs. Pen C §1026(a). If the defendant is found not guilty, there is no trial on the NGI plea. Pen C §1026(a).

- *Death penalty* (Pen C §190.2). The question of the defendant's guilt or innocence is tried to a verdict. If a guilty verdict is reached, evidence concerning the death penalty is presented. Pen C §190.1.

Proof of, and defenses to, prior convictions that must be pleaded and proven or admitted during trial are presented and tried in an order determined by the court. See Pen C §1093.

The broad discretion of the trial judge to regulate the order of proof has repeatedly been upheld. See, *e.g., Taylor v Bell* (1971) 21 CA3d 1002, 98 CR 855 (on its own motion, court may reopen case to take additional evidence even after case has been submitted).

§3.9 V. RULING ON ORDER OF PROOF IS NOT RULING ON ADMISSIBILITY

Counsel should not confuse a court ruling on the order of proof with an order excluding evidence. Even if the court does not allow certain evidence to be presented at a particular time, the court may admit that evidence at another time. In *LeCyr v Dow* (1939) 30 CA2d 457, 86 P2d 900, the plaintiff was precluded, over objection, from introducing certain evidence when offered. On appeal, the court rejected the plaintiff's contention that the trial court's ruling on the order of proof was actually an order excluding the evidence.

4
Objecting to Evidence

I. INTRODUCTION
    A. Importance of Weighing Alternatives   §4.1
    B. Reasons for Objecting   §4.2
    C. Reasons for Not Objecting
        1. Danger of Alienating Jury   §4.3
        2. Danger of Highlighting Harmful Evidence   §4.4
        3. Negligible Harm Threatened   §4.5
        4. Reversal on Appeal Unlikely   §4.6
        5. When Trial Judge's Questions Are Objectionable   §4.7
    D. Waiver; Invited Error   §4.8

II. ALTERNATIVES TO OBJECTING
    A. Not Objecting   §4.9
    B. Combining Series of Objections
        1. Introduction   §4.10
        2. Continuing Objections   §4.11
        3. Adoptive Objections   §4.12
        4. Summary Objections   §4.13
    C. Impeaching the Witness   §4.14

III. MAKING THE OBJECTION
    A. Statutory Requirements   §4.15
    B. Timeliness   §4.16
    C. Form
        1. Wording   §4.17
        2. Specific Ground Essential   §4.18
        3. General Objection Insufficient   §4.19
    D. Obtaining a Ruling   §4.20

I. INTRODUCTION

§4.1   A. Importance of Weighing Alternatives

    This chapter assumes that evidence has been offered that is subject to objection and that a valid ground exists for excluding it. The discussion analyzes the split-second decision that opposing counsel must make: whether to object, whether to refrain from objecting, or whether to follow an alternative course. In making this decision, counsel should determine whether admission of the evidence will hurt the case and, if so, how badly.

One of the hallmarks of an effective trial attorney is knowing when and when not to object. The obvious alternative to objecting is not objecting. The primary reasons for choosing this course are considered in §§4.3-4.7; the most likely consequence, waiver, is discussed in §4.8. Other alternatives to stating an objection whenever one is technically permissible include framing the objection in continuing, adoptive, or summary form (see §§4.11-4.13); impeaching the witness (see §4.14); and presenting evidence in rebuttal (see §4.15).

§4.2   B. Reasons for Objecting

Before considering the alternatives to objecting, it may be helpful to review the principal reasons for making objections:

- To exclude improper evidence, *i.e.,* to keep from the trier of fact potentially harmful facts that are inadmissible or could be ruled inadmissible under Evid C §352;

- To make a record for appeal, *i.e.,* to present the issue of the admissibility of the offered evidence in such a way that, if the trial judge rules incorrectly, the error can be used as a ground for appeal;

- To protect one's witness from undue harassment or embarrassment (see Evid C §765);

- To expose the opposing party's unfair tactics, *e.g.,* leading the witness (see chap 13), assuming facts that are in dispute or not in evidence (see chap 15), or using the question to insinuate that inadmissible evidence exists; and

- To prevent confusing the jury and to make the interrogation as effective as practicable (see Evid C §765).

Some attorneys use objections to rattle inexperienced opposing counsel, to improperly convey argument to the jury, or to throw a lifeline to a friendly witness. Such practices are potentially unethical and may subject offenders to sanctions for misconduct (see §29.15).

C. Reasons for Not Objecting

§4.3   1. Danger of Alienating Jury

The primary aim of any attorney trying a jury case is to persuade the jurors to return a verdict that is favorable to the client. Counsel's persuasiveness depends to a large degree on the attorney's credibility, *i.e.,* whether counsel impresses the jury as an attorney who is "playing fair" and not trying to hide the facts. When deciding whether to object, counsel must therefore evaluate the effect that the objection will have on the jury. For an appellate court commentary on the possible tactical advantage of choosing not to object, see *People v Garrison* (1966) 246 CA2d 343, 54 CR 731.

Because the jury often wants to hear witnesses tell their story without interruption, jurors might regard objections as part of a tedious, time-consuming game played by the attorneys and the judge, with an appalling disregard for getting to the bottom of things. The instinctive reaction of jurors who observe an attorney constantly raising objections is that the attorney is trying to keep them from learning the truth by throwing technical roadblocks in the opponent's path. An attorney who elicits such a reaction from the jury limits the ability to persuade. On how to overcome this reaction, see §4.2.

Trial counsel can partially obviate this problem through motions in limine (see §1.3) or sidebar objections. To the extent that counsel can convince the trial judge that material is inadmissible, the jury will be less inclined to conclude that counsel is simply being an obstructionist.

No matter how emphatically the judge admonishes the jury that it must draw no adverse inferences from the statement of an objection (or the invoking of any privilege), the unfavorable impression that counsel has made cannot be entirely dispelled.

In a nonjury case, the tactical disadvantages of objections are less pronounced. Even a fair-minded judge, however, will resent repeated objections on relatively unimportant points.

§4.4   2. Danger of Highlighting Harmful Evidence

At times it is better to allow harmful evidence to be introduced without comment than to highlight the evidence by raising an objection. For example, if counsel challenges the qualifications of an expert witness in front of the jury, the jurors may conclude that the witness's testimony must be of great consequence. If the judge rules that the expert may testify, the jurors are apt to give undue weight to that testimony. Moreover, the jurors may interpret the judge's ruling as an implied endorsement of what the expert has to say.

If it is necessary to challenge the qualifications of an expert to give an opinion, counsel should make these challenges as a motion in limine outside the presence of the jury. If possible, the motion should be made before selection of the jury so that counsel will know what evidence will be permitted and which witnesses will testify. The same is true of any challenge to the admissibility of a test or other matter under the *Kelly* test. See *People v Kelly* (1976) 17 C3d 24, 130 CR 144; *People v Leahy* (1994) 8 C4th 587, 34 CR2d 663.

§4.5   3. Negligible Harm Threatened

Although the most important reason for objecting to evidence is to keep improper and harmful evidence from being considered by the jury, some evidence presented at trial has no practical effect, or a negligible effect, on the outcome. Experienced trial counsel seldom object to evidence that is not likely to make a difference in the case.

Deciding, often in a split second, whether proposed evidence is both improper and potentially harmful requires preparation. Most trials can be boiled down to a few significant issues that will be recognized through proper discovery proceedings. The evidence likely to be offered on these key issues can usually be identified, and appropriate objections can be made by motion in limine before trial.

§4.6   4. Reversal on Appeal Unlikely

Another important reason for objecting is to protect the record for appeal. The most effective tool is proper preparation, *i.e.,* a thorough knowledge of the law and how it applies to the facts. Counsel should be able to immediately recognize the pertinent objections available as the evidence develops. Counsel should keep up to date on the types of error that result in reversal.

Defense counsel in criminal cases will be more prone to object than counsel in civil cases because of the numerous categories of objections that, despite their limited success during trial, have resulted in the reversal of convictions on appeal. For example, counsel in criminal cases tend to be especially diligent in raising the issue of illegally obtained admissions or confessions because the probability of obtaining a reversal on appeal on this ground is relatively high.

If the chances of reversal are slight, counsel's decision is more difficult—particularly for matters within the trial court's discretion. In addition, before reversing a judgment in a civil case, the reviewing court must agree that any erroneous admission of evidence constitutes a miscarriage of justice. In criminal cases, some errors are reversible unless found harmless beyond a reasonable doubt, and a few are prejudicial per se and require automatic reversal regardless of other evidence of guilt. Evid C §353. See Appeals and Writs in Criminal Cases §1.168 (2d ed Cal CEB 2000).

On the requirement that the trial court's determination under Evid C §352 be set forth in the record, see §2.2.

§4.7   5. When Trial Judge's Questions Are Objectionable

A practical problem may arise when an attorney believes that a question that the judge has asked a witness is objectionable. It is entirely proper for the judge to intervene in the examination of witnesses to "aid in bringing out the truth or in preventing a misunderstanding." *Bell v Moloney* (1917) 175 C 366, 371, 165 P 917. See Evid C §765; Pen C §1044. See also *McCartney v Commission on Judicial Qualifications* (1974) 12 C3d 512, 533, 116 CR 260; *People v Campbell* (1958) 162 CA2d 776, 329 P2d 82. In doing so, however, the judge may elicit objectionable testimony. If an attorney's objection is overruled by the judge, jurors may attach particular importance to the question and give undue weight to the answer. Even if the judge sustains the objection, the jury is likely to speculate about what the answer might have been despite all instructions to the contrary. Thus, it is prudent to refrain from objecting to the judge's questions unless the evidence sought will significantly harm the case. If counsel decides to object, counsel should approach the bench and make the objection or a motion to strike the evidence. On when the judge abuses the inherent power to examine witnesses, see §29.23; *McCartney v Commission on Judicial Qualifications, supra*; 3 Witkin, California Evidence, *Presentation at Trial* §§80-82 (4th ed 2000).

If the judge repeatedly interrupts or asks questions, counsel should raise the issue with the judge outside the presence of the jury. If the problem persists and counsel believes that the judge is going into matters that counsel has strategically avoided, counsel should make a record for appeal. Even if the judge does not relent, counsel will have preserved the ground for appeal.

§4.8   D. Waiver; Invited Error

A general objection that does not specifically state the legal ground on which it is based is insufficient to preserve the issue on appeal. See §§4.19- 4.20. If counsel allows inadmissible evidence to be received without a timely objection, or fails to make a motion to strike or exclude, the error is usually waived and may not be used as a basis for a new trial or an appeal. Evid C §353(a). See, *e.g., Heiner v Kmart* (2000) 84 CA4th 335, 346, 100 CR2d 854 (defendant waived objection to damages for plaintiff's lost profits by failing to make offer of proof or timely and specific objection at trial); *Russell v Geis* (1967) 251 CA2d 560, 569, 59 CR 569 (failure to object during defamation action to evidence concerning prior criminal action defeated claim of error on appeal).

In egregious cases, exceptions have been made to the waiver rule. For example, failing to object is excusable when a change in the law occurs. *People v Williams* (1976) 16 C3d 663, 667 n4, 128 CR 888, superseded by statute (Evid C §1294) on other grounds as stated in *People v Martinez* (2003) 113 CA4th 400, 408, 7 CR3d 49. An exception also occurs when misconduct is egregious. See *Garden Grove Sch. Dist. v Hendler* (1965) 63 C2d 141, 143, 45 CR 313 (attorney's misconduct so egregious that failure to object and request admonition did not defeat reversal on appeal).

Defendants in criminal actions avoid the waiver rule if they can show on appeal that the failure to object was due to the incompetence of counsel (*In re Jones* (1996) 13 C4th 552, 54 CR2d 52; *People v Pope* (1979) 23 C3d 412, 152 CR 732) or that a retraction or an admonition would not have obviated the prejudicial effect of counsel's failure to object in a prosecutorial misconduct case (see *People v Green* (1980) 27 C3d 1, 28, 164 CR 1). The record must not show that counsel's alleged neglect was a tactical decision.

When both a timely objection and a request for a jury admonition are required to preserve an objection for appeal, counsel's failure to press the court for an admonition after securing a favorable ruling may be deemed a waiver or an abandonment of the objection, even though admonishment may in fact be futile in that particular case. *People v Heldenburg* (1990) 219 CA3d 468, 268 CR 255. To justify a reversal, appellate courts seeking to reverse a decision will seize on counsel's failure to follow such procedures.

A party does not waive the right to cite as error an objection that was overruled by later cross-examining a witness or introducing rebuttal evidence on the point. *Warner Constr. Corp. v City of Los Angeles* (1970) 2 C3d 285, 303, 85 CR 444. Nor is this right waived when defense counsel fails to renew the objection when the judge asks whether there is any objection to introducing certain exhibits into evidence. *People v Gibson* (1976) 56 CA3d 119, 137, 128 CR 302. See §4.11 on continuing objections.

A party who is responsible for the introduction of evidence cannot claim on appeal that the evidence was erroneously admitted because the party "invited" the error. *People v Moran* (1970) 1 C3d 755, 762, 83 CR 411 (direct examination); *Zarafonitis v Yellow Cab Co.* (1932) 127 CA 607, 16 P2d 141 (cross-examination).

The "doctrine of invited error" does not bar a party from appealing the lower court decision when plaintiffs did nothing to mislead the trial court when they entered into a stipulated judgment solely for the purpose of expediting the trial process. *Norgart v Upjohn Co.* (1999) 21 C4th 383, 402, 87 CR2d 453.

II. ALTERNATIVES TO OBJECTING

§4.9 A. Not Objecting

An alternative that trial counsel should always consider when the opponent offers evidence that is technically objectionable is to refrain from objecting. The principal reasons for not stating an objection, although one is available, are summarized in §§4.3–4.7. These reasons must be weighed against the possible benefits to be gained from objecting (see §4.2) and the possible consequences of waiving the error (see §4.8).

B. Combining Series of Objections

§4.10 1. Introduction

An attorney who makes repeated objections inevitably creates a negative impression on the jury. Sometimes the law relieves counsel from having to continually object. If an objection to a question is overruled and the question is then repeated, the objection need not be renewed. *Balcom v Growers Warehouse Co.* (1921) 55 CA 474, 482, 204 P 39 (supreme court's denial of hearing). An objection to one question may also preserve the right to claim error in failing to object to other questions on the same subject.

For example, in *Green v Southern Pac. Co.* (1898) 122 C 563, 565, 55 P 577, the trial court admitted, over the plaintiff's objection, the testimony of a witness to the effect that the plaintiff had no property of her own from which to support herself. Later in the trial, the plaintiff testified, without objection, to substantially the same fact. The plaintiff argued on appeal that, by not objecting to later testimony on the point, the defendant had waived the error. The supreme court rejected this argument, holding that if a party has once formally taken exception to a certain line or character of evidence, there is no requirement to renew the objection at each recurrence. If counsel anticipates that, having lost the objection, the opponent will continue with the same line of questioning on the same subject, counsel should simply ask the judge to consider the objection a continuing one on that subject matter and obtain a ruling on the record.

What constitutes a substantially similar question is not always evident. In *W.C. Cook & Co. v White Truck & Transfer Co.* (1932) 124 CA 721, 729, 13 P2d 549, the issue was how much the plaintiff's products had been damaged by water. When the plaintiff's sales manager was called to testify on this point, the defense objected to the first question put to the witness on the subject of damages, on the ground that it called for an inadmissible opinion. The objection was overruled. The witness then testified at length about damages, without further objections being made. The appellate court held that defense counsel's failure to object precluded the defendant from attacking on appeal the competency of the witness or the relevancy of the evidence. See 3 Witkin, California Evidence, *Presentation at Trial* §381 (4th ed 2000).

§4.11   2. Continuing Objections

The Comment to Evid C §353 states that, as under pre-Code case law, "the use of a continuing objection to a line of questioning would be proper." The purpose of this rule is to keep from prolonging the trial and cluttering the record with repeated objections and rulings on essentially similar points. For example, the judge in a personal injury case may rule, over the objection of defense counsel, that a witness called by the plaintiff may testify concerning statements overheard at the scene of the accident. Defense counsel may disagree with the judge's decision that these statements qualify under the spontaneous declaration exception to the hearsay rule. When plaintiff's counsel then commences to ask a series of questions relating to these statements, defense counsel is faced with the prospect of interrupting after each question to voice the objection.

The alternative is to make one continuing objection, using the following form:

> Objection, Your Honor. _ _[State ground, e.g., The question calls for hearsay]_ _.

[Add if judge overrules objection]

> Your Honor, it appears that counsel is about to ask this witness a series of questions that will raise the same point of law. So that I need not

interrupt counsel's examination, may it be understood that I am making a continuing objection to this entire line of questioning, on the ground just stated, and that Your Honor is making a similar ruling on each question?

> [Judge signifies agreement with counsel's
> question for the record]

A motion in limine before trial might be the best way to handle this issue. See chap 2.

§4.12 3. Adoptive Objections

A somewhat similar but less obtrusive technique for making objections to a series of questions is the use of adoptive objections. When the objection just stated exactly fits the next question, opposing counsel may make an adoptive objection by stating:

> Same objection, Your Honor.

§4.13 4. Summary Objections

A common vice of trial attorneys is to continue asking leading questions during direct examination of their own witnesses even after completing questions on preliminary matters. See §13.5. When confronted with this practice, opposing counsel should refrain from objecting at first and then, at the point when the questions start probing into damaging matters, assert a summary objection. Although the summary objection is technically an objection only to the last question asked, it also refers to the preceding series of questions and thus carries added weight on leading questions, see chap 13.

For example, when the examiner has been leading the witness on direct examination, the opposing attorney may say:

> Objection, Your Honor. Counsel has been asking leading questions ever since this witness took the stand. I have not objected until now because I do not like to interrupt. However, the jury is entitled to hear what the witness has to say without having counsel suggest the answers to her. I therefore object to the last question on the ground that it is leading and request that counsel be instructed to stop leading the witness.

Note that this objection contains argument, which many local rules prohibit. See Los Angeles Super Ct R 8.76. If the judge does not favor such objections, counsel should refrain from objecting until it appears that the questions themselves are improper and are causing damage.

The advantages of such a summary objection are that:

- It emphasizes the objector's restraint and helps to show that counsel is not trying to obstruct;

- It conveys the message to the jury that the witness may simply be following the answers being suggested by the questioner; and
- It usually puts an end to the improper practice at which it is aimed, *e.g.,* leading the witness.

The primary disadvantage of this technique is that, by waiting, counsel risks having the witness unexpectedly recount damaging testimony that a timely objection would have excluded.

§4.14   C. Impeaching the Witness

A tactic sometimes used as an alternative to objecting is to let the witness answer without objection and then demonstrate, through cross-examination or other evidence, that the witness is wrong or lying. On what constitutes proper impeachment, see chap 22.

III. MAKING THE OBJECTION

§4.15   A. Statutory Requirements

Once counsel has decided to object, the requirements for a valid objection must be met. These are set forth in Evid C §353:

> A verdict or finding shall not be set aside, nor shall the judgment or decision based thereon be reversed, by reason of the erroneous admission of evidence unless:
>
> (a) There appears of record an objection to or a motion to exclude or to strike the evidence that was timely made and so stated as to make clear the specific ground of the objection or motion; and
>
> (b) The court which passes upon the effect of the error or errors is of the opinion that the admitted evidence should have been excluded on the ground stated and that the error or errors complained of resulted in a miscarriage of justice.

§4.16   B. Timeliness

To be timely, an objection to inadmissible evidence must be made at the earliest opportunity. Evid C §353(a); 3 Witkin, California Evidence, *Presentation at Trial* §372 (4th ed 2000). In the case of tangible evidence, this means at the time it is first offered into evidence. *McFeely v IAC* (1923) 65 CA 45, 223 P 413 (letters and reports). An objection to testimony usually must be raised before the improper question is answered. *Price v Northern Elec. Ry.* (1914) 168 C 173, 142 P 91. Opposing counsel may not speculate on obtaining a favorable answer to an improper question and then object if the answer proves unfavorable. *Hastings v Serleto* (1943) 61 CA2d 672, 692, 143 P2d 956. Similarly, a party may not sit through voir dire examination of the jury without objecting and complain only after receiving an unfavorable verdict. See §§6.15–6.18. Privileges, too, must be claimed at the earliest practicable opportunity. See §§34.4–34.5, 34.8.

Counsel is not expected to object to a question before it is answered if it is not apparent until the answer that the evidence is inadmissible. On hearing the answer, counsel must move to strike the evidence immediately. Evid C §353(a). *Rodriguez v McDonnell Douglas Corp.* (1978) 87 CA3d 626, 659, 151 CR 399. Sometimes a witness will answer before opposing counsel can interpose an objection. To avoid waiving the error in this situation, opposing counsel must immediately object to the question and move to strike the answer. Evid C §353(a). See *Wysock v Borchers Bros.* (1951) 104 CA2d 571, 232 P2d 531. See also §52.5 (motion to strike). If the motion to strike is granted, counsel should request that the judge admonish the jury to disregard the answer. If the witness (perhaps wrongfully coached to do so) persists in giving rapid-fire replies, opposing counsel should request the judge to direct the witness to pause before answering to allow for possible objections.

To stop the witness from answering too quickly, counsel can attract the witness's attention by raising a hand and then rising to state the objection. It may be appropriate under some circumstances to say something like "Wait, please" to stop the witness before the answer is stated.

Counsel must also react promptly if the witness, in responding to a proper question, injects damaging inadmissible matter in the answer. See *People v Perry* (1972) 7 C3d 756, 103 CR 161 (counsel may not wait to see whether answer is favorable). If the answer is nonresponsive, counsel should move to strike the nonresponsive parts of the answer. Evid C §766. See discussion of nonresponsive answers in §§52.5–52.4. Counsel should also specify the ground that makes the answer improper (see §52.11) and request that the jury be admonished to disregard that part of the answer that is stricken (see §§52.1–52.3). If the witness refuses to answer a question, the entire testimony may be stricken. See *People v Hathcock* (1973) 8 C3d 599, 616, 105 CR 540. See also §52.5.

C. Form

§4.17   1. Wording

The Evidence Code does not specify the particular form in which an objection must be made. See Comment to Evid C §353. Local rules often prohibit speaking objections. Although practices vary, counsel clearly must make a statement that contains the following two elements:

(1) A declaration to the effect that an objection is being made; and
(2) An identification of the specific ground or grounds (see §4.18).

The wording suggested throughout this book is:

> Objection, Your Honor. _ _[*State objection, e.g., The question calls for inadmissible opinion*]_ _.

In objecting to a judge's question, counsel might ask for a bench conference or say:

> I must object to the question on the ground that _ _[state ground]_ _.

However the objection is phrased, it should be made on specific grounds and in an undramatic manner. For suggested wording of continuing, adoptive, and summary objections, see §§4.11-4.13.

§4.18   2. Specific Ground Essential

Every objection must be stated to clearly specify the ground of the objection. Evid C §353(a). This requirement enables the trial judge to consider and rule on the exact point raised. See *People v Morris* (1991) 53 C3d 152, 187, 279 CR 720. For an analysis of possible grounds for objecting to questions asked of jurors during voir dire (*e.g.,* a question that is not related to any ground of challenge for cause or to intelligently exercise a peremptory challenge, a question that asks the jurors to prejudge the evidence), see chaps 15-17. On the most common grounds for objecting to the form of questions (*e.g.,* a question that is ambiguous or leading), see chaps 7, 13. The most common grounds for objecting to the introduction of offered evidence (*e.g.,* a question that calls for hearsay, a question that calls for an inadmissible opinion) are analyzed in chaps 19-20.

If the question is objectionable on several grounds, each should be distinctly specified. In addition, counsel should clearly identify the specific evidence being challenged. Similarly, a motion to strike should state not only the legal grounds on which it is based but the particular evidence to be stricken. See §51.10. This gives opposing counsel an opportunity to meet the objection or motion and frames the issue on which the trial judge will make a ruling. For example, in *People v Nugent* (1971) 18 CA3d 911, 96 CR 209, the defendant objected at trial only that the question called for a narrative answer and depended on the witness's ability to remember the victim's testimony. Consequently, counsel could not argue on appeal that the question called for a conclusion. 18 CA3d at 917.

§4.19   3. General Objection Insufficient

A general objection that does not specifically state the legal ground on which it is based is legally insufficient. Trial counsel who merely state "I object," "Objection," or "I object on the ground that this evidence is inadmissible" are effectively waiving the defect.

The Comment to Evid C §353 declares that a general objection is "insufficient," citing 1 Witkin, California Evidence §§703-709 (1958). The cited discussion (which corresponds to 3 Witkin, California Evidence, *Presentation at Trial* §§375-382 (4th 2000)) includes the following illustrations of futile general objections: "I want to call your attention to [former] section 1880 of the Code of Civil Procedure" (see *Estate of Wahlefeld* (1930) 105 CA 770, 772, 288 P 870), and "I object to its being introduced in evidence in respect to this case" (see *People v Jacobs* (1925) 73 CA 334, 345, 238 P 770). See also *Fellom v Adams* (1969) 274 CA2d 855, 863, 79 CR 633 ("I'll object, Your Honor").

The general objection that the evidence is "incompetent, irrelevant, and immaterial" is insufficient. In *Short v Frink* (1907) 151 C 83, 90 P 200, a general objection was effective on appeal because the evidence was inadmissible for any purpose. In view of the clear language of Evid C §353(a) and the condemnation of general objections that appears in the Comment to §353(a), the phrase "incompetent, irrelevant, and immaterial" should no longer be in the vocabulary of trial attorneys. When irrelevancy is the basis for the objection, that should be the specific ground stated. For a fuller discussion of this point, see §17.8. If only part of the evidence is admissible, counsel must specify what evidence is inadmissible and that counsel objects to its introduction. *People v Harris* (1978) 85 CA3d 954, 957, 149 CR 860.

The record must show the specific objection. In *People v Boehm* (1969) 270 CA2d 13, 17, 75 CR 590, defense counsel's only objection on the record was, "I wish to make the strongest objection. I want to make it at the bench." Counsel then approached the bench, but the record failed to disclose what was said there (the question had been answered before the objection was made and, because nothing further was on the record, the effect was to overrule the objection). The appellate court ruled that the objection was insufficiently general. The appellate court in dictum speculated about what the "strongest objection" might have been and concluded that overruling it was not error. 270 CA2d at 19.

§4.20 D. Obtaining a Ruling

After stating an objection, counsel must pursue it until the trial judge makes a ruling. Frequently counsel argue the merits of an objection, but the argument is left unresolved. If counsel lets the matter drop without requesting a formal ruling, counsel is considered to have abandoned the objection and cannot raise the matter on appeal. *Fibreboard Paper Prods. Corp. v East Bay Union of Machinists* (1964) 227 CA2d 675, 698, 39 CR 64; 3 Witkin, California Evidence, *Presentation at Trial* §389 (4th ed 2000). If the judge's response to counsel's request is to reserve ruling on the objection, absent a showing of prejudicial error, the judge's subsequent failure to act on the question may be treated on appeal as an implied overruling of the objection. See *Stanwood v Carson* (1915) 169 C 640, 644, 147 P 562; *Raymond v Glover* (1898) 122 C 471, 476, 55 P 398 (reversible error because if judge had advised counsel of ruling, counsel could have introduced evidence to rebut evidence admitted); 3 Witkin, Evidence, *Presentation at Trial* §387 (4th ed 2000). See also *Monogram Indus. v Sar Indus.* (1976) 64 CA3d 692, 703, 134 CR 714.

The safer course is for counsel to persist, even in this situation. To be sure of preserving the objection, counsel should again request a ruling when counsel's opponent rests his or her case. If the judge, at that point, sustains the objection, counsel should move to strike the evidence that was admitted earlier (see §52.16). If the judge still does not make a ruling, counsel should point out that the appellate courts prefer that such rulings are on the record so that there is no question of prejudice by failing to do so. Evid C §353(a). See *Stanwood v Carson, supra*; *Estate of Horman* (1968) 265 CA2d 796, 805, 71 CR 780.

When counsel does not understand the ruling, counsel should request clarification before proceeding. Ambiguous rulings are construed by appellate courts to support the verdict. *Goodale v Thorn* (1926) 199 C 307, 315, 249 P 11.

It is not necessary to state a formal exception to a ruling sustaining or overruling an objection to evidence. Code of Civil Procedure §647 provides that such rulings are "deemed excepted to." For further discussion of rulings on objections, see California Trial Practice: Civil Procedure During Trial §§15.66-15.69 (3d ed Cal CEB 1995).

5
Responding to Objections

I. CHECKLIST OF RESPONSES §5.1

II. INVOKING EXCEPTIONS TO EXCLUSIONARY RULES §5.2

III. CONDITIONAL ADMISSION OF EVIDENCE §5.3

IV. OFFERS OF PROOF
    A. Nature and Function; Proving Substance, Purpose, and Relevancy §5.4
    B. When Offer of Proof Is Not Required
        1. During Cross-Examination §5.5
        2. After Broad Exclusionary Ruling §5.6
        3. If Question Contains Necessary Elements §5.7
        4. If Necessary Elements Otherwise Apparent §5.8
    C. Procedure for Offer of Proof
        1. Out of Jury's Presence §5.9
        2. Substance of Offered Evidence §5.10
        3. Purpose of Offered Evidence §5.11
        4. Relevancy of Offered Evidence §5.12
        5. Availability of Offered Evidence §5.13
    D. Objections to Offers of Proof §5.14

V. RESPONSES
    A. Counsel's Duty to Seek Other Methods of Proof §5.15
    B. Rephrasing the Question §5.16
    C. Presenting Other Proof §5.17

§5.1 I. CHECKLIST OF RESPONSES

If a party offers evidence and the opposing party objects, the proponent of the evidence may respond in various ways:

- Attack the objection itself by arguing that it does not apply;

- Obviate the objection by demonstrating that an exception applies (see §5.2);

- Request that the evidence be admitted conditionally, postponing a determination of its admissibility (see §5.3);

- If the objection is sustained and opposing counsel considers the ruling to be erroneous, make an offer of proof to demonstrate admissibility and make a record for appeal (see §§5.4-5.14);

- If the objection is sustained, seek to prove the facts by alternative methods (see §§5.15-5.17);
- If the facts justify it (*i.e.*, multi-party case), argue that the evidence, although inadmissible against one party or for one purpose, is admissible against another party or for a different purpose (see Evid C §355; see also chap 52); or
- Ascertain whether opposing counsel has "opened the door" (see §§26.5-26.7).

Opposing counsel may make evidence admissible as trial develops if other evidence is produced or new issues are framed.

§5.2   II. INVOKING EXCEPTIONS TO EXCLUSIONARY RULES

One way to overcome an objection is to invoke an exception to the applicable exclusionary rule. This ordinarily raises a preliminary issue of fact under Evid C §403 or §405. See chap 21. The burden of proof on this preliminary issue is usually on the party seeking to invoke the exception. For example, the party offering hearsay evidence must prove the existence of circumstances warranting an exception to the hearsay rule, *e.g.*, the spontaneousness of the declaration (Evid C §1240) or the trustworthiness of a business record (Evid C §1271).

§5.3   III. CONDITIONAL ADMISSION OF EVIDENCE

Evidence that appears to be objectionable may become admissible by the introduction of other evidence as a foundation. The most common example is evidence that initially appears to be irrelevant. An objection can be obviated by interrupting the examination of the witness then on the stand and offering to introduce the necessary foundational evidence. An alternative response is to request that the foundational evidence be postponed so that the examination of the witness can be completed normally after an appropriate offer of proof.

In certain situations, the Evidence Code authorizes the trial judge to permit this alternative procedure and to admit evidence conditionally, subject to proof of the preliminary fact later at the trial. Evid C §403(b). The Code specifically authorizes such conditional admission if relevance depends on the existence of the preliminary fact or if the preliminary fact is the authenticity of a writing or the identity of a declarant. Evid C §403(a)(1), (3)-(4). See §21.11. The Code prohibits conditional admission of testimony against an objection that the witness's personal knowledge of the subject matter has not been shown. Evid C §403(a)(2), (b); §702. The possibility that other types of preliminary facts may be admitted in evidence conditionally is suggested by Evid C §§320 (judge's power to regulate order of proof) and 772(b) (judge's power to direct departures from usual order of examination of witnesses).

To counter the objection, the party offering the evidence must remember to introduce proof of the foundational facts before resting. Failure to do so will render the conditionally admitted evidence subject to a motion to strike, charges of misconduct, or a motion for mistrial—all based on how damaging the admitted but now inadmissible evidence is to the case. To avoid potential problems that result from the conditional admission of evidence (*e.g.,* confusing the jury or having to recall earlier witnesses), counsel normally will have witnesses needed to establish preliminary facts testify first.

A somewhat similar situation arises when a party offers tangible evidence, such as a document, the relevancy of which is challenged. The trial judge may allow the document to be marked for identification but at the same time may rule against its admission at that time. It is not enough for counsel offering the document merely to present foundational proof later in the trial that the item is relevant. Counsel must also remember, before resting, to again formally offer the document in evidence because when the court defers ruling on admitting evidence, it is under no duty to do so later, sua sponte, even after sufficient evidence has been presented to justify admission. It is the offering party's responsibility to press for admission. See *People v Prince* (1968) 268 CA2d 398, 74 CR 197.

IV. OFFERS OF PROOF

§5.4 A. Nature and Function; Proving Substance, Purpose, and Relevancy

An offer of proof is a disclosure, made out of the hearing of the jury, of the substance, purpose, and relevancy of evidence the offering party seeks to introduce. Offers of proof are made under various circumstances, including the following:

- Opposing counsel has objected to a question or to the introduction of a document, and the trial judge has not yet ruled. The purpose of an offer of proof in this situation would be to persuade the judge to overrule the objection based on the judge's hearing the substance, purpose, and relevancy of the evidence. See Evid C §354(a).

- Opposing counsel has moved to strike certain testimony, and the trial judge has not yet ruled. The purpose of an offer of proof in this situation would be to make a showing by the offer of proof of the substance, purpose, and relevancy of the evidence. See Evid C §354(a).

- The opposing party claims a privilege, and the trial judge has not yet ruled. The opposing party's offer of proof in this situation would be designed to persuade the judge to deny the privilege (*e.g.,* exception to privilege applies). See Evid C §354(a); see also §34.24.

- The trial judge has just ruled, sustaining an objection to the introduction of evidence, granting a motion to strike, or granting a claim of privilege.

An offer of proof in this situation would have either or both of the following objectives:

- (1) To show the substance, purpose, and relevancy of the proffered evidence, or why an exception to admissibility applies. See *In re Mark C.* (1992) 7 CA4th 433, 8 CR2d 856; *Pugh v See's Candies, Inc.* (1988) 203 CA3d 743, 758, 250 CR 195. Judges frequently rule on objections summarily, without hearing argument. This is especially true of objections based on the ground of relevancy. An offer of proof places before the judge all the facts bearing on the admissibility of the excluded evidence and allows contextual consideration of the evidence in its specific form. Many judges will allow argument, hear offers of proof, or otherwise allow you to make a record at a regularly scheduled break in the proceedings. Even in the situations (discussed in §§5.5-5.8) in which Evid C §354 makes an offer of proof unnecessary to preserve a party's right to base an appeal on the judge's error, it may be advisable to make an offer of proof. The offer may persuade the judge to reverse the ruling, which may avoid both the necessity of an appeal and great expense to all involved.

- (2) To avoid waiver of the right to appeal the exclusion of evidence that may result from failure to make an offer of proof. Evid C §354. See *People v Cox* (1991) 53 C3d 618, 664, 280 CR 692. A judgment may not be reversed on appeal on the ground of an erroneous evidentiary ruling unless it appears that the error was prejudicial (*i.e.*, resulted in a "miscarriage of justice" (Cal Const art VI, §13)), except in criminal cases, in which some errors are prejudicial per se and require automatic reversal regardless of other evidence of guilt. See Appeals and Writs in Criminal Cases §1.168 (2d ed Cal CEB 2000). Unless certain exceptions (discussed in §§5.5-5.8) apply, it must also appear of record that the substance, purpose, and relevancy of the excluded evidence was made known to the trial judge by means of an offer of proof. Evid C §354(a) ("or by any other means"; see §5.8).

For a reviewing court to determine whether there was error, the record must show both the intended purpose of the offered evidence and that such purpose was proper. See *Beckett v Kaynar Mfg. Co.* (1958) 49 C2d 695, 699, 321 P2d 749; §5.11. See also *Gherman v Colburn* (1977) 72 CA3d 544, 586, 140 CR 330 (on appeal, appellants cannot raise new grounds to justify offer of proof that was properly rejected by trial court on basis of showing made at trial); *People v Rodriquez* (1969) 274 CA2d 770, 777, 79 CR 240 (when issue on appeal is sustaining of hearsay objection, record must show that party made offer of proof of purpose of testimony; otherwise ruling on objection will be considered proper).

See generally California Trial Practice: Civil Procedure During Trial §§15.53-15.60 (3d ed Cal CEB 1995); 3 Witkin, California Evidence, *Presentation at Trial* §§401-405 (4th ed 2000).

B. When Offer of Proof Is Not Required

§5.5　1. During Cross-Examination

Evidence Code §354(c) provides that an offer of proof is not required during cross-examination. *Tossman v Newman* (1951) 37 C2d 522, 525, 233 P2d 1; *Gallaher v Superior Court* (1980) 103 CA3d 666, 672, 162 CR 389. This exception recognizes that (103 CA3d at 672):

- The effectiveness of most cross-examinations would be lost if the examiner were required to divulge the purpose of the questions beforehand; and

- Counsel may not know what to expect when cross-examining a witness for impeachment purposes or eliciting additional facts.

Despite the Evid C §354(c) exception, the judge may require the cross-examiner to explain the purpose of a line of questions before the witness answers. In this situation, the cross-examiner may ask the court's permission to make an offer of proof. If explaining the purpose of the questions will "tip off" the witness to counsel's cross-examination strategy (see *People v Burton* (1961) 55 C2d 328, 344, 11 CR 65), counsel should ask the judge to hear this explanation outside the witness's presence. If the judge allows counsel to continue the line of questions, counsel should ask the judge to admonish opposing counsel not to discuss the ruling with the witness.

An offer of proof may also be necessary to obtain appellate reversal of an improperly sustained objection to a question asked during cross-examination or recross-examination. *People v Coleman* (1970) 8 CA3d 722, 730, 87 CR 554. In the absence of an offer of proof, an appellate court may uphold a trial court's improper sustaining of an objection to a cross-examiner's question if the question concerned an area of evidence or an issue of which the trial judge was unaware or the relevancy of which was apparently overlooked. *People v Coleman, supra*. See, *e.g., People v Burton, supra*, (although requiring offer of proof would have been unreasonable, counsel's failure to tell judge the theory on which the question was based resulted in ruling being upheld on appeal). A "contrary rule would enable a party secretly to reserve a means of reversal in case the judgment went against him." *People v Lancaster* (1957) 148 CA2d 187, 196, 306 P2d 626. See also *People v Alfaro* (1976) 61 CA3d 414, 132 CR 356 (cross-examiner required to make offer of proof to show that theory was not based on speculation).

§5.6　2. After Broad Exclusionary Ruling

An offer of proof need not be made when it clearly would be a futile gesture. If the trial judge has already ruled that an entire class of evidence is inadmissible, or that no evidence may be introduced on a certain issue, offers of proof regarding such evidence are obviously futile. The proponent may therefore refrain from making an offer of proof without fear of waiving any grounds for appeal. See Evid C §354(b).

§5.7 3. If Question Contains Necessary Elements

No offer of proof is necessary if an objection has been sustained to a question that clearly reveals on its face the substance, purpose, and relevancy of the excluded evidence. Evid C §354(a).

§5.8 4. If Necessary Elements Otherwise Apparent

If the substance, purpose, and relevancy of excluded evidence was made known to the trial judge "by any other means, the proponent need not make an offer of proof. . . ." Evid C §354(a). In *People v McGee* (1947) 31 C2d 229, 242, 187 P2d 706, the court held that an offer of proof was not necessary

> because the questions themselves, *together with colloquies with the trial judge,* in the light of previously introduced testimony, clearly disclosed their purpose, and since they were directed to defendant's own witness they indicate that the answers were expected to be favorable to defendant. [Emphasis added.]

See also *Delta Dynamics, Inc. v Arioto* (1968) 69 C2d 525, 528 n1, 72 CR 785 (pretrial conference order made reason for offered evidence known to trial judge); *People v Duane* (1942) 21 C2d 71, 81, 130 P2d 123 (judge erroneously excluded defense witness's testimony; purpose of witness's testimony was apparent from other testimony).

C. Procedure for Offer of Proof

§5.9 1. Out of Jury's Presence

The offer of proof should be made out of the jury's presence, with the court reporter present. Obviously, the jury should not hear evidence that the judge has excluded. Counsel therefore should request that the jury be excused while counsel makes the offer or that the matter be heard in chambers. See *People v Francis* (1957) 156 CA2d 1, 6, 319 P2d 103 (trial judge refused to allow offer of proof; held no error, partly because there was no request that the offer be made out of the presence of the jury). If making the offer of proof can be delayed until the jury recesses for a break, for lunch, or for the day, without disrupting the orderly presentation of counsel's case, the trial judge and the jury will appreciate counsel's consideration. Some judges allow or encourage offers of proof to be made in the jury's presence if the matter does not take too long, is not too complex, and is not prejudicial.

§5.10 2. Substance of Offered Evidence

Unless it is otherwise apparent, the offer of proof should clearly describe the substance of the evidence sought to be introduced. Evid C §354(a). This entails disclosing the specific evidentiary facts to be proved; it is insufficient merely to refer to conclusions, summaries, or ultimate facts. *Stickel v San*

Diego Elec. Ry. (1948) 32 C2d 157, 162, 195 P2d 416; *United Sav. & Loan Ass'n v Reeder Dev. Corp.* (1976) 57 CA3d 282, 293, 129 CR 113.

For example, in *Moore v Rogers* (1958) 157 CA2d 192, 195, 320 P2d 524, counsel stated:

> I want to introduce evidence to show that no consideration was given for this release[;] this evidence is going to show that it was given for specific purposes other than a general release. I want to offer proof that it was the intention of both parties at the time this waiver was executed that it was not to be a general release but, rather, a release for a special and specific purpose, to wit, to secure a title policy and for no other purpose at all, and it was not the intention of either party that it should operate as a general release.

The trial judge refused to allow the offer. In affirming the judgment, the appellate court observed (157 CA2d at 197):

> [T]he offer to prove that it was the intention of the parties that this release should be effective for the special purpose named, and not that it should have the effect of a general release, was merely the expression of a desire to offer some proof on the issue which the court was to decide, without disclosing in any way the nature of any proposed evidence or stating what the evidence would be whereby the fact in issue might be proved. In effect, it was an offer by counsel to prove his contentions with respect to the issue before the court, without stating anything concerning what evidence he desired to produce. There was no offer to prove any fact which would support counsel's expressed conclusion or tend to show any deception, misrepresentation or misunderstanding in connection with the execution of the waiver.

See also *Estate of Fries* (1963) 221 CA2d 725, 729, 34 CR 749 (sufficient offer of proof).

In addition to stating the specific testimony that would be given under oath, counsel should also indicate the answers expected to other questions asked on the subject. The substance of documentary evidence is ordinarily apparent from its face. However, with a voluminous or complex document, or with a proposed exhibit such as a file or a tape recording, the offer of proof should include the specific content sought to be admitted.

As an alternative to this method of presenting an offer of proof, counsel often asks the trial judge for permission to question the witness out of the jury's presence so that the judge can hear the intended questions and answers in context and under oath. For crucial evidence that counsel anticipates having difficulty in introducing, counsel should consider preparing carefully written offers of proof in advance. Such a practice would also save the court's time in listening to a narrative by counsel and the record would only need to show that the court had received and considered the written offer of proof.

§5.11   3. Purpose of Offered Evidence

Because the admissibility of evidence depends on the purpose for which it is offered, an offer of proof must disclose that purpose if it would not otherwise be apparent. Evid C §354(a).

If the evidence in question is offered for more than one purpose, counsel should make separate offers of proof identifying each specific purpose separately. If only one offer of proof is made and it contains both admissible and inadmissible matter, the trial judge under Evid C §352 may reject the entire offer. See *Hutton v Brookside Hosp.* (1963) 213 CA2d 350, 357, 28 CR 774; *Eaton v Brock* (1954) 124 CA2d 10, 16, 268 P2d 58.

§5.12 4. Relevancy of Offered Evidence

An offer of proof must demonstrate the relevancy of the evidence to a disputed issue if it would not otherwise be apparent. Evid C §354(a). See *Moore v Rogers* (1958) 157 CA2d 192, 197, 320 P2d 524 (analyzed in §5.10). The relevancy of evidence often depends on proof of preliminary facts. See discussion of Evid C §403(a)(1) in §§17.4 (relevancy) and 21.4 (laying foundation for relevancy). In this situation, the offer of proof should describe in detail the preliminary facts that will be proved to demonstrate relevancy and the specific evidence (*e.g.,* testimony, exhibits) that will be presented to prove those facts.

§5.13 5. Availability of Offered Evidence

An offer of proof must show that the disputed evidence is available at trial. With documentary or other tangible evidence, the proper procedure is to produce the item, ask that it be marked for identification, and describe it fully for the record. With testimony, the conclusive method to demonstrate its availability is to call the witness and proceed by question and answer to elicit the evidence. An alternative is to identify the witness, establish to the judge's satisfaction that the witness is currently available to testify, and declare that, if called as a witness and sworn, "this witness would testify under oath as follows. . . ."

An illustration of the wrong way to make an offer of proof appears in *Douillard v Woodd* (1942) 20 C2d 665, 128 P2d 6. In this case, defense counsel offered to prove by testimony of the defendant and "by other witnesses" that the plaintiffs previously took positions inconsistent with their claims in court. Counsel failed to name these other witnesses or to describe the specific facts to which any witness would testify. In affirming the judgment for the plaintiffs, the court stated the applicable rule as follows (20 C2d at 670):

> A mere general offer of proof without producing the witness or stating the evidence whereby the fact in issue is to be proved, or, if the witness be present, without putting a question to him in such form as to give opportunity for objection, is not correct trial procedure and it affords no ground for appeal.

§5.14   D. Objections to Offers of Proof

Offers of proof, which are usually made in response to objections, may also be the target of objections challenging the admissibility of the evidence described in the offer of proof.

An offer of proof may also be objectionable because it fails to disclose sufficient information to enable the opposing party and the trial judge to determine whether the offered evidence will be admissible. On the necessary formal elements, see §§5.10 (substance), 5.11 (purpose), 5.12 (relevancy), and 5.13 (availability).

As indicated in *Douillard v Woodd* (1942) 20 C2d 665, 670, 128 P2d 6 (see §5.13), the offer of proof must be in a form specific enough to provide an opportunity for opposing counsel to object to the substance of the offered evidence. See also *Stickel v San Diego Elec. Ry.* (1948) 32 C2d 157, 162, 195 P2d 416 (defendant's vague offer to prove that plaintiff was intoxicated at time of accident held insufficient); *Sena v Turner* (1961) 195 CA2d 487, 495, 15 CR 857 (witness on stand not asked question that was later subject of rejected offer of proof).

V. RESPONSES

§5.15   A. Counsel's Duty to Seek Other Methods of Proof

Rules of evidence are designed to exclude unreliable forms of proof—not to exclude the truth. If counsel offers evidence to prove a fact, and opposing counsel's objection to that evidence is sustained, counsel should seek other methods of proof. Too often in these circumstances, trial attorneys abandon important evidence that could be proved by following another route.

§5.16   B. Rephrasing the Question

When an objection to the form of a question (for examples, see chaps 7–16) is sustained, counsel can usually restate the question in a proper manner. An ambiguous question (see chap 7) can be clarified; a compound question (see chap 8) can be broken down into separate questions; a question that is too general (see chap 9) can be rephrased to limit the witness to a specific answer on a specific subject; an improper leading question (see chap 13) can be followed by a question on the same point that does not suggest the desired answer.

In certain circumstances, it may be necessary to postpone repeating the question. If an objection that a question assumes facts in dispute is sustained, counsel should call a witness, if possible, and put the facts in evidence.

§5.17   C. Presenting Other Proof

When an objection to the substance of a question (for examples, see chaps 17–30) is sustained, counsel should examine the possibilities of proving the facts by alternative methods. If counsel has properly prepared for the trial, counsel will have anticipated that such an objection might be raised and sustained and will have planned an alternative course. For example, to prove the balance due on a bank loan, counsel may ask an officer of the bank how much remains unpaid. If the question is excluded as calling for hearsay, counsel should be prepared to establish the balance from the bank's business records, in compliance with Evid C §1271. Similarly, if counsel asks a question during cross-examination that is excluded as exceeding the scope of the direct examination (see chap 26), the question need not be lost. Counsel may:

- Obtain leave to interrupt the cross-examination to ask the question as if counsel had called the witness on direct examination (Evid C §772(c); see §3.5);

- Call the witness later in the trial (under Evid C §776) and repeat the question if the witness is an adverse party or an adverse witness;

- Find some other way to prove the facts.

The important point to remember is that objections to evidence, even when well taken, should not deter the proponent of the evidence from gaining its admission by other methods, *e.g.*, amending the foundation, using additional witnesses, seeking a continuance.

6
Objections to Jury Voir Dire

I. SCOPE OF CHAPTER §6.1

II. PRE-VOIR DIRE PROCEDURES
    A. Challenges for Cause to Panel as a Whole
        1. When Challenge Is Available §6.2
        2. Procedure §6.3
        3. Differences Between Civil and Criminal Cases §6.4
    B. Pre-Voir Dire Conference
        1. Civil §6.5
        2. Criminal §6.6
    C. Objections at Pre-Voir Dire Conference §6.7
        1. Motions in Limine §6.8
        2. Trial Brief §6.9
        3. Juror Questionnaire §6.10

III. METHODS OF SEATING JURORS FOR QUESTIONING AND CHALLENGING §6.11
    A. "Jury Box" Method §6.12
    B. "Six Pack" or "Struck Juror" Method §6.13

IV. QUESTIONING BY TRIAL JUDGE AND COUNSEL §6.14
    A. Civil §6.15
    B. Criminal §6.16

V. CHALLENGES
    A. Challenges for Cause
        1. Grounds for Challenge §6.17
            a. General Disqualification §6.18
            b. Implied Bias §6.19
            c. Actual Bias §6.20
        2. Both Court and Counsel May Exercise Challenge §6.21
        3. How and When to Exercise Challenge §6.22
        4. Trial of Challenge for Cause §6.23
    B. Peremptory Challenges
        1. How and When to Exercise Challenges §6.24
        2. Number of Challenges Permitted
            a. Civil §6.25
            b. Criminal §6.26
        3. Discriminatory Use of Peremptory Challenges: *Wheeler-Elem* Rule
            a. Discriminatory Use of Peremptory Challenges Prohibited in Both Civil and Criminal Trials §6.27

b. Proving Prima Facie Case §6.28
c. Rebutting Prima Facie Case §6.29
d. Proof Currently Accepted at Hearing §6.30
e. Determination by Court §6.31
f. Appellate Review §6.32

VI. GROUNDS FOR OBJECTING TO IMPROPER VOIR DIRE QUESTIONS
   A. Question Attempts to Indoctrinate Jurors on Law
      1. Nature of Objection §6.33
      2. Stating the Objection §6.34
   B. Question Based on Incorrect Statement of Law
      1. Nature of Objection §6.35
      2. Stating the Objection §6.36
   C. Question Asks Jurors to Prejudge Evidence
      1. Nature of Objection §6.37
      2. Stating the Objection §6.38
   D. Question Introduces Prejudicial Matter
      1. Nature of Objection §6.39
      2. Stating the Objection §6.40
   E. Question Improper if Not Related to Challenge for Cause (Special Rule for Criminal Cases)
      1. Nature of Objection §6.41
      2. Stating the Objection §6.42
      3. Response to Objection: Connect Question to Basis for Challenge §6.43
   F. Question Prohibited by Judicial Administrative Standards §6.44
   G. Question in Improper Form §6.45

VII. HOW TO OBJECT TO IMPROPER VOIR DIRE EXAMINATION
   A. Objection to Examination by Judge §6.46
   B. Objection to Examination by Counsel; "Speaking Objections" §6.47
   C. Motion for Mistrial §6.48

VIII. WAIVER OF OBJECTION §6.49

IX. ISSUES ON APPEAL §6.50

X. SELECTED RULES OF COURT AND STATUTES
   A. Civil
      1. California Rules of Court §6.51
      2. Code of Civil Procedure §6.52
   B. Criminal
      1. California Rules of Court §6.53
      2. Code of Civil Procedure §6.54

§6.1 I. SCOPE OF CHAPTER

This chapter focuses on challenges and objections raised during jury selection and on responses to such challenges and objections. Issues requiring a challenge or an objection may arise either before or during voir dire examination. Specifically, counsel may face jury selection issues concerning the following items:

- The composition of the jury panel as a whole (see §6.2);

- Opposing counsel's motions in limine concerning voir dire questions and procedures (see §6.8);

- Opposing counsel's jury questionnaire (see §6.10);

- Opposing counsel's written statement of the case to be read to jurors at the beginning of the voir dire process (see §§6.5-6.6);

- Opposing counsel's written questions for prospective jurors (see §§6.5-6.6);

- Challenges for cause, especially in multiparty cases (see §§6.2-6.4, 6.17-6.23);

- Misconduct of jurors, *e.g.*, in concealing bias (see §§29.33-29.35);

- Peremptory challenges, especially in multiparty cases (see §§6.24-6.32);

- Grounds for objecting to improper voir dire questions (see §§6.15-6.16, 6.33-6.45); and

- Waiver of challenges and objections (see §§6.3, 6.27, 6.49).

A general discussion of jury selection and the examination of prospective jurors is beyond the scope of this book. For such a discussion, see, *e.g.*, California Trial Practice: Civil Procedure During Trial §§8.19-8.77 (3d ed Cal CEB 1995); 1 Wegner, Fairbank & Epstein, California Practice Guide, Civil Trials and Evidence, chap 5 (1993); Bennett, Hirschhorn & Dimitrius, Bennett's Guide to Jury Selection and Trial Dynamics in Civil and Criminal Litigation (1994); California Criminal Law Procedure and Practice, chap 28 (7th ed Cal CEB 2004); 7 Witkin, California Procedure, *Trial* §§133-160 (4th ed 1997); Ginger, Jury Selection in Civil and Criminal Trials (2d ed 1984-1985); Starr Litigation Services, Jury Selection: Sample Voir Dire Questions (2000 ed); Gobert, Jury Selection, The Law Art and Science of Selecting a Jury (2d ed 1990); Frederick, Mastering Voir Dire and Jury Selection, Gaining an Edge in Questioning a Jury; McCormick, Jury Selection, 2000 Cumulative Supplement (2d ed); Levine on Trial Advocacy, Jury Selection (1996).

Objections that apply to jury voir dire in death penalty cases are also beyond the scope of this book. For information on death penalty cases, see Crim Law, chap 28, §§55.25-55.29. See also 1-3 California Attorneys for Criminal Justice, California Death Penalty Defense Manual (1986).

Jury voir dire practice is essentially statutory and involves analysis of the Code of Civil Procedure, the California Rules of Court, local rules, and rules established by particular judges. To aid the reader in finding key statutory provisions without searching elsewhere, this chapter includes relevant statutes and rules of court. See §§6.51-6.54. Because local rules vary, counsel should obtain them from the court clerk when the case is assigned.

II. PRE-VOIR DIRE PROCEDURES

A. Challenges for Cause to Panel as a Whole

§6.2 **1. When Challenge Is Available**

A "challenge" is an objection to the trial jurors that may be made by any party. CCP §225. A challenge for cause can be made to the entire panel in both civil and criminal cases. CCP §225(a)(1)-(3). Although this challenge is made more frequently in criminal cases, it is available to counsel whenever there is systematic exclusion of a cognizable group. *People v Buford* (1982) 132 CA3d 288, 182 CR 904. See CCP §§197(a) (random selection required), 203 (persons not qualified to serve as jurors), 204(a) (no exemption based on "occupation, race, color, religion, sex, national origin, or economic status, or sexual orientation, or for any other reason"). Code of Civil Procedure §204(b) allows the exclusion of eligible persons for "undue hardship, upon themselves or upon the public, as defined by the Judicial Council").

Common challenges to the panel as a whole include the following:

- The jury selection process denied equal protection of the laws. See US Const amends V, XIV; Cal Const art I, §7.

- The jury panel does not contain a representative cross-section of the community. See US Const amend VI; Cal Const art I, §16. See *Williams v Superior Court* (1989) 49 C3d 736, 263 CR 503.

- The entire panel has been prejudiced irreversibly by the remarks of other jurors. See *People v Nguyen* (1994) 23 CA4th 32, 28 CR2d 140 (court of appeal upheld trial court ruling that prospective juror's stated fear of retaliation or retribution for serving on jury did not taint entire jury, because prospective juror who made the comments was excused). See also *People v Martinez* (1991) 228 CA3d 1456, 279 CR 858 (court of appeal upheld trial court's refusal to dismiss entire panel on basis of cause and rejected defendant's claim that prejudicial answers from excused jurors created hostile atmosphere).

A defendant in a criminal case does not have the right to a petit jury that mirrors the demographic composition of the population, that necessarily includes members of his or her own group, or that is composed of any particular group of individuals. A defendant is, however, constitutionally entitled to a jury panel from which the defendant's jury will be chosen that is as near an approximation of an ideal cross-section of the community as the process of random drawing permits. *Thiel v Southern Pac. Co.* (1946) 328 US 217, 220, 90 L Ed 1181, 66 S Ct 984; *People v Wheeler* (1978) 22 C3d 258, 148 CR 890. See *Di Donato v Santini* (1991) 232 CA3d 721, 283 CR 751.

The following groups can be excluded:

- Resident aliens and ex-felons (*People v Pride* (1992) 3 C4th 195, 227, 10 CR2d 636; *People v Karis* (1988) 46 C3d 612, 631, 250 CR 659);
- Hearing-impaired persons (*People v Fauber* (1992) 2 C4th 792, 9 CR2d 24); and
- Peace officers (CCP §219(b)).

To establish a prima facie violation of the fair cross-section requirement, three elements must be satisfied (*Duren v Missouri* (1979) 439 US 357, 58 L Ed 2d 579, 99 S Ct 664; *Williams v Superior Court* (1989) 49 C3d 736, 263 CR 503):

- The group alleged to have been excluded is a "distinctive" group in the community;
- The representation of this group in panels from which juries are selected is not fair and reasonable in relation to the number of such persons in the community; and
- The under-representation is due to systematic exclusion of the group in the jury selection process.

The systematic exclusion element is particularly difficult to establish. The proponent must demonstrate that criteria were applied in a constitutionally impermissible way that caused the disparity. If constitutionally permissible jury selection criteria are applied in a neutral manner, there can be no "systematic exclusion"—even when it is established that the percentage of the distinctive group in the community represented on jury panels is consistently less than the percentage of that group in the community. *People v Bell* (1989) 49 C3d 502, 530, 262 CR 1. See also *People v Breaux* (1991) 1 C4th 281, 3 CR2d 81.

The appropriate definition of "community" for cross-section analysis is the judicial district in which the case is tried rather than the county as a whole. See *Williams v Superior Court, supra*.

§6.3   2. Procedure

Under CCP §225(a)(1), the challenge to the entire panel must:

- Be made before the jury is sworn;
- Be in writing; and
- State plainly and distinctly the facts constituting the grounds for the challenge.

Counsel making the challenge must give reasonable notice of the challenge by serving a copy on all parties and the jury commissioner. CCP §225(a)(2).

NOTE➤ Regardless of the requirement under CCP §225 relating to challenges for cause, such a challenge should also exist if trial counsel first learns of the defect later in the proceedings under the Sixth Amendment right to a fair and impartial trial.

Counsel should check local rules for additional requirements for motions to challenge a jury selection system or discovery motions related to such challenges.

§6.4   3. Differences Between Civil and Criminal Cases

When considering a challenge to the jury panel as a whole, counsel should note the differences between civil and criminal cases. The data on which a challenge of the entire panel is made is often the subject of expert investigation and opinion. See *People v Horton* (1995) 11 C4th 1068, 47 CR2d 516.

Code of Civil Procedure §223 requires, in criminal cases, an initial examination of prospective jurors by the court, after which counsel for each party may conduct additional examination, by oral and direct questioning, of prospective jurors. See Cal Rules of Ct App Div 1, §8.5 for procedures to follow, questions by judge, and improper questions. Juror questionnaires may be used to help determine whether a fair cross-section of the population is represented. In addition to the juror questionnaires required by the jury commissioner (CCP §205(a)), other questionnaires may be used if directed by the trial judge. See CCP §205(c); Cal Rules of Ct 4.200(b). For further discussion of juror questionnaires, see §6.10.

For further discussion of challenges to the jury panel as a whole, including procedures for challenging the panel, see California Criminal Law Procedure and Practice §§28.1, 28.3–28.7 (7th ed Cal CEB 2004); National Jury Project, Jurywork: Systematic Techniques, chap 5 (2d ed 1983).

B. Pre-Voir Dire Conference

§6.5   1. Civil

In civil trials, the trial judge "should" confer with counsel before the voir dire examination with a court reporter present to discuss "specific questions or areas of inquiry." Cal Rules of Ct App Div I, §8(b). The judge usually will ask counsel to submit in writing voir dire questions that they wish the judge to ask in addition to those specific questions set forth in Cal Rules of Ct App Div I, §8(c)–(d). Eminent domain questions are set forth in Cal Rules of Ct App Div 1, §8.5(d). See Cal Rules of Ct 228.

The trial judge should allow counsel to conduct voir dire examination without requiring prior submission of the questions they plan to ask "unless a particular counsel engages in improper questioning." CCP §222.5. See the questions proscribed by Cal Rules of Ct App Div I, §8(f). On improper questions, see §§6.15-6.16, 6.33, 6.35, 6.37, 6.39, 6.41, 6.44-6.45. If any questions are unusual or potentially troublesome (*e.g.,* questions about insurance), the judge may ask counsel to submit them at the pre-voir dire conference.

The judge may limit the scope and length of counsel's voir dire examination, but the limits imposed must be reasonable. See CCP §222.5. To educate the jurors about the case, the judge should obtain from counsel a brief outline of the nature of the case and a list of witnesses. See Cal Rules of Ct App Div I, §§8(b), 8(c)(4), (6). See also local rules, *e.g.,* Los Angeles Super Ct R 8.20(a)-(b). In multi-party cases, the number of peremptory challenges and how they are to be exercised should be determined before trial in the pre-voir dire conference. See CCP §231(c).

Counsel should check local rules and the particular judge's own rules for additional requirements regarding the pre-voir dire conference. In San Francisco, for example, deadlines for motions in limine are set forth in San Francisco Uniform Local R 6.2, which states that all motions in limine must be in writing, with copies mailed to all parties at least ten days before the trial date or hand-delivered at least five days before trial.

§6.6   2. Criminal

The trial judge must hold a conference before trial during which the following issues should be discussed:

- The nature of the case;

- The names of persons whom counsel intends to call as witnesses;

- The prosecution and defense theories of the case (although the defense has the right not to disclose defense theories);

- Procedures for deciding requests for jury exemptions based on undue hardship and challenges for cause;

- Areas of inquiry and specific questions to be asked during voir dire examination by the court and (if permitted) by counsel; and

- Time limits on counsel's examination of potential jurors, either per juror or in the aggregate. Code of Civil Procedure §223 provides for direct examination of prospective jurors by counsel in criminal trials and states that the court's discretion in limiting questioning by counsel is not grounds for reversal of a conviction absent a miscarriage of justice as described in Cal Const art VI, §13.

Cal Rules of Ct 4.200(a)-(b) (superior court).

If the questions are asked by written questionnaire, the questionnaire should be submitted to the court and opposing counsel before the pre-voir dire conference. Cal Rules of Ct 4.200.

§6.7 C. Objections at Pre-Voir Dire Conference

Whether the trial is civil or criminal, the pre-voir dire conference provides the first opportunity to challenge proposed subjects or questions on the record. See Cal Rules of Ct App Div I, §§8(f) (civil), 8.5(d) (criminal), which set forth questions that are not allowed except in unusual circumstances. This conference may also be counsel's best opportunity to persuade the judge to delineate proper and improper subjects or questions. This delineation will prevent opposing counsel from attempting to precondition or preinstruct the jury. Voir dire is not the time for counsel to begin argument or to precondition or educate the jurors as to particular facts.

When responding to opposing counsel's contention that a question or subject is improper, counsel should explain why it is proper or that unusual circumstances justify its use. The judge has broad discretion to determine when unusual circumstances exist. Cal Rules of Ct App Div I, §§8(f) (civil), 8.5(d) (criminal). The trial judge must consider "any unique or complex elements, legal or factual" that might allow the question to be asked. Cal Rules of Ct App Div I, §8(a)(2) (civil).

By court rule, it is improper to question jurors about applicable law. CCP §222.5; Cal Rules of Ct App Div 1, §8(f) (civil); Cal Rules of Ct App Div I, §8.5(c). Note that it is dangerous for a judge to allow counsel during voir dire questioning to preinstruct potential jurors about the applicable law. See *People v Love* (1960) 53 C2d 843, 852, 3 CR 665.

Counsel should not leave the pre-voir dire conference without being certain how the trial judge wants counsel to handle objections during voir dire, *e.g.*, whether the trial judge wants arguments regarding objections decided at sidebar. See Cal Rules of Ct App Div I, §8(b) (civil); Cal Rules of Ct 4.200. On procedures for objections, see §§6.46–6.48.

Counsel who wish to object to any questions that the trial judge proposes to ask during voir dire should request during the pre-voir dire conference to be allowed to object on the record and explain the basis for the objection. If unreasonable limits are placed on voir dire examination, counsel should object to these limits before the jury is sworn to avoid waiving this objection. *Bly-Magee v Budget Rent-A-Car Corp.* (1994) 24 CA4th 318, 29 CR2d 330; *Rousseau v West Coast House Movers* (1967) 256 CA2d 878, 881, 64 CR 655.

A separate voir dire examination is not held on each issue in a bifurcated trial. *Bly-Magee v Budget Rent-A-Car Corp., supra* (counsel's attempt to reopen voir dire when second phase of bifurcated trial began contemplated a procedure not provided by California law).

§6.8 1. Motions in Limine

During the pre-voir dire conference, counsel should be prepared to object orally to, or file appropriate written motions in limine regarding, any objectionable portions of the following items:

- Proposed voir dire questions of the trial judge or opposing counsel;

- Jury questionnaires proposed by opposing counsel;
- Voir dire questions that might be obviated by the court's rulings on in limine motions; and
- Proposed outlines of the case drafted by the court or opposing counsel to be read to prospective jurors at the beginning of the voir dire process.

§6.9   2. Trial Brief

Whenever possible, counsel should use a trial brief at the pre-voir dire conference both to raise objections and to respond to anticipated objections to voir dire questions. For example, the brief may:

- Clarify the significance of questions proposed to be asked by counsel, in juror questionnaires, or by the judge;
- Address the need for sequestered voir dire in appropriate circumstances, *e.g.,* if prospective jurors might be embarrassed to answer personal questions in open court or discussing certain death penalty issues; and
- Deal with pretrial publicity issues that might have already prejudiced the jury and provided grounds for challenges for cause.

§6.10   3. Juror Questionnaire

Juror questionnaires are permitted in both civil trials (CCP §§205(d), 222.5, 228) and criminal trials (CCP §§205(c), (d), 223; Cal Rules of Ct 4.201). Under CCP §205(d), the judge may direct a prospective juror to complete additional questionnaires proposed by counsel to assist the voir dire process. If counsel requests the use of questionnaires, the court has discretion to determine their content. In civil trials, the court should not "arbitrarily or unreasonably refuse to submit reasonable written questionnaires" when requested by counsel. CCP §222.5.

If counsel plans to use a juror questionnaire, counsel should try to obtain a stipulation with opposing counsel for its use. It may be helpful to meet and confer with opposing counsel regarding a joint questionnaire. If a stipulation is not reached, counsel should prepare a written motion requesting use of the proposed questionnaire. A copy of the questionnaire should be attached to the motion, which should be prepared before the pre-voir dire conference and must be timely filed and served. Counsel should check local rules for specific deadlines for filing and service and for any additional requirements.

An attorney-prepared juror questionnaire is often a key topic during the pre-voir dire conference. Any unresolved objections or responses to objections regarding the questionnaire should be addressed at the pre-voir dire conference. For an excellent discussion of the use of jury questionnaires in both civil and criminal trials, see Larrabee & Drucker, *Adieu Voir Dire: The Jury Questionnaire,* 21 Litig 37 (Fall 1994).

For a sample criminal jury questionnaire form, see California Criminal Law Forms Manual §28.2 (Cal CEB 1995). Questionnaire depositories may be available from litigation specialty groups such as the American College of Trial Lawyers and The American Board of Trial Advocates.

§6.11 III. METHODS OF SEATING JURORS FOR QUESTIONING AND CHALLENGING

Once the jury panel has been sworn, prospective jurors are selected at random and seated in the jury box. There are two ways to seat, question, and challenge prospective jurors:

- The "jury box" method (see §6.12); and
- The "six pack" or "struck juror" method (see §6.13).

§6.12 A. "Jury Box" Method

In the "jury box" method of seating jurors, the trial court clerk randomly calls 12 or more prospective jurors. A lesser number may be called if the number is agreed on by the parties in civil and misdemeanor trials. Cal Const art I, §16; CCP §220. As few as six jurors may be seated in felony trials if both the defense and the prosecution waive the right to 12 jurors. *People v Trejo* (1990) 217 CA3d 1026, 266 CR 266.

The judge questions the potential jurors before the attorneys are allowed to do so. In civil cases, plaintiff's counsel usually goes first. In criminal cases, defense counsel goes first.

After 12 prospective jurors have been questioned, the defense exercises its challenges for cause, followed by the plaintiff or the People. CCP §226(d). The prospective jurors are replaced until 12 qualified jurors remain. Both sides then exercise peremptory challenges. A juror removed by peremptory challenge is replaced by another juror, who is questioned and then may be challenged both for cause and peremptorily. This procedure continues until peremptories have been expended or waived. *People v Morris* (1991) 53 C3d 152, 185, 279 CR 720.

§6.13 B. "Six Pack" or "Struck Juror" Method

Under the "six pack" method of seating jurors, replacement jurors (usually four or more) are randomly selected and listed in the order in which they will be called as replacements. These replacements are examined at the same time as the 12 jurors seated in the jury box. When one of the original jurors is excused, the next replacement juror in order takes the empty seat in the jury box. If all replacement jurors are used, another group of replacement jurors is called and examined separately.

A variation of the six pack method is the "struck juror" (*i.e.,* "challenge") method. See *People v Wright* (1990) 52 C3d 367, 395, 276 CR 731 (trial judge instructed attorneys to question and challenge 21 prospective jurors before anyone was seated in jury box). If after each side exercises its strikes more than 12 persons remain on the list, the trial judge must decide which 12 will constitute the jury. In *Wright,* defense counsel objected, claiming that the struck juror method improperly diluted the right to exercise peremptory challenges. Defense counsel reasoned that the strategic use of a peremptory challenge against any prospective juror requires knowledge of the personalities of the remaining jurors. Former Pen C §1088 (which applied to the trial in *Wright*) allowed each party the right to have the panel full before exercising any peremptory challenge. The supreme court agreed that although the struck juror method may have caused counsel to exercise less informed peremptory challenges, reversal was not required because no prejudice was shown in this case. Nevertheless, the court acknowledged that the potential for prejudice from using the struck juror method exists. 52 C3d at 397.

§6.14   IV. QUESTIONING BY TRIAL JUDGE AND COUNSEL

In all civil and criminal jury trials, it is the trial judge's duty to examine prospective jurors so that a fair and impartial jury is selected. CCP §222.5 (civil); Cal Rules of Ct 228 (superior court; civil). See also Cal Rules of Ct App Div I, §§8(f) (civil), 8.5(d) (criminal). The rules governing the trial judge's involvement in jury selection differ, however, depending on whether the trial is civil or criminal.

§6.15   A. Civil

In civil trials, judges are authorized by statute to perform the initial juror examination. CCP 222.5. Many judges follow the list of specific questions and areas of inquiry set forth in Cal Rules of Ct App Div I, §8(c)-(d).

When the initial examination by the judge has been completed, counsel for each party have the right to conduct a reasonable examination in order to "intelligently exercise both peremptory challenges and challenges for cause." CCP §222.5; See Cal Rules of Ct 228. The trial judge must keep this examination within "reasonable limits." CCP §222.5. When ruling on the form and subject matter of a question asked by counsel, the judge may take the following issues into consideration:

- Any unique or complex legal or factual elements of the trial; and

- Individual responses or conduct of potential jurors evincing unsuitability to serve as fair and impartial jurors.

The judge must give counsel wide latitude to ask questions of prospective jurors that are calculated to discover bias or prejudice. CCP §222.5. See *Bly-Magee v Budget Rent-A-Car Corp.* (1994) 24 CA4th 318, 324, 29 CR2d 330 (trial court must "allow counsel liberal and probing examination to discover bias and prejudice within the circumstances of each case").

The fact that the trial judge has questioned jurors about a topic does not preclude counsel from asking different questions about the same area. CCP §222.5. The court may also permit counsel to examine prospective jurors outside a judge's presence, if counsel for all the parties agree to such an examination. CCP §222.5; Cal Rules of Ct 228 (superior court).

Under CCP §222.5, improper voir dire questions by counsel include those:

- Whose "dominant purpose" is to "precondition the prospective jurors to a particular result";

- That indoctrinate the prospective jurors;

- That question the prospective jurors about the pleadings; or

- That question the prospective jurors about the law.

§6.16 B. Criminal

Beginning January 1, 2001, CCP §223 requires, in criminal cases, that the court conduct an initial examination of prospective jurors, after which counsel for each party may conduct additional examination of prospective jurors, by oral and direct questioning. The court may, in the exercise of discretion, limit the oral and direct questioning of prospective jurors and counsel. The court may specify the maximum amount of time that counsel for each party may question an individual juror, or may specify an aggregate amount of time for each party, which can then be allocated among the prospective jurors by counsel. Examination of prospective jurors shall be conducted only in aid of the exercise of challenges for cause. CCP §223.

The court's exercise of discretion in the manner in which voir dire is conducted, including any limitation on the time allowed for direct questioning of prospective jurors by counsel and any determination that a question is not in aid of the exercise of challenges for cause, shall not cause any conviction to be reversed unless the exercise of that discretion has resulted in a miscarriage of justice as specified in Cal Const art VI, §13. CCP §223. Under former law, Proposition 115 (the "Crime Victims Justice Reform Act"), passed on June 5, 1990, provided that the judge conduct the voir dire examination of prospective jurors and that counsel be allowed to supplement voir dire only on a showing of good cause. Only voir dire questions that assist in the exercise of challenges for cause are allowed. See CCP §223 (prior to amendment by Stats 2000, ch 192).

The amendments to CCP §223 do not appear to affect the list of specific questions and areas of inquiry that are set forth in Cal Rules of Ct App Div I, Standards of Judicial Administration §8.5(b).

Improper questions by counsel in criminal cases include attempts to precondition prospective jurors to a particular result and comments on the personal lives and families of the parties or counsel. Cal Rules of Ct App Div I, §8.5(c). Except in unusual circumstances, the following are also improper under §8.5(c):

- Questions about the pleadings;
- Questions about the applicable law and the meaning of particular words or phrases; and
- Questions about the comfort of jurors.

The court is not constitutionally required to ask open-ended questions; questions calling for "yes" or "no" responses are allowed. The form and number of questions probing into sensitive areas such as racial bias are within the court's discretion. *People v Taylor* (1992) 5 CA4th 1299, 7 CR2d 676.

The routine exclusion of the press and public during voir dire examination in both civil and criminal cases was disapproved by the United States Supreme Court in *Press-Enterprise Co. v Superior Court* (1984) 464 US 501, 78 L Ed 2d 629, 104 S Ct 819. See also *People v Harris* (1992) 10 CA4th 672, 12 CR2d 758 (trial court's procedure for expediting jury selection process (peremptory challenges were exercised in chambers and outside presence of public) violated defendant's constitutional right to public trial).

Proposition 115 also addresses the issue of individual, sequestered voir dire. A goal of Proposition 115 was to limit the cases involving protracted individual sequestered voir dire of each prospective juror called to the jury box. "Voir dire of any prospective jurors shall, where practicable, occur in the presence of the other jurors in all criminal cases, including death penalty cases." CCP §223. Before Proposition 115, the California Supreme Court exercising its supervisory authority over California criminal procedure, enacted a rule of criminal procedure to allow individual sequestered "death qualification" voir dire (*i.e.*, could the juror impose the death penalty in a cause such as that presently before the potential juror; would the juror always impose the death penalty or never impose the death penalty in the case before the juror) in all death penalty cases. This type of voir dire procedure, known as "*Hovey* voir dire," avoided the potentially prejudicial effect of an open voir dire on jurors' views and willingness to reveal their views about capital punishment. See *Hovey v Superior Court* (1980) 28 C3d 1, 80, 168 CR 128; *People v Clark* (1990) 50 C3d 583, 596, 268 CR 399; *People v Visciotti* (1992) 2 C4th 1, 47, 5 CR2d 495. Since the trial court was required to go through the effort of individually questioning each potential juror on the issue of death qualification, the subject matter soon expanded to include *all* voir dire of the juror.

Because the supreme court's decision in *Hovey* was merely a rule created under the court's supervisory authority over California criminal procedure and not constitutionally based, it is arguable that the passage of Proposition 115 and the language in CCP §223 supersede the *Hovey* rule of criminal procedure.

Code of Civil Procedure §223 requires that "voir dire of any prospective jurors shall, where practicable, occur in the presence of the other jurors in all criminal cases." Typical circumstances where it is not practicable include:

- Cases that have generated such publicity, *e.g.*, murder, rape, child molestation, drunk driving, that it needs to be determined whether prospective jurors might be influenced by that publicity and taint the rest of the panel members who have no knowledge of the case; and

- Cases in which the issues are such that, to obtain a juror's true attitudes and to uncover any bias, the prospective juror needs to be voir dired in a manner that avoids being tainted by other prospective jurors' attitudes and that makes the juror feel comfortable enough for candid expression.

This approach may also be warranted simply because a prospective juror wants to discuss an isolated subject in a more private setting out of the presence of the other jurors (*e.g.*, the case involves child molestation and the juror was a molest victim; the charge is murder and the prospective juror's son is currently in prison convicted of murder).

The pre-voir dire conference (see Cal Rules of Ct 4.200) gives the attorney an opportunity to show the judge that, in a particular criminal case with its unique circumstances, it is not practicable to allow voir dire in front of the other jurors. The language of §223 (requiring juror voir dire in the presence of the other jurors "where practicable") combined with the California Rules of Court and Standards of Judicial Administration (starting at §8.5), enacted to deal with the passage of Proposition 115 and changes to §223, provide authority for attorneys, when special circumstances exist, to request that a *Hovey* process be followed. See Cal Rules of Ct App Div I, §8.5(a)(2) ("the examination of prospective jurors in a criminal case should include all questions necessary to insure the selection of a fair and impartial jury"). Also, Cal Rules of Ct App Div I, §8.5(a)(2) allows the trial judge, for good cause, to permit supplemental examination calculated to discover possible bias or prejudice with regard to the circumstances of the case relevant to a challenge for cause

In all criminal cases, a trial judge who refuses to grant a motion for in chambers voir dire with counsel present (including a motion for "*Hovey* voir dire" in a death penalty case) is subject to reversal for an abuse of discretion that results in a miscarriage of justice. See CCP §223.

With regard to application of *Hovey* procedures, counsel should take note that the practice of California trial court judges varies. Counsel should check to determine local practice.

For further discussion of voir dire in criminal cases, including death penalty cases, see California Criminal Law Procedure and Practice §§28.19-28.20, 55.25-55.29 (7th ed Cal CEB 2004).

V. CHALLENGES

A. Challenges for Cause

§6.17   **1. Grounds for Challenge**

The grounds for challenging a juror for cause in both civil and criminal cases are stated in CCP §225(b)(1)(A)-(C). Under this section, a juror may be challenged for one of the following reasons:

- General disqualification (see §6.18);
- Implied bias (see §6.19); or
- Actual bias (see §6.20).

§6.18   a. General Disqualification

The grounds for challenging a juror for cause in both civil and criminal cases are stated in CCP §225. A general disqualification challenge is made on the ground that a juror is not statutorily qualified to serve as a juror. CCP §225(b)(1)(A). Attorneys usually do not question jurors about these requirements, however, because most prospective jurors are screened by the jury commissioner before being allowed on the qualified juror list. See CCP §205.

A prospective juror is not qualified to serve in either a civil or a criminal case if the juror is:

- An alien (CCP §203(a)(1));
- A minor (CCP §203(a)(2));
- Not domiciled in the State of California (CCP §203(a)(3));
- Not a resident of the jurisdiction from which the prospective jurors were summoned (CCP §203(a)(4));
- A felon whose civil rights have not been restored (CCP §203(a)(5));
- A person convicted of malfeasance in office (CCP §203(a)(5));
- Without sufficient knowledge of the English language (CCP §203(a)(6));
- Currently serving as a juror (CCP §203(a)(7));
- The subject of a conservatorship (CCP §203(a)(8)); or
- Incapable of performing the duties of a juror due to a disability, *e.g.*, loss of hearing (CCP §228(b)).

Interestingly, CCP §228 conflicts with CCP §203(a)(6), which declares that no person is incompetent to serve as a juror solely because of a disability that impedes the person's ability to communicate (*e.g.*, loss of hearing) or impairs or interferes with the person's mobility. There is no statutory basis for a challenge for cause to a disabled person who can perform the duties of a juror with the aid of an attendant. When an individual juror requires a sign language interpreter, reader, or speech interpreter to facilitate communication because of a disability and a party does not cause the juror's removal by challenge, the party is required to stipulate to the presence of a "service provider" in the jury room during jury deliberations and to prepare and deliver to the court proposed jury instructions to the "service provider." CCP §224.

Hearing-impaired persons (and probably those with other disabilities) are not a "distinctive" or cognizable group within the community for purposes of a fair cross-section challenge. *People v Fauber* (1992) 2 C4th 792, 9 CR2d 24. See §6.2.

§6.19   b. Implied Bias

A prospective juror can be challenged for cause if there is a showing of implied bias. CCP §§225(b)(1)(B), 229. Implied bias arises when facts demonstrate that a prospective juror is presumed to be biased as a matter of law and the prospective juror falls into any of the eight categories specified in CCP §229. CCP §225(b)(1)(B). No further proof of prejudice is required; it is inferred as a matter of law. See *People v Wheeler* (1978) 22 C3d 258, 148 CR 890.

Eight categories of implied bias are set forth in CCP §229.

- The juror is related by blood or marriage within the fourth degree to a party or an alleged witness or victim in the case;
- The juror is related to any party or officer of a corporate party or is a business partner with either party;
- The juror has served as a trial or grand juror or has been a witness in a previous or pending civil or criminal action between the same parties;
- The juror has an interest in the litigation, with the exception of the juror's interest as a resident, citizen, or taxpayer;
- The juror has an unqualified opinion or belief regarding the merits of the action based on knowledge of material facts;
- The juror is biased for or against either party;
- The juror is a party to the action pending in the court for which the juror is drawn, which is set for trial before the panel of which the juror is a member; or
- The offense charged is punishable with death, and the juror entertains "conscientious opinions that would preclude the juror [from] finding the defendant guilty."

On misconduct of jurors in concealing bias, discovery of the misconduct during trial, remedies, and waiver, see §§29.33-29.35.

§6.20   c. Actual Bias

Code of Civil Procedure §225(b)(1)(C) defines "actual bias" as

> the existence of a state of mind on the part of the juror in reference to the case, or to any of the parties, which will prevent the juror from

acting with entire impartiality and without prejudice to the substantial rights of any party.

The following are examples of disqualification of prospective jurors or jurors for actual bias:

- The juror (1) cannot assure the court that he or she would decide the case by reference strictly to the law and the evidence or (2) admits that there is a significant likelihood that extraneous matters will enter into the decision-making process. See *Lombardi v California St. Ry. Co.* (1899) 124 C 311, 314, 57 P 66 (prospective juror intimately acquainted with plaintiff and stated that, if testimony were equally balanced, would find for plaintiff and go to biggest verdict); *People v Hecker* (1990) 219 CA3d 1238, 1243, 268 CR 884 (juror properly excused midtrial when she was unable to give assurance that she could decide case without reference to having seen defendant join church the week before); *Leibman v Curtis* (1955) 138 CA2d 222, 226, 291 P2d 542 (prospective juror hostile to claim and would require more evidence than preponderance to render verdict for plaintiff).

- The juror states that it would be difficult to keep an open mind because of the nature of the case. See *People v Compton* (1971) 6 C3d 55, 59, 98 CR 217 (belated discovery during trial that alternate juror told barber that it would be hard to keep an open mind because defendant was charged with lewd conduct with a child); *Smith v Smith* (1935) 7 CA2d 271, 46 P2d 232 (action to enforce property settlement agreement; prospective juror's religious beliefs on divorce and remarriage are relevant and proper subjects of inquiry).

- The juror admits bias for or against a group involved in the case. See *Lawlor v Linforth* (1887) 72 C 205, 13 P 496 (in action for rent, prospective juror hostile to all landlords); *People v Buyle* (1937) 22 CA2d 143, 70 P2d 955.

- The juror admits having settled opinions about issues in the case. See *People v Williams* (1988) 199 CA3d 469, 245 CR 61 (prospective juror made conflicting statements about his ability to remain impartial); *People v Sullivan* (1922) 59 CA 633, 211 P 467.

§6.21   2. Both Court and Counsel May Exercise Challenge

A challenge for cause is usually made by a party as authorized by CCP §§225 and 227. The trial court has the power, however, to excuse a juror for cause sua sponte, based on the court's duty to ensure the selection of a fair and impartial jury. *People v Jiminez* (1992) 11 CA4th 1611, 15 CR2d 268 (juror admitted that she would be lenient). According to the court in *Jiminez,* the trial judge should use this power sparingly.

§6.22   3. How and When to Exercise Challenge

After all sides have questioned a group of prospective jurors, the judge will commonly ask each side if it wants to exercise any challenges for cause or if it will pass. Challenges for cause must be exercised before peremptory challenges. CCP §226(c). All challenges to an individual juror must be taken first by the defendant and then by the plaintiff or People. CCP §226(d). A challenge for cause should be exercised as soon as the ground for the challenge is discovered.

At the pre-voir dire conference, counsel should ask the judge how challenges for cause will be handled and determine whether any local rules govern such challenges. See, *e.g.,* Los Angeles Super Ct R 8.32 (challenge must be made outside hearing of prospective jurors).

If the judge's practice is to have counsel make a challenge in open court, obviously counsel should not disparage the juror by declaring, "I challenge Mrs. Smith!" Instead, counsel should simply say quietly that, *e.g.,* the plaintiff will excuse for cause Mrs. Smith (or Juror No. 7), and thank the juror for participating in the examination. The judge will simply excuse the juror without any explanation.

§6.23   4. Trial of Challenge for Cause

Challenges for cause are generally heard orally, although they may be in writing (CCP §226(b)). The court "tries" (think of it as a mini-trial) the challenge (CCP §230), and the Evidence Code applies. See Evid C §300. If the judge needs more information from the prospective juror before ruling on the challenge, the court may question the juror and "any other person" to ascertain potential bias. CCP §230. The judge decides whether the challenge for cause will be heard out of the other jurors' presence (*e.g.,* in chambers or at sidebar conference) or in open court. A court reporter should be present during this questioning.

The qualification of jurors challenged for cause is within the court's discretion. *People v Kelly* (1992) 1 C4th 495, 3 CR2d 677; *People v Kaurish* (1990) 52 C3d 648, 276 CR 788. See *People v Bittaker* (1989) 48 C3d 1046, 259 CR 630. In both a civil and a criminal trial, if the judge denies the challenge for cause, counsel must exhaust all peremptory challenges to preserve the issue for appeal. *People v Kelly, supra; People v Price* (1991) 1 C4th 324, 3 CR2d 106; *Kimbley v Kaiser Found. Hosp.* (1985) 164 CA3d 1166, 1169, 211 CR 148. Moreover, if the trial court erroneously denies a party's challenge for cause, reversal is required if the challenging party wanted to excuse another juror, because the erroneous denial forced counsel to use a peremptory challenge that would have been available to excuse another juror. See *Leibman v Curtis* (1955) 138 CA2d 222, 226, 291 P2d 542.

If the judge denies a challenge for cause, counsel should make a record of this denial. Counsel may later run out of peremptory challenges and want to reargue the lost challenge for cause. In the interests of a fair trial, the judge may give both sides one additional peremptory challenge. If this request is denied, the lost challenge may be grounds for a new trial in retrospect or for appeal. *Leibman v Curtis, supra*. The court may refuse to grant additional peremptory challenges unless counsel makes a showing that, in the absence of such additional challenges, the defendant is reasonably likely to receive an unfair trial. See *People v Bonin* (1989) 47 C3d 808, 254 CR 298; *Leibman v Curtis, supra*.

There is no limit to the number of challenges for cause that may be exercised under CCP §230. There are limits, however, on the number of peremptory challenges in both civil and criminal actions. Code of Civil Procedure §231 provides for a specific number of challenges for each "side"; in multiparty cases, the judge determines "sides." Discretion for additional challenges is also allowed.

B. Peremptory Challenges

§6.24   1. How and When to Exercise Challenges

Peremptory challenges occur after voir dire is completed, challenges for cause have been made and decided, and replacement jurors have been questioned and passed for cause. See CCP §226(c). See also CCP §231(d). A peremptory challenge is an objection to a prospective juror that may be made without any explanation when exercised in both civil and criminal cases. CCP §226(b). It is a "guess" challenge by the parties' attorneys that is available to remove jurors who were not found disqualified for cause. See *Austin v Lambert* (1938) 11 C2d 73, 79, 77 P2d 849. Counsel may simply state, *e.g.*, "We excuse, with thanks, Juror No. 7." But check local rules, *e.g.*, Los Angeles Super Ct R 8.34 (statement requesting excusal of a prospective juror should be made to the court; counsel should not "excuse" juror).

Code of Civil Procedure §231(d) states that "each party shall be entitled to have the panel full before exercising any peremptory challenge." In actual practice, this is the case if the "jury box" method of jury selection is used. See *People v Wright* (1990) 52 C3d 367, 396, 276 CR 731. On the differences between the jury box and the "six pack" or "struck juror" methods of juror selection, see §§6.12-6.13.

The right to exercise peremptory challenges begins with counsel for plaintiff (in civil cases) or the People (in criminal cases) and then alternates between counsel until all peremptory challenges have been exhausted or both sides pass. See CCP §231(d). The selection of alternate jurors to replace discharged jurors is governed by CCP §§233-234.

Peremptory challenges may not be used to exclude jury members of an identifiable racial, religious, ethnic, or similar group solely because of a presumed group bias. *People v Sanders* (1990) 51 C3d 471, 497, 273 CR 537. See §6.27.

2. Number of Challenges Permitted

§6.25 a. Civil

When there are only two parties in a civil case, each party is entitled to six peremptory challenges. CCP §231(c). When there are more than two parties, the court must divide the parties into two or more sides "according to their respective interests in the issues." Each side is then entitled to eight peremptory challenges. CCP §231(c).

When there are several parties on one side, the court must divide the eight challenges among the parties as equally as possible. When there are more than two sides, the court must grant additional peremptory challenges to a side in the "interests of justice"; the peremptory challenges of one side, however, may not exceed the aggregate number of peremptory challenges of all other sides. CCP §231(c). If a party on a side does not use that party's full share of peremptory challenges, any other party or parties on the same side may use the unused challenges. CCP §231(c).

The number of sides, the number of peremptory challenges to be exercised by each party, and the sequence for exercising them should be determined during the pre-voir dire conference. See, *e.g.,* Los Angeles Super Ct R 8.20(f), 8.33.

§6.26 b. Criminal

In criminal cases, if the offense charged is punishable with a maximum term of imprisonment of 90 days or less, each side is entitled to six peremptory challenges. If more than one defendant is tried in such a case, the People are entitled to six peremptory challenges and the codefendants to six joint challenges. In addition, each defendant is entitled to four independent peremptory challenges. The prosecution is entitled to as many additional peremptory challenges as are allowed all defendants. CCP §231(b). For special rules regarding the number of peremptory challenges available in death penalty cases and cases of life imprisonment, see CCP §231(a).

3. Discriminatory Use of Peremptory Challenges: *Wheeler-Elem* Rule

§6.27 a. Discriminatory Use of Peremptory Challenges Prohibited in Both Civil and Criminal Trials

The *Wheeler* rule. Peremptory challenges are ordinarily exercised without stating a reason. See CCP §226(b). There is an exception: peremptory challenges may not be used intentionally to excuse prospective jurors because they are "members of an identifiable group distinguished on racial, religious, ethnic, or similar grounds." *People v Wheeler* (1978) 22 C3d 258, 276, 148 CR 890 ("*Wheeler*" rule); *People v Silva* (2001) 25 C4th 345, 106 CR2d 93; *People v Garcia* (2000) 77 CA4th 1269, 1276, 92 CR2d 339 (adding sexual orientation). But see *People v Martin* (1998) 64 CA4th 378, 385, 75 CR2d

147 (peremptory challenge of juror based on juror's relevant personal values not improper even though those views may be founded in juror's religious beliefs).

The *Wheeler* rule originated in a criminal case. The prosecutor there excluded a number of African-American prospective jurors over the objection of the African-American defendant. The California Supreme Court held that it is illegal for a party to presume "that certain jurors are biased merely because they are members of an identifiable group distinguished on racial, religious, ethnic, or similar grounds." 22 C3d at 276. The court said it is still acceptable for members of such an identifiable group to be challenged peremptorily on grounds that do not rise to the level of a challenge for cause; however, those grounds must reasonably relate to the case, parties, or witnesses. The court rested its decision on the constitutional right to an impartial jury made up of a representative cross-section, based on the court's interpretation of Cal Const art I, §16.

The *Wheeler* rule applies both to the defense and prosecution in criminal cases. *People v Pagel* (1986) 186 CA3d Supp 1, 232 CR 104.

A party may challenge systematic exclusion of prospective jurors who are in a protected group even though the party is not a member of that group. *People v Johnson* (1989) 47 C3d 1194, 1217 n3, 255 CR 569 (African-American defendant objected to exclusion of African-American, Jewish, and Asian prospective jurors); *People v Garcia* (2000) 77 CA4th 1269, 1277, 92 CR2d 339 (gays and lesbians); see also CCP §204 barring exemption from jury service on basis of sexual orientation.

Procedures established by *Wheeler*. The *Wheeler* court established procedures for objecting to the discriminatory use of peremptory challenges. They are summarized here and discussed in more detail in §§6.29–6.31. Problems involved in the proof offered in these hearings are discussed in §6.30.

- Counsel must object in a timely fashion and request a hearing. See *People v Perez* (1996) 48 CA4th 1310, 56 CR2d 299. Counsel should make as complete a record of the circumstances as possible, including establishing that the persons excluded are members of a protected group. (The court used the wording "members of a cognizable group within the meaning of the representative cross-section rule." 22 C3d at 280.) Counsel making the objection must prove a prima facie case of discrimination to the satisfaction of the court. The requirements of proving a prima facie case are not clear; the *Wheeler* court discussed them in several ways. A prima facie case requires proof of "a strong likelihood that such persons are being challenged because of their group association rather than because of any specific bias." *People v Wheeler, supra*. The court also said that the trial court must "determine whether a reasonable inference arises that peremptory challenges are being used on the ground of group bias alone." 22 C3d at 281; *People v Garcia, supra*.

- The court must determine whether a prima facie case has been proven.
- If the court finds that a prima facie case has been proven, the burden shifts to opposing counsel to establish that the peremptory challenges in question were not based on group bias alone. Opposing counsel must satisfy the court that the peremptories in question were exercised on grounds "reasonably relevant to the particular case on trial or its parties or witnesses *i.e.,* for reasons of specific bias." *People v Wheeler* (1978) 22 C3d 258, 282, 148 CR 890. The nature of this burden is not completely clear, however, because the court also held that there is a presumption that peremptory challenges are exercised on constitutionally permissible grounds. 22 C3d at 278.
- The court, after taking evidence from both parties, rules. If the court finds that there was a *Wheeler* violation, the court must strike the entire jury panel and begin jury selection again with a new panel.

The *Wheeler* rule applies to civil cases. The *Wheeler* rule originated in a criminal case, but it also applies in civil trials. See *Di Donato v Santini* (1991) 232 CA3d 721, 283 CR 751. The *Di Donato* opinion relied on *Edmonson v Leesville Concrete Co.* (1991) 500 US 614, 114 L Ed 2d 660, 111 S Ct 2077, and *Holley v J & S Sweeping Co.* (1983) 143 CA3d 588, 192 CR 74.

The court in *Di Donato* based its ruling on both the Fourteenth Amendment to the United States Constitution and the right to a jury drawn from a representative cross-section of the community under Cal Const art I, §§7, 16, as implemented by CCP §§191, 197(a), 204. The court in *Edmonson* based its holding on the equal protection component of US Const amend V's due process clause.

The *Wheeler* rule applies to both parties in civil cases. *Di Donato v Santini, supra.*

Application of U.S. Constitution in criminal and civil cases. The *Wheeler* court based its holding on Cal Const art I, §16. 22 C3d at 276. The use of peremptory challenges to discriminate against members of certain protected groups also violates the equal protection clause of the Fourteenth Amendment to the United States Constitution. *Purkett v Elem* (1995) 514 US 765, 131 L Ed 2d 834, 115 S Ct 1769; *J.E.B. v Alabama ex rel T.B.* (1994) 511 US 127, 128 L Ed 2d 89, 114 S Ct 1419; *Batson v Kentucky* (1986) 476 US 79, 90 L Ed 2d 69, 106 S Ct 1712. This is true in both civil and criminal cases. See *J.E.B. v Alabama ex rel T.B., supra*; *Batson v Kentucky, supra.*

So far, the United States Supreme Court has found only race and gender to be protected under the Fourteenth Amendment for purposes of exercising peremptory challenges. See *Batson v Kentucky, supra* (race); *J.E.B. v Alabama ex rel T.B., supra* (gender). Based on dicta in *J.E.B. v Alabama ex rel T.B.* (1994) 511 US 127, 145, 128 L Ed 2d 89, 107, 114 S Ct 1419, however, it appears that ethnicity will be included in the future:

> Equal opportunity to participate in the fair administration of justice is fundamental to our democratic system. It not only furthers the goals of

the jury system. It reaffirms the promise of equality under the law that all citizens, regardless of race, *ethnicity,* or gender, have the chance to take part directly in our democracy. [Emphasis added.]

Some lower federal courts have extended *Batson* protection to include certain ethnic groups. See, *e.g., U.S. v Biaggi* (2d Cir 1988) 853 F2d 89 (Italian-Americans). For discussion of other groups that may be entitled to equal protection under the United States Constitution, see Bray, *Comment: Reaching the Final Chapter in the Story of Peremptory Challenges,* 40 UCLA L Rev 517 (1992).

The rule that prohibits discrimination in the exercise of peremptory challenges under the United States Constitution applies both to the defense and the prosecution in criminal cases and to both parties in civil cases, as under *Wheeler. Georgia v McCullum* (1992) 505 US 42, 120 L Ed 2d 33, 112 S Ct 2348 (criminal); *J.E.B. v Alabama ex rel T.B., supra* (civil). As under *Wheeler,* a party may challenge systematic exclusion of a juror even though the party is not a member of that group. *Powers v Ohio* (1991) 499 US 400, 113 L Ed 2d 411, 111 S Ct 1364. See also *U.S. v De Gross* (9th Cir 1992) 960 F2d 1433.

While the intent of both the United States and California Supreme Court decisions is to prohibit discrimination with regard to certain protected groups in the exercise of peremptory challenges, the procedures prescribed are quite different. See §6.28.

Trial court may make *Wheeler* objection sua sponte. The trial court may make a *Wheeler* objection sua sponte. *People v Lopez* (1991) 3 CA4th Supp 11, 5 CR2d 775.

§6.28   b. Proving Prima Facie Case

Definition of a prima facie case of protected group bias. To challenge group bias in the exercise of peremptory challenges, counsel must prove a prima facie case. *People v Wheeler* (1978) 22 C3d 258, 148 CR 890; *Batson v Kentucky* (1986) 476 US 79, 90 L Ed 2d 69, 106 S Ct 1712. A prima facie case under the California Constitution requires proof that certain prospective jurors were challenged because of their group association rather than because of any specific bias related to the case, parties, or witnesses. *People v Wheeler, supra.* Under the United States Constitution, counsel must prove "purposeful discrimination." *Batson v Kentucky* (1986) 476 US 79, 96, 90 L Ed 2d 69, 87, 106 S Ct 1712. The fact that counsel does not attempt to remove all members of a particular group is not dispositive as to whether, under the facts and circumstances, an inference of the exclusion on the basis of race is raised. See *Turner v Marshall* (9th Cir 1995) 63 F3d 807, overruled on other grounds in 182 F3d at 677. See also *People v Horton* (1995) 11 C4th 1068, 47 CR2d 516. In a criminal case, counsel may not establish a prima facie case simply by stating that all members of a cognizable class have been excluded. In one case, however, counsel made a prima facie case by showing that there was no apparent legitimate reason to excuse one of three African-American male jurors. *People v Gray* (2001) 87 CA4th 781, 788, 104 CR2d 848.

Whether the action is criminal or civil, the procedures for proving a prima facie case are the same under the California constitution. See *Di Donato v Santini* (1991) 232 CA3d 721, 733, 283 CR 751 (civil); *Holley v J & S Sweeping Co.* (1983) 143 CA3d 588, 592, 192 CR 74 (civil); *People v Wheeler, supra* (criminal). The procedures for showing a prima facie case under the federal constitution are somewhat different from those under the California Constitution. See *Purkett v Elem* (1995) 514 US 765, 131 L Ed 2d 834, 115 S Ct 1769. The text that follows applies under both the state and federal constitutions unless a difference is noted.

How to prove the objection. The usual practice in making the objection is for counsel either to rise and state that counsel wishes to make a *Wheeler* objection (legalspeak for an objection based on Cal Const art I, §16), or a *Wheeler-Elem* objection (meaning an objection based both on Cal Const art I, §16 and on the Fourteenth Amendment), or to ask to approach the bench to make the objection there. Some judges prefer having counsel approach the bench to avoid any possibility that a prospective juror may understand the grounds for the objection. Prospective jurors are excused from the courtroom during the hearing on the objection. Counsel should then:

- Object in a timely manner. Under *Wheeler*, this means that the objection must be made before the jury is empanelled, after the completion of jury selection. See *Di Donato v Santini* (1991) 232 CA3d 721, 740, 283 CR 751. See also *People v Gore* (1993) 18 CA4th 692, 22 CR2d 435 (jury selection not complete until alternates sworn, even though alternates selected after 12 regular trial jurors sworn to hear case). The United States Supreme Court looks to state requirements to determine the timeliness of these claims. In *Ford v Georgia* (1991) 498 US 411, 422, 112 L Ed 2d 935, 948, 111 S Ct 850, the court upheld a Georgia rule that required the objection to be raised after jury selection began, and before the jury was sworn.

- Set forth the grounds to establish a prima facie case, based on the state or United States Constitution, or on both constitutions. To establish a prima facie case of discriminatory use of peremptory challenges, the objecting party should:

    (1) Establish the identity of the persons excluded, and that they are members of a cognizable group within the meaning of the representative cross-section rule (under the California Constitution), or within the equal protection clause of the Fourteenth Amendment. It is not required that counsel ask the juror his or her race, etc., because this may antagonize the juror. If opposing counsel disagrees with counsel's unsworn statement concerning a juror's race, etc., counsel may wish to submit that information in a declaration. See *People v Motton* (1985) 39 C3d

596, 217 CR 416. In addition, the juror may have written the relevant information on the jury questionnaire completed at the beginning of jury service (assuming the jury commissioner form asks for such information; some do not, and some make such information optional). See CCP §205 on use of the jury commissioner's forms. Some trial judges routinely supply these forms to counsel for use during voir dire.

(2) Under the California Constitution, present proof establishing that there is a strong likelihood that such persons are being challenged because of their group association rather than because of any specific bias (see *People v Wheeler, supra*; see *People v Gray* (2001) 87 CA4th 781, 788, 104 CR2d 848). Under the United States Constitution, present proof of "purposeful" discrimination. *Purkett v Elem* (1995) 514 US 765, 131 L Ed 2d 834, 115 S Ct 1769. In *Wade v Terhune* (9th Cir 2000) 202 F3d 1190, the Ninth Circuit criticized California's continued use of the *Wheeler* "strong likelihood" test for establishing a prima facie case, holding that "the *Wheeler* standard, as currently used by California courts does not satisfy the constitutional requirements laid down in *Batson*." 202 F3d at 1197. The court found, however, that the *Wheeler* opinion had used both "strong likelihood" and *Batson*'s "reasonable inference" of bias to mean the same thing. 202 F3d at 1196.

- Present any other evidence that will support a prima facie case, *e.g.*:

    (1) The jurors in question share only one characteristic: membership in a protected group;

    (2) The party who excused the jurors asked them very few questions;

    (3) The party challenging the jury is a member of the same group as the excused jurors;

    (4) The victim or party who excused the jurors is of the same group as the remaining jurors;

    (5) Abuse of peremptories by the same attorney in other cases;

    (6) Remaining jurors do not contain members of the target group;

    (7) Opposing counsel did not challenge other similar jurors who were not in the target group; and

    (8) Any case authority similar to the facts of the case.

- Under the California Constitution, challenge the entire jury panel and request a new panel. See *People v Wheeler* (1978) 22 C3d 258, 148 CR 890. United States Supreme Court cases do not prescribe procedures, leaving them to the states. See *Batson v Kentucky* (1986) 476 US 79, 90 L Ed 2d 69, 106 S Ct 1712. Because *Wheeler* requires that the entire jury panel be challenged, this procedure is recommended. Compare *People v Smith* (1993) 21 CA4th 342, 25 CR2d 850 (counts tried by jury reversed because trial court's remedy was to just reseat excused juror after granting *Wheeler* motion), with *People v Williams* (1994) 26 CA4th Supp 1, 9, 31 CR2d 769 (juror may be reinstated when it is prosecution that made successful *Wheeler* challenge, and prosecution waives right to have new panel). Objecting only on *Wheeler* grounds has been deemed a waiver of the federal aspect of the claim on appeal. *People v McPeters* (1992) 2 C4th 1148, 1174, 9 CR2d 834.

Court may wish to make express finding and have complete record made. Although it is not required, appellate courts have urged trial courts to make an express finding about whether a prima facie case of discrimination in the exercise of challenges has been established. See, *e.g., People v Ferro* (1993) 21 CA4th 1, 25 CR2d 747. Once the prima facie case has been established, the burden of justification shifts to the other party to provide a race-neutral explanation for the peremptory challenge. See *People v Fuentes* (1991) 54 C3d 707, 286 CR 792. However, once a prima facie showing has been refuted, it is incumbent on the moving party to make a new prima facie showing with regard to any subsequent *Wheeler* motion pertaining to different jurors of the identified group from the venire. Subsequent *Wheeler* motions may be based on evidence presented in prior *Wheeler* motions to the extent necessary to establish a discriminatory pattern of peremptory challenges. *People v Irvin* (1996) 46 CA4th 1340, 54 CR2d 450. See also §6.29.

Some trial judges make a practice of having both sides present evidence, even when the court finds no prima facie case, to make a better record for appellate review.

§6.29   c. Rebutting Prima Facie Case

If the court finds that the party objecting has established a prima facie case, the opponent has the opportunity to rebut the charge. *People v Clair* (1992) 2 C4th 629, 652, 7 CR2d 564; *People v Johnson* (1989) 47 C3d 1194, 1216, 255 CR 569; *Di Donato v Santini* (1991) 232 CA3d 721, 740, 283 CR 751; *Holley v J & S Sweeping Co.* (1983) 143 CA3d 588, 592, 192 CR 74; *Purkett v Elem* (1995) 514 US 765, 131 L Ed 2d 834, 115 S Ct 1769.

Before the decision by the United States Supreme Court in *Purkett v Elem, supra,* California cases assumed that the state test (under Cal Const art I, §16) and the federal test (under US Const amend XIV) were the same for determining whether a cognizable group of jurors had been systematically excluded on the basis of an impermissible group bias. See *People v Crittenden* (1994) 9 C4th 83, 115, 36 CR2d 474. There appear to be differences, however, between the requirements of the United States Supreme Court in *Purkett v Elem, supra,* and those of the California cases.

The court in *Purkett v Elem, supra,* stated that there are three steps in making a ruling on a challenge of systematic exclusion: (1) the challenger must state a prima facie case; (2) the party who excluded the jurors must "come forward with a race-neutral explanation"; and (3) "if a race-neutral explanation is tendered, the trial court must then decide whether the opponent of the strike has proved purposeful racial discrimination." *Purkett v Elem, supra*.

In California, under *People v Wheeler* (1978) 22 C3d 258, 282, 148 CR 890, the second and third steps discussed above appear to be merged. Once the court finds that a prima facie case has been made, the burden shifts to the opponent to

> satisfy the court that he exercised such peremptories on grounds that were reasonably relevant to the particular case on trial or its parties or witnesses i.e., for reasons of specific bias as defined herein. If the court finds that the burden of justification is not sustained as to any of the questioned peremptory challenges, the presumption of their validity is rebutted.

The United States Supreme Court in *Purkett v Elem, supra*, defined the second step as shifting the burden of production

> to the proponent of the strike to come forward with a race-neutral explanation ... the second step of this process does not demand an explanation that is persuasive, or even plausible. 'at this [second] step of the inquiry, the issue is the facial validity of the prosecutor's explanation. Unless a discriminatory intent is inherent in the prosecutor's explanation, the reason offered will be deemed race-neutral.'"

It appears, therefore, that it may be more difficult to justify a strike under *Wheeler* than under *Elem* once the court finds that a prima facie case has been made, because California courts can decide that the justification is unreasonable at the second step. Under *Elem*, the justification necessary in the second step does not even have to be "plausible."

In a case decided based on *Wheeler, People v Johnson* (1989) 47 C3d 1194, 1217, 255 CR 569, the court discussed some subjective explanations that may justify why particular jurors were excused. These descriptions of jurors, which follow, would also appear to pass the second step test of *Elem*:

- Was very nervous;
- Looked tired;
- Unconventional lifestyle;
- Record of prior arrests;
- Complained of police harassment;
- Victim of crime;
- Relatives in law enforcement;
- Excessive respect for authority;
- Smiled or glared at one party or attorney;

- Body language (disapproving *People v Trevino* (1985) 39 C3d 667, 217 CR 652);
- Manner of answering questions (disapproving *People v Trevino, supra*);
- Appeared more friendly to the opposing party;
- Appeared to have a great rapport with opposing counsel;
- Was "weird";
- Did not appear to be willing to commit to promises to make a decision based on the evidence;
- Is a type of person that counsel is "unable to relate to";
- Was overweight and poorly groomed and, thus, possibly "not . . . in the mainstream of people's thinking"; and
- Did not come to court on two occasions when asked to by the clerk.

The California Supreme Court has held that a trial court erred in finding that a prosecutor's peremptory challenges against Hispanic prospective jurors did not show purposeful racial discrimination. The trial court failed to ask probing questions about the prosecutor's reasoning and to point out numerous inconsistencies between the prosecutor's explanation and the record of the jurors' actual responses in voir dire. When the prosecutor's stated reasons are unsupported by the record or inherently implausible, the trial court must question the prosecutor and make detailed findings. *People v Silva* (2001) 25 C4th 345, 384, 106 CR2d 93.

On how the *Wheeler-Elem* rule may be exploited by inventive counsel articulating subjective reasons for peremptory challenges, see Younger, *Unlawful Peremptory Challenges*, 7 Litig 23 (Fall 1980).

§6.30   d. Proof Currently Accepted at Hearing

The "proof" currently allowed at *Wheeler* hearings is frequently of questionable validity. Universal practice in California state courts appears to be for all proof to come from counsels' unsworn statements to the court. These presentations are commonly misnamed "offers of proof." Among a list of problems with these misnamed "offers of proof," we identify only the more obvious:

- Taking unsworn testimony from trial lawyers is not evidence or proof. *People v Belton* (1979) 23 C3d 516, 524, 153 CR 195.
- Requiring attorneys to state their thought processes concerning why they did something has definite intrusive work product implications. See CCP §2018(c); Pen C §1054.6 (work product).
- If the *Wheeler/Elem* procedures call for a hearing, then witnesses should be sworn and subject to cross-examination. See *People v Belton, supra* (testimony means statements made under oath); Evid C §773 (right to

cross-examine witness who has given direct examination). Certainly when appellate courts uniformly speak of burden of proof (see *Purkett v Elem* (1995) 514 US 765, 131 L Ed 2d 834, 115 S Ct 1769), a full and fair hearing is implied. See *U.S. v Thompson* (9th Cir 1987) 827 F2d 1254 (case reversed in which trial court heard prosecutor's reasons for challenging jurors without defense counsel present after defense made *Batson* objection). The fact that the third step in *Purkett v Elem, supra,* ascribes to counsel making the *Elem* objection the burden of proving purposeful discrimination may result in more future requests to examine and cross-examine witnesses in state courts.

- Because many peremptory challenges today in high profile cases are based on jury consultants' opinions, should they be called as witnesses?

§6.31   e. Determination by Court

Trial court should rule immediately. The court should take evidence from the parties and rule immediately on objections on the grounds of the systematic exclusion of a protected group, rather than deferring that process until the conclusion of voir dire. Delaying the determination could result in an inadequate evaluation and violate a party's right to a trial by a jury drawn from a representative cross-section of the community. See, *e.g., People v Fuentes* (1991) 54 C3d 707, 286 CR 792; *Di Donato v Santini* (1991) 232 CA3d 721, 283 CR 751.

Trial court's rulings. Under both the California and United States Constitutions, the trial court first must determine whether a prima facie case of improper exclusion has been made by the person objecting. The prima facie case is discussed in §6.28. The trial judge has broad discretion to distinguish valid reasons to exercise peremptory challenges from false excuses. *People v Wright* (1990) 52 C3d 367, 399, 276 CR 731 (defendant failed to establish prima facie case solely on observation that one challenged juror was member of defendant's racial group); *Johnson v Campbell* (9th Cir 1996) 92 F3d 951 (plaintiff failed to establish prima facie case of purposeful discrimination based on observation that juror excused by defense was "obviously gay"; but see *People v Garcia* (2000) 77 CA4th 1269, 92 CR2d 339, discussed in §6.27). If the court finds that a prima facie case has been made, the court asks the attorney who made the challenges to present reasons for having excused the jurors in question. See §6.29.

Under *People v Wheeler* (1978) 22 C3d 258, 282, 148 CR 890, if the court finds that a prima facie case has been established, the court, after hearing the rebuttal evidence, decides whether that evidence has met its burden of justification—that the peremptories were exercised "on grounds that were reasonably relevant to the particular case on trial or its parties or witnesses, i.e., for reasons of specific bias as defined herein."

Under *Purkett v Elem* (1995) 514 US 765, 131 L Ed 2d 834, 115 S

Ct 1769, if the court finds that a prima facie case of discrimination was established (the first step), the court then asks the opponent to give reasons for having made the challenges. After hearing those reasons, the court determines whether they were neutral (the second step). If the court finds that the reasons were neutral, it determines the persuasiveness of the justification and whether the opponent of the strike has carried the burden of proving purposeful discrimination (the third step). "[A]t that stage, implausible or fantastic justifications may (and probably will) be found to be pretexts for purposeful discrimination."

Remedy. Until recently, if the objection under *Wheeler* had been sustained, the trial court would have declared a mistrial, dismissing the entire venire and beginning jury selection with a new panel. *People v Wheeler* (1978) 22 C3d 258, 282, 148 CR 890 (states rule); *People v Smith* (1993) 21 CA4th 342, 25 CR2d 850 (counts tried by jury reversed because trial court's remedy after granting *Wheeler* motion was merely to reseat excused juror). This customary remedy, however, permitted lawyers who chose to engage in deliberate misconduct the opportunity to manipulate jury selection when they encountered a panel not to their liking. Paradoxically, the sole remedy could result in rewarding and encouraging the very party engaged in the misconduct.

In *People v Willis* (Apr. 4, 2002; S096349) 2002 Cal LEXIS 2011, the California Supreme Court reviewed this anomalous result and held that when a nonoffending party elects to waive or consent to proceed with jury selection in the face of a *Wheeler* violation, the trial court has discretion to invoke procedures and sanctions to mitigate the *Wheeler* errors and continue with the trial. In *Willis*, the defendant's lawyer was found to have excluded white jurors based on group bias. Relying on *Wheeler*, the defendant's lawyer then moved for a mistrial, asking that the entire venire be dismissed—a result he evidently desired from the outset of jury selection. The prosecution objected to a mistrial on the grounds that there were other remedies available to the court that were less drastic and costly and that would not, in effect, benefit the lawyer committing the misconduct. The supreme court agreed, holding that giving the trial judge discretion to deal with the problem without declaring a mistrial was not constitutionally prohibited by *Wheeler* and that, in California, a trial judge has discretion to fashion appropriate alternative remedies that would not require a mistrial or dismissal of the venire. The court gave examples of various procedures for passing on *Wheeler* objections and sanctions that might be invoked by the trial court when confronted by *Wheeler* misconduct (after waiver or consent by the innocent party), such as requiring sidebar conferences in advance of peremptory challenges or ordering that counsel privately advise each other of intended peremptory challenges so that objections, when necessary, can be made to the court outside the presence of the jury; reseating the challenged juror; disallowing the peremptory challenge; or allotting additional peremptory challenges to the innocent party. Monetary sanctions are also proper. See *People v Williams* (1994) 26 CA4th Supp 1, 31 CR2d 769 (using sidebar for *Wheeler* objections); but note *People v Harris* (1992) 10 CA4th

672, 12 CR2d 758 (conducting all peremptory challenges in chambers violates defendant's right to public trial).

§6.32   f. Appellate Review

When the trial court finds no *Wheeler* violation, the appellate court must give great deference to the trial court's ruling. *People v Davenport* (1995) 11 C4th 1171, 47 CR2d 800; *People v Dunn* (1995) 40 CA4th 1039, 47 CR2d 638; *People v Johnson* (1989) 47 C3d 1194, 1221, 255 CR 569. However, if the appellate court rules that *Wheeler* error occurred (see *People v Wheeler* (1978) 22 C3d 258, 148 CR 890), it is prejudicial per se error; the conviction or judgment, therefore, must be reversed. 22 C3d at 283; *Holley v J & S Sweeping Co.* (1983) 143 CA3d 588, 594, 192 CR 74.

A different procedure is followed when the error consists of failing to recognize that a prima facie case was made in the trial court and not requiring an explanation of challenges. In that event, the case must be remanded to the trial court to allow the prosecutor to explain the reasons for excluding the prospective jurors in question. *Batson v Kentucky* (1986) 476 US 79, 90 L Ed 2d 69, 106 S Ct 1712. Although the California Supreme Court has not absolutely rejected or endorsed that remedy, it declined to adopt it in two cases in which the lapse of time made it unrealistic to expect the prosecution to recall the details of the case or the court to assess the manner in which the challenges had been exercised. See *People v Snow* (1987) 44 C3d 216, 242 CR 477 (lapse of six years); *People v Hall* (1983) 35 C3d 161, 197 CR 71 (lapse of three years).

Paradoxically, looking back at this area, we are troubled by the present lack of fair trial constitutional guaranties in the presentation of proof at hearings that have as their objective fair trial constitutional guaranties. See §6.30.

VI. GROUNDS FOR OBJECTING TO IMPROPER VOIR DIRE QUESTIONS

A. Question Attempts to Indoctrinate Jurors on Law

§6.33   1. Nature of Objection

Counsel should consider moving in limine at the pre-voir dire conference (with a court reporter present) to exclude all areas of inquiry or questions relating to applicable propositions of law unless opposing counsel makes a showing that the purpose of such inquiry or questions is not solely related to indoctrinating the jury.

Questions concerning the pleadings or applicable law may be objectionable under CCP §222.5 and Cal Rules of Ct App Div I, §8(f) (civil) or §8.5(d) (criminal). A question may be objectionable if it includes a correct statement of the law but is taken out of context. (It may also be objectionable as a misstatement of the law (see §6.35) if it is a correct statement of the law but leaves out essential elements.)

In exercising discretion, a trial judge may restrict voir dire examination from being used to preindoctrinate the jurors on one attorney's view of the law to ensure that such questioning does not mislead the jurors. From counsel's viewpoint, any tactical advantage gained by preindoctrinating the jurors on a rule of law is likely to be dispelled by objections and appropriate admonitions. To ferret out bias, however, it is often desirable for counsel to remind prospective jurors of key legal principles such as reasonable doubt.

§6.34   2. Stating the Objection

> Objection, Your Honor. _ _[The purpose of the question is to pre-indoctrinate the jurors _ _[on counsel's view of the law/of what is not the law]_]_ _. _ _[The law will come from the Court, not counsel]_ _.

B. Question Based on Incorrect Statement of Law

§6.35   1. Nature of Objection

In civil or criminal actions, jury voir dire questions on propositions of law are often vulnerable to the objection that the proposition stated is not legally correct. Like questions that attempt to indoctrinate jurors on the law, a question based on an incorrect statement of the law may be objectionable under CCP §222.5 or Cal Rules of Ct App Div I, §8(f) (civil) or §8.5(d) (criminal). Although a question that attempts to indoctrinate jurors on the law is usually a correct statement of law that is taken out of context (see §6.33), questions that incorrectly state the law are usually missing essential elements. By pointing out the missing legal element in the examiner's statement of the law and by objecting, opposing counsel can convey the impression that the examiner was trying to mislead the prospective jurors.

Serious misstatement of the law may be a ground for a new trial or reversal on appeal if it is not remedied at the time of questioning. See *Kelly v Trans Globe Travel Bureau, Inc.* (1976) 60 CA3d 195, 203, 131 CR 488. In a criminal case, for example, it is improper to ask whether a prospective juror will follow an instruction that, for the jury to acquit the defendant, it is only "necessary for the defendant to establish evidence sufficient to raise a reasonable doubt in your mind as to the truth of the charge." *People v Tibbetts* (1929) 102 CA 787, 789, 283 P 830. This question is defective in omitting essential aspects of the prosecution's burden of proof, *e.g.*, that reasonable doubt must be determined from all the evidence rather than just the evidence produced by the defendant. See Pen C §1096.

One way to ensure that the law will be properly stated is to ask the judge at the pre-voir dire conference to read the relevant BAJI or CALJIC instructions during the voir dire examination and ask the prospective jurors whether they will apply the law as instructed by the trial court whether they agree with it or not. See *People v Williams* (1981) 29 C3d 392, 410, 174 CR 317 (proper to ask prospective jurors to promise to apply law as instructed whether they agree with it or not). See also *People v Tolbert* (1969) 70 C2d 790, 812, 76 CR 445. It is improper to ask prospective jurors whether they agree with a law. Such a question is argumentative. See *People v Mitchell* (1964) 61 C2d 353, 366, 38 CR 726. However, a well-crafted, open-ended question may invoke an expression of dissatisfaction with a law that would trigger a peremptory or cause challenge.

§6.36   2. Stating the Objection

> Objection, Your Honor. The question does not correctly state the law and seeks to precommit the juror to counsel's view of the law.

C. Question Asks Jurors to Prejudge Evidence

§6.37   1. Nature of Objection

Voir dire questions are improper if they call for a promise that is inconsistent with a juror's duty to hear the evidence with an open mind and to refrain from forming or expressing an opinion until the case is submitted for a verdict. See CCP §222.5; Cal Rules of Ct App Div I, §§8(f) (civil), 8.5(d) (criminal).

Prospective jurors cannot be asked to state their reactions to particular evidence or to promise to give weight to the testimony of a particular witness. *People v Warner* (1905) 147 C 546, 552, 82 P 196 (improper to ask whether prospective juror would give weight to testimony of defendant that "was reasonable, not contradicted, and not impeached"). See *People v Fowler* (1918) 178 C 657, 174 P 892 (improper to ask whether juror could give same credit to defendant's testimony as to testimony of any other witness, considering defendant's interest in result; question omits other considerations affecting credibility). Jurors can be asked, however, whether they will exclude improper factors from consideration in weighing testimony or deciding on the verdict.

§6.38   2. Stating the Objection

> Objection, Your Honor. The question asks the juror to _ _[prejudge the evidence/precommit to evidence]_ _.

D. Question Introduces Prejudicial Matter

§6.39   1. Nature of Objection

Asking a prospective juror a question containing or suggesting inadmissible and prejudicial matter is not only improper but also constitutes misconduct. It is misconduct to introduce during jury voir dire examination the kinds of improper matters that give rise to misconduct when introduced in the opening statement, examination of witnesses, or closing argument (see §§29.5-29.7). These matters include:

- *Religious beliefs.* It is generally improper to ask a prospective juror about religious beliefs. See Cal Const art I, §4. *Estate of Malavasi* (1929) 96 CA 204, 210, 273 P 1097. But see *Smith v Smith* (1935) 7 CA2d 271, 46 P2d 232 (prospective juror's religious beliefs on divorce and remarriage are proper topics for inquiry in action to enforce property settlement agreement when defense was molestation).

- *Insurance.* It is improper to ask repeated questions about insurance to convey the impression that the defendant is insured against liability for negligence. *Swift v Winkler* (1957) 148 CA2d 927, 307 P2d 666. See also Evid C §1155; *Scally v PG&E* (1972) 23 CA3d 806, 813, 100 CR 501.

- *Financial interest in insurance company.* An unresolved issue that may be appropriate for a motion in limine is whether counsel may ask prospective jurors whether they or family members have a financial interest in any insurance company. Compare *Hart v Wielt* (1970) 4 CA3d 224, 230, 84 CR 220 (juror's financial interest in insurance company may be ground for disqualification, but counsel should not leave impression with prospective jurors that defendant is insured), with *Scally v PG&E, supra* (naive to suggest that jurors would not assume that party is insured).

If the misconduct seems so prejudicial as to eliminate any possibility of selecting an impartial jury from the prospective jurors who are then in the courtroom, counsel may decide that it is appropriate to move for a mistrial.

For further discussion of attorney misconduct, see §§29.2-29.20. On remedies for misconduct, see §§29.10-29.20. On misconduct of jurors in concealing bias, discovery of the misconduct during trial, remedies (including motion for mistrial), and waiver, see §§29.33-29.35.

§6.40   2. Stating the Objection

> Objection, Your Honor. Counsel's question introduces inadmissible matter and constitutes misconduct. I _ _[*request that the prospective jurors be admonished to disregard it/move for a mistrial on the ground that the prejudicial effect of this misconduct makes a fair trial now impossible*]_ _.

E. Question Improper if Not Related to Challenge for Cause (Special Rule for Criminal Cases)

§6.41   1. Nature of Objection

In criminal cases, the examination of prospective jurors "shall be conducted only in aid of the exercise of challenges for cause." CCP §223. See §§6.16-6.23.

The trial court may ask the prospective jurors broad questions about their impartiality and their willingness to apply the applicable law as instructed. See, *e.g.,* Cal Rules of Ct App Div I, §8.5(b).

§6.42   2. Stating the Objection

Objection, Your Honor. The question is not related to any ground of challenge for cause.

§6.43   3. Response to Objection: Connect Question to Basis for Challenge

If the objection is made, the burden is on counsel who asked the question to inform the court of the question's relevance to a challenge for cause. See CCP §223 (criminal). Examples of questions relevant to challenges for cause may be found in the decisions cited in §§29.35–29.44 (juror misconduct to conceal information relevant to challenge for cause in answering voir dire question).

Reasonable inquiry into specific legal prejudice on controversial matters material to the trial must be permitted as a basis for a challenge for cause. *People v Balderas* (1985) 41 C3d 144, 183, 222 CR 184. See also *People v Fuentes* (1985) 40 C3d 629, 638, 221 CR 440. It is also proper to ask prospective jurors for their promise to apply the law as instructed by the trial court whether they agree with it or not. See *People v Tolbert* (1969) 70 C2d 790, 812, 76 CR 445. See also CCP §222.5.

If counsel is not sure that these questions will be allowed or wants to restrict or preclude opposing counsel's questions, counsel should discuss them at the pre-voir dire conference and seek a ruling on the record at that time.

§6.44   F. Question Prohibited by Judicial Administrative Standards

Certain types of voir dire questions are prohibited by the Standards of Judicial Administration in both civil and criminal cases. See Cal Rules of Ct App Div I, §§8(f) (civil), 8.5(d) (criminal). Except in unusual circumstances, counsel may not ask questions that (Cal Rules of Ct App Div I, §§8(f), 8.5(d)):

- Precondition the prospective jurors to a particular result;
- Comment on the personal lives and families of the parties or their attorneys;
- Are related to the pleadings, the applicable law, or the meaning of particular words and phrases; or
- Are related to the comfort of the jurors.

§6.45 G. Question in Improper Form

Most objections to the form of questions to witnesses (*e.g.,* that the question is ambiguous, compound, or argumentative) can also be made to the form of questions asked of prospective jurors during voir dire examination. See, *e.g., People v Mitchell* (1964) 61 C2d 353, 366, 38 CR 726 (argumentative question).

The trial judge has discretion to permit leading questions. See *People v Ah Lee Doon* (1893) 97 C 171, 31 P 933. Hypothetical questions may be allowed (see *Kramm v Stockton Elec. R.R. Co.* (1913) 22 CA 737, 746, 136 P 523), but the judge has discretion to exclude hypotheticals that are unfocused or abstract (see *People v Williams* (1981) 29 C3d 392, 410, 174 CR 317).

On objections to the form of questions, see chaps 7–16.

VII. HOW TO OBJECT TO IMPROPER VOIR DIRE EXAMINATION

§6.46 A. Objection to Examination by Judge

Counsel must object in a timely fashion to any improper voir dire examination by the court. Failure to make a timely objection will preclude a subsequent attack on appeal. *Rousseau v West Coast House Movers* (1967) 256 CA2d 878, 64 CR 655. If allowed, this type of objection should be made at sidebar. For detailed discussion of the proper procedure for objecting at trial, see chap 4.

The following examination by the court may be properly objected to by counsel:

- The judge attempts to improperly indoctrinate and precondition the jury in its determination of facts (see *Kelly v Trans Globe Travel Bureau, Inc.* (1976) 60 CA3d 195, 131 CR 488); and

- The judge improperly personally selects the jury foreperson (see *Dorshkind v Harry N. Koff Agency, Inc.* (1976) 64 CA3d 302, 134 CR 344).

For other examples, see §§29.21–29.27.

Reversible error will only be found, however, if there is a showing of prejudice. See, *e.g., People v Hernandez* (1979) 94 CA3d 715, 156 CR 572 (judicial error in not allowing counsel sufficient time for voir dire was not prejudicial, because counsel did not exercise all peremptory challenges allowed). See also CCP §222.5 (time limits cannot be unreasonable in civil cases).

§6.47 B. Objection to Examination by Counsel; "Speaking Objections"

An objection should be made to any type of question that attempts to inject improper considerations or argument into the case (*e.g.,* settlement negotiations, hatred of attorneys, possibility of insurance coverage, racial bias, prior felonies).

Counsel should stifle the urge to object to improper but harmless questions. Needless objections and continuous interruptions of the examination frustrate and antagonize the judge and jurors and hurt the client.

Counsel objecting to an improper voir dire question must satisfy the following two requirements to preserve the right to argue error on appeal. Counsel must:

- Make a timely and proper objection. See Evid C §353; *Neumann v Bishop* (1976) 59 CA3d 451, 468 n3, 130 CR 786; *Hart v Wielt* (1970) 4 CA3d 224, 84 CR 220. See also *Leibman v Curtis* (1955) 138 CA2d 222, 291 P2d 542 (counsel who makes position clear in timely manner reserves automatic exception and need not repeat objection to court's ruling or seek to have it reversed).

- Request that a curative admonition be given. *Sabella v Southern Pac. Co.* (1969) 70 C2d 311, 318, 74 CR 534.

If the damage done is irremediable, a mistrial must be considered.

If the subject of the objection is crucial, counsel should not argue it in front of the jury but instead request permission for a sidebar conference with a court reporter present. Because the proper manner of exercising objections now varies from court to court, counsel should check local rules and ascertain the judge's preference on this matter before jury selection begins. The following are examples of typical objections that counsel might make:

> Objection, Your Honor. Counsel's question constitutes improper voir dire. May we approach the bench?

> Objection, Your Honor. This area was addressed in chambers.

> Objection, Your Honor. I object to counsel's question as argumentative.

The request for a curative admonition may be stated along the following lines:

> I also ask that the court inform the jury to disregard the question and any insinuations that may be drawn from it and that counsel be warned to end this line of questioning.

Although "speaking objections" are not textbook practice, they are often used by counsel in retaliation for an improper question. For example, instead of objecting to a question as "argumentative," counsel using a speaking objection might say:

> Your Honor, I object to counsel's question. Counsel is starting an early final argument.

Speaking objections are usually not allowed by local rules.

§6.48   C. Motion for Mistrial

When opposing counsel engages in highly improper voir dire questioning, counsel may consider making a motion for mistrial. A mistrial is rarely necessary, however, and such a motion will be granted only when the questions are particularly outrageous and the bias created cannot be cured by an admonition. See *Sabella v Southern Pac. Co.* (1969) 70 C2d 311, 74 CR 534; *Neumann v Bishop* (1976) 59 CA3d 451, 130 CR 786.

On motion for mistrial because of juror misconduct occurring during the selection process, see §29.35.

§6.49   VIII. WAIVER OF OBJECTION

Unless counsel objects to unreasonable limits placed on voir dire examination before the jury is sworn, the objection is waived. *Bly-Magee v Budget Rent-A-Car Corp.* (1994) 24 CA4th 318, 324, 29 CR2d 330; *Rousseau v West Coast House Movers* (1967) 256 CA2d 878, 881, 64 CR 655. Such an objection should be made on the record as early as possible out of the jury's hearing.

Objections to voir dire questions are waived unless made as soon as practicable after the question is asked. A party may not sit silently through the trial, gambling on the verdict, and then raise the objection only after suffering a defeat. *Richmond v Moore* (1930) 103 CA 173, 178, 284 P 681 (plaintiff's voir dire improperly revealed that defendant was insured; no objection until motion for new trial after unfavorable verdict).

On waiver of challenge for juror misconduct occurring during the selection process, see §29.35.

§6.50   IX. ISSUES ON APPEAL

In civil cases, reversals based on voir dire rulings usually depend on whether substantial prejudice results from the ruling. See, *e.g., Swift v Winkler* (1957) 148 CA2d 927, 307 P2d 666 (reversible error for trial judge to fail to sustain objections to repeated questions implying that defendants were insured). In criminal cases, CCP §223 states that the

> trial court's exercise of its discretion in the manner in which voir dire is conducted shall not cause any conviction to be reversed unless the exercise of that discretion has resulted in a miscarriage of justice, as specified in Section 13 of Article VI of the California Constitution.

On the standard of review of alleged error under *People v Wheeler* (1978) 22 C3d 258, 283, 148 CR 890, see §6.32.

X. SELECTED RULES OF COURT AND STATUTES

A. Civil

§6.51   1. California Rules of Court

- California Rules of Court 228, on the examination of prospective jurors, states:

    > This rule applies to all civil jury trials. To select a fair and impartial jury, the trial judge shall examine the prospective jurors orally, or by written questionnaire, or by both methods. The Juror Questionnaire for Civil Cases (Judicial Council form MC-001) may be used. Upon completion of the initial examination, the trial judge shall permit counsel for each party who so requests to submit additional questions which the judge shall put to the jurors. Upon request of counsel, the trial judge shall permit counsel to supplement the judge's examination by oral and direct questioning of any of the prospective jurors. The scope of the additional questions or supplemental examination shall be within reasonable limits prescribed by the trial judge in the judge's sound discretion.
    >
    > The court may, upon stipulation by counsel for all parties appearing in the action, permit counsel to examine the prospective jurors outside a judge's presence.

- California Rules of Court App Div I, §8(a) states:

    > (1) The examination of prospective jurors in a civil case may be oral, or by written questionnaire, or by both methods, and should include all questions necessary to ensure the selection of a fair and impartial jury. The Juror Questionnaire for Civil Cases (Judicial Council form MC-001) may be used. During any supplemental examination conducted by counsel for the parties, the trial judge should permit liberal and probing examination calculated to discover possible bias or prejudice with regard to the circumstances of the particular case.
    >
    > (2) When counsel requests to be allowed to conduct a supplemental voir dire examination, the trial judge should permit counsel to conduct such examination without requiring prior submission of the questions to the judge unless a particular counsel has demonstrated unwillingness to avoid the type of examination proscribed in subdivision (f) of this section. In exercising his or her sound discretion as to the form and subject matter of voir dire questions, the trial judge should consider, among other criteria: (a) any unique or complex elements, legal or factual, in the case, and (b) the individual responses or conduct of jurors which may evince attitudes inconsistent with suitability to serve as a fair and impartial juror in the particular case. Questions regarding personal relationships of jurors should be relevant to the subject matter of the case.

- California Rules of Court App Div I, §8(b), on the pre-voir dire conference, states:

Before the examination the trial judge should, outside the prospective jurors' hearing and with a court reporter present, confer with counsel, at which time specific questions or areas of inquiry may be proposed that the judge in his discretion may inquire of the jurors. Thereafter the judge should advise counsel of the questions or areas to be inquired into during the examination and the voir dire procedure. He should also obtain from counsel the names of the witnesses whom counsel then plan to call at trial and a brief outline of the nature of the case, including any alleged injuries or damages and, in an eminent domain action, the respective contentions of the parties concerning the value of the property taken and any alleged severance damages and special benefits.

- California Rules of Court App Div I, §8(c), on the examination of jurors, states:

  (c) Except as otherwise provided in (d), the trial judge's examination of prospective jurors should include the following areas of inquiry and any other matters affecting their qualifications to serve as jurors in the case:

  (1) *(To the entire jury panel after it has been sworn and seated)* I am now going to question the prospective jurors who are seated in the jury box concerning their qualifications to serve as jurors in this case. All members of this jury panel. however, should pay close attention to my questions, making note of the answers you would give if these questions were put to you personally. If and when any other member of this panel is called to the jury box, he will be asked to give his answers to these questions.

  (2) In the trial of this case the parties are entitled to have a fair, unbiased and unprejudiced jury. If there is any reason why any of you might be biased or prejudiced in any way, you must disclose such reason when you are asked to do so. It is your duty to make this disclosure.

  (3) *(In lengthy trials)* This trial will likely take _____ days to complete, but it may take longer. Will any of you find it difficult or impossible to participate for this period of time?

  (4) The nature of this case is as follows: (Describe briefly, including any alleged injuries or damages and, in an eminent domain action, the name of the condemning agency, a description of the property being acquired and the particular public project or purpose of the condemnation.)

  (5) The parties to this case and their respective attorneys are: (Specify.) Have you heard of or been acquainted with any of these parties or their attorneys?

  (6) During the trial of this case, the following witnesses may be called to testify on behalf of the parties. These witnesses are: (Do not identify the party on whose behalf the witnesses might be called.) Have any of you heard of or been otherwise acquainted with any of the witnesses just named? The parties are not required

and might not wish to call all of these witnesses, and they may later find it necessary to call other witnesses.

(7) Have any of you heard of, or have you any knowledge of, the facts or events in this case? Are any of you familiar with the place(s) or property mentioned in this case?

(8) Do any of you believe that a case of this nature should not be brought into court for determination by a jury?

(9) Do any of you have any belief or feeling toward any of the parties, attorneys or witnesses that might be regarded as a bias or prejudice for or against any of them? Do you have any interest, financial or otherwise, in the outcome of this case?

(10) Have any of you served as a juror or witness involving any of these parties, attorneys or witnesses?

(11) Have any of you served as a juror in any other case? (If so, was it a civil or criminal case?) You must understand that there is a basic difference between a civil case and a criminal case. In a criminal case a defendant must be found guilty beyond a reasonable doubt; in a civil case such as this, you need only find that the evidence you accept as the basis of your decision is more convincing, and thus has the greater probability of truth than the contrary evidence.

In the following questions I will be using the terms "family", "close friend", and "anyone with whom you have a significant personal relationship." The term "anyone with whom you have a significant personal relationship" means a domestic partner, life partner, former spouse, or anyone with whom you have an influential or intimate relationship that you would characterize as important.

(12) *(If a corporation or "company" is a party)*
(i) Have you, or to your knowledge, any member of your family, a close friend, or anyone with whom you have a significant personal relationship, ever had any connection with, or any dealings with, the _____ corporation (or company)?

(ii) Are any of you or them related to any officer, director or employee of this corporation (or company) to your knowledge?

(iii) Do you or they own any stock or other interest in this corporation (or company) to your knowledge?

(iv) Have you or they ever done business as a corporation or company?

(v) The fact that a corporation (or company) is a party in this case must not affect your deliberations or your verdict. You may not discriminate between corporations (or companies) and natural individuals. Both are persons in the eyes of the law and both are entitled to have a fair and impartial trial based upon the same legal standards. Do any of you have any belief or feeling for or against corporations (or companies) that might prevent you from being a completely fair and impartial juror in this case?

(13) Have you, or to your knowledge, any member of your family, a close friend, or anyone with whom you have a significant personal relationship, ever sued anyone, or presented a claim against anyone, in connection with a matter similar to this case? (If so, did the matter terminate satisfactorily so far as you were concerned?)

(14) Has anyone ever sued, or presented a claim against you, or to your knowledge, against any member of your family, a close friend, or anyone with whom you have a significant personal relationship, in connection with a matter similar to this case? (If so, did the matter terminate satisfactorily so far as you were concerned?)

(15) Are you, or to your knowledge, any member of your family, a close friend, or anyone with whom you have a significant personal relationship, presently involved in a lawsuit of any kind?

(16) *(When appropriate)* It may appear that one or more of the parties, attorneys or witnesses come from a particular national, racial or religious group (or may have a life style different than your own). Would this in any way affect your judgment or the weight and credibility you would give to their testimony?

(17) Have you, or to your knowledge, any member of your family, a close friend, or anyone with whom you have a significant personal relationship, had any special training in: (Describe briefly the fields of expertise involved in the case, such as law, medicine, nursing or any other branch of the healing arts.)

(18) *(In personal injury or wrongful death cases)*
   (i) You may be called upon in this case to award damages for personal injury, pain and suffering. Do any of you have any religious or other belief that pain and suffering are not real or any belief that would prevent you from awarding damages for pain and suffering if liability for them is established?
   (ii) Are there any of you who would not employ a medical doctor?
   (iii) Have you, or to your knowledge, any member of your family, a close friend, or anyone with whom you have a significant personal relationship, ever engaged in investigating or otherwise acting upon claims for damages?
   (iv) Have you or they, to your knowledge, ever been in an accident with the result that a claim for personal injuries or for substantial property damage was made by someone involved in that accident, whether or not a lawsuit was filed?
   (v) Have you or they, to your knowledge, ever been involved in an accident in which someone died or received serious personal injuries whether or not a lawsuit was filed?
   (vi) Are there any of you who do not drive an automobile? (If so, have you ever driven an automobile, and if you have, give your reason for not presently driving.) Does your spouse, or anyone with whom you have a significant personal relationship, drive an automobile? (If that person does not drive but did so in the past, why did they stop?)

(vii) Plaintiff (or cross-complainant) _____ is claiming injuries to his (or her): (Describe briefly the general nature of the alleged injuries.) Do you, or to your knowledge, does any member of your family, a close friend, or anyone with whom you have a significant personal relationship, suffer from similar injuries? Have you or they, to your knowledge, suffered from similar injuries in the past? (If so, would that fact affect your point of view in this case to the extent that you might not be able to render a completely fair and impartial verdict?)

(19) It is important that I have your assurance that you will, without reservation, follow my instructions and rulings on the law and will apply that law to this case. To put it somewhat differently, whether you approve or disapprove of the court's rulings or instructions, it is your solemn duty to accept as correct these statements of the law. You may not substitute your own idea of what you think the law ought to be. Will all of you follow the law as given to you by me in this case?

(20) Each of you should now state your:
(i) Name;
(ii) Children's ages and the number of children, if any;
(iii) Occupation;
(iv) Occupational history; and
(v) Present employer.

And for your spouse or anyone with whom you have a significant personal relationship, their:
(vi) Names;
(vii) Occupations;
(viii) Occupational histories; and
(ix) Present employers.

Please begin with juror number one.

(21) Do you know of any other reason, or has anything occurred during this question period, that might make you doubtful you would be a completely fair and impartial juror in this case? If there is, it is your duty to disclose the reason at this time.

- California Rules of Court App Div I, §8(e), on the subsequent conference and examination of jurors, states:

    Upon completion of the initial examination and upon request of counsel for any party that the trial judge put additional questions to the jurors, the judge should, outside the jurors' hearing and with a court reporter present, confer with counsel, at which time additional questions or areas of inquiry may be proposed that the judge may inquire of the jurors.

- California Rules of Court App Div I, §8(f), on improper questions, states:

    When any counsel examines the prospective jurors, the trial judge should not permit counsel to attempt to precondition the prospective jurors to a particular result or allow counsel to comment on the personal lives and families of the parties or their attorneys. Nor should he allow counsel to question the jurors concerning the pleadings, the applicable law, the meaning of particular words and phrases, or the comfort of the jurors, except in unusual circumstances, where, in the trial judge's sound discretion, such questions become necessary to insure the selection of a fair and impartial jury.

§6.52   2. Code of Civil Procedure

- Code of Civil Procedure §191, on state policy regarding jury service, states:

> The Legislature recognizes that trial by jury is a cherished constitutional right, and that jury service is an obligation of citizenship.
>
> It is the policy of the State of California that all persons selected for jury service shall be selected at random from the population of the area served by the court; that all qualified persons have an equal opportunity, in accordance with this chapter, to be considered for jury service in the state and an obligation to serve as jurors when summoned for that purpose; and that it is the responsibility of jury commissioners to manage all jury systems in an efficient, equitable, and cost-effective manner, in accordance with this chapter.

- Code of Civil Procedure §197, on sources for the selection of jurors, states:

> (a) All persons selected for jury service shall be selected at random, from a source or sources inclusive of a representative cross section of the population of the area served by the court. Sources may include, in addition to other lists, customer mailing lists, telephone directories, or utility company lists.
>
> (b) The list of registered voters and the Department of Motor Vehicles' list of licensed drivers and identification cardholders resident within the area served by the court, are appropriate source lists for selection of jurors. These two source lists, when substantially purged of duplicate names, shall be considered inclusive of a representative cross section of the population within the meaning of subdivision (a).
>
> (c) The Department of Motor Vehicles shall furnish the jury commissioner of each county with the current list of the names, addresses, and other identifying information of persons residing in the county who are age 18 years or older and who are holders of a current driver's license or identification card issued pursuant to Article 3 (commencing with Section 12800) of, or Article 5 (commencing with Section 13000) of, Chapter 1 of Division 6 of the Vehicle Code. The conditions under which these lists shall be compiled semiannually shall be determined by the director, consistent with any rules which may be adopted by the Judicial Council. This service shall be provided by the Department of Motor Vehicles pursuant to Section 1812 of the Vehicle Code. The jury commissioner shall not disclose the information

furnished by the Department of Motor Vehicles pursuant to this section to any person, organization, or agency.

- Code of Civil Procedure §204, on exemption from jury service, states:

    (a) No eligible person shall be exempt from service as a trial juror by reason of occupation, race, color, religion, sex, national origin, or economic status, or sexual orientation, or for any other reason. No person shall be excused from service as a trial juror except as specified in subdivision (b).

    (b) An eligible person may be excused from jury service only for undue hardship, upon themselves or upon the public, as defined by the Judicial Council.

- Code of Civil Procedure §205, on juror questionnaires, states:

    (a) If a jury commissioner requires a person to complete a questionnaire, the questionnaire shall ask only questions related to juror identification, qualification, and ability to serve as a prospective juror.

    (b) Except as ordered by the court, the questionnaire referred to in subdivision (a) shall be used solely for qualifying prospective jurors, and for management of the jury system, and not for assisting in the courtroom voir dire process of selecting trial jurors for specific cases.

    (c) The court may require a prospective juror to complete such additional questionnaires as may be deemed relevant and necessary for assisting in the voir dire process or to ascertain whether a fair cross section of the population is represented as required by law, if such procedures are established by local court rule.

    (d) The trial judge may direct a prospective juror to complete additional questionnaires as proposed by counsel in a particular case to assist the voir dire process.

- Code of Civil Procedure §222.5, on examining prospective jurors in civil trials, states:

    To select a fair and impartial jury in civil jury trials, the trial judge shall examine the prospective jurors. Upon completion of the judge's initial examination, counsel for each party shall have the right to examine, by oral and direct questioning, any of the prospective jurors in order to enable counsel to intelligently exercise both peremptory challenges and challenges for cause. During any examination conducted by counsel for the parties, the trial judge should permit liberal and probing examination calculated to discover bias or prejudice with regard to the circumstances of the particular case. The fact that a topic has been included in the judge's examination should not preclude additional nonrepetitive or nonduplicative questioning in the same area by counsel.

    The scope of the examination conducted by counsel shall be within reasonable limits prescribed by the trial judge in the judge's sound discretion. In exercising his or her sound discretion as to the form and subject matter of voir dire questions, the trial judge should consider, among other criteria, any unique or complex elements, legal or factual, in the case and the individual responses or conduct of jurors which may evince attitudes inconsistent with suitability to serve as a fair and impartial juror in the particular case. Specific unreasonable or arbitrary time limits shall not be imposed.

The trial judge should permit counsel to conduct voir dire examination without requiring prior submission of the questions unless a particular counsel engages in improper questioning. For purposes of this section, an "improper question" is any question which, as its dominant purpose, attempts to precondition the prospective jurors to a particular result, indoctrinate the jury, or question the prospective jurors concerning the pleadings or the applicable law. A court should not arbitrarily or unreasonably refuse to submit reasonable written questionnaires, the contents of which are determined by the court in its sound discretion, when requested by counsel.

In civil cases, the court may, upon stipulation by counsel for all the parties appearing in the action, permit counsel to examine the prospective jurors, outside a judge's presence.

- Code of Civil Procedure §225, on challenges, states:

    A challenge is an objection made to the trial jurors that may be taken by any party to the action, and is of the following classes and types:

    (a) A challenge to the trial jury panel for cause.

    (1) A challenge to the panel may only be taken before a trial jury is sworn. The challenge shall be reduced to writing, and shall plainly and distinctly state the facts constituting the ground of challenge.

    (2) Reasonable notice of the challenge to the jury panel shall be given to all parties and to the jury commissioner, by service of a copy thereof.

    (3) The jury commissioner shall be permitted the services of legal counsel in connection with challenges to the jury panel.

    (b) A challenge to a prospective juror by either:

    (1) A challenge for cause for one of the following reasons:
        (A) General disqualification—that the juror is disqualified from serving in the action on trial.
        (B) Implied bias—as, when the existence of the facts as ascertained, in judgment of law disqualifies the juror.
        (C) Actual bias—the existence of a state of mind on the part of the juror in reference to the case, or to any of the parties, which will prevent the juror from acting with entire impartiality, and without prejudice to the substantial rights of any party.

    (2) A peremptory challenge to a prospective juror.

- Code of Civil Procedure §226, on challenges to individual jurors, states:

(a) A challenge to an individual juror may only be made before the jury is sworn.

(b) A challenge to an individual juror may be taken orally or may be made in writing, but no reason need be given for a peremptory challenge, and the court shall exclude any juror challenged peremptorily.

(c) All challenges for cause shall be exercised before any peremptory challenges may be exercised.

(d) All challenges to an individual juror, except a peremptory challenge, shall be taken, first by the defendants, and then by the people or plaintiffs.

- Code of Civil Procedure §227, on order of challenges, states:

    The challenges of either party for cause need not all be taken at once, but they may be taken separately, in the following order, including in each challenge all the causes of challenge belonging to the same class and type:

    (a) To the panel.

    (b) To an individual juror, for a general disqualification.

    (c) To an individual juror, for an implied bias.

    (d) To an individual juror, for an actual bias.

- Code of Civil Procedure §228, on general disqualification and grounds, states:

    Challenges for general disqualification may be taken on one or both of the following grounds, and for no other:

    (a) A want of any of the qualifications prescribed by this code to render a person competent as a juror.

    (b) A loss of hearing, or the existence of any other incapacity which satisfies the court that the challenged person is incapable of performing the duties of a juror in the particular action without prejudice to the substantial rights of the challenging party.

- Code of Civil Procedure §229, on challenges for implied bias, states:

    A challenge for implied bias may be taken for one or more of the following causes, and for no other:

    (a) Consanguinity or affinity within the fourth degree to any party, to an officer of a corporation which is a party, or to any alleged witness or victim in the case at bar.

    (b) Standing in the relation of, or being the parent, spouse, or child of one who stands in the relation of, guardian and ward, conservator and conservatee, master and servant, employer and clerk, landlord and tenant, principal and agent, or debtor and creditor, to either party or to an officer of a corporation which is a party, or being a member of the family of either party; or a partner in the business with either party; or surety on any bond or obligation for either party, or being the holder of bonds or shares of capital stock of a corporation which is a party; or having stood within one year previous to the filing of the complaint in the relation of attorney and client with either party or with the attorney for either party. A depositor of a bank or a holder of a savings account in a savings and loan association shall not be deemed a creditor of that bank or savings and loan association for the purpose of this paragraph solely by reason of his or her being a depositor or account holder.

(c) Having served as a trial or grand juror or on a jury of inquest in a civil or criminal action or been a witness on a previous or pending trial between the same parties, or involving the same specific offense or cause of action; or having served as a trial or grand juror or on a jury within one year previously in any criminal or civil action or proceeding in which either party was the plaintiff or defendant or in a criminal action where either party was the defendant.

(d) Interest on the part of the juror in the event of the action, or in the main question involved in the action, except his or her interest as a member or citizen or taxpayer of a county, city and county, incorporated city or town, or other political subdivision of a county, or municipal water district.

(e) Having an unqualified opinion or belief as to the merits of the action founded upon knowledge of its material facts or of some of them.

(f) The existence of a state of mind in the juror evincing enmity against, or bias towards, either party.

(g) That the juror is a party to an action pending in the court for which he or she is drawn and which action is set for trial before the panel of which the juror is a member.

(h) If the offense charged is punishable with death, the entertaining of such conscientious opinions as would preclude the juror finding the defendant guilty; in which case the juror may neither be permitted nor compelled to serve.

- Code of Civil Procedure §230, on challenges for cause, states:

    Challenges for cause shall be tried by the court. The juror challenged and any other person may be examined as a witness in the trial of the challenge, and shall truthfully answer all questions propounded to them.

- Code of Civil Procedure §231(a)-(b), on peremptory challenges in criminal trials, is quoted in §6.54.

- Code of Civil Procedure §231(c)-(e), on peremptory challenges in civil trials, states:

    (c) In civil cases, each party shall be entitled to six peremptory challenges. If there are more than two parties, the court shall, for the purpose of allotting peremptory challenges, divide the parties into two or more sides according to their respective interests in the issues. Each side shall be entitled to eight peremptory challenges. If there are several parties on a side, the court shall divide the challenges among them as nearly equally as possible. If there are more than two sides, the court shall grant such additional peremptory challenges to a side as the interests of justice may require; provided that the peremptory challenges of one side shall not exceed the aggregate number of peremptory challenges of all other sides. If any party on a side does not use his or her full share of peremptory challenges, the unused challenges may be used by the other party or parties on the same side.

(d) Peremptory challenges shall be taken or passed by the sides alternately, commencing with the plaintiff or people; and each party shall be entitled to have the panel full before exercising any peremptory challenge. When each side passes consecutively, the jury shall then be sworn, unless the court, for good cause, shall otherwise order. The number of peremptory challenges remaining with a side shall not be diminished by any passing of a peremptory challenge.

(e) If all the parties on both sides pass consecutively, the jury shall then be sworn, unless the court, for good cause, shall otherwise order. The number of peremptory challenges remaining with a side shall not be diminished by any passing of a peremptory challenge.

- Code of Civil Procedure §233, on discharge of jurors and substitution of alternates, states:

    If, before the jury has returned its verdict to the court, a juror becomes sick or, upon other good cause shown to the court, is found to be unable to perform his or her duty, the court may order the juror to be discharged. If any alternate jurors have been selected as provided by law, one of them shall then be designated by the court to take the place of the juror so discharged. If after all alternate jurors have been made regular jurors or if there is no alternate juror, a juror becomes sick or otherwise unable to perform the juror's duty and has been discharged by the court as provided in this section, the jury shall be discharged and a new jury then or afterwards impaneled, and the cause may again be tried. Alternatively, with the consent of all parties, the trial may proceed with only the remaining jurors, or another juror may be sworn and the trial begin anew.

- Code of Civil Procedure §234, on the selection and role of alternate jurors, states:

    Whenever, in the opinion of a judge of a superior or municipal court about to try a civil or criminal action or proceeding, the trial is likely to be a protracted one, or upon stipulation of the parties, the court may cause an entry to that effect to be made in the minutes of the court and thereupon, immediately after the jury is impaneled and sworn, the court may direct the calling of one or more additional jurors, in its discretion, to be known as "alternate jurors."

    These alternate jurors shall be drawn from the same source, and in the same manner, and have the same qualifications, as the jurors already sworn, and shall be subject to the same examination and challenges. However, each side, or each defendant, as provided in Section 231, shall be entitled to as many peremptory challenges to the alternate jurors as there are alternate jurors called.

The alternate jurors shall be seated so as to have equal power and facilities for seeing and hearing the proceedings in the case, and shall take the same oath as the jurors already selected, and shall, unless excused by the court, attend at all times upon the trial of the cause in company with the other jurors, but shall not participate in deliberation unless ordered by the court, and for a failure to do so are liable to be punished for contempt.

They shall obey the orders of and be bound by the admonition of the court, upon each adjournment of the court; but if the regular jurors are ordered to be kept in the custody of the sheriff or marshal during the trial of the cause, the alternate jurors shall also be kept in confinement with the other jurors; and upon final submission of the case to the jury, the alternate jurors shall be kept in the custody of the sheriff or marshal who shall not suffer any communication to be made to them except by order of the court, and shall not be discharged until the original jurors are discharged, except as provided in this section.

If at any time, whether before or after the final submission of the case to the jury, a juror dies or becomes ill, or upon other good cause shown to the court is found to be unable to perform his or her duty, or if a juror requests a discharge and good cause appears therefor, the court may order the juror to be discharged and draw the name of an alternate, who shall then take his or her place in the jury box, and be subject to the same rules and regulations as though he or she has been selected as one of the original jurors.

All laws relative to fees, expenses, and mileage or transportation of jurors shall be applicable to alternate jurors, except that in civil cases the sums for fees and mileage or transportation need not be deposited until the judge directs alternate jurors to be impaneled.

B. Criminal

§6.53 1. California Rules of Court

- California Rules of Court 4.200, on the pre-voir dire conference, states:

    (a) Before a jury selection begins in criminal cases, the court shall conduct a conference with counsel to determine:

    (1) a brief outline of the nature of the case, including a summary of the criminal charges;

    (2) the names of persons counsel intend to call as witnesses at trial;

    (3) the People's theory of culpability and the defendant's theories;

    (4) the procedures for deciding requests for excuse for hardship and challenges for cause; and

(5) the areas of inquiry and specific questions to be asked by the court and, as permitted by the court, by counsel and any time limits on counsel's examination.

The judge shall, if requested, excuse the defendant from then disclosing any defense theory.

(b) The court may require that all questions to be asked of prospective jurors, either orally or by written questionnaire, shall be submitted to the court and opposing counsel in writing before the conference.

- California Rules of Court 4.201, on supplemental examination, states:

In criminal jury trials, after completion of the initial examination, on request of counsel or on the court's own motion and on a showing of good cause, the court may conduct or permit counsel to conduct supplemental questioning as the court deems proper.

- California Rules of Court App Div I, §8.5(a) states:

(1) This standard applies in all criminal cases.

(2) The examination of prospective jurors in a criminal case should include all questions necessary to insure the selection of a fair and impartial jury.

The trial judge may, upon a showing of good cause, permit supplemental examination calculated to discover possible bias or prejudice with regard to the circumstances of the particular case, relevant to a challenge for cause.

- California Rules of Court App Div I, §8.5(b), on the trial judge's examination of jurors in criminal trials, states:

(b) The trial judge's examination of prospective jurors in criminal cases should include the following areas of inquiry and any other matters affecting their qualifications to serve as jurors in the case:

(1) (*To the entire jury panel after it has been sworn and seated*): I am now going to question the prospective jurors who are seated in the jury box concerning their qualifications to serve as jurors in this case. All members of this jury panel, however, should pay close attention to questions, making note of the answers you would give if these questions were put to you personally. If and when any other member of this panel is called to the jury box, he or she will be asked to answer these questions.

(2) (*To the prospective jurors seated in the jury box*): In the trial of this case each side is entitled to have a fair, unbiased and unprejudiced jury. If there is any fact or any reason why any of you might be biased or prejudiced in any way, you must disclose such reasons when you are asked to do so. It is your duty to make this disclosure.

(3) (*In lengthy trials*): This trial will likely take _____ days to complete. but it may take longer. Will any of you find it difficult or impossible to participate for this period of time?

(4) Ladies and gentlemen of the jury: This is a criminal [case] entitled The People of the State of California v. _____. The (defendant is) (defendants are) seated _____.

    (a) (Mr.) (Ms.) (defendant), please stand and face the prospective jurors in the jury box and in the audience seats. (Defendant complies.) Is there any member of the jury panel who is acquainted with the defendant or who may have heard (his) (her) name prior to today? If your answer is yes. please raise your hand.

    (b) The defendant, _____, is represented by (his) (her) attorney, _____, who is seated _____. (Mr.) (Ms.) (defense attorney), would you please stand? Is there any member of the jury panel who knows or who has seen (Mr.) (Ms.) _____ prior to today?

    (c) (*If there is more than one defendant, repeat (a) and (b) for each codefendant.*)

(5) The people are represented by _____, Deputy District attorney, who is seated _____. (Mr.) (Ms.) (district attorney), would you please stand? Is there any member of the jury panel who knows or who has seen (Mr.) (Ms.) _____ prior to today?

(6) The defendant is charged by an (information) (indictment) filed by the district attorney with having committed the crime of _____, in violation of section _____ of the _____ Code, it being alleged that on or about _____ in the County of _____ the defendant did (describe the offense). To (this charge) (these charges) the defendant has pleaded not guilty, and it will be the question of whether the defendant's guilt has been proved beyond a reasonable doubt that you will be asked to decide if you are selected as a trial juror in this case. Having heard the charge(s) which (has) (have) been filed against the defendant, is there any member of the jury panel who feels that he or she cannot give this defendant a fair trial because of the nature of the charge(s) against (him) (her)?

(7) Have any of you heard of, or have you any prior knowledge of, the facts or events in this case?

(8) During the trial of this case, the following persons may be called as witnesses to testify on behalf of the parties: (*The defendant may be excused from disclosing the name of any witness. Do not identify the side on whose behalf the witnesses might be called.*) Have any of you heard of or otherwise been acquainted with any of the witnesses just named? You should note that the parties are not required and might not wish to call all of these witnesses, and they may later find it necessary to call other witnesses.

(9) Do any of you have any belief or feeling toward any of the parties, attorneys or witnesses that would make it impossible, or difficult, for you to act fairly and impartially, both as to the defendant and the People? Do any of you have any interest in the outcome of this case?

(10) How many of you have served previously as jurors in a criminal case?

(*To each person whose hand is raised*):

    (a) (Mr.) (Ms.)_____, you indicated you have been a juror in a criminal case. What was the nature of the charge in that case? (Response.)

    (b) Do you feel you can put aside whatever you heard in that case and decide this case on the evidence to be presented and the law as I shall state it to you? (Response.)

(11) May I see the hands of those jurors who have served on civil cases, but who have never served on a criminal case? (Response.) You must understand that there are substantial differences in the rules applicable to the trial of criminal cases from those applicable to the trial of civil cases. This is particularly true respecting the burden of proof which is placed upon the People. In a civil case we say that the plaintiff must prove his case by a preponderance of the evidence. In a criminal case, the defendant is presumed to be innocent, and before he may be found guilty, the People must prove his guilt beyond a reasonable doubt. If the jury has a reasonable doubt, the defendant must be acquitted. Will each of you be able to set aside the instructions which you received in your previous cases and try this case on the instructions given by me in this case?

(12) The fact that the defendant is in court for trial, or that charges have been made against (him) (her), is no evidence whatever of (his) (her) guilt. The jurors are to consider only evidence properly received in the courtroom in determining the guilt or innocence of the defendant. The defendant has been arraigned and has entered a plea of "not guilty," which is a complete denial, making it necessary for the People, acting through the district attorney, to prove beyond a reasonable doubt the case against the defendant. Until and unless this is done, the presumption of innocence prevails.

In the following questions I will be using the terms "family", "close friend", and "anyone with whom you have a significant personal relationship." The term "anyone with whom you have a significant personal relationship" means a domestic partner, life partner, former spouse, or anyone with whom you have an influential or intimate relationship that you would characterize as important.

(13) Have you, or to your knowledge, any member of your family, close friend, or anyone with whom you have a significant relationship, ever been arrested for or charged with an offense similar to that in this case?

(14) Have you, or to your knowledge, any member of your family, close friends, or anyone with whom you have a significant relationship, ever been a complaining witness or a victim in a case of this kind?

(15) Have you, or to your knowledge, any member of your family, any close friend, or anyone with whom you have a significant relationship, had any law enforcement training or experience or been a member of or been employed by any law enforcement

agency? By law enforcement agency, I include any police department, sheriff's office, highway patrol, district attorney's office, city attorney's office, attorney general's office, United States attorney's office, FBI, etc.? (*If so, elicit the details of the experience or connection.*)

(16) Would you be able to listen to the testimony of a police or other peace officer and measure it by the same standards that you use to test the credibility of any other witness?

(17) Would you have any difficulty or embarrassment in returning a verdict for or against the side which had a police or other peace officer as a witness?

(18) (*When appropriate*) It may appear that one or more of the parties, attorneys or witnesses come from a particular national, racial or religious group (or may have a life style different than your own). Would this in any way affect your judgment or the weight and credibility you would give to their testimony?

(19) It is important that I have your assurance that you will, without reservation, follow my instructions and rulings on the law and will apply that law to this case. To put it somewhat differently, whether you approve or disapprove of the court's rulings or instructions, it is your solemn duty to accept as correct these statements of the law. You may not substitute your own idea of what you think the law ought to be. Will all of you follow the law as given to you by me in this case?

(20) Each of you should now state your:
    (i) Name;
    (ii) Children's ages and the number of children, if any;
    (iii) Occupation;
    (iv) Occupational history; and
    (v) Present employer.

And for your spouse or anyone with whom you have a significant personal relationship, their:
    (vi) Names;
    (vii) Occupations;
    (viii) Occupational histories; and
    (ix) Present employers.

Please begin with juror number one. Please begin with juror number one. [sic]

(21) Do you know of any other reason, or has anything occurred during this question period, that might make you doubtful you would be a completely fair and impartial juror in this case or why you should not be on this jury? If there is, it is your duty to disclose the reason at this time.

(22) (*At this point the court asks each side to exercise any challenges for cause.*)

(*At this point the court calls on each side, alternately, to exercise any peremptory challenges.*)

(23) (*When a new prospective juror is seated, the court should ask (him) (her)*):

(i) Have you heard my questions to the other prospective jurors?

(ii) Have any of the questions I have asked raised any doubt in your mind as to whether you could be a fair and impartial juror in this case?

(iii) Can you think of any other reason why you might not be able to try this case fairly and impartially to both the prosecution and defendant, or why you should not be on this jury?

(iv) Give us the personal information requested concerning your occupation, that of your spouse or anyone with whom you have a significant personal relationship, your prior jury experience.

(*Thereupon, as to each new juror seated, the court should ask counsel whether it has adequately covered the proper subjects of inquiry, ask such additional questions as the court determines are proper, and permit counsel, upon a showing of good cause, to ask supplemental questions and proceed with challenges as above.*)

§6.54 2. Code of Civil Procedure

- Code of Civil Procedure §191, on state policy regarding jury service, is quoted in §6.52.

- Code of Civil Procedure §197, on sources for the selection of jurors, is quoted in §6.52.

- Code of Civil Procedure §204, on exemption from jury service, is quoted in §6.52.

- Code of Civil Procedure §205, on juror questionnaires, is quoted in §6.52.

- Code of Civil Procedure §223, on examining prospective jurors in criminal trials, states:

    In a criminal case, the court shall conduct the initial examination of prospective jurors. The court may submit to prospective jurors additional questions requested by the parties as it deems proper. Upon completion of the court's examination, counsel for each party shall have the right to examine, by oral and direct questioning, any or all of the prospective jurors. The court may, in the exercise of discretion, limit the oral and direct questioning of prospective jurors by counsel. The court may specify the maximum amount of time that counsel for each party may question an individual juror, or may specify an aggregate amount of time for each part, which can then be allocated among the prospective jurors by counsel. Voir dire of any prospective jurors shall, where practicable, occur in the presence of other jurors in all criminal cases, including death penalty cases.

Examination of prospective jurors shall be conducted only in aid of the exercise of challenges for cause.

The trial court's exercise of its discretion in the manner in which voir dire is conducted, including any limitation on the time which will be allowed for direct questioning of prospective jurors by counsel and any determination that a question is not in aid of the exercise of challenges for cause, shall not cause any conviction to be reversed unless the exercise of that discretion has resulted in a miscarriage of justice, as specified in Section 13 of Article VI of the California Constitution.

- Code of Civil Procedure §225, on challenges, is quoted in §6.52.
- Code of Civil Procedure §226, on challenges to individual jurors, is quoted in §6.52.
- Code of Civil Procedure §227, on order of challenges, is quoted in §6.52.
- Code of Civil Procedure §228, on general disqualification and grounds, is quoted in §6.52.
- Code of Civil Procedure §229, on challenges for bias, is quoted in §6.52.
- Code of Civil Procedure §230, on challenges for cause, is quoted in §6.52.
- Code of Civil Procedure §231(c), on peremptory challenges in civil trials, is quoted in §6.52. Code of Civil Procedure §231(a)-(b), (d)-(e) states:

    (a) In criminal cases, if the offense charged is punishable with death, or with imprisonment in the state prison for life, the defendant is entitled to 20 and the people to 20 peremptory challenges. Except as provided in subdivision (b), in a trial for any other offense, the defendant is entitled to 10 and the state to 10 peremptory challenges. When two or more defendants are jointly tried, their challenges shall be exercised jointly, but each defendant shall also be entitled to five additional challenges which may be exercised separately, and the people shall also be entitled to additional challenges equal to the number of all the additional separate challenges allowed the defendants.

    (b) If the offense charged is punishable with a maximum term of imprisonment of 90 days or less, the defendant is entitled to six and the state to six peremptory challenges. When two or more defendants are jointly tried, their challenges shall be exercised jointly, but each defendant shall also be entitled to four additional challenges which may be exercised separately, and the state shall also be entitled to additional challenges equal to the number of all the additional separate challenges allowed the defendants.

    (d) Peremptory challenges shall be taken or passed by the sides alternately, commencing with the plaintiff or people; and each party shall be entitled to have the panel full before exercising any peremptory challenge. When each side passes consecutively, the jury shall then be sworn, unless the court, for good cause, shall otherwise order. The number of peremptory challenges remaining with a side shall not be diminished by any passing of a peremptory challenge.

(e) If all the parties on both sides pass consecutively, the jury shall then be sworn, unless the court, for good cause, shall otherwise order. The number of peremptory challenges remaining with a side shall not be diminished by any passing of a peremptory challenge.

- Code of Civil Procedure §233, on discharge of jurors and substitution of alternates, is quoted in §6.52.
- Code of Civil Procedure §234, on selection and role of alternate jurors, is quoted in §6.52.

7

Question Is Ambiguous or Unintelligible

I. DEFINITION §7.1

II. DANGERS PRESENTED §7.2

III. ANALYSIS §7.3

IV. SPEAKING OBJECTIONS §7.4

V. STATUTE §7.5

VI. STATING THE OBJECTION §7.6

§7.1 I. DEFINITION

If a question cannot be understood or as posed may be misunderstood by the witness, it is objectionable on the ground that it is ambiguous or unintelligible. See Evid C §765, discussed in §7.5.

§7.2 II. DANGERS PRESENTED

The dangers presented by ambiguous and unintelligible questions are that:

- The witness (and therefore the jury) will be confused or misled. In this case, the objection is made to prevent the witness from inadvertently giving incorrect, erroneous, or uncalled-for testimony.

- The record will not accurately reflect the witness's testimony. For example, counsel may be examining a witness about one document, hand the witness a second document, and ask the witness to identify the date on which it was signed. Although the question itself is not ambiguous, the witness's reply may appear to refer to the first document.

§7.3 III. ANALYSIS

When examining a witness, counsel should ask questions that are intelligently phrased, concise, and clear in meaning. The witness, the court, and counsel should not have to guess at the meaning of a question. If the question cannot be understood, counsel should object that it is ambiguous or unintelligible. This objection normally results in a rephrasing of the question.

Instead of ruling, the judge may ask the witness whether the question is understood. If the witness understands the question, the judge will instruct the witness to answer it.

The "ambiguous/unintelligible" objection is often overlooked. A witness may unknowingly give mistaken testimony in response to a poorly worded question if no objection is made. This objection can be abused by counsel. For example, it may be used as a way to alert the witness to a danger presented by the examination or to present what is in effect a brief argument to the jury. Although it is difficult to prevent isolated abuses, persistent abuse should be brought to the attention of the court with a request that such "speaking objections" cease. See §7.4. Local rules and court practices may require that only one objection be made and that the ground (*e.g.*, "ambiguous") be stated.

This objection should be distinguished from the objection that a question is too general, *i.e.*, permits the witness to respond with irrelevant or otherwise inadmissible matter (see chap 9). In brief, each question must be comprehensible and call for specific answers. Even if the witness understands the question, counsel should object to the question if counsel does not understand it. For this reason, counsel may object to a question on the ground that it is ambiguous "to me," regardless of whether the witness understands the question.

Attorneys often object to questions as being "vague and ambiguous." There is no difference between these two criteria. The objection should be that the question is ambiguous.

§7.4 IV. SPEAKING OBJECTIONS

Objections that include argument of counsel in the presence of the jury are called "speaking objections." Although such objections were common until the early 1960s, they are now strongly disfavored as objections that waste time, create bias, and result in argument back and forth by counsel. If there is a dire need to argue an objection, counsel should do this at sidebar, in chambers, or otherwise outside the jury's presence. If the trial judge does not enforce this rule, the trial will quickly get out of control.

§7.5 V. STATUTE

Evidence Code §765(a) provides the statutory authority for the "ambiguous/unintelligible" objection:

> (a) The court shall exercise reasonable control over the mode of interrogation of a witness so as to make such interrogation as rapid, as distinct, and as effective for the ascertainment of the truth, as may be, and to protect the witness from undue harassment or embarrassment.

§7.6 VI. STATING THE OBJECTION

Objection, Your Honor. The question is ambiguous.

8
Question Is Compound

I. DEFINITION §8.1

II. DANGERS PRESENTED §8.2

III. ILLUSTRATIONS §8.3

IV. STATUTE §8.4

V. ALTERNATIVES TO OBJECTING §8.5

VI. STATING THE OBJECTION §8.6

§8.1   I. DEFINITION

A question is objectionable on the ground that it is compound if it joins two or more questions with the disjunctive "or" or the conjunctive "and."

§8.2   II. DANGERS PRESENTED

The dangers presented by compound questions are that:

- The testimony of a witness may be inaccurate because the witness is confused by the multiple nature of the question;
- The testimony of a witness is confusing because it cannot be determined which part of the question the witness is answering;
- Part of the question may call for inadmissible evidence; or
- An appellate court may construe the answer to support the judgment when the answer, if understood as intended by the witness, would have had the opposite effect.

§8.3   III. ILLUSTRATIONS

If the witness answers "yes" to the following compound questions, it will be unclear whether the witness's reply refers to one or all of the questions:

- "Does Pearce Plastics or did Pearce Plastics, at the time of this accident, produce items that your company would be likely to purchase?" See *Wiese v Rainville* (1959) 173 CA2d 496, 506, 343 P2d 643. The answer to such a question, especially if it is "yes," raises the danger that the witness does not intend to reply to both questions. In *Wiese,* the appellate court held that the objection to this compound question had been properly sustained; furthermore, the part of the question that related to the present time was irrelevant (see chap 17).

- "Officer, when you arrived at the scene of the accident, did you or to your knowledge did any of your fellow officers take any steps to determine the point of impact?"

§8.4 IV. STATUTE

Evidence Code §765 provides the statutory authority for the "compound" objection. The statute allows the trial judge wide discretion in controlling the examination of witnesses. Thus, although the statute does not specifically mention compound questions, §765 authorizes the judge to sustain the objection.

Evidence Code §765(a) states:

> The court shall exercise reasonable control over the mode of interrogation of a witness so as to make such interrogation as rapid, as distinct, and effective for the ascertainment of the truth, as may be, and to protect the witness from undue harassment or embarrassment.

§8.5 V. ALTERNATIVES TO OBJECTING

If it appears that the answer to a compound question will not be harmful, counsel should refrain from objecting. Technically, most questions of any length are compound, but this does not necessarily make them harmful. If the answer is nonresponsive, counsel can move to strike it on that ground. Evid C §766. See §§52.2-52.4. If the answer is ambiguous, it can be clarified on cross-examination. For discussion of alternatives to objecting, see §§4.9-4.14.

To dispel any doubts about whether counsel is trying to obstruct the trial's progress or prevent the jury from hearing the evidence, counsel might add after objecting to a compound question: "I have no objection to having the question rephrased." Some judges may disapprove of this additional statement as constituting a "speaking objection." See §7.4. In practice, objections to compound questions are usually sustained, and the witness is then asked the questions separately. Counsel should balance the benefits of objecting against the harm that could result. When compound questions are involved, the judge will at times intervene and ask counsel to restate the question so that it is not a compound question.

§8.6 VI. STATING THE OBJECTION

Objection, Your Honor. The question, as phrased, is compound.

[Add if appropriate]

I have no objection to having the question rephrased, Your Honor.

9
Question Is Too General

I. DEFINITION §9.1

II. DANGERS PRESENTED §9.2

III. ILLUSTRATION §9.3

IV. STATUTE §9.4

V. STATING THE OBJECTION §9.5

§9.1 I. DEFINITION

A question is too general if it permits the witness to respond with irrelevant or otherwise inadmissible matter. Each question should limit the witness to a specific answer on a specific subject. The test is whether it can be determined from the question what specific admissible testimony is being sought; if not, the question is objectionable. See chap 10.

§9.2 II. DANGERS PRESENTED

General questions, when asked of unfriendly witnesses, may prove dangerous. If counsel cannot infer from the question the specific testimony that is being sought, counsel may be unable to object in time to prevent the jury from hearing inadmissible or argumentative answers. When this happens, counsel is forced to move to strike the answer from the record and ask the judge to admonish the jury to disregard it. Because such admonitions may serve to emphasize inadmissible evidence, many trial attorneys consider them to be of little value.

Unfriendly witnesses, especially if they are experienced (*e.g.,* experts), are often poised to exploit the freedom given to them by general questions and interject into their answers harmful matter that would otherwise not be admissible. Thus, it is axiomatic that the general question "Why?" should not be used without a reason on cross-examination. Similarly, open-ended questions like "How?" and "Please explain" should be asked only in those few cases in which they are strategically advantageous. Because open-ended questions elicit open-ended answers, counsel may lose control over the questioning process.

Impeachment examination should always be conducted with short leading questions. See chap 13.

§9.3 III. ILLUSTRATION

The following question is too general: "What happened after Mr. Rodenback left on that day?" See *Schuur v Rodenback* (1901) 133 C 85, 89, 65 P 298, in which the court held that it was proper to sustain an objection to this question because it was too general and "from it the court could not say whether an answer to it would be pertinent to the subject under inquiry."

In most situations, a lay witness is allowed to testify only about facts that the witness personally perceived. See Evid C §702. As with a narrative question, a question that is too general may allow a witness to interject evidence not personally known or observed by the witness.

§9.4 IV. STATUTE

The statutory authority for this objection is primarily Evid C §765. See §7.5. The trial judge has wide discretion, however, in controlling the examination of witnesses.

§9.5 V. STATING THE OBJECTION

Objection, Your Honor. The question is too general.

10

Question Calls for Narrative Answer

I. DEFINITION §10.1

II. DANGERS PRESENTED §10.2

III. ILLUSTRATIONS §10.3

IV. TRIAL JUDGE'S ROLE §10.4

V. STATUTE §10.5

VI. STATING THE OBJECTION §10.6

§10.1 I. DEFINITION

The "narrative answer" objection is appropriate when a question invites the witness to narrate a series of occurrences. The objection is closely related to the objection that a question is too general, *i.e.,* permits the witness to respond with irrelevant or otherwise inadmissible matter. See chap 9.

§10.2 II. DANGERS PRESENTED

Narrative answers often include inadmissible matter, *e.g.,* hearsay (see chap 19), inadmissible opinion (see chap 20), or argument. When an improper question calls for a factual answer that will be damaging to one's case, counsel can make a timely objection before the witness responds. When a question calls for a narrative answer, however, the response may include unexpected damaging testimony. Counsel should object to any questions that call for narrative answers if the answer could contain information that counsel may prefer the jury not to hear. This rule is particularly important when a witness is unknown or unfriendly. Experienced expert witnesses are quick to take advantage of an open-ended question that calls for a narrative answer.

§10.3 III. ILLUSTRATIONS

The following questions call for narrative answers:

- "Now tell us what everyone said and did at that point."
- "What happened that night?"

- "How did the accident happen?"

§10.4 IV. TRIAL JUDGE'S ROLE

Under the broad powers granted to the trial judge by Evid C §765, the court may sustain objections to questions, such as those illustrated above, to keep the jury from hearing inadmissible matter. The judge has wide discretion, however, to allow witnesses to give narrative answers. For example, in *Silva v Dias* (1941) 46 CA2d 662, 116 P2d 496, the appellate court rejected the claim that the trial judge erred in permitting the defendant to testify in narrative form instead of by question and answer, observing that "such questions are primarily addressed to the sound discretion of the trial court, and unless prejudice is shown, it can scarcely be said that such action amounted to an abuse of discretion." 46 CA2d at 664. See also *People v Belcher* (1961) 189 CA2d 404, 407, 11 CR 175.

One rationale for permitting narrative answers is that they tend to present the facts more accurately and completely than specific answers to specific questions and are easier for the jury to follow. Another rationale is that witnesses are more at ease and more likely to tell what they know in their own words if interruptions are kept to a minimum. This is especially true if the witness is a child. See *People v Davis* (1907) 6 CA 229, 230, 91 P 810.

Although the judge may tend to allow more narrative testimony when a litigant is in pro per, the judge may properly require that testimony be presented in question-and-answer form. "A lay person . . . who exercises the privilege of trying his own case must expect and receive the same treatment as if represented by an attorney—no different, no better, no worse." See *Taylor v Bell* (1971) 21 CA3d 1002, 1009, 98 CR 855. To protect the right to object, counsel faced with an unrepresented party should ask the judge to insist that the witness proceed by questions and answers. Similarly, if for some reason an attorney with no co-counsel present testifies, the attorney-witness should be made to proceed by question and answer.

§10.5 V. STATUTE

Evidence Code §765 provides the basis for the "narrative answer" objection. See §7.5.

§10.6 VI. STATING THE OBJECTION

Objection, Your Honor. The question calls for a narrative answer.

11

Question Has Been Asked and Answered

    I. DEFINITION   §11.1

    II. DANGERS PRESENTED   §11.2

    III. ANALYSIS   §11.3

    IV. STATUTE   §11.4

    V. ALTERNATIVES TO OBJECTING   §11.5

    VI. STATING THE OBJECTION   §11.6

§11.1   I. DEFINITION

A question may be objectionable on the ground that the witness has already answered a substantially similar question on the same subject matter. This objection must be distinguished from the objection that proposed evidence is cumulative, *i.e.*, merely adds to other similar evidence on a point (*e.g.*, calling for several expert witnesses to give similar testimony; see chap 31). The "asked and answered" objection applies when a question is repeated after having been previously asked of the witness.

§11.2   II. DANGERS PRESENTED

The dangers presented by a question that has been asked and answered are that:

- Repetition may give important evidence undue emphasis. Counsel sometimes attempts to highlight favorable testimony by covering the same matter more than once. As with repetitive jury instructions, repetitive testimony is argumentative and potentially prejudicial because it isolates and therefore emphasizes selected evidence. This frequently occurs on redirect examination, when counsel attempts to emphasize matters previously covered on direct examination. This repetition violates Evid C §774, which provides that "a witness once examined cannot be reexamined as to the same matter without leave of the court."

- Repetition may consume an undue amount of time. See Evid C §352, discussed in chap 31.

§11.3 III. ANALYSIS

Whether to allow a question to be repeated is entirely within the discretion of the trial judge. *Robinson v Kelly* (1949) 95 CA2d 320, 326, 212 P2d 921. The test is whether the truth can be better ascertained by allowing repetition. See Evid C §765(a). The trial judge may allow counsel to ask a question that is substantially similar to one that has already been asked and answered, *e.g.*, when witnesses have difficulty expressing themselves. This situation often arises when a witness testifies to a lack of recollection:

> PROSECUTOR: Did you tell the police officer that the knife the officer found was yours?
>
> DEFENDANT: I don't remember.
>
> PROSECUTOR: Do you deny telling the officer that?
>
> DEFENSE COUNSEL: Objection, Your Honor. The witness has already answered that question.
>
> PROSECUTOR: Your Honor, it's not clear from the answer whether the witness denies saying it or whether the witness merely doesn't remember at this time saying it.

The prosecutor's repetition of the first question is permissible to clarify the defendant's answer; the second question asks for slightly different information than was asked in the first question. Defense counsel may object to the second question in the manner indicated above only when speaking objections are allowed. For the objection to apply, a question must have the same import as one previously asked. *People v Hatfield* (1933) 129 CA 162, 166, 18 P2d 366. See also *People v Walker* (1948) 33 C2d 250, 256, 201 P2d 6 (repetition of question in slightly different form objectionable). The prosecutor's response to defense counsel's objection might be considered argument, which usually is not allowed in a jury trial.

Similarly, to promote "the ascertainment of the truth" (see Evid C §765), trial judges normally permit greater latitude for repetition during cross-examination. For example, to lay the foundation for the introduction of a prior inconsistent statement, a series of questions like the following is common and usually permitted:

> PROSECUTOR:
>
> Did you have anything to drink that evening before the accident?
>
> DEFENDANT:
>
> I had two beers, and that's all.

PROSECUTOR:

That's all?

DEFENDANT:

That's all.

PROSECUTOR:

You're sure of that?

DEFENDANT:

Yes.

PROSECUTOR:

Didn't you tell officer Jones at the police station on the night of the accident that you had four beers?

Only under exceptional circumstances would such repetition be allowed during direct or redirect examination.

Sometimes trial counsel will abuse this objection by asserting it to try to alert the witness that he or she is giving, or is in danger of giving, an answer inconsistent with previous testimony. Such maneuvers should be objected to and, if opposing counsel persists, an admonition should be requested.

Counsel who has truly forgotten the similar question or answer should simply ask the trial judge for permission to ask the question again. Or counsel may ask the court reporter for the previous question and answer that has been alleged as "asked and answered" at the next recess.

§11.4   IV. STATUTE

Evidence Code §§765 (see §7.5) and 774 provide the statutory bases for this objection. The trial judge has discretion in controlling the examination of witnesses. See Evid C §352 (excluding cumulative evidence in judge's discretion). Repeating questions may produce cumulative evidence.

§11.5   V. ALTERNATIVES TO OBJECTING

On possible alternatives to objecting, see §§4.9–4.14.

§11.6   VI. STATING THE OBJECTION

Objection, Your Honor. The question has been asked and answered.

12

Question Misquotes Witness

I. DEFINITION §12.1

II. ILLUSTRATIONS §12.2

III. ADDITIONAL REMEDIES §12.3

IV. STATUTE §12.4

V. STATING THE OBJECTION §12.5

§12.1 I. DEFINITION

This objection is self-explanatory: The question misstates the evidence or misquotes the testimony of a witness. The misquoting generally occurs in a prefatory statement before the question is asked rather than in the question itself. A related error is misquoting a witness in argument. See §§29.3-29.8. Misleading the trier of fact by such misquoting violates Cal Rules of Prof Cond 5-200(B)-(C).

If there is any uncertainty about the witness's actual statement, the judge—not counsel—should ask that the court reporter read the disputed answer. Although this procedure tends to deter the offender from further misquoting, it can be time-consuming for the reporter to find the answer if the witness's testimony was given long before the misquote. Instead, the judge will usually admonish the jurors that they are the final judges of what has or has not been said at trial.

§12.2 II. ILLUSTRATIONS

The following are illustrations of the misquoting of a witness:

- When the accused testified that a Mr. G had threatened him in order to keep certain information from the prosecutor, counsel made it appear while questioning the accused that the accused had admitted threatening the prosecutor. See *Berger v U.S.* (1935) 295 US 78, 84, 79 L Ed 1314, 1319, 55 S Ct 629. Although the trial judge had sustained objections to some of the prosecutor's improper questions and had instructed the jury to disregard them, the Supreme Court concluded that these measures were too mild (295 US at 85, 79 L Ed at 1320):

> [T]he situation was one which called for stern rebuke and repressive measures and, perhaps, if these were not successful, for the granting of a mistrial.

- When the witness testified that she was not sure whether anyone had taken a gun, counsel made it appear that she had stated that she had seen someone taking the gun: "You have testified that you observed a man taking a gun. Is that man here in the courtroom?"

§12.3   III. ADDITIONAL REMEDIES

As an alternative to or in addition to simply objecting to a question that misstates what a witness has said, counsel may find it necessary to invoke other remedies such as the following:

- Object to the practice as misconduct and request the judge to admonish the jury to disregard the prefatory statement. See §§29.6, 29.12, 29.14. Some judges respond to this request by merely reminding the jury that what the attorney says is not evidence. Such an admonition bypasses the real issue and fails to convey the necessary corrective message. The judge should exercise discretion under Evid C §765 because this method of questioning is not "effective for the ascertainment of the truth."

- Ask the judge to admonish counsel to stop the practice if the misquotation is repetitive and clearly intentional. See chap 31.

§12.4   IV. STATUTE

Evidence Code §§765 (see §7.5) and 774 provide the statutory bases for this objection. The judge has discretion in controlling the examination of witnesses.

§12.5   V. STATING THE OBJECTION

> Objection, Your Honor. Counsel is misquoting the witness.

13

Question Is Leading

I. DEFINITION §13.1

II. ILLUSTRATIONS
   A. Leading Questions §13.2
   B. Questions Not Leading §13.3

III. PROPER LEADING QUESTIONS DURING DIRECT OR REDIRECT EXAMINATION
   A. Introduction §13.4
   B. To Establish Preliminary Matters §13.5
   C. To Refresh Recollection §13.6
   D. To Aid Witnesses Requiring Assistance in Testifying §13.7
   E. To Question Expert Witnesses §13.8
   F. To Question Hostile Witnesses §13.9
   G. To Question Witnesses Who Have Changed Their Stories §13.10
   H. To Identify Exhibits §13.11

IV. IMPROPER LEADING QUESTIONS DURING CROSS- OR RECROSS-EXAMINATION §13.12

V. STATUTE §13.13

VI. ALTERNATIVES TO OBJECTING §13.14

VII. STATING THE OBJECTION §13.15

§13.1 I. DEFINITION

A leading question is one that suggests to the witness the answer desired by the examining party. Evid C §764. The danger in permitting the leading question is that the witness may acquiesce in a false suggestion.

Leading questions are objectionable on direct or redirect examination (Evid C §767(a)(1)), except as noted in §§13.4–13.11, but proper on cross- or recross-examination (Evid C §767(a)(2)), except as noted in §13.12. Special rules apply to children under age 14 and those under age ten in child abuse cases. Essentially, the judge has discretion to determine the propriety of asking a child leading questions; the interests of the child are paramount. Evid C §§765(b), 767(b)(2).

II. ILLUSTRATIONS

§13.2   A. Leading Questions

The following questions are leading:

- "It extends clear across the street, doesn't it?"
- "Did he then raise his fist and strike his wife?"
- "Was this followed by a terrific explosion?"
- "She appeared to be perfectly competent when she signed this will, didn't she?"

A commonly encountered form of leading question begins, "Isn't it a fact that . . ." (*e.g.,* "Isn't it a fact that the manhole cover was missing?"). Another commonly used form of question that can be leading begins, "Would it be __[*fair/correct/accurate*]__ to say that . . ." (*e.g.,* "Well, would it be accurate to say that you were experiencing severe pain during your stay in the hospital?").

§13.3   B. Questions Not Leading

In *Estate of Melvin* (1927) 85 CA 691, 696, 259 P 980, the issue was whether the testator had been of sound mind when he executed his will. The trial judge sustained objections to the following two questions on the ground that they were leading:

(1) "How was he as to being able to carry on a connected conversation, whether he would talk about one thing connectedly straight through or whether he would branch off on other subjects?"

(2) "In these several conversations, what is the fact as to whether or not he would repeat about the same line of conversation each time?"

The appellate court ordered the judgment reversed, observing that each of these questions gave the witness an equal choice between two alternatives, without any apparent suggestion that the witness should choose one over the other. It was error, therefore, to classify these questions as leading.

A suggestion that the witness should give a particular answer may come not only from the phrasing of the question but also from the examiner's manner or vocal inflection. When such nonverbal elements are present, the objection should include a description of the pertinent details for the record (*e.g.,* that counsel was nodding his or her head up and down) so that a reviewing court may correctly assess what occurred.

Asking the witness to state "whether or not" a recited fact is true (see the second question above) often keeps the question from being classified as leading. Not every question that calls for a "yes" or "no" answer is leading. *People v Calloway* (1954) 127 CA2d 504, 508, 274 P2d 497. An example of this kind of question by plaintiff's counsel is, "Did you see plaintiff after the accident?" Even though the answer desired by the examiner is clear from the question, this is not the test of whether a question is leading. The test is whether a reasonable person would infer from the context of the question that the examiner desires one answer rather than another. See 3 Witkin, California Evidence, *Presentation at Trial* §165 (4th ed 2000); Cleary, McCormick on Evidence §6 (3d ed 1984).

III. PROPER LEADING QUESTIONS DURING DIRECT OR REDIRECT EXAMINATION

§13.4   A. Introduction

The Comment to Evid C §767 states that the statute continues prior law permitting leading questions on direct or redirect examination if there is little danger of improper suggestion or such questions are necessary to obtain relevant evidence. These exceptions to the rule comprise "special circumstances" that are mandated by the "interests of justice." Evid C §767. See §13.13 for the complete statutory language.

Five examples of the exceptions to the rule given in the Comment are discussed in §§13.5–13.9. Other possible exceptions are described in §§13.10–13.11.

§13.5   B. To Establish Preliminary Matters

To save time, the judge may allow leading questions that pertain to preliminary matters. See Evid C §765; Comment to Evid C §767. Introductory facts that are not in dispute (*e.g.,* the name, address, and occupation of the witness) may be sought by leading questions. The location of the witness at the time of the relevant event is also usually established by this method. Leading questions are allowed if they pertain to preliminary facts because they "lead the witness more quickly to matters which are material to the issues." *People v Orona* (1947) 79 CA2d 820, 827, 180 P2d 694.

A question using the following introductory language effectively accomplishes this purpose: "Mr. _ _[name of witness]_ _, directing your attention to the events that occurred at _ _[location]_ _ on _ _[time and date]_ _, _ _[state question]_ _."

§13.6   C. To Refresh Recollection

Although a witness being interviewed before trial may be able to recount the exact details of an event, the witness may quite innocently forget important matters while testifying in the courtroom. When this occurs, the judge may allow leading questions to refresh the witness's recollection. Comment to Evid C §767.

§13.7   D. To Aid Witnesses Requiring Assistance in Testifying

It is the duty of the trial judge to exercise control over the mode of interrogation to make it "effective for the ascertainment of the truth." Evid C §765. If the witness is having difficulty testifying (*e.g.,* because of age, illness, limited intelligence, or difficulty with the language), the judge may permit leading questions. See Evid C §767(b); *People v Augustin* (2003) 112 CA4th 444, 449, 5 CR3d 171; *Stewart v Marvin* (1956) 139 CA2d 769, 294 P2d 114; Comment to Evid C §767.

Some witnesses find it difficult to testify if the subject matter is offensive. For example, a girl who was testifying about having been raped was properly asked leading questions by the examiner to help her overcome her embarrassment and to disclose the facts. See *People v Jackson* (1954) 124 CA2d 787, 789, 269 P2d 17.

The special circumstances that make it necessary to use leading questions are usually known to counsel before trial. It is wise to review these circumstances with the judge in chambers before the witness is called to testify. The judge can then make a preliminary determination, if desired, by questioning the witness outside the presence of the jury.

§13.8   E. To Question Expert Witnesses

Leading questions may properly be used during the interrogation of an expert witness. *People v Campbell* (1965) 233 CA2d 38, 44, 43 CR 237; *Chula v Superior Court* (1952) 109 CA2d 24, 38, 240 P2d 398; Comment to Evid C §767.

As a practical matter, non-court-appointed expert witnesses are often retained to support a party's position. For that reason, any expert witness may be susceptible to the examiner's suggestion, and some judges will automatically sustain a leading question objection. If a particular expert witness is known to the court or to counsel as always partisan either toward plaintiffs or toward defendants, a judge who might otherwise allow leading questions may refuse to allow them of that expert. Furthermore, leading an expert witness may be harmful from a tactical standpoint because it gives the jury the impression that the attorney rather than the expert is testifying.

§13.9   F. To Question Hostile Witnesses

The rule restricting leading questions on direct or redirect examination presupposes that the witness is friendly and will be influenced by the suggested answer. Occasionally, a party is obliged to call a hostile witness to the stand to prove the case. On a showing that the witness is hostile, the examiner may ask leading questions. A preliminary showing of hostility may be made on the basis of the identity of the witness, the witness's connection with the case, or the nature of the proposed testimony. Through discovery, the factual basis for claiming hostility can usually be determined before trial. Hostility may also appear from the demeanor of the witness in court or from the witness's answers. See Evid C §§776, 767(a). See also Evid C §785 ("[t]he credibility of a witness may be attached or supported by any party, including the party calling him").

If the witness is an adverse party, or a "person identified with" an adverse party (see Evid C §776(d)), the examiner clearly may ask leading questions. In this situation, when the witness is called to testify, counsel should point out to the judge that Evid C §776 is being invoked. That section permits the witness to be examined "as if under cross-examination." Evid C §776(a). The purpose of §776 is discussed in *Gerhard v Stephens* (1968) 68 C2d 864, 911, 69 CR 612.

Sometimes a witness is called under Evid C §776, when in fact the witness is friendly toward the party calling the witness. For example, an employee plaintiff in an action against his employer may call as an adverse witness a co-employee who is actually friendly to the plaintiff and hostile to the employer. If both the party calling the witness and the witness are identified with the same opposing party, Evid C §776(e) permits leading questions by the opposing party on cross-examination of the witness. This rule is designed to eliminate the unfairness of barring leading questions on cross-examination in situations in which the "adverse" witness is not actually adverse and yet can be asked leading questions on direct examination. Comment to Evid C §776.

If a witness is truly adverse, leading questions should be permitted during direct, cross-, redirect, or recross-examination.

§13.10   G. To Question Witnesses Who Have Changed Their Stories

The prohibition against leading questions on direct or redirect examination is qualified by the phrase "except under special circumstances where the interests of justice otherwise require." See Evid C §767(a). This phrase appears to cover testimony by a witness that differs substantially from statements that the witness previously made out of court.

Any party may impeach any witness. Evid C §785. One method of impeachment is by proof that the witness previously made a statement that is inconsistent with the present testimony. Evid C §780(h). This ordinarily requires asking the witness to explain or deny the inconsistent statement. Evid C §770(a).

Evidence Code §765 requires the trial judge to control the mode of interrogation to make it "effective for the ascertainment of the truth." When a witness has a changed story, the most effective way to disclose the truth may be to allow leading questions to be asked, even by the attorney who called the witness. As indicated above, the language of Evid C §767 suggests that this procedure is appropriate under such "special circumstances."

§13.11   H. To Identify Exhibits

Leading questions that relate solely to the identification of exhibits are freely permitted. *People v Campbell* (1965) 233 CA2d 38, 44, 43 CR 237; *People v Wilson* (1941) 46 CA2d 218, 224, 115 P2d 598.

§13.12 IV. IMPROPER LEADING QUESTIONS DURING CROSS-OR RECROSS-EXAMINATION

The objective of cross-examination is often to test the veracity of a hostile witness. Leading questions are allowed if the witness is hostile, because the danger is relatively slight that the witness will give false answers suggested by the cross-examiner. If the witness is friendly to the cross-examiner's side, this danger is just as present as under normal direct examination, and leading questions are prohibited.

In *People v Grey* (1972) 23 CA3d 456, 100 CR 245, the defendant's fiancée testified for the prosecution under a grant of immunity. Noting that the witness's demeanor on direct examination indicated that she was favoring the defense as much as possible, the trial court ordered defense counsel to refrain from using leading questions in his cross-examination of her. The appellate court upheld the trial court's ruling because it was "the exact situation envisaged by the official comment to section 767 of the Evidence Code and by Dean Wigmore." 23 CA3d at 464. See 3 Wigmore, Evidence in Trials at Common Law §773 (3d ed 1940) (cited in Comment to Evid C §767); Anno, 38 ALR2d 952 (1954).

The fact that another party called the witness to the stand as an adverse witness does not necessarily entitle the examiner to pose leading questions. Coparties may cross-examine one another's witnesses, but if the coparties' interests are not adverse, leading questions are restricted by the rules governing direct examination. See Evid C §773(b). Without this prohibition, counsel for one coparty could conduct a sketchy direct examination, leaving it to counsel for the other coparty to develop the case by asking leading questions under the cover of cross-examination. This type of prohibited examination has been characterized as a "sweetheart cross-examination."

Leading questions, however, may be asked during cross-examination of a witness who, although technically not adverse, has given testimony that is "antagonistic" to the position of the examining party. Comment to Evid C §773.

A person who has been properly called to testify and is examined as an adverse witness under Evid C §776 clearly may not be asked leading questions when cross-examined by a friendly side. Comment to Evid C §776. The Evid C §767(a) rules and limitations governing redirect examinations apply. Evid C §776(b).

Under special circumstances and in the interests of justice, the trial judge may forbid leading questions during cross- or recross-examination. See Evid C §767. The test is whether the witness is biased in favor of the cross-examiner and would be unduly susceptible to giving answers suggested by the cross-examiner. Comment to Evid C §767.

§13.13   V. STATUTE

Evidence Code §767 states:

(a) Except under special circumstances where the interests of justice otherwise require:

(1) A leading question may not be asked of a witness on direct or redirect examination.

(2) A leading question may be asked of a witness on cross-examination or recross-examination.

(b) The court may in the interests of justice permit a leading question to be asked of a child under 10 years of age in a case involving a prosecution under Section 273a, 273d, or 288 of the Penal Code.

§13.14   VI. ALTERNATIVES TO OBJECTING

On possible alternatives to objecting, see §§4.9–4.14.

§13.15   VII. STATING THE OBJECTION

Objection, Your Honor. The question is leading.

14

Question Is Argumentative

I. DEFINITION §14.1

II. ILLUSTRATION §14.2

III. STATUTE §14.3

IV. STATING THE OBJECTION §14.4

§14.1   I. DEFINITION

A question is argumentative and therefore objectionable if it:

- Is asked for the purpose of creating improper bias rather than for eliciting admissible evidence; or
- Calls for an argument in answer to an argument in the question.

Both argumentative questions and argumentative answers are objectionable. See *Seidenberg v George* (1946) 76 CA2d 306, 309, 172 P2d 891. The examiner should move to strike such an answer on the grounds that it is nonresponsive and argumentative. On motions to strike, see chap 52.

An attorney is bound by the standards of conduct set out in Bus & P C §§6000–6159.2 (particularly Bus & P C §6068) to refrain from argumentative questions and answers. See §29.2. If counsel's conduct constitutes undue harassment or embarrassment of the witness, the court should sustain an objection on those grounds or act on its own to protect the witness. Evid C §765.

§14.2   II. ILLUSTRATION

The following question is argumentative: "How is it you can recollect a date so long ago as that, and you cannot remember the day of the week?"

§14.3   III. STATUTE

The statutory authority for this objection is Evid C §765. See §7.5. Note the trial judge's wide discretion in controlling the examination of witnesses.

§14.4   IV. STATING THE OBJECTION

Objection, Your Honor. The question is argumentative.

15

Question Assumes Fact in Dispute or Not in Evidence

I. DEFINITION §15.1

II. DANGERS PRESENTED §15.2

III. ANALYSIS
   A. Direct Examination §15.3
   B. Cross-Examination §15.4

IV. ILLUSTRATIONS §15.5

V. CONDITIONAL ADMISSION OF EVIDENCE §15.6

VI. ADDITIONAL REMEDIES §15.7

VII. STATUTE §15.8

VIII. STATING THE OBJECTION §15.9

§15.1   I. DEFINITION

A question that assumes an unproved fact is objectionable. Such a question usually falls into one of two categories:

(1) It asserts or assumes that a fact in dispute has been proved; or
(2) It asserts or assumes a fact for which no evidence has been introduced.

§15.2   II. DANGERS PRESENTED

The dangers presented by questions that assume facts in dispute or not in evidence include the following:

- The question may bring before the jury facts that counsel is unable to prove. "The inherent vice of the matter lies in the attempt to bring before the jury in a round-about way facts which could not be proved and which from all appearances may have been entirely false." See *McDonald v Price* (1947) 80 CA2d 150, 152, 181 P2d 115.

- The question may trap the witness into impliedly affirming the truth of the assumed fact, without meaning to do so.

III. ANALYSIS

§15.3 A. Direct Examination

When asked on direct or redirect examination, a question that assumes facts in dispute or not in evidence is usually objectionable on the additional ground that it is leading. See Evid C §767(a). See also §§13.1–13.2. Such a question is leading because it asks the witness to affirm a suggested fact and misleading because it implies that this fact is already in evidence or has been proved.

§15.4 B. Cross-Examination

During cross-examination, trial counsel may not state facts that have not been proved and perhaps cannot be proved. On improper impeachment, see §22.7; on scope of cross-examination, see §§26.2–26.4. Cross-examiners often resort to such questions to prompt a witness into saying something unintentionally.

When an expert witness has been asked a complicated hypothetical question, it may be difficult to ascertain whether the question assumes facts in dispute or facts not in evidence. At the chambers conference before trial, counsel should consider asking the court to require that all hypothetical questions be circulated to the court and counsel for review and discussion before they are asked of a witness. See California Expert Witness Guide §§11.32, 12.8, 14.4 (2d ed Cal CEB 1991).

§15.5 IV. ILLUSTRATIONS

The following questions assume facts in dispute or not in evidence:

- "When did you stop beating your wife?"

- "Did you know their business dropped 50% and some went broke and closed up?" See *People ex rel Dep't of Pub. Works v Lillard* (1963) 219 CA2d 368, 379, 33 CR 189. This question, asked during cross-examination in a condemnation case, referred to the effect on certain businesses of a freeway bypass in their part of town. The appellate court held that the trial court properly sustained an objection to this question on the ground that it assumed matter not in evidence. The appellate court observed that such "did you know that" questions have been repeatedly condemned as being outside the wide latitude permitted the questioner on cross-examination, because they are "designed not to obtain information or test adverse testimony but to afford cross-examining counsel a device by which his own unsworn statements can reach the ears of the jury and be accepted by them as proof. . . ." *People ex rel Dep't of Pub. Works v Lillard, supra.*

- "Did you know that in April of 1937 he pled guilty to a charge of burglary and served six months in the road camp . . . ? Did you know that in May of 1939 he was charged with three counts of petty theft to which he pled guilty?" See *McDonald v Price* (1947) 80 CA2d 150, 151, 181 P2d 115. Asked during cross-examination of the plaintiff, the decedent's wife in a wrongful death action, these questions related to crimes allegedly committed by the decedent. After the judge overruled counsel's objections to each of these questions, the witness answered "no." Although the trial judge had instructed the jury to consider the questions only on the issue of damages (the value of the decedent's life to his family), the appellate court concluded that it was "highly probable" that the plaintiff had been prejudiced. The defendant had neither proved, nor offered to prove, the truth of the assumed convictions. On this ground alone, the appellate court ordered the judgment reversed. On the issue of the decedent's contributory negligence, the appellate court observed that the case was "close." The jury returned a verdict for the defendant. As pointed out by the appellate court (80 CA2d at 153), whether the witness knew of the alleged conviction was irrelevant. See chap 17.

- "In the survey of Ted Woodward, do you recall that in all the cases, there were twenty-nine cases studied by him in which twenty-six resulted in aplastic anemia, one in severe anemia, two in thrombocytopenia, and twenty-one of the twenty-nine patients were already dead before his survey was completed. Do you remember that?" See *Love v Wolf* (1964) 226 CA2d 378, 390, 38 CR 183. This question was asked during cross-examination of a witness for a drug company being sued for personal injuries. In asking the question, plaintiff's counsel appeared to be reading from a document that the jury would have assumed to be Dr. Woodward's survey. When opposing counsel demanded production of the document, examining counsel denied that he had been reading from that survey. The witness answered that he was certain that Dr. Woodward had made no such finding. No evidence was produced supporting the truth of the matter stated in the question; no proof was presented that such a survey was ever made. In another "did you know that" series of questions, trial counsel stated that several California counties had enacted legislation prohibiting use of the drug except in hospitals. "Having asserted over and over that this was not a misstatement, and he would prove its truth, *no such evidence was in fact produced.*" (Emphasis added by court.) 226 CA2d at 390. Concluding that these questions, among others, amounted to prejudicial misconduct by plaintiff's counsel, the appellate court ordered the $334,046 judgment reversed. The court's italicized declaration suggests that if the fact in question is later proved, that may cancel any claim that the misconduct was prejudicial. See §29.9. Although the misconduct of counsel in *Love v Wolf, supra,* resulted in reversal by the appellate court, the four instances of trial counsel's alleged misconduct in *Bigboy v County of San Diego* (1984) 154 CA3d 397, 411, 201 CR 226, did not warrant reversal, because they were not blatant, continuous, or contrived to inflame the jury. See also *Dominguez v Pantalone* (1989) 212 CA3d 201, 260 CR 431.

- "How long after you purchased the goods were they handed over to Mr. Hand?" See *Hand v Scodeletti* (1900) 128 C 674, 676, 61 P 373. This question was asked during cross-examination of a witness for the plaintiff, who was testifying in an action for wrongful conversion of goods. The trial court sustained the defense counsel's objection to the question on the ground that it assumed facts that had not been proved (*i.e.*, that the witness had sold or given those goods to the plaintiff). The witness had previously denied having given the goods to the plaintiff, and whether the witness had sold them was pivotal to the plaintiff's proving that the defendant had converted the goods. The appellate court ruled that the question was "unfair and improper" because it assumed "that the witness admitted as a fact what he denied. . . ." 128 C at 676.

Although the "did you know that" type of question is generally objectionable on either direct examination or cross-examination when it refers to facts not in evidence (see *Simmons v Southern Pac. Transp. Co.* (1976) 62 CA3d 341, 356, 133 CR 42), questions asked during cross-examination that begin, "Isn't it a fact," may be allowed if they allude to disputed facts that were admitted into evidence (see *Marcus v Palm Harbor Hosp.* (1967) 253 CA2d 1008, 1015, 61 CR 702).

§15.6 V. CONDITIONAL ADMISSION OF EVIDENCE

The trial judge has the power to permit evidence to be introduced conditionally, subject to proof of a foundational fact being supplied later at the trial. See §3.6. The judge also has broad discretion to regulate the order of proof. Evid C §320.

It is therefore appropriate for the judge to overrule an objection that a question assumes the truth of a fact, on the examining counsel's representation that counsel will subsequently prove the assumed fact. The judge may allow the witness's answer to be received subject to that condition. See §5.3.

If the examining counsel rests without supplying proof of the existence of the assumed fact, counsel's opponent should move to have the conditionally admitted answer stricken. See §§21.11, 21.13, 52.7. The additional sanctions outlined in §15.7 may also be appropriate.

§15.7 VI. ADDITIONAL REMEDIES

In addition to objecting to a question that assumes a fact not in evidence, counsel may find it necessary to invoke other sanctions such as the following:

- Object to the practice as misconduct and request that the judge admonish the jury to disregard the matter (see §§29.12, 29.14);

- Request that the judge order counsel to stop this practice if the improper suggestive wording of the question was clearly intentional (see §29.14); or

- Move for a mistrial if the question's undue prejudicial effect has caused irremediable harm that prevents a fair trial (see §29.16).

§15.8 VII. STATUTE

Evidence Code §765 is the statutory authority for objecting that a question assumes a fact in dispute or not in evidence. See §7.5. Note the trial judge's wide discretion in controlling the examination of witnesses.

§15.9 VIII. STATING THE OBJECTION

Objection, Your Honor. The question assumes facts _ _[in dispute/not in evidence]_ _. I ask that the jury be instructed that counsel's statements are _ _[in dispute/not in evidence]_ _ and that the jurors should disregard the question and what it suggests.

16

Question Calls for Speculation

I. DEFINITION §16.1

II. ILLUSTRATIONS §16.2

III. ANALYSIS §16.3
   A. Lay Witnesses: Opinion Testimony versus Speculation §16.4
   B. Expert Witnesses: Speculation §16.5

IV. STATUTE §16.6

V. STATING THE OBJECTION §16.7

§16.1 I. DEFINITION

A question that invites the witness to answer on the basis of conjecture is one that asks the witness to speculate and is therefore objectionable.

§16.2 II. ILLUSTRATIONS

The following questions call for speculation by the witness:

- "How much of the top soil on your land was washed away by reason of the rain being diverted onto it from the road?" See *County of San Mateo v Christen* (1937) 22 CA2d 375, 379, 71 P2d 88 (held speculative).

- "Is it possible, Miss Smith, that there could have been other meetings?" See *People v Glancy* (1956) 142 CA2d 669, 680, 299 P2d 18. The court held that the trial court properly sustained an objection to this question on the ground that it called for speculation. On lack of personal knowledge, see Evid C §§702, 800(a).

§16.3 III. ANALYSIS

Testimony falls into one of two categories:

(1) A witness states facts based on personal knowledge (*i.e.,* acquired through one's own senses); or

(2) A witness states an opinion (*i.e.,* an inference, a conclusion, or another subjective statement) drawn from facts that may or may not be within that witness's personal perception.

If a witness is not qualified to give an opinion, the opinion would be considered speculation.

§16.4   A. Lay Witnesses: Opinion Testimony versus Speculation

A lay witness is allowed to state an opinion only about matter that has been personally perceived and only if it is helpful to understand the testimony. Evid C 702, 800. See §§20.2–20.5.

Evidence Code §800 is statutory recognition of the desirability of opinion testimony on many matters that are within the common experience of lay witnesses and that are most accurately described through the opinion of the witness.

Some types of permissible opinion testimony include questions of identity, handwriting, quantity, value, weight, measure, time, distance, velocity, form, size, age, strength, heat, cold, sickness, and health. Questions about an individual's mental and moral characteristics (*e.g.,* disposition, temper, anger, fear, excitement, intoxication, veracity, general character) are also permissible opinion testimony. See generally *Manney v Housing Auth.* (1947) 79 CA2d 453, 459, 180 P2d 69; Comment to Evid C §800. See also *Wheeler v St. Joseph Hosp.* (1976) 63 CA3d 345, 361, 133 CR 775 (whether plaintiff signed document without reading it); *People v Moreno* (1973) 32 CA3d Supp 1, 108 CR 338 (whether defendant provoked altercation with police); *People v Harris* (1969) 270 CA2d 863, 872, 76 CR 130 (whether defendant was trying to break up altercation); *People v Ruiz* (1968) 265 CA2d 766, 773, 71 CR 519 (defendant's intoxication); *People v Chrisman* (1967) 256 CA2d 425, 434, 64 CR 733 (narcotics addict allowed to testify about nature of substance involved).

In deciding whether a lay witness may give opinion testimony, the court must consider the following:

- Whether the witness has adequate personal knowledge on which to form the requested opinion (see Evid C §802); and

- Whether the opinion testimony will help the trier of fact come to a clear understanding of the matter perceived by the witness (Evid C 800; see §20.4).

When a lay witness is asked to express an opinion based on ambiguous matter that is not within the common experience of lay persons, the question is objectionable because it calls for inadmissible opinion and it is speculative. See §§20.3–20.4.

§16.5   B. Expert Witnesses: Speculation

After a proper foundation is established proving that a particular expert is properly qualified, the expert witness may state an opinion within proven scientific areas of expertise even without personal knowledge of the facts. Evid C §801. See §§20.6–20.18. Under certain circumstances, an expert may base an opinion on assumptions related to the expert in the form of hypothetical questions, on the opinions or statements of others, or on independent studies or texts. What is a permissible foundation for an expert's opinion depends on the facts of each case. Comment to Evid C §801. The test is whether the matter "is of a type that reasonably may be relied upon by an expert in forming an opinion upon the subject." Evid C §801(b). See chap 20.

Whether an expert's opinion is based on permissible matter is a preliminary question for the trial judge to decide. Evid C §§405, 802. See §§21.8, 21.15 (foundations). If the judge rules that the opinion would be speculative and excludes it, the decision will not be reversed unless there is a showing that the party offering the evidence was thereby denied a fair opportunity to present a case. *Reynolds v Natural Gas Equip.* (1960) 184 CA2d 724, 740, 7 CR 879. Compare *People v Gamez* (1991) 235 CA3d 957, 967, 286 CR 894 (police officers qualified as experts on gang activity because their opinions were based on their own investigations and observations), with *People v Price* (1991) 1 C4th 324, 420, 3 CR2d 106 (trial court properly excluded proffered expert testimony on prison gangs by defense witness who did not base his testimony on personal knowledge, frustrated cross-examination on his qualifications and credibility, and refused to reveal persons whose statements formed basis of his opinions).

Under no circumstances may an expert base an opinion on speculative matter. Comment to Evid C §801. If the data on which an expert bases an opinion includes so many varying or uncertain factors that the expert is required to guess, surmise, or conjecture about that data, then the expert's opinion is speculative. For example:

- In *Waller v Southern Cal. Gas Co.* (1959) 170 CA2d 747, 339 P2d 577, the appellate court found no factual basis for an expert witness's assumption that a truck was making a right turn. The court therefore held that the trial judge had erred in admitting an opinion of the expert that was based on that speculative assumption.

- In *Eisenmayer v Leonardt* (1906) 148 C 596, 600, 84 P 43, the alleged value of stock that would have been issued to the plaintiff was sought as damages for breach of contract to organize a corporation. An expert was asked for an opinion of what that value would have been. The court held that the trial court properly excluded evidence of that "fanciful value."

§16.6   IV. STATUTE

Evidence Code §§702 (set out in §18.21), 800 (set out in §20.5), and 801 (set out in §20.22) provide the statutory bases for this objection.

§16.7 V. STATING THE OBJECTION

Objection, Your Honor. The question calls for speculation by the witness.

Some judges prefer a more precisely worded objection that explains its statutory basis, *e.g.*, "Objection, Your Honor. The matter is not within the witness's personal knowledge" or "There is an insufficient foundation for this opinion." One advantage of the more precisely worded objection is that the record then shows the specific legal ground raised.

17

Irrelevant Evidence

I. STATUTORY PROVISIONS §17.1

II. RELEVANCY
   A. Under Evidence Code §17.2
   B. Admissibility of Evidence to Which Opposing Counsel Offers to Stipulate §17.3
   C. Relevancy in Criminal Actions §17.4
   D. Admissibility of Prior Convictions §17.5
   E. Admissibility of Evidence to Support "Third Party Defense" §17.6

III. LAYING FOUNDATION FOR RELEVANCY §17.7

IV. "INCOMPETENT, IRRELEVANT, AND IMMATERIAL" §17.8

V. FAILURE TO OBJECT TO IRRELEVANT EVIDENCE §17.9

VI. ALTERNATIVES TO OBJECTING §17.10

VII. STATING THE OBJECTION §17.11

§17.1   I. STATUTORY PROVISIONS

The statutory provisions that form the basis for the "irrelevant" objection are found in the Evidence Code. "Relevant evidence" means "evidence, including evidence relevant to the credibility of a witness or hearsay declarant," that tends "to prove or disprove any disputed fact that is of consequence to the determination of the action." Evid C §210. No evidence is admissible except relevant evidence. Evid C §350. Generally, unless otherwise provided by statute, all relevant evidence is admissible. Evid C §351. See chaps 18–32.

The Comment to Evid C §351 lists some of the provisions of the Evidence Code and various other Codes that form the basis for exclusion of relevant evidence.

II. RELEVANCY

§17.2   A. Under Evidence Code

Under Evid C §210, set out in §17.1, two elements must be present for evidence to be classified as relevant:

(1) The evidence must have some probative value, *i.e.,* it must tend to prove or disprove a fact that is of consequence to the action. See *People v Snow* (2003) 30 C4th 43, 84, 132 CR2d 271; *People v Hall* (1980) 28 C3d 143, 167 CR 844. This is the traditional concept of relevancy. See 1 Witkin, California Evidence, *Circumstantial Evidence* §4 (4th ed 2000); Cleary, McCormick on Evidence §185 (3d ed 1984). Under Evid C §350, the court cannot admit irrelevant evidence over objection. See *Fuentes v Tucker* (1947) 31 C2d 1, 7, 187 P2d 752; *People v Slone* (1978) 76 CA3d 611, 631, 143 CR 61.

(2) The fact that the evidence tends to prove or disprove must be disputed in the action. This is the traditional concept of relevancy (McCormick's Handbook §185). If a fact is not genuinely disputed, evidence offered to prove the fact is irrelevant and inadmissible. See *Fuentes v Tucker, supra* (because defendant in wrongful death action admitted liability, circumstances of accident should not have been admitted).

The fact regarding which the evidence is offered need not be an ultimate fact. The Comment to Evid C §210 makes it clear that this element is satisfied if the evidence tends to prove or disprove a fact from which an ultimate fact in dispute may be presumed or inferred or if the evidence relates to the credibility of witnesses or hearsay declarants. See *People v Thompson* (1980) 27 C3d 303, 315, 165 CR 289. In arguing the merits of an objection on the ground of relevancy, the parties should address themselves to the presence or absence of these two component elements. In ascertaining whether evidence tends to prove a disputed fact, the court will examine whether the evidence offered serves "logically, naturally and by reasonable inference" to establish the fact. 27 C3d at 316.

A trial court is vested with wide discretion in determining relevance. *People v Babbitt* (1988) 45 C3d 660, 681, 248 CR 69; *People v Green* (1980) 27 C3d 1, 19, 164 CR 1; Evid C §350. Although there is no universal test of relevancy, the general rule in criminal cases might be stated as the court did in *People v Freeman* (1994) 8 C4th 450, 491, 34 CR2d 558:

> whether or not the evidence tends logically, naturally, and by reasonable inference to establish any fact material for the prosecution or to overcome any material matter sought to be proved by the defense. [Citation.] Evidence is relevant when no matter how weak it may be, it tends to prove the issue before the jury.

§17.3 B. Admissibility of Evidence to Which Opposing Counsel Offers to Stipulate

If counsel stipulates to a fact because of its potentially damaging effect on the case, opposing counsel may not present evidence on that fact, because it is not in dispute.

If the facts that a party has admitted or about which a party offers to stipulate has probative value relating to other issues, evidence of those facts may be introduced. Evid C §355. For example, if the action is not for wrongful death damages but for personal injury damages, the circumstances of the accident are admissible to show the seriousness of the injury as it relates to the extent of damages suffered. See *Krouse v Graham* (1977) 19 C3d 59, 79, 137 CR 863 (defendant stipulated to liability, but not to seriousness of plaintiff's injuries, and eyewitness testimony and photograph of accident scene were admissible on that issue); *Martin v Miqueu* (1940) 37 CA2d 133, 136, 98 P2d 816 (defendant stipulated to liability, but nature and extent of defendant's admissions were unclear).

§17.4   C. Relevancy in Criminal Actions

Under Proposition 8 (Cal Const art I, §28(d)), commonly called the "truth-in-evidence" provision, relevant evidence may not be excluded in any criminal proceeding with the following exceptions: "evidence relating to privilege or hearsay, or Evidence Code, Sections 352, 782 or 1103." Also excludable is evidence that is inadmissible under the United States Constitution. See *People v Cudjo* (1993) 6 C4th 585, 611, 25 CR2d 390.

Not only does the federal constitution protect defendants by keeping certain evidence from being admitted against them, but the converse is true as well. The admissibility of evidence by criminal defendants is protected by the federal constitution under certain circumstances. See, *e.g., Rock v Arkansas* (1987) 483 US 44, 97 L Ed 2d 37, 107 S Ct 2704 (defendant's testimony admissible at trial even though he had been hypnotized and state rule excluded testimony of previously hypnotized witnesses).

Even when no statutory exclusion is available, certain state constitutional rights may allow some other remedy, *e.g.*, a judicial instruction or comment belittling the weight of the evidence. See *Raven v Deukmejian* (1990) 52 C3d 336, 354, 276 CR 326, in which the court held that a provision of Proposition 115 (amending Cal Const art I, §24), characterizing state rights as the same as federal rights, is unconstitutional and has no effect. For example, if a pre-complaint lineup were held, evidence of identification might be admissible only when accompanied by a cautionary instruction.

In criminal cases, a defendant may offer to stipulate to an issue to foreclose the prosecution from offering relevant evidence on that issue. See §17.3. In *People v Washington* (1979) 95 CA3d 488, 157 CR 58, for example, the defendant was charged with selling heroin packaged in a yellow balloon. Defense counsel offered to stipulate that the defendant was "familiar with heroin, the way it is packaged and the way it is sold" but not that he "knew the contents of the yellow balloon in the prosecution's case." 95 CA3d at 490. The appellate court reversed the trial court's decision because the trial court did not accept the stipulation offered by defense counsel and instead admitted evidence of other narcotics activity by the defendant to prove knowledge of the narcotic nature of heroin. Ruling that courts must accept such stipulations to avoid unnecessarily prejudicing the accused, the appellate court held that exceptions to this rule apply when the stipulation would impair the effectiveness of the prosecutor's case and foreclose his options to obtain a conviction under differing theories. 95 CA3d at 488. See *People v Hall* (1980) 28 C3d 143, 152, 167 CR 844; *People v McClellan* (1969) 71 C2d 793, 800, 80 CR 31.

For the primary Evidence Code differences between criminal and civil cases, see §1.10. For further discussion of Proposition 8, see §1.6.

§17.5   D. Admissibility of Prior Convictions

The prosecution cannot be forced to accept a defendant's stipulation to a prior conviction that is an element of the offense; the prosecution has the right to prove this type of prior to the jury. Cal Const art I, §28(f) (applies only to prior convictions that are "an element of any felony offense"). For priors that are not an element of the offense, the defense may waive a jury and have them tried to the court after the trial on the underlying offense. See Pen C §1025. Alternatively, defendants appear to be entitled to bifurcate the trial of the underlying offense from the trial of the prior conviction. The jury first hears and decides the underlying crime. If there is a guilty verdict, a trial on the priors is held. See *People v Garcia* (1996) 45 CA4th 1242, 53 CR2d 256.

Evidence that a defendant committed a crime or other bad act may be admissible to prove a fact other than the defendant's disposition to commit the crime charged. The common issues on which bad acts may be admissible are to prove motive, opportunity, intent, plan, identity, and absence of mistake or accident. See Evid C §1101(b). In a case where the defendant is accused of a sexual offense, evidence of the defendant's commission of another sexual offense is admissible if the evidence is not inadmissible under Evid C §352. See Evid C §1108. However, such evidence must be disclosed to the defendant at least 30 days before the scheduled trial date. Evid C §1108(b). See California Criminal Law Procedure and Practice §§35.52-35.55 (7th ed Cal CEB 2004).

§17.6   E. Admissibility of Evidence to Support "Third Party Defense"

The admissibility of evidence to support a "third party defense" in a criminal action was modified and clarified in *People v Hall* (1986) 41 C3d 826, 833, 226 CR 112. In this case, the court held that a defendant is entitled to offer evidence that reasonably tends to show that a third person perpetrated the crime, subject to the application of Evid C §352. To be admissible, the evidence must be capable of raising a reasonable doubt of the defendant's guilt. It need not show substantial proof of a probability that the third person committed the act.

This rule does not require the trial court to admit any evidence, however remote; evidence is not relevant when it shows only the third person's motive and opportunity to commit the crime. There must be direct or circumstantial evidence linking the third person to the actual perpetration of the crime. See, e.g., *People v Huggins* (1986) 182 CA3d 828, 832, 227 CR 547 (statement of victim's neighbor showing opportunity to commit crime was not admissible). See also *People v Babbitt* (1988) 45 C3d 660, 248 CR 69, discussed in §16.3.

§17.7 III. LAYING FOUNDATION FOR RELEVANCY

The relevancy of evidence is normally apparent without reference to other evidence. Under some circumstances, however, the relevancy of proposed evidence depends on a "foundation," *i.e.*, on the existence of a "preliminary fact." Evid C §§400, 403(a)(1).

The Comment to Evid C §403(a) discusses the following examples:

- Suing the defendant for breach of an alleged agreement, the plaintiff offers evidence of negotiations with A. This evidence is irrelevant and therefore inadmissible unless the plaintiff proves the preliminary fact that A was the defendant's agent. See *Brown v Spencer* (1912) 163 C 589, 126 P 493.

- The defendant is charged with criminal responsibility for the acts of C because the two were allegedly conspirators. Evidence of C's acts is inadmissible unless the preliminary fact of conspiracy is proved. See *People v Steccone* (1950) 36 C2d 234, 238, 223 P2d 17.

The party offering evidence has the burden of producing foundational evidence on the existence of the preliminary fact sufficient to sustain a finding that the offered evidence is relevant. Evid C §403(a)(1). On proving a foundation, see §21.4. If, after considering this foundational evidence, the judge determines that no jury could reasonably find that the offered evidence is relevant, the judge must exclude that evidence. Comment to Evid C §403.

The judge may, however, admit proffered evidence conditionally, subject to establishing a proper foundation later in the trial. See Evid C §403(b). See §21.11. If the party that offered the evidence rests without having proved its relevancy, the opposing party should move to have the conditionally admitted evidence stricken. See §§21.13, 52.7. When the foundational fact is the witness's personal knowledge, that knowledge must be shown before the witness may testify about the matter. The judge may not admit the offered evidence conditionally before the witness's personal knowledge is shown.

§17.8 IV. "INCOMPETENT, IRRELEVANT, AND IMMATERIAL"

The general objection that evidence is "incompetent, irrelevant, and immaterial" is misconceived and misused by some attorneys to attack evidence for defects of every conceivable sort.

The Evidence Code makes it clear that a general objection of this sort is "insufficient." See Comment to Evid C §353.

- *Incompetent.* It is improper to speak of evidence as being incompetent.

Under the Evidence Code, only a witness may be incompetent, *i.e.,* disqualified from testifying (see §18.1). Technically, the trial judge can overrule the objection "incompetent, irrelevant, and immaterial" on this ground alone. Nevertheless, some courts still refer to evidence as being incompetent. See, *e.g., Samson v Transamerica Ins. Co.* (1981) 30 C3d 220, 234, 178 CR 343.

- *Irrelevant.* Irrelevancy remains a proper ground for objection, as described in §17.2. The objection should not be defeated by coupling it with such extraneous elements as incompetency.

- *Immaterial.* Before enactment of the Evidence Code, materiality was recognized as a separate concept (see former CCP §§1867–1868), and the line between relevancy and materiality was a difficult one to draw (see 1 Witkin, California Evidence, *Circumstantial Evidence* §3 (4th ed 2000); Cleary, McCormick on Evidence §185 (3d ed 1984)). The Evidence Code has solved this problem by merging the concept of materiality into the concept of relevancy. The single objection that evidence is irrelevant now effectively covers both, although courts sometimes still refer to "materiality" as if it were a separate element.

§17.9   V. FAILURE TO OBJECT TO IRRELEVANT EVIDENCE

Counsel's failure to object to inadmissible evidence does not "open the door" to the admission of related but otherwise inadmissible evidence. See *People v Gambos* (1970) 5 CA3d 187, 192, 84 CR 908. This general rule has been applied to the admission without objection of evidence characterized by the court as irrelevant. See *People v Johnson* (1964) 229 CA2d 162, 168, 40 CR 105 (evidence introduced without objection on direct examination used on cross-examination to introduce highly prejudicial evidence); *Fortner v Bruhn* (1963) 217 CA2d 184, 190, 31 CR 503 (legitimate cross-examination does not extend to matters improperly admitted on direct examination).

§17.10   VI. ALTERNATIVES TO OBJECTING

On possible alternatives to objecting, see §§4.9–4.14.

§17.11   VII. STATING THE OBJECTION

> Objection, Your Honor. The question calls for an answer that is irrelevant.

18
Incompetent Witness

I. GENERAL DESCRIPTION
   A. Definition §18.1
   B. Statutory Grounds §18.2
   C. Statute §18.3

II. ANALYSIS OF STATUTORY GROUNDS
   A. Inability to Communicate
      1. Definition §18.4
      2. Ruling on Objection §18.5
      3. Statute §18.6
      4. Alternatives to Objecting §18.7
      5. Stating the Objection §18.8
   B. Inability to Understand Duty to Tell Truth
      1. Definition §18.9
      2. Ruling on Objection §18.10
      3. Statute §18.11
      4. Alternatives to Objecting §18.12
      5. Stating the Objection §18.13
   C. Attorney as Witness
      1. Definition §18.14
      2. Statute; Rule of Professional Conduct §18.15
      3. Stating the Objection §18.16
   D. Judge as Witness
      1. Definition §18.17
      2. Statute §18.18
      3. Stating the Objection §18.19
   E. Juror as Witness §18.20
   F. Lack of Personal Knowledge
      1. Definition §18.21
      2. Illustrations §18.22
      3. Ruling on Objection §18.23
      4. Statute §18.24
      5. Alternatives to Objecting §18.25
      6. Stating the Objection §18.26
   G. Juror Impeaching Verdict
      1. Discussion §18.27
      2. Alternatives to Objecting §18.28
      3. Stating the Objection §18.29
   H. Testimony Based on Use of Speedtrap
      1. Discussion; Statute §18.30
      2. Alternatives to Objecting §18.31
      3. Stating the Objection §18.32

I. GENERAL DESCRIPTION

§18.1 A. Definition

Except as otherwise provided by statute, every person is qualified to be a witness, irrespective of age, and no person is disqualified to testify on any matter. Evid C §700. The statutory grounds that make a person incompetent to be a witness, or incompetent to testify about a particular matter, are analyzed in §§18.4–18.32. The principal grounds appear in Evid C §§700–704, which comprise chapter 1 ("Competency") of division 6 of the Evidence Code. It is the witness, not the evidence, that is incompetent. On misapplying the term "incompetent" to evidence, see §17.8.

Incompetency, which may disqualify a witness from testifying, must be distinguished from privilege (see §34.1), which may prevent even a competent witness from testifying.

Counsel studying this chapter should also review chaps 20–21 on the failure to establish a sufficient foundation before introducing evidence. Incompetence to testify and insufficient foundation are overlapping concepts. For example, a witness lacking personal knowledge of a matter (as required by Evid C §702(a)) is not competent to testify. See §§18.21, 21.5. Even if a witness has such knowledge, however, the witness can be barred from testifying on the ground of lack of foundation if sufficient knowledge is not shown. Evid C §403(a)(2). See §§21.3, 21.5. Often a witness is asked, "Do you know whether . . . ?" Unless personal knowledge as required by Evid C §702(a) is shown, counsel should object first on foundational grounds. Once a foundation is shown, counsel may be able to make an objection on competence or hearsay grounds.

Counsel should make an offer of proof when a witness's testimony has been erroneously excluded on the ground that the witness is incompetent. See §5.4.

§18.2 B. Statutory Grounds

Grounds for incompetency fall into the following two classes:

(1) *Grounds making a person incompetent to be a witness.* A person is incompetent to be a witness if the individual:

- Cannot express himself or herself "so as to be understood" (Evid C §701(a)(1); see §§18.4–18.8);

- Cannot understand the duty to tell the truth (Evid C §701(a)(2); see §§18.9–18.13);

- Is the attorney in the case and has not obtained the informed, written consent of the client (Cal Rules of Prof Cond 5-210; see §§18.14–18.16);

- Is the judge in the case, and a party objects (Evid C §703(b); see §§18.17–18.19); or

- Is a juror in the case, and a party objects (Evid C §704(b); see §18.20).

(2) *Grounds making a witness incompetent to testify about a particular matter.* A person, although competent to be a witness, is incompetent to testify about a particular matter if the individual:

- Has no personal knowledge of the matter (Evid C §702(a); see §§18.21-18.26);
- Is a juror being asked to give evidence about subjective thought processes to impeach the jury's verdict (Evid C §1150; see §§18.27-18.29); or
- Is being asked to give testimony in a prosecution for speeding, based on the use of a speedtrap (Veh C §40804; see §§18.30-18.32).

§18.3 C. Statute

Under Evid C §700, except as otherwise provided by statute, every person is qualified to be a witness, irrespective of age, and no person is disqualified to testify on any matter.

II. ANALYSIS OF STATUTORY GROUNDS

A. Inability to Communicate

§18.4 1. Definition

A person is disqualified to be a witness if unable to express himself or herself "so as to be understood." Evid C §701(a).

The court determines competency on the basis of a person's capacity to understand the oath and to perceive, recollect, and communicate regarding the events in question. Comment to Evid C §701. The accuracy of the witness's perception is a question of credibility to be resolved by the trier of fact.

§18.5 2. Ruling on Objection

This objection raises an issue of fact: whether the witness is capable of expressing himself or herself about the subject matter so as to be understood. See Evid C §§400, 402, 701(a)(1). This issue is decided as a preliminary foundational matter by the judge. Evid C §405(a). A witness is presumed to be competent. Evid C §701; Comment to Evid C §405.

Proof that a witness lacks capacity to testify often depends on what the objecting party has been able to discover about the witness. If the case is a sexual assault prosecution, the court is prohibited by statute from ordering a psychiatric or psychological examination of a witness. Pen C §1112. By implication perhaps, a court may, under Cal Const art I, §28(d), order such examinations in prosecutions other than for sexual assault. The argument against such an order is that the discovery statutes (Pen C §§1054-1054.7) are the exclusive means of discovery in criminal cases. Pen C §1054(e) ("no discovery shall occur in criminal cases except as provided by this chapter, other express statutory provisions, or as mandated by the Constitution of the United States"). California Constitution art I, §28(d) does not fit within any of the exceptions in Pen C §1054(e).

There may also be a right to discover psychiatric, psychological, medical, or other records that may show a lack of competence, particularly in a criminal case in which the defendant's constitutional right to the production of such evidence is weighed against the witness's statutory right against their production. See *Rubio v Superior Court* (1988) 202 CA3d 1343, 1348, 249 CR 419; *People v Boyette* (1988) 201 CA3d 1527, 1531, 247 CR 795; *People v Reber* (1986) 177 CA3d 523, 531, 223 CR 139, disapproved on other grounds in *People v Hammon* (1997) 15 C4th 1117, 1120, 65 CR2d 1; California Criminal Law Procedure and Practice §11.26 (7th ed Cal CEB 2004). See also *People v Hammon* (1997) 15 C4th 1117, 1120, 65 CR2d 1 (disapproving *Reber, supra*, regarding pretrial discovery of psychiatric records, but agreeing that discovery of records during trial allowable).

The offering party may present evidence, in rebuttal, demonstrating that the witness is able to express himself or herself so as to be understood. This evidence can be presented by questioning the witness. The issue to be resolved by the judge is whether the witness can communicate what the witness knows, either directly or through interpretation. Evid C §701(a). The judge often takes the initiative in this situation, posing questions to test the witness's capacity. On interpreters, see Evid C §§750–752, 754. Evidence Code §701(a) provides that an interpreter who understands the witness can, in effect, make the witness competent. Evidence Code §751(a) provides the form of oath for the interpreter.

If a party questions the interpreter's qualifications, an Evid C §402 preliminary fact hearing may be held to determine whether the testimony may be admitted. Interpreters may be somewhat suspect if they have not filed an oath with the clerk showing their certification under the Government Code. See Evid C §751(d). Each defendant in a criminal case must have an interpreter separate from the person who is interpreting for the witness. *People v Aguilar* (1984) 35 C3d 785, 200 CR 908; *People v Resendes* (1985) 164 CA3d 812, 210 CR 609.

§18.6   3. Statute

Under Evid C §701(a), a person is disqualified to be a witness if "[i]ncapable of expressing himself or herself concerning the matter so as to be understood, either directly or through interpretation by one who can understand him."

§18.7   4. Alternatives to Objecting

On possible alternatives to objecting, see §§4.9–4.14. If counsel is aware before trial that a prospective witness may be incompetent to testify, this matter should be brought to the court's attention as soon as possible, *e.g.,* by a motion in limine. See chap 2.

§18.8   5. Stating the Objection

> Your Honor, may we approach the bench? [At sidebar, state:] Objection, Your Honor. This person is incompetent to be a witness because _ _[he/she]_ _ cannot express _ _[himself/herself]_ _ so as to be understood.

B. Inability to Understand Duty to Tell Truth

§18.9   1. Definition

A person is disqualified to be a witness if the person is incapable of understanding the duty of a witness to tell the truth. Evid C §701(a)(2).

The court determines a person's competency on the basis of the capacity to understand the oath and to perceive, recollect, and communicate regarding the events in question. Comment to Evid C §701. The accuracy of the witness's perception is a question of credibility to be resolved by the trier of fact.

The objecting party has the burden of proving the prospective witness's lack of capacity. See *People v Knox* (1979) 95 CA3d 420, 431, 157 CR 238; Comment to Evid C §405.

The issue that the judge must resolve is whether the witness understands the nature of an oath, realizes the moral duty to tell the truth, and understands the prospect of being punished for a falsehood. *People v Burton* (1961) 55 C2d 328, 11 CR 65 (seven-year-old child found competent to be witness); *People v Berry* (1968) 260 CA2d 649, 67 CR 312 (child need not have detailed understanding of oath; merely that some earthly evil will occur for lying). See also *People v Liddicoat* (1981) 120 CA3d 512, 515, 174 CR 649, in which the court held that the trial court properly introduced the transcript of a four-year-old witness's preliminary examination even though she was not found competent at the time of trial. The court determined that there was substantial evidence to support the magistrate's finding at the preliminary examination that the witness was competent. The judge often takes the initiative in this situation, posing questions to test the witness's capacity.

§18.10   2. Ruling on Objection

This objection raises an issue of fact: whether the witness is capable of understanding the duty to tell the truth. Evid C §§400, 402, 701(a)(2). This issue is decided as a foundational matter by the judge. Evid C §405(a). In the absence of a clear abuse of discretion, the trial court's decision will not be reversed. *People v Blagg* (1970) 10 CA3d 1035, 89 CR 446 (evidence of victim's ability, a mentally disordered sex offender, to testify about being attacked in his jail cell deemed adequately presented to trial judge).

§18.11 3. Statute

Under Evid C §701(a)(2), a person is disqualified to be a witness if "incapable of understanding the duty of a witness to tell the truth."

§18.12 4. Alternatives to Objecting

On possible alternatives to objecting, see §§4.9–4.14.

§18.13 5. Stating the Objection

> Your Honor, may we approach the bench? [At sidebar, state:] Objection, Your Honor. This person is incompetent to be a witness because _ _[he/she]_ _ cannot understand _ _[his/her]_ _ duty to tell the truth.

C. Attorney as Witness

§18.14 1. Definition

Although an attorney is competent under Evid C §700 to testify at a trial while acting as counsel for one of the parties, this general rule is qualified by Cal Rules of Prof Cond 5-210. Under Rule 5-210(C), in a jury trial, a party's attorney may be a witness if the client's informed written consent is obtained first. This is just one of the problems facing an attorney who chooses to be a witness.

Counsel should therefore interview witnesses in the presence of a third party, who can later be called as a witness if necessary. To avoid waiving any applicable privileges, counsel should select a third party who is an investigator for the attorney or a member of counsel's own law firm.

Rule 5-210(C) applies when the attorney knows or should know that he or she ought to be called to testify before a jury. The rule does not apply to another attorney in the firm who will be a witness. See Drafter's Notes (1992) to Rule 5-210(C).

Assuming the role of both advocate and witness may impair credibility (as a witness) and diminish effectiveness (as an advocate). See *Comden v Superior Court* (1978) 20 C3d 906, 912, 145 CR 9 (decided under former Cal Rule of Prof Cond 2-111(A)(4)) (requiring withdrawal of law firm when member of firm was likely to be called as witness); *Reich v Club Universe* (1981) 125 CA3d 965, 178 CR 473 (decided under former Cal Rules of Prof Cond 2-111(A)(4), as amended; discussing the amendment and criticism of the former *Comden* rule). Even if the client gives informed consent, counsel who testifies before the jury may risk disqualification if there is "a convincing demonstration of detriment to the opponent or injury to the integrity of the judicial process." See *Lyle v Superior Court* (1981) 122 CA3d 470, 482, 175 CR 918 (decided under former Cal Rules of Prof Cond 2-111(A)(4), as amended; when deciding whether attorney can testify, court will resolve close case in favor of client's right to representation by attorney of choice).

In a criminal case, precluding an attorney from testifying might be a denial of due process. See *People v Goldstein* (1982) 130 CA3d 1024, 1030, 182 CR 207 (decided under former Cal Rules of Prof Cond 2-111(A)(4), as amended). See also *People v Smith* (1970) 13 CA3d 897, 91 CR 786 (under inherent power to control trial, court may force competent testifying attorney to discontinue representing client for ethical violation; decided under former Cal Rules of Prof Cond 2-111(A)(4)).

§18.15   2. Statute; Rule of Professional Conduct

Under Evid C §700, "[e]xcept as otherwise provided by statute, every person, irrespective of age, is qualified to be a witness, and no person is disqualified to testify on any matter."

Under Cal Rules of Prof Cond 5-210:

> A member shall not act as an advocate before a jury which will hear testimony from the member unless:
>
> (A) The testimony relates to an uncontested matter; or
>
> (B) The testimony relates to the nature and value of legal services rendered in the case; or
>
> (C) The member has the informed, written consent of the client. If the member represents the People or a governmental entity, the consent shall be obtained from the head of the office or a designee of the head of the office. . . . by which the member is employed and shall be consistent with principles of recusal.

Drafter's Notes (1992) to Rule 5-210 states:

> Rule 5-210 is intended to apply to situations in which the member knows or should know that he or she ought to be called as a witness in litigation in which there is a jury. This rule is not intended to encompass situations in which the member is representing the client in an adversarial proceeding and is testifying before a judge.

§18.16   3. Stating the Objection

> Your Honor, may we approach the bench? [At sidebar, state:] I object, Your Honor, to opposing counsel's being a witness in this action. There has been no showing that counsel has the client's informed written consent.

In these circumstances, counsel may choose not to object because of the difficult situation in which opposing counsel is being placed by being an advocate-witness.

D. Judge as Witness

§18.17 1. Definition

The judge presiding at a trial is incompetent to be a witness at that trial if a party objects. Evid C §703(b). See also Evid C §703.5, which provides that no person who presided at a judicial or quasi-judicial proceeding, and no arbitrator or mediator, can testify in or in conjunction with any later civil proceeding about any statement or conduct that occurred at the prior proceeding, except under circumstances outlined in the statute. This section does not apply, however, to a mediator with regard to any mediation under Fam C §§3160-3186.

§18.18 2. Statute

Evidence Code §703 governs the competency of a judge to testify at a trial over which the judge presides:

> (a) Before the judge presiding at the trial of an action may be called to testify in that trial as a witness, he shall, in proceedings held out of the presence and hearing of the jury, inform the parties of the information he has concerning any fact or matter about which he will be called to testify.
>
> (b) Against the objection of a party, the judge presiding at the trial of an action may not testify in that trial as a witness. Upon such objection, the judge shall declare a mistrial and order the action assigned for trial before another judge.
>
> (c) The calling of the judge presiding at a trial to testify in that trial as a witness shall be deemed a consent to the granting of a motion for mistrial, and an objection to such calling of a judge shall be deemed a motion for mistrial.
>
> (d) In the absence of objection by a party, the judge presiding at the trial of an action may testify in that trial as a witness.

§18.19 3. Stating the Objection

> Your Honor, may we approach the bench? [At sidebar, state:] I object, Your Honor, to your being a witness to this action.

§18.20 E. Juror as Witness

A person sworn and impaneled as a juror at a trial is incompetent to be a witness before the jury at that trial if a party objects. Evid C §704(b). "A juror is incompetent to give evidence as to matters that might impeach his verdict." Comment to Evid C §1150. However, in *People v Hutchinson* (1969) 71 C2d 342, 349, 78 CR 196, the supreme court interpreted Evid C §1150(a) to permit a party seeking to impeach a verdict to present juror affidavits or declarations to show overt conduct, conditions, events, and statements. The subjective reasoning processes of a jury may not be shown by such an affidavit. See §18.27.

F. Lack of Personal Knowledge

§18.21   1. Definition

Unless a witness has personal knowledge of facts, the witness is incompetent to testify. Evid C §702(a). Personal knowledge means a present recollection of an impression derived from the exercise of the witness's own senses. Comment to Evid C §702. To have personal knowledge, the witness must be physically or mentally capable of observing or recollecting the matter about which the witness proposes to testify. Evid C §702. See *People v St. Andrew* (1980) 101 CA3d 450, 457 n3, 161 CR 634. However a witness's testimony cannot be based solely on the witness's memory resulting from hypnosis. *Schall v Lockheed Missiles & Space Co.* (1995) 37 CA4th 1485, 44 CR2d 191. See §§19.11, 20.13.

If an objection is made to the witness's capacity to observe or recollect the matter, that capacity must be shown before the witness may be permitted to testify. Evid C §702(a). Further, a witness who has been hypnotized is not incompetent when questioned on topics unrelated to the events that were the topic of the hypnotic session. Evid C §795; *People v Shirley* (1982) 31 C3d 18, 181 CR 243.

Expert witnesses having certain qualifications (see §20.6) may give opinion testimony without "personal knowledge." Evid C §801. With this exception, the requirement of personal knowledge applies to all witnesses. Comment to Evid C §702.

§18.22   2. Illustrations

In the following cases, the courts considered whether a witness was being asked to testify on matters without personal knowledge:

- In *Fildew v Shattuck & Nimmo Warehouse Co.* (1918) 39 CA 42, 46, 177 P 866, counsel asked a witness "for what purpose the guard-rails around this elevator shaft were originally put there?" The court held that the trial court properly sustained an objection to this question on the ground of insufficient foundation, because no foundation had been laid showing that the witness had any personal knowledge of the matter. See *People v Southern Cal. Edison Co.* (1976) 56 CA3d 593, 606, 128 CR 697 (motion to strike State Forestry Department auditor's answer granted because no showing that he had personal knowledge about reasons for expenses set forth in report).

- In *People v St. Andrew* (1980) 101 CA3d 450, 458, 161 CR 634, before Mrs. S., the rape victim, testified, the defense objected that she was incompetent under Evid C §§701–702. A court-appointed psychiatrist testified at a chambers hearing that Mrs. S. might not have had the capacity to correctly observe or remember the events on the night of the rape. The trial judge did not question the psychiatrist, examined Mrs. S. only about whether she understood the difference between truth and falsehood (see Evid C §701(a)(2) requirement for competence), and said that he was not concerned with Evid C §702. The appellate court held that permitting Mrs. S. to testify was error because the trial court did not follow the correct legal standard of determining her competence to testify under Evid C §702.

§18.23   3. Ruling on Objection

The objection raises an issue of fact: whether the witness has personal knowledge about the matter. Evid C §§400, 402, 702. The party offering the testimony has the burden of producing evidence sufficient to sustain a finding that the witness has the required personal knowledge. Evid C §403(a)(2). See §21.5.

Merely asking whether the witness has personal knowledge of the matter is not sufficient. Opposing counsel should cross-examine the witness on this foundational issue before allowing the witness to testify. See Evid C §702(a).

If, after considering this evidence, the judge determines that no jury could reasonably find that the witness had such knowledge, the judge must exclude the proposed testimony. Comment to Evid C §403; Comment to Evid C §701. See §21.11.

This objection is important because witnesses testify without personal knowledge with some regularity and it is easy for them to conceal that they are doing so. Thus, the opponent of the evidence should be alert to object on foundation grounds if a question is phrased in such a way that the witness's personal knowledge of the answer appears unlikely (*e.g.,* "Did such and such occur, if you know?"). When the foundational questions are asked, it may become clear that the answer is based on hearsay or speculation.

§18.24   4. Statute

Evidence Code §702 governs the competency of a witness to testify on matters about which the person has no personal knowledge:

> (a) Subject to Section 801, the testimony of a witness concerning a particular matter is inadmissible unless he has personal knowledge of the matter. Against the objection of a party, such personal knowledge must be shown before the witness may testify concerning the matter.
>
> (b) A witness' personal knowledge of a matter may be shown by any otherwise admissible evidence, including his own testimony.

§18.25   5. Alternatives to Objecting

On possible alternatives to objecting, see §§4.9–4.14.

The absence of the requisite foundation may be raised at any time. For example, if a witness has given harmful testimony, counsel may be able to show by cross-examination that the witness's knowledge of the matter was acquired by hearsay rather than through the witness's perception. If so, counsel should move to strike the testimony and request that the jury be instructed to disregard it. In *Sneed v Marysville Gas & Elec. Co.* (1906) 149 C 704, 707, 87 P 376, the court held that the trial judge erroneously denied such a motion to strike after lack of personal knowledge was shown on cross-examination. Under similar circumstances in *Parker v Smith* (1854) 4 C 105, the court held that the trial judge, on his own motion, properly ordered a witness's testimony stricken from the record. The Comment to Evid C §702 cites these two cases as still expressing the law. Such a motion to strike is appropriate after lack of knowledge has been shown "if there is no reasonable opportunity to object before the testimony is given." Comment to Evid C §702.

Because the effectiveness of an instruction to the jury to disregard stricken testimony is questionable (see §52.3), counsel should make every effort to determine whether there is an adequate foundation for an adverse witness's testimony before the witness is allowed to testify.

§18.26   6. Stating the Objection

> Objection, Your Honor. This witness is incompetent to testify about this matter because it has not been shown that _ _[he/she]_ _ has personal knowledge of it.

G. Juror Impeaching Verdict

§18.27   1. Discussion

In *People v Hutchinson* (1969) 71 C2d 342, 349, 78 CR 196, the California Supreme Court interpreted Evid C §1150(a) to permit a party seeking to impeach a verdict to present juror affidavits or declarations to show overt conduct, conditions, events, and statements. The subjective reasoning processes of a jury may not be shown by such an affidavit. See also *In re Stankewitz* (1985) 40 C3d 391, 396, 220 CR 382 (declarations of two jurors admissible to show that third juror advised jury (incorrectly) on law of robbery based on his 20-year experience as police officer); *People v Hord* (1993) 15 CA4th 711, 19 CR2d 55 (affidavits that jurors discussed (a) fact that defendant did not testify and (b) possible sentence were admissible to show overt acts relevant to juror misconduct); *People v Hall* (1980) 108 CA3d 373, 378, 166 CR 578 (court rejected attempt to show that jurors mistakenly believed that they were voting for lesser-included offense rather than felony for which defendant was convicted; affidavit showed only jurors' state of mind).

The reason for such a distinction is that overt acts can be corroborated. This rule was applied to civil cases in *Clemens v Regents of Univ. of Cal.* (1970) 8 CA3d 1, 19, 87 CR 108. Juror counter-declarations are likewise admissible if they refer to objective behavior. *Hasson v Ford Motor Co.* (1982) 32 C3d 388, 414, 185 CR 654, interpreting *People v Deegan* (1891) 88 C 602, 26 P 500, cited in Comment to Evid C §1150.

People v Hutchinson, supra, was cited with approval in *People v Hill* (1992) 3 CA4th 16, 26, 4 CR2d 258, disapproved on other grounds in 16 C4th at 582 n5, in which the court held that Cal Const art I, §28(d) did not abrogate Evid C §1150(a). Because evidence of a juror's subjective reasoning process is not material to an inquiry into the validity of a verdict, it is not relevant evidence within the meaning of Evid C §210 and Cal Const art I, §28(d). 3 CA4th at 28.

A juror's affidavit may also be used to prove that a juror gave false answers during voir dire examination (see cases cited in Comment to Evid C §1150; see §29.35), a juror was mentally incompetent to serve as a juror (see Comment to Evid C §1150, citing *Church v Capital Freight Lines* (1956) 141 CA2d 246, 296 P2d 563), or the verdict was reached by chance (CCP §657(2); see §29.45).

At the hearing on a motion for new trial, evidence to prove or rebut a claim of jury misconduct is limited in civil cases to affidavits; testimony of witnesses is not allowed, and an objection to the introduction of such testimony is proper. *Linhart v Nelson* (1976) 18 C3d 641, 134 CR 813 (interpreting CCP §§657–658 as it applies to civil cases). In criminal cases, jury misconduct may be shown by actual testimony of jurors because CCP §§657–658 (requiring affidavits) do not apply in criminal cases. *People v Hedgecock* (1990) 51 C3d 395, 272 CR 803; *People v Hayes* (1999) 21 C4th 1211, 1255, 91 CR2d 211. The trial court has discretion to determine whether such evidence will be received and should allow it only if necessary to resolve material, disputed issues of fact; no "fishing expeditions" should be allowed. *People v Hardy* (1992) 2 C4th 86, 174, 5 CR2d 796; *People v Cox* (1991) 53 C3d 618, 697, 280 CR 692; *People v Hayes, supra*.

§18.28   2. Alternatives to Objecting

On possible alternatives to objecting, see §§4.9–4.14.

§18.29   3. Stating the Objection

> Your Honor, may we approach the bench? [At sidebar, state:] Objection, Your Honor. As a juror, this witness is incompetent to give subjective evidence to impeach the verdict.

H. Testimony Based on Use of Speedtrap

§18.30   1. Discussion; Statute

The use of radar to support a speeding violation is unlawful unless supported by an engineering and traffic study that supports the posted speed limit. *People v Goulet* (1992) 13 CA4th Supp 1, 17 CR2d 801. Further, a mere summary of an engineering and traffic survey justifying the posted speed limit is not sufficient; either the original survey or a certified copy is required. *People v Ellis* (1995) 33 CA4th Supp 25, 40 CR2d 111. Vehicle Code §40805 provides that

> every court shall be without jurisdiction to render a judgment of conviction against any person for a violation of this code involving the speed of a vehicle if the court admits any evidence or testimony secured in violation of, or which is inadmissible under this article.

Because of the specific provisions of Veh C §40808, Proposition 8 (Cal Const art I, §28) does not affect "speed trap" evidence. *People v Munoz* (1992) 11 CA4th 1190, 15 CR2d 21. See *People v Goulet, supra.*

An officer or other person is incompetent as a witness if the testimony is based on use or maintenance of a speed trap when there has been no traffic study. Veh C §40804(a).

§18.31 2. Alternatives to Objecting

On possible alternatives to objecting, see §§4.9–4.14.

§18.32 3. Stating the Objection

[Option 1: Witness is incompetent to testify]

Your Honor, may we approach the bench? [At sidebar state:] Objection, Your Honor. The witness is incompetent to testify about this matter because _ _[e.g., _ _[his/her]_ _ testimony is based on the use of a speed trap/at the time of the arrest _ _[he/she]_ _ was not wearing a full distinctive officer's uniform/at the time of the arrest _ _[he/she]_ _ was not using a vehicle painted the required distinctive color]_ _.

[Option 2: Traffic study not admissible]

Objection, Your Honor. The traffic study used by the prosecution to avoid the speed trap law is not admissible based on _ _[hearsay/no foundation]_ _.

19

Hearsay

I. DEFINITION §19.1

II. HEARSAY RULE §19.2

III. WHAT IS HEARSAY?
   A. Out-of-Court Statement §19.3
   B. Out-of-Court Statement Offered to Prove Truth of Matter Stated §19.4

IV. WHAT IS NOT HEARSAY?
   A. Statement Offered as Circumstantial Evidence §19.5
   B. Statement Offered to Prove That Statement Was Made §19.6
   C. Statement Offered to Prove Knowledge or Belief §19.7

V. EXCEPTIONS TO HEARSAY RULE: ADMISSIBLE HEARSAY
   A. Major Categories §19.8
   B. Important Considerations Regarding Exceptions
      1. Other Exclusionary Rules May Apply §19.9
      2. Proponent Must Lay Foundation §19.10
      3. Declarant Is Unavailable §19.11
      4. Statement Is Untrustworthy §19.12
   C. Descriptive Catalog of Exceptions
      1. Confessions and Admissions
         a. Admissions of Parties §19.13
         b. Adoptive Admissions §19.14
         c. Authorized Admissions §19.15
         d. Admissions of Co-Conspirators §19.16
      2. Statements Under Evid C §§1231–1231.4 §19.16A
      3. Statements Under Evid C §§1224–1228 §19.17
      4. Declarations Against Interest §19.18
      5. Prior Statements of Witnesses
         a. Statement Inconsistent With Present Testimony §19.19
         b. Prior Consistent Statements Offered Under Evid C §1236 §19.20
         c. Past Recollection Recorded §19.21
         d. Prior Statement Identifying Persons §19.22
      6. Spontaneous, Contemporaneous, and Dying Declarations §19.23
      7. Statements of Mental or Physical State §19.24
      8. Statements Relating to Wills or to Claims Against Estates §19.25
      9. Business Records §19.26
      10. Official Records and Other Official Writings §19.27

11. Former Testimony
    a. Former Testimony Defined (Evid C §1290) **§19.28**
    b. Party Same in Former Action (Evid C §1291) **§19.29**
    c. Party Different in Former Action (Evid C §1292) **§19.30**
    d. Minor Child in Dependency Action (Evid C §1293) **§19.31**
    e. Inconsistent Statement (Evid C §1294) **§19.31A**
12. Judgments **§19.32**
13. Family History **§19.33**
14. Reputation or Statements Concerning Community History, Property Interests, or Character **§19.34**
15. Dispositive Instruments or Ancient Writings **§19.35**
16. Statements in Commercial, Scientific, or Similar Publications **§19.36**
17. Bills Offered to Corroborate Other Evidence **§19.37**
18. Testimony Given at Preliminary Hearing in Criminal Case **§19.38**

VI. IMPEACHING HEARSAY DECLARANT **§19.39**

VII. COMMON MISCONCEPTIONS ABOUT HEARSAY RULE
　A. "Self-Serving" Is Not an Objection **§19.40**
　B. "Res Gestae" Is Not an Exception **§19.41**

VIII. CHECKLIST: HEARSAY PROBLEMS **§19.42**

IX. STATUTE **§19.43**

X. ALTERNATIVES TO OBJECTING **§19.44**

XI. STATING THE OBJECTION **§19.45**

§19.1　I. DEFINITION

Hearsay evidence is "evidence of a statement that was made other than by a witness while testifying at the hearing and that is offered to prove the truth of the matter stated." Evid C §1200(a). The component parts of this definition are analyzed in §§19.3-19.4.

§19.2　II. HEARSAY RULE

"Hearsay evidence" is defined in Evid C §1200. Evid C §150. Unless an exception is "provided by law" (see §19.8), hearsay evidence is inadmissible. Evid C §1200(b). "Law" includes constitutional, statutory, and decisional law. Evid C §160. Therefore, the People, the Legislature, and the California Supreme Court are free to create additional exceptions. Exceptions, of course, are still subject to constitutional limitations. See *Lilly v Virginia* (1999) 527 US 116, 144 L Ed 2d 117, 119 S Ct 1887 (hearsay exception subject to constitutionally protected right to confrontation).

For a catalog of exceptions, see §§19.8-19.27.

III. WHAT IS HEARSAY?

§19.3   A. Out-of-Court Statement

To be hearsay, evidence must be a statement made outside the current proceeding (*i.e.*, made "out of court"). Evidence Code §225 defines "statement" broadly to include:

- Oral or written verbal expressions; or
- Nonverbal conduct intended by the actor as a substitute for oral or written verbal expression, *e.g.*, sign language, symbols, or signals.

The conduct must be assertive in character, *i.e.*, there must be an intent to communicate some fact. See Comment to Evid C §1200. For example, in *People v Mayfield* (1972) 23 CA3d 236, 100 CR 104, a witness pointed to the defendant's picture in response to police questioning about who sold narcotics to the witness. The pointing was hearsay evidence. By contrast, flight after the commission of a crime is not hearsay, because there is no intent to use flight as communication. Flight is nonassertive conduct even though the act itself may indicate a consciousness of guilt. CALJIC 2.52. Another example of nonverbal nonassertive conduct appears in *People v Clark* (1970) 6 CA3d 658, 86 CR 106. A wife fainted when asked by her defendant husband, while he was being interrogated by police, whether he owned the type of coat identified as having been worn by the murderer. The fainting was held to be nonverbal, nonassertive conduct that was admissible as nonhearsay evidence (and relevant) to prove that her husband owned such a coat.

People v Sundlee (1977) 70 CA3d 477, 138 CR 834, is the first California decision to examine the hearsay character of an electronic recording of out-of-court statements made by a nonparty. The court held that such a recording made by a surveillance team has no more sanctity than any other evidence of an out-of-court statement offered to prove the truth of the matter stated. The recording is simply another form of such a statement, which constitutes hearsay.

§19.4   B. Out-of-Court Statement Offered to Prove Truth of Matter Stated

Evidence of an out-of-court statement is not hearsay unless it is offered, either expressly or by implication, to prove the truth of the matter stated, *i.e.*, that what was said is true. See *People v Archer* (2000) 82 CA4th 1380, 1391, 99 CR2d 230.

The primary reason for excluding hearsay is that such evidence is unreliable because the declarant's veracity, accuracy of perception, or recollection cannot be tested before the current trier of fact. Such matters concerning the declarant, however, are not relevant unless the truth of the declarant's statement is an issue. If evidence of such an out-of-court statement is offered for an asserted nonhearsay purpose (*e.g.*, to show the declarant's state of mind), its relevance to any issue in the case must be established before it is admissible. Evid C §350 (see §1.4).

IV. WHAT IS NOT HEARSAY?

§19.5   A. Statement Offered as Circumstantial Evidence

If the issue is the declarant's sanity, evidence that he declared, "I am the Emperor Napoleon," would obviously not be offered to prove that the declarant is Emperor Napoleon. The statement may be admissible to prove the declarant's mental state but would not be classified as hearsay, because the out-of-court statement would be offered only as circumstantial evidence of insanity or simulated insanity.

Similarly, in a civil suit for malicious prosecution for public drunkenness, statements made by the plaintiff at the time of arrest may be used to show that he or she was not intoxicated (see *Sandoval v Southern Cal. Enters.* (1950) 98 CA2d 240, 219 P2d 928); and, in an action for false arrest, evidence of statements made by unidentified informants near the scene of the alleged crime may be admitted to prove that the arresting officers acted reasonably and with probable cause to arrest (see *Dussault v Condon* (1959) 170 CA2d 693, 339 P2d 896). Whether the statements themselves are true is not the purpose for which they are being offered.

For example, evidence of a defendant's flight from the crime scene is not hearsay when offered as circumstantial evidence of consciousness of guilt (see *People v Hedrington* (1985) 171 CA3d 517, 521, 217 CR 754), and out-of-court statements and a note from the victim accusing the defendant of molesting her can be admitted (see *People v Fair* (1988) 203 CA3d 1303, 250 CR 486). The court in *Fair* observed that such evidence is subject to the hearsay exception in the "fresh" or recent-complaint doctrine. See Evid C §1228. A defendant's conflicting and arguably false statements regarding his or her whereabouts at the time of the crime are admissible as circumstantial evidence of consciousness of guilt. See *People v Zack* (1986) 184 CA3d 409, 417, 229 CR 317.

Out-of-court statements have been admitted as circumstantial evidence in prosecutions for bookmaking. To prove that certain premises were used for bookmaking, police officers who answered incoming telephone calls on the premises have been allowed to testify that the callers said that they wanted to place bets. Because this testimony was not offered for the purpose of proving the truth of what the callers said, it was not hearsay. *People v Warner* (1969) 270 CA2d 900, 907, 76 CR 160. In addition, the testimony would not be classified as hearsay because the callers did not intend to communicate anything about the use of the premises. See Comment to Evid C §1200; §19.3.

Out-of-court statements are also admissible when offered to prove good faith as a defense to a charge of malicious prosecution. See *Weber v Leuschner* (1966) 240 CA2d 829, 840, 50 CR 86 (statements were offered to prove that they were made by district attorney to defendant and that defendant was justified in relying on them). See also *Tennessee v Street* (1985) 471 US 409, 417, 85 L Ed 2d 425, 432, 105 S Ct 2078 (accomplice's confession admissible for nonhearsay purpose of rebutting defendant's testimony that defendant's confession was coercively derived from accomplice's statement).

NOTE▶ Out-of-court statements expressing sympathy or benevolence to the relative of an accident victim are not admissible as admissions of liability. Evid C §1160.

§19.6 B. Statement Offered to Prove That Statement Was Made

The issue in some cases is whether certain words were actually spoken. For example, under the objective theory of contract formation, out-of-court statements of offer and acceptance are not hearsay, because such statements are offered to prove that certain things were said and not that the statements were true or false. *Bank of America v Taliaferro* (1956) 144 CA2d 578, 301 P2d 393.

In *Bumb v Bennett* (1958) 51 C2d 294, 301, 333 P2d 23, an assignment of property was executed by one partner on behalf of a partnership. The issue was whether the partner was authorized to bind the partnership. Testimony was offered that the two partners had discussed the assignment and that the nonsigning partner had said "Go ahead." The statement "go ahead" is not hearsay, because it is not an assertion, which is susceptible to being true or false, but merely an instruction. This testimony was held to be admissible because its purpose was to prove that a statement of authorization had in fact been made. Similarly, evidence of statements made to an owner about a dangerous condition on his premises is admissible when offered to prove that the owner had notice of that condition. See *Hickman v Arons* (1960) 187 CA2d 167, 9 CR 379.

Another typical example of nonhearsay is evidence of an allegedly slanderous remark. If offered only to prove that the defendant made a particular remark, the evidence is not hearsay. The plaintiff's purpose in offering the remark is obviously not to prove the truth of the matter stated. See, *e.g., Stoneking v Briggs* (1967) 254 CA2d 563, 62 CR 249. In *Weathers v Kaiser Found. Hosps.* (1971) 5 C3d 98, 95 CR 516, the plaintiffs moved for a new trial based on alleged juror misconduct. In support of the motion, they offered declarations of jurors stating that the foreman had described the plaintiff as a "black woman" and added that, where he came from, "they don't even let a black woman into the courtroom." 5 C3d at 107. The declarations also alleged that another juror had made comments about the high quality of the defendant hospital. The court held that the declarations evidence was admissible because the statements had not been offered to show that black people were excluded from courtrooms or that the defendant hospital was of high quality, but to show the speakers' biases in making the statements. See also *People v Montgomery* (1976) 61 CA3d 718, 733, 132 CR 558 (statements admissible to show police officer's state of mind when defense was entrapment); §19.4. If declarations or affidavits are used in any court proceeding, counsel should review the documents for any inadmissible matters and move to strike them orally at the hearing.

§19.7   C. Statement Offered to Prove Knowledge or Belief

People v Roberson (1959) 167 CA2d 429, 334 P2d 666, contains one of many examples of the nonhearsay use of a statement offered to prove state of mind. The defendant was prosecuted for making a sale of heroin to an undercover police officer. After the defendant denied making the sale, the defense called his girlfriend to testify that a week before the alleged sale she told the defendant that she had heard that the buyer was an undercover narcotics officer. The appellate court held that this testimony was admissible nonhearsay to show, as circumstantial evidence, that defendant did not make and would not have made the alleged sale of heroin to the police officer.

Another example is evidence of statements made by informants to a police officer, which is offered for the nonhearsay purpose of establishing probable cause for arrest or issuance of search warrants. See *People v Magana* (1979) 95 CA3d 453, 462, 157 CR 173. Such statements by informants are not offered to prove the truth of the matter asserted in the statement but instead to show that regardless of whether the facts in the statements were true or false, the police officer or issuing magistrate reasonably believed them to be correct and that he or she had probable cause to arrest, search, or issue the warrant.

V. EXCEPTIONS TO HEARSAY RULE: ADMISSIBLE HEARSAY

§19.8   A. Major Categories

There are 16 broad categories of exceptions to the hearsay rule under the Evidence Code:

   (1) Confessions and admissions (see Evid C §§1220-1228; §§19.13-19.16);
   (2) Declarations against interest (see Evid C §1230; §19.18);
   (3) Prior statements of witnesses (see Evid C §§1235-1238; §§19.19-19.22);
   (4) Spontaneous, contemporaneous, and dying declarations (see Evid C §§1240-1242; §19.23);
   (5) Statements of mental or physical state (see Evid C §§1250-1252; §19.24);
   (6) Statements relating to wills or to claims against estates (see Evid C §§1260-1261; §19.25);
   (7) Business records (see Evid C §§1270-1272; §19.26);
   (8) Official records and other official writings (see Evid C §§1280-1284; §19.27);
   (9) Former testimony (see Evid C §§1290-1293; §§19.28-19.31A);

(10) Judgments (see Evid C §§1300-1302; §19.32);

(11) Family history (see Evid C §§1310-1316; §19.33);

(12) Reputation or statements concerning community history, property interests, and character (see Evid C §§1320-1324; §19.34);

(13) Dispositive instruments and ancient writings (see Evid C §§1330-1331; §19.35);

(14) Commercial, scientific, and similar publications (see Evid C §§1340-1341; §19.36);

(15) Statements under Evid C §§1231-1231.4 (criminal prosecution of gang-related crimes; see §19.16A); and

(16) Statements under Evid C §§1224-1228 (various statements of declarants involved in actions; see §19.17).

In addition to the Evidence Code exceptions, there are two other hearsay exceptions found in case law and in the California Constitution and Penal Code:

(17) Bills offered to corroborate evidence (see §19.37); and

(18) Preliminary hearing testimony in criminal cases (see §19.38).

Although the courts cannot expand the hearsay rule (see Evid C §351), they can diminish it by creating new exceptions by interpretation of its application in individual cases. See, *e.g.*, *In re Carmen O.* (1994) 28 CA4th 908, 921, 33 CR2d 848 (child dependency hearsay exception). In developing new exceptions to the hearsay rule, courts must proceed with caution. The general rule that hearsay evidence is inadmissible because it is inherently unreliable is of venerable common law pedigree. *People v Ayala* (2000) 23 C4th 225, 268, 96 CR2d 682; *In re Cindy L.* (1997) 17 C4th 15, 27, 69 CR2d 803.

B. Important Considerations Regarding Exceptions

§19.9   1. Other Exclusionary Rules May Apply

Each hearsay exception in the Evidence Code is introduced by a phrase similar to the following: "Evidence of a statement is not made inadmissible by the hearsay rule if. . . ." This language serves as a constant reminder that other rules of evidence may make the evidence inadmissible or excludable. For example, an out-of-court declaration that qualifies under an exception to the hearsay rule (admissible hearsay) may nevertheless be inadmissible because:

- It is irrelevant (Evid C §350), will confuse the issues (Evid C §352), or contains inadmissible opinion (Evid C §§800-803);

- The declarant had no personal knowledge of the subject matter (Evid C §702); or

- A privilege has been invoked (see Evid C §§911-1070).

Even if hearsay evidence in a criminal case falls within an exception to the hearsay rule, it may nevertheless be inadmissible for constitutional reasons. Evid C §1204. For example, if a criminal defendant confesses to a crime or makes an incriminating admission under circumstances violating the Fifth Amendment (privilege against self-incrimination) or Sixth Amendment (right to counsel) to the United States Constitution, the confession or admission must be excluded even though it is excepted from the hearsay rule. *Minnick v Mississippi* (1990) 498 US 146, 112 L Ed 2d 489, 111 S Ct 486; *Miranda v Arizona* (1966) 384 US 436, 16 L Ed 2d 694, 86 S Ct 1602. See also *Dickerson v U.S.* (2000) 530 US 428, 147 L Ed 2d 405, 120 S Ct 2326 (reaffirming *Miranda*).

The confrontation clause of the Sixth Amendment may bar the use of testimonial evidence against a defendant unless the defendant had a prior opportunity to cross-examine the unavailable witness. *Crawford v Washington* (2004) ___ US ___, 158 L Ed 2d 177, 124 S Ct 1354. The Supreme Court held that issues related to trustworthiness and reliability were not sufficient to satisfy constitutional guarantees when testimonial statements were at stake. The court declined to spell out a comprehensive definition of what constitutes "testimonial" evidence in *Crawford*.

§19.10   2. Proponent Must Lay Foundation

The party offering hearsay has the burden of establishing a foundation that proves an exception to the hearsay rule. Evid C §§403, 405.

The threshold preliminary foundation issue is whether the evidence is relevant. This determination must be made initially by the judge under Evid C §403(a)(1). If the next preliminary issue is the identity of the hearsay declarant (*i.e.,* whether the alleged declarant was the person who made the statement), or the existence of a relationship (*e.g.,* agency or conspiracy) that makes the declarant's statement admissible against a party, the Evid C §403 procedure also governs, and the judge decides only whether there has been a prima facie showing of the preliminary fact. The jury must make the final decision on the existence of the fact. See Comment to Evid C §403. See also §§21.1-21.14. All other foundational issues relating to hearsay are governed by Evid C §405, by which the trial judge determines whether a proper foundation for the exception has been laid. See §§21.8, 21.15, 21.18.

§19.11   3. Declarant Is Unavailable

The following exceptions to the hearsay rule apply if the declarant is unavailable as a witness:

- Declarations against interest (Evid C §1230);
- Former testimony (Evid C §§1291-1292);
- Statements concerning family history (Evid C §§1310-1311);
- Statements of the declarant's previously existing mental or physical state (Evid C §1251);
- Statements about the decedent's will (Evid C §1260); and

- Statements concerning land boundaries (Evid C §1323).

Evidence Code §240 defines "unavailable as a witness" quite broadly. In addition to physical unavailability (*e.g.,* the declarant has died or is beyond the reach of the court's process), the term includes situations in which the declarant is prevented from testifying or chooses not to testify on legal grounds (*e.g.,* privilege). See, *e.g., People v Fuentes* (1998) 61 CA4th 956, 961, 72 CR2d 237 (declarant who asserts Fifth Amendment privilege not to testify is "unavailable").

The question of what constitutes "unavailability" can present problems. This is especially true in criminal cases in which, under Evid C §240(a)(5), the prosecutor's reasonable diligence in trying to procure the absent witness is at issue. See *People v Smith* (2003) 30 C4th 581, 608, 134 CR2d 1 (prosecutor made reasonable efforts to procure witness's presence at trial); *People v Williams* (1973) 9 C3d 24, 106 CR 622 (supreme court agreed with trial judge that prosecution had sustained its burden of showing that a diligent search was made as a prerequisite for introducing preliminary hearing testimony); *People v Enriquez* (1977) 19 C3d 221, 236, 137 CR 171 (reversible error to receive prior recorded testimony of absent witness when prosecutor displayed "casual indifference" by making only slight efforts to locate witness, whose testimony was critical to prosecution's case). See also 1 Witkin, California Evidence, *Hearsay* §§27–29 (4th ed 2000).

In *People v Louis* (1986) 42 C3d 969, 990, 232 CR 110, the prosecution's key witness in a murder prosecution, a highly unreliable person with a criminal history, was released on his own recognizance after testifying at a preliminary examination and then promptly disappeared. The court held that the prosecutor's lack of diligence in securing the witness's attendance at trial rendered the preliminary hearing transcript testimony inadmissible at trial. Compare *Louis* with *People v Guiterrez* (1991) 232 CA3d 1624, 1640, 284 CR 230 (preliminary hearing testimony was permitted at trial when prosecutor exercised due diligence to locate unavailable witness by leaving subpoenas at home of witness's parents and making thorough inquiries to locate witness), disapproved on another ground in *People v Cromer* (2003) 24 C4th 889, 901 n3, 103 CR2d 23, *People v Watson* (1989) 213 CA3d 446, 261 CR 635 (absent witness's preliminary hearing testimony was properly admitted when prosecution demonstrated diligence by serving subpoena on witness and advising him that relocation to foreign country coupled with failure to appear at trial could subject him to arrest on return to United States), and *People v Rivera* (1986) 186 CA3d 251, 230 CR 533 (witness's preliminary hearing testimony was admitted at trial even though prosecution had not resorted to interstate or international process to secure attendance, because witness's location was unknown and witness was clearly being evasive).

When unavailability of a witness is predicated on a mental or physical condition, the incapacity must be of extreme severity; determination of the degree of severity is a matter within the trial court's discretion. See *Schall v Lockheed Missiles & Space Co.* (1995) 37 CA4th 1485, 44 CR2d 191 (plaintiff incompetent to testify in sexual harassment case because her sole memory of the harassment occurred as a result of being hypnotized by a therapist); *People v Shirley* (1982) 31 C3d 18, 72 n60, 181 CR 243 (victim, who purportedly had perceived events of crime but whose memory was enhanced by hypnosis after preliminary examination but before being called to testify at trial, was unavailable under Evid C §240(a)(2) because she was "disqualified from testifying to the matter" to which her testimony would apply under Evid C §240(a)(2)); *People v Rojas* (1975) 15 C3d 540, 125 CR 357 (although present in court and invoking no claim of privilege, declarant unavailable because his justified fear for his and his family's safety induced "mental infirmity" required by Evid C §240(a)(3)); *People v Reed* (1996) 13 C4th 217, 52 CR2d 106 (preliminary hearing transcripts containing hearsay were admissible under the unavailable witness exception (Evid C §1291(a)), because witnesses were legally unavailable as matter of law as prosecution was precluded by judicial rule from presenting any evidence outside record of conviction to prove circumstances of prior crime). In *People v Reed, supra,* the court found that, although Evid C §240 defines "unavailable witness," the rule barring live testimony was not specifically mentioned. Courts have not interpreted Evid C §§240 and 1291 so strictly as to preclude unlisted variants of unavailability.

Application of the rule established in *People v Shirley, supra*, has been restricted by Evid C §795. In a criminal proceeding, the testimony of a witness who has previously undergone hypnosis for the purpose of recalling events that are the subject of the witness's testimony is admissible if the detailed conditions of the statute are met. Evid C §795(a). Before admitting the testimony, the court must hold an Evid C §402 hearing at which the proponent must prove by clear and convincing evidence that the hypnosis did not make the witness's prehypnosis recollection unreliable or substantially impair the witness's ability to be cross-examined on the recollection. Evid C §795(a)(4). The admissible testimony at trial is limited to matters that the witness recalled and related and of which a written record, an audiotape, or a videotape was made before the hypnosis. Evid C §795(a)(1)-(2). The hypnosis must have been conducted according to prescribed procedures, including the videotaping of the hypnotic session. Evid C §795(a)(3). Note, however, that Evid C §795 cannot be invoked to prevent a defendant from testifying. See *Rock v Arkansas* (1987) 483 US 44, 97 L Ed 2d 37, 107 S Ct 2704 (state statute regarding admissibility of defendant's testimony after having been hypnotized was unconstitutional).

In *People v Alcala* (1992) 4 C4th 742, 15 CR2d 432, the California Supreme Court held that a witness was properly found to be "unavailable" when she testified at the defendant's first trial but then lost all memory of the events because of a stress-related disability. The witness, who the trial judge found to be credible, was thoroughly questioned at the second trial about her memory of prior testimony.

Another definition of "unavailability of a witness" can be found in Evid

C §240(c). An alleged crime victim witness is unavailable as a witness when expert testimony establishes that harm caused by the alleged crime was of sufficient severity that the witness is physically unable to testify or is unable to testify without suffering substantial trauma. Evid C §240(c). Evidence Code §240(c) is apparently a partial codification of the holding in *People v Stritzinger* (1983) 34 C3d 505, 194 CR 431.

Under Evid C §1350, in a criminal proceeding charging a serious felony, a statement of an unavailable declarant is not inadmissible as hearsay if all of the following are true:

- There is clear and convincing evidence that the declarant's unavailability was knowingly caused, aided, or solicited by the party against whom the statement is offered for the purpose of preventing arrest or prosecution, and the unavailability is the result of death by homicide or kidnapping of the declarant.

- There is no evidence that the party offering the statement caused, aided, solicited, or procured the declarant's unavailability.

- The statement has been memorialized in a tape recording made by a law enforcement official, or in a written statement prepared by a law enforcement official and signed by the declarant and notarized in the presence of the law enforcement official, prior to the death or kidnapping of the declarant.

- The statement was made under circumstances that indicate its trustworthiness and was not the result of promise, inducement, threat, or coercion.

- The statement is relevant to the issues to be tried.

- The statement is corroborated by other evidence that tends to connect the party against whom the statement is offered with the commission of the serious felony with which the party is charged. The corroboration is not sufficient if it merely shows the commission of the offense or the circumstances thereof.

If the defendant did not have an earlier opportunity to cross-examine the unavailable witness, the testimonial evidence may be barred by the confrontation clause of the Sixth Amendment. See *Crawford v Washington* (2004) ___ US ___, 158 L Ed 2d 177, 124 S Ct 1354, discussed in §19.9.

§19.12   4. Statement Is Untrustworthy

A hearsay exception does not apply if the circumstances under which an out-of-court statement was made indicate that it lacks trustworthiness. The trial judge can exclude otherwise admissible hearsay if the judge determines that the evidence is not reliable. See, *e.g.*, Evid C §1252. If the judge determines that a hearsay statement concerning mental state was made with a motive to misrepresent, the judge may exclude the statement as being untrustworthy. Comment to Evid C §1252.

In a personal injury action, the plaintiff's family and co-workers may testify that the plaintiff constantly complained about his or her physical and mental condition following an accident. Such statements are usually admissible in personal injury actions to prove the plaintiff's condition before and after the accident, which is at issue as part of the claim for damages. Such statements are usually not admissible in a criminal action, however, because the defendant may be motivated to falsify, *e.g.*, statements to a police officer about his grief-stricken state after hearing of his wife's death. Note that under Evid C §1252, the court determines the trustworthiness of the hearsay statement rather than that of the testimony of the witness who relates it. *People v Spencer* (1969) 71 C2d 933, 80 CR 99.

The trustworthiness restriction applies to the following:

- Testimony regarding the declarant's mental or physical state (see Evid C §§1250–1252);

- Statements about the declarant's will (see Evid C §1260);

- Statements of a decedent offered in an action against the decedent's estate (see Evid C §1261);

- Statements concerning family history (see Evid C §§1310–1311); and

- Statements concerning land boundaries (see Evid C §1323).

A showing of trustworthiness is also required to invoke the business-records exception to the hearsay rule. The proponent must make an affirmative showing that the "sources of information and method and time of preparation were such as to indicate its trustworthiness." Evid C §1271(d). A similar affirmative showing must be made to invoke the exception for entries in official records. Evid C §1280(c)

In each of these situations, the Evidence Code requires the trial judge to make a preliminary determination regarding the element of trustworthiness. See Comments to Evid C §§405, 1271.

The Supreme Court has held that issues related to trustworthiness and reliability were not sufficient to satisfy constitutional guarantees when testimonial statements were at stake in a criminal case. *Crawford v Washington* (2004) ___ US ___, 158 L Ed 2d 177, 124 S Ct 1354. The court held that the confrontation clause of the Sixth Amendment may bar the use of testimonial evidence against a defendant unless the defendant had a prior opportunity to cross-examine the unavailable witness, but declined to spell out a comprehensive definition of what constitutes "testimonial" evidence.

C. Descriptive Catalog of Exceptions

1. Confessions and Admissions

§19.13   a. Admissions of Parties

Exceptions to the hearsay rule for the admissions of parties are governed by Evid C §1220. Even an unverified pleading is presumed to be filed with the party's consent and is thus regarded as an admission. *Valerio v Andrew Youngquist Constr.* (2002) 103 CA4th 1264, 1271, 127 CR2d 436 (admission in pleading is waiver of proof of fact by conceding its truth). A superseded pleading is no longer admissible as direct evidence to establish a fact, but it may be offered for impeachment. *Staples v Hoefke* (1987) 189 CA3d 1397, 1412, 235 CR 165. See also *Uram v Abex Corp.* (1990) 217 CA3d 1425, 1433, 266 CR 695 (defendant moving for summary judgment may rely on allegations in complaint as judicial admissions).

Although a pleading in a prior civil proceeding may be offered as an evidentiary admission in a subsequent proceeding, the party against whom the admission is offered may show that the statements were inadvertently made. *Magnolia Square Homeowners Ass'n v Safeco Ins. Co.* (1990) 221 CA3d 1049, 1060, 271 CR 1. See also *Simon v Steelman* (1990) 224 CA3d 1002, 274 CR 218 (plaintiff's testimony concerning corporate ownership given in paternity action was properly admitted in later action for involuntary dissolution of corporation).

The admissions of a defendant in a criminal case are governed by a number of rules that are not found in civil cases. For example, a statement may be excluded if the defendant was not properly *Miranda*-ized (see *Miranda v Arizona* (1966) 384 US 436, 16 L Ed 2d 694, 86 S Ct 1602. See also *Dickerson v U.S.* (2000) 530 US 428, 147 L Ed 2d 405, 120 S Ct 2326 (reaffirming *Miranda*). Defendant's statement may also be excluded if the statement was the product of an unlawful search and seizure, detention, or arrest (see *People v Takencareof* (1981) 119 CA3d 492, 496, 174 CR 112) or coercive police conduct (see *People v Hall* (2000) 78 CA4th 232, 92 CR2d 687). For a detailed discussion, see California Criminal Law Procedure and Practice, chap 30 (7th ed Cal CEB 2004).

Defendant's statement made after an alleged murder that he would get rid of a body by dumping it in Los Angeles was admissible as a party admission. It was offered as consciousness of guilt and to prove circumstantially that defendant had recently dumped the body of another woman in Los Angeles in an attempt to get rid of the body. *People v Robinson* (2000) 85 CA4th 434, 445, 102 CR2d 179. In another case, the party admission was in the form of defendant's handwritten document listing the his murder victims. See *People v Kraft* (2000) 23 C4th 978, 1032, 99 CR2d 1.

The defendant's statements in a criminal case need not be incriminatory to be admissions; they may even be exculpatory if they are believed. *People v Zack* (1986) 184 CA3d 409, 416, 229 CR 317 (defendant's conflicting statement on his whereabouts at time of crime offered to show consciousness of guilt). Such admission or confession comes under Evid C §1220 (admission-of-a-party exception) rather than Evid C §1230 (declaration against penal interest). Evidence Code §1230 requires both that the declarant be unavailable and that the statement have been made against penal interest. Neither of these conditions is required by Evid C §1220.

Even if a defendant's admission is inadmissible during the prosecution's case in chief, a statement that was voluntary is admissible to impeach the defendant if he or she chooses not to testify. *People v May* (1988) 44 C3d 309, 243 CR 369.

§19.14   b. Adoptive Admissions

Exceptions to the hearsay rule for adoptive admissions are governed by Evid C §1221. A party who has knowledge of the contents of a statement manifests his or her adoption or belief in its truth by words or other conduct. *People v Riel* (2000) 22 C4th 1153, 1189, 96 CR2d 1. See Jefferson's California Evidence Benchbook §§3.23–3.30 (3d ed CJA-CEB 1997).

The declarant of an adoptive admission need not expressly acknowledge the correctness of a statement made; an evasion, equivocal reply, or even silence is more typical of such an admission. *People v Riel* (2000) 22 C4th 1153, 1189, 96 CR2d 1; *People v Humphries* (1986) 185 CA3d 1315, 1335, 230 CR 536. For example, in a murder prosecution, evidence that the defendant smiled while listening to an accomplice describe their participation in a murder was held sufficient to be submitted to the jury as an adoptive admission under Evid C §1221. See *People v Silva* (1988) 45 C3d 604, 623, 247 CR 573. See also *People v Medina* (1990) 51 C3d 870, 891, 274 CR 849, aff'd on other grounds in 505 US 437, 120 L Ed 2d 353, 112 S Ct 2572 (treating defendant's silence in response to sister's statement as adoptive admission did not unconstitutionally penalize defendant's right to remain silent).

§19.15   c. Authorized Admissions

Exceptions to the hearsay rule for authorized admissions are governed by Evid C §1222. Authorized admissions are contingent on foundational evidence of the party's having authorized the declarant to make a statement for the party concerning the subject matter.

§19.16   d. Admissions of Co-Conspirators

Exceptions to the hearsay rule for the admissions of co-conspirators are governed by Evid C §1223. Requirements include the following (*People v Herrera* (2000) 83 CA4th 46, 59, 98 CR2d 911):

- The statement must have been made by the declarant while participating in the conspiracy;

- The statement must have been made in furtherance of the conspiracy's objective; and
- The statement must have been made before or during the time that the party was participating in the conspiracy.

See Jefferson's California Evidence Benchbook §§3.39–3.49 (3d ed CJA-CEB 1997).

The defendant need not be charged with co-conspiracy to apply the co-conspirator exception to the hearsay rule. Thus, admissions by prostitutes that implicate their pimp are admissible against the pimp under the co-conspirator exception. *People v Ambrose* (1986) 183 CA3d 136, 139, 227 CR 885.

In order for a declaration to be admissible under the co-conspirator exception to the hearsay rule, the proponent must proffer sufficient evidence to allow the trier of fact to determine that the conspiracy exists by a preponderance of the evidence. A prima facie showing of a conspiracy for the purposes of admissibility of a co-conspirator's statement under Evid C §1223 simply means that a reasonable jury could find it more likely than not that the conspiracy existed at the time the statement was made. *People v Herrera* (2000) 83 CA4th 46, 59, 98 CR2d 911.

§19.16A   2. Statements Under Evid C §§1231–1231.4

Exceptions to the hearsay rule in criminal proceedings exist for a prior statement made by a declarant under penalty of perjury if the declarant is deceased and the statement is relevant to a criminal prosecution of a gang-related crime. The proponent inducing the statement must establish each of the following:

- The statement relates to acts or events relevant to a criminal prosecution under provisions of the California Street Terrorism Enforcement and Prevention Act. Evid C §1231(a).
- A verbatim transcript, copy, or record of the statement exists. A record may include a statement preserved by means of an audio or video recording or equivalent technology. Evid C §1231(b).
- The statement relates to acts or events within the personal knowledge of the declarant. Evid C §1231(c).
- The statement was made under oath of affirmation in an affidavit or was made at a deposition, preliminary hearing, grand jury hearing, or other proceeding in compliance with law, and was made under the penalty of perjury. Evid C §1231(d).
- The declarant died of natural causes. Evid C §1231(e).
- The statement was made under circumstances that would indicate its trustworthiness and render the declarant's statement particularly worthy of belief. See Evid C §1231(f).

A statement is admissible under Evid C §1231 only if the proponent of the statement makes known to the adverse party the intention to offer the statement and the particulars of the statement sufficiently in advance of the proceedings to provide the adverse party with a fair opportunity to prepare to meet the statement. Evid C §1231.1.

A peace officer may administer and certify oaths for the purpose of this section. Evid C §1231.2.

Any law enforcement officer testifying as to any hearsay statement under Evid C §1231 shall either have five years of law enforcement experience or have completed a training course certified by the Commission on Peace Officer Standards and Training that includes training in investigation and reporting of cases and testifying at preliminary hearings and trials. Evid C §1231.3.

If evidence of a prior statement is introduced under this section, the jury may not be told that the declarant died from other than natural causes, but merely that the declarant is unavailable. Evid C §1231.4.

The Supreme Court has held that the confrontation clause of the Sixth Amendment bars use of testimonial evidence of an unavailable witness at a criminal trial unless the defendant had a prior opportunity to cross-examine the unavailable witness. *Crawford v Washington* (2004) ___ US ___, 158 L Ed 2d 177, 124 S Ct 1354. It is unclear to what extent *Crawford* may limit the hearsay exceptions described in this section.

Counsel should note that the California Street Terrorism Enforcement and Prevention Act will not affect other evidentiary requirements including, but not limited to, Evid C §§351 and 352. This act will not impair a party's right to attack the credibility of the declarant under Evid C §1202, will not affect the defendant's right to discovery for purposes of producing rebuttal evidence attacking the declarant's credibility, and must not be used in a manner inconsistent with the defendant's right to due process and to confront witnesses under the United States or California Constitution. See Stats 1997, ch 499, §2.

§19.17   3. Statements Under Evid C §§1224–1228

An exception to the hearsay rule exists for the following statements:

- Statements of declarants when liabilities, obligations, or duties of the parties are based on liabilities, obligations, or duties of the declarants. Evid C §1224. See Jefferson's California Evidence Benchbook §3.50 (3d ed CJA-CEB 1997).

- Statements of declarants whose rights or titles are at issue. Evid C §1225. See Evidence Benchbook §3.60.

- Statements of minor children when offered against parents who are plaintiffs in actions for injuries to their children. Evid C §1226.

- Statements by deceased persons when offered against plaintiffs in actions for wrongful death. Evid C §1227.

- Statements of minor children under age 12 that describe the minor as a victim of sexual abuse. Evid C §1228. See also *In re Lucero L.* (2000) 22 C4th 1227, 1239, 96 CR2d 56; *In re Cindy L.* (1997) 17 C4th 15, 18, 69 CR2d 803; *In re Carmen O.* (1994) 28 CA4th 908, 921, 33 CR2d 848. These cases set forth the child dependency hearsay exception, which allows, under certain conditions, admission of out-of-court statements by alleged victims of child sexual abuse during juvenile court dependency hearings.

§19.18   4. Declarations Against Interest

Statements by unavailable declarants (who had sufficient knowledge of the subject) are not made inadmissible by the hearsay rule if the statements are so contrary to the declarant's pecuniary or proprietary interests, subject them to such risks of civil or criminal liability, tend to render claims they have against others invalid, or create such a risk of making the declarants objects of hatred, ridicule, or social disgrace in the community that reasonable persons would not have made the statements unless they believed them to be true. Evid C §1230; *People v Wheeler* (2003) 105 CA4th 1423, 1427, 129 CR2d 916 (statement of defendant's wife that she was having affair with victim admissible as declaration against social interest).

If a nonparty witness asserts the privilege against self-incrimination, his or her extrajudicial declarations do not automatically become admissible as statements against penal interest and are thus excepted from the hearsay objection under Evid C §1230. *People v Johnson* (1974) 39 CA3d 749, 114 CR 545. The test is whether the nonparty declarant realized or should have realized that the statements were distinctly against a penal interest at the time they were made.

Admission of a declaration against penal interest is predicated on the basic trustworthiness of such a declaration. The court must determine whether a statement is truly against interest and, therefore, is sufficiently trustworthy. The court should take into account the circumstances surrounding the statement, including the declarant's possible motivation and relationship to the defendant. The determination requires the court to apply to the facts of each case its knowledge of and appreciation for the ways in which people conduct themselves. *People v Duarte* (2000) 24 C4th 603, 610, 101 CR2d 701; *People v Frierson* (1991) 53 C3d 730, 745, 280 CR 440.

5. Prior Statements of Witnesses

§19.19   a. Statement Inconsistent With Present Testimony

Under Evid C §1235, a prior inconsistent statement may be used as substantive evidence of the truth of its contents, as well as for impeachment of the witness's credibility, if it is offered in compliance with the Evid C §770 requirements of (1) giving the witness an opportunity to explain or deny the statement while testifying or (2) not excusing the witness from giving further testimony.

Prior inconsistent statements are admissible in criminal cases for purposes of impeachment and also as substantive evidence if the declarant testifies in person and is at trial subject to cross-examination. *People v Chavez* (1980) 26 C3d 334, 352, 161 CR 762 (general application of Evid C §1235 does not violate California's confrontation clause, Cal Const art I, §15). See 1 Witkin, California Evidence, *Hearsay* §§157–160 (4th ed 2000).

Only if the witness testifies at a hearing (including the trial at which the question of admissibility arises) is there a basis for applying Evid C §1235 and introducing a prior statement that is inconsistent with that testimony.

§19.20   b. Prior Consistent Statements Offered Under Evid C §1236

Prior consistent statements offered under Evid C §1236 are admissible as exceptions to the hearsay rule, as long as they are offered in compliance with Evid C §791, to rehabilitate or support the credibility of a witness. These requirements include the following:

- That the witness's credibility has been attacked by admission of a prior inconsistent statement or by an express or implied charge that the testimony at the hearing is recently fabricated or influenced by bias or other improper motive; and

- That the prior consistent statement was made before the prior inconsistent statement was made or before such bias or motive arose.

A prior consistent statement may be used as substantive evidence of the truth of its contents as well as for rehabilitation of the witness's credibility. *People v Cannady* (1972) 8 C3d 379, 105 CR 129. On rehabilitation, see chap 23.

In *People v Bunyard* (1988) 45 C3d 1189, 249 CR 71, a murder case, the court held that, under Evid C §791, a witness's sister was properly allowed to testify to prior consistent statements made to her by her brother before any implied improper motive was alleged to have arisen. Similarly, in *People v Andrews* (1989) 49 C3d 200, 260 CR 583, the court held that a prior statement by an accomplice was properly admitted to refute the defendant's charge of recent fabrication motivated by a favorable plea bargain deal made by the accomplice.

§19.21   c. Past Recollection Recorded

Exceptions to the hearsay rule for past recollection recorded are governed by Evid C §1237. The record of past recollection need not have been made by the witness or under the witness's direction or by someone else for the purpose of recording the statement at the time it was made. See *People v Miller* (1996) 46 CA4th 412, 53 CR2d 773, disapproved on other grounds in 18 C4th at 1240. The statute contains many detailed requirements for this exception, which should not be confused with using a writing to refresh recollection. The latter is governed by Evid C §771.

§19.22   d. Prior Statement Identifying Persons

An exception to the hearsay rule exists for prior statements identifying persons (*e.g.,* as participants in crimes) if:

- The statement would have been admissible if made by the witness while testifying (Evid C §1238);

- The statement is an identification of a party or another person who participated in a crime or other occurrence (Evid C §1238(a));

- The statement was made when the occurrence was fresh in the witness's memory (Evid C §1238(b)); and

- The witness testifies at the trial that he or she made the prior identifying statements and that they were a true reflection of the witness's memory (Evid C §1238(c)).

§19.23   6. Spontaneous, Contemporaneous, and Dying Declarations

An exception to the hearsay rule exists for the following declarations:

- Spontaneous declarations relating to an event while under the stress of excitement caused by perception. Evid C §1240(b). *People v Farmer* (1989) 47 C3d 888, 901, 254 CR 508, overruled on other grounds in *People v Waidla* (2000) 22 C4th 690, 724 n6, 94 CR2d 396 (statements made by victim to police dispatcher were thus spontaneous, even though they were responses to questions); *People v Gallego* (1990) 52 C3d 115, 175, 276 CR 679 (spontaneous statement triggered by facial slap and bizarre circumstances); *Rufo v Simpson* (2001) 86 CA4th 573, 590, 103 CR2d 492 (battered woman's statements to police after violent incidents occurred); *People v Gutierrez* (2000) 78 CA4th 170, 177, 92 CR2d 626 (piece of paper handed to victim moments after robbery that contained license plate number of robber); *People v Provencio* (1989) 210 CA3d 290, 299, 258 CR 330 (child's cry triggered by exciting event, while mood of attendant crowd was anxious and expectant, was properly admitted as spontaneous statement). In *People v Miron* (1989) 210 CA3d 580, 258 CR 494, the court held that *People v Farmer, supra,* did not change the rule that opinion testimony may properly be excluded even when the rest of the statement meets the requirements of Evid C §1240.

- Contemporaneous statements offered to explain, qualify, or make understandable the declarant's conduct while he or she was engaged in that conduct. Evid C §1241. The Comment to Evid C §1241 does not characterize such evidence but merely declares that it is not made inadmissible by the hearsay rule. The court in *People v Marchialette* (1975) 45 CA3d 974, 979, 119 CR 816, followed the Comment by admitting into evidence, as verbal acts explaining certain relevant conduct, a conversation between the declarant and the testifying witness while the declarant was being murdered. The court did not try to decide whether the conversation was hearsay and admissible under Evid C §1241 or whether it was not hearsay. 45 CA3d at 980. If counsel is unsure how to characterize a statement, it may be better to ask that the statement be admitted under Evid C §1241 rather than to argue over whether the statement is hearsay. The critical issue is the purpose for which the statement is being offered rather than whether it is or is not hearsay.

- Dying declarations about the cause and circumstances of the declarant's death, based on his or her personal knowledge and made under a sense of immediately impending death. Evid C §1242. This exception applies in all civil and criminal cases—not only in prosecutions for homicide. The tests for application of the dying-declaration exception are discussed in *People v Tahl* (1967) 65 C2d 719, 56 CR 318. When a dying declaration is properly admitted, it is an erroneous invasion of the jury's province for the court to instruct the jury that the statement has a substantial guarantee of trustworthiness. *People v Smith* (1989) 214 CA3d 904, 263 CR 155 (statement of dying shooting victim to police officer at scene of crime).

§19.24   7. Statements of Mental or Physical State

An exception to the hearsay rule exists for the following statements:

- Statements of a declarant's then-existing state of mind, emotion, or physical sensation if one of those factors is itself at issue or if the statement is offered to prove or explain acts or conduct of the declarant. Evid C §1250; *People v Cox* (2003) 30 C4th 916, 958, 135 CR2d 272. See *Rufo v Simpson* (2001) 86 CA4th 573, 591, 103 CR2d 492 (murdered woman's phone call to battered women's shelter, diary entries, and letters); *Estate of Sheldon* (1977) 75 CA3d 364, 375, 142 CR 119. See also *People v Ortiz* (1995) 38 CA4th 377, 44 CR2d 914 (statements showing victim's state of mind regarding past conduct by defendant may be admitted). Before applying this complex exception, counsel should study the Comment to Evid C §1250. See Evid C §§1250(b) (excluding statements of memory or belief to prove fact remembered or believed), 1252 (requires judge to weigh trustworthiness in determining admissibility). Evidence of a defendant's statement regarding possible future criminal conduct in a hypothetical situation falls within the state-of-mind exception to the hearsay rule. *People v Karis* (1988) 46 C3d 612, 635, 250 CR 659; see also *People v Lang* (1989) 49 C3d 991, 1013, 264 CR 386 (after Evid C §352 analysis, trial court properly admitted defendant's generic threat of using gun against anyone "that screws with me" on question of preexisting intent to kill).

- Statements by an unavailable declarant of his or her prior state of mind, emotion, or physical sensation if offered solely to prove that prior state when it is at issue. Evid C §1251. See *Estate of Truckenmiller* (1979) 97 CA3d 326, 332, 158 CR 699; *Gillette v WCAB* (1971) 20 CA3d 312, 321, 97 CR 542. Before applying this complex exception, counsel should study the Comment to Evid C §1251. See Evid C §1252 (requires judge to weigh trustworthiness in determining admissibility). See also *People v Bunyard* (1988) 45 C3d 1189, 1203, 249 CR 71 (in murder case, trial court erred in admitting statements made by victim to physician concerning her fear of defendant and manner in which she received bruises when such statements were not necessary for proper diagnosis or treatment).

§19.25 8. Statements Relating to Wills or to Claims Against Estates

An exception to the hearsay rule exists for the following statements:

- Statements by an unavailable declarant that the declarant has or has not made a will or has not revoked a will, or statements that identify the will. Evid C §1260(a). See *Estate of Morrison* (1926) 198 C 1, 7, 242 P 939. See also Evid C §1260(b) (requires judge to weigh trustworthiness in determining admissibility).

- Statements offered in an action on a claim or demand against the declarant's estate, which were made on the declarant's personal knowledge when the matters had been recently perceived by the declarant and while his or her recollection was clear. Evid C §1261(a). See *Adams v Young* (1967) 255 CA2d 145, 158, 62 CR 877. See also Evid C §1261(b) (requires judge to weigh trustworthiness in determining admissibility).

§19.26 9. Business Records

Evidence of a writing made as a record of an act, a condition, or an event is excepted from the hearsay rule when offered to prove the act, condition, or event, if (Evid C §1271):

- The writing was made in the regular course of a business;

- The writing was made at or near the time of the act, condition, or event;

- The custodian or other qualified witness testifies to its identity and the mode of its preparation; and

- The sources of information, and method and time of preparation, indicate its trustworthiness.

Evidence of the absence of business records is similarly excepted from the hearsay rule if the requisite conditions are satisfied. Evid C §1272.

"Business" is defined broadly to include every kind of business, profession, occupation, or calling; government activities; and various operations of for-profit and nonprofit institutions. Evid C §1270. See, *e.g., People v Aguilar* (1971) 16 CA3d 1001, 1005, 94 CR 492 (police department).

Although business records may qualify under an exception to the hearsay rule, the statements in those records may be subject to other objections, such as the following:

- Violations of constitutional protections (see Evid C §1204; chap 28). See *People v Dickinson* (1976) 59 CA3d 314, 319, 130 CR 561 (business records excluded in criminal case because admission would violate defendant's right of confrontation; not enough information in affidavit to find information trustworthy). But see *People v Aguilar* (1971) 16 CA3d 1001, 94 CR 492, in which the court held that whether a particular business record is admissible depends on the trustworthiness of the evidence, which the court determines on a case-by-case basis from the circumstances surrounding the making of the offered record. Thus, admission of a business record in a criminal trial as an exception to the hearsay rule does not necessarily violate the defendant's Sixth Amendment right of confrontation.

- Lack of personal knowledge by the person making the record or furnishing the recorded information under the business duty. See *People v Blagg* (1968) 267 CA2d 598, 609, 73 CR 93 (hospital records admissible if properly authenticated and proper foundation laid). See also *People v Hernandez* (1997) 55 CA4th 225, 63 CR2d 769 (computer data contained in an in-house police sex crimes data base not admissible as circumstantial evidence to prove defendant's identity and guilt).

- Irrelevancy. See Evid C §350.

- Violations of the rules relating to opinion evidence. See Evid C §§702, 800–801.

- Violations of privileges. See Evid C §§911–1070.

- That the probative value is substantially outweighed by the danger of creating undue prejudice, confusing the issues, or misleading the jury. See Evid C §352.

If a writing fails to qualify as a business record, and the person who furnished the information it contains is available to testify, counsel should consider reading the writing into evidence as the witness's past recollection recorded. See Evid C §1237. The writing may also prove helpful in refreshing a witness's present recollection. Evid C §771.

Whenever a business record is offered into evidence, opposing counsel should consider whether the person who made it (or, being under a business duty to do so, supplied the information from which it was made) could have testified to the contents of that record in court over objection. If not, the record is inadmissible. See Comment to Evid C §1271. In *Hoel v City of Los Angeles* (1955) 136 CA2d 295, 309, 288 P2d 989, the appellate court held that the trial court's admission into evidence of a police officer's accident investigation report was sufficient error to warrant granting a new trial. The court noted that

> [e]ssentially accident reports, especially those compiled by police at the scene of an accident—based on statements of participants, bystanders, measurements, deductions and conclusions of their own—fail to qualify as admissible official records or business records.

Because all accident reports required by the Vehicle Code are now also confidential (Veh C §20012), the use of such reports as evidence is now prohibited (Veh C §20013).

In *McGowan v City of Los Angeles* (1950) 100 CA2d 386, 392, 223 P2d 862, the court explained that the business-records exception to the hearsay rule

> does not change the rules of competency or relevancy with respect to recorded facts. It does not make that proof which is not proof. It merely provides a method of proof of an admissible "act, condition, or event." It does not make the record admissible when oral testimony of the same facts would be inadmissible.

See also Comment to Evid C §1271. In *Taggart v Super Seer Corp.* (1995) 33 CA4th 1697, 40 CR2d 56, the court held that helmet safety test reports were inadmissible under the business records exception because of insufficient foundation. Even though the custodian's declaration conformed to the requirements of Evid C §§1560 and 1561, it was inadequate to establish the foundational requirements of Evid C §1271 because it provided no assurance of competency, reliability, or trustworthiness. See also *Levy-Zentner Co. v Southern Pac. Transp. Co.* (1977) 74 CA3d 762, 142 CR 1 (all Evid C §1271 requirements were satisfied by accident report made in usual course of defendant's business, based on observations of defendant's employees that they reported to supervisor who prepared report); *Behr v County of Santa Cruz* (1959) 172 CA2d 697, 704, 342 P2d 987 (fire ranger's official report regarding origin of fire inadmissible because not based on personal knowledge); *Reisman v Los Angeles City Sch. Dist.* (1954) 123 CA2d 493, 506, 267 P2d 36 (applying test stated in *McGowan v City of Los Angeles, supra,* to public records).

Hospital records that qualify under the business-records exception to the hearsay rule often contain inadmissible matter, *e.g.*, the medical opinion of a technician who would not be qualified to give such an opinion if he or she were testifying in court. See *Hutton v Brookside Hosp.* (1963) 213 CA2d 350, 28 CR 774. See also *People v Williams* (1960) 187 CA2d 355, 9 CR 722; §§20.6–20.18 (expert opinion evidence). Even if rendered by fully qualified experts, opinions sometimes fall outside the scope of the business-records exception because they are conclusions and not records of acts, conditions, or events. Compare *People v Reyes* (1974) 12 C3d 486, 502, 116 CR 217 (excluding psychiatrist's opinion as conclusion; opponent could not cross-examine on basis of and qualifications for opinion), and *People v Terrell* (1955) 138 CA2d 35, 57, 291 P2d 155 (excluding doctor's notation of diagnosis of "probable criminal abortion"), with *McDowd v Pig 'n' Whistle Corp.* (1945) 26 C2d 696, 160 P2d 797 (admitting diagnosis of plaintiff's condition and nature and extent of her injuries).

A frequent problem with hospital records is determining the admissibility of the case history of the accident related by the patient to the physician when offered to prove the truth of the facts stated in the report. The patient's hearsay statement is not made admissible merely because it is included in a hospital record. *Johnson v Aetna Life Ins. Co.* (1963) 221 CA2d 247, 252, 34 CR 484. To be admissible, the record must be introduced under some other exception to the hearsay rule, *e.g.*, as a prior inconsistent statement (Evid C §§770, 1235), a prior consistent statement (Evid C §§791, 1236), a statement of the patient's prior physical or mental state (Evid C §1251), or business records of the patient's admission to the hospital (Evid C §1271). A hearsay statement may be used to prove a hearsay statement but only if both statements qualify under exceptions to the hearsay rule. Evid C §1201 (multiple hearsay).

The record of a patient's statement about the injury may be admissible not as hearsay but for some purpose other than to prove the truth of the facts stated, *e.g.*, as a partial basis for the physician's opinion, diagnosis, and prescribed treatment (Evid C §801). *Johnson v Aetna Life Ins. Co., supra*; *People v Williams, supra*. See also *People v Piper* (1980) 103 CA3d 102, 112, 162 CR 833. In such a case, the judge should be requested to give an instruction to the jury that explains the limited purpose for which the evidence is received. *Kelley v Bailey* (1961) 189 CA2d 728, 737, 11 CR 448. See §53.5. An interesting problem arises when counsel wishes to admit into evidence a statement about how an accident happened, given to the physician or hospital staff by a patient who becomes a party in a personal injury action. If opposing counsel can independently establish the statement, it is admissible as a party admission. Evid C §1220. If the adversary must rely on the notation in the medical record, counsel can object that such information is not usually included in such records and therefore is not made in the ordinary course of business.

The fact that a hospital or other business record contains some inadmissible matter does not make the entire record inadmissible. *Barr v Scott* (1955) 134 CA2d 823, 286 P2d 552. The objecting party should specify the portions that are inadmissible. The judge will then allow the record to be introduced into evidence with the inadmissible parts deleted or with an instruction to the jury to disregard the inadmissible portions. See *People v Gorgol* (1953) 122 CA2d 281, 300, 265 P2d 69.

On the use of computer printouts as business records, see *Huber, Hunt & Nichols, Inc. v Moore* (1977) 67 CA3d 278, 295, 136 CR 603 (exclusion of potentially confusing printout (under Evid C §352) upheld in absence of explanatory testimony). See also *People v Cohen* (1976) 59 CA3d 241, 130 CR 656 (computer printout admitted as business record in case involving theft of library books).

Courts have held, however, that the foundation for the admission of a business record does not necessarily require the testimony of the person who made the record. Under Evid C §1271(c), that foundation may be furnished by the testimony of an "other qualified witness" such as the person in charge of the department. *Aguimatang v California State Lottery* (1991) 234 CA3d 769, 797, 286 CR 57 (computer printouts properly admitted through declarations of lottery employees and director of company that provided computer services to lottery); *People v Martinez* (2000) 22 C4th 106, 91 CR2d 687 (supreme court affirmed admission, under official records exception (see §19.27), of uncertified computer printouts as evidence that defendant was habitual offender); *County of Sonoma v Grant W.* (1986) 187 CA3d 1439, 232 CR 471 (blood test report was properly admitted in paternity case under testimony of director of paternity testing department of laboratory). See also *People v Lugashi* (1988) 205 CA3d 632, 641, 252 CR 434 (credit card fraud investigator familiar with computer equipment, credit card sales, sales recordation, and other procedures was qualified to offer foundation evidence under Evid C §1271).

§19.27   10. Official Records and Other Official Writings

An exception to the hearsay rule exists for the following official writings:

- An entry in the public records, when offered in any civil or criminal proceeding, if made by and within the scope of duty of a public employee at or near the time of the act, condition, or event recorded. The sources of information and method and time of preparation must be such as to indicate its trustworthiness. Evid C §1280. See *People v Martinez* (2000) 22 C4th 106, 119, 91 CR2d 687 (admission, under official records exception, of uncertified computer printouts as evidence that defendant was habitual offender). This exception is similar to the business-records exception (see Evid C §1271; §19.26) in that it requires the proponent to lay a foundation of the sources of information and method and time of preparation showing the trustworthiness of the writing (Evid C §1280(c)). This foundation is usually laid by asking the judge to take judicial notice of the writing's trustworthiness or by offering other independent proof of the writing's trustworthiness. The exception under Evid C §1280 is unlike the business-records exception in that the custodian or other qualified witness need not testify about the identity and mode of preparation of the writing itself. See Comment to Evid C §1280; Jefferson's California Evidence Benchbook §§5.1–5.11 (3d ed CJA-CEB

1997). The definitions in Evid C §§195 and 200 make the exception applicable to the records of any foreign or domestic public entity.

- A postal receipt offered to show cancellation of an insurance policy before a fire loss was admissible under Evid C §1280 (writings by public employees) because it was filled out by a postal employee at the time of mailing and was officially stamped. Such a showing shifts the burden of proof of trustworthiness to the party objecting to the admission of the evidence. *Preis v American Indem. Co.* (1990) 220 CA3d 752, 269 CR 617.

- Writings recording vital statistics. Evid C §1281. This exception applies to records of jurisdictions outside California. Official reports of births, deaths, and marriages occurring in California are admitted under Health & S C §103550. See *Romero v Volunteer State Life Ins. Co.* (1970) 10 CA3d 571, 580, 88 CR 820.

- Writings containing findings of presumed death, made by authorized federal employees. Evid C §1282.

- Official reports or records, made by federal employees, that persons are missing, captured, or the like. Evid C §1283.

- Admission of qualifying court records to prove fact of criminal conviction and that the offense reflected in the record occurred. Evid C §452.5(b). See *People v Duran* (2002) 97 CA4th 1448, 119 CR2d 272.

11. Former Testimony

§19.28   a. Former Testimony Defined (Evid C §1290)

An exception to the hearsay rule exists for former testimony, defined in Evid C §1290 as testimony given under oath in:

- Another action or a former hearing or trial of the same action (Evid C §1290(a));

- A proceeding to determine a controversy conducted by or under the supervision of an agency that has the power to determine such a controversy and is an agency of the United States or a public entity in the United States (Evid C §1290(b));

- A deposition taken in compliance with law in another action (Evid C §1290(c)); or

- An arbitration proceeding if the evidence of such former testimony is a verbatim transcript of it (Evid C §1290(d)).

§19.29   b. Party Same in Former Action (Evid C §1291)

An exception to the hearsay rule exists for former testimony when the parties are the same in the former action if:

- The former testimony is offered against a person who offered it in evidence in his or her own behalf on the former occasion or against the successor in interest of such person (Evid C §1291(a)(1)); or

- The party against whom the former testimony is offered was a party to the action or proceeding in which the testimony was given and had the right and opportunity to cross-examine the declarant with an interest and motive similar to that which he or she has at the hearing (Evid C §1291(a)(2)).

In *People v Lepe* (1997) 57 CA4th 977, 982, 67 CR2d 525, the court of appeal rejected the defendant's claim that Cal Const art I, §30, added by Proposition 115 to allow hearsay evidence at preliminary hearings, so changed the preliminary hearing that testimony at that hearing no longer meets the requirements of Evid C §1291(a)(2).

The admissibility of former testimony under Evid C §1291 is subject to the same limitations and objections as though the declarant were testifying at the hearing, except that former testimony offered under this section is not subject to (Evid C §1291(b)):

- Objections to the form of the question that were not made at the time the former testimony was given (Evid C §1291(b)(1)); and

- Objections based on competency or privilege that did not exist at the time the former testimony was given (Evid C §1291(b)(2)).

In *People v Rojas* (1975) 15 C3d 540, 125 CR 357, the court held that a witness, who testified at a preliminary hearing and a prior trial but refused to testify at the second trial because he feared for his safety, was "unavailable" and therefore that his testimony was admissible at the hearing under Evid C §1291. See *People v Reed* (1996) 13 C4th 217, 52 CR2d 106. See also Evid C §1350 (when statements of declarants in previous felony cases are admissible).

Admission of the former testimony of a prosecution witness violates a defendant's right to confrontation unless the witness is "actually unavailable" (see *Barber v Page* (1968) 390 US 719, 725, 20 L Ed 2d 255, 260, 88 S Ct 1318; *People v Sandoval* (2001) 87 CA4th 1425, 1443, 105 CR2d 504) and there was an adequate opportunity for cross-examination at the prior hearing (*Pointer v Texas* (1965) 380 US 400, 13 L Ed 2d 923, 85 S Ct 1065; *People v Sandoval* (2001) 87 CA4th 1425, 1434, 105 CR2d 504). The prosecution must establish that reasonable diligence was used to procure the witness for trial. *People v Mendieta* (1986) 185 CA3d 1032, 1036, 230 CR 162. See also *People v Price* (1991) 1 C4th 324, 3 CR2d 106. In order to satisfy the requirements of the confrontation clause, the prosecution must make a reasonable, good faith effort to obtain the witness's presence at trial. *People v Sandoval* (2001) 87 CA4th 1425, 1443, 105 CR2d 504 (reasonable good faith effort not made to obtain witness who resided in Mexico). When these requirements are not met, California courts have held this testimony to be inadmissible. See, *e.g., People v Sandoval* (2001) 87 CA4th 1425, 1444, 105 CR2d 504; *People v Williams* (1979) 93 CA3d 40, 155 CR 414; *People v Gibbs* (1967) 255 CA2d 739, 63 CR 471. Counsel must recognize that admission of such testimony in a criminal case always raises a constitutional question. See §19.9. See also §19.19 on the need for cross-examination regarding witnesses' prior statements.

Testimony of a defendant given at his first trial is admissible impeachment at his second trial when he makes himself unavailable by invoking his Fifth Amendment right not to testify at his second trial. *People v Malone* (2003) 112 CA4th 1241, 1243, 5 CR3d 741.

§19.30   c. Party Different in Former Action (Evid C §1292)

An exception to the hearsay rule exists for former testimony when the parties are different in the former action if (*Rufo v Simpson* (2001) 86 CA4th 573, 605, 103 CR2d 492):

- The declarant is unavailable as a witness (Evid C §1292(a)(1));
- The former testimony is offered in a civil action (Evid C §1292(a)(2)); and
- The issue is such that the party to the action or proceeding in which the former testimony was given had the right and opportunity to cross-examine the declarant with an interest and motive similar to that which the party against whom the testimony is offered has at the hearing (Evid C §1292(a)(3)).

The admissibility of former testimony under Evid C §1292 is subject to the same limitations and objections as though the declarant were testifying at the hearing, except that former testimony offered under this section is not subject to objections based on competency or privilege that did not exist at the time the former testimony was given. Evid C §1292(b). In a wrongful death action, former testimony of a police officer was not admissible when plaintiffs in the present action had no opportunity to cross-examine the officer; a prior cross-examination by the prosecution in a related criminal case was not a substitute for the right to cross-examine in the present case. *Rufo v Simpson* (2001) 86 CA4th 573, 605, 103 CR2d 492.

§19.31   d. Minor in Child Dependency Action (Evid C §1293)

An exception to the hearsay rule exists for former testimony made at a preliminary examination by a minor child who was the complaining witness if:

- The testimony is offered to declare the minor a dependent child of the court (Evid C §1293(a)(1));

- The defendant in the prior proceeding was given the right and opportunity to cross-examine the minor with an interest and motive similar to that which the parent or guardian against whom the testimony is offered has at the proceeding to declare the minor a dependent child of the court (Evid C §1293(a)(2));

- The admissibility of the testimony is subject to the same limitations and objections as though the minor were testifying at the proceeding to declare the minor a dependent child of the court (Evid C §1293(b)); and

- The attorney for the parent or guardian or, if none, the parent or guardian makes a motion to challenge the admissibility of the former testimony on a showing that new, substantially different issues are present in the proceeding to declare the minor a dependent child than were present in the preliminary examination (Evid C §1292(c)).

In *In re Elizabeth T.* (1992) 9 CA4th 636, 12 CR2d 10, the court held that Evid C §1293, authorizing the use in a juvenile dependency proceeding of the transcript of a minor's testimony at a preliminary hearing on a child molestation charge, did not violate the parent's constitutional due process rights, although the statute did not require any showing of the child's unavailability as a witness.

§19.31A   e. Inconsistent Statement (Evid C §1294)

Under Evid C §1294, in a criminal case, the prior inconsistent statements of a witness from a preliminary hearing or trial may be admissible hearsay if:

- The witness is unavailable;
- The witness's former testimony was admitted under Evid C §1291;
- The inconsistent statement was properly admitted at a preliminary hearing or other proceeding under Evid C §1235; and
- The party against whom the statement is introduced has an opportunity to cross-examine any witness who testified to the inconsistent statement at the other proceeding.

If the defendant has not had a full opportunity to cross-examine the witness about the statement, admission of the statement for its truth violates the defendant's Sixth Amendment right to confrontation. *People v Martinez* (2003) 113 CA4th 400, 410, 7 CR3d 49.

§19.32   12. Judgments

An exception to the hearsay rule exists for evidence of the following judgments:

- Judgments of conviction of crimes punishable as felonies when offered in a civil action to prove facts essential to the judgment. The plea may have been either guilty or nolo contendere. Evid C §1300. Note that when the crime involved is a misdemeanor or the plea was nolo contendere, the plea and any admissions that are the basis for the plea may not be used against the defendant as an admission in a civil action arising from the judgment of conviction. Pen C §1016(3).

- Judgments against persons entitled to indemnity when offered by such persons in actions against their indemnitors or warrantors. Evid C §1301.

- Judgments determining a third person liability, obligation, or duty that is at issue in a civil action. Evid C §1302.

The above three exceptions, which make evidence of judgments admissible, should be distinguished from the doctrines of res judicata and estoppel, which give conclusive effect to judgments. See Comment to Evid C §1300.

§19.33   13. Family History

An exception to the hearsay rule exists for the following:

- Statements of an unavailable declarant concerning the declarant's family history. Evid C §1310. See Evid C §1310(b) (requires judge to weigh trustworthiness in determining admissibility).

- Statements of an unavailable declarant concerning the family history of a relative or an intimate associate. Evid C §1311. See Evid C §1311(b) (requires judge to weigh trustworthiness in determining admissibility).

- Entries in family records or the like. Evid C §1312.

- Reputation in family concerning family history. Evid C §1313.

- Reputation in community concerning resident's family history. Evid C §1314.

- Church records of customarily recorded facts about family history, if admissible under the requirements of Evid C §1271 for admitting business records. Evid C §1315. On Evid C §1271, see §19.26.

- Marriage, baptismal, or similar certificates. Evid C §1316.

§19.34   14. Reputation or Statements Concerning Community History, Property Interests, or Character

An exception to the hearsay rule exists for the following:

- Reputation concerning community history. Evid C §1320.

- Reputation concerning public interests in property. Evid C §1321.

- Reputation concerning boundaries or customs affecting land. Evid C §1322.

- Statements concerning boundaries by an unavailable declarant who had sufficient knowledge of the subject. Evid C §1323 (judge required to weigh trustworthiness in determining admissibility).

- Community reputation concerning person's character. Evid C §1324.

§19.35 15. Dispositive Instruments or Ancient Writings

An exception to the hearsay rule exists for the following instruments and writings:

- Recitals in writing affecting property (*e.g.*, deeds or wills) if relevant to the purpose and subject matter of the writing and consistent with subsequent dealings relating to the property. The recital must also be relevant to an issue concerning an interest in the property. Evid C §1330. See *Russell v Langford* (1902) 135 C 356, 67 P 331.

- Statements in writings over 30 years old that have been generally acted on as true by persons having an interest in the matter. Evid C §1331. The rationale for adopting a broader interpretation is that the unbiased writings of persons having no financial interest in litigation are usually more reliable than testimony given by expert witnesses.

§19.36 16. Statements in Commercial, Scientific, or Similar Publications

An exception to the hearsay rule exists for statements in the following publications:

- Statements, other than opinions, in tabulations, lists, directories, registers, or other published compilations that are generally used and relied on as accurate in the course of a business as defined in Evid C §1270. Evid C §1340. It is sometimes possible to use a published reference work as a basis for requesting the trial judge to take judicial notice of a fact not reasonably subject to dispute. See Evid C §452(h).

- Statements in historical works, books of science or art, or published maps or charts if made by neutral persons and offered to prove facts of general notoriety and interest. Evid C §1341. Judicial decisions have interpreted this provision narrowly, *e.g.*, to exclude medical texts in negligence cases. Legal commentators have disagreed with this interpretation of §1341, urging one that permits wider use of books of "science or art." See, *e.g.*, Cleary, McCormick on Evidence §321 (3d ed 1984).

- In *People v Smith* (1989) 215 CA3d 19, 263 CR 678, the court held that, even though the trial court did not hold a complete *Kelly* hearing (see *People v Kelly* (1976) 17 C3d 24, 130 CR 144), it properly took judicial notice of transcripts and findings of previous hearings held in the same county for the purpose of concluding that electrophoretic analysis of dried bloodstains is a reliable scientific technique. In *Nguyen v Scott* (1988) 206 CA3d 725, 736, 253 CR 800, the court recognized that a trial court may take judicial notice of relevant criteria promulgated by a private professional association (ethics of a real estate broker who switches status from agent to principal).

§19.37   17. Bills Offered to Corroborate Other Evidence

In *PG&E v G.W. Thomas Drayage & Rigging Co.* (1968) 69 C2d 33, 69 CR 561, the California Supreme Court created an exception to the hearsay rule by holding that a repair bill or invoice is admissible as corroborative evidence if the party testifies that he or she incurred the obligation and paid the bill. These documents are then admissible to show that the charges were incurred or paid and that they were reasonable. This case is important for attorneys who handle cases in which it is impracticable to have the person who rendered the bill testify at trial.

In a personal injury case, *Rodgers v Kemper Constr. Co.* (1975) 50 CA3d 608, 627, 124 CR 143, the court applied the *Drayage* holding to admit medical bills showing that a physician's charges were reasonable under the corroborative-evidence hearsay exception. In *Rodgers*, the plaintiff identified his medical bills, described what they were for, and testified that he paid them.

§19.38   18. Testimony Given at Preliminary Hearing in Criminal Case

Exceptions to the hearsay rule exist in the California Constitution and Penal Code for testimony given at a preliminary hearing in a criminal case. Under Cal Const art I, §30(b).

> In order to protect victims and witnesses in criminal cases, hearsay evidence shall be admissible at preliminary hearings, as prescribed by the Legislature or by the people through the initiative process.

Penal Code §872 allows law enforcement officers to testify in the form of hearsay when certain conditions are met. These law enforcement officers must have five years of law enforcement experience or have completed a training course certified by the Commission on Peace Officer Standards and Training that includes training in the investigation and reporting of cases and in testifying at preliminary hearings. The officer may relate the statements of declarants that were made out of court. Those statements may be offered for the truth of the matter asserted, and a holding order may be based on them. See *People v Dawkins* (1992) 10 CA4th 565, 12 CR2d 633. This exception applies only to single-level hearsay. *People v Miranda* (2000) 23 C4th 340, 354, 96 CR2d 758. See *People v Correa* (2002) 27 C4th 444, 117 CR2d 27 (out-of-court contemporaneous translations offered to police officers by unbiased bystanders is permissible hearsay when offered as testimony by police officers in preliminary hearing).

Neither Cal Const art I, §30 nor Pen C §872 addresses the issue of whether such hearsay testimony is admissible at trial in place of an unavailable witness. Because the witness neither testifies under oath nor is cross-examined by defense counsel when the Pen C §872 hearsay procedure is used, such testimony would not be admissible at trial. The confrontation clauses of the California Constitution and the U.S. Constitution would obviously be violated, because no opportunity to cross-examine ever existed. *Crawford v Washington* (2004) ___ US ___, 158 L Ed 2d 177, 124 S Ct 1354 (use of testimonial evidence of unavailable witness barred by confrontation clause of Sixth Amendment if defendant had no opportunity to cross-examine witness). It seems likely after *Crawford* that testimonial evidence given in preliminary hearings will not be admissible at trial if the witness is unavailable for the criminal trial, absent some other opportunity for the defendant to confront the witness.

Defense counsel may not call and cross-examine these hearsay declarants at the preliminary hearing. Evidence Code §1203.1 does not allow defense counsel to call and examine an adverse party as if under cross-examination (see Evid C §1203) when the hearsay statement is offered under Pen C §872.

In *Whitman v Superior Court* (1991) 54 C3d 1063, 2 CR2d 160, the court held that a finding of probable cause cannot be based on the hearsay testimony of a noninvestigating officer or "reader" who has no personal knowledge of the case. The court reasoned that provisions of Pen C §872(b) that permit a properly qualified law enforcement officer to relate the hearsay statements of victims or witnesses, including other law enforcement officers, require the testifying officer to have sufficient knowledge of the crime or the circumstances under which the hearsay statement was made to enable the officer to assist the magistrate in determining the reliability of the statement.

§19.39 VI. IMPEACHING HEARSAY DECLARANT

The hearsay declarant may ordinarily be called as a witness and examined as if under cross-examination by any adverse party. Evid C §1203. This kind of examination was formerly precluded by the rule that a witness called by a party is his or her witness and may not be cross-examined by him or her. See Comment to Evid C §1203. Evidence Code §1203 does not apply if the hearsay statement was admitted as a confession or an admission (Evid C §§1220–1228; see §§19.13–19.16), as a prior statement of a witness (Evid C §§1235–1238; see §§19.19–19.22), as a final judgment (Evid C §§1300–1302; see §19.32), or in a situation in which it would be inappropriate to examine a hearsay declarant as if under cross-examination (Evid C §1203(b)-(c); Comment to Evid C §1203). Under Evid C §1203.1, however, §1203 does not apply if the hearsay statement is offered at a preliminary examination, as provided in Pen C §872(b).

Even if the hearsay declarant is not called as a witness, the declarant may be impeached (*e.g.,* by extrinsic evidence) on the basis the declarant had no personal knowledge about the subject matter of his or her statement. Evid C §1202. Impeachment and rehabilitation evidence is admissible on the same basis as it would be if the out-of-court declarant were a witness at the trial, except for one difference: Impeachment by proof that the out-of-court declarant made a statement inconsistent with the one that has been admitted into evidence is permissible even though the declarant has no opportunity to explain or deny the inconsistent statement in court. Evid C §1202. The deponent of a deposition taken in the action in which it is offered into evidence may be impeached or rehabilitated under Evid C §1202 like any other hearsay declarant.

The hearsay exceptions allowing prior inconsistent or consistent statements of witnesses to be used as substantive evidence (Evid C §§1235–1236) do not apply to prior statements of hearsay declarants (Comment to Evid C §1202).

VII. COMMON MISCONCEPTIONS ABOUT HEARSAY RULE

§19.40   A. "Self-Serving" Is Not an Objection

Trial counsel sometimes object to the introduction of evidence of an out-of-court statement on the ground that it is "self-serving." This objection is meaningless. All evidence offered is self-serving; otherwise, it would not be offered.

The term "self-serving" does not appear in the Evidence Code, and there is no indication that this is an available objection to evidence. The proper objection is simply that the out-of-court statement is inadmissible hearsay.

§19.41   B. "Res Gestae" Is Not an Exception

The Evidence Code does not use the term "res gestae." It has been used to cover a wide variety of situations, most frequently to "embody the notion that evidence of any concededly relevant act or condition might bring in likewise the words which accompanied it." Cleary, McCormick on Evidence §288 (3d ed 1984).

If a person's conduct is equivocal, the words that accompanied it are admissible to explain that conduct. The proper reference, when justifying the introduction of evidence about such accompanying words, is not to res gestae but to the contemporaneous statement rule of Evid C §1241. See §19.23. Similarly, when introducing an out-of-court statement made under the stress of excitement caused by an event, counsel should invoke the spontaneous-statement exception to the hearsay rule (Evid C §1240) rather than the confusing general term "res gestae." See §19.16. See *People v Gutierrez* (2000) 78 CA4th 170, 180 n10, 92 CR2d 626 ("res gestae is the now outdated name of the hearsay exception that is currently called spontaneous declaration"); *People v Orduno* (1978) 80 CA3d 738, 744 n1, 145 CR 806 ("Res gestae has now gone the way of the great auk, the passenger pigeon and high button shoes. It was in its time a handy gadget. When an attorney can think of no other reason for the introduction of hearsay, he would simply utter the magic words 'res gestae' and, often as not, get the testimony in.").

§19.42 VIII. CHECKLIST: HEARSAY PROBLEMS

When evaluating the admissibility of relevant evidence, counsel may wish to use the following checklist to disclose hearsay problems:

___ 1. Is the evidence hearsay?
    ___ a. Is it an out-of-court statement?
    ___ b. Is there any intent to communicate?
    ___ c. Is it offered to prove the truth of the matter stated?
___ 2. If the evidence is hearsay, does an exception to the hearsay rule apply?
___ 3. If an exception to the hearsay rule applies, is the evidence made inadmissible by some other rule?

§19.43 IX. STATUTE

Under Evid C §1200(a), hearsay evidence is "evidence of a statement that was made other than by a witness while testifying at the hearing and that is offered to prove the truth of the matter stated." Hearsay evidence is inadmissible "except as provided by law." Evid C §1200(b). Evidence Code §1200 "shall be known and may be cited as the hearsay rule." Evid C §1200(c).

§19.44 X. ALTERNATIVES TO OBJECTING

On possible alternatives to objecting, see §§4.9–4.14.

§19.45 XI. STATING THE OBJECTION

Objection, Your Honor. The question calls for hearsay.

20
Inadmissible Opinion

I. DEFINITION §20.1

II. ADMISSIBLE OPINION BY LAY WITNESS
   A. Introduction §20.2
   B. Lay Opinion Permitted on Certain Subject Matter §20.3
   C. Lay Opinion Otherwise Permitted §20.4
   D. Statute §20.5

III. ADMISSIBLE OPINION BY EXPERT WITNESS
   A. Qualification as Expert §20.6
   B. Special Type of Subject Matter Beyond Common Experience §20.7
   C. Basis of Expert Opinion §20.8
      1. Expert May Rely on Inadmissible Matter §20.9
      2. Scientific Evidence §20.10
         a. *Kelly-Frye* Standard §20.11
         b. California's *Kelly* Test
            (1) Establishing General Acceptance of New Scientific Technique or Theory §20.12
            (2) Applying *Kelly* Test to Scientific Evidence
               (a) Techniques That Passed Test §20.13
               (b) Techniques That Did Not Pass Test §20.14
         c. Federal Courts' *Daubert* Test
            (1) *Daubert I* §20.15
            (2) *Daubert II* §20.16
         d. Impact of *Daubert* in California: *People v Leahy* §20.17
         e. Psychological Opinion §20.18
   D. Hypothetical Questions
      1. Use §20.19
      2. General Rules of Framing §20.20
   E. Appointment of Experts §20.21
   F. Statutes §20.22

IV. PROCEDURES FOR TESTING OPINION TESTIMONY
   A. Foundational Examination Before Opinion Stated §20.23
   B. Voir Dire Examination of Expert §20.24
   C. Cross-Examination After Opinion Stated §20.25
   D. Impeachment of Expert by Extrinsic Evidence §20.26
   E. Cross-Examination of Third Person if Expert's Opinion Is Based on Hearsay §20.27

V. OPINION ON ULTIMATE ISSUE IS PERMISSIBLE §20.28

VI. ALTERNATIVES TO OBJECTING §20.29

VII. STATING THE OBJECTION
   A. Lay Witness §20.30
   B. Expert Witness §20.31

VIII. RESPONSE: MOTION TO STRIKE §20.32

§20.1   I. DEFINITION

The Evidence Code defines "opinion" to include all opinions, inferences, conclusions, and other subjective statements made by a witness. Comment to Evid C §§800–805. Opinions are based on matter either personally observed by a witness or communicated to the witness. Evid C §§800(a), 801(b). In practice, it is often impossible to distinguish between fact and opinion. Most factual testimony includes elements of inference and opinion. For instance, a witness's declaration that a photograph accurately represents what the witness saw is a mixture of fact and opinion.

Opinion evidence comes from two sources: lay witnesses (Evid C §800; see §§20.2–20.5) and expert witnesses (Evid C §801; see §§20.6–20.22). Its admissibility is governed by a tangled set of rules and standards that differ from state to state and circuit to circuit and may befuddle the most intelligent trial practitioners. When uncertainty exists, admissibility is likely to turn on the trustworthiness (*i.e.,* reliability) and probative value (*i.e.,* relevance) of the opinion. Relevant evidence is judged by its probative worth to the issues involved.

II. ADMISSIBLE OPINION BY LAY WITNESS

§20.2   A. Introduction

Many attorneys mistakenly assume that a lay witness may never testify in the form of an opinion. Such testimony, however, is admissible if it is rationally based on a witness's perception, helpful to a clear understanding of the witness's testimony, or otherwise permitted by law. See Evid C §800(a)–(b).

Admissible opinion testimony includes the following:

- Testimony concerning certain specific subjects (see §20.3); and

- Testimony based on a witness's personal perception of matter subject to uniform interpretation, which the witness can give in the form of an opinion (see §20.4).

§20.3   B. Lay Opinion Permitted on Certain Subject Matter

Evidence Code §800 codifies what is proper subject matter for an opinion by a lay witness without any special foundational requirements such as those described in §20.4. Comment to Evid C §800. For example, a lay witness may usually give an opinion on the following:

- *Sanity.* See *Estate of Holloway* (1925) 195 C 711, 733, 235 P 1012 (subscribing witness's testimony on condition of testator's mind). See also *Estate of Schwartz* (1945) 67 CA2d 512, 520, 155 P2d 76.

- *Value of services.* See *Donahue v Ziv Television Programs, Inc.* (1966) 245 CA2d 593, 609, 54 CR 130 ("value of his services" in disclosing idea for television screenplay).

- *Value of property owned by witness.* See *Schroeder v Auto Driveaway Co.* (1974) 11 C3d 908, 921, 114 CR 622 (owner's opinion on value of personal property is competent evidence of its value and usually sufficient to support judgment based on that value); *Holmes v Southern Cal. Edison Co.* (1947) 78 CA2d 43, 53, 177 P2d 32 (value of personal effects and furniture destroyed in fire). See also Evid C §§813, 815, 817, 822; *Sacramento & San Joaquin Drainage Dist. v Goehring* (1970) 13 CA3d 58, 65, 91 CR 375 (owner's opinion on value of real property admissible only if opinion based on proper matter).

- *Value of estate property.* See *Crail v Blakely* (1973) 8 C3d 744, 754, 106 CR 187 (estate administrator has sufficient personal knowledge to give opinion on value of estate; extension of rule allowing owner to give opinion on value of property).

- *Witness's own intent, motive, or knowledge.* See *Cope v Davison* (1947) 30 C2d 193, 200, 180 P2d 873 (on issue of willful misconduct, defendant allowed to testify that he thought he was acting in safe manner). See also *Larson v Solbakken* (1963) 221 CA2d 410, 418, 34 CR 450 (defendant's comment about prior similar driving experience should have been admitted to show state of mind before accident).

- *Personal health or injury.* See *Waite v Godfrey* (1980) 106 CA3d 760, 764, 163 CR 881 (opinion testimony by plaintiff about her own physical condition).

Lay witnesses may not express opinions interpreting such relationships as employment or agency and such issues as authority, control, or the existence of a contract when such matters are at issue. For example, a lay witness may not answer questions such as "Was your employer a subsidiary company to the defendant company?" or "Did you delegate authority to your sister to act as your agent?" (see *Parker v Otis* (1900) 130 C 322, 62 P 571, aff'd in 187 US 606, 47 L Ed 323, 23 S Ct 168) or "By whom was the Central Labor Council controlled at that time?" (see *People v Ware* (1924) 67 CA 81, 226 P 956). See also Evid C §405.

§20.4 C. Lay Opinion Otherwise Permitted

Opinion testimony by lay witnesses is permitted, regardless of the subject matter, if the following three elements are present:

(1) *Matter personally perceived by witness*. The lay witness must have personally perceived the fact or facts on which the opinion is based. Evid C §800(a). Personal knowledge is a prerequisite to any lay witness's competency to give testimony about any matter. Evid C §702. See *Smith v Lockheed Propulsion Co.* (1967) 247 CA2d 774, 56 CR 128. To be "perceived" by the witness, the event must be observed with the witness's senses. For example, if a witness was physically present at an automobile accident but did not see it occur, the defense attorney should object if plaintiff's counsel asks the witness whether the witness knows or has personal knowledge of whether either the plaintiff or the defendant ran a red light. It has not been shown that the witness is competent to testify to that matter (*i.e.,* has personal knowledge of the matter), because a foundation has not been laid showing that the witness "perceived" with the witness's senses either party running the red light. The witness would only be competent to testify to what was heard, *e.g.,* screeching brakes. For an interesting application of this rule, see *People v Perry* (1976) 60 CA3d 608, 131 CR 629 (witness's personal knowledge of defendant's appearance permitted opinion testimony that person in photograph taken during robbery was defendant).

(2) *Matter subject to commonly understood interpretation*. Evidence Code §800(a) codifies prior law with respect to an additional requirement: The perception that permits a lay opinion must be "rationally based," *i.e.,* subject to a commonly understood and accepted interpretation. The perception cannot mean different things to different people. In *McNeil v Yellow Cab Co.* (1978) 85 CA3d 116, 118, 147 CR 733, the injured plaintiff was allowed to testify that he could not find seat belts in the defendant company's taxicab and that not wearing a seat belt was the proximate cause of his injury in a collision. The court held that testifying on this matter was not beyond a layman's common experience. But see *Truman v Vargas* (1969) 275 CA2d 976, 982, 80 CR 373. In contrast to *McNeil,* an experiment by a robbery victim to try to open her apartment door from the outside by using her hands to unlatch the chain was considered beyond a layman's common experience in *People v Allen* (1976) 65 CA3d 426, 436, 135 CR 276. The evidence was disallowed on the ground that the victim's inability to unchain the door with her hands did not establish a reasonable inference that the chain could not be unlatched by one with knowledge and skill in the method of unlatching a chain. 65 CA3d at 436.

(3) *Opinion helpful to understanding testimony*. Having the witness testify in the form of an opinion must be "helpful to a clear understanding of [the witness's] testimony." Evid C §800(b); *People v Maglaya* (2003) 112 CA4th 1604, 1608, 6 CR3d 155 (officer's lay opinion comparing defendant's shoe and prints found at crime scene helpful to jury). The rule requires that witnesses express themselves at the "lowest possible level of abstraction." *People v Hurlic*

(1971) 14 CA3d 122, 127, 92 CR 55. Often it is impossible to explain observations other than by stating an opinion. Even though conclusions should be left to the fact-trier whenever feasible, an observation can involve too many complex or subtle elements to permit a straightforward factual description. 14 CA3d at 126 (officer's opinion that suspect "indicated" or "acknowledged" that he waived *Miranda* rights).

Accordingly, opinion testimony by lay witnesses has been held admissible on such subjects as:

- *Speed, distance, amount of illumination, or size.* See *Albrecht v Broughton* (1970) 6 CA3d 173, 181, 85 CR 659 (court allowed testimony to show how dark out it was in response to following question: "Would you need to turn on your headlights to see?"); *Dean v Feld* (1946) 77 CA2d 327, 330, 175 P2d 278 (11-year-old girl allowed to testify that car was "pretty close"; discussion of allowing opinion on matters such as "speed, distance, weight and the like").

- *A person's appearance or demeanor.* See *People v Medina* (1990) 51 C3d 870, 886, 274 CR 849, aff'd on other grounds in 505 US 437, 120 L Ed 2d 353, 112 S Ct 2572; *People v Harris* (1969) 270 CA2d 863, 872, 76 CR 130 (witness's opinion that it looked as if defendant was trying to break up fight should have been admitted); *Pfingst v Goetting* (1950) 96 CA2d 293, 304, 215 P2d 93 (opinion allowed that deceased understood what was explained to her; discussion of decisions addressing this issue).

- *Intoxication.* See *People v Williams* (1988) 44 C3d 883, 915, 245 CR 336 (drug intoxication); *People v Garcia* (1972) 27 CA3d 639, 643, 104 CR 69 (defendant's wife should have been allowed to testify that he was drunk); *People v Ravey* (1954) 122 CA2d 699, 702, 265 P2d 154 (officer allowed to testify that defendant appeared drunk). But see *People v Navarette* (2003) 30 C4th 458, 493, 133 CR2d 89 (witness's opinion that defendant seemed high on cocaine inadmissible because witness admitted she had not seen anyone on drugs before).

- *Pain or suffering of another.* See *People v McAlpin* (1991) 53 C3d 1289, 1307, 283 CR 382.

- *Dangerous condition at site.* See *Osborn v Mission Ready Mix* (1990) 224 CA3d 104, 125, 273 CR 457 ("open and obvious").

- *Identity of persons.* See *People v Perry, supra* (witness viewing robbery film allowed to identify defendant from it). See also *People v Ingle* (1986) 178 CA3d 505, 223 CR 723; *In re Corey* (1964) 230 CA2d 813, 826, 41 CR 379.

- *Age or parentage.* See *People v Caldwell* (1921) 55 CA 280, 295, 203 P 440 (adoptive parents allowed to give opinion of child's age).

- *Competence.* Evid C §870. See *Estate of Martin* (1969) 270 CA2d 506, 514, 75 CR 911.

- *Damage to a person's reputation.* See *Weller v American Broadcasting Co.* (1991) 232 CA3d 991, 1008, 283 CR 644.

- *Who provoked a fight.* See *People v Moreno* (1973) 32 CA3d Supp 1, 8, 108 CR 338.

- *Speed of a vehicle.* See *Seaton v Spence* (1963) 215 CA2d 761, 765, 30 CR 510.

The requirement that the opinion must be "helpful to a clear understanding" of the testimony gives the trial judge wide discretion in that the judge need not find that opinion testimony is necessary but merely that it would be helpful. Because the misperceptions on which opinions are based can be effectively tested by cross-examination, trial judges tend to admit lay opinion rather than to exclude it.

A party failing to object to the opinion testimony of a witness will be considered to have waived the objection on appeal. *In re Joseph G.* (1970) 7 CA3d 695, 700, 87 CR 25.

§20.5   D. Statute

Under Evid C §800, if a witness is not testifying as an expert, his or her testimony in the form of an opinion is limited to an opinion "permitted by law," including but not limited to an opinion that is:

- Rationally based on the perception of the witness; and

- Helpful to a clear understanding of the witness's testimony.

Evidence Code §802 states:

> A witness testifying in the form of an opinion may state on direct examination the reasons for the opinion and the matter on which it is based (including, in the case of an expert, special knowledge, skill, experience, training, and education), unless he or she is precluded by law from using such reasons or matter as a basis for the opinion. The court in its discretion may require that, before testifying in the form of an opinion, a witness first be examined concerning the matter on which the opinion is based.

Evidence Code §803 states:

> The court may, and on objection shall, exclude testimony in the form of an opinion that is based in whole or in significant part on matter that is not a proper basis for such an opinion. If a proper basis for the opinion remains, the witness may then state that opinion after excluding from consideration the matter determined to be improper.

III. ADMISSIBLE OPINION BY EXPERT WITNESS

§20.6   A. Qualification as Expert

A witness may state an opinion on certain subjects (see §20.7) if the witness qualifies as an expert on those subjects. To qualify as an expert, a person must have special knowledge, skill, experience, training, or education about the subject of the testimony. Evid C §720(a). If a party objects, these special qualifications must be shown to the satisfaction of the trial judge before the witness testifies as an expert. Evid C §§405, 720(a). See *People v Roberts* (1992) 2 C4th 271, 6 CR2d 276, in which government investigators were permitted to testify on the practices and rules of the prison gang to which the defendant belonged because the defendant never challenged the expert witnesses' qualifications and their opinions were based on personal investigation. See *People v Killbrew* (2002) 103 CA4th 644, 126 CR2d 876 (police officer's expert opinion testimony regarding subjective knowledge and intent of defendant's gang conspiracy prosecution inadmissible); *In re Nathaniel C.* (1991) 228 CA3d 990, 1003, 279 CR 236 (rejecting expert testimony that offense was part of "pattern of criminal gang activity" when witness's opinion was based only on hearsay).

The qualification of an expert witness is left to the sound discretion of the trial court. *People v Bloyd* (1987) 43 C3d 333, 233 CR 368 (ballistic expert's testimony properly based on analyzed observations). For example, in *People v Davenport* (1995) 11 C4th 1171, 47 CR2d 800, the trial court's exclusion of a homicide investigator's expert opinion as to whether the victim had been impaled by a stake before or after death was proper because the expert lacked the qualifications necessary to render such an opinion. A foundation must be established that the expert is an expert in the field in which the opinion is rendered. *People v Bonin* (1989) 47 C3d 808, 846, 254 CR 298 (trial court failed to obtain requisite foundation for ligature mark comparison; testing conditions were insufficient). But see *People v Knights* (1985) 166 CA3d 46, 53, 212 CR 307, in which the court upheld the admission of expert testimony on footprint identification, including expert opinion comparing a sample of the defendant's footprint to photographs of footprints taken at the murder scene. The main objection to the testimony was other anthropologists' inability to verify or replicate the expert witness's measurements because her only publication on footprint analysis did not define the reference points from which the measurements had been made. The expert explained, however, that the published article was the result of a paper presented in conjunction with slides that had not been incorporated into the published article. With the addition of the slide presentation shown to the court and jury, all the measurements relied on could be verified by the jury.

The trial judge has wide discretion in deciding whether a person qualifies as an expert, and that determination will seldom be disturbed on appeal. *Putensen v Clay Adams, Inc.* (1970) 12 CA3d 1062, 91 CR 319. But see *Naples*

Restaurant, Inc. v Coberley Ford (1968) 259 CA2d 881, 884, 66 CR 835 (trial court's exclusion of Chrysler salesman's testimony on value of Ford Thunderbird reversed as prejudicial error).

Although the most commonly used experts are professionals such as doctors and engineers, a university degree is not a prerequisite for a witness to be considered an expert. *People v Smith* (1956) 142 CA2d 287, 292, 298 P2d 540. Expertness depends on the subject matter. For instance, the most logical person to give expert testimony about the proper method of unloading a boxcar is a worker whose regular job is to unload boxcars. See *Fonts v Southern Pac. Co.* (1916) 30 CA 633, 159 P 215.

For an excellent and humorous discussion on the entire subject of expert witnesses, read Richard H. Underwood *"X-Spurt" Witness*, 19 American Journal of Trial Advocacy 344–409 (1996).

§20.7   B. Special Type of Subject Matter Beyond Common Experience

The subject matter about which the expert testifies must be "sufficiently beyond common experience that the opinion of an expert would assist the trier of fact." Evid C §801(a). According to the Comment to Evid C §801, this section codifies the rule stated in *People v Cole* (1956) 47 C2d 99, 103, 301 P2d 854. See also *Campbell v General Motors Corp.* (1982) 32 C3d 112, 124, 184 CR 891 (expert testimony not required to determine whether bus was defectively designed because it lacked a grab bar within reach of plaintiff's seat). The test is whether the witness, because of experience, training, and education, is better qualified to render an opinion than a person without that background.

If the field of inquiry is "one of such common knowledge" that persons "of ordinary education could reach a conclusion as intelligently" as the expert witness, then expert opinion testimony is inadmissible. *Smith v Lockheed Propulsion Co.* (1967) 247 CA2d 774, 783, 56 CR 128. Compare *McNeil v Yellow Cab Co.* (1978) 85 CA3d 116, 118, 147 CR 733, in which the court permitted the plaintiff to testify that the defendant company's failure to provide visible seatbelts was the proximate cause of injuries suffered in a collision, with *Truman v Vargas* (1969) 275 CA2d 976, 982, 80 CR 373, in which expert testimony was required to establish what injuries would have been prevented by the plaintiff's wearing a seatbelt in a car traveling 40 miles an hour when it crashed into another vehicle and stopped suddenly. See also *People v Son* (2000) 79 CA4th 224, 240, 93 CR2d 871 (trial court acted within discretion in excluding proffered expert testimony on false confessions); *Loth v Truck-A-Way Corp.* (1998) 60 CA4th 757, 767, 70 CR2d 571 (plaintiff's loss of enjoyment of life is not subject sufficiently beyond common experience that expert opinion would assist trier of fact); *People v Johnson* (1993) 19 CA4th 778, 786, 23 CR2d 703 (court did not abuse discretion in excluding defendants' proffered expert testimony concerning prison inmates' propensity to lie when testifying).

Although an expert witness may properly testify on custom and practice in the industry, the witness will not be permitted to state an opinion as to whether a statute, an ordinance, or a safety regulation promulgated under a statute applies to a certain type of project. Opinions on the interpretation and scope of the law are reserved for the court. See *Summers v A.L. Gilbert Co.* (1999) 69 CA4th 1155, 82 CR2d 162 (although expert can give opinion on ultimate issue there is a prohibition against an opinion on a question of law); *Elder v Pacific Tel. & Tel. Co.* (1977) 66 CA3d 650, 664, 136 CR 203 (architect testified as expert in construction industry).

The following examples show the wide variety of subject matter that expert opinion encompasses:

- Lawyers and doctors on standards of care within the professions. See *Osborn v Irwin Mem. Blood Bank* (1992) 5 CA4th 234, 7 CR2d 101; *Lysick v Walcom* (1968) 258 CA2d 136, 65 CR 406; *Stephenson v Kaiser Found. Hosps.* (1962) 203 CA2d 631, 21 CR 646.

- Experiments and scientific evidence. See *People v Bonin* (1989) 47 C3d 808, 254 CR 298.

- Seat belt use. See *Franklin v Gibson* (1982) 138 CA3d 340, 343, 188 CR 23.

- Insurance "bad faith." See *Neal v Farmers Ins. Exch.* (1978) 21 C3d 910, 148 CR 389.

- Automobile manufacturer acted in "conscious disregard" of passenger safety. See *Hasson v Ford Motor Co.* (1982) 32 C3d 388, 403, 185 CR 654.

- Product was defective. See *Self v General Motors Corp.* (1974) 42 CA3d 1, 6, 116 CR 575, overruled on other grounds in 8 C4th at 580.

- Tax consequences. See California Expert Witness Guide §6.8 (2d ed Cal CEB 1991).

- Adequacy of warnings by traffic safety engineer. See *New v Consolidated Rock Prods. Co.* (1985) 171 CA3d 681, 217 CR 522.

- Foundation by expert for hypnosis. Evid C §795(a).

- Ultimate issue. Evid C §805.

- DNA. See *People v Venegas* (1998) 18 C4th 47, 74 CR2d 262.

- Paternity (HLA blood test). Evid C §895, subject to Evid C §352. See *County of Sonoma v Grant W.* (1986) 187 CA3d 1439, 232 CR 471.

- Footprint identification. See *People v Knights* (1985) 166 CA3d 46, 53, 212 CR 307.

- Gangs. See *People v Williams* (1997) 16 C4th 153, 194, 66 CR2d 123; *People v Manriquez* (1999) 72 CA4th 1486, 1492, 86 CR2d 69.

Passage of Proposition 8 (the "truth-in-evidence" provision; Cal Const art I, §28(d)) did not affect the rule in California that admissibility of evidence based on a new scientific technique is determined under the *Kelly* rule (see *People v Kelly* (1976) 17 C3d 24, 130 CR 144). *People v Leahy* (1994) 8 C4th 587, 598, 34 CR2d 663; *People v Harris* (1989) 47 C3d 1047, 1094, 255 CR 352. But see Justice Baxter's dissent in *Leahy*, arguing that *Kelly* "excludes relevant evidence which this court does not have the power to render inadmissible by perpetuation of a court-made rule of evidence." *People v Leahy* (1994) 8 C4th 587, 624, 34 CR2d 663.

§20.8   C. Basis of Expert Opinion

Opinions are based on matter either personally observed by the witness or communicated to the witness. As used in the Evidence Code, the term "matter" includes facts, data, the witness's knowledge or experience, statements and opinions of others, and "other intangibles," *i.e.,* every conceivable basis for an opinion. Comment to Evid C §§800–805. The matter on which the expert witness bases an opinion must be of a type that (1) may reasonably be relied on by an expert forming an opinion on the subject to which his or her testimony relates and (2) is not precluded by law from consideration. Evid C §801(b).

What is permissible as a basis for an expert opinion varies from case to case. See Comment to Evid C §801; *Board of Trustees v Porini* (1968) 263 CA2d 784, 793, 70 CR 73. Special rules apply to experts who base their opinions on the statements or opinions of others. See Evid C §802. For example, a physician or an appraiser may usually state an opinion even though the opinion is based on the statements and opinion of others. A fireman testifying on the cause of a fire, however, may be precluded from basing an opinion on statements of bystanders. See *Behr v County of Santa Cruz* (1959) 172 CA2d 697, 342 P2d 987, cited in Comment to Evid C §801.

Clearly, an expert may not base an opinion on irrelevant or speculative matters. *People v Luis* (1910) 158 C 185, 110 P 580, overruled on other grounds in 27 C4th 444 (expert based opinion of feeblemindedness on person's exterior appearance); *Roscoe Moss Co. v Jenkins* (1942) 55 CA2d 369, 130 P2d 477 (expert compared wells drilled by plaintiff with other wells without laying proper foundation for comparison). See Comment to Evid C §801. See also *City of San Diego v Sobke* (1998) 65 CA4th 379, 395, 76 CR2d 9 (expert's opinion testimony about existence and loss of goodwill founded on matter insufficient to form proper basis for that opinion); *Solis v Southern Cal. Rapid Transit Dist.* (1980) 105 CA3d 382, 389, 164 CR 343 (accident reconstruction expert's attempt to recreate accident from experiment conducted two years after accident involved too many variables to be reliable). In such cases, opposing counsel should object on the ground that a proper foundation for an expert opinion has not been laid. But see *Staples v Hoefke* (1987) 189 CA3d 1397, 1416, 235 CR 165, in which the court held that experimental evidence is admissible when it (1) is relevant, (2) was obtained under conditions substantially similar to those to which it is sought to be applied, and (3) will not unduly delay the trial or confuse the jury.

If the judge determines that the expert is basing the opinion in significant part on improper matter, the judge may exclude that opinion; on objection, the judge must exclude it. Evid C §803. The judge should then determine whether a proper basis remains for an opinion without the improper matter. For example, an expert witness on automobile accident reconstruction may have based an opinion regarding the point of impact partly on a bystander's statement, which is an improper basis. See Comment to Evid C §801. If a proper basis for an opinion on the point of impact remains after excluding the bystander's statement from consideration, the witness may express that opinion. See Evid C §803.

Counsel should be alert to the use of an expert simply as a method for smuggling inadmissible hearsay into the record. A hearing outside the jury's presence is the safest way to determine whether hearsay is part or all of the basis for the opinion. Counsel should move to strike the opinion of an expert if, after the opinion is stated, it becomes apparent that the basis for the opinion is improper matter. See Evid C §803. See *People v Szeto* (1981) 29 C3d 20, 32, 171 CR 652. See also *People v Coleman* (1985) 38 C3d 69, 211 CR 102, in which the court held to be reversible error the cross-examination of an expert witness that elicited testimony on otherwise-inadmissible hearsay statements (letters written by the deceased victim). A limiting instruction directing the jury not to consider the letters for the truth of the matter asserted was not enough to cure the error.

§20.9   1. Expert May Rely on Inadmissible Matter

The matter on which experts base their opinions need not itself be admissible into evidence. Evid C §801(b). The opinion must be based on "reliable matter, whether or not admissible, of a type that may reasonably be used in forming an opinion on the subject to which [the] expert testimony relates." Comment to Evid C §801. Thus, in cases involving the possession of illegal drugs, such as marijuana or heroin, an experienced police officer may give an opinion that the narcotics are held for the purpose of sale based on such matters as quantity, packaging, and normal use by an individual. *People v Carter* (1997) 55 CA4th 1376, 64 CR2d 747. Before offering opinion testimony, counsel should consider the necessity and relative reliability of the matter on which the opinion is based. See *Buckwalter v Airline Training Ctr.* (1982) 134 CA3d 547, 553, 184 CR 659. For example, a doctor may rely on a patient's case history, even though the medical history would be inadmissible if offered to prove the facts stated. Comment to Evid C §801. The court may at times give an appropriate limiting instruction to the jury, *e.g.,* that the medical history is the basis for the doctor's opinion and is not being admitted to prove the facts in the history stated by the patient. See CACI 218; *People v Montiel*

(1993) 5 C4th 877, 918, 21 CR2d 705 (expert may explain reasons for opinion, including matters considered in forming it, if reasons fall within recognized hearsay exception).

Expert witnesses may, however, reasonably take into account hearsay in arriving at an opinion. *Genrich v State* (1988) 202 CA3d 221, 248 CR 303 (plaintiff's expert properly based opinion on alleged hazardous intersection on statistical information in government report that was hearsay); *Mosesian v Pennwalt Corp.* (1987) 191 CA3d 851, 236 CR 778 (expert plant pathologist's reasonable use of hearsay while testifying on other expert's opinions on pesticide's capacity to cause chemical burns); *Conservatorship of Isaac O.* (1987) 190 CA3d 50, 235 CR 133 (psychiatrist permitted to rely on hearsay concerning person's mental capacities). The test is whether the hearsay on which the opinion is based relates to the subject on which the expert is testifying. See Evid C §801(a); *Isaacs v Huntington Mem. Hosp.* (1985) 38 C3d 112, 133, 211 CR 356.

The California Supreme Court has held, however, that a plaintiff in a medical malpractice action may not subpoena an expert to testify when the expert's conclusions are substantially based on hospital peer review committee records the expert reviewed as part of his official duties for a public agency. Hospital peer review records are immune from discovery under Evid C §1157(a). *Fox v Kramer* (2000) 22 C4th 531, 535, 93 CR2d 497.

§20.10   2. Scientific Evidence

Although traditional evidentiary rules continue to apply to most expert opinion in civil and criminal actions (see Evid C §720; qualification as an expert witness), the foundation for admitting opinions based on new scientific techniques and theories requires the application of special rules and a special foundation hearing. See Federal Judicial Center, Reference Manual of Scientific Evidence (2d ed 2000).

Because jurors give considerable weight to the opinion of experts, the court must determine whether any new scientific techniques and theories on which the opinion is based may be reasonably relied on by an expert in forming an opinion. Before any opinion is stated, an Evid C §402 or §405 foundation hearing must be held to determine the admissibility of the opinion. This hearing is usually held in limine outside the presence of the jury. Evid C §§402, 405.

Admissibility standards and criteria with respect to new scientific evidence differ in California and federal law. See *People v Leahy* (1994) 8 C4th 587, 612, 34 CR2d 663. California courts apply the standard developed in *Frye v U.S.* (DC Cir 1923) 293 F 1013 and *People v Kelly* (1976) 17 C3d 24, 130 CR 144. *People v Leahy, supra.* Federal courts apply the standard developed in *Daubert v Merrell Dow Pharmaceuticals, Inc.* (1993) 509 US 579, 125 L Ed 2d 469, 113 S Ct 2786. See Fed R Evid 702.

§20.11 a. *Kelly-Frye* Standard

In 1923, the court in *Frye v U.S.* (DC Cir 1923) 293 F 1013 held that, to be admissible, any "new scientific technique" on which an expert bases an opinion must be sufficiently established to have gained "general acceptance" in the relevant scientific community. Although the *Frye* standard was criticized for being too "conservative" and "uncertain," in 1976 the California Supreme Court reaffirmed its long use of the *Frye* rule in *People v Kelly* (1976) 17 C3d 24, 130 CR 144.

The *Kelly* court discussed the foundation hearing necessary for establishing the general acceptance test for voiceprint evidence produced by a technique used to identify voices by spectrographic analysis. After analyzing the *Frye* standard, the *Kelly* court "reaffirmed allegiance" to its cautious but reliable general acceptance test. 17 C3d at 32. See *People v Fierro* (1991) 1 C4th 173, 214, 3 CR2d 426; *People v Morris* (1991) 53 C3d 152, 206, 279 CR 720. Practitioners in California refer to the *Frye* standard as the "*Kelly* test." See *People v Leahy* (1994) 8 C4th 587, 591, 34 CR2d 663 (supreme court refers to *Kelly-Frye* standard as "now more accurately, the *Kelly* formulation"). For the types of tests admitted under *Kelly*, see §20.13.

The *Kelly* test is considered by some to be a "nose-counting" standard that "penalizes crime victims" and is contrary to the liberal intent of the Evidence Code (which allows "all admissible relevant evidence" except as otherwise prohibited by statute) and Cal Const art I, §28(d) (which allows "all relevant evidence ... unless barred by the Federal Constitution or §§352, 782 or 1103 of the evidence code"). There is no question that, contrary to the legislative intent of the Evidence Code and Cal Const art I, §28(d), the *Kelly* test excludes relevant evidence. Nevertheless, it continues to be followed in California courts. See *People v Leahy, supra*.

The *Frye* test continued to be followed in federal courts until the decision in *Daubert v Merrell Dow Pharmaceuticals, Inc.* (1993) 509 US 579, 125 L Ed 2d 469, 113 S Ct 2786. In *Daubert*, the United States Supreme Court rejected the *Frye* test in favor of a new balancing test. See §§20.15-20.16.

b. California's *Kelly* Test

§20.12 (1) Establishing General Acceptance of New Scientific Technique or Theory

If an expert's opinion is based on the application of a new scientific technique or theory, the test for determining the admissibility of the opinion is whether the technique or theory on which it is based is "sufficiently established to have gained general acceptance in the particular field in which it belongs." See *Frye v U.S.* (DC Cir 1923) 293 F 1013, 1014, quoted in *People v Kelly* (1976) 17 C3d 24, 30, 130 CR 144. Under this so-called *Kelly* test, "general acceptance" in the scientific community is established if the technique or theory is generally accepted by a cross-section of the relevant scientific community.

People v Leahy (1994) 8 C4th 587, 612, 34 CR2d 663; *People v Kelly, supra*. Thus, any evidence relevant to such an inquiry is admissible unless it is barred by other exclusionary rules, *e.g.,* Evid C §352. A majority of the scientific community need not accept the scientific technique or theory for the opinion on which it is based to be admissible. The opinion may be admitted if the technique or theory on which it is based is accepted by a "reliable" segment of the scientific community. See *People v Leahy, supra*; *People v Coleman* (1988) 46 C3d 749, 251 CR 83; *People v Kelly, supra*; *People v Wallace* (1993) 14 CA4th 651, 17 CR2d 721; *People v Pizarro* (1992) 10 CA4th 57, 12 CR2d 436. See also *People v Allen* (1999) 72 CA4th 1093, 85 CR2d 655 (testimony of a single expert witness is sufficient to establish general acceptance in the scientific community).

A *Kelly* showing is not necessary if the court determines that the scientific technique or theory is not new or novel. *People v Pride* (1992) 3 C4th 195, 238, 10 CR2d 636 (hair comparison); *People v Stoll* (1989) 49 C3d 1136, 1156, 265 CR 111 (standardized test relied on by psychologist). An expert's testimony that the use of methamphetamine in greater than therapeutic dosages results in impaired driving did not involve a novel process or new scientific technique or device. The expert's opinion was based on epidemiological studies and published papers, which are common, valid, and accepted tools of scientific research in use in the scientific community for the past 200 years. *People v Bui* (2001) 86 CA4th 1187, 1195, 103 CR2d 908.

For reasons of judicial economy, courts are also allowed to do the following:

- Take judicial notice of conclusions reached by proceedings in the same court (*People v Smith* (1989) 215 CA3d 19, 25, 263 CR 678); or

- Use published writings in scholarly treatises and journals in lieu of live testimony (*People v Shirley* (1982) 31 C3d 18, 55, 181 CR 243) or stipulated evidence concerning similar foundational issues (*People v Fierro* (1991) 1 C4th 173, 214 n11, 3 CR2d 426).

See also *People v Pizarro, supra* (court considered "rate of error," existence and maintenance of standards, and "relationship with other types of scientific techniques . . . routinely admitted into evidence").

The *Kelly* test applies to a California administrative hearing. *Seering v Department of Social Servs.* (1987) 194 CA3d 298, 239 CR 422.

(2) Applying *Kelly* Test to Scientific Evidence

§20.13 (a) Techniques That Passed Test

The *Kelly* test has been applied to a variety of forensic techniques in civil and criminal cases. Those found to pass the test include the following:

- Agglutination-inhibition blood testing. See *People v Morganti* (1996) 43 CA4th 643, 50 CR2d 837; *People v Yorba* (1989) 209 CA3d 1017, 257 CR 641; *People v Riel* (2000) 22 C4th 1153, 1191, 96 CR2d 1.

- Detection of child abuse by reports of abuse and observations of child with anatomically correct dolls. See *In re Amber B.* (1987) 191 CA3d 682, 236 CR 623; *In re Christine C.* (1987) 191 CA3d 676, 236 CR 630.

- Electrophoretic testing of dried blood stains. See *People v Morganti, supra*; *People v Fierro* (1991) 1 C4th 173, 3 CR2d 426; *People v Morris* (1991) 53 C3d 152, 279 CR 720; *People v Reilly* (1987) 196 CA3d 1127, 242 CR 496.

- Horizontal gaze nystagmus field sobriety test. See *People v Leahy* (1994) 8 C4th 587, 34 CR2d 663.

- Hypnosis (limited admissibility under Evid C §795). See *People v Hayes* (1989) 49 C3d 1260, 265 CR 132; *Schall v Lockheed Missiles & Space Co.* (1995) 37 CA4th 1485, 44 CR2d 191 (opinion relied on *People v Shirley* (1982) 31 C3d 18, 181 CR 243).

- Matching bite marks with dentition. See *People v Marx* (1975) 54 CA3d 100, 126 CR 350 (opinion relied on *Frye v U.S.* (DC Cir 1923) 293 F 1013).

- DNA. *People v Venegas* (1998) 18 C4th 47, 89, 74 CR2d 262 (statistical probability calculations of random matches of DNA profiles admissible, provided they are computed under National Research Council's proposed "modified ceiling method"). See also *People v Soto* (1999) 21 C4th 512, 88 CR2d 34 (evidence of statistical probabilities using the "unmodified" ceiling method as applied in DNA forensic analysis also meet the *Kelly* standard for admissibility); *People v Hill* (2001) 89 CA4th 48, 60, 107 CR2d 110 ("Profiler Plus" DNA test kit uses accepted PCR and STR testing methods). But see *People v Pizarro* (2003) 110 CA4th 530, 557, 3 C3d 21 (failure to follow proper scientific procedures renders evidence inadmissible).

§20.14 (b) Techniques That Did Not Pass Test

The *Kelly* test has been applied to a variety of forensic techniques in civil and criminal cases. Those found not to pass the test include the following:

- Evidence of child sexual abuse accommodation syndrome or rape trauma syndrome. Such evidence is not admissible under *People v Kelly* (1976) 17 C3d 24, 130 CR 144, to prove abuse or rape. Such evidence is admissible, however, to explain certain behavioral reactions of the victim. See *People v Bledsoe* (1984) 36 C3d 236, 203 CR 450.

- Penile plethysmograph test. See *People v John W.* (1986) 185 CA3d 801, 229 CR 783.

- Polygraph (also called a "lie detector" test). See *People v Price* (1991)

1 C4th 324, 419, 3 CR2d 106. The results of a polygraph examination are admissible, however, on stipulation of the parties. Evid C §351.1.

- Population subgrouping used in DNA profiling. See *People v Pizarro* (1992) 10 CA4th 57, 12 CR2d 436.

- Posthypnotic testimony, except under the limited circumstances set out in Evid C §795. See *People v Shirley* (1982) 31 C3d 18, 181 CR 243.

- Voiceprint identification through spectrographic analysis. See *People v Kelly, supra.*

- Testimony to the truth of a memory refreshed by sodium amytal and of allegedly recovered repressed memories of sexual abuse recalled after a sodium amytal interview. See *Ramona v Superior Court* (1997) 57 CA4th 107, 115, 66 CR2d 766. But see *Wilson v Phillips* (1999) 73 CA4th 250, 86 CR2d 204 (expert testimony on repressed memory of sexual abuse allowed without *Kelly* hearing because no reliance on scientific technique or procedure).

c. Federal Courts' *Daubert* Test

§20.15 (1) *Daubert I*

In *Daubert v Merrell Dow Pharmaceuticals, Inc.* (1993) 509 US 579, 125 L Ed 2d 469, 113 S Ct 2786 (*Daubert I*), the United States Supreme Court rejected the "general acceptance" test of *Frye v U.S.* (DC Cir 1923) 293 F 1013 in favor of a more liberal balancing test that was soon labeled the "*Daubert* test." California courts continue to apply the test established in *People v Kelly* (1976) 17 C3d 24, 130 CR 144, but federal courts follow the standard developed in *Daubert I*.

Daubert I involved claims that Bendectin, taken by pregnant women for nausea, caused birth defects. In reversing an order granting summary judgment, the Supreme Court held that a foundation hearing should have been held under Fed R Evid 702 to determine the admissibility of certain statistical evidence of birth defect causation. According to the Court, rather than focusing on the Frye test of whether the scientific theory or technique on which the evidence is based is generally accepted in the scientific community, this hearing should focus on the reliability and trustworthiness of the evidence. See *Lust v Merrell Dow Pharmaceuticals, Inc.* (9th Cir 1996) 89 F3d 594.

The United States Supreme Court has expanded *Daubert's* balancing test to include not only scientific evidence but also testimony based on "technical" and "other specialized" matters within its scope. *Kumho Tire Co. v Carmichael* (1999) 526 US 137, 143 L Ed 2d 238, 119 S Ct 1167. In *Kumho* the Supreme Court, in a near unanimous decision (Stevens, J., dissenting in part), held that a federal judge's gatekeeping role under Fed R Evid 702, ensuring that an expert witness's testimony rests on a reliable foundation and is relevant, applies not only to scientific knowledge but also to all expert testimony based on technical and other specialized knowledge. 143 L Ed 2d 250. The Court further refined *Daubert's* balancing formula holding that, in determining admissibility of evidence, "a trial court should consider the specific factors identified in *Daubert* where they are reasonable measures of the reliability of expert testimony." 143 L Ed 2d 252. Hence, a trial judge is granted "broad latitude" to consider one or more of the specific *Daubert* factors, without having to satisfy all the factors, in helping to determine the testimony's reliability. 143 L Ed 2d at 253.

In a discussion of the *Daubert I* test, the court in *Bradley v Brown* (7th Cir 1994) 42 F3d 434, 437, noted that trial courts should take the following factors into consideration at the foundation hearing:

> (1) whether a theory or technique can be or has been tested; (2) whether the theory or technique has been subjected to peer review and publication; (3) the known or potential rate of error [of the theory or technique]; and (4) the "general acceptance" of the [technique or] theory.

Thus, according to the *Bradley* court, although the Supreme Court recognized the *Frye* general acceptance test, it was considered merely one factor in a more complex balancing test.

The U.S. Court of Appeals for the Ninth Circuit has upheld the admission of expert testimony on the gang code of silence to impeach exculpatory testimony of a codefendant who was also a gang member. By admitting the testimony, the trial court properly applied its "gatekeeping" function under *Daubert I* and *Kumho Tire Co. v Carmichael* (1999) 526 US 137, 143 L Ed 2d 238, 119 S Ct 1167. *U.S. v Hankey* (9th Cir 2000) 203 F3d 1160, 1167.

A separate pretrial hearing, outside the jury's presence, is not required before expert testimony may be admitted at trial. Given the trial court's broad discretion and the absence of authority mandating such a hearing, the district court acted well within its discretion when it refused a pretrial hearing, but instead allowed the plaintiff to explore the prosecution's expert's qualifications at trial via voir dire. The district court did not abandon its "gatekeeping" function by doing so. *U.S. v Alatorre* (9th Cir 2000) 222 F3d 1098, 1099.

§20.16 (2) *Daubert II*

Daubert v Merrell Dow Pharmaceuticals, Inc. (1993) 509 US 579, 125 L Ed 2d 469, 113 S Ct 2786 (*Daubert I*), was remanded to the Ninth Circuit Court of Appeals. In *Daubert v Merrell Dow Pharmaceuticals, Inc.* (9th Cir 1995) 43 F3d 1311 (*Daubert II*), plaintiff's counsel argued that the case should be remanded to the trial court for the foundation hearing described by the Supreme Court. Instead, the court of appeals ruled on the foundational issues from the record below, finding that the statistical evidence of birth defect causation could not prove causation by a preponderance of the evidence.

Commenting that "federal judges, ruling on the admissibility of expert scientific evidence, face a far more complex and daunting task in the post-Daubert world than before," the *Daubert II* court described a two-part analysis that courts must conduct after *Daubert I* (43 F3d at 1315):

> First, we must determine nothing less than whether the experts' testimony reflects "scientific knowledge," whether their findings are "derived by the scientific method," and whether their work product amounts to "good science." . . . Second, we must ensure that the proposed expert testimony is "relevant to the task at hand," . . . *i.e.,* that it logically advances a material aspect of the proposing party's case.

According to the court (43 F3d at 1316), federal judges must perform a "gatekeeping role" by satisfying

> themselves that scientific evidence meets a certain standard of reliability before it is admitted. This means that the expert's bald assurance of validity is not enough. Rather, the party presenting the expert must show that the expert's findings are based on sound science, and this will require some objective, independent validation of the expert's methodology.

It appears that trial judges should go about this task in the same way that scientists conduct their research and reach their conclusions.

In *Joiner v General Elec. Co.* (ND Ga 1994) 864 F Supp 1310, Robert Joiner claimed his small-cell lung cancer resulted from exposure to chemicals, in addition to his eight-year habit of smoking up to a pack of cigarettes a day and childhood exposure to second-hand smoke. In support of the claim, Joiner's experts extrapolated from existing research to conclude that there was a causal link between the chemicals and the cancer. Before excluding the testimony of Joiner's experts, the trial court conducted a hearing to determine whether the testimony was relevant and scientifically valid, as required by *Daubert I*. Because Joiner's expert based his opinion on studies that did not involve humans, did not involve the relevant chemicals, and were inconclusive, the trial court found the expert testimony was too unconnected and unreliable and thus inadmissible. The court, therefore, granted summary judgment for General Electric.

On appeal, in *Joiner v General Elec. Co.* (11th Cir 1996) 78 F3d 524, 529, the Eleventh Circuit addressed the standard to be applied when reviewing the results of a *Daubert* hearing. The court reasoned that a decision to admit scientific testimony should be reversed only for an abuse of discretion, but a decision to exclude such testimony should be independently reviewed under the "particularly stringent" review standard.

On review, the United States Supreme Court, in *General Elec. Co. v Joiner* (1997) 522 US 136, 139 L Ed 2d 508, 118 S Ct 512, resolved the conflict over the level of scrutiny that should be applied to admissibility rulings made after a *Daubert* hearing. The Court disagreed with the Eleventh Circuit in three significant areas. First, the Court held that the same standard should be applied to all evidentiary decisions under *Daubert*, whether the ruling was to admit or exclude evidence. Second, it held that the proper standard to apply is "abuse of discretion." Finally, the Court echoed the district court's criticism of *Joiner*'s scientific evidence, reversed the Eleventh Circuit decision, and re-entered the summary judgment for the manufacturer.

In making its determination that an abuse of discretion standard should be applied to all rulings on scientific evidence, the Supreme Court obviously rejected the "preference for admissibility" that the Eleventh Circuit found so compelling. The Supreme Court recognized that, in the absence of conclusive scientific proof, "experts commonly extrapolate from existing data" to reach new conclusions. However, the Court also cautioned against the blind acceptance of such conclusions: "[N]othing in either Daubert or the Federal Rules of Evidence requires a district court to admit opinion evidence which is connected to existing data only by the *ipse dixit* of the expert. A court may conclude that there is simply too great an analytical gap between the data and the opinion proffered." 139 L Ed 2d at 519. By upholding the district court's exclusion of the opinion testimony, the Court reinforced the notion that there must be an adequate scientific foundation for any opinions an expert might ultimately express. See also *Kumho Tire Co. v Carmichael* (1999) 526 US 137, 143 L Ed 2d 238, 256, 119 S Ct 1167, discussed in §20.15.

The tests described in *Daubert II* and *Bradley v Brown* (7th Cir 1994) 42 F3d 434 (see §20.15) are illustrative rather than exhaustive. 43 F3d at 1317.

§20.17   d. Impact of *Daubert* in California: *People v Leahy*

In *People v Leahy* (1994) 8 C4th 587, 34 CR2d 663, the California Supreme court rejected the balancing test established in *Daubert v Merrell Dow Pharmaceuticals, Inc.* (1993) 509 US 579, 125 L Ed 2d 469, 113 S Ct 2786, in favor of the general acceptance test of *Frye v U.S.* (DC Cir 1923) 293 F 1013.

Defense counsel in *Leahy* moved in limine to exclude the HGN (eye-ball bounce) field sobriety test used by street police officers for over 30 years. Holding that the trial court erroneously admitted this test without requiring the prosecution to make a *Kelly-Frye* foundational showing, the appellate court reversed the conviction and remanded the case to the trial court for the necessary *Kelly* hearing. The appellate court used these facts to analyze whether the recent federal *Daubert* test should be used in California instead of the *Kelly* test. For a thorough analysis of the use of new scientific evidence in a California courtroom, see *People v Leahy, supra.*

For further discussion of the admissibility of new scientific evidence, see *Daubert v Merrell Dow, The Supreme Court Tackles Scientific Evidence in the Courtroom*, 270 JAMA 24 (1993); Annas, *Scientific Evidence in the Courtroom: The Death of the Frye Rule*, 330 New Eng J Med 14 1018 (1993); Walker, *"Chicken Little's" Revenge: Strict Judicial Scrutiny of Scientific Evidence*, 41 Clev St L Rev 717 (1993). See also *Casey v Ohio Med. Prods.* (ND Cal 1995) 877 F Supp 1380.

§20.18   e. Psychological Opinion

Psychological opinion based on personal examination and an analysis of accepted psychological tests may be admitted as character evidence to show that an individual was or was not likely to have committed a particular act. The admissibility of such testimony is not subject to the *Kelly* test for the admissibility of new scientific techniques. *People v Stoll* (1989) 49 C3d 1136, 265 CR 111 (psychological tests admitted to show that defendant charged with committing lewd and lascivious acts on children showed no signs of "deviance" or "abnormality"). See 1 Witkin, California Evidence, *Opinion Evidence* §58 (4th ed 2000). See also *People v Kelly* (1976) 17 C3d 24, 130 CR 144; *Frye v U.S.* (DC Cir 1923) 293 F 1013.

Although drug-induced testimony regarding recovered repressed memories of sexual abuse is subject to the *Kelly* test, expert medical testimony by a psychologist on childhood sexual abuse and repressed memory is not. *Wilson v Phillips* (1999) 73 CA4th 250, 86 CR2d 204. See §20.14.

Psychological testimony assessing a criminal defendant's potentiality as a sexually violent predator is not subject to the *Kelly* test. In *People v Ward* (1999) 71 CA4th 368, 83 CR2d 828, the court held that, while Welf & I C §6601(d) requires a potentially violent predator to be psychologically evaluated, the testimony of the psychologist or psychiatrist is not subject to the *Kelly* test because of the distinction between expert medical opinion and scientific evidence. 71 CA4th at 368.

Additionally, a psychologist may testify to the effect that circumstances may have on a person's perception. Thus, in *People v Vu* (1991) 227 CA3d 810, 278 CR 153, the court recognized as proper testimony (from a psychologist on the defendant's behalf) statements about the effects of stress and expectation on the defendant's perception of the situation. Expert testimony that an alleged rape victim suffers from "rape trauma syndrome" is not admissible, however, to prove that the alleged victim was raped. See *People v Bledsoe* (1984) 36 C3d 236, 203 CR 450. See also *In re Amber B.* (1987) 191 CA3d 682, 236 CR 623, in which the court thoroughly analyzed *Bledsoe* as well as the *Kelly* test.

The psychological technique of diagnosing child sexual abuse by observing a child's behavior with anatomically correct dolls and analyzing the child's reports of sexual abuse is inadmissible without a showing that this new scientific method of proof has been generally accepted as reliable in the relevant scientific community. See *Seering v Department of Social Servs.* (1987) 194 CA3d 298, 239 CR 422, in which the appellate court held that the trial court erroneously admitted a psychiatrist's opinion that child molestation had occurred because the theory on which the opinion was based (the "child sexual abuse accommodation syndrome") was not generally accepted as reliable in the relevant scientific community. Under the specific facts of the case, the court held that the error was harmless.

In a related matter, admission of an expert's testimony regarding common reactions of child sexual abuse victims was held proper for the purpose of explaining the victim's behavior when the defense had attacked the victim's credibility, in contrast to the improper purpose of proving that the victim had been molested. See *People v Harlan* (1990) 222 CA3d 439, 449, 271 CR 653.

D. Hypothetical Questions

§20.19   1. Use

If an expert witness lacks personal knowledge of the specifics of the subject matter that is the basis for the opinion, such specifics must be "made known" to the expert in the form of a hypothetical question. See Evid C §801(b).

For strategic reasons, some counsel may put all hypothetical questions in writing and deliver copies to the judge and opposing counsel before calling the expert to the stand. Each question can then be reviewed in chambers and revised if it is unduly slanted or too complex for the jury to understand. This practice will allow opposing counsel to obtain a copy of the hypothetical questions, which will alert opposing counsel to possible objections. See California Expert Witness Guide §14.4 (2d ed Cal CEB 1991).

§20.20   2. General Rules of Framing

The exact form that a hypothetical question may take is largely within the court's discretion. See *Estate of Collin* (1957) 150 CA2d 702, 310 P2d 663; *Graves v Union Oil Co.* (1918) 36 CA 766, 173 P 618. Case law suggests the following general rules:

- Each assumed fact stated in the hypothetical question must be supported by evidence. *Rowe v Such* (1901) 134 C 573, 66 P 862. If an assumed fact is not supported by evidence, opposing counsel should object on the ground that the question assumes a fact that is not in evidence. Counsel may also object on the ground of insufficient foundation. Whether the expert's opinion may be considered as evidence depends on a finding by the trier of fact that the assumed facts exist. See Comment to Evid C §802.

- The hypothetical question need not state all the pertinent evidence (*Perkins v Sunset Tel. & Tel. Co.* (1909) 155 C 712, 103 P 190) if the assumed facts are "within the limits of the evidence" (*People v Wilson* (1944) 25 C2d 341, 349, 153 P2d 720). For a case stating that hypothetical questions used in cross-examination of expert witnesses must be fair in scope and fairly relate to the state of the evidence, see *Dincau v Tamayose* (1982) 131 CA3d 780, 798, 182 CR 855. See also *Barajas v USA Petroleum Corp.* (1986) 184 CA3d 974, 990, 229 CR 513, in which the court observed that appellate courts place great reliance on trial courts' exercise

- The question may be framed to reflect only the examiner's theory of the case. *Coogan Fin. Corp. v Beatcher* (1932) 120 CA 278, 7 P2d 695. Trial counsel tend to exploit this freedom, which is the primary reason for the frequent criticism of the use of hypothetical questions. Hypothetical questions have been held subject to exclusion, however, under Evid C §352 grounds. See, *e.g., People v Clark* (1980) 109 CA3d 88, 167 CR 51.

- Failure to object to an omission or a misstatement in a hypothetical objection and require that the question be framed correctly waives the defect on appeal. *Waller v Southern Pac. Co.* (1967) 66 C2d 201, 210, 57 CR 353.

§20.21   E. Appointment of Experts

On the appointment of expert witnesses by the court, see Evid C §§730–733. When an expert appointed by the court is called as a witness and examined by the trial judge, each party to the action may cross-examine that witness as if the witness had been called as a witness by an adverse party, and each party may object to the questions asked and to the evidence given. Evid C §§732, 775. Counsel should make a motion to strike and request an admonition.

§20.22   F. Statutes

Evidence Code §§801–804 apply to the admissibility of opinion testimony.

- Evidence Code §801 states:

    If a witness is testifying as an expert, his testimony in the form of an opinion is limited to such an opinion as is:

    (a) Related to a subject that is sufficiently beyond common experience that the opinion of an expert would assist the trier of fact; and

    (b) Based on matter (including his special knowledge, skill, experience, training, and education) perceived by or personally known to the witness or made known to him at or before the hearing, whether or not admissible, that is of a type that reasonably may be relied upon by an expert in forming an opinion upon the subject to which his testimony relates, unless an expert is precluded by law from using such matter as a basis for his opinion.

- Evidence Code §802 states:

    A witness testifying in the form of an opinion may state on direct examination the reasons for his opinion and the matter (including, in the case of an expert, his special knowledge, skill, experience, training, and education), upon which it is based, unless he is precluded by law from using such reasons or matter as a basis for his opinion. The court in its discretion may require that a witness before testifying in the form of an opinion be first examined concerning the matter upon which his opinion is based.

- Evidence Code §803 states:

   The court may, and upon objection shall, exclude testimony in the form of an opinion that is based in whole or in significant part on matter that is not a proper basis for such an opinion. In such case, the witness may, if there remains a proper basis for his opinion, then state his opinion after excluding from consideration the matter determined to be improper.

- Evidence Code §804 states:

   (a) If a witness testifying as an expert testifies that his opinion is based in whole or in part upon the opinion or statement of another person, such other person may be called and examined by any adverse party as if under cross-examination concerning the opinion or statement.

   (b) This section is not applicable if the person upon whose opinion or statement the expert witness has relied is (1) a party, (2) a person identified with a party within the meaning of subdivision (d) of Section 776, or (3) a witness who has testified in the action concerning the subject matter of the opinion or statement upon which the expert witness has relied.

   (c) Nothing in this section makes admissible an expert opinion that is inadmissible because it is based in whole or in part on the opinion or statement of another person.

   (d) An expert opinion otherwise admissible is not made inadmissible by this section because it is based on the opinion or statement of a person who is unavailable for examination pursuant to this section.

IV. PROCEDURES FOR TESTING OPINION TESTIMONY

§20.23   A. Foundational Examination Before Opinion Stated

Before a witness states an opinion, the witness will normally be asked to describe the matter on which it is based. Such a foundation is not always required. See Evid C §802. It is usually within the judge's discretion to require that the witness be examined about the basis for the opinion before it may be stated. Evid C §802. If the opinion is based on assumed facts and not on personal observation, testimony concerning the basis for the opinion is necessary to establish the opinion's admissibility under Evid C §405. See Comment to Evid C §802.

In three situations, a preliminary foundation is mandatory *before* an opinion may be stated. Against the objection of a party:

- A lay witness must be shown to have personally observed the facts before the witness testifies (Evid C §702; see §§18.26, 21.11);
- An expert witness's special qualifications must be shown before the witness states an opinion (Evid C §720(a)); and
- A *Kelly* foundation hearing must be held if an expert opinion is based on new scientific techniques (see §§20.10–20.14, 20.17).

§20.24 B. Voir Dire Examination of Expert

After the foundational phase of questioning, opposing counsel may cross-examine an expert witness to ascertain whether the witness is sufficiently qualified to testify. This questioning is commonly called a "voir dire examination."

Although voir dire examination may be a useful means of learning the basis for a witness's opinion, counsel should weigh the tactical risks before beginning such cross-examination in the jury's presence. It will be obvious to the jurors that counsel is trying to keep the opinion out of evidence. Should the judge ultimately rule that a proper foundation has been laid and admit the opinion testimony, the jury will observe counsel's unsuccessful attempt to block the witness from giving an opinion and may misinterpret the court's ruling as an implied endorsement of the witness. In addition, voir dire may unduly emphasize the subject matter and highlight the expert's qualifications.

To minimize these risks, counsel may request that the voir dire examination be conducted out of the jury's presence. See Evid C §402(b). On motions in limine, see chap 2. As an alternative, counsel may wait until the direct examination is completed and then discredit the witness's qualifications and opinion by cross-examination or extrinsic evidence. If the opinion relates to an important issue, however, and the witness clearly lacks the necessary qualifications, counsel is well advised to proceed with a voir dire examination before the opinion is stated.

If opposing counsel is using voir dire examination to improperly question the witness, counsel should object on the ground of improper voir dire. For instance, counsel might state:

> Objection, Your Honor. With this line of questioning, counsel is starting an early cross-examination and breaking up the logical sequence of my case.

If speaking objections are not allowed (which is usually the case), counsel should simply state the objection and the ground.

§20.25 C. Cross-Examination After Opinion Stated

Cross-examination is the usual method of testing opinion testimony. A witness who renders an opinion as an expert is exposed to much broader cross-examination than is usually permitted. Comment to Evid C §721. Questions about the following matters are all proper: qualifications (see *People v Andrews* (1972) 23 CA3d Supp 1, 7, 100 CR 276), the source of the expert's knowledge, the reasons for the opinion, the specific matter on which it is based, what the witness took into consideration in forming the opinion (Evid C §722(b)), and prior testimony that the witness may have given in other trials. See *People v Nye* (1969) 71 C2d 356, 78 CR 467; *Hope v Arrowhead & Puritas Waters, Inc.* (1959) 174 CA2d 222, 230, 344 P2d 428. When hypothetical questions are used on cross-examination to test the expert's credibility, the requirement that they be based on facts in evidence is relaxed if not eliminated. See *People v Busch* (1961) 56 C2d 868, 16 CR 898; California Expert Witness Guide §§15.29–15.30 (2d ed Cal CEB 1991).

It is improper to impeach an expert witness by cross-examining the witness about a scientific, technical, or professional publication unless

- the witness referred to, considered, or relied on that publication in forming an opinion,
- that publication has been admitted into evidence, or
- the publication has been established as a reliable authority by the testimony or admission of the witness, by other expert testimony, or by judicial notice.

If such evidence is admitted, relevant portions of the publication may be read into evidence but may not be received as exhibits. Evid C §721(b). Counsel commonly try to smuggle hearsay into evidence through the use of learned texts, but this type of cross-examination requires a foundational showing that the expert "referred to," "considered," or "relied on" the text before it may be mentioned.

§20.26   D. Impeachment of Expert by Extrinsic Evidence

A common method of impeaching an expert witness is the use of extrinsic evidence proving that the expert relied on inaccurate data. The facts on which the expert based the opinion may also be attacked by introducing extrinsic evidence that a different opinion is warranted.

One rarely finds a subject about which all experts agree. It is therefore quite common for the opinions of experts to be defeated by testimony from stronger experts with contrary opinions. See California Expert Witness Guide §§15.24–15.25 (2d ed Cal CEB 1991).

§20.27   E. Cross-Examination of Third Person if Expert's Opinion Is Based on Hearsay

If an expert witness's opinion is based in whole or in part on the opinion or statement of another, opposing counsel may call that third person and examine the person as if under cross-examination. Evid C §804. The purpose of this rule is to allow the opinion to be fully tested. Certain exceptions to this rule apply if the third person is a party to the action, is a representative of a party, or has already testified. Evid C §804(b).

§20.28 V. OPINION ON ULTIMATE ISSUE IS PERMISSIBLE

It is not proper to object to a question on the ground that it calls for an opinion on an ultimate issue. Evid C §805. Other exclusionary rules may apply, however, that make the opinion inadmissible. For example:

- Asking a witness to state an opinion on whether the defendant was negligent, whether the arrest was valid, or whether first-degree murder was committed is objectionable but on grounds other than that the question relates to the ultimate issue. See *Summers v A.L. Gilbert Co.* (1999) 69 CA4th 1155, 82 CR2d 162 (although expert can give opinion on ultimate issue there is a prohibition against an opinion on a question of law).

- An opinion on an ultimate issue is frequently made inadmissible by one of the rules restricting opinion evidence, *e.g.,* because the lay witness has no personal knowledge of the facts or because the witness, although an expert on some subjects, is not qualified on the specific subject at issue.

- An opinion on the ultimate issue may also be excluded under a general provision such as Evid C §352, which authorizes the judge to exclude evidence if its probative value will be outweighed by the risk that, *e.g.,* the jury will be misled.

- In *Paez v Alcoholic Beverage Control Appeals Bd.* (1990) 222 CA3d 1025, 272 CR 272, an administrative law judge correctly allowed an officer to testify regarding his opinion on the ultimate issue of whether a customer of a board licensee was "obviously intoxicated" when served an alcoholic beverage.

Special rules govern opinion testimony about the following issues:

- Value, damages, and benefits in eminent domain and inverse condemnation cases. See Evid C §§810–824; *South Bay Irr. Dist. v California-American Water Co.* (1976) 61 CA3d 944, 133 CR 166 (court's discretionary handling of conflicting valuation methods in eminent domain case). See also Jefferson's California Evidence Benchbook §§29.60A–29.66 (3d ed CJA-CEB 1997).

- Sanity. See Evid C §870; Evidence Benchbook §29.3.

- Paternity based on blood tests. See Fam C §§7550–7557.

- Character. See Evid C §§1100–1104; Evidence Benchbook, chap 33.

- Handwriting. See Evid C §§1416, 1418; Evidence Benchbook §30.2.

§20.29   VI. ALTERNATIVES TO OBJECTING

On possible alternatives to objecting, see §§4.9–4.14.

VII. STATING THE OBJECTION

§20.30   A. Lay Witness

Objection, Your Honor. The question calls for inadmissible opinion.

§20.31   B. Expert Witness

[Option 1: No foundation]

Objection, Your Honor. A foundation has not been established showing that the witness is qualified to give such an opinion.

[Option 2: Improper subject matter]

Objection, Your Honor. This is not a proper subject matter for expert testimony.

[Option 3: Opinion based on improper matter]

Objection, Your Honor. The witness will be basing _ _[his/her]_ _ opinion on improper matter.

§20.32   VIII. RESPONSE: MOTION TO STRIKE

If the court allows the witness to give the opinion testimony, counsel should move, out of the presence of the jury and after cross-examination, to strike the evidence. If counsel's motion is successful, counsel should request an appropriate jury admonition.

21

Insufficient Foundation

I. INTRODUCTION §21.1

II. DETERMINING TYPE OF FOUNDATIONAL PROBLEM PRESENTED
   A. Determining Proper Classification (Evid C §§403, 405) §21.2
   B. When Evid C §403 Applies
      1. Introduction §21.3
      2. Relevancy §21.4
      3. Personal Knowledge §21.5
      4. Authenticity of Writing §21.6
      5. Identity §21.7
   C. When Evid C §405 Applies §21.8

III. COMPARING PROCEDURAL RULES
   A. Presence of Jury §21.9
   B. Procedure Under Evid C §403
      1. Judge Determines Only Whether Prima Facie Showing Made §21.10
      2. Conditional Admission if No Prima Facie Showing Made §21.11
      3. Cautionary Instructions to Jury Under Evid C §403 Only §21.12
      4. Exclusion of Evidence on Redetermination §21.13
      5. Statute §21.14
   C. Procedure Under Evid C §405
      1. Judge Alone Determines Admissibility §21.15
      2. No Evid C §405 Conditional Admission §21.16
      3. Separating Jury's Role if Preliminary Fact Is Also Ultimate Fact §21.17
      4. Statute §21.18

IV. RESPONSES TO OBJECTION §21.19

V. STATING THE OBJECTION §21.20

§21.1 I. INTRODUCTION

In many situations, the admissibility or inadmissibility of proffered evidence depends on proof of a "preliminary fact." See Evid C §§400–401. Laying a foundation is the procedure for presenting proof of the existence of the preliminary fact.

"Proffered evidence" (*i.e.,* proposed evidence) is evidence that requires, before it is admissible, preliminary proof (*i.e.,* a foundation) of the existence or nonexistence of a preliminary fact. Evid C §401. Types of proffered evidence that may be dependent on proof of a preliminary fact include:

- Relevance;
- Personal knowledge of a witness;
- Authenticity of a writing;
- Hearsay;
- Privilege;
- Identity; and
- Opinion (lay or expert).

See Evid C §403.

A hearsay declaration is not normally admissible. Such a declaration becomes admissible, however, if a foundation is established that it falls within an exception to the hearsay rule or that a particular privilege applies.

II. DETERMINING TYPE OF FOUNDATIONAL PROBLEM PRESENTED

§21.2   A. Determining Proper Classification (Evid C §§403, 405)

When a foundational problem is presented, the initial step under the Evidence Code is one of classification. Counsel should first determine whether the required foundation is a "§403 type" or a "§405 type." As indicated in §§21.9-21.18, the procedure that governs if Evid C §403 applies differs substantially from the procedure that governs if Evid C §405 applies. For the §403 type of foundational problem, the judge decides only whether there has been a prima facie showing of the existence of the preliminary fact; the final decision on the existence or nonexistence of the preliminary fact is made by the jury. For the §405 type of foundational problem, the judge alone decides the foundational question.

B. When Evid C §403 Applies

§21.3   1. Introduction

Evidence Code §403 applies only if one of the following four problems is presented:

(1) Relevancy (see §21.4);
(2) Personal knowledge (see §21.5);
(3) Authenticity of a writing (see §21.6); or
(4) Identity (see §21.7).

In the limited situations in which §403 governs, the judge determines whether there is enough evidence to sustain a finding by the jury of the existence of the preliminary fact. If there is enough evidence, the proposed evidence is admitted, and the jury makes the final determination of whether the preliminary fact exists. See §21.10.

As with other evidence attempted to be introduced, the burden of proof rests with the party offering the evidence. Evid C §403(a). See *People v Collins* (1975) 44 CA3d 617, 628, 118 CR 864.

§21.4   2. Relevancy

The Evid C §403 procedure (*i.e.,* the jury makes the final determination) applies if the relevancy of the proposed evidence depends on the existence of a preliminary fact. Evid C §403(a)(1). For example, if the plaintiff sues the defendant on an alleged agreement and offers evidence of negotiations with A, that evidence is not relevant unless A was the defendant's agent. The evidence must therefore be excluded on objection unless the plaintiff presents sufficient foundational evidence to support a finding of the preliminary fact that A was the defendant's agent. Comment to Evid C §403(a). Similarly, when evidence of conviction of a felony is offered to attack credibility (Evid C §788), a preliminary fact to be decided is whether the witness is actually the person who was convicted. This fact bears on the relevancy of the evidence of the conviction. Under Evid C §403(a)(1), if there is enough evidence of identity to support a finding, the judge may admit the evidence and the jury will make the final decision of whether the witness was the person who was convicted. Comment to Evid C §403(a). (Of course, the judge has the option of exclusion under Evid C §352.)

The supreme court has determined that a trial court's discretion under Evid C §352 to exclude evidence of prior felony convictions offered for impeachment of any witness has survived the passage of Cal Const art I, §28(f) (added by Proposition 8). See *People v Castro* (1985) 38 C3d 301, 306, 211 CR 719. The court also held, however, that the trial court must find that the prior conviction involves moral turpitude to be relevant to credibility.

In *People v Wheeler* (1992) 4 C4th 284, 14 CR2d 418, the supreme court determined that, if past criminal conduct amounting to a misdemeanor has some logical bearing on the veracity of a witness in a criminal proceeding, evidence of that conduct is admissible, subject to the trial court's discretion, as "relevant" evidence under Cal Const art I, §28(d) (added by Proposition 8). Evidence of the conviction itself is not admissible, because it is hearsay.

§21.5   3. Personal Knowledge

The Evid C §403 foundational procedure (*i.e.,* the jury makes the final determination) applies if the preliminary fact is the personal knowledge of a witness concerning the subject matter of the testimony. Evid C §403(a)(2). A lay witness is competent to testify only if the witness has personal knowledge of the subject matter, *i.e.,* a present recollection of an impression derived from the exercise of the witness's own senses. Evid C §702. See §§18.18-18.23. For example, if the proposed evidence is testimony of a witness that a car went through a red light, a foundation must be established that the witness was present and observed the fact.

The Evidence Code differentiates the personal knowledge foundation from foundational situations in which the judge may admit evidence conditionally, subject to having it "connected up" by proof of the preliminary fact later in the trial. By objecting, any party can require that the foundation of personal knowledge be established before the witness testifies. Evid C §702(a). The required foundation need only be sufficient for the judge to conclude that the jury could reasonably find from that evidence that the witness has personal knowledge. See *People v Jones* (1971) 19 CA3d 437, 449, 96 CR 795 (deputy allowed to testify that documents were those seized, although he had placed no identification marks on them and was unable to recall their contents verbatim); *People v Blagg* (1970) 10 CA3d 1035, 1040, 89 CR 446 (conflict in evidence about whether witness had capacity to have personal knowledge of testimony admitted). Whether the trial judge is personally convinced that the witness has personal knowledge is immaterial; that question is for the jury to decide.

§21.6   4. Authenticity of Writing

The Evid C §403 procedure (*i.e.,* the jury makes the final determination) applies if the preliminary fact is that a "writing" is authentic, *i.e.,* that it was made or signed by its purported maker. Evid C §403(a)(3). The term "writing" in this context has a broad meaning: It includes letters, words, pictures, sounds, symbols, or combinations of these, "and any record thereby created, regardless of the manner in which the record has been stored." Evid C §250.

Authentication of a writing is required before it, or evidence of its contents, may be received in evidence. Evid C §1401. See *People v Miller* (2000) 81 CA4th 1427, 1445, 97 CR2d 684. To lay this foundation, sufficient evidence must be introduced to sustain a finding that it is the writing that the proponent claims it to be. Evid C §1400; Comment to Evid C §403(a). *People v Miller,* supra. For example, if the proposed evidence is a photograph of the scene of a homicide, the foundation must be established that it is an accurate representation of what it portrays. Methods of proving authenticity are described in Evid C §§1402, 1410-1421. Such proof is distinct from the requirements of the secondary evidence rule. See §24.2. Authentication is a prerequisite to the admission of a writing before it may be received in evidence. Evid C §1401(a). On admitting writings conditionally before authentication, see §21.11.

Inadequate authentication resulted in the exclusion of a tape-recorded telephone conversation in *O'Laskey v Sortino* (1990) 224 CA3d 241, 273 CR 674, disapproved on other grounds in *Flanagan v Flanagan* (2002) 27 C4th 766, 776 n4, 117 CR2d 574. The court held that the tape, purporting to show an admission by a defendant in a personal injury case, was not authenticated because (a) the admission was supported by the affidavit of plaintiff's counsel rather than the investigator who actually made the telephone call and (b) the transcript did not contain sufficient identifying information to show the circumstances under which the tape was made.

Despite the Evid C §1401 requirement, the lack of authentication may not serve as the basis for an appeal if there is no objection at trial. *People v Jones* (1970) 7 CA3d 48, 86 CR 717.

§21.7   5. Identity

The Evid C §403 procedure (*i.e.,* the jury makes the final determination) applies if the proposed evidence is of a statement or other conduct of a particular person and the preliminary fact is whether that person made the statement or acted in that manner. Evid C §403(a)(4). For example, the proposed evidence in a murder case may be testimony that the witness overheard the statement "I'm going to kill Joe" after seeing several men, including the defendant, enter a room. The statement may be admissible as a voluntary admission (under Evid C §1220) if a foundation is laid that the defendant was the one who made it. Similarly, preliminary proof of identity may be required to invoke such other exceptions to the hearsay rule as (Comment to Evid C §403(a)):

- Adoptive and authorized admissions (Evid C §§1221–1222);
- Admissions of co-conspirators (Evid C §1223);
- Admissions of a third person whose liability, breach of duty, or right is at issue (Evid C §§1224–1227); and
- Prior inconsistent or consistent statements (Evid C §§1235–1236).

For discussion of these hearsay exceptions, see chap 19.

§21.8   C. When Evid C §405 Applies

Evidence Code §405 is a catch-all section. It applies to all preliminary fact determinations not governed by Evid C §403 (relevancy, personal knowledge, authenticity, identity) or by Evid C §404 (privilege against self-incrimination; see chap 45).

If §405 applies, the judge alone decides whether the preliminary fact exists. If the fact exists, the judge admits the proposed evidence; if not, it is excluded. The foundational question is not decided preliminarily by the judge and then referred to the jury. See §21.15.

Counsel should study the Comment to Evid C §405, which lists some of the situations in which Evid C §405 is most frequently invoked and indicates who has the burden of proof on the preliminary issue. Applications of §405 are discussed below:

- *Claiming a privilege.* Evid C §§900-1070. On privileges, see §§34.13, 34.22. The party claiming a privilege must prove the preliminary facts showing that the privilege applies. *San Diego Prof. Ass'n v Superior Court* (1962) 58 C2d 194, 199, 23 CR 384. The party offering the evidence against which a privilege has been claimed has the burden of proving that an exception to the privilege exists or that the privilege has been waived. The party may also have the burden, expressly imposed by Evid C §917, of proving nonconfidentiality. See §§34.14-34.15, 34.23.

- *Introducing hearsay evidence.* Evid C §§1200-1350. The identity of a hearsay declarant is a preliminary question governed by Evid C §403 (jury makes final determination). See §21.7. Evidence Code §405 (judge alone decides) governs foundational questions raised in connection with hearsay. See *People v Chapman* (1975) 50 CA3d 872, 123 CR 862 (trial judge exclusively determines voluntariness of confession, spontaneity of allegedly spontaneous declaration, presence of sense of impending death at time of alleged dying declaration, and trustworthiness of declaration against penal interest). The party offering hearsay evidence has the burden of proving the existence of circumstances warranting an exception to the hearsay rule, *e.g.,* spontaneousness of a declaration (Evid C §1240; see §19.23) or the trustworthiness of a business record (Evid C §1271; see §19.26). In a criminal case, for example, the judge must make a foundational determination under Evid C §405 on the corpus delicti before receiving in evidence an alleged confession or admission. See §27.6. An admission of criminal conduct is a preliminary fact that must be proved before a hearsay statement can be admitted as a statement against penal interest. *People v Huggins* (1986) 182 CA3d 828, 831, 227 CR 547.

- *Introducing opinion testimony.* Evid C §§720, 870, 1415. The foundational requirements for opinion testimony are discussed in §20.12. Note especially the rules that the proponent of expert opinion testimony must establish that the witness is a qualified expert on the subject matter of the question and that a lay witness is competent to testify about a matter only if the lay witness has personal knowledge concerning it.

- *Introducing evidence of experiments.* When a party seeks to introduce evidence of experiments, the party must show, as a preliminary fact, that the conditions under which the experiments were conducted were "substantially identical" to the conditions giving rise to the facts that the party sought to test. *Culpepper v Volkswagen of Am., Inc.* (1973) 33 CA3d 510, 521, 109 CR 110 (film admitted showing simulated automobile speed and turning).

- *Introducing secondary evidence of a writing.* Evid C §§1520-1523, effective January 1, 1999. Presumably the opponent of such evidence will have the burden of proving that one of the exceptions to admissibility in Evid C §1521(a) applies. See chap 24.

- *Including admissions made during settlement negotiations.* Evid C §§1152, 1154. The party seeking to keep the evidence out must prove that the admissions occurred during such negotiations. See §§32.2-32.3.

- *Proving incompetency of witness because of lack of mental capacity.* Evid C §701. The objecting party has the burden of proving either that the witness is incapable of expressing himself or herself so as to be understood (see §18.4) or that the witness is incapable of understanding the duty to tell the truth (see §18.9).

III. COMPARING PROCEDURAL RULES

§21.9   A. Presence of Jury

Under both Evid C §§403 and 405, the judge may hear matters relating to preliminary facts out of the presence of the jury. Evid C §402(b). See *Mize v Atchison, T. & S.F. R.R.* (1975) 46 CA3d 436, 448, 120 CR 787. If a danger exists that the jury may be exposed to potentially damaging information while the foundational question is being considered, counsel should request that the jury be excused.

The judge will generally meet with counsel in chambers before the trial begins to consider evidentiary problems that are likely to arise. See chap 2. Motions in limine give counsel an excellent opportunity to describe evidence that the attorney anticipates the opponent will attempt to introduce without being able to lay a sufficient foundation. Counsel should point out the danger of undue prejudice if the judge does not rule on all matters relating to that foundation before the jury hears evidence on the subject. An offer of proof is often necessary to overcome foundation issues. See chap 21.

If requested by a party, the judge must hear and determine the admissibility of a confession or an admission of a criminal defendant out of the presence and hearing of the jury. Evid C §402(b). See *People v Carroll* (1970) 4 CA3d 52, 58, 84 CR 60.

B. Procedure Under Evid C §403

§21.10   1. Judge Determines Only Whether Prima Facie Showing Made

In the four limited situations in which Evid C §403 governs, the judge determines whether the proponent has presented enough evidence to sustain a finding by the jury that the preliminary fact exists. If not enough evidence has been presented, the proposed evidence will be excluded; if enough evidence has been presented, it will be admitted. The jury will make the final decision, however, of whether the preliminary fact exists.

§21.11   2. Conditional Admission if No Prima Facie Showing Made

In cases governed by Evid C §403, the judge may admit the proposed evidence conditionally, subject to evidence of the preliminary fact being supplied later in the trial. Evid C §403(b).

In such a situation, the proponent of the evidence should respond to the Evid C §403 objection of improper foundation as follows:

> Your Honor, we ask that this evidence be admitted conditionally under Evidence Code section 403. We will present evidence later in the trial establishing the necessary foundation.

If personal knowledge of the witness is at issue, the proposed evidence may not be admitted conditionally. See Evid C §§403(a)(2), (b); 702. On objection that a proper foundation has not been laid showing that the witness has personal knowledge of the subject matter, sufficient evidence to support a finding of personal knowledge must be introduced before the witness testifies. See Evid C §§403(b), 702(a). For example, before a witness may testify that a car went through a red light, a foundation must be established that the witness was present and observed the fact. See §§18.18–18.23.

If evidence has been admitted conditionally, and the party that offered the evidence rests, opposing counsel should determine whether the required foundation was in fact supplied, *e.g.*, whether foundational evidence was introduced showing that the conditionally admitted evidence is relevant. If no such evidence was introduced, counsel should move to strike the conditionally admitted evidence and should request a cautionary instruction to the jury to disregard that evidence. Under such circumstances, Evid C §403(c)(2) makes this instruction mandatory. See §52.7 (motion to strike).

§21.12   3. Cautionary Instructions to Jury Under Evid C §403 Only

If the judge admits the proposed evidence in an Evid C §403 situation, the judge may (and, if requested, must) instruct the jury to determine whether the preliminary fact exists and to disregard the proposed evidence unless the jury finds that the preliminary fact does exist. Evid C §403(c)(1).

To make sure that this instruction is given, objecting counsel should prepare and submit an appropriate request for an instruction, in keeping with the following illustration:

> **The Court has preliminarily admitted evidence of** _ _[e.g., the alleged declaration of A]_ _ **that** _ _[e.g., she was an agent of P]_ _. **In admitting this evidence, the Court determined preliminarily that** _ _[e.g., the declaration could be admitted in evidence but only if you, the jury, determine that A was in fact an agent of P]_ _.
>
> **If you determine that** _ _[e.g., A was an agent of P]_ _, **then you must**

consider that determination, along with all other evidence, to arrive at your verdict. If you decide that _ _[e.g., A was not an agent of P]_ _, then you must disregard _ _[e.g., the declaration]_ _ in your deliberations.

§21.13 4. Exclusion of Evidence on Redetermination

If the judge admits the proffered evidence but subsequently determines that a jury could not reasonably find that the preliminary fact exists, the judge must instruct the jury to disregard the specific evidence admitted. Evid C §403(c)(2). See, *e.g.,* CACI 106 and 5003 (motion to strike testimony). For example, a blueprint of a building may have been admitted on the testimony of the architect that it accurately represents the details of the structure. If later evidence shows beyond reasonable dispute that the building was extensively remodeled after the architect completed the work, the judge must instruct the jury to disregard the blueprint.

§21.14 5. Statute

Evidence Code §403 states:

> (a) The proponent of the proffered evidence has the burden of producing evidence as to the existence of the preliminary fact, and the proffered evidence is inadmissible unless the court finds that there is evidence sufficient to sustain a finding of the existence of the preliminary fact, when:
>
> (1) The relevance of the proffered evidence depends on the existence of the preliminary fact;
>
> (2) The preliminary fact is the personal knowledge of a witness concerning the subject matter of his testimony;
>
> (3) The preliminary fact is the authenticity of a writing; or
>
> (4) The proffered evidence is of a statement or other conduct of a particular person and the preliminary fact is whether that person made the statement or so conducted himself.
>
> (b) Subject to Section 702, the court may admit conditionally the proffered evidence under this section, subject to evidence of the preliminary fact being supplied later in the course of the trial.
>
> (c) If the court admits the proffered evidence under this section, the court:
>
> (1) May, and on request shall, instruct the jury to determine whether the preliminary fact exists and to disregard the proffered evidence unless the jury finds that the preliminary fact does exist.
>
> (2) Shall instruct the jury to disregard the proffered evidence if the court subsequently determines that a jury could not reasonably find that the preliminary fact exists.

C. Procedure Under Evid C §405

§21.15 1. Judge Alone Determines Admissibility

When the existence of a preliminary fact governed by Evid C §405 is disputed, the judge must first indicate which party has the burden of producing evidence and the burden of proof on the issue. Evid C §405(a). The rules governing the burden of proof in various situations are discussed in the Comment to Evid C §405. See §21.8. For most preliminary fact issues, the burden of proof is preponderance of the evidence in agreement with Evid C §115, which defines "burden of proof." See also *People v Jimenez* (1978) 21 C3d 595, 604, 147 CR 172.

The judge will then receive evidence on the issue and decide whether to admit or exclude the proposed evidence. Evid C §405(a). The question is not referred to the jury; the judge's ruling on the question of admissibility is final. The judge's ruling that evidence is admissible does not, however, preclude any party from introducing evidence relevant to the weight or credibility that the jury should give to the proposed evidence. Evid C §406. For example, even if a statement has been admitted as a spontaneous declaration, opposing counsel may cross-examine freely to show that the circumstances under which the statement was made render it untrustworthy.

§21.16 2. No Evid C §405 Conditional Admission

There is no provision in Evid C §405 comparable to Evid C §403(b), which allows the judge to admit proposed evidence on the condition that the required foundation be supplied later in the trial. Evidence Code §§320 (judge's power to regulate order of proof) and 772(b) (judge's power to direct departures from usual order of examination of witnesses) have been interpreted by most trial judges as giving them the discretionary power to admit evidence conditionally in cases governed by §405.

As a practical matter, this question will probably not be clarified in a case in which the missing foundational fact is proved later during the trial, because the fact of such proof will ordinarily negate any claim of prejudicial error. Without prejudicial error, there can be no reversal on appeal. Cal Const art VI, §13; Evid C §353(b). Clarification will probably come, if at all, in a case in which the proponent fails to prove the missing foundational fact. In this situation, the opponent is presumably entitled to an order striking the conditionally admitted evidence and an instruction to the jury to disregard that evidence, as in the analogous situation governed by Evid C §403. See §21.11. The opponent may argue, however, that the judge committed error in admitting the evidence conditionally without statutory authority and that the judge's failure to exclude it initially as required by Evid C §405(a) was prejudicial. The basis for the claim of prejudice would be the burden imposed on the opponent of having to erase from the jurors' minds harmful matter that the jurors should not have been allowed to hear in the first place. Note that in criminal cases there is a higher standard of review on appeal, *e.g.,* concerning the admissibility of a confession.

§21.17   3. Separating Jury's Role if Preliminary Fact Is Also Ultimate Fact

If the existence of the preliminary fact is also one of the ultimate facts to be determined by the jury, the jury must not be told how the judge ruled. Evid C §405(b).

§21.18   4. Statute

Evidence Code §405 states:

> With respect to preliminary fact determinations not governed by Section 403 or 404:
>
> > (a) When the existence of a preliminary fact is disputed, the court shall indicate which party has the burden of producing evidence and the burden of proof on the issue as implied by the rule of law under which the question arises. The court shall determine the existence or nonexistence of the preliminary fact and shall admit or exclude the proffered evidence as required by the rule of law under which the question arises.
> >
> > (b) If a preliminary fact is also in issue in the action:
> >
> > > (1) The jury shall not be informed of the court's determination as to the existence or nonexistence of the preliminary fact.
> > >
> > > (2) If the proffered evidence is admitted, the jury shall not be instructed to disregard the evidence if its determination of the fact differs from the court's determination of the preliminary fact.

§21.19   IV. RESPONSES TO OBJECTION

The objection must be specific enough for the trial judge to determine what is lacking and for the party offering the evidence to recognize and attempt to correct the defect. In *Parlier Fruit Co. v Fireman's Fund Ins. Co.* (1957) 151 CA2d 6, 15, 311 P2d 62, for example, an expert was asked to base an opinion concerning the origin of a fire on certain hypothetical questions. The objection made was simply that "no foundation was laid." On appeal, the objecting party pointed out for the first time that the hypothetical questions had omitted certain essential facts. The appellate court held that the testimony had been properly admitted, declaring that the specific omitted facts "should have been pointed out in the objection." See also *Cramer v Morrison* (1979) 88 CA3d 873, 886, 153 CR 865.

Whenever this objection is made, opposing counsel should respond by asking that the objecting attorney be required to specify exactly what preliminary facts are missing for a sufficient foundation. Under certain circumstances, the missing element is so obvious that the objecting party is excused from having to be so specific. For example, if a witness is asked to state an opinion as an expert, the simple objection that a sufficient foundation has not been laid is specific enough to indicate that the qualifications of the witness as an expert have not been shown. *Lemley v Doak Gas Engine Co.* (1919) 40 CA 146, 154, 180 P 671.

Although this term is usually identified with jury selection, it also refers to attacking foundational evidence before the proffered evidence is admitted. When evidence requires a foundation and foundational evidence is admitted, opposing counsel may at that time interrupt the witness's testimony and ask to "voir dire" the witness, *i.e.,* cross-examine the witness to show that the necessary foundation is lacking. This often results in a mini-trial on the adequacy of the foundation and on whether the judge or jury should hear the proffered evidence. Attacking foundations usually occurs with the expert witness's being called to render opinions. See California Expert Witness Guide §§14.4–14.6 (2d ed Cal CEB 1991). The procedure applies to most foundations, however. Whether the foundational attack occurs in or out of the jury's presence depends on the circumstances. Counsel should be alert that this procedure may be used to start an early improper cross-examination of the witness, which is not a proper use of "voir dire." Similarly, when it appears that opposing counsel is using the procedure merely to interrupt the flow of coherent testimony, counsel should object on the ground that this is an improper use of the procedure. See Expert Witness §14.6.

§21.20   V. STATING THE OBJECTION

> Objection, Your Honor. There is no foundation showing _ _ [state required preliminary fact, e.g., that the witness has personal knowledge of the matter]_ _.

22

Improper Impeachment

I. INTRODUCTION §22.1

II. WIDE LATITUDE ALLOWED FOR IMPEACHMENT
   A. Increased Freedom to Impeach §22.2
   B. Impeachment on Collateral Matter Permitted §22.3
   C. Impeachment by Cross-Examination Not Limited to Scope of Direct Examination §22.4
   D. Impeachment by Prior Inconsistent Statement
      1. Determination of Inconsistency §22.5
      2. Permitted Without Showing Statement to Witness §22.5A
      3. Permitted, in Judge's Discretion, Even if Witness Has No Opportunity to Explain §22.6

III. LIMITATIONS ON IMPEACHMENT
   A. Rules of General Applicability §22.7
   B. Rules Specifically Limiting Impeachment
      1. Character Evidence §22.8
      2. Absence of Religious Belief §22.9
      3. Use of Texts for Impeachment §22.10
      4. Noncompliance With CCP §2034 Expert Witness List §22.11
      5. Judicial Arbitration §22.11A

IV. STATUTE §22.12

V. ALTERNATIVES TO OBJECTING §22.13

VI. STATING THE OBJECTION §22.14

§22.1 I. INTRODUCTION

To impeach a witness means to attack that person's credibility in order to discredit that person as a witness. A party may impeach any witness, regardless of who called the witness. Evid C §785. See *Matthews v Superior Court* (1988) 201 CA3d 385, 394, 247 CR 226. (The old rule that counsel "vouchsafes" for witnesses has been rejected for a new rule allowing impeachment of a witness by any party.) This is accomplished either directly, by cross-examination, or indirectly, by production of extrinsic evidence, *e.g.,* the testimony of other witnesses. The following are the most commonly used lines of attack (see Evid C §780):

- Showing the witness's bias, interest, or motive.
- Showing a prior inconsistent statement or prior inconsistent conduct (see §§22.5–22.6).
- Showing that the witness lacks the ability to observe, remember, or recount. A witness lacking this ability may be incompetent to testify (see §18.18).
- Showing that the witness has a poor character for honesty or veracity.
- Introducing contradictory evidence.

Even if not called as a witness, a hearsay declarant may be impeached similarly as if a witness at the trial. Evid C §1202. See §19.28.

II. WIDE LATITUDE ALLOWED FOR IMPEACHMENT

§22.2   A. Increased Freedom to Impeach

The Evidence Code allows a party extremely wide latitude in impeaching a witness. As indicated in §§22.3–22.6, the Code specifically repudiates a number of grounds that have been invoked to limit impeachment in the past.

California Constitution art I, §28(f) (added by Proposition 8) has been interpreted by the supreme court to allow in criminal actions prior convictions to attack the credibility of a witness if the conviction is one that necessarily involves moral turpitude, subject to the trial court's discretion under Evid C §352. See *People v Castro* (1985) 38 C3d 301, 306, 211 CR 719 (felony convictions). For cases defining crimes that involve moral turpitude, see §22.8. Note that Proposition 8 does not apply to civil cases. *Robbins v Wong* (1994) 27 CA4th 261, 32 CR2d 337.

Evidence that has been excluded in a criminal case on the basis of a constitutional violation may nonetheless be used to impeach. See *Harris v New York* (1971) 401 US 222, 28 L Ed 2d 1, 91 S Ct 643; *People v Williams* (2000) 79 CA4th 1157, 94 CR2d 727.

§22.3   B. Impeachment on Collateral Matter Permitted

In determining the credibility of a witness, the judge or jury may consider "any matter that has any tendency in reason to prove or disprove the truthfulness of his testimony. . . ." Evid C §780. See *People v Lavergne* (1971) 4 C3d 735, 742, 94 CR 405.

Before enactment of the Evidence Code, a witness could not be impeached on "collateral matter" (*i.e.,* evidence that was not independently relevant to one of the issues in the case), on the theory that evidence on collateral matter always consumes too much time and confuses the jury about the issues. The Evidence Code eliminates this inflexible rule. Impeachment using any matter relevant to credibility, including a collateral matter, is now permitted, subject to the judge's discretion. Comment to Evid C §780. The trial judge may exclude collateral evidence if its probative value is substantially outweighed by the risk that it will consume too much time, cause undue prejudice, confuse the issues, or mislead the jury. Evid C §352. See *People v Lavergne, supra*; *People v Humphries* (1986) 185 CA3d 1315, 1337, 230 CR 536. See also §22.7; chap 32. The usual response to counsel's impeaching on a collateral matter is to object and invoke the provisions of Evid C §352.

§22.4   C. Impeachment by Cross-Examination Not Limited to Scope of Direct Examination

There are fundamentally two types of cross-examination:
(1) Examination conducted for the purpose of bringing out additional facts; and
(2) Examination conducted for the purpose of impeachment.

Many attorneys do not realize that 80 percent of all cross-examination is conducted to bring out additional facts, while only 20 percent of cross-examination is conducted for impeachment purposes.

The rule in Evid C §§761 and 773(a), which normally limits cross-examination to matter within the scope of the direct examination, applies only to the first type of cross-examination. It does not apply to questions asked for the purpose of impeachment. Judicial decisions have established that the cross-examiner testing such matters as the witness's capacity to observe, recollect, and recount, the witness's character traits, or showing the witness's bias, has considerable freedom to exceed the scope of the direct examination. See §26.3.

D. Impeachment by Prior Inconsistent Statement
§22.5   1. Determination of Inconsistency

Unless the statement is truly inconsistent, it is not admissible. *People v Newton* (1970) 8 CA3d 359, 385, 87 CR 394. What constitutes a prior inconsistent statement may be difficult to determine when the current testimony that is used for the comparison is implied. See, *e.g., People v Green* (1971) 3 C3d 981, 988, 92 CR 494 (witness's evasive answers and memory lapses during testimony amounted to statement inconsistent with prior statement). "I-don't-remember" answers may amount to a lack of testimony for purposes of comparison with earlier statements. See *People v Sam* (1969) 71 C2d 194, 210, 77 CR 804. But see contrary implication in *People v Parks* (1971) 4 C3d 955, 961, 95 CR 193.

> **NOTE➤** Evidence Code §1235 makes evidence of a witness's prior inconsistent statement admissible not only for the purpose of impeachment but also as evidence of the truth of the matter stated. Under the secondary evidence rule, the content of a writing can generally be proven without producing the original. Evid C §1521, discussed in chap 24.

§22.5A 2. Permitted Without Showing Statement to Witness

When a witness is being examined about a prior inconsistent written statement, it is not a ground for objection that "the statement has not been shown to the witness." Evidence Code §769 permits a witness to be interrogated about a prior oral or written inconsistent statement, without requiring any preliminary disclosure about the statement. Before enactment of the Evidence Code, the witness was entitled to see a written statement before answering. This requirement deprived the impeaching examiner of the valuable element of surprise. Comment to Evid C §769. See *People v Fatone* (1985) 165 CA3d 1164, 1181, 211 CR 288.

Even though disclosure need not be made to the witness, opposing counsel is entitled to the information in certain circumstances. See *Kadelbach v Amaral* (1973) 31 CA3d 814, 821, 107 CR 720 (tape recording of factual information from other witnesses to accident intended for use to impeach witness's testimony should have first been shown to opposing counsel on request because Evid C §769 applies only to witnesses). On request, however, the court can forbid communication between the witness and opposing counsel until the cross-examination is completed. 31 CA3d at 822.

§22.6 3. Permitted, in Judge's Discretion, Even if Witness Has No Opportunity to Explain

Extrinsic evidence that a witness made a prior statement that is inconsistent with present testimony is admissible under Evid C §770(b) if the witness (a) has not been excused from giving further testimony in the action, and therefore can be recalled and given an opportunity to explain or deny the statement, or (b) had that opportunity before the prior inconsistent statement is introduced. *People v Strickland* (1974) 11 C3d 946, 954, 114 CR 632.

Moreover, Evid C §770 gives the trial judge broad discretion. If "the interests of justice" require, the trial judge is empowered to admit, for impeachment purposes, evidence of an inconsistent statement of a witness, even though the witness had no opportunity to explain or deny the statement and has been excused from testifying further.

III. LIMITATIONS ON IMPEACHMENT

§22.7 A. Rules of General Applicability

Objections applicable to the introduction of evidence generally also apply to evidence offered for the purpose of impeachment. The following rules of general applicability are especially pertinent to impeachment:

- *Most normal exclusionary rules apply.* The rules governing objections to impeachment examinations differ in two principal respects from the rules of general applicability:
  - (1) The objection that the evidence is irrelevant will not be sustained

if the matter in question has any tendency to impeach the witness, even if it relates only to a "collateral" issue (see §22.3); and

- (2) The objection that cross-examination exceeds the scope of the direct examination will not be sustained if the purpose of the cross-examination is to impeach (see §§22.4, 26.3).

• With these exceptions, a question asked for the purpose of impeachment is subject to the various objections to substance or form that may be made to any question.

• Similarly, privileges may be invoked against impeachment evidence. For example, a prior inconsistent statement may be excluded if it was made under circumstances in which the attorney-client privilege applies. See chap 35. Note also that a witness's previous claim of privilege cannot be used for impeachment. See Evid C §913. See also §34.17.

• Counsel engaged in impeachment frequently include in their questions facts that have not been, and perhaps cannot be, proved. On proper objection, this type of cross-examination may be sanctionable by the court as a violation of Cal Rules of Prof Cond 5-200. See also CCP §128; Cal Rules of Ct 227. See chap 14 (argumentative questions). The commonly held belief that it is permissible to assume during cross-examination facts in dispute or not in evidence is erroneous. See §15.4. The objection that the question assumes the truth of matter that is not in evidence applies during an impeachment examination just as it does during any other examination of a witness.

• *Probative value outweighed by risks.* The court in its discretion may exclude otherwise admissible evidence under Evid C §352 if its probative value is substantially outweighed by the risk that the evidence will:

- (1) Consume an undue amount of time;
- (2) Create undue prejudice;
- (3) Confuse the issues; or
- (4) Mislead the jury.

• There are limitations, however, on the judge's power to exclude impeachment evidence under Evid C §352. See, *e.g., People v Mayfield* (1972) 23 CA3d 236, 243, 100 CR 104 (trial judge erroneously excluded evidence under §352 when wide latitude should have been afforded counsel to test witness's credibility).

• In view of the latitude allowed during an impeachment examination (see §§22.2–22.6), proper use of the grounds listed in Evid C §352 is especially important to any attorney concerned with keeping the impeachment within reasonable bounds. Judges seldom exercise the discretionary power granted by §352 to exclude evidence on their own. Trial counsel must therefore be prepared to take the initiative. For example, if character evidence is offered to show that the witness has a reputation for dishonesty, the opposing attorney might invoke §352 by pointing out the amount of time that will be consumed by opening up the subject and creating a mini-trial just to cover that issue. Counsel might describe the number of witnesses that will need to be called for the purpose of rehabilitation and the time that each will consume. Counsel invoking §352 to limit impeachment should ask that the matter be discussed out of the jury's presence.

- *Questions asked in improper manner.* Another general limitation that is especially pertinent to impeachment is that cross-examiners may not unduly harass or embarrass the witness. In their zeal to impeach, some trial attorneys stand close to the witness, shout, or even interrupt, berate, or bully the witness. Opposing counsel should promptly object to such tactics. Evidence Code §765 requires the judge to exercise reasonable control over the mode of interrogation of witnesses in order to protect them from such conduct.

- *Denial of opportunity to impeach is subject to harmless error analysis.* The constitutionally improper denial of an accused person's opportunity to impeach a witness for bias is not grounds for the automatic reversal of a conviction. If the denial was harmless beyond a reasonable doubt, the conviction may be upheld. *Delaware v Van Arsdall* (1986) 475 US 673, 89 L Ed 2d 674, 106 S Ct 1431.

B. Rules Specifically Limiting Impeachment

§22.8   1. Character Evidence

There are three categories of character evidence: personal opinion, reputation, and specific instances of conduct. See Evid C §1100. The rules concerning use of these types of character evidence are complex. See Effective Introduction of Evidence in California, chaps 14-16 (2d ed Cal CEB 2000).

Following are the most common objections to character evidence in civil cases:

- Character traits, other than honesty or veracity or their opposites, or specific acts that are relevant only to prove a character trait may not be used to attack or support credibility but may be used to show some other fact, *e.g.,* bias, interest, or other motive. See Evid C §§786-787. See also Evid C §780. But Evid C §788 allows impeachment by prior felony convictions of the witness. See *People v Jacobs* (2000) 78 CA4th 1444, 1446, 93 CR2d 783; *People v Mendoza* (2000) 78 CA4th 918, 925, 93 CR2d 216.

- Evidence of a person's character trait is not admissible to prove conduct. Comment to Evid C §1101. All three methods of proving a person's character trait are available when that person's character is at issue. Comment to Evid C §1100.

- In civil cases alleging sexual harassment, assault, or battery, specific instances of the plaintiff's sexual conduct are not admissible to prove the plaintiff's consent or absence of injury (except injury caused by loss of consortium). Evidence of the plaintiff's sexual conduct with the alleged perpetrator is admissible as rebuttal to any such evidence offered by the plaintiff or the plaintiff's witness. Evid C §1106. The proponent of evidence to attack the plaintiff's credibility in these types of cases must comply with the procedural requirements of Evid C §783.

- Neither misdemeanor convictions nor the facts underlying a misdemeanor conviction may be used to impeach a witness in a civil case because there is no authority for admitting this type of hearsay. Impeachment with the facts underlying a misdemeanor conviction is allowed in criminal cases. *People v Wheeler* (1992) 4 C4th 284, 299, 14 CR2d 418. See California Criminal Law Procedure and Practice, chap 35 (7th ed Cal CEB 2004).

- Felony convictions may not be used to impeach when the witness has obtained a pardon based on innocence (Evid C §788(a)); a certificate of rehabilitation and pardon has been granted (Evid C §788(b), (d)); or the charge was dismissed under Pen C §1203.4 or, in another jurisdiction, under a procedure similar to Pen C §1203.4 (Evid C §788(c)-(d)).

The following are the most common objections to character evidence in criminal cases:

- In cases involving the sexual conduct described in Evid C §1103(c), special rules govern the introduction of evidence of the victim's sexual conduct with anyone other than the defendant to prove consent. The defendant is allowed to attack the victim's credibility under Evid C §782. Evid C §1103(c)(5).

- Specific acts concerning the conduct of a party, witness, or anyone else when that person's conduct or state of mind is in issue may be used if the evidence is offered to prove an issue other than character. See Evid C §1101(b) for a nonexhaustive list of such issues, *e.g.*, motive, intent, identity. See also Evid C §§1102 (character evidence of criminal defendant), 1103 (character of victim of crime), 1108 (prior commission of sexual offense), and 1109 (evidence of defendant's prior acts of domestic violence or prior abuse of an elder or dependent adult).

- Evidence of character or a trait of character is not admissible to prove a victim's consent. Evid C §1103(c). That evidence becomes admissible, however, for rebuttal if a prosecution witness gives testimony or evidence relating to such conduct. Evid C §1103(c)(4).

- Prior misdemeanor convictions are not admissible to impeach a witness; however, evidence is admissible concerning the underlying facts of the misdemeanor. *People v Wheeler* (1992) 4 C4th 284, 299, 14 CR2d 418.

- Opposing counsel must comply with the procedural requirements of Evid C §782 when intending to introduce evidence of sexual conduct of the complaining witness to attack credibility under Evid C §780 in cases involving violation of Pen C §§261 (rape), 262 (spousal rape), 264.1 (aiding and abetting rape), 286 (sodomy), 288 (lewd and lascivious acts involving children), 288a (oral copulation), 288.5 (continuous sexual abuse of child), or 289 (penetration by foreign object).

- Prior felony convictions are not admissible to impeach if they do not involve moral turpitude (*People v Collins* (1986) 42 C3d 378, 389, 228 CR 899); the risk of undue prejudice from impeachment substantially outweighs its probative value, based on Evid C §352 (*People v Castro* (1985) 38 C3d 301, 211 CR 719); they are constitutionally invalid (*Loper v Beto* (1972) 405 US 473, 483, 31 L Ed 2d 374, 381, 92 S Ct 1014); the defendant has been pardoned based on innocence (Evid C §788(a), (d)); or the charge was dismissed under Pen C §1203.4 or, in another jurisdiction, under a procedure similar to Pen C §1203.4 (Evid C §788(c)-(d)). If the prior felony is being used to impeach someone other than a defendant in a criminal case, it cannot be used if the witness has been granted a certificate of rehabilitation and pardon. Evid C §788(b), (d). For further discussion of impeachment with prior convictions in criminal cases, see Crim Law §§35.45-35.51.

- A plaintiff's prior felony conviction based on a nolo contendere plea may be admitted into evidence for impeachment purposes in a suit brought under 42 USC §1983 (civil action against police officers for deprivation of constitutional rights based on use of excessive force). *Brewer v City of Napa* (9th Cir 2000) 210 F3d 1093.

§22.9   2. Absence of Religious Belief

A witness may not be impeached by evidence showing absence of religious beliefs. Evid C §789. This statute may be inconsistent with Cal Const art I, §28(d) (the "truth-in-evidence" provision of Proposition 8) if the religious beliefs are deemed relevant to the action and may be admissible, subject to Evid C §352.

§22.10   3. Use of Texts for Impeachment

Traditionally in California an expert witness giving opinion testimony could not be impeached by cross-examination about a text (*e.g.,* a scientific, technical, or professional journal or similar publication) unless the expert "referred to, considered, or relied upon" that text in forming the opinion or the text has been previously admitted into evidence. Evid C §721(b). The traditional rule was significantly broadened in 1997 when Evid C §721(b) was amended to adopt an approach similar, but not identical, to the learned treatise exception found in Federal Rules of Evidence 803(18). The new rule now provides that cross-examination may go forward with a text not previously relied upon when the publication "has been established as a reliable authority by the testimony or admission of the witness or by other expert testimony or by judicial notice." Evid C §721(b)(3).

Cases decided under federal and similar state rules provide that the burden of establishing that a text qualifies for admission as a learned treatise rests with the party offering the text into evidence. That party has the burden of proving not only that the proffered publication is reliable, but also that the material sought to be used during impeachment is relevant to the facts of the case.

Under the new rule, a learned treatise should not be used for impeachment until the trial judge is satisfied that the publication is a "reliable authority." Evid C §721(b)(3). Many jurisdictions describe this element as the "authoritativeness" of the text. See *Shaw v Bolduc* (Me 1995) 658 A2d 229. Counsel should not assume that the written word will automatically amount to a "reliable authority"; publication is not synonymous with authoritativeness. Authoritativeness is not only one expert's opinion, but also a showing of general acceptance of views expressed in the treatise by the out-of-court author in the profession as a whole. *Meschino v North Am. Drager, Inc.* (1st Cir 1988) 841 F2d 429.

Any expert may establish that a publication is a reliable authority at trial. The federal and state rules do not require that an opposing expert recognize a particular text before cross-examination, thereby avoiding the possibility that an opponent's expert may block cross-examination by refusing to concede a publication's authoritativeness. Evid C §721(b)(3).

The party with the burden of proof must also overcome any objections regarding the relevancy of the text in question. It is not enough that an expert has established the reliability or authoritativeness of a treatise. The expert must also tie the statements or theories set forth in the proffered publication to the facts of the case. See *Mercado v Ahmed* (7th Cir 1992) 974 F2d 863. Even when relevancy of a text is established (and especially when it is attenuated), counsel seeking to keep a publication out of evidence should consider the availability of an Evid C §352 objection on the grounds that the probative value of the passages referred to in the text might create undue prejudice, confuse the issues, or mislead the jury. Similar arguments have been accepted at both the state and federal level. See *Ellis v International Playtex, Inc.* (4th Cir 1984) 745 F2d 292.

Section 721(b)(3) provides that: "If admitted, relevant portions of the publication may be read into evidence but may not be received as exhibits." In this regard, the language and effect of California's new rule and the federal rule are nearly identical. The rationale for this portion of the rule is to keep often voluminous learned treatises out of the jury room where they might receive undue attention or emphasis. See *Maggipinto v Reichman* (ED Penn 1979) 481 F Supp 547. Statements may be read into evidence, but may not be received in the form of text, excerpts from texts, or similar exhibits. See *Ferguson v Williams* (NC App 1991) 399 SE2d 389.

As a practical matter, admission of a learned treatise at trial should begin with motions in limine brought by either party to require their opponent to disclose to the court, outside of the presence of the jury, any proposed text that counsel expects to use when conducting cross-examination under the new amendment. Such a motion would assure counsel the opportunity to conduct an Evid C §402 hearing to probe whether the proffered treatise qualifies as authoritative and whether the material being offered is relevant to the facts of the case. Counsel should be prepared to object to the use of a text when these foundational requirements are not established.

The amendment to Evid C §721 leaves intact the traditional rule that impeachment by cross-examination may proceed when an expert "referred to, considered or relied upon" a text in forming any opinions or when the text has been admitted into evidence. Evid C §721(b)(1). Under this portion of the rule, unless the text in question has been admitted into evidence, it may be used only to impeach; it may not be quoted to prove facts in the case because it is hearsay (see chap 19). Cross-examiners often try to circumvent this rule by attempting, under the guise of impeaching the witness, to bring before the jury helpful statements made by absent authors. See Comment to Evid C §721. To guard against this abuse, the attorney who called the expert should request that the judge give a cautionary instruction to the jury explaining that the text (if allowed) is being used only for the limited purpose of impeachment. Counsel should also object to any attempts by the cross-examiner to go beyond the specific impeaching material in the text.

§22.11 4. Noncompliance With CCP §2034 Expert Witness List

An expert witness list includes percipient witnesses. For example, if an expert is a percipient witness and the examiner also intends to use the expert to elicit opinion testimony, that fact must be included on the CCP §2034 expert witness list or the expert will be limited to what has been perceived. *Province v Center for Women's Health & Family Birth* (1993) 20 CA4th 1673, 1683, 25 CR2d 667. If CCP §2034 has not been complied with, exclusion of the expert's testimony is mandatory. Note, however, that a treating physician does not become a retained expert witness within the meaning of CCP §2034(a)(2), requiring the submission of an expert witness declaration under CCP §2034(f)(2), when that physician gives opinion testimony. In *Schreiber v Estate of Kiser* (1999) 22 C4th 31, 91 CR2d 293, the California Supreme Court held that a treating physician does not become a retained expert under CCP §2034(a)(2), even though the treating physician is a percipient witness. The court decided that, due to the unique nature of the physician-patient relationship, the physician is not retained for the purpose of forming and expressing an opinion but instead learns of the patient's injuries and medical history because of the underlying relationship. Therefore, the requirements of CCP §2034(a)(2), (f)(2) are not relevant to a treating physician.

A party must submit an expert witness declaration that fully complies with CCP §2034(f) or face preclusion of expert witness testimony not previously described in the party's declaration. *Bonds v Roy* (1999) 20 C4th 140, 83 CR2d 289; *Fish v Guevana* (1993) 12 CA4th 142, 15 CR2d 329; see also *Jones v Moore* (2000) 80 CA4th 557, 565, 95 CR2d 216 (expert witness's testimony excluded under CCP §2034 as beyond scope of opinions expressed in deposition).

Under CCP §2034(j), on the objection of any party who has made a complete and timely compliance with CCP §2034(f), the trial court must exclude from evidence the expert opinion of any witness that is offered by any party who has unreasonably failed to do any of the following:

- List that witness as an expert under CCP §2034(f);
- Submit an expert witness declaration;
- Produce reports and writings of expert witnesses under CCP §2034(g); or
- Make that expert available for a deposition under CCP §2034(i).

Note that an exception is provided for an undesignated expert who is called to impeach the testimony of another expert on whether foundational facts are false or nonexistent. CCP §2034(m). See *Bonds v Roy, supra.*

§22.11A 5. Judicial Arbitration

A witness's testimony from a judicial arbitration proceeding is not admissible for impeachment purposes in a subsequent trial. *Jimena v Alesso* (1995) 36 CA4th 1028, 43 CR2d 18. Under Cal Rules of Ct 1616(c), no reference may be made during trial to any aspect of arbitration proceedings or evidence adduced at the arbitration hearing, and none of the foregoing may be used as affirmative evidence for impeachment or any other purpose at trial.

§22.12 IV. STATUTE

Evidence Code §780 states:

> Except as otherwise provided by statute, the court or jury may consider in determining the credibility of a witness any matter that has any tendency in reason to prove or disprove the truthfulness of his testimony at the hearing, including but not limited to any of the following:
>
> (a) His demeanor while testifying and the manner in which he testifies.
>
> (b) The character of his testimony.

(c) The extent of his capacity to perceive, to recollect, or to communicate any matter about which he testifies.

(d) The extent of his opportunity to perceive any matter about which he testifies.

(e) His character for honesty or veracity or their opposites.

(f) The existence or nonexistence of a bias, interest, or other motive.

(g) A statement previously made by him that is consistent with his testimony at the hearing.

(h) A statement made by him that is inconsistent with any part of his testimony at the hearing.

(i) The existence or nonexistence of any fact testified to by him.

(j) His attitude toward the action in which he testifies or toward the giving of testimony.

(k) His admission of untruthfulness.

Under Evid C §785, the credibility of a witness may be attacked or supported by any party, including the party calling the witness.

§22.13 V. ALTERNATIVES TO OBJECTING

On possible alternatives to objecting, see §§4.9–4.14.

§22.14 VI. STATING THE OBJECTION

Objection, Your Honor. This attempt to impeach the witness is improper because _ _[state reasons]_ _.

23

Improper Rehabilitation

I. INTRODUCTION §23.1

II. WIDE LATITUDE ALLOWED FOR REHABILITATION §23.2

III. LIMITATIONS ON REHABILITATION
   A. Rules of General Applicability §23.3
   B. Rules Specifically Limiting Rehabilitation §23.4

IV. STATUTE §23.5

V. ALTERNATIVES TO OBJECTING §23.6

VI. EFFECT OF FAILURE TO REHABILITATE §23.7

VII. STATING THE OBJECTION §23.8

§23.1 I. INTRODUCTION

To rehabilitate a witness means to support the witness's credibility after it has been attacked. Any party may rehabilitate any witness. See Evid C §785. Rehabilitation is usually accomplished by introducing evidence that rebuts prior impeaching evidence introduced by the opposing party. Before rehabilitation evidence can be offered, there generally must be evidence in the record impeaching the witness. See §23.4. See discussion of impeachment in chap 22.

Even if a hearsay declarant is not called as a witness, the absent witness may be rehabilitated in substantially the same way as if called as a witness at trial. Evid C §1202. See §19.28.

§23.2 II. WIDE LATITUDE ALLOWED FOR REHABILITATION

Wide latitude is allowed in rehabilitating a witness. In determining a witness's credibility, the judge or jury may consider "any matter that has any tendency in reason to prove or disprove the truthfulness of his testimony." Evid C §780. See also *Grudt v City of Los Angeles* (1970) 2 C3d 575, 593, 86 CR 465 (admission of evidence offered to show bias within sound discretion of court). Under Evid C §§352 and 780, the trial court may allow or exclude relevant evidence of a collateral nature offered to prove or attack the credibility of a witness. See Comment to Evid C §780; *People v Hernandez* (1976) 63 CA3d 393, 405, 133 CR 745; *People v Eisenberg* (1968) 266 CA2d 606, 615, 72 CR 390.

If the plaintiff in a civil action introduces evidence of the plaintiff's sexual conduct, the defendant may cross-examine the witness who gives the evidence and offer relevant evidence, which must be limited specifically to rebuttal of the plaintiff's evidence. Evid C §1106(c).

A defendant who has been impeached by evidence of a felony conviction is entitled to introduce evidence of rehabilitation, *e.g.,* that there has been no further arrest. *People v Marsh* (1985) 175 CA3d 987, 995, 221 CR 311.

III. LIMITATIONS ON REHABILITATION

§23.3   A. Rules of General Applicability

Most normal exclusionary rules apply to rehabilitation evidence. During rehabilitation examination, the objection "irrelevant" is appropriate only if the evidence has no tendency whatsoever to support the witness's credibility. See Evid C §§210, 351, 780. With this exception, a question asked for the purpose of rehabilitation is subject to the various objections that may be made to any question, *e.g.,* that it is hearsay or that the information is privileged.

The court in its discretion may exclude otherwise-admissible rehabilitation evidence under Evid C §352 when its probative value is substantially outweighed by the risk that the evidence will:

- Consume an undue amount of time;
- Create undue prejudice;
- Confuse the issues; or
- Mislead the jury.

When evidence is offered for the purpose of rehabilitation, there is an especially acute risk that the time consumed will substantially outweigh the probative value of the evidence. Because judges seldom exercise this discretionary power on their own initiative, the attorney should object with a request that the judge invoke Evid C §352 and exclude such evidence. See chap 31. The trial judge will often limit the number of witnesses who may be called for rehabilitation purposes, depending on the gravity of the disputed point.

§23.4   B. Rules Specifically Limiting Rehabilitation

Until a witness has been impeached, there is no need for rehabilitation. See, *e.g., People v Andrews* (1970) 14 CA3d 40, 45, 92 CR 49.

In civil actions, evidence of a witness's "good character for honesty and veracity" is admissible to prove or support credibility only if the witness's credibility has first been impeached. In criminal actions, a criminal defendant may introduce evidence of "good character for honesty and veracity" whether or not the witness's good character for honesty and veracity has been attacked. *People v Harris* (1989) 47 C3d 1047, 1081, 255 CR 352.

Note that the supreme court held that Evid C §§786–787 and 790 were abrogated in criminal cases by Cal Const art I, §28(d) (the "truth-in-evidence" provision of Proposition 8). See *People v Harris, supra*. Because Evid C §790 restrictions no longer apply in criminal cases, evidence of a witness's good character for honesty and veracity is admissible (subject to the court's discretion under Evid C §352) to support credibility, even when the witness's credibility has not been impeached with evidence of bad character. See *People v Taylor* (1986) 180 CA3d 622, 631, 225 CR 733.

The Evidence Code limits the admission of rehabilitation evidence based on prior consistent statements. Under Evid C §791, evidence of a statement previously made by the witness that is consistent with the witness's testimony is inadmissible to support credibility unless it is offered after:

- Evidence of a statement made by the witness that is inconsistent with any part of the witness's testimony has been admitted for the purpose of attacking credibility, and the statement was made before the alleged inconsistent statement (Evid C §791(a)); or

- An express or implied charge has been made that the witness's testimony is recently fabricated or is influenced by bias or other improper motive, and the statement was made before the bias, motive for fabrication, or other improper motive is alleged to have arisen (Evid C §791(b)).

Under Evidence Code §1236, evidence of a statement previously made by a witness is not made inadmissible by the hearsay rule if the prior statement is consistent with the witness's testimony and is offered in compliance with Evid C §791.

Once bias has been admitted by a witness, the trial court should not allow rehabilitation by inquiry into the witness's reasons for the bias, but the judge has discretion under Evid C §352 to admit or exclude such evidence. *People v Pierce* (1969) 269 CA2d 193, 205, 75 CR 257.

§23.5   IV. STATUTE

Under Evid C §785, the credibility of a witness may be attacked or supported by any party, including the party calling the witness.

§23.6   V. ALTERNATIVES TO OBJECTING

On possible alternatives to objecting, see §§4.9–4.14.

§23.7   VI. EFFECT OF FAILURE TO REHABILITATE

A defendant in a criminal case who is given the opportunity to rehabilitate a witness whose damaging extrajudicial statement has been admitted, and who fails to do so, waives any objection to the admission of the testimony under the confrontation clause of the sixth amendment to the United States Constitution. *People v Green* (1971) 3 C3d 981, 990, 92 CR 494. See also *People v Chavez* (1980) 26 C3d 334, 360, 161 CR 762.

§23.8   VII. STATING THE OBJECTION

Objection, Your Honor. This attempt to rehabilitate the witness is improper because _ _[state reason]_ _.

24

Excluding Secondary Evidence

I. REPEAL OF BEST EVIDENCE RULE §24.1

II. SECONDARY EVIDENCE RULE §24.2

III. ADDITIONAL GROUND FOR EXCLUSION OF SECONDARY EVIDENCE IN CRIMINAL ACTION §24.3

IV. ORAL TESTIMONY OF CONTENT OF WRITING GENERALLY NOT ADMISSIBLE §24.4

V. PRINTED REPRESENTATIONS OF COMPUTER INFORMATION OR PROGRAM, OR OF VIDEO OR DIGITAL IMAGES, PRESUMED ACCURATE §24.5

VI. STATUTE §24.6

VII. ALTERNATIVES TO OBJECTING §24.7

VIII. STATING THE OBJECTION §24.8

§24.1   I. REPEAL OF BEST EVIDENCE RULE

Effective January 1, 1999, the legislature repealed the longstanding "best evidence rule" (see former Evid C §1500) and replaced it with the "secondary evidence rule" (see Evid C §1521; §24.2). The best evidence rule required the content of a writing to be proved by the original of the writing itself unless a statute authorized admission of secondary evidence. See former Evid C §1500. The best evidence rule generally precluded a party from proving the content of a writing with secondary evidence (*i.e.,* testimony or a copy) if the original writing was available. The secondary evidence rule, on the other hand, generally allows the content of a writing to be proved with secondary evidence.

§24.2   II. SECONDARY EVIDENCE RULE

The content of a writing may be proved by an otherwise admissible original. Evid C §1520. On the meaning of "original," see Evid C §255. Under the "secondary evidence rule," however, the content of a writing may also generally be proved by otherwise admissible secondary evidence. See Evid C §1521(a), (d). Nevertheless, the court must exclude secondary evidence of the content of a writing if the court determines that either:

- A genuine dispute exists concerning material terms of the writing and justice requires the exclusion (Evid C §1521(a)(1)); or
- Admission of the secondary evidence would be unfair (Evid C §1521(a)(2)).

The act that includes the secondary evidence rule (Stats 1998, ch 100) applies, effective January 1, 1999, to any action, regardless of when the action commenced. If an evidentiary determination made before January 1, 1999, in an action that is still pending on that date ruled evidence inadmissible under the former statutes, the proponent of the evidence may, before entry of judgment, make a new request for admission based on the new statutes. Stats 1998, ch 100, §9.

The Evidence Code gives "writing" a broad definition by including (Evid C §250):

> handwriting, typewriting, printing, photostating, photographing, photocopying, transmitting by electronic mail or facsimile, and every other means of recording upon any tangible thing any form of communication or representation, including letters, words, pictures, sounds, or symbols, or combinations thereof, and any record thereby created, regardless of the manner in which the record has been stored.

Thus, all tangible items bearing any form of communication are writings.

Note that the secondary evidence rule applies only to evidence offered to prove the content of a writing, not to evidence offered to prove some other fact. See *Crail v Blakely* (1973) 8 C3d 744, 754, 106 CR 187 (although witness's testimony on value of estate may have been evidence inferior to decree of distribution and inventory, best evidence rule did not apply because testimony was not offered to prove content of any particular writing). Although *Crail* was a pre-1999 case and therefore addressed the former best evidence rule (former Evid C §1500), the same analysis would apply to determine applicability of the secondary evidence rule.

The secondary evidence rule does not excuse compliance with Evid C §1401 (authentication). Evid C §1521(c).

The secondary evidence rule does not apply to preliminary hearings in criminal cases. Pen C §872.5.

§24.3 III. ADDITIONAL GROUND FOR EXCLUSION OF SECONDARY EVIDENCE IN CRIMINAL ACTION

In addition to excluding secondary evidence of the content of a writing on the grounds provided by the secondary evidence rule (Evid C §1521; see §24.2), the court in a criminal action must exclude such secondary evidence if the court determines that the original is in the proponent's possession, custody, or control, and the proponent has not made the original reasonably available for inspection at or before trial. Evid C §1522. This rule does not apply, however, to any of the following:

- A duplicate (for definition, see Evid C §260) (Evid C §1522(a)(1));
- A writing that is not closely related to the controlling issues in the action (Evid C §1522(a)(2));
- A copy of a writing in the custody of a public entity (Evid C §1522(a)(3)); or
- A copy of a writing recorded in public records, if the record or a certified copy of it is made evidence of the writing by statute (Evid C §1522(a)(4)).

Note that in a criminal action tried to a jury, any request to exclude secondary evidence of the content of a writing must be made out of the jury's presence. Evid C §1522(b).

§24.4 IV. ORAL TESTIMONY OF CONTENT OF WRITING GENERALLY NOT ADMISSIBLE

Oral testimony is generally not admissible to prove the content of a writing. See Evid C §1523(a). Section 1523(a) does not, however, make oral testimony of the content of a writing inadmissible when:

- The proponent does not have possession or control of a copy of the writing and the original is lost or has been destroyed without fraudulent intent on the proponent's part (Evid C §1523(b));
- The proponent does not have possession or control of the original or a copy of the writing and (a) neither the writing nor a copy was reasonably procurable by the proponent by court process or other available means, or (b) the writing is not closely related to the controlling issues and it would be inexpedient to require its production (Evid C §1523(c)); or
- The writing consists of numerous accounts or other writings that cannot be examined in court without great loss of time and the evidence sought from them is only the general result of the whole (Evid C §1523(d)).

§24.5 V. PRINTED REPRESENTATIONS OF COMPUTER INFORMATION OR PROGRAM, OR OF VIDEO OR DIGITAL IMAGES, PRESUMED ACCURATE

A printed representation of computer information or a computer program or of images stored on a video or digital medium is presumed to be an accurate representation of the information, program, or images it purports to represent. This presumption is one affecting the burden of producing evidence. If a party introduces evidence that such a printed representation is inaccurate or unreliable, the proponent has the burden of proving, by a preponderance of evidence, that the printed representation is an accurate representation of the content of that it purports to represent. Evid C §§1552-1553.

§24.6 VI. STATUTE

Evidence Code §1521 states:

(a) The content of a writing may be proved by otherwise admissible secondary evidence. The court shall exclude secondary evidence of the content of writing if the court determines either of the following:

(1) A genuine dispute exists concerning material terms of the writing and justice requires the exclusion.

(2) Admission of the secondary evidence would be unfair.

(b) Nothing in this section makes admissible oral testimony to prove the content of a writing if the testimony is inadmissible under Section 1523 (oral testimony of the content of a writing).

(c) Nothing in this section excuses compliance with Section 1401 (authentication).

(d) This section shall be known as the "Secondary Evidence Rule."

§24.7 VII. ALTERNATIVES TO OBJECTING

An objection to the admissibility of secondary evidence should not be made unless there is a genuine dispute about the accuracy of the secondary evidence on an important point. On possible alternatives to objecting, see §§4.9-4.14.

§24.8 VIII. STATING THE OBJECTION

Objection, Your Honor. This secondary evidence is not admissible because _ _[state reason]_ _.

25
Inadmissible Parol Evidence

I. DEFINITION §25.1

II. STATUTORY BASIS §25.2

III. WHEN RULE APPLIES; CONCEPT OF INTEGRATION §25.3

IV. WHO MAY INVOKE RULE §25.4

V. EXCEPTIONS TO RULE
    A. To Prove Mistake, Illegality, or Fraud §25.5
    B. To Prove Invalidity §25.6
    C. To Explain Terms §25.7
    D. To Resolve Ambiguity §25.8
    E. Several Writings Constituting Agreement §25.9
    F. Consistent Additional Terms §25.10
    G. Subsequent Modifications §25.11

VI. REQUIREMENT OF PROMPT OBJECTION §25.12

VII. STATING THE OBJECTION §25.13

§25.1 I. DEFINITION

The parol evidence rule prohibits the introduction of oral or written extrinsic evidence of prior or contemporaneous agreements to vary the terms of an integrated written instrument, *i.e.,* a writing intended by the parties as a complete and final expression of their agreement. See CCP §§1856–1866.

Unlike the secondary evidence rule (see chap 24), the parol evidence rule is not designed to bar unreliable secondary proof. It is a rule of substantive law (not an evidence rule) declaring that terms contradicting those included in an integrated instrument simply have no legal effect. Counsel should also distinguish the parol evidence rule from the statute of frauds, which makes some types of contracts unenforceable unless evidenced by writings. See CC §1624; Com C §§1206, 2201, 8113, 9203.

Extrinsic evidence that is inconsistent with an integrated instrument is irrelevant and cannot support a judgment. *Delucchi v County of Santa Cruz* (1986) 179 CA3d 814, 824, 225 CR 43; *BMW of N. Am. v New Motor Vehicle Bd.* (1984) 162 CA3d 980, 990, 209 CR 50. Whether the instrument is integrated is an Evid C §405 decision made by the judge alone; it is not a question of fact for the jury to decide. CCP §1856(d); Evid C §405.

§25.2   II. STATUTORY BASIS

The parol evidence rule is stated in CCP §1856, which provides:

> (a) Terms set forth in a writing intended by the parties as a final expression of their agreement with respect to such terms as are included therein may not be contradicted by evidence of any prior agreement or of a contemporaneous oral agreement.
>
> (b) The terms set forth in a writing described in subdivision (a) may be explained or supplemented by evidence of consistent additional terms unless the writing is intended also as a complete and exclusive statement of the terms of the agreement.
>
> (c) The terms set forth in a writing described in subdivision (a) may be explained or supplemented by course of dealing or usage of trade or by course of performance.
>
> (d) The court shall determine whether the writing is intended by the parties as a final expression of their agreement with respect to such terms as are included therein and whether the writing is intended also as a complete and exclusive statement of the terms of the agreement.
>
> (e) Where a mistake or imperfection of the writing is put in issue by the pleadings, this section does not exclude evidence relevant to that issue.
>
> (f) Where the validity of the agreement is the fact in dispute, this section does not exclude evidence relevant to that issue.
>
> (g) This section does not exclude other evidence of the circumstances under which the agreement was made or to which it relates, as defined in Section 1860, or to explain an extrinsic ambiguity or otherwise interpret the terms of the agreement, or to establish illegality or fraud.
>
> (h) As used in this section, the term agreement includes deeds and wills, as well as contracts between parties.

The parol evidence rule applies to written agreements intended by the parties to be the final expression of their agreement. CCP §1856(a). Thus, the parol evidence rule applies to deeds, wills, and promissory notes as well as to contracts. CCP §1856(h). See *Coast Bank v Holmes* (1971) 19 CA3d 581, 590, 97 CR 30. The Commercial Code contains special parol evidence rules governing contracts for the sale of goods, as defined in Com C §§2102, 2105(1), and 2106(1). Regarding such contracts, Com C §2202 provides:

> Terms with respect to which the confirmatory memoranda of the parties agree or which are otherwise set forth in a writing intended by the parties as a final expression of their agreement with respect to such terms as are included therein may not be contradicted by evidence of any prior agreement or of a contemporaneous oral agreement but may be explained or supplemented:

(a) By course of dealing or usage of trade (Section 1205) or by course of performance (Section 2208); and

(b) By evidence of consistent additional terms unless the court finds the writing to have been intended also as a complete and exclusive statement of the terms of the agreement.

The principal differences between the extrinsic evidence allowed under CCP §1856 and that allowed under Com C §2202 are pointed out in §§25.7, 25.8, and 25.10. For a detailed description of the rule in the context of the Commercial Code, see California UCC Sales and Leases §§6.31-6.53 (Cal CEB 2002). On the parol evidence rule generally, see 2 Witkin, California Evidence, *Documentary Evidence* §§59-112 (4th ed 2000).

§25.3 III. WHEN RULE APPLIES; CONCEPT OF INTEGRATION

In determining whether to make a parol evidence objection, counsel's threshold consideration is whether the written agreement is "integrated," *i.e.,* whether the terms in the writing were "intended by the parties as a final expression of their agreement with respect to such terms as are included therein." CCP §1856(a). If the written agreement contains an "integration clause" (*i.e.,* a clause stating that the writing constitutes the entire contract and that there are no agreements or representations other than those in the writing), it is considered to be integrated. See *Salyer Grain & Milling Co. v Henson* (1970) 13 CA3d 493, 501, 91 CR 847. In that situation, it is proper for counsel to object to the introduction of extrinsic evidence proffered to vary the terms of the written agreement on the ground that the evidence violates the parol evidence rule.

Ascertaining the parties' intent may be difficult, however, if the writing contains neither an integration clause nor an express statement that the parties intend the writing as an integration. In California, the courts have traditionally held that (a) whether a document is integrated must be decided solely from the face of the document and (b) the question for the court is whether the document appears to be a complete agreement. See, *e.g., Ferguson v Koch* (1928) 204 C 342, 346, 268 P 342; *Thoroman v David* (1926) 199 C 386, 389, 249 P 513. In *Masterson v Sine* (1968) 68 C2d 222, 65 CR 545, however, the California Supreme Court rejected that view and adopted a broader rule based on trustworthiness of the evidence. Quoting from 9 Wigmore, Evidence in Trials at Common Law §2431 (3d ed 1940), the court stated (68 C2d at 226):

> The conception of a writing as wholly and intrinsically self-determinative of the parties' intent to make it a sole memorial of one or seven or twenty-seven subjects of negotiation is an impossible one.

Thus, the parties' intentions must be the ultimate test for determining whether a written agreement is integrated. 68 C2d at 225. In making this determination, the trial court (under Evid C §405) must examine (a) the written instrument, (b) the facts and circumstances surrounding the preparation and execution of the written instrument, and (c) evidence of the collateral agreement. See *Coast Bank v Holmes* (1971) 19 CA3d 581, 589, 97 CR 30; Jefferson's California Evidence Benchbook, chap 32 (3d ed CJA-CEB 1997). Evidence of oral negotiations and of the surrounding circumstances may be introduced for the purpose of determining whether a writing was intended to constitute the entire contract. See *Schwartz v Shapiro* (1964) 229 CA2d 238, 251 n8, 40 CR 189.

A two-fold test is used under *Masterson v Sine* (1968) 68 C2d 222, 227, 65 CR 545, to determine whether a prior or contemporaneous agreement is admissible to show that the written agreement was not intended to be integrated:

(1) Is the collateral agreement one that might naturally be made as a separate agreement by parties similar to those that entered into the written agreement?

(2) Is the collateral agreement not one that, if made, certainly would have been included in the written agreement?

Even under the liberal *Masterson* rule, evidence of an oral collateral agreement that directly contradicts the written instrument is not admissible. 68 C2d at 227; *American Nat'l Ins. Co. v Continental Parking Corp.* (1974) 42 CA3d 260, 266, 116 CR 801 (written lease for parking structure, providing that lessor was not required to make improvements to premises; objection sustained to proffered evidence of oral agreement entered into when lease was executed that landlord would build office building above parking structure).

§25.4   IV.   WHO MAY INVOKE RULE

Before the 1978 amendment to CCP §1856, the parol evidence rule applied only in an action between the parties to an agreement, their representatives, and their successors in interest. This limitation was removed by the 1978 amendment. Accordingly, any litigant may apparently invoke the parol evidence rule regardless of whether the action is between parties to the agreement (or their successors) or involves third parties. See *Garcia v Truck Ins. Exch.* (1984) 36 C3d 426, 204 CR 435. See also *Neverkovec v Fredericks* (1999) 74 CA4th 337, 350 n8, 87 CR2d 856. The Commercial Code also contains no limitation on application of the parol evidence rule. See Com C §2202.

V. EXCEPTIONS TO RULE

§25.5   A. To Prove Mistake, Illegality, or Fraud

Extrinsic evidence of mistake, illegality, or fraud is excepted from the parol evidence rule (CCP §1856) because it is offered to prove that the document at issue has no legal effect rather than to contradict its terms. A common setting for such evidence is in an action to rescind or reform a contract. See *Munchow v Kraszewski* (1976) 56 CA3d 831, 836, 128 CR 762. Extrinsic evidence is inadmissible, however, when offered to prove a false promise allegedly made to induce the complaining party to enter into a contract if the evidence relates to terms covered by the instrument. For example, the guarantor of a corporation's promissory note may not introduce parol evidence to show that she was assured that she would not be held personally liable. *Bank of America v Lamb Fin. Co.* (1960) 179 CA2d 498, 3 CR 877. See also *Glendale Fed. Sav. & Loan Ass'n v Marina View Heights Dev. Co.* (1977) 66 CA3d 101, 160, 135 CR 802.

Parol evidence is admissible to prove fraud in the inducement, even though the contract recites that all conditions and representations are contained in the contract (integration clause). *Ron Greenspan Volkswagen, Inc. v Ford Motor Land Dev.* (1995) 32 CA4th 985, 38 CR2d 783.

When a general release contains an integration clause and states that the release applies to "all claims known and unknown," parol evidence has been allowed when the question is whether a general release extends to unknown injuries and is a question of fact to be determined by evidence of intent independent of the language in the release. *Casey v Proctor* (1963) 59 C2d 97, 28 CR 307. *Casey* stands for the proposition that "boilerplate language in agreements is not always conclusive." *Ron Greenspan Volkswagen, Inc. v Ford Motor Land Dev., supra*. But see *Edwards v Comstock Ins. Co.* (1988) 205 CA3d 1164, 252 CR 807, in which the court (1) affirmed summary judgment for the insurer when its insureds executed a general release of all claims including unfair settlement practices and (2) rejected parol evidence of the insureds' undisclosed intention to waive only personal injury damages and not bad faith claims.

§25.6 B. To Prove Invalidity

Introduction of extrinsic evidence is expressly permitted by CCP §1856(f) "where the validity of the agreement is the fact in dispute." Such evidence must be offered to prove that the document is invalid, rather than to vary its terms, because the parol evidence rule does not affect a contention that an agreement is invalid. Extrinsic evidence is offered to prove only that the agreement itself is unenforceable. This exception covers such defects as absence of consideration (see *Ruess v Baron* (1932) 217 C 83, 17 P2d 119) and failure of consideration (see *Coast Bank v Holmes* (1971) 19 CA3d 581, 590, 97 CR 30). The exception also covers the situation in which the agreement was not intended to become effective until the occurrence of some condition precedent. *Coast Bank v Holmes, supra*; *Harper v French* (1938) 29 CA2d 214, 84 P2d 216.

§25.7 C. To Explain Terms

Evidence of the "circumstances" under which the agreement was made or to which it relates (as defined by CCP §1860), if offered to explain rather than to vary its terms, is not excluded by CCP §1856. Section 1860 provides:

For the proper construction of an instrument, the circumstances under which it was made, including the situation of the subject of the instrument, and of the parties to it, may also be shown, so that the Judge be placed in the position of those whose language he is to interpret.

Even if the words of a written instrument appear to be clear and unambiguous, extrinsic evidence is admissible if it "is relevant to prove a meaning to which the language of the instrument is reasonably susceptible." *PG&E v G.W. Thomas Drayage & Rigging Co.* (1968) 69 C2d 33, 37, 69 CR 561. The purpose of this exception is to give effect to the meaning of the instrument intended by the parties. See application of this rule in *Brawthen v H & R Block, Inc.* (1972) 28 CA3d 131, 136, 104 CR 486.

Extrinsic evidence may be admissible to interpret a written insurance contract unless it would not persuade a reasonable person that the instrument meant anything other than the ordinary meaning of its words. *Producer's Dairy Delivery Co. v Sentry Ins. Co.* (1986) 41 C3d 903, 226 CR 558. Even when the uncertainty of a written contract goes to "the precise act which is to be done," extrinsic evidence is admissible to determine the intent of the parties. *Okun v Morton* (1988) 203 CA3d 805, 819, 250 CR 220. See also *Edwards v Comstock Ins. Co.* (1988) 205 CA3d 1164, 252 CR 807, in which the court affirmed:

- Summary judgment for an insurer when its insureds executed a general release of all claims including unfair settlement practices; and

- Rejection of parol evidence of the insureds' undisclosed intention to waive only personal injury and not bad faith claims.

Under the Commercial Code, the written terms of a sales contract may be explained or supplemented by evidence of the parties' previous course of dealing with each other. Com C §§1205(1), (3)-(4); 2202(a). This exception applies even to written terms that are unambiguous on their face. See Official Comment 1(c) to Com C §2202; California UCC Sales and Leases §6.47 (Cal CEB 2002).

California law provides that a written contract supersedes all prior or contemporaneous oral agreements. Further, there cannot be a valid express contract and an implied-in-fact contract on the same subject that would require a different result. *Anderson v Savin Corp.* (1988) 206 CA3d 356, 254 CR 627 (allegations of implied-in-fact contract for continuing employment and termination only for good cause do not rebut status of at-will employment embodied in written contract). See also *Slivinsky v Watkins-Johnson Co.* (1990) 221 CA3d 799, 270 CR 585; *Wagner v Glendale Adventist Med. Ctr.* (1989) 216 CA3d 1379, 265 CR 412.

For a thorough analysis of the parol evidence rule, its scope of application, and policy considerations, see *Banco Do Brazil, S.A. v Latian, Inc.* (1991) 234 CA3d 973, 285 CR 870.

§25.8   D. To Resolve Ambiguity

Parol evidence is admissible "to explain an extrinsic ambiguity." CCP §1856(g). In the past, judicial opinions made much of the supposed distinction between a latent ambiguity (*e.g.,* the document refers to a property at 15 Main Street when there is no such address) and a patent ambiguity appearing on the face of the document (*e.g.,* the document refers to a single piece of property as 16 Main Street and also as 17 Main Street). Although for many years parol evidence was held inadmissible to explain patent ambiguities (perhaps because the statute refers only to extrinsic, or latent, ambiguities), many courts now permit extrinsic evidence to resolve a patent ambiguity. See, *e.g., Steele v Langmuir* (1976) 65 CA3d 459, 463, 135 CR 426 (trial court should have admitted letter identifying wife's death as date of termination of support, referred to only as "the death" in dissolution agreement). See also *Beneficial Fire & Cas. Ins. Co. v Kurt Hitke & Co.* (1956) 46 C2d 517, 525, 297 P2d 428 (evidence of custom and usage held admissible to explain special meaning of words even though they had another unambiguous ordinary meaning).

The Commercial Code, like CCP §1856, allows evidence of "course of dealing," "usage of trade," or "course of performance" to explain or supplement the terms of a contract for the sale of goods. Com C §2202(a). Testimony of an attorney about the circumstances and negotiations of the parties to a contract that the attorney drafted, and about the intention of the attorney's client concerning the contract, is admissible. *Garcia v Truck Ins. Exch.* (1984) 36 C3d 426, 435, 204 CR 435.

Special rules apply to the resolution of ambiguities in wills (Prob C §103).

§25.9   E. Several Writings Constituting Agreement

Parol evidence is allowed to show that two or more writings were intended to serve as a single agreement. *Torrey v Shea* (1916) 29 CA 313, 155 P 820. See also *Roberts v Reynolds* (1963) 212 CA2d 818, 824, 28 CR 261.

§25.10   F. Consistent Additional Terms

Extrinsic evidence may be introduced to prove that the parties agreed to additional terms that were not incorporated in the writing as long as these additional terms are not inconsistent with those stated in the writing. CCP §1856(b); *Spurgeon v Buchter* (1961) 192 CA2d 198, 13 CR 354. Commercial Code §2202(b) expressly allows evidence of consistent additional terms.

When parol evidence of consistent additional terms is offered, the trial judge must determine as a matter of law whether the parties intended the instrument to be an integration, *i.e.,* a complete expression of their agreement. CCP §1856(d); *Mobil Oil Corp. v Handley* (1978) 76 CA3d 956, 961, 143 CR 321. The procedure set forth in Evid C §405 (see chap 21) relating to preliminary fact determinations applies to this determination. The Commercial Code version of the parol evidence rule adopts the assumption that the parties did not intend a fully integrated agreement. Official Comment 1(a) to Com C §2202. See California UCC Sales and Leases §6.35 (Cal CEB 2002).

For an exhaustive description of instances in which extrinsic evidence is admissible notwithstanding the parol evidence rule, see 2 Witkin, California Evidence, *Documentary Evidence* §§74–110 (4th ed 2000).

§25.11   G. Subsequent Modifications

Although evidence of subsequent modifications often arises in the context of parol evidence, it is subject to the rules provided in CC §1698 rather than the parol evidence rule. Under §1698, oral modification evidence is admissible to prove rescission or novation. Written contracts usually include language in the integration clause that any subsequent modifications must be in writing and signed by the parties. *Marani v Jackson* (1986) 183 CA3d 695, 228 CR 518 (oral subsequent modifications inadmissible).

§25.12   VI. REQUIREMENT OF PROMPT OBJECTION

Because the parol evidence rule is one of substantive law, its application is not subject to the principles of objection and waiver codified in Evid C §353. Although the party failing to object cannot attack on appeal the trial court's receipt of extrinsic evidence, it may nonetheless be argued that the extrinsic evidence conflicts with any interpretation to which the instrument is reasonably susceptible, is therefore irrelevant, and as a matter of substantive law does not support the judgment. *Tahoe Nat'l Bank v Phillips* (1971) 4 C3d 11, 92 CR 704, modifying *Lee v Gregoriou* (1958) 50 C2d 502, 506, 326 P2d 135. Nevertheless, when potentially harmful evidence is offered, counsel should promptly interpose an objection if that evidence violates the parol evidence rule and is irrelevant.

If a parol-evidence rule objection is anticipated before trial begins, a motion in limine at the chambers conference should be used to have the matter settled. See chap 2. If the need for the objection arises during a jury trial, counsel should request that the evidence be considered at a hearing outside the jury's presence. See *Brawthen v H & R Block, Inc.* (1972) 28 CA3d 131, 137, 104 CR 486.

§25.13   VII. STATING THE OBJECTION

> Objection, Your Honor. The evidence is inadmissible parol evidence because allegedly the proposed testimony expressly contradicts the terms of the written agreement at issue.

26

Cross-Examination Exceeds Scope of Direct Examination

I. TYPES OF CROSS-EXAMINATION §26.1

II. STATEMENT OF RULE
   A. Statutory Provisions Establishing Restricted Scope §26.2
   B. Unlimited Scope for Impeachment Cross-Examination §26.3
   C. Determining "Scope" §26.4

III. "OPENING THE DOOR" EXCEPTION
   A. Limited Nature of Exception §26.5
   B. When "Curative Admissibility" Exception Applies
      1. Offsetting Highly Prejudicial Evidence: Curative Admissibility §26.6
      2. Putting Evidence in Proper Context: Rule of Completeness §26.7

IV. ADDITIONAL PROTECTION BASED ON CONSTITUTIONAL PRIVILEGE AGAINST SELF-INCRIMINATION §26.8

V. RELATED OBJECTIONS TO RECROSS- AND REDIRECT EXAMINATION §26.9

VI. ALTERNATIVES TO OBJECTING §26.10

VII. STATING THE OBJECTION §26.11

§26.1   I. TYPES OF CROSS-EXAMINATION

There are two distinct types of cross-examination:

(1) Cross-examination conducted for the purpose of impeachment, which is designed either to discredit the witness's testimony (*e.g.*, by attacking the ability of the witness to observe, remember, or recount) or to discredit the witness as a witness (*e.g.*, by showing bias or that the witness has made a prior inconsistent statement). The objection considered in this chapter does not apply to this type of cross-examination. See §26.3.

(2) Cross-examination conducted for the purpose of bringing out additional facts. The objection considered in this chapter applies only to this type of cross-examination.

See Effective Direct & Cross-Examination (Cal CEB 1986).

II. STATEMENT OF RULE

§26.2 A. Statutory Provisions Establishing Restricted Scope

"Cross-examination" is the examination of a witness by a party other than the direct examiner on a matter that is within the scope of the direct examination of the witness. Evid C §761.

Under Evid C §773:

> (a) A witness examined by one party may be cross-examined upon any matter within the scope of the direct examination by each party to the action in such order as the court directs.
>
> (b) The cross-examination of a witness by any party whose interest is not adverse to the party calling him is subject to the same rules that are applicable to the direct examination.

In most jurisdictions throughout the United States, the courts restrict cross-examination to matters within the scope of the direct examination unless it is for impeachment purposes. See §26.3; 3 Witkin, California Evidence, *Presentation at Trial* §231 (4th ed 2000). This rule enables the parties to proceed in a definite sequence: The party bringing the action presents all the plaintiff's or the prosecution's proof, after which the defendant presents the opposing proof. On order of proof, see CCP §§607, 631.7; Pen C §§1093–1094; Evid C §320.

Keeping the proof separate, rather than letting the respective presentations overlap, theoretically enables the trier of fact to maintain a better focus on the issues. It also enables counsel to follow a more orderly plan in presenting proof. See *Haines v Snedigar* (1895) 110 C 18, 42 P 462; *Manuel v Flynn* (1907) 5 CA 319, 90 P 463. See also *Butler v Stratton* (1949) 95 CA2d 23, 212 P2d 43.

Although the scope of cross-examination is restricted in California, the Evidence Code provides a method for completing the examination of a witness when first testifying. In the discretion of the judge, counsel may switch from cross-examination to direct examination and question the witness on matters outside the scope of previous direct examination. Evid C §772(c). Whether the judge will exercise this discretion depends on such matters as the witness's availability to appear for further examination when the examining party presents his or her case and the difficulty of determining the exact scope of the direct examination.

The extent to which the examiner may ask leading questions is a consideration separate from the scope of the examination (see Evid C §767) that depends primarily on whether the witness is adverse or hostile to the examiner's position (Comment to Evid C §767). See chap 13 (leading questions).

When a witness is called to testify as an adverse party or adverse witness in a civil action under Evid C §776, the witness is examined "as if under cross-examination" but without limitation on scope. When the witness's own counsel, or counsel for a party toward whom the witness is not adverse, then examines the witness, the examination must be carried out "only as if under redirect examination." Evid C §776(b). This rule means that the scope of examination is limited to matters covered during the adverse party's "776 examination" of the witness; it also means that leading questions are prohibited. Comment to Evid C §776. The rule does not apply when the party who called the adverse witness for examination under §776 is "identified with the same party . . ." (Evid C §776(e)(1)) or is the "personal representative, heir, successor, or assignee of a person identified with the same party with whom the witness is identified" (Evid C §776(e)(2)). The ensuing cross-examination is no longer limited to examination as if under redirect examination. This means that the cross-examiner may ask leading questions. Comment to Evid C §776. See §13.12.

The permissible scope of cross-examination is unaffected by Evid C §776(e). Section 776(e) appears to apply only when a witness was improperly called under Evid C §776, *i.e.*, by a party "identified with the same party with whom the witness is identified."

§26.3 B. Unlimited Scope for Impeachment Cross-Examination

It is firmly established in California case law that the rule restricting cross-examination to the scope of the direct examination does not apply to cross-examination for the purpose of impeachment. *Daggett v Atchison, T. & S.F. Ry.* (1957) 48 C2d 655, 663, 313 P2d 557; *Estate of Kasson* (1900) 127 C 496, 500, 59 P 950; *People v Jackson* (1960) 183 CA2d 332, 340, 6 CR 505. See 3 Witkin, California Evidence, *Presentation at Trial* §238 (4th ed 2000).

The latitude allowed during impeachment cross-examination is especially wide when the witness is:

- *A party to the action.* See *Stromerson v Averill* (1940) 39 CA2d 118, 125, 102 P2d 571. The broad scope of this cross-examination is illustrated in *Smith v Lewis* (1975) 13 C3d 349, 363, 118 CR 621, disapproved on other grounds in 15 C3d at 851. In this case, the plaintiff sued an attorney for malpractice for failing to assert, in marital dissolution proceedings, his client's community interest in her husband's federal and state retirement benefits. The defendant testified that he always sought the best possible results for his clients. The plaintiff called a witness to testify that the defendant had represented the witness in an unrelated divorce action and had strongly advised her against asserting a community interest in her husband's state retirement fund. Citing Evid C §§776 and 780, the court held that even though the testimony of the plaintiff's witness was related to a collateral matter, it was legitimate impeachment showing that the defendant had conducted himself in an inconsistent manner.

- *An expert.* See *Laird v I.W. Mather, Inc.* (1958) 51 C2d 210, 219, 331

P2d 617; *Grimshaw v Ford Motor Co.* (1981) 119 CA3d 757, 796, 174 CR 348. This rule is codified in Evid C §§721(a), 722(b). See §20.13.

- *A witness against the defendant in a criminal case.* See *People v Watson* (1956) 46 C2d 818, 827, 299 P2d 243.

The Evidence Code neither codifies nor rejects the principle that impeachment cross-examination may exceed the scope of the direct examination. The Code clearly grants the party attempting to impeach a witness broader latitude than was allowed before its enactment. For example, Evid C §780 eliminates the rule that prohibited use of impeachment evidence on "collateral matter" (see Comment to Evid C §780; §22.3), and Evid C §785 permits the credibility of a witness to be attacked "by any party," eliminating the prior restriction against impeaching one's own witness (see Comment to Evid C §785; §22.4).

§26.4 C. Determining "Scope"

The decisions in this field provide the trial judge with only vague criteria for determining the scope of direct examination for the purposes of cross-examination. For example, it has been held that cross-examination is permitted:

- On any matter covered during direct examination (see *Sharp v Hoffman* (1889) 79 C 404, 408, 21 P 846; *Payette v Sterle* (1962) 202 CA2d 372, 375, 21 CR 22);

- On all relevant matter necessarily implied in the direct examination (see *People v Pike* (1962) 58 C2d 70, 90, 22 CR 664; *People v Zerillo* (1950) 36 C2d 222, 229, 223 P2d 223);

- On any matter about which the witness has been examined during the case in chief (see *People v Gardner* (1954) 128 CA2d 1, 7, 274 P2d 908);

- On any matter having a logical tendency to rebut an unfavorable inference that might be drawn from the direct examination (see *Sandoval v Southern Cal. Enters.* (1950) 98 CA2d 240, 246, 219 P2d 928); and

- On any matter relevant to the subject matter of the direct examination (see *Laursen v Tidewater Assoc. Oil Co.* (1954) 123 CA2d 813, 816, 268 P2d 104).

The task of applying these criteria to define the proper scope of cross-examination "is committed to the sound discretion of the trial court, and its ruling thereon will not be disturbed on appeal in the absence of a clear showing of abuse of that discretion." *Garcia v Hoffman* (1963) 212 CA2d 530, 536, 28 CR 98. See also *People v Lavergne* (1971) 4 C3d 735, 742, 94 CR 405; *Kadelbach v Amaral* (1973) 31 CA3d 814, 822, 107 CR 720.

III. "OPENING THE DOOR" EXCEPTION

§26.5   A. Limited Nature of Exception

It is a "popular fallacy" that if testimony is given on a subject during direct examination, this will "open the door" to unrestricted cross-examination about that matter and make evidence admissible that would otherwise be inadmissible. *People v McDaniel* (1943) 59 CA2d 672, 677, 140 P2d 88. See *People v Matlock* (1970) 11 CA3d 453, 461, 89 CR 862.

A party does not ordinarily open the door to otherwise inadmissible evidence by introducing evidence on a subject during direct examination. *Buchanan v Nye* (1954) 128 CA2d 582, 585, 275 P2d 767 (judgment for defendants reversed because defendants, "under the guise of cross-examination" of plaintiff's witness, read into evidence a written statement that, although related to subject of direct examination, should have been excluded as hearsay). See also *People v Odom* (1980) 108 CA3d 100, 115, 166 CR 283. The fact that the evidence introduced during direct examination was itself excludable (*e.g.,* because it violated the hearsay rule) does not give the cross-examiner license to present inadmissible evidence. As the court stated in *People v McDaniel, supra*:

> [L]egitimate cross-examination does not extend to matters improperly admitted on direct examination. Failure to object to improper questions on direct examination may not be taken advantage of on cross-examination to elicit immaterial or irrelevant testimony.

Similarly, failure to object to improper questions on direct examination may not be used to elicit highly prejudicial evidence on cross-examination. *People v Matlock* (1970) 11 CA3d 453, 89 CR 862; *People v Johnson* (1964) 229 CA2d 162, 168, 40 CR 105. See also *Fortner v Bruhn* (1963) 217 CA2d 184, 189, 31 CR 503 (in personal injury action, irrelevant question on direct examination about whether passenger in defendant's car was good companion for injured minor did not permit question on cross-examination about passenger's sexual proclivities).

Only in two special situations, described in §§26.6–26.7, can it accurately be said that the door is opened. Even in these situations, the extent to which the door is opened to otherwise inadmissible matter is quite narrow.

B. When "Curative Admissibility" Exception Applies

§26.6   1. Offsetting Highly Prejudicial Evidence: Curative Admissibility

Under certain exceptional circumstances, the cross-examiner may introduce otherwise inadmissible evidence to offset the effect of highly prejudicial evidence that might have been excluded on direct examination. For example, in *Travis v Southern Pac. Co.* (1962) 210 CA2d 410, 420, 26 CR 700, an action for damages resulting from a collision between a car and a train, the driver of the car volunteered the declaration, during his direct examination on the subject of the car's speed, that he was always conscious of speed laws. To counteract the prejudicial effect of this broad declaration, the court held that it was proper to question him during cross-examination about his prior arrests for speeding. Ordinarily, this evidence would have been excluded as being irrelevant or on Evid C §352 grounds.

Similarly, if the defendant in a criminal case volunteers that he or she never committed an offense like the one charged, the door is opened to questions, that would otherwise be improper, about prior conduct. See *People v Crume* (1976) 61 CA3d 803, 812, 132 CR 577, disapproved on other grounds in *People v Gaston* (1978) 20 C3d 476, 485 n11, 143 CR 205; *People v Lindsey* (1949) 90 CA2d 558, 566, 203 P2d 572. For discussion of this "curative admissibility" exception, see 3 Witkin, California Evidence, *Presentation at Trial* §§353-354 (4th ed 2000).

§26.7 2. Putting Evidence in Proper Context: Rule of Completeness

Occasionally, evidence presented during direct examination is distorted by being taken out of context. The cross-examiner can counteract such distortions by putting the evidence in its proper context. Evidence Code §356 provides:

> Where part of an act, declaration, conversation, or writing is given in evidence by one party, the whole on the same subject may be inquired into by an adverse party; when a letter is read, the answer may be given; and when a detached act, declaration, conversation, or writing is given in evidence, any other act, declaration, conversation, or writing which is necessary to make it understood may also be given in evidence.

In *Rosenberg v Wittenborn* (1960) 178 CA2d 846, 3 CR 459, a police officer called by the plaintiff testified that the defendant had told him that he had gone through the intersection at 30 miles per hour while the light was red. Under former CCP §1854 (the predecessor of Evid C §356), it was held proper on cross-examination to elicit from the police officer that the defendant had also immediately stated that he had experienced a brake failure. By introducing evidence of part of what the defendant had told the officer as an admission against the defendant, the plaintiff opened the door to the defendant's evidence of the remainder of his statement, even though the defendant's use of that statement would ordinarily have been barred by the hearsay rule. See also *People v Barrick* (1982) 33 C3d 115, 131, 187 CR 716.

A closely related principle permits the trial judge to require that an entire transaction be covered on direct examination. For example, in *Conderback, Inc. v Standard Oil Co.* (1966) 239 CA2d 664, 48 CR 901, counsel introduced only a portion of an answer from a deposition. The trial judge required that the entire answer be read at that time and his ruling was upheld as a proper protection against giving the jury a false first impression.

Section 356, quoted above, "only makes admissible such parts of an act, declaration, conversation, or writing as are relevant to the part thereof, previously given in evidence." Comment to Evid C §356. It does not necessarily follow that because a portion of a writing was introduced on direct examination all the remaining portions can be read into the record on cross-examination. A portion omitted during direct examination should be excluded on cross-examination if it is not necessary to put the direct examination in its true context. See *People v McCoy* (1944) 25 C2d 177, 187, 153 P2d 315; *Magee v Wyeth Labs.* (1963) 214 CA2d 340, 355, 29 CR 322. Section 356 also provides that the witness may be cross-examined on independent acts, declarations, conversations, or writings in order to clarify the act, declaration, conversation, or writing testified to on direct examination.

§26.8 IV. ADDITIONAL PROTECTION BASED ON CONSTITUTIONAL PRIVILEGE AGAINST SELF-INCRIMINATION

The defendant in a criminal case has a privilege not to be called as a witness and, if called, to refuse to testify. In fact, any witness in a civil or criminal action may refuse to answer questions that will tend to subject the witness to criminal prosecution. US Const amend V; Cal Const art I, §15; Evid C §§930, 940. See discussion of this privilege in chaps 46–47.

The defendant's privilege not to be called as a witness imposes an additional restriction on the scope of cross-examination of defendants in criminal cases. In a civil matter, or in a criminal trial when the witness is not the defendant, the judge has discretion to permit counsel to "interrupt his cross-examination, redirect examination, or recross-examination of a witness in order to examine the witness upon a matter not within the scope of a previous examination of the witness." Evid C §772(c). When such interruption is permitted, the examiner makes the witness "his or her own," *i.e.*, the examiner examines the witness as if on direct examination. But a defendant in a criminal case can never be examined under direct examination by any party, even temporarily, without giving consent. Evid C §772(d). When the defendant testifies, the privilege is waived only with respect to matters within the scope of the direct examination. See §47.5. The privilege to refuse to testify remains in effect on all other matters. *People v Robinson* (1964) 61 C2d 373, 393, 38 CR 890; *People v Doebke* (1969) 1 CA3d 931, 936, 81 CR 391.

For example, if the defendant testifies about his weight to enable a blood alcohol expert to make certain calculations (the situation presented in *People v Mortenson* (1966) 241 CA2d 137, 50 CR 269), he may be cross-examined only on the subject of his weight. The defendant forfeits much of the constitutional protection described above, however, if he takes the stand and generally denies that he committed the crime of which he is accused. Such a denial leaves the defendant open to extensive cross-examination. *People v Citrino* (1956) 46 C2d 284, 294 P2d 32; *People v Toth* (1960) 182 CA2d 819, 827,

6 CR 372. For example, in *People v Lynn* (1971) 16 CA3d 259, 271, 94 CR 16, the defendants denied the charges, which included attempted escape. The prosecutor was allowed extensive cross-examination about events that had occurred long before the alleged crime. The court held that such evidence tended to show a planned escape scheme.

Thus, if a defendant testifies to matters inconsistent with the prosecution's evidence, the defendant may be examined about facts or denials implied in his or her testimony. Cross-examination will not be limited even though the defendant did not directly testify on the relevant point. *People v Cartwright* (1980) 107 CA3d 402, 415, 166 CR 37. For any point about which the defendant has voluntarily testified, the cross-examination may range over "any matter which may tend to overcome or qualify the effect of the testimony given by him." *People v Zerillo* (1950) 36 C2d 222, 228, 223 P2d 223. See also *People v Lanphear* (1980) 26 C3d 814, 834, 163 CR 601, opinion restated at 28 C3d 463, 171 CR 505; *People v Pike* (1962) 58 C2d 70, 90, 22 CR 664.

Similarly, if the defendant in a criminal case volunteers a statement during cross-examination, the defendant loses the privilege to remain silent about the subject matter of that statement and may be fully cross-examined about it even though the subject matter was not covered during the direct examination. *People v Robinson* (1964) 61 C2d 373, 410, 38 CR 890; *People v Peete* (1946) 28 C2d 306, 321, 169 P2d 924. Neither the ordinary restriction limiting cross-examination to the scope of the direct examination nor the constitutional privilege protects the defendant in this situation.

A defendant in a criminal case may call witnesses to testify to the defendant's good character if the traits to be shown are relevant to the charge. Evid C §1102. A character witness can state an opinion of the defendant's character as well as testify to the defendant's reputation in the community for the relevant trait of character. Evid C §§1101–1102.

If the witness states, as witnesses are allowed to do under Evid C §§1101–1102, that in his or her opinion the defendant's character for the disputed trait is good, the cross-examiner may test that opinion as freely as the opinion testimony of any lay witness (Evid C §§800, 802), including probing into the witness's source of knowledge (*i.e.,* acquaintance with the defendant) and the data on which the opinion is based. See §§20.12–20.15.

Subject to the trial court's discretion to exclude evidence under Evid C §352, witnesses who give opinions of the defendant's good character (as contrasted with reputation evidence) may be cross-examined concerning the defendant's prior misconduct, even though they had no knowledge of the misconduct. *People v Hempstead* (1983) 148 CA3d 949, 954, 196 CR 412.

"Good faith" is demanded of prosecutors in asking character witnesses "Have you heard" questions. The matters implied in the questions should be supported by the facts, and the prosecutor must have good reason to anticipate affirmative responses. The prosecutor may not try to insinuate what is not true or cannot be proved. *People v Kramer* (1968) 259 CA2d 452, 467, 66 CR 638 (trial judge should conduct inquiry about prosecutor's good faith outside presence of jury). See also *People v Hurd* (1970) 5 CA3d 865, 880, 85 CR 718. For a case discussing the types of questions allowed, see *People v Wagner* (1975) 13 C3d 612, 618, 119 CR 457.

§26.9 V. RELATED OBJECTIONS TO RECROSS- AND REDIRECT EXAMINATION

Just as cross-examination is restricted in scope to matters covered during direct examination, each subsequent examination (*i.e.,* redirect, recross-, re-redirect) may not exceed the scope of the examination it follows. Evid C §772(c). See Comment to Evid C §772. See also 3 Witkin, California Evidence, *Presentation at Trial* §§256–257 (4th ed 2000).

A closely related limitation on the scope of re-examination appears in Evid C §774, which declares that once a party has examined a witness about a matter, the witness may not be re-examined about the same matter without the court's permission. Compare this objection with the objection to a question that has already been asked and answered (see chap 11).

§26.10 VI. ALTERNATIVES TO OBJECTING

On possible alternatives to objecting, see §§4.9–4.14.

§26.11 VII. STATING THE OBJECTION

> Objection, Your Honor. This question exceeds the scope of the _ _[e.g., direct examination/cross-examination/redirect examination]_ _.

27

Corpus Delicti Not Proved

I. INTRODUCTION §27.1

II. ELEMENTS OF CRIME §27.2

III. ILLUSTRATIONS §27.3

IV. PROOF REQUIRED §27.4

V. PROCEDURE
   A. Separate Determination by Judge and Jury §27.5
   B. Judge's Determination Regarding Corpus Delicti §27.6
   C. Jury's Determination
      1. Separate Determination Required §27.7
      2. Determination Regarding Corpus Delicti §27.8
      3. Determination Regarding Guilt §27.9
      4. Difficulty of Separating Jury's Determinations §27.10
   D. Admitting Confessions or Admissions Conditionally §27.11

VI. STATING THE OBJECTION §27.12

§27.1   I. INTRODUCTION

In a criminal action, the "corpus delicti" rule means that evidence of a confession or an admission made by the defendant is inadmissible when offered before the prosecution has presented independent proof of the elements of the crime, unless the judge allows the evidence to be introduced conditionally. *People v Diaz* (1992) 3 C4th 495, 528, 11 CR2d 353; *People v Jennings* (1991) 53 C3d 334, 368, 279 CR 780.

The elements of the crime are established when the prosecution has proved that a crime has been committed by someone. *People v Cobb* (1955) 45 C2d 158, 161, 287 P2d 752; *People v Manson* (1977) 71 CA3d 1, 41, 139 CR 275. The purpose of the corpus delicti rule is to guard against a defendant's confessing to a crime that was never committed.

Even if the corpus delicti rule is satisfied, defense counsel may be able to prevent the introduction in evidence of the confession or admission by demonstrating that it was illegally obtained, *e.g.,* that it was the product of an illegal search or that it was obtained by coercion or without giving the accused the warnings required by the constitution. See California Criminal

Law Procedure and Practice, chap 30 (7th ed Cal CEB 2004); 4 Witkin & Epstein, California Criminal Law, *Illegally Obtained Evidence* §§22-23 (3d ed 2000). Although it can be argued that Cal Const art I, §28(d) has abrogated the corpus delicti rule (see the concurring opinion of Timlin, J., in *People v Culton* (1992) 11 CA4th 363, 373, 14 CR2d 189), the California Supreme Court has continued to recognize the rule. See, *e.g., People v Diaz, supra.*

§27.2 II. ELEMENTS OF CRIME

The elements or body (corpus) of the crime (delicti) that must be proved independently of the extrajudicial statements of the accused are:

- The injury, loss, or harm; and

- The existence of a criminal agency as its cause.

See *People v Cantrell* (1973) 8 C3d 672, 679, 105 CR 792, overruled in part on other grounds in *People v Flannel* (1979) 25 C3d 668, 685 n12, 160 CR 84, and *People v Wetmore* (1978) 22 C3d 318, 327 n7, 149 CR 265; 1 Witkin & Epstein, California Criminal Law, *Elements* §§45, 47-49 (3d ed 2000). Proof of "criminal agency" means evidence from which it might be concluded that the injury or harm resulted from the intentional act of a human being. *People v Wong* (1973) 35 CA3d 812, 839, 111 CR 314.

Until these elements have been proved, defense counsel should object to the introduction of any confession or admission against the defendant. If counsel fails to make this objection, this silence may be treated as an implied concession by the defendant that the requisite elements exist. See *People v Peters* (1950) 96 CA2d 671, 216 P2d 145. See also *In re Frances W.* (1974) 42 CA3d 892, 903, 117 CR 277.

Penal Code §190.41, added as part of Proposition 115, provides that the corpus delicti of any of the felony-based special circumstances listed in Pen C §190.2(a)(17) need not be proved independent of a defendant's extrajudicial statement. This provision nullifies the holding in *People v Mattson* (1984) 37 C3d 85, 93, 207 CR 278, that to sustain a felony-murder special circumstance, the corpus delicti of the underlying felony must be established. Section 190.41 returns the law to that in existence before *Mattson*: It is necessary only to show prima facie evidence of a murder (*i.e.,* the death of the victim with some criminal agency as the cause) before the defendant's statements are admissible in a homicide prosecution involving the felony-murder rule (*People v Cantrell* (1973) 8 C3d 672, 680, 105 CR 792, overruled in part on other grounds in *People v Flannel* (1979) 25 C3d 668, 685 n12, 160 CR 84, and *People v Wetmore* (1978) 22 C3d 318, 327 n7, 149 CR 265).

§27.3 III. ILLUSTRATIONS

Counsel should object to the admission of evidence in the following circumstances:

291 • Corpus Delicti Not Proved §27.4

- A defendant being prosecuted for receiving stolen goods confesses that he committed the crime. The prosecution offers the confession into evidence before presenting any proof that the goods were stolen.

- In a prosecution for driving while under the influence of alcohol, the defendant's admission that she was drunk is offered before there has been any proof that she was driving on a public street.

- The defendant has confessed to battery with a deadly weapon. The confession is offered before any proof that the victim's injury was caused by human agency.

- In a prosecution for murder, a husband has admitted putting poison into his wife's food. The prosecution offers evidence of this admission before proving the cause of death.

§27.4   IV. PROOF REQUIRED

Proof of the corpus delicti does not require proof that the defendant was the one who committed the crime. Every element of the crime, however, must be proved. See *People v Borchers* (1958) 50 C2d 321, 328, 325 P2d 97; *People v Francisco* (1964) 228 CA2d 355, 358, 39 CR 503. See also *People v Gentry* (1968) 257 CA2d 607, 610, 65 CR 235. To lay the foundation for the introduction of a confession or an admission, the prosecution need not prove the elements of the crime beyond a reasonable doubt; a prima facie showing is sufficient. *People v Rupp* (1953) 41 C2d 371, 378, 260 P2d 1; *People v Mehaffey* (1948) 32 C2d 535, 545, 197 P2d 12. See also *In re Quintas W.* (1981) 120 CA3d 640, 645, 175 CR 30.

The elements to be proved must be elements of the crime charged against the defendant, not simply elements of *a* crime even though the latter may closely relate to the one charged. *People v Martinez* (1972) 27 CA3d 131, 103 CR 451 (in prosecution for receiving stolen property, defendant's confession to that charge was barred when prosecution proved the existence of stolen property but failed to offer independent proof of receipt of property, a necessary element of the crime of receiving stolen property).

The corpus delicti may be established by circumstantial evidence—even in a murder case. *People v Cullen* (1951) 37 C2d 614, 624, 234 P2d 1. Corpus delicti means "body of the crime" rather than the "body of the deceased," as it is frequently mistranslated. The rule does not require the production of the dead body to prove that a homicide has been committed. *People v Watters* (1927) 202 C 154, 259 P 442; *People v Scott* (1959) 176 CA2d 458, 489, 1 CR 600. See also *People v Manson* (1977) 71 CA3d 1, 2, 139 CR 275, in which the court held that, under the facts of the case, the fact that the body was never recovered would justify an inference that death was caused by criminal agency.

The following are not part of the corpus delicti:

- The identity of the perpetrator of the crime. *People v Cullen, supra.* See also *Ernst v Municipal Court* (1980) 104 CA3d 710, 718, 163 CR 861. For the purpose of proving the corpus delicti, it is not even necessary to connect the defendant with the crime. *People v Leary* (1946) 28 C2d 740, 172 P2d 41; *Jones v Superior Court* (1979) 96 CA3d 390, 393, 157 CR 809.

- Motive. *People v Cullen, supra*; *People v Manson* (1977) 71 CA3d 1, 43, 139 CR 275.

- Venue (*i.e.*, the locus of the crime), which subsequently may be established by the defendant's extrajudicial statements. *People v Garcia* (1970) 4 CA3d 904, 911, 84 CR 624.

The corpus delicti rule is reviewed in *People v Manson* (1977) 71 CA3d 1, 41, 139 CR 275, and in *People v Wong* (1973) 35 CA3d 812, 839, 111 CR 314. See Comment, *California's Corpus Delicti Rule: The Case for Review and Clarification*, 20 UCLA L Rev 1055 (1973). See also §27.2.

V. PROCEDURE

§27.5   A. Separate Determination by Judge and Jury

To understand the practical effect of the corpus delicti rule, it is important to recognize what the California Supreme Court characterized in *People v McMonigle* (1947) 29 C2d 730, 738, 177 P2d 745, as the "sharp distinction" between the rule's two aspects:

- First, the corpus delicti rule specifies what the judge must find before a confession or an admission may be admitted into evidence. This aspect is discussed in §27.6.

- Second, the corpus delicti rule specifies what the jury must find before it may convict. This aspect is discussed in §§27.7–27.10.

§27.6   B. Judge's Determination Regarding Corpus Delicti

When the prosecution offers an alleged confession or admission by the defendant in evidence and the defendant objects on the ground that the corpus delicti has not been proved, a preliminary question is presented for the trial judge to decide. If the trial judge determines that the prosecution has previously presented sufficient evidence to constitute prima facie proof that a crime was committed, and that no other rule of evidence requires the judge to exclude it, the court will permit the confession or admission to be introduced in evidence. If the judge determines that the corpus delicti has not yet been established, the court will rule that the confession or admission is inadmissible or only conditionally admissible (see §27.11). Evidence Code §405 governs the trial court's determination concerning the corpus delicti. If a question is raised concerning the identity of the person who made the confession or admission, that is determined under Evid C §403.

Defense counsel should raise the issue outside the jury's presence at the earliest opportunity, preferably at the chambers conference before trial (see chap 2) and before the prosecution's attempt to introduce the alleged confession or admission. See §§21.15-21.18.

On the trial judge's duty to instruct the jury on what it must determine to satisfy the corpus delicti rule, see §27.7.

C. Jury's Determination

§27.7   1. Separate Determination Required

The judge's ruling that the defendant's confession or admission is admissible (see §27.6) allows the jury to consider it as evidence. The jury may not, however, render a verdict of guilty on the basis of the confession or admission alone. In this respect, the corpus delicti rule is similar to the rules requiring more than the testimony of a single witness to convict a person of certain crimes, *e.g.,* treason (US Const art III, §3; Cal Const art I, §18), solicitation to commit a felony (Pen C §653f). See Comment to Evid C §411; 3 Witkin, California Evidence, *Presentation at Trial* §§96-98, 102, 107 (4th ed 2000).

This aspect of the corpus delicti rule is summarized as follows in CALJIC 2.72:

> No person may be convicted of a criminal offense unless there is some proof of each element of the crime independent of any [confession] [or] [admission] made by [him] [her] outside of this trial.
>
> The identity of the person who is alleged to have committed a crime is not an element of the crime [nor is the degree of the crime]. Such identity [or degree of the crime] may be established by [a] [an] [confession] [or] [admission].

Whether or not requested to do so, the trial judge must give the CALJIC 2.72 instruction to the jury in every criminal case in which the defendant's confession or admission is introduced in evidence. Failure to do so constitutes error. See *People v Beagle* (1972) 6 C3d 441, 455, 99 CR 313; *People v Carpenter* (1997) 15 C4th 312, 63 CR2d 1. This error may not be considered prejudicial, however, if the record contains sufficient evidence (other than the confession or admission) to establish the corpus delicti. *People v Beagle, supra* (although it is error for court not to instruct, on its own, that corpus delicti must be proved independently of confession or admission, error will not be grounds for reversal unless it is reasonably probable that result more favorable to defendant would have been reached in absence of error); *People v Starr* (1970) 11 CA3d 574, 583, 89 CR 906 (error prejudicial).

The practical effect of the instruction is that the jury must make two essentially separate determinations (described in §§27.8-27.9) whenever the defendant's confession or admission has been admitted into evidence.

§27.8   2. Determination Regarding Corpus Delicti

Before it may consider the question of the defendant's guilt, the jury must decide whether there is sufficient evidence, other than the confession or admission, to establish the corpus delicti. If the jury finds that the corpus delicti has not been established, it must acquit the defendant. If the jury finds (to paraphrase the language of CALJIC 2.72, quoted in §27.7) that there has been proof, independent of the confession or admission, that the crime in question was committed, it may proceed to the issue of whether the defendant is guilty.

§27.9   3. Determination Regarding Guilt

Having determined that the corpus delicti was independently established, the jury considers the question of the defendant's guilt as in any other criminal case. Once the defendant's confession or admission is admitted, it may be considered along with all other evidence by the jury in its determination of whether all the elements of the crime and the defendant's connection to it have been established beyond a reasonable doubt. *People v Selby* (1926) 198 C 426, 437, 245 P 426; *People v Manson* (1977) 71 CA3d 1, 42, 139 CR 275.

Once admitted, the confession itself may be sufficient to raise the quantity of proof to proof beyond a reasonable doubt. See *People v Manson, supra*. If the evidence, including the confession or admission, does not persuade the jury beyond a reasonable doubt that the defendant is guilty, the defendant is entitled to an acquittal. Pen C §1096.

§27.10   4. Difficulty of Separating Jury's Determinations

The average juror is unlikely to be able to differentiate the finding expected to be made regarding the corpus delicti, described in §27.8, from the finding expected to be made on the issue of guilt, described in §27.9. As Judge Learned Hand remarked about a system similar to California's in *U.S. v Dennis* (2d Cir 1950) 183 F2d 201, 230, aff'd (1951) 341 US 494: "[I]t is a practical impossibility for laymen, and for that matter for most judges, to keep their minds in the isolated compartments that this requires." For further criticism of the type of system in California that requires the jury to make a separate determination regarding the corpus delicti, see *People v Starr* (1970) 11 CA3d 574, 89 CR 906 (dissenting opinion of Gustafson, J.).

§27.11   D. Admitting Confessions or Admissions Conditionally

Under the court's power to regulate the order of proof (Pen C §1094; Evid C §320), the trial judge may exercise discretion by allowing evidence of an out-of-court confession or admission to be introduced on the condition that the prosecution must prove the corpus delicti later in the trial. *People v Wade* (1959) 53 C2d 322, 330, 1 CR 683, overruled on another ground in *People v Carpenter* (1997) 15 C4th 312, 381, 63 CR2d 1. To avoid the risk of prejudicing the defendant's case, trial judges normally require the corpus delicti to be proved in advance. See 1 Witkin & Epstein, California Criminal Law, *Introduction to Crimes* §46 (3d ed 2000).

If the judge has permitted the confession or admission to be introduced conditionally and the prosecution rests without having established the necessary elements of the crime, defense counsel should move to strike the confession or admission and for a mistrial or a judgment of acquittal (Pen C §§1118-1118.1).

§27.12   VI. STATING THE OBJECTION

> Objection, Your Honor. This evidence should not be admitted, because the corpus delicti has not been proved.

28
Illegally Obtained Evidence

I. SCOPE OF CHAPTER §28.1

II. SUMMARY §28.2

III. SEARCH AND SEIZURE EXCLUSIONARY RULE
   A. Constitutional Provisions §28.3
   B. Applicability
      1. Civil Cases §28.4
      2. Quasi-Criminal Cases §28.5
      3. Administrative Proceedings §28.6

IV. EXCLUDING EVIDENCE UNDER EVID C §352 §28.7

V. EXCLUDING EVIDENCE OBTAINED BY FRAUD AND DECEIT §28.8

VI. EXCLUDING EVIDENCE OBTAINED BY OUTRAGEOUS OR SHOCKING METHODS §28.9

VII. EXCLUDING ILLEGALLY OBTAINED CONFESSIONS AND ADMISSIONS §28.10

VIII. EXCLUDING EVIDENCE OBTAINED DURING ADMINISTRATIVE INSPECTIONS §28.11

IX. PROCEDURE §28.12

X. STATING THE OBJECTION
   A. Illegal Search and Seizure §28.13
   B. Illegally Obtained Confessions and Admissions §28.14
   C. Other Illegally Obtained Evidence §28.15

§28.1   I. SCOPE OF CHAPTER

This chapter discusses search and seizure motions in quasi-criminal cases. It does not discuss the exclusion of illegally obtained evidence in criminal cases or in proceedings ancillary to criminal cases, *e.g.,* probation and parole revocation hearings. For detailed discussion of these matters, see Bell, Bell's Searches, Seizures and Bugging Compendium (1970); LaFave, Search and Seizure: A Treatise on the Fourth Amendment (3d ed 1996).

This chapter also does not discuss objecting in criminal cases to illegally obtained confessions or admissions or incriminating evidence obtained in a manner that shocks the conscience. For detailed discussion of these topics, see Witkin & Epstein, California Criminal Law (3d ed 2000). See also California Criminal Law Procedure and Practice, chaps 20 (search and seizure), 30 (confessions and admissions) (7th ed Cal CEB 2004). On the privilege against self-incrimination, see chaps 46–47.

§28.2   II. SUMMARY

Objections in California state courts concerning illegal search and seizure are based on the Fourth Amendment to the United States Constitution (applied to the states through US Const amend XIV) and Cal Const art I, §13. Under the exclusionary rule, both constitutions guarantee the right of the People to be secure in their persons, houses, papers, and effects against unreasonable searches and seizures. No warrants may issue except on probable cause, supported by oath or affirmation. A warrant must specify the place to be searched and the persons or things to be seized.

"A 'search' is a governmental intrusion upon, or invasion of, a citizen's personal security in an area in which he has a reasonable expectation of privacy." *People v Mayberry* (1982) 31 C3d 335, 341, 182 CR 617, quoted in *Conservatorship of Susan T.* (1994) 8 C4th 1005, 1014, 36 CR2d 40.

Search and seizure law is most frequently applied in criminal cases. Its application to civil cases has been only to quasi-criminal cases. In determining whether a particular case is quasi-criminal, the courts have considered whether there is a close identity to the aims and objectives of criminal law enforcement, balancing the deterrent effect of the rule with its social cost. *Conservatorship of Susan T., supra.* See also *U.S. v Janis* (1976) 428 US 433, 447, 49 L Ed 2d 1046, 1057, 96 S Ct 3021. But see *Soldal v Cook County* (1992) 506 US 56, 67, 121 L Ed 2d 450, 462, 113 S Ct 538 (Fourth Amendment applied to 42 USC §1983 lawsuit; court stated in dicta that "the Amendment's protection applies in the civil context as well").

III. SEARCH AND SEIZURE EXCLUSIONARY RULE

§28.3   A. Constitutional Provisions

The Fourth Amendment to the United States Constitution guarantees the right of the People to be secure in their persons, houses, papers, and effects against unreasonable searches and seizures. The amendment declares that no warrants may issue except on probable cause, supported by oath or affirmation, and particularly describing the place to be searched and the persons or things to be seized. California Constitution art I, §13 provides:

> The right of the people to be secure in their persons, houses, papers, and effects against unreasonable seizures and searches may not be violated; and a warrant may not issue except on probable cause, supported by

oath or affirmation, particularly describing the place to be searched and the persons and things to be seized.

The Fourth Amendment applies to the states through US Const amend XIV. *Mapp v Ohio* (1961) 367 US 643, 6 L Ed 2d 1081, 81 S Ct 1684. The Fourth Amendment has been interpreted to apply only to searches conducted or instigated by the government. *Walter v U.S.* (1980) 447 US 649, 65 L Ed 2d 410, 100 S Ct 2395; *Burdeau v McDowell* (1921) 256 US 465, 65 L Ed 1048, 41 S Ct 574. See also Note, *Private Searches and Seizures: An Application of the Public Function Theory*, 48 Geo Wash L Rev 433 (1980).

B. Applicability

§28.4   1. Civil Cases

The exclusionary rule of US Const amend XIV has been interpreted to apply only to criminal and quasi-criminal cases: "In the complex and turbulent history of the [exclusionary] rule, the Court never has applied it to exclude evidence from a civil proceeding, federal or state." *U.S. v Janis* (1976) 428 US 433, 447, 49 L Ed 2d 1046, 1057, 96 S Ct 3021. See *Conservatorship of Susan T.* (1994) 8 C4th 1005, 1017, 36 CR2d 40. See also *NLRB v South Bay Daily Breeze* (9th Cir 1969) 415 F2d 360, 364. But see *Soldal v Cook County* (1992) 506 US 56, 67, 121 L Ed 2d 450, 462, 113 S Ct 538 (Fourth Amendment to United States Constitution applied to 42 USC §1983 lawsuit; court stated in dicta that "the Amendment's protection applies in the civil context as well").

§28.5   2. Quasi-Criminal Cases

The exclusionary rule of US Const amend XIV has been interpreted to apply only to criminal and quasi-criminal cases. See §28.4. When deciding whether a particular type of civil proceeding is quasi-criminal, the courts generally examine two issues:

(1) Whether there is a close identity to the aims and objectives of criminal law enforcement (see *Emslie v State Bar* (1974) 11 C3d 210, 227, 113 CR 175); and

(2) Whether the deterrent effect of the rule is weighed against the social cost (*Conservatorship of Susan T.* (1994) 8 C4th 1005, 1012, 36 CR2d 40).

See *In re Ruffalo* (1968) 390 US 544, 551, 20 L Ed 2d 117, 122, 88 S Ct 1222 (administrative proceedings that concern deprivation of license to practice one's profession are usually considered to be quasi-criminal); *Webster v Board of Dental Examiners* (1941) 17 C2d 534, 537, 110 P2d 992 (ordinary disciplinary proceedings and proceedings involving applications for permits and licenses are not considered to be quasi-criminal).

In *Emslie v State Bar, supra,* the court described the balancing test to be used in deciding whether the exclusionary rule applies to a particular proceeding:

- Whether the purposes of the proceeding are similar to the goals of criminal law enforcement;
- Whether the exclusionary rule would deter persons effecting searches or seizures in this type of case;
- The social consequences of applying the exclusionary rule; and
- The effect on the integrity of the judicial process.

Despite these guidelines, the outcome of individual cases is not predictable.

The same search and seizure laws that are applied in criminal cases should apply to quasi-criminal cases in which the exclusionary rule is applied. See *Elder v Board of Med. Examiners* (1966) 241 CA2d 246, 266, 50 CR 304 (court applied federal rule excluding evidence that was "fruit of the poisonous tree"; see §28.4); *Knoll Assocs. v FTC* (7th Cir 1968) 397 F2d 530, 536 (court applied Fourth Amendment to United States Constitution; see §28.4).

§28.6   3. Administrative Proceedings

It has been suggested that exclusion of illegally seized evidence is required in administrative proceedings when its admission would be "inconsistent with the dignity of [the] proceedings and the fair administration of justice." See *Patty v Board of Med. Examiners* (1973) 9 C3d 356, 364, 107 CR 473 (recognizing defense of entrapment in administrative hearing concerning deprivation or suspension of license to practice one's profession); California Administrative Hearing Practice §§7.78–7.82 (2d ed Cal CEB 1997). But see *Wong v State Bar* (1975) 15 C3d 528, 530, 125 CR 482 (*Patty* not applied to State Bar disciplinary proceeding, because attorney was not entrapped by agents of State Bar).

In the following cases, the courts found that the exclusionary rule did not apply:

- *INS v Lopez-Mendoza* (1984) 468 US 1032, 82 L Ed 2d 778, 104 S Ct 3479 (exclusionary rule did not apply to deportation proceeding, which is a purely civil action).
- *Emslie v State Bar* (1974) 11 C3d 210, 230, 113 CR 175 (exclusionary rule did not apply to State Bar disciplinary proceedings).
- *Finkelstein v State Personnel Bd.* (1990) 218 CA3d 264, 271, 267 CR 133 (exclusionary rule did not apply to briefcase search conducted by supervisor of public employee; search was motivated by desire to prepare office for move rather than to uncover evidence damaging to employee; application of rule would have had no deterrent effect).
- *Pating v Board of Med. Quality Assur.* (1982) 130 CA3d 608, 624, 182

CR 20 (exclusionary rule did not apply to administrative proceeding against medical doctor when protection of public's physical well-being was at stake and application would have had no deterrent effect).

- *Governing Bd. v Metcalf* (1974) 36 CA3d 546, 111 CR 724 (exclusionary rule did not apply in proceeding for revoking teaching credential based on moral grounds).

In the following cases, the courts held that the exclusionary rule did apply:

- *Dyson v State Personnel Bd.* (1989) 213 CA3d 711, 262 CR 112 (exclusionary rule applied in dismissal hearing of school youth counselor because unconstitutional search had "tight nexus" with school that sought to profit from it). See also dicta in *Governing Bd. v Metcalf* (1974) 36 CA3d 546, 551, 111 CR 724, which left open the possibility that the exclusionary rule may apply to revocation of teaching credentials on other than moral grounds.

- *Elder v Board of Med. Examiners* (1966) 241 CA2d 246, 50 CR 304 (exclusionary rule assumed to apply in proceeding to revoke medical license, although court found no violation of that rule).

- *Knoll Assocs. v FTC* (7th Cir 1968) 397 F2d 530, involving a Clayton Act violation (15 USC §13(a)) (documents stolen by employee to assist FTC counsel in pending case against employer were excluded because theft and use of documents violated Fourth Amendment to United States Constitution). But see criticism of *Knoll* in *Morale v Grigel* (D NH 1976) 422 F Supp 988, 1000.

§28.7 IV. EXCLUDING EVIDENCE UNDER EVID C §352

One case suggests that counsel may use an Evid C §352 objection in place of a search and seizure objection to accomplish the same purpose. See *Tanuvasa v City & County of Honolulu* (Haw App 1981) 626 P2d 1175 (civil action against police officer for damages arising from plaintiff's arrest; gun and marijuana, illegally seized at time of arrest, suppressed because prejudice to plaintiff outweighed any remote relevance). For further discussion of Evid C §352, see chap 31.

§28.8 V. EXCLUDING EVIDENCE OBTAINED BY FRAUD AND DECEIT

In *Redner v WCAB* (1971) 5 C3d 83, 95 CR 447, the California Supreme Court approved exclusion, in a workers' compensation proceeding, of a movie obtained by the fraudulent inducements of private investigators. The court found that the investigators' inducements caused the applicant to engage in the filmed activities. The same objection presumably may be made in other quasi-criminal or administrative proceedings, subject to the balancing test discussed in *Emslie v State Bar* (1974) 11 C3d 210, 227, 113 CR 175 (see §28.6).

§28.9 VI. EXCLUDING EVIDENCE OBTAINED BY OUTRAGEOUS OR SHOCKING METHODS

Dicta in two California cases state that some investigatory conduct may be so shocking to the conscience as to require exclusion. See *Emslie v State Bar* (1974) 11 C3d 210, 229, 113 CR 175; *Patty v Board of Med. Examiners* (1973) 9 C3d 356, 107 CR 473. See also §28.6.

§28.10 VII. EXCLUDING ILLEGALLY OBTAINED CONFESSIONS AND ADMISSIONS

An involuntary or coerced confession is inadmissible at trial for any purpose. *People v Neal* (2003) 31 C4th 63, 79, 1 CR3d 650.

The same balancing test that is used for illegally seized evidence can probably be used to determine whether an illegally obtained confession or admission can be challenged in an administrative proceeding. See *Emslie v State Bar* (1974) 11 C3d 210, 113 CR 175, in which the court in dicta included the *Miranda* exclusionary rule in its discussion of applying a particular balancing test to illegally seized evidence. See *Miranda v Arizona* (1966) 384 US 436, 16 L Ed 2d 694, 86 S Ct 1602, and *Dickerson v U.S.* (2000) 530 US 428, 147 L Ed 2d 405, 120 S Ct 2326 (reaffirming *Miranda*).

On the privilege against self-incrimination, see chaps 46–47.

§28.11 VIII. EXCLUDING EVIDENCE OBTAINED DURING ADMINISTRATIVE INSPECTIONS

The Fourth Amendment to the United States Constitution prohibits unreasonable searches of residential and commercial property without a warrant, whether the search is for criminal or civil reasons. *See v City of Seattle* (1967) 387 US 541, 18 L Ed 2d 943, 87 S Ct 1737; *Camara v Municipal Court* (1967) 387 US 523, 18 L Ed 2d 930, 87 S Ct 1727.

Warrants have been required for routine searches by agents of the Occupational Safety and Health Administration (OSHA) (*Marshall v Barlow's, Inc.* (1978) 436 US 307, 56 L Ed 2d 305, 98 S Ct 1816), housing code inspectors (*Camara v Municipal Court, supra*), social workers making early morning raids on the homes of welfare recipients (*Parrish v Civil Serv. Comm'n* (1967) 66 C2d 260, 57 CR 623), and fire department inspectors (*See v City of Seattle, supra*). Absent consent or exigent circumstances, administrative searches into the cause or origin of a fire are subject to the warrant requirement of the Fourth Amendment. *Michigan v Clifford* (1984) 464 US 287, 78 L Ed 2d 477, 104 S Ct 641. See *Smith v Board of Supervisors* (2002) 104 CA4th 1104, 128 CR2d 700, in which the court distinguished *Parrish v Civil Serv. Comm'n, supra,* and found adequate Fourth Amendment protections because applicants were provided notice of the visits and the visits have rehabilitative and fraud-prevention purposes.

Courts have found certain searches made without a warrant to be reasonable when the business searched was pervasively regulated by the government (*U.S. v Biswell* (1972) 406 US 311, 314, 32 L Ed 2d 87, 91, 92 S Ct 1593) or had long been subject to close supervision and inspection (*Colonnade Catering Corp. v U.S.* (1970) 397 US 72, 75, 25 L Ed 2d 60, 63, 90 S Ct 774). Warrants have not been required of inspectors making routine searches of mines under the Federal Mine Safety and Health Act of 1977 (30 USC §813(a)) (*Donovan v Dewey* (1981) 452 US 594, 69 L Ed 2d 262, 101 S Ct 2534), routine inspections of gun shops under the Gun Control Act of 1968 (18 USC §§921-928) (*U.S. v Biswell, supra*), or routine nonforceable inspections of liquor dealers under IRC §§5146(b) and 7606 (*Colonnade Catering Corp. v U.S., supra*).

Under Proposition 8 (Cal Const art I, §28(d)), a student's right to object, in a juvenile or criminal court proceeding, to evidence illegally seized by school authorities must be raised under federal law and not under the California Constitution. *In re Bobby B.* (1985) 172 CA3d 377, 381, 218 CR 253. Under federal law, the legality of searching a student does not depend on probable cause to believe that the student has violated or is violating the law but rather on the reasonableness of the search under all the circumstances. In determining whether a search is reasonable, the court must consider whether the action was justified at its inception and whether the search as actually conducted was reasonably related in scope to the circumstances that originally justified the interference. *New Jersey v T.L.O.* (1985) 469 US 325, 341, 83 L Ed 2d 720, 734, 105 S Ct 733, followed by the court in *In re Bobby B., supra*. See also *In re William G.* (1985) 40 C3d 550, 221 CR 118, decided under pre-Proposition 8 law. In contrast, the exclusionary rule has been held not to apply in high school disciplinary proceedings, even when such proceedings are brought in part to punish the offending student. *Gordon J. v Santa Ana Unified Sch. Dist.* (1984) 162 CA3d 530, 544, 208 CR 657 (affirming one-year suspension for possession of marijuana on campus).

In discussing the less stringent standards required for constitutional searches of students at schools, compared with normal search and seizure standards, the court in *In re William G.* (1985) 40 C3d 550, 562 n13, 221 CR 118, noted that the warrant and probable cause requirements have also been relaxed for searches conducted in military institutions, on the national border, aboard vessels within the United States or its coastal waters, at certain licensed businesses, or at the site of other regulated activities.

In *Skinner v Railway Labor Executives' Ass'n* (1989) 489 US 602, 103 L Ed 2d 639, 109 S Ct 1402, the United States Supreme Court held that safety regulations of the Federal Railroad Administration mandating or authorizing alcohol and drug tests of employees, without individualized suspicion or warrants, did not violate the Fourth Amendment. The court held that even though the Fourth Amendment applies to alcohol and drug tests under the regulations, the tests were reasonable because the government interest in promoting safety outweighs employees' privacy concerns.

A traveler at an international border may be detained beyond the scope of a routine customs search and inspection, if customs agents reasonably suspect that the traveler is smuggling contraband in his or her alimentary canal. The border officials must have a particularized and objective basis for that suspicion. *U.S. v Montoya de Hernandez* (1985) 473 US 531, 87 L Ed 2d 381, 105 S Ct 3304.

For further discussion, see California Administrative Hearing Practice §§7.78-7.83 (2d ed Cal CEB 1997).

§28.12   IX. PROCEDURE

There is no statutory procedure in quasi-criminal or administrative cases for objecting to illegally seized evidence. Counsel should check local court rules or practice. In administrative hearings, counsel should contact the agency or hearing officer to find out what procedure to follow. Whether or not there is a separate proceeding before trial on the issue of the illegally seized evidence, counsel may object to its use at trial. See *Conservatorship of Susan T.* (1994) 8 C4th 1005, 36 CR2d 40 (objection to photographs apparently made for first time during trial); *People v Berger* (1955) 44 C2d 459, 463, 282 P2d 509 (in criminal cases before enactment of Pen C §1538.5 (statute that regulates criminal search and seizure hearings), no statewide requirement that search and seizure motion be made before trial; if motion made before trial and denied, motion could be made de novo in trial court). If the motion is not made at the hearing, the issue is waived. *Savoy Club v Board of Supervisors* (1970) 12 CA3d 1034, 91 CR 198.

Prudent practice dictates that counsel make search and seizure motions in writing, describing the evidence to be excluded and setting forth points and authorities stating both the legal and factual grounds for exclusion. The motion should be made as early as possible after notice is given to the court and opposing parties. If made during trial, the motion should be raised out of the jury's presence. On motions in limine, see chap 2.

X. STATING THE OBJECTION

§28.13   A. Illegal Search and Seizure

Your Honor,

[Option 1: Before trial]

I move to suppress _ _[state particular evidence to be suppressed]_ _

[Option 2: During trial]

I object to _ _[state objection]_ _

[Continue]

on the ground that the evidence was illegally obtained by unreasonable search and seizure in violation of the Fourth and Fourteenth amendments to the United States Constitution

[Add if objection is made on state constitutional ground]

and Article I, section 13, of the California Constitution because _ _[state legal reason that requires suppression]_ _.

[Add if objection is based on Evid C §352]

Your Honor,

[Option 1: Before trial]

I also move to suppress this evidence

[Option 2: During trial]

I object to _ _[state objection]_ _

[Continue]

on the ground that admission of this evidence would _ _[be unduly inflammatory/consume an undue amount of time/create undue prejudice/confuse the issues/mislead the jury]_ _ under Evidence Code section 352.

§28.14 B. Illegally Obtained Confessions and Admissions

Your Honor, I object to this evidence on the ground that _ _[state reason, e.g. it was involuntary/it was obtained in the absence of Miranda warnings]_ _.

§28.15 C. Other Illegally Obtained Evidence

Your Honor, I object to this evidence on the ground that

[Option 1: Objection made on Patty grounds; see §28.6]

its admission would be inconsistent with the dignity of these proceedings and the fair administration of justice.

[Option 2: Objection made because evidence was obtained by fraud and deceit]

it was obtained by fraud and deceit.

[Option 3: Objection made because evidence was obtained by outrageous or shocking methods]

it was obtained by methods so shocking to the conscience under the Fourth Amendment to the United States Constitution that it must be excluded.

29

Objecting to Misconduct

I. SCOPE OF CHAPTER §29.1

II. MISCONDUCT OF COUNSEL
   A. Definition §29.2
   B. Examples of Misconduct of Counsel
      1. Primary Categories §29.3
      2. Misconduct Before Trial or During Voir Dire Examination §29.4
      3. Misconduct During Opening Statement §29.5
      4. Misconduct During Examination of Witnesses §29.6
      5. Misconduct During Argument §29.7
      6. Misconduct After Trial §29.8
   C. Determining Prejudicial Effect §29.9
   D. Remedies
      1. Objection
         a. Purpose §29.10
         b. Timeliness §29.11
         c. Objecting to Misconduct §29.12
         d. Laying Foundation for Misconduct That Occurred Without Judge's Knowledge §29.13
      2. Requesting Curative Admonition §29.14
      3. Contempt §29.15
      4. Motion for Mistrial §29.16
      5. Motion for New Trial §29.17
      6. Appeal §29.18
   E. Alternatives to Objecting §29.19
   F. Stating the Objection §29.20

III. MISCONDUCT OF JUDGE
   A. Standards of Conduct §29.21
   B. Examples of Misconduct of Judge §29.22
      1. Abuse of Power to Comment on Evidence §29.23
      2. Abuse of Power to Examine Witnesses or Prospective Witnesses §29.24
      3. Interference With Production of Proof §29.25
      4. Coercive Actions §29.26
      5. Disparagement of Counsel, Witness, or Party §29.27
   C. Remedies
      1. Objection §29.28
      2. Motion for Mistrial §29.29
      3. Motion for New Trial §29.30
      4. Appeal §29.31

D. Alternatives to Objecting §29.32
E. Stating the Objection §29.33

IV. MISCONDUCT OF JURORS
   A. Standards of Conduct §29.34
   B. Examples of Misconduct of Jurors
      1. Concealing Information During Voir Dire Examination §29.35
      2. Receiving Evidence Out of Court
         a. General Restrictions §29.36
         b. Specific Prohibitions
            (1) Independent Investigations §29.37
            (2) Independent Experiments §29.38
            (3) Unauthorized Discussions §29.39
            (4) Personal Knowledge of Facts §29.40
            (5) Personal Knowledge of Law §29.41
            (6) Unauthorized Matter in Jury Room §29.42
      3. Arriving at Verdict by Chance or by Quotient §29.43
      4. Inattentiveness During Trial §29.44
      5. Failure to Deliberate §29.44A
   C. Remedies
      1. Before Verdict Rendered §29.45
      2. After Verdict Rendered §29.46
   D. Alternatives to Objecting §29.47
   E. Stating the Objection
      1. Before Verdict Rendered §29.48
      2. After Verdict Rendered §29.49

§29.1   I. SCOPE OF CHAPTER

A general discussion of misconduct is beyond the scope of a book on trial objections. The purpose of this chapter is to aid the trial attorney in recognizing what constitutes misconduct and how to respond to it. Misconduct of trial counsel is described in §§29.2-29.20. Less frequently encountered are misconduct of the trial judge, discussed in §§29.21-29.33, and misconduct of jurors, discussed in §§29.34-29.44.

II. MISCONDUCT OF COUNSEL

§29.2   A. Definition

More than ever before, judges and the public closely examine attorney misconduct during litigation. To foster civility, prevent delay, and discourage "Rambo" tactics during discovery and at trial, many courts strictly limit attorneys from carrying advocacy beyond what was originally intended by the concept. Cal Rules of Prof Cond 5-200.

With respect to a trial, misconduct of counsel has been defined as the disregard of rules of evidence or procedure for the purpose and with the effect of prejudicing the adverse party's claim or defense before the trier of fact. See 7 Witkin, California Procedure, *Trial* §223 (4th ed 1997). Misconduct has also been defined as a dishonest act or the attempt to persuade the court or jury using deceptive or reprehensible methods. See *People v Rhinehart* (1973) 9 C3d 139, 154, 107 CR 34, disapproved by *People v Bolton* (1979) 23 C3d 208, 213, 152 CR 141; *People v Jenkins* (1974) 40 CA3d 1054, 1057, 115 CR 622.

Many errors amounting to misconduct occur because counsel does not know or understand the rules of evidence. In addition to becoming familiar with the Evidence Code, trial counsel should understand the statutes and rules that govern an attorney's behavior and form the basis for disciplinary proceedings. See Bus & P C §§6000-6172 (particularly Bus & P C §6068 on an attorney's duties) and the State Bar of California Rules of Professional Conduct (in West's Annotated California Codes: Professional Rules, vol 23, pt 2; and Deering's California Codes Annotated: Rules of Court, State Bar Rules). See also *People v Ballard* (1980) 104 CA3d 757, 761, 164 CR 81 (conduct of California attorneys governed by California Rules of Professional Conduct). On the standard of conduct of prosecutors, see *In re Ferguson* (1971) 5 C3d 525, 531 96 CR 594 (duty to fully and fairly present evidence material to charge against defendant); *People v Gionis* (1995) 9 C4th 1196, 40 CR2d 456.

Attorneys may use only such "means" as are consistent with the truth (Cal Rules of Prof Cond 5-200(A)) and "shall not seek to mislead the judge, judicial officer or jury by an artifice or false statement of fact or law" (Cal Rules of Prof Cond 5-200(B)). Attorneys may not suppress any evidence that they or their clients have a legal obligation to reveal or produce. Cal Rules of Prof Cond 5-220. In addition, deceiving the court or collusion may constitute a misdemeanor. Bus & P C §6128(a). Any attorney who is or has participated in litigation cannot make an extrajudicial statement that a reasonable person would expect to be disseminated by a public communication if that attorney reasonably knows that the communication will have a substantial likelihood of materially prejudicing the proceeding. Cal Rules of Prof Cond 5-120.

Draconian measures such as striking pleadings, issues, or defenses may seem unfair to clients, but judges often impose severe sanctions on attorneys for discovery abuse and inappropriate trial conduct. More common sanctions include specific warnings to counsel in the presence of the jury, carefully worded curative admonitions to jurors regarding misconduct, assessment of costs and attorney fees against the offending attorney, exclusion of evidence or the testimony of witnesses, initiation of contempt proceedings, or the granting of a mistrial. All these sanctions are within the trial judge's discretion to impose.

A court that orders reversal of a judgment based even in part on attorney misconduct is required to report the matter to the State Bar, which will investigate the appropriateness of instituting disciplinary action. Bus & P C §6086.7. This reporting requirement is enforced more frequently than in the past.

B. Examples of Misconduct of Counsel

§29.3 1. Primary Categories

The examples of misconduct in §§29.3-29.20 are not exhaustive. For additional examples, see California Trial Practice: Civil Procedure During Trial, chap 16 (3d ed Cal CEB 1995); 7 Witkin, California Procedure, *Trial* §§227-237 (4th ed 1997).

The primary categories of misconduct by counsel during trial are:

- Attempting to bring inadmissible matter before the jury;

- Asking a witness questions, not for the answer that might be given but rather for the purpose of presenting facts, references, or insinuations that cannot be supported by the record;

- Willfully concealing evidence;

- Referring in argument to facts that are not in evidence;

- Appealing to the jurors' sympathy or prejudice by, *e.g.*, referring to the wealth or poverty of the parties or to their race, religion, or national origin;

- Making impermissible references to insurance;

- Referring to a party's settlement with other persons or offers to settle;

- Making derogatory remarks to or about opposing counsel, a party, or a witness;

- Making unauthorized communications with or attempts to influence the jury; and

- Making certain motions in the jury's presence.

See Civil Trials Benchbook §10.14.

§29.4 2. Misconduct Before Trial or During Voir Dire Examination

The following may constitute attorney misconduct before trial or during voir dire examination of jurors:

- Interviewing potential jurors. See Cal Rules of Prof Cond 5-320.

- Acting in a manner that suggests or encourages a witness not to testify or to testify falsely. See Cal Rules of Prof Cond 5-310.

- Unnecessarily emphasizing the fact that the defendant is insured. *Swift v Winkler* (1957) 148 CA2d 927, 307 P2d 666. See §6.38. See also *Scally v PG&E* (1972) 23 CA3d 806, 814, 100 CR 501.

- Interjecting prejudicial matter in voir dire questions. See §6.38.

- Intimidating witnesses. *People v Hill* (1998) 17 C4th 800, 834, 72 CR2d 656 (prosecutor threatened defense witness before trial with perjury prosecution).

§29.5   3. Misconduct During Opening Statement

The following may constitute attorney misconduct during opening statement:

- Stating matter that counsel knows will not be received in evidence. See *Isaac Upham Co. v United States Fid. & Guar. Co.* (1922) 59 CA 606, 211 P 809. See also *Smith v Covell* (1980) 100 CA3d 947, 958, 161 CR 377.

- Making false or inflammatory statements. See, *e.g., Love v Wolf* (1964) 226 CA2d 378, 385, 38 CR 183 ("[a]fter [defendant] started to use this [drug] all over the country came reports of people dying from it"). See also *Simmons v Southern Pac. Transp. Co.* (1976) 62 CA3d 341, 351, 133 CR 42 (suggesting that defendant would commit perjury and that defendant company did not care about pedestrian safety).

- Stating matters known to be unsupported by the evidence. *Malkasian v Irwin* (1964) 61 C2d 738, 40 CR 78. See also Cal Rules of Prof Cond 5-200.

- Stating matters of personal belief. Cal Rules of Prof Cond 5-200(E); ABA Model Rules of Prof Cond 3.4(e).

- Engaging in prejudicial argument. *Love v Wolf, supra.*

- Making impossible promises of proof. See, *e.g., Love v Wolf, supra* ("[t]here isn't a bigger con outfit in the world than [defendant], and I will prove it before I get through with this case").

- Improperly referring to the defendant's insurance. See, *e.g., Neumann v Bishop* (1976) 59 CA3d 451, 473, 130 CR 786 (by using term "defense interests").

- Addressing individual jurors. See, *e.g., Neumann v Bishop, supra* (calling a juror by name and making a comment about her; singling out another juror and implying that he had a closed mind).

- Discussing the law without court permission. See *Williams v Goodman* (1963) 214 CA2d 856, 29 CR 877.

- Improperly referring to settlement and dismissal of action with former defendants. *Granville v Parsons* (1968) 259 CA2d 298, 301, 66 CR 149.

- Improperly referring to the defendant's financial or corporate status to appeal to jurors' sympathies. *Brokopp v Ford Motor Co.* (1977) 71 CA3d 841, 860, 139 CR 888.

- Appealing to jurors to calculate damages as an amount that they or their loved ones would expect if they were in the plaintiff's position (the so-called Golden Rule argument). *Brokopp v Ford Motor Co., supra.*

§29.6 4. Misconduct During Examination of Witnesses

The following may constitute attorney misconduct during the examination of witnesses:

- Repeating questions ruled out by the judge. *McCollum v Barr* (1918) 38 CA 411, 429, 176 P 463. See also *Simmons v Southern Pac. Transp. Co.* (1976) 62 CA3d 341, 133 CR 42. Such questions may be allowed, however, based on an offer of proof.

- Repeatedly questioning a witness on a subject about which the witness has denied having knowledge. *Estate of Martin* (1915) 170 C 657, 669, 151 P 138.

- Assuming and asserting facts not in evidence (Bus & P C §6068(d); Cal Rules of Prof Cond 5-200), *e.g.,* engaging in the "do you know" type of examination to bring before the jury facts that have not been proved (see *Love v Wolf* (1964) 226 CA2d 378, 38 CR 183; *Dastagir v Dastagir* (1952) 109 CA2d 809, 241 P2d 656; *McDonald v Price* (1947) 80 CA2d 150, 181 P2d 115). See also *Simmons v Southern Pac. Transp. Co.* (1976) 62 CA3d 341, 356, 133 CR 42. Compare these improper "do you know" questions with proper "isn't it a fact" questions asked during cross-examination about disputed facts that have already been admitted into evidence. See *Marcus v Palm Harbor Hosp.* (1967) 253 CA2d 1008, 1015, 61 CR 702.

- Fraternizing with jurors or attempting to curry favor with them. *Garden Grove Sch. Dist. v Hendler* (1965) 63 C2d 141, 45 CR 313. See Cal Rules of Prof Cond 5-320.

- Asking question calling for inadmissible evidence, *e.g.,* inquiring in a civil case about the witness's previous plea of no contest to a criminal charge. Pen C §1016.

- Displaying prejudicial material in plain view of jurors. See, *e.g., Richardson v Employers Liab. Assur. Corp.* (1972) 25 CA3d 232, 242, 102 CR 547 (in action against liability insurer for refusing to settle claim, newspaper with headline "Didn't Settle in Policy Limits" left on counsel table during jury recess and allowed to remain there while jurors in jury box).

- Arguing the merits of a case on the pretense of objecting to the offered evidence and making self-serving and gratuitous remarks. *Continental Dairy Equip. Co. v Lawrence* (1971) 17 CA3d 378, 384, 94 CR 887.

- Asking questions designed to arouse ethnic (*Kolaric v Kaufmann* (1968) 261 CA2d 20, 28, 67 CR 729) or sexual (*People v Fosselman* (1983) 33 C3d 572, 580, 189 CR 855) prejudices.

- Questioning one defendant about the inadequate insurance so that the jury understands that the other defendant, a large corporation, would be the only party able to satisfy a large judgment. *Self v General Motors Corp.* (1974) 42 CA3d 1, 12, 116 CR 575.

§29.7   5. Misconduct During Argument

Counsel has wide latitude during final argument. *People v Boyd* (1990) 222 CA3d 541, 571, 271 CR 738; *Rogers v Foppiano* (1937) 23 CA2d 87, 72 P2d 239. There are limits to this rule, however. In *People v Espinoza* (1992) 3 C4th 806, 820, 12 CR2d 682, the California Supreme Court summarized the rules relating to prosecutorial misconduct in criminal cases:

> A prosecutor's rude and intemperate behavior violates the federal Constitution when it comprises a pattern of conduct "so egregious that it infects the trial with such unfairness as to make the conviction a denial of due process." [*People v Harris* (1989) 47 C3d 1047, 1084, 255 CR 352, citing *Donnelly v DeChristoforo* (1974) 416 US 637, 642, 40 L Ed 2d 431, 446, 94 S Ct 1868.] But conduct by a prosecutor that does not render a criminal trial fundamentally unfair is prosecutorial misconduct under state law only if it involves "the use of deceptive or reprehensible methods to attempt to persuade either the court or the jury." [*People v Haskett* (1982) 30 C3d 841, 866, 180 CR 640, quoting *People v Strickland* (1974) 11 C3d 946, 955, 114 CR 632.] Included within the deceptive or reprehensible methods we have held to constitute prosecutorial misconduct are personal attacks on the integrity of opposing counsel. [*People v Bell* (1989) 49 C3d 502, 538, 262 CR 1.]

Generally, an appellate court will not review a claim of misconduct in the absence of an objection and request for admonition at trial. To preserve for appeal a claim of prosecutorial misconduct, the defense must make a timely objection at trial and request an admonition. Otherwise, the point is reviewable only if an admonition would not have cured the harm caused by the misconduct. See also *People v Rowland* (1992) 4 C4th 238, 274, 14 CR2d 377; *People v Gionis* (1995) 9 C4th 1196, 40 CR2d 456.

The following behavior has been held to be prejudicial misconduct:

- Making remarks intended to play on the jurors' emotions of sympathy, shock, and horror (*Horn v Atchison, T. & S.F. Ry.* (1964) 61 C2d 602, 39 CR 721) or to arouse ethnic prejudices (*Kolaric v Kaufmann* (1968) 261 CA2d 20, 25, 67 CR 729). For example, in *People v Pitts* (1990) 223 CA3d 606, 273 CR 757, the court examined various instances of misconduct and overturned the verdict because the prosecutor improperly appealed to the jurors' self-interest by arguing that their time would be wasted if one juror failed to vote for conviction, used religious references to "turn Christ into an unsworn witness," and generally attempted to play on the passions and prejudices of the jurors. See also *People v Siripongs* (1988) 45 C3d 548, 247 CR 729 (error for prosecutor to make reference to victims' families in penalty phase argument to jury; error was harmless because trial court promptly admonished jury); *Du Jardin v City of Oxnard* (1995) 38 CA4th 174, 45 CR2d 48 (attorney's warning to jurors that verdict in favor of plaintiff could result in loss of social services in the community constituted misconduct and requires retrial).

- Denouncing opposing counsel with or without justification. *People v Hill* (1998) 17 C4th 800, 832, 72 CR2d 656 (prosecutor commits misconduct if he or she attacks integrity of defense counsel or casts aspersions on defense counsel); *Peacock v Levy* (1931) 114 CA 246, 299 P 790. See also Bus & P C §6068(f). Bus & P C §6068(f); *Simmons v Southern Pac. Transp. Co.* (1976) 62 CA3d 341, 352, 133 CR 42. For example, in *People v Lindsey* (1988) 205 CA3d 112, 252 CR 96, the court held that it was prejudicial error for the trial court to allow the prosecutor, during closing argument, to condemn defense counsel for not disclosing an alibi defense before trial. In *People v Hawthorne* (1992) 4 C4th 43, 14 CR2d 133, the supreme court held that the trial court erred in permitting the prosecutor in a death penalty case to read to the jury from a dissenting United States Supreme Court opinion stating that defense counsel in a criminal case should act as an advocate for the defendant and not as a seeker of the truth. The court held, however, that such remarks were not prejudicial. But see *People v Morris* (1988) 46 C3d 1, 36, 249 CR 119, in which the court held that the prosecutor did not impermissibly comment on the defendant's failure to testify by commenting on the state of the evidence (*e.g.,* "not a shred of evidence to suggest anybody else did the killing") or the defense's failure to introduce evidence or call witnesses.

- Charging willful suppression of evidence because opposing counsel has failed to call a witness when opposing counsel is under no duty to call that witness. *Keena v United R.R.* (1925) 197 C 148, 239 P 1061.

- Alleging collusion between the defendant and a codefendant without any support in the record. *Beecher v Stafford* (1927) 83 CA 408, 256 P 870.

- Making untrue inflammatory statements. See, *e.g., Jonte v Key Sys.* (1949) 89 CA2d 654, 201 P2d 562 (stating that defendant bus company consistently repudiates legitimate claims against it); *People v Stanley* (1986) 187 CA3d 248, 254, 232 CR 22, disapproved on another ground in *People v Bennett* (1991) 54 C3d 1032, 1038, 2 CR2d 8 (erroneously arguing matters of law did not create reversible error, because defense raised no objection, which would have resulted in trial court admonition curing any error). See also *People v Bell* (1989) 49 C3d 502, 539, 262 CR 1.

- Alluding to large verdicts awarded in other similar cases. *Salgo v Leland Stanford Jr. Univ. Bd. of Trustees* (1957) 154 CA2d 560, 317 P2d 170.

- Alluding to prejudicial newspaper articles. *People v Purvis* (1963) 60

C2d 323, 33 CR 104, overruled on other grounds in *People v Morse* (1964) 60 C2d 631, 36 CR 201.

- Misstating evidence. *People v Hill* (1998) 17 C4th 800, 823, 72 CR2d 656; *People v Purvis, supra.* See Cal Rules of Prof Cond 5-200.

- Referring to facts not in evidence. *People v Hill* (1998) 17 C4th 800, 827, 72 CR2d 656; *City of Los Angeles v Decker* (1977) 18 C3d 860, 870, 135 CR 647; *Malkasian v Irwin* (1964) 61 C2d 738, 40 CR 78. See Cal Rules of Prof Cond 5-200.

- Misstating law. *People v Hill* (1998) 17 C4th 800, 829, 72 CR2d 656 (improper for prosecutor to misstate law generally and particularly to attempt to absolve prosecution from its prima facie obligation to overcome reasonable doubt on all elements).

- Referring to the parties' wealth or poverty. *Hoffman v Brandt* (1966) 65 C2d 549, 553, 55 CR 417; *Alberts v Lytle* (1934) 1 CA2d 682, 37 P2d 705. See also *Seimon v Southern Pac. Transp. Co.* (1977) 67 CA3d 600, 606, 136 CR 787; 1 Witkin, California Evidence, *Circumstantial Evidence* §§138-139 (4th ed 2000). Note that such reference is permissible when punitive damages are sought. See, *e.g., Roemer v Retail Credit Co.* (1975) 44 CA3d 926, 941, 119 CR 82. See also CC §3295 (allowing trial court to require plaintiff to produce evidence of prima facie case of liability for punitive damages before introducing evidence of defendant's financial condition).

- Appealing to jurors' self-interest as taxpayers. *Brokopp v Ford Motor Co.* (1977) 71 CA3d 841, 861, 139 CR 888.

- Referring to the extent of liability insurance coverage. Evid C §1155. See *Curtis v McAuliffe* (1930) 106 CA 1, 288 P 675; 1 Witkin, Evidence, *Circumstantial Evidence* §§133-137 (4th ed 2000).

- Engaging in improper argument to retaliate for improper argument by opposing counsel. *Luflin v City of Bakersfield* (1933) 131 CA 21, 20 P2d 788.

- Using material not admitted into evidence to support argument. See, *e.g., Weisbart v Flohr* (1968) 260 CA2d 281, 291, 67 CR 114 (toys).

- Expressing a personal belief on the reliability of a witness. *People v Gates* (1987) 43 C3d 1168, 1188, 240 CR 666. Compare *Gates* with *People v Adcox* (1988) 47 C3d 207, 236, 253 CR 55 (prosecutor's use of pronoun "I" in argument to jury was proper because it was intended to convey deductions and inferences warranted by evidence; prosecutor may use appropriate "epithets" warranted by evidence). See also *People v Brown* (1989) 212 CA3d 1409, 1423, 261 CR 262, disapproved on other grounds in *People v Hayes* (1990) 52 C3d 577, 628 n10, 276

CR 874 (prosecutor's statement of belief about defendant's guilt did not imply possession of proof of guilt beyond that examined by jury). In *People v Fauber* (1992) 2 C4th 792, 9 CR2d 24, no prejudicial error was committed by the prosecutor in reading to the jury a prosecution witness's plea agreement containing language that could have implied that the prosecution was "vouching" for the witness's credibility, because the prosecutor's determination of witness credibility was irrelevant to the witness's veracity at trial. See also *People v Gionis* (1995) 9 C4th 1196, 40 CR2d 456 (no reversible error for prosecutor to quote many sources saying in various ways that lawyers are liars).

- Reliance on biblical doctrine. The California Supreme Court has repeatedly condemned the reliance by prosecutors on biblical scripture to support a death penalty. See *People v Hill* (1998) 17 C4th 800, 836, 72 CR2d 656; *People v Wash* (1993) 6 C4th 215, 261, 24 CR2d 421; *People v Montiel* (1993) 5 C4th 877, 934, 21 CR2d 705; *People v Sandoval* (1992) 4 C4th 155, 192, 14 CR2d 342.

§29.8 6. Misconduct After Trial

The following may constitute attorney misconduct after trial:

- Attempting to influence jurors by conducting direct or indirect investigation of jurors. See Cal Rules of Prof Cond 5-320(D)-(E).

- Attempting to tamper with reporter's transcript. See Pen C §132 (felony to offer in evidence as true any, *e.g.*, paper, document that has been altered); Cal Rules of Prof Cond 5-200(B) (may not seek to mislead a judge).

§29.9 C. Determining Prejudicial Effect

In ruling on an objection or a motion based on misconduct, the trial judge's primary concern is the degree of prejudice caused by the misconduct. It is immaterial for this purpose whether the misconduct resulted from inadvertence, negligence, or willful design. See, *e.g.*, *People v Bolton* (1979) 23 C3d 208, 214, 152 CR 141 (prosecutor's misconduct need not be intentional to constitute reversible error). The prejudicial error standard of review applies (see *People v Watson* (1956) 46 C2d 818, 836, 299 P2d 243) unless a federal constitutional error was involved. In that event, the *Chapman* test applies (see *Chapman v California* (1967) 386 US 18, 17 L Ed 2d 705, 87 S Ct 824; *Neder v U.S.* (1999) 527 US 1, 144 L Ed 2d 35, 119 S Ct 1827). The judge weighs such factors as the type of case, the nature of the misconduct, and its probable effect on the jury's determination of the issues. Misconduct that is prejudicial in the setting of one trial may not be deemed prejudicial in a different trial.

The judge decides whether conduct is improper and the degree or prejudicial effect of the misconduct by considering:

- The setting in which the misconduct occurred;
- Whether the court had previously warned counsel;
- The likelihood that the prejudice will affect the jury and to what extent; and
- Whether a curative admonition will be sufficient under the circumstances.

The trial judge has wide discretion in determining whether misconduct is prejudicial in the context of a motion for a new trial. If the judge grants a new trial on the ground of prejudicial misconduct (see §29.17), the order will ordinarily be affirmed on appeal even though the degree of prejudice shown falls short of that required for reversal of a judgment on the verdict. *Malkasian v Irwin* (1964) 61 C2d 738, 40 CR 78. See also *Seimon v Southern Pac. Transp. Co.* (1977) 67 CA3d 600, 604, 136 CR 787; *Laboa v Calderon* (2000) 224 F3d 972; *Lowery v Anders* (2000) 225 F3d 833 (federal habeas corpus review; Ninth Circuit applied harmless error standard of *Brecht v Abrahamson* (1993) 507 US 619, 638, 123 L Ed 2d 353, 373, 113 S Ct 1710; see California Criminal Law Procedure and Practice §43.34 (7th ed Cal CEB 2004)).

Similarly, if a motion for a new trial based on alleged misconduct was made and denied at the trial level, the appellate court will give considerable weight to the trial judge's conclusion that no prejudice resulted, because "the trial judge is in a better position . . . to determine whether the jury was prejudicially influenced." *Vogt v McLaughlin* (1959) 172 CA2d 498, 504, 342 P2d 481. See also *Grimshaw v Ford Motor Co.* (1981) 119 CA3d 757, 793, 174 CR 348.

Occasionally, however, an appellate court will reverse a judgment on the ground of misconduct of counsel, even though the trial judge denied a motion for a new trial based on this ground, ruling in effect that the judge erroneously concluded that the misconduct was not prejudicial. See, *e.g., City of Los Angeles v Decker* (1977) 18 C3d 860, 135 CR 647. For example, in *People v Evans* (1952) 39 C2d 242, 246 P2d 636, a prosecution for lewd conduct with a child, the only evidence regarding the identity of the assailant was the testimony of the victim. In an effort to corroborate this evidence, the prosecutor asked various witnesses leading questions primarily designed to present prejudicial matter that could not be proved. The defendant was convicted, and his motion for a new trial was denied. Observing that the main issue of identity was "closely balanced," the California Supreme Court reversed the trial court decision because the misconduct "could not have had any other effect upon the jury than to tip the scales against the accused." 39 C2d at 252. See also *People v Wagner* (1975) 13 C3d 612, 119 CR 457 (effect of prosecutor's misconduct was to impair defendant's credibility).

In *People v Adams* (1960) 182 CA2d 27, 5 CR 795, the defendant had been convicted of five counts of kidnapping and robbery, and his motion for a new trial was denied. On three of these counts, the case hinged on the veracity of certain prosecution witnesses who had taken, and presumably passed, lie detector tests. In his argument to the jury, the prosecuting attorney stated that to disbelieve these witnesses would be to impugn the integrity of the police officers who administered the tests and of the district attorney who called these witnesses to testify. Noting that the issue on which these witnesses testified was "a matter of fine balance," the appellate court held that the prosecutor's misconduct in throwing "the reputations of the police and the district attorney into the scales" resulted in a miscarriage of justice. 182 CA2d at 37. Although the appellate court reversed the defendant's conviction on the three counts discussed above, it affirmed his conviction on the two remaining counts. In his argument regarding these two counts, the prosecuting attorney had made improper comments about the defendant's prior convictions. Emphasizing that there was "strong evidence" of the defendant's guilt on these counts, "not dependent upon the inferences and conclusions which [the attorney's comments] would invoke in the minds of the jurors," the appellate court ruled that, under the circumstances, this particular misconduct had not been prejudicial. 182 CA2d at 38.

The applicability of these principles to civil actions is illustrated by *Hoffman v Brandt* (1966) 65 C2d 549, 550, 55 CR 417. Defense counsel's improper comment during argument that an adverse verdict would put the defendant in a home for the indigent was held sufficiently prejudicial to warrant reversal of the judgment inasmuch as "the question of liability was very close."

In *Garden Grove Sch. Dist. v Hendler* (1965) 63 C2d 141, 45 CR 313, a condemnation suit, the only issue was the value of the condemned property. The jury awarded a sum considerably below what the defendant property owner contended it was worth. Reversing the trial court decision, the California Supreme Court concluded that the defendant would have received a more favorable verdict but for prejudicial statements made by plaintiff's counsel during the trial and in his summation to the jury (*e.g.,* asserting as a fact that the defendant had bought the property for speculation knowing it was to be condemned, although there was no evidence of that fact). In applying this "but for" test to assess prejudice, the supreme court emphasized that plaintiff's counsel had interjected improper statements repeatedly throughout the trial and not just in a few isolated instances. See also *Stone v Foster* (1980) 106 CA3d 334, 355, 164 CR 901 (misconduct prejudicial because court could not find that jury was not influenced by impropriety in deciding amount of award).

D. Remedies

1. Objection

§29.10 a. Purpose

A timely objection to misconduct coupled with a request for a curative admonition on the misconduct is usually a prerequisite to a later motion for mistrial (see §29.16) or an appeal (see §29.18). See §29.14.

On arguing the objection out of the jury's presence, see §29.12.

§29.11 b. Timeliness

The objection to misconduct must be asserted promptly together with a request that the jury be admonished to disregard the conduct. Unless an objection is made immediately, the misconduct is waived in most situations. *Horn v Atchison, T. & S.F. Ry.* (1964) 61 C2d 602, 39 CR 721. See also *People v Fosselman* (1983) 33 C3d 572, 580, 189 CR 855; *Warner Constr. Corp. v City of Los Angeles* (1970) 2 C3d 285, 85 CR 444. This rule is based on the premise that the injurious effect of an attorney's misconduct can usually be cured if the judge admonishes the jury to disregard what occurred. See *Nelson v Gaunt* (1981) 125 CA3d 623, 644, 178 CR 167; *Barlin v Barlin* (1957) 156 CA2d 143, 319 P2d 87.

A waiver resulting from failure to object promptly or from failure to accompany the objection with a request for an admonition (see §29.14) eliminates any right to complain of the misconduct on appeal. See, *e.g., People v Green* (1980) 27 C3d 1, 164 CR 1; *Grimshaw v Ford Motor Co.* (1981) 119 CA3d 757, 798, 174 CR 348. The trial judge, however, has the power to disregard this waiver and grant a motion for a new trial based on the misconduct. *Malkasian v Irwin* (1964) 61 C2d 738, 747, 40 CR 78. See also *Seimon v Southern Pac. Transp. Co.* (1977) 67 CA3d 600, 604, 136 CR 787.

An exception to the waiver rule is recognized when the misconduct was so prejudicial that it could not have been cured by a timely admonition to the jury. *People v Green* (1980) 27 C3d 1, 34, 164 CR 1; *Balistreri v Turner* (1964) 227 CA2d 236, 244, 38 CR 553; *Dastagir v Dastagir* (1952) 109 CA2d 809, 819, 241 P2d 656. See also *Simmons v Southern Pac. Transp. Co.* (1976) 62 CA3d 341, 358, 133 CR 42; *People v McDaniel* (1976) 16 C3d 156, 176, 127 CR 467; *People v Andrews* (1970) 14 CA3d 40, 48, 92 CR 49. When egregious attorney misconduct occurs, counsel should consider immediately moving for a mistrial. See §29.16.

Another exception to the waiver rule applies when counsel persists in repeated misconduct but the trial judge overrules opposing counsel's objections. If it is clear that further objections to that misconduct would be futile, opposing counsel may refrain from objecting without waiving any rights. *People v Hill* (1998) 17 C4th 800, 820, 72 CR2d 656 (when counsel's continual misconduct was coupled with court's failure to rein in counsel's excesses, opposing counsel excused from obligation to continually object, state grounds, and ask that jury be admonished, and all of asserted grounds for misconduct preserved for appeal); *Peacock v Levy* (1931) 114 CA 246, 299 P 790. See also *Simmons v Southern Pac. Transp. Co.* (1976) 62 CA3d 341, 359, 133 CR 42 (appellate court recognized that repeated objections and requests for admonitions to repeated and flagrant misconduct would have overemphasized objectionable material and that admonitions "would not have unrung the bell").

§29.12 c. Objecting to Misconduct

In the past, counsel objecting to misconduct would "assign" the improper statement or conduct as misconduct. Depending on strategy, this is done either outside the presence of the jury or in open court. Following the modern practice of using plain English, most counsel today "object" to misconduct in this manner:

> Objection, Your Honor. I object as misconduct counsel's _ _[describe conduct, e.g., counsel's showing that photograph to the jury after Your Honor has ruled that it is inadmissible]_ _.

Ordinarily, this statement should be coupled with a request for a curative admonition to the jury. See §29.14. If the misconduct is egregious, the objection should be accompanied by a motion for mistrial (see §29.16) or, when circumstances permit, a request for a finding of contempt (see §29.15).

Whenever the misconduct is clearly intentional, counsel should consider adding the following request:

> I further request that counsel be warned to stop this repeated and intentional misconduct on pain of being held in contempt.

If the misconduct continues, this request may prompt the judge to invoke sua sponte the more drastic measure of initiating contempt proceedings. See §29.15.

If counsel does not wish the statement or conduct that is the basis for assigning misconduct to be repeated or emphasized before the jury, counsel may object to it without describing it at that time (*e.g.*, "I object as misconduct counsel's last remarks") and then request to approach the bench to place the impropriety and relief sought on the record outside the jury's presence.

§29.13 d. Laying Foundation for Misconduct That Occurred Without Judge's Knowledge

An act of misconduct may occur outside the judge's presence. For example, counsel may be seen talking with a juror outside the courtroom. See *Garden Grove Sch. Dist. v Hendler* (1965) 63 C2d 141, 45 CR 313. Misconduct may even occur in the courtroom in the judge's presence without the judge's knowledge. For example, stage whispers may be overheard by the jury but not by the judge. If the judge has no personal knowledge of the acts constituting the misconduct, counsel must make a foundational showing to the judge that proves what happened. The type of proof required depends on the circumstances of each case. On some occasions, testimony may be necessary; on others, written declarations may suffice.

To lay a foundation for proving misconduct, counsel should fully describe what occurred so that it will be part of the record.

§29.14   2. Requesting Curative Admonition

Counsel objecting to misconduct must request that the judge give a curative admonition (instruction) to the jury. This request provides the judge with an opportunity to obviate the prejudicial effect of the misconduct and to prevent additional prejudice caused by further misconduct. See *Horn v Atchison, T. & S.F. Ry.* (1964) 61 C2d 602, 39 CR 721. See also *Whitfield v Roth* (1974) 10 C3d 874, 892, 112 CR 540. The following is a typical request for a curative admonition:

> Your Honor, I request that the jury be admonished [or instructed] to disregard that photograph.

The courts have uniformly held that a prompt admonition is a sufficient cure for misconduct except in "extreme" cases. See, *e.g., Tingley v Times Mirror Co.* (1907) 151 C 1, 23, 89 P 1097. See also *Whitfield v Roth, supra.*

In *People v Riel* (2000) 22 C4th 1153, 1212, 96 CR2d 1, defense counsel argued on appeal that the prosecutor committed many acts of misconduct but counsel had not objected at trial. The appeals court held that "[b]ecause an admonition could easily have cured any harm from any misconduct, the contentions are not cognizable on appeal."

This premise is unrealistic when severe misconduct occurs. As trial lawyers say, it is impossible to "unring the bell" or "unscramble the egg," *i.e.,* cure the misconduct, in extreme situations; a mistrial is necessary. See §53.3. Although many judges merely advise the jury to disregard the objectionable matter (see CACI 106 and 5003 (formerly BAJI 1.02)), a more effective instruction can be adapted from the California Supreme Court's suggested language in *People v Bolton* (1979) 23 C3d 208, 215 n5, 152 CR 141. Even though *Bolton* was a criminal case involving prosecutorial misconduct, the suggested language should be appropriate in a civil matter because both types of cases may necessitate the strong rebuke of counsel. A possible adaptation of the suggestion in *Bolton* follows:

> Ladies and Gentlemen of the jury, counsel for the _ _[plaintiff/defendant]_ _ has just _ _[e.g., made improper remarks about the _ _[defendant/plaintiff]_ _ /shown you a photograph that I have ruled inadmissible]_ _. I want you to know that counsel _ _[e.g., has absolutely no evidence to present to you to back up those remarks/acted improperly in showing you something that is not to be considered by you in reaching a decision]_ _. Counsel's actions are an attempt to prejudice you against the _ _[plaintiff/defendant]_ _. Were you to _ _[e.g., believe these unwarranted remarks/rely on what is depicted in the photograph in finding against the _ _[plaintiff/defendant]_]_ _, I would have to declare a mistrial. Therefore, you are instructed to disregard [*the conduct detailed*].

Before counsel objects and seeks a curative admonition, consideration should be given to whether the impropriety has actually prejudiced the client's case.

Counsel should also be familiar with the particular trial judge's attitude toward citing an attorney for misconduct. Unless counsel is certain of the prejudice and confident that the judge will grant the request, the benefit of objecting may not outweigh the damage that a denied objection may cause. In considering whether to object, counsel should also remember that the right to claim the misconduct as an error on appeal will be waived if counsel does not make a timely objection and request for a curative admonition. See §29.11. Note that an attorney who secures a favorable ruling on an objection of prosecutorial misconduct, and then fails to inform the court that no admonition to the jury has been made, may waive the defendant's right to raise the issue on appeal. *People v Heldenburg* (1990) 219 CA3d 468, 474, 268 CR 255.

Many judges are reluctant to cite an attorney for misconduct and admonish the jury because of the prejudicial impact of this action on the jury. In deciding whether to grant counsel's request, the judge will balance the prejudicial effect of the impropriety against the prejudicial impact of citing misconduct and admonishing the jury. If opposing counsel commits minor improprieties that do not warrant a formal objection and request for an admonition, counsel may ask to approach the bench or have a chambers conference during a jury recess to request that the judge warn opposing counsel to stop violating the rules or risk a mistrial.

§29.15 3. Contempt

If an attorney's misconduct is willful and repeated despite clear warnings, the trial judge may find the attorney in contempt of court. CCP §§128(a)(5), 1209(a). See *Gallagher v Municipal Court* (1948) 31 C2d 784, 192 P2d 905, discussed in chap 57. See also *Hawk v Superior Court* (1974) 42 CA3d 108, 116 CR 713. In an extreme case, an attorney's willful and repeated disobedience may result in suspension or disbarment. Bus & P C §6103.

For a comprehensive discussion of the types of attorney misconduct that warrant contempt, see 7 Witkin, California Procedure, *Trial* §§202-211 (4th ed 1997). On the differences between "direct" (occurring in the judge's immediate view or presence), "indirect" (not occurring in the judge's immediate view or presence), and "hybrid" (occurring in the judge's presence but possibly excusable because of events occurring outside the courtroom) contempt, see California Criminal Law Procedure and Practice, chap 51 (7th ed Cal CEB 2004). For the distinction between civil (CCP §1209(a)) and criminal (Pen C §166) contempt, see Crim Law §51.4. See also §57.3.

§29.16 4. Motion for Mistrial

The prejudicial effect of most types of attorney misconduct presumably can be cured by a prompt admonition to the jury. See §29.14. Because certain incidents cannot be effectively erased from the jurors' minds, however, a mistrial should be requested when proceeding with the trial would deprive the injured party of his or her right to a fair trial. To move for a mistrial, counsel should add the following statement to the assignment of misconduct (see §29.12):

> I move for a mistrial on the ground that the effect of this misconduct is so prejudicial that a fair trial is now impossible.

For the same reasons that counsel might decide to ask to approach the bench to object to misconduct (see §29.12) and request a curative admonition (see §29.14), counsel might also wish to move for a mistrial out of the jurors' presence. This procedure prevents their repeated exposure to the misconduct and precludes their becoming aware of an adverse ruling on the motion. The motion, and the judge's reasons for granting or rejecting it, should be made on the record.

For further discussion of this remedy, see chap 56. Note that a motion for mistrial is not a prerequisite to a later motion for a new trial or an appeal. See 1 Stanbury, California Trial and Appellate Practice §570 (1958).

§29.17   5. Motion for New Trial

In civil actions, a new trial may be ordered on all or part of the issues if, as a result of the misconduct, a party was "prevented from having a fair trial." CCP §657(1); *City of Los Angeles v Decker* (1977) 18 C3d 860, 870, 135 CR 647. To make such a motion, counsel must serve and file a written notice of intention to move for a new trial within 15 days after notice of entry of judgment is mailed by the clerk or served by a party and in any event no later than 180 days after entry of judgment. CCP §659. Counsel must serve and file all declarations supporting the motion within ten days after service of the notice of motion, unless the trial judge grants an extension of time, which may not exceed an additional 20 days. CCP §659a. For a suggested form, see California Trial Practice: Civil Procedure During Trial §§25.92–25.95 (3d ed Cal CEB 1995).

In criminal cases, a new trial may be granted "when the district attorney or other counsel prosecuting the case has been guilty of prejudicial misconduct during the trial thereof before a jury." Pen C §1181(5). The prosecution does not have a corresponding right to a new trial following an acquittal based on the misconduct of defense counsel. The trial judge, however, may punish such misconduct through contempt proceedings. See §29.15. In a criminal case, an "application" for a new trial (Pen C §1181) may be made by either oral or written motion. *People v Simon* (1989) 208 CA3d 841, 847, 256 CR 373. The motion for a new trial must be made before judgment, before the granting of probation, before commitment of a defendant for observation as a mentally disordered sex offender, or before commitment of a defendant for narcotics addiction or insanity. Pen C §1182. For discussion of the applicable procedure, see California Criminal Law Procedure and Practice §§34.12–34.13 (7th ed Cal CEB 2004); 4, 6 Witkin & Epstein, California Criminal Law,

Introduction to Criminal Procedure §8; *Criminal Judgment* §§111-125 (3d ed 2000).

A party injured by opposing counsel's misconduct should state a prompt objection rather than planning to use the misconduct as a basis for a motion for a new trial in the event of an unfavorable verdict. Although the trial judge can overlook the waiver and grant a new trial (*Malkasian v Irwin* (1964) 61 C2d 738, 747, 40 CR 78), counsel should not risk being foreclosed from making a successful motion for a new trial. Even if a prior objection is overruled, it may help convince the judge, when the motion for a new trial is made, that the moving party was genuinely injured by the misconduct because it influenced the verdict. If the prior objection was sustained and the judge instructed the jury to disregard the misconduct, the judge may nevertheless grant a motion for a new trial based on the misconduct. *Baroni v Rosenberg* (1930) 209 C 4, 284 P 1111.

In ruling on the motion for a new trial, the judge must examine the entire record and decide whether the attorney's misconduct "resulted in a miscarriage of justice." Cal Const art VI, §13. See Evid C §353. To make this determination, the judge must assess the degree of prejudice caused by the misconduct. See §29.9.

§29.18   6. Appeal

Ultimately, the injured party may appeal from the judgment. When the error that occurred does not implicate the federal constitution, a reversal will be ordered only if the appellate court, after making its own independent "examination of the entire cause, including the evidence," decides that there was a "miscarriage of justice." Cal Const art VI, §13. See, *e.g., People v Green* (1980) 27 C3d 1, 34, 164 CR 1. See Evid C §353. When federal constitutional error is involved, the *Chapman* standard of review applies (see *Chapman v California* (1967) 386 US 18, 17 L Ed 2d 705, 87 S Ct 824; *Neder v U.S.* (1999) 527 US 1, 144 L Ed 2d 35, 119 S Ct 1827). *People v Bolton* (1979) 23 C3d 208, 214, 152 CR 141. For examples of such reversals, see *People v Purvis* (1963) 60 C2d 323, 33 CR 104 (prosecutor persisted in improper behavior despite repeated admonitions by trial judge); *Love v Wolf* (1964) 226 CA2d 378, 382, 38 CR 183 (appellate court termed misconduct "egregious beyond any in our experience"). Compare *Love* to *Bigboy v County of San Diego* (1984) 154 CA3d 397, 412, 201 CR 226, in which the appellate court reinstated the jury's verdict for the plaintiff and reversed the trial court's conditional new trial order despite the defendant's claim of an excessive award and misconduct by plaintiff's counsel. The applicable test is whether it is reasonably probable that a different verdict would have been reached had the misconduct not occurred. *People v Castaldia* (1959) 51 C2d 569, 573, 335 P2d 104. See, *e.g., Stone v Foster* (1980) 106 CA3d 334, 355, 164 CR 901 (misconduct held prejudicial because it was not possible to decide that jury was not influenced by misconduct in amount of award). Cases analyzing the prejudicial effect of misconduct by counsel under various circumstances are discussed in §29.9.

The trial court's determination of whether the misconduct was prejudicial is accorded great weight by the appellate court. *Stevens v Parke, Davis & Co.* (1973) 9 C3d 51, 72, 107 CR 45. Compare *Grimshaw v Ford Motor Co.* (1981) 119 CA3d 757, 793, 174 CR 348 (trial court's determination upheld), with *City of Los Angeles v Decker* (1977) 18 C3d 860, 135 CR 647 (trial court's determination not upheld).

In the absence of a defense objection to claimed prosecutorial misconduct in a criminal action, the court must first determine whether a timely objection and admonition would have cured the harm. If it would have, the contention of misconduct must be rejected; if it would not have, the court must determine, on the basis of the entire record, whether error occurred under the relevant standard of review. See *People v Gionis* (1995) 9 C4th 1196, 40 CR2d 456; *People v Martinez* (1987) 191 CA3d 1372, 237 CR 219; *People v Hutton* (1986) 187 CA3d 934, 232 CR 263.

§29.19 E. Alternatives to Objecting

On possible alternatives to objecting, see §§4.9–4.14.

§29.20 F. Stating the Objection

> Objection, Your Honor. I object as misconduct to _ _[*describe objectionable conduct, e.g., counsel's showing that photograph to the jury after Your Honor has ruled that it is inadmissible*]_ _, and

> [Option 1: Motion for mistrial; see §29.16, chap 56]

> I move for a mistrial on the ground that the effect of this misconduct is so prejudicial that a fair trial is now impossible.

> [Option 2: Motion for mistrial is not made or has been denied]

> I request that the jury be admonished _ _[*e.g., to disregard that photograph*]_ _.

> [Add if misconduct was clearly intentional]

> I further request that counsel be admonished to stop repeatedly committing this type of misconduct on pain of being held in contempt.

III. MISCONDUCT OF JUDGE

§29.21   A. Standards of Conduct

It is the duty of a trial judge to maintain a judicial attitude during trial, *i.e.,* to be temperate, attentive, patient, impartial, and courteous to counsel, witnesses, parties, and court staff and personnel. See Code of Judicial Ethics Canon 3(B)(4). See also *People v Campbell* (1958) 162 CA2d 776, 787, 329 P2d 82; *People v Williams* (1942) 55 CA2d 696, 703, 131 P2d 851. In *People v Fatone* (1985) 165 CA3d 1164, 211 CR 288, the court held that the cumulative impact of the judge's consistent and unjustified abuse of defense counsel before the jury, combined with a number of mistaken legal rulings in favor of the prosecution, deprived the defendant of the basic right to a fair trial. For further discussion, see §§29.26–29.27.

Although the trial judge has the power to comment on the evidence (see §29.22), the court must refrain from making remarks that

> deflect the minds of jurors from the evidence actually before them and cause them to reach conclusions based upon feeling, bias, and prejudice, rather than upon the evidence which has been properly received and from which alone they should arrive at verdicts under the law.

People v Williams, supra. A trial judge must be particularly mindful that lay jurors are deeply impressed and easily swayed by statements from the bench. See *Forte v Schiebe* (1956) 145 CA2d 296, 301, 302 P2d 336. See also *People v Cook* (1983) 33 C3d 400, 407, 189 CR 159, overruled in part by *People v Rodriguez* (1986) 42 C3d 730, 770, 230 CR 667. Measured against this obligation of neutrality is the duty of a trial judge to conduct an orderly trial and to protect the rights of litigants. See Code of Judicial Ethics Canon 3(B)(1)–(8). According to the Commentary to Code of Judicial Ethics Canon 3(B)(8), the judge's duty to hear all proceedings fairly and with patience is not inconsistent with the duty to dispose promptly of the business of the court. Courts can be efficient and businesslike while being patient and deliberate.

§29.22   B. Examples of Misconduct of Judge

The examples of misconduct in §§29.21–29.33 are not exhaustive. For other examples, see 7 Witkin, California Procedure, *Trial* §§256–265 (4th ed 1997).

§29.23   1. Abuse of Power to Comment on Evidence

The trial judge has the power to comment on the evidence and on the testimony and credibility of any witness. Cal Const art VI, §10. See also Pen C §§1093, 1127. The California Supreme Court has recommended a wide use of this power by stating that this provision makes the judge

> a real factor in the administration of justice, rather than a mere referee.... [H]e is no longer confined to a colorless recital of the evidence but may analyze the testimony and express his views with respect to its credibility.

See *People v Friend* (1958) 50 C2d 570, 577, 327 P2d 97 (contrary dicta on another point criticized in *People v Cook* (1983) 33 C3d 400, 413 n13, 189 CR 159). The judge may restrict comments to only certain portions of the evidence, or to the credibility of only certain witnesses, and is not obliged to sum up all the testimony. *People v Ivy* (1966) 244 CA2d 406, 411, 53 CR 47; *People v Welborn* (1966) 242 CA2d 668, 51 CR 644. See also *Clark v Laughlin* (1977) 68 CA3d 506, 513, 137 CR 354 (trial judge may comment on portion of testimony in malpractice action and express a fair opinion on negligence when instruction explains that his comments are advisory and can be disregarded by jury).

The trial judge's power to comment on the evidence has limitations, but it is difficult to precisely distinguish comments that are authorized by Cal Const art VI, §10 from those that are not. The test for determining whether the comments are proper examines "the context and extent of the comments and the peculiar circumstances under which comment is made." *People v Cook* (1983) 33 C3d 400, 408, 189 CR 159, overruled in part by *People v Rodriguez* (1986) 42 C3d 730, 770, 230 CR 667. For example, the trial judge "may not withdraw material evidence from the jury's consideration or distort the testimony, and his comments should be temperately and fairly made." *People v Friend, supra*. See also *People v Cook, supra*. In addition, the judge may not do the following:

- Comment on the exercise of a privilege unless requested to give an instruction dispelling unfavorable inferences that might be drawn because a privilege was exercised. Evid C §913. See §34.17.

- Comment on the failure of the defendant in a criminal case to explain or deny evidence. *Griffin v California* (1965) 380 US 609, 14 L Ed 2d 106, 85 S Ct 1229. See 2 Witkin, California Evidence, *Witnesses* §§432–443 (4th ed 2000); §34.26. See also chap 46 (privilege against self-incrimination), chap 47 (privilege not to be called as a witness and not to testify).

- Express his or her views on the ultimate question of an accused's guilt or innocence. *People v Cook* (1983) 33 C3d 400, 413, 189 CR 159, overruled in part by *People v Rodriguez* (1986) 42 C3d 730, 770, 230 CR 667.

In *Lewis v Robertson & Sons* (1984) 162 CA3d 650, 654, 208 CR 699, the appellate court found judicial misconduct in a trial court's comments on the evidence and the issue of proximate cause in a slip and fall case, despite the trial court's admonition that these comments were advisory and nonbinding. The appellate court noted that the trial court effectively removed the verdict from the jury when it stated that there was no evidence of a defect in the premises causing injury and when it misrepresented that the plaintiff had produced no evidence showing that he had suffered permanent injuries. 162 CA3d at 657.

The comment's timing is important in determining whether it has a prejudicial impact on the jury. For example, comments made when a jury in a criminal case is deadlocked can constitute error and may result in reversal of a conviction (*People v Cook* (1983) 33 C3d 400, 419, 189 CR 159, overruled in part by *People v Rodriguez* (1986) 42 C3d 730, 770, 230 CR 667), but comment made as part of the court's instructions before submitting the case to the jury is more likely to be permitted (33 C3d at 409 n8). Because the constitutional right to a fair trial is the basis for prohibiting comment when a jury is deadlocked, the *Cook* rule should apply equally to civil cases.

Although not directly an example of judicial misconduct by abuse of the judge's power to comment on evidence, an interesting analogous situation arose in *Dorshkind v Harry N. Koff Agency, Inc.* (1976) 64 CA3d 302, 308, 134 CR 344. The trial judge appointed a juror as foreman, an act held by the appellate court to be an improper violation of Cal Const art I, §16 (right to jury trial). Implicit in the appellate court's decision is the concern that the trial judge's action constituted an attempt to influence the jury's deliberations—the same consideration underlying the decisions finding judicial misconduct when the judge oversteps the bounds of fair comment.

Whenever a trial judge finds it necessary to comment on the evidence, the judge should give a cautionary admonition to the jurors that they are the exclusive triers of all questions of fact and the credibility of all witnesses. CACI 5000 and 5003–5004 (formerly BAJI 15.21) (civil); CALJIC 17.32 (criminal). See, *e.g., Clark v Laughlin* (1977) 68 CA3d 506, 512, 137 CR 354.

§29.24 2. Abuse of Power to Examine Witnesses or Prospective Witnesses

Although it is the right and sometimes the duty of a trial judge to examine witnesses, it is misconduct for the judge to ask questions that convey to the jury an opinion regarding the credibility of a witness. See *McCartney v Commission on Judicial Qualifications* (1974) 12 C3d 512, 533, 116 CR 260; *People v Rigney* (1961) 55 C2d 236, 10 CR 625. See also *People v Gates* (1979) 97 CA3d Supp 10, 13, 158 CR 759. The rationale for this rule was stated in *Karvoski v Grant* (1938) 30 CA2d 171, 177, 85 P2d 944, as follows:

> It needs no citation to convince any unbiased observer that a jury has both ears and eyes open for any little word or act of the trial judge from which they may gather enough to read his mind and get his opinion of the merits of the issues under investigation. Trial judges therefore would better leave any interrogation of witnesses upon their part until the conclusion of the examination by counsel, direct, cross, redirect and recross, and then, if anything, in the judgment of the trial court, remains obscure, which may be material for the jury to know, and it seems desirable that an examination of the witness should be further pressed, then the trial judge may, and indeed should, intervene, so that the ends of justice may be subserved.

It is misconduct for the judge to examine prospective expert witnesses outside of court. *People v Archerd* (1970) 3 C3d 615, 638, 91 CR 397.

§29.25 3. Interference With Production of Proof

It is misconduct for a trial judge to exclude evidence simply because he or she has heard enough (*Caldwell v Caldwell* (1962) 204 CA2d 819, 22 CR 854), desires to limit proof to certain years (*Del Ruth v Del Ruth* (1946) 75 CA2d 638, 171 P2d 34), or feels that small children should not be called to testify in a divorce case (*Bole v Bole* (1946) 76 CA2d 344, 172 P2d 936), or because the evidence is "nauseating to sit here and listen to" (*National Auto. Ins. Co. v Fraties* (1941) 46 CA2d 431, 433, 115 P2d 997). Under some circumstances, repeatedly nagging counsel to hurry may constitute misconduct. *Murr v Murr* (1948) 87 CA2d 511, 197 P2d 369. Setting time and witness limit rules before trial begins, however, is common.

On the right to present evidence, see chap 1.

§29.26 4. Coercive Actions

It is misconduct for a trial judge to coerce compliance with personal preferences through pressures, threats, or intimidation. Examples of such misconduct include the following:

- Coercing counsel to waive argument (*Shippy v Peninsula Rapid Transit Co.* (1925) 197 C 290, 240 P 785);

- Coercing settlement in a nonjury case by indicating that the judge will not hear further evidence with an open mind, *e.g.,* advising counsel to "tell your clients that in my opinion it would be to their best interests to settle" (*Rosenfield v Vosper* (1941) 45 CA2d 365, 368, 114 P2d 29); or

- Pressuring the parties to dismiss a cause of action for separate maintenance (*Del Ruth v Del Ruth* (1946) 75 CA2d 638, 171 P2d 34).

§29.27 5. Disparagement of Counsel, Witness, or Party

It is misconduct for a judge to insult, ridicule, or otherwise disparage counsel, witnesses, or parties. *McCartney v Commission on Judicial Qualifications* (1974) 12 C3d 512, 533, 116 CR 260. See also *Gonzalez v Commission on Judicial Performance* (1983) 33 C3d 359, 371, 188 CR 880 (disparagement directed toward counsel, jurors, parties, and other judges). For example, in *People v Williams* (1942) 55 CA2d 696, 131 P2d 851, a prosecution for rape, the prosecuting attorney referred to one of the defendants as "the gentleman on the right." The judge interrupted with the comment that the word "gentleman" was unnecessary and inappropriate and remarked that he could think of a better name for the defendants, which made it obvious to the jury that he was convinced the defendants were guilty. This, coupled with other prejudicial errors, caused the appellate court to order a new trial. See also *Catchpole v Brannon* (1995) 36 CA4th 237, 42 CR2d 440 (trial court's finding that employee in a sexual harassment action was not believable rested on stereotyped thinking about women and misconceptions of the social and economic realities many women confront and therefore reflected a predetermined disposition by the court to rule against the employee based on her status as a woman).

It is also improper for a judge to advise the jury of negative personal views concerning the competence, honesty, or ethics of the attorneys in a trial. *People v Fatone* (1985) 165 CA3d 1164, 1174, 211 CR 288. Disparaging statements such as those described above must be distinguished from statements made by the trial judge for the purpose of admonishing counsel, witnesses, or parties guilty of misconduct. To preserve the order and dignity of the proceedings, the judge may properly reprimand offenders, even in the presence of the jury. *Hickambottom v Cooper Transp. Co.* (1960) 186 CA2d 479, 486, 9 CR 276.

The judge should avoid intemperate remarks when administering a reprimand. For a case in which the judge's excessive rebuke of an attorney was held to have been a contributing factor in denying a fair trial, see *People v Burns* (1952) 109 CA2d 524, 543, 241 P2d 308.

C. Remedies

§29.28   1. Objection

Counsel must immediately object to judicial misconduct or the error is waived and cannot be used as a ground for appeal. *People v Corrigan* (1957) 48 C2d 551, 310 P2d 953; *Karvoski v Grant* (1938) 30 CA2d 171, 179, 85 P2d 944. See also *People v Archerd* (1970) 3 C3d 615, 636, 91 CR 397. Counsel is not allowed to sit back in silence and "speculate on the verdict by deliberately failing to call the court's attention to a matter which could be remedied during the trial." *People v Corrigan* (1957) 48 C2d 551, 556, 310 P2d 953.

A statutory exception to this rule applies when the trial judge exercises the power of commenting on the evidence. See §29.22. Such comments are "deemed excepted to." CCP §647. Another exception applies when the prejudicial effect of the misconduct cannot be cured by proper admonition. *Estate of Golden* (1935) 4 C2d 300, 311, 48 P2d 962; *Forte v Schiebe* (1956) 145 CA2d 296, 301, 302 P2d 336. See also *People v Terry* (1970) 2 C3d 362, 398, 85 CR 409, overruled on another ground in *People v Carpenter* (1997) 15 C4th 312, 381, 63 CR2d 1; *People v Hefner* (1981) 127 CA3d 88, 95, 179 CR 336. A third exception to the waiver rule applies when a pattern of misconduct by the judge clearly makes further objection futile. Commenting on this exception, the court in *People v Robinson* (1960) 179 CA2d 624, 638, 4 CR 50, declared:

> We do not believe it would have been in the interests of [defense counsel's] client to interpose continuous objections or to otherwise express disapproval or criticism of the court's actions and thus run the risk of incurring the disfavor of the jurors, and perhaps of the court. We do not doubt that to utter a protest every time the defense was hurt by an answer

to the court's questions or to insist that the court desist from its procedure would have been a tactical mistake.

It is clear that the prejudicial effect of judicial misconduct cannot be cured by any admonition when the judge's abuse of counsel is so consistent and extreme that "it permeates the record and defies a finding of no prejudice." *People v Fatone* (1985) 165 CA3d 1164, 1176, 211 CR 288 (conviction reversed for judicial abuse of defense counsel even though it does not appear that counsel ever objected on that ground).

The objection to judicial misconduct may be accompanied by a request for an admonition to the jury to disregard the judge's actions. Although such a request is necessary to avoid waiver of attorney misconduct (see §29.10), it is not necessary to protect the injured party's right to base an appeal on judicial misconduct. *Delzell v Day* (1950) 36 C2d 349, 351, 223 P2d 625; *Berguin v Pacific Elec. Ry.* (1928) 203 C 116, 121, 263 P 220.

§29.29 2. Motion for Mistrial

If misconduct of the judge is so prejudicial that it deprives the client of a fair trial, counsel should add a motion for mistrial to the objection. See §29.27. To obtain a mistrial, counsel must prove to the trial judge that the judge's conduct was improper and that the effect of the misconduct cannot be remedied by an admonition to the jury to disregard it.

For a description of the applicable procedure, see chap 56.

§29.30 3. Motion for New Trial

In a civil action, the trial judge's misconduct may constitute an "irregularity in the proceedings" that warrants the granting of a new trial under CCP §657(1). See *Webber v Webber* (1948) 33 C2d 153, 199 P2d 934. The moving party must serve and file a written notice of intention to move for a new trial within 15 days after notice of entry of judgment is mailed by the clerk or served by a party and in any event no later than 180 days after entry of judgment. CCP §659. Counsel must serve and file all declarations supporting the motion within ten days after service of the notice of motion, unless the trial judge grants an extension of time, which may not exceed an additional 20 days. CCP §659a. For a suggested form, see California Trial Practice: Civil Procedure During Trial §§25.92, 25.93 (3d ed Cal CEB 1995). On orders denying that motion, see Civ Proc During Trial §25.69.

Misconduct of the judge is not among the grounds listed in Pen C §1181 for a new trial in a criminal case; however, the grounds enumerated in that section are not exclusive. See *People v Fosselman* (1983) 33 C3d 572, 582, 189 CR 855 (new trial allowed on ground of incompetence of defense counsel, a ground that is not covered in §1181). To support a nonstatutory ground for a motion for a new trial, counsel must show that the error denied the defendant a fair trial and that there were no earlier opportunities to raise the issue. *People v Mayorga* (1985) 171 CA3d 929, 940, 218 CR 830.

A criminal defendant who successfully challenged a judge under CCP §170.6(3) and was transferred to another judge, and then again transferred "inexplicably" back to the originally challenged judge's court, was granted a new trial because a "judgment rendered by a judge who is subject of a timely challenge is void...." *In re Jenkins* (1999) 70 CA4th 1162, 1165, 83 CR2d 232.

§29.31   4. Appeal

Appeal from the judgment is the most commonly used remedy to rectify misconduct by the trial judge. The cumulative impact of the judge's consistent, persistent, and unjustified abuse of counsel, in the presence of the jury, may result in the denial of the basic right to a fair trial—especially when combined with mistaken legal rulings. *People v Fatone* (1985) 165 CA3d 1164, 1167, 211 CR 288.

Ordinarily, the appellate court's principal concern, as dictated by Cal Const art VI, §13, is whether "after an examination of the entire cause, including the evidence," it appears that the misconduct complained of resulted in "a miscarriage of justice." *Webber v Webber* (1948) 33 C2d 153, 155, 199 P2d 934. Translated into practice, this test requires the appellate court to determine, after reviewing the entire record, whether it is reasonably probable that a result more favorable to the appealing party would have been reached in the absence of the judge's misconduct. *Delzell v Day* (1950) 36 C2d 349, 351, 223 P2d 625. See also *Newman v First Cal. Co.* (1975) 47 CA3d 60, 68, 120 CR 494. A less restrictive statement of the applicable test appears in *Etzel v Rosenbloom* (1948) 83 CA2d 758, 761, 189 P2d 848, in which the appellate court declared:

> [A]ny misconduct on the part of the trial judge from which it may be rightfully deduced that the jury was influenced in rendering its verdict constitutes prejudicial error.

See also *Estate of Buchman* (1954) 123 CA2d 546, 559, 267 P2d 73.

The effect of the judge's misconduct may be examined and evaluated only in the light of the setting and circumstances of the particular trial. What may be extremely prejudicial in the context of one trial may have relatively little effect on the outcome of a different trial. In determining the extent of prejudice, the appellate court will consider a number of factors, including the cumulative effect of a number of errors (*Delzell v Day, supra*; *People v Burns* (1952) 109 CA2d 524, 552, 241 P2d 308), the closeness of the case (*People v Burns, supra*), whether there was comparable treatment of both sides (*Germ v City & County of San Francisco* (1950) 99 CA2d 404, 415, 222 P2d 122), and the nature and type of misconduct.

See generally California Civil Appellate Practice §§5.23-5.39 (3d ed Cal CEB 1996).

§29.32   D. Alternatives to Objecting

On possible alternatives to objecting, see §§4.9–4.14.

§29.33   E. Stating the Objection

> I object to Your Honor's _ _[describe misconduct, e.g., remarks]_ _ and ask that the jury be admonished appropriately.
>
> [Add if prejudicial effect of judge's misconduct is so severe that client is deprived of fair trial]
>
> I move for a mistrial on the ground that the effect of this misconduct is so prejudicial that a fair trial is now impossible.

IV. MISCONDUCT OF JURORS

§29.34   A. Standards of Conduct

Before the voir dire examination begins, prospective jurors are required to take the following oath, which is administered by the court clerk (CCP §232(a)):

> Do you, and each of you, understand and agree that you will accurately and truthfully answer, under penalty of perjury, all questions propounded to you concerning your qualifications and competency to serve as a trial juror in the matter pending before this court; and that failure to do so may subject you to criminal prosecution.

As soon as the selection of the jury has been completed, each juror takes an oath to render a true verdict according to the evidence and the instructions of the court. For statutory provisions governing selection and qualifications of jurors, see CCP §§190–237. Following is the required acknowledgment and agreement to be obtained from the trial jurors when the selection of the trial jury is complete (CCP §232(b)):

> Do you, and each of you, understand and agree that you will well and truly try the cause now pending before this court, and a true verdict render according only to the evidence presented to you and to the instructions of the court.

The specific standard of conduct jurors must follow is derived from these oaths and from the various admonitions and instructions given to the jurors by the trial judge during trial. The instructions most commonly used in civil and in criminal cases are collected in Judicial Council of California Civil Jury Instructions (2003-2004) (CACI) (replacing Book of Approved Jury Instructions (9th ed 1994) (BAJI)) and California Jury Instructions, Criminal (6th ed 1996) (CALJIC), respectively.

Whenever the court is put on notice that cause may exist to discharge a juror, it must conduct an inquiry to determine the facts. *People v Hoover* (1986) 187 CA3d 1074, 1086, 231 CR 203 (trial court properly rejected contention of juror nonparticipation in jury deliberations). The court must conduct such an inquiry when it is put on notice that "improper or external influences were brought to bear on a juror" (*People v Burgener* (1986) 41 C3d 505, 518, 224 CR 112, disapproved on other grounds in 19 C4th at 239). See also *People v Kaurish* (1990) 52 C3d 648, 694, 276 CR 788 (court need not conduct inquiry when record did not show juror's derogatory remark resulted from improper influences or from serious bias).

B. Examples of Misconduct of Jurors

§29.35   1. Concealing Information During Voir Dire Examination

The concealment by a juror through false answers during voir dire examination of a matter that prevents the juror from acting impartially constitutes misconduct. See CCP §232(a) (jurors' agreement under penalty of perjury to answer voir dire questions truthfully, set out in §29.34); *Weathers v Kaiser Found. Hosps.* (1971) 5 C3d 98, 107, 95 CR 516 (one juror intentionally concealed bias against plaintiff because of her race; two other jurors intentionally concealed bias in favor of defendant; new trial granted after 9–3 verdict, with biased jurors comprising minority); *Clemens v Regents of Univ. of Cal.* (1970) 8 CA3d 1, 16, 87 CR 108 (in medical malpractice action, retired dentist concealed former profession and bias against medical malpractice plaintiffs).

Ordinarily, a juror's disqualifications relate to beliefs, personal knowledge of the facts relevant to the litigation, acquaintanceship with the parties or their counsel, or other special circumstances that may cause the juror to be consciously or unconsciously inclined to favor one side over the other. See CCP §§203, 225, 228, 229.

In *People v Diaz* (1984) 152 CA3d 926, 936, 200 CR 77, the appellate court reversed the defendant's conviction because of juror misconduct although it was not clear whether the misconduct was intentional. The juror, who ultimately was elected foreperson, failed to disclose when directly queried on voir dire that she had been a victim of an assault with a deadly weapon, the crime alleged against the defendant. When this was brought to the court's attention during the trial and before commencement of the jury's deliberations, the trial judge asked for the parties to stipulate to a jury of 11 because no alternates had been chosen. Because the defense attorney refused the stipulation, the court refused to discharge the juror. 152 CA3d at 931. The appellate court held that when a prospective juror fails to respond to a direct question, the factors relevant to a trial court's determination on a motion for a new trial are:

- Whether the question propounded was relevant to the voir dire examination;

- Whether the question was unambiguous; and

- Whether the juror had substantial knowledge of the information sought to be elicited.

A new trial should be ordered if the answer to these three questions is "yes," and prejudice may reasonably be inferred from the juror's failure to respond. 152 CA3d at 935.

Even when the juror's concealment is not intentional, the trial judge has discretion to rely on this conduct as a basis for granting a new trial. See *Shipley v Permanente Hosp.* (1954) 127 CA2d 417, 425, 274 P2d 53, disapproved on another ground in 50 C2d at 773. In *People v Kelly* (1986) 185 CA3d 118, 229 CR 584, the court held that the defendant was not denied a fair trial when a juror failed to disclose during voir dire that she had been sexually approached as a child by a step-uncle. The court concluded that the nondisclosure was unintentional and concerned a minor offense when compared to the crime with which the defendant was charged.

If the judge does not grant a new trial, however, the juror's concealment must have been intentional to be a ground for reversal on appeal. For example, in *Philbrick v Weinberger* (1964) 228 CA2d 681, 39 CR 617, a juror was asked during voir dire whether he knew the defendant's attorney or any member of his law firm. Although the juror answered "no" at that time, during the course of the trial he remembered having met the defense attorney's father (also an attorney) several years before. On learning this after the verdict had been rendered in the defendant's favor, plaintiff's counsel moved to set the verdict aside, partly on the basis of the juror's alleged misconduct. The appellate court ruled that "without an affirmative showing of both willful falsity and prejudice, no ground for a new trial exists." 228 CA2d at 688.

It follows from this rule that, to constitute reversible error, the grounds for disqualification must exist at the time the juror is questioned as opposed to arising later during the trial. *Crespo v Cook* (1959) 168 CA2d 360, 336 P2d 31; *Estate of Mesner* (1947) 77 CA2d 667, 676, 176 P2d 70. In addition, the false answer must relate to a fact that would have supported a challenge for cause (see *Castro v Fowler Equip. Co.* (1965) 233 CA2d 416, 43 CR 589) or the intelligent exercise of a peremptory challenge (see *People v Williams* (1981) 29 C3d 392, 174 CR 317). See §6.5. The false answer must be a direct response to a specific question. *Ross v Lighter* (1956) 139 CA2d 756, 294 P2d 59.

Typically, the grounds for disqualification are inferred from remarks made by the juror during the jury's deliberations. For example, in *Williams v Bridges* (1934) 140 CA 537, 35 P2d 407, a juror who had stated on voir dire that she knew absolutely nothing about the facts of the case, declared in the jury room that she knew about the accident, had passed the place where it occurred, and was not surprised that the fence fell because she had noticed that it was poorly constructed. On the basis of this misconduct, the appellate court ordered a new trial. See also *Smith v Covell* (1980) 100 CA3d 947, 161 CR 377 (concealment of bias by silence).

The examples of juror misconduct in this section are not exhaustive. For further discussion and examples, see 7 Witkin, California Procedure, *Trial* §§337-344 (4th ed 1997).

2. Receiving Evidence Out of Court

§29.36   a. General Restrictions

It is fundamental that all evidence must be presented in open court so that each party to the controversy may have knowledge of the evidence and can defend against it if necessary. *Higgins v Los Angeles Gas & Elec. Co.* (1911) 159 C 651, 656, 115 P 313. See also *Wagner v Doulton* (1980) 112 CA3d 945, 950, 169 CR 550. By statute, jurors must be admonished whenever they separate that it is their duty not to receive evidence out of court. CCP §611; Pen C §1122. This is usually worded along the following lines:

> It is your duty as jurors not to converse with or allow yourselves to be addressed by any person on any subject of the trial. You are not to conduct any independent investigation of any matters being considered during this trial. You are not to read news commentary about this case or use the Internet for information about this trial or its subject matter or its attorneys. You are not to go to the scene. It is your duty not to form or express any opinion regarding the merits of this case until it is finally submitted to you for your verdict.

In the past, many judges secured a stipulation from counsel that this admonition need not be given to the jurors at each separation but only at the commencement of trial. In *People v Jacobson* (1965) 63 C2d 319, 326, 46 CR 515, the California Supreme Court criticized this practice as an "inappropriate judicial shortcut in criminal cases." In view of the strict wording of CCP §611, it does not seem appropriate to omit the admonition, regardless of the type of case.

Specific applications of the prohibition against receiving evidence out of court are analyzed in §§29.37-29.42.

b. Specific Prohibitions

§29.37   (1) Independent Investigations

Jurors may not conduct independent investigations concerning the facts. For example, it is misconduct for a juror to consult with his or her personal physician in order to determine the physician's opinion about a medical issue in the case. *Walter v Ayvazian* (1933) 134 CA 360, 25 P2d 526. It is similarly misconduct for a juror to make an independent visit to the scene of the accident (see *Maffeo v Holmes* (1941) 47 CA2d 292, 117 P2d 948) or of the alleged crime (see *People v Tedesco* (1934) 1 C2d 211, 34 P2d 467) or to read newspaper accounts of the case (see *People v Lambright* (1964) 61 C2d 482, 39 CR 209).

§29.38 (2) Independent Experiments

It is misconduct for a juror to conduct independent experiments in an attempt to resolve factual issues. Such experiments constitute prejudicial error, however, only when "new" evidence is generated as a result. *People v Cooper* (1979) 95 CA3d 844, 853, 157 CR 348 (alleged reenactment of defendant's disposal of contraband not prejudicial, because it simply repeated testifying officer's demonstration). See also *People v Castro* (1986) 184 CA3d 849, 229 CR 280 (juror's use of binoculars to test identification testimony; prosecution failed to rebut presumed prejudice); *Wagner v Doulton* (1980) 112 CA3d 945, 950, 169 CR 550 (juror, who was engineer and drew diagram in jury room of scene of accident based solely on evidence heard in court, acted properly in rendering "pictorial representation" of such evidence). But see *McDonald v Southern Pac. Transp. Co.* (1999) 71 CA4th 256, 83 CR2d 734 (juror's presentation in jury room of expert opinion not based on trial evidence constitutes misconduct).

In *People v Conkling* (1896) 111 C 616, 44 P 314, the distance between the deceased and the defendant when the fatal shot was fired was a key issue. The clothing of the deceased, which was introduced in evidence, had no powder marks on it. To determine at what distance a rifle shot would leave powder marks on cloth, two jurors borrowed a rifle and experimented with it outside the courtroom during a recess in the trial. Because of this misconduct, the California Supreme Court reversed the conviction and ordered a new trial.

Compare *Conkling* with *People v Phillips* (1981) 122 CA3d 69, 81, 175 CR 703, in which a juror conducted at-home experiments concerning the solubility of sodium bicarbonate in a case in which a parent defendant was accused of murdering a child by administering a sodium compound into food. Although the juror's act constituted misconduct, the appellate court found insufficient prejudice to reverse the conviction, because the experiment's finding was not inconsistent with evidence presented at trial. See Anno, Tests or Experiments in Jury Room, 95 ALR2d 351 (1964). See also *Wagner v Doulton, supra*.

Counsel should ask the judge to warn the jury (see §29.37) against conducting improper experiments that go beyond the scope of the evidence when taking exhibits that are susceptible of experimentation into the jury room. .

Cases conflict on the effect of a juror's reference to a dictionary during deliberations. Compare *Glage v Hawes Firearms* (1990) 226 CA3d 314, 323, 276 CR 430 (use of dictionary to look up "preponderance" was serious misconduct in light of restricted legal meaning of word and broader scope of common definition), with *People v Karis* (1988) 46 C3d 612, 250 CR 659 (trial court did not err in denying motion for new trial based on alleged prejudicial jury misconduct of one juror's consulting a dictionary for definition of "mitigating" and another juror's asking a librarian whether county public library contained books written by expert witness called by defense).

§29.39 (3) Unauthorized Discussions

It is misconduct for a juror to converse with anyone about the pending case. CCP §611; Pen C §1122. Even discussion with a fellow juror is prohibited until the case has been submitted to the jury for decision. See CCP §611; Pen C §1122. Any private communication during the trial between a juror and a party (*Wright v Eastlick* (1899) 125 C 517, 58 P 87) or counsel (*Garden Grove Sch. Dist. v Hendler* (1965) 63 C2d 141, 45 CR 313) is "serious misconduct," regardless of the subject discussed.

Conversations between jurors and others about the case also constitute misconduct. *People v Pierce* (1979) 24 C3d 199, 207, 155 CR 657 (jury foreperson discussed case with policeman during trial); *Andrews v County of Orange* (1982) 130 CA3d 944, 958, 182 CR 176, disapproved on other grounds in *People v Nesler* (1997) 16 C4th 561, 582 n5, 66 CR2d 454 (inverse condemnation action in which jury was to decide on loss of market value of plaintiffs' homes; juror told other jurors about hearing from real estate broker that price on house was "not unusual"); *Forman v Alexander's Mkts.* (1956) 138 CA2d 671, 292 P2d 257 (automobile accident case; juror discussed question of skid marks with her husband, who was a truck driver, and used that information during deliberations to argue that plaintiff was clearly negligent); *People v Goodale* (1939) 33 CA2d 80, 91 P2d 163 (juror conversed about evidence with bystander in courthouse hallway during recess).

It is error for jurors to speak with a testifying witness, particularly about matters related to the case. *People v Ryner* (1985) 164 CA3d 1075, 1083, 211 CR 140 (no reversal); *City of Los Angeles v Lowensohn* (1976) 54 CA3d 625, 637, 127 CR 417.

It does not, however, constitute juror misconduct when a juror prepares a written statement summarizing his or her view of the evidence and then reads that statement to the jury when it reconvenes if the juror has not refused to deliberate, has not consulted outside sources, and has not included any facts outside the evidence presented. *Bormann v Chevron USA, Inc.* (1997) 56 CA4th 260, 65 CR2d 321.

In addition to the admonition required by CCP §611 (see §29.37), counsel might request that the judge advise the jurors that it is their duty not to converse with or be addressed by anyone about the trial and that transgressions and irregularities must be immediately reported to the court.

§29.40 (4) Personal Knowledge of Facts

Penal Code §1120 provides:

> If a juror has any personal knowledge respecting a fact in controversy in a cause, he must declare the same in open Court during the trial. If, during the retirement of the jury, a juror declare[s] a fact which could be evidence in the cause, as of his own knowledge, the jury must return into Court. In either of these cases, the juror making the statement must be sworn as a witness and examined in the presence of the parties in

order that the Court may determine whether good cause exists for his discharge as a juror.

This provision applies whether or not the juror in question is asked during voir dire examination if he or she has any personal knowledge about the matter being litigated. The trial court must conduct a hearing sufficiently complete to determine whether facts exist to discharge the juror for good cause.

In *People v Nesler* (1997) 16 C4th 561, 66 CR2d 454, during a break in the sanity phase of the trial, a juror heard a woman at a bar, who claimed to have worked for the defendant as a babysitter, discussing the defendant's drug use and her neglect of her children, and the juror interjected this information into the sanity phase deliberations. The supreme court reversed and remanded for a new trial on the defendant's sanity.

§29.41 (5) Personal Knowledge of Law

Erroneous legal advice given by a juror to other jurors during deliberations constitutes serious misconduct. *In re Stankewitz* (1985) 40 C3d 391, 402, 220 CR 382 (juror gave his opinion on elements of robbery based on his experience as police officer). See also *Young v Brunicardi* (1986) 187 CA3d 1344, 1351, 232 CR 588 (retired police officer juror asserted during deliberations that defendant could not have been negligent in absence of receiving citation for Vehicle Code offense).

§29.42 (6) Unauthorized Matter in Jury Room

Code of Civil Procedure §612 specifies what the jurors in a civil case may take with them when they retire to the jury room for deliberation:

> Upon retiring for deliberation the jury may take with them all papers, which have been received as evidence in the cause, except depositions, or copies of such papers as ought not, in the opinion of the court, to be taken from the person having them in possession; and they may also take with them any exhibits which the court may deem proper, notes of the testimony or other proceedings on the trial, taken by themselves or any of them, but none taken by any other person.

Code of Civil Procedure §612.5 and Pen C §109(f) provide that the judge must instruct a jury in a civil or criminal trial that a written copy of jury instructions is available and must supply the jury with a copy if it requests one. Even if the jurors do not request a copy, the court may give them one.

Although no express provision allows exhibits in the jury room in criminal cases (see Pen C §§1093, 1137), case law allows exhibits that are in evidence to be brought to the jury at its request. See *People v Hogan* (1982) 31 C3d 815, 849, 183 CR 817, disapproved on other grounds in *People v Cooper* (1991) 53 C3d 771, 836, 281 CR 90; *People v Horowitz* (1945) 70 CA2d 675, 704, 161 P2d 833.

It is misconduct for jurors to take unauthorized matter into the jury room, even through inadvertence. *People v Hogan* (1982) 31 C3d 815, 844, 183 CR 817, disapproved on other grounds in *People v Cooper* (1991) 53 C3d 771, 836, 281 CR 90 (tape of conversation, including inadmissible portion); *Davenport v Waite* (1959) 175 CA2d 623, 346 P2d 501 (deposition); *Newton v Thomas* (1955) 137 CA2d 748, 768, 291 P2d 503 (exhibit marked for identification but not admitted in evidence). It is misconduct for a juror to take material into the jury room even though it would have been admitted into evidence if offered by either the prosecution or defense. *People v Martinez* (1978) 82 CA3d 1, 22, 147 CR 208 (foreman brought maps into jury room to help jury evaluate evidence; misconduct, but not prejudicial because maps did not contradict evidence).

To avoid any potential problems about what is sent to the jury room, counsel should request that before argument the judge and all counsel discuss, with a court reporter present, what materials will be permitted in the jury room. For making such a recommendation to trial judges, see Los Angeles Super Ct R §§8.37, 8.66-8.68.

The need to act promptly is illustrated by the decision in *Newton v Thomas* (1955) 137 CA2d 748, 291 P2d 503, in which police reports were inadvertently taken into the jury room when the jury retired for deliberation of the case. The reports had been marked for identification but were not received in evidence. The trial judge asked the complaining counsel at what time he became aware of the error. Counsel replied that he noticed that all the exhibits for identification were missing about 20 or 25 minutes after the jury retired. He did not object until after the verdict was rendered. Noting that the jury was out for approximately two hours, the reviewing court declared (137 CA2d at 769):

> [C]ounsel should have called the situation to the court's attention the moment he suspected that the jury had the exhibit. The court could have immediately demanded its return and could have admonished the jury, if they had examined the exhibit, to disregard its contents.

The judgment was affirmed.

§29.43   3. Arriving at Verdict by Chance or by Quotient

It is misconduct for jurors in a civil action to "resort to the determination of chance." CCP §657(2). A chance verdict is one reached by tossing a coin, drawing lots, or any other form of gambling. See *People v Decker* (1954) 122 CA2d 447, 265 P2d 41. A quotient verdict is one in which the jurors agree in advance to be bound by an average of their views and do not discuss or deliberate further on the question. See *Diamond Springs Lime Co. v American River Constructors* (1971) 16 CA3d 581, 605, 94 CR 200 (having each juror state a figure for verdict, combining figures of all jurors, and dividing by number of jurors to reach quotient does not necessarily result in prohibited chance verdict unless result is adopted without subsequent discussion and balloting). See also *Bardessono v Michels* (1970) 3 C3d 780, 795, 91 CR 760;

CACI 5001 (formerly BAJI 15.33) (forbidding jurors to agree in advance to arrive at amount of damages to be awarded by, *e.g.,* totaling jurors' independent estimates and averaging it to reach a verdict). The statute expressly allows such misconduct to be proved in a civil case by affidavit (or declaration under penalty of perjury; CCP §2015.5) of any one of the jurors. CCP §657(2). See 7 Witkin, California Procedure, *Trial* §§384-390 (4th ed 1997).

In a criminal case, a new trial will be granted if the verdict was "decided by lot, or by any means other than a fair expression of opinion on the part of all jurors." Pen C §1181(4). That the verdict was reached by chance or by lot in a criminal case may also be shown by jurors' affidavits (or declarations; CCP §2015.5). See *People v Hall* (1980) 108 CA3d 373, 380, 166 CR 578; *People v Hutchinson* (1969) 71 C2d 342, 347, 78 CR 196; California Criminal Law Procedure and Practice §34.5 (7th ed Cal CEB 2004).

§29.44 4. Inattentiveness During Trial

It is misconduct for jurors not to pay attention to the evidence presented at trial by, *e.g.,* reading books or doing crossword puzzles. *Hasson v Ford Motor Co.* (1982) 32 C3d 388, 410, 185 CR 654.

Consumption of alcohol by jurors during the trial or deliberations is misconduct if it appears that the alcohol affected the jurors' ability to perform their duties. See *People v Burgener* (1986) 41 C3d 505, 521, 224 CR 112, disapproved on other grounds in 19 C4th at 239 (failure to investigate foreman's charge that juror was intoxicated was error but not reversible for lack of adequate record of misconduct); *People v Trevino* (1985) 39 C3d 667, 693 n27, 217 CR 652, disapproved on other grounds in 47 C3d at 1291 (record insufficient to show that juror's abilities were impaired).

Courts will not order a new trial on the basis of jurors' sleeping during the proceedings "in the absence of convincing proof that the jurors were actually asleep during material portions of the trial." *People v Bradford* (1997) 15 C4th 1229, 1349, 65 CR2d 145.

§29.44A 5. Failure to Deliberate

Failure to deliberate can constitute juror misconduct. See CALJIC 17.40 (criminal); CACI 5001 (formerly BAJI 15.30) (civil). It is not an abuse of the court's discretion if the court fails to investigate new information obtained during trial regarding accusations of a juror's failure to deliberate. However, the court's failure to inquire into new allegations by the juror who was accused of failing to deliberate, raising the possibility of misconduct by the original complaining juror, is a prejudicial abuse of the court's discretion which will result in reversal on appeal. See *People v Castorena* (1996) 47 CA4th 1051, 55 CR2d 151.

It does not constitute juror misconduct when a jury begins its deliberation by taking a straw vote and reaches a verdict without further discussion. Although the preferred procedure is for the jury to discuss the case (see CACI 5001 (formerly BAJI 15.30-15.31)), the constitutional right to a jury trial does not include the right to compel discussion of the issues. See *Vomaska v City of San Diego* (1997) 55 CA4th 905, 64 CR2d 492.

C. Remedies

§29.45   1. Before Verdict Rendered

If juror misconduct is not discovered until after the jury is sworn but before or during the selection of alternates, the court may reopen jury selection. *People v Armendariz* (1984) 37 C3d 573, 580, 209 CR 664; *Lindemann v San Joaquin Cotton Oil Co.* (1936) 5 C2d 480, 496, 55 P2d 870. It is unclear when the reopening of jury selection in criminal cases is possible without violating the double jeopardy clause. See discussion of this issue in *People v Johnson* (1988) 200 CA3d 1553, 247 CR 767.

If juror misconduct is discovered while the trial is in progress, this must immediately be brought to the judge's attention or the error is waived. See *Weathers v Kaiser Found. Hosps.* (1971) 5 C3d 98, 103, 95 CR 516; *Zibbell v Southern Pac. Co.* (1911) 160 C 237, 253, 116 P 513. "[A] party may not sit by in silence, taking chances of a favorable verdict, and after a hostile verdict, then, for the first time, be heard to complain." 160 C at 253. For analogous cases, see §29.35.

Once a jury panel in a civil case has been sworn, a juror may be excused for good cause. CCP §233. Once the jury has been sworn in a criminal case, a retrial is barred unless there is legal necessity for the discharge or the defendant or defense counsel consent to the discharge. Cal Const art I, §15; *Larios v Superior Court* (1979) 24 C3d 324, 155 CR 374 (no legal necessity shown).

When a juror's competence is called into question during trial, the judge is required to conduct a hearing to determine whether good cause (civil trials) or legal necessity (criminal trials) exists to discharge the juror. A court reporter should be at the hearing. Under compelling circumstances, it is an abuse of discretion to fail to make that inquiry. *People v Wright* (1990) 52 C3d 367, 403 n9, 276 CR 731 (court's failure to conduct "full-blown formal hearing" was harmless error when court made sincere attempt to determine juror's fitness and decision to leave juror on jury was supported by substantial evidence). See also *People v Burgener* (1986) 41 C3d 505, 519, 224 CR 112, disapproved on other grounds in 19 C4th at 239 (failure to conduct inquiry on foreperson's statement that juror was intoxicated).

When the court has reason to believe that other jurors are not aware of the misconduct of one juror, the usual procedure is for the judge to examine the juror believed to have committed misconduct—on the record, under oath, and out of the presence of the other jurors—to determine the facts relating to the alleged misconduct. If the judge discovers that the improperly obtained information may already been transmitted to other jurors, the judge may poll the jurors to determine whether they are aware of the misconduct. Under some circumstances, it may constitute error to refuse to take such a poll when requested to do so. For example, in *People v Lambright* (1964) 61 C2d 482, 39 CR 209, an article appeared in a local newspaper during the trial that, if read by the jurors, could have caused serious prejudice. Defense counsel requested that the jury be polled to ascertain whether any jurors had read the article, but the judge refused to do so. The trial judge had previously instructed the jury that it was permissible for them to read newspaper accounts of the trial. Under these circumstances, the California Supreme Court held that the request to poll the jury should have been granted. But in *People v Lanphear* (1980) 26 C3d 814, 835, 163 CR 601, opinion restated at 28 C3d 463, 171 CR 505, additional polling was not required because the trial judge had admonished the jury not to read newspaper accounts of the trial and there was no evidence that any juror had failed to heed the admonishment.

If the judge determines that a juror has acted improperly and that there is good cause (civil trials) or legal necessity (criminal trials), the judge may order that the juror be discharged and replaced by an alternate juror, if one was selected. See CCP §234; Pen C §1089; *Garden Grove Sch. Dist. v Hendler* (1965) 63 C2d 141, 45 CR 313. See §29.35 for discussion of stipulating to select alternate jurors. If an alternate juror is substituted for a regular juror during deliberations, the jury must be instructed to disregard all past deliberations and begin deliberating anew unless counsel has stipulated to the silent presence of alternates during the original deliberations. See *People v Valles* (1979) 24 C3d 121, 154 CR 543.

If the court does not find good cause or legal necessity, it may decide that an admonition to the juror involved is sufficient. When the entire jury is aware of the misconduct, or participated in it, the court should admonish the jury to disregard the misconduct. See *Horn v Atchison, T. & S.F. Ry.* (1964) 61 C2d 602, 39 CR 721; *Whitfield v Roth* (1974) 10 C3d 874, 892, 112 CR 540.

In civil cases, if the court rules not to excuse a juror who has been guilty of misconduct, and counsel believes that there is good cause for excusing the juror, counsel in a civil case must move for a mistrial or the misconduct is waived. *Sepulveda v Ishimaru* (1957) 149 CA2d 543, 308 P2d 809. See also *Miller v National Am. Life Ins. Co.* (1976) 54 CA3d 331, 346, 126 CR 731. Counsel may not gamble by holding back to see whether the verdict is favorable. See chap 6.

In criminal cases, a defendant who successfully moves for a mistrial is usually considered to have consented to a retrial and to have waived the protection of the double jeopardy clause. See *Oregon v Kennedy* (1982) 456 US 667, 72 L Ed 2d 416, 102 S Ct 2083. But compare *Weston v Kernan* (1995) 50 F3d 633 (court of appeal held that state trial court abused its discretion in granting a mistrial without prejudice over defense objections, and thus retrial violated double jeopardy clause).

A party moving for a mistrial must show, usually by affidavit (CCP §568) or declaration (CCP §2015.5), that misconduct or irregularity occurred and that the misconduct or irregularity is prejudicial to a fair trial and cannot be otherwise remedied at that stage of the proceeding. See §56.2.

§29.46 2. After Verdict Rendered

Usually a juror's misconduct is not discovered until after the verdict has been rendered, when it is brought to the attention of the losing party by a concerned juror. The appropriate remedy at this stage is a motion for new trial. In a civil case, such a motion lies under CCP §§657(2) (misconduct of jury) and 657(1)) (irregularity in jury proceedings). In a criminal case, the defendant may move for a new trial when:

- "[T]he jury has received any evidence out of court, other than that resulting from a view of the premises, or of personal property" (Pen C §1181(2); see, *e.g., People v Lambright* (1964) 61 C2d 482, 486, 39 CR 209);

- The verdict was decided by lot or other similar method (Pen C §1181(4)); or

- The jury has separated without leave of court after beginning to deliberate, or has been guilty of any misconduct that prevented a fair consideration of the case (Pen C §1181(3)).

Juror affidavits (CCP §658) or declarations (CCP §2015.5) can be used to prove this type of misconduct but only as proof of overt conduct, conditions, events, and statements. *People v Hutchinson* (1969) 71 C2d 342, 349, 78 CR 196; Evid C §1150(a). See also *Hasson v Ford Motor Co.* (1982) 32 C3d 388, 414, 185 CR 654. Affidavits or declarations showing the mental processes of the jurors or the effect of a statement, conduct, a condition, or an event on a juror that influenced the juror to vote for or against the verdict may not be used. See *Hasson v Ford Motor Co., supra*; *People v Hutchinson, supra*; *People v Stevenson* (1970) 4 CA3d 443, 445, 84 CR 349. In criminal cases, Cal Const art I, §28(d) (the "truth-in-evidence" provision of Proposition 8) did not remove the limitations on the use of affidavits to show the effect of, *e.g.,* a statement or conduct on the mental processes of jurors with regard to jury misconduct. *People v Hill* (1992) 3 CA4th 16, 32, 4 CR2d 258, disapproved on other grounds in *People v Nesler* (1997) 16 C4th 561, 582 n5. See §18.24. For additional cases showing proper and improper uses of juror affidavits, see 7 Witkin, California Procedure, *Trial* §§391–394, 396 (4th ed 1997). The usual procedures for making a motion for a new trial apply. See §29.36.

On the requirement that only affidavits or declarations may be used to support a motion for a new trial on the ground of juror misconduct, see *Linhart v Nelson* (1976) 18 C3d 641, 644, 134 CR 813, discussed in §18.24. On the effect of oral testimony received without objection on a motion for a new trial, see *Bardessono v Michels* (1970) 3 C3d 780, 793, 91 CR 760 (oral testimony received without objection held not to taint procedure with jurisdictional defect). Because a record is needed to appeal this type of error, a motion for a new trial is necessary before the misconduct can be relied on as a ground for reversal on appeal. See *Crespo v Cook* (1959) 168 CA2d 360, 336 P2d 31.

To make a motion for new trial in a civil case, counsel must serve and file a written notice of intention to move for a new trial within 15 days after notice of entry of judgment is mailed by the clerk or served by a party or within 180 days after entry of judgment, whichever is earlier. CCP §659. Counsel must serve and file all declarations supporting the motion within ten days after service of the notice of motion, unless the trial judge grants an extension of time, which may not exceed an additional 20 days. CCP §659a. For a suggested form, see California Trial Practice: Civil Procedure During Trial §§25.92-25.95 (3d ed Cal CEB 1995). For further discussion of procedural requirements of a motion for a new trial and supporting documents, see 8 Witkin, California Procedure, *Attack on Judgment in Trial Court* §§67-68 (4th ed 1997).

In a criminal case, a motion for new trial must be made before judgment, the granting of probation, commitment of a defendant for observation as a mentally disordered sex offender, or commitment of a defendant for narcotics addiction or insanity. Pen C §1182. Defense counsel makes an "application" for a new trial. Pen C §1181. This statute has been interpreted to mean either an oral or a written motion. *People v Simon* (1989) 208 CA3d 841, 847, 256 CR 373. Counsel should follow any local rules for form, notice, service, and filing requirements.

When jury misconduct involves information given by a juror during the voir dire examination, the following information should be included in the affidavits or declarations:

- That misconduct or irregularity occurred.

- That the misconduct or irregularity is prejudicial to a fair trial and cannot be otherwise remedied. In most cases, a declaration is prepared to establish that the juror's answer was false at the time it was given and that a true answer would have provided the basis for a challenge for cause. If the concealment was intentional, the declaration should also establish that fact. See §29.34. Customarily, this declaration is made by one of the other jurors, who reports what the offending juror said and did during the jury's deliberations that indicated concealment of a ground for disqualification during voir dire. *Bardessono v Michels* (1970) 3 C3d 780, 794, 91 CR 760; *Smith v Covell* (1980) 100 CA3d 947, 953, 161 CR 377. Sometimes the falsity of the juror's answer can be established by someone who is not on the jury. See, *e.g., Deward v Clough* (1966) 245 CA2d 439, 54 CR 68 (bystander's affidavit regarding offending juror's statement overheard during recess). A declaration containing only hearsay information concerning the misconduct, however, is insufficient. The statements must be based on personal knowledge. *Weathers v Kaiser Found. Hosps.* (1971) 5 C3d 98, 105, 95 CR 516; *Richards v Gemco* (1963) 217 CA2d 858, 863, 32 CR 65. See generally Evid C §1150; §18.24.

- That neither the moving party nor that party's counsel knew about the misconduct until after the verdict. *Weathers v Kaiser Found. Hosps.* (1971) 5 C3d 98, 103, 95 CR 516 (no prior knowledge requirement; affidavits or declarations from both party and counsel needed). If counsel files an affidavit or a declaration alleging that neither counsel nor the client knew of the misconduct before the verdict, counsel has substantially complied with the no-prior-knowledge requirement. This requirement does not apply if the misconduct occurs after jury deliberations have started and is not discovered until after the verdict, in which case neither counsel nor client could possibly have known of the misconduct before the verdict was returned. *Krouse v Graham* (1977) 19 C3d 59, 18, 137 CR 863.

The motion for new trial should be accompanied by a transcript of the voir dire question-and-answer exchange during which the misconduct was committed. The transcript is usually prepared by the court reporter.

In ruling on a motion for new trial, the trial court must determine, after making "an examination of the entire cause, including the evidence," whether the juror's misconduct "resulted in a miscarriage of justice." Cal Const art VI, §13. See also *Olinger v Pacific Greyhound Lines* (1935) 7 CA2d 484, 46 P2d 774, and Evid C §353. For a form of an order denying a motion for a new trial, see California Trial Practice: Civil Procedure During Trial §§25.92–25.95 (3d ed Cal CEB 1995).

If the court *orders* a new trial, the party that opposed the motion may appeal, but the appellate court will not disturb the judge's determination that prejudicial error occurred unless there was a manifest abuse of discretion. *Abercrombie v Thomsen* (1943) 59 CA2d 331, 346, 138 P2d 701. See also *Weathers v Kaiser Found. Hosps.* (1971) 5 C3d 98, 109, 95 CR 516; *Andrews v County of Orange* (1982) 130 CA3d 944, 955, 182 CR 176, disapproved on other grounds in 16 C4th at 582 n5. The court in *Miller v National Am. Life Ins. Co.* (1976) 54 CA3d 331, 126 CR 731, said that a trial court's *granting* of a new trial can even be upheld when the party making the motion, during trial, failed to object or invited the error on which the new trial motion is based.

If the court *denies* a new trial, the court's order is usually reviewable only on appeal from the judgment on the verdict. See Pen C §1237; CCP §§904.1–904.2, 906; Civ Proc During Trial §19.30. The appellate court, in reviewing *denial* of a new trial motion, determines independently whether the juror's misconduct was prejudicial. *Deward v Clough* (1966) 245 CA2d 439, 445, 54 CR 68. See also *Hasson v Ford Motor Co.* (1982) 32 C3d 388, 417 n10, 185 CR 654; *City of Los Angeles v Decker* (1977) 18 C3d 860, 872, 135 CR 647.

When a new trial motion has been denied, there is a presumption of prejudice on appeal from any juror misconduct. *Hasson v Ford Motor Co.* (1982) 32 C3d 388, 416, 185 CR 654; *People v Honeycutt* (1977) 20 C3d 150, 141 CR 698. This presumption applies in both civil and criminal cases. *Hasson v Ford Motor Co., supra*. The presumption of prejudice, however, is not conclusive; it (32 C3d at 417):

> may be rebutted by an affirmative evidentiary showing that prejudice does not exist or by a reviewing court's examination of the entire record to determine whether there is a reasonable probability of actual harm to the complaining party resulting from the misconduct.

Relevant factors used in determining the prejudicial effect of jury misconduct include the type of case and the closeness of the issues. See *Weathers v Kaiser Found. Hosps.* (1971) 5 C3d 98, 110, 95 CR 516 (foreman's remark that plaintiff was "black woman" and that "where he came from, they don't even let a black woman into the courtroom" and another juror's comments about high quality of defendant hospital; 9-3 verdict meant that disqualification of one juror for concealing bias on voir dire could have resulted in different verdict); *People v Castaldia,* (1959) 51 C2d 569, 335 P2d 104 (juror's concealment of hostility toward bookmakers); *Smith v Covell, supra* (juror's statements about impact of personal injury litigation on insurance rates); *Irvin v Padelford* (1954) 127 CA2d 135, 140, 273 P2d 539 (because only nine votes were necessary for verdict, 10-2 verdict meant that result would have been same even if juror in question had voted for defendant); *George v City of Los Angeles* (1942) 51 CA2d 311, 321, 124 P2d 872 (no prejudice from juror's concealment of fact that her husband had been slightly injured in automobile accident many years earlier).

§29.47 D. Alternatives to Objecting

On possible alternatives to objecting, see §§4.9–4.14.

E. Stating the Objection

§29.48 1. Before Verdict Rendered

Your Honor, I object as misconduct _ _[e.g., based on the private visit to the scene of the accident yesterday evening by two of the jurors]_ _.

[Option 1: Motion for mistrial]

I move for a mistrial on the ground that this misconduct is so prejudicial that a fair trial is now impossible.

[Option 2: Motion for mistrial is not made or has been denied]

I request that the jury be admonished _ _[e.g., to disregard all information obtained concerning the private visit to the scene of the accident by two of the jurors.]_ _.

§29.49 2. After Verdict Rendered

To assert juror misconduct after the verdict has been rendered, the appropriate remedy is a motion for a new trial. See discussion of new trial motions in §§29.17, 29.30.

30

Unduly Inflammatory

I. DEFINITION §30.1

II. ANALYSIS §30.2

III. TACTICS; PROCEDURE §30.3

IV. ILLUSTRATIONS
   A. Discretion Upheld §30.4
   B. Abuse of Discretion §30.5

V. STATUTE §30.6

VI. STATING THE OBJECTION §30.7

§30.1   I. DEFINITION

Evidence is objectionable if by its very nature it is so shocking that its inflammatory effect on the jury substantially outweighs its probative value.

The objection that evidence is unduly inflammatory must be distinguished from the request that the judge exercise discretion under Evid C §352 by excluding evidence because its prejudicial effect substantially outweighs its probative value. See chap 31. Section 352 is the statutory authority for both the objection and the request, but the objection is based on a separate ground. Evidence that is prejudicial need not be inflammatory.

§30.2   II. ANALYSIS

The trial judge may exclude shocking or unduly prejudicial evidence if the court determines that "its probative value is substantially outweighed by the probability that its admission will ... create substantial danger of undue prejudice." Evid C §352. It is clearly erroneous for the judge to admit inflammatory evidence that has no probative value whatsoever.

In *People v Burns* (1952) 109 CA2d 524, 541, 241 P2d 308, the defendant was accused of hitting the deceased repeatedly with his fists, causing her death. Defense counsel claimed that the deceased's fatal injuries resulted from her falling down. Over defense counsel's objection, three photographs of the deceased were admitted into evidence. Taken after the autopsy, these photographs were particularly gruesome because they showed the deceased's head completely shaved and with large incisions that had been made for the autopsy. Bruises and abrasions could only be faintly seen on the head, neck, and arms. Observing that potentially inflammatory post-autopsy photographs of a deceased have been held admissible when there is some necessity for exhibiting the wounds, the appellate court noted that the prosecution in *Burns* raised no question about the deceased's bruises and abrasions. Because "a view of them was of no particular value to the jury, it is obvious that the only purpose of exhibiting them was to inflame the jury's emotions against defendant." The appellate court ruled that admitting the photographs over defense counsel's objection constituted an abuse of the trial judge's discretion. Because this error, coupled with others committed by the trial judge, had denied the defendant a fair trial, the appellate court ordered the judgment of conviction reversed. See also *People v Heard* (2003) 31 C4th 946, 976, 4 CR3d 131 (photos that are graphic and unpleasant to consider not unduly prejudicial when they portray the results of defendant's violent conduct); *People v Smith* (1973) 33 CA3d 51, 69, 108 CR 698, overruled on other grounds in 22 C3d at 327 n7 (abuse of discretion but not miscarriage of justice to admit gruesome photographs).

A gruesome photograph may be admissible if it constitutes important evidence on significant, contested issues. In *People v Coleman* (1988) 46 C3d 749, 776, 251 CR 83, the court recognized that such a photograph is properly admitted if the evidence is "highly relevant" to factual issues or if the photograph would clarify the testimony of a medical examiner. Similarly, in *People v Turner* (1990) 50 C3d 668, 706, 268 CR 706, the court held that the trial court properly admitted a videotape of the crime scene, including the victim's body as found by police, because divergent theories on how the homicide occurred were based on details of physical and circumstantial evidence. See *People v Riel* (2000) 22 C4th 1153, 1193, 96 CR2d 1. See also *People v Hendricks* (1987) 43 C3d 584, 238 CR 66 (photograph of person killed not relevant because identity was not at issue, but error in admitting photograph was harmless); *People v Allen* (1986) 42 C3d 1222, 1255, 232 CR 849 (no abuse of discretion in admitting into evidence photographs of murder victims even though they were cumulative and corroborated uncontested testimony).

In admitting six photographs of a crime scene and victims, the supreme court stated that at the penalty phase, the trial court's discretion to exclude circumstances-of-the-crime evidence as unduly prejudicial is more circumscribed than at the guilt phase. During the guilt phase, there is a legitimate concern that crime scene photographs can produce a visceral response that unfairly tempts jurors to find the defendant guilty of the charged crimes. Such concerns are greatly diminished at the penalty phase because the defendant has been found guilty of the charged crimes; the jury's discretion is focused on the circumstances of those crimes solely to determine the defendant's sentence. *People v Box* (2000) 23 C4th 1153, 1201, 99 CR2d 69.

Photographs of a victim while still alive were held admissible in the penalty phase of a murder trial as relevant to questions of age, size, and vulnerability. See *People v Frank* (1990) 51 C3d 718, 274 CR 372. See also *People v Anderson* (1990) 52 C3d 453, 474, 276 CR 356 (admission may be error but under circumstances was not prejudicial); *People v Kelly* (1990) 51 C3d 931, 963, 275 CR 160 (admission, in guilt phase, of photographs of victims while still alive was arguably inappropriate but harmless).

To obtain a reversal, the appellant must show that (a) the evidence was inflammatory, (b) its admission amounted to an abuse of discretion, and (c) its admission resulted in a miscarriage of justice. In *People v Cavanaugh* (1955) 44 C2d 252, 268, 282 P2d 53, a murder case, the California Supreme Court found the first two of these elements present but not the third. To emphasize the horrible condition in which the victim's body had been left, the prosecution introduced the severed fingers of the deceased, preserved in alcohol. The supreme court found that this served no useful purpose other than to inflame the jury and, citing *People v Burns, supra*, held that its admission was improper and erroneous. After reviewing all the evidence, however, the court concluded that this error had not resulted in a miscarriage of justice (see Cal Const art VI, §13; Evid C §353(b)), which would have deprived the defendant of a fair trial and required a reversal of the judgment of conviction. Compare *People v Smith, supra* (trial court should have excluded color photographs of mutilated bodies), with *People v Milan* (1973) 9 C3d 185, 193, 107 CR 68 (under similar facts, trial court found not to have abused discretion in allowing photographs), and *People v Jentry* (1977) 69 CA3d 615, 626, 138 CR 250 (gruesome and inflammatory photographic enlargements properly admitted because highly probative of intent, malice, and felony (mayhem-murder issues)).

§30.3   III. TACTICS; PROCEDURE

Because of the difficulty of securing a reversal on the ground that the court abused its discretion, counsel must anticipate, through discovery, whether and how opposing counsel will try to introduce inflammatory evidence. Counsel should make a motion in limine before trial (see chap 2) to avoid the irreversible prejudicial effect that the inflammatory evidence will have on the jury, even with a cautionary instruction. The motion should show how the danger of prejudice outweighs the possible probative value of the evidence. If the motion is made and granted before trial, opposing counsel will be effectively barred from asking any questions relating to the inflammatory evidence and from referring to that evidence during the opening statement or voir dire of the jury.

The trial judge is required under *People v Green* (1980) 27 C3d 1, 24, 164 CR 1, to indicate factually for the record the balancing process that he or she went through and the reasons for admitting or excluding evidence under Evid C §352. In *People v Farmer* (1989) 47 C3d 888, 906, 254 CR 508, overruled on other grounds in *People v Waidla* (2000) 22 C4th 690, 724 n6, 94 CR2d 396, the supreme court acknowledged that admission of a tape-recorded telephone conversation of a victim in distress (audible groans) was inflammatory and that the preferred form of such probative evidence is a transcript. The court held, however, that the error was nonprejudicial. See also *Kessler v Gray* (1978) 77 CA3d 284, 291, 143 CR 496. To avoid the risk of waiving this issue on appeal, counsel must make sure that the judge states on the record what factors were weighed and the reasons for the decision.

The procedure for moving under Evid C §352 to exclude evidence of a prior felony conviction offered for impeachment purposes in a criminal case is discussed in California Criminal Law Procedure and Practice §§35.45–35.51 (7th ed Cal CEB 2004)

IV. ILLUSTRATIONS

§30.4   A. Discretion Upheld

In the following cases, the trial court's admission of inflammatory evidence was upheld:

- *People v Robles* (1970) 2 C3d 205, 214, 85 CR 166 (photographs aided understanding of pathologist's testimony);

- *People v Brawley* (1969) 1 C3d 277, 295, 82 CR 161 (admission of color photographs upheld because they showed wounds more clearly than black and white photographs and were circumstantial evidence of malice);

- *People v Stanworth* (1969) 71 C2d 820, 838, 80 CR 49 (photos relevant to issue of aggravation of crime and penalty);

- *People v Nye* (1969) 71 C2d 356, 369, 78 CR 467 (photographs showing 37 wounds relevant to issue of malice);

- *People v Reeves* (1980) 105 CA3d 444, 448, 164 CR 426 (hundreds of nude photographs of complaining witness boy and other boys admissible in lewd and lascivious conduct case because they were part of offense and tended to discredit defendant);

- *People v Moran* (1974) 39 CA3d 398, 411, 114 CR 413 (inflammatory photographs and film of exhumation of body within court's discretion to admit);

- *People v Dacy* (1970) 5 CA3d 216, 221, 85 CR 57 (photographs showing injuries of kidnap victim admissible); and

- *People v Seastone* (1969) 3 CA3d 60, 64, 82 CR 907 (gruesome photographs of murdered infant admissible to show malice and sexual molestation).

§30.5   B. Abuse of Discretion

In the following cases, admission of inflammatory evidence was held to be an abuse of the trial court's discretion:

- *People v Cardenas* (1982) 31 C3d 897, 906, 184 CR 165 (inflammatory effect of testimony on defendant's drug use and addiction substantially outweighed its slight probative value as to motive for attempted robbery and should have been excluded);

- *People v Vindiola* (1979) 96 CA3d 370, 384, 158 CR 6 (admission of cumulative evidence of prior booking photographs error because it indicated defendant's prior arrests and convictions);

- *People v Gibson* (1976) 56 CA3d 119, 134, 128 CR 302 (gruesome photos were cumulative evidence and should have been excluded because they were of slight relevancy and constituted "blatant appeal to the jury's emotions"); and

- *People v Smith* (1973) 33 CA3d 51, 69, 108 CR 698, overruled on other grounds in 22 C3d at 327 n7 (error to admit several color photographs of mutilated bodies of female victims after detailed autopsy testimony showing exact location and nature of wounds).

§30.6   V. STATUTE

Evidence Code §352 states:

> The court in its discretion may exclude evidence if its probative value is substantially outweighed by the probability that its admission will (a) necessitate undue consumption of time or (b) create substantial danger of undue prejudice of confusing the issues, or of misleading the jury.

§30.7   VI. STATING THE OBJECTION

Objection, Your Honor. This evidence is unduly inflammatory, and its resulting undue prejudice outweighs its slight probative value.

31

Excluding Relevant Evidence Under Evid C §352

I. INTRODUCTION §31.1

II. APPLICABILITY §31.2
   A. Unduly Prejudicial
      1. Civil Trials §31.3
      2. Criminal Trials §31.4
   B. Unduly Time Consuming §31.5
   C. Cumulative Evidence §31.6
      1. Analysis §31.7
      2. Illustrations §31.8
      3. Tactics §31.9
      4. Stating the Objection §31.10
   D. Confuses Issue or Misleads Jury §31.11

III. DURING TRIAL
   A. Court's Balancing Factors §31.12
   B. Responses
      1. Motion to Strike §31.13
      2. Offer of Proof §31.14
      3. Argument §31.15
      4. Record for Appeal §31.16

IV. PROCEDURE §31.17

V. STATUTE §31.18

VI. INVOKING JUDGE'S AUTHORITY §31.19

§31.1 I. INTRODUCTION

The trial court has the authority to exclude relevant evidence under Evid C §352 when it is unduly inflammatory (see chap 30). This chapter discusses the other circumstances in which counsel may ask the court to invoke its authority under §352 to exclude evidence. Note that counsel *asks* the court to invoke its discretion under §352; counsel does not *object* to the evidence's introduction under that section.

Section 352 allows a trial court to exclude relevant evidence when the court determines that the probative value of the proffered evidence is substantially outweighed by the probability that its admission will cause undue consumption of time, create a substantial danger of undue prejudice, confuse the issue, or mislead the jury.

Section 352 is the most frequently used section in the Evidence Code for excluding relevant evidence. It makes the trial judge the final "gatekeeper" when evidence is otherwise admissible. Because §352 is a safety net for trial attorneys "when all else fails," they must understand how the section is invoked, what type of showing must be made, and how to respond to an opponent who seeks §352 protection.

California courts are acutely aware of "trial management" problems and, whenever possible, try to streamline trials and narrow the issues before trial. The courts try to prevent "mini-trials" at the whim of counsel and laborious nit-picking witness examinations that consume valuable time and go nowhere. Section 352 aids the trial judge in controlling the flow, extent, and substance of otherwise-relevant evidence. Appellate courts have encouraged judges to use §352 in addition to their inherent power to control proceedings. See, *e.g., People v Jackson* (1971) 18 CA3d 504, 509, 95 CR 919.

§31.2   II. APPLICABILITY

Trial counsel are often confronted with a situation in which the opposition offers evidence that has only slight probative value but that raises a substantial risk of unduly prejudicing, confusing, or misleading the jury, or simply consuming an undue amount of time. The evidence is relevant, and none of the recognized grounds for objecting apply. In this situation, counsel can ask the trial judge to exercise the court's discretionary power under Evid C §352 to exclude the evidence.

Section 352 has tremendous potential as a means of keeping certain practices within reasonable bounds. See *People v Jackson* (1971) 18 CA3d 504, 509, 95 CR 919 (suggesting that trial courts exercise this discretion more often). For example, during cross-examination, counsel may question a witness about any matter that tends to impeach the witness, even if that matter is irrelevant to the main issues. Evid C §720. The Comment to Evid C §780 points out that the effect of the provision (together with Evid C §351) is to eliminate the former inflexible rule that all such "collateral" evidence is inadmissible. The Comment emphasizes, however, that such evidence may still be excluded (*i.e.,* kept within reasonable bounds) under the "substantial discretion" vested in the trial judge by §352.

Under Evid C §352, relevant evidence should be excluded in the following four circumstances:

- When the danger of undue prejudice to a party from the evidence exceeds its probative value;

- When the danger that the evidence will confuse the issues exceeds its probative value;

- When the danger of the jury's being misled by the evidence exceeds its probative value; and

- When undue consumption of time is required to admit the evidence.

See, *e.g., Wagner v Benson* (1980) 101 CA3d 27, 36, 161 CR 516 (evidence of fraud and deceit in cattle-raising scheme properly excluded because probative value of evidence was outweighed by danger of confusing and prejudicing jury); *Marocco v Ford Motor Co.* (1970) 7 CA3d 84, 94, 86 CR 526 (evidence of unrelated defects in manufacturing process not properly admitted, because it created dangers of prejudice, confusing issues, and misleading jury; error held harmless). Even in a strict products liability case, the court had discretion under §352 to exclude evidence of the addition of safety equipment after an accident occurred when that evidence was offered to show that a design change was feasible. See *Aguayo v Crompton & Knowles Corp.* (1986) 183 CA3d 1032, 1040, 228 CR 768.

A. Unduly Prejudicial

§31.3   1. Civil Trials

The trial judge may exclude evidence under Evid C §352 that may cause "undue" prejudice, which means that the evidence carries with it a danger of evoking an unfair or overwhelming personal bias while having little probative value. *People v Gionis* (1995) 9 C4th 1196, 40 CR2d 456; *People v Karis* (1988) 46 C3d 612, 638, 250 CR 659. Evidence that is likely to "inflame the passions" has been excluded under §352. See *People v Hoze* (1987) 195 CA3d 949, 954, 241 CR 14. In *Vorse v Sarasy* (1997) 53 CA4th 998, 1008, 62 CR2d 164, the court expounded at length on the test for prejudice:

> "Prejudice" as contemplated by section 352 is not so sweeping as to include any evidence the opponent finds inconvenient. Evidence is not prejudicial, as that term is used in a section 352 context, merely because it undermines the opponent's position or shores up that of the proponent. The ability to do so is what makes evidence relevant. The code speaks in terms of *undue* prejudice. Unless the dangers of undue prejudice, confusion, or time consumption "substantially outweigh'" the probative value of relevant evidence, a section 352 objection should fail. [Citation omitted.] "'The "prejudice" referred to in Evidence Code section 352 applies to evidence which uniquely tends to invoke an emotional bias against the defendant as an individual and which has very little effect on the issues. In applying section 352, "prejudicial" is not synonymous with "damaging." [Citations omitted.] The prejudice that section 352 "'is designed to avoid is not the prejudice or damage to a defense that naturally flows from relevant, probative evidence.' [Citations omitted.] 'Rather, the statute uses the word in its etymological sense of "prejudging a person or cause on the basis of extraneous factors."'" [Citations omitted.] In other words, evidence should be excluded as unduly prejudicial when it is of such nature as to inflame the emotions of the jury, motivating them to use the information, not to logically evaluate the point upon which it

is relevant, but to reward or punish one side because of the juror's emotional reaction. In such a circumstance, the evidence is unduly prejudicial because of the substantial likelihood the jury will use it for an illegitimate purpose.

The evidence subject to exclusion may be testimonial evidence, writings, or material objects. Evid C §140. For example, if a letter incidentally impeaching a witness contains prejudicial material, the trial judge may exclude it. *O'Gan v King City Joint Union High Sch. Dist.* (1970) 3 CA3d 641, 645, 83 CR 795.

Because evidence that is excluded as unduly prejudicial may also be excluded on other §352 grounds, trial counsel should cite all possible grounds. Judges may consider that a companion §352 ground is more appropriate or that several but not all grounds apply. See *Wagner v Benson* (1980) 101 CA3d 27, 161 CR 516.

§31.4   2. Criminal Trials

The "prejudice" referred to in Evid C §352 applies to evidence that uniquely tends to evoke an emotional bias against defendant as an individual and has very little effect on the issues. In applying §352, "prejudicial" is not synonymous with "damaging." *People v Coddington* (2000) 23 C4th 529, 588, 97 CR2d 528, overruled on other grounds in *Price v Superior Court* (2001) 25 C4th 1046, 1069 n13, 108 CR2d 409.

In criminal cases, Evid C §352 has historically been the basis for allowing the court to exclude evidence of prior felony convictions offered under Evid C §788 to impeach a witness if the risk of undue prejudice outweighs the probative value of the evidence. *People v Castro* (1985) 38 C3d 301, 211 CR 719.

For a prior felony conviction to be considered a potential source of impeachment, the conviction must involve moral turpitude. *People v Castro, supra.* Offenses involving moral turpitude include not only those showing dishonesty or lack of integrity but also those showing a "general readiness to do evil." Although the latter class of moral turpitude offenses should not weigh as heavily in favor of admission as offenses involving dishonesty, they are nonetheless relevant and may be considered by the trial court in determining the appropriate exercise of discretion under §352. 38 C3d at 314.

The court in *Castro* held that, although simple possession of heroin does not necessarily demonstrate moral turpitude, possession of heroin for sale does. Although possession of heroin for sale does not demonstrate dishonesty, it does demonstrate the intent to corrupt others. 38 C3d at 317.

Whether a prior conviction involves moral turpitude is a question of law that depends on the elements of the crime in the abstract and not on the underlying facts of the conviction. *People v Collins* (1986) 42 C3d 378, 390, 228 CR 899. In *Collins,* the court held that the four circumstances (see §31.2) in which relevant evidence should be excluded under Evid C §352 remain relevant to its application after adoption of Proposition 8, which sought to broaden the admissibility of evidence in certain areas of criminal law (Cal Const art I, §28(f)). The four factors should be considered as guiding rather than restraining the trial court's discretion to apply §352. The court should further consider any other relevant circumstances. 42 C3d at 391. See also *People v Martinez* (1985) 175 CA3d 881, 221 CR 258.

Whether to admit evidence of similar bad acts should be based on an analysis of Evid C §352. In *Andrews v City & County of San Francisco* (1988) 205 CA3d 938, 252 CR 716, the plaintiff brought a civil action against a police officer for false imprisonment, wrongful arrest, and assault and battery. After completing a §352 analysis, the court allowed evidence of the officer's prior alleged acts of misconduct. The evidence was offered to prove intent and was admissible under Evid C §110(b). Moreover, the officer had put his intent at issue.

When codefendants in a criminal case are being tried together, it is reversible error for the court to invoke §352 to exclude evidence of significant probative value as to one defendant because of potential substantial prejudice to a codefendant. *People v Reeder* (1978) 82 CA3d 543, 553, 147 CR 275. The appellate court in *Reeder* recommended that the trial judge, on the request of the codefendant's counsel, should have either given a limiting instruction on use of the evidence (Evid C §355) or offered the codefendant who wished to exclude evidence the right to move for a mistrial if he considered the evidence sufficiently prejudicial to preclude a fair trial. 82 CA3d at 555.

Citing *People v Castro, supra,* the supreme court in *People v Wheeler* (1992) 4 C4th 284, 14 CR2d 418, noted that a court, when determining under Evid C §352 whether to admit evidence of similar bad acts, must always consider the factors traditionally deemed pertinent in this area, *e.g.,* whether there is some basis for inferring that the person who committed a crime involving moral turpitude is more likely to be dishonest than a witness who has not committed such a crime or about whom no such thing is known.

Using an Evid C §352-type of analysis to determine whether the proffered evidence was unduly time consuming, prejudicial, confusing, or misleading, the supreme court in *People v Bonin* (1989) 47 C3d 808, 849, 254 CR 298, stated that testimony in a murder trial by the victims' parents should not have been admitted. See also *People v Brown* (1988) 46 C3d 432, 442, 250 CR 604 (use of mannequin to illustrate testimony was proper); *People v Siripongs* (1988) 45 C3d 548, 573, 247 CR 729 (admission of telephone conversation recording in Thai and of both Thai and English transcription of recording was not abuse of discretion).

In a trial involving rape, the trial court has the discretion to exclude the victim's address and telephone number if the probative value of this evidence is outweighed by "the creation of substantial danger to the victim." Evid C §352.1.

§31.5 B. Unduly Time Consuming

If admitting evidence will unnecessarily extend the length of the trial, cause "mini-trials" on collateral issues, or waste court time when compared with the probative value of the evidence, Evid C §352 applies. *Hinson v Clairemont Community Hosp.* (1990) 218 CA3d 1110, 267 CR 503, disapproved in part on other grounds in *Alexander v Superior Court* (1993) 5 C4th 1218, 1228 n10, 23 CR2d 397. But see *Andrews v City & County of San Francisco* (1988) 205 CA3d 938, 252 CR 716 (excluding police officer's prior misconduct was abuse of discretion, based on time involved). An attack by a defendant on an accuser's credibility is considered fundamental evidence and is not outweighed by the time consumed. *People v Mayfield* (1972) 23 CA3d 236, 100 CR 104.

The "consumption of time" ground brings into play other Evidence Code sections involving impeachment cross-examination. For example, during cross-examination, counsel may question a witness about any matter that tends to impeach that witness, even if the matter is irrelevant to the main issues. Evid C §780. The Comment to Evid C §780 points out that the effect of Evid C §780 (together with Evid C §351) is to eliminate the former, inflexible rule that all "collateral" evidence is inadmissible. The Comment emphasizes that such evidence may still be excluded (*i.e.*, kept within reasonable bounds) under the "substantial discretion" vested in the trial judge by §352.

In complex cases, essential facts cannot be excluded simply because of the time required to present the evidence. *Andrews v City & County of San Francisco, supra.*

§31.6 C. Cumulative Evidence

Cumulative evidence is evidence that repeats the substance of evidence that was previously introduced. Repeating the substance of such evidence may give it undue emphasis and consume undue time. Note, however, that photographs of a murder victim or of a crime scene are not cumulative simply because testimony also has been introduced to prove the facts that the photographs are intended to establish. *People v Box* (2000) 23 C4th 1153, 1199, 99 CR2d 69.

The trial judge should stop the introduction of cumulative evidence if its probative value is substantially outweighed by the probability that its admission will consume an undue amount of time or create undue prejudice. Evid C §352. The "cumulative evidence" objection must be distinguished from the "asked and answered" objection discussed in chap 11, which applies to a witness and arises when a question is repeated after the witness has already answered it.

§31.7 1. Analysis

The power to exclude cumulative evidence is both inherent in the court and provided by statute. Evid C §§352, 723, 765; *Peat, Marwick, Mitchell & Co. v Superior Court* (1988) 200 CA3d 272, 286, 245 CR 873 (court has inherent power to preclude evidence to cure abuses or overreaching involving confidential information); *Weller v Chainarria* (1965) 233 CA2d 234, 43 CR 364. The court has wide discretion in this regard, and reversal on appeal is rare. *Horn v General Motors Corp.* (1976) 17 C3d 359, 371, 131 CR 78; *People v Albert* (1960) 182 CA2d 729, 6 CR 473. See also *People v Szeto* (1981) 29 C3d 20, 30, 171 CR 652 (because proposed stipulation was inadequate, evidence introduced on facts that were subject of stipulation was not cumulative).

Under Evid C §352, the judge weighs the probative value of the evidence against various dangers, such as the risk that repeating the evidence will give it undue emphasis and consume an undue amount of time. *Cubic Corp. v Marty* (1986) 185 CA3d 438, 229 CR 828. If the judge finds that these dangers substantially outweigh the probative value of the evidence, the judge will sustain the objection. The record must show that the court engaged in this weighing process when making the decision. *People v Green* (1980) 27 C3d 1, 24, 164 CR 1. Counsel should take care to protect the record by asking the court to refer specifically to §352 when making this ruling.

§31.8   2. Illustrations

In the following cases, the courts considered whether to exclude cumulative evidence:

- In a condemnation case, undisputed evidence had been introduced that property could be subdivided for residential purposes. The judge properly excluded as cumulative the proposed expert testimony to prove the same point. See *McCarthy v City of Manhattan Beach* (1953) 41 C2d 879, 895, 264 P2d 932.

- In a criminal case, evidence of prior crimes committed by a prosecution witness and her boyfriend, who was also a prosecution witness, was properly excluded as cumulative on the issue of the witness's credibility in view of other evidence of the close relationship between the witnesses. See *People v Burgener* (1986) 41 C3d 505, 525, 224 CR 112, disapproved on other grounds in 19 C4th at 239.

- In a products liability case, a witness for the plaintiff was not allowed to testify about his personal observations at the scene of an accident, the crashworthiness of the defendant's aircraft, or the efficacy of certain safety features of the aircraft. The trial court excluded the evidence as cumulative of evidence presented by other witnesses for the plaintiff. Reversing the judgment on other grounds, the appellate court stated that on retrial that the witness should be allowed to testify because, as the only observer to investigate the scene of the crash and review the wreckage, his testimony would be "unique" and not cumulative of other testimony. See *McGee v Cessna Aircraft Co.* (1983) 139 CA3d 179, 192, 188 CR 542.

- In a products liability case, the court had discretion to exclude evidence of a change in the product's design on the ground that it was cumulative of expert testimony on the feasibility of such a change. See *Aguayo v Crompton & Knowles Corp.* (1986) 183 CA3d 1032, 1040, 228 CR 768.

- In a criminal case, the prosecution introduced rebuttal evidence that was cumulative of earlier direct testimony by the same witness about the distance between the gun and the victim when he was shot. Although cumulative, this evidence was properly admitted because it fortified a part of the case-in-chief that had been attacked by defense evidence. *People v Graham* (1978) 83 CA3d 736, 741, 149 CR 6, disapproved on other grounds in 18 C4th at 569.

§31.9   3. Tactics

The judge may be primarily concerned about the amount of time that it will take to present cumulative evidence, but counsel should focus on the effect that the evidence may have on the jury. An objection to presenting cumulative evidence may be appropriate whenever it may damage the client's case. For example, defense counsel may want to object to the repetitive presentation of a series of gruesome photographs of the victim.

Although repeated questioning of a witness on a particular subject may emphasize significant points, counsel should take care not to bore the jury. A series of hypothetical questions can be used to summarize favorable evidence without appearing to repeat it. To prevent opposing counsel from profiting from this tactic, counsel may want to object that the evidence is cumulative. If the evidence is being introduced during cross-examination, the court may be reluctant to sustain the objection. Judges tend to allow counsel wide latitude on cross-examination as long as the questions are within the scope of the direct examination or are for impeachment purposes. Before objecting to cumulative evidence, counsel should consider that the jury may construe the objection as an implied admission that the evidence has been proved as fact. Whenever possible, counsel should object to cumulative evidence outside the jury's presence. Through discovery proceedings, settlement discussions, and pretrial conferences, counsel usually knows before the start of trial what evidence opposing counsel intends to offer. If it appears that the evidence will be cumulative, counsel should move in limine to exclude it.

The problem of cumulative evidence often arises with expert witnesses. Each side may propose to call a roster of experts on a particular subject. In this situation, Evid C §723 specifically empowers the judge "at any time before or during the trial" to limit the number of expert witnesses that a party may call. In *Horn v General Motors Corp.* (1976) 17 C3d 359, 371,

131 CR 78, the trial court refused to allow a fifth expert witness to testify to the same facts testified to by four previous experts. The California Supreme Court upheld the trial court's discretion to exclude cumulative testimony under Evid C §352 as well as to limit the number of expert witnesses under Evid C §723.

Note that the courts today commonly impose "time limits" during trial, *e.g.*, limits on presentation of evidence, jury selection, witness examinations, or final arguments, that seek to make the trial process more efficient.

§31.10   4. Stating the Objection

> Objection, Your Honor. The proposed evidence is cumulative because it merely repeats _ _[e.g., similar testimony already given by _ _[name]_]_ _, and I therefore move to exclude it under Evidence Code section 352.

§31.11   D. Confuses Issues or Misleads Jury

Subject to the court's discretion, evidence that would confuse the issues or mislead the jury is properly excluded. *People v Milner* (1988) 45 C3d 227, 238, 246 CR 713.

In *Ehrhardt v Brunswick, Inc.* (1986) 186 CA3d 734, 740, 231 CR 60, a products liability case, the appellate court held that the trial court properly excluded a videotaped demonstration of a possible cause of a water-skiing accident because the tape was inconsistent with all eyewitnesses' testimony and the record provided no support for the assumptions on which the tape was based. See 1 Witkin, California Evidence, *Circumstantial Evidence* §23 (4th ed 2000).

III. DURING TRIAL

§31.12   A. Court's Balancing Factors

The trial judge must balance the probative value of the offered evidence against its potential prejudicial effect, undue consumption of time, and the likelihood that the admission of such evidence might cause confusion. This process requires consideration of the relation between the actual evidence and any inferences that can be drawn from it. The trial judge must consider whether the evidence is relevant to the main issue or only to collateral issues, the necessity of the evidence to the proponent's case, and other reasons described in Evid C §352. *Rufo v Simpson* (2001) 86 CA4th 573, 599, 103 CR2d 492; *Kessler v Gray* (1978) 77 CA3d 284, 291, 143 CR 496.

When invoked, §352 allows the court to weigh the probative value of specific evidence: Is the evidence relevant to central issues or only to a collateral matter? Is the evidence necessary to the party's case? Is it important or merely "side-show" evidence? Do any of the §352 grounds for exclusion apply? *Hinson v Clairemont Community Hosp.* (1990) 218 CA3d 1110, 1124, 267 CR 503, disapproved in part on other grounds in *Alexander v Superior Court* (1993) 5 C4th 1218, 1228 n10, 23 CR2d 397. The specific circumstances of the case are critical. Perhaps the best test for counsel, when balancing the circumstances against the proffered evidence, is whether it might exasperate the judge, which is a common reason for a judge to sustain this objection.

The trial judge must show on the record the factors involved in the exercise of discretion in sustaining the objection. *People v Green* (1980) 27 C3d 1, 25, 164 CR 1; *People v Meacham* (1984) 152 CA3d 142, 199 CR 586 (abuse of discretion; "weighing" not shown on record). Some evidence is obviously subject to exclusion under §352, *e.g.,* cumulative gruesome photographs in a murder case. See chap 30.

If it becomes necessary to request a §352 ruling, counsel should seek to have the matter heard outside the jury's presence. See *Hrnjak v Graymar, Inc.* (1971) 4 C3d 725, 733, 94 CR 623; *Acosta v Southern Cal. Rapid Transit Dist.* (1970) 2 C3d 19, 26, 84 CR 184 (counsel's failure to accept trial court's offer to hear §352 matter outside jury's presence was proper ground for court's decision to deny counsel's request to have matter heard before jury and to exclude evidence). Because jurors often complain about trial delays caused by frequent recesses to discuss matters outside the jury's presence, counsel should try to avoid appearing to the jury to be the cause of those delays and should try to have the matter heard during a recess or before or at the end of the trial day.

If evidence is admitted despite a request for exclusion under §352, the record must affirmatively show that the court weighed the risk of undue prejudice against the probative value of the evidence and that the court explicitly found that the evidentiary value outweighed the risk of undue prejudice. The record should be sufficient to permit meaningful review of any claim of abuse of discretion. Evid C §§353–354; *People v Clair* (1992) 2 C4th 629, 7 CR2d 564; *People v Montiel* (1985) 39 C3d 910, 924, 218 CR 572; *People v Navarez* (1985) 169 CA3d 936, 948, 215 CR 519.

Failure to make such a record is not necessarily reversible error, however, especially if the judge must also indicate on the record the reasons for a particular ruling under §352. *People v Green, supra.*

B. Responses

§31.13   1. Motion to Strike

If evidence deleterious to a party is admitted either because the question is answered too fast or counsel is unaware of the Evid C §352 danger, a motion to strike the evidence is proper. If it is sustained, the motion should be followed by a motion for cautionary instructions to the jury. See chaps 52–53.

§31.14 2. Offer of Proof

When confronted by opposing counsel with a motion to exclude evidence under Evid C §352, the party offering the evidence should make an appropriate offer of proof that will demonstrate to the judge the substance, purpose, and relevance of the offered evidence. Evid C §354(a); *United Sav. & Loan Ass'n v Reeder Dev. Corp.* (1976) 57 CA3d 282, 293, 129 CR 113.

§31.15 3. Argument

Counsel offering evidence to which an Evid C §352 motion to exclude is made should demonstrate to the court, through oral argument, why the offered evidence is not unduly prejudicial, cumulative, time consuming, or will not confuse the issues or mislead the jury. Counsel's argument should be complete in every detail.

§31.16 4. Record for Appeal

If all else fails, counsel should be sure that there is an adequate record for appeal. A trial court's ruling under Evid C §352 will not be overruled without a showing of "a clear abuse of discretion." See *Andrews v City & County of San Francisco* (1988) 205 CA3d 938, 252 CR 716.

§31.17 IV. PROCEDURE

Obviously, counsel cannot compel the court to exclude evidence under Evid C §352. Remember that counsel asks the court to invoke its discretion under §352; counsel does not object to the evidence's introduction under that section. If the court declines to exercise its discretionary power under that section, counsel will be able to successfully assert that failure as an error on appeal only if there is a clear showing on the record that the trial court abused its discretion. See *Wagner v Benson* (1980) 101 CA3d 27, 36, 161 CR 516.

In most instances, the trial court's ruling will be upheld as an appropriate exercise of discretion, but the courts have held to the contrary in certain cases. See, *e.g., Hrnjak v Graymar, Inc.* (1971) 4 C3d 725, 729, 94 CR 623 (trial court failed to weigh probative value versus prejudicial effect of admitting evidence of insurance to show motive to malinger); *Thor v Boska* (1974) 38 CA3d 558, 567, 113 CR 296 (in malpractice action, trial court erroneously excluded evidence of defendant's destruction of treatment records when highly probative of defendant's guilty state of mind).

All relevant evidence that points to a defendant's guilt is prejudicial to the defendant's defense. The stronger the evidence, the more it is prejudicial. The prejudice referred to in §352 applies to evidence that uniquely tends to evoke an emotional bias against the defendant as an individual and that has little effect on the issues.

Counsel should make sure that the record reflects the fact that the court weighed the risk of undue prejudice generated by the evidence against its probative value on the issues in dispute. See *People v Lankford* (1989) 210 CA3d 227, 241, 258 CR 322. There is no requirement, however, that the judge make an affirmative finding; it is sufficient if the record shows that the judge weighed prejudice against probative value. See *Continental Airlines v McDonnell Douglas Corp.* (1989) 216 CA3d 388, 412, 264 CR 779.

Ordinarily, counsel's purpose in raising §352 is to call to the judge's attention the fact that the probative value of the proffered evidence is outweighed by a serious risk. For example, if defense counsel offers evidence to show that the plaintiff has a reputation for dishonesty (see Evid C §1324), plaintiff's counsel might respond by pointing out the excessive amount of time that this matter would consume, by enumerating the witnesses that the plaintiff would be obliged to call in support (see Evid C §790; chap 23), and by estimating the amount of time that each witness would consume. Plaintiff's counsel would seek to demonstrate that the time consumed by allowing both sides to present evidence on the subject would substantially outweigh the probative value of that evidence, and that therefore all evidence relating to the plaintiff's reputation for honesty should be excluded under §352.

Counsel should anticipate (*e.g.,* through discovery) whether a §352 request will be needed and, if possible, should bring an in limine motion at the chambers conference (see chap 2). If successful, the motion will prevent opposing counsel from referring to the excluded evidence during both the opening statement and the jury voir dire. By presenting the issue to the court before trial, the judge will have more time to engage in the weighing process that *People v Green* (1980) 27 C3d 1, 25, 164 CR 1, requires to be put on the record.

On appeal, a showing must be made that a timely objection was made on the §352 ground and that the judge weighed the §352 factors involved. Evid C §§352, 353(a), 354.

The court may invoke §352 sua sponte. *Gherman v Colburn* (1977) 72 CA3d 544, 581, 140 CR 330.

Because this "objection" (*i.e.,* the motion to exclude) can usually be anticipated through discovery proceedings, counsel should raise an objection under §352 through a motion in limine. See chap 2. If the court overrules this "objection," the objection must be renewed at trial. Also, from a tactical standpoint, the judge may have a better context during trial to make a ruling. In limine motions also allow the court to prevent counsel from referring to the evidence during voir dire, opening statement, or the trial.

§31.18   V. STATUTE

Evidence Code §352 states:

> The court in its discretion may exclude evidence if its probative value is substantially outweighed by the probability that its admission will (a) necessitate undue consumption of time or (b) create substantial danger of undue prejudice, of confusing the issues, or of misleading the jury.

§31.19 VI. INVOKING JUDGE'S AUTHORITY

Objection, Your Honor. The probative value of the proffered evidence is slight because _ _[state reason]_ _ and is outweighed by the fact that this evidence will _ _[consume an undue amount of time/create undue prejudice/confuse the issues/mislead the jury]_ _. I request that it be excluded under Evidence Code section 352.

32

Other Policy Exclusions of Evidence

I. INTRODUCTION §32.1

II. EVIDENCE OF SETTLEMENT NEGOTIATIONS
    A. Offer of Compromise Payment in Civil Cases §32.2
    B. Acceptance of Compromise Payment in Civil Cases §32.3
    C. Offer to Plead Guilty §32.4

III. EVIDENCE OF SUBSEQUENT SAFETY MEASURES §32.5

IV. EVIDENCE REGARDING LIABILITY INSURANCE §32.6

V. EVIDENCE OF SIMILAR ACTS OR OCCURRENCES §32.7

VI. LIMITED ADMISSIBILITY INSTRUCTION §32.8

VII. MISCELLANEOUS OTHER STATUTES §32.9

VIII. ALTERNATIVES TO OBJECTING §32.10

IX. STATING THE OBJECTION §32.11

§32.1 I. INTRODUCTION

When objecting to the introduction of evidence, counsel must make the specific ground of the objection clear. See §4.19. Evid C §353(a). Counsel must also cite the specific statutory or constitutional authority establishing that ground as a valid basis for objecting. See Evid C §351. Section 351 states that "except as otherwise provided by statute, all relevant evidence is admissible." The word "statute" in this context includes constitutional provisions (Evid C §230; Comment to Evid C §351). On what constitutes relevant evidence, see chap 17.

The list of available objections to offered evidence discussed in this book is not exhaustive. The focus in chaps 17–31 is on objections most frequently used and misused. This chapter summarizes several grounds for objection that appear in the Evidence Code but are less frequently used.

II. EVIDENCE OF SETTLEMENT NEGOTIATIONS

§32.2   A. Offer of Compromise Payment in Civil Cases

Evidence Code §1152 states:

>   (a) Evidence that a person has, in compromise or from humanitarian motives, furnished or offered or promised to furnish money or any other thing, act, or service to another who has sustained or will sustain or claims that he or she has sustained or will sustain loss or damage, as well as any conduct or statements made in negotiation thereof, is inadmissible to prove his or her liability for the loss or damage or any part of it.
>
>   (b) In the event that evidence of an offer to compromise is admitted in an action for breach of the covenant of good faith and fair dealing or violation of subdivision (h) of Section 790.03 of the Insurance Code, then at the request of the party against whom the evidence is admitted, or at the request of the party who made the offer to compromise that was admitted, evidence relating to any other offer or counteroffer to compromise the same or substantially the same claimed loss or damage shall also be admissible for the same purpose as the initial evidence regarding settlement. Other than as may be admitted in an action for breach of the covenant of good faith and fair dealing or violation of subdivision (h) of Section 790.03 of the Insurance Code, evidence of settlement offers shall not be admitted in a motion for a new trial, in any proceeding involving an additur or remittitur, or on appeal.
>
>   (c) This section does not affect the admissibility of evidence of any of the following:
>
>   (1) Partial satisfaction of an asserted claim or demand without questioning its validity when such evidence is offered to prove the validity of the claim.
>
>   (2) A debtor's payment or promise to pay all or a part of his or her preexisting debt when such evidence is offered to prove the creation of a new duty on his or her part or a revival of his or her preexisting duty.

Evidence Code §1152(a) permits an offer of compromise to be considered by the trier of fact as an admission of liability if it is presented without objection. See Comment to Evid C §1152.

The pre-Evidence Code distinction between offers and other types of admissions made during settlement negotiations was eliminated by Evid C §1152(a). Evidence of "any conduct or statements made in negotiation" is inadmissible. The statement of a party against whom a claim is pending that the party is willing to settle the claim, when not connected with an offer of compromise, may, however, be received in evidence as a party's admission. The party's intent is dispositive in deciding whether the statement is an admission or offer to compromise. *Moving Picture Mach. Operators Union v Glasgow Theatres, Inc.* (1970) 6 CA3d 395, 402, 86 CR 33 (admission made after settlement negotiations had terminated).

The phrase "to another" in Evid C §1152(a) codifies the rule of *Brown v Pacific Elec. Ry.* (1947) 79 CA2d 613, 180 P2d 424, that evidence of compromise negotiations and settlements with others who are not parties to the present action is inadmissible. See also *Shepherd v Walley* (1972) 28 CA3d 1079, 1083, 105 CR 387. Disclosure to the jury of sliding scale recovery agreements is within the court's discretion under Evid C §352. See CCP §877.5. See also Ins C §11582 (settlement of automobile liability claim). See 1 Witkin, California Evidence, *Circumstantial Evidence* §§150–151 (4th ed 2000).

Evidence Code §1152 does not prohibit the introduction of evidence that may be circumstantial evidence of other relevant facts. *Lemer v Boise Cascade, Inc.* (1980) 107 CA3d 1, 11, 165 CR 555 (settlement offer admitted to show good faith). For a case in which a purported settlement or compromise was admitted for proof of other relevant facts, see *Carney v Santa Cruz Women Against Rape* (1990) 221 CA3d 1009, 271 CR 30. In this action for libel, the court held that an apology letter from a purported victim was properly admitted because it bore on the truth or falsity of statements in a newsletter as opposed to constituting evidence of settlement or compromise. Even if the court admits evidence of settlement negotiations or offers of compromise, the appellate courts will not reverse unless a different result would have been likely had the evidence been excluded. *Warner Constr. Corp. v City of Los Angeles* (1970) 2 C3d 285, 299, 85 CR 444 (appellate court found no prejudice). Finally, in insurance litigation, the language of Evid C §1152 does not preclude the introduction of settlement negotiations if offered not to prove liability for the original loss but to prove failure to process the claim fairly and in good faith. *Shade Foods, Inc. v Innovative Products Sales and Mktg.* (2000) 78 CA4th 847, 915, 93 CR2d 364.

§32.3   B. Acceptance of Compromise Payment in Civil Cases

Evidence Code §1154 states:

> Evidence that a person has accepted or offered or promised to accept a sum of money or any other thing, act, or service in satisfaction of a claim, as well as any conduct or statements made in negotiation thereof, is inadmissible to prove the invalidity of the claim or any part of it.

Section 1154 is the companion provision to Evid C §1152(a), discussed in §32.2.

§32.4   C. Offer to Plead Guilty

Evidence Code §1153 states:

> Evidence of a plea of guilty, later withdrawn, or of an offer to plead guilty to the crime charged or to any other crime, made by the defendant in a criminal action is inadmissible in any action or in any proceeding of any nature, including proceedings before agencies, commissions, boards, and tribunals.

Penal Code §1192.4 has substantially the same effect. A related statute,

Evid C §1153.5, provides that an offer for civil resolution of a criminal matter under CCP §33, or admissions made during discussion of such an offer, are not admissible in any action. Penal Code §1192.4 and Evid C §1153, as applied to criminal cases, may have been abrogated by Cal Const art I, §28(d) (the "truth-in-evidence" provision of Proposition 8). If Proposition 8 applies, counsel may argue that the evidence of a withdrawn plea is excludable under Evid C §352. Because of the risk that this evidence will be admitted, defense counsel who wishes to keep such evidence from the trier of fact should obtain a stipulation in writing from opposing counsel that all settlement negotiations are confidential and will not be revealed at trial in the case in chief, as impeachment, or in rebuttal.

§32.5 III. EVIDENCE OF SUBSEQUENT SAFETY MEASURES

Evidence Code §1151 states:

> When, after occurrence of an event, remedial or precautionary measures are taken, which, if taken previously, would have tended to make the event less likely to occur, evidence of such subsequent measures is inadmissible to prove negligence or culpable conduct in connection with the event.

For instance, evidence of an insurer's subsequent revisions of an exclusionary clause in a policy is inadmissible. *State Farm Fire & Cas. Co. v Eddy* (1990) 218 CA3d 958, 972, 267 CR 379. See *Morehouse v Taubman* (1970) 5 CA3d 548, 555, 85 CR 308. Additionally, in a medical malpractice action, post-event hospital peer review evidence is inadmissible to prove negligence. *Fox v Kramer* (2000) 22 C4th 531, 535, 93 CR2d 497.

Without this provision, defendants would tend to postpone making repairs and taking desirable precautionary measures as long as these acts could be used against them as admissions of fault. See *Daggett v Atchison, T. & S.F. Ry.* (1957) 48 C2d 655, 660, 313 P2d 557; *Sappenfield v Main St. & Agric. Park R.R.* (1891) 91 C 48, 61, 27 P 590. See also *Westbrook v Gordon H. Ball, Inc.* (1967) 248 CA2d 209, 215, 56 CR 422.

The policy considerations of Evid C §1151 do not apply to subsequent remedial measures taken by a third person who is not a party to the litigation. Thus, evidence of post-accident modifications of equipment made by the plaintiff's employer are admissible to show that the product was defective. *Magnante v Pettibone-Wood Mfg. Co.* (1986) 183 CA3d 764, 767, 228 CR 420.

Evidence of subsequent safety measures may under certain circumstances be offered for a limited purpose such as impeachment, *i.e.*, to show prior inconsistent acts or statements. *Daggett v Atchison, T. & S.F. Ry.* (1957) 48 C2d 655, 665, 313 P2d 557; *Hatfield v Levy Bros.* (1941) 18 C2d 798, 809, 117 P2d 841; *Inyo Chem. Co. v City of Los Angeles* (1936) 5 C2d 525, 543, 55 P2d 850. For an interesting application of admission of evidence to impeach a witness, see *Wilson v Gilbert* (1972) 25 CA3d 607, 615, 102 CR 31 (evidence admitted that physician received medical training after alleged negligence and referred similar cases to other physicians). This type of impeachment, however, is permitted only if the witness has testified that the condition existing before the change was safe or free from defect and if "the witness *himself* authorized, recommended, approved, directed, or supervised the making, or himself made the subsequent repair, alteration or change of procedure." *Pierce v J.C. Penney Co.* (1959) 167 CA2d 3, 8, 334 P2d 117. See Comment to Evid C §1151. See also *Sanchez v Bagues & Sons Mortuaries* (1969) 271 CA2d 188, 76 CR 372 (discussion of weighing process involved in admitting impeachment evidence). The proponent of the evidence has the burden of showing its admissibility. 271 CA2d at 190.

Evidence Code §1151 does not apply to cases based on strict products liability. See *Ault v International Harvester Co.* (1974) 13 C3d 113, 118, 117 CR 812. The court in *Ault* held that such cases do not involve issues of "culpable conduct" and that the manufacturer's self-interest is in continuing to make product improvements without regard to the possible use of remedial conduct as evidence of the defective nature of the original product. *Ault* created the potential for a substantial exception to Evid C §1151 in products liability litigation. See, *e.g., Burke v Almaden Vineyards, Inc.* (1978) 86 CA3d 768, 771, 150 CR 419.

A trial court's refusal to allow evidence of product improvements in a strict products liability case, notwithstanding the holding in *Ault v International Harvester Co., supra*, was held not to be reversible error in *Finn v G.D. Searle Co.* (1984) 35 C3d 691, 200 CR 870. The supreme court held that evidence of the post-accident warning excluded by the trial court was cumulative in light of other evidence heard by the jury that, following the plaintiff's injury, warnings describing effects similar to those experienced by the plaintiff had been inserted by the manufacturer in its drug containers. 35 C3d at 703.

In *Aguayo v Crompton & Knowles Corp.* (1986) 183 CA3d 1032, 1040, 228 CR 768, the appellate court took a similar approach in holding that even in a products liability case the court has discretion under Evid C §352 to exclude evidence of the addition of safety equipment after the accident. The court reasoned that *Ault v International Harvester Co., supra*, does not mandate the admission of such evidence but merely permits it to the extent consistent with other rules of evidence. See also *Santelli v Otis Elevator Co.* (1989) 215 CA3d 210, 263 CR 496, in which the court observed that although Evid C §1151 does not apply to strict liability, when a nonparty's liability predicated on negligence could be adversely affected by evidence of post-accident safety measures, such evidence is properly excluded.

Post-accident consumer warnings are admissible in strict liability cases. *Schelbauer v Butler Mfg. Co.* (1984) 35 C3d 442, 450, 198 CR 155. Other exceptions allowing subsequent safety measures evidence include:

- Evidence offered for impeachment purposes (*Daggett v Atchison, T. & S.F. Ry.* (1957) 48 C2d 655, 313 P2d 557);
- Evidence of the duty to take safety precautions (*Baldwin Contracting Co. v Winston Steel Works* (1965) 236 CA2d 565, 46 CR 421);

- Evidence on the feasibility of a safety measure (*Baldwin Contracting Co. v Winston Steel Workers, supra*);

- Evidence on the denial of control of premises (*Morehouse v Taubman, supra*);

- Evidence of third party repairs (*Magnante v Pettibone-Wood Mfg. Co., supra*);

- Evidence showing willful disregard in a punitive damage case in which subsequent remedial action was not taken (*Hilliard v A.H. Robins Co.* (1983) 148 CA3d 374, 401, 196 CR 117);

- Evidence showing knowledge, control, and discussions regarding repair (*Alpert v Villa Romano Homeowners' Ass'n* (2000) 81 CA4th 1320, 1341, 96 CR2d 364); and

- Evidence proving ownership (see 1 Witkin, California Evidence, *Circumstantial Evidence* §164 (4th ed 2000)).

§32.6   IV. EVIDENCE REGARDING LIABILITY INSURANCE

Evidence Code §1155 states:

> Evidence that a person was, at the time a harm was suffered by another, insured wholly or partially against loss arising from liability for that harm is inadmissible to prove negligence or other wrongdoing.

Under Evid C §1155, evidence of a defendant's insurance is inadmissible to prove the defendant's negligence or other wrongdoing. Such evidence is regarded as both irrelevant and prejudicial to the defendant. *Staples v Hoefke* (1987) 189 CA3d 1397, 1410, 235 CR 165. Thus, reference in the jury's presence to the extent of liability insurance coverage, like references to a party's wealth or poverty, may also be assigned as misconduct, often warranting a mistrial or reversal of the judgment. See §§1.7, 29.4.

Evidence of liability insurance may be admissible, however, if it is an integral part of other admissible evidence of substantial probative value. For example, proof of a plaintiff's receipt of liability insurance proceeds may be admissible as evidence of a motive to malinger. *Hrnjak v Graymar, Inc.* (1971) 4 C3d 725, 732, 94 CR 623. Before such evidence may be admitted, the defendant must make a foundational showing in a hearing out of the presence of the jury "that the evidence of collateral source receipts establishes a strong inference that plaintiff was motivated by the insurance receipts rather than by the actual disabling extent of his injuries." 4 C3d at 733.

In a proper case, a witness may be cross-examined to show bias even though the cross-examination discloses that insurance exists. *Hart v Wielt* (1970) 4 CA3d 224, 231, 84 CR 220 (witness was insurance investigator). In Federal Employees Liability Act cases, such evidence is never admissible. *Eichel v New York Cent. R.R.* (1963) 375 US 253, 11 L Ed 2d 307, 84 S Ct 316;

Morse v Southern Pac. Transp. Co. (1976) 63 CA3d 128, 133 CR 577. There is a statutory exception to the so-called collateral source rule. In an action against a health care provider for professional negligence, the defendant can elect to introduce evidence that the plaintiff received insurance benefits. CC §3333.1.

§32.7   V. EVIDENCE OF SIMILAR ACTS OR OCCURRENCES

As an exception to the general rule that character evidence is inadmissible to prove a party's conduct on a specific occasion (Evid C §1101(a); see *People v Archer* (2000) 82 CA4th 1380, 1394, 99 CR2d 230), evidence of other acts is admissible when relevant to prove some fact (*e.g.,* motive, opportunity, intent, preparation, plan, knowledge, identity, or absence of mistake or accident) other than the party's disposition to commit such acts (Evid C §1101(b)). However, the use of evidence of a defendant's commission of sexual offenses is permitted when the defendant is accused of a sexual offense. Evid C §1108(a). Also, evidence in a domestic violence or elder or dependent adult abuse case of a defendant's commission of other acts of domestic violence or elder or dependent adult abuse is permitted. Evid C §§1109(a), 1101(a). See *People v Jennings* (2000) 81 CA4th 1301, 1309, 97 CR2d 727 (upholding constitutionality of Evid C §1109 under federal and state due process clauses). These similar acts are commonly called "similars," "bad acts," or "other crimes evidence." The following are examples of the use of such evidence:

- In *People v Falsetta* (1999) 21 C4th 903, 89 CR2d 847, the California Supreme Court held that introduction of certain "propensity" evidence under Evid C §1108(a) is constitutionally valid, allowing evidence of uncharged sex crimes to be introduced in a sex offense case. See *People v Waples* (2000) 79 CA4th 1389, 1395, 95 CR2d 45; see *People v Regalado* (2000) 78 CA4th 1056, 1059, 93 CR2d 83 (Evid C §352 provides safeguard against unrestricted application of Evid C §1108); *People v Vichroy* (1999) 76 CA4th 92, 97, 90 CR2d 105. But see *People v McFarland* (2000) 78 CA4th 489, 495, 92 CR2d 884 (expert testimony must be limited to prior sexual acts; psychiatrist's opinion that defendant harbored abnormal sexual interest in child is opinion on defendant's character and thus inadmissible).

- In an action for wrongful discharge brought by an employee, the court held that similar acts of misconduct were admissible to show that the employee was unfit for the job. See *Pugh v See's Candies, Inc.* (1988) 203 CA3d 743, 756, 250 CR 195.

- Evidence of alleged prior misconduct by a police officer against other suspects was held admissible in *Andrews v City & County of San Francisco* (1988) 205 CA3d 938, 947, 252 CR 716, a civil action against the officer for assault, battery, false arrest, and false imprisonment. The court reasoned that such prior conduct was probative, especially after the officer on direct examination testified that he generally handled prisoners with patience.

- In a criminal case, *People v Gordon* (1990) 50 C3d 1223, 1238, 270 CR 451, evidence of similar uncharged robberies was properly admitted because distinctive circumstances between the prior and current robberies bore on the issue of intent. See also *People v Miller* (2000) 81 CA4th 1427, 1448, 97 CR2d 684 (other crimes evidence admissible when proof of defendant's intent is ambiguous or to show common scheme or plan).

- In a criminal case, *People v Erving* (1998) 63 CA4th 652, 659, 73 CR2d 815, 40 uncharged arson fires and seven charged arson fires and attempted arson fires were sufficiently similar for evidence of the uncharged fires to be admissible to show the defendant's identity as the arsonist, a common plan to commit arson, and her intent in setting fires.

Evidence of similar bad acts is inadmissible if its only purpose is to prove prior criminality. See *People v Kronemyer* (1987) 189 CA3d 314, 346, 234 CR 442, in which the trial court improperly admitted evidence of similar uncharged acts of embezzlement. Because the evidence was not offered to prove a fact other than the propensity to commit a specific crime, its admission violated Evid C §1101(b).

If the subject of the uncharged offense does not deny that the similar act occurred, the court, before allowing the jury to hear evidence of the uncharged offense, must determine that the evidence has substantial probative value that "clearly outweighs its inherent prejudicial effect." *People v Bean* (1988) 46 C3d 919, 938, 251 CR 467. In reaching this decision, the court must consider the materiality of the fact to be proved or disproved, the probative value of the other crimes evidence, and the existence of any rule or policy requiring exclusion even if the evidence is relevant. *People v Daniels* (1991) 52 C3d 815, 856, 277 CR 122.

If the subject of the similar offense claims not to have committed it, or disputes part of the evidence to be presented concerning the similar offense, the court first makes an Evid C §403 determination concerning the preliminary factual issues and then decides whether to allow the jury to hear the evidence, as described above. If the judge decides that evidence of the offense is admissible, the jurors must also determine the questions of fact raised by the subject of the similar offense before being able to consider the offense in their deliberations. *People v Wade* (1959) 53 C2d 322, 330, 1 CR 683, overruled on another ground in *People v Carpenter* (1997) 15 C4th 312, 381, 63 CR2d 1; *People v Simon* (1986) 184 CA3d 125, 134, 228 CR 855.It appears that the burden of proof concerning a similar offense is by a preponderance of the evidence. In two earlier California Supreme Court cases, however, the court applied the clear and convincing standard. See *People v Simon, supra*. Evidence of uncharged offenses is still admissible in criminal cases after passage of Cal Const art I, §28(d) because the legislature reenacted Evid C §1101 by a two-thirds' vote, thus making it exempt from §28(d). See *People v Scott* (1987) 194 CA3d 550, 239 CR 588.

For further discussion of similar acts of misconduct in criminal cases, see California Criminal Law Procedure and Practice §§35.52-35.55 (7th ed Cal CEB 2004).

Evidence of habit or custom is admissible to prove conduct on a specified occasion in conformity with the habit or custom. *Jenkins v Tuneup Masters* (1987) 190 CA3d 1, 13, 235 CR 214 (in unlawful detainer action, testimony of tenant company's officer concerning company's habit and custom in preparation and sending of lease renewal options was enough to support finding that renewal notice was properly mailed). Included within this exception are other prior and subsequent accidents at the same or a similar location, prior subsequent conditions or acts, and evidence of other crimes. See 1 Witkin, California Evidence, *Circumstantial Evidence* §§101, 109, 117, 120, 122, 130 (4th ed 2000). An objection is proper, however, when no recognized exception applies, *e.g.*, to evidence of a prior accident that is offered only to show a propensity for negligent acts. *Downing v Barrett Mobile Home Transp.* (1974) 38 CA3d 519, 524, 113 CR 277.

§32.8 VI. LIMITED ADMISSIBILITY INSTRUCTION

When evidence is admissible for one purpose only but not for other purposes, the judge should be requested to give the jury instructions regarding the limited purpose for which the evidence is being offered. See CACI 206 (formerly BAJI 2.05). Evid C §355; *Wilson v Gilbert* (1972) 25 CA3d 607, 615, 102 CR 31.

§32.9 VII. MISCELLANEOUS OTHER STATUTES

A partial catalog of other California statutes that may result in the exclusion of relevant evidence is set forth in the Comment to Evid C §351. The following is a list of some other statutes that may result in the exclusion of evidence:

- Ed C §72621 (confidential data);
- Evid C §1042 (confidential informant);
- Evid C §1121 (mediator's report) (see *Foxgate Homeowners' Ass'n v Bramalea Cal., Inc.* (2001) 26 C4th 1, 10, 108 CR2d 642);
- Fam C §§1818 (family conciliation court; private proceedings), 8718 (appearance and examination of parties);
- Fin C §8754 (public audit of documents);
- Fish & G C §7923 (confidential records);
- Govt C §§7460-7493 (California Right to Financial Privacy Act), 15619 (unlawful divulgence of information), 18573 (confidential information),

18934 (forms not open to inspection), 18952 (confidential written appeals), 20134 (confidential nature of data), 31532 (confidential nature of statements and records);

- Health & S C §§100330 (confidential nature of patient's identity), 103990 (confidential reports on disorders characterized by lapses of consciousness);

- Ins C §§735 (examination of private records), 855 (writings as public records), 10381.5 (exclusion of application from admittance);

- Pen C §§290(i) (records not open for inspection except by peace or other law enforcement officer), 631 (unauthorized recording of telephone calls), 938 (secrecy of transcript), 3046 (confidential statements and recommendations), 11105 (duty to furnish information);

- Pub Res C §3234 (inspection of records);

- Un Ins C §§1094 (privacy of information; exception), 2111 (private information private; punishment), 2714 (medical records);

- Veh C §§1808 (exception to availability of Department of Motor Vehicles information), 16005 (partial disclosure of confidential information), 20012-20015 (disclosure of confidential information), 40803 (speed trap evidence), 40804 (testimony based on speed trap), 40832 (suspension or revocation);

- Wat C §1251 (unauthorized confidential information); and

- Welf & I C §§827 (limitation on inspection right), 5328 (confidentiality of information and records obtained to provide mental health services with specified exceptions), 10850 (confidential grants-in-aid records).

§32.10 VIII. ALTERNATIVES TO OBJECTING

On possible alternatives to objecting, see §§4.9-4.14.

§32.11 IX. STATING THE OBJECTION

Usually, objection will be made by motion in limine or before the witness testifies:

> Objection, Your Honor. _ _[State reason for objection, e.g., This evidence is prohibited by Evidence Code section 1155]_ _.

33

Privileges: General Rules and Considerations

I. INTRODUCTION
   A. Overview of Privileges §33.1
   B. Applicability §33.2
   C. Exclusively Statutory Basis §33.3
   D. Confidentiality Distinct From Privilege §33.3A

II. EXERCISING PRIVILEGES
   A. Determining Who Can Invoke or Waive
      1. Meaning of "Holder" §33.4
      2. Claim or Assertion §33.5
      3. Waiver §33.6
      4. Remedies for Erroneous Denial §33.7
   B. Privileges in Preparing for Trial
      1. Role of Counsel §33.8
      2. Discovery Proceedings §33.9
      3. Selection of Privileges To Be Invoked §33.10
   C. Assertion of Privilege at Trial
      1. Claim of Privilege §33.11
      2. Use of Privileged Writing to Refresh Memory §33.12
      3. Avoiding Need to Claim Privilege Before Jury §33.13
      4. Exclusion of Privileged Information in Absence of Claimant
         a. Privileges Covered by Exclusion Procedure §33.14
         b. Evid C §916 Requirements for Exclusion of Information Subject to Claim §33.15
         c. Exceptions §33.16
   D. Upholding Privilege Contested at Trial
      1. Procedure for Ruling on Privilege §33.17
      2. Burden of Proof §33.18
      3. Offer of Proof §33.19
   E. Evid C §913 Protection Against Comment and Inference §33.20
   F. Remedies for Erroneous Denial of Privilege
      1. Party's Assertion of Error §33.21
      2. Seeking Extraordinary Writ
         a. Privilege Claimed by Witness §33.22
         b. Privilege Claimed by Person Other Than Witness §33.23
      3. Objection to Subsequent Use of Erroneously Compelled Disclosure §33.24

III. OPPOSITION TO PRIVILEGES
    A. Before Trial §33.25
    B. Response to Assertion of Privilege at Trial
        1. Controverting Privilege §33.26
        2. Offer of Proof §33.27
    C. Subsequent Admission of Evidence Excluded as Privileged in Absence of Claimant §33.28
    D. Comment on Opponent's Failure to Explain or Deny Evidence §33.29
    E. Remedy for Erroneous Allowance of Privilege §33.30

IV. STATUTES §33.31

I. INTRODUCTION

§33.1 A. Overview of Privileges

Evidence, even though relevant, may be excluded if it is privileged. See Evid C §351 (all relevant evidence is admissible unless otherwise provided by statute). The general areas of concern with regard to privileges are:

- What are the requirements for application of the privilege to this witness?
- Who is the holder of the privilege?
- Who may assert the privilege?
- Has the privilege been waived?
- Do any precautions need to be taken to preserve the privilege?
- What procedures should be used to assert the privilege in court?
- When should the privilege be asserted?

The existence of a privilege results from a value judgment that the interests protected by the privilege are more important than the possible contribution of the privileged information to the ascertainment of truth. See Comment to Evid C §910; 2 Witkin, California Evidence, *Witnesses* §§59–60 (4th ed 2000). Similar societal and policy considerations govern the application of the numerous other privileges discussed in this chapter.

Although most privileges can be used to prevent disclosure of information regardless of its probative value in the particular proceeding, four of the Evidence Code privileges are sometimes conditioned on a preliminary determination by the trial judge that the interests protected by the privilege outweigh the importance of the offered evidence in arriving at the truth: counselor-domestic violence victim (Evid C §1037.5; see §39.10), official information (Evid C §1040(b)(2); see §43.6), identity of informer (Evid C §1041(a)(2); see §44.6), and trade secret (Evid C §1060; see §45.3). See Comment to Evid C §915.

The trial judge's determination is made under Evid C §§405 (foundational evidence) and 915(b). See §33.17.

Privileges apply only to prevent the use of testimony in a judicial proceeding—not to prevent the giving of information to law enforcement agencies to aid in prosecution. *U.S. v Davies* (7th Cir 1985) 768 F2d 893 (information given to FBI by defendant's daughter was not privileged).

The "truth-in-evidence" provision of Proposition 8 (Cal Const art I, §28(d)) expressly leaves the Evidence Code privileges sections untouched. Counsel can therefore continue to base arguments concerning privileges on the California Constitution in criminal as well as civil cases.

§33.2   B. Applicability

Division 8 of the Evidence Code (§§900–1070), governing privileges, has broader application than other provisions of the Code. Most of the other provisions usually apply only to proceedings in court (Evid C §300; for exceptions, see Comment to Evid C §300), but Division 8 applies to all proceedings in which testimony can be compelled, including judicial, legislative, administrative, and arbitration proceedings, even though the proceeding may be exempted by statute from the rules of evidence (Evid C §§901, 910). Thus, the privileges of the Code may be asserted in judicial, quasi-judicial, and nonjudicial proceedings. See Comment to Evid C §910; 2 Witkin, California Evidence, *Witnesses* §1073 (4th ed 2000).

All privileges, including those outside the Evidence Code (see §33.3), apply to discovery proceedings. CCP §2017(a); Pen C §1054.6; see 2 Witkin, Evidence, *Discovery* §12. Note that unless a specific privilege objection is timely made, the privilege may be waived. See CCP §§2025(m)(1), 2028(d)(2) (civil). See also *Rodriguez v Superior Court* (1993) 14 CA4th 1260, 1271, 18 CR2d 120 (criminal). The discussion of privileges in this book focuses on their use at trial, however, and deals only incidentally with discovery. See §§33.6 (waiver by failure to assert privilege during discovery), 33.25 (use of discovery to attack or test privileges).

§33.3   C. Exclusively Statutory Basis

All privileges now are statutory; courts cannot recognize a privilege unless it is in a statute or a constitutional provision and cannot enlarge the privilege beyond the scope of these provisions. Evid C §911. See also *Dickerson v Superior Court* (1982) 135 CA3d 93, 99, 185 CR 97 (courts may not limit privilege by creating their own nonstatutory exception); Evid C §§230 ("'statute' includes a treaty and a constitutional provision"), 351 (all relevant evidence admissible except as provided by statute); *In re Terry W.* (1976) 59 CA3d 745, 130 CR 913 (rejecting claim of parent-child privilege but noting that some parent-child communications qualify for lawyer-client, physician-patient, or psychotherapist-patient privilege (Evid C §§952, 992, 1012)).

There are some statutory provisions outside the Evidence Code that create, restrict, or enlarge privileges. Evid C §920. For examples of the privileges outside the Evidence Code, see Comments to Evid C §§920, 1040; 2 Witkin, California Evidence, *Witnesses* §§60, 64, 529 (4th ed 2000).

Article I, section 1 of the California Constitution creates a state constitutional right to privacy. Although not strictly a privilege, the state right to privacy may be raised to prevent disclosure of certain records that might or might not be privileged at trial. Usually the court will engage in a balancing test if a motion to quash production of the records is brought when their discovery is sought. See, *e.g., Valley Bank v Superior Court* (1975) 15 C3d 652, 125 CR 553. See generally *Hill v NCAA* (1994) 7 C4th 1, 26 CR2d 834.

Some privileges are described in general terms, leaving interpretation of their bounds to the courts. For example, the Code provides for the privilege against self-incrimination and the privilege of a defendant in a criminal proceeding not to testify or to be called as a witness simply by declaring that a witness or a defendant has these privileges to the extent that they exist under the United States or the California Constitutions. Evid C §§930, 940. See chaps 46-47. Other provisions also leave the courts with leeway to develop the details of a privilege. See, *e.g.,* Evid C §1060. See also chap 45 (trade secrets). But most aspects of privileges are regulated by the Code in such detail that analysis of a privilege problem often requires continual reference to its statutory text. To facilitate this reference, the Code provisions applicable to privileges in general (Evid C §§900-920) are set out in §33.31, and those applicable to specific privileges are set out in the sections entitled "Statutes" in chaps 34-51.

§33.3A D. Confidentiality Distinct From Privilege

Disclosures made to a mediator in the course of mediation, just as any disclosure to a third party, will waive the privilege. The scope of waiver would be determined as in any case of waiver. As a practical matter, however, the discovery of the waiver would be a difficult matter, because the mediator as a matter of course respects confidentiality, and Evid C §1119 directs that all discussions and disclosures made in the course of mediation must remain confidential unless all the parties agree to disclosure as provided in Evid C §§1122 and 1126. In a major case, however, one party may choose to notice the mediator for deposition to discuss the disclosures, and issues of waiver might become the subject of discovery. See §34.10A for discussion.

The law concerning protections for confidentiality in mediations is still very much in development. One approach to addressing the issue of mediation confidentiality is a comprehensive mediation agreement, to be executed by the parties and the mediator before the mediation session begins. The agreement could call for liquidated damages in the event of its breach, although the agreement would not bind nonparties who might seek discovery of the agreement. The enforceability of such an agreement may be questionable in some circumstances, such as when a governmental entity is a party and information exchanged in the mediation is subject to public disclosure requirements. There is already some case law to support an action for breach of a confidentiality agreement; see, *e.g., Cohen v Cowles Media Co.* (1991) 501 US 663, 115 L Ed 2d 586, 111 S Ct 2513 (promissory estoppel theory upheld for breach of promise to keep identity confidential). It is possible that a confidentiality agreement could be found to be against public policy (and therefore unenforceable) on any number of possible grounds; for example, a court might construe it as an agreement to suppress evidence. In an extreme case in which confidentiality is crucial, consider obtaining a protective order in advance of the mediation, which would allow disclosure of protected information to occur in an effort to resolve litigation without trial, yet provide significant protection against the compelled disclosure of the information in another forum.

II. EXERCISING PRIVILEGES

A. Determining Who Can Invoke or Waive

§33.4   1. Meaning of "Holder"

The Evidence Code uses the term "holder of the privilege" to refer to persons having the power to invoke or waive a privilege. Although the power to waive a privilege is usually confined to the holder of the privilege and authorized representatives, the power to claim a privilege is held by holders and nonholders alike.

The "holder" of the attorney-client, physician-patient, psychotherapist-patient, sexual assault victim-counselor, and domestic violence victim-counselor privileges is expressly defined in Evid C §§953, 993, 1013, and 1035.6. See §§34.11, 36.5, 37.5, 38.5, 39.5. These definitions do not include all persons entitled to claim the privilege. For example, even though an attorney, a physician, a psychotherapist, or a counselor are not holders, they must claim the privilege on behalf of the client or patient. See Evid C §§954–955, 994–995, 1013, 1015, 1036. See also §§34.12, 36.6, 37.6, 38.6, 39.6. For other types of privileges, the Evidence Code simply specifies who "has a privilege" of a particular description (see Evid C §§930, 940, 977, 980, 1033–1034, 1040–1041, 1050, 1060); the person who "has" the privilege is the holder. For example, Evid C §1060 specifies only the owner of a trade secret as one who has the trade secret privilege; therefore, only the owner is a holder even though agents and employees share the power to claim the privilege. See §§45.4–45.5.

§33.5   2. Claim or Assertion

Usually, a privilege can be claimed by the witness from whom the privileged information is sought. When the witness entitled to claim a privilege is a party, the witness's attorney can claim the privilege on the witness's behalf.

When the privilege is one that entitles its holder to "prevent another from disclosing" (see, *e.g.,* Evid C §954), it can be claimed on behalf of the holder to prevent the witness's disclosure of privileged information. For a list of these privileges, see §33.14. Counsel for a party entitled to claim one of these privileges can interpose the claim when the witness is asked to make such a disclosure.

If a witness is called in violation of the privilege of a party's spouse or of a defendant in a criminal proceeding not to be called as a witness, the claim of privilege is asserted by an objection or a motion by the party's counsel. See §§42.10, 47.5.

When offered evidence is subject to a privilege but that privilege can be claimed only by someone who is neither a witness nor a party, Evid C §916 provides for exclusion of the privileged information by the judge on a party's motion. For the requisites and exceptions to this form of exclusion, see §§33.14–33.16, 33.28.

§33.6   3. Waiver

Unlike the right to claim or to assert a privilege, the power to waive a privilege appears to be confined to the holder. Evidence Code §912 expressly provides that the holder of certain privileges can waive them by specified conduct. See §§35.8 (attorney-client), 36.20 (physician-patient), 37.17 (psychotherapist-patient), 38.9 (counselor-sexual assault victim), 39.9 (counselor-domestic violence victim) 40.17 (marital communications), 50.8 (penitent), 51.8 (cleric).

Certain other privileges, not referred to in Evid C §912, may also be waived only by the conduct of a holder. See §§45.5 (trade secret), 46.19 (self-incrimination), 47.7 (defendant in criminal case), 48.6 (voter). Waiver of the official information and informer identity privileges seems to require authorization from the public entity that holds the privilege. See §§43.12, 44.8. Waiver of the two privileges of spouses not to testify or to be called as witnesses against each other is governed by the complex provisions of Evid C §973. See §§41.17–41.21, 42.14–42.16.

If disclosure is ordered despite a valid claim of privilege, neither the disclosure nor a failure to seek review of the order constitutes a waiver. Evid C §919(b).

§33.7   4. Remedies for Erroneous Denial

If a privilege is denied, a party cannot predicate error on this denial (*e.g.,* as a basis for a new trial or reversal on appeal) unless the party is a holder of the privilege (subject to an exception for the spousal privileges not to testify or be called). Evid C §918. See §33.21. But an extraordinary writ to prevent a trial court from compelling disclosure of privileged information may be granted to any person entitled to claim the privilege, whether or not a holder. See §§33.22–33.23.

B. Privileges in Preparing for Trial

§33.8   1. Role of Counsel

Counsel preparing for trial should consider both the privileges that may impede efforts to obtain or present evidence and privileges that may be available to the client or to friendly witnesses (*e.g.,* the client's spouse, employee, or doctor) to prevent interrogation by the other side. If counsel represents a prospective witness who is not a party to the proceeding, counsel should advise the witness of the applicable privileges not to be called, not to testify, and not to answer questions on particular matters.

If counsel foresees advantageous trial use of evidence against which the client or a friendly witness could claim a privilege, it may be better to waive the privilege during discovery so as to avoid obstacles to using the evidence at trial. See §§33.6, 33.25. Apart from intentional waiver, however, caution should be the rule. To preserve a privilege, the holder must assert it at the first opportunity. Because that opportunity is not always obvious, it is better to err on the side of over-assertion. Generally, this position offers the client maximum protection and can be revised if appropriate. As long as potentially privileged information is not revealed, all applicable privileges should survive. But see §33.9 on possible consequences of asserting the privilege during discovery and attempting to waive it at trial.

§33.9   2. Discovery Proceedings

Questions concerning which privileges should be invoked are likely to arise first during discovery proceedings. On applicability of privileges to discovery, see §33.2. Usually, a failure to claim a privilege to prevent disclosure of confidential matter in a deposition, in an answer to an interrogatory, or in other response to discovery waives the privilege for all subsequent actions and proceedings (see Evid C §912(a)). There are two exceptions to this rule:

(1) Deposition testimony waives the privilege of a spouse not to testify or be called as a witness only for the trial or other subsequent stage of the same action (see Evid C §973(a); see also §41.17).

(2) Waiver of the privilege against self-incrimination during discovery is not a waiver for the trial. See §§46.11, 47.7.

Nevertheless, this privilege cannot be used at the trial to exclude admissible testimony or evidence that was produced during discovery. Moreover, if a witness claims the privilege at trial, the claim may create a basis for admitting the deposition testimony into evidence by making the witness "unavailable as a witness." Evid C §240(a)(1); CCP §2025(u). See 1 Witkin, California Evidence, *Hearsay* §§19–21 (4th ed 2000).

Thus, claiming a privilege during discovery preserves the option to claim it at trial. If the privilege is waived at trial, the fact that it was claimed during discovery cannot be a subject for adverse comment or inference. See Evid C §913. See also §33.20.

If a party withholds testimony by claiming a privilege during discovery and then waives the privilege at trial, that waiver may take the adverse party by surprise, justifying a continuance (see chap 54), or may even trigger provisions of a discovery order excluding the testimony from the trial. See §33.25 (use of discovery to test or attack privileges). For example, when counsel asserts the privilege before trial, opposing counsel might invoke an estoppel theory if counsel attempts to waive at trial. Opposing counsel could argue that the assertion of the privilege led the opponent to believe that there would be no need to be prepared to rebut that specific type of information. If, as a result, the opponent failed to investigate possible rebuttal information, that change of position might give rise to an estoppel.

§33.10   3. Selection of Privileges To Be Invoked

Each of the chapters covering a specific privilege (see chaps 34–51) enumerates the (a) requirements, (b) eligible claimants, (c) exceptions, and (d) rules on termination and waiver that should be considered in deciding whether to invoke that privilege. Sometimes there is a choice of privileges or an opportunity to invoke more than one privilege at the same time. For example:

- A witness asked to testify to a confidential communication with a spouse may invoke the marital communications privilege (Evid C §980; see chap 40) and, if the opponent may block that privilege with the exception for communications in aid of a crime or fraud (Evid C §981; see §40.8), also claim the privilege against self-incrimination (Evid C §940; see chap 46). A witness who is still married to the communicating spouse may be able to avoid testifying altogether by claiming the privilege not to testify against one's spouse (Evid C §970; see chap 41) or, if the other spouse is a party, by invoking the privilege not to be called as a witness by an adverse party (Evid C §971; see chap 42).

- Counsel who has sent the client to a physician for examination may be able to exclude the physician's report or testimony by having the client invoke the physician-patient privilege (Evid C §994; see chap 36), the attorney-client privilege (see Evid C §954; *People v Lines* (1975) 13 C3d 500, 119 CR 225 (examination by doctor employed by attorney covered by attorney-client privilege, which still applied when there was exception to psychotherapist-patient privilege); see also chap 34), or both. If it applies, the attorney-client privilege is more advantageous than the physician-patient privilege because its use is less restrictive. See, *e.g.,* the exception to use of the physician-patient privilege in criminal proceedings (Evid C §998; see §36.1) or for personal injury or death claims (Evid C §996; see §36.9).

Sometimes there are reasons for not invoking an available privilege, *e.g.,* the need to fill gaps in proof or extralegal repercussions such as a witness's

C. Assertion of Privilege at Trial

§33.11 1. Claim of Privilege

Most privileges are available only if the privilege is claimed in response to a question or other demand for privileged information. For exceptions, see §33.14. On who can claim, see §33.4. To avoid waiver, the claim must be made at the first opportunity. See Evid C §912(a) (applies to specified privileges).

If information demanded from a witness is subject to a privilege that can be claimed by the witness, but not by any party whom counsel represents, counsel may request the court to advise the witness of the witness's rights under the privilege. For example, when a female is charged with prostitution, defense counsel should request that the male witness-participant, who could also be prosecuted (Pen C §647(b)), be advised of the right to claim the privilege against self-incrimination (Evid C §940; see chap 46).

Usually counsel for the party to whose advantage it would be to have the witness claim the privilege will request that the witness be advised of existing rights to claim the privilege. As an officer of the court, counsel is in the position of reminding the court of its obligations under Evid C §916. Because testifying in court might intimidate the witness (which would violate the defendant's due process rights in a criminal case), the court should appoint an attorney to advise the witness when there is a colorable issue that the witness's testimony may be privileged. *People v Schroeder* (1991) 227 CA3d 784, 278 CR 237; *People v Warren* (1984) 161 CA3d 961, 207 CR 912. See discussion of representing witnesses in California Criminal Law Procedure and Practice, chap 49 (7th ed Cal CEB 2004).

§33.12 2. Use of Privileged Writing to Refresh Memory

When a witness uses a "writing" (Evid C §250) to refresh memory "either while testifying or prior thereto," the writing must be produced at the request of the adverse party, who may introduce it in evidence. Evid C §771. The only exceptions in Evid C §771 are (Evid C §771(c)):

- Production is excused if the writing is not in the possession or control of the witness or party who produced testimony concerning the matter; and

- Production is excused if the writing was not reasonably procurable by the witness or party who produced testimony concerning the matter.

Cases conflict on whether there is also an attorney-client/work product exception to Evid C §771. Compare *Sullivan v Superior Court* (1972) 29 CA3d

64, 67, 105 CR 241 (privilege upheld despite use of writing to refresh recollection before deposition), with *Kerns Constr. Co. v Superior Court* (1968) 266 CA2d 405, 411, 72 CR 74 (use of writing at deposition constitutes waiver).

§33.13 3. Avoiding Need to Claim Privilege Before Jury

Use of a privilege to exclude evidence in a jury trial always presents a danger of creating an unfavorable impression on the jury. It is therefore desirable for counsel to make any assertion of a privilege, or any objection based on a privilege, outside the hearing of the jury, by a motion in limine or by sidebar conference. When a privilege is claimed by a witness instead of by counsel, however, the jury is almost always aware of it, and the resulting adverse effect is offset only by the rule against comment or influence and by the right to a curative instruction. See Evid C §913. See also §33.20.

In criminal actions, if counsel knows that a witness is going to claim the privilege against self-incrimination, that privilege can be claimed in a pretestimonial hearing. There is no right to have the witness claim the privilege in front of the jury. *People v Hill* (1992) 3 C4th 959, 13 CR2d 475, overruled on other grounds in *Price v Superior Court* (2001) 25 C4th 1046, 1069 n13, 108 CR2d 409.

Two privileges in the Evidence Code, the privilege of a defendant in a criminal proceeding not to be called as a witness (Evid C §930; see chap 47) and the privilege of a party's spouse not to be called as a witness by an adverse party (Evid C §971; see chap 42), are worded to protect the witness from being called and forced to claim the privilege in front of the jury. Either of these privileges is violated by merely calling the witness. See §§42.10, 47.5. If a party's spouse intends to rely on the privilege not to be called, all adverse parties should be put on notice of the marital relationship. See §42.11.

For privileges that arise only if they are claimed, counsel is usually entitled to put a question to a witness in front of the jury even though counsel expects that the witness will invoke the privilege. A possible exception is a prosecutor's questioning a witness whose anticipated invocation of the privilege against self-incrimination is likely to create inferences against the defendant. See *Namet v U.S.* (1963) 373 US 179, 10 L Ed 2d 278, 83 S Ct 1151. If the question asked is clearly similar to questions asked when the witness has already invoked the privilege in front of the jury, counsel seeking to protect the witness should object to this tactic as misconduct. See chap 29.

Even though opposing counsel is legally entitled in specific cases to force a party or a witness to claim the privilege, it may be possible to deflect this tactic by putting counsel on notice, during a chambers conference, that any attempt to inquire into specified matters with a particular witness will be met with a claim of a specified privilege. If the judge informally indicates that the privilege will be upheld, opposing counsel may be reluctant to antagonize the judge by deliberately forcing the claim of privilege in front of the jury, unless counsel has a good faith basis for disputing the availability of the privilege. See §2.3.

4. Exclusion of Privileged Information in Absence of Claimant

§33.14 **a. Privileges Covered by Exclusion Procedure**

Evidence Code §916 creates a procedure for the exclusion of privileged information when at least one person eligible to claim the privilege exists, but none of the eligible claimants is a witness or party. This procedure cannot be used for privileges that must be claimed by the witness from whom the information is demanded, *e.g.*, the privilege against self-incrimination. It is available only for privileges that can be claimed by one person to prevent disclosure by another person. See Comment to Evid C §916.

Evidence Code §916 applies to the following privileges:

- Attorney-client (Evid C §954; see chap 34);
- Physician-patient (Evid C §994; see chap 36);
- Psychotherapist-patient (Evid C §1014; see chap 37);
- Counselor-sexual assault victim (Evid C §1035.8; see chap 38);
- Counselor-domestic violence victim (Evid C §§1037–1037.7; see chap 39);
- Marital communications (Evid C §980; see chap 40);
- Official information (Evid C §1040; see chap 43);
- Identity of informer (Evid C §1041; see chap 44);
- Trade secret (Evid C §1060; see chap 45); and
- Penitent (Evid C §1033; see chap 50).

§33.15 **b. Evid C §916 Requirements for Exclusion of Information Subject to Claim**

The trial judge is required to exclude privileged information sua sponte or on the motion of any party, if the requirements for exclusion are met (Evid C §916(a)), unless exclusion is precluded by one of two exceptions (Evid C §916(b)), which are discussed in §33.16. A motion for exclusion may raise preliminary questions of fact; if it does, they must be decided under Evid C §§400–402 and 405 (procedure for determining preliminary facts). See §§33.17–33.19.

The first requirement for exclusion is that the excluded evidence be "subject to a claim of privilege." Evid C §916(a). This requirement raises the same issues that would be presented if the privilege were actually claimed. The burden of proof on these issues is allocated between the party seeking exclusion and the proponent of the evidence in the same way that it would be between the claimant and the opponent of the privilege. See §33.18.

The second requirement for excluding privileged information from evidence under Evid C §916 is that neither the witness nor any party to the proceeding can be authorized to claim the privilege. Evid C §916(a)(1)–(2). Thus, if a witness or a party can claim the privilege but chooses not to do so, the information apparently cannot be excluded even though an absent person could claim the privilege if a witness or party. This requirement that all potential claimants be absent seems to create an anomaly, causing Evid C §916 to fall short of its stated purpose "to protect the holder of a privilege when he is not available to protect his own interest" (Comment to Evid C §916). For example, when a husband and wife are both before the court and one of them is asked to reveal a confidential marital communication, the marital communications privilege can be claimed by either of them. Evid C §980. See §40.5. But if the nontestifying spouse is absent, Evid C §916 apparently is not available to prevent the witness-spouse from violating the confidence, because the witness is "a person authorized to claim the privilege" (Evid C §916(a)(1)).

Despite this apparent gap in Evid C §916, the courts are likely to find ways of enforcing privileges that witnesses fail to claim. Thus, the court in *People v Flores* (1977) 71 CA3d 559, 564, 139 CR 546, held that "inherent" in the "mandate" of Evid C §916 is "the obligation that the court, when aware that a witness is without advice of counsel and uninformed, inform such witness of his right to assert the privilege." In *People v Vargas* (1975) 53 CA3d 516, 126 CR 88, counsel for the absent defendant violated Evid C §955 (see §34.12) by disclosing confidential conversations at a hearing on whether the absence was voluntary under Pen C §1043(b). Citing Evid C §916, the appellate court held that the disclosure should have been excluded from evidence. 53 CA3d at 527.

In other situations, Evid C §916 unquestionably fulfills its purpose. It can be used to prevent an attorney's secretary from revealing a confidential attorney-client communication when both the attorney and client are absent, because the secretary is not a person authorized to claim the privilege. See Comment to Evid C §916. See also §34.10. It can also be used to prevent testimony by an eavesdropper against which only an absent holder could claim a privilege. See, *e.g.*, §§34.10 (attorney-client), 40.4 (marital communication). A cleric can be prevented, under Evid C §916, from revealing a penitential communication in the absence of the penitent because no one is present who can claim the penitent's privilege (Evid C §1033; see §50.6) even though the cleric could claim the cleric's privilege (Evid C §1034; see §51.6).

§33.16   c. Exceptions

Privileged information cannot be excluded under Evid C §916 if either of two exceptions applies:

(1) The trial judge has been "instructed" not to exclude the evidence as

privileged "by a person authorized to permit disclosure." Evid C §916(b)(1). If the judge has received such an instruction and it is unclear whether the person from whom the judge received it had this authority, the burden of proving the authority is presumably on the proponent of the evidence. On use of this exception, see §33.8.

(2) "The proponent of the evidence establishes that there is no person authorized to claim the privilege in existence." Evid C §916(b)(2). For example, if exclusion is sought on the basis that the evidence is a confidential communication between an attorney, a physician, or a psychotherapist and his or her client or patient, the exclusion can be prevented by showing that the client or patient is dead and has no executor or administrator. See §§34.20, 36.19, 37.16. Nonexistence of any potential claimant of the privilege can also be established by showing that each person who could otherwise claim the privilege has waived it. On defeating exclusion by obtaining express waiver, see §33.25.

D. Upholding Privilege Contested at Trial

§33.17   1. Procedure for Ruling on Privilege

When the existence of a privilege is disputed at trial, questions of fact arising out of the dispute are determined by the trial judge under a procedure that the Evidence Code provides for determining the existence of a "preliminary fact, i.e., foundation." See Evid C §402(a) (disputed preliminary facts must be determined under Evid C §§400–406). Evidence Code §400 defines a preliminary fact as one on which "the admissibility or inadmissibility of evidence" depends, including "the existence or nonexistence of a privilege." All questions of fact necessary for rulings on privileges are decided under Evid C §405 (judge decides alone) except the question of whether offered evidence has an incriminating tendency sufficient to support a claim of the privilege against self-incrimination. This determination is governed by Evid C §404. See §46.2. Privilege questions are never decided under Evid C §403. On the procedure usually applicable to rulings on privileges (Evid C §405), see §§21.8, 21.15 (laying a foundation).

Except as provided in Evid C §915(b), the judge may not require disclosure of information claimed to be privileged in order to rule on the claim Evid C §915(a). This provision prevents the judge from compelling unwilling disclosure of the information covered by the claim until the claim is overruled by the court. Thus, a witness who responds to a question by claiming a privilege cannot be required to answer before the judge rules on the validity of the claim.

The Evidence Code does not state whether, in ruling on one of the privileges claimed by one person to prevent disclosure by another (see list in §33.14), the judge can permit an opponent of the privilege to make a disclosure that the claim was asserted to prevent. Arguably the judge cannot permit such disclosure, because the underlying purpose of Evid C §915(a) is to provide the claimed protection of a privilege until the claim is overruled.

The only statutory exceptions to this rule against disclosure for purposes of ruling on the claim are provided by Evid C §915(b), under which the trial judge may require confidential disclosure in chambers of information claimed to be within the privilege for official information (see §43.13), for identity of an informer (see §44.10), for trade secrets (see §45.6), or for attorney work product (see §35.9), if the court is unable to rule without receiving this information. A 1979 amendment to Evid C §915(a) extends the Evid C §915(b) procedure to hearings under Pen C §1524(c) to determine a claim of privilege against a search warrant for documentary evidence, interposed by an attorney (Evid C §950), a physician (Evid C §990), a psychotherapist (Evid C §1010), or a cleric (Evid C §1030) who is not reasonably suspected of criminal activity related to the evidence sought.

The disclosure may be required only in chambers with no one present except the judge, the witness, the person authorized to claim the privilege, and anyone that person is willing to have present, *e.g.,* his or her attorney. If the judge rules that the information is privileged, neither the judge nor anyone else may ever reveal what was disclosed in chambers without the consent of a person authorized to permit disclosure. Evid C §915(b). When the allegedly privileged information is documentary, the judge may be able to rule in camera simply from examining the document; whether to also hear confidential in-chambers testimony in support of the claim of privilege is discretionary. *In re Muszalski* (1975) 52 CA3d 475, 125 CR 281. In proceeding under this provision in the absence of opposing counsel, it is unethical for an attorney to discuss or argue any matters except those to be determined through the confidential disclosure. See Cal Rules of Prof Cond 5-300; *People v Lam Choi* (2000) 80 CA4th 476, 482 n4, 94 CR2d 922.

In case any appeal on the issue is necessary, counsel for the party opposing the privilege should request the presence of a reporter in chambers and that the transcript be sealed. Diligent counsel may furnish a list of topics or questions for the court to consider as relevant to the ruling.

An additional exception to Evid C §915(a)'s proscription of compelled disclosure arises from the suggestion in *In re Lifschutz* (1970) 2 C3d 415, 437 n23, 85 CR 829, that confidential disclosure of a communication claimed to be within the psychotherapist-patient privilege may be required when examination of its contents is necessary to determine whether it falls within an exception to the privilege. See *Mavroudis v Superior Court* (1980) 102 CA3d 594, 606, 162 CR 724 (ordering confidential disclosure as suggested in *Lifschutz*); 2 Witkin, California Evidence, *Witnesses* §§87-91 (4th ed 2000).

Questions of law raised by a dispute over the applicability of a privilege are determined by the trial judge, and the procedure for determining preliminary facts does not then apply. Evid C §310(a). For example, none of the spousal privileges (see chaps 40-42) is available in a criminal proceeding in which one spouse is charged with certain types of family crimes. Evid C §§972(e), 985. See §§40.15, 41.13. The applicability of this exception is presumably determinable as a matter of law without the necessity for any preliminary determination of fact.

§33.18   2. Burden of Proof

As a general rule, the claimant or other person asserting a privilege has the burden of proving that the requirements of the privilege exist, and the opponent of the privilege (proponent of the offered evidence) has the burden of proving that the privilege is made invalid by an exception or waiver. See Comment to Evid C §405. However, communications between attorney and client (see §34.10), physician and patient (see §36.22), psychotherapist and patient (see §37.19), husband and wife (see §40.19), and cleric and penitent (see §§50.10, 51.10) are presumed to have been made in confidence, and the burden of proving nonconfidentiality is on the opponent of the privilege. Evid C §917.

§33.19   3. Offer of Proof

If the judge prematurely disallows a claim of privilege before the claimant has been fully heard in support of the privilege claim, there may not be a sufficient record on which to assert error unless the claimant formally offers to prove the elements of the privilege on which the claimant has the burden. On offers of proof when evidence is excluded, see §§5.4-5.14, 33.27.

§33.20   E. Evid C §913 Protection Against Comment and Inference

Whenever a privilege is exercised, counsel must not comment on that fact, no presumption arises from it, and the trier of fact must not draw any inference from it. The trial judge is also prohibited from commenting, except that, if requested to do so by any party who would be adversely affected by an unfavorable inference, the judge must instruct the jury that no presumption arises from the exercise of the privilege and that they may draw no inference from it. Evid C §913. See §53.7 (jury admonitions). Because of this prohibition against drawing inferences, a witness's previous claim of a privilege cannot be proved for purposes of impeachment. See Comment to Evid C §913; *Hubbard v Calvin* (1978) 83 CA3d 529, 535, 147 CR 905.

The effectiveness of this protection against comment and inference is sometimes reduced by the opposing party's right to comment on the protected party's failure to explain or deny evidence or to produce stronger evidence. See §33.29.

The protection does not apply to a newsperson's claim of immunity from contempt under Evid C §1070. See §48.5.

F. Remedies for Erroneous Denial of Privilege

§33.21 1. Party's Assertion of Error

Evidence Code §918 precludes a party from predicating error (*e.g.,* as a basis for appeal or motion for new trial) on a trial judge's denial of a claim of privilege unless:

- The party is "the holder of the privilege"; or
- The denial is of the privilege of the party's spouse to refuse to testify against him or her (Evid C §970; see chap 41) or not to be called as a witness by an adverse party (Evid C §971; see chap 42).

For example, if a trial judge erroneously denies a nonparty witness's claim of the privilege against self-incrimination and compels the witness to testify, a party adversely affected by the testimony cannot complain of the error on appeal because the party is not a holder of the privilege. See §46.7. On who is holder of each privilege, see §33.4.

A party can never predicate error on the trial judge's failure to exclude privileged information from evidence on motion under Evid C §916 (discussed in §§33.14-33.16). See Comment to Evid C §916. In all cases in which Evid C §916 requires exclusion, none of the parties can have standing under either of the provisions of Evid C §918 to assert error for failure to exclude. A party cannot be a "holder of the privilege" (Evid C §918), because the exclusion procedure applies only if "there is no party to the proceeding who is a person authorized to claim the privilege" (Evid C §916(a)(2); see §33.15). The right of a party under Evid C §918 to base error on a denial of the spouse's privilege not to testify or not to be called as a witness (Evid C §§970-973) cannot apply to a failure to exclude under Evid C §916, because the exclusion procedure does not apply to those privileges. See §33.14.

2. Seeking Extraordinary Writ

§33.22 a. Privilege Claimed by Witness

If a witness's claim of privilege is improperly denied, the witness may be able to prevent the trial judge from compelling testimony by obtaining an extraordinary writ from an appellate court.

The trial judge's ruling is usually enforced by contempt proceedings. See 2 Witkin, California Evidence, *Witnesses* §§28-32 (4th ed 2000). If a witness is imprisoned as a result of being adjudged in contempt for refusal to testify, an appellate court may review the contempt order by issuing a writ of habeas corpus. See *In re Clarke* (1899) 126 C 235, 58 P 546 (contempt for nonproduction of subpoenaed books at trial).

If the witness is not imprisoned or does not seek release from imprisonment, an appellate court may review a contempt order against the witness by issuing a writ of certiorari. Thus, if the trial judge gives the witness a choice of paying a fine or going to jail as punishment for contempt, the witness may pay the fine under protest and obtain review of the contempt order through certiorari. See *Dreher v Superior Court* (1932) 124 CA 469, 12 P2d 671 (contempt for failure to obey subpoena for deposition). If enforcement of the contempt order is delayed, a writ of prohibition against enforcement may be obtainable. See *Cohen v Superior Court* (1959) 173 CA2d 61, 343 P2d 286.

It is unclear whether a witness who is ordered to testify at a trial after a claim of privilege is denied can obtain review of the order by extraordinary writ before being held in contempt. At least under earlier decisions of the California Supreme Court, the writ of prohibition is not available for this purpose. See, *e.g., C.S. Smith Metro. Mkt. Co. v Superior Court* (1940) 16 C2d 226, 105 P2d 587. This restrictive rule may have been relaxed by later decisions granting extraordinary writs against improper orders in discovery proceedings. In *Roberts v Superior Court* (1973) 9 C3d 330, 107 CR 309, the court issued a writ of prohibition barring discovery of records of psychiatric treatment privileged under Evid C §1014. On the propriety of the remedy, the court explained (9 C3d at 336):

> The need for the availability of the prerogative writs in discovery cases[,] where an order of the trial court granting discovery allegedly violates a privilege of the party against whom discovery is granted, is obvious. The person seeking to exercise the privilege must either succumb to the court's order and disclose the privileged information, or subject himself to a charge of contempt for his refusal to obey the court's order pending appeal. The first of these alternatives is hardly an adequate remedy and could lead to disruption of a confidential relationship. The second is clearly inadequate as it would involve the possibility of a jail sentence and additional delay in the principal litigation during review of the contempt order. Thus, the use of the prerogative writ in a case such as this is proper. (See Code Civ. Proc., §§1086, 1103).

See *Sav-On Drugs, Inc. v Superior Court* (1975) 15 C3d 1, 5, 123 CR 283 (following *Roberts*). When a petitioner is uncertain of which writ is correct, the petitioner may properly plead in the alternative, *e.g.,* "for certiorari, prohibition, mandamus or other appropriate writ." *Peck's Liquors, Inc. v Superior Court* (1963) 221 CA2d 772, 775, 34 CR 735. On use of writs to review discovery proceedings, see 2 Witkin, California Evidence, *Discovery* §§242–248 (4th ed 2000).

There is no apparent reason why the considerations underlying the availability of writs of prohibition and mandamus to prevent disclosure of privileged information during discovery should not also support the use of these writs against orders to testify or produce evidence at trial after a claim of privilege has been improperly denied. In an opinion denying a writ of prohibition sought by a defendant in a criminal case to prevent the introduction of illegally obtained evidence, the California Supreme Court declared that "neither a writ of prohibition nor a writ of mandate may be used to resolve an issue as to the admissibility of evidence." *Ballard v Superior Court* (1966) 64 C2d 159, 164, 49 CR 302.

This broad statement appears to be based on the court's conclusion that, in *Ballard,* appeal was an adequate remedy. Reversal on appeal often cannot correct the harm resulting from improper denial of a privilege, *e.g.,* the disclosure of confidential information or the creation of marital discord by forcing one spouse to testify against the other. If the improperly denied privilege is not one of those precluding testimony by a spouse (Evid C §§970-971; see chaps 41-42) and is held only by a nonparty witness, the ruling cannot even be reviewed on appeal (Evid C §918; see §33.21). Therefore, prohibition or mandamus should be available at least in these situations for relief against an order to testify in violation of a privilege.

§33.23   b. Privilege Claimed by Person Other Than Witness

The Evidence Code permits some privileges (listed in §33.14) to be claimed by one person to prevent disclosure of confidential information by another person. For example, an attorney or a client can claim the attorney-client privilege to prevent an eavesdropper from revealing an attorney-client communication (see §34.10), and a married person may claim the marital communications privilege to prevent a spouse from revealing a confidential communication between them (see §40.4). In these situations, a denial of the privilege usually cannot be tested through contempt proceedings, because the witness is uninterested in enforcing the privilege and therefore is unlikely to risk being held in contempt. But when the trial judge indicates an intention to deny the claim of privilege, counsel for the nonwitness party who claimed it may be able to obtain a continuance of the trial (see chap 54) long enough to enable seeking a writ from an appellate court to prevent the judge from permitting the witness to testify in violation of the privilege. The petition for the writ may pray in the alternative for certiorari, prohibition, or other appropriate writ. *Peck's Liquors, Inc. v Superior Court* (1963) 221 CA2d 772, 34 CR 735. Based on the authorities discussed in §33.21, an appellate court may grant such a writ if it is convinced that the claim of privilege is proper, that the trial judge intends to deny the claim, and that irreparable harm will result if the witness discloses the privileged information. The California Supreme Court has criticized the decision in *Peck's,* however, and warned against using "prerogative writs as the normal instruments for reviewing discovery orders." See *Pacific Tel. & Tel. Co. v Superior Court* (1970) 2 C3d 161, 169, 84 CR 718.

§33.24   3. Objection to Subsequent Use of Erroneously Compelled Disclosure

If privileged information is erroneously admitted into evidence because a valid claim of privilege was disallowed or because of a failure to exclude the evidence on motion under Evid C §916 (see §§33.14-33.16), evidence of the disclosure is inadmissible against a holder of the privilege. Evid C §919. On who is a holder, see §33.4. This exclusionary rule usually applies at a subsequent proceeding in which the record of the evidence in the earlier proceeding is offered under an exception to the hearsay rule, *e.g.,* as "former testimony" (Evid C §§1290-1292; see also §19.21). The rule can be invoked even though the erroneous denial of the claim of privilege was not challenged by refusing disclosure or by seeking review of the order. Disclosure under those circumstances "is one made under coercion" (Evid C §919(b)) and is therefore not a waiver of the privilege (Evid C §912(a)).

A party can validly object to privileged information from an earlier proceeding only if the party holds the privilege at the time of the objection. Evid C §919.

If the former testimony was compelled in violation of one of the privileges that a holder can claim to prevent disclosure by another person (see list in §33.14), an objection under Evid C §919 should be accompanied by a claim of the privilege itself. The hearsay exceptions for former testimony permit such a claim if the privilege existed when the testimony was given. Evid C §§1291(b)(2), 1292(b). Thus, if an eavesdropper has given testimony in a previous proceeding of a confidential husband-wife communication that the court should have excluded under Evid C §916, the husband, as holder of the privilege, can both object to the former testimony under Evid C §919 and claim the marital communications privilege against it (Evid C §980; see §40.5). But if this privilege is eliminated from the present proceeding by an exception (*e.g.,* if the litigation is between the husband and a claimant to his wife's estate (Evid C §984(b); see §40.12)), the husband is not presently a holder of the privilege and therefore can neither claim the privilege nor object.

A party cannot object under Evid C §919 to former testimony that violated only a privilege held by another person. Thus, if a wife was compelled to testify despite her valid claim of the privilege not to testify against her husband (Evid C §970; see chap 41), the husband cannot object to the former testimony on that ground, because only the wife holds the privilege. See §41.17.

A holder of a privilege cannot object to former testimony under Evid C §919 on the sole ground that the holder would have been entitled to claim the privilege if the holder had been a party to the earlier proceeding. For example, if a wife voluntarily testifies to a confidential marital communication in a proceeding to which her husband is not a party and subsequently her testimony is introduced against the husband in another proceeding, he is prevented from objecting under Evid C §919 by the fact that she could have claimed the marital communications privilege and therefore her testimony was not erroneously compelled (see Evid C §919(a)). Instead of objecting, the husband can claim the marital communications privilege against her former testimony. His right to do so is not impaired by her waiver. Evid C §912(b). See §40.15.

The procedure for ruling on an objection under Evid C §919 is the same as that for ruling on a claim of privilege. See §§33.17, 33.19. The objector, being a holder of the privilege, has the same burden of proof that rests on a claimant of the privilege.

III. OPPOSITION TO PRIVILEGES

§33.25 A. Before Trial

One of the uses of discovery is to test which claims of privilege will be made by adverse parties and witnesses. All privileges are available as defenses to discovery. CCP §2017(a); Pen C §1054.6. See CCP §§2025(m)(1), 2028(d)(2). Whatever information is obtained on discovery without being met by a claim of privilege usually cannot be blocked by a privilege at the trial. Failure to claim the privilege during discovery usually waives it for the trial. If it does not, the claim of privilege at the trial may facilitate introduction into evidence of deposition testimony or other discovery matter. See §33.6.

If an adverse party or witness claims a privilege during discovery proceedings, counsel should consider possible grounds for attacking the privilege by disproving its requirements or by establishing an exception, termination, or waiver. These grounds of attack can be developed through further discovery or other investigation and then used either to compel discovery of the information claimed to be privileged or to meet a claim of privilege at trial.

An adverse party or witness who refuses on a ground of privilege to testify to certain matters on deposition may waive the privilege at the trial and testify to those matters under direct examination. This possibility must be considered in preparing for cross-examination. If the waiver opens up new matters on which additional evidence must be obtained, it may furnish a ground for continuance. See chap 54. A witness's previous claim of privilege for matters on which the witness freely testifies at trial cannot be used to impeach the witness or even be commented on. Evid C §913. See §33.20.

B. Response to Assertion of Privilege at Trial

§33.26 1. Controverting Privilege

Privileges may be asserted at a trial by a claim of privilege (see §33.11), a motion for exclusion of privileged information (Evid C §916; see §§33.14-33.16), an objection to the calling of a party's spouse or a criminal defendant as a witness (see §33.10), or an objection to evidence of a disclosure compelled in violation of a privilege asserted in an earlier proceeding (Evid C §919; see §33.24).

If the proponent of the evidence wishes to contest any of these assertions of privilege, the proponent should immediately state his or her opposition and the reasons why the privilege does not apply. If these reasons raise questions of fact, the statement of opposition will require the trial judge to follow the statutory procedure for ruling on disputed questions of preliminary fact necessary for determining the existence or nonexistence of a privilege. See Evid

C §§400-402, 404-405. Expression of opposition is necessary because this procedure applies only "when the existence of a preliminary fact is disputed." Evid C §§402(a), 405(a).

Questions of law governing privileges are decided by the trial judge under Evid C §310(a). See §§33.17-33.19.

§33.27   2. Offer of Proof

If evidence is excluded as privileged, the proponent of the evidence may be required to make two types of offers of proof to preserve the right to predicate error on the ruling. If the proponent was not permitted to complete a showing against the privilege, the proponent may have to offer to prove matters that the proponent has the burden of proving to defeat the privilege, *e.g.,* an exception or waiver. In addition, the proponent may be required to show the substance, purpose, and relevance of the excluded evidence. See Evid C §354. See §§5.4-5.14 (offer of proof).

§33.28   C. Subsequent Admission of Evidence Excluded as Privileged in Absence of Claimant

If privileged information is properly or improperly excluded from evidence under Evid C §916 (see §§33.14-33.16), the proponent of the evidence may be able to have it admitted later in the trial by obtaining one or both of the following from each holder of the privilege:

- An express waiver of the privilege or the holder's express consent to disclosure of the information, which is equivalent to a waiver. This waiver or consent defeats exclusion of the evidence by establishing "that there is no person authorized to claim the privilege in existence." Evid C §916(b)(2).

- An affirmative request by the holder to the trial judge to permit disclosure of specified matters. This request defeats exclusion under Evid C §916(b)(1), which provides that the judge may not exclude the privileged information if "he is otherwise instructed by a person authorized to permit disclosure." See §33.16.

This waiver, request, or combination of both can be presented to the judge in a letter or other written statement signed by each holder of the privilege. An authorized representative may sign on the holder's behalf, but counsel should then be prepared to prove the representative's authority. If the authenticity of the statement may be questioned, it should be acknowledged before a notary public or counsel should be prepared to otherwise prove authenticity. See Evid C §1451.

Usually there is only one holder of a privilege, so only one signature is normally required. If the privilege is held by two or more persons (*e.g.,* an attorney-client privilege held by joint clients or a marital communications privilege held by both spouses), each should sign the same statement or separate statements. On determining who is holder of privilege, see §33.4.

Evidence Code §916(b)(1), which directs the trial judge not to exclude the privileged information if so "instructed by a person authorized to permit disclosure," is not likely to be construed as authorizing one joint holder of a privilege to permit disclosure without the consent of the other holders. Requiring all joint holders to consent is consistent with Evid C §912(b), which provides that a waiver of the attorney-client, physician-patient, psychotherapist-patient, counselor-sexual assault victim, counselor-domestic violence victim, or marital communications privilege by one joint holder does not affect the right of the other holders to claim the privilege.

§33.29   D. Comment on Opponent's Failure to Explain or Deny Evidence

Except for a right to cautionary jury instructions, the Evidence Code prohibits any comment on, or the drawing of any inference from, the exercise of a privilege. Evid C §913. See §33.20. But the Code also provides that weaker and less satisfactory evidence should be viewed with distrust when offered by a party having power to produce stronger and more satisfactory evidence (Evid C §412), and that the trier of fact may base inferences against a party for failure to explain or deny particular evidence through testimony. Evid C §413.

The Comment to Evid C §412 explains that there is no inconsistency between §913 and §§412–413. Section 913, on the one hand, deals only with inferences that may be drawn from the exercise of a privilege; it does not purport to deal with the inferences that may be drawn from the evidence in the case. Sections 412 and 413, on the other hand, deal with the inferences to be drawn from the evidence in the case; the fact that a privilege has been relied on is irrelevant to the application of these sections.

These Code sections and the official comments were drafted before the United States Supreme Court held that if a defendant in a criminal case exercises the privilege to refuse to testify, the United States Constitution prohibits court and counsel from commenting on the defendant's failure to explain or deny the contrary evidence. *Griffin v California* (1965) 380 US 609, 14 L Ed 2d 106, 85 S Ct 1229. See §46.5. After this decision, the Law Revision Commission decided not to recommend amendment of Evid C §412 or §413, partly because of uncertainty over the extent of the *Griffin* rule. See 8 Cal L Rev'n Comm'n Reps 113 (1966). It is now settled, however, that *Griffin* does not preclude comment on a defendant's failure to introduce relevant evidence or to call logical witnesses. See *People v Mitcham* (1992) 1 C4th 1027, 5 CR2d 230; *People v Szeto* (1981) 29 C3d 20, 171 CR 652.

The *Griffin* rule has not been extended to protect a party who exercises the privilege against self-incrimination in a civil proceeding from comment on the failure to explain or deny the contrary evidence. In *Shepherd v Superior*

Court (1976) 17 C3d 107, 117, 130 CR 257, the California Supreme Court reaffirmed its holdings in *Nelson v Southern Pac. Co.* (1937) 8 C2d 648, 67 P2d 682, and *Fross v Wotton* (1935) 3 C2d 384, 44 P2d 350, that unfavorable inferences may be drawn from the claim of the privilege against self-incrimination in a civil case. The authority of that reaffirmation may be questioned, however, because it overlooks Evid C §913 and the Comment to Evid §913, which states that §913 modifies the holdings in *Nelson* and *Fross*.

The *Griffin* rule does not appear to affect the other privileges. When the exercise of one of the other privileges causes gaps in a party's case, opposing counsel is free to comment on the party's failure to explain or deny the contrary evidence or to produce stronger favorable evidence, to the same extent that prosecutors were free to comment on the silence of defendants in criminal proceedings before the *Griffin* decision. See Comment to Evid C §913. Permissible limits of such comment are stated in *People v Modesto* (1965) 62 C2d 436, 42 CR 417 (decided two months before *Griffin*). For example, if a party avoids having to testify in explanation or denial of certain evidence against the party by exercising the attorney-client or marital communications privilege, opposing counsel may point out that the evidence is uncontradicted even though counsel may not comment on the party's exercise of the privilege. There can be no comment, however, on the exercise of a constitutional right. *Wainwright v Greenfield* (1986) 474 US 284, 88 L Ed 2d 623, 106 S Ct 634 (comment on post-*Miranda* silence); *People v Fabert* (1982) 127 CA3d 604, 179 CR 702; *People v Schindler* (1980) 114 CA3d 178, 170 CR 461 (comment on exercise of right to counsel). Therefore, if the claim of privilege involves a constitutional right, comment should be prevented.

§33.30 E. Remedy for Erroneous Allowance of Privilege

If a privilege is erroneously allowed, the resulting exclusion of evidence entitles the proponent to assert error (*e.g.,* on appeal or on motion for new trial) just as if the evidence had been excluded by the sustaining of an objection. The proponent must have preserved the record by making a sufficient showing in opposition to the privilege at the time it was asserted. See §33.26. It may be necessary for this showing to include one or more offers of proof. See §33.27.

§33.31 IV. STATUTES

Evidence Code §§900–920 apply to a number of privileges or to privileges generally. Provisions applicable to particular privileges are set out in the sections entitled "Statutes" in chaps 35–40, 42–50.

- Evidence Code §900 states:

    Unless the provision or context otherwise requires, the definitions in §§900–905 govern the construction of [Evid C §§900–1070]. They do not govern the construction of any other division.

- Evidence Code §901 states:

    "Proceeding" means any action, hearing, investigation, inquest, or inquiry (whether conducted by a court, administrative agency, hearing officer, arbitrator, legislative body, or any other person authorized by law) in which, pursuant to law, testimony can be compelled to be given.

- Evidence Code §902 states:

    "Civil proceeding" means any proceeding except a criminal proceeding.

- Evidence Code §903 states:

    "Criminal proceeding" means:

    (a) A criminal action; and

    (b) A proceeding pursuant to [Govt C §§3060-3074] to determine whether a public officer should be removed from office for willful or corrupt misconduct in office.

- Evidence Code §905 states:

    "Presiding officer" means the person authorized to rule on a claim of privilege in the proceeding in which the claim is made.

- Evidence Code §910 states:

    Except as otherwise provided by statute, the provisions of this division [Div 8, Evid C §§900-1070] apply in all proceedings. The provisions of any statute making rules of evidence inapplicable in particular proceedings, or limiting the applicability of rules of evidence in particular proceedings, do not make this division inapplicable to such proceedings.

- Evidence Code §911 states:

    Except as otherwise provided by statute:

    (a) No person has a privilege to refuse to be a witness.

    (b) No person has a privilege to refuse to disclose any matter or to refuse to produce any writing, object, or other thing.

    (c) No person has a privilege that another shall not be a witness or shall not disclose any matter or shall not produce any writing, object, or other thing.

- Evidence Code §912 states:

    (a) Except as otherwise provided in this section, the right of any person to claim a privilege provided by Section 954 (lawyer-client privilege), 980 (privilege for confidential marital communications), 994 (physician-patient privilege), 1014 (psychotherapist-patient privilege), 1033 (privilege of penitent), 1034 (privilege of clergyman), 1035.8 (sexual assault victim-counselor privilege) or 1037.5 (domestic violence victim-counselor privilege) is waived with respect to a communication protected by the privilege if any holder of the privilege, without coercion, has disclosed a significant part of the communication or has consented to such disclosure made by anyone. Consent to disclosure is manifested by any statement or other conduct of the holder of the privilege indicating consent to the disclosure, including failure to claim the privilege in any proceeding in which the holder has the legal standing and opportunity to claim the privilege.

(b) Where two or more persons are joint holders of a privilege provided by Section 954 (lawyer-client privilege), 994 (physician-patient privilege), 1014 (psychotherapist-patient privilege), 1035.8 (sexual assault victim-counselor privilege) or 1037.5 (domestic violence victim-counselor privilege), a waiver of the right of a particular joint holder of the privilege to claim the privilege does not affect the right of another joint holder to claim the privilege. In the case of the privilege provided by Section 980 (privilege for confidential marital communications), a waiver of the right of one spouse to claim the privilege does not affect the right of the other spouse to claim the privilege.

(c) A disclosure that is itself privileged is not a waiver of any privilege.

(d) A disclosure in confidence of a communication that is protected by a privilege provided by Section 954 (lawyer-client privilege), 994 (physician-patient privilege), 1014 (psychotherapist-patient privilege), 1035.8 (sexual assault victim-counselor privilege) or 1037.5 (domestic violence victim-counselor privilege), when disclosure is reasonably necessary for the accomplishment of the purpose for which the lawyer, physician, psychotherapist, sexual assault counselor or domestic violence counselor was consulted, is not a waiver of the privilege.

- Evidence Code §913 states:

    (a) If in the instant proceeding or on a prior occasion a privilege is or was exercised not to testify with respect to any matter, or to refuse to disclose or to prevent another from disclosing any matter, neither the presiding officer nor counsel may comment thereon, no presumption shall arise because of the exercise of the privilege, and the trier of fact may not draw any inference therefrom as to the credibility of the witness or as to any matter at issue in the proceeding.

    (b) The court, at the request of a party who may be adversely affected because an unfavorable inference may be drawn by the jury because a privilege has been exercised, shall instruct the jury that no presumption arises because of the exercise of the privilege and that the jury may not draw any inference therefrom as to the credibility of the witness or as to any matter at issue in the proceeding.

- Evidence Code §914 is omitted because it applies to privileges claimed other than in court.

- Evidence Code §915 states:

    (a) Subject to subdivision (b), the presiding officer may not require disclosure of information claimed to be privileged under this division or attorney work product under [CCP §2018(c)] in order to rule on the claim of privilege; provided, however, that in any hearing conducted pursuant to [Pen C §1524(c)] in which a claim of privilege is made and the court determines that there is no other feasible means to rule on the validity of such claim other than to require disclosure, the court shall proceed in accordance with subdivision (b).

(b) When a court is ruling on a claim of privilege under [Evid C §§1040-1047] (official information and identity of informer) or under Section 1060 (trade secret) or under [CCP §2018(b)] (attorney work product) and is unable to do so without requiring disclosure of the information claimed to be privileged, the court may require the person from whom disclosure is sought or the person authorized to claim the privilege, or both, to disclose the information in chambers out of the presence and hearing of all persons except the person authorized to claim the privilege and such other persons as the person authorized to claim the privilege is willing to have present. If the judge determines that the information is privileged, neither he nor any other person may ever disclose, without the consent of a person authorized to permit disclosure, what was disclosed in the course of the proceedings in chambers.

- Evidence Code §916 states:

    (a) The presiding officer, on his own motion or on the motion of any party, shall exclude information that is subject to a claim of privilege under this division if:

    (1) The person from whom the information is sought is not a person authorized to claim the privilege; and

    (2) There is no party to the proceeding who is a person authorized to claim the privilege.

    (b) The presiding officer may not exclude information under this section if:

    (1) He is otherwise instructed by a person authorized to permit disclosure; or

    (2) The proponent of the evidence establishes that there is no person authorized to claim the privilege in existence.

- Evidence Code §917 states:

    (a) Whenever a privilege is claimed on the ground that the matter sought to be disclosed is a communication made in confidence in the course of the lawyer-client, physician-patient, psychotherapist-patient, clergyman-penitent, husband-wife, sexual assault victim-counselor, or domestic violence victim-counselor relationship, the communication is presumed to have been made in confidence and the opponent of the claim of privilege has the burden of proof to establish that the communication was not confidential.

    (b) A communication between persons in a relationship listed in subdivision (a) does not lose its privileged character for the sole reason that it is communicated by electronic means or because persons involved in the delivery, facilitation, or storage of electronic communication may have access to the content of the communication.

(c) For purposes of this section, "electronic" has the same meaning provided in section 1632 of the civil code.

- Evidence Code §918 states:

    A party may predicate error on a ruling disallowing a claim of privilege only if he is the holder of the privilege, except that a party may predicate error on a ruling disallowing a claim of privilege by his spouse under Section 970 or 971.

- Evidence Code §919 states:

    (a) Evidence of a statement or other disclosure of privileged information is inadmissible against a holder of the privilege if:

    (1) A person authorized to claim the privilege claimed it but nevertheless disclosure erroneously was required to be made; or

    (2) The presiding officer did not exclude the privileged information as required by Section 916.

    (b) If a person authorized to claim the privilege claimed it, whether in the same or a prior proceeding, but nevertheless disclosure erroneously was required by the presiding officer to be made, neither the failure to refuse to disclose nor the failure to seek review of the order of the presiding officer requiring disclosure indicates consent to the disclosure or constitutes a waiver and, under these circumstances, the disclosure is one made under coercion.

- Evidence Code §920 states:

    Nothing in this division shall be construed to repeal by implication any other statute relating to privileges.

34

Attorney-Client Privilege

I. NATURE AND PURPOSE §34.1

II. DISTINGUISHING BETWEEN ATTORNEY-CLIENT PRIVILEGE AND WORK PRODUCT DOCTRINE §34.2

III. REQUIREMENTS
  A. Attorney-Client Relationship
    1. Professional Consultation §34.3
    2. Who Is the Client?
      a. Individual as Client §34.4
      b. Corporation as Client §34.5
        (1) Current and Former Corporate Employees §34.6
        (2) *Upjohn* Decision §34.7
    3. Who Is the Attorney? §34.8
  B. Communication §34.9
  C. Confidentiality §34.10
  D. Mediation Confidentiality §34.10A

IV. WHO CAN CLAIM THE PRIVILEGE
  A. Client or Client's Representative §34.11
  B. Attorney's Duty to Claim §34.12
  C. Judge May Exclude Information §34.13

V. EXCEPTIONS §34.14
  A. Based on Nature of Attorney-Client Relationship
    1. Assistance in Crime or Fraud §34.15
    2. Breach of Attorney-Client Duty §34.16
    3. Subsequent Litigation Between Joint Clients §34.17
  B. Claims Through Deceased Client
    1. Issues Between Claimants §34.18
    2. Deceased Client's Written Instrument §34.19

VI. TERMINATION BY DEATH, DISSOLUTION, OR WAIVER
  A. Effect of Client's Death §34.20
  B. Effect of Organization Client's Dissolution §34.21
  C. Waiver
    1. Disclosure of Significant Part of Communication §34.22
    2. Failure to Claim Privilege §34.22A
    3. Disclosure and Joint Defense Agreements §34.22B

VII. RULING ON PRIVILEGE
  A. Procedure §34.23
  B. Burden of Proof §34.24

VIII. STATUTES §34.25

IX. ILLUSTRATIONS OF PRIVILEGE §34.26

X. STATING CLAIM OF PRIVILEGE
  A. By Client-Witness §34.27
  B. By Attorney-Witness §34.28
  C. By Trial Counsel §34.29

§34.1 I. NATURE AND PURPOSE

The attorney-client privilege prevents compulsory disclosure of confidential communications between an attorney and the client. Its purpose is to promote freedom of consultation, to encourage clients to be completely truthful, and thus to assist the attorney in giving competent legal advice. See *Solin v O'Melveny & Myers* (2001) 89 CA4th 451, 107 CR2d 456; *Glade v Superior Court* (1978) 76 CA3d 738, 743, 143 CR 119. Although plainly an obstruction to ascertaining the truth, the privilege is nevertheless so rooted in public policy that its lineage may be traced from the time of Elizabeth I, when a lawyer refused to inform on his client. If an attorney's lawsuit is incapable of complete resolution without breaching the attorney-client privilege, the suit may not proceed. *Solin v O'Melveny & Myers, supra*.

Evidence Code §§950–962 govern the attorney-client privilege. An attorney also has an independent duty under Bus & P C §6068(e) to preserve the client's secrets, unless the attorney reasonably believes disclosure is necessary to prevent a criminal act likely to result in death or substantial bodily harm. See §34.12. An attorney may not, however, suppress any evidence that the attorney or the attorney's client has a legal obligation to reveal or to produce. Cal Rules of Prof Cond 5-220.

§34.2 II. DISTINGUISHING BETWEEN ATTORNEY-CLIENT PRIVILEGE AND WORK PRODUCT DOCTRINE

The protection against disclosure afforded by the attorney-client privilege overlaps somewhat with the protection provided by the work product doctrine. An attorney's opinions are protected by both the privilege and the doctrine. "While the lawyer-client privilege is prompted by the need for confidentiality of the *client,* the work product doctrine is designed to satisfy the *attorney's* requirement for privacy." *American Mut. Liab. Ins. Co. v Superior Court* (1974) 38 CA3d 579, 594, 113 CR 561. See California Civil Discovery Practice §§3.5–3.64A (3d ed Cal CEB 1998).

Two types of protection for work product of an attorney are recognized in California courts in civil cases:

- A qualified protection against discovery for an attorney's general work product. No discovery is allowed of such work product unless denial will (a) unfairly prejudice the party seeking discovery and preparing that party's claim or defense or (b) result in an injustice. CCP §2018(b).

- An absolute protection for a writing reflecting the attorney's "impressions, conclusions, opinions, or legal research or theories." CCP §2018(c).

Code of Civil Procedure §2018(b) does not define "work product" that is subject to the qualified protection. The courts are left to determine the protection on a case-by-case basis. *In re Jeanette H.* (1990) 225 CA3d 25, 32, 275 CR 9. See, *e.g., City of Long Beach v Superior Court* (1976) 64 CA3d 65, 134 CR 468 (qualified work product protection during pretrial discovery for identity of intended trial nonexpert witnesses); Jefferson's California Evidence Benchbook, chaps 40, 41 (3d ed CJA-CEB 1997); 2 Witkin, California Evidence, *Witnesses* §§137–152 (4th ed 2000); California Expert Witness Guide §8.10 (2d ed Cal CEB 1991).

See chap 35 for a thorough discussion of the work product doctrine.

III. REQUIREMENTS

A. Attorney-Client Relationship

§34.3   1. Professional Consultation

The attorney-client privilege requires the existence of an attorney-client relationship, which arises only if the client consults the attorney in the attorney's professional capacity. The purpose of the consultation can be to enable the attorney to provide the client with legal advice or representation or merely to decide whether the client will retain the attorney. Evid C §951. The relationship exists even when the attorney does not expect to be compensated or declines to represent the client after hearing the client's problem. The relationship does not arise, however, when the attorney is consulted in other than a professional capacity. *People v Gionis* (1995) 9 C4th 1196, 40 CR2d 456 (during attorney's visit to home of friend who shared business relationship, incriminating disclosures made by friend after attorney refused to undertake representation in marital dissolution proceedings); *Montebello Rose Co. v ALRB* (1981) 119 CA3d 1, 32, 173 CR 856 (communication between employer and attorney acting as labor negotiator not privileged unless its "dominant purpose" was to "secure or render legal service or advice"). See 2 Witkin, California Evidence, *Witnesses* §§113–118 (4th ed 2000).

The attorney-client privilege does not apply when the attorney acts only as a negotiator for the client, gives business advice, or otherwise acts as a business agent. *Chicago Title Ins. Co. v Superior Court* (1985) 174 CA3d

1142, 1151, 220 CR 507 (discussing functions of house counsel). See also *Aetna Cas. & Sur. Co. v Superior Court* (1984) 153 CA3d 467, 475, 200 CR 471 (attorney retained to investigate insurance claim and to ascertain coverage was acting in professional capacity as attorney).

The privilege may also be deemed impliedly waived if the dual functions of the attorney as a business adviser and as legal counsel are so intertwined that it is impossible to clearly distinguish the two roles. *Chicago Title Ins. Co. v Superior Court* (1985) 174 CA3d 1142, 1154, 220 CR 507.

2. Who Is the Client?

§34.4   a. Individual as Client

The attorney may be consulted by the client personally or by the client's authorized representative. A person who is under a guardianship or conservatorship because of minority or mental or physical impairment becomes a client when the person consults with the attorney. Evid C §951 ("client"). See Comment to Evid C §953 (underage client). When the client has a guardian or conservator, the guardian or conservator is the "holder of the privilege" authorized to claim or waive the attorney-client privilege. Evid C §§953(b), 954, 912; *De Los Santos v Superior Court* (1980) 27 C3d 677, 682, 166 CR 172 (guardian ad litem).

The client may be any "person." Evid C §951. A person is either a natural person or an organization, *e.g.,* corporation, partnership, unincorporated association, or public entity. See Evid C §175. "Public entity" includes every form of foreign or domestic public authority. Evid C §200.

§34.5   b. Corporation as Client

With the myriad legal issues confronting corporate officers, they naturally turn to in-house and outside counsel for legal advice. When a corporation is under government investigation or is charged with federal or state violations, its board of directors commonly hires its own independent counsel to report to it regarding an in-house investigation of the merits of civil or criminal charges. This situation raises issues that are beyond the scope of this book, but one thing is clear: Corporations, officers, and employees should ascertain their disclosure protection and duties and, if necessary, make sure that all corporate practices comply with federal and state laws.

Clearly, a corporation may be a client and invoke the attorney-client privilege. *D.I. Chadbourne, Inc. v Superior Court* (1964) 60 C2d 723, 736, 36 CR 468. See *Smith v Laguna Sur Villas Community Ass'n* (2000) 79 CA4th 639, 643, 94 CR2d 321. Focusing on the corporation's intention to keep communications confidential, the court in *Chadbourne* noted the following:

- If an employee of a defendant corporation is also a defendant and makes statements about the facts at issue, obtained by a representative of the corporation and delivered to an attorney for the employee and/or the corporation, the privilege applies.

- If the employee is not a codefendant, the communication is not privileged unless the employee is the "natural person to be speaking for the corporation" and would ordinarily communicate with the corporation's attorney.

- If an employee is simply a witness to an incident, the simple fact that the employer requires the employee to make a statement to the corporation's attorney does not make the statement privileged.

- If the employee's statement is required in the ordinary course of the corporation's business and the employee's connection with the matter arises from the scope of the employment, the employee is not an independent witness and the statement is that of the employer.

- If making the statement is part of the employee's responsibility, on a regular basis, to make a report, the report may be privileged if the employer's purpose is for confidential reasons.

- If there is more than one purpose for directing an employee to make a report, the primary purpose controls unless the secondary use is such that the confidentiality is waived.

- A communication does not lose its privilege merely because it was obtained by an agent of the employer, with the knowledge and consent of the employer.

- When an employee was not expressly directed by the employer to make a statement and does not know that the statement is to be confidential, the intent of the party receiving and transmitting the statement does not affect applicability of the privilege.

See also *Alpha Beta Co. v Superior Court* (1984) 157 CA3d 818, 825, 203 CR 752.

When attorneys are called as witnesses during discovery or trial, claims of the attorney-client privilege usually arise. California follows the federal rule established in *Shelton v American Motors Corp.* (8th Cir 1986) 805 F2d 1323, 1327, in requiring a foundation when opposing counsel is deposed:

- The information sought must be relevant and nonprivileged;

- There must be no other means of obtaining the information sought; and

- The information sought must be critical to preparing or presenting the party's case.

See *Spectra-Physics, Inc. v Superior Court* (1988) 198 CA3d 1487, 1494, 244 CR 258.

§34.6 (1) Current and Former Corporate Employees

Former employees present special problems: Are former employees holders of the attorney-client privilege? Can adversary attorneys contact them? Does the work product doctrine apply when the attorney-client privilege applies?

Under Cal Rules of Prof Cond 2-100, ex parte contact with employees or former employees of an entity's opponent without the consent of the entity's attorney is permissible if the employees are not or were not members of the corporation's "control group," *i.e.*, officers, directors, managing agents, or partners. See *Triple A Mach. Shop v State* (1989) 213 CA3d 131, 139, 261 CR 493; *Bobele v Superior Court* (1988) 199 CA3d 708, 712, 245 CR 144.

§34.7 (2) *Upjohn* Decision

In *Upjohn Co. v U.S.* (1981) 449 US 383, 392, 66 L Ed 2d 584, 593, 101 S Ct 677, the United States Supreme Court ruled that the former upper management "control group" test (see §34.6) was too narrow. Quoting from Burnham, *The Attorney-Client Privilege in the Corporate Arena*, 24 Bus L 901, 913 (1969), the Court observed:

> The narrow scope given the attorney-client privilege by the court below not only makes it difficult for corporate attorneys to formulate sound advice when their client is faced with a specific legal problem but also threatens to limit the valuable efforts of corporate counsel to ensure their client's compliance with the law. In light of the vast and complicated array of regulatory legislation confronting the modern corporation, corporations, unlike most individuals, "constantly go to lawyers to find out how to obey the law."

Upjohn involved an investigation by in-house and outside counsel concerning a typed questionnaire sent by the chairman of Upjohn Co. and returned to inside counsel. The court concluded that the communications by Upjohn employees to counsel were covered by the attorney-client privilege.

§34.8 3. Who Is the Attorney?

The attorney may be an individual, a law corporation, or a member of the state bar employed by a law corporation that is licensed, or that the client believes to be licensed, to practice law in any state or nation. The client is permitted to rely on reasonable appearances without having to inquire about the "lawyer's" license to practice. Evid C §950. On law corporations, see Evid C §954; 9 Witkin, Summary of California Law, *Corporations* §33 (9th ed 1989). See also *Welfare Rights Org. v Crisan* (1983) 33 C3d 766, 190 CR 919 (Welf & I C §10950 implies privilege for communications between welfare applicants and lay representatives similar to attorney-client privilege).

§34.9 B. Communication

A communication protected by the privilege can be (1) any information transmitted between client and attorney, including statements of the client or the client's representative and the advice of the attorney, and (2) the attorney's uncommunicated legal opinion, including impressions and conclusions. Evid C §952. See Cal L Rev Comm'n Comment to 1967 amendment to Evid C §952. See also *People v Canfield* (1974) 12 C3d 699, 704, 117 CR 81 (statement was privileged because accused gave it to public defender to establish financial eligibility for latter's services). Even the fact of communication may be privileged. See *In re Navarro* (1979) 93 CA3d 325, 330, 155 CR 522 (attorney properly refused to disclose whether she had shown her client a robbery arrest report).

Knowledge independent of an attorney-client communication is usually not privileged, however. See *Coy v Superior Court* (1962) 58 C2d 210, 220, 23 CR 393 (client compelled to state when he first consulted attorney on particular matter); *People v Bolden* (1979) 99 CA3d 375, 160 CR 268 (attorney's opinion on client's mental competence to stand trial (Pen C §1368) not privileged); *Grand Lake Drive In, Inc. v Superior Court* (1960) 179 CA2d 122, 126, 3 CR 621 (attorney's observations of client's appearance not privileged).

A means of conveying information (*e.g.,* drawings, photographs, videotapes, written statements) can be a communication. Evid C §952; *Suezaki v Superior Court* (1962) 58 C2d 166, 23 CR 368; *Holm v Superior Court* (1954) 42 C2d 500, 50, 267 P2d 1025, disapproved on another ground in *Suezaki v Superior Court* (1962) 58 C2d 166, 176, 23 CR 368.

The privilege covers all forms of communication, including transmittal of documents. Nevertheless, the privilege does not cover every document turned over to an attorney by the client. Documents prepared independently by a party, including witness statements, do not become privileged communications or work product merely because they are turned over to counsel. Similarly, reports prepared by police officers in the performance of their duties are public records and are not protected by the attorney-client privilege, even though the reports were sent to their attorney. *Green & Shinee v Superior Court* (2001) 88 CA4th 532, 536, 105 CR2d 886.

If the attorney refers the client to an expert consultant (*e.g.,* physician, accountant), the attorney-client privilege may protect the client's communications with the consultant and the consultant's reports to the attorney. See Comment to Evid C §952; *City & County of San Francisco v Superior Court* (1951) 37 C2d 227, 234, 231 P2d 26; *Torres v Municipal Court* (1975) 50 CA3d 778, 784, 123 CR 553; 2 Witkin, California Evidence, *Witnesses* §§122–123 (4th ed 2000). Similarly, a client's statement made to the client's guardian ad litem for transmission to the attorney is privileged whether or not the attorney receives it in full. *De Los Santos v Superior Court* (1980) 27 C3d 677, 685, 166 CR 172. But information that has been gathered for an independent purpose and would not be privileged in the client's hands cannot become privileged simply by being delivered to the attorney. Thus, a report to the attorney by the client's treating doctor (as distinct from a doctor to whom the attorney has referred the client for examination) is not within the attorney-client privilege. *San Francisco Unified Sch. Dist. v Superior Court* (1961) 55 C2d 451, 456, 11 CR 373. See 2 Witkin, Evidence, *Witnesses* §1134.

The applicability of the privilege to communications transmitted directly or indirectly between a corporate client's employees and its attorneys depends on the "dominant purpose" of the communication. The dominant purpose rule is discussed in *D.I. Chadbourne, Inc. v Superior Court* (1964) 60 C2d 723, 36 CR 468. See *Scripps Health v Superior Court* (2003) 109 CA4th 529, 534, 135 CR2d 126; *Alpha Beta Co. v Superior Court* (1984) 157 CA3d 818, 203 CR 752; *Rodriguez v North Am. Rockwell Corp.* (1972) 28 CA3d 441, 449, 104 CR 678; 2 Witkin, Evidence §§1138-1139. The privilege does not entitle the attorney to refuse disclosure of the client's identity except in unusual circumstances. *Brunner v Superior Court* (1959) 51 C2d 616, 335 P2d 484. An attorney may, however, rely on the privilege in refusing to identify a client who would be incriminated by being named. *In re McDonough* (1915) 170 C 230, 149 P 566. Relying on *McDonough,* the Ninth Circuit Court of Appeals held that an attorney could not be compelled to name the clients who had employed him to send money to the Internal Revenue Service for their unpaid taxes. *Baird v Koerner* (9th Cir 1960) 279 F2d 623, 632. But the broad language of *Baird* has been criticized and considered by some to be unreliable. See 1 McCormick, Evidence §90 (5th ed 1999). See also *In re Subpoena to Testify Before the Grand Jury (Alexiou)* (9th Cir 1994) 39 F3d 973; *Tornay v U.S.* (9th Cir 1988) 840 F2d 1424, 1428. In *In re Osterhoudt* (9th Cir 1983) 722 F2d 591, 593, the court of appeals, distinguishing *Baird,* held that fee arrangements between attorney and client are usually not privileged, because they reveal no confidential professional communication. See 2 Witkin, Evidence §1120 The court in *Willis v Superior Court* (1980) 112 CA3d 277, 293, 169 CR 301, recognized the *McDonough* exception but ordered disclosure of clients' names and addresses (as well as fee arrangements), stating that the existence of the privilege depended on "the potential for harm to the client." See also *U.S. v Gray* (9th Cir 1989) 876 F2d 1411, 1415 (attorney's communication to defendant of his sentencing date had no confidential nature).

§34.10   C. Confidentiality

A communication protected by the privilege must not, to the knowledge of the client, be seen or heard by a third person except one who is assisting the client or the attorney in the matter. The privilege is not destroyed by the client's knowledge that the communication is accessible to persons who assist with the consultation or are present to further the client's interest for the attorney, *e.g.,* a secretary, an accountant, a physician, or the client's relative or business associate. The privilege can be asserted to prevent disclosure by an eavesdropper unless the client knew that the information would become known to an eavesdropper or other unauthorized person. Evid C §§952, 954. See Comments to Evid C §§952, 954.

The courts have broadly defined the classes of third persons to whom the communication can be disclosed without destroying confidentiality. See *Benge v Superior Court* (1982) 131 CA3d 336, 182 CR 275 (statements at closed meeting of 65 union members with attorney giving advice on union's and members' rights); *Insurance Co. of N. Am. v Superior Court* (1980) 108 CA3d 758, 166 CR 880 (legal advice to wholly owned subsidiary disclosed to officer of parent corporation); *Cooke v Superior Court* (1978) 83 CA3d 582, 147 CR 915 (attorney's letters about marital dissolution proceeding sent to persons concerned with client's family business).

If a communication has two purposes, however, one of which is unrelated to the attorney-client relationship, confidentiality is lost. See *Gonzales v Municipal Court* (1977) 67 CA3d 111, 118, 136 CR 475 (police officer's statement to city attorney's investigator to (1) assist legal defense of possible suit against officer for excessive force during arrest and (2) uncover any grounds for disciplining officer).

There is a presumption of confidentiality, which shifts the burden of proof on this issue to the opponent of the privilege. Evid C §917.

§34.10A D. Mediation Confidentiality

Evidence Code §1152 precludes evidence of an offer of settlement from being used at trial, but does not address the question of whether a statement made by an attorney or party in the course of a mediation, to the mediator or others, can vitiate the attorney-client or work product privilege. The simple answer seems to be that disclosure to the mediator, just as any disclosure to a third party, will waive the privilege. The scope of waiver would presumably be determined as in any case of waiver. As a practical matter, however, the discovery of the waiver would be difficult because the mediator usually respects confidentiality, *i.e.*, to the extent a party directs that a particular communication should be maintained in confidence, the mediator will respect that request. In addition, Evid C §1119 directs that all discussions and disclosures made in the course of mediation must remain confidential unless all the parties agree to disclosure as provided in Evid C §§1122 and 1126. In a major case, however, in which one party may sense a victory in the case if these disclosures and their subject matter can be ordered fair game for discovery and possible use at trial, a party may choose to notice the mediator for deposition to discuss the disclosures, and issues of waiver might become the subject of discovery.

In *Foxgate Homeowners' Ass'n v Bramalea Cal., Inc.* (2001) 26 C4th 1, 108 CR2d 642, the supreme court held that Evid C §§1119 and 1121 barred the use of a report written by a mediator in conjunction with a motion for sanctions based on one party's failure to participate in good faith in court-ordered mediation. The court refused to create a judicial exception to the otherwise unambiguous statutory scheme of confidentiality. In *Eisendraft v Superior Court*

(2003) 109 CA4th 351, 134 CR2d 716, the court addressed the issue of whether one party to a mediation could depose the mediator in conjunction with a motion to correct a spousal support agreement. One party claimed that she was willing to waive her confidentiality rights in connection with the mediation and that the other party had constructively waived his confidentiality rights by discussing the issue in his declaration attached to his motion to correct. The court held that there is no implied waiver to the confidentiality of mediation discussions. 109 CA4th at 360. Absent agreement by all parties, communications made in the course of mediation remain confidential. 109 CA4th at 359; Evid C §1122(a).

The law is not sufficiently developed to allow the trial lawyer to assume that Evid C §§1119–1128 will completely protect from disclosure all information disclosed in a mediation setting, or related information in the same subject area. It is clear that disclosure of documents in a mediation is not sufficient to imbue the documents with confidentiality, thus rendering them unavailable in the litigation. In fact, the easy and inexpensive "discovery" of facts, documents, theories, and strategies that takes place in a mediation is one of the strengths (or one of the weaknesses, depending on your perspective) of mediations generally. In practice, the trial lawyer should guard against improper use of matters divulged in a mediation through:

- Exercise of great care in divulging any matter that could reasonably be construed as trade secrets, attorney-client communications, or attorney work product, with a potential for a broad waiver of privilege in that subject matter;

- Consideration of a confidentiality agreement, signed by all parties to the mediation and the mediator, providing for liquidated damages when appropriate; and

- Consideration of a court order, entered in advance of the mediation by stipulation, providing explicit protection for otherwise privileged or protected matters that may be divulged at the mediation in an effort to promote settlement.

The more important the case (monetarily speaking) and the greater the potential harm from broad disclosure of the information, the further counsel should go in seeking advance protection against the consequences of disclosure.

IV. WHO CAN CLAIM THE PRIVILEGE

§34.11   A. Client or Client's Representative

Only the holder of the attorney-client privilege can claim it. Evid C §954(a). If the client is a natural person, the client is the holder and can make the claim personally unless the client is under a guardianship or conservatorship because of minority or disability (see §34.4); in that situation, only the guardian or conservator is the holder and can make the claim. Evid C §953(a)-(b);

De Los Santos v Superior Court (1980) 27 C3d 677, 682, 166 CR 172 (guardian ad litem). The Evidence Code has no provision that allows a client under a guardianship or conservatorship to claim the privilege personally, even for communications with a separate attorney who advises or represents the client because of a conflict of interest with the guardian or conservator. (This situation might arise, for example, if separate attorneys for a guardian and a minor were appointed under Welf & I C §634 in a juvenile proceeding.) On waiver of a client's privilege by a guardian or conservator, see §34.22. After the client's death, the client's personal representative becomes the holder and can claim the privilege. Evid C §953(c).

The holder may authorize a representative to claim the privilege. Evid C §954(b). If the client is an organization (*e.g.,* corporation, partnership, unincorporated association, or public entity (see §§34.5–34.7)), its claim is necessarily made through a representative. If the organization ceases to exist but is succeeded by another entity, the successor becomes the holder and can claim the privilege. This transfer of the privilege may occur when, for example, a partnership incorporates or a corporation sells its assets as a going concern. If an organization's assets pass to a trustee in dissolution, the trustee becomes the holder and can claim the privilege. Evid C §953(d).

§34.12   B. Attorney's Duty to Claim

The attorney who received or made the privileged communication has a duty to claim the privilege on the client's behalf if both of the following conditions are met:

- The attorney is "present when the communication is sought to be disclosed." Evid C §955. Being "present" presumably includes any opportunity to claim the privilege as witness, party, or trial counsel.

- The attorney has authority to claim the privilege on the client's behalf. Evid C §955. Evidence Code §954(c) gives the attorney this authority unless the privilege has been terminated by death or dissolution (see §§34.20–34.21) or the holder authorized to waive the privilege instructs the attorney not to claim it or otherwise waives it (see §34.22).

The attorney's duty to claim the privilege is complemented by the attorney's professional obligation "to maintain inviolate the confidence, and at every peril to himself or herself to preserve the secrets, of his or her client." Bus & P C §6068(e)(1). Effective July 1, 2004, Bus & P C §6068(e) has been amended to permit an attorney to disclose confidential information to the extent the attorney reasonably believes the disclosure is necessary to prevent a criminal act that the attorney reasonably believes is likely to result in death or substantial bodily harm to an individual. Bus & P C §6068(e)(2).

Breach of the obligation may give rise to a malpractice claim. See generally 1 Witkin, California Procedure, *Attorneys* §§257–286 (4th ed 1997); California Trial Practice: Civil Procedure During Trial §11.152 (3d ed Cal CEB 1995).

The extent of the obligation is illustrated by *People v Kor* (1954) 129 CA2d 436, 277 P2d 94, in which the court reversed a criminal conviction because defense counsel had been erroneously compelled to testify to a privileged communication under threat of being held in contempt if he refused. A concurring opinion, adopted by two of the three justices, declared that "[d]efendant's attorney should have chosen to go to jail and take his chances of release by a higher court." 129 CA2d at 447. See also *Littlefield v Superior Court* (1982) 136 CA3d 477, 482, 186 CR 368 (communication between former codefendant and his counsel about prosecution evidence when codefendant later testified as prosecution witness protected by attorney-client privilege).

When the communication was made to or by the client's former attorney, trial counsel may be authorized to claim the privilege under Evid C §954(c) but have no duty to do so under Evid C §955.

§34.13   C. Judge May Exclude Information

When neither the witness nor a party can claim the privilege, Evid C §916(a) may require the judge to exclude privileged information on the court's own motion or the motion of a party. See *Lemelle v Superior Court* (1978) 77 CA3d 148, 158, 143 CR 450.

§34.14   V. EXCEPTIONS

Most of the exceptions to the attorney-client privilege stated in the Evidence Code are based on pre-Code case law. The former provision for the privilege contained no express exceptions. See former CCP §1881(2).

A. Based on Nature of Attorney-Client Relationship

§34.15   1. Assistance in Crime or Fraud

There is no attorney-client privilege "if the services of the attorney were sought or obtained to enable or aid anyone to commit or plan to commit a crime or a fraud." Evid C §956; *Jasmine Networks, Inc. v Marvell Semiconductor, Inc.* (2004) 117 CA4th 794, 806, ___ CR3d ___ (sufficient evidence for prima facie showing of crime-fraud exception to attorney-client privilege). This exception does not deprive the client of the privilege if the client merely mentions to counsel that he or she is going to commit a crime or fraud, but if the client tries to obtain assistance in planning or committing it, the privilege is lost. This exception is narrower than the corresponding crime or tort exceptions to the physician-patient and psychotherapist-patient privileges (Evid C §§997, 1018; see §§36.15, 37.11).

The privilege is also lost in the following situations:

- When the only assistance sought is for a tort not amounting to a crime or fraud. See *Dickerson v Superior Court* (1982) 135 CA3d 93, 100,

185 CR 97; *Nowell v Superior Court* (1963) 223 CA2d 652, 657, 36 CR 21.

- When the attorney misuses the client's information to defraud others without the client's knowledge or intention of any wrongdoing. *Glade v Superior Court* (1978) 76 CA3d 738, 746, 143 CR 119.

- When a client seeks the attorney's assistance to escape detection or apprehension after committing a wrong. See *People v Lee* (1970) 3 CA3d 514, 526, 83 CR 715 (if defendant delivers incriminating physical object to attorney, privilege may cover fact of delivery but not object itself).

See generally 2 Witkin, California Evidence, *Witnesses* §§153-156, 158 (4th ed 2000). On proving the exception, see §34.23.

For special privilege problems in criminal cases, see California Criminal Law Procedure and Practice §§18.24, 18.26, 30.53-30.55 (7th ed Cal CEB 2004).

§34.16 2. Breach of Attorney-Client Duty

The attorney-client privilege does not protect communications relevant to issues of either the attorney's or the client's breach of a duty arising from the attorney-client relationship. Evid C §958. This exception applies in an action against the client to collect the attorney's fee and in an action against the attorney for malpractice. *People v Vargas* (1975) 53 CA3d 516, 525, 126 CR 88; *Carlson, Collins, Gordon & Bold v Banducci* (1967) 257 CA2d 212, 228, 64 CR 915.

This exception also removes the privilege as a barrier to the attorney's testifying in defense of charges of professional impropriety, *e.g.*, in a state bar disciplinary proceeding or in a criminal case in which a convicted client claims that the attorney did not properly defend the client. Although an attorney has a duty to cooperate and participate in any state bar investigation or proceeding against the attorney, that duty does not deprive the attorney of constitutional or statutory privileges. Bus & P C §6068(i). Business and Professions Code §6068(i) offers further protections to attorneys subject to investigation. In addition to protection of an attorney's constitutional and statutory privileges, reasonable time limitations on requests for information are considered, based on an attorney's time constraints. Further, the exercise by an attorney of any constitutional or statutory privileges cannot be used against the attorney in any disciplinary or regulatory proceeding against him or her. See Comment to Evid C §958; 2 Witkin, California Evidence, *Witnesses* §§161-162 (4th ed 2000).

§34.17 3. Subsequent Litigation Between Joint Clients

If two or more clients retain or consult an attorney on a matter of common interest, none of their communications with the attorney is privileged in subsequent civil litigation between any of the clients or their successors in interest. Evid C §962; *Houston Gen. Ins. Co. v Superior Court* (1980) 108 CA3d 958, 964, 166 CR 904 (exception inapplicable without evidence that insurer's attorney had also represented insured); *Glacier Gen. Assur. Co. v Superior Court* (1979) 95 CA3d 836, 157 CR 435 (in suit by insured's assignee against insurer for bad faith failure to defend, joint-client exception applied to litigation file of attorney who had represented both insured and insurer). See 2 Witkin, California Evidence, *Witnesses* §§165-168 (4th ed 2000).

B. Claims Through Deceased Client

§34.18   1. Issues Between Claimants

The attorney-client privilege does not protect communications relevant to an issue between parties claiming through the same deceased client. Each party's claim may be by testate or intestate succession or by inter vivos transfer. Evid C §957. See 2 Witkin, California Evidence, *Witnesses* §160 (4th ed 2000).

§34.19   2. Deceased Client's Written Instrument

Three exceptions to the attorney-client privilege pertain to writings executed by deceased clients. If the attorney was an attesting witness to a document executed by the client, the privilege does not prevent disclosure of attorney-client communications relevant to the document's execution or attestation or to the client's competence or intentions when the document was executed. Evid C §959. This exception applies to witnessed wills and other instruments attested by subscribing witnesses. See Evid C §§870 (competence of subscribing witness to give opinion on sanity), 1411-1413 (authentication by subscribing witnesses). According to the Comment to Evid C §959, the exception supersedes prior case law, which provided a broader exception when the attorney was an attesting witness.

The other two exceptions for deceased clients' writings (not limited to attested documents) apply when a deceased client executed a deed, will, or other instrument purporting to affect an interest in property. There is no privilege for communications relevant to the decedent's intention or relevant to an issue of the invalidity of the written instrument. Evid C §§960-961.

On problems of establishing the exception by proving that the communication is relevant to a particular subject, see §34.24.

VI. TERMINATION BY DEATH, DISSOLUTION, OR WAIVER

§34.20   A. Effect of Client's Death

The guardian or conservator of a client who dies loses authority to act for the client, presumably including the authority under Evid C §953(b) as the holder of the client's privilege, because death terminates the guardianship or conservatorship. See Prob C §§1600(a), 1860(a); *Estate of Kelley* (1920) 184 C 448, 194 P 4. After a client's death, the privilege passes to the client's personal representative, *i.e.*, the client's executor or administrator. Evid C §953(c). The privilege terminates when the estate is finally distributed and the representative discharged. See Comment to Evid C §954.

During the period between death and appointment of the personal representative, there apparently is no holder of the privilege, which is therefore suspended. See Evid C §§953–954, 916(b)(2). The court may, however, exert the privilege on its own motion or the motion of any party if the person from whom the information is sought is not a party authorized to claim the privilege and no party to the proceeding is authorized to claim it. Evid C §916(a)(2). If appointment of an executor or administrator is delayed, this period may be shortened by the immediate appointment of a special administrator. See Prob C §§8481, 8524, 8540–8547; 1 California Decedent Estate Practice §§7.25–7.43 (Cal CEB 1986). Even after final distribution of the estate and discharge of the personal representative, it may be possible to revive the privilege by reopening the estate and having a personal representative again appointed. See Prob C §12252.

Between death and the appointment of a personal representative, the attorney's professional duty "[t]o maintain inviolate the confidence, and at every peril to himself to preserve the secrets, of his or her client" (Bus & P C §6068(e)(1)) may require the attorney to refuse to disclose communications with a deceased client whose affairs are not yet settled. Probably Evid C §954(c), which eliminates the attorney's power to claim the privilege "if there is no holder of the privilege in existence," will be construed to continue this power (and thus the duty under Evid C §955) if it appears likely that a personal representative of the deceased client (who becomes the holder under Evid C §953(c)) will be appointed. See §34.12 on an attorney's duty to claim the privilege.

§34.21 B. Effect of Organization Client's Dissolution

If a corporation, partnership, public entity, or other organization client ceases to exist, the privilege passes to its successor, assignee, trustee in dissolution, or similar representative. Evid C §953(d). The privilege terminates in the hands of this representative when settlement of the organization's affairs is complete. The privilege cannot pass to the representative while the organization still exists. If the organization leaves no such representative, its privilege terminates when the organization goes out of existence. See §§34.5 (organizations as clients), 34.11 (claim of privilege by organization client).

C. Waiver

§34.22 1. Disclosure of Significant Part of Communication

The text of Evid C §912, governing waiver of the attorney-client privilege, is set out in §33.31. The privilege is waived whenever the holder discloses, or consents to disclosure of, a significant part of the privileged communication. Evid C §912(a). Thus, a client who is a natural person can waive the privilege unless he has a guardian or conservator; in that situation, only the guardian or conservator, as the holder of the privilege, can waive it. Evid C §953(a)-(b). See §34.4 (status of client under guardianship or conservatorship). The Evidence Code contains no provision that enables the client or the client's counsel to prevent the client's guardian or conservator from waiving the client's privilege when the client has separate counsel because of a conflict of interest with the guardian or conservator. If the client has died, the client's personal representative can waive the privilege. Evid C §953(c).

The privilege of an organization client can be waived by its authorized representative or by its successor, assignee, or trustee in dissolution after the organization ceases to exist. Evid C §953(d); *Jasmine Networks, Inc. v Marvell Semiconductor, Inc.* (2004) 117 CA4th 794, 802, ___ CR3d ___ (inadvertent voicemail message left on plaintiff's system containing disclosures made by defendant company's attorneys and officers waived defendant's attorney-client privilege as to those communications; no intent to disclose or waive privilege required). On protection against waiver through representation by an attorney who ought to testify for the client, see California Trial Practice: Civil Procedure During Trial §16.38 (3d ed Cal CEB 1995) (discussing former Cal Rules of Prof Cond 2-111(A)(4)).

If the privilege is held jointly (*e.g.*, two or more clients have consulted the attorney on a matter of common interest), waiver by one joint holder does not impair the privilege of other joint holders. Evid C §912(b). A general guardian or conservator of a client's estate presumably holds the privilege jointly with a general guardian or conservator of the client's person (see Comment to Evid C §953), and a guardian ad litem (CCP §§372-373; Prob C §1607) presumably holds the privilege jointly with a general guardian or conservator. A waiver by the client's general guardian of a privilege that is held jointly with the client's guardian ad litem does not impair the guardian ad litem's right to claim the privilege. But if a general guardian waives the client's privilege before the guardian ad litem is appointed, the latter appears to be bound by the waiver under Evid C §912.

If a party designates himself as an expert witness in his own case and then withdraws that designation before disclosure of any confidential information, there is no waiver of the attorney-client privilege. *Shooker v Superior Court* (2003) 111 CA4th 923, 928, 4 CR3d 334. In *Shooker*, the plaintiff designated himself as an expert witness and was called to testify as such at a deposition. When the defendant attempted to elicit information about communications between the plaintiff and his attorneys, the plaintiff objected on the basis of the attorney-client privilege and terminated the deposition shortly thereafter. The plaintiff withdrew his designation of himself as an expert and moved for a protective order. The appellate court held that the privilege was not waived merely by the designation; because the designation was withdrawn before any significant disclosure of confidential communications, there had been no waiver of the privilege.

There is no waiver if the holder acts under coercion (Evid C §912(a)) or if disclosure is protected by another privilege, *e.g.,* is made in confidence to the holder's physician or spouse (Evid C §912(c)). Confidential disclosure to third persons reasonably necessary to the purpose for which the attorney was consulted does not constitute a waiver. Evid C §912(d).

§34.22A 2. Failure to Claim Privilege

The most common form of waiver is the holder's failure to claim the privilege whenever the opportunity arises. Thus, waiver may occur from prelitigation disclosure to an investigative agency, from failure to claim the privilege on discovery (see §33.9), or, even if it is claimed then, from failure to claim it at trial. If the holder testifies, or permits another to testify, to a significant part of the privileged communication, the holder's right to claim the privilege is lost, not only for the current proceeding but for all future purposes. Evid C §912(a). Thus, waiver may occur if the client answers a question calling for facts by referring to a communication with the attorney. Nonprivileged disclosure of facts to third persons does not waive the privilege for subsequent communication of those facts to an attorney. *Miller v Superior Court* (1980) 111 CA3d 390, 168 CR 589 (attorney malpractice suit); *Lohman v Superior Court* (1978) 81 CA3d 90, 146 CR 171 (issuing subpoena for privileged records is not disclosure or waiver).

The attorney-client privilege is impliedly waived when a party has placed in issue a communication that goes to the heart of the claim in controversy. *Chicago Title Ins. Co. v Superior Court* (1985) 174 CA3d 1142, 1149, 220 CR 507 (counsel for plaintiff title company was only person who could thoroughly testify to relevant knowledge of title company in its action for fraud).

If the holder claims the privilege and the claim is improperly overruled, the information disclosed is inadmissible against the holder in later proceedings. Evid C §919(a)-(b). See Comment to Evid C §919(b). Similarly, the privilege is not waived by disclosure in a proceeding in which there is no legal standing to claim it; thus, disclosure under the exception for litigation between joint clients (Evid C §962) does not waive the privilege for a later proceeding between one client and another party (Evid C §912(a)). An attorney's failure to claim the privilege as required by Evid C §§954(c) and 955 is not a waiver, because the attorney is not the holder. Evid C §953.

§34.22B 3. Disclosure and Joint Defense Agreements

Joint defense agreements are increasingly common in civil litigation, and inevitably include the express intention to share privileged information and work product in working together toward joint goals (*e.g.,* defeating class

§34.22B

certification, conducting cost-efficient discovery, etc.). The generalized term "joint defense privilege" (or "common interest privilege") is often used by parties to such agreements. The agreements are treated, in effect, as if multiple parties have elected, for certain specific purposes enumerated in the agreement, to hire the same otherwise unaffiliated group of attorneys to represent them. The law governing exercise of privileges and waiver in operating under these agreements is limited, as tests are rare. These agreements are typically analyzed for application of privileges under precisely the same rules applicable to any attorney-client relationship. One problem, however, is that parties ordinarily expressly disavow the existence of any attorney-client relationship arising out of these agreements.

There is no "joint defense" privilege in California law. *Raytheon Co. v Superior Court* (1989) 208 CA3d 683, 689, 256 CR 425. Privileges are statutorily based (Evid C §911) and courts have no power to expand a privilege or to recognize implied exceptions to it. *Wells Fargo Bank v Superior Court* (2000) 22 C4th 201, 206, 91 CR2d 716. The issue of whether disclosure of otherwise privileged attorney-client communications among some parties is a waiver of the privilege is governed by Evid C §§912(d) and 952. The issue of joint defense agreements and their potential for waiver of the attorney-client privilege has been analyzed by two recent appellate court decisions.

In *Oxy Resources California LLC v Superior Court* (2004) 115 CA4th 874, 9 CR3d 621, two oil and gas companies, in the course of negotiating a business transaction, entered into a formal Joint Defense Agreement to protect the confidentiality of privileged communications shared between them, in the event they were sued in the future. After completion of their negotiations, a third party sued the companies and moved to compel disclosure of more than 200 documents purportedly protected by the Joint Defense Agreement. In its analysis, the appellate court noted that the issue is more appropriately characterized as a nonwaiver doctrine, rather than as a "privilege" or an extension of the attorney-client privilege. 115 CA4th at 890. The court stated that a party seeking to invoke the nonwaiver doctrine must first demonstrate that the communicated information would otherwise be protected from disclosure by a claim of privilege; then the court must determine whether disclosure to a party outside the attorney-client relationship waived any privileges. The court found that the Joint Defense Agreement evidenced the parties' expectations that the communications would remain confidential, but could not serve as a basis for withholding disclosure of the documents without reference to any underlying privileges. 115 CA4th at 892. The court further held that an in-camera review of the documents claimed to be privileged would allow the court to determine whether the prelitigation disclosure of privileged documents between the companies was reasonably necessary to accomplish the purpose for which the parties had consulted their attorneys. 115 CA4th at 894.

In *McKesson HBOC, Inc. v Superior Court* (2004) 115 CA4th 1229, 9 CR3d 812, the appellate court was asked to determine whether disclosure of a corporation's privileged communications to the SEC and the U.S. Attorney's Office constituted a waiver. The corporation claimed that its disclosures of an internal audit report and interview memoranda were necessary to accomplish the purpose for which it had hired its attorneys and furthered a common interest or purpose with the government to investigate and root out the source of accounting improprieties at HBOC. The court found no real alignment between the government agencies and the entities under investigation, and likened the situation to that of a defendant who shares privileged information with one plaintiff but not another. 115 CA4th at 1238.

A growing number of cases in other jurisdictions and under federal law recognize a "joint defense" or "common interest" exception to the waiver of privilege. See, e.g., *U.S. v Stewart* (SD NY 2003) 287 F Supp 2d 461; *U.S. v Bergonzi* (ND Cal 2003) 216 FRD 487; *Gulf Islands Leasing, Inc. v Bombardier Capital, Inc.* (SD NY 2003) 215 FRD 466.

As a practical matter, be sure to respect absolutely any confidential information conveyed to you by your client, even when you are operating under a joint defense agreement, and limit your disclosure of attorney-client confidences and work product to those necessary to fulfill the purposes of the agreement.

VII. RULING ON PRIVILEGE

§34.23   A. Procedure

When the attorney-client privilege is claimed, its existence and applicability may raise questions of preliminary fact that must be heard and decided by the judge as a threshold issue under Evid C §405. Evid C §914. The parties may present evidence on these issues, which usually consists of further examination and cross-examination of the witness already on the stand.

Evidence Code §915(a) prevents the judge from requiring disclosure of information claimed to be within the privilege for purposes of ruling on the claim. Once the information has already been disclosed, then Evid C §915(a) is inapplicable. *Jasmine Networks, Inc. v Marvell Semiconductor, Inc.* (2004) 117 CA4th 794, 805, ___ CR3d ___. If it is necessary for the court to determine whether there is an exception to or a waiver of the privilege, then the court may order an in-camera review of the information, using a discovery referee if necessary. *Oxy Resources California LLC v Superior Court* (2004) 115 CA4th 874, 894, 9 CR3d 621.

§34.24   B. Burden of Proof

The claimant of the privilege has the burden of proving the existence of the attorney-client relationship and that the offered evidence is a communication within that relationship. The claimant also has the burden of proving standing to claim the privilege. Evid C §§953–954.

The opponent of the privilege (proponent of the offered evidence) has the burden of proving that the communication or information was not confidential. Evid C §917 (establishing presumption of confidentiality; for text, see §33.31). On the requirement of confidentiality, see §34.10. If the contention is that the privilege has been waived or is excluded by an exception, the opponent of the privilege has the burden of proving this contention. Comment to Evid C §405.

The opponent's burden of proving an exception may present difficulties when the exception depends on the contents of the allegedly privileged information, because the opponent is not entitled to have the information disclosed for purposes of obtaining a ruling on the claim. Evid C §915(a). Therefore, an opponent of the privilege can establish the exception only by convincing the judge, from circumstantial evidence or the nature of the question, that the exception applies to the information sought. For example, an attorney-witness may be asked if the client ever consulted him for advice in carrying out a particular fraudulent scheme. The judge may deny the claim of privilege to this question on the ground that an affirmative answer will necessarily refer to communications within the exception and a negative answer will reveal nothing privileged. If the answer is affirmative, examining counsel can then explore the time, place, circumstances, and contents of the nonprivileged communications. But see *Dickerson v Superior Court* (1982) 135 CA3d 93, 100, 185 CR 97 (dictum that prima facie showing of fraudulent purpose is sufficient).

On burden of proof on issues raised by motion under Evid C §916 to have the court exclude at the outset privileged information in the absence of anyone entitled to claim the privilege, see §§33.14-33.16.

§34.25   VIII. STATUTES

Evidence Code §§950-962, referred to in these provisions as "this article," apply to the attorney-client privilege.

- Evidence Code §950 states:

    As used in this article, "lawyer" means a person authorized, or reasonably believed by the client to be authorized, to practice law in any state or nation.

- Evidence Code §951 states:

    As used in this article, "client" means a person who, directly or through an authorized representative, consults a lawyer for the purpose of retaining the lawyer or securing legal service or advice from him in his professional capacity, and includes an incompetent (a) who himself so consults the lawyer or (b) whose guardian or conservator so consults the lawyer in behalf of the incompetent.

- Evidence Code §952 states:

    As used in this article, "confidential communication between client and lawyer" means information transmitted between a client and his or her lawyer in the course of that relationship and in confidence by a means which, so far as the client is aware, discloses the information to no third persons other than those who are present to further the interest of the client in the consultation or those to whom disclosure is reasonably necessary for the transmission of the information or the accomplishment of the purpose for which the lawyer is consulted, and includes a legal opinion formed and the advice given by the lawyer in the course of that relationship.

- Evidence Code §953 states:

    As used in this article, "holder of the privilege" means:

    (a) The client when he has no guardian or conservator.

    (b) A guardian or conservator of the client when the client has a guardian or conservator.

    (c) The personal representative of the client if the client is dead.

    (d) A successor, assign, trustee in dissolution, or any similar representative of a firm, association, organization, partnership, business trust, corporation, or public entity that is no longer in existence.

- Evidence Code §954 states:

    Subject to Section 912 [on waiver] and except as otherwise provided in this article, the client, whether or not a party, has a privilege to refuse to disclose, and to prevent another from disclosing, a confidential communication between client and lawyer if the privilege is claimed by:

    (a) The holder of the privilege;

    (b) A person who is authorized to claim the privilege by the holder of the privilege; or

    (c) The person who was the lawyer at the time of the confidential communication, but such person may not claim the privilege if there is no holder of the privilege in existence or if he is otherwise instructed by a person authorized to permit disclosure.

    The relationship of attorney and client shall exist between a law corporation as defined in [Bus & P C §§6160-6172] and the persons to whom it renders professional services, as well as between such persons and members of the State Bar employed by such corporation to render services to such persons. The word "persons," as used in this subdivision includes partnerships, corporations, limited liability companies, associations and other groups and entities.

- Evidence Code §955 states:

    The lawyer who received or made a communication subject to the privilege under this article shall claim the privilege whenever he is present when the communication is sought to be disclosed and is authorized to claim the privilege under subdivision (c) of Section 954.

- Evidence Code §956 states:

    There is no privilege under this article if the services of the lawyer were sought or obtained to enable or aid anyone to commit or plan to commit a crime or fraud.

- Evidence Code §956.5 (effective until July 1, 2004) states:

    There is no privilege under this article if the lawyer reasonably believes that disclosure of any confidential communication relating to representation of a client is necessary to prevent the client from committing a criminal act that the lawyer believes is likely to result in death or substantial bodily harm.

- Evidence Code §956.5 (effective July 1, 2004) states:

    There is no privilege under this article if the lawyer reasonably believes that disclosure of any confidential communication relating to representation of a client is necessary to prevent a criminal act that the lawyer reasonably believes is likely to result in death of, or substantial bodily harm to, an individual.

- Evidence Code §957 states:

    There is no privilege under this article as to a communication relevant to an issue between parties all of whom claim through a deceased client, regardless of whether the claims are by testate or intestate succession or by inter vivos transaction.

- Evidence Code §958 states:

    There is no privilege under this article as to a communication relevant to an issue of breach, by the lawyer or by the client, of a duty arising out of the lawyer-client relationship.

- Evidence Code §959 states:

    There is no privilege under this article as to a communication relevant to an issue concerning the intention or competence of a client executing an attested document of which the lawyer is an attesting witness, or concerning the execution or attestation of such a document.

- Evidence Code §960 states:

    There is no privilege under this article as to a communication relevant to an issue concerning the intention of a client, now deceased, with respect to a deed of conveyance, will, or other writing, executed by the client, purporting to affect an interest in property.

- Evidence Code §961 states:

    There is no privilege under this article as to a communication relevant to an issue concerning the validity of a deed of conveyance, will, or other writing, executed by a client, now deceased, purporting to affect an interest in property.

- Evidence Code §962 states:

    > Where two or more clients have retained or consulted a lawyer upon a matter of common interest, none of them, nor the successor in interest of any of them, may claim a privilege under this article as to a communication made in the course of that relationship when such communication is offered in a civil proceeding between one of such clients (or his successor in interest) and another of such clients (or his successor in interest).

§34.26 IX. ILLUSTRATIONS OF PRIVILEGE

The privilege may be available for the following questions:

- "What did your client tell you when the interview took place in jail?"
- "Didn't you tell your attorney that there was another witness when you first talked with him?"
- "Did your attorney tell you to refuse to answer?"
- "What did you say to your attorney?"

X. STATING CLAIM OF PRIVILEGE

§34.27 A. By Client-Witness

Your Honor, I claim the attorney-client privilege.

§34.28 B. By Attorney-Witness

Your Honor, that question calls for disclosure of a confidential communication with my client, and I claim the attorney-client privilege on behalf of my client.

§34.29 C. By Trial Counsel

Trial counsel should preferably make this statement outside the jury's presence:

> Your Honor, that question calls for disclosure of a privileged confidential communication between attorney and client.

> [Option 1: Counsel represents party entitled to claim privilege]

> On behalf of _ _[name of party]_ _, I claim the privilege and object to the question on that ground.

[Option 2: Witness holds privilege and is
not represented by counsel]

I request that Your Honor advise the witness of the right to refuse to answer on the ground of privilege.

[Option 3: Neither witness nor party may claim
privilege (Evid C §916)]

I move that Your Honor exclude the answer as privileged.

35

Work Product Doctrine

I. DEFINITION AND PURPOSE §35.1

II. DISTINGUISHING BETWEEN WORK PRODUCT DOCTRINE AND ATTORNEY-CLIENT PRIVILEGE §35.2

III. TYPES OF WORK PRODUCT
  A. Civil Cases §35.3
  B. Criminal Cases §35.4

IV. WHO MAY CLAIM PROTECTION §35.5

V. DURATION AND AVAILABILITY OF PROTECTION §35.6

VI. EXCEPTIONS §35.7

VII. WAIVER §35.8

VIII. IN CAMERA REVIEW IN CIVIL AND CRIMINAL CASES §35.9

IX. STATUTES §35.10

X. STATING THE CLAIM §35.11

§35.1   I. DEFINITION AND PURPOSE

The work product doctrine provides attorneys with protection from disclosure of the "work" they create and assemble as they prepare cases for trial. CCP §2018(a). Like the attorney-client privilege, the work product doctrine allows an attorney to represent a client diligently without fear of intrusion by discovery rules or government subpoena.

The work product doctrine is designed to prevent opposing counsel from taking advantage of an attorney's efforts to investigate both the favorable and the unfavorable aspects of a case. CCP §2018(a). This doctrine provides an attorney with a "degree of privacy" (CCP §2018(a)) within which to think, plan, form opinions, investigate facts, weigh facts and legal theories, interview witnesses, and prepare a case for trial. *Hickman v Taylor* (1947) 329 US 495, 510, 91 L Ed 451, 462, 67 S Ct 385.

The issue of work product protection usually does not arise during trial. Because the protected information is normally sought in pretrial discovery, the issue is commonly resolved before trial. Troublesome problems in maintaining work product protection are most likely to surface in the following circumstances:

- One attorney represents joint clients or enters into a joint cooperation agreement with another attorney representing a different client who has the same interest;

- An attorney represents a corporation but not certain employees of that corporation; or

- An attorney representing a corporation needs to maintain work product protection (particularly during discovery) of information resulting from internal investigations conducted within the corporation.

See California Expert Witness Guide, chap 8 (2d ed Cal CEB 1991). For a description of the types of protection offered by the work product doctrine in civil and criminal cases, see §§35.3-35.4.

Instead of identifying everything that is arguably work product as evidence that need not be disclosed at trial, counsel should analyze each item of proffered evidence to determine whether the absolute or conditional work product protection applies. See §35.3.

For a practical, detailed analysis of the work product doctrine and practice guidelines, see Canter, Cabillot, Immel, & Pahre, *Attorney Client Privilege and Attorney Work Product Doctrine As Applied to Corporations*, 15 CEB Civ Litigation Rep 261 (Part One, Aug. 1993), 346 (Part Two, Sept. 1993); 2 Weil & Brown, Jr., California Practice Guide: Civil Procedure Before Trial, chap 8 (1983); 2 Civil Practice and Litigation in Federal and State Courts §8 (8th ed 1998).

§35.2 II. DISTINGUISHING BETWEEN WORK PRODUCT DOCTRINE AND ATTORNEY-CLIENT PRIVILEGE

The work product doctrine must be distinguished from the attorney-client privilege. Whereas the work product doctrine protects the attorney's work product from discovery (CCP §2018), the attorney-client privilege protects an attorney's confidential communication with a client (Evid C §§952, 954). According to the court in *American Mut. Liab. Ins. Co. v Superior Court* (1974) 38 CA3d 579, 594, 113 CR 561.

> While the lawyer-client privilege is prompted by the need for confidentiality of the *client,* the work product rule is designed to satisfy the *attorney's* requirement for privacy.

Dual protection from disclosure may arise from an overlap between the work product doctrine and the attorney-client privilege. For example, a writing may be protected by both the doctrine and the privilege. See *BP Alaska Exploration, Inc. v Superior Court* (1988) 199 CA3d 1240, 1258, 245 CR 682 (fact that client does not object to disclosure does not prevent attorney from asserting work product protection in contents of writing after delivery to client); *Kerns Constr. Co. v Superior Court* (1968) 266 CA2d 405, 72 CR 74 (any dual protection waived for employee's investigation and accident reports given to employer during deposition).

III. TYPES OF WORK PRODUCT

§35.3   A. Civil Cases

Two types of protection for work product of an attorney are recognized in California courts in civil cases:

- A qualified protection against discovery for an attorney's general work product. No discovery is allowed of such work product unless denial will (1) unfairly prejudice the party seeking discovery and preparing that party's claim or defense or (2) result in an injustice. CCP §2018(b).

- An absolute protection for a writing reflecting the attorney's "impressions, conclusions, opinions, or legal research or theories." CCP §2018(c); see *Wells Fargo Bank v Superior Court* (2000) 22 C4th 201, 214, 91 CR2d 716.

Code of Civil Procedure §2018(b) does not define "work product" that is subject to the qualified protection. The courts are left to determine the protection on a case-by-case basis. *In re Jeanette H.* (1990) 225 CA3d 25, 32, 275 CR 9. See, e.g., *City of Long Beach v Superior Court* (1976) 64 CA3d 65, 134 CR 468 (qualified work product protection during pretrial discovery for identity of intended trial nonexpert witnesses); Jefferson's California Evidence Benchbook §§41.2–41.26 (3d ed CJA-CEB 1997); 2 Witkin, California Evidence, *Witnesses* §§137–152 (4th ed 2000); California Expert Witness Guide §8.10 (2d ed Cal CEB 1991).

§35.4   B. Criminal Cases

In criminal cases, neither the defense nor the prosecution is required to disclose materials or information that are defined as "work product" in CCP §2018(c) or that are privileged under an express statutory provision or the United States Constitution. Pen C §1054.6. Thus, work product in criminal cases extends only to "[a]ny writing that reflects an attorney's impressions, conclusions, opinions, or legal research or theories." CCP §2018(c). Work product protection of such writings is absolute; California criminal law does not embrace the qualified work product protection of CCP §2018(b).

Only limited work product protection applies to witness statements and interviews that reflect what a witness said. Such statements and interviews are protected by the work product doctrine only to the extent that they reflect the attorney's thought processes. A list of witnesses intended to be called is not protected by the doctrine. *Hobbs v Municipal Court* (1991) 233 CA3d

670, 284 CR 655, disapproved on other grounds in 18 C4th at 295. See Pen C §1054.3. See also *People v Superior Court* (Sturm) (1992) 9 CA4th 172, 11 CR2d 652.

§35.5   IV. WHO MAY CLAIM PROTECTION

Code of Civil Procedure §2018 does not state who holds or may claim work product protection. Because the doctrine exists for the attorney's benefit, the attorney is most likely to be considered the "holder" of the protection. In the absence of the attorney, however, the client has standing to assert work product protection on behalf of the attorney. *BP Alaska Exploration, Inc. v Superior Court* (1988) 199 CA3d 1240, 1258, 245 CR 682. See also *Dowden v Superior Court* (1999) 73 CA4th 126, 86 CR2d 180 (litigant appearing in pro per may assert work product protection under CCP §2018).

As the arguable holder of the privilege, an attorney has been held able to assert the work product doctrine against the client. *Lasky, Haas, Cohler & Munter v Superior Court* (1985) 172 CA3d 264, 278, 218 CR 205. The court in *Lasky* did not consider the extent to which an attorney may assert work product protection against a client seeking a former attorney's work product in preparation of a case against that attorney. 172 CA3d at 279. After the decision in *Lasky*, however, CCP §2018(f) was added to provide that no work product protection exists in an action between an attorney and a client or former client if the "work product is relevant to an issue of breach by the attorney of a duty to the attorney's client arising out of the attorney-client relationship."

For further discussion of who holds or may claim work product protection, see California Civil Discovery Practice §§3.61-3.62 (3d ed Cal CEB 1998).

§35.6   V. DURATION AND AVAILABILITY OF PROTECTION

Work product protection extends "beyond termination of the action." It does not cease with termination of the litigation in which the protection is afforded. See *Popelka, Allard, McCowan & Jones v Superior Court* (1980) 107 CA3d 496, 501, 165 CR 748.

When a party affirmatively tenders an issue, the party waives the work product protection as to evidence relevant to that issue. 107 CA3d at 502. See also §35.8. The protection remains, however, for a defendant who, rather than producing witnesses on an issue, waits for the plaintiff to come forward with evidence on the issue. 107 CA3d at 503.

Because a party may call as a trial witness an expert not previously designated by that party if the expert was designated by another party and deposed under CCP §2034(i) (CCP §2034(m)(1)), counsel should not expect the court to sustain an objection to the opinion of this expert on work product grounds if the expert is called by opposing counsel. Section 2034(m)(1) codified the decision in *Lunghi v Clark Equip. Co.* (1984) 153 CA3d 485, 490, 200 CR

387, in which the appellate court ruled that the trial court erroneously excluded an expert's opinions, apparently believing them to be protected by the work product doctrine.

There is conflicting authority on whether work product protection is available at the time of trial to prevent the otherwise-admissible testimony of a witness. Appellate courts concluding that work product protection does not apply at trial reason that such protection is not found in the Evidence Code and is available only to limit pretrial discovery. See *Jasper Constr., Inc. v Foothill Jr. College Dist.* (1979) 91 CA3d 1, 16, 153 CR 767; *Brokopp v Ford Motor Co.* (1977) 71 CA3d 841, 857, 139 CR 888 (dicta; case involved notes of party's expert; protection waived in any event because expert testified); *Mize v Atchison, T. & S.F. RR.* (1975) 46 CA3d 436, 448, 120 CR 787 (similar dicta and facts as in *Brokopp*; agent was investigator rather than expert). But see *Rodriguez v McDonnell Douglas Corp.* (1978) 87 CA3d 626, 648, 151 CR 399, in which Justice Jefferson stated: "The attorney's work-product privilege is applicable at trial as well as at pretrial discovery proceedings." In *Rodriguez,* the work product doctrine was held to protect an investigator's notes at trial.

California state law is generally more liberal than federal law in granting work product protection. Federal Rules of Civil Procedure 26(b)(3), for example, applies only to work product prepared in anticipation of litigation. California work product doctrine, however, applies to work product of an attorney generated in any nonlitigation legal capacity. See *Rumac, Inc. v Bottomley* (1983) 143 CA3d 810, 815, 192 CR 104 (work product generated in role of counselor during lease negotiations). Similarly, federal law allows "opinion work product [to] be penetrated under exceptional circumstances," but California's CCP §2018 forbids discovery "under any circumstance." *BP Alaska Exploration, Inc. v Superior Court* (1988) 199 CA3d 1240, 1250, 245 CR 682 (crime-fraud exception to attorney-client privilege (Evid C §956) does not apply to documents protected by absolute work product rule).

§35.7 VI. EXCEPTIONS

Work product protection extends only to *attorney* work product. Counsel may not adopt the independent work of others after the fact and convert it into attorney work product. See *Jasper Constr., Inc. v Foothill Jr. College Dist.* (1979) 91 CA3d 1, 153 CR 767. To avoid being penalized by this prohibition, attorneys should ensure that they, rather than their clients, hire all experts and that all expert opinions, conclusions, and reports are transmitted directly to counsel. These steps will ensure that any legal work based on the expert opinion is protected by the work product doctrine. During discovery, counsel should also explore the issues of opposing counsel's retention of experts and transmittal of information between opposing counsel and opposing counsel's retained experts. See California Expert Witness Guide §§8.9–8.10 (2d ed Cal CEB 1991).

An attorney retained for nonlegal work cannot assert work product protection (*Watt Indus. v Superior Court* (1981) 115 CA3d 802, 171 CR 503), but an attorney retained both to investigate and to provide legal assistance may assert the protection if the work requires the attorney's legal skills and knowledge (see *Rumac, Inc. v Bottomley* (1983) 143 CA3d 810, 815, 192 CR 104). The court may have to review the file in camera to determine which documents reflect investigative work and which reflect the rendering of legal advice. See *Aetna Cas. & Sur. Co. v Superior Court* (1984) 153 CA3d 467, 478, 200 CR 471. See also §35.9.

Generally, the work product doctrine will not prevent production of statements taken from witnesses if good cause can be shown for discovery. *Christy v Superior Court* (1967) 252 CA2d 69, 60 CR 85 (good cause shown for obtaining copies of witness's statement to refresh recollection of what was contained in written statement previously given to adversary). For examples of when the protection is available and unavailable, see California Civil Discovery Practice §§3.50–3.64(A) (3d ed Cal CEB 1998).

The attorney-client privilege does not apply if the attorney was used to help in a crime or fraud. Evid C §956. This exception does not apply to writings protected by the absolute work product rule. *BP Alaska Exploration, Inc. v Superior Court* (1988) 199 CA3d 1240, 1250, 245 CR 682.

§35.8   VII. WAIVER

If information sought in pretrial discovery is subject to work product protection, the protection is waived if counsel fails to object at that time. See CCP §2033(k). An attorney, as holder of the protection, may also waive it by disclosure to a person who has no interest in maintaining confidentiality. Waiver occurs even though the attorney's action is contrary to the client's desire. See *Lohman v Superior Court* (1978) 81 CA3d 90, 101, 146 CR 171.

The protection is waived when a party uses an expert as a witness. See *Brokopp v Ford Motor Co.* (1977) 71 CA3d 841, 857, 139 CR 888. Waiver may also occur when protected material is used by a witness to refresh recollection. *Mize v Atchison, T. & S.F. R.R.* (1975) 46 CA3d 436, 449, 120 CR 787 (protection waived when investigator witness used report to refresh recollection). See *Kerns Constr. Co. v Superior Court* (1968) 266 CA2d 405, 411, 72 CR 74 (protection waived when adverse witness used report he had previously prepared to refresh recollection before testifying on cross-examination).

A party who affirmatively tenders an issue may waive the protection as to evidence relevant to that issue. See *Popelka, Allard, McCowan & Jones v Superior Court* (1980) 107 CA3d 496, 502, 165 CR 748.

The report of an expert who is retained by an attorney as a consultant may not be discovered if the expert is not deposed and is not called as a witness at trial. See *County of Los Angeles v Superior Court* (Hernandez) (1990) 222 CA3d 647, 271 CR 698 (report of defense's consulting expert protected, and plaintiff's counsel disqualified for improper contact). Moreover, communications made to a potential expert in a retention interview are confidential and subject to protection from disclosure even though the expert is not retained if there is a reasonable expectation of confidentiality. See *Shadow Traffic Network v Superior Court* (1994) 24 CA4th 1067, 29 CR2d 693 (law firm retained by defendant disqualified for retaining expert accounting firm previously interviewed by plaintiff for same lawsuit).

There is a growing trend in civil litigation toward the use of joint defense agreements, which inevitably include the express intention to share work product in working together toward common goals (*e.g.*, defeating class certification, conducting cost-efficient discovery, etc.). Although the generalized term "joint defense privilege" (or "common interest privilege") is often used by parties to such agreements, one court has noted that the issue is more appropriately characterized as a nonwaiver doctrine, rather than as a "privilege" or an extension of the attorney-client privilege. *Oxy Resources California LLC v Superior Court* (2004) 115 CA4th 874, 890, 9 CR3d 621. The issue often arises in connection with the attorney-client privilege. See *Oxy Resources California LLC v Superior Court, supra*, and *McKesson HBOC, Inc. v Superior Court* (2004) 115 CA4th 1229, 9 CR3d 812, for analyses of the doctrine and its application to waiver of the work product privilege. See §34.22B for further discussion.

Attorneys seeking publicity by holding press conferences, responding to media inquiries, or acting as television consultants should be aware that the work product doctrine may be waived by disclosure. See *City of Los Angeles v Superior Court* (Friedman) (1985) 170 CA3d 744, 754, 216 CR 311.

See §35.6 on circumstances in which work product protection is not waived at trial.

§35.9   VIII. IN CAMERA REVIEW IN CIVIL AND CRIMINAL CASES

In civil cases, the court may conduct an in camera review to determine whether documents are protected by the work product doctrine. See Evid C §915(b); *Oxy Resources California LLC v Superior Court* (2004) 115 CA4th 874, 894, 9 CR3d 621; *Aetna Cas. & Sur. Co. v Superior Court* (1984) 153 CA3d 467, 200 CR 471. In camera hearings may be necessary to decide which material in an attorney's file is subject to CCP §2018(b) (qualified protection) and CCP §2018(c) (absolute protection).

In criminal cases, required disclosures are supposed to be made at least 30 days before trial. If a witness's recorded statement includes counsel's impressions, conclusions, or opinions, counsel should consider requesting an in camera hearing that excludes opposing counsel in order to decide whether the nondiscoverable portions can be excised. The hearing is recorded, sealed, preserved, and made available to an appellate court in the event of an appeal or a writ. See Pen C §1054.7. When the issue arises for the first time at trial, an in camera hearing is also generally used. See Evid C §915(b).

§35.10   IX. STATUTES

The work product doctrine is stated in CCP §2018. Penal Code §1054.6 applies CCP §2018(c) to criminal cases.

- Code of Civil Procedure §2018 states:

    (a) It is the policy of the state (1) to preserve the rights of attorneys to prepare cases for trial with that degree of privacy necessary to encourage them to prepare their cases thoroughly and to investigate not only the favorable but the unfavorable aspects of those cases; and (2) to prevent attorneys from taking undue advantage of their adversary's industry and efforts.

    (b) Subject to subdivision (c), the work product of an attorney is not discoverable unless the court determines that denial of discovery will unfairly prejudice the party seeking discovery in preparing that party's claim or defense or will result in an injustice.

    (c) Any writing that reflects an attorney's impressions, conclusions, opinions, or legal research or theories shall not be discoverable under any circumstances.

    (d) This section is intended to be a restatement of existing law relating to protection of work product. It is not intended to expand or reduce the extent to which work product is discoverable under existing law in any action.

    (e) The State Bar may discover the work product of an attorney against whom disciplinary charges are pending when it is relevant to issues of breach of duty by the lawyer, subject to applicable client approval and to a protective order, where requested and for good cause, to ensure the confidentiality of work product except for its use by the State Bar in disciplinary investigations and its consideration under seal in State Bar Court proceedings. For purposes of this section, whenever a client has initiated a complaint against an attorney, the requisite client approval shall be deemed to have been granted.

    (f) In an action between an attorney and his or her client or former client, no work product privilege under this section exists if the work product is relevant to an issue of breach by the attorney of a duty to the attorney's client arising out of the attorney-client relationship.

- Penal Code §1054.6 states:

    Neither the defendant nor the prosecuting attorney is required to disclose any materials or information which are work product as defined in subdivision (c) of Section 2018 of the Code of Civil Procedure, or which are privileged pursuant to an express statutory provision, or are privileged as provided by the Constitution of the United States.

§35.11   X. STATING THE CLAIM

In civil cases, counsel may object under either the qualified protection of CCP §2018(b) or the absolute protection of CCP §2018(c). In criminal cases, counsel may object only under the absolute protection of CCP §2018(c) and Pen C §1054.6. The need for claiming work product protection usually arises in pretrial discovery or in limine proceedings.

> Your Honor, may we approach the bench?
>
> [Add at sidebar]
>
> I object under the work product doctrine. The question calls for information that is protected, either qualifiedly or absolutely.

36

Physician-Patient Privilege

I. NATURE AND PURPOSE §36.1

II. REQUIREMENTS
    A. Physician-Patient Relationship §36.2
    B. Communication or Information §36.3
    C. Confidentiality §36.4

III. WHO CAN CLAIM
    A. Patient or Patient's Representative §36.5
    B. Physician's Duty to Claim §36.6
    C. Judge May Exclude Information §36.7

IV. EXCEPTIONS §36.8
    A. Patient-Litigant §36.9
    B. Criminal and Quasi-Criminal
        1. Criminal Proceedings §36.10
        2. Civil Damages for Patient's Conduct §36.11
        3. Disciplinary Proceedings §36.12
        4. Child Abuse §36.13
    C. When Patient's Competence Is at Issue §36.14
    D. Nature of Physician-Patient Relationship
        1. Assistance in Crime or Tort §36.15
        2. Breach of Physician-Patient Duty §36.16
    E. Claims Through Deceased Patient §36.17
    F. Public Record §36.18

V. TERMINATION BY DEATH OR WAIVER
    A. Effect of Patient's Death §36.19
    B. Waiver §36.20

VI. RULING ON PRIVILEGE
    A. Procedure §36.21
    B. Burden of Proof §36.22

VII. STATUTES §36.23

VIII. ILLUSTRATIONS OF PRIVILEGE §36.24

IX. STATING CLAIM OF PRIVILEGE
    A. By Witness §36.25
    B. By Trial Counsel §36.26

§36.1 I. NATURE AND PURPOSE

The physician-patient privilege prevents compulsory disclosure of confidential information transmitted between physician and patient. The privilege is intended to encourage patients to reveal medical information to their physicians by relieving the patient's apprehension that the information, or the physician's diagnoses or advice, will be disclosed without the patient's consent. See Evid C §§990-1007, set out in §36.23. The privilege also promotes patient privacy. See *Britt v Superior Court* (1978) 20 C3d 844, 864, 143 CR 695. Because of the numerous exceptions to the privilege, the protection it affords is in many cases illusory. Most frequently applicable are the patient-litigant exception and the exception for criminal proceedings. See Evid C §§996, 998, discussed in §§36.9-36.10. On exceptions, termination, and waiver of privilege, see §§36.8-36.20.

When an exception eliminates the patient-physician privilege, another privilege may apply. If the patient was being seen for a mental or emotional condition by a physician who qualifies as a "psychotherapist" (Evid C §1010), the confidential information may be protected by the psychotherapist-patient privilege. See chap 37. If the information emanated from a medical examination made at the request of the patient's attorney, the attorney-client privilege may apply. See Comment to Evid C §952; *People v Lines* (1975) 13 C3d 500, 510, 119 CR 225; *City & County of San Francisco v Superior Court* (1951) 37 C2d 227, 234, 231 P2d 26; 2 Witkin, California Evidence, *Witnesses* §§122-123 (4th ed 2000). See also §34.9.

II. REQUIREMENTS

§36.2 A. Physician-Patient Relationship

The physician-patient privilege protects information arising from purely diagnostic examinations as well as from consultations for preventive or curative treatment. The condition for which the patient is seen may be physical, mental, or emotional. Evid C §991. See 2 Witkin, California Evidence, *Witnesses* §201 (4th ed 2000).

The physician may be either licensed to practice medicine in any state or nation or reasonably believed by the patient to be so licensed. The patient is permitted to rely on reasonable appearances without having to inquire about the extent of the "physician's" license to practice. Evid C §990.

A medical or podiatry corporation, as well as its physician employees, has a physician-patient relationship with its patients. Evid C §994. See 9 Witkin, Summary of California Law, *Corporations* §33 (9th ed 1989).

§36.3 B. Communication or Information

Although the Evidence Code provides that the privilege applies to a "confidential communication between patient and physician" (Evid C §994), it defines this term broadly to include information obtained from examining the patient but not ordinarily thought of as "communications," *e.g.*, laboratory reports, X rays, or the physician's notes of his or her findings. This term also applies to photographs of a patient's ailments, even if the patient's identity is not disclosed. *Binder v Superior Court* (1987) 196 CA3d 893, 898, 242 CR 231 (in wrongful death medical malpractice action, defendant doctor successfully opposed disclosure of photographs of patient's ailments on grounds that it would violate physician-patient privilege and patient's right of privacy under Cal Const art I, §1). The physician-patient privilege also includes communications between physician and patient in the more usual sense, *e.g.*, the patient's statements of medical history or the physician's advice. Evid C §992; *Carlton v Superior Court* (1968) 261 CA2d 282, 289, 67 CR 568 (privilege applies to doctor's notes, orders, and comments, and to records of examinations, observations, and tests). See Comment to 1967 amendment to Evid C §992 (amendment assures protection of uncommunicated diagnosis); 2 Witkin, California Evidence, *Witnesses* §§201-203 (4th ed 2000).

Mere disclosure of patients' names that reveals nothing of their ailments does not violate the privilege. *Ascherman v Superior Court* (1967) 254 CA2d 506, 515, 62 CR 547. The privilege applies, however, if the disclosure would reveal ailments even indirectly, *e.g.*, by indicating tests or treatment given to the patient. *Rudnick v Superior Court* (1974) 11 C3d 924, 933 n13, 114 CR 603 (summarizing rules); *Blue Cross v Superior Court* (1976) 61 CA3d 798, 132 CR 635; *Marcus v Superior Court* (1971) 18 CA3d 22, 95 CR 545.

§36.4   C. Confidentiality

The information protected by the privilege must not, to the knowledge of the patient, be seen or heard by a third person except one who is assisting the patient or physician in the matter. The privilege is not destroyed by the patient's knowledge that the information is accessible to persons who assist with examinations or treatment or are present to further the patient's interest, *e.g.*, nurses, technicians, secretaries, consulting physicians. Evid C §992; Comments to Evid C §§952, 992; *Rudnick v Superior Court* (1974) 11 C3d 924, 930, 114 CR 603 (physician's disclosure to drug manufacturer of patient's reaction to its product in order to obtain assistance in treatment); *Blue Cross v Superior Court* (1976) 61 CA3d 798, 132 CR 635 (disclosure to health plan operator for purpose of paying doctor's fee).

The privilege can be asserted to prevent disclosure by any witness unless the patient was aware that the information would become known to an eavesdropper or other unauthorized person. See Comments to Evid C §§954, 994.

There is a presumption of confidentiality, which shifts the burden of proof on this issue to the opponent of the privilege. Evid C §917. See §36.22.

III. WHO CAN CLAIM

§36.5 A. Patient or Patient's Representative

The patient can claim the privilege only as a holder. Evid C §994(a). The patient is a holder and can claim it personally unless the patient is under a guardianship or conservatorship because of minority or disability; then only the guardian or conservator is a holder and can make the claim. Evid C §993(b). On applicability of this provision to the guardianship of minors, see Comment to Evid C §953.

If the patient has two guardians or conservators, one for his or her person and the other for his or her estate, the two are joint holders of the privilege and each can claim it. See Comment to Evid C §993. A guardian ad litem (CCP §§372-373; Prob C §1003) is also a holder. *De Los Santos v Superior Court* (1980) 27 C3d 677, 682, 166 CR 172.

The Evidence Code contains no provision that allows a patient under a guardianship or conservatorship to claim the privilege personally, even when the patient has a conflict of interest with the guardian or conservator and is therefore represented by separate counsel. See §35.7 (attorney-client privilege). On waiver of patient's privilege by guardian or conservator, see §36.20.

After the patient dies, the decedent's executor or administrator becomes a holder and can claim the privilege. Evid C §993(c). Any holder can authorize a representative to claim the privilege. Evid C §994(b). A person to whom disclosure is made in furtherance of examination or treatment has implied authority to make the claim. *Rudnick v Superior Court* (1974) 11 C3d 924, 932, 114 CR 603 (drug manufacturer); *Blue Cross v Superior Court* (1976) 61 CA3d 798, 132 CR 635 (health plan operator).

§36.6 B. Physician's Duty to Claim

The physician has a duty to claim the privilege on behalf of the patient if both the following conditions are met:

- The physician is "present when the communication is sought to be disclosed." Evid C §995. Being "present" presumably includes any opportunity to claim the privilege as a witness or a party.

- The physician has authority to claim the privilege on behalf of the patient. Evid C §995. Evidence Code §994(c) gives the physician this authority unless the privilege has been terminated by death (see §36.19) or unless a holder authorized to waive the privilege instructs the physician not to claim it or otherwise waives it (see §36.20).

The duty to claim the privilege on the patient's behalf is imposed on each person who is the patient's physician (Evid C §992) "at the time of the confidential communication" (Evid C §994(c)). Presumably, the duty extends to consulting physicians even though they were not in charge of the patient's case.

§36.7 C. Judge May Exclude Information

When neither the witness nor a party can claim the privilege, Evid C §916 may require the judge to exclude privileged information on the judge's own motion or the motion of a party. See §§33.5–33.7.

§36.8 IV. EXCEPTIONS

Broad exceptions to the physician-patient privilege frequently make it unavailable. When this is so, counsel for the claimant should consider whether the psychotherapist-patient or attorney-client privilege is available. See §§34.9, 37.1.

§36.9 A. Patient-Litigant

The physician-patient privilege does not protect information relevant to an issue concerning the condition of the patient if this issue is tendered either by the patient or by any party asserting a claim based on the patient's injury, disability, or death. Evid C §996.

The patient-litigant exception extends to actions in which claimants raise issues based on the patient's condition, *e.g.*, an action by an insurance beneficiary against the patient's life insurer for benefits payable on the death of the patient. See Evid C §996(c). The exception also appears to apply when an issue concerning a patient's condition is raised by the employer or employer's insurance carrier in a subrogation action against a third party for reimbursement of workers' compensation benefits paid to the patient for injuries caused by the third party. See Evid C §996(b). But see *Jones v Superior Court* (1981) 119 CA3d 534, 545, 174 CR 148 (exception in Evid C §996(b)-(c) does not apply to privilege of mother whose daughter sues for injuries from mother's ingestion of drugs during pregnancy).

For purposes of the plaintiff-litigant exception, the party who seeks relief on account of the patient's injury, disability, or death tenders all issues of the patient's condition relevant to liability or damages, but not issues arising out of affirmative defenses. Thus, the exception does not allow the defendant to explore medical conditions other than the injuries claimed by the plaintiff in order to establish that the damages are unrelated to the alleged tort. *Britt v Superior Court* (1978) 20 C3d 844, 862, 143 CR 695; *Hallendorf v Superior Court* (1978) 85 CA3d 553, 149 CR 564. Similarly, the exception probably does not eliminate the privilege of a plaintiff-driver in an automobile accident case to withhold medical evidence relevant solely to the defense of contributory negligence, *e.g.*, plaintiff's visual acuity at the time of the accident. See California Personal Injury Proof §6.4 (Cal CEB 1970).

The patient-litigant exception does not apply to information on issues of a defendant's medical condition unless the defendant raises them. Thus, if the plaintiff advances a theory that the defendant was negligent in driving with a known physical impairment and attempts to call the defendant's doctor to support this theory, the defendant may invoke the privilege. *Carlton v Superior Court* (1968) 261 CA2d 282, 289, 67 CR 568. The plaintiff may, however, be able to obtain the information under Evid C §999 by showing good cause. See §36.11.

If the defendant tenders an issue of the defendant's own condition, the patient-litigant exception applies. For example, if the defendant-driver claims that an accident occurred when the defendant-driver lost control of the car after experiencing a totally unexpected epileptic seizure and calls a doctor to testify in support of this theory, plaintiff's counsel may not only cross-examine that doctor but may also introduce other medical testimony on the issue free of the privilege, *e.g.*, to show that the defendant had suffered similar seizures before the accident and knew better than to drive. See 6 Cal L Rev'n Comm'n Reps 236, 412 (1964).

The patient-litigant exception does not apply unless the information is "relevant" to the tendered issues of the patient's condition. This rule appears to limit the scope of permissible discovery. To be "relevant," evidence must meet the standard of relevancy required for its admission at trial. Evid C §§350–351. See chap 17. Although discovery extends to evidence inadmissible at trial if it is relevant to the subject matter or reasonably calculated to lead to admissible evidence, discovery is expressly limited by privileges and the work product rule. CCP §§2018, 2030(a), (n), 2031(a).

Thus, a patient who sues for damages for a broken leg may invoke the privilege against discovery of records on an illness unrelated to the accident or injury. *Britt v Superior Court, supra*; *Hallendorf v Superior Court, supra*. If, however, the plaintiff claims that the broken leg kept the plaintiff from working, the fact that the plaintiff had some other injury or condition that was the cause of the inability to work would be relevant.

On proving relevancy under the patient-litigant exception, see §36.22.

B. Criminal and Quasi-Criminal

§36.10   1. Criminal Proceedings

There is no physician-patient privilege in a criminal proceeding. Evid C §998. Criminal proceedings include prosecutions for crime and certain proceedings for removal of public officers for misconduct in office. Evid C §§130, 903; Pen C §683.

If a defendant's mental or emotional condition is relevant to the defendant's guilt, the defendant may fare better if treatment has been in the hands of a psychotherapist instead of a physician not specializing in psychiatry because the defendant may be able to claim the psychotherapist-patient privilege in criminal proceedings. See §37.1. The blanket exclusion of the physician-patient privilege from criminal proceedings may benefit the accused, however, by precluding claims of privilege by other persons. See Evid C §1103 (permitting defendant to prove victim's character traits in certain instances).

§36.11 2. Civil Damages for Patient's Conduct

When damages are sought for a patient's conduct, a communication relevant to the patient's condition is not within the physician-patient privilege if good cause is shown for its disclosure. Evid C §999. This exception may apply to the privilege of a defendant or to that of a person for whose conduct the defendant is liable, *e.g.,* an employee. The requirement of good cause permits the court to protect the defendant against a fishing expedition. See Comment to Evid C §999. The exception does not apply to patients whose conduct, even though relevant to the issues, is not the basis for the damage claim.

§36.12 3. Disciplinary Proceedings

There is no physician-patient privilege in a proceeding brought by a public entity to terminate or limit anyone's right, authority, license, or privilege. This exception specifically includes proceedings to terminate public employment. Evid C §1007. The proceedings covered by this exception are considered to be "comparable to criminal proceedings, *i.e.,* proceedings brought for the purpose of imposing discipline of some sort." Comment to Evid C §1007.

§36.13 4. Child Abuse

Penal Code §§11164–11174.3 (the Child Abuse and Neglect Reporting Act) require physicians, members of the clergy, and other practitioners to report suspected instances of child abuse or neglect to local authorities. Penal Code §11171.2(b) provides that the information reported is not subject to the physician-patient privilege in any court proceeding or administrative hearing.

In *People v Stritzinger* (1983) 34 C3d 505, 513, 194 CR 431, however, the supreme court limited the operation of Pen C §§11164–11174.3 and held that not all communications to psychotherapists need be disclosed. In *Stritzinger,* the psychotherapist treated both the alleged child molestation victim and her stepfather, the alleged molester. The psychotherapist's first session was with the victim, and the substance of the victim's revelations was properly reported and admitted as evidence. The psychotherapist divulged statements made by the stepfather during a subsequent session about the same transgressions as a result of misrepresentations by a deputy sheriff that the statements were exempt from the psychotherapist-patient privilege. The court held that the psychotherapist's duty was fulfilled by the initial disclosure and that the evidence adduced as a result of the deputy sheriff's misrepresentations should have been excluded. For further discussion of *Stritzinger,* see §19.11. See also *People v John B.* (1987) 192 CA3d 1073, 237 CR 659 (information concerning child abuse, given to psychiatrist in second session but not reported under Child Abuse and Neglect Reporting Act, was subject to psychotherapist-patient privilege even if there was duty to report information).

§36.14   C. When Patient's Competence Is at Issue

There is no physician-patient privilege in proceedings to commit the patient as mentally ill or to put the patient under a guardianship or conservatorship because of mental or physical condition. Evid C §1004. Nor is there a privilege in a proceeding brought by or on behalf of a patient to establish competence. Evid C §1005 (identical to psychotherapist-patient exception of Evid C §1025; see §§37.8, 37.20).

The reason given for these exceptions is the unfairness of permitting a patient to withhold evidence in proceedings being conducted for the patient's benefit. See Comments to Evid C §§1004–1005. The exceptions could be liberally construed as applying to anyone's privilege, enabling the subject of the proceedings to use the exceptions in attacking the mental condition of a person seeking to commit the patient or to establish incompetence. Adoption of that construction, however, seems unlikely. The Comments apparently regard the exceptions as applying only to the privilege of the patient whose competence is at issue, and no policy reason appears to exist for extending them further.

D. Nature of Physician-Patient Relationship

§36.15   1. Assistance in Crime or Tort

There is no physician-patient privilege if the physician's services were sought or obtained to help plan, commit, or escape detection or arrest for a crime or tort. Evid C §997. This exception is similar to the psychotherapist-patient exception (Evid C §1018) and broader than the corresponding exceptions to the attorney-client privilege (chap 34) and the marital communications privilege (chap 40), which apply only if help was sought to commit or plan a crime or fraud and do not cover attempts to hide or escape. See Evid C §§956, 981. See also §37.11.

§36.16   2. Breach of Physician-Patient Duty

The physician-patient privilege does not protect information relevant to an issue of either the physician's or the patient's breach of a duty arising out of the physician-patient relationship. Evid C §1001. This exception applies in an action against the patient to collect the physician's fee. In an action against the physician for malpractice, this exception will usually have the same effect as the patient-litigant exception. See §36.9. On the problem of proving relevancy necessary for this exception, see §36.22.

§36.17   E. Claims Through Deceased Patient

The physician-patient privilege does not protect information relevant to an issue between parties claiming through the same deceased patient. Each litigant's claim may be by testate or intestate succession or by inter vivos transfer.

Evid C §1000. In most of the situations covered by this exception, the plaintiff-litigant exception also applies. See Evid C §996(b). See also §36.9.

Two other exceptions apply when a deceased patient has executed a deed, a will, or another instrument purporting to affect an interest in property: There is no privilege for information relevant to an issue of the decedent's intention (Evid C §1002) or for information relevant to an issue of the validity of the written instrument (Evid C §1003).

On problems of proving relevancy under these three exceptions, see §36.22. Similar exceptions to the attorney-client and psychotherapist-patient privileges are provided by Evid C §§957, 960–961, 1019, 1021–1022. See chaps 34, 37.

§36.18   F. Public Record

The physician-patient privilege does not protect information that is required to be made a matter of public record. Evid C §1006. There is a similar exception to the psychotherapist-patient privilege. See Evid C §1026.

V. TERMINATION BY DEATH OR WAIVER

§36.19   A. Effect of Patient's Death

The guardian or conservator of a patient who dies loses authority to act for the patient, presumably including his or her authority under Evid C §993(b) as holder of the patient's privilege, because the death terminates the guardianship or conservatorship. See Prob C §§1600(a), 1860(a); *Estate of Kelley* (1920) 184 C 448, 194 P 4. After a patient's death, the privilege passes to his or her personal representative, *i.e.,* the executor or administrator. Evid C §993(c). The privilege terminates when the estate is finally distributed and the representative is discharged. See Comment to Evid C §993.

Because there apparently is no holder of the privilege during the period between death and the appointment of the personal representative, the privilege is suspended during that time. See Evid C §§993–994. See also Evid C §916(b)(2). If appointment of a regular executor or administrator is delayed, this period may be shortened by the immediate appointment of a special administrator. See Prob C §§8481, 8524, 8540–8547; 1 California Decedent Estate Practice §§7.25–7.43 (Cal CEB 1986). Even after final distribution of the estate and discharge of the personal representative, it may be possible to revive the privilege by reopening the estate and having a personal representative again appointed. See Prob C §12252.

A physician's duty to claim the privilege on behalf of the patient may possibly be held to continue after the patient's death while a personal representative of the patient's estate (a holder under Evid C §993(c)) is likely to be appointed. Evidence Code §994(c) eliminates the physician's power to claim the privilege (and thus the duty to so do under Evid C §995) "if there is no holder of the privilege in existence." See §36.6 (physician's duty).

A similar suspension problem exists for the attorney-client, psychotherapist-patient, and sexual assault victim-counselor privileges between death and the appointment of a personal representative. See §§34.20, 37.16, 39.8.

§36.20 B. Waiver

The physician-patient privilege is waived whenever a holder discloses, or consents to disclosure of, a significant part of the privileged communication. Evid C §912(a). Thus, a patient can waive the privilege unless the patient has a guardian or conservator; if the patient has a guardian or conservator, only that person can waive the privilege. See Evid C §993(a)-(b); *Jones v Superior Court* (1981) 119 CA3d 534, 546, 174 CR 148. The text of Evid C §912, governing waiver of the physician-patient privilege, is set out in §33.31.

The Evidence Code contains no provision that enables the patient or the patient's counsel to prevent the patient's guardian or conservator from waiving the patient's privilege when the patient has separate counsel because of a conflict of interest with the guardian or conservator. See §§34.11-34.13 (related problem under provisions for claim of attorney-client privilege). If the patient has died, the privilege can be waived by a personal representative. Evid C §993(c).

If there are joint holders of the privilege (*e.g.,* a husband and wife consulting a physician about a marital problem), waiver by one joint holder does not impair the other joint holder's privilege. Evid C §912(b). A general guardian or conservator of a patient's estate holds the privilege jointly with a general guardian or conservator of the patient's person (see Comment to Evid C §993), and presumably a guardian ad litem (CCP §§372-373; Prob C §1003) holds the privilege jointly with a general guardian or conservator. See §36.5. A waiver by the patient's general guardian of a privilege that the patient holds jointly with the guardian ad litem does not impair the guardian ad litem's right to claim the privilege. But if a general guardian waives the patient's privilege before the guardian ad litem is appointed, the guardian ad litem appears to be bound by the waiver under Evid C §912.

There is no waiver if the holder acts under coercion (Evid C §912(a)) or if disclosure is protected by another privilege, *e.g.,* is made in confidence to the holder's attorney or spouse (Evid C §912(c)). Confidential disclosure to third persons reasonably necessary to the purpose for which the physician was consulted is not a waiver. Evid C §912(d); *Rudnick v Superior Court* (1974) 11 C3d 924, 930, 114 CR 603. On confidentiality as a requisite of the privilege, see Evid C §992. See also §36.4. Disclosure to an in-hospital medical or medical-dental staff committee engaged in research on reducing morbidity or mortality is not a waiver. The information disclosed is inadmissible in evidence in civil proceedings, and the patient's identity is protected from discovery. Evid C §1156.

The most common form of waiver is the holder's failure to claim the privilege whenever the opportunity arises. Thus, waiver may occur from failure to claim the privilege on discovery (see §33.9) or, even if the privilege is claimed then, from failure to claim it at the trial. If a holder testifies, or permits another to testify, to a significant part of the privileged information, the right to claim the privilege is destroyed—not only for the current proceeding but for all future purposes. Evid C §912(a); *Jones v Superior Court, supra*. But if the holder claims the privilege and the claim is improperly overruled, the holder can claim error at the trial if the holder is a party (Evid C §918; see §33.21), and the disclosure is inadmissible against the holder in later proceedings (Evid C §919(a); see §33.24) whether or not the holder sought review of the order requiring disclosure (Evid C §919(b); see Comment to Evid C §919(b)).

Similarly, the privilege is not waived by disclosure in a proceeding in which there is no legal standing to claim it, *e.g.,* when it is excluded by an exception; the privilege remains available in later proceedings to which no exception applies. Evid C §912(a). A physician's failure to claim the privilege, as required by Evid C §§994(c) and 995 (see §36.20), is not a waiver, because the physician is not a holder of the privilege. Evid C §993; *Roberts v Superior Court* (1973) 9 C3d 330, 341, 107 CR 309.

On waiver as a bar to exclusion of privileged information by a judge under Evid C §916, see §§33.16, 33.28.

VI. RULING ON PRIVILEGE

§36.21   A. Procedure

When the privilege is claimed, its existence and applicability may present questions of preliminary fact that must be heard and decided by the judge as an independent issue. Evid C §§400–402, 405. The parties may present evidence on these issues. The evidence typically consists of further examination and cross-examination of the witness already on the stand.

Evidence Code §915(a) ordinarily prevents the judge from requiring disclosure of information claimed to be within the physician-patient privilege for purposes of ruling on the claim. Decisions in which the courts applied the psychotherapist-patient privilege indicate, however, that the judge may be entitled to require confidential disclosure in order to rule on an exception to the physician-patient privilege that depends on the content of the communication. See §37.21.

Penal Code §1524(c) provides for a hearing on claims of privilege against a search warrant for documentary evidence in the possession of a physician who is "not reasonably suspected of engaging or having engaged in criminal activity related to the documentary evidence for which a warrant is requested." Evidence Code §915(a) provides that if in such a hearing the court determines that there are "no other feasible means to rule on the validity" of the claim of privilege, the court must proceed under Evid C §915(b), which provides for confidential disclosure in chambers (see §33.17).

§36.22 B. Burden of Proof

The claimant of the privilege has the burden of proving the existence of the physician-patient relationship and that the offered evidence is a communication within that relationship. On these requisites, see §§36.2–36.3. The claimant also has the burden of proving standing to claim the privilege. On who can claim, see Evid C §§993–994. See also §§36.5–36.6.

The opponent of the privilege (the proponent of the offered evidence) has the burden of proving that the communication or information was not confidential. Evid C §917 (establishing presumption of confidentiality; for statutory text, see §33.31). On the requisite of confidentiality, see §36.4. The opponent also has the burden of proving that the privilege has been waived and, ordinarily, that it is excluded by an exception. See Comment to Evid C §405. Because the patient-litigant exception depends on the relevancy of the communication's content to the alleged condition of the patient (see Evid C §996; see also §36.9), however, the burden of proving that exception apparently rests on the patient. *In re Lifschutz* (1970) 2 C3d 415, 436, 85 CR 829 (psychotherapist-patient privilege). Meeting that burden may require confidential disclosure of the communication to the judge. See §§36.22, 37.19.

When confidential disclosure is unavailable, the opponent must meet the burden of proving an exception dependent on the communication's content by other means. For example, the opponent may inquire whether a witness has medical information on specified matters relevant to an issue within the exception. The judge may deny the claim of privilege to this question on the grounds that an affirmative answer will necessarily refer to information within the exception and that a negative answer will reveal nothing privileged. If the answer is affirmative, the defendant can then explore the time, place, circumstances, and contents of the unprivileged information.

On the burden of proof on issues raised by a motion under Evid C §916 to have the judge exclude privileged information in the absence of anyone entitled to claim privilege, see §§33.15–33.16.

§36.23 VII. STATUTES

Evidence Code §§990–1007, referred to in these provisions as "this article," apply to the physician-patient privilege.

- Evidence Code §990 states:

    As used in this article, "physician" means a person authorized, or reasonably believed by the patient to be authorized, to practice medicine in any state or nation.

- Evidence Code §991 states:

    As used in this article, "patient" means a person who consults a physician or submits to an examination by a physician for the purpose of securing a diagnosis or preventive, palliative, or curative treatment of his physical or mental or emotional condition.

- Evidence Code §992 states:

   As used in this article, "confidential communication between patient and physician" means information, including information obtained by an examination of the patient, transmitted between a patient and his physician in the course of that relationship and in confidence by a means which, so far as the patient is aware, discloses the information to no third persons other than those who are present to further the interest of the patient in the consultation or those to whom disclosure is reasonably necessary for the transmission of the information or the accomplishment of the purpose for which the physician is consulted, and includes a diagnosis made and the advice given by the physician in the course of that relationship.

- Evidence Code §993 states:

   As used in this article, "holder of the privilege" means:

   (a) The patient when he has no guardian or conservator.

   (b) A guardian or conservator of the patient when the patient has a guardian or conservator.

   (c) The personal representative of the patient if the patient is dead.

- Evidence Code §994 states:

   Subject to Section 912 [on waiver] and except as otherwise provided in this article, the patient, whether or not a party, has a privilege to refuse to disclose, and to prevent another from disclosing, a confidential communication between patient and physician if the privilege is claimed by:

   (a) The holder of the privilege;

   (b) A person who is authorized to claim the privilege by the holder of the privilege; or

   (c) The person who was the physician at the time of the confidential communication, but such person may not claim the privilege if there is no holder of the privilege in existence or if he or she is otherwise instructed by a person authorized to permit disclosure.

   The relationship of physician and patient shall exist between a medical or podiatry corporation as defined in the Medical Practice Act and the patient to whom it renders professional services, as well as between such patients and licensed physicians and surgeons employed by such corporation to render services to such patients. The word "persons" as used in this subdivision includes partnerships, corporations, limited liability companies, associations, and other groups and entities.

- Evidence Code §995 states:

   The physician who received or made a communication subject to the privilege under this article shall claim the privilege whenever he is present when the communication is sought to be disclosed and is authorized to claim the privilege under subdivision (c) of Section 994.

- Evidence Code §996 states:

    There is no privilege under this article as to a communication relevant to an issue concerning the condition of the patient if such issue has been tendered by:

    (a) The patient;

    (b) Any party claiming through or under the patient;

    (c) Any party claiming as a beneficiary of the patient through a contract to which the patient is or was a party; or

    (d) The plaintiff in an action brought under Section 376 or 377 of the Code of Civil Procedure for damages for the injury or death of the patient.

- Evidence Code §997 states:

    There is no privilege under this article if the services of the physician were sought or obtained to enable or aid anyone to commit or plan to commit a crime or a tort or to escape detection or apprehension after the commission of a crime or a tort.

- Evidence Code §998 states:

    There is no privilege under this article in a criminal proceeding.

- Evidence Code §999 states:

    There is no privilege under this article as to a communication relevant to an issue concerning the condition of the patient in a proceeding to recover damages on account of the conduct of the patient if good cause for disclosure of the communication is shown.

- Evidence Code §1000 states:

    There is no privilege under this article as to a communication relevant to an issue between parties all of whom claim through a deceased patient, regardless of whether the claims are by testate or intestate succession or by inter vivos transaction.

- Evidence Code §1001 states:

    There is no privilege under this article as to a communication relevant to an issue of breach, by the physician or by the patient, of a duty arising out of the physician-patient relationship.

- Evidence Code §1002 states:

    There is no privilege under this article as to a communication relevant to an issue concerning the intention of a patient, now deceased, with respect to a deed of conveyance, will, or other writing, executed by the patient, purporting to affect an interest in property.

- Evidence Code §1003 states:

    There is no privilege under this article as to a communication relevant to an issue concerning the validity of a deed of conveyance, will, or other writing, executed by a patient, now deceased, purporting to affect an interest in property.

- Evidence Code §1004 states:

    There is no privilege under this article in a proceeding to commit the patient or otherwise place him or his property, or both, under the control of another because of his alleged mental or physical condition.

- Evidence Code §1005 states:

    There is no privilege under this article in a proceeding brought by or on behalf of the patient to establish his competence.

- Evidence Code §1006 states:

    There is no privilege under this article as to information that the physician or the patient is required to report to a public employee, or as to information required to be recorded in a public office, if such report or record is open to public inspection.

- Evidence Code §1007 states:

    There is no privilege under this article in a proceeding brought by a public entity to determine whether a right, authority, license, or privilege (including the right or privilege to be employed by the public entity or to hold a public office) should be revoked, suspended, terminated, limited, or conditioned.

§36.24   VIII. ILLUSTRATIONS OF PRIVILEGE

The privilege may be available in the following situations in a civil action for damages from an automobile accident. In the first three illustrations, the privilege might be circumvented by a showing of good cause. Evid C §999. See §36.11.

- A doctor is asked by the plaintiff to reveal electrocardiogram readings performed on the defendant-driver.

- The defendant-driver's doctor is asked what the defendant told her about the accident during a consultation for a nervous condition.

- A defendant-driver alleged to have been intoxicated at the time of an accident is asked: "Didn't your doctor warn you on many occasions not to mix tranquilizers with alcohol?"

- After a witness testifies to events that occurred 300 yards away, the witness's ophthalmologist is subpoenaed and asked about the witness's vision.

IX. STATING CLAIM OF PRIVILEGE

§36.25   A. By Witness

Your Honor, I claim the physician-patient privilege.

§36.26   B. By Trial Counsel

If possible, this objection by trial counsel should be made outside the presence of the jury. In stating the claim, counsel may properly refer to the privileged matter as a "communication" even though it is an X ray, a laboratory report, or another type of information that was not consciously transmitted or received by the patient. See Evid C §992 (definition of "confidential communication between patient and physician"). See also §36.3.

Your Honor, that question calls for disclosure of a privileged confidential communication between patient and physician.

[Option 1: Counsel represents party entitled to claim privilege]

On behalf of _ _[name of party]_ _, I claim the privilege and object to the question on that ground.

[Option 2: Witness holds privilege and is not represented by counsel]

I request that you advise the witness of _ _[his/her]_ _ right to refuse to answer on the ground of privilege.

[Option 3: Neither witness nor party can claim privilege (Evid C §916)]

I move that you exclude the answer as privileged.

37

Psychotherapist-Patient Privilege

I. NATURE AND PURPOSE   §37.1

II. REQUIREMENTS
   A. Psychotherapist-Patient Relationship   §37.2
   B. Communication or Information   §37.3
   C. Confidentiality   §37.4

III. WHO CAN CLAIM
   A. Patient or Patient's Representative   §37.5
   B. Psychotherapist's Duty to Claim   §37.6
   C. Judge May Exclude Information   §37.7

IV. EXCEPTIONS
   A. Patient-Litigant
      1. Civil Trials   §37.8
      2. Criminal Trials   §37.9
   B. Psychotherapist Considers Patient To Be Dangerous   §37.10
   C. Nature of Psychotherapist-Patient Relationship
      1. Assistance in Crime or Tort   §37.11
      2. Breach of Psychotherapist-Patient Duty   §37.12
   D. Claims Through Deceased Patient   §37.13
   E. Public Record   §37.14
   F. Child Abuse   §37.15

V. TERMINATION BY DEATH OR WAIVER
   A. Effect of Patient's Death   §37.16
   B. Waiver   §37.17

VI. RULING ON PRIVILEGE
   A. Procedure   §37.18
   B. Burden of Proof   §37.19

VII. STATUTES   §37.20

VIII. ILLUSTRATIONS OF PRIVILEGE   §37.21

IX. STATING CLAIM OF PRIVILEGE
   A. By Witness   §37.22
   B. By Trial Counsel   §37.23

§37.1 I. NATURE AND PURPOSE

The psychotherapist-patient privilege prevents compulsory disclosure of confidential information transmitted between psychotherapist and patient. Its purpose is to encourage the patient to give the psychotherapist information necessary for psychotherapeutic diagnosis, treatment, or research, by relieving the patient's apprehension that the information will be disclosed without consent. See Comment to Evid C §1014. The text of Evid C §§1010–1027, governing the psychotherapist-patient privilege, is set out in §37.20.

The psychotherapist-patient privilege covers both licensed psychologists and physicians practicing psychiatry and has been extended to include certain other licensees (see §37.2). The privilege is restricted by certain exceptions not applicable to the attorney-client privilege.

The psychotherapist-patient privilege is not subject to the blanket physician-patient exceptions for criminal and quasi-criminal proceedings (see §§36.10–36.13). Counsel should note that Cal Const art I, §28(d) (the "truth-in-evidence" provision of Proposition 8) expressly leaves the Evidence Code privileges sections untouched in criminal actions. Also, unlike the physician-patient privilege, it is sometimes available in commitment and guardianship proceedings (see §37.12).

When an exception eliminates the psychotherapist-patient privilege, but the confidential communication emanated from a psychiatric examination made at the request of the patient's attorney, the attorney-client privilege may apply. See Comment to Evid C §952; *People v Lines* (1975) 13 C3d 500, 510, 119 CR 225; 2 Witkin, California Evidence, *Witnesses* §§122–123 (4th ed 2000). See also §34.9.

II. REQUIREMENTS

§37.2 A. Psychotherapist-Patient Relationship

To qualify for the psychotherapist-patient privilege, the therapist must be a person who is, or is reasonably believed by the patient to be (Evid C §1010)

- A person licensed to practice medicine in any state or nation who devotes a substantial portion of time to the practice of psychiatry;

- A psychologist licensed under Bus & P C §§2900–2989;

- A licensed clinical social worker engaged in applied psychotherapy of a nonmedical nature;

- A credentialed school psychologist;

- A licensed marriage and family therapist;

- A registered psychological assistant under the supervision of a licensed psychologist or board-certified psychiatrist;

- A registered marriage, family, and child therapist intern or a registered apprentice clinical social worker under the supervision of a licensed marriage, family, and child therapist;

- A licensed clinical social worker;
- A licensed psychologist;
- A licensed physician certified in psychiatry;
- A psychological intern;
- A person exempt from the psychology licensing law under Bus & P C §2909(d);
- A trainee, as defined in Bus & P C §4980.03, who is fulfilling the supervised practicum required by Bus & P C §4980.40(b); or
- A person licensed as a registered nurse who has a master's degree in psychiatric-mental health nursing and is listed as a psychiatric-mental health nurse by the Board of Registered Nurses.

The privilege may also arise out of the relationship between a patient and a psychological corporation or licensed clinical social workers corporation (Evid C §1014) or out of treatment or counseling of minors age 12 or over by certain professional persons who might not otherwise qualify as psychotherapists (Fam C §6924(b); see §37.5). A person whom the patient reasonably believes to be a licensed physician practicing psychiatry (even though the belief is mistaken) is also a "psychotherapist" for purposes of the privilege. If, however, the patient reasonably believes that the person in whom he or she confides is another type of psychotherapist (*e.g.,* a licensed psychologist), a psychotherapist-patient relationship is not created for purposes of the privilege if that person is in fact not qualified. Evid C §1010. In a criminal proceeding, the privilege includes psychologists; physicians practicing psychiatry and persons whom the patient reasonably believes to be such physicians; clinical social workers; school psychologists; and marriage, family, and child therapists. See Pen C §1102; Evid C §1010. Evidence Code §1010.5 provides that a communication between a patient and an educational psychologist is privileged to the same extent as a communication between a patient and a psychotherapist. See §37.20.

The relationship can arise out of a consultation or an examination for the diagnosis, prevention, or treatment of the patient's mental or emotional condition. It can also arise when the patient is examined "for the purpose of scientific research on mental or emotional problems." Evid C §1011. Only a limited type of research qualifies under this provision: An interview by a licensed psychologist for a commercial marketing research project presumably does not create a psychotherapist-patient relationship.

The California Supreme Court has held that motive for participating in psychotherapy "is largely, if not totally, immaterial" in determining whether the psychotherapist-patient privilege attaches from the relationship. *Menendez v Superior Court* (1992) 3 C4th 435, 454, 11 CR2d 92. There appears to be a split, however, in the courts of appeal as to whether the psychotherapist-patient privilege arises when a party is ordered by the court to undergo psychotherapy. In earlier cases courts have held that communications are privileged only if the predominant purpose is to secure treatment or a diagnosis as specified in Evid C §1011. *In re Tabatha G.* (1996) 45 CA4th 1159, 1168, 53 CR2d 93 (bonding study not protected by psychotherapist-patient privilege because mother sought study to show termination of her parental rights was precluded); *People v Cabral* (1993) 12 CA4th 820, 15 CR2d 866 (defendant's letter to psychotherapist admitting molestation held not privileged because defendant's purpose in writing letter was to obtain probation). More recently, however, in *Story v Superior Court* (2003) 109 CA4th 1007, 135 CR2d 532, the court held that the defendant's motive in seeking psychotherapy was immaterial in determining whether the psychotherapist-patient privilege applied, holding that the "dispositive fact is *what* the participants do, not *why*." 109 CA4th at 1016.

§37.3   B. Communication or Information

The privilege applies to a "confidential communication between patient and psychotherapist." This term is defined broadly to include information obtained from examining the patient, *e.g.,* the psychotherapist's diagnosis and observations and the results of psychological tests. Evid C §1012. The term also includes the patient's statements, the psychotherapist's advice, and communications from intimate members of the patient's family. See *Grosslight v Superior Court* (1977) 72 CA3d 502, 508, 140 CR 278 (privilege covers family member communications); Comment to 1967 amendment to Evid C §1012 (uncommunicated diagnosis). Communications by patients to persons to whom disclosure is reasonably necessary to assist psychiatrists and psychologists in the patient's treatment come within the privilege. *Luhdorff v Superior Court* (1985) 166 CA3d 485, 489, 212 CR 516 (communications to unlicensed clinical social worker who was under supervision of psychologist).

When the existence of a psychotherapist-patient relationship has been kept confidential, the privilege protects a psychotherapist in refusing to name the patient or a patient in refusing to reveal whether he or she has consulted a psychotherapist. Despite diminution of the stigma formerly associated with psychotherapy, disclosure of the fact of consultation with a psychotherapist may be harmful to the patient. Confidentiality for that fact is derived from rules governing the physician-patient privilege, which is violated by disclosure of the relationship only if it results in revelation of the ailment. See *Rudnick v Superior Court* (1974) 11 C3d 924, 933 n13, 114 CR 603. See also §36.3.

Thus, the fact of a psychotherapist-patient relationship is privileged because its disclosure necessarily would reveal consultation for a "mental or emotional condition" (Evid C §1011). *Smith v Superior Court* (1981) 118 CA3d 136,

173 CR 145; *City of Alhambra v Superior Court* (1980) 110 CA3d 513, 519, 168 CR 49. In *County of Alameda v Superior Court* (1987) 194 CA3d 254, 239 CR 400, the court limited its decision of *Smith v Superior Court, supra. County of Alameda* was a personal injury action brought against a county by a woman alleging that she had been raped by a fellow patient in a locked psychiatric facility operated by the county, which sought to prevent the discovery of the name, address, and telephone number of the male patient. Narrowly confining its holding to the specific facts, the court allowed the disclosure because the plaintiff would have been unable to obtain the information to establish her case. The court held that the *Smith* rule should not apply rigidly in every case and that, in extraordinary cases of need for disclosure, a court retains discretion to order the patient's identity revealed.

§37.4   C. Confidentiality

The information protected by the privilege must not, to the knowledge of the patient, be seen or heard by a third person except one who is assisting the patient or collaborating with the psychotherapist in the matter. The privilege is not destroyed by the patient's knowledge that the information is accessible to persons who assist with the patient's examination or treatment, who are present to further the patient's interest (*e.g.,* a member of the family invited by the psychotherapist) or to whom disclosure is necessary for "the accomplishment of the purpose for which the psychotherapist is consulted." Evid C §1012; *Grosslight v Superior Court* (1977) 72 CA3d 502, 508, 140 CR 278 (privilege covers communications to "psychiatric personnel," *e.g.,* secretaries who record case histories); *In re Edward D.* (1976) 61 CA3d 10, 132 CR 100 (privilege of mother who consented to being psychiatrically examined in parental fitness proceeding was not destroyed by psychotherapist's report to judge, because report was necessary to accomplish purpose of consultation).

The privilege can be asserted to prevent disclosure by any witness unless the patient was aware that the information would become known to an eavesdropper or other unauthorized person. Evid C §§1012, 1014. See Comment to Evid C §954; *People v Henderson* (1977) 19 C3d 86, 97, 137 CR 1 (no confidentiality for arrestee's voluntary statements to psychotherapist he knew was sent by district attorney). In *Menendez v Superior Court* (1992) 3 C4th 435, 11 CR2d 92, the supreme court held that the psychotherapist-patient privilege (Evid C §1012) can cover a communication that was never, in fact, confidential if the communication was made in confidence. The court noted that the communication need only comprise information transmitted between the patient and the psychotherapist in the course of that relationship, in confidence by a means that, as far as the patient is aware, discloses the information to no outside third person. 3 C4th at 447.

There is a presumption of confidentiality, which shifts the burden of proof on the issue to the opponent of the privilege. Evid C §917. See §§37.19, 37.22.

III. WHO CAN CLAIM

§37.5   A. Patient or Patient's Representative

The patient can claim the privilege only as a "holder." Evid C §1014(a). The patient is a holder unless the patient is under a guardianship or conservatorship because of minority or disability. In that case, only the guardian or conservator can make the claim as a holder. Evid C §1013(a)-(b). On the applicability of this provision to the guardianship of minors, see Comment to Evid C §953. If the patient has two guardians or conservators, one for his or her person and the other for the estate, the two are joint holders of the privilege and either can claim it. See Comment to Evid C §993. A special guardian (*i.e.,* a guardian ad litem (CCP §§372-373; Prob C §1003) is also a holder. See *De Los Santos v Superior Court* (1980) 27 C3d 677, 682, 166 CR 172.

The Evidence Code contains no provision that allows a patient under a guardianship or conservatorship to claim the privilege personally even when the patient has a conflict of interest with the guardian or conservator and is therefore represented by separate counsel. See §34.11 (attorney-client privilege). On waiver of the patient's privilege by a guardian or conservator, see §37.17. After the patient dies, the executor or administrator becomes a holder and can claim the privilege. Evid C §1013(c). Any holder can authorize a representative to claim the privilege. Evid C §1014(b).

Family Code §6924(b) lists professional persons authorized to give mental health treatment or counseling to minors who are at least 12 years old and deemed dangerous or victims of child abuse, without the consent or notification of the minor's parent or guardian. Under Evid C §1014(c), the professional person rendering that treatment or counseling "has" the psychotherapist-patient privilege. That person appears to be an additional holder of the privilege, even though the definition of "holder" (Evid C §1013) has not been expressly enlarged.

§37.6   B. Psychotherapist's Duty to Claim

The psychotherapist has a duty to claim the privilege on behalf of the patient if both of the following conditions are met:

- The psychotherapist is "present when the communication is sought to be disclosed." Evid C §1015. Being "present" includes any opportunity to claim the privilege as a witness or a party.

- The psychotherapist has authority to claim the privilege on behalf of the patient. Evid C §1015. Evidence Code §1014(c) gives the psychotherapist this authority unless the privilege has been terminated by death (see §37.16) or unless a holder authorized to waive the privilege instructs the psychotherapist not to claim it or otherwise waives it (see §37.17).

With respect to treatment or counseling of certain minors, the psychotherapist "has" the privilege and presumably can claim it as a holder. Evid C §1014(c);

Fam C §6924(b). See §37.5. See also *Reynaud v Superior Court* (1982) 138 CA3d 1, 10, 187 CR 660 (psychiatrist being investigated for criminal fraud barred from claiming patients' privilege for allegedly fraudulent insurance claims that purported to contain confidential diagnostic conclusions).

§37.7   C. Judge May Exclude Information

When neither the witness nor a party can claim the privilege, Evid C §916 may require the judge to exclude privileged information on the court's own motion or the motion of a party. See §§33.14-33.17.

IV. EXCEPTIONS

A. Patient-Litigant

§37.8   1. Civil Trials

The psychotherapist-patient privilege does not protect information relevant to an issue concerning the mental or emotional condition of the patient, if this issue is tendered either by the patient or by any party asserting a claim based on the patient's injury, disability, or death. Evid C §1016. Thus, the plaintiff in a personal injury suit cannot use the privilege to conceal evidence relevant to a mental or emotional condition on which a claim for damages depends.

When the psychotherapist-patient privilege is ruled out by an exception, the attorney-client privilege may be available. See §§37.1, 34.4. In civil cases, this exception operates in a manner similar to the patient-litigant exception to the physician-patient privilege. See Evid C §996. See also §36.9.

The exception usually is narrowly construed. It does not apply to issues tendered only by the patient's adversary. *Simek v Superior Court* (1981) 117 CA3d 169, 172 CR 564 (father sought visitation rights; mother's claim that he was emotionally unstable did not allow her to examine his psychiatrist); *Grey v Superior Court* (1976) 62 CA3d 698, 133 CR 318 (on life insurance claim for accidental death, insurer's assertion of suicide did not permit it to examine decedent's psychotherapist; concurring opinion emphasized that claimant had not tendered issue of decedent's mental condition). The exception covers only communications that are directly relevant to a specific mental or emotional condition that the patient (or a party claiming through the patient) has placed at issue. See *In re Lipschutz* (1970) 2 C3d 415, 431, 85 CR 829.

Thus, the allegation that an automobile accident rendered the plaintiff "sick, sore, lame, and disabled" is insufficient to allow the defendant to inquire into the plaintiff's prior communications with psychotherapists. See *Roberts v Superior Court* (1973) 9 C3d 330, 107 CR 309. See also *Huelter v Superior Court* (1978) 87 CA3d 544, 151 CR 138 (wife's allegation of physical inability to support herself did not enable husband to inquire into her psychiatric treatment). Similarly, in *Vinson v Superior Court* (1987) 43 C3d 833, 239 CR

292, the supreme court held that the plaintiff, by asserting a claim for sexual harassment and intentional infliction of emotional distress, waived her right to privacy concerning her mental state. By doing so, however, the plaintiff did not waive her right to privacy concerning her sexual history and practices.

§37.9   2. Criminal Trials

The psychotherapist-patient privilege is available in criminal proceedings when the psychotherapist is, or is reasonably believed by the patient to be, a physician or a licensed psychologist, licensed social worker or apprentice, family therapist, psychiatric nurse, or psychological intern. See *Nielsen v Superior Court* (1997) 55 CA4th 1150, 64 CR2d 566. For a complete list, see Evid C §1010(a)–(*l*) or §37.2.

The patient-litigant exception generally does not arise in criminal proceedings, because the physician-patient privilege is completely excluded from criminal proceedings by another exception. See Evid C §998. The patient-litigant exception does arise, however, when the defendant pleads insanity or seeks to disprove guilt by evidence of mental or emotional condition. Because the defendant tenders these issues, the exception prevents the accused from claiming the privilege for information relevant to them. See Comments to Evid C §§1014, 1017. On insanity issues, see §37.10 (discussing narrower exception under Evid C §1023).

Communications between the appointed psychotherapist and the person examined are privileged if the appointment was made on the request of criminal defense counsel to help counsel obtain information needed for advising the defendant on whether to enter or withdraw a plea of insanity or to present a defense based on mental or emotional condition. Evid C §1017. According to the Comment to Evid C §1017, the purpose of leaving the privilege intact when the psychotherapist was appointed to assist defense counsel is to protect confidentiality if the defendant decides not to tender an issue of mental or emotional condition.

If the trial court doubts the defendant's competence to stand trial, the court must appoint a psychiatrist or licensed psychologist to examine the defendant. If the defendant does not seek to be found incompetent to stand trial, the court must appoint two psychotherapists. Pen C §1369(a). There is no privilege concerning the psychotherapists' work on the competency issue with regard to the competency proceeding. See Evid C §§1016–1017, 1023. The defendant's statements to a psychotherapist determining competency are not admissible, however, in the trial of the underlying criminal case. *People v Arcega* (1982) 32 C3d 504, 186 CR 94. See *Powell v Texas* (1989) 492 US 680, 106 L Ed 2d 551, 109 S Ct 3146.

If the defendant enters a plea of not guilty by reason of insanity, the court must appoint two or three psychotherapists to examine the defendant. Pen C §1027(a). The psychotherapist-patient privilege does not apply to the court-appointed psychotherapists. Evid C §1017. Statements made to the psychotherapists are inadmissible in the guilt phase, however, unless the defendant places mental state at issue. *In re Spencer* (1965) 63 C2d 400, 441, 46 CR 753.

§37.10   B. Psychotherapist Considers Patient to Be Dangerous

The psychotherapist-patient privilege cannot be used if the psychotherapist has reasonable cause to believe that (Evid C §1024):

- The patient's mental or emotional condition makes the patient dangerous to himself or herself or to other persons or their property; and

- Disclosure of the confidential communication is necessary to prevent the threatened danger.

For example, if a psychotherapist has heard a defendant in a criminal case make confidential admissions relevant to the defendant's prosecution, the psychotherapist may be able to invoke the exception by determining that the patient is sufficiently dangerous to warrant disclosure of the admissions for the purpose of obtaining conviction and removal from society. Moreover, a psychotherapist may incur civil liability for failing to warn the intended victim of violent assault by a dangerous patient. *Tarasoff v Regents of Univ. of Cal.* (1976) 17 C3d 425, 131 CR 14 (because of Evid C §1024, psychotherapist-patient privilege does not preclude such warning); see *People v One Ruger.22 Caliber Pistol* (2000) 84 CA4th 310, 314, 100 CR2d 780. See *Menendez v Superior Court* (1992) 3 C4th 435, 11 CR2d 92 (privilege applied to an audiotape of a psychotherapist's notes of a session with two patients). See also *Bellah v Greenson* (1978) 81 CA3d 614, 622, 146 CR 535 (no duty to warn of threatened suicide even though Evid C §1024 would permit warning). For the court to invoke the dangerous patient exception (Evid C §1024), evidence of the patient's suicidal feelings must indicate a danger to other persons. *Luhdorff v Superior Court* (1985) 166 CA3d 485, 494, 212 CR 516.

The privilege of Evid C §1014 does not apply when a therapist has made a disclosure to a third person, in a communication that is not itself privileged. After disclosure, the reason for the privilege—protection of the patient's right to privacy—no longer exists. *People v Clark* (1990) 50 C3d 583, 620, 268 CR 399. This exception, however, applies only to statements of the defendant that triggered the therapist's warning. *People v Wharton* (1991) 53 C3d 522, 554, 280 CR 631. The rationale of *People v Clark, supra,* however, has been criticized for ignoring the Evidence Code requirement that a party must properly establish waiver of a privilege or an exception to the privilege in order to negate the privilege. See Imwinkelried, Wydick & Hogan, California Evidentiary Foundation (4th ed 1998).

The psychotherapist thus has more leeway and more responsibility than the attorney with an obviously dangerous client. The attorney can urge the client to disclose, or to permit the attorney to disclose, their confidential communications, but both the attorney-client privilege and professional ethics forbid counsel from breaching the client's confidence by making a disclosure without the client's consent. See §34.12 (attorney's duty to claim privilege).

C. Nature of Psychotherapist-Patient Relationship

§37.11   1. Assistance in Crime or Tort

There is no psychotherapist-patient privilege if the psychotherapist's services were sought or obtained to help plan, commit, or escape detection or arrest for a crime or tort. Evid C §1018. This exception is similar to the physician-patient exception (Evid C §997) and broader than the corresponding exceptions to the attorney-client privilege and marital communications privilege, which apply only if help was sought to commit or plan a crime or fraud and do not cover attempts to hide or escape. See Evid C §§956, 981. See also §§34.15, 40.9.

§37.12   2. Breach of Psychotherapist-Patient Duty

The psychotherapist-patient privilege does not protect information relevant to an issue of either the psychotherapist's or the patient's breach of a duty arising out of their professional relationship with each other. Evid C §1020. This exception applies in an action against the patient to collect the psychotherapist's fee. In an action against the psychotherapist for malpractice, this exception will usually have the same effect as the patient-litigant exception. See §37.9. See §36.22 on the problem of proving the relevancy necessary for this exception, which is similar to the problem under the physician-patient exception.

§37.13   D. Claims Through Deceased Patient

The psychotherapist-patient privilege does not protect information relevant to an issue between parties claiming through the same deceased patient. Each litigant's claim may be by testate or intestate succession or by inter vivos transfer. Evid C §1019. In most of the situations covered by this exception, the patient-litigant exception also applies. See Evid C §1016. See also §37.8.

Two other exceptions apply when a deceased patient has executed a deed, will, or other instrument purporting to affect an interest in property: No privilege exists for information relevant to an issue of the decedent's intention (Evid C §1021) or for information relevant to an issue of the validity of the written instrument (Evid C §1022). Exceptions similar to these three apply to the attorney-client and physician-patient privileges. See Evid C §§957, 960–961, 1000, 1002–1003. See also §§34.18–34.19, 36.17.

On problems of proving the relevancy necessary for these three exceptions, see §36.22 (similar problem under physician-patient exceptions).

§37.14   E. Public Record

The psychotherapist-patient privilege does not protect information that is required to be made a matter of public record. Evid C §1026.

There is a similar exception to the physician-patient privilege. See Evid C §1006.

§37.15 F. Child Abuse

There is no psychotherapist-patient privilege if the patient is a child under age 16 and the psychotherapist has reasonable cause to believe that the patient has been the victim of a crime and that disclosure of the communication is in the child's best interest. Evid C §1027.

Penal Code §§11164–11174.3 require physicians, psychiatrists, psychologists, and other practitioners to report suspected instances of child abuse to local authorities. Penal Code §11171.2(b) provides that the information reported is not subject to the psychotherapist-patient privilege in any court proceeding or administrative hearing. See §36.13 on the supreme court decision in *People v Stritzinger* (1983) 34 C3d 505, 194 CR 431.

The child abuse or neglect reporting exception to the psychotherapist-patient privilege, contained in the Child Abuse and Neglect Reporting Act (Pen C §11171(b)), applies to information reported under the Act in a civil action for damages brought by a husband against his former wife, alleging false statements to her therapist. See *Roe v Superior Court* (1991) 229 CA3d 832, 280 CR 380.

V. TERMINATION BY DEATH OR WAIVER

§37.16 A. Effect of Patient's Death

The guardian or conservator of a patient who dies loses the authority to act for the patient, presumably including the authority under Evid C §993(b) as holder of the patient's privilege, because death terminates guardianship or conservatorship. See Prob C §§1600, 1860(a); *Estate of Kelley* (1920) 184 C 448, 194 P 4. After a patient's death, the privilege passes to the personal representative, *i.e.*, the executor or administrator. Evid C §1013(c). The privilege terminates when the estate is finally distributed and the representative is discharged. See Comment to Evid C §993.

During the period between death and the appointment of the personal representative, the privilege is suspended because there apparently is no holder. See Evid C §§916(b)(2), 1013–1014. If appointment of a regular executor or administrator is delayed, this period may be shortened by the immediate appointment of a special administrator. See Prob C §§8481, 8524, 8540–8547; 1 California Decedent Estate Practice §§7.25–7.43 (Cal CEB 1986). Even after final distribution of the estate and discharge of the personal representative, it may be possible to revive the privilege by reopening the estate and having a personal representative appointed. See Prob C §12252.

The psychotherapist's duty to claim the privilege on behalf of the patient may possibly be held to continue after the patient's death while a personal representative of the patient's estate (a holder under Evid C §1013(c)) is likely to be appointed. Evidence Code §1014(c) eliminates the psychotherapist's power to claim the privilege (and thus his or her duty to do so under Evid C §1015) "if there is no holder of the privilege in existence." See §37.6 on psychotherapist's duty.

A similar suspension problem exists for the attorney-client, physician-patient, and counselor-sexual assault victim privileges between death and the appointment of a personal representative. See §§34.11, 36.19, 38.8.

§37.17   B. Waiver

The text of Evid C §912, governing waiver of the psychotherapist-patient privilege, is set out in §33.31.

The privilege is waived whenever a holder discloses, or consents to disclosure of, a significant part of the privileged communication. Evid C §912(a); *Roberts v Superior Court* (1973) 9 C3d 330, 341, 107 CR 309 (psychotherapist cannot waive because not holder). It may also be waived when the patient voluntarily discloses otherwise confidential information or tenders his or her mental state as an issue. The waiver must be a voluntary and knowing act done with sufficient awareness of the relevant circumstances and likely consequences. *Roberts v Superior Court* (1973) 9 C3d 330, 340, 343, 107 CR 309; *San Diego Trolley, Inc. v Superior Court* (2001) 87 CA4th 1083, 1092, 105 CR2d 476. Notwithstanding a waiver, any disclosure of confidential or private information must be supported by a showing of compelling need and accomplished in a manner that protects, insofar as it is practical, the patient's privacy. 87 CA4th at 1093.

A "significant part of the communication" must be disclosed to establish waiver. Evid C §912(a). Thus, consent to disclosure of medical records may not be a waiver if it omits specific reference to mental or emotional condition or to psychotherapy. *Grey v Superior Court* (1976) 62 CA3d 698, 133 CR 318. Nor is the privilege necessarily waived by disclosure of the existence of a psychotherapist-patient relationship (*Roberts v Superior Court* (1973) 9 C3d 330, 340, 107 CR 309; *San Diego Trolley, Inc. v Superior Court* (2001) 87 CA4th 1083, 1092, 105 CR2d 476), of its general purpose (*Roberts v Superior Court, supra; San Diego Trolley, Inc. v. Superior Court, supra*), or of the substance of the consultation (*People v Perry* (1972) 7 C3d 756, 783, 103 CR 161).

There is no waiver if the holder acts under coercion (Evid C §912(a)) or if the disclosure is protected by another privilege, *e.g.*, is made in confidence to the holder's attorney or spouse (Evid C §912(c)). Confidential disclosure to third persons that is reasonably necessary to the purpose for which the psychotherapist was consulted is not a waiver. See Evid C §912(d); *Huelter v Superior Court* (1978) 87 CA3d 544, 548, 151 CR 138 (transmission of psychotherapist's records to patient's physician is not waiver). On confidentiality as a requisite of the privilege, see Evid C §1012. See also §37.4. Disclosure to an in-hospital medical staff committee engaged in research on reducing morbidity or mortality is not a waiver. The information disclosed is inadmissible in evidence in civil proceedings and the patient's identity is protected from discovery. Evid C §1156.

The most common form of waiver is the holder's failure to claim the privilege whenever the opportunity arises. Thus, waiver may occur from failure to claim the privilege during discovery (see §33.9) or, even if the privilege is claimed then, from failure to claim it at the trial. If a holder testifies, or permits another to testify, to a significant part of the privileged information, the right to claim the privilege is terminated—not only for the current proceeding but for all future purposes. Evid C §912(a). But if the privilege is claimed and the claim is improperly overruled, the holder can claim error at the trial if the holder is a party (Evid C §918; see §33.21) and the disclosure is inadmissible against the holder in later proceedings (Evid C §919(a); see §33.24). Similarly, the privilege is not waived by disclosure in a proceeding in which there is no legal standing to claim it, *e.g.*, when the privilege yields to an exception. The privilege remains available in later proceedings to which no exception applies. Evid C §912(a). A psychotherapist's failure to claim the privilege, as required by Evid C §1014(c) (see §37.6), is not a waiver because the psychotherapist is not a holder of the privilege. See Evid C §1013.

A patient can waive the privilege unless the patient has a guardian or conservator, in which case only that person can waive the privilege. See Evid C §1013(a)-(b). The Evidence Code contains no provision that enables the patient or the patient's counsel to prevent the patient's guardian or conservator from waiving the patient's privilege when the patient has separate counsel because of a conflict of interest with the guardian or conservator. See §§34.11, 34.22 (related problem under provisions for claim of attorney-client privilege). If the patient has died, the privilege can be waived by the personal representative. See Evid C §1013(c). If there are joint holders of the privilege (*e.g.*, members of the same family receiving psychotherapy in a group), a waiver by one joint holder does not impair the privilege of other joint holders. Evid C §912(b).

A general guardian or conservator of a patient's estate holds the privilege jointly with a general guardian or conservator of the patient's person (see Comment to Evid C §993); presumably, a guardian ad litem (CCP §§372-373; Prob C §1003) holds the privilege jointly with a general guardian or conservator. See §37.5. A waiver by the patient's general guardian of a privilege that is held jointly with the patient's guardian ad litem does not impair the guardian ad litem's right to claim the privilege. But if a general guardian waives the patient's privilege before the guardian ad litem is appointed, the guardian ad litem appears to be bound by the waiver under Evid C §912.

On waiver as a bar to the exclusion of privileged information by a judge under Evid C §916, see §§33.15-33.16.

VI. RULING ON PRIVILEGE

§37.18 A. Procedure

When the psychotherapist-patient privilege is claimed, its existence and applicability may present questions of preliminary fact that must be heard and decided by the judge as an independent issue. Evid C §§402, 405. The parties may present evidence on these issues; the evidence typically consists of further examination and cross-examination of the witness already on the stand.

Evidence Code §915(a) normally prevents the judge from requiring disclosure of a communication claimed to be within the psychotherapist-patient privilege for purposes of ruling on the claim. But the judge may be entitled to require confidential disclosure in order to rule on an exception to the privilege that depends on the content of the communication. *In re Lifschutz* (1970) 2 C3d 415, 437 n23, 85 CR 829 (patient-litigant exception; Evid C §1016; see §§37.8-37.9); *Mavroudis v Superior Court* (1980) 102 CA3d 594, 606, 162 CR 724 (dangerous patient exception; Evid C §1024; see §37.10).

Penal Code §1524(c) provides for a hearing on claims of privilege against a search warrant for documentary evidence in the possession of a psychotherapist who is "not reasonably suspected of engaging or having engaged in criminal activity related to the documentary evidence for which a warrant is requested . . . ." If, in such a hearing, the court determines that there are "no other feasible means to rule on the validity" of the claim of privilege, the court must proceed under Evid C §915(b), which provides for confidential disclosure in chambers (see §37.17). Evid C §915(a).

§37.19 B. Burden of Proof

The claimant of the privilege has the burden of proving the existence of the psychotherapist-patient relationship and that the offered evidence is a communication within that relationship. On these requisites, see §§37.2-37.3. The claimant also has the burden of proving foundational standing to claim the privilege. On who can claim, see Evid C §§1013-1014. See also §§37.5-37.6.

The opponent of the privilege (the proponent of the offered evidence) has the burden of proving that the communication or information was not confidential. Evid C §917 (establishing presumption of confidentiality; for statutory text, see §33.31). On the requisite of confidentiality, see §37.4. The opponent also has the burden of proving that the privilege has been waived and, ordinarily, that it is excluded by an exception. See Comment to Evid C §405. Because the patient-litigant exception depends on the relevancy of the communication's content to the mental or emotional condition asserted by the patient (see Evid C §1016), however, the burden of proving that exception rests on the patient (*In re Lifschutz* (1970) 2 C3d 415, 436, 85 CR 829). Meeting that burden may require confidential disclosure of the communication to the judge. See §37.19. For a suggested means of establishing exception without such disclosure, see §36.22 (physician-patient privilege).

On the burden of proof on issues raised by a motion under Evid C §916 to have the judge exclude privileged information in the absence of anyone entitled to claim privilege, see §§33.15-33.16.

§37.20 VII. STATUTES

Evidence Code §§1010-1027, referred to in these provisions as "this article," apply to the psychotherapist-patient privilege.

Evidence Code §1010 states:

> As used in this article, "psychotherapist" means a person who is, or is reasonably believed by the patient to be:
>
> (a) A person authorized, or reasonably believed by the patient to be authorized, to practice medicine in any state or nation who devotes, or is reasonably believed by the patient to devote, a substantial portion of his or her time to the practice of psychiatry.
>
> (b) A person licensed as a psychologist under Chapter 6.6 (commencing with Section 2900) of Division 2 of the Business and Professions Code.
>
> (c) A person licensed as a clinical social worker under Article 4 (commencing with Section 4996) of Chapter 14 of Division 2 of the Business and Professions Code, when he or she is engaged in applied psychotherapy of a nonmedical nature.
>
> (d) A person who is serving as a school psychologist and holds a credential authorizing such service issued by the state.
>
> (e) A person licensed as a marriage and family therapist under Chapter 13 (commencing with Section 4980) of Division 2 of the Business and Professions Code.
>
> (f) A person registered as a psychological assistant who is under the supervision of a licensed psychologist or board certified psychiatrist as required by Section 2913 of the Business and Professions Code, or a person registered as a marriage and family therapist intern who is under the supervision of a licensed marriage and family therapist, a licensed clinical social worker, a licensed psychologist, or a licensed physician certified in psychiatry, as specified in Section 4980.44 of the Business and Professions Code.
>
> (g) A person registered as an associate clinical social worker who is under the supervision of a licensed clinical social worker, a licensed psychologist, or a board certified psychiatrist as required by Section 4996.20 of the Business and Professions Code.
>
> (h) A person exempt from the Psychology Licensing Law pursuant to subdivision (d) of Section 2909 of the Business and Professions Code.
>
> (i) A psychological intern as defined in Section 2911 of the Business and Professions Code who is under the supervision of a licensed psychologist or board certified psychiatrist.

(j) A trainee, as defined in subdivision (c) of Section 4980.03 of the Business and Professions Code, who is fulfilling his or her supervised practicum required by subdivision (b) of Section 4980.40 of the Business and Professions Code and is supervised by a licensed psychologist, board certified psychiatrist, a licensed clinical social worker, or a licensed marriage, family and child counselor.

(k) A person licensed as a registered nurse pursuant to Chapter 6 (commencing with Section 2700) of Division 2 of the Business and Professions Code, who possesses a master's degree in psychiatric-mental health nursing. and is listed as a psychiatric-mental health nurse by the Board of Registered Nurses.

(*l*) An advanced practice nurse who is certified as a clinical nurse specialist pursuant to Article 9 (commencing with Section 2838) of Chapter 6 of Division 2 of the Business and Professions Code and who participates in expert clinical practice in the specialty of psychiatric-mental health nursing.

(m) A person rendering mental health treatment or counseling services as authorized pursuant to Section 6924 of the Family Code.

- Evidence Code §1010.5 states:

    A communication between a patient and an educational psychologist, licensed under Article 5 (commencing with Section 4986) of Chapter 13 of Division 2 of the Business and Professions Code, shall be privileged to the same extent, and subject to the same limitations, as a communication between a patient and a psychotherapist described in subdivisions (c), (d), and (e) of Section 1010.

- Evidence Code §1011 states:

    As used in this article, "patient" means a person who consults a psychotherapist or submits to an examination by a psychotherapist for the purpose of securing a diagnosis or preventive, palliative, or curative treatment of his mental or emotional condition or who submits to an examination of his mental or emotional condition for the purpose of scientific research on mental or emotional problems.

- Evidence Code §1012 states:

    As used in this article, "confidential communication between patient and psychotherapist" means information, including information obtained by an examination of the patient, transmitted between a patient and his psychotherapist in the course of that relationship and in confidence by a means which, so far as the patient is aware, discloses the information to no third persons other than those who are present to further the interest of the patient in the consultation, or those to whom disclosure is reasonably necessary for the transmission of the information or the accomplishment of the purpose for which the psychotherapist is consulted, and includes a diagnosis made and the advice given by the psychotherapist in the course of the relationship.

- Evidence Code §1013 states:

    As used in this article, "holder of the privilege" means:

(a) The patient when he has no guardian or conservator.

(b) A guardian or conservator of the patient when the patient has a guardian or conservator.

(c) The personal representative of the patient if the patient is dead.

- Evidence Code §1014 states:

Subject to Section 912 and except as otherwise provided in this article, the patient, whether or not a party, has a privilege to refuse to disclose, and to prevent another from disclosing, a confidential communication between patient and psychotherapist if the privilege is claimed by:

(a) The holder of the privilege;

(b) A person who is authorized to claim the privilege by the holder of the privilege; or

(c) The person who was the psychotherapist at the time of the confidential communication, but the person may not claim the privilege if there is no holder of the privilege in existence or if he is otherwise instructed by a person authorized to permit disclosure.

The relationship of a psychotherapist and patient shall exist between a psychological corporation as defined in Article 9 (commencing with Section 2995) of Chapter 6.6 of Division 2 of the Business and Professions Code, a marriage and family therapy corporation as defined in Article 9 (commencing with Section 4987.5) of Chapter 13 of Division 2 of the Business and Professions code, or a licensed clinical social workers corporation as defined in Article 5 (commencing with Section 4998) of Chapter 14 of Division 2 of the Business and Professions Code, and the patient to whom it renders professional services, as well as between such patients and psychotherapists employed by those corporations to render services to such patients. The word "persons" as used in this subdivision includes partnerships, corporations, limited liability companies, associations and other groups and entities.

- Evidence Code §1015 states:

The psychotherapist who received or made a communication subject to the privilege under this article shall claim the privilege whenever he is present when the communication is sought to be disclosed and is authorized to claim the privilege under subdivision (c) of Section 1014.

- Evidence Code §1016 states:

There is no privilege under this article as to a communication relevant to an issue concerning the mental or emotional condition of the patient if such issue has been tendered by:

(a) The patient;

(b) Any party claiming through or under the patient;

(c) Any party claiming as a beneficiary of the patient through a contract to which the patient is or was a party; or

(d) The plaintiff in an action brought under Section 376 or 377 of the Code of Civil Procedure for damages for the injury or death of the patient.

- Evidence Code §1017 states:

    (a) There is no privilege under this article if the psychotherapist is appointed by order of a court to examine the patient, but this exception does not apply where the psychotherapist is appointed by order of the court upon the request of the lawyer for the defendant in a criminal proceeding in order to provide the lawyer with information needed so that he or she may advise the defendant whether to enter or withdraw a plea based on insanity or to present a defense based on his or her mental or emotional condition.

    (b) There is no privilege under this article if the psychotherapist is appointed by the Board of Prison Terms to examine a patient pursuant to the provisions of Article 4 (commencing with Section 2960) of Chapter 7 of Title 1 of Part 3 of the Penal Code.

- Evidence Code §1018 states:

    There is no privilege under this article if the services of the psychotherapist were sought or obtained to enable or aid anyone to commit or plan to commit a crime or a tort or to escape detection or apprehension after the commission of a crime or a tort.

- Evidence Code §1019 states:

    There is no privilege under this article as to a communication relevant to an issue between parties all of whom claim through a deceased patient, regardless of whether the claims are by testate or intestate succession or by inter vivos transaction.

- Evidence Code §1020 states:

    There is no privilege under this article as to a communication relevant to an issue of breach, by the psychotherapist or by the patient, of a duty arising out of the psychotherapist-patient relationship.

- Evidence Code §1021 states:

    There is no privilege under this article as to a communication relevant to an issue concerning the intention of a patient, now deceased, with respect to a deed of conveyance, will, or other writing, executed by the patient, purporting to affect an interest in property.

- Evidence Code §1022 states:

    There is no privilege under this article as to a communication relevant to an issue concerning the validity of a deed of conveyance, will, or other writing, executed by a patient, now deceased, purporting to affect an interest in property.

- Evidence Code §1023 states:

    There is no privilege under this article in a proceeding under Chapter 6 (commencing with Section 1367) of Title 10 of Part 2 of the Penal Code initiated at the request of the defendant in a criminal action to determine his sanity.

    Penal Code §1367.1 establishes procedures for determining whether a misdemeanor defendant is mentally disordered and incompetent to stand trial. This statute also provides that if counsel informs the court that he or she believes that the defendant is or may be mentally disordered, the court must order that the defendant be referred for evaluation and treatment in accordance with Pen C §4011.6. If counsel does not believe that the defendant is mentally disordered, the court may nonetheless require such an evaluation. The judge may also order the facility providing evaluation and treatment to give the court a copy of the discharge summary at the conclusion of evaluation and treatment.

- Evidence Code §1024 states:

    There is no privilege under this article if the psychotherapist has reasonable cause to believe that the patient is in such mental or emotional condition as to be dangerous to himself or to the person or property of another and that disclosure of the communication is necessary to prevent the threatened danger.

- Evidence Code §1025 states:

    There is no privilege under this article in a proceeding brought by or on behalf of the patient to establish his competence.

- Evidence Code §1026 states:

    There is no privilege under this article as to information that the psychotherapist or the patient is required to report to a public employee or as to information required to be recorded in a public office, if such report or record is open to public inspection.

- Evidence Code §1027 states:

    There is no privilege under this article if all of the following circumstances exist:

    (a) The patient is a child under the age of 16.

    (b) The psychotherapist has reasonable cause to believe that the patient has been the victim of a crime and that disclosure of the communication is in the best interest of the child.

§37.21 VIII. ILLUSTRATIONS OF PRIVILEGE

The psychotherapist-patient privilege may be available for the following questions:

- "Did you tell your psychiatrist that you intended to kill the victim?"

- "What did you say to your psychologist?"
- "In your opinion, would your patient have felt the need to consult you at that time if in fact she did not recall what happened?"

IX. STATING CLAIM OF PRIVILEGE

§37.22　A. By Witness

Your Honor, I claim the psychotherapist-patient privilege.

§37.23　B. By Trial Counsel

If possible, trial counsel should make this statement outside the presence of the jury. In stating the claim, counsel may properly refer to the privileged matter as a "communication" even though it is information that was not consciously transmitted or received by the patient, *e.g.*, the psychotherapist's observations. See Evid C §1012 (definition of "confidential communication between patient and psychotherapist"). See also §37.3.

Your Honor, that question calls for disclosure of a privileged confidential communication between patient and psychotherapist.

[Option 1: Counsel represents party
entitled to claim privilege]

On behalf of _ _[name of party]_ _, I claim the privilege and object to the question on that ground.

[Option 2: Witness holds privilege and
is not represented by counsel]

I request that you advise the witness of _ _[his/her]_ _ right to refuse to answer on the ground of privilege.

[Option 3: Neither witness nor party can
claim privilege (Evid C §916)]

I move that you exclude the answer as privileged.

38
Counselor-Sexual Assault Victim Privilege

I. NATURE AND PURPOSE §38.1

II. REQUIREMENTS
    A. Counselor-Victim Relationship §38.2
    B. Communication or Information §38.3
    C. Confidentiality §38.4

III. WHO CAN CLAIM
    A. Victim or Victim's Representative §38.5
    B. Counselor's Duty to Claim §38.6
    C. Judge May Exclude Information §38.7

IV. TERMINATION BY DEATH OR WAIVER
    A. Effect of Victim's Death §38.8
    B. Waiver §38.9

V. RULING ON PRIVILEGE
    A. Dispute Over Nature of Communication; Procedure §38.10
    B. Other Issues §38.11
    C. Burden of Proof §38.12

VI. STATUTES §38.13

VII. ILLUSTRATIONS OF PRIVILEGE §38.14

VIII. STATING CLAIM OF PRIVILEGE
    A. By Witness §38.15
    B. By Trial Counsel §38.16

§38.1   I. NATURE AND PURPOSE

The counselor-sexual assault victim privilege (Evid C §§1035–1036.2) prevents compulsory disclosure of confidential information transmitted between counselor and victim. Its purpose is to encourage victims to give counselors all the information necessary for providing advice and assistance following a sexual assault, by relieving the victim's apprehension of disclosure to outsiders without the victim's consent. Creation of the privilege in 1980 reflected growth in awareness of the trauma caused by sexual assaults and of the need to protect the victim's ability to obtain treatment of that trauma. The privilege is narrower than the psychotherapist-patient privilege in that it covers more limited subject matter, but broader in that counselors include not only psychotherapists but also other trained persons.

The privilege appears to be intended primarily to prevent disclosure to which the victim has not consented, in criminal prosecutions for sexual assaults, of information about the victim's sexual conduct or reputation that is not relevant to the charged offense. Note that Cal Const art I, §28(d) (the "truth-in-evidence" provision of Proposition 8) expressly leaves the Evidence Code privileges sections untouched.

The text of Evid C §§1035-1036.2, governing the counselor-sexual assault victim privilege, is quoted in §38.13.

II. REQUIREMENTS

§38.2 A. Counselor-Victim Relationship

The privilege requires the sexual assault victim counselor to have a certificate of training in the counseling of sexual assault victims from a counseling center meeting certain requirements. The counselor must meet one of the following requirements:

- Be a psychotherapist as defined in Evid C §1010 (see §37.2);
- Have a master's degree in counseling or a related field;
- Have one year of supervised counseling experience, at least six months of which is in rape crisis counseling; or
- Have 40 hours of training under a person qualified under the first three categories (Evid C §1035.2; see Health & S C §§1598-1598.5; Pen C §13837).

The counselor-victim relationship arises when the victim consults the counselor to secure advice or assistance concerning a mental, physical, or emotional condition caused by a sexual assault. Evid C §1035. A sexual assault may consist of one or more of the criminal acts listed in Evid C §1036.2(a)-(i) or an attempt to commit any of those acts (Evid C §1036.2(j)).

§38.3 B. Communication or Information

The privilege applies to a confidential communication between counselor and victim in the course of their relationship. The communication may pertain to the victim's sexual conduct before or after the assault or to opinions about the victim's sexual conduct or reputation. The communication is also protected by the privilege to the extent that it reflects the facts and circumstances of the alleged sexual assault and includes advice on potential testimony. Evid C §1035.4. See Evid C §917.

The court may compel disclosure of confidential communications when they involve evidence relevant to the assault of which the victim complains and for which a defendant is being prosecuted, if the probative value of the information outweighs the effect on the victim, the treatment relationship, and the treatment services. See Evid C §1035.4, quoted in §38.13. A special procedure is provided for cases in which the court finds that the probative value of the communication outweighs the need for confidentiality. Evid C §1035.4. See §38.10.

§38.4 C. Confidentiality

The information protected by the privilege must not, to the knowledge of the victim, be seen or heard by a third person except one who is assisting the victim or the counselor in the matter. The privilege is not destroyed by the victim's knowledge of disclosures reasonably necessary to transmit the information or to accomplish the purpose of the consultation. Evid C §1035.4. The privilege can be asserted to prevent disclosure by any witness unless the victim was aware that the information would become known to an eavesdropper or other unauthorized person. Evid C §§1035.4, 1035.8. See Comment to Evid C §954.

III. WHO CAN CLAIM

§38.5 A. Victim or Victim's Representative

The privilege can be claimed by a holder or a person authorized by the holder. Evid C §1035.8(a)-(b). The victim is the holder unless the victim is under a guardianship or conservatorship because of minority or disability, in which case the guardian or conservator is the holder. If the victim is dead, the privilege is held by the victim's personal representative. Evid C §1035.6.

The physician-patient privilege rule that a person to whom disclosure is made in furtherance of the consultation has implied authority to claim the privilege (see §36.5) is likely to be applied to the counselor-sexual assault victim privilege.

§38.6 B. Counselor's Duty to Claim

The counselor has a duty to claim the privilege on behalf of the victim if the following conditions are met:

- The counselor is "present when the communication is sought to be disclosed." Evid C §1036. Being "present" presumably includes any opportunity to claim the privilege as a witness or a party.

- The counselor has authority to claim the privilege on behalf of the victim. Evid C §1036. Evidence Code §1035.8(c) gives the counselor this authority unless the privilege has been terminated by death (see §38.8) or unless a holder authorized to waive the privilege instructs the counselor not to claim it or otherwise waives it (see §38.9).

§38.7 C. Judge May Exclude Information

When neither the witness nor a party can claim the privilege, Evid C §916 may require the judge to exclude privileged information on the court's own motion or the motion of a party. See §§34.11–34.13.

IV. TERMINATION BY DEATH OR WAIVER

§38.8 A. Effect of Victim's Death

After a victim dies, the privilege passes to the personal representative, *i.e.,* executor or administrator. Evid C §1035.6(c). The privilege terminates when the estate is finally distributed and the representative is discharged. See Comment to Evid C §993.

During the period between death and the appointment of the personal representative, the privilege is suspended because there is apparently no holder. See Evid C §§916(b)(2), 1035.8, 1036.6. For discussion of this hiatus, see §§34.20 (attorney-client privilege), 36.19 (physician-patient privilege), 37.16 (psychotherapist-patient privilege).

§38.9 B. Waiver

The text of Evid C §912, governing waiver of privileges, is quoted in §33.31. The privilege is waived whenever a holder discloses, or consents to disclosure of, a significant part of the privileged communication. Evid C §912(a). Thus, a victim who has no guardian or conservator can waive the privilege; if there is a guardian or conservator, only that person can waive the privilege. See Evid C §1035.6(a)-(b). The Evidence Code contains no provision that enables the victim or victim's counsel to prevent the victim's guardian or conservator from waiving the victim's privilege when the victim has separate counsel because of a conflict of interest with the guardian or conservator. See §§34.11, 34.17-34.19 (related problem under provisions for claim of attorney-client privilege).

If the victim has died, the privilege can be waived by the victim's personal representative. See Evid C §1035.6(c). If there are joint holders of the privilege (*e.g.,* victims of a single course of conduct who consulted the counselor together), a waiver by one joint holder does not impair the privilege of the others. Evid C §912(b).

There is no waiver if the holder acts under coercion (Evid C §912(a)) or if the disclosure is protected by another privilege (Evid C §912(c)). Confidential disclosure to third persons that is reasonably necessary to the purpose for which the counselor was consulted is not a waiver. Evid C §912(d). On confidentiality as requisite of privilege, see Evid C §1035.4. See also §38.4.

The most common form of waiver is the holder's failure to claim the privilege whenever the opportunity arises. The privilege of a holder who testifies, or permits another to testify, to a significant part of the privileged information is destroyed—not only for the current proceeding but for all future purposes.

Evid C §912(a). A holder whose claim of the privilege is improperly overruled can claim error at the trial if the holder is a party (Evid C §918; see §33.21) and in any event is entitled to exclusion of the disclosure in later proceedings (Evid C §919; see §33.24). A counselor's failure to claim the privilege, as required by Evid C §1036 (see §38.6), is not a waiver, because the counselor is not a holder of the privilege (Evid C §1035.6).

On waiver as a bar to exclusion of privileged information by the judge under Evid C §916, see §§33.16, 33.28.

V. RULING ON PRIVILEGE

§38.10 A. Dispute Over Nature of Communication; Procedure

Evidence Code §1035.4 directs the court in the criminal proceeding concerning the sexual assault to weigh the probative value of the evidence against the effect on the victim, the treatment relationship, and the treatment services. After balancing these matters, if the court finds that the information should be disclosed, the court must do the following (Evid C §1035.4(1)-(3)):

- Advise the defendant of the nature of the information subject to disclosure;

- Order a hearing to allow questioning of the counselor out of the jury's presence; and

- Rule at the conclusion of the hearing on what information may be disclosed, what evidence may be introduced, and the nature of the questions that will be permitted.

Admission of evidence of the complaining witness's sexual conduct is subject to Evid C §§352, 782, and 1103. Evid C §1035.4(3).

§38.11 B. Other Issues

A claim of the privilege may present other issues, *e.g.*, the qualifications of the counselor (Evid C §1035.2), questions of preliminary fact that must be heard and decided by the judge independently (Evid C §§400-402, 405). The parties may present evidence on these issues. The evidence typically consists of further examination and cross-examination of the witness already testifying.

Subject to the special procedure under Evid C §1035.4 (see §38.10), Evid C §915(a) prevents the judge from requiring disclosure of information claimed to be within the counselor-sexual assault victim privilege for the purpose of ruling on it. See §33.17.

§38.12 C. Burden of Proof

Subject to the special procedure under Evid C §1035.4 (see §38.10), the claimant of the privilege has the burden of proving the existence of the counselor-sexual assault victim relationship, standing to claim the privilege, and that the offered evidence is a communication within that relationship. Effective January 1, 2003, Evid C §917 has been amended to extend its presumption of confidentiality to the counselor-victim privilege. On the burden of proof of the claimant and opponent respectively, see generally Comment to Evid C §405.

On the burden of proof on issues raised by a motion under Evid C §916 to have the judge exclude privileged information in the absence of anyone entitled to claim privilege, see §§33.15–33.16.

§38.13   VI. STATUTES

Evidence Code §§1035–1036.2, referred to in these provisions as "this article," apply to the counselor-sexual assault victim privilege.

- Evidence Code §1035 states:

    As used in this article, "victim" means a person who consults a sexual assault victim counselor for the purpose of securing advice or assistance concerning a mental, physical, or emotional condition caused by a sexual assault.

- Evidence Code §1035.2 states:

    As used in this article, "sexual assault victim counselor" means any of the following:

    (a) A person who is engaged in any office, hospital, institution, or center commonly known as a rape crisis center, whose primary purpose is the rendering of advice or assistance to victims of sexual assault and who has received a certificate evidencing completion of a training program in the counseling of sexual assault victims issued by a counseling center that meets the criteria for the award of a grant established pursuant to Section 13837 of the Penal Code and who meets one of the following requirements:

    (1) Is a psychotherapist as defined in Section 1010; has a master's degree in counseling or a related field; or has one year of counseling experience, at least six months of which is in rape crisis counseling.

    (2) Has 40 hours of training as described below and is supervised by an individual who qualifies as a counselor under paragraph (1). The training supervised by a person qualified under subdivision (1) shall include, but not be limited to, the following areas: law, medicine, societal attitudes, crisis intervention and counseling techniques, role playing, referral services, and sexuality.

    (b) A person who is employed by any organization providing the programs specified in Section 13835.2 of the Penal Code, whether financially compensated or not, for the purpose of counseling and assisting sexual assault victims, and who meets one of the following requirements:

(1) Is a psychotherapist as defined in Section 1010; has a master's degree in counseling or a related field; or has one year of counseling experience, at least six months of which is in rape assault counseling.

(2) Has the minimum training for sexual assault counseling required by guidelines established by the employing agency pursuant to subdivision (c) of Section 13835.10 of the Penal Code, and is supervised by an individual who qualifies as a counselor under paragraph (1). The training, supervised by a person qualified under paragraph (1), shall include, but not be limited to, the following areas: law, victimology, counseling techniques, client and system advocacy, and referral services.

- Evidence Code §1035.4 states:

As used in this article, "confidential communication between the sexual assault counselor and the victim" means information transmitted between the victim and the sexual assault counselor in the course of their relationship and in confidence by a means which, so far as the victim is aware, discloses the information to no third persons other than those who are present to further the interests of the victim in the consultation or those to whom disclosures are reasonably necessary for the transmission of the information or an accomplishment of the purposes for which the sexual assault counselor is consulted. The term includes all information regarding the facts and circumstances involving the alleged sexual assault and also includes all information regarding the victim's prior or subsequent sexual conduct, and opinions regarding the victim's sexual conduct or reputation in sexual matters.

The court may compel disclosure of information received by the sexual assault counselor which constitutes relevant evidence of the facts and circumstances involving an alleged sexual assault about which the victim is complaining and which is the subject of a criminal proceeding if the court determines that the probative value outweighs the effect on the victim, the treatment relationship, and the treatment services if disclosure is compelled. The court may also compel disclosure in proceedings related to child abuse if the court determines the probative value outweighs the effect on the victim, the treatment relationship, and the treatment services if disclosure is compelled.

When a court is ruling on a claim of privilege under this article, the court may require the person from whom disclosure is sought or the person authorized to claim the privilege, or both, to disclose the information in chambers out of the presence and hearing of all persons except the person authorized to claim the privilege and such other persons as the person authorized to claim the privilege is willing to have present. If the judge determines that the information is privileged and must not be disclosed, neither he or she nor any other person may ever disclose, without the consent of a person authorized to permit disclosure, what was disclosed in the course of the proceedings in chambers.

If the court determines certain information shall be disclosed, the court shall so order and inform the defendant. If the court finds there is a reasonable likelihood that particular information is subject to disclosure pursuant to the balancing test provided in this section, the following procedure shall be followed:

(1) The court shall inform the defendant of the nature of the information which may be subject to disclosure.

(2) The court shall order a hearing out of the presence of the jury, if any, and at the hearing allow the questioning of the sexual assault counselor regarding the information which the court has determined may be subject to disclosure.

(3) At the conclusion of the hearing, the court shall rule which items of information, if any, shall be disclosed. The court may make an order stating what evidence may be introduced by the defendant and the nature of questions to be permitted. The defendant may then offer evidence pursuant to the order of the court. Admission of evidence concerning the sexual conduct of the complaining witness is subject to Sections 352, 782, and 1103.

- Evidence Code §1035.6 states:

    As used in this article, "holder of the privilege" means:

    (a) The victim when such person has no guardian or conservator.

    (b) A guardian or conservator of the victim when the victim has a guardian or conservator.

    (c) The personal representative of the victim if the victim is dead.

- Evidence Code §1035.8 states:

    A victim of a sexual assault, whether or not a party, has a privilege to refuse to disclose, and to prevent another from disclosing, a confidential communication between the victim and a sexual assault victim counselor if the privilege is claimed by:

    (a) The holder of the privilege;

    (b) A person who is authorized to claim the privilege by the holder of the privilege; or

    (c) The person who was the sexual assault victim counselor at the time of the confidential communication, but such person may not claim the privilege if there is no holder of the privilege in existence or if he is otherwise instructed by a person authorized to permit disclosure.

- Evidence Code §1036 states:

    The sexual assault victim counselor who received or made a communication subject to the privilege under this article shall claim the privilege whenever he is present when the communication is sought to be disclosed and is authorized to claim the privilege under subdivision (c) of Section 1035.8.

- Evidence Code §1036.2 states

    As used in this article, "sexual assault" includes all of the following:

    (a) Rape, as defined in Section 261 of the Penal Code.

    (b) Unlawful sexual intercourse, as defined in Section 261.5 of the Penal Code.

    (c) Rape in concert with force and violence, as defined in Section 264.1 of the Penal Code.

    (d) Rape of a spouse, as defined in Section 262 of the Penal Code.

    (e) Sodomy, as defined in Section 286 of the Penal Code, except a violation of subdivision (e) of that section.

    (f) A violation of Section 288 of the Penal Code.

    (g) Oral copulation, as defined in Section 288a of the Penal Code, except a violation of subdivision (e) of that section.

    (h) Sexual penetration as defined in Section 289 of the Penal Code.

    (i) Annoying or molesting a child under 18, as defined in Section 647a of the Penal Code.

    (j) Any attempt to commit any of the above acts.

§38.14 VII. ILLUSTRATIONS OF PRIVILEGE

The counselor-sexual assault victim privilege may be available for the following questions:

- "What did you tell the counselor at the rape crisis center?"
- "What did Ms. Sanderson tell you when she came to the center?"
- "What advice did you give to Mr. Edwards when he came to the center?"

VIII. STATING CLAIM OF PRIVILEGE

§38.15 A. By Witness

Your Honor, I claim the counselor-sexual assault victim privilege.

§38.16 B. By Trial Counsel

Trial counsel should preferably make this statement outside the presence of the jury:

   Your Honor, that question calls for disclosure of a privileged confidential communication between counselor and sexual assault victim.

[Option 1: Counsel represents party
entitled to claim privilege]

On behalf of _ _[name of party]_ _, I claim the counselor-sexual assault victim privilege and object to the question on that ground.

[Option 2: Witness holds privilege and is not
represented by counsel]

I request that you advise the witness of _ _[his/her]_ _ right to refuse to answer on the ground of the counselor-sexual assault victim privilege.

[Option 3: Neither witness nor party can claim
privilege (Evid C §916)]

I move that you exclude the answer as privileged.

39

Counselor-Domestic Violence Victim Privilege

I. NATURE AND PURPOSE §39.1

II. REQUIREMENTS
    A. Counselor-Victim Relationship §39.2
    B. Communication or Information §39.3
    C. Confidentiality §39.4

III. WHO CAN CLAIM
    A. Victim or Victim's Representative §39.5
    B. Counselor's Duty to Claim §39.6
    C. Judge May Exclude Information §39.7

IV. TERMINATION BY DEATH OR WAIVER
    A. Effect of Victim's Death §39.8
    B. Waiver §39.9

V. RULING ON PRIVILEGE
    A. Court-Compelled Disclosure; Procedure §39.10
    B. Other Issues §39.11
    C. Burden of Proof §39.12

VI. STATUTES §39.13

VII. ILLUSTRATIONS OF PRIVILEGE §39.14

VIII. STATING CLAIM OF PRIVILEGE
    A. By Witness §39.15
    B. By Trial Counsel §39.16

§39.1 I. NATURE AND PURPOSE

The counselor-domestic violence victim privilege (Evid C §§1037–1037.7) prevents compulsory disclosure of confidential information transmitted between counselor and victim. Its purpose is to encourage victims to give counselors the information necessary for providing advice and assistance following an act of domestic violence by relieving the victim's apprehension of disclosure to outsiders without the victim's consent. Creation of the privilege in 1986 reflected increased awareness of the trauma caused by domestic violence and the desirability of encouraging victims to obtain treatment for that trauma.

The privilege is narrower than the psychotherapist-patient privilege in that it covers more limited subject matter, but broader in that the definition of "counselor" includes not only psychotherapists but also other trained persons.

The privilege seems intended primarily to prevent disclosures to which the victim has not consented in criminal prosecutions for acts of domestic violence. These disclosures include information about the victim or the children of the victim or abuser that is not relevant to the offense charged. See §39.10. Note that Cal Const art I, §28(d) (the "truth-in-evidence" provision of Proposition 8) expressly leaves the Evidence Code privileges sections untouched.

The text of Evid C §§1037–1037.7, governing the counselor-domestic violence victim privilege, is set out in §39.13.

II. REQUIREMENTS

§39.2   A. Counselor-Victim Relationship

The counselor-domestic violence victim privilege requires that the counselor be employed by an organization providing the services listed in Welf & I C §18294. Evid C §1037.1. To qualify, a counselor must (Evid C §1037.1):

- Have a master's degree in counseling or a related field;
- Have one year of counseling experience, at least half of which is in domestic violence counseling; or
- Have 40 hours of training under specified persons.

The counselor-victim relationship apparently arises when the victim consults the counselor to secure advice or assistance concerning domestic violence. "Domestic violence" is defined as abuse against a spouse or former spouse, a cohabitant or former cohabitant, a person whom the respondent is dating or engaged to, a coparent, a child, or a second-degree relation. See Evid C §1037.7; Fam C §6211.

§39.3   B. Communication or Information

The privilege applies to a confidential communication between counselor and victim in the course of their relationship. Effective January 1, 2003, Evid C §917 was amended to extend its presumption of confidentiality to communications between a counselor and domestic violence victim.

§39.4   C. Confidentiality

The information protected by the privilege must not, to the knowledge of the victim, be seen or heard by a third person except one who is assisting the victim or the counselor in the matter. The privilege is not destroyed by the victim's knowledge of disclosures reasonably necessary to transmit the information or to accomplish the purpose of the consultation. Evid C §1037.2. The privilege can be asserted to prevent disclosure by any witness unless the victim was aware that the information would become known to an eavesdropper or other unauthorized person. See Evid C §§1037.2, 1037.5.

III. WHO CAN CLAIM

§39.5   A. Victim or Victim's Representative

The privilege can be claimed by a holder or a person authorized by the holder. Evid C §1037.5(a)-(b). The victim is the holder unless the victim is under a guardianship or conservatorship because of minority or disability, in which case the guardian or conservator is the holder. Evid C §1037.4.

The physician-patient privilege rule that a person to whom disclosure is made in furtherance of the consultation has implied authority to claim the privilege (see §36.3) appears to apply to the counselor-domestic violence victim privilege.

§39.6   B. Counselor's Duty to Claim

The counselor has a duty to claim the privilege on behalf of the victim if both of the following conditions are met:

- The counselor is "present when the communication is sought to be disclosed." Evid C §1037.6. Being "present" presumably includes any opportunity to claim the privilege as a witness or a party.

- The counselor has authority to claim the privilege on behalf of the victim. Evid C §1037.6. Evidence Code §1037.5(c) gives the counselor this authority unless the privilege has been terminated by death (see §39.8) or unless a holder authorized to waive the privilege instructs the counselor not to claim it or otherwise waives the privilege (see §39.9).

§39.7   C. Judge May Exclude Information

When neither the witness nor a party can claim the privilege, Evid C §916 may require the judge to exclude privileged information on the court's own motion or the motion of a party. See §§33.14-33.16.

IV. TERMINATION BY DEATH OR WAIVER

§39.8   A. Effect of Victim's Death

Unlike the counselor-sexual assault victim privilege, the counselor-domestic violence victim privilege does not pass on the victim's death to the victim's personal representative. See Evid C §1037.4. Evidence Code §1037.5(b), however, authorizes a person authorized by the victim to claim the privilege. Unlike the counselor (see Evid C §1037.5(c)), the person authorized by the victim does not appear to lose that authority when the victim dies. Compare Evid C §1037.5(b) with Evid C §1037.5(c).

§39.9 B. Waiver

Evidence Code §§1037–1037.7 do not provide for waiver, and, unlike other privileges, the counselor-domestic violence victim privilege is not covered by the general provisions of Evid C §912. Nevertheless, the privilege does not apply if the victim (and perhaps any other holder of the privilege under Evid C §1037.5) does not comply with the statutory requisites for claiming the privilege. If, for example, the victim makes a nonconfidential communication of the facts, it appears that the privilege is waived. Similarly, if no holder of the privilege claims the privilege, it appears to be waived.

A holder whose claim of the privilege is improperly overruled can claim error at the trial if the holder is a party (Evid C §918; see §33.21) and is entitled to exclusion of the disclosure in later proceedings (Evid C §919; see §33.24). A counselor's failure to claim the privilege, as required by Evid C §1037.6 (see §39.6), is not a waiver, because the counselor is not a holder of the privilege (see Evid C §1037.4).

On waiver as a bar to exclusion of privileged information by the judge under Evid C §916, see §§33.16, 33.28.

V. RULING ON PRIVILEGE

§39.10 A. Court-Compelled Disclosure; Procedure

Under Evid C §1037.2, the court may compel disclosure of information received by the domestic violence counselor in the following situations:

- The information is related to child abuse proceedings or relevant evidence of the facts and circumstances of a crime against the victim or a member of the household, and its probative value outweighs the effect of its disclosure on the victim, the counseling relationship, and the counseling services; or
- The victim is dead or is not the complaining witness in a criminal action against the perpetrator.

When ruling on the privilege, the court may require disclosure of the information in chambers and then order whether it may be disclosed. If the court determines that the information is reasonably likely to be subject to the balancing test described above, it must follow the procedure stated in Evid C §1035.4(1)–(3), described in §38.13.

§39.11 B. Other Issues

Claiming the privilege may raise other issues (*e.g.*, the qualifications of the counselor (see Evid C §1037.1)) that are questions of preliminary fact to be heard and decided by the judge independently. Evid C §§400–402, 405. The parties may present evidence on these issues. The evidence typically consists of further examination and cross-examination of the witness already on the stand.

Subject to the special procedure under Evid C §1037.2 (see §39.13), Evid C §915(a) prevents the judge from requiring disclosure of information claimed to be within the counselor-domestic violence victim privilege for the purpose of ruling on it. See §33.17.

§39.12 C. Burden of Proof

Subject to the special procedure under Evid C §1037.2 (see §39.13), the claimant of the privilege has the burden of proving the existence of the counselor-domestic violence victim relationship, standing to claim the privilege, and that the offered evidence is a communication within that relationship. Effective January 1, 2003, Evid C §917 was amended to extend its presumption of confidentiality to communications between a counselor and domestic violence victim. On the burden of proof of the claimant and opponent respectively, see generally Comment to Evid C §405.

On the burden of proof on issues raised by a motion under Evid C §916 to have the judge exclude privileged information in the absence of anyone entitled to claim privilege, see §§33.15–33.16.

§39.13 VI. STATUTES

Evidence Code §§1037–1037.7, referred to in these provisions as "this article," and Fam C §6211 apply to the counselor-domestic violence victim privilege.

- Evidence Code §1037 states:

    As used in this article, "victim" means any person who suffers domestic violence, as defined in Section 1037.7.

- Evidence Code §1037.1 states:

    As used in this article, "domestic violence counselor" means any of the following:

    (a) A person who is employed by any organization providing the programs specified in Section 18294 of the Welfare and Institutions Code, whether financially compensated or not, for the purpose of rendering advice or assistance to victims of domestic violence, who has received specialized training in the counseling of domestic violence victims, and who meets one of the following requirements:

    (1) Has a master's degree in counseling or a related field; or has one year of counseling experience, at least six months of which is in the counseling of domestic violence victims.

    (2) Has at least 40 hours of training as specified in this paragraph and is supervised by an individual who qualifies as a counselor under paragraph (1); or is a psychotherapist, as defined in Section 1010. The training provided by a person qualified under paragraph (1) shall include, but need not be limited to, the following areas: history of domestic violence, civil and criminal law as it

relates to domestic violence, societal attitudes towards domestic violence, peer counseling techniques, housing, public assistance and other financial resources available to meet the financial needs of domestic violence victims, and referral services available to domestic violence victims.

(b) A person who is employed by any organization providing the programs specified in Section 13835.2 of the Penal Code, whether financially compensated or not, for the purpose of counseling and assisting victims of domestic violence, and who meets one of the following requirements:

(1) Is a psychotherapist as defined in Section 1010; has a master's degree in counseling or a related field; or has one year of counseling experience, at least six months of which is in counseling victims of domestic violence.

(2) Has the minimum training for counseling victims of domestic violence required by guidelines established by the employing agency pursuant to subdivision (c) of Section 13835.10 of the Penal Code, and is supervised by an individual who qualifies as a counselor under paragraph (1). The training, supervised by a person qualified under paragraph (1), shall include, but not be limited to, the following areas: law, victimology, counseling techniques, client and system advocacy, and referral services.

- Evidence Code §1037.2 states:

    As used in this article, "confidential communication" means information transmitted between the victim and the counselor in the course of their relationship and in confidence by a means which, so far as the victim is aware, discloses the information to no third persons other than those who are present to further the interests of the victim in the consultation or those to whom disclosures are reasonably necessary for the transmission of the information or an accomplishment of the purposes for which the domestic violence counselor is consulted. It includes all information regarding the facts and circumstances involving all incidences of domestic violence, as well as all information about the children of the victim or abuser and the relationship of the victim with the abuser.

    The court may compel disclosure of information received by a domestic violence counselor which constitutes relevant evidence of the facts and circumstances involving a crime allegedly perpetrated against the victim or another household member and which is the subject of a criminal proceeding, if the court determines that the probative value of the information outweighs the effect of disclosure of the information on the victim, the counseling relationship, and the counseling services. The court may compel disclosure if the victim is either dead or not the complaining witness in a criminal action against the perpetrator. The court may also compel disclosure in proceedings related to child abuse if the court determines that the probative value of the evidence outweighs the effect of the disclosure on the victim, the counseling relationship, and the counseling services.

When a court rules on a claim of privilege under this article, it may require the person from whom disclosure is sought or the person authorized to claim the privilege, or both, to disclose the information in chambers out of the presence and hearing of all persons except the person authorized to claim the privilege and such other persons as the person authorized to claim the privilege consents to have present. If the judge determines that the information is privileged and shall not be disclosed, neither he nor she nor any other person may disclose, without the consent of a person authorized to permit disclosure, any information disclosed in the course of the proceedings in chambers.

If the court determines that information shall be disclosed, the court shall so order and inform the defendant in the criminal action. If the court finds there is a reasonable likelihood that any information is subject to disclosure pursuant to the balancing test provided in this section, the procedure specified in subdivisions (1), (2), and (3) of Section 1035.4 shall be followed.

- Evidence Code §1037.3 states:

    Nothing in this article shall be construed to limit any obligation to report instances of child abuse as required by Section 11166 of the Penal Code.

- Evidence Code §1037.4 states:

    As used in this article, "holder of the privilege" means:

    (a) The victim when he or she has no guardian or conservator.

    (b) A guardian or conservator of the victim when the victim has a guardian or conservator.

- Evidence Code §1037.5 states:

    A victim of domestic violence, whether or not a party to the action, has a privilege to refuse to disclose, and to prevent another from disclosing, a confidential communication between the victim and a domestic violence counselor if the privilege is claimed by any of the following persons:

    (a) The holder of the privilege.

    (b) A person who is authorized to claim the privilege by the holder of the privilege.

    (c) The person who was the domestic violence counselor at the time of the confidential communication. However, that person may not claim the privilege if there is no holder of the privilege in existence or if he or she is otherwise instructed by a person authorized to permit disclosure.

- Evidence Code §1037.6 states:

    The domestic violence counselor who received or made a communication subject to the privilege granted by this article shall claim the privilege whenever he or she is present when the communication is sought to be disclosed and he or she is authorized to claim the privilege under subdivision (c) of Section 1037.5.

- Evidence Code §1037.7 states:

    As used in this article, "domestic violence" means "domestic violence" as defined in Section 6211 of the Family Code.

- Family Code §6211 states:

    "Domestic violence" is abuse perpetrated against any of the following persons:

    (a) A spouse or former spouse.

    (b) A cohabitant or former cohabitant, as defined in Section 6209.

    (c) A person with whom the respondent is having or has had a dating or engagement relationship.

    (d) A person with whom the respondent has had a child, where the presumption applies that the male parent is the father of the child of the female parent under the Uniform Parentage Act (Part 3 (commencing with Section 7600) of Division 12).

    (e) A child of a party or a child who is the subject of an action under the Uniform Parentage Act, where the presumption applies that the male parent is the father of the child to be protected.

    (f) Any other person related by consanguinity or affinity within the second degree.

§39.14 VII. ILLUSTRATIONS OF PRIVILEGE

The counselor-domestic violence victim privilege may be available for the following questions:

- "What did you tell the counselor at the domestic violence center?"
- "What did Ms. Manwaring tell you when she came to the center?"
- "What advice did you give to Mr. Schmidt when he came to the center?"

VIII. STATING CLAIM OF PRIVILEGE

§39.15   A. By Witness

Your Honor, I claim the counselor-domestic violence victim privilege.

§39.16   B. By Trial Counsel

Trial counsel should preferably make this statement outside the presence of the jury:

Your Honor, that question calls for disclosure of a privileged confidential communication between counselor and domestic violence victim.

[Option 1: Counsel represents party
entitled to claim privilege]

On behalf of _ _[name of party]_ _, I claim the counselor-domestic violence victim privilege and object to the question on that ground.

[Option 2: Witness holds privilege and is not
represented by counsel]

I request that you advise the witness of _ _[his/her]_ _ right to refuse to answer on the ground of the counselor-domestic violence victim privilege.

[Option 3: Neither witness nor party can claim
privilege (Evid C §916)]

I move that you exclude the answer as privileged.

40

Privilege for Confidential Marital Communications

I. NATURE AND PURPOSE §40.1

II. REQUIREMENTS
   A. Valid Marriage §40.2
   B. Communication §40.3
   C. Confidentiality §40.4

III. WHO CAN CLAIM
   A. Either Spouse §40.5
   B. Guardian or Conservator §40.6
   C. Judge May Exclude Information §40.7

IV. EXCEPTIONS
   A. Assistance in Crime or Fraud §40.8
   B. Communication Offered by Defendant Spouse in Criminal Proceeding §40.9
   C. Particular Proceedings §40.10
      1. Spouse's Competence Is at Issue §40.11
      2. Litigation Between Spouses §40.12
      3. Litigation Between Surviving Spouse and Claimant Through Deceased Spouse §40.13
      4. Juvenile Court Proceedings §40.14
      5. Spouse Charged With Certain Crimes §40.15

V. TERMINATION BY DEATH OR WAIVER
   A. Effect of Spouse's Death §40.16
   B. Waiver §40.17

VI. RULING ON PRIVILEGE
   A. Procedure §40.18
   B. Burden of Proof §40.19

VII. STATUTES §40.20

VIII. ILLUSTRATIONS OF PRIVILEGE §40.21

IX. STATING CLAIM OF PRIVILEGE
   A. By Witness §40.22
   B. By Trial Counsel §40.23

§40.1   I. NATURE AND PURPOSE

The privilege for confidential marital communications prevents compulsory disclosure of a communication made in confidence between husband and wife. The purpose of the privilege is to enhance marital relationships by enabling spouses to communicate freely with each other without fearing disclosure of their confidences to outsiders.

The text of Evid C §§980–987, governing the confidential marital communications privilege, is set out in §40.20. Note that Cal Const art I, §28(d) (the "truth-in-evidence" provision of Proposition 8) expressly leaves the Evidence Code privileges sections untouched.

The privilege discussed in this chapter should be distinguished from the privileges under Evid C §§970–973 not to testify against one's spouse or to be called as a witness (sometimes referred to as the "marital testimonial privileges"). Whereas the marital communications privilege applies to either spouse and requires a valid marriage when the communication is made (see §40.2), the testimonial privileges apply to a witness spouse only and require a valid marriage at the time the testimony is sought (see chaps 41–42).

II. REQUIREMENTS

§40.2   A. Valid Marriage

For the confidential marital communications privilege to apply, the communicating spouses must have a valid marriage at the time of the communication; a purported marriage that is legally void, or a marriage performed after the communication, is insufficient. See *People v Mabry* (1969) 71 C2d 430, 439, 78 CR 655; *People v Delph* (1979) 94 CA3d 411, 415, 156 CR 422; 2 Witkin, California Evidence, *Witnesses* §§171–173, 187 (4th ed 2000). However, California does recognize the validity of a marriage contracted in another state that is valid under the laws of that state (*e.g.*, common-law marriages). Fam C §308; *People v Badgett* (1995) 10 C4th 330, 41 CR2d 635. After termination of the marriage, the privilege continues to protect communications made during the marriage. Evid C §980; *People v Dorsey* (1975) 46 CA3d 706, 717, 120 CR 508.

§40.3   B. Communication

The privilege is applicable to any communication between spouses, subject only to the exception for communications in aid of crime or fraud (Evid C §981; see §40.8). The privilege protects only the contents of a communication; it does not exclude evidence that the spouses communicated or had other dealings at a particular time or place. *People v Bradford* (1969) 70 C2d 333, 342 n2, 74 CR 726; *People v Saidi-Tabatabai* (1970) 7 CA3d 981, 986, 86 CR 866. See 2 Witkin, California Evidence, *Witnesses* §190 (4th ed 2000).

§40.4   C. Confidentiality

To be privileged, the communication must be "made in confidence between" the spouses. Evid C §980; *People v Dorsey* (1975) 46 CA3d 706, 718, 120 CR 508. The knowledge of only one spouse that a third party is overhearing an oral communication probably does not make it nonconfidential for the other spouse or destroy the other spouse's privilege. This construction of Evid C §980 is consistent with the provision that one spouse's subsequent disclosure of the communication to an outsider does not waive the privilege for the other spouse. See Evid C §912(b). See §40.17. Each spouse can assert the privilege to prevent disclosure by any person, including an eavesdropper or the other spouse. See Comment to Evid C §980.

The marital privilege of Evid C §980 applies to written as well as oral communications. *Rubio v Superior Court* (1988) 202 CA3d 1343, 249 CR 419 (sexual acts by husband and wife recorded on videotape are privileged). The privilege does not apply, however, to communications not made in confidence. *People v Mickey* (1991) 54 C3d 612, 286 CR 801 (defendant did not have reasonable expectation of privacy for letters written and sent to wife while he was incarcerated in Japan).

Confidentiality of conversations between jail and prison inmates and their spouses depends on whether the spouse claiming the privilege had a reasonable expectation of privacy. In *North v Superior Court* (1972) 8 C3d 301, 311, 104 CR 833, an inmate's privilege was sustained because police had lulled him and his wife into believing that their conversation would be private, but the court added that "an ordinary jailhouse conversation between spouses could not be deemed to have been 'made in confidence' " under Evid C §980. The supreme court later held, however, that Pen C §§2600–2601 (on rights of state prisoners) precludes jail officials from monitoring conversations between detainees and their visitors except as necessary for institutional security or public protection. See *De Lancie v Superior Court* (1982) 31 C3d 865, 183 CR 866, superseded by statute as stated in *People v Loyd* (2002) 27 C4th 997, 1008, 119 CR2d 360. In *People v White* (1984) 161 CA3d 246, 251, 207 CR 266, the appellate court observed that *De Lancie* does not prevent a judicial order permitting the monitoring of conversations between a defendant and visitors, except for defense counsel, for the purpose of investigating threats made to prosecution witnesses. See also *People v McCaslin* (1986) 178 CA3d 1, 223 CR 587 (court permitted the interception and reading of intrajail mail).

In *People v Loyd* (2002) 27 C4th 997, 119 CR2d 360, *De Lancie* was expressly overruled. The court in *Loyd* held that 1994 amendments to Pen C §§2600–2601 abrogated the *De Lancie* holding limiting surreptitious recording of prisoner-visitor conversations. The court held that those amendments adopted the view of the United State Supreme Court's decision in *Turner v Safely* (1987) 482 US 78, 96 L Ed 2d 64, 107 S Ct 2254, which held that a prisoner's constitutional rights may be impinged when "it is reasonably related to legitimate penological interests." 27 C4th at 1008. Law enforcement officers are permitted to secretly monitor and record conversations between inmates and visitors solely for the purpose of gathering evidence in criminal prosecutions.

A presumption of confidentiality shifts the burden of proof on the issue to the opponent of the privilege. Evid C §917. See §40.19.

III. WHO CAN CLAIM

§40.5   A. Either Spouse

The privilege can be claimed by either spouse. Under Evid C §980, a spouse can claim the privilege to avoid testifying to a communication as well as to prevent disclosure by any other witness (including the other spouse). See Comment to Evid C §980.

§40.6   B. Guardian or Conservator

The guardian or conservator of a spouse can claim the privilege on the spouse's behalf. Evid C §980. In contrast to certain other privileges, however, the fact that a spouse has a guardian or conservator apparently does not prohibit the spouse from personally claiming the marital communications privilege. For privileges with a different rule, see Evid C §§953(a)-(b), 954(a) (attorney-client; see also §34.11); Evid C §§993(a)-(b), 994(a) (physician-patient; see also §36.5); Evid C §§1013(a)-(b), 1014(a) (psychotherapist-patient; see also §37.5); Evid C §§1035.6(a)-(b), 1035.8(a) (counselor-sexual assault victim; see also §38.5). When a spouse dies, no one can claim the marital communications privilege on behalf of the decedent, but the surviving spouse retains the privilege. See Comment to Evid C §980. See also §40.16.

§40.7   C. Judge May Exclude Information

When neither the witness nor a party can claim the privilege, Evid C §916 may require the judge to exclude privileged information on the court's own motion or the motion of a party. See §§33.14-33.16.

IV. EXCEPTIONS

§40.8   A. Assistance in Crime or Fraud

There is no marital communications privilege "if the communication was made, in whole or in part, to enable or aid anyone to commit or plan to commit a crime or a fraud." Evid C §981. This exception may apply if there is a conspiracy between a husband and wife or if one spouse asks the other to assist in planning or perpetrating a crime or fraud. *People v Baker* (1978) 88 CA3d 115, 121, 151 CR 362 (attempt to induce other spouse to suppress evidence and testify falsely). A confidential communication that merely reveals a plan to commit a crime or fraud is not affected by the exception and remains privileged. See Comment to Evid C §981; *People v Dorsey* (1975) 46 CA3d 706, 718, 120 CR 508. The scope of this exception is similar to that of the corresponding exception to the attorney-client privilege (see §34.15) and is narrower than the corresponding exceptions to the physician-patient and psychotherapist-patient privileges (see §§36.15, 37.11).

There is no similar exception to the privileges not to be called as a witness and not to testify against one's spouse (Evid C §§970–973; see chaps 41–42). Thus, a married person may be able to avoid interrogation on marital communications in aid of crime or fraud by refusing to take the stand or to testify against the spouse. See Comment to Evid C §981.

§40.9   B. Communication Offered by Defendant Spouse in Criminal Proceeding

The marital communications privilege does not apply to an interspousal communication offered in evidence by one of the spouses as a defendant in a criminal proceeding. Evid C §987. This exception prevents the spouse of such a defendant from invoking the privilege to withhold information vital to the defendant's acquittal. In civil litigation, however, the exception does not apply and does not prevent a married person whom his or her spouse calls as a witness from refusing to testify to a confidential marital communication.

§40.10   C. Particular Proceedings

The exceptions discussed in §§40.11–40.15 (see Evid C §§982–986) exclude the marital communications privilege from specific types of proceedings. The privileges not to be called as a witness and not to testify against one's spouse (which apply only during the marriage) are also excluded from these same proceedings by Evid C §972.

§40.11   1. Spouse's Competence Is at Issue

There is no marital communications privilege in a proceeding to commit either spouse as mentally ill or to put either spouse under a guardianship or conservatorship on the ground of mental or physical condition. Evid C §982. See also Comment to Evid C §1004 (similarly worded exception includes "such cases as the appointment of a conservator"). Nor is there a privilege in a proceeding brought by or on behalf of either spouse to establish competence. Evid C §983. The reason for these exceptions is the vital importance of such proceedings to society and to the spouse whose competence is in question. See Comment to Evid C §982.

§40.12   2. Litigation Between Spouses

There is no marital communications privilege in a proceeding between spouses. Evid C §984(a).

§40.13 3. Litigation Between Surviving Spouse and Claimant Through Deceased Spouse

There is no marital communications privilege in a proceeding between a surviving spouse and a person claiming through a deceased spouse. The claim may be by testate or intestate succession or by inter vivos transaction. Evid C §984(b).

§40.14 4. Juvenile Court Proceedings

There is no marital communications privilege in a proceeding under the Arnold-Kennick Juvenile Court Law (Welf & I C §§200-987). Evid C §986.

§40.15 5. Spouse Charged With Certain Crimes

There is no marital communications privilege in a criminal proceeding in which one spouse is charged with any of the following offenses:

- A crime committed at any time against the person or property of the other spouse, the other spouse's child, or the defendant's child (Evid C §985(a));

- A crime against a third person or his or her property, committed at any time in the course of a crime against the other spouse's person or property (Evid C §985(b));

- Bigamy (Evid C §985(c)); or

- Failure to provide support for one's spouse or child (Pen C §§270-270a; Evid C §985(d)).

The exceptions that require a charge of crime against "the other spouse" (Evid C §985(a)-(b)) presumably refer to the spouse with whom the marital communication is made. Thus, if the defendant has been married twice and is charged with a crime against the first spouse, these exceptions do not affect the privilege for marital communications with the second spouse.

V. TERMINATION BY DEATH OR WAIVER

§40.16 A. Effect of Spouse's Death

On the death of one spouse, the privilege can be claimed only by the surviving spouse or the surviving spouse's guardian or conservator. When both spouses die, the privilege terminates. See Comment to Evid C §980.

§40.17 B. Waiver

The text of Evid C §912(a)-(c), governing waiver of the marital communications privilege, is set out in §33.31. Holders of the privilege are each spouse and the guardian or conservator of each spouse. Evid C §980. See §33.4.

The privilege is waived whenever the holder discloses, or consents to disclosure of, a significant part of the privileged communication. Evid C §912(a); *People v Worthington* (1974) 38 CA3d 359, 365, 113 CR 322 (defendant's statement to police, accusing his wife of homicide described in detail, waived his privilege against her testimony of his confession to her, by which he described same details but admitted that he, not she, committed crime). A waiver by one spouse does not impair the other spouse's right to claim the privilege. Evid C §912(b).

There is no waiver if the holder acts under coercion (Evid C §912(a)) or if the disclosure is protected by another privilege, *e.g.,* is made in confidence to the holder's attorney or physician (Evid C §912(c)). Any disclosure that is voluntary and not privileged is a waiver; the marital communications privilege is not one of those specified in Evid C §912(d) as subject to the rule that a confidential disclosure reasonably necessary to the purpose of certain types of privileged communications is not a waiver.

The most common form of waiver is the holder's failure to claim the privilege whenever the opportunity arises. Thus, waiver may result from failure to claim the privilege on discovery (see §33.6) or, even if it is claimed then, from failure to claim it at the trial. *People v Mabry* (1969) 71 C2d 430, 439, 78 CR 655. If a holder testifies, or permits another to testify, to a significant part of the privileged information, the right to claim the privilege is destroyed—not only for the current proceeding but for all future purposes. Evid C §912(a); *Feldman v Allstate Ins. Co.* (2003) 322 F3d 660, 667. (The other spouse's privilege may nevertheless persist under Evid C §912(b).)

If the privilege is claimed and the claim is improperly overruled, a holder who is a party to the action can claim error at the trial (Evid C §918; see §33.21), and the disclosure is inadmissible against the holder in later proceedings (Evid C §919(a); see §33.24). Similarly, the privilege is not waived by disclosure in a proceeding in which there is no legal standing to claim it; thus, disclosure under the exception for litigation between spouses (see Evid C §984; see also §40.12) does not waive the privilege for a later proceeding between one of the spouses and a third party (Evid C §912(a)).

On waiver as a bar to the exclusion of privileged information by the judge under Evid C §916, see §§33.16, 33.28.

VI. RULING ON PRIVILEGE

§40.18   A. Procedure

When the privilege is claimed, its existence and applicability may present questions of preliminary fact that must be heard and decided by the judge as independent issues. Evid C §§400-402, 405.

Evidence Code §915(a) prevents the trial judge from requiring disclosure of information claimed to be within the marital communications privilege for purposes of ruling on the claim. The judge arguably is also precluded from permitting disclosure in violation of a claim of the marital communications privilege for the purpose of ruling on it. See §34.14. On the ruling procedure generally, see §§21.8, 21.15, 33.17-33.19, 33.25-33.26.

§40.19   B. Burden of Proof

The claimant of the privilege has the burden of proving the existence of a valid marriage between the spouses at the time of the communication. If the claimant is a spouse's guardian or conservator, the claimant also has the burden of proving standing to claim the privilege in that capacity. On these requirements, see §§40.2 (marriage), 40.6 (guardian or conservator).

The opponent of the privilege (the proponent of the offered evidence) has the burden of proving that the marital communication was not confidential. Evid C §917 (establishing presumption of confidentiality; for statutory text, see §33.31). On the requisite of confidentiality, see §40.4. If the opponent contends that the privilege has been waived or is excluded by an exception, the opponent has the burden of proving these contentions. The claimant's and opponent's respective burdens of proof are discussed in the Comment to Evid C §405.

The opponent's burden of proving the exception for marital communications in aid of crime or fraud (Evid C §981; see §40.8) may present difficulties because the opponent is not entitled to have the contents of the communication disclosed for the purpose of obtaining a ruling on whether it is privileged. Evid C §915. See §§33.17, 40.18. For discussion of this problem under the similar exception to the attorney-client privilege, see §34.24.

On the burden of proof on issues raised by a motion under Evid C §916 to have the judge exclude privileged information in the absence of anyone entitled to claim privilege, see §§33.15-33.16.

§40.20   VII. STATUTES

Evidence Code §§980-987, referred to in these provisions as "this article," apply to the privilege for confidential marital communications.

- Evidence Code §980 states:

    Subject to Section 912 [on waiver] and except as otherwise provided in this article, a spouse (or his guardian or conservator when he has a guardian or conservator), whether or not a party, has a privilege during the marital relationship and afterwards to refuse to disclose, and to prevent another from disclosing, a communication if he claims the privilege and the communication was made in confidence between him and the other spouse while they were husband and wife.

- Evidence Code §981 states:

    There is no privilege under this article if the communication was made, in whole or in part, to enable or aid anyone to commit or plan to commit a crime or fraud.

- Evidence Code §982 states:

    There is no privilege under this article in a proceeding to commit either spouse or otherwise place him or his property, or both, under the control of another because of his alleged mental or physical condition.

- Evidence Code §983 states:

    There is no privilege under this article in a proceeding brought by or on behalf of either spouse to establish his competence.

- Evidence Code §984 states:

    There is no privilege under this article in:

    (a) A proceeding brought by or on behalf of one spouse against the other spouse.

    (b) A proceeding between a surviving spouse and a person who claims through the deceased spouse, regardless of whether such claim is by testate or intestate succession or by inter vivos transaction.

- Evidence Code §985 states:

    There is no privilege under this article in a criminal proceeding in which one spouse is charged with:

    (a) A crime committed at any time against the person or property of the other spouse or of a child of either.

    (b) A crime committed at any time against the person or property of a third person committed in the course of committing a crime against the person or property of the other spouse.

    (c) Bigamy.

    (d) A crime defined by Section 270 or 270a of the Penal Code.

- Evidence Code §986 states:

    There is no privilege under this article in a proceeding under the Juvenile Court Law, Chapter 2 (commencing with Section 200) of Part 1 of Division 2 of the Welfare and Institutions Code.

- Evidence Code §987 states:

    There is no privilege under this article in a criminal proceeding in which the communication is offered in evidence by a defendant who is one of the spouses between whom the communication was made.

§40.21 VIII. ILLUSTRATIONS OF PRIVILEGE

The confidential marital communications privilege may be available in the following situations:

- In a prosecution for driving under the influence of alcohol, the prosecutor asks the defendant's wife if her husband admitted to her that he had been drinking heavily before the accident.

- A personal letter from the plaintiff to his wife is offered in evidence by the defendant to impeach the plaintiff.

IX. STATING CLAIM OF PRIVILEGE

§40.22   A. By Witness

> Your Honor, I claim the privilege for confidential communications between husband and wife.

§40.23   B. By Trial Counsel

Trial counsel should preferably make this statement outside the presence of the jury:

> Your Honor, that question calls for disclosure of a privileged confidential marital communication.

[Option 1: Counsel represents party entitled to claim privilege]

> On behalf of _ _[name of party]_ _, I claim the privilege and object to the question on that ground.

[Option 2: Witness holds privilege and is not represented by counsel]

> I request that you advise the witness of _ _[his/her]_ _ right to refuse to answer on the ground of privilege.

[Option 3: Neither witness nor party can claim privilege (Evid C §916)]

> I move that you exclude the answer as privileged.

41

Privilege Not to Testify Against Spouse

I. NATURE AND PURPOSE §41.1

II. REQUIREMENTS
    A. Valid Marriage §41.2
    B. Demand for Testimony "Against" Spouse
        1. Testimony "For" Spouse Not Privileged §41.3
        2. Testimony "Against" Party Spouse
            a. Two-Party Action §41.4
            b. Multiple Parties Including One Spouse §41.5
            c. Both Spouses Are Parties §41.6
        3. Testimony "Against" Nonparty Spouse §41.7

III. ONLY WITNESS SPOUSE CAN CLAIM §41.8

IV. EXCEPTIONS §41.9
    A. Litigation Between Spouses §41.10
    B. Spouse's Competence Is at Issue §41.11
    C. Juvenile Court Proceedings §41.12
    D. Spouse Charged With Certain Crimes §41.13
    E. Criminal Act Occurred Before Marriage of Spouses §41.14
    F. Certain Proceedings Brought by One Spouse Against Other or to Enforce Child Support Obligations §14.15

V. TERMINATION BY DISSOLUTION OF MARRIAGE OR BY WAIVER
    A. Dissolution of Marriage §41.16
    B. Waiver
        1. Waiver by Testimony §41.17
            a. Testimony for Spouse §41.18
            b. Testimony Against Party Spouse §41.19
            c. Testimony Against Nonparty Spouse §41.20
            d. Extent of Waiver §41.21
        2. Action or Defense for Immediate Benefit of Spouse §41.22

VI. RULING ON PRIVILEGE
    A. Procedure §41.23
    B. Burden of Proof §41.24

VII. STATUTES §41.25

VIII. ILLUSTRATIONS OF PRIVILEGE §41.26

IX. STATING CLAIM OF PRIVILEGE
  A. If Witness's Spouse Is Party
    1. By Witness §41.27
    2. By Trial Counsel for Party Spouse §41.28
  B. If Particular Question Calls for Testimony Against Witness's Nonparty Spouse
    1. By Witness §41.29
    2. By Trial Counsel §41.30

§41.1   I. NATURE AND PURPOSE

A married person has a privilege not to testify against his or her spouse. Evid C §970. The purpose of this privilege is to avoid the impairment of the marital relationship that is likely to result from such testimony. Comment to Evid C §970.

The text of Evid C §§970-973, governing both the privilege not to testify against one's spouse (discussed in this chapter) and the privilege not to be called as a witness against one's spouse (see chap 42), is set out in §41.25.

Whenever the potential witness's spouse is a party to the proceeding, counsel must consider the privilege not to testify in conjunction with the complementary privilege not to be called as a witness by a party adverse to the party spouse (Evid C §971). The two privileges (sometimes referred to as the "marital testimonial privileges") are closely interrelated—not only in their similarity of purpose (see §42.1) but also because both are subject to the same statutory exceptions and waiver provisions (see Evid C §§972-973; see also §§41.9-41.13, 41.15-41.20). The operation of both privileges is especially complicated when there are multiple parties. See §§41.5, 42.8.

Unlike the privilege not to be called as a witness, the privilege not to testify is available in proceedings to which the spouse against whom the testimony is sought is not a party. In such a proceeding, the privilege can be claimed against particular questions calling for testimony adverse to the witness's spouse. See §41.7. When the witness's spouse is a party, however, the privilege not to testify cannot be used selectively against only certain questions, because the privilege is waived as soon as the witness testifies at all. Evid C §973(a). See §§41.5-41.6.

The testimonial privileges discussed in this chapter and chap 42 should be distinguished from the marital communications privilege under Evid C §980 (see chap 40). Whereas the testimonial privileges apply to a witness spouse only and require a valid marriage at the time the testimony is sought (see §41.2), the marital communications privilege applies to either spouse and requires a valid marriage when the communication is made (see §40.2). Each privilege acts independently of the others. *People v Dorsey* (1975) 46 CA3d 706, 717, 120 CR 508.

II. REQUIREMENTS

§41.2 A. Valid Marriage

For the privilege to apply, a valid marriage must exist at the time the privilege is claimed between the witness and the spouse against whom the witness is asked to testify. A voidable marriage that has not yet been annulled is sufficient, but a purported marriage that is legally void is not sufficient. See 2 Witkin, California Evidence, *Witnesses* §§171–173 (4th ed 2000). On termination of the privilege by dissolution of marriage, see §41.16.

B. Demand for Testimony "Against" Spouse

§41.3 1. Testimony "For" Spouse Not Privileged

A witness has no privilege to refuse to testify at the request of a spouse, because such a privilege would probably not be claimed except for "mercenary or spiteful motives." See the Comment to the repeal of former CCP §1881 in 7 Cal L Rev'n Comm'n Reps 1303 (1965). See also *People v Coleman* (1969) 71 C2d 1159, 1167, 80 CR 920, overruled on other grounds in 14 C4th at 966 (prosecutor may comment on failure of defendant's spouse to testify, because spouse has no privilege to refuse).

Although a witness cannot refuse to testify at all when called by a spouse, the witness can, when called in a civil proceeding, claim the marital communications privilege (Evid C §980) and refuse to testify to a confidential marital communication between spouses. See §40.5. But a witness cannot claim the marital communications privilege when called as a witness for the defense of a spouse in a criminal proceeding. Evid C §987. See §40.9.

2. Testimony "Against" Party Spouse

§41.4 a. Two-Party Action

If there are only two parties to an action, and a witness is married to one of them, any interrogation of that witness by a spouse's adversary presumably calls for testimony "against" the spouse, and the testimony is therefore privileged under Evid C §970. It is usually unnecessary to rely on this privilege in this situation because the witness can first invoke the privilege not to be called as a witness (see §§42.5–42.9). The witness can exercise the privilege not to testify against a spouse (Evid C §970), however, if the privilege not to be called is unavailable because the adversary was unaware of the marital relationship or the witness consented to be called but has since decided not to testify.

§41.5 b. Multiple Parties Including One Spouse

When there are multiple parties (*e.g.*, coplaintiffs, codefendants, or one or more cross-defendants), it is probable that not all the issues concern all the parties. If, in such a multiparty proceeding, the nonparty spouse of one party is called as a witness by any other party, the privilege not to testify against the party spouse should be available only if the testimony sought from the witness would affect the interests of the party spouse and not relate solely to issues among other parties. But if the party calling the witness and the party spouse are adverse parties (either under the pleadings or because their interests in the proceedings are adverse, both the privilege not to testify (Evid C §970) and the privilege not to be called (Evid C §971) appear to be available regardless of the nature of the testimony sought.

If this rule did not govern the privilege not to testify against one's spouse, the adverse party, by requiring the witness to answer a question not affecting his or her spouse, could force the witness to waive the privilege under Evid C §973(a), which provides that a witness waives the privilege when the witness "testifies in a proceeding to which his spouse is a party." (On this form of waiver, see §41.17.) Having obtained the waiver, the adverse party could proceed with questions that did affect the party spouse. The courts are not likely to permit this circumvention of the privilege.

If the party calling the nonparty spouse as a witness is not adverse to the party spouse, the applicability of the privilege not to testify (Evid C §970) is unclear. If the privilege is not immediately available and the witness testifies, a single answer that is unprivileged because it is harmless to the party spouse's interests will waive the privilege for subsequent testimony that may be harmful (see Evid C §973(a); see also §41.17). The witness should arguably be allowed to claim the privilege when called, however, by showing that some part of the anticipated examination (direct or cross) would call for testimony "against" the party spouse (Evid C §970).

§41.6 c. Both Spouses Are Parties

Usually the privilege not to testify against one's spouse is not available when both spouses are parties to a civil proceeding. If they are parties on opposite sides, an exception applies (Evid C §972(a); see §41.10); if they are parties on the same side, they are usually treated as having waived the privileges under Evid C §973(b) by suing or defending for the immediate benefit of each other. See §41.20. But if there are party spouses on the same side to whom Evid C §973(b) does not apply, the application of the privilege raises difficult problems.

The waiver rules applicable to the privilege appear to preclude applying it selectively to a particular type of testimony, as was done with the former privilege of a party to prevent the spouse from testifying for or against him or her (see former CCP §1881(1)). The former privilege could be used to exclude the testimony of one of two party spouses if the testimony affected the other party spouse, but not if it affected only the spouse who was testifying. See *Stein v Superior Court* (1959) 174 CA2d 21, 344 P2d 406 (allowing privilege); *Dean v Superior Court* (1951) 103 CA2d 892, 230 P2d 362 (disallowing privilege). This differentiation based on the content of the testimony is impracticable in applying the privilege not to testify against one's spouse (Evid C §970) because counsel for the adverse party could simply ask the witness an "unprivileged" question (*i.e.,* one not affecting the other spouse) and the witness's answer would waive the privilege for all subsequent questions. Evid C §973(a). Hence, the privilege not to testify against a party spouse apparently must be allowed against any interrogation by the adverse party or not allowed at all. Yet allowing a party spouse to use the privilege against a question affecting only his or her own rights and liabilities and not those of the other party spouse extends the privilege beyond its underlying purpose of protecting the marital relationship.

A similar problem is presented when both spouses are parties, by the privilege not to be called as a witness against one's spouse. See §42.9. Thus, both privileges appear to be unavailable in practically every civil case in which the spouses are parties on the same side. This problem is not likely to arise when the spouses are codefendants in a criminal proceeding, because each defendant is protected from being called by the privilege of a defendant (Evid C §930; see chap 46) regardless of the privileges as a spouse.

§41.7 3. Testimony "Against" Nonparty Spouse

When a witness's spouse is not a party, the witness can exercise the privilege not to testify against the spouse, but only in response to particular questions calling for testimony that may adversely affect the spouse, *e.g.,* tend to incriminate that spouse or to harm the spouse's legal position or interests as a party to some other civil or criminal proceeding. Allowance of the privilege for some questions but not others is possible when the spouse is not a party because of a distinction in the waiver provisions of Evid C §973(a). When a witness's spouse is a party, the spouse waives the privilege simply by testifying and so cannot claim it for particular questions. See §§41.5–41.6. But if the spouse is not a party, the witness waives the privilege only if the witness "testifies against his spouse. . ." (Evid C §973(a)). Therefore, the witness can answer questions not adverse to the witness's spouse and still retain the privilege for adverse questions. See §41.18.

In grand jury proceedings, "no person has the status of a party defendant." *In re Lemon* (1936) 15 CA2d 82, 85, 59 P2d 213. Thus, a grand jury witness can exercise the privilege only when questions call for testimony against the witness's spouse. See Comment to Evid C §971. In proceedings between parties a witness (whether or not a party) who is married to a nonparty can exercise the privilege to avoid testimony adverse to the spouse. For example, the sole defendant in a tort suit can use the privilege to avoid giving testimony that would expose the spouse to liability. On proving and ruling on possible adverse effect of testimony, see §§41.18–41.19.

§41.8 III. ONLY WITNESS SPOUSE CAN CLAIM

Only the married person called as a witness can claim the privilege not to testify against one's spouse. Formerly, a party to a criminal or civil proceeding had a privilege to prevent his or her spouse from testifying for or against the party. Former Pen C §1322; former CCP §1881(1). A party can still prevent a spouse from testifying for the party by not calling the spouse as a witness. However, to prevent the spouse from testifying against the party, the party must prevail on the spouse to exercise the privilege not to testify or the privilege not to be called as a witness (see chap 42). If the spouse refuses to claim such a privilege, the marriage probably has already deteriorated so far that no evidentiary privilege will contribute to its preservation. See the Comment to the repeal of former CCP §1881 in 7 Cal L Rev'n Comm'n Reps 1303 (1965). A different privilege enables the party to prevent the spouse from revealing confidential marital communications. Evid C §980. See §40.5.

The witness can claim the privilege not to testify against the witness's spouse on deposition as well as at trial. Failure to claim it for a deposition waives it for the trial but not if there is an independent action. See §41.19.

The witness presumably can claim the privilege not to testify even though the witness previously consented to being called and so waived the privilege not to be called as a witness.

Although a party cannot claim the privilege to prevent a spouse from testifying, the party can predicate error on a ruling by the court disallowing the spouse's claim of the privilege. Evid C §918.

§41.9 IV. EXCEPTIONS

Exceptions provided by Evid C §972 eliminate both the privilege not to testify against one's spouse and the privilege not to be called as a witness against one's spouse from specified kinds of proceedings. These exceptions are discussed in relation to both privileges in §§41.9-41.15. Evidence Code §§982-986 provide similar exceptions to the privilege for confidential marital communications. See §§40.8-40.15.

There is no exception for compelling a spouse to testify while the marriage still exists but is no longer viable. *Jurcoane v Superior Court* (2001) 93 CA4th 886, 897, 113 CR2d 483. Thus, in *Jurcoane*, although the wife had not seen her husband in the 17 years since he had allegedly committed the crimes, she could not be compelled to testify against him. Because privileges and exceptions are statutory creations, courts may not imply unwritten exceptions to them. 93 CA4th at 895.

§41.10 A. Litigation Between Spouses

The privileges not to testify and not to be called as a witness against one's spouse are not available in a proceeding brought by or on behalf of one spouse against the other. Evid C §972(a). This exception forestalls any attempt by one spouse to invoke either privilege when called by the other spouse to testify as an adverse party under Evid C §776. The privilege to refuse to testify "against" one's spouse cannot be claimed on the theory that testimony given under §776 is "against" the party calling the witness.

The exception also prevents a spouse from using either privilege to avoid testifying when called as a witness by his or her coplaintiff or codefendant. For example, if a husband brings a quiet title action against his wife and others and the defendant wife is called to testify by a codefendant, she cannot invoke the privilege to avoid testifying against her husband.

This exception under Evid C §972(a), which applies when the spouses are opposing parties, should be distinguished from elimination of the privileges under Evid C §973(b), which occurs when the spouses are parties on the same side. See §41.19. Such elimination of the privilege is regarded as a "waiver" rather than an "exception." Compare Comment to Evid C §972 with Comment to Evid C §973.

§41.11   B. Spouse's Competence Is at Issue

The privileges not to testify and not to be called as a witness against one's spouse cannot be exercised in a proceeding to commit the spouse as mentally ill or to put the spouse under a guardianship or conservatorship on the ground of his or her mental or physical condition. Evid C §972(b). See Comment to Evid C §1004 (similarly worded exception includes "such cases as the appointment of a conservator"). Nor is either privilege available in a proceeding brought by or on behalf of a spouse to establish competence. Evid C §972(c). The reason for these exceptions is the vital importance of such proceedings to society and to the spouse whose competence is in question. See Comment to Evid C §982.

§41.12   C. Juvenile Court Proceedings

The privileges not to testify and not to be called as a witness against one's spouse are not available in a proceeding under the Arnold-Kennick Juvenile Court Law (Welf & I C §§200-987). Evid C §972(d).

§41.13   D. Spouse Charged With Certain Crimes

The privileges not to testify and not to be called as a witness against one's spouse cannot be exercised in prosecutions for certain crimes involving harm to the defendant's spouse or child. Evid C §972(e). This exception, derived from former Pen C §1322, prevents a privilege designed to preserve family harmony from being used to thwart punishment for crimes that disrupt the family. It applies when a spouse is charged with one of the following offenses:

- A crime committed at any time against the person or property of the other spouse, a parent, a relative, or a cohabitant as well as a child of either spouse (Evid C §972(e)(1));

- A crime against a third person or that person's property, committed at any time in the course of a crime against the other spouse's person or property (Evid C §972(e)(2); *People v Sinohui* (2002) 28 C4th 205, 212, 120 CR2d 783 (no requirement that accusation also charge crime against spouse); see *Fortes v Municipal Court* (1980) 113 CA3d 704, 170 CR 292 (prima facie showing of offense giving rise to exception required));

- Bigamy (Evid C §972(e)(3)); or

- Failure to provide support for one's spouse or child (Evid C §972(e)(4); see Pen C §§270-270a).

The usual effect of eliminating from the proceedings the privilege to refuse to testify (Evid C §970) is to prevent the defendant's spouse from claiming the privilege to avoid testifying against the defendant. But the exception applies in criminal proceedings in which "one spouse" is charged with a specified offense; therefore, it is possible to interpret the exception as also preventing the defendant spouse, when testifying in his or her own behalf, from claiming the privilege for testimony usable against the nonparty spouse, *e.g.*, to implicate the nonparty spouse in a crime.

§41.14 E. Criminal Act Occurred Before Marriage of Spouses

Evidence Code §972(f) adds a further exception to the privilege not to testify against a spouse. A spouse may be required to testify in a proceeding resulting from a criminal act that occurred before the legal marriage of the spouses to each other, regarding knowledge acquired before that marriage if, before the legal marriage, the witness spouse was aware that the spouse had been arrested for or had been formally charged with the crime(s) about which the witness spouse is called to testify. See §41.25 for the exact text of Evid C §972(f).

§41.15 F. Certain Proceedings Brought by One Spouse Against Other or to Enforce Child Support Obligations

Evidence Code §972(g) adds, as an exception to the privilege not to testify against a spouse, a proceeding brought against the spouse by a former spouse (1) before the property and debts of the marriage have been adjudicated or (2) to establish, modify, or enforce a child, family, or spousal support obligation arising from the marriage to the former spouse. Evidence Code §972(g) also includes the following exceptions:

- A proceeding brought against a spouse by the other parent to establish, modify, or enforce a child support obligation for a child of a nonmarital relationship of the spouse; and

- A proceeding brought against a spouse by the guardian of a child of that spouse to establish, modify, or enforce a child support obligation of the spouse.

The married person does not have a privilege under Evid C §972(g) to refuse to provide information relating to the issues of income, expenses, assets, debts, and employment of either spouse, but he or she may assert the privilege as otherwise provided in Evid C §§970-973 if other information is requested by the former spouse, guardian, or other parent of the child. Any person demanding the otherwise privileged information made available by Evid C §972(g), for whom an order to establish, modify, or enforce child support is sought, waives the marital privilege to the same extent as the spouse as provided in Evid C §972(g).

V. TERMINATION BY DISSOLUTION OF MARRIAGE OR BY WAIVER

§41.16   A. Dissolution of Marriage

The privilege is terminated by any dissolution of the marriage between the witness and the spouse against whom the testimony is called for. The dissolution may be by annulment, final judgment of divorce, or death of either spouse. See also §41.2 (valid marriage as requisite of privilege).

Dissolution of the marriage destroys the privilege because the purpose of the privilege is to protect the marriage from disruption through the spouse's adverse testimony. In contrast, the marital communications privilege survives dissolution of the marriage (for communications made during the marriage) because the purpose of that privilege is to encourage frank communication between the spouses by assuring them against future violation of confidences. See Comment to Evid C §980. See also §§40.1-40.2.

B. Waiver

§41.17   1. Waiver by Testimony

Evidence Code §973(a) prescribes circumstances under which a witness's act of testifying causes loss of both the privilege not to testify against one's spouse and the privilege not to be called as a witness against one's spouse (see chap 42). This waiver provision is discussed in relation to both privileges in §§41.17-41.19.

In *People v Resendez* (1993) 12 CA4th 98, 15 CR2d 575, the trial court did not err in compelling a wife to testify against her husband, who was being prosecuted for attempted murder. Even though the wife was not aware of her privilege not to testify under Evid C §973, the court held that she had waived this privilege by testifying at the preliminary hearing.

§41.18 a. Testimony for Spouse

A married person waives both privileges when the witness spouse testifies in any proceeding to which the other spouse is a party; therefore, a waiver occurs when a spouse testifies as a witness for the party spouse. Evid C §973(a). See Comment to Evid C §973. Because a witness has no privilege to refuse to testify for the spouse (see §41.3), this form of waiver is controlled by the party spouse who calls on the witness to testify.

§41.19 b. Testimony Against Party Spouse

A witness who is not a party but is married to a party presumably can exercise either privilege if called by a party adverse to the party spouse. See §§41.3-41.7 (privilege not to testify), 41.5-41.9 (privilege not to be called). If the witness testifies without attempting to exercise either privilege, both are waived. But if the witness attempts to exercise one of the privileges and is erroneously compelled to testify, there is no waiver. Evid C §973(a). See *People v Lankford* (1976) 55 CA3d 203, 210, 127 CR 408 (waiver upheld because trial court found, on substantial evidence, that it was voluntary and not coerced).

If the witness is called by a party not adverse to the party spouse, the witness cannot claim the privilege not to be called (Evid C §971; see §41.8) and may be unable to claim the privilege not to testify (Evid C §970; see §41.5). If unable to exercise either privilege, the witness loses both of them as soon as testimony begins because the spouse is a party to the proceeding. Evid C §973(a). The Comment to Evid C §973(a) calls this loss of the privileges a "waiver" even though both the witness and the spouse are powerless to prevent it.

A party who is not adverse to the party spouse should realize that forcing the witness spouse to testify will leave the witness unable to use either privilege to avoid testifying later if called by a party who is adverse to the party spouse.

When both spouses are parties, either spouse who testifies waives both privileges unless the testimony is erroneously compelled despite the exercise of a privilege. Evid C §973(a). Usually neither privilege can be exercised when both spouses are parties to a civil proceeding. See §41.6. In *People v Resendez* (1993) 12 CA4th 98, 15 CR2d 575, a defendant's wife was deemed to have waived her privilege not to testify against her spouse because she (1) had testified against him at the preliminary hearing; (2) had failed to establish that her prior testimony was "erroneously compelled"; and (3) the court was not required to advise the wife of the privilege not to testify or the loss of that privilege.

§41.20 c. Testimony Against Nonparty Spouse

A witness whose spouse is not a party to the proceeding waives the privilege not to testify only if he or she "testifies against his spouse." Evid C §973(a).

To waive the privilege in this way, a witness must give testimony that may adversely affect the spouse, *e.g.*, by tending to incriminate the spouse or harm the spouse's legal position or interests in a civil or criminal proceeding. See §41.7. If the nonparty spouse is later joined as a party to the proceeding, this form of waiver also eliminates the witness's privilege not to be called as a witness by a party adverse to his or her spouse (see chap 42).

§41.21   d. Extent of Waiver

A waiver by testimony destroys both privileges for "the proceeding in which such testimony is given" but not for any other proceeding. Evid C §973(a). "Proceeding" includes a civil or criminal action (Evid C §§105, 901), *i.e.*, everything from initial complaint to final judgment, not merely a particular trial, deposition, or other part of an action. See Comment to Evid C §973; *People v Lankford* (1976) 55 CA3d 203, 210, 127 CR 408 (testimony at preliminary hearing waived privilege at trial). Thus, if the privileges are waived by testimony on deposition, they cannot be claimed at the trial of the same action.

A waiver by testimony in one action is not a waiver for another action even when the two actions are closely related in subject matter. But even if one of the privileges enables a married person to avoid testifying in the second action, neither privilege can be invoked in the second action to prevent the introduction into evidence of a transcript of that person's testimony from the first action under one of the hearsay exceptions, *e.g.*, the exceptions for former testimony (Evid C §§1291-1292; see §§19.28-19.31).

If testimony is erroneously compelled despite a valid claim of either privilege by a party's spouse, it is doubtful whether the party could object to its admission in another action. The party would not have standing to object as a "holder of the privilege" (Evid C §919; see §§33.7, 33.25, 42.10, 42.12), and the right to "predicate error on a ruling disallowing a claim of privilege by his spouse" (Evid C §918; see §§33.21, 41.8) appears to be limited to post-judgment review in the same action. The courts may, however, construe Evid C §§918-919 in light of their underlying policies to permit the objection.

§41.22   2. Action or Defense for Immediate Benefit of Spouse

Evidence Code §973(b) eliminates both the privilege not to testify against one's spouse and the privilege not to be called as a witness against one's spouse (see chap 42) from any "civil proceeding brought or defended by a married person for the immediate benefit of his spouse or of himself and his spouse."

If a married person brings or defends a civil action for the "immediate benefit" of the spouse, the spouse to be benefited (as well as the party spouse) can be called and cross-examined by the adverse party under Evid C §776(a), (d)(1). The adverse party can also take the benefited spouse's deposition and use it at trial as if that spouse were a party. See CCP §2020(h). See also

CCP §§2023(a)-(b), 2025(h), (j)(2), (*l*)(1), 2030(k)-(*l*), 2032(f), (h), (j). The witness spouse in these situations has no privilege not to testify or not to be called as a witness for or against the party spouse because the bringing or defense of a civil proceeding by one spouse for the immediate benefit of the other spouse, or of both spouses, waives these privileges for both of them. Evid C §973(b).

When both spouses are parties, the operation of this form of waiver appears to depend on whether the witness spouse's interest as a party to the proceeding would be enhanced by the successful prosecution or defense of the other spouse's interest. According to the Comment to Evid C §973, the waiver provision of Evid C §973(b) reflects a principle that

> has seemingly been developed by the case law to prevent a spouse from refusing to testify as to matters which affect his own interest on the ground that such testimony would also be "against" his spouse.

The case law, however, seems to have limited the waiver of the former privilege not to testify (former CCP §1881(1)) to cases in which the spouses affirmatively asserted and sought adjudication of a common claim or interest. See 2 Witkin, California Evidence, *Witnesses* §§264-268 (4th ed 2000). Spouses who were joined as defendants and simply prayed that the plaintiff take nothing did not waive the privilege. In *Stein v Superior Court* (1959) 174 CA2d 21, 344 P2d 406, a husband and wife were sued for personal injuries allegedly resulting from negligent maintenance of their property and filed an answer pleading denials and contributory negligence. The privilege was successfully asserted to prevent the plaintiff from taking the wife's deposition. A contrary result presumably would have been reached under the waiver provision of Evid C §973(b), which appears to operate even when the spouses seek no affirmative relief. Thus, the spouses in *Stein* could not have asserted the privileges of Evid C §§970-971, because each spouse stood to benefit from the successful defense of the other spouse.

This broad scope of Evid C §973(b) is indicated not only by its own language and the related prior case law but also by its relationship to other provisions of the Evidence Code. The combination of the exception for litigation between spouses (Evid C §972(a); see §41.10) and the waiver provision of Evid C §973(b) apparently is intended to eliminate the privileges in practically all cases in which both spouses are parties. Allowing either privilege when both spouses are parties raises difficult problems for which the Code does not provide satisfactory solutions. This absence of solutions seems to indicate that the privileges are not intended to be available when both spouses are parties. For discussion of these problems, see §§41.6, 41.10.

VI. RULING ON PRIVILEGE

§41.23   A. Procedure

When the witness spouse claims the privilege, its existence and applicability may present questions of preliminary fact that must be heard and decided by the judge as an independent issue. Evid C §§402, 405. The parties may present evidence on these issues. See *People v Lankford* (1976) 55 CA3d 203, 210, 127 CR 408. In ruling on whether testimony sought from a witness would adversely affect the spouse (see §41.7) the judge is forbidden to require disclosure of information claimed to be privileged. Evid C §915(a). On the burden of proof on this issue, see §41.22.

§41.24   B. Burden of Proof

The claimant of the privilege (*i.e.,* the witness or the party supporting the witness's claim) has the burden of proving a present valid marriage between the spouses. On this requisite, see §41.2. If the witness's spouse is a party, the claimant also has the burden of proving any facts necessary to establish that the testimony sought is "against" the party spouse, in that the party calling the witness is an adverse party. This requisite is ordinarily determinable as a matter of law. See §§41.4–41.6.

If the witness's spouse is not a party, and the privilege therefore depends on whether the content of the testimony would adversely affect a spouse (see §41.7), the claimant has the burden of proving this adverse effect. Because the claimant cannot be required to reveal the answer in order to establish the privilege (Evid C §915(a)), the claimant's burden will presumably be to show that there could be an answer that would have the requisite adverse effect. Compare the similar test governing the privilege against self-incrimination, discussed in §46.12.

The opponent of the privilege (the proponent of the offered testimony) has the burden of proving any preliminary fact necessary to establish an exclusion of the privilege by an exception or a waiver. The nature of these exceptions and forms of waiver, however, makes them usually determinable as a matter of law. See §§41.9–41.22.

The claimant's and opponent's respective burdens of proof are discussed in the Comment to Evid C §405.

§41.25   VII. STATUTES

Evidence Code §§970–973, referred to in these provisions as "this article," apply both to the privilege not to testify against one's spouse and to the privilege not to be called as a witness against one's spouse (see chap 42).

- Evidence Code §970 states:

    Except as otherwise provided by statute, a married person has a privilege not to testify against his spouse in any proceeding.

- Evidence Code §971 states:

    Except as otherwise provided by statute, a married person whose spouse is a party to a proceeding has a privilege not to be called as a witness by an adverse party to that proceeding without the prior express consent of the spouse having the privilege under this section unless the party calling the spouse does so in good faith without knowledge of the marital relationship.

- Evidence Code §972 states:

    A married person does not have a privilege under this article in:

    (a) A proceeding brought by or on behalf of one spouse against the other spouse.

    (b) A proceeding to commit or otherwise place his or her spouse or his or her spouse's property, or both, under the control of another because of the spouse's alleged mental or physical condition.

    (c) A proceeding brought by or on behalf of a spouse to establish his or her competence.

    (d) A proceeding under the Juvenile Court Law, Chapter 2 (commencing with Section 200) of Part 1 of Division 2 of the Welfare and Institutions Code.

    (e) A criminal proceeding in which one spouse is charged with:

    (1) A crime against the person or property of the other spouse or of a child, parent, relative, or cohabitant of either, whether committed before or during marriage.

    (2) A crime against the person or property of a third person committed in the course of committing a crime against the person or property of the other spouse, whether committed before or during marriage.

    (3) Bigamy.

    (4) A crime defined by Section 270 or 270a of the Penal Code.

    (f) A proceeding resulting from a criminal act which occurred prior to legal marriage of the spouses to each other regarding knowledge acquired prior to that marriage if prior to the legal marriage the witness spouse was aware that his or her spouse had been arrested for or had been formally charged with the crime or crimes about which the spouse is called to testify.

    (g) A proceeding brought against the spouse by a former spouse so long as the property and debts of the marriage have not been adjudicated, or in order to establish, modify, or enforce a child, family or spousal support obligation arising from the marriage to the former spouse; in a proceeding brought against a spouse by the other parent in order to establish, modify, or enforce a child support obligation for a child of a nonmarital relationship of the spouse; or in a proceeding brought against a spouse by the guardian of a child of that spouse in order to establish, modify, or enforce a child support obligation of the spouse. The married person does not have a privilege under this subdivision to refuse to provide information relating to the issues of income, expenses, assets, debts, and employment of either spouse, but may assert the privilege as otherwise provided in this article if other information is requested by the former spouse, guardian, or other parent of the child.

Any person demanding the otherwise privileged information made available by this subdivision, who also has an obligation to support the child for whom an order to establish, modify, or enforce child support is sought, waives his or her marital privilege to the same extent as the spouse as provided in this subdivision.

- Evidence Code §973 states:

    (a) Unless erroneously compelled to do so a married person who testifies in a proceeding to which his spouse is a party, or who testifies against his spouse in any proceeding, does not have a privilege under this article in the proceeding in which such testimony is given.

    (b) There is no privilege under this article in a civil proceeding brought or defended by a married person for the immediate benefit of his spouse or of himself and his spouse.

§41.26 VIII. ILLUSTRATIONS OF PRIVILEGE

The privilege not to testify against one's spouse may be available for the following situations. The first three situations may also constitute violations of the privilege not to be called as a witness against one's spouse (see chap 42):

- In a prosecution of a sole defendant for driving under the influence of alcohol, the prosecutor calls the defendant's husband to the stand.

- In a prosecution of several defendants for bank robbery, one defendant calls another defendant's wife to the stand and asks her where her husband was at the alleged time of the crime.

- In a personal injury suit, the plaintiff attempts to depose the sole defendant's husband.

- In an employee's personal injury suit in which a fellow employee apparently participated in the events leading to the accident but is not a party, the defendant deposes the fellow-employee's wife, asking how many rounds of drinks she saw her husband and the plaintiff consume before they went on the job.

IX. STATING CLAIM OF PRIVILEGE

A. If Witness's Spouse Is Party

§41.27   1. By Witness

Your Honor, I claim the privilege not to testify against my _ _[wife/husband]_ _.

§41.28 2. By Trial Counsel for Party Spouse

Trial counsel should preferably make this statement outside the presence of the jury:

> Your Honor, any examination of this witness by counsel will violate the witness's privilege not to testify against _ _[his wife/her husband]_ _. I request that you advise the witness of _ _[his/her]_ _ right to refuse to answer questions by counsel.

B. If Particular Question Calls for Testimony Against Witness's Nonparty Spouse

§41.29 1. By Witness

> Your Honor, I claim the privilege not to testify against my _ _[wife/husband]_ _.

§41.30 2. By Trial Counsel

Trial counsel should preferably make this statement outside the presence of the jury:

> Your Honor, that question violates the witness's privilege not to testify against _ _[his wife/her husband]_ _.
>
> [Option 1: Counsel represents witness]
>
> On behalf of _ _[name of witness]_ _, I claim the privilege and object to the question on that ground.
>
> [Option 2: Witness holds privilege and is not represented by counsel]
>
> I request that you advise the witness of _ _[his/her]_ _ right to refuse to answer on the ground of privilege.

42

Privilege Not To Be Called as Witness Against Spouse

I. NATURE AND PURPOSE §42.1

II. EFFECT OF MULTIPLE PARTIES §42.2

III. REQUIREMENTS
    A. Valid Marriage §42.3
    B. Witness's Spouse Must Be Party §42.4
    C. Witness Called by Adverse Party
        1. Criminal Actions
            a. Witness Called by Prosecutor §42.5
            b. Witness Called by Codefendant §42.6
        2. Civil Actions
            a. Two-Party Action §42.7
            b. Multiple Parties Including One Spouse §42.8
            c. Both Spouses Are Parties §42.9

IV. EXERCISE OF PRIVILEGE §42.10

V. EXCEPTIONS
    A. Witness Called in Good Faith Ignorance of Marital Relationship §42.11
    B. Proceedings in Which Privilege Is Not Available §42.12

VI. TERMINATION BY DISSOLUTION OF MARRIAGE OR BY WAIVER
    A. Dissolution of Marriage §42.13
    B. Waiver
        1. Acquiescence in Being Called by Adverse Party §42.14
        2. Waiver by Testimony §42.15
        3. Action or Defense for Immediate Benefit of Spouse §42.16

VII. RULING ON PRIVILEGE
    A. Procedure §42.17
    B. Burden of Proof §42.18

VIII. STATUTES §42.19

IX. ILLUSTRATIONS OF PRIVILEGE §42.20

X. STATING CLAIM OF PRIVILEGE
    A. By Witness §42.21
    B. By Trial Counsel for Party Spouse §42.22

§42.1   I. NATURE AND PURPOSE

A married person whose spouse is a party to a proceeding has a privilege not to be called as a witness by any adverse party. Evid C §971. This privilege is considered necessary to avoid prejudice to the party spouse that is likely to result from the other spouse's being called as a witness and being required to exercise in front of the jury the privilege under Evid C §970 not to testify against the party spouse. See Comment to Evid C §971. The purpose of both privileges (sometimes referred to as "marital testimonial privileges") is to protect the marital relationship from disruption through the witness spouse's adverse testimony. See Comment to Evid C §970.

The text of Evid C §§970–973, governing both the privilege not to be called as a witness against one's spouse (discussed in this chapter) and the privilege not to testify against one's spouse (see chap 41), is set out in §41.25.

The privilege not to be called as a witness, like the privilege not to testify, belongs to the witness spouse to invoke. The litigant spouse has no privilege to present the voluntary testimony of a spouse. Evid C §970; *People v Dorsey* (1975) 46 CA3d 706, 716, 120 CR 508.

The privilege not to be called as a witness against one's spouse is similar to the privilege of a defendant in a criminal proceeding not to be called as a witness (Evid C §930; see chap 47), in that a violation of the privilege occurs as soon as the married person or the defendant is called as a witness and before any claim of privilege or objection is made. In discovery proceedings, the privilege prevents a party from even noticing the deposition of the adversary's spouse. See §42.10.

The party spouse can protect the privilege against any claim of exception for good faith ignorance of the marriage (Evid C §971; see §42.10) by putting all adverse parties on notice of the marital relationship.

The testimonial privileges discussed in this chapter and chap 41 should be distinguished from the marital communications privilege under Evid C §980. While the testimonial privileges apply to a witness spouse only and require a valid marriage at the time the testimony is sought (see §42.3, chap 41), the marital communications privilege applies to either spouse and requires a valid marriage when the communication is made (see §40.2).

§42.2   II. EFFECT OF MULTIPLE PARTIES

The presence of multiple parties in an action may lead to complications in the operation of the privilege not to be called as a witness (Evid C §971) and the privilege not to testify (Evid C §970).

Both privileges may be available when there are multiple parties even though neither privilege could be asserted if the dispute between each pair of adverse parties were litigated separately. For example, if a plaintiff has causes of action against *A* and *B* but sues *A* alone, neither privilege can prevent the plaintiff from calling Mrs. *B* as a witness and obtaining her testimony on matters that are relevant to the cause of action against *A* and do not adversely affect *B*. If, however, the plaintiff joins *A* and *B* in the same action and wants to call Mrs. *B* for the same testimony, plaintiff presumably can be prevented from calling Mrs. *B* by her privilege not to be called as a witness by a party adverse to her spouse (see §42.8) and from questioning her by her privilege not to testify against her spouse (see §41.5).

The presence of multiple parties may force a party's spouse to waive a privilege that could otherwise be claimed. For example, if in a single action a plaintiff sues both *A* and *B*, whose interests are not adverse, Mrs. *B* has no privilege against being called as a witness by *A* (see §42.8) and, if called, may have no privilege to refuse to testify on matters that are relevant to *A*'s defense against the plaintiff and do not adversely affect *B*. See §41.5. But if Mrs. *B* testifies for *A* without being "erroneously compelled to do so" (Evid C §973(a)), Mrs. *B* presumably waives both privileges for the entire proceeding and so cannot avoid being called by the plaintiff to testify against her husband, *B*. See §41.6. This waiver could not occur if the claim against *B* were litigated in a separate action.

Usually, neither privilege is available when both spouses are parties. If they are parties on opposite sides, an exception to both privileges applies. Evid C §972(a). See §41.10. If they are parties on the same side, the privileges are usually considered to be waived. Evid C §973(b). See §41.20. For possible exceptions, see §42.9. On the one hand, it may be advantageous for a married person's adversary to join both spouses as parties to eliminate the privileges. On the other hand, it may be advantageous for a married person who has a claim or defense that does not affect the spouse (*e.g.*, one pertaining solely to the separate property) to assert this claim or defense in a proceeding to which the spouse is not a party so that both privileges will remain available.

III. REQUIREMENTS

§42.3   A. Valid Marriage

At the time the privilege operates, a valid marriage must exist between the person to be called as a witness and the party spouse adverse to the party calling the witness. A voidable marriage not yet annulled is sufficient, but a purported marriage that is legally void is insufficient. See *People v Delph* (1979) 94 CA3d 411, 156 CR 422; 2 Witkin, California Evidence, *Witnesses* §§171–173 (4th ed 2000). However, a common-law marriage that is recognized as valid in another state will be recognized as valid in California. Fam C §308; *People v Badgett* (1995) 10 C4th 330, 41 CR2d 635. On termination of the privilege by dissolution of marriage, see §42.13.

§42.4   B. Witness's Spouse Must Be Party

The privilege applies only if the witness's spouse is a party to the proceeding. Evid C §971. If the spouse is not a party, the witness may be entitled to invoke the privilege not to testify against one's spouse (see chap 41) or the privilege for confidential marital communications (see chap 40) but not the privilege not to be called as a witness. In grand jury proceedings, the privilege not to be called as a witness is never available, because "no person has the status of a party defendant." *In re Lemon* (1936) 15 CA2d 82, 85, 59 P2d 213. See Comment to Evid C §971.

C. Witness Called by Adverse Party

1. Criminal Actions

§42.5   a. Witness Called by Prosecutor

When a spouse is the only defendant in a criminal action, the privilege (unless eliminated by an exception or a waiver) prohibits the prosecutor from calling the defendant's spouse as a witness. Evid C §971. But see *People v Villarino* (1970) 7 CA3d 56, 86 CR 338 (prosecutor allowed to subpoena defendant's wife to (1) ask merely whether she is married to defendant and (2) enable witness to identify her as person who passed checks allegedly forged by defendant).

Evidence of one spouse's statements made to police during interrogation is not admissible against the other spouse at his criminal trial, because such evidence violates the confrontation clause of the Sixth Amendment. *Crawford v Washington* (2004) ___ US ___, 158 L Ed 2d 177, 124 S Ct 1354.

On criminal proceedings in which this privilege is unavailable, see §42.12.

§42.6   b. Witness Called by Codefendant

If there are two or more defendants in a criminal action, the applicability of the privilege to the calling by one defendant of another defendant's spouse as a witness depends on whether the two defendants are adverse parties. They may be considered adverse if testimony connecting one of them with the alleged crime may tend to exculpate the other. See, *e.g., People v Zingarelli* (1934) 137 CA 61, 29 P2d 905. See also §42.8 (adversity between civil co-parties). If co-parties are considered adverse, the privilege (unless eliminated by exception or waiver) prohibits one defendant from calling the spouse of the other.

On the similar relation between the adversity of parties and the privilege not to testify against a spouse, see §41.5.

2. Civil Actions

§42.7   a. Two-Party Action

If there is only one plaintiff and one defendant, the privilege (unless eliminated by an exception or a waiver) prohibits either party from calling the spouse of the other as a witness. See Evid C §970.

§42.8 b. Multiple Parties Including One Spouse

If there are multiple parties, a party adverse to a party spouse may be litigating separate issues with another party, *e.g.*, a cross-defendant, coplaintiff, or codefendant. In this situation, the privilege can be invoked to prohibit the adverse party from calling the nonparty spouse not only for testimony affecting the party spouse but also for any other purpose, including a purpose that affects only another party. The privilege does not, however, protect a witness married to one party from being called by another party who is not adverse to the party spouse.

Parties may be adverse even when they are co-parties who do not plead for relief against each other, *e.g.*, two coplaintiffs, two codefendants, or a plaintiff and a cross-defendant. Thus, a personal injury plaintiff may advance a theory of the accident under which the coplaintiff's recovery would be diminished by contributory negligence, and a breach of contract defendant may contend that the plaintiff agreed to look solely to the codefendant for payment. See, *e.g., Koeberle v Friganza* (1924) 66 CA 323, 327, 226 P 35. If there is actual adversity between two parties, each party's spouse has a privilege not to be called by the other party just as if their adversity were established by the pleadings.

On the similar relation between the adversity of parties and the privilege not to testify against a spouse, see §41.5.

§42.9 c. Both Spouses Are Parties

If the spouses are parties on opposite sides, the privilege is eliminated by an exception. Evid C §972(a). See §§41.9–41.10. If they are parties on the same side (*e.g.*, coplaintiffs, codefendants), they are usually treated as having waived the privilege under Evid C §973(b) by suing or defending for the benefit of each other. See §41.22. If no such waiver occurs, however, Evid C §971 appears to prevent a party adverse to the party spouses from calling either spouse under Evid C §776 even for testimony unrelated to the interests of the other spouse. The wording of Evid C §971 furnishes no basis for confining the use of the privilege to the prevention of testimony that would adversely affect the other spouse. Yet allowing a party spouse to use the privilege to avoid giving testimony that would affect only his or her separate rights and liabilities seems to extend the privilege beyond its underlying purpose of protecting the marital relationship.

A similar problem is presented by the privilege not to testify against one's spouse. See §41.6. Thus, both privileges appear to be unavailable in practically every civil case in which spouses are parties on the same side. See §41.22. This problem is not likely to arise when spouses are codefendants in a criminal proceeding, because each defendant is protected from being called by the privilege of a defendant (Evid C §930); see chap 47) regardless of the privileges as a spouse (see §§42.5–42.6).

§42.10 IV. EXERCISE OF PRIVILEGE

The privilege exists only if a married person whose spouse is a party is called as a witness by an adverse party "without the prior express consent of the spouse having the privilege." Evid C §971. Because the witness spouse (not the litigant spouse) "has" the privilege (Evid C §971), a married party cannot prevent the spouse from voluntarily giving this express consent and being called by the adversary. See §42.14.

The privilege takes effect without being expressly claimed. If the adversary has not obtained the witness spouse's consent and is not excused by the exception for good faith ignorance of the marriage (see §42.11) or by some other exception or waiver, counsel violates the privilege as soon as the witness is called. See Comment to Evid C §971.

A witness called in violation of the privilege is entitled to object to the violation and presumably also to claim the privilege not to testify (see §41.8). The party whose spouse is called also has standing to object to the violation of the privilege not to be called and to predicate error on a failure of the court to sustain the objection or grant other necessary relief. See Evid C §918. See also §33.21. If the privilege is violated at the trial, forcing an objection from the witness or party spouse, the aggrieved party can pursue remedies for misconduct, *e.g.*, with a motion for mistrial. See chap 56.

The privilege is violated before trial by the noticing of the witness's deposition. See CCP §2017(a). See also §33.9 (privileges apply to discovery). This violation entitles the witness or party spouse to move for an order that the deposition not be taken. CCP §2025(i).

If the witness testifies because of the failure of the witness or party spouse to pursue these remedies either on deposition or at trial, the privilege is waived. Evid C §973(a). See §§41.19, 41.21.

V. EXCEPTIONS

§42.11 A. Witness Called in Good Faith Ignorance of Marital Relationship

There is no privilege if the party calling the witness spouse "does so in good faith without knowledge of the marital relationship." Evid C §971. A married party anticipating that the spouse may be called as a witness can eliminate this exception by giving the adverse party express notice of the marriage. Even if the adverse party has no actual knowledge of the marriage, the requirement of good faith presumably imposes a duty of reasonable inquiry if circumstances (*e.g.*, identical last names) suggest the possibility of a marital relationship.

The good faith exception eliminates only the privilege not to be called; the witness spouse may still exercise the privilege not to testify. See §42.14.

§42.12 B. Proceedings in Which Privilege Is Not Available

Exceptions provided by Evid C §972 eliminate both the privilege not to be called as a witness against one's spouse and the privilege not to testify against one's spouse (see chap 41) from specified kinds of proceedings. These exceptions are discussed in relation to both privileges in the following sections of chap 41:

- Litigation between spouses (Evid C §972(a)); see §41.10);
- Spouse's competence at issue (Evid C §972(b)-(c)); see §41.11);
- Juvenile court proceedings (Evid C §972(d)); see §41.12); and
- Spouse charged with certain crimes (Evid C §972(e)); see §41.13).

VI. TERMINATION BY DISSOLUTION OF MARRIAGE OR BY WAIVER

§42.13 A. Dissolution of Marriage

The privilege is terminated by dissolution of the marriage between the witness and the party spouse against whom the witness is called. Dissolution may be by annulment, final judgment of divorce, or the death of either spouse. See also §42.3 (valid marriage as requisite of privilege).

Dissolution of the marriage destroys the privilege because the purpose of the privilege is to protect the marriage from disruption through the spouse's adverse testimony. In contrast, the marital communications privilege survives dissolution of the marriage (for communications made during the marriage) because the purpose of that privilege is to encourage frank communication between the spouses by assuring them against future violation of confidences. See Comment to Evid C §980. See also §§40.1-40.2.

B. Waiver

§42.14 1. Acquiescence in Being Called by Adverse Party

A person whose spouse is a party waives the privilege not to be called as a witness by giving prior express consent to being called. Evid C §971. See §42.10. The privilege is presumably restored if the witness expressly revokes the consent before being called. Even if the privilege not to be called is waived because the consent is unrevoked, this waiver apparently does not prevent the witness from a change of mind and claiming the privilege not to testify against the party spouse (see §41.8) upon reaching the witness stand. Similarly, a witness who fails to object to being called for a deposition, but gives no deposition testimony, may still claim the privilege not to be called as a trial witness.

If the witness has not waived the privilege not to be called, it is violated by the mere act of calling the witness. To avoid a subsequent waiver by testimony, however, the witness or the aggrieved party spouse must bring the violation to the court's attention by objection or other means (see §42.10) as soon as the witness is called and before any testimony is given. If the court then erroneously compels the witness to testify despite the assertion of privilege, the testimony is not a waiver of either privilege. Evid C §973(a). See §41.19.

§42.15   2. Waiver by Testimony

Evidence Code §973(a) prescribes circumstances under which the act of testifying causes a person to lose both the privilege not to be called as a witness against one's spouse and the privilege not to testify against one's spouse (see chap 41). This waiver provision is discussed in relation to both privileges in the following sections of chap 41:

- Testimony for spouse (see §41.18);
- Testimony against party spouse (see §41.19);
- Testimony against nonparty spouse (see §41.20); and
- Extent of waiver (see §41.21).

§42.16   3. Action or Defense for Immediate Benefit of Spouse

Evidence Code §973(b) eliminates both the privilege not to be called as a witness against one's spouse and the privilege not to testify against one's spouse (see chap 41) from any "civil proceeding brought or defended by a married person for the immediate benefit of his spouse or of himself and his spouse." This provision is discussed for both privileges in §41.22.

VII. RULING ON PRIVILEGE

§42.17   A. Procedure

The privilege may be brought into question by the witness's objection to being called or by the party spouse's objection or motion. See §42.10. The existence and applicability of the privilege may then present questions of preliminary fact that must be heard and decided by the judge as an independent issue. Evid C §§402, 405. The parties may present evidence on these issues. See generally §§21.8, 21.15, 33.14-33.16, 33.22-33.23.

§42.18   B. Burden of Proof

The witness or party relying on the privilege has the burden of proving a present valid marriage between the spouses. On this requisite, see §42.3. The proponent of the privilege also has the burden of proving any facts necessary to establish that the witness's spouse is a party adverse to the party calling the witness, although this requisite is ordinarily determinable as a matter of law. See §§42.5-42.9.

The opponent of the privilege (the adverse party calling the witness) has the burden of proving that the opponent called the witness in good faith without knowledge of the marriage or that the witness gave prior express consent to being called. See Evid C §971. See also §§42.11, 42.14. The opponent also has the burden of proving any facts necessary to establish other exceptions or forms of waiver, but these are usually determinable as a matter of law. See §§41.9-41.21.

The respective burdens of proof of claimants and opponents of privileges are discussed in the Comment to Evid C §405.

§42.19   VIII. STATUTES

The text of Evid C §§970-973, governing both the privilege not to be called as a witness against one's spouse and the privilege not to testify against one's spouse, is set out in §41.25.

§42.20   IX. ILLUSTRATIONS OF PRIVILEGE

The privilege not to be called as a witness against one's spouse would presumably be violated by calling a witness in the following situations:

- The prosecutor in a criminal action calls the defendant's wife as a witness.
- The plaintiff in a civil action notices the deposition of defendant's husband.
- In a personal injury action, defendant Smith, who contends that plaintiff's injuries were caused solely by the negligence of codefendant Jones, calls Mrs. Jones as a witness.

X. STATING CLAIM OF PRIVILEGE

§42.21   A. By Witness

> Your Honor, I object to being called as a witness because it violates my privilege not to be called as a witness by a party adverse to my _ _[wife/husband]_ _.

§42.22   B. By Trial Counsel for Party Spouse

Trial counsel should preferably make this statement outside the presence of the jury:

> Your Honor, I object to the calling of this witness on the ground that it violates _ _[his/her]_ _ privilege not to be called as a witness by a party adverse to _ _[his wife/her husband]_ _.
>
> [Add if appropriate]
>
> I object to counsel's calling of this witness as misconduct, and I _ _[request/move]_ _ that _ _[describe appropriate remedy]_ _.

On the similar relation between the adversity of parties and the privilege not to testify against a spouse, see §41.5.

43

Privilege for Official Information

I. NATURE OF PRIVILEGE §43.1

II. REQUIREMENTS
    A. Information Acquired by Public Employee §43.2
    B. Confidentiality §43.3
    C. Grounds for Nondisclosure
        1. Federal or California Statute §43.4
        2. Military and State Secrets §43.5
        3. Balancing of Necessities §43.6

III. WHO CAN CLAIM §43.7

IV. EFFECT IN CRIMINAL PROCEEDINGS
    A. Order or Finding Adverse to Prosecution §43.8
    B. Exceptions to Adverse Finding Rule
        1. Privilege Invoked by Non-California Public Entity §43.9
        2. Federal Statute Forbidding Disclosure §43.10
        3. Information to Support Search Warrant §43.11

V. TERMINATION AND WAIVER §43.12

VI. RULING ON PRIVILEGE
    A. Procedure §43.13
    B. Burden of Proof §43.14

VII. STATUTES §43.15

VIII. ILLUSTRATIONS OF PRIVILEGE §43.16

IX. STATING CLAIM OF PRIVILEGE
    A. By Witness §43.17
    B. By Trial Counsel §43.18

X. MOTION FOR ORDER OR FINDING ADVERSE TO PROSECUTION §43.19

§43.1   I. NATURE OF PRIVILEGE

The privilege for official information prohibits compulsory disclosure of "information acquired in confidence by a public employee in the course of his duty and not open, or officially disclosed, to the public." Evid C §1040(a). The privilege applies when disclosure is prohibited by a statute or when the trial judge determines that the public interest in confidentiality outweighs the necessity for disclosure in the interest of justice to the litigants who are before the court. Evid C §1040(b)(2). See §43.6. The privilege does not, however, affect the right of access to medical or psychological histories that are otherwise available under the patient-litigant exception to the physician-patient privilege (Evid C §996; see §36.9) or the psychotherapist-patient privilege (Evid C §1016; see §37.9). Evid C §1044.

Only a public entity can claim the privilege, but the Evidence Code did not repeal other statutes giving private persons a privilege not to disclose reports they have made to the government. See Comment to Evid C §1040. See also §43.7.

The privilege is an exception to the general rule, declared in the California Public Records Act (Govt C §§6250-6268), that public records are open to inspection by all citizens (Govt C §§6250, 6253-6253.1). But the exemption of certain records from the right of inspection provided by the Act (see Govt C §§6254-6255) does not establish that those records are privileged. The Act does not affect discovery rights (Govt C §6260), and Evid C §1040 "represents the exclusive means by which a public entity may assert a claim of governmental privilege based on the necessity for secrecy" (*Pitchess v Superior Court* (1974) 11 C3d 531, 540, 113 CR 897; see *County of Orange v Superior Court* (2000) 79 CA4th 759, 94 CR2d 261 (Evid C §1040 barred production of county sheriffs' criminal investigative file in civil rights action); *Shepherd v Superior Court* (1976) 17 C3d 107, 123, 130 CR 257). See also *Times Mirror Co. v Superior Court* (1991) 53 C3d 1325, 283 CR 893, which held that Govt C §6255 protected the Governor's appointment calendars and schedules from disclosure, ruling that the public interest in facilitating the frank discussion of policy within the executive branch outweighed the public interest in disclosure. A similar "executive" or "deliberative process" privilege applies to federal agencies under 5 USC §552(b)(5).

The privilege for official information is wholly statutory (*Pitchess v Superior Court, supra* (codified in Pen C §§832.7-832.8 and Evid C §§1043-1045)) and is distinct from the related governmental privilege to withhold the identity of an informer (see Evid C §1041; chap 44). The use of either privilege against a defendant in a criminal proceeding sometimes subjects the prosecution to adverse consequences. See Evid C §1042. See also §§43.8-43.11.

II. REQUIREMENTS

§43.2   A. Information Acquired by Public Employee

The privilege for official information protects only information that is acquired by a public employee "in the course of his or her duty," *i.e.,* in the employee's official, not private, capacity. Evid C §1040(a). The employee may be an officer, agent, or employee of any "public entity." See Evid C §195. The public entity may be any form of foreign or domestic public authority, including a nation, state, city, county, district, public corporation, or public agency. See Evid C §200. The holder of the privilege is the public entity, not its employee. Evid C §1040(b). See §43.7.

§43.3 B. Confidentiality

The public employee must acquire the information "in confidence," *i.e.,* under a duty not to reveal it to the public. Evid C §1040(a). This duty can be based on any legal prohibition of disclosure or any public interest in confidentiality (see §§43.4–43.6) and does not require an express understanding with the informant that the information will not be disclosed (see *Jessup v Superior Court* (1957) 151 CA2d 102, 108, 311 P2d 177 (discussing former privilege that probably would have been unavailable under Evid C §1040(b)(2); see §43.6).

Unless the information becomes officially available to the public, the privilege can be used to prevent its disclosure by any person acquiring it from official sources. The privilege cannot, however, prevent (1) disclosure of the personal knowledge of the person who transmitted the information to the government or (2) anyone from disclosing information acquired through purely private channels. See Comment to Evid C §1040.

In one case, plaintiffs sued the county for defamation based on police public statements that they were suspects in the murder of their son. The plaintiffs sought to discover the contents of the police investigative file. They argued that their own statements to the police, as well as statements made by other witnesses, were not acquired in confidence. Similarly, photos, sketches, and police reports concerning the crime scene were not acquired in confidence because the scene itself was "a ravine open to the public." The court of appeal stated that, viewed individually, many of the pieces of information in the file may not have been "acquired in confidence" in the literal sense of that term. But simply because the public may observe the police gathering evidence at a crime scene, or interviewing witnesses, it does not follow that the information obtained is public. Evidence gathered by police as part of an ongoing criminal investigation is by its nature confidential. *County of Orange v Superior Court* (2000) 79 CA4th 759, 763, 94 CR2d 261.

C. Grounds for Nondisclosure

§43.4 1. Federal or California Statute

If disclosure of official information is forbidden by an act of Congress or by a California statute or constitutional provision, the privilege is absolute. Evid C §1040(b)(1). See Evid C §230 ("statute" includes constitutional provision); *County of Los Angeles v Superior Court* (1975) 13 C3d 721, 119 CR 631 (courts lack constitutional power to inquire into legislators' motives in enacting legislation); *City of Santa Cruz v Superior Court* (1995) 40 CA4th 1146, 48 CR2d 216 (legislative privilege that prevents judiciary from inquiring into legislators' motives applies to nonlegislators as long as questioning goes to legislators' thought processes). If the trial judge finds that the information is within the statute and that disclosure has not been officially authorized, the privilege must be sustained.

The following are examples of information protected by state statute:

- Tax returns (see 2 Witkin, California Evidence, *Witnesses* §§255-260 (4th ed 2000));

- Public social services records (Welf & I C §10850);

- Compulsory vehicle accident reports (Veh C §§20012-20014; see *Edgar v Superior Court* (1978) 84 CA3d 430, 148 CR 687 (confidentiality of reports does not preclude discovery of existence and number of accidents at particular location)); and

- Stale or remote matter (Evid C §1045(b)(1)), investigative conclusions (Evid C §1045(b)(2)), and peace and custodial officer personnel files concerning citizen complaints against them (see Evid C §1045(e)).

Edgar v Superior Court, supra, has been disapproved to the extent that it is inconsistent with *Davies v Superior Court* (1984) 36 C3d 291, 300, 204 CR 154. In *Davies,* the supreme court held that Veh C §§20012-20014 protect the confidentiality of accident reports but do not establish a privilege. Thus, computer data that does not reveal or compromise the identity or privacy interests of reporting parties is discoverable and admissible, even though it has been compiled from accident reports. 36 C3d at 298.

Moreover, in *State ex rel Dep't of Transp. v Superior Court* (Hall) (1985) 37 C3d 847, 855, 210 CR 219, the supreme court held that a defendant charged with a crime arising from an automobile accident has a proper interest within the meaning of Veh C §20012 in the discovery of reports of other accidents at the same site. On a proper showing, an accused is thus entitled to the reports if data identifying the reporting parties has been deleted. 37 C3d at 857.

The privilege may also be based on a federal order or regulation authorized by statutory or constitutional provision. See *People v Parham* (1963) 60 C2d 378, 33 CR 497. There may be no absolute privilege, however, if the statute makes the information available to a party before the court. See *Saulter v Municipal Court* (1977) 75 CA3d 231, 142 CR 266 (if exception in federal Privacy Act of 1974 allows disclosure on request of state law enforcement agency (5 USC §§552a(b)(7), (11)), prosecutor must make such request to satisfy defendant's right to discovery). But see *People v Superior Court (Barrett)* (2000) 80 CA4th 1305, 1319, 96 CR2d 264 (continued viability of *Saulter* doubtful in light of Proposition 115's statutory criminal discovery scheme).

Additionally, a police officer has a conditional privilege in his or her police personnel records. See Evid C §1043. The privilege must be balanced against the right of the litigant to obtain information material to the subject matter of the litigation. *Rosales v City of Los Angeles* (2000) 82 CA4th 419, 424, 98 CR2d 144. See §43.6.

§43.5   2. Military and State Secrets

The federal executive branch appears to have a constitutional absolute privilege for military and state secrets. *U.S. v Nixon* (1974) 418 US 683, 710, 41 L Ed 2d 1039, 1065, 94 S Ct 3090. If the information is sufficiently important in a case, however, the court may require the government to make a reasonable showing that the information is of the sensitive nature claimed.

In *U.S. v Reynolds* (1953) 345 US 1, 97 L Ed 727, 73 S Ct 528, a claim of privilege by the Secretary of the Air Force on grounds of military secrecy was held sufficient to deny discovery of an official report of a military plane crash, because the plaintiffs, who were suing the government for deaths in the crash, had made only a "dubious showing of necessity" of the information for proving their claims. The court stated (345 US at 11, 97 L Ed at 734):

> In each case, the showing of necessity which is made will determine how far the court should probe.... [W]here there is a strong showing of necessity, the claim of privilege should not be lightly accepted, but even the most compelling necessity cannot overcome the claim of privilege if the court is ultimately satisfied that military secrets are at stake.

See 2 Witkin, California Evidence, *Witnesses* §§249–250 (4th ed 2000).

§43.6   3. Balancing of Necessities

The official information privilege, once asserted, should not be sustained unless the court is presented with a showing that the information sought to be protected is covered by the privilege. There are, no doubt, circumstances where this is self-evident, or nearly so. But if it is not, the party claiming the privilege must either show in open court why the matter is privileged or declare that doing so would compromise the privilege. If it appears to the trial court, based on this representation, that the claim cannot be determined in open court without "disclosure of the information claimed to be privileged," the court may call for that disclosure in chambers pursuant to Evid C §915(b). *Torres v Superior Court* (2000) 80 CA4th 867, 873, 95 CR2d 686.

If disclosure of the official information is not forbidden by California statute or federal law, the privilege can exist only if disclosure "is against the public interest because there is a necessity for preserving the confidentiality of the information that outweighs the necessity for disclosure in the interest of justice." Evid C §1040(b)(2). The "consequences to the public of disclosure" must be weighed against the "consequences to the litigant of nondisclosure." Comment to Evid C §1040. This balancing of necessities is the duty of the judge. See *Shepherd v Superior Court* (1976) 17 C3d 107, 125, 130 CR 257 (analysis of weighing process); *Marylander v Superior Court* (2000) 81 CA4th 1119, 1126, 97 CR2d 439. See also §§43.13-43.14.

Various considerations weigh in favor of keeping official information confidential. For example, the Board of Prison Terms (Pen C §5078), formerly the Adult Authority, has an interest in maintaining institutional security that creates a qualified privilege under Evid C §1040. *In re Olson* (1974) 37 CA3d 783, 787, 112 CR 579. See also 2 Witkin, California Evidence, *Witnesses* §§264-268 (4th ed 2000). Confidentiality is important to many types of public entities because it encourages private persons to supply them with full and accurate information. See *City & County of San Francisco v Superior Court* (1951) 38 C2d 156, 162, 238 P2d 581; see also *County of Orange v Superior Court* (2000) 79 CA4th 759, 768, 94 CR2d 261 (criminal investigative file). 2 Witkin, Evidence, *Witnesses* §§262-263§§262-263269. Licensing agency information concerning complaints and investigations should also be kept confidential for the protection of licensees against unfounded charges. See *Chronicle Publishing Co. v Superior Court* (1960) 54 C2d 548, 567, 7 CR 109 (complaints to State Bar that do not result in discipline held privileged); 2 Witkin, Evidence, *Witnesses* §270.

The privilege for official information can be claimed by a public entity of another state or a foreign country. See Evid C §200. See also §§43.2, 43.7. Although such a claimant cannot rely on a statute of its own jurisdiction as creating an absolute privilege under Evid C §1040(b)(1), the trial judge presumably should give weight to the statute as a reason for keeping the information confidential.

The necessity for disclosure in the interest of justice (which offsets factors favoring confidentiality) depends on the importance of the information as evidence in the case and the availability of alternative means of proof. As pointed out in the Comment to Evid C §1040, the public has an interest not only in official secrecy but also "in seeing that justice is done in the particular cause." In a criminal proceeding, however, the necessity for disclosure in the interest of justice may be eliminated when sustaining the privilege results in a finding that is adverse to the prosecution under Evid C §1042(a) (see §§43.8-43.11).

In determining the necessity for keeping the information confidential, the trial judge must not consider the public entity's interest as a party to the proceeding. Evid C §1040(b)(2). Thus, in a condemnation action the condemning agency is not entitled to conceal its own appraisers' reports of the property's fair market value on the ground that disclosure would be against the public interest (see *Oceanside Union Sch. Dist. v Superior Court* (1962) 58 C2d 180, 23 CR 375), but the information held by the governmental party may be protected by the attorney-client privilege (see *Jessup v Superior Court* (1957) 151 CA2d 102, 311 P2d 177 (former attorney-client privilege protected information that would have been helpful to public entity as party; application of former public officer's privilege seems contrary to rule of Evid C §1040(b)(2) for official information privilege)). On protection by the attorney-client privilege, see §34.4.

§43.7 III. WHO CAN CLAIM

The holder of the privilege for official information is the public entity (Evid C §1040(b)) by whom the information was "acquired in confidence" (Evid C §1040(a)). See §34.4 (meaning of "holder"). The holder can be any foreign or domestic governmental body, whether national, state, or local. See Evid C §200.

The privilege must be "claimed by a person authorized by the public entity to do so." Evid C §1040(b). If a public employee is called as a witness and asked to disclose privileged official information, the employee may claim the privilege if the employee has authority to do so. The public entity may claim the privilege through its attorney, regardless of the witness's authority, if it is a party to the proceeding. Even if the entity is not a party, it may authorize counsel for a party to make the claim. If neither the witness nor any party is authorized to claim the privilege, Evid C §916 may require the trial judge on the judge's own motion or the motion of a party to exclude the official information from evidence as "information that is subject to a claim of privilege." See §§34.11-34.13. Exclusion may be required, for example, when a witness obtains unauthorized access to privileged official information and is about to reveal it in court, and the public entity itself is not represented in the proceeding.

The privilege for military or state secrets, based on federal law (see §43.5), must be formally claimed "by the head of the department which has control over the matter, after actual personal consideration by that officer." *U.S. v Reynolds* (1953) 345 US 1, 8, 97 L Ed 727, 733, 73 S Ct 528. Federal departmental regulations may channel all applications for official information to the head of the department by requiring approval for its release. A subordinate employee is entitled to refuse disclosure in reliance on such a regulation. See *U.S. ex rel Touhy v Ragen* (1951) 340 US 462, 95 L Ed 417, 71 S Ct 416 (Department of Justice); *U.S. v Allen* (10th Cir 1977) 554 F2d 398, 406 (Department of Justice).

Only a public entity that is both a party and "the holder of the privilege" has standing to claim error when the privilege is erroneously disallowed. Evid C §918. See §33.21.

Any holder, party or nonparty, may be entitled to an extraordinary writ as a remedy for erroneous denial of the privilege. See §§33.22-33.23. An extraordinary writ may also be available to a private party who has disclosed affairs in confidence to a public agency and seeks to challenge a ruling that erroneously compels disclosure. But see *City & County of San Francisco v Superior Court* (1951) 38 C2d 156, 161, 238 P2d 581 (reserving question regarding whether private employer, as well as city, could challenge order for disclosure of confidential information given to city).

California statutes other than the Evidence Code may entitle private persons to claim a privilege to prevent disclosure of official information. For instance, a taxpayer has a privilege under Rev & T C §§19542-19566 to refuse disclosure of his or her own copies of federal and state income tax returns. *Webb v Standard Oil Co.* (1957) 49 C2d 509, 512, 319 P2d 621; but see, conversely, *McCabe v Snyder* (1999) 75 CA4th 337, 89 CR2d 315 (disclosure of DMV records barred in individual's action seeking names and addresses of those paying smog impact fee for class refund action challenging constitutionality of fee). See also *Sav-On Drugs, Inc. v Superior Court* (1975) 15 C3d 1, 6, 123 CR 283 (sales tax returns (Rev & T C §7056)); *Sammut v Sammut* (1980) 103 CA3d 557, 562, 163 CR 193 (W-2 form); *Brown v Superior Court* (1977) 71 CA3d 141, 139 CR 327 (W-2 form). But see *Miller v Superior Court* (1977) 71 CA3d 145, 149, 139 CR 521, in which the court relied on former Rev & T C §19286.5 (which has since been repealed and replaced by Rev & T C §19553) in holding that the privilege for official information is not available in a proceeding to enforce child support payments. The court stated that the "policy favoring the confidentiality of tax returns must give way to the greater public policy of enforcing child support obligations."

IV. EFFECT IN CRIMINAL PROCEEDINGS

§43.8   A. Order or Finding Adverse to Prosecution

In a criminal proceeding under California law, if the trial judge sustains a claim of the privilege for official information asserted by the State of California or another California public entity, the judge must make an appropriate order or finding of fact adverse to the prosecution on any issue dependent on the excluded information. Evid C§1042(a). This requirement presumably also applies when the judge, under Evid C §916, excludes information that is subject to such a claim of privilege. The remedial order should be no broader than necessary to assure a fair trial. See *Dell M. v Superior Court* (1977) 70 CA3d 782, 144 CR 418 (in prosecution for interference with police officer (Pen C §148), police department's withholding of officer's personnel records required suppressing evidence of scuffle between defendant and officer but not dismissal, because charge was provable by other evidence); *People v Superior Court* (Biggs) (1971) 19 CA3d 522, 97 CR 118 (before ordering dismissal, court should have considered whether prosecutor's offer of partial disclosure would fulfill defendant's needs).

This provision prevents the state from prosecuting a defendant and at the same time using its governmental privilege in a way that deprives the defendant of evidence that is material to the defense. See *People v McShann* (1958) 50 C2d 802, 330 P2d 33; 2 Witkin, California Evidence, *Witnesses* §§252-254 (4th ed 2000). (The provision also applies to the companion privilege not to disclose the identity of an informer (Evid C §1041).)

An area of official information privilege law that arises more frequently involves motions to discover a law enforcement officer's or custodial officer's personnel file, sometimes referred to as *Pitchess* motions (see *Pitchess v Superior Court* (1974) 11 C3d 531, 113 CR 897, codified in Pen C §§832.7-832.8

and Evid C §§1043-1045). See *Rosales v City of Los Angeles* (2000) 82 CA4th 419, 98 CR2d 144 (violation of *Pitchess* statutory disclosure procedures did not give rise to private cause of action by affected former police officer). These motions are discussed in detail in California Criminal Law Procedure and Practice §§11.18-11.22 (7th ed Cal CEB 2004).

B. Exceptions to Adverse Finding Rule

§43.9   1. Privilege Invoked by Non-California Public Entity

An order or finding adverse to the prosecution is required only when the privilege is claimed by "the state or a public entity in this state" (Evid C §1042(a)), *i.e.,* by a California public entity (see Evid C §220, defining "state"). Therefore, if the privilege for official information is claimed by a federal or other non-California public entity, the exclusion of the information does not require the adverse order or finding (see Comment to Evid C §1042), at least when no showing has been made that the local agency withheld evidence or conspired with the federal agency to do so (see *In re Pratt* (1980) 112 CA3d 795, 882, 170 CR 80).

Thus, if a prosecution witness's written statement to the FBI is excluded on a claim of privilege by the United States Department of Justice, the defendant is not entitled to have the witness's testimony stricken on the ground that the issue of credibility must be resolved adversely to the prosecution (see *People v Parham* (1963) 60 C2d 378, 33 CR 497); the court may require the prosecution to exercise its federal right to obtain the information to satisfy the defendant's discovery right (*Saulter v Municipal Court* (1977) 75 CA3d 231, 142 CR 266). But see *People v Superior Court (Barrett)* (2000) 80 CA4th 1305, 1319, 96 CR2d 264 (continued viability of *Saulter* doubtful in light of Proposition 115's statutory criminal discovery scheme).

§43.10   2. Federal Statute Forbidding Disclosure

If a claim of the privilege is based on a federal statute that prohibits disclosure of the information, the requirement of an order or a finding adverse to the prosecution does not apply. Evid C §1042(a). Any issue depending on the excluded evidence is then determined as though the evidence had not been introduced.

§43.11   3. Information to Support Search Warrant

The prosecution is not required to reveal official information to establish the legality of a search warrant that is valid on its face. Evid C §1042(b). This exception usually arises when a defendant objects to the prosecution's evidence as having been obtained through an illegal search, in that the search warrant was not supported by a sufficient showing of probable cause. See chap 28 (objection to illegally obtained evidence).

If insufficiency cannot be established without disclosure of official information to the defendant by the prosecution, Evid C §1042(b) requires that the legality of the search be treated as established without disclosure. To invoke this provision, the prosecution need only show that the warrant is valid on its face and that the undisclosed information is official information under Evid C §1040(a), *i.e.*, information acquired and kept in confidence by a police department or other public entity.

The defense may seek disclosure of information claimed to be privileged under Evid C §1040. The procedures for making that challenge are discussed in §§43.13-43.14.

§43.12 V. TERMINATION AND WAIVER

The privilege for official information terminates when the information is opened or officially disclosed to the public. Evid C §1040(a).

Unless disclosure is forbidden by a federal or California statute, the privilege is waived when an authorized person consents to disclosure of the information in the proceeding. This authority must be given by the public entity that holds the privilege. Evid C §1040(b). See *Richards v Superior Court* (1968) 258 CA2d 635, 65 CR 917 (personal injury plaintiff's consent to defendants' discovery of records of her medical examination, ordered by Department of Employment to determine her disability claim, did not affect Department's right to claim absolute privilege under Un Ins C §§2111, 2714). An employee who has been given access to the privileged information or who has authority to claim the privilege may not have received authority to waive it. Compare *Procunier v Superior Court* (Losoya) (1973) 35 CA3d 207, 110 CR 529 (Attorney General authorized to claim privilege for prison records), with *Procunier v Superior Court* (Herth) (1973) 35 CA3d 211, 110 CR 531 (Attorney General's failure to claim privilege for such records did not waive it).

A disclosure of privileged information erroneously required by an unchallenged court order is not a waiver of the official information privilege. See Evid C §919(b); Comment to 1973 amendment to Evid C §919. On waiver as a bar to the exclusion of privileged information by the judge under Evid C §916, see §§33.6, 33.14.

A taxpayer who has a privilege for copies of his or her tax returns (see §43.7) may waive it by contract (*Crest Catering Co. v Superior Court* (1965) 62 C2d 274, 42 CR 110 (employer's promise to furnish information to trustee under union welfare agreement waived privilege against trustee's discovery of employment tax returns); *Marriage of Parks* (1982) 138 CA3d 346, 188 CR 26 (husband's earlier agreement to furnish certain information constituted waiver of privilege for copies of W-2P forms (naval retirement pay)) or by placing the content of the return at issue (*Wilson v Superior Court* (1976) 63 CA3d 825, 134 CR 130 (suit by taxpayer against her accountant for improper advice concerning her 1972 income tax waived her privilege for returns from 1965 through 1973)). But see *Brown v Superior Court* (1977) 71 CA3d 141,

139 CR 327 (claim of lost income for personal injuries did not waive privilege for W-2 forms).

VI. RULING ON PRIVILEGE

§43.13   A. Procedure

The privilege may be brought into issue by the public entity's claiming it or by a motion by any party that the trial judge act under Evid C §916. See §43.7. The existence and applicability of the privilege may then present questions of preliminary fact that must be heard and decided by the judge as an independent issue. Evid C §§400–402, 405. The parties may present evidence on these issues.

If the judge cannot rule on the privilege without disclosure of the official information in question, the judge may require confidential disclosure in chambers by either the witness or a person authorized to claim the privilege. No other person may be present except a court reporter who has been deemed necessary to preserve a record for any appeal. *People v Hertz* (1980) 103 CA3d 770, 780, 163 CR 233 (trial court's dismissal of charges based on Pen C §995 motion held proper because of lack of record of in camera hearing on official information privilege). If the privilege is sustained, no person may disclose what was said in chambers, unless an authorized person consents to such presence or disclosure. Evid C §915(b). This procedure may be appropriate for deciding whether the information is of the kind required to be kept confidential by a statute or by the federal Constitution (see Evid C §1040(b)(1); see also §43.4), or whether the necessity for confidentiality outweighs the necessity for disclosure in the interest of justice (Evid C §1040(b)(2); *People v Woolman* (1974) 40 CA3d 652, 115 CR 324; see §43.6). The procedure should not, however, be the sole basis for sustaining a claim of privilege without consideration of other possibilities for resolving the issue, *e.g.,* a determination that other available evidence is an adequate substitute for the information claimed to be privileged. See *People v Superior Court* (Biggs) (1971) 19 CA3d 522, 530, 97 CR 118. See generally 2 Witkin, California Evidence, *Witnesses* §§249–250 (4th ed 2000).

Disclosure of peace officer and custodial officer personnel files or of records of citizen complaints against police agencies requires a written motion with ten days' notice to the agency, which must notify the officer whose records are sought. The motion must identify the proceedings, the records sought, and the officer to whom the records pertain; the motion must be supported by affidavits showing good cause for disclosure. Evid C §1043. See *Dominguez v Superior Court* (1980) 101 CA3d 6, 161 CR 407 (requirements of Evid C §1043 were satisfied by discovery motion against city under former CCP §2034). Confidential examination of the records in camera is mandatory, and certain stale or remote matter, investigative conclusions, and information available from agency records other than individual personnel files, must be excluded. Evid C §1045(a)-(c). The court may make protective orders and must forbid use of the records outside court. Evid C §1045(d)-(e).

A party seeking disclosure of peace or custodial officer personnel files or of records of citizen complaints against peace or custodial officers must, when alleging excessive force by a peace officer during arrest of that party or conduct by custodial officer alleged to have occurred within a jail facility, include a copy of the police report of the circumstances of the arrest or a copy of the crime report of the circumstances of the conduct alleged to have occurred within a jail facility. Evid C §1046. Records of peace or custodial officers, including supervisorial officers, who either were not present during the arrest or had no contact with the party seeking disclosure, or who were not present at the time the conduct is alleged to have occurred at the jail facility, are not subject to disclosure. Evid C §1047. See §43.15.

§43.14   B. Burden of Proof

If the privilege is based on a statute (see §43.4), the claimant or party relying on the privilege has the burden of proving facts necessary to establish that the information claimed to be privileged is within the class of information protected by the statute. If the privilege requires the trial judge to balance the necessities for confidentiality and disclosure, the claimant or party relying on the privilege has the burden of proving the nature and extent of the public interest in confidentiality. On balancing necessities, see Evid C §1040(b)(2).

The opponent of the privilege (the proponent of the evidence) has the burden of proving the necessity for disclosure of the information in the interest of justice. This necessity may be based on the relevance and importance of the information as evidence in the case and the nonavailability of adequate substitute means of proof. The opponent of the privilege also has the burden of proving any contention that the privilege has been terminated or waived by official disclosure or consent to disclosure.

See Comment to Evid C §405 (burdens of proof on privileges).

§43.15   VII. STATUTES

Evidence Code §§1040, 1042-1045, referred to in these provisions as "this article," apply to the privilege for official information.

- Evidence Code §1040 states:

    (a) As used in this section, "official information" means information acquired in confidence by a public employee in the course of his or her duty and not open, or officially disclosed, to the public prior to the time the claim of privilege is made.

    (b) A public entity has a privilege to refuse to disclose official information, and to prevent another from disclosing official information, if the privilege is claimed by a person authorized by the public entity to do so and:

(1) Disclosure is forbidden by an act of the Congress of the United States or a statute of this state; or

(2) Disclosure of the information is against the public interest because there is a necessity for preserving the confidentiality of the information that outweighs the necessity for disclosure in the interest of justice; but no privilege may be claimed under this paragraph if any person authorized to do so has consented that the information be disclosed in the proceeding. In determining whether disclosure of the information is against the public interest, the interest of the public entity as a party in the outcome of the proceeding may not be considered.

- Evidence Code §1041, which pertains to the privilege for the identity of an informer, is set out in §44.12.

- Evidence Code §1042(a)-(b) states:

    (a) Except where disclosure is forbidden by an act of the Congress of the United States, if a claim of privilege under this article by the state or a public entity in this state is sustained in a criminal proceeding, the presiding officer shall make such order or finding of fact adverse to the public entity bringing the proceeding as is required by law upon any issue in the proceeding to which the privileged information is material.

    (b) Notwithstanding subdivision (a), where a search is made pursuant to a warrant valid on its face, the public entity bringing a criminal proceeding is not required to reveal to the defendant official information or the identity of an informer in order to establish the legality of the search or the admissibility of any evidence obtained as a result of it.

- Evidence Code §1042(c)-(d), which pertains to the privilege for the identity of an informer, is set out in §44.12.

- Evidence Code §1043 states:

    (a) In any case in which discovery or disclosure is sought of peace or custodial officer personnel records or records maintained pursuant to Section 832.5 of the Penal Code or information from those records, the party seeking the discovery or disclosure shall file a written motion with the appropriate court or administrative body upon written notice to the governmental agency which has custody and control of the records. The written notice shall be given at the times prescribed by subdivision (b) of Section 1005 of the Code of Civil Procedure. Upon receipt of the notice the governmental agency served shall immediately notify the individual whose records are sought.

    (b) The motion shall include all of the following:

        (1) Identification of the proceeding in which discovery or disclosure is sought, the party seeking discovery or disclosure, the peace or custodial officer whose records are sought, the governmental agency which has custody and control of the records, and

the time and place at which the motion for discovery or disclosure shall be heard.

(2) A description of the type of records or information sought.

(3) Affidavits showing good cause for the discovery or disclosure sought, setting forth the materiality thereof to the subject matter involved in the pending litigation and stating upon reasonable belief that the governmental agency identified has the records or information from the records.

(c) No hearing upon a motion for discovery or disclosure shall be held without full compliance with the notice provisions of this section except upon a showing by the moving party of good cause for noncompliance, or upon a waiver of the hearing by the governmental agency identified as having the records.

- Evidence Code §1044 states:

    Nothing in this article shall be construed to affect the right of access to records of medical or psychological history where such access would otherwise be available under Section 996 or 1016.

- Evidence Code §1045 states:

    (a) Nothing in this article shall be construed to affect the right of access to records of complaints, or investigations of complaints, or discipline imposed as a result of those investigations, concerning an event or transaction in which the peace officer or custodial officer, as defined in Section 831.5 of the Penal Code, participated, or which he or she perceived, and pertaining to the manner in which he or she performed his or her duties, provided that information is relevant to the subject matter involved in the pending litigation.

    (b) In determining relevance, the court shall examine the information in chambers in conformity with Section 915, and shall exclude from disclosure:

    (1) Information consisting of complaints concerning conduct occurring more than five years before the event or transaction that is the subject of the litigation in aid of which discovery or disclosure is sought.

    (2) In any criminal proceeding the conclusions of any officer investigating a complaint filed pursuant to Section 832.5 of the Penal Code.

    (3) Facts sought to be disclosed that are so remote as to make disclosure of little or no practical benefit.

    (c) In determining relevance where the issue in litigation concerns the policies or pattern of conduct of the employing agency, the court shall consider whether the information sought may be obtained from other records maintained by the employing agency in the regular course of agency business which would not necessitate the disclosure of individual personnel records.

(d) Upon motion seasonably made by the governmental agency which has custody or control of the records to be examined or by the officer whose records are sought, and upon good cause showing the necessity thereof, the court may make any order which justice requires to protect the officer or agency from unnecessary annoyance, embarrassment or oppression.

(e) The court shall, in any case or proceeding permitting the disclosure or discovery of any peace or custodial officer records requested pursuant to Section 1043, order that the records disclosed or discovered may not be used for any purpose other than a court proceeding pursuant to applicable law.

- Evidence Code §1046 states:

    In any case, otherwise authorized by law, in which the party seeking disclosure is alleging excessive force by a peace officer or custodial officer, as defined in Section 831.5 of the Penal Code, in connection with the arrest of that party or for conduct alleged to have occurred within a jail facility, the motion shall include a copy of the police report setting forth the circumstances under which the party was stopped and arrested, or a copy of the crime report setting forth the circumstances under which the conduct is alleged to have occurred within a jail facility.

- Evidence Code §1047 states:

    Records of peace officers or custodial officers, as defined in Section 831.5 of the Penal Code, including supervisorial peace officers, who either were not present during the arrest or had no contact with the party seeking disclosure from the time of the arrest until the time of booking, or who were not present at the time the conduct is alleged to have occurred within a jail facility, shall not be subject to disclosure.

§43.16   VIII. ILLUSTRATIONS OF PRIVILEGE

The privilege for official information may be available in the following situations:

- A police detective is asked the names of suspected participants in a criminal conspiracy who have not been indicted or charged.

- A county assessor is asked to produce a taxpayer's annual written property statement.

IX. STATING CLAIM OF PRIVILEGE

§43.17   A. By Witness

[Option 1: Witness is authorized to claim privilege]

Your Honor, on behalf of _ _[name of public entity]_ _, I claim the privilege for official information.

[Option 2: Witness is not authorized to claim privilege]

> Your Honor, that question calls for privileged official information held in confidence by _ _[name of public entity]_ _. I am not authorized to disclose it

[Add if appropriate]

without permission from _ _[name and title of authorized official]_ _.

§43.18 B. By Trial Counsel

Trial counsel should preferably make this statement outside the presence of the jury:

> Your Honor, that question calls for privileged official information held in confidence by _ _[name of public entity]_ _.

[Option 1: Counsel is authorized by public entity to claim privilege]

On its behalf, I claim the privilege for official information.

[Option 2: Public entity is not a party, and neither counsel nor witness is authorized to claim privilege (Evid C §916)]

I move that Your Honor exclude the information as privileged.

§43.19 X. MOTION FOR ORDER OR FINDING ADVERSE TO PROSECUTION

This motion, which is made by defense counsel in a criminal proceeding, should preferably be made outside the presence of the jury:

> Your Honor, I move that if you _ _[sustain this claim of privilege/exclude this information as privileged]_ _, you also _ _[describe appropriate finding or order to be made by judge, e.g., strike all the testimony of _ _[name]_]_ _. I also move that you admonish the jurors to disregard the stricken matter and to treat it as if they had never known it.

44
Privilege for Identity of Informer

I. NATURE OF PRIVILEGE §44.1

II. PRETRIAL PROCEDURES CONCERNING PRIVILEGE FOR IDENTITY OF INFORMER §44.2

III. PROCEDURES WHEN INFORMER PRIVILEGE ARISES DURING TRIAL
   A. Information From Informer
      1. Purported Disclosure of Law Violation §44.3
      2. Recipient of Information §44.4
      3. Confidentiality §44.5
   B. Grounds for Nondisclosure of Identity §44.6
   C. Who Can Claim §44.7
   D. Termination and Waiver §44.8
   E. Hearings and Ruling on Privilege
      1. Privilege Raised §44.9
      2. In-Camera Hearing; Final Hearing §44.10
      3. Burden of Proof §44.11

IV. STATUTES §44.12

V. ILLUSTRATIONS OF PRIVILEGE §44.13

VI. STATING CLAIM OF PRIVILEGE
   A. By Witness §44.14
   B. By Prosecutor §44.15

VII. DEFENSE COUNSEL'S MOTION FOR ORDER OR FINDING ADVERSE TO PROSECUTION §44.16

§44.1 I. NATURE OF PRIVILEGE

The privilege for identity of an informer prevents compulsory disclosure of the identity of a person who informs a law enforcement agency of an apparent violation of California or federal law. The privilege applies when disclosure is prohibited by a statute (Evid C §1041) or when the trial judge determines that the informer is a material witness on the issue of guilt who could give evidence that might exonerate the defendant (see Evid C §1042). See §§44.5–44.6. Only a public entity can claim the privilege. Evid C §1041(a); see §44.7.

The privilege for the identity of the informer is most commonly raised in criminal cases. It is usually litigated before trial because defense counsel is usually alerted to the existence of an informer in the affidavit to a search warrant in the case. See the overview of pretrial procedures for making the motion in criminal cases in §44.2.

The privilege for identity of an informer is distinct from the related privilege for official information. See Evid C §1040; chap 43. The use of either privilege against a defendant in a criminal proceeding sometimes subjects the prosecution to adverse consequences. See Evid C §1042. See also §§44.2, 44.9. For further discussion of the informer privilege, see California Criminal Law Procedure and Practice, chap 21 (7th ed Cal CEB 2004).

§44.2 II. PRETRIAL PROCEDURES CONCERNING PRIVILEGE FOR IDENTITY OF INFORMER

Defense counsel in a criminal case is usually alerted to the existence of an informer through reading the affidavit to a search warrant in the case. In that event, the defense makes a pretrial written motion to discover the identity of the informer. At the hearing on that motion, the prosecution may (a) concede the motion and disclose the identity of the informer or (b) oppose the motion. If the prosecution opposes the motion, it usually argues that the law as applied to the facts of the case does not require the informer's identity to be disclosed. *Twiggs v Superior Court* (1983) 34 C3d 360, 194 CR 152; *People v Otte* (1989) 214 CA3d 1522, 1535, 263 CR 393.

If the court rules against the defendant, that is the end of the matter. Evid C §1042(c). If the court finds a reasonable possibility that the informer is material on the issue of guilt and can give evidence that might exonerate the defendant, defense counsel should ask the court to order the prosecutor to disclose the informer's identity. *People v Rodgers* (1976) 54 CA3d 508, 517, 126 CR 719. The prosecution can then disclose the informer's identity or ask for an in camera hearing that excludes the defense (Evid C §1042(d)).

At the in camera hearing, the prosecution presents evidence to support a finding that nondisclosure would not deprive the defendant of a fair trial. *Williams v Superior Court* (1974) 38 CA3d 412, 112 CR 485. Following the in camera hearing, the court holds a hearing in open court at which it makes its ruling on the motion. If the court rules in favor of the defense, the prosecution can either disclose the informer's identity or refuse to disclose it. If the prosecution refuses disclosure, defense counsel should ask the court to dismiss all counts that depend on the informer's information. See Evid C §1042(a); *People v Rodgers, supra.*

III. PROCEDURES WHEN INFORMER PRIVILEGE ARISES DURING TRIAL

A. Information From Informer

§44.3 **1. Purported Disclosure of Law Violation**

The privilege protects an informer's identity only if he or she furnishes information purporting to disclose a violation of federal or California law. Evid C §1041(a). The California law may be either a law of the state (*e.g.,* a statute) or a law of a public entity within the state (*e.g.,* a city or county ordinance). For definitions, see Evid C §§160 ("law"), 200 ("public entity"), 230 ("statute").

§44.4 **2. Recipient of Information**

The privilege applies only if the informer furnishes the information for transmission to either a "law enforcement officer" (Evid C §1041(b)(1)) or "a representative of an administrative agency charged with the administration or enforcement of the law alleged to be violated . . ." (Evid C §1041(b)(2)). A law enforcement officer is a person designated by statute as a peace officer or having equivalent powers to make arrests. See, *e.g.,* Pen C §830.6 (reserve, auxiliary, or deputy officers); Pen C §§830.7, 831-831.5 (persons having powers of arrest); 18 USC §§3055-3056 and Pen C §830.8 (federal officials).

The powers of some types of peace officers may be limited to enforcement of particular laws or to other special situations. See, *e.g.,* Pen C §§830-830.5.

The requirement of Evid C §1041(b)(2) (covering information given to administrative agency representatives) that the recipient be charged with administering or enforcing the law alleged to be violated is inapplicable under Evid C §1041(b)(1) (covering information given to law enforcement officers). Thus, the privilege apparently can arise even when a law enforcement officer is informed of a violation beyond enforcement powers, *e.g.,* when a fish and game warden is informed of a conspiracy to rob a bank. See 6 Cal L Rev'n Comm'n Reps 258 (1964). Penal Code §830.1(b) classifies some officials having limited enforcement duties (*e.g.,* special agents and Attorney General investigators) as peace officers for all purposes, along with police officers, deputy sheriffs, and others.

The privilege applies whether the informer gives the information to a police officer or other qualified recipient directly or gives it to a go-between for transmittal to a qualified recipient. Evid C §1041(b)(3).

§44.5 **3. Confidentiality**

The privilege applies only if the informer furnishes the information "in confidence." Evid C §1041(b). The officer receiving the information must be under a duty not to reveal the informer's identity to the public. This duty may be based on a legal prohibition against disclosure or on a public interest in confidentiality. See §44.6.

The privilege cannot be used to prevent informers from disclosing their own identity (Evid C §1041(c)), but it can be used to prevent disclosure of their identity by any other person (Evid C §1041(a)).

§44.6   B. Grounds for Nondisclosure of Identity

If disclosure of the informer's identity is forbidden by an act of Congress or by a California statute or constitutional provision, the privilege must be sustained. Evid C §1041(a)(1). See Evid C §230 ("statute" includes constitutional provision). The privilege also must be sustained if it is based on a federal order or regulation that is authorized by federal statute or constitutional provision. See §43.4 (official information privilege).

A defendant who knows the identity of the informer will ordinarily not be prejudiced by a refusal to disclose that identity. *People v McShann* (1958) 50 C2d 802, 807, 330 P2d 33. See also *People v Hardeman* (1982) 137 CA3d 823, 829, 187 CR 296 (disclosure of informer's identity not required when defendant claimed that informer was one of a group on defendant's lawn, giving defendant right "as licensor or invitor" to subpoena members of group). The public entity's interest in the outcome of the proceeding in which the privilege is claimed (*e.g.,* in obtaining a conviction) cannot be weighed in favor of the privilege. Evid C §1041(a)(2).

§44.7   C. Who Can Claim

The holder of the privilege for identity of an informer may be any "public entity," *i.e.,* a domestic or foreign governmental body (Evid C §200). See §34.4 (meaning of "holder"). Because the privilege applies only if the informer has furnished information of a purported violation of federal or California law, the claimant will usually be either a federal entity or a state or local California entity. See Evid C §1041(a).

The privilege must be "claimed by a person authorized by the public entity to do so." Evid C §1041(a). If a public employee (*e.g.,* a police officer) is called as a witness and asked to disclose the identity of an informer, the employee may claim the privilege if the employee has authority to do so. The witness may be accompanied by an official or attorney who has this authority. See *People v Parham* (1963) 60 C2d 378, 33 CR 497 (subpoenaed FBI agent appeared with assistant United States attorney). If the public entity holding the privilege is a party, or has authorized a party (*e.g.,* the "People") to claim the privilege, the entity may make the claim through the prosecuting attorney. If neither the witness nor any party is authorized to claim the privilege, Evid C §916 may require the trial judge, on the judge's own motion or the motion of a party, to exclude the informer's identity from evidence as "information that is subject to a claim of privilege." Exclusion may be required, for example, if a witness is about to reveal the identity of an informer and the public entity holding the privilege is not represented in the proceeding.

Federal departmental regulations may channel all applications for official information to the head of the department to obtain approval for its release. A subordinate employee is entitled to refuse disclosure in reliance on such a regulation. See *U.S. ex rel Touhy v Ragen* (1951) 340 US 462, 95 L Ed 417, 71 S Ct 416 (Department of Justice); *People v Parham, supra*.

Only a public entity that is both a party and "the holder of the privilege" has standing to claim error if the privilege is erroneously disallowed. Evid C §918. See §33.21. Any holder, party or nonparty, may be entitled to an extraordinary writ as a remedy for erroneous denial of the privilege. See §§33.22-33.23.

§44.8   D. Termination and Waiver

Unless disclosure is forbidden by a federal or California statute, the privilege terminates when a person authorized to do so consents to disclosure of the informer's identity in the proceeding. Evid C §1041(a)(2). The authority for this disclosure presumably must come from the public entity that holds the privilege.

E. Hearings and Ruling on Privilege

§44.9   1. Privilege Raised

The burden is on the defense to demonstrate a reasonable possibility that the informer could give evidence on the issue of guilt that might result in the defendant's exoneration. *People v Borunda* (1974) 11 C3d 523, 527, 113 CR 825; *People v Hardeman* (1982) 137 CA3d 823, 828, 187 CR 296. It is easiest to show materiality when the informer was in a position to have observed the crime or some event related to it. The further removed the informer is from the scene of the crime, the less likely the informer will be considered a material witness. See *People v Hardeman, supra*. Defense counsel may be required to demonstrate "an articulable actual relationship" between the charged crime and the need for the informer's identity "as shown by the specific facts in evidence." 137 CA3d at 831. Even if not required, it is better practice for the defense to provide the judge with grounds for making a preliminary finding that the informer is a material witness on the issue of guilt.

If the defense meets this burden and the prosecutor refuses to disclose the informer's identity, the defendant should demand that the prosecutor elect between disclosure and an adverse order or finding under Evid C §1042(a). See *Coy v Superior Court* (1959) 51 C2d 471, 334 P2d 569; *People v Rodgers* (1976) 54 CA3d 508, 517, 126 CR 719.

If the public employee, usually a police officer, claims the privilege, the trial judge must first determine whether the privilege is properly claimed. The essential three elements to be considered are:

- Whether the officer received the information in the normal course of business, *i.e.,* whether the information is official (see Evid C §1040);

- Whether the information was received in confidence so that the informer clearly intended that the privilege be claimed (see Evid C §1041(b)); and

- Whether there is some interest at the time the privilege is claimed in maintaining confidentiality, *e.g.*, a risk of harm to the informer (see *People v Towler* (1982) 31 C3d 105, 116 n4, 181 CR 391) or to other current investigations.

§44.10   2. In-Camera Hearing; Final Hearing

If the defense succeeds in showing materiality, and the prosecution claims the privilege for identity of the informer, the prosecution should then request an in-camera hearing under Evid C §1042(d). The in-camera hearing may be held in chambers or in any other location where the informer's presence presumably will go unnoticed, *e.g.*, the district attorney's office, police station, or county jail. The only persons entitled to be present at the hearing are the judge, the court reporter, the prosecutor, the informer, and the law enforcement officer claiming the privilege. The defendant cannot demand that the informer be present at the hearing, but the prosecution should consider including the informer at the hearing because, without that testimony, the judge may compel disclosure because the informer could possibly give exonerating evidence.

An illustration of what may take place at an in-camera hearing follows. In this typical situation, the informer gave information leading to the obtaining of a search warrant. The defendant claims that the informer is a material witness on the issue of guilt (see §44.12):

- The judge or court reporter swears in the witnesses.

- The prosecutor calls the officer to testify and questions that person on the basis for the claim of privilege, *i.e.*, whether the officer obtained a signed warrant, whether the information that was the basis for the warrant was received from the informer in confidence, and whether there was a need to preserve that confidence. After the basis for the claim of privilege is established, the prosecutor asks the officer what information was received and asks the officer to identify whether the person present at the hearing was the informer who provided the information.

- The prosecutor calls the person identified by the officer as the informer to testify and asks the person's name and address. The prosecutor also asks whether the information in question was information given in confidence and whether there was a need to preserve that confidence (again showing the basis for the claim of privilege). The prosecutor then produces physical evidence (*e.g.*, a photograph of the defendant) to establish whether there is any relationship between the informer and the accused. For example, if the informer does not recognize the defendant, the informer is unlikely to be able to help the prosecutor on the issue of guilt.

- The better practice is for the prosecutor to conduct a full hearing on the extent of the informer's information about the defendant and the charged offense. Because of the rule requiring disclosure if there is a reasonable possibility that the informer is a material witness on the issue of guilt (*People v Borunda* (1974) 11 C3d 523, 527, 113 CR 825; §44.12), the prosecutor must show that the informer will help convict, rather than exonerate, the defendant. See, *e.g., People v McCarthy* (1978) 79 CA3d 547, 144 CR 822 (nondisclosure proper because informer's in-camera testimony was not exculpatory). A less than full hearing also exposes the prosecutor to the charge that the defendant was deprived of the constitutional right to a fair trial. To ensure a full hearing, the prosecutor should ask the informer any questions requested by the defendant or the court, *e.g.,* whether there is any information bearing on the defendant's proffered theory of how the informer is a material witness.

- At the in-camera hearing, the prosecutor should ask the court to state on the record whether the witnesses were credible and whether nondisclosure would deprive the defendant of a fair trial. See *People v Flannery* (1985) 164 CA3d 1112, 210 CR 899. One copy of the transcribed record of the hearing is sealed, together with any physical evidence produced at it, and delivered to the court in a sealed condition. The seal is not opened except on order of the court. Evid C §1042(d).

After the in-camera hearing is concluded, the court sets a date on which it will announce its ruling to the defense. Both parties are notified to attend. If the judge rules affirmatively, either the prosecutor discloses the informer's identity or the relevant counts of the information are dismissed (see §§44.2, 44.9).

§44.11   3. Burden of Proof

If the privilege is based on a statute or a federal regulation (see §44.6), the claimant or party relying on the privilege (usually the prosecution) has the burden of proving facts necessary to establish that disclosure of the informer's identity is within the prohibition of the statute or regulation. If the privilege requires the trial judge to balance the necessities for confidentiality and disclosure, the claimant or party relying on the privilege has the burden of proving the nature and extent of the public interest in confidentiality, *e.g.,* that disclosure of the informer's identity would subject the informant to acts of revenge or would cut off an important source of information to a police department. On balancing necessities, see Evid C §1041(a)(2).

The opponent of the privilege (usually a defendant seeking to interrogate the informer) has the burden of proving a reasonable possibility that nondisclosure of the informer's identity might deprive the defendant of a fair trial.

§44.12 IV. STATUTES

Evidence Code §§1041-1042 apply to the privilege for the identity of an informer.

- Evidence Code §1041 states:

    (a) Except as provided in this section, a public entity has a privilege to refuse to disclose the identity of a person who has furnished information as provided in subdivision (b) purporting to disclose a violation of a law of the United States or of this state or of a public entity in this state, and to prevent another from disclosing such identity, if the privilege is claimed by a person authorized by the public entity to do so and:

    (1) Disclosure is forbidden by an act of the Congress of the United States or a statute of this state; or

    (2) Disclosure of the identity of the informer is against the public interest because there is a necessity for preserving the confidentiality of his identity that outweighs the necessity for disclosure in the interest of justice; but no privilege may be claimed under this paragraph if any person authorized to do so has consented that the identity of the informer be disclosed in the proceeding. In determining whether disclosure of the identity of the informer is against the public interest, the interest of the public entity as a party in the outcome of the proceeding may not be considered.

    (b) This section applies only if the information is furnished in confidence by the informer to:

    (1) A law enforcement officer;

    (2) A representative of an administrative agency charged with the administration or enforcement of the law alleged to be violated; or

    (3) Any person for the purpose of transmittal to a person listed in paragraph (1) or (2).

    (c) There is no privilege under this section to prevent the informer from disclosing his identity.

- Evidence Code §1042 states:

    (a) Except where disclosure is forbidden by an act of the Congress of the United States, if a claim of privilege under this article by the state or a public entity in this state is sustained in a criminal proceeding, the presiding officer shall make such order or finding of fact adverse to the public entity bringing the proceeding as is required by law upon any issue in the proceeding to which the privileged information is material.

    (b) Notwithstanding subdivision (a), where a search is made pursuant to a warrant valid on its face, the public entity bringing a criminal proceeding is not required to reveal to the defendant official information or the identity of an informer in order to establish the legality of the search or the admissibility of any evidence obtained as a result of it.

(c) Notwithstanding subdivision (a), in any preliminary hearing, criminal trial, or other criminal proceeding, any otherwise admissible evidence of information communicated to a peace officer by a confidential informant, who is not a material witness to the guilt or innocence of the accused of the offense charged, is admissible on the issue of reasonable cause to make an arrest or search without requiring that the name or identity of the informant be disclosed if the judge or magistrate is satisfied, based upon evidence produced in open court, out of the presence of the jury, that such information was received from a reliable informant and in his discretion does not require such disclosure.

(d) When, in any such criminal proceeding, a party demands disclosure of the identity of the informant on the ground the informant is a material witness on the issue of guilt, the court shall conduct a hearing at which all parties may present evidence on the issue of disclosure. Such hearing shall be conducted outside the presence of the jury, if any. During the hearing, if the privilege provided for in Section 1041 is claimed by a person authorized to do so or if a person who is authorized to claim such privilege refuses to answer any question on the ground that the answer would tend to disclose the identity of the informant, the prosecuting attorney may request that the court hold an in camera hearing. If such a request is made, the court shall hold such a hearing outside the presence of the defendant and his counsel. At the in camera hearing, the prosecution may offer evidence which would tend to disclose or which discloses the identity of the informant to aid the court in its determination whether there is a reasonable possibility that nondisclosure might deprive the defendant of a fair trial. A reporter shall be present at the in camera hearing. Any transcription of the proceedings at the in camera hearing, as well as any physical evidence presented at the hearing, shall be ordered sealed by the court, and only a court may have access to its contents. The court shall not order disclosure, nor strike the testimony of the witness who invokes the privilege, nor dismiss the criminal proceeding, if the party offering the witness refuses to disclose the identity of the informant, unless, based upon the evidence presented at the hearing held in the presence of the defendant and his counsel and the evidence presented at the in camera hearing, the court concludes that there is a reasonable possibility that nondisclosure might deprive the defendant of a fair trial.

§44.13   V. ILLUSTRATIONS OF PRIVILEGE

The privilege for the identity of an informer may be available in the following situations:

- The defendant in a narcotics case asks the investigating police officer to name the person who told the police that the defendant was selling narcotics.

- After a police officer testifies to having received information from an FBI agent that the defendant participated in a bank robbery, the defendant subpoenas the FBI agent and asks who gave him that information.

VI. STATING CLAIM OF PRIVILEGE

§44.14   A. By Witness

[Option 1: Witness authorized to claim privilege]

Your Honor, on behalf of _ _[name of public entity]_ _, I claim the privilege for identity of an informer.

[Option 2: Witness authorized to claim privilege only with permission]

Your Honor, that question calls for privileged information on the identity of an informer held in confidence by _ _[name of public entity]_ _. I am not authorized to disclose it

[Add if appropriate]

without permission from _ _[name and title of authorized official]_ _.

§44.15   B. By Prosecutor

Your Honor, that question calls for privileged information on the identity of an informer held in confidence by _ _[name of public entity]_ _.

[Option 1: Counsel is authorized by public entity to claim privilege]

On its behalf, I claim the privilege for identity of an informer.

[Option 2: Public entity is not a party, and neither counsel nor witness is authorized to claim privilege (Evid C §916)]

I move that Your Honor exclude the information as privileged.

§44.16   VII. DEFENSE COUNSEL'S MOTION FOR ORDER OR FINDING ADVERSE TO PROSECUTION

Your Honor, I move that if you _ _[sustain this claim of privilege/exclude this information as privileged]_ _, you also _ _[describe appropriate finding or order to be made by judge]_ _.

45

Trade Secrets Privilege

I. NATURE OF PRIVILEGE §45.1

II. REQUIREMENTS
   A. Trade Secret §45.2
   B. Privilege Allowed Only if No Injustice Will Result §45.3

III. WHO MAY CLAIM §45.4

IV. TERMINATION AND WAIVER §45.5

V. RULING ON PRIVILEGE
   A. Procedure §45.6
   B. Burden of Proof §45.7

VI. STATUTE §45.8

VII. STATING CLAIM OF PRIVILEGE
   A. By Witness §45.9
   B. By Trial Counsel §45.10

§45.1 I. NATURE OF PRIVILEGE

A conditional privilege protects owners of trade secrets from compulsory disclosure of a secret if the disclosure would injure the owner's business and is not essential to a determination of the rights of the parties. Evid C §1060. The trade secrets privilege was recognized in *Willson v Superior Court* (1924) 66 CA 275, 225 P 881, and is reflected in the courts' statutory power to make protective orders against discovery of trade secrets. CCP §2019(d).

However, when a plaintiff's proper invocation of the trade secrets privilege prevents a defendant from examining the basis for the plaintiff's damage claim, the trial court may properly bar the plaintiff's damage evidence at trial. *Steiny & Co. v California Elect. Supply Co.* (2000) 79 CA4th 285, 288, 93 CR2d 920.

II. REQUIREMENTS

§45.2   A. Trade Secret

In 1984, the Uniform Trade Secrets Act was enacted in California as CC §§3426-3426.11. "Trade secret" is defined in CC §3426.1(d) as

> information, including a formula, pattern, compilation, program, device, method, technique, or process, that:
> (1) Derives independent economic value, actual or potential, from not being generally known to the public or to other persons who can obtain economic value from its disclosure or use; and
>
> (2) Is the subject of efforts that are reasonable under the circumstances to maintain its secrecy.

The privilege may apply to a secret formula, pattern, device, or compilation if it is used in the owner's business and enables the owner to obtain a competitive business advantage. Typical examples are customer lists, manufacturing processes, chemical formulas, and mechanical designs. To be protected, the trade secret must not be generally known or accessible to others in the trade. See *Uribe v Howie* (1971) 19 CA3d 194, 206, 96 CR 493; *Futurecraft Corp. v Clary Corp.* (1962) 205 CA2d 279, 289, 23 CR 198; Competitive Business Practices §§4.9, 4.37 (2d ed Cal CEB 1991); Trade Secrets Practice in California §4.2 (2d ed Cal CEB 1996). See also Pen C §499c(a)(3) (defining trade secret subject to theft); Govt C §6254.7(d) (defining trade secrets excluded from air pollution control data accessible to public).

Trade secret protection requires continuous use; involvement in a single business transaction is insufficient. *California Francisco Inv. Corp. v Vrionis* (1971) 14 CA3d 318, 322, 92 CR 201. Examples of information not considered to be trade secrets are terms of a secret bid for a contract, employee salaries, security investments, or the date for announcing new policy. 14 CA3d at 322.

A trade secret may be a process or device that is patentable, but patentability is not required for trade secret protection. *Rigging Int'l Maintenance Co. v Gwin* (1982) 128 CA3d 594, 613, 180 CR 451. In fact, patented ideas cannot be trade secrets. See *Sinclair v Aquarius Elec.* (1974) 42 CA3d 216, 223, 116 CR 654. Unlike a patent, a trade secret need not be novel or unanticipated by prior art; in the broad sense, it consists of any unpatented idea that may be used for industrial and commercial purposes. 42 CA3d at 222. A trade secret remains the private property of the owner until the owner discloses it. 42 CA3d at 223.

The court may consider the following factors in determining whether the privilege applies (*Uribe v Howie* (1971) 19 CA3d 194, 208, 96 CR 493):

- The extent to which the information is known outside the business;
- The extent to which the information is known by employees and others inside the business;
- The measures taken to protect the secrecy of the information;

- The value of the information to competitors as well as to the party;
- The expense and effort spent in developing the information; and
- The difficulty of duplicating the information by others.

§45.3   B. Privilege Allowed Only if No Injustice Will Result

The privilege is available only if its allowance "will not tend to conceal fraud or otherwise work injustice." Evid C §1060. If disclosure is essential to establish a party's substantive rights, the claim of privilege must be denied. See *Willson v Superior Court* (1924) 66 CA 275, 225 P 881 (plaintiff, injured from explosion of flare, was entitled to disclosure of secret formula for its manufacture). If a reasonable alternative means of proof not requiring disclosure is available, the privilege must be allowed. On the procedure for ruling on a claim of privilege, see §45.6.

§45.4   III. WHO MAY CLAIM

The privilege may be claimed by the owner of the trade secret (*i.e.,* the owner of the business in which the trade secret is used) or by the owner's agent or employee. Evid C §1060. The employee needs no authority to claim the privilege other than his or her status as an employee in the owner's business. Because only the owner is a holder of the privilege, the employee's claim is on the owner's behalf. See §33.4. A proper claim and allowance of the privilege entitles the owner "to refuse to disclose the secret and to prevent another from disclosing it." Evid C §1060.

An employee usually has not only a right but also a duty to claim the privilege because of the "implied obligation not to divulge or use confidential information which he acquires by reason of his employment." *By-Buk Co. v Printed Cellophane Tape Co.* (1958) 163 CA2d 157, 164, 329 P2d 147. See *Greenly v Cooper* (1978) 77 CA3d 382, 391, 143 CR 514; Competitive Business Practices §§4.20-4.21 (2d ed Cal CEB 1991). Because of this obligation, Evid C §1060 will probably be construed as empowering a former employee to claim the privilege for trade secrets learned during the former employee's employment.

If neither the witness nor any party has standing or authority to claim the privilege, Evid C §916 may require the trial judge to exclude the trade secret from evidence on the judge's own motion or on the motion of a party. See §§33.14-33.16.

§45.5   IV. TERMINATION AND WAIVER

The privilege is terminated when the information in question ceases to meet the qualifications for a trade secret. Thus, the owner of a trade secret waives the privilege if the owner permits the secret to become generally known or accessible to others in the trade. See §45.2. Disclosure by an agent or employee in violation of a duty to the owner (see §45.4) presumably does not waive the owner's right to claim the privilege, although the disclosure may lead to destruction of the trade secret by making it generally known. The privilege is held only by the owner, not by the agent or employee. See §33.4. For analogous provisions for waiver by holders of certain other privileges, see Evid C §912.

V. RULING ON PRIVILEGE

§45.6   A. Procedure

The privilege may be brought into question through a claim by the owner or an agent or employee or by a motion under Evid C §916. The existence and applicability of the privilege may then present questions of preliminary fact that must be heard and decided by the judge as an independent issue. Evid C §§400–402, 405. The parties may present evidence on these issues.

The court's ability to protect trade secrets is embodied in CC §3426.5, which provides:

> In an action under this title, a court shall preserve the secrecy of an alleged trade secret by reasonable means, which may include granting protective orders in connection with discovery proceedings, holding in-camera hearings, sealing the records of the action, and ordering any person involved in the litigation not to disclose an alleged trade secret without prior court approval.

If the judge cannot rule on the privilege without disclosure of the trade secret, the judge may require confidential disclosure in camera by either the witness or the person authorized to claim the privilege. No other person may be present. If the privilege is sustained, no person may disclose what was said in chambers unless an authorized person consents to such presence or disclosure. Evid C §915(b). See §33.17. For the text of Evid C §915(b), see §33.31. A trial judge may be reluctant to rely on this form of ex parte information to sustain the privilege unless adverse information (which the other side has no opportunity to present) would clearly not affect the ruling. If the judge remains in doubt, the court may determine that the privilege will be denied unless the claimant extends authority for confidential disclosure to certain persons, *e.g.*, a court-appointed expert (Evid C §730) or to opposing counsel under a pledge not to tell his or her client. The judge may also consider a partial allowance of the privilege, *e.g.*, in a products liability case, ordering disclosure of the ingredients but not the manufacturing process of the compound alleged to have caused the harm.

If the privilege is claimed by a party and the judge indicates that the privilege will be denied because all or part of the trade secret is essential to the opposing party's proof of a material issue, the claimant of the privilege may prefer to concede the issue rather than to disclose the trade secret. For example, the manufacturer of a cleaning compound may consider it so important not to reveal the formula to competitors that the manufacturer is willing to concede that use of the compound proximately caused a plaintiff's injury. If the claimant offers this concession, the privilege should be allowed because its allowance will no longer "work injustice." Evid C §1060.

§45.7 B. Burden of Proof

The claimant of the privilege has the burden of proving that the information in question qualifies as a trade secret (see §45.2). The claimant also may have the burden of proving matters that the trial judge determines cannot be decided without a confidential disclosure of the trade secret to the court (see §45.6). The opponent of the privilege (the proponent of the evidence) has the burden of proving that disclosure is essential to establishing the case. On the claimant's and opponent's respective burdens of proof, see Comments to Evid C §405.

§45.8 VI. STATUTE

The statutory basis for the trade secrets privilege is Evid C §1060, which states:

> If he or his agent or employee claims the privilege, the owner of a trade secret has a privilege to refuse to disclose the secret, and to prevent another from disclosing it, if the allowance of the privilege will not tend to conceal fraud or otherwise work injustice.

VII. STATING CLAIM OF PRIVILEGE

§45.9 A. By Witness

> Your Honor, I claim the privilege for trade secrets.

§45.10 B. By Trial Counsel

Trial counsel should preferably make this statement outside the presence of the jury:

> Your Honor, that question calls for disclosure of a privileged trade secret.
>
> [Option 1: Counsel represents party entitled to claim privilege]
>
> On behalf of _ _[name of party]_ _, I claim the privilege and object to the question on that ground.
>
> [Option 2: Witness owns trade secret and is not represented by counsel]
>
> I request that Your Honor advise the witness of _ _[his/her]_ _ right to refuse to answer on the ground of privilege.

[Option 3: Witness is agent or employee of
owner of trade secret]

I request that Your Honor advise the witness of _ _[his/her]_ _ right and duty to refuse to answer on the ground of privilege.

[Option 4: Neither witness nor party can
claim privilege (Evid C §916)]

I move that Your Honor exclude the answer as privileged.

46

Privilege Against Self-Incrimination

I. SCOPE OF CHAPTER §46.1

II. NATURE AND CONSTITUTIONAL BASIS §46.2

III. REQUIREMENTS
    A. Demand for Testimony or Communication Belonging to Witness §46.3
    B. Criminal Penalties Threatened §46.4
    C. Connection Between Evidence and Punishable Act §46.5

IV. WRITINGS THAT QUALIFY §46.6

V. CLAIM OF PRIVILEGE
    A. Who Can Claim §46.7
    B. Form of Claim §46.8
    C. When to Raise Privilege; Questioning Before Jury §46.9
    D. Court's Duty to Warn Unrepresented Witness of Privilege §46.10

VI. RESPONSES OF PARTY OPPOSING PRIVILEGE IN CIVIL CASE §46.11

VII. RULE AGAINST COMMENT ON OR INFERENCE FROM EXERCISE OF PRIVILEGE §46.12

VIII. TERMINATION OF PRIVILEGE
    A. Prosecution Barred §46.13
    B. Immunity
        1. Principal Immunity Provisions §46.14
            a. Transactional and Use Immunity in Criminal Proceedings §46.15
            b. Immunity in Civil Cases §46.16
        2. Other Immunity Provisions §46.17
        3. Criminal Defense Witness Immunity §46.18
    C. Waiver §46.19

IX. BURDEN OF PROOF AND RULING; WRIT REVIEW §46.20

X. STATING CLAIM OF PRIVILEGE AGAINST SELF-INCRIMINATION §46.21

§46.1 I. SCOPE OF CHAPTER

This chapter discusses the privilege of a person, other than a criminal defendant, to refuse to give self-incriminating testimony or to produce self-incriminating communications in any civil or criminal proceeding. See chap 47 for discussion of the privilege of the defendant in a criminal proceeding not to be called as a witness and not to testify.

The privilege against self-incrimination and the constitutional right to counsel form the basis for rules excluding from evidence in criminal proceedings the statements that a defendant made during in-custody interrogation without first being adequately warned of his or her constitutional rights. *Miranda v Arizona* (1966) 384 US 436, 16 L Ed 2d 694, 86 S Ct 1602; *Dickerson v U.S.* (2000) 530 US 428, 147 L Ed 2d 405, 120 S Ct 2326 (reaffirming *Miranda*). For further discussion, see California Criminal Law Procedure and Practice, chap 30 (7th ed Cal CEB 2004); 2 Witkin, California Evidence, chap IX, *Witnesses* (4th ed 2000).

California rules relating to self-incrimination in criminal discovery were drastically changed by the passage of Proposition 115. See *Izazaga v Superior Court* (1991) 54 C3d 356, 285 CR 231. See also Crim Law, chap 11.

§46.2   II. NATURE AND CONSTITUTIONAL BASIS

The Fifth Amendment to the United States Constitution provides that "no person . . . shall be compelled in any criminal case to be a witness against himself." The privilege against self-incrimination entitles witnesses to refuse to give testimony or evidence (*e.g.*, documents) that may tend to incriminate them. *U.S. v White* (1944) 322 US 694, 699, 88 L Ed 1542, 1546, 64 S Ct 1248. Because this privilege applies any time the witness is placed in peril of incrimination, it may be invoked even if the incriminatory material is not true. The privilege does not apply, however, to evidence that is not "of a testimonial or communicative nature" (*Schmerber v California* (1966) 384 US 757, 761, 16 L Ed 2d 908, 914, 86 S Ct 1826; §46.6) or to corporations or other collective entities (*Bellis v U.S.* (1974) 417 US 85, 40 L Ed 2d 678, 94 S Ct 2179; *U.S. v White, supra*).

Evidence Code §§940 and 404 govern the privilege against self-incrimination:

- Under Evid C §940, a person has a privilege, to the extent that such a privilege exists under the federal or state constitution, to refuse to disclose any matter that may tend to incriminate him or her.

- Under Evid C §404, whenever the proffered evidence is claimed to be privileged under Evid C §940, the person claiming the privilege has the burden of showing that the proffered evidence might tend to incriminate him or her. The proffered evidence is inadmissible unless it clearly appears to the court that the proffered evidence cannot possibly tend to incriminate the person claiming the privilege.

Federal standards govern the privilege against self-incrimination in state courts as well as in federal courts because the Fourteenth Amendment to the

United States Constitution requires the states to enforce the privilege provided by the Fifth Amendment. *Malloy v Hogan* (1964) 378 US 1, 12 L Ed 2d 653, 84 S Ct 1489. Federal rules concerning the judicially created remedy of the exclusion of statements taken in violation of *Miranda* apply in California state criminal cases. *People v May* (1988) 44 C3d 309, 243 CR 369.

The following examples illustrate questions to which the privilege may apply:

- A district attorney asks a nonimmunized witness before the grand jury whether she owned the gun previously identified as the murder weapon.

- In a civil action for damages from an automobile accident, the plaintiff's attorney asks the defendant driver how much he had to drink before the accident.

Although the privilege to refuse to testify applies only to the accused in criminal cases, the privilege to refuse to disclose self-incriminating information is available to witnesses in both criminal and civil proceedings. *Kastigar v U.S.* (1972) 406 US 441, 32 L Ed 2d 212, 92 S Ct 1653. For example, the privilege against self-incrimination may be asserted during civil depositions (*Shepherd v Superior Court* (1976) 17 C3d 107, 130 CR 257), State Bar disciplinary proceedings (*Segretti v State Bar* (1976) 15 C3d 878, 886, 126 CR 793 (rule stated, but prior immunized testimony before a United States Senate committee admitted because State Bar disciplinary proceedings not criminal)), civil commitment hearings (*Cramer v Tyars* (1979) 23 C3d 131, 138, 151 CR 653), hearings before the Commission on Judicial Performance (*McComb v Superior Court* (1977) 68 CA3d 89, 137 CR 233), investigative hearings conducted by the Director of Agriculture (*Fielder v Berkeley Props. Co.* (1972) 23 CA3d 30, 99 CR 791), and hearings to commit a person who is in imminent danger of becoming a narcotics addict (*People v Whelchel* (1967) 255 CA2d 455, 63 CR 258).

III. REQUIREMENTS

§46.3   A. Demand for Testimony or Communication Belonging to Witness

The privilege against self-incrimination applies to testimony that may incriminate a witness. The privilege does not apply to testimony that may incriminate others (*e.g.,* friends or relatives; see Evid C §918), although this testimony may be covered by other privileges. Similarly, documents are not protected unless they are held by the person they might incriminate. See *U.S. v Helina* (9th Cir 1977) 549 F2d 713.

If documents sought from witnesses may tend to incriminate them but are held by them only in a representative capacity (*e.g.,* as an officer of a corporation or an association), the privilege does not exempt them from being compelled to produce the documents (see *Braswell v U.S.* (1988) 487 US 99, 101 L Ed 2d 98, 108 S Ct 2284; *Bellis v U.S.* (1974) 417 US 85, 40 L

Ed 2d 678, 94 S Ct 2179; *Curcio v U.S.* (1957) 354 US 118, 1 L Ed 2d 1225, 77 S Ct 1145; *DeCamp v First Kensington Corp.* (1978) 83 CA3d 268, 280, 147 CR 869) but may entitle them to refuse to testify to the contents or whereabouts of the documents (see *Fisher v U.S.* (1976) 425 US 391, 412 n12, 48 L Ed 2d 39, 57 n12, 96 S Ct 1569). Note that other privileges (*e.g.,* the attorney-client privilege) may protect them.

In *Federal Sav. & Loan Ins. Corp. v Rodrigues* (ND Cal 1988) 717 F Supp 1424, the court held that the required records exception to the Fifth Amendment to the United States Constitution applied to an individual's income tax records subpoenaed by the Federal Savings and Loan Insurance Corporation in an investigation of whether conflict-of-interest regulations had been violated.

When business records have been voluntarily prepared, the Fifth Amendment privilege against self-incrimination does not apply to the content of the records, but when the act of producing the records requires testimonial self-incrimination, the privilege applies to that act. *U.S. v Doe* (1984) 465 US 605, 79 L Ed 2d 552, 104 S Ct 1237. When documents that provide evidence of the commission of a crime (*e.g.,* a diary or letters voluntarily created by a defendant) are obtained by the prosecution by means that do not involve testimonial self-incrimination of the defendant, the privilege does not apply. *People v Sanchez* (1994) 24 CA4th 1012, 30 CR2d 111.

§46.4   B. Criminal Penalties Threatened

The privilege against self-incrimination is available if the testimony or evidence might subject the witness to any form of criminal or quasi-criminal penalty. Thus, the privilege protects the witness from being compelled to furnish evidence that might lead to any of the following forms of incrimination:

- Prosecution for a crime. See *People v Coleman* (1975) 13 C3d 867, 876, 120 CR 384.

- Punishment for contempt. See *In re Leainitt* (1959) 174 CA2d 535, 345 P2d 75 (questions about witness's default under alimony judgment).

- A civil action by the government for a penalty or forfeiture of a criminal nature. See *U.S. v U.S. Coin & Currency* (1971) 401 US 715, 28 L Ed 2d 434, 91 S Ct 1041.

- Juvenile delinquency proceedings under Welf & I C §602. See *In re Gault* (1967) 387 US 1, 49, 18 L Ed 2d 527, 558, 87 S Ct 1428.

The criminal or quasi-criminal prosecution need not be imminent. A claim of privilege is proper unless it is "perfectly clear" that the witness's answer "cannot possibly" incriminate him or her. *Hoffman v U.S.* (1951) 341 US 479, 486, 95 L Ed 1118, 71 S Ct 814; *Prudhomme v Superior Court* (1970) 2 C3d 320, 326, 85 CR 129; *Cohen v Superior Court* (1959) 173 CA2d 61, 68, 343 P2d 286. The privilege does not entitle a witness to withhold evidence because of possible incrimination of a third person. See §46.7.

The privilege does not protect a witness from many of the possible extra judicial effects of exercising the privilege, *e.g.,* loss of employment. See *Coleman v Galinin* (1947) 78 CA2d 313, 177 P2d 606. The United States Supreme Court, however, has restricted the operation of statutes providing for the discharge of public employees who exercise the privilege. See *Garrity v New Jersey* (1967) 385 US 493, 17 L Ed 2d 562, 87 S Ct 616 (grand jury testimony of police officers who under statute would have lost their jobs if they remained silent held inadmissible against them in subsequent prosecution). See also *Gardner v Broderick* (1968) 392 US 273, 20 L Ed 2d 1082, 88 S Ct 1913 (police officer before grand jury can be fired for refusing to testify about performance of his duties but cannot be fired for refusing to waive *Garrity* immunity); *Williams v City of Los Angeles* (1988) 47 C3d 195, 252 CR 817 (police officer discipline). In *Spevack v Klein* (1967) 385 US 511, 514, 17 L Ed 2d 574, 577, 87 S Ct 625, the court held that it was unconstitutional to impose on an attorney "the dishonor of disbarment and the deprivation of a livelihood as a price for asserting" the privilege in a disciplinary proceeding against him.

The privilege protects a witness in a California court against incrimination under either California or federal law. For example, the witness's privilege can be based on a possibility of prosecution for falsifying a federal income tax return. In a federal court, the privilege protects witnesses against incrimination under either federal law or the law of any state. *Murphy v Waterfront Comm'n* (1964) 378 US 52, 75, 12 L Ed 2d 678, 693, 84 S Ct 1594, overruled on other grounds in *U.S. v Balsys* (1998) 524 US 666, 688, 141 L Ed 2d 575, 118 S Ct 2218. The privilege probably also protects a witness in a California court against incrimination under the law of a sister state. The privilege does not extend to protection from fear of a foreign prosecution. *U.S. v Balsys* (1998) 524 US 666, 141 L Ed 2d 575, 118 S Ct 2218.

The United States Supreme Court held that the privilege against self-incrimination under the Fifth Amendment to the United States Constitution does not apply when a probationer reveals incriminating information to a probation officer instead of timely asserting the Fifth Amendment privilege. See *Minnesota v Murphy* (1984) 465 US 420, 79 L Ed 2d 409, 104 S Ct 1136. The rule is the same in California. *People v Pacchioli* (1992) 9 CA4th 1331, 1340, 12 CR2d 156; *People v Goodner* (1992) 7 CA4th 1324, 1332, 9 CR2d 543. The court in *Murphy* found that, unlike the defendant in *Garrity v New Jersey, supra,* the defendant in *Murphy* did not reasonably fear that a penalty would have been imposed had he exercised his privilege against self-incrimination.

§46.5   C. Connection Between Evidence and Punishable Act

Evidence is incriminatory, for the purpose of the privilege, not only if it could support a conviction of the witness but also if it could furnish a link in the chain of evidence necessary to establish guilt. The privilege must be sustained if there is any possibility that the evidence that the witness is asked to furnish (*e.g.,* a responsive answer to the question asked) would tend to incriminate him or her. Even the seemingly harmless question, "Do you know Mr. X?," may be incriminatory by this test. *Malloy v Hogan* (1964) 378 US 1, 11, 12 L Ed 2d 653, 661, 84 S Ct 1489; *Cohen v Superior Court* (1959) 173 CA2d 61, 343 P2d 286.

A claim of incrimination was deemed trifling and speculative, however, when it involved questions about criminal conduct that was apparently barred in a criminal prosecution by the statute of limitations. A claim that the criminal conduct might be used as "other crimes" evidence (see Evid C §1101(b)) was deemed too remote. *Blackburn v Superior Court* (1993) 21 CA4th 414, 27 CR2d 204.

The judge's determination of whether the evidence might tend to incriminate the witness is governed by Evid C §404, discussed in §46.20.

§46.6 IV. WRITINGS THAT QUALIFY

In general, the privilege against self-incrimination does not apply to records and reports that a witness is required, by regulatory statute, to keep and to disclose for enforcement purposes. *Craib v Bulmash* (1989) 49 C3d 475, 261 CR 686; *De la Cruz v Quackenbush* (2000) 80 CA4th 775, 784, 96 CR2d 92. This is commonly called the "required records doctrine." However, some regulatory statutes that require the submission of information that might subject the person making the submission to prosecution have been invalidated by the constitutional protection against self-incrimination. See *Marchetti v U.S.* (1968) 390 US 39, 19 L Ed 2d 889, 88 S Ct 697 (registration and taxation of gambling activities); *Albertson v Subversive Activities Control Bd.* (1965) 382 US 70, 15 L Ed 2d 165, 86 S Ct 194 (registration of Communist Party members); Note, *Self-Incrimination and the Federal Excise Tax on Wagering*, 76 Yale LJ 839 (1967). Statutes other than the Evidence Code may protect such records if they are disclosed in confidence to a government official. See §43.7 (tax returns). Note that when tax records are conveyed to a tax preparer or attorney, the records may be subject to subpoena. See *Fisher v U.S.* (1976) 425 US 391, 48 L Ed 2d 39, 96 S Ct 1569. See also CCP §1985.3 (subpoena duces tecum and motion to quash procedure for production of personal records of consumers, *e.g.,* bank and telephone company records).

The California Supreme Court fashioned a judicial remedy to allow continued enforcement of Veh C §20002 (requiring information after causing property damage with a vehicle) and yet protect citizens from incriminating themselves. The court ruled that citizens who comply with Veh C §20002 automatically have use immunity (discussed in §46.15) for communications required by that statute. *Byers v Justice Court* (1969) 71 C2d 1039, 1050, 80 CR 553, vacated on other grounds (1971) 402 US 424, 29 L Ed 2d 9, 91 S Ct 1535.

Statutes that require individuals to give evidence that is not of a testimonial or communicative nature do not require "self-incrimination." *U.S. v Dionisio* (1973) 410 US 1, 6, 35 L Ed 2d 67, 74, 93 S Ct 764; *Schmerber v California*

(1966) 384 US 757, 761, 16 L Ed 2d 908, 914, 86 S Ct 1826. One example of such a statute is Veh C §13353, which provides for suspension or revocation of the driver's license for refusal to take a blood, urine, or breath test. See *Quintana v Municipal Court* (1987) 192 CA3d 361, 365, 237 CR 397 (defendant's refusal to submit to blood-alcohol test not protected by self-incrimination privilege).

The following also do not violate the privilege against self-incrimination:

- Compulsory physical testing, *i.e.*, "field sobriety tests." See *Whalen v Municipal Court* (1969) 274 CA2d 809, 79 CR 523; §§46.14-46.17 (statutes that compel testimony after grants of immunity).

- Voice identification testimony not protected by self-incrimination privilege. See *People v Ellis* (1966) 65 C2d 529, 533, 55 CR 385.

- Nontestimonial, physical evidence such as a defendant's appearance as manifested in a lineup. See *U.S. v Wade* (1967) 388 US 218, 221, 18 L Ed 2d 1149, 1153, 87 S Ct 1926. Evidence of a defendant's refusal to participate in a lineup is admissible at trial. *People v Johnson* (1992) 3 C4th 1183, 1221, 14 CR2d 702; *People v Huston* (1989) 210 CA3d 192, 216, 258 CR 393 (defendant's refusal was no more or less probative because attorney misled him as to its appropriateness); *People v Smith* (1970) 13 CA3d 897, 910, 91 CR 786 (defendant's refusal, during show-up at police station, to don jacket and cap allegedly worn by robber not protected by self-incrimination privilege).

V. CLAIM OF PRIVILEGE

§46.7   A. Who Can Claim

The privilege against self-incrimination may be claimed only by the witness or by the witness and the attorney who personally represents the witness in the proceeding. *Fisher v U.S.* (1976) 425 US 391, 404, 48 L Ed 2d 39, 52, 96 S Ct 1569; *In re Marcario* (1970) 2 C3d 329, 85 CR 135. See also *Robinson v McAbee* (1923) 64 CA 709, 222 P 871 (witness claimed privilege through own attorney, who represented no party at trial; validity of claim not determined on appeal).

Counsel for a party may request the trial judge to advise a nonparty witness of his or her rights under the privilege (see §33.8; *People v Warren* (1984) 161 CA3d 961, 967, 207 CR 912), but a party cannot predicate error on a ruling that compels a nonparty to testify after making a valid claim of the privilege (see *Robinson v McAbee, supra*). Only a holder of the privilege may predicate error on a ruling disallowing the claim. Evid C §918; *People v Wheeler* (1966) 243 CA2d 340, 52 CR 508. See also §34.21.

The privilege cannot be claimed on behalf of a corporation, partnership, labor union, or other organization of an institutional or impersonal nature. *Braswell v U.S.* (1988) 487 US 99, 104, 101 L Ed 2d 98, 106, 108 S Ct

2284; *U.S. v White* (1944) 322 US 694, 88 L Ed 1542, 64 S Ct 1248. See also §46.3 on corporations and associations.

§46.8   B. Form of Claim

The federal and state constitutional bases for the privilege against self-incrimination are somewhat different. See §46.2. The surest way to preserve both federal and state rights is to refer expressly to the privilege against self-incrimination granted by the Fifth and Fourteenth Amendments to the United States Constitution and Cal Const art I, §15. An attorney stating or supporting a claim of privilege should expressly refer to these constitutional provisions. Less formality may be required of a lay witness. In *Malloy v Hogan* (1964) 378 US 1, 3, 12 L Ed 2d 653, 662, 84 S Ct 1489, the United States Supreme Court granted federal relief to a witness who, in a court of a state (Connecticut) having its own privilege against self-incrimination, refused to answer certain questions simply "on the ground it may tend to incriminate me." This form of claim also appears sufficient under Evid C §§404, 940.

The Evidence Code may provide a witness with the following way to claim the privilege without indicating that the witness fears self-incrimination: "I decline to answer on the grounds stated in Section 940 of the Evidence Code." Such a statement seems appropriate even though its legal sufficiency has not yet been tested. Concealing from the jury the exact ground of the witness's refusal to answer is consistent with the policy, underlying Evid C §913 and the *Griffin* rule (see *Griffin v California* (1965) 380 US 609, 14 L Ed 2d 106, 85 S Ct 1229), of not permitting the jury to draw unfavorable inferences from the exercise of the privilege. The statement's reference to Evid C §940 would fully inform the judge of the exact privilege being claimed, while ensuring that the jury is not influenced. Because Evid C §940 expressly refers to both the United States and California Constitutions, the statement seems sufficient to invoke both federal and state grounds.

See §46.21 for the exact form of the claim. On the burden of proof and ruling, see §46.20.

§46.9   C. When to Raise Privilege; Questioning Before Jury

The witness who wishes to refuse to answer questions based on the privilege against self-incrimination may raise the privilege out of the presence of the jury or may assert it in response to questions on the witness stand. It is preferable, however, for the court to determine outside the jury's presence whether the privilege against self-incrimination applies. See *People v Hill* (1992) 3 C4th 959, 991, 13 CR2d 475, overruled on other grounds in *Price v Superior Court* (2001) 25 C4th 1046, 1069 n13, 108 CR2d 409; *People v Brown* (1971) 14 CA3d 334, 339, 92 CR 370. The court may also determine the applicability of the privilege at an in limine hearing. *People v Johnson* (1974) 39 CA3d

749, 114 CR 545 (disapproving dictum to the contrary in *People v Chandler* (1971) 17 CA3d 798, 95 CR 146).

The witness cannot rely on a pretrial claim of the privilege but must also appear and assert the privilege at trial. *People v Frohner* (1976) 65 CA3d 94, 105, 135 CR 153.

A witness intending to claim the privilege against self-incrimination cannot make a blanket refusal to answer any questions on the ground of the privilege. The privilege must be asserted for each question asked unless the court determines that the witness can properly invoke the privilege concerning all questions that relate to a particular event or matter. *People v Cornejo* (1979) 92 CA3d 637, 658, 155 CR 238. See also *People v Hill, supra.*

When a witness able to claim the privilege against self-incrimination is to be granted immunity (see §§46.14–46.17), the privilege must be claimed either for each question or for each general area specified in the immunity order. Immunity for one question ordinarily removes the need to assert the privilege for other questions on the same subject because immunity under Pen C §1324 extends to use of "testimony or other information compelled under the order or any information directly or indirectly derived from" that testimony or information, and immunity under Pen C §1324.1 extends to any fact or act concerning which the witness is required to testify or produce evidence. See *People v Keller* (1963) 212 CA2d 210, 219, 27 CR 805.

§46.10 D. Court's Duty to Warn Unrepresented Witness of Privilege

Judges in civil and criminal cases are required to advise unrepresented witnesses of the privilege against self-incrimination. See *People v Thomas* (1974) 43 CA3d 862, 118 CR 226 (inquiry mandated only when criminal defendant is unrepresented; in this case, defendant was represented by counsel). See also *People v Schroeder* (1991) 227 CA3d 784, 278 CR 237 (intimidation of witness when judge argued that witness, who was willing to waive, should take privilege against self-incrimination); *People v Superior Court* (Barker) (1965) 232 CA2d 178, 42 CR 651 (judge in criminal case erroneously ordered witness not to answer questions even though witness waived privilege; court may admonish witness but may not forbid witness to testify).

On a criminal defendant's right not to be called as a witness and not to testify, see chap 47.

§46.11 VI. RESPONSES OF PARTY OPPOSING PRIVILEGE IN CIVIL CASE

A plaintiff in a civil action does not waive the privilege against self-incrimination by filing a lawsuit placing the plaintiff's own conduct at issue. In California state courts, however, if the plaintiff invokes the privilege, the defendant may request dismissal of the action. *Fremont Indem. Co. v Superior*

Court (1982) 137 CA3d 554, 187 CR 137 (plaintiff who brought lawsuit against insurer to recover under fire insurance policy was then charged with arson and refused to answer any deposition questions until after completion of criminal case; appellate court ordered plaintiff to answer questions and ordered trial court to dismiss case if plaintiff failed to do so); *Newson v City of Oakland* (1974) 37 CA3d 1050, 112 CR 890 (personal injury case in which plaintiff invoked privilege at trial when asked to produce income tax returns; court of appeal ruled that plaintiff would have to either withdraw his claim for lost earnings or waive his privilege).

In federal court cases involving loss of a professional license or of employment, it has been argued that dismissals against parties because they invoked the privilege against self-incrimination are a form of penalty burdening the exercise of a constitutional right and are therefore available only as a last resort, based on *Spevack v Klein* (1967) 385 US 511, 17 L Ed 2d 574, 87 S Ct 625 (attorney cannot be disbarred for invoking privilege during a disciplinary hearing), and *Garrity v New Jersey* (1967) 385 US 493, 17 L Ed 2d 562, 87 S Ct 616 (police officers cannot be fired for claiming privilege during departmental investigation). See *Wehling v Columbia Broadcasting Sys.* (5th Cir 1979) 608 F2d 1084, 1087 (remedies less burdensome than dismissal should be tried first); *Campbell v Gerrans* (9th Cir 1979) 592 F2d 1054 (dismissal was abuse of discretion). This issue remains unsettled in the federal courts. See *Mertsching v U.S.* (D Colo 1982) 547 F Supp 124, aff'd without published opinion (10th Cir 1983) 716 F2d 907 (citing split in authorities). See generally Comment, *Plaintiff as Deponent: Invoking the Fifth Amendment*, 48 U Chi L Rev 158 (1981).

If a witness invoking the Fifth Amendment to the United States Constitution has testified in an earlier hearing and is a party to the action, counsel can introduce the earlier testimony as:

- Former testimony recorded because the witness is unavailable (see Evid C §1291; *People v Maxwell* (1979) 94 CA3d 562, 569, 156 CR 630 (preliminary examination testimony of victim in criminal case read to jury));

- As an admission (Evid C §§1220 (statement of party offered against him or her), 1204 (constitutional requirements for introduction of statements of criminal defendant); see *People v Dub* (1930) 110 CA 631, 637, 294 P 496 (preliminary examination testimony admitted as admission); *People v Canard* (1967) 257 CA2d 444, 465, 65 CR 15 (grand jury testimony wrongfully admitted as admission; testimony was coerced));

- As a statement against penal interests (Evid C §1230; *People v Coble* (1976) 65 CA3d 187, 135 CR 199, disapproved on other grounds in 61 CA4th at 969 (uncharged accomplice statement improperly admitted)).

The trier of fact may not be asked to draw an unfavorable inference when a civil litigant, whether a plaintiff or defendant, invokes the privilege against self-incrimination. See Comment to Evid C §913. The rule is to the contrary in the federal courts. See *Baxter v Palmigiano* (1976) 425 US 308, 318, 47 L Ed 2d 810, 821, 96 S Ct 1551 ("Fifth Amendment does not forbid adverse inferences against parties to civil actions when they refuse to testify in response to probative evidence offered against them"). See also *Shepherd v Superior Court* (1976) 17 C3d 107, 117, 130 CR 257.

The opposing party in California state court may move to strike the entire testimony of a witness who answers questions concerning aspects of a case but refuses to answer others based on the privilege against self-incrimination. See *Newson v City of Oakland* (1974) 37 CA3d 1050, 1056, 112 CR 890.

A possible sanction against civil parties who invoke the privilege during pretrial discovery is to preclude them from testifying at trial about the matters for which the privilege was asserted. See *A&M Records, Inc. v Heilman* (1977) 75 CA3d 554, 142 CR 390 (defendant asserted privilege).

§46.12 VII. RULE AGAINST COMMENT ON OR INFERENCE FROM EXERCISE OF PRIVILEGE

If the privilege against self-incrimination is exercised by a witness, counsel cannot comment on that fact, no presumption arises from it, and the trier of fact must not draw any adverse inference. Evid C §913; *In re Scott* (2003) 29 C4th 783, 816, 129 CR2d 605. The trial judge is also prohibited from comment, except that on the request of any party who would be adversely affected by an unfavorable inference, the trial judge must instruct the jury that no presumption arises from the exercise of the privilege and that the jury may draw no inference from it. Evid C §913. This rule against comment or inference applies in civil as well as criminal cases. See Comment to Evid C §913.

Section 913 prohibits comment on and inference from a witness's exercise of the privilege against self-incrimination on a past occasion as well as during a current or pending proceeding. For example, a witness who chooses to testify at trial cannot be impeached by showing that he or she claimed the privilege when asked the same questions in an earlier proceeding. See Comment to Evid C §913.

In prohibiting comment on an exercise of the privilege, Evid C §913 is not intended to deny counsel the freedom to comment on an adverse party's failure to produce the strongest evidence available to him or her (Evid C §412) or failure to explain or deny the evidence against him or her (Evid C §413). See Comments to Evid C §§412, 913. See also *Griffin v California* (1965) 380 US 609, 14 L Ed 2d 106, 85 S Ct 1229 (improper for prosecutor to comment on defendant's failure to testify); *Doe v Glanzer* (9th Cir 2000) 232 F3d 1258, 1264 (court properly denied admission of defendant's alleged invocation of privilege during deposition, preventing jury from drawing negative inference).

VIII. TERMINATION OF PRIVILEGE

§46.13 A. Prosecution Barred

There is no privilege against self-incrimination when the witness has an absolute defense to any incrimination to which the witness might be exposed, *e.g.,* if the statute of limitations has run or the witness has already been convicted, acquitted, put in jeopardy, or accepted a pardon for all crimes with which the evidence might connect him or her. See *In re Cohen* (1894) 104 C 524, 528, 38 P 364. On statutes of limitations, see Pen C §§799–803; California Criminal Law Procedure and Practice §14.13 (7th ed Cal CEB 2004). On defense of former jeopardy, see 1 Witkin & Epstein, California Criminal Law, *Defenses* §§103–187 (3d ed 2000). The privilege still exists after a conviction, however, if the case is on appeal. *People v Lopez* (1980) 110 CA3d 1010, 168 CR 378.

Counsel should not assume, however, that incrimination is not possible simply because the question asked of the witness pertains directly to offenses for which prosecution is barred. For example, the question may relate to a misdemeanor for which the statute of limitations is one year (Pen C §801), but the same evidence may also expose the witness to prosecution for conspiracy to commit the misdemeanor, which is a felony (Pen C §182) for which the statutory period is three years (Pen C §800). See *Peck's Liquors, Inc. v Superior Court* (1963) 221 CA2d 772, 776, 34 CR 735. The question may ask for identification of persons and circumstances surrounding a crime for which the witness has already been convicted, but the privilege may persist because a responsive answer could also connect the witness with a more recent crime. See *Malloy v Hogan* (1964) 378 US 1, 12, 12 L Ed 2d 653, 84 S Ct 1489.

A grant of either transactional or use immunity (see §46.15) also terminates the privilege (*Kastigar v U.S.* (1972) 406 US 441, 32 L Ed 2d 212, 92 S Ct 1653; *Daly v Superior Court* (1977) 19 C3d 132, 143, 137 CR 14). A California grant of immunity gives use immunity from federal prosecution. *Nelson v Municipal Court* (1972) 28 CA3d 889, 105 CR 46. A federal grant of immunity gives use immunity from state prosecution. See *Murphy v Waterfront Comm'n* (1964) 378 US 52, 79, 12 L Ed 2d 678, 695, 84 S Ct 1594, overruled on other grounds in *U.S. v Balsys* (1998) 524 US 666, 688, 141 L Ed 2d 575, 118 S Ct 2218.

A grant of immunity does not protect a witness from prosecution for perjury if the witness lies while testifying. *People v Hathcock* (1971) 17 CA3d 646, 95 CR 221.

B. Immunity

§46.14 1. Principal Immunity Provisions

A witness can be compelled to give self-incriminating evidence, despite claiming the privilege, if a judge grants the witness immunity. See *In re Critch-*

low (1938) 11 C2d 751, 756, 81 P2d 966. See also *People v Campbell* (1982) 137 CA3d 867, 187 CR 340.

The two major types of immunity are transactional and use immunity. Transactional immunity provides broader protection from later prosecution than does use immunity. See discussion in §46.15. Federal law provides for grants of use immunity. 18 USC §§6001–6005. California provides use immunity in felony cases, unless the prosecutor requests transactional immunity. Pen C §1324. In misdemeanor cases, California provides transactional immunity. Pen C §1324.1. See discussion of Pen C §§1324, 1324.1 in §46.15.

The prosecuting attorney may "at any time before the defendants have gone into their defense" move the trial court for an order discharging any co-defendant to testify for the prosecution. Pen C §1099. If the motion is granted, the remaining defendants can request the court to inform the jury of the reason for the discharge so that the jury can consider it in assessing the witness's credibility. *People v Frahm* (1930) 107 CA 253, 290 P 678. Dismissal under Pen C §1099 is an acquittal that bars another prosecution for the same offense, whether a misdemeanor or a felony. Pen C §1101.

In civil cases, trial judges may take advantage of CCP §2025(i) to frame protective orders that are the equivalent of grants of use immunity. *Daly v Superior Court* (1977) 19 C3d 132, 137 CR 14 (trial court may grant equivalent of use immunity to party in civil action after notice to, and absence of objection from, state and federal prosecutors). See §46.16 for discussion of the procedures that civil litigants must follow to obtain a protective order under CCP §2025(i).

Counsel representing a witness who will be immunized should check with all relevant prosecution agencies (*e.g.*, other counties) to be sure that the client receives as much protection as possible from future prosecution relating to the testimony to be immunized.

§46.15   a. Transactional and Use Immunity in Criminal Proceedings

Use immunity protects only against use of the compelled testimony itself and its fruits. *Kastigar v U.S.* (1972) 406 US 441, 32 L Ed 2d 212, 92 S Ct 1653. Transactional immunity provides broader protection: it provides immunity from later prosecution related to any matter about which the individual testified. Transactional immunity is not limited to later use of the testimony itself, or its fruits. See *Nelson v Municipal Court* (1972) 28 CA3d 889, 105 CR 46.

In felony cases, California provides use immunity unless the prosecution requests transactional immunity. Pen C §1324. Because the language concerning use immunity in Pen C §1324 was modeled after the federal immunity statute, 18 USC §6002 (see Committee Analysis, AB 988, July 7, 1996), the judicial construction of 18 USC §6002 may serve as a basis for interpreting Pen C §1324. See *ACLU v Deukmejian* (1982) 32 C3d 440, 447, 186 CR 235 (court looked to federal Freedom of Information Act to construe California Public Records Act because California act was modeled on federal act).

A grant of immunity in a felony case under Pen C §1324 requires an order of the superior court in response to the prosecutor's written request that the witness be compelled to answer specified questions or to produce specified evidence. The prosecutor cannot make this request until the witness has claimed the privilege, and the judge must give the witness an opportunity to oppose the request in a hearing on an order to show cause. The court will not order a witness to give self-incriminating evidence under this procedure if it finds that to do so "would be clearly contrary to the public interest, or could subject the witness to a criminal prosecution in another jurisdiction." Pen C §1324.

The court should disclose on the record the terms and extent of the immunity grant. If the court orders the witness to furnish the requested testimony or evidence after granting immunity, the witness must testify on pain of contempt. Pen C §1324.

The prosecutor has the inherent power to grant immunity even when the procedure set forth in Pen C §1324 has not been followed. *People v Superior Court* (Crook) (1978) 83 CA3d 335, 339, 147 CR 856. In *People v Brunner* (1973) 32 CA3d 908, 108 CR 501, the appellate court, in sustaining a defendant's claim that he had received transactional immunity (which was the only immunity provided by Pen C §1324 at that time), held that the prosecution was estopped from arguing noncompliance with the section; the prosecutor had promised immunity to the defendant and had substantially received the benefit of his bargain. The prosecutor may, however, limit the immunity to particular crimes; the defendant cannot take unfair advantage of an immunity grant by spontaneously confessing to an unrelated crime. See *People v Superior Court* (Crook) (1978) 83 CA3d 335, 340, 147 CR 856 (informal offer of immunity for one series of crimes did not cover unrelated burglary to which defendant voluntarily confessed). Section 1324 specifically provides that there is no immunity "for any perjury, false swearing or contempt."

In misdemeanor cases, California provides transactional immunity. Pen C §1324.1. Under Pen C §1324.1, immunity can be granted in exchange for testimony only if the witness agrees. This is different from felony proceedings, in which the court can *compel* a witness to testify in exchange for immunity. See Pen C §1324. Penal Code §1324.1 provides that, in misdemeanor proceedings, if a person refuses to answer a question or produce evidence on the ground of self-incrimination, the person may agree in writing with the prosecuting attorney to testify voluntarily in exchange for a grant of immunity from prosecution, penalty, or forfeiture. Thereafter, on the prosecuting attorney's written request, the court must approve the agreement unless it finds "that to do so would be clearly contrary to the public interest." Pen C §1324.1. The witness's failure to testify following such an agreement merely results in loss of immunity. Pen C §1324.1.

Under federal law, a witness may be granted use immunity (see 18 USC §§6001-6005), which prevents authorities from using the testimony or evidence obtained under the grant of immunity, or evidence derived from it, in a subsequent prosecution of that witness. Use immunity is sometimes referred to as "use and derivative use" immunity. See *Nelson v Municipal Court* (1972) 28 CA3d 889, 893, 105 CR 46. Though narrower than transactional immunity, it is sufficient to terminate the privilege against self-incrimination. *Kastigar v U.S.* (1972) 406 US 441, 32 L Ed 2d 212, 92 S Ct 1653. Although use immunity is the only statutorily recognized type of immunity in federal proceedings, government informal promises may be obtained through agreement with a federal prosecutor, *e.g.,* a letter agreement, a promise not to prosecute or indict, or a plea bargain arrangement. Federal courts enforce these agreements between the parties in federal proceedings. See *U.S. v Librach* (8th Cir 1976) 536 F2d 1228; *U.S. v Pellon* (SD NY 1979) 475 F Supp 467. These informal agreements, however, are not enforceable by federal courts against a state in state court proceedings. See Federal Procedure: Lawyer's Edition, vol. 33A, §80:281, p. 356 (Lawyers Cooperative Publishing 1995).

Immunity granted by California courts gives use immunity from later federal prosecution. *Murphy v Waterfront Comm'n* (1964) 378 US 52, 79, 12 L Ed 2d 678, 695, 84 S Ct 1594, overruled on other grounds in *U.S. v Balsys* (1998) 524 US 666, 688, 141 L Ed 2d 575, 118 S Ct 2218. A federal grant of use immunity applies to a California prosecution. *Nelson v Municipal Court, supra.* Federal law probably also prohibits a state from using testimony compelled under immunity granted by another state in a subsequent prosecution of the immunized witness. See *Murphy v Waterfront Comm'n* (1964) 378 US 52, 77, 12 L Ed 2d 678, 694, 84 S Ct 1594. The witness cannot be ordered to testify under Pen C §1324, however, if federal law does not have this effect and the compelled testimony could subject the witness to prosecution under the laws of another state.

If a prosecutor pursues prosecution of a witness who has given testimony or evidence after a grant of use immunity, the prosecutor must show that it comes from an independent, legitimate source wholly independent of the compelled testimony. 378 US at 79 n18, 12 L Ed 2d at 695 n18; *Kastigar v U.S.* (1972) 406 US 441, 460, 32 L Ed 2d 212, 226, 92 S Ct 1653; *Daly v Superior Court* (1977) 19 C3d 132, 138, 137 CR 14. Hearings at which the prosecution must show an independent, legitimate source are called *Kastigar* hearings after *Kastigar v U.S., supra.* See *U.S. v North* (DC Cir 1990) 910 F2d 843, 854 (case reversed for failure to hold *Kastigar* hearing).

For an example of when transactional immunity did not protect against a conviction, see *In re Tracy L.* (1992) 10 CA4th 1454, 1466, 13 CR2d 593.

Courts differ on how immunized testimony may be used for nonevidentiary purposes. See the list of cases, and their holdings, in *U.S. v North* (DC Cir 1990) 910 F2d 843, 857, modified on other grounds (DC Cir 1990) 920 F2d 940.

To prove that criminal charges brought at a later time concerning a crime covered by a grant of immunity are based on an independent, legitimate source, prosecutors sometimes seal evidence gathered before hearing the testimony of the immunized witness and file the evidence with the court. Counsel for an immunized witness later prosecuted for a crime covered by the grant of immunity should demand to see this sealed evidence.

Witnesses who refuse to testify after receiving use or transactional immunity are subject to contempt. *U.S. v Wilson* (1975) 421 US 309, 44 L Ed 2d 186, 95 S Ct 1802. Witnesses testifying under a grant of immunity are not immune from prosecution for perjury if they testify falsely. Pen C §1324; *People v Hathcock* (1971) 17 CA3d 646, 95 CR 221.

A grant of immunity that is conditioned on the witness's promise to testify in a particular way in a criminal proceeding may deny the defendant's right to a fair trial. *People v Medina* (1974) 41 CA3d 438, 116 CR 133. See also *People v Badgett* (1995) 10 C4th 330, 367, 41 CR2d 635 (concurring opinion of Mosk, J.). Pressure on a witness by the prosecution to echo earlier testimony or statements in order to receive the benefit of a bargain, however, is not considered to be an improper inducement unless there is a specific condition that the later testimony must match the earlier statement or testimony. See *People v Garrison* (1989) 47 C3d 746, 768, 254 CR 257.

If immunity is granted only for designated crimes committed within a specified period, the witness may claim the privilege against self-incrimination on testimony about other matters and other times. *People v Label* (1974) 43 CA3d 766, 774, 119 CR 522.

For further discussion, see §46.8 (raising claim of privilege). See generally 2 Witkin, California Evidence, *Witnesses* §§470–494 (4th ed 2000).

§46.16 b. Immunity in Civil Cases

The court in civil cases, either on the judge's own motion or a party's motion, may order that "certain matters not be inquired into" (CCP §2025(i)(9)) and may "make any other order which justice requires to protect any party, deponent, or other natural person or organization from unwarranted annoyance, embarrassment, or oppression, or undue burden or expense" (CCP §2025(i)). Good cause must be shown. This section gives judges in civil cases the ability to fashion protective orders that effectively grant use immunity sufficient to force the witness to testify. *Daly v Superior Court* (1977) 19 C3d 132, 137 CR 14; *People v Superior Court (Kaufman)* (1974) 12 C3d 421, 115 CR 812; *Gonzales v Superior Court* (1980) 117 CA3d 57, 178 CR 358.

Because the grant of use immunity could hamper subsequent criminal prosecutions or interfere with prosecutorial discretion, the California Supreme Court has defined a procedure requiring prior notice to state and federal prosecutors. On receipt of notice, a prosecutor can object to the granting of immunity. The required declarations supporting the objection must show that the prosecutor is familiar with the notice and has reasonable ground to believe that the proposed grant of immunity might unduly hamper the prosecution. An objection conclusively establishes that an immunity order cannot be granted. *Daly v Superior Court, supra. Daly* and *Rysdale v Superior Court* (1978) 81 CA3d 280, 146 CR 633, provide illuminating discussions of the granting of use immunity in civil cases under former CCP §2019 and the factors that an appellate court must consider in reviewing the trial court's granting of such a protective order. See also *Gonzales v Superior Court, supra*; *Smith v Superior Court* (1980) 110 CA3d 422, 168 CR 24.

The judge's grant of immunity under CCP §2025(i) should specify exactly what testimony is covered because only the testimony itself and its fruits are protected by the order (see *People v Superior Court (Kaufman)* (1974) 12 C3d 421, 115 CR 812).

§46.17 2. Other Immunity Provisions

A number of statutes grant immunity to persons compelled to testify in certain noncourt proceedings: Govt C §9410 (proceedings before the California Senate or Assembly or their committees); Ins C §12924(b) (investigations by the insurance commissioner); Wat C §1106 (State Water Resources Control Board investigations); Welf & I C §355.1(f) (testimony of parents or other custodians in child dependency proceedings). These statutes do not require the witness to claim the privilege; by their language, however, they specifically confer immunity on those testifying under compulsion in a proceeding to which the statute applies. See *People v King* (1967) 66 C2d 633, 58 CR 571 (Ins C §12924).

The following statutes provide for immunity only if the witness first claims the privilege: Corp C §25531(e), concerning investigations by the Corporations Commissioner; Govt C §§18676-18677, governing State Personnel Board hearings; and Pen C §1324, the principal statute governing immunity grants in felony criminal proceedings (discussed in §46.15).

Use immunity applies to the information required to be disclosed by Veh C §20002 when property damage results from a vehicular accident. See *Byers v Justice Court* (1969) 71 C2d 1039, 1050, 80 CR 553, vacated on other grounds (1971) 402 US 424, 29 L Ed 2d 9, 91 S Ct 1535. See also *Bailey v Superior Court* (1970) 4 CA3d 513, 84 CR 436 (applying same rule in Veh C §20001 cases), and *People v Superior Court* (Kaufman) (1974) 12 C3d 421, 428, 115 CR 812 (summarizing and relying on *Byers* in another context).

Juvenile court judges may grant immunity in proceedings under Welf & I C §§300 and 601 without the prosecutor's consent. Note, however, that a prosecutor's consent is required in Welf & I C §602 proceedings. Cal Rules of Ct 1421.

California courts have exercised their inherent powers to grant use immunity in limited circumstances. See *Ramona R. v Superior Court* (1985) 37 C3d 802, 806, 210 CR 204 (statements made by minor to probation officer in preparation of juvenile fitness hearing may not be used as substantive evidence at subsequent criminal trial—but see *People v Macias* (1997) 16 C4th 739, 743, 66 CR2d 659 (*Ramona R.* does not extend to impeachment of inconsistent testimony minor defendant volunteers during adult criminal trial)); *People v Coleman* (1975) 13 C3d 867, 120 CR 384 (testimony at probation revocation hearing scheduled before trial); *In re Jessica B.* (1989) 207 CA3d 504, 520, 254 CR 883 (statements of parents in child dependency proceedings); *People v Dennis* (1986) 177 CA3d 863, 876, 223 CR 236 (statements of defendant supporting motion for new trial on ground of ineffectiveness of trial counsel); *Tarantin v Superior Court* (1975) 48 CA3d 465, 122 CR 61 (statements made during psychiatric evaluation to determine defendant's competence to stand trial may not be used on issue of guilt in pending trial). See also *Simmons v U.S.* (1968) 390 US 377, 394, 19 L Ed 2d 1247, 1259, 88 S Ct 967 (statements of defendant at pretrial motion to suppress evidence).

Other courts have rejected requests to grant use immunity in other situations. See *People v Cooke* (1993) 16 CA4th 1361, 1369, 20 CR2d 506 (testimony of defendant to rebut other acts of misconduct offered under Evid C §1101(b)); *People v Harris* (1992) 8 CA4th 104, 108, 10 CR2d 42 (testimony of defendant in first phase of bifurcated trial); *People v Baumann* (1985) 176 CA3d 67, 84, 222 CR 32 (testimony at post-trial restitution hearing); *People v O'Connell* (1984) 152 CA3d 548, 554, 199 CR 542 (defendant's prior testimony used in subsequent proceeding against him).

§46.18 3. Criminal Defense Witness Immunity

A defendant who has reason to believe that a witness claiming the privilege against self-incrimination actually committed the crime with which the defendant is charged cannot compel the court to grant immunity to force the witness to testify. Penal Code §1324 applies only to potential prosecution witnesses. The prosecution is therefore under no obligation to make a witness available to testify for a defendant by granting the witness statutory immunity. *People v Pineda* (1973) 30 CA3d 860, 106 CR 743.

The court in *Daly v Superior Court* (1977) 19 C3d 132, 137 CR 14, cited *People v Pineda, supra*, with approval for the proposition that Pen C §1324 permits immunity orders only on the district attorney's request. See also *People v Sutter* (1982) 134 CA3d 806, 812, 184 CR 829, in which the appellate court rejected the defendant's contention that the trial court should have granted use immunity to a co-participant.

For criticism of the *Pineda* and *Sutter* rule, see Note, *The Public Has A Claim to Every Man's Evidence: The Defendant's Constitutional Right to Witness Immunity*, 30 Stan L Rev 1211 (1978); Note, *The Sixth Amendment Right to Have Use Immunity Granted to Defense Witnesses*, 91 Harv L Rev 1266 (1978). For support of the rule, see Note, *The Case Against A Right to Defense Witness Immunity*, 83 Colum L Rev 139 (1983).

In *People v Hunter* (1989) 49 C3d 957, 974, 264 CR 367, the supreme court stated:

> [I]t is possible to hypothesize cases where a judicially conferred use immunity might possibly be necessary to vindicate a criminal defendant's rights to compulsory process and a fair trial. . . .

This statement was found to be dictum by one court of appeal, which held that use immunity for a defendant should be granted only by the state's highest court. See *People v Cooke* (1993) 16 CA4th 1361, 20 CR2d 506.

§46.19   C. Waiver

Parties who testify on their own behalf waive the privilege against self-incrimination for all proper cross-examination within the scope of direct examination of that party, whether or not the testimony they actually gave during their direct examination could have incriminated them. *Brown v U.S.* (1958) 356 US 148, 2 L Ed 2d 589, 78 S Ct 622. But parties who are called by the adverse party, and witnesses who are subpoenaed, do not control the scope of their direct testimony and therefore do not waive the privilege unless they actually give self-incriminating testimony without claiming the privilege. See 356 US at 155, 2 L Ed 2d at 597.

If witnesses give self-incriminating evidence without claiming the privilege, they waive the privilege not only for that evidence but also for additional information concerning the transaction that their evidence has disclosed. Thus, a witness who, without claiming the privilege, discloses his or her failure to file an income tax return, waives the privilege for questions about his or her reasons for failing to file. See *Regents of Univ. of Cal. v Superior Court* (1962) 200 CA2d 787, 798, 19 CR 568. See also *Rogers v U.S.* (1951) 340 US 367, 374, 95 L Ed 344, 71 S Ct 438 (no possibility of increasing danger of prosecution based on facts of case); 2 Witkin, California Evidence, *Witnesses* §§498–499 (4th ed 2000).

When an individual who is called to testify as a witness before the grand jury voluntarily reveals information that is self-incriminating, the government is not deemed to have compelled the incrimination even if the most damning admissions are made. *U.S. v Swacker* (9th Cir 1980) 628 F2d 1250.

Unlike the waiver of most privileges, a waiver of the privilege against self-incrimination is effective only for the particular stage of the proceeding at which it occurs. A waiver by testimony before the beginning of trial or on voir dire outside the presence of the jury does not preclude a claim of the privilege at the trial itself. See *People v Lawrence* (1959) 168 CA2d 510, 517, 336 P2d 189 (voir dire by court to determine whether witness called by defendant could properly refuse to answer questions based on Fifth Amendment; witness's answers did not waive privilege); *In re Sales* (1933) 134 CA 54, 60, 24 P2d 916 (waiver before grand jury; witness may claim fifth at trial); 2 Witkin, Evidence, *Witnesses* §500. If the witness testified before trial but asserts the privilege against self-incrimination at trial, the prior testimony is admissible because the witness is now "unavailable" under Evid C §240(a)(1). See Evid C §§1291–1292 (hearsay exception for former testimony); CCP §2016(d)(3) (admissibility of deposition). See also *People v Maxwell* (1979) 94 CA3d 562, 573, 156 CR 630 (testimony at preliminary examination); *In re Sales, supra* (grand jury testimony).

Note that in criminal cases, the defendant's constitutional right of confrontation (US Const amends VI and XIV; Cal Const art I, §15) requires that the defendant have had the full opportunity to cross-examine the unavailable witness with an interest and motive similar to that at trial. *California v Green* (1970)

399 US 149, 165, 26 L Ed 2d 489, 501, 90 S Ct 1930. Evidence Code §1291(a)(2), dealing with former testimony, also requires that there have been an opportunity to cross-examine with a similar interest and motive.

If a party's testimony was erroneously compelled over a claim of privilege and is being offered against him or her, the party can object under Evid C §919. See §33.24.

§46.20   IX. BURDEN OF PROOF AND RULING; WRIT REVIEW

Under Evid C §404, a person claiming the privilege against self-incrimination "has the burden of showing that the proffered evidence might tend to incriminate him." For further discussion, see §§46.4 (criminal penalties threatened), 46.5 (connection between evidence and punishable act).

The burden of proof does not require claimants of the privilege to produce admissible evidence to support their claim, but they must point out circumstances indicating a possibility that a responsive answer to the question, or production of the evidence demanded, could subject them to prosecution. Claimants may, for example, point out the implications of the question, the setting in which it is asked, circumstances subjecting them to suspicion of crime, or other circumstances affecting the likelihood of their being criminally punished as a result of their answers. See Comment to Evid C §404; *People v Maxwell* (1979) 94 CA3d 562, 571, 156 CR 630 (witness's refusal to testify because her testimony might conflict with previous testimony given at preliminary hearing, thus subjecting her to possible perjury charge, was sufficient to establish privilege). The federal constitutional standard may require the court to consider some of these circumstances even when the witness does not point them out, if they are within the court's judicial knowledge or are apparent from the record. See *Malloy v Hogan* (1964) 378 US 1, 12, 12 L Ed 2d 653, 662, 84 S Ct 1489.

After considering the relevant circumstances, the court must exclude the evidence claimed to be privileged "unless it clearly appears to the court that the proffered evidence cannot possibly have a tendency to incriminate the person claiming the privilege." Evid C §404.

Apart from the requirements of Evid C §404, the procedure for ruling on the privilege against self-incrimination is generally the same as for ruling on other privileges. See §§21.8, 21.15, 33.17-33.19, 33.26-33.27.

Extraordinary writ review may be available to test not only a denial of the privilege (see §33.22) but also a refusal to circumvent a claim of the privilege by a grant of immunity (see §46.18).

§46.21 X. STATING CLAIM OF PRIVILEGE AGAINST SELF-INCRIMINATION

[Option 1: Claim made to ensure preservation of federal and state rights]

I claim the privilege against self-incrimination under Evidence Code section 940, the fifth and fourteenth amendments to the United States Constitution, and California Constitution article I, section 15.

[Option 2: Claim appears to be sufficient but is untested]

I decline to answer on the grounds stated in Evidence Code section 940.

[Option 3: Claim made by unrepresented witness]

I decline to answer on the ground that my answer might tend to incriminate me.

47

Privilege of Defendant in Criminal Case Not To Be Called and Not To Testify

I. NATURE AND CONSTITUTIONAL BASIS §47.1

II. REQUIREMENTS
   A. Criminal Prosecution of Defendant §47.2
   B. Testimonial or Communicative Evidence §47.3

III. DECIDING WHETHER TO TESTIFY §47.4

IV. ASSERTION OF PRIVILEGE §47.5

V. RULE AGAINST COMMENT ON OR INFERENCE FROM FAILURE TO TESTIFY §47.6

VI. WAIVER §47.7

VII. RULING ON PRIVILEGE §47.8

VIII. STATUTE §47.9

IX. STATING OBJECTIONS BASED ON PRIVILEGE §47.10

§47.1 I. NATURE AND CONSTITUTIONAL BASIS

A defendant in a criminal prosecution has the privilege not to be called as a witness and, if called, to refuse to testify. The privilege applies not only when the prosecutor calls the defendant as a witness but also, in a prosecution of codefendants, when one calls the other as a witness. See *People v Haldeen* (1968) 267 CA2d 478, 73 CR 102.

The Evidence Code does not define the scope of the privilege. Evidence Code §930 states:

> To the extent that such privilege exists under the Constitution of the United States or the State of California, a defendant in a criminal case has a privilege not to be called as a witness and not to testify.

Thus, the Code recognizes the existence of the privilege under the federal and state constitutions. The Fifth Amendment to the United States Constitution provides that "no person . . . shall be compelled in any criminal case to be a witness against himself. . . ." Similar language appears in Cal Const art I,

§15. The same constitutional provisions also create the privilege against self-incrimination, *i.e.,* the privilege of any witness to refuse to give testimony or evidence that may tend to incriminate the witness. Evid C §940. See also chap 46.

The Fourteenth Amendment to the United States Constitution makes the federal privilege granted by the Fifth Amendment applicable in state as well as federal courts. *Griffin v California* (1965) 380 US 609, 14 L Ed 2d 106, 85 S Ct 1229; *Malloy v Hogan* (1964) 378 US 1, 12 L Ed 2d 653, 84 S Ct 1489.

The privilege entitles the defendant not only to refuse to testify but also not to be called as a witness. Evid C §930. See also Evid C §772(d). Before enactment of the Evidence Code, the right not to be called as a witness was attributed both to Cal Const art I, §15 and to former Pen C §1323.5, which declared defendants incompetent to testify except at their own request. See *People v Talle* (1952) 111 CA2d 650, 662, 245 P2d 633 (applying statute that preceded former Pen C §1323.5). Although Pen C §1323.5 was repealed when the Evidence Code was enacted, a criminal defendant continues to have a constitutional privilege not to be called as a witness before the jury and forced to claim the privilege not to testify. See Comment to Evid C §930; Comment to repeal of Pen C §1323.5; 2 Witkin, California Evidence, *Witnesses* §§355–502 (4th ed 2000).

The right not to be called as a witness is also part of the federal constitutional privilege. *U.S. v Echeles* (7th Cir 1965) 352 F2d 892. On asserting the right not to be called as a witness, see §47.5. Note that Cal Const art I, §28(d) (the "truth-in-evidence" provision of Proposition 8) expressly leaves the Evidence Code privileges sections untouched. Therefore, counsel can continue to rely on the California Constitution in criminal as well as civil proceedings with regard to privileges.

The privilege against self-incrimination and the constitutional right to counsel form the basis for rules excluding from evidence, in criminal proceedings, a defendant's incriminating statements made during in-custody interrogation without adequate warning of the defendant's constitutional rights. *Miranda v Arizona* (1966) 384 US 436, 16 L Ed 2d 694, 86 S Ct 1602; *Dickerson v U.S.* (2000) 530 US 428, 147 L Ed 2d 405, 120 S Ct 2326 (reaffirming *Miranda*). For further discussion, see California Criminal Law Procedure and Practice, chap 30 (7th ed Cal CEB 2004); 2 Witkin, Evidence, *Witnesses* §§355–502.

Because the defendant's privilege not to be called and not to testify is guaranteed by the United States Constitution, its erroneous denial must be treated as a ground for reversal on appeal unless the appellate court finds that the error was harmless beyond a reasonable doubt. *Chapman v California* (1967) 386 US 18, 17 L Ed 2d 705, 87 S Ct 824 (prosecutor's comment on defendant's failure to testify held reversible error even though nonreversible under California law); *People v Modesto* (1967) 66 C2d 695, 711, 59 CR 124 (although prosecutor referred in closing argument to defendant's failure to testify, reference was held to be harmless error because prosecutor proved beyond reasonable doubt that error did not contribute to verdict). A denial of the privilege may also furnish grounds for review by the federal courts. See Appeals and Writs in Criminal Cases, chaps 3 (review in United States Supreme Court), 4 (federal habeas corpus review of state criminal cases) (2d ed Cal CEB 2000).

II. REQUIREMENTS

§47.2   A. Criminal Prosecution of Defendant

The privilege not to be called as a witness and not to testify may be claimed by the defendant in any proceeding in which the defendant is being prosecuted on a criminal charge. See *Cramer v Tyars* (1979) 23 C3d 131, 137, 151 CR 653; *Black v State Bar* (1972) 7 C3d 676, 685, 103 CR 288. See also Pen C §16 (crimes and public offenses include felonies, misdemeanors, and infractions). In addition, the privilege is applicable in contempt proceedings (*In re Leainitt* (1959) 174 CA2d 535, 345 P2d 75; *Killpatrick v Superior Court* (1957) 153 CA2d 146, 314 P2d 164, overruled on other grounds at 29 C4th 1210 (contempt proceeding for nonsupport)) and civil actions by the government for a penalty or forfeiture of a criminal nature (*U.S. v U.S. Coin & Currency* (1971) 401 US 715, 718, 28 L Ed 2d 434, 437, 91 S Ct 1041; but see *People v Superior Court (Kaufman)* (1974) 12 C3d 421, 430 n6, 115 CR 812).

Proceedings that are not considered to be criminal proceedings for purposes of the privilege of a criminal defendant not to be called as a witness include proceedings before the Commission on Judicial Performance inquiring into the performance of a judge (*McComb v Superior Court* (1977) 68 CA3d 89, 137 CR 233), Welf & I C §§6500-6512 proceedings to commit persons who are a danger to themselves or others to an institution for the mentally retarded (*Cramer v Tyars* (1979) 23 C3d 131, 151 CR 653), and a habeas corpus action instituted by a convicted defendant to challenge the results of a previous criminal case (*In re Scott* (2003) 29 C4th 783, 815, 129 CR2d 605).

A person does not have the privilege to refuse to be called as a witness in administrative proceedings to suspend or revoke that person's license, because they are not considered to be criminal proceedings for purposes of the defendant's right not to be called. *Black v State Bar* (1972) 7 C3d 676, 684, 103 CR 288; *West Coast Home Improvement Co. v Contractor's State License Bd.* (1945) 72 CA2d 287, 300, 164 P2d 811.

Similarly, the privilege cannot be claimed in a grand jury proceeding, even by a person who is under investigation and is a prospect for indictment. *In re Lemon* (1936) 15 CA2d 82, 59 P2d 213. See *U.S. v Washington* (1977) 431 US 181, 189, 52 L Ed 2d 238, 246, 97 S Ct 1814. Of course, a witness in a grand jury proceeding, and in many administrative hearings (see §46.4), can claim the privilege against self-incrimination (see chap 46) in response to particular questions. See Evid C §§901, 910, 940; *Fielder v Berkeley Props. Co.* (1972) 23 CA3d 30, 99 CR 791.

If a criminal defendant's case is being appealed, the defendant may refuse to be called to testify by codefendants at a separate trial, even though the defendant's trial has been completed. *People v Lopez* (1980) 110 CA3d 1010, 168 CR 378. Because a codefendant at a separate trial might waive the privilege, a defendant may have to make the effort to subpoena and call the codefendant to avoid comment by the prosecution about the failure to call a logical witness. *People v Ford* (1988) 45 C3d 431, 247 CR 121. An alternative may be to seek a stipulation or pretrial ruling to avoid such comment. 45 C3d at 447 n8.

§47.3   B. Testimonial or Communicative Evidence

The privilege not to be called and not to testify applies only to "evidence of a testimonial or communicative nature." *Schmerber v California* (1966) 384 US 757, 761, 16 L Ed 2d 908, 914, 86 S Ct 1826. Therefore, the privilege does not protect an accused from being fingerprinted (*People v Williams* (1969) 71 C2d 614, 79 CR 65) or photographed (*People v Smith* (1956) 142 CA2d 287, 298 P2d 540). The defendant can be compelled to cooperate actively in reasonable identification procedures, *e.g.*, by speaking or furnishing handwriting samples. *Gilbert v California* (1967) 388 US 263, 18 L Ed 2d 1178, 87 S Ct 1951 (handwriting samples); *People v Ellis* (1966) 65 C2d 529, 55 CR 385 (voice identification). The defendant can also be compelled to submit to reasonable nonbrutal body examinations using approved medical procedures, including the taking of specimen body fluids. *Schmerber v California, supra* (blood alcohol test); *People v Sudduth* (1966) 65 C2d 543, 55 CR 393 (breathalyzer test). See §46.6.

The use of surgery or brutality to extract nontestimonial evidence from a defendant is prohibited—not by the privilege against self-incrimination and not to testify as a defendant, but by the right of personal integrity, derived from the constitutional right of due process. See *Planned Parenthood v Casey* (1992) 505 US 833, 120 L Ed 2d 674, 112 S Ct 2791; see also *Rochin v California* (1952) 342 US 165, 96 L Ed 183, 72 S Ct 205 (stomach pump); *People v Scott* (1978) 21 C3d 284, 145 CR 876 (involuntary ejaculation); *People v Matteson* (1964) 61 C2d 466, 469, 39 CR 1 (coerced handwriting exemplars); *People v Cahill* (1993) 5 C4th 478, 523, 20 CR2d 582 (coerced confession). But see *People v Haeussler* (1953) 41 C2d 252, 260 P2d 8 (use of emetic acceptable; *Rochin v California, supra,* distinguished). See also *People v Browning* (1980) 108 CA3d 117, 166 CR 293 (surgery on victim to recover bullet not allowed); *Winston v Lee* (1985) 470 US 753, 84 L Ed 2d 662, 105 S Ct 1611 (involuntary surgery to extract bullet as evidence of suspect's guilt is unreasonable search under Fourth Amendment to United States Constitution). Compare *Winston v Lee, supra,* with *Skinner v Railway Labor Executives' Ass'n* (1989) 489 US 602, 103 L Ed 2d 639, 109 S Ct

1402, discussed in §28.11 (Federal Railroad Administration safety regulations that mandated or authorized use of employee alcohol and drug tests without warrants or individual suspicion did not violate Fourth Amendment). See also *Perkey v DMV* (1986) 42 C3d 185, 228 CR 169 (applicant required to give fingerprints to obtain driver's license, but DMV use of prints limited by court); *Bibeau v Pacific Northwestern Research Found.* (9th Cir 1999) 188 F3d 1105 (testicular radiation experiments on consenting prison inmate not violative of due process personal integrity right).

§47.4 III. DECIDING WHETHER TO TESTIFY

Although defense counsel must advise the defendant of the merits and possible detriments of testifying, the ultimate decision remains with the defendant. *People v Robles* (1970) 2 C3d 205, 214, 85 CR 166. See also *People v Douglas* (1990) 50 C3d 468, 519, 268 CR 126.

The personal right of a defendant to choose to testify includes the right to decide to offer evidence on a diminished capacity defense. Counsel cannot properly refuse to honor the defendant's clearly expressed desire to present that defense at the guilt phase of a capital case, even though counsel believes that the better trial tactic is to withhold that evidence until the penalty phase. *People v Frierson* (1985) 39 C3d 803, 218 CR 73. But see *People v Burton* (1989) 48 C3d 843, 258 CR 184 (no error when defense counsel failed to accede to defendant's desire to present defense at guilt phase of trial because record did not show that any defense that defendant wished to present had credible evidentiary support; defendant did not allege that he wanted a particular piece of evidence or defense to be presented or that he wanted to testify himself).

The court is not required to obtain an on-the-record personal waiver from the defendant of the right against self-incrimination, right to a jury trial, and right to confront adverse witnesses whenever defense counsel chooses to rest without putting on a defense. *People v Hendricks* (1987) 43 C3d 584, 238 CR 66.

There is disagreement over whether it is generally better for defendants to testify or not to testify. Regardless of counsel's factual and philosophical preference, there are a number of legal and tactical considerations. Some of the more important ones follow:

- *Will the defendant be able to take the stand without committing perjury or confessing?* Counsel whose client insists on taking the stand and committing perjury may have to withdraw from the case. Counsel may be able to avoid withdrawing from the case by having the client present testimony in a narrative manner without counsel's participation and by not discussing the defendant's testimony during closing argument. *People v Gadson* (1993) 19 CA4th 1700, 24 CR2d 219. On representing a defendant who says that he or she will commit perjury or who does so, see

Wolfram, *Client Perjury*, 50 S Cal L Rev 809 (1977). Knowingly aiding a client in perjuring himself or herself violates Cal Rules of Prof Cond 3-700. See also *In re Jones* (1971) 5 C3d 390, 96 CR 448 (attorney suspended for soliciting perjury).

- *Will the defendant be a good witness?* Before making the decision to call or not to call the defendant, counsel should observe the defendant's responses while role playing direct and cross-examinations.

- *Will the trier of fact be a judge or a jury?* Some defenses may be more acceptable to a judge and others to a jury.

- *Has the defendant been convicted of a felony?* If the defendant testifies and has previously been convicted of a felony, it may be possible to impeach the defendant with it. Evid C §788. A trial court's discretion under Evid C §352 to exclude evidence of a prior felony conviction offered under Evid C §788 to impeach a witness was not abrogated by Cal Const art I, §28(f) (added by Proposition 8). *People v Castro* (1985) 38 C3d 301, 306, 211 CR 719. See also *People v Wheeler* (1992) 4 C4th 284, 14 CR2d 418; §31.3.

- *Has the defendant committed a similar act of misconduct?* Although acts of misconduct found similar, under Evid C §1101, to the criminal act that the defendant is accused of committing are admissible whether or not the defendant testifies, the defendant's testimony may be such that it permits the prosecutor to introduce evidence of similar or dissimilar acts of misconduct as impeachment that otherwise would be inadmissible. See *People v Ewoldt* (1994) 7 C4th 380, 27 CR2d 646.

- *Will the defendant's testimony correct deficiencies in the prosecutor's case-in-chief?* Although the defendant's testimony should have no effect on appellate review of a motion for judgment of acquittal under Pen C §1118 (court trial) or §1118.1 (jury trial) (*People v Belton* (1979) 23 C3d 516, 519, 153 CR 195), it may convince the judge or jury beyond a reasonable doubt of the defendant's guilt.

- *Will the judge deem the defendant's testimony untruthful and therefore impose a more severe sentence?* See *People v Redmond* (1981) 29 C3d 904, 176 CR 780.

- *Has there been a strong prosecution case?* If so, the defendant may have little to lose by taking the stand. If not, it may be best to "stand on the state of the evidence." See CALJIC 2.61.

§47.5　IV. ASSERTION OF PRIVILEGE

The defendant's privilege not to take the stand and not to testify exempts the defendant from being called as a witness. If the prosecutor nevertheless calls the defendant, the privilege is immediately violated, and the defendant may not only object to being called but also may pursue remedies for misconduct. See *People v Talle* (1952) 111 CA2d 650, 664, 245 P2d 633.

The privilege protects the defendant from being called to testify for a codefendant as well as for the prosecution. One defendant's need to call another defendant as a witness may be a ground for ordering a separate trial. See *U.S. v Martinez* (5th Cir 1973) 486 F2d 15, 23; *U.S. v Echeles* (7th Cir 1965) 352 F2d 892; *People v Massie* (1967) 66 C2d 899, 59 CR 733; *People v Isenor* (1971) 17 CA3d 324, 330, 94 CR 746.

Assertion of the privilege is usually the responsibility of defense counsel. If a defendant is not represented by counsel and is not aware of the privilege, the court is required to advise the defendant of the right not to testify. One line of cases holds such error to be reversible per se (see, *e.g., People v Solomos* (1978) 83 CA3d 945, 148 CR 248), and the other applies the test developed in *Chapman v California* (1967) 386 US 18, 17 L Ed 2d 705, 87 S Ct 824, for review (see, *e.g., People v Cervantes* (1978) 87 CA3d 281, 290, 150 CR 819). See *People v Spencer* (1984) 153 CA3d 931, 945, 200 CR 693.

§47.6 V. RULE AGAINST COMMENT ON OR INFERENCE FROM FAILURE TO TESTIFY

In a criminal case, counsel for the People cannot comment on the defendant's failure to testify, and the trier of fact cannot draw any inference from it. The Fifth and Fourteenth Amendments to the United States Constitution prohibit any comment on the defendant's failure to explain or deny evidence. *Griffin v California* (1965) 380 US 609, 14 L Ed 2d 106, 85 S Ct 1229; *People v Modesto* (1967) 66 C2d 695, 711, 59 CR 124. The trial judge is also prohibited from comment, except to instruct the jury against drawing any inference from the defendant's failure to testify if the defendant requests such an instruction. Evid C §913. See CALJIC 2.60. It is error for the judge to give this instruction over the defense's objection. *People v Molano* (1967) 253 CA2d 841, 847, 61 CR 821. See CALJIC 2.61. Case law is divided on whether it is error under *Griffin* for the court, on its own motion or on the request of the prosecutor and without objection by the defendant, to instruct the jury on the defendant's right not to testify. See cases collected in *People v Cooper* (1970) 10 CA3d 96, 88 CR 919.

Violation of the *Griffin* rule is reversible error unless held to be harmless beyond a reasonable doubt (see *Chapman v California* (1967) 386 US 18, 17 L Ed 2d 705, 87 S Ct 824). *People v Stout* (1967) 66 C2d 184, 198, 57 CR 152. The identity of the speaker may make a difference, however, in whether the comment is found to be harmless beyond a reasonable doubt. *People v Hardy* (1992) 2 C4th 86, 157, 5 CR2d 796. For example, in *Hardy,* the court noted that a comment that would require reversal if made by a prosecutor might be harmless if made by a codefendant's counsel because of the institutional role the prosecutor plays in a criminal trial. Moreover, a defendant's right to freedom from adverse comment regarding the defendant's silence must be balanced against a codefendant's right to a full and vigorous defense. Thus, oblique or indirect references to a defendant's silence by a codefendant's counsel do not require reversal.

The prosecutor cannot comment on the defendant's exercise of the privilege on a past occasion. For example, if the defendant takes the stand at a second trial for the same offense, the prosecutor cannot ask why the defendant failed to testify at the first trial. See *People v Sharer* (1964) 61 C2d 869, 40 CR 851 (reversal because prosecutor was allowed to impeach defendant by showing that he had claimed self-incrimination privilege before grand jury).

Although defense counsel attempts to justify to the jury the defendant's failure to testify, the doctrine of invited error does not allow the prosecutor to commit *Griffin* error in reply. *People v Stout, supra*. But see *People v Davenport* (1966) 240 CA2d 341, 49 CR 575 (contrary ruling made before decision in *Stout* not expressly overruled). Neither is the defendant precluded from objecting to the court's comment or unrequested instruction by the invited-error doctrine. *People v Davenport, supra*.

§47.7   VI. WAIVER

If the defendant testifies at trial, this waives the privilege not to be called and not to testify concerning matters within the scope of the direct examination. See Evid C §§761, 773. Cross-examination may reach any matter that the defendant has stated or implied on direct examination; if the defendant has denied guilt, the permissible scope of cross-examination is quite broad. *People v Perez* (1967) 65 C2d 615, 55 CR 909 (defendant's denial of one robbery count during direct examination justified cross-examination on another count to disclose common pattern); *People v Ing* (1967) 65 C2d 603, 55 CR 902 (defendant's general denial of offenses charged on direct examination did not preclude cross-examination on collateral offenses). Further, an instruction under CALJIC 2.62 (failure of a witness to explain or deny evidence) may be given under certain circumstances with reference to the defendant's testimony. *People v Saddler* (1979) 24 C3d 671, 678, 156 CR 871.

If the defendant refuses to answer questions on cross-examination that properly fall within the scope of direct examination, the prosecutor may move to strike all the defendant's testimony. *People v Kadison* (1966) 243 CA2d 162, 167, 52 CR 114. If cross-examination exceeds the scope of the defendant's direct testimony, however, the privilege is violated. *People v Sims* (1958) 165 CA2d 108, 114, 331 P2d 799. See *People v Fauber* (1992) 2 C4th 792, 859, 9 CR2d 24. Further, prosecution comment on what the defendant failed to say when testifying may violate the *Griffin* rule (see *Griffin v California* (1965) 380 US 609, 14 L Ed 2d 106, 85 S Ct 1229). *People v Tealer* (1975) 48 CA3d 598, 604, 122 CR 144.

The cross-examiner may impeach the defendant's testimony by any permissible method, *e.g.,* by showing prior conviction of a felony (Evid C §788).

Codefendants may also cross-examine the defendant (see Evid C §773(a)), except that a codefendant "whose interest is not adverse" to the defendant may not ask leading questions (Evid C §773(b)). See Comment to Evid C §773. To prevent the prosecution or a codefendant from making the defendant his or her own witness for the purpose of examination beyond the scope of the defendant's direct testimony, Evid C §772(d) provides that the defendant "may not, without his consent, be examined under direct examination by another party."

Unlike the waiver of most privileges, a waiver of the defendant's privilege not to be called and not to testify, or of the privilege against self-incrimination, is effective only for the particular stage of the proceeding at which it occurs. A waiver by testifying at a preliminary examination or before the grand jury does not preclude the defendant from exercising the privilege not to be called or not to testify at the trial itself. *People v Thourwald* (1920) 46 CA 261, 267, 189 P 124. The defendant cannot, however, use the privilege at trial to prevent introduction of the prior testimony into evidence, *e.g.*, as an admission (Evid C §1220; see §§19.9, 19.18). See *People v Finch* (1963) 213 CA2d 752, 771, 29 CR 420 (admission at trial of defendant's self-incriminating testimony given before prosecution against her began). See also *People v Marwell* (1979) 94 CA3d 562, 570, 156 CR 630 (prosecution witness's testimony at preliminary examination admitted at trial although her basis for invoking Fifth Amendment at trial was that she would subject herself to possible perjury charges because her testimony at trial would be at variance with her earlier testimony). The defendant can object to the admission of prior testimony, however, if it was compelled after erroneous denial of the privilege. Evid C §919. See §33.24. See also Evid C §1204.

It may be reversible error for the judge to allow a defendant appearing in propria persona to be called to testify without having been advised of the right to refrain from testifying. For further discussion, see §47.5.

§47.8 VII. RULING ON PRIVILEGE

Questions raised at a criminal trial concerning the defendant's privilege not to testify are usually determinable as a matter of law. If the defendant has not testified, the court may have to rule on objections or motions for remedies arising from the prosecutor's attempts to draw attention to the defendant's failure to testify. See §§47.5–47.6. If the defendant waived the privilege by testifying, rulings on the extent of the waiver must be made on objection that questions asked by other parties exceed the permissible scope of cross-examination. See §47.7.

§47.9 VIII. STATUTE

The statutory basis for the privilege not to be called and not to testify is Evid C §930, which provides:

To the extent that such privilege exists under the Constitution of the United States or the State of California, a defendant in a criminal case has a privilege not to be called as a witness and not to testify.

§47.10   IX. STATING OBJECTIONS BASED ON PRIVILEGE

The form for assigning misconduct in §29.48 may be used with any of the following objections. All of them should be made outside the presence of the jury:

[Option 1: Defendant called as witness by
prosecution or codefendant]

Your Honor, I object to the defendant's being called as a witness on the ground that it violates _ _[his/her]_ _ privilege not to be called and not to testify as a witness under the fifth and fourteenth amendments to the United States Constitution; article I, section 15 of the California Constitution; and Evidence Code section 930.

[Option 2: Defendant testifies, and question on
cross-examination exceeds scope of direct examination]d

Your Honor, I object to that question as exceeding the scope of the defendant's testimony on direct examination and violating _ _[his/her]_ _ privilege not to testify under the fifth and fourteenth amendments to the United States Constitution; article I, section 15 of the California Constitution; and Evidence Code section 930.

[Option 3: Prosecutor or counsel for codefendant
comments on defendant's failure to testify]

Your Honor, I object to counsel's statement as violating the defendant's privilege not to testify under the fifth and fourteenth amendments to the United States Constitution; article I, section 15 of the California Constitution; and Evidence Code section 930.

[Add, if appropriate, to any objection]

I object to counsel's _ _[calling of the defendant/question/comment]_ _ as misconduct and _ _[request or move for appropriate remedy, e.g., mistrial, admonition to jury]_ _.

48

Journalist's Immunity From Contempt

I. NATURE OF JOURNALIST'S "SHIELD LAW" §48.1
   A. Federal and State Constitutional Basis for Privilege Not to Disclose Information
      1. Historical Development of Privilege §48.2
      2. Showing Required to Compel Testimony of Journalist §48.3
      3. Guidelines for Issuing Subpoenas to Journalists §48.4
      4. Interpretation of Privilege by California Supreme Court §48.5
   B. Constitutional and Statutory Sources for California's Immunity From Contempt §48.6
      1. Requirements
         a. Who Is Considered a "Journalist" §48.7
         b. Information Covered by Immunity §48.8
         c. When Immunity May Be Claimed §48.9
      2. Scope of Immunity
         a. Civil Trials §48.10
         b. Criminal Trials §48.11

II. ASSERTION OF PRIVILEGE OR CLAIM OF IMMUNITY §48.12
   A. Civil Trials §48.13
   B. Criminal Trials
      1. Triggering *Delaney* Protection §48.14
      2. Applying *Delaney* Balancing Test §48.15
      3. Hypothetical Case History §48.16

III. WAIVER §48.17

IV. STATING THE OBJECTION §48.18

V. RESPONSE IF JOURNALIST IS CITED FOR CONTEMPT §48.19

VI. CALIFORNIA CONSTITUTION; STATUTE §48.20

§48.1 I. NATURE OF JOURNALIST'S "SHIELD LAW"

When a litigant seeks to compel testimony from a journalist about either confidential sources or unpublished information, two competing public interests are implicated:

- The free flow of information, which is promoted by journalistic confidentiality and independence; and

- The integrity of the trial process, which may be enhanced by full disclosure.

These interests are reflected in potentially conflicting constitutional and statutory principles, which are frequently tested by journalists willing to face jail for contempt rather than to reveal information they consider to be sensitive. This chapter focuses on the approach to resolution of this conflict that has developed in California.

Journalists often use the term "shield law" to refer to any protection against compelled disclosure; California's legal writers tend to refer only to a journalist's "immunity from contempt." To avoid confusion, this book uses the terms "privilege" to refer to the constitutional right not to disclose information and "immunity" to refer to a journalist's protection against contempt.

A. Federal and State Constitutional Basis for Privilege Not to Disclose Information

§48.2   1. Historical Development of Privilege

A qualified privilege against compelled testimony has been recognized by the courts arising under the First Amendment to the United States Constitution and the parallel free expression provision of Cal Const art I, §2(a). No authority suggests that the scope of the journalist's privilege is different under the federal and state constitutions.

Journalists have argued for many years that their ability to gather the news depends on the right to keep their sources' identities confidential and that the independence of the editorial process depends on the right not to disclose even nonconfidential unpublished information. The United States Supreme Court first dealt with these constitutional claims in *Branzburg v Hayes* (1972) 408 US 665, 33 L Ed 2d 626, 92 S Ct 2646. Although no majority opinion was written in that case, the four dissenting justices and Justice Powell, concurring, supported a First Amendment right not to disclose information under some circumstances.

Most federal circuit courts considering this issue after *Branzburg* have found a qualified journalist's privilege against compelled disclosure of information. See, *e.g.*, *U.S. v Burke* (2d Cir 1983) 700 F2d 70, 77; *Zerilli v Smith* (DC Cir 1981) 656 F2d 705, 710; *Bruno & Stillman, Inc. v Globe Newspaper Co.* (1st Cir 1980) 633 F2d 583, 595; *Miller v Transamerican Press* (5th Cir 1980) 621 F2d 721, 725; *Riley v City of Chester* (3d Cir 1979) 612 F2d 708, 714; *Silkwood v Kerr-McGee Corp.* (10th Cir 1977) 563 F2d 433, 436; *U.S. v Steelhammer* (4th Cir 1976) 539 F2d 373, 375, rev'd in part on reh'g en banc (4th Cir 1977) 561 F2d 539; *Farr v Pitchess* (9th Cir 1975) 522 F2d 464, 468; *Cervantes v Time, Inc.* (8th Cir 1972) 464 F2d 986, 992. But see *U.S. v King* (ED Va 2000) 194 FRD 569 (finding no qualified privilege in *Branzburg* and questioning *Steelhammer, supra*).

Slightly different standards have been developed for the protection of confidential sources and nonconfidential unpublished information. See §48.3.

§48.3 2. Showing Required to Compel Testimony of Journalist

Although courts have stated the showing required to compel journalistic testimony differently in various decisions, the following questions are generally the focus of attention:

- How central is the information to the case?
- Will disclosure of the information affect the outcome of the case?
- Is the information available from a nonjournalistic source?

The test applicable to confidential source information was described in *Shoen v Shoen* (9th Cir 1995) 48 F3d 412, 416, as follows:

> [D]isclosure may be ordered only upon a clear and specific showing that the information is: highly material and relevant, necessary or critical to the maintenance of the claim, and not obtainable from other available sources.

The court established a similar but slightly less demanding test for compelling non-confidential information (*Shoen v Shoen, supra*):

> [W]here information sought is not confidential, a civil litigant is entitled to requested discovery notwithstanding a valid assertion of the journalist's privilege by a nonparty only upon a showing that the requested material is: (1) unavailable despite exhaustion of all reasonable alternative sources; (2) noncumulative; and (3) clearly relevant to an important issue in the case.

Although the *Shoen* decision approached the issue in a civil case, a similar analysis has been applied in criminal cases. See, *e.g., U.S. v Cuthbertson* (3d Cir 1980) 630 F2d 139.

§48.4 3. Guidelines for Issuing Subpoenas to Journalists

The United States Attorney General has established guidelines that government attorneys must follow before issuing subpoenas to members of the media. See 28 CFR §50.10. "[I]ntended to provide protection for the news media from forms of compulsory process, whether civil or criminal, which might impair the news gathering function," the guidelines acknowledge that "the prosecutorial power of the government should not be used in such a way that it impairs a reporter's responsibility to cover as broadly as possible controversial public issues." 28 CFR §50.10.

Under these guidelines, no subpoena can be issued to a journalist without the express authorization of the Attorney General. 28 CFR §50.10(e). In requesting the Attorney General's authorization for a subpoena, the attorney requesting the subpoena must (28 CFR §50.10(a)–(c)):

- Balance First Amendment considerations against the public interest "in effective law enforcement and the fair administration of justice";

- Make "all reasonable attempts" to obtain information from alternative sources; and

- Negotiate to "accommodate the interests of the trial or grand jury" with the interests of the media.

Before a subpoena can be issued to a journalist in a civil case, reasonable grounds must exist, based on nonmedia sources, to believe that the information sought is essential to the successful completion of the litigation "in a case of substantial importance." 28 CFR §50.10(f)(2). In criminal cases, the government must have information obtained from nonmedia sources that a crime has occurred and that the information sought from the journalist is essential to a successful investigation, "particularly with reference to directly establishing guilt or innocence." 28 CFR §50.10(f)(1).

In both civil and criminal cases, a subpoena issued by the Attorney General "should not be used to obtain peripheral, nonessential, or speculative information." 28 CFR §50.10(f)(1)-(2).

§48.5   4. Interpretation of Privilege by California Supreme Court

The California Supreme Court interpreted the qualified constitutional privilege for journalists in *Mitchell v Superior Court* (1984) 37 C3d 268, 208 CR 152. California's provision for a journalist's immunity from contempt did not play a significant role in the court's analysis, because the journalist in that case was a party and testimony may be compelled from a party without resort to contempt. See §48.10.

The *Mitchell* court held that the First Amendment to the United States Constitution and Cal Const art I, §2(a) provide a "qualified privilege to withhold disclosure of the identity of confidential sources and of unpublished information supplied by such sources." 37 C3d at 279. The scope of the privilege in a particular case depends on the following factors (37 C3d at 279):

- The nature of the litigation and whether the journalist is a party;

- The relevance of the information sought to the plaintiff's case;

- Whether the party seeking the journalist's testimony has exhausted all alternative sources for obtaining the information;

- The importance of protecting confidentiality in the case at hand; and

- In a libel case, whether the plaintiff has made a prima facie case that the alleged defamatory statements are false.

In nonlibel cases, the factual issue of whether alternative sources exist for obtaining the information frequently determines whether a journalist must divulge unpublished information or sources. In libel cases, the final factor listed above is usually the primary focus of inquiry. In all cases, the journalist's privilege should be asserted in a motion in limine before voir dire. To develop an effective voir dire examination, the attorney must know whether the journalist will be testifying at trial. See *Anti-Defamation League of B'nai B'rith v Superior Court* (1998) 67 CA4th 1072, 79 CR2d 597 (non-defamation case outlining *Mitchell* factors).

§48.6 B. Constitutional and Statutory Sources for California's Immunity From Contempt

In addition to the constitutional qualified privilege for journalists, California provides for a journalist's immunity from contempt in both Cal Const art I, §2(b) and Evid C §1070. Application of this immunity (which the courts sometimes refer to as a privilege) depends on whether the case is civil or criminal and whether the journalist is a party to the litigation or a nonparty witness.

Evidence Code §1070, enacted in 1965, expands the protection formerly provided by former CCP §1881(6), which was enacted in 1872 and repealed in 1965. The Evidence Code addresses the issue of journalistic confidentiality by prohibiting the courts from adjudging a journalist in contempt for declining to reveal either confidential sources or unpublished information. By focusing on punishment rather than discovery or admissibility, §1070 stands in contrast to all traditional privileges in the Evidence Code.

Although the phrasing of §1070 is comprehensive and absolute, the appellate courts limited its scope significantly by holding that the legislature could not interfere with the courts' power to control their own proceedings. See *Rosato v Superior Court* (1975) 51 CA3d 190, 206, 124 CR 427; *Farr v Superior Court* (1971) 22 CA3d 60, 69, 99 CR 342. The substantive provisions of §1070 were placed before the voters in 1980 as a constitutional amendment to invalidate *Rosato, Farr,* and similar cases. The amendment was adopted by the voters and now appears as Cal Const art I, §2(b). See §48.20.

1. Requirements

§48.7 a. Who Is Considered a "Journalist"

The journalist's immunity from contempt is available to the following:

- "A publisher, editor, reporter, or other person connected with or employed upon a newspaper, magazine, or other periodical publication, or by a press association or wire service" (Cal Const art I, §2(b); Evid C §1070(a));

- "[A] radio or television news reporter or other person connected with or employed by a radio or television station" (Cal Const art I, §2(b); Evid C §1070(b)); and

- "[A]ny person who has been so connected or employed" (Cal Const art I, §2(b); Evid C §1070(a)–(b)).

Organizations (*e.g.,* corporations, partnerships, associations) and natural persons may claim the immunity. See Evid C §175 (defining "person"); *CBS, Inc. v Superior Court* (1978) 85 CA3d 241, 249, 149 CR 421, disapproved on other grounds in *Delaney v Superior Court* (1990) 50 C3d 785, 804, 268 CR 753 (recognizing corporation's claim of immunity). Freelance writers qualify for the protection. *People v Von Villas* (1992) 10 CA4th 201, 13 CR2d 62. The Ninth Circuit accorded protection for a book author under the California immunity provision. See *Shoen v Shoen* (9th Cir 1993) 5 F3d 1289, 1293. See also *Shoen v Shoen* (9th Cir 1995) 48 F3d 412, discussed in §48.3.

Even a person who is unquestionably a journalist, however, may not claim protection for all information in his or her possession. Article I, §2(b) provides no protection for information obtained by a journalist who was not directly engaged in gathering, receiving, or processing news. *Delaney v Superior Court* (1990) 50 C3d 785, 797 n8, 268 CR 753. See §48.11. See also *Anti-Defamation League of B'nai B'rith v Superior Court* (1998) 67 CA4th 1072, 79 CR2d 597 (protection limited only to extent information sought to be discovered was used and disseminated for legitimate journalistic purposes).

§48.8   b. Information Covered by Immunity

Article I, §2(b) of the California Constitution protects the identity of confidential sources and confidential or "off the record" information. The immunity from contempt goes further by also protecting nondisclosure of unpublished information obtained or prepared in gathering, receiving, or processing information for communication to the public. Unpublished information may consist of notes, outtakes, photographs, tapes, or other data. It is unpublished if the person seeking immunity has not disseminated it to the public, whether or not other related or derivative information has been disseminated.

Protection of unpublished material promotes the flow of information to the public by preventing detection of sources from clues in the raw data. See *Miller v Superior Court* (1999) 21 C4th 883, 897, 89 CR2d 834; *Hammarley v Superior Court* (1979) 89 CA3d 388, 396, 153 CR 608, disapproved on other grounds in *Delaney v Superior Court* (1990) 50 C3d 785, 268 CR 753. It also assures independence of the editorial press.

§48.9   c. When Immunity May Be Claimed

The journalist's immunity from contempt must be claimed in response to a question or demand that calls for disclosure of protected information. See *CBS, Inc. v Superior Court* (1978) 85 CA3d 241, 149 CR 421, disapproved on other grounds in *Delaney v Superior Court* (1990) 50 C3d 785, 804, 268 CR 753 (claim by corporation in response to subpoena served on its custodian of records). See §48.18 on stating the objection.

2. Scope of Immunity

§48.10 a. Civil Trials

In *New York Times Co. v Superior Court* (1990) 51 C3d 453, 273 CR 98, the California Supreme Court clarified three aspects of the protection against contempt provided by Cal Const art I, §2(b) in civil cases:

- The scope of the information protected by the provision is quite broad. It includes all unpublished information whether that information is confidential or not. It includes photographs and direct observations, not just information from sources. 51 C3d at 458 n4.

- The protection against contempt is absolute rather than qualified. No evidentiary showing can overcome the immunity (except in cases in which the party seeking to compel disclosure has a federal constitutional right to the evidence). 51 C3d at 461. See §48.11.

- Article I, §2(b) does not create a privilege. Thus, the trial court may impose any sanction other than contempt without violating that section. In effect, the section provides virtually absolute protection for nonparty witnesses when the only remedy against nondisclosure is contempt. Because a full range of court sanctions other than contempt is available against parties, the section affords little protection to journalists who are parties. 51 C3d at 462.

§48.11 b. Criminal Trials

In *Delaney v Superior Court* (1990) 50 C3d 785, 268 CR 753, the California Supreme Court comprehensively considered the scope of the journalist's immunity from contempt in criminal trials. Concluding that US Const amend VI's guaranty of a fair trial limits the literal enforcement of Cal Const art I, §2(b) in criminal cases when the defendant seeks the information, the court established procedural and substantive standards to govern efforts by defendants to compel journalists' testimony and claims for immunity under the California Constitution in criminal trials. In *Miller v Superior Court* (1999) 21 C4th 883, 901, 89 CR2d 834, the California Supreme Court addressed the issue left unanswered by *Delaney*—whether the prosecution in a criminal proceeding has a constitutional interest sufficient to require the disclosure of information otherwise protected by the shield law. Holding that the shield law protection of Cal Const art I, §2(b) is virtually absolute and may only yield to a conflicting federal constitutional right, the court decided that the People's right to due process of law incorporated in Cal Const art I, §29 is not a constitutional interest sufficient to overcome the shield law. 21 C4th at 897. The court further held that there is not conflict between the shield law and the subsequently enacted People's "right to truth-in-evidence" under Cal Const art I, §28(d) because the latter, by its own terms, does not effect "any existing statutory or constitutional right of the press." 21 C4th at 894. Finding no conflict between the shield law and the People's "right to due process of law," the court held that there was no need to engage in the balancing of interests prescribed by *Delaney.* 21 C4th at 895. See §§48.14–48.15.

§48.12   II. ASSERTION OF PRIVILEGE OR CLAIM OF IMMUNITY

Generally, an objection to giving testimony or producing unpublished material will be made on the basis of both the qualified privilege not to disclose information and the immunity from contempt. The determination of whether the privilege or immunity applies involves questions of both fact and law that can best be addressed in a foundational hearing out of the presence of the jury under Evid C §405.

Because the availability of alternative sources must be ascertained, witnesses other than the journalist may need to be called. If it is necessary to hear the reporter's disputed information to resolve the privilege or immunity issue, that information should be reviewed in camera. Otherwise, the court would destroy the protection in order to rule on it. To avoid confusion, save time, and preserve the continuity of the trial, the court should conduct the §405 hearing and rule on the objection before the jury is empaneled. If the hearing is conducted at this time, extended proceedings outside the presence of the jury may be avoided and a petition for extraordinary relief may be filed to challenge the trial court's ruling, as outlined in *New York Times Co. v Superior Court* (1990) 51 C3d 453, 273 CR 98, without risking a midtrial stay of proceedings. See §§48.8–48.9.

§48.13   A. Civil Trials

In a civil case in which the immunity is properly claimed by a nonparty journalist, the trial judge could theoretically order the witness to answer but stop short of actually enforcing the order through a contempt citation. This procedure technically honors the prohibition against contempt but may create the appearance of the trial judge's ineffectiveness and engender disrespect for the court, particularly if the order and the journalist's refusal to answer occur in the presence of the jury. The better procedure, therefore, is for the court to rule in response to a proper claim under Cal Const art I, §2(b) that the journalist need not answer the question.

B. Criminal Trials

§48.14   1. Triggering *Delaney* Protection

When a criminal defendant seeks to compel a journalist's testimony, the journalist can trigger the procedural and substantive protection under *Delaney v Superior Court* (1990) 50 C3d 785, 268 CR 753, by a prima facie showing that the testimony would require the disclosure of either a confidential source or unpublished information. In *Miller v Superior Court* (1999) 21 C4th 883,

901, 89 CR2d 834, the California Supreme Court further refined the *Delaney* holding, deciding that "the absoluteness of the immunity embodied in the media shield law only yields to a conflicting federal, or perhaps, state constitutional right." See §48.11.

To overcome the journalist's prima facie showing, the criminal defendant must show "a reasonable possibility the information will materially assist his defense." 50 C3d at 808. The showing "need not be detailed or specific, but it must rest on more than mere speculation." 50 C3d at 809. This threshold showing does not entitle the defendant to the journalist's testimony. Rather, it triggers the balancing of competing interests by the court. See *People v Sanchez* (1995) 12 C4th 1, 47 CR2d 843; §48.3.

Delaney provides one additional procedural safeguard. If the trial court determines that the journalist's claim of confidentiality or sensitivity is "colorable," the trial court must receive the journalist's testimony in camera to apply the balancing test. 50 C3d at 814. See §48.15.

In a case of first impression, one court held that when, in a criminal trial, a defense witness protected under the shield law resists proper cross-examination on the basis of that law, the testimony of that witness on direct examination, though it did not consist of unpublished information protected by the shield law, may on an appropriate motion by the People be barred or stricken unless the defendant can show that the refusal of the court to receive such evidence would deprive him or her of a federal constitutional right to a fair trial and that, in the circumstances, his or her right transcends that of the witness under the shield law. If the defendant makes such showings, the testimony of the witness on direct may be received by the trier of fact and the journalist may be held in contempt of court for refusing to respond to proper cross-examination seeking information that would otherwise be protected under the shield law. *Fost v Superior Court* (2000) 80 CA4th 724, 732, 95 CR2d 620.

§48.15   2. Applying *Delaney* Balancing Test

In *Delaney v Superior Court* (1990) 50 C3d 785, 268 CR 753, the court identified four factors to be balanced by the trial court in determining whether the federal constitutional interest of the criminal defendant in the journalist's testimony is sufficient to overcome the journalist's rights under Cal Const art I, §2(b):

- Whether the unpublished information is confidential or sensitive;
- Whether nondisclosure will serve the interests sought to be protected by the shield law;
- The importance of the information to the criminal defendant; and
- Whether an alternative source for the unpublished information exists.

In some federal court cases, the existence of an alternative source for the information is enough to preclude the journalist's testimony regardless of other factors. The *Delaney* court, however, did not consider this factor to be dispositive in itself; it must be weighed along with the others listed above. See §48.11.

§48.16   3. Hypothetical Case History

The following hypothetical case history will illustrate some of the issues that may face trial attorneys and the court in this area:

- A journalist interviews witnesses at a crime scene. One of them, whose name is known to both the police and the defendant, makes a statement to the journalist that was not made to police investigators. The journalist checks with confidential sources and concludes that the statement is reliable. Parts of the statement are published in the local newspaper. The prosecution subpoenas the journalist to testify to the published information. The journalist moves to quash the subpoena. This motion will be denied because there is no showing that information protected by either the qualified privilege not to disclose information or the journalist's immunity from contempt is implicated. The protection exists for certain types of information; it is not a privilege against appearing in court.

- At trial, the prosecution asks the journalist what the witness said. Defense counsel chooses not to object for tactical reasons, and the journalist's attorney objects on the grounds of hearsay. This objection will probably be overruled on the grounds that the journalist has standing only to object on privilege and immunity grounds and that only the parties can raise other objections.

- The prosecution asks the journalist to authenticate the published material. The journalist's attorney objects. Such a question will usually not be viewed as invading the qualified privilege. Because the question does not ask for unpublished information, the immunity from contempt is not implicated.

- On cross-examination, defense counsel asks what else the witness said that was not published. The journalist testifies that the answer will involve unpublished information. To trigger the balancing test required by *Delaney v Superior Court* (1990) 50 C3d 785, 268 CR 753, the defendant must now show that the answer will materially assist the defense. At this juncture, the trial judge faces a particularly difficult decision. If the defendant's only showing in support of the question is that it might provide impeachment, the showing is based on "mere speculation" and is insufficient to overcome the journalist's constitutional protection. Without the ability to explore unpublished information, however, cross-examination is limited. *Delaney* leaves little doubt that, on these facts, the cross-examination cannot be permitted. If the defense sought information about the statements from the confidential sources, the ruling would be even more clear. To preclude the potential for prejudice to the defense, one possibility is for the trial judge to rule that the prosecution cannot call the journalist under these circumstances, even to establish the published information.

§48.17   III. WAIVER

Both the qualified privilege not to disclose information and the journalist's immunity from contempt belong to the journalist rather than to the source. *Los Angeles Memorial Coliseum Comm'n v National Football League* (CD Cal 1981) 89 FRD 489, 494. Unlike the attorney-client and physician-patient privileges, the journalist's privilege and immunity may not be waived by the source over the objection of the professional.

Publication or broadcast of some information does not waive the protection for other related information that is not published. *Playboy Enters. v Superior Court* (1984) 154 CA3d 14, 201 CR 207. See §48.4. Although the case law offers little guidance on the issue, disclosure of unpublished information or the name of a confidential source to someone outside the journalistic process may waive the right not to reveal the same information in court.

The most difficult waiver issue arises when a question is asked at trial that may or may not call for unpublished information. Does the reporter risk a finding of waiver by answering? The attorney representing the journalist witness can avoid this risk by requiring a court order before answering borderline questions so that the answer is not voluntary and does not constitute a waiver. If this situation is likely to arise, the attorney should alert the trial judge in advance to avoid confusion and state the objection as follows:

> Your Honor, I object to the question on the ground that an answer might be construed as a waiver of rights protected by the First Amendment to the United States Constitution; California Constitution article I, section 2(a) and 2(b); and Evidence Code section 1070. I therefore advise the witness not to answer unless ordered to do so by the Court.

§48.18   IV. STATING THE OBJECTION

An objection may usually be stated to raise both the qualified privilege not to disclose information and the journalist's immunity from contempt, as follows:

> Your Honor, I object on the ground that the question calls for information protected by the First Amendment to the United States Constitution; California Constitution article I, section 2(a) and 2(b); and Evidence Code section 1070.

If the objection is overruled and the journalist wishes to preserve the issue for appellate review, the journalist may decline to answer, as follows:

> Your Honor, I respectfully decline to answer because I cannot answer the question without revealing information protected by the First Amendment to the United States Constitution; California Constitution article I, section 2(a) and 2(b); and Evidence Code section 1070.

After the issue is first raised and stated on the record, subsequent questions may be dealt with in either of the following ways:

> Your Honor, I object on the ground previously stated.

> Your Honor, I respectfully decline to answer for the reasons previously stated.

§48.19 V. RESPONSE IF JOURNALIST IS CITED FOR CONTEMPT

If the objection is overruled and the journalist is cited for contempt, appellate review is available by petition for extraordinary writ. A petition for writ is premature unless the journalist has been cited for contempt. The California Supreme Court has made it clear that a stay of the contempt by the trial judge is appropriate to permit appellate review and that if the trial court does not grant a stay, the appellate court should do so while it is considering whether or not to issue the extraordinary writ. See *Miller v Superior Court* (1999) 21 C4th 883, 89 CR2d 834; *New York Times Co. v Superior Court* (1990) 51 C3d 453, 273 CR 98. It is, of course, important for the attorney representing the journalist to formally request the stay on the record.

§48.20 VI. CALIFORNIA CONSTITUTION; STATUTE

The following constitutional amendment was adopted by the voters in 1980 and is now set forth in Cal Const art I, §2(b). Only minor immaterial changes in current Evid C §1070 appear in the constitutional provision:

> A publisher, editor, reporter, or other person connected with or employed upon a newspaper, magazine, or other periodical publication, or by a press association or wire service, or any person who has been so connected or employed, shall not be adjudged in contempt by a judicial, legislative, or administrative body, or any other body having the power to issue subpoenas, for refusing to disclose the source of any information procured while so connected or employed for publication in a newspaper, magazine or other periodical publication, or for refusing to disclose any unpublished information obtained or prepared in gathering, receiving or processing of information for communication to the public.

> Nor shall a radio or television news reporter or other person connected with or employed by a radio or television station, or any person who has been so connected or employed, be so adjudged in contempt for refusing to disclose the source of any information procured while so connected or employed for news or news commentary purposes on radio or television, or for refusing to disclose any unpublished information

obtained or prepared in gathering, receiving or processing of information for communication to the public.

As used in this subdivision, "unpublished information" includes information not disseminated to the public by the person from whom disclosure is sought, whether or not related information has been disseminated and includes, but is not limited to, all notes, outtakes, photographs, tapes or other data of whatever sort not itself disseminated to the public through a medium of communication, whether or not published information based upon or related to such material has been disseminated.

49

Voter's Privilege

    I. NATURE AND PURPOSE §49.1

    II. REQUIREMENTS
        A. Public Election; Secret Ballot §49.2
        B. Tenor of Vote Permitted §49.3

    III. WHO CAN CLAIM §49.4

    IV. EXCEPTION FOR ILLEGAL VOTE §49.5

    V. WAIVER THROUGH DISCLOSURE §49.6

    VI. RULING ON PRIVILEGE
        A. Procedure §49.7
        B. Burden of Proof §49.8

    VII. STATUTE §49.9

    VIII. ILLUSTRATIONS OF PRIVILEGE §49.10

    IX. STATING CLAIM OF PRIVILEGE
        A. By Witness §49.11
        B. By Trial Counsel §49.12

§49.1 I. NATURE AND PURPOSE

Persons who legally cast a secret ballot at a public election have a privilege not to disclose how they voted. Evid C §1050. The purpose of this privilege is to preserve the secrecy of the ballot. The scope of the privilege is limited:

- It does not entitle the voter to prevent other persons from disclosing their vote (see §49.4);

- It does not apply to illegal voting (see §49.5); and

- It is waived if the voter makes an unprivileged disclosure of how he or she voted (see §49.6).

The text of Evid C §1050, governing the voter's privilege, is set out in §49.9.

II. REQUIREMENTS

§49.2   A. Public Election; Secret Ballot

The voter's privilege covers voting in "a public election where the voting is by secret ballot." Evid C §1050. Although the California Constitution requires that voting be secret (Cal Const art II, §7), this provision applies only to "elections held in the ordinary course of civil government, and not necessarily to all public elections." See *Alden v Superior Court* (1963) 212 CA2d 764, 770, 28 CR 387 (inapplicable to election for formation of water district). A public election by secret ballot presumably exists, for which the privilege is available, if:

- The election is held to implement the organization or operation of a public entity;

- Voting is open to all persons of a stated class (as distinct from a vote among particular persons, *e.g.*, the members of a legislative body); and

- The voting is required to be, or is in fact, conducted by secret ballot.

See Evid C §1050.

§49.3   B. Tenor of Vote Permitted

The voter's privilege permits disclosure of the "tenor" of a person's vote. Evid C §1050. Voters may refuse (1) to disclose how they voted at a particular election on a ballot measure or on candidates for an office or (2) to answer more general questions on how they voted, *e.g.*, whether they ever voted for candidates of a particular party. The privilege does not, however, relieve them from answering questions about other aspects of their vote, *e.g.*, whether they voted at all or the time, place, or circumstances of their voting.

§49.4   III. WHO CAN CLAIM

Only the voter can claim the privilege. Evid C §1050. The right to claim it arises when a voter is asked to disclose the vote by testifying or furnishing documents. A voter cannot invoke the privilege to exclude proof through another witness of the identity or contents of the voter's ballot. Therefore, the procedure of Evid C §916, under which the judge may exclude privileged information in the absence of any claimant of the privilege, does not apply to the voter's privilege. See Comment to Evid C §916.

§49.5   IV. EXCEPTION FOR ILLEGAL VOTE

The privilege does not apply to a vote cast illegally, *e.g.*, by an ineligible or improperly registered voter. Thus, in an election contest, the privilege does not prevent the contestant from proving that particular persons voted illegally for the opponent (*Singletary v Kelley* (1966) 242 CA2d 611, 51 CR 682), but the privilege against self-incrimination (Evid C §940; see chap 46) is available to a witness whose answer to a question might subject them to prosecution for voting illegally.

§49.6 V. WAIVER THROUGH DISCLOSURE

The voter's privilege is not available if the voter "previously made an unprivileged disclosure of the tenor of his vote." Evid C §1050. A privileged disclosure (*e.g.*, to the voter's attorney or spouse (see chaps 34, 40) is not a waiver. Even the voter's unprivileged statement of how he or she voted may not always be a waiver. The requirement of ballot secrecy is intended to enable a voter to indicate to other persons that he or she is voting one way and actually to vote another. See *Smith v Thomas* (1898) 121 C 533, 536, 54 P 71. The courts may hold that an unsworn statement by a voter who does not wish or intend to reveal the true vote is not a "disclosure of the tenor of his vote" and thus is not a waiver.

A person who testifies to a personal vote without claiming the privilege waives it. Compelled testimony by the court does not constitute a waiver. Evid C §919(b). See Comment to 1974 amendment to Evid C §919.

VI. RULING ON PRIVILEGE

§49.7 A. Procedure

When the voter's privilege is claimed, its existence and applicability may present questions of preliminary fact that must be decided by the judge as an independent issue. Evid C §405. The parties may present evidence on these issues, but the court cannot require the claimant to reveal the tenor of the vote for the purpose of ruling on the privilege. Evid C §915(a).

§49.8 B. Burden of Proof

The voter claiming the privilege has the burden of establishing that the vote was cast at a public election at which the voting was done by secret ballot. See §49.2. The opponent of the privilege (the proponent of the offered evidence) has the burden of proving that the vote was cast illegally (see §49.5) or that the privilege has been waived by disclosure (see §49.6).

§49.9 VII. STATUTE

Evidence Code §1050 states:

> If he claims the privilege, a person has a privilege to refuse to disclose the tenor of his vote at a public election where the voting is by secret ballot unless he voted illegally or he previously made an unprivileged disclosure of the tenor of his vote.

§49.10 VIII. ILLUSTRATIONS OF PRIVILEGE

The voter's privilege may be available for the following questions:

- "For whom did you vote for district attorney?"
- "Did you vote for 187?"
- "Have you ever voted for a Republican?"

IX. STATING CLAIM OF PRIVILEGE

§49.11 A. By Witness

Your Honor, I claim the voter's privilege.

§49.12 B. By Trial Counsel

Trial counsel should preferably make this statement outside the presence of the jury:

> Your Honor, that question calls for disclosure of the tenor of a vote by secret ballot at a public election.

[Option 1: Counsel represents witness entitled to claim privilege]

> On behalf of _ _[name of party]_ _, I claim the voter's privilege and object to the question on that ground.

[Option 2: Witness holds privilege and is not represented by counsel]

> Your Honor, I request that you advise the witness of _ _[his/her]_ _ right to refuse to answer on the ground of the voter's privilege under Evidence Code section 1050.

50

Penitent's Privilege

I. NATURE OF PRIVILEGE §50.1

II. REQUIREMENTS
   A. Cleric §50.2
   B. Penitent §50.3
   C. Communication §50.4
   D. Confidentiality §50.5

III. WHO CAN CLAIM §50.6

IV. TERMINATION AND WAIVER
   A. Death of Penitent §50.7
   B. Waiver §50.8

V. RULING ON PRIVILEGE
   A. Procedure §50.9
   B. Burden of Proof §50.10

VI. STATUTE §50.11

VII. ILLUSTRATIONS OF PRIVILEGE §50.12

VIII. STATING CLAIM OF PRIVILEGE
   A. By Witness §50.13
   B. By Trial Counsel §50.14

§50.1 I. NATURE OF PRIVILEGE

A penitent is any person who makes a "penitential communication" to a cleric. A penitential communication is one that a cleric receives in confidence in the course of clerical duties and is required to keep secret by the discipline of a religious organization. Evid C §1032. A penitent has a privilege to refuse to disclose the communication and to prevent others (including a cleric) such disclosure it. Evid C §1033. See Evid C §1031. See generally *In re Lifschutz* (1970) 2 C3d 415, 427, 85 CR 829 (explaining purpose of cleric's privilege); 2 Witkin, California Evidence, *Witnesses* §§238-240 (4th ed 2000).

The penitent's privilege is distinct from the privilege of the clergy (see Evid C §1034), discussed in chap 51.

The text of Evid C §§1030-1033, governing the penitent's privilege, is set out in §50.11. These sections replace the earlier "confessions" privilege in former CCP §1881(3). When researching cases decided under former §1881(3), counsel should be aware that the former requirements were somewhat different from those in Evid C §§1030–1033.

II. REQUIREMENTS

§50.2   A. Cleric

For the penitent's privilege to apply, the penitential communication must be made to a cleric ("member of the clergy" in the statute). Evid C §1032. "Member of the clergy" is broadly defined as "a priest, minister, religious practitioner, or similar functionary of a church or of a religious denomination or religious organization." See Evid C §1030. But unlike an attorney (Evid C §950; see §34.8), a physician (Evid C §990), or a psychotherapist (see Evid C §1010(a); see also §§36.2, 37.2), the cleric must be actually qualified. The privilege cannot be based on a penitent's reasonable but mistaken belief that the person receiving the communication is a cleric.

§50.3   B. Penitent

A penitent is anyone who makes a penitential communication to a cleric. Evid C §1031. No legal requirement seems to exist that the penitent belong to the cleric's religious organization or be personally seeking religious aid. See *Cimijotti v Paulsen* (ND Iowa 1963) 219 F Supp 621 (confidential statements to priest to corroborate another person's application for church sanctions held privileged).

§50.4   C. Communication

The Evidence Code does not restrict the possible content of a privileged penitential communication. It may relate to any matter that the cleric is authorized or accustomed to hear and required to keep secret under the rules of the church or religious organization to which the cleric belongs. Evid C §1032. See *People v Johnson* (1969) 270 CA2d 204, 75 CR 605 (statement to cleric by stranger fleeing from police was not privileged in absence of showing that cleric had authority to hear statement and duty to keep it secret). See also *People v Edwards* (1988) 203 CA3d 1358, 1364, 248 CR 53 (cleric-penitent privilege held not to apply in prosecution for grand theft, because defendant did not seek absolution but only asked for help in preventing bad checks from bouncing); *People v Thompson* (1982) 133 CA3d 419, 425, 184 CR 72 (confession to Church of Scientology ethics officer not privileged, because officer not authorized to hear confession and keep it secret).

§50.5   D. Confidentiality

The communication must be "made in confidence, in the presence of no third person so far as the penitent is aware." Evid C §1032. See *People v Thompson* (1982) 133 CA3d 419, 422, 184 CR 72 (confession not privileged, because no showing of confidentiality). If an eavesdropper whose presence is unknown to the penitent overhears the information, the privilege can be asserted to prevent disclosure. Evid C §1033.

The presence of a third party known to the penitent apparently destroys the privilege even though the third person's presence may be consistent with religious rules or practice. Thus, the privilege apparently cannot apply to a married couple's joint consultation with a cleric, even though either spouse can disclose to the other what he or she alone has said to a clergy member without waiving the privilege, because the marital communications privilege attaches to the conversation between the spouses. See Evid C §912(c) (privileged disclosure not a waiver). On the marital communications privilege, see chap 40.

A presumption of confidentiality shifts the burden of proof on this issue to the opponent of the privilege. See Evid C §917, discussed in §50.10.

§50.6 III. WHO CAN CLAIM

If the penitent is asked to disclose the privileged communication, the communication is privileged. A penitent may also claim it if present or represented in the proceeding when the cleric or another person is asked to disclose the privileged communication. Evid C §1033. If the penitent is not a witness or party, the judge may be required to exclude the privileged communication under Evid C §916.

IV. TERMINATION AND WAIVER

§50.7 A. Death of Penitent

Because the penitent is the only person entitled to claim the penitent's privilege (see Evid C §1033), the privilege is terminated by the penitent's death. The penitent's death does not, however, prevent a claim of the cleric's privilege for the same communication. See Evid C §1034. Similarly, the cleric's death does not prevent a claim of the penitent's privilege.

§50.8 B. Waiver

The penitent, as holder of the privilege (see §33.4), waives the privilege if the penitent discloses, or consents to disclosure of, a significant part of the privileged communication. See *People v Johnson* (1969) 270 CA2d 204, 75 CR 605 (claimant of privilege waived it by tacitly consenting to cleric's repeating to police what claimant had told cleric). The text of Evid C §912(a), (c), governing waiver of the penitent's privilege, is set out in §33.31.

A common form of waiver is the penitent's failure to claim the privilege whenever the opportunity arises. Thus, waiver may occur from failure to claim the privilege on discovery (see §33.6) or, even if it is claimed then, from failure to claim it at the trial. If the penitent testifies, or permits another to testify, to the contents of the privileged communication, the privilege terminates—not only for the current proceeding but for all future purposes. Evid C §912(a). A court's improper overruling of a party-penitent's claim of the privilege is error (Evid C §918), and the disclosure is inadmissible in later proceedings (Evid C §919).

No waiver exists if the penitent makes or consents to the disclosure under coercion (Evid C §912(a)) or if the disclosure is protected by another privilege, *e.g.,* the attorney-client or marital communications privilege (Evid C §912(c)).

Because the penitent's privilege and the cleric's privilege are treated separately by Evid C §912(a) for purposes of waiver, the waiver of either privilege does not waive the other with respect to a particular communication. See also Comment to Evid C §1034.

If no holder is present to claim the privilege, the judge may be required to exclude the information under Evid C §916.

V. RULING ON PRIVILEGE

§50.9   A. Procedure

When the penitent's privilege is claimed and contested, its existence and applicability present questions of preliminary fact that must be heard and decided by the judge alone. See Evid C §405.

Penal Code §1524(c) and Evid C §915(b) provide a special procedure for determining claims of privilege for documents seized under a search warrant issued against a cleric. Although the penitent is unlikely to be a party to the proceeding, the court may be required to exclude items subject to the penitent's privilege under Evid C §916.

§50.10   B. Burden of Proof

The claimant of the penitent's privilege has the burden of proving that:

- The person who received the communication was a cleric (see Evid C §1030, discussed in §50.2); and

- The cleric received the communication in the course of the discipline and practice of a "church, denomination or organization" and was required by that discipline to keep the communication secret (see Evid C §1032, discussed in §50.4).

The opponent of the privilege (the proponent of the offered evidence) has the burden of proving the following:

- That the penitent did not make a "penitential communication" (Evid C §1032; see *People v Edwards* (1988) 203 CA3d 1358, 248 CR 53);

- That the penitent did not make the communication in confidence (Evid

C §§917, 1032 (establishing the presumption of confidentiality); see *People v Johnson* (1969) 270 CA2d 204, 75 CR 605 (presumption overcome by evidence that claimant tacitly consented to cleric's repeating to police what claimant had told cleric)); and

- Waiver.

§50.11   VI. STATUTE

Evidence Code §§1030-1033, referred to in these provisions as "this article," apply to the penitent's privilege. Section 1034, set out in §51.11, is also part of "this article."

- Evidence Code §1030 states:

    As used in this article, a "member of the clergy" means a priest, minister, religious practitioner, or similar functionary of a church or of a religious denomination or religious organization.

- Evidence Code §1031 states:

    As used in this article, "penitent" means a person who has made a penitential communication to a member of the clergy.

- Evidence Code §1032 states:

    As used in this article, "penitential communication" means a communication made in confidence, in the presence of no third person so far as the penitent is aware, to a member of the clergy who, in the course of the discipline or practice of the clergy member's church, denomination, or organization, is authorized or accustomed to hear such communications and, under the discipline or tenets of his or her church, denomination, or organization, has a duty to keep those communications secret.

- Evidence Code §1033 states:

    Subject to Section 912 [on waiver], a penitent, whether or not a party, has a privilege to refuse to disclose, and to prevent another from disclosing, a penitential communication if he or she claims the privilege.

§50.12   VII. ILLUSTRATIONS OF PRIVILEGE

The penitent's privilege may be available to keep confidential an answer that might otherwise have been required in response to the following questions:

- "Didn't you tell your priest that you voluntarily submitted to the defendant's sexual advances?"
- "What did the defendant tell you, Father McFeeley?"
- "Did you hear the defendant tell Rabbi Loeb that he was the murderer?"

VIII. STATING CLAIM OF PRIVILEGE

§50.13   A. By Witness

Your Honor, I claim the privilege of a penitent.

§50.14   B. By Trial Counsel

Trial counsel should preferably make this statement outside the presence of the jury:

> Your Honor, that question calls for disclosure of a privileged penitential communication to a cleric.

>> [Option 1: Counsel represents party entitled to claim privilege]

> On behalf of _ _[name of party]_ _, I claim the penitent's privilege and object to the question on that ground.

>> [Option 2: Witness holds privilege and is not represented by counsel]

> Your Honor, I request that you advise the witness of _ _[his/her]_ _ right to refuse to answer on the ground of the penitent's privilege.

>> [Option 3: Neither witness nor party can claim privilege (Evid C §916)]

> I move that Your Honor exclude the answer as privileged.

51

Cleric's Privilege

I. NATURE OF PRIVILEGE §51.1

II. REQUIREMENTS
   A. Cleric §51.2
   B. Penitent §51.3
   C. Communication §51.4
   D. Confidentiality §51.5

III. WHO CAN CLAIM §51.6

IV. TERMINATION AND WAIVER
   A. Death of Cleric §51.7
   B. Waiver §51.8

V. RULING ON PRIVILEGE
   A. Procedure §51.9
   B. Burden of Proof §51.10

VI. STATUTE §51.11

VII. ILLUSTRATIONS OF PRIVILEGE §51.12

VIII. STATING CLAIM OF PRIVILEGE
   A. By Witness §51.13
   B. By Trial Counsel §51.14

§51.1   I. NATURE OF PRIVILEGE

A cleric who receives a "penitential communication" has a privilege to refuse to disclose it. Evid C §1034. A penitential communication is one that a cleric receives in confidence in the course of clerical duties and is required to keep secret by the discipline of a religious organization. Evid C §1032. On the purpose of the privilege, see *Trummel v U.S.* (1980) 445 US 40, 53, 63 L Ed 2d 186, 196, 100 S Ct 906; *In re Lifschutz* (1970) 2 C3d 415, 427, 85 CR 829.

The cleric's privilege is distinct from the privilege of the penitent (Evid C §1033), which is discussed in chap 50. These two privileges supersede the "confessions" privilege in former CCP §1881(3).

Note that Cal Const art I, §28(d) (the "truth-in-evidence" provision of Proposition 8) expressly leaves the Evidence Code privileges sections untouched.

II. REQUIREMENTS

§51.2   A. Cleric

For the cleric's privilege to apply, the penitential communication must be received by a cleric ("member of the clergy" in the statute). Evid C §1032. A "member of the clergy" is broadly defined as "a priest, minister, religious practitioner, or similar functionary of a church or of a religious denomination or religious organization." See Evid C §1030. But unlike an attorney (Evid C §950; see §34.8) or a physician (Evid C §990; see Evid C §1010(a); §§36.2, 37.2), the cleric must be actually qualified. A noncleric cannot claim the privilege even if the penitent reasonably believed him or her to be a cleric.

§51.3   B. Penitent

A penitent is anyone who makes a penitential communication to a cleric. Evid C §1031. There seems to be no legal requirement that the penitent be a member of the cleric's religious organization or be personally seeking religious aid. See *Cimijotti v Paulsen* (ND Iowa 1963) 219 F Supp 621 (confidential statements to priest to corroborate another person's application for church sanctions held privileged).

§51.4   C. Communication

The Evidence Code does not restrict the possible content of a privileged penitential communication. It may relate to any matter that the cleric is authorized or accustomed to hear and required to keep secret under the rules of the church or religious organization. Evid C §1032. See *People v Johnson* (1969) 270 CA2d 204, 75 CR 605 (statement to cleric by stranger fleeing from police was not privileged in absence of showing that cleric had authority to hear statement and duty to keep it secret). See also *People v Thompson* (1982) 133 CA3d 419, 425, 184 CR 72 (confession to Church of Scientology ethics officer not privileged, because officer not authorized to hear confession and keep it secret). See generally Jefferson's California Evidence Benchbook §§39.1–39.10 (3d ed CJA-CEB 1997).

§51.5   D. Confidentiality

The communication must be "made in confidence, in the presence of no third person so far as the penitent is aware." Evid C §1032. See *People v Thompson* (1982) 133 CA3d 419, 427, 184 CR 72 (confession not privileged, because no showing of confidentiality). If an eavesdropper whose presence is unknown to the penitent overhears the information, the cleric can continue to claim the privilege for his or her own testimony even though the cleric's privilege (unlike the penitent's privilege) cannot be asserted against the testimony of the eavesdropper.

The presence of a third person known to the penitent apparently destroys the cleric's privilege even though the third person's presence may be consistent with religious rules or practice. Thus, the privilege apparently cannot apply to two penitents' joint consultation with a cleric.

A presumption of confidentiality shifts the burden of proof on this issue to the opponent of the privilege. See Evid C §917, discussed in §51.10.

§51.6　III. WHO CAN CLAIM

A cleric can claim the privilege if asked to disclose the privileged communication. The cleric cannot claim it to prevent disclosure by the penitent or by any other person. Evid C §1034.

A cleric has no legal duty to claim the privilege. Although a cleric necessarily receives the communication under a religious duty of secrecy (Evid C §1032), the cleric is legally free to use his or her own judgment about disclosure. See Comment to Evid C §1034.

If a cleric fails to claim the privilege, the penitent may be entitled to stop him or her from disclosure by claiming the penitent's privilege (Evid C §1033). If the penitent is not a party, the judge may be required to exclude the cleric's disclosure under Evid C §916.

IV. TERMINATION AND WAIVER

§51.7　A. Death of Cleric

Because a cleric is the only person entitled to claim the cleric's privilege (see Evid C §1034, discussed in §51.6), the privilege is terminated by the cleric's death. The cleric's death does not, however, prevent a claim of the penitent's privilege for the same communication. See Evid C §1033. Similarly, the penitent's death does not prevent a claim of the cleric's privilege.

§51.8　B. Waiver

The cleric, as holder of the privilege, waives the privilege if the cleric discloses or consents to disclosure of a significant part of the privileged communication. The text of Evid C §912(a), (c), governing waiver of the cleric's privilege, is set out in §33.31.

A common form of waiver is the cleric's failure to claim the privilege whenever the opportunity arises. Thus, waiver may occur from failure to claim the privilege on discovery or, even if it is claimed then, from failure to claim it at the trial. If the cleric testifies to the contents of a privileged communication, the privilege is destroyed—not only for the current proceeding but for all future purposes. Evid C §912(a).

There is no waiver if the cleric makes or consents to the disclosure under coercion (Evid C §912(a)) or if the disclosure is protected by another privilege (Evid C §912(c)). Because the cleric's privilege and the penitent's privilege are treated separately by Evid C §912(a) for purposes of waiver, the waiver of either privilege does not waive the other with respect to a particular communication. See also Comment to Evid C §1034.

V. RULING ON PRIVILEGE

§51.9   A. Procedure

When the cleric's privilege is claimed and contested, its existence and applicability present questions of preliminary fact that must be heard and decided by the judge as independent issues. Evidence on these fact issues is presented under Evid C §§400–402 and 405 when the existence of a preliminary fact is disputed.

Evidence Code §915(a) prevents the judge from requiring disclosure of information claimed to be within the cleric's privilege for purposes of ruling on the claim.

Penal Code §1524(c) provides for a hearing on claims of privilege against a search warrant for documentary evidence in the possession of a cleric who is "not reasonably suspected of engaging or having engaged in criminal activity related to the documentary evidence for which a warrant is requested." If the court determines in such a hearing that there are "no other feasible means to rule on the validity" of the claim of privilege, the court must proceed under Evid C §915(b), which provides for confidential disclosure in chambers (see §33.17). Evid C §915(a).

§51.10   B. Burden of Proof

The claimant of the cleric's privilege has the burden of proving:

- Status as a cleric when the communication was received (see Evid C §1030); and

- That the communication was received in the course of the discipline and practice of the religious organization and was required by that discipline to keep the communication secret (see Evid C §1032).

The opponent of the privilege (the proponent of the offered evidence) has the burden of proving that the penitent did not make the communication in confidence. Evid C §917 (establishing the presumption of confidentiality; for statutory text, see §33.31). This burden of disproving confidentiality does not, however, include refuting the cleric's general duty of secrecy imposed by religious discipline. That duty must be proved by the claimant in proving the cleric-penitent relationship. On the requirement of confidentiality, see §51.5.

The opponent of the privilege also has the burden of proving waiver. See §51.8.

The claimant's and opponent's respective burdens of proof are discussed in the Comment to Evid C §405.

§51.11 VI. STATUTE

The text of Evid C §1034, set out below, applies to the cleric's privilege. The text of Evid C §§1030-1033, on the penitent's privilege, is set out in §50.11.

> Subject to Section 912 [on waiver], a member of the clergy, whether or not a party, has a privilege to refuse to disclose a penitential communication if he or she claims the privilege.

§51.12 VII. ILLUSTRATIONS OF PRIVILEGE

The cleric's privilege may be available to keep confidential a response that might otherwise have been required in answer to the following questions:

- "What did the defendant tell you, Rabbi Loeb?"
- "Father McFeeley, didn't the defendant tell you during confession that she was the murderer?"

VIII. STATING CLAIM OF PRIVILEGE

§51.13 A. By Witness

> Your Honor, I claim the privilege of a cleric.

§51.14 B. By Trial Counsel

Trial counsel should preferably make this statement outside the presence of the jury:

> Your Honor, that question calls for disclosure of a privileged penitential communication to a cleric.

> [Option 1: Counsel represents party entitled to claim cleric's privilege]

> On behalf of _ _[name of party]_ _, I claim the cleric's privilege and object to the question on that ground.

> [Option 2: Witness holds privilege and is not represented by counsel]

> Your Honor, I request that you advise the witness of _ _[his/her]_ _ right to refuse to answer on the ground of the cleric's privilege.

[Option 3: Neither witness nor party can claim privilege (Evid C §916)]

I move that Your Honor exclude the answer as privileged.

52

Motion to Strike

I. NATURE AND PURPOSE §52.1

II. WHO CAN MAKE MOTION TO STRIKE; USES OF MOTION §52.2

III. WHEN MOTION TO STRIKE IS PROPER
    A. Nonresponsive Answer to Proper Question §52.3
    B. Improper Question Answered Too Quickly for Objection §52.4
    C. Failure to Prove Foundation for Conditionally Admitted Evidence §52.5
    D. Admissible Evidence That Becomes Inadmissible §52.6

IV. HOW MOTION MUST BE MADE
    A. Timeliness; Request for Admonition §52.7
    B. Specification of Particular Evidence To Be Stricken §52.8
    C. Specification of Grounds §52.9
    D. Striking by Judge on Own Motion §52.10

V. POSSIBLE SANCTIONS: ADMONITION, MISCONDUCT, MISTRIAL §52.11

VI. EFFECT ON TRIAL RECORD OF STRIKING EVIDENCE §52.12

VII. WAIVER
    A. Failure to Make Proper Motion §52.13
    B. Failure to Obtain Ruling §52.14

VIII. DECIDING WHETHER TO MAKE MOTION
    A. Tactical Advantages and Disadvantages §52.15
    B. Alternatives to Motion to Strike §52.16

IX. EFFECT AT TRIAL OF FAILURE TO OBJECT TO NONRESPONSIVE ANSWER GIVEN DURING DEPOSITION §52.17

X. STATING MOTION AND REQUEST FOR ADMONITION §52.18

§52.1 I. NATURE AND PURPOSE

Like objections and motions to exclude, a motion to strike is a procedure for attacking inadmissible evidence. Evid C §353(a). If a motion to strike is necessary, waiver often occurs for failure to preserve the evidentiary issue.

As with all challenges to the admission of evidence, the motion must be timely made and indicate the specific ground on which it is based.

Evidence Code §353 provides that a verdict or finding may not be set aside, and the judgment or decision based on it reversed, because of the erroneous admission of evidence unless:

- The record shows that an objection to the evidence, or a motion to exclude or strike the evidence, was timely made and clearly specified the specific ground of the objection or motion; and
- The court reviewing the effect of the error rules that the admitted evidence should have been excluded on the ground stated and that the error resulted in a miscarriage of justice.

In addition to attacking testimony, motions to strike may also attack writings, statements of counsel, and demonstrative evidence or experiments. Motions to strike may also be used to strike:

- Witness answers when there is no opportunity to object, the answer contains inadmissible parts, or the answer is given before the court can rule;
- Conditionally admitted evidence when the foundation is not established (Evid C §403(b));
- Evidence admitted "subject to" a motion to strike (Evid C §403(b));
- Evidence when a witness testifies "out of order" (Evid C §320) and preliminary facts are not established to strike the entire testimony (Evid C §403(c)(2));
- The insinuation of facts that counsel is unable to prove;
- False or unsupportable representations of fact during opening statement;
- False statements during closing argument, including insinuation or suggestions not supported by the evidence; and
- Demonstrative or scientific evidence admitted but later found to be inadmissible.

A motion to strike may also be used as a sanction against specific types of misconduct, *e.g.,* learning during trial that evidence has been wrongfully withheld during discovery.

Motions to strike often require counsel to request cautionary admonitions or limiting instructions to the jurors at the same time. See CACI 106 and 5003 (formerly BAJI 1.02); CALJIC 2.50; Evid C §§320, 403(c). See also §52.13.

§52.2 II. WHO CAN MAKE MOTION TO STRIKE; USES OF MOTION

Both counsel examining a witness and other counsel in a multi-party trial may make a motion to strike. The judge, sua sponte, also has the power to strike inadmissible evidence. See *People v Neustice* (1972) 24 CA3d 178, 189, 100 CR 783.

Counsel examining a witness may move to strike nonresponsive answers for the following reasons:

- To confine the scope of the examination of the witness and thus the permissible scope of the opponent's subsequent examination (see Evid C §§773(a), 774); and

- To make clear counsel's right to repeat the question, in the hope of obtaining a responsive answer, without meeting the objection that it has already been asked and answered (see chap 11).

Opposing counsel frequently uses a motion to strike a nonresponsive argumentative answer that is inadmissible and damaging. Sometimes these volunteered responses are the result of coaching. If a witness continually volunteers information, it may be a good strategy to stop the argumentative answers, move to strike the answer, request that the judge admonish the witness to answer only the question asked, and request that the jury be admonished to disregard the improper argument.

III. WHEN MOTION TO STRIKE IS PROPER

§52.3 A. Nonresponsive Answer to Proper Question

"A witness must give responsive answers to questions, and answers that are not responsive shall be stricken on motion of any party." Evid C §766. If part of the answer is responsive, only the nonresponsive part should be stricken on this ground. *Bates v Newman* (1953) 121 CA2d 800, 804, 264 P2d 197.

If a witness's answer is responsive to a proper question but contains inadmissible matter, a motion to strike any inadmissible part of the answer may be made. Because the question was proper (*i.e.*, an answer to it could have been both responsive and admissible), opposing counsel had no reasonable opportunity to object before the question was answered. See, *e.g.*, *Johnston v Beadle* (1907) 6 CA 251, 91 P 1011; 3 Witkin, California Evidence, *Presentation at Trial* §385 (4th ed 2000).

§52.4 B. Improper Question Answered Too Quickly for Objection

Failure to object promptly to an improper question waives the objection and precludes a motion to strike an answer that is responsive to the question. A motion to strike is proper, however, if the question is answered so quickly that an objection cannot be interposed.

Counsel may be able to obviate the need for a motion to strike by preventing the witness from answering before an objection can be stated. For example, if counsel's own witness is being cross-examined and an improper question is asked, counsel may signal the witness by raising a hand as a warning not to answer before counsel has time to make an objection. If an opponent's witness is testifying, and counsel wants to object before the witness answers, the same approach may be effective, or counsel may prevent the answer by stating, "Just a moment!" If a witness repeatedly answers too quickly, the judge should be requested to warn the witness to pause before answering to allow counsel an opportunity to object. See also §4.17 (timeliness of objection).

Counsel should be aware that expert witnesses are prone to load their answers with argumentative or other inadmissible matter.

§52.5   C. Failure to Prove Foundation for Conditionally Admitted Evidence

Circumstances such as the availability of witnesses often make it impracticable to introduce evidence in logical or legal sequence. The judge may regulate the order of proof. Evid C §320. See chap 3. The judge also has the power to admit evidence conditionally, despite valid objections of irrelevancy or insufficient foundation, "subject to evidence of the preliminary fact being supplied later in the course of the trial" (Evid C §403(b)).

Opposing counsel should object to the conditional admission of evidence unless counsel knows that the foundational evidence undoubtedly will be supplied. When the judge allows the conditional admission of evidence, opposing counsel should request a specific offer of proof of the necessary preliminary fact and ask the court to specify in its ruling the conditions of admissibility.

Evidence can be admitted when later proof will establish the following:

- A fact necessary to establish relevancy (Evid C §403(a)(1));
- The authenticity of a document (Evid C §403(a)(3)); or
- The identity of the person who made the statement or committed the act that the evidence is being offered to prove (Evid C §403(a)(4)).

If objection is made, however, the procedure cannot be used to defer proof of a witness's personal knowledge of the matter to which the witness is testifying. Evid C §702(a). See §21.11 (objection of insufficient foundation).

If this procedure is permitted, counsel should request the court to require the proponent to indicate, and the court reporter to note, where this conditionally admitted evidence begins and ends. If such evidence is subsequently stricken on motion, the record will be clear and the jury can be advised of the specific evidence to be disregarded.

If the proponent fails to fulfill the condition of admissibility by resting without supplying proof of the necessary preliminary fact, the opponent should move to strike the conditionally admitted evidence. Failure to move to strike the evidence waives any error in its admission; the opponent's right to assert error in admitting the evidence is not preserved even though counsel's objection led to the conditional admission. *Estate of Wempe* (1921) 185 C 557, 564, 197 P 949. Further, the motion to strike must state the correct legal ground. *Walker v Nitzberg* (1970) 13 CA3d 359, 365, 91 CR 526. See also 3 Witkin, California Evidence, *Presentation at Trial* §388 (4th ed 2000). But see *Schwartz v Shapiro* (1964) 229 CA2d 238, 247, 40 CR 189 (trial court's apparent acceptance of blanket reservation of rights at end of trial held sufficient to avoid waiver).

To avoid inadvertently omitting the motion, counsel should keep a record of all conditionally admitted evidence in trial notes for review when the opponent rests. If evidence is conditionally admitted and then stricken on motion in a jury trial, counsel should consider asking the judge for an immediate instruction to the jury to disregard the stricken evidence. See Evid C §403(c)(1)–(2). Counsel should also consider whether the jury's exposure to the stricken evidence was sufficiently prejudicial to warrant moving for a mistrial or other sanctions.

§52.6   D. Admissible Evidence That Becomes Inadmissible

After evidence is admitted, grounds for excluding it may appear that were not available when it was admitted. In a condemnation case, for example, an expert's opinion on damages may seem unobjectionable when given on direct examination, but cross-examination may reveal that the opinion was based on improper considerations. This revelation entitles the cross-examiner to move to strike the original opinion testimony from the record. *People v Dunn* (1956) 46 C2d 639, 297 P2d 964. In a criminal case, when a prosecution witness refuses to answer questions on cross-examination, the entire testimony must be stricken. See *Gallaher v Superior Court* (1980) 103 CA3d 666, 673, 162 CR 389. A mistrial may also be possible. *People v Woodberry* (1970) 10 CA3d 695, 708, 89 CR 330.

IV. HOW MOTION MUST BE MADE

§52.7   A. Timeliness; Request for Admonition

A motion to strike, like an objection, must be "timely made." Evid C §353(a). To be timely, the motion should be made at the earliest opportunity. If directed at an answer that is nonresponsive, comes too quickly for objection, or contains inadmissible matter, the motion should be made during or immediately following the answer. If directed against evidence that was admitted conditionally, the motion should be made when it is demonstrated that the condition will not be met, *i.e.,* when the proponent rests without having supplied evidence of the necessary preliminary fact. A motion to strike evidence that appeared admissible, but is later (*e.g.,* on cross-examination) shown to be inadmissible, should be made when the inadmissibility is demonstrated.

When the proponent of evidence was successful in having it admitted conditionally but then fails to provide the foundation for that evidence, opposing counsel should ask the court to instruct jurors to disregard the evidence. On request, the judge must give such an admonition. Evid C §403(c)(1). The judge is required to give an admonition without a request if the court finds that the jurors could not reasonably find that the preliminary fact exists. Evid C §403(c)(2).

When counsel moves to strike testimony or evidence because of opposing counsel's misconduct, a jury admonition should be repeated.

Certain general instructions warn the jury to ignore particular evidence. See CACI 106 and 5003 (formerly BAJI 1.02); CALJIC 1.02, 2.09. It is preferable, however, for counsel who wants the jury admonished to ask the judge to give a specific admonition at the time the judge strikes the evidence.

§52.8   B. Specification of Particular Evidence to Be Stricken

A motion to strike must be directed with precision to the specific matter sought to be stricken. If evidence that is subject to a motion to strike because of its admissibility is intermingled with admissible evidence, a motion to strike the whole should be denied as too broad. *Rose v State* (1942) 19 C2d 713, 742, 123 P2d 505. Similarly, a motion to strike an answer as nonresponsive is too broad if part of the answer is responsive. The burden is on counsel making the motion to state the exact portion of the evidence to be stricken. See *Orange County Flood Control Dist. v Sunny Crest Dairy, Inc.* (1978) 77 CA3d 742, 753, 143 CR 803; 3 Witkin, California Evidence, *Presentation at Trial* §383 (4th ed 2000). Before moving to strike an entire answer, counsel should be sure that all parts of the answer are properly subject to the motion.

§52.9   C. Specification of Grounds

The motion to strike must state the specific legal ground or grounds on which the evidence should be stricken. Evid C §353(a). If this is not done, the motion can properly be denied. *People v Brown* (1962) 200 CA2d 111, 116, 19 CR 36; *Toomes v Nunes* (1938) 24 CA2d 395, 75 P2d 94. A ground of inadmissibility should be stated in the same manner as in an objection on the same ground, *e.g.,* that the evidence is irrelevant, is hearsay, or calls for inadmissible opinion. If the ground is nonresponsiveness, it may be sufficient to state as the ground simply that the answer is nonresponsive. See Evid C §766. Stating the ground properly raises a legal issue and also enables opposing counsel to offer other evidence that would avoid the ground of the motion.

§52.10   D. Striking by Judge on Own Motion

The trial judge has the power to strike inadmissible evidence on the court's own motion. See *People v Neustice* (1972) 24 CA3d 178, 189, 100 CR 783; *Eaugharn v Chamberlain* (1934) 139 CA 601, 34 P2d 756. When highly prejudicial evidence is offered in a criminal case, the judge has the power, and may have a duty, to protect the defendant by excluding or striking the evidence despite the absence of an objection or a motion from counsel. See *People v Johnson* (1964) 229 CA2d 162, 170, 40 CR 105; *People v Arends* (1957) 155 CA2d 496, 508, 318 P2d 532.

§52.11   V. POSSIBLE SANCTIONS: ADMONITION, MISCONDUCT, MISTRIAL

As indicated in §53.4, it is usually advantageous in a jury trial to couple a motion to strike with a request that the judge admonish the jury to disregard the stricken evidence. This admonition is customarily given immediately after the motion is granted; it is normally considered sufficient to cure any error in its admission. See *Arneson v Webster* (1964) 226 CA2d 370, 377, 38 CR 88.

If the impropriety and prejudicial effect of introducing the evidence are sufficiently clear, it may also be appropriate to object to its introduction as misconduct and ask the judge to sanction opposing counsel and admonish counsel not to refer further to the matter. When the question is objected to as misconduct, counsel must request an admonition. See *People v Washington* (1968) 263 CA2d 814, 817, 70 CR 80. If the witness has volunteered the improper matter, the judge may also be asked to admonish the witness.

If a "ring-wise" expert witness is involved and the court determines that the inappropriate answer was intentional, the court may first warn the witness. If the practice continues, the court may impose sanctions against the witness. Counsel should consider a motion for a mistrial if the improper response is so prejudicial that its disclosure makes a fair trial impossible.

Before granting either a motion to strike or a motion for mistrial, the court should ask the party offering such evidence to state the purpose for eliciting the evidence. If counsel's reason is proper (*e.g.*, proof of insurance is offered to prove some other issue in the case), the evidence is admissible. 1 Witkin, California Evidence, *Circumstantial Evidence* §134 (4th ed 2000); *Turner v Mannon* (1965) 236 CA2d 134, 45 CR 831; *Mullanix v Basich* (1945) 67 CA2d 675, 155 P2d 130. Counsel may, however, be required to make a proper offer of proof. *Helfend v Southern Cal. Rapid Transit Dist.* (1970) 2 C3d 1, 16, 84 CR 173.

§52.12   VI. EFFECT ON TRIAL RECORD OF STRIKING EVIDENCE

When evidence is ordered stricken, the order is simply noted in the record; the stricken matter is not physically deleted. If post-trial review is sought against a party who successfully moved to strike, the reviewing court may examine the stricken evidence in the record to determine whether striking it was error and, if so, whether the error was sufficiently prejudicial to warrant reversal under Evid C §354 and Cal Const art VI, §13 (formerly Cal Const art VI, §4½).

If the party who successfully moved to strike attacks the verdict or judgment as not supported by sufficient evidence, the other party can attack the granting of the motion to strike and, if granting it was erroneous, can rely on the stricken evidence in support of the verdict or judgment. *Gray v Southern Pac. Co.* (1944) 23 C2d 632, 644, 145 P2d 561. See also *Watenpaugh v State Teachers' Retirement* (1959) 51 C2d 675, 681, 336 P2d 165.

VII. WAIVER

§52.13   A. Failure to Make Proper Motion

The right to have evidence stricken may be waived by failure to make an objection or, if there was no reasonable opportunity to object, a timely motion to strike. Even a timely motion does not prevent waiver if the moving party does not specify the exact evidence to be stricken and the particular grounds for the motion.

§52.14   B. Failure to Obtain Ruling

After making a motion to strike, counsel should be sure that the judge rules. Counsel's failure to insist on a ruling before the trial proceeds to other matters is usually considered an abandonment of the motion and precludes raising it on appeal. See *Bennett v Hoge* (1930) 108 CA 180, 183, 291 P 444; 3 Witkin, California Evidence, *Presentation at Trial* §2031 (4th ed 2000). The judge's express reservation or postponement of the ruling, however, may be treated on appeal as a denial of the motion if the court takes no further action. See 3 Witkin, Evidence, *Presentation at Trial* §387; §4.20 (obtaining ruling on objection). Note that an express reservation of ruling must not be confused with a ruling conditionally admitting evidence, which requires the party seeking to exclude the evidence, or later seeking to question its admissibility on appeal, to move to strike it if the condition is not fulfilled.

It is preferable for counsel to insist on an immediate ruling. A delayed ruling may not only be improperly based on or influenced by subsequent evidence, it may also be confusing or misleading to the jury when it is made out of context. If the judge persists in too many "dangling rulings," counsel should request a chambers session with the judge and opposing counsel to challenge the procedures being followed.

VIII. DECIDING WHETHER TO MAKE MOTION

§52.15   A. Tactical Advantages and Disadvantages

The usual purpose of a motion to strike is to prevent the jury from considering evidence harmful to one's case. A decision on whether to move to strike should be based on what the motion may accomplish, the harm it may cause, and the available alternatives for accomplishing the same ends. To be able to act wisely and promptly during the heat of trial on the basis of all these factors requires thorough pretrial preparation of the facts and applicable law.

Counsel usually should move to strike evidence that may significantly affect an important issue in the case if moving to strike it will keep the trier of fact from considering it. Counsel usually should not move to strike testimony legally subject to being stricken, because it will have little effect on the outcome even though left in the record. Moving that such unimportant testimony be stricken and that the jury be admonished to disregard it usually serves only to highlight the evidence and encourage the jury to speculate on its possible importance or on why counsel considers it harmful. "Object only when it hurts" applies equally to motions to strike.

Even though the motion is granted, it does not always result in eliminating the substance of the stricken evidence from the record. For example, if an answer is stricken as nonresponsive, opposing counsel may be able to ask the witness additional questions that will introduce substantially the same evidence into the record. If hearsay testimony is stricken, opposing counsel may be able readily to establish an exception to the hearsay rule and reintroduce the testimony. The net effect of moving to strike evidence that will eventually be admitted is simply to highlight the subject.

To have the desired effect on the factfinder, therefore, motions to strike should be confined to evidence that:

- May seriously affect the jury's decision regarding an important factual issue; and

- If stricken, is not likely to be circumvented by the later admission of equivalent evidence on the same issue.

§52.16   B. Alternatives to Motion to Strike

A motion to strike that results in the elimination from the record of adverse evidence on an important point may not completely accomplish its objective. Despite an admonition to disregard the stricken evidence, jurors may be unable to erase it from their minds or, if they have forgotten the stricken evidence, may believe they are being asked to disregard what they never heard in the first place. In addition, they may regard the motion as a technical roadblock or a sign of weakness in the moving party's case.

At times, therefore, it may be advantageous to refrain from attacking the evidence by a motion to strike and to meet the evidence problem head-on by cross-examining the witness, impeachment, or presenting other evidence in rebuttal. On alternatives to objecting, see §§4.9–4.14.

§52.17 IX. EFFECT AT TRIAL OF FAILURE TO OBJECT TO NONRESPONSIVE ANSWER GIVEN DURING DEPOSITION

Code of Civil Procedure §2025(m)(2) provides that errors or irregularities in the form of deposition questions or answers are "waived" unless a timely objection is made at the deposition. Although overlooked by many practitioners, failure to object to a nonresponsive answer given at a deposition could lead to denial of a motion to strike and admission of the answer at trial.

§52.18 X. STATING MOTION AND REQUEST FOR ADMONITION

> Your Honor, I move to strike _ _[specify exact evidence to be stricken, e.g., all of the last answer after the words _ _[specify]_]_ _ on the ground that _ _[state exact ground for motion]_ _.

> [Add if appropriate]

> I request that you admonish the jurors to disregard the stricken matter and to treat it as if they had never heard it.

53

Jury Admonitions

I. ADMONITIONS
   A. During Trial §53.1
   B. As Part of Jury Instructions §53.2

II. COMMON USE OF ADMONITIONS
   A. Misconduct §53.3
   B. Stricken or Excluded Evidence §53.4
   C. Evidence Admitted for Limited Purpose
      1. Counsel's Request for Limiting Admonition or Instruction §53.5
      2. Sample Limiting Instructions §53.6
   D. Exercise of Privilege §53.7

I. ADMONITIONS

§53.1   A. During Trial

The judge often gives the jury timely oral admonitions (cautionary instructions) during trial that should not wait until the final charge. Admonitions are frequently used to obviate the effect of improper matter that has come before jurors by instructing them to disregard it. There are also other kinds of admonitions. Judges frequently admonish jurors at the start of trial not to investigate the case on their own. See CACI 100 (formerly BAJI 1.00.5). Code of Civil Procedure §611 requires the judge to admonish jurors, each time they leave the courtroom, not to discuss "any subject of the trial" and "not to form or express an opinion thereon until the case is finally submitted to them." The judge may also instruct jurors during the course of the trial on how to consider certain evidence, *e.g.*, by giving a limiting instruction advising jurors that they should consider certain evidence for a specified purpose only. Evid C §355.

It is important for the judge to give jurors immediate guidance during trial on matters that might otherwise be improperly considered by them. Jurors are less likely to give improper consideration to a matter or an occurrence if they are warned against doing so immediately rather than during jury instruction at the close of the trial. Although the judge may give an immediate admonition either at the request of counsel or on the court's own motion, it is counsel's responsibility to request specific admonitions. Among the subjects on which these admonitions may be given are misconduct of counsel, excluded or stricken evidence, evidence admitted for a limited purpose, and the exercise of a privilege.

The court is not required sua sponte to give limiting or cautionary instructions during trial. *People v Richards* (1976) 17 C3d 614, 618, 131 CR 537; *Grimshaw v Ford Motor Co.* (1981) 119 CA3d 757, 789, 174 CR 348. Although the court may comment on the evidence during trial, usually with respect to the credibility of the witness testimony (Cal Const art VI, §10), this is rarely done in either civil or criminal actions.

A common format for an admonition follows:

> The motion to strike is granted. The witness's last answer is stricken. Ladies and gentlemen, you are instructed to disregard the answer in its entirety and treat it as if you had never heard it.

See *People v Jones* (1970) 7 CA3d 48, 54 n2, 86 CR 717.

§53.2 B. As Part of Jury Instructions

Cautionary instructions (admonitions) that have been given during the course of the trial are usually repeated at the conclusion of trial as part of jury instructions, either in response to the written requests of counsel or on the judge's own motion. CCP §§607a-609; Pen C §§1093.5, 1127. See Pen C §1093(6) (judge must charge jury in criminal case on relevant points of law if requested by either party). They may also be reiterated in more generalized form. For example, instead of referring to specific misconduct or specific evidence that was excluded or admitted for a limited purpose, the charge usually tells the jury not to treat any statement of counsel, other than admissions and stipulations, as evidence; to disregard all rejected or stricken evidence; or to follow previous instructions limiting evidence to particular purposes. See, *e.g.,* CACI 106, 206, and 5003 (formerly BAJI 1.02 and 2.05); CALJIC 1.02, 2.07-2.08.

In civil cases, the court usually has no duty to give sua sponte instructions, *i.e.,* instructions that were not requested by counsel. *Willden v Washington Nat'l Ins. Co.* (1976) 18 C3d 631, 135 CR 69. The court does, however, have the obligation to instruct sua sponte on the controlling legal principles that apply to the case. *Thomas v Buttress & McClellan, Inc.* (1956) 141 CA2d 812, 819, 297 P2d 768 (trial court decision reversed because court should have instructed on its own motion on measure of recovery to be used if plaintiff's version of facts was adopted). Because the court usually has no duty to instruct sua sponte in civil cases, it is important for counsel to submit proposed instructions to the court in writing.

In criminal cases, the court has a greater duty to give sua sponte instructions than in civil cases. For example, the judge must instruct jurors on the court's own motion concerning certain defenses. See Use Note to CALJIC 4.60. Even so, counsel should submit proposed cautionary instructions to the court in writing to help ensure that they are given. Trial counsel should not rely on a reversal on appeal; the appellate court may not agree that a particular instruction should have been given sua sponte and may uphold the client's conviction. See, *e.g., People v Hood* (1969) 1 C3d 444, 82 CR 618 (trial court committed prejudicial error in failing to instruct on its own motion with respect to lesser-included offense).

Counsel should object to the giving of instructions not supported by evidence (*LeMons v Regents of Univ. of Cal.* (1978) 21 C3d 869, 148 CR 355) or that have not been discussed with counsel (see CCP §607a, which requires the judge, on request, to inform counsel before argument begins of all instructions to be given).

II. COMMON USE OF ADMONITIONS

§53.3   A. Misconduct

At various stages of the trial, counsel may commit misconduct by, *e.g.,* asking questions not for the answers that might be given but for the purpose of presenting facts, inferences, and suggestions that cannot be supported by the record or anticipated evidence. On attorney misconduct, see §§29.2-29.20. If opposing counsel objects to the misconduct, the judge must be requested to admonish the jury to disregard the improper matter. If counsel does not request an admonition or instruction in addition to objecting, the misconduct is waived unless it is so extreme as to be held incurable by any admonition. See *People v Perry* (1972) 7 C3d 756, 790, 103 CR 161 (criminal); *Simmons v Southern Pac. Transp. Co.* (1976) 62 CA3d 341, 355, 133 CR 42 (civil).

The efficacy of an admonition for curing or obviating misconduct depends not only on the seriousness of the misconduct but also on the forcefulness of the admonition. A general admonition to "try the case on the evidence only" may be insufficient as a specific admonition to disregard improper remarks. Admonitions should be directed to the specific problem confronting the court and phrased in language that the jury will understand. Even specific admonitions, regardless of how they are phrased, may not be able to "unring the bell." See *Stevenson v Link* (1954) 128 CA2d 564, 574, 275 P2d 782 (plaintiff brought his acquittal on criminal charges related to civil suit to jurors' attention; judge's specific admonition inadequate to cure misconduct).

§53.4   B. Stricken or Excluded Evidence

A motion to strike evidence normally should be coupled with a request that the jury be admonished to disregard the stricken evidence. If the judge grants the motion, he or she usually gives the requested warning immediately. If an objection to a question or an exhibit is sustained, the possibility of prejudice may warrant the judge's giving an immediate specific admonition to the jury not to speculate on the possible answers to the question, contents of the exhibit, or reasons for the objection. See chap 52.

C. Evidence Admitted for Limited Purpose

§53.5 1. Counsel's Request for Limiting Admonition or Instruction

If evidence is admissible for one purpose but not another, and an objection to it is sustained because the apparent purpose of its being offered is the improper one, the party making the offer cannot complain of the ruling unless counsel explains the proper purpose. See Evid C §354(a). If the evidence is then admitted, the burden is on the opponent to request that the judge order its admission for the limited purpose only and give the jury a limiting admonition or instruction. Evid C §355. See *Larson v Solbakken* (1963) 221 CA2d 410, 422 n7, 34 CR 450. If counsel fails to request a limiting instruction, the evidence may be considered as if it had been admitted without objection. See *Wicktor v County of Los Angeles* (1960) 177 CA2d 390, 405, 2 CR 352; 1 Witkin, California Evidence, *Circumstantial Evidence* §33 (4th ed 2000).

Examples of evidence that may be admitted for a limited purpose follow:

- Offered evidence may be admissible against only one of several parties, *e.g.*, a hearsay statement by a declarant speaking as the agent of one party but not of any other party. See Evid C §1222.

- Evidence may be admissible in relation to only one issue. See, *e.g.*, *Allen v Toledo* (1980) 109 CA3d 415, 167 CR 270, a wrongful death and negligent entrustment suit against a father and son arising out of an automobile accident in which the son, while driving his father's car, killed a woman. Testimony that the son had been in three prior automobile accidents was admissible to show negligent entrustment by the father but not admissible to show that the son was negligent in driving the car when the woman was killed. 109 CA3d at 419.

§53.6 2. Sample Limiting Instructions

The following instruction could be given to limit the use of evidence against particular defendants:

> This witness's testimony of the conversation with _ _[name]_ _ has been admitted only as evidence against defendant _ _[name]_ _. In deciding the issues of this case for or against any other defendant, you must not consider this testimony as evidence but must completely disregard it.

The following instruction could be given to limit the use of evidence to fewer than all causes of action (in civil cases) or counts (in criminal cases):

> The testimony of witnesses *X, Y,* and *Z* has been admitted only as evidence against the defendant on Count 1 of the Information charging _ _[specify]_ _. You must not consider this testimony as evidence on the remaining counts of the Information.

The following instructions may be given to limit the use of evidence to particular purposes:

> This letter, Exhibit 1, has been admitted only as evidence of the defendant's knowledge of its contents and not as evidence of whether the statements in the letter are true. If you find from the other evidence before you that any statement in the letter is true, you may consider this exhibit on the issue of whether the defendant had knowledge of that statement. You are not to consider the exhibit for any other purpose.

> The blackboard drawing made by witness X, marked Exhibit 2, has been admitted into evidence only for the limited purpose of allowing witness X to explain testimony. You are not to consider the exhibit for any other purpose.

§53.7 D. Exercise of Privilege

Both the trial judge and counsel are prohibited from commenting on the exercise of a privilege. Evid C §913(a). The purpose of this prohibition is to avoid any argument or suggestion to the jury that the person who exercised the privilege did so because the evidence excluded by the privilege would be adverse. If trial counsel believes, however, that the jury is likely to speculate or assume that the excluded evidence would be adverse to the client, Evid C §913(b) gives counsel the right to have the judge

> instruct the jury that no presumption arises because of the exercise of the privilege and that the jury may not draw any inference therefrom as to the credibility of the witness or as to any matter at issue in the proceeding.

Counsel should ask the judge to give this admonition in plain English when the privilege is invoked. Giving the instruction at the close of the trial may do more harm than good by recalling and emphasizing the issue just before the jurors begin their deliberations. See also §33.20 (commenting on privileges).

54
Motion for Continuance

I. INTRODUCTION §54.1

II. GOOD CAUSE REQUIRED
   A. Civil Trials §54.2
   B. Criminal Trials §54.3

III. CONTINUANCE BASED ON SURPRISE EVIDENCE
   A. Surprise Must Be Genuine §54.4
   B. Relevant Opposing Evidence Must Be Available §54.5
   C. Opposing Evidence Must Be Disputed §54.6

IV. PROCEDURE
   A. Civil Cases
      1. Form of Motion §54.7
      2. Stipulation to Avoid Continuance §54.8
      3. Factors Considered by Judge in Ruling on Continuance Motion §54.9
      4. Allowing Depositions §54.10
      5. Awarding Costs §54.11
      6. Jury Fees §54.12
      7. Consideration of Ruling on Appeal §54.13
      8. Effect of Failure to Make Motion for Continuance on Motion for New Trial §54.14
   B. Criminal Cases §54.15
      1. Conditional Examination of Witnesses §54.16
      2. Writ Review §54.17

§54.1 I. INTRODUCTION

During trial, a motion for continuance may be granted on an affirmative showing of good cause that is timely made. Usually the motion for continuance (or recess) will have resulted from some emergency that could not be avoided or anticipated or, at the time the motion is made, could not be obviated by some alternative remedy. In determining whether good cause exists to grant the motion, the court considers the relevant circumstances, including declarations and sworn testimony. Cal Rules of Ct 375(c); CCP §§473 (pleading amendment), 594(a) (court's sua sponte motion), 595 (party, attorney, or principal witness is member of legislature), 595.4 (absence of evidence based on affidavit). See also local court rules, especially Los Angeles Superior Court R 7.12(a) ("civility in litigation recommendations") and Cal Rules of Ct 227.

In determining whether to grant a motion for continuance in criminal cases, the court must also consider constitutional guaranties such as the right to a speedy trial. See California Criminal Law Procedure and Practice, chap 15 (7th ed Cal CEB 2004).

This area of law has been largely developed by case law because the showing of good cause is largely based on the circumstances of each case. See, *e.g., Nebraska Press Ass'n v Stuart* (1976) 427 US 539, 563, 49 L Ed 2d 683, 96 S Ct 2791 (continuance to allow publicity to subside). A motion for a continuance, however, is disfavored by statute. CCP §375(c).

For a thorough discussion of motions for continuances during trial in civil cases, see California Trial Practice: Civil Procedure During Trial §§6.6-6.25 (3d ed Cal CEB 1995).

II. GOOD CAUSE REQUIRED

§54.2   A. Civil Trials

Continuances during trial in civil cases are disfavored. Cal Rules of Ct 375(c). No continuance may be granted during the trial of a civil case except on an affirmative showing of good cause. Circumstances indicating good cause include (Cal Rules of Ct 375(c)(1)-(7)):

- The unavailability of a witness, party, or trial attorney;

- The substitution of a trial attorney required in the interests of justice;

- The addition of a new party, which affects a reasonable opportunity for discovery and trial preparation;

- A party's excused inability to obtain essential evidence; or

- Some significant unanticipated change that results in the case not being ready for trial.

The court must also consider the relevant facts and circumstances listed in Cal Rules of Ct 375(d) in ruling on the motion for continuance. See also Cal Rules of Ct 154 (small claims cases in superior court). Although CCP §595.2 provides that on written stipulation of all parties the court "shall postpone a trial for up to 30 days," trial court policy may be against granting continuances even if all the parties agree. See Cal Rules of Ct 375(a); *County of San Bernardino v Doria Mining & Eng'g Corp.* (1977) 72 CA3d 776, 140 CR 383. The trial court must approve a continuance during trial.

In addition, case law has recognized specific circumstances that usually require a continuance, *e.g.,* a material witness is unavailable (see CCP §595.4). For a catalog of grounds specifically allowed in published cases, see 7 Witkin, California Procedure, *Trial* §§13-31 (4th ed 1997).

For a sample continuance motion and a declaration supporting the motion, see California Civil Procedure Before Trial §§54.19-54.20 (3d ed Cal CEB 1990) and California Civil Litigation Forms Manual §§42.6-42.7 (Cal CEB 1980).

§54.3   B. Criminal Trials

During a criminal trial, a party seeking a continuance must also show good cause. Pen C §1050(b), (f). See also Cal Rules of Ct 4.113 (continuance of trial must be required by the ends of justice). The parties may not stipulate to good cause. Pen C §1050(e). Good cause is also required to continue a jurisdictional hearing in a juvenile case under Welf & I C §300 (Cal Rules of Ct 1422(a)) or Welf & I C §601 or §602 (Cal Rules of Ct 1422(b)).

Some Penal Code sections specify that certain issues involve good cause:

- Section 1050 specifically states that there is good cause for a continuance in cases involving either murder as defined in Pen C §187(a) or allegations that a violation of one or more of the sections specified in Pen C §11165.1(a) or §11165.6 or domestic violence as defined in Pen C §13700 has occurred, if the prosecutor assigned to the case has another trial, a preliminary hearing, or a motion to suppress in progress. A maximum of ten additional court days may be granted. Pen C §1050(g)(2), (3).

- Members of the legislature are entitled to a maximum 30-day continuance when the legislature is in session and in certain other specified circumstances. Pen C §1050(h).

- The prosecution may obtain a continuance whenever a defense witness (including the defendant) unexpectedly testifies, unless the prosecutor knew or should have known of that witness. Pen C §1051. A continuance granted because of the defendant's testimony may not exceed one day. Pen C §1051.

- The trial judge is prevented from appearing by death, illness, or inability. Pen C §1053.

- Counsel is taken by surprise by testimony or evidence during trial because of opposing counsel's failure to provide required discovery. Pen C §1054.5(b) (continuance is one of several possible sanctions).

- The defendant in a felony case is not present. A felony trial cannot be started if the defendant is not present, unless the defendant has waived his or her presence. Pen C §1043(b)(2).

- The charging instrument is amended. Pen C §1009.

- The defendant has not been given at least five calendar days to prepare for trial between the time of entering a plea and the trial. Pen C §1049; Veh C §40306.

- A judge or magistrate for good cause continues the case of one of several codefendants charged in the same complaint, indictment, or information. The continuance of one of their cases constitutes good cause for continuing the case of the other codefendants on motion of the prosecutor. Pen C §1050.1.

Good cause for a continuance during trial was found in the following cases for a variety of reasons:

- Incapacity of defense counsel. See *People v Crovedi* (1966) 65 C2d 199, 53 CR 284 (illness). See also *People v Mickey* (1991) 54 C3d 612, 660, 286 CR 801 (motion properly denied because defense counsel was present in court and stated that he did not feel well but did not indicate that his illness would make him unavailable).

- Incapacity of prosecutor during trial. See *People v McJimson* (1982) 135 CA3d 873, 881, 185 CR 605. A prosecutor's incapacity should require a continuance of only two or three days. During that time, the prosecutor should find a replacement if he or she will be unable to return.

- Material witness is unavailable. See *People v Iocca* (1974) 37 CA3d 73, 79, 112 CR 102.

- Defendant is brought into court, over objection, in jail clothes. See *People v Taylor* (1982) 31 C3d 488, 183 CR 64.

Penal Code §1048 requires a showing of good cause to obtain a continuance in the following circumstances:

- A case involves a minor;
- A person age 70 or older is the alleged victim;
- A minor is detained as a material witness; or
- The crime charged involves certain specified violent sex offenses.

Although this statute adds nothing to the requirement that good cause be shown to support a continuance, its existence probably indicates that courts will give serious consideration to motions for continuance in these types of cases and regarding these types of witnesses.

III. CONTINUANCE BASED ON SURPRISE EVIDENCE

§54.4 A. Surprise Must Be Genuine

The opposing party's surprise at the introduction of the evidence must be genuine. In *Specht v Keitel* (1961) 190 CA2d 332, 343, 12 CR 95, the plaintiff produced a handwriting expert who testified that in his opinion the assignment under which the defendant claimed the disputed property was a forgery. The defendant's attorney, professing surprise, requested a one-week continuance to obtain another handwriting expert to controvert this testimony. The trial judge denied the request, pointing out that the pretrial order explicitly stated that the plaintiff claimed that the document was forged. The appellate court affirmed, observing that "the record more than negates any contention of 'surprise.'"

In contrast, the court should have granted a continuance in *Crosby v Martinez* (1958) 159 CA2d 534, 539, 324 P2d 26. The issue in *Crosby* was whether the plaintiff had run a red light just before his car collided with the defendant's car. A police officer called by the defendant was allowed to testify, over the plaintiff's objection, that the defendant had informed him that an alleged eyewitness named Harris had told the defendant that he had seen the plaintiff's car run the red light. Surprised at the admission of this hearsay evidence, plaintiff's counsel requested a continuance for several hours to enable him to call Harris as a witness. The appellate court held that, under the circumstances, the continuance should have been granted. The plaintiff "had no reason to anticipate" the judge's erroneous ruling in allowing such "unadulterated hearsay." See also *Hays v Viscome* (1953) 122 CA2d 135, 141, 264 P2d 173 ("[n]o lawyer can foresee or predict all the vicissitudes that will occur in the course of a contested trial, which often consist of unpredictable rulings of the court").

§54.5 B. Relevant Opposing Evidence Must Be Available

Before granting a continuance based on surprise evidence, the trial judge may require a showing that the party requesting the continuance has a reasonable expectation of being able to produce opposing evidence. If such evidence will not be available when the trial resumes, a postponement is pointless. See *Hillman v Stults* (1968) 263 CA2d 848, 877, 70 CR 295 (civil); *People v Mendoza* (1974) 37 CA3d 717, 722, 112 CR 565 (criminal).

If the evidence to be offered is relevant and sufficiently probative to affect the outcome of the case, a continuance should be granted. See CCP §595.4; *Hurley v Kazantzis* (1947) 82 CA2d 378, 186 P2d 434; *Young v Evans* (1944) 62 CA2d 365, 373, 144 P2d 651. If, however, the evidence will be merely cumulative or admissible only for impeachment purposes, the trial judge may justifiably deny the continuance. See *People v Laursen* (1972) 8 C3d 192, 203, 104 CR 425; *People v Hill* (1976) 64 CA3d 16, 34, 134 CR 443.

§54.6 C. Opposing Evidence Must Be Disputed

If, in a civil case, the evidence in question is undisputed, a continuance will usually be unnecessary. After the party requesting the continuance describes the evidence that he or she expects to obtain, the adverse party can forestall a postponement by admitting, for the record, that such evidence would be acceptable and stipulating that it be considered as if it had been given at the trial. CCP §595.4.

IV. PROCEDURE

A. Civil Cases

§54.7   1. Form of Motion

Continuance motions must be in writing, with notice to all parties. Cal Rules of Ct 375(b). The motion should be accompanied by declarations (or affidavits; see CCP §2015.5, which allows either to be filed) that show the basis for a good cause finding. Cal Rules of Ct 375(c). Counsel should make the motion at the earliest practicable moment because, in making a decision on good cause, the court will consider counsel's diligence in making the motion. Cal Rules of Ct 375(b).

§54.8   2. Stipulation to Avoid Continuance

Adverse counsel in a civil case may avoid a continuance sought to secure a witness by offering to stipulate to that person's testimony. CCP §595.4. There is no comparable statutory provision for criminal cases.

§54.9   3. Factors Considered by Judge in Ruling on Continuance Motion

Suggestions of issues that the court may consider in arriving at a decision on a motion for continuance are listed in Cal Rules of Ct 375(d):

- The proximity of the trial or hearing date;
- Whether there were any previous continuances, extensions of time, or other delay attributable to any party;
- The length of the continuance requested;
- The availability of alternative means to address the problem that gave rise to the request for a continuance;
- The prejudice that parties or witnesses will suffer as a result of the continuance;
- If the case is entitled to a preferential trial setting, the reasons for that status and whether the need for the continuance outweighs the need to avoid delay;
- The condition of the court's calendar and the availability of an earlier trial or hearing date if the matter is ready for trial or hearing;
- Whether the trial attorney is engaged in another trial;
- Whether all parties have stipulated to a continuance;
- Whether the interests of justice are best served by a continuance, by the trial or hearing of the matter, or by imposing conditions on its continuance; and

- Any other fact or circumstance relevant to a fair determination of the motion.

It is ordinarily left to the trial judge's discretion whether to grant or deny a request for continuance, "unless it appears that a denial of the continuance motion [would result] in the denial of a full and fair hearing." *Cade v Mid-City Hosp. Corp.* (1975) 45 CA3d 589, 599, 119 CR 571. For example, in *People v Lynch* (1971) 14 CA3d 602, 607, 92 CR 411, the appellate court found no error in the trial court's refusal to allow the appellant a continuance. The appellant had told the trial court on a Thursday that he hoped to call a particular witness, but when that witness's testimony was needed the following Monday, the witness was unavailable. The appellant apparently had not subpoenaed him. Similarly, in *Lipman v Ashburn* (1951) 106 CA2d 616, 620, 235 P2d 627, the trial judge denied a short continuance requested to enable the plaintiff to produce a witness who had been subpoenaed and then excused. "There is a hazard in excusing a witness to appear on call which counsel should anticipate," observed the appellate court, concluding that "in the absence of a clear abuse of discretion it cannot be said that justice has miscarried."

Although the trial judge's discretionary power to grant or deny continuances during the course of a trial is extremely broad, it does have limits. If a party who has been genuinely surprised by evidence or by a ruling requests a continuance to obtain rebuttal evidence, it may be an abuse of discretion to deny the request. *Crosby v Martinez* (1958) 159 CA2d 534, 324 P2d 26, illustrates this principle, which is analyzed in §54.4. In this case, it was clear that (a) the party requesting the continuance could not have anticipated the need for the evidence that he sought to present in rebuttal; (b) the witness was readily available (see §54.4); and (c) his testimony would be relevant (see §54.5). Under these circumstances, the denial of a continuance amounted to an abuse of discretion.

§54.10 4. Allowing Depositions

In a civil case, parties opposing a request for a continuance based on a witness's unavailability need not arrange for their witnesses to appear again when the trial is resumed. At the request of such a party, the testimony of these witnesses will be taken by deposition. This testimony may then be read at the trial "with the same effect, and subject to the same objections, as if the witnesses were produced." CCP §596.

§54.11 5. Awarding Costs

In civil cases, the trial judge has discretion to require, as a condition to granting a continuance, that the party requesting one pay the resulting expenses. CCP §1024. Compare that section with CCP §473 (when continuance granted to amend pleadings, court may condition amendment on paying adverse party "such costs as may be just").

The expenses that may be ordered under CCP §1024 are not limited to costs that are ordinarily taxable. However, these "expenses" do not include attorney fees. *Levine v Pollack* (1995) 37 CA4th 129, 43 CR2d 491. In *Levine* the court states that attorney fees are "costs" and not "expenses" and concludes that when the legislature amended CCP §1024 to change "costs" to "expenses" it intended that a court should not have discretion to award attorney fees. The *Levine* court thus distinguished and overruled *McFaddin v H. S. Crocker Co.* (1963) 219 CA2d 585, 595, 33 CR 389.

Nevertheless, there are procedures for obtaining attorney fees when improper conduct is employed. See, for example, CCP §128.7. See also Cal Rules of Ct 227.

§54.12   6. Jury Fees

When a party in a civil case has deposited jury fees and that party waives a jury, a continuance is granted, or the case is settled, the court may retain that deposit if it finds that there has been insufficient time to notify jurors that the trial will not proceed at the scheduled time. CCP §631.3.

§54.13   7. Consideration of Ruling on Appeal

The trial judge's error in a civil case will support a reversal on appeal only if the error was prejudicial and resulted in a miscarriage of justice. Cal Const art VI, §13 (formerly §4½); Evid C §354. The test, as stated in *Crosby v Martinez* (1958) 159 CA2d 534, 542, 324 P2d 26, is whether it is "reasonably probable that a result more favorable to appellants would have been reached" in the absence of the error.

If the trial judge has granted a continuance, appellate courts have appeared reluctant to find the "clear abuse of discretion" necessary to reverse the judgment. See, *e.g., Larson v Solbakken* (1963) 221 CA2d 410, 429, 34 CR 450. No reported California case has been found in which the granting of a continuance was held to be reversible error. Witkin notes that it is practically impossible to show prejudicial error in the granting of a continuance. See 7 Witkin, California Procedure, *Trial* §10 (4th ed 1996). Current trial court practice, however, seems to be against granting continuances. See *County of San Bernardino v Doria Mining & Eng'g Corp.* (1977) 72 CA3d 776, 140 CR 383 (appellate court repudiated view that trial court should exercise great liberality in granting continuances, finding such liberality wholly inconsistent with former Cal Rules of Ct 375(a) and former Cal Rules of Ct App Div I, §9).

§54.14   8. Effect of Failure to Make Motion for Continuance on Motion for New Trial

Failure to make a timely request for a continuance may preclude the party against whom the evidence is received from seeking relief at a later stage. Code of Civil Procedure §657(3) authorizes a new trial to be granted on the ground of "surprise, which ordinary prudence could not have guarded against." In *Kauffman v De Matiis* (1948) 31 C2d 429, 432, 189 P2d 271, the plaintiff subpoenaed a witness who failed to appear. Although surprised, the plaintiff proceeded without the witness and without requesting a continuance. After the jury found for the defendant, the plaintiff moved for a new trial under CCP §657(3). This motion was granted. On appeal, the California Supreme Court reversed the order granting a new trial, declaring that a plaintiff may not "speculate on a favorable verdict."

§54.15   B. Criminal Cases

Motions to continue the trial of a criminal case are disfavored and should be denied unless the moving party, under Pen C §1050, presents affirmative proof in open court that the ends of justice require a continuance. Cal Rules of Ct 4.113.

To continue any hearing in a criminal proceeding, including a trial, a written motion must be filed and served on all parties at least two court days before the hearing, together with affidavits or declarations detailing specific facts showing that a continuance is necessary. A party is not considered to be served until that party has actually received a copy of the documents, unless service is waived. Regardless of who makes the motion, the prosecuting attorney must notify prosecution witnesses, and the defense attorney must notify defense witnesses, of the motion, the date of hearing, and the right of the witnesses to be heard by the court. Pen C §1050(b). These requirements must be met, or the court is justified in denying the motion. See *People v Navarro* (1933) 135 CA 535, 538, 27 P2d 652 (trial judge properly denied defendant's oral continuance motion for failure to file declarations supporting motion and failure to produce evidence; there was therefore no adequate showing on which to base continuance order).

A party may move for a continuance without complying with these requirements, but the court may impose sanctions under Pen C §1050.5 unless the moving party shows good cause, at a hearing, for noncompliance. Sanctions on the moving party for failure to comply with the requirements concerning continuance motions may include a fine not exceeding $1000 and a report filed with an appropriate disciplinary committee. These sanctions apply to the moving party whether it is the prosecution or the defense. Pen C §1050.5.

A motion for continuance may not be granted if the moving party is unable to show good cause for failure to give notice. Pen C §1050(c)–(d), (f). If good cause is found at the hearing, the court must state on the record the facts proved that justify its finding, and the statement of facts must be entered in the minutes.

Neither the convenience of the parties nor a stipulation of the parties is in itself good cause for a continuance in a criminal case. Pen C §1050(e).

In deciding the good cause issue, the court must consider the general convenience and prior commitments of all witnesses, including peace officers. Those factors must also be considered in selecting a continuance date if the motion is granted. The facts on inconvenience or prior commitments may be offered by the witness or by a party to the case. Pen C §1050(g)(1). For purposes of Pen C §1050, good cause includes, but is not limited to, cases involving either murder as defined in Pen C §187(a) or allegations that a violation of one or more of the sections specified in Pen C §11165.1(a) or §11165.6 or domestic violence as defined in Pen C §13700 has occurred, if the prosecutor assigned to the case has another trial, a preliminary hearing, or a motion to suppress in progress. A continuance under Pen C §1050(g) is limited to a maximum of ten additional court days. Pen C §1050(g)(2), (3).

A continuance may be granted only for the period necessary, and the facts justifying that period must also be stated on the record and entered in the minutes. Pen C §1050(i).

For a sample motion for continuance in a criminal case, see California Criminal Law Forms Manual §15.1 (Cal CEB 1995).

§54.16   1. Conditional Examination of Witnesses

In a criminal case, there is statutory authority for a deposition of a material witness for the defendant or the People. Pen C §§1335-1336. This procedure, termed "conditional examination of a material witness," is strictly confined to criminal cases that involve (Pen C §1336):

- A material witness who is about to leave the state, or is so sick or infirm as to afford reasonable grounds for apprehension that he or she will be unable to attend the trial, or is a person 70 years of age or older, or is a dependent adult, or

- A prosecution witness whose life is in jeopardy.

The deposition is made by application for court order with supporting affidavit. Pen C §1337.

Acting under a constitutional grant (Cal Const art I, §15), the legislature has clearly declined to extend deposition procedures beyond the confines of Pen C §1336. Thus, it is inappropriate for a court acting under the guise of its plenary powers to manage the trial before it to broaden the provisions of Pen C §1336. *People v Municipal Court* (Runyan) (1978) 20 C3d 523, 143 CR 609.

If the requirements of Pen C §1336 are met during trial, the court may grant a continuance based on good cause shown for such a deposition. For good cause requirements, see §§54.2-54.3.

Although conditional examination depositions are usually taken before trial, a short continuance during trial may be granted to take such depositions on a showing of good cause.

§54.17 2. Writ Review

Proposition 115 added Pen C §871.6, which allows either the prosecution or the defense to file a petition for writ of mandate or prohibition in the superior court to challenge the granting of a continuance of a preliminary hearing without good cause.

Penal Code §1512 gives the prosecution the right to seek writ review of the grant of either discovery or a continuance to the defense. Proposition 115 also added Pen C §1511, which provides that if the superior court sets the trial of a felony case beyond the period specified in Pen C §1049.5 (in violation of Pen C §1049.5) or continues the hearing of any matter without good cause (when good cause is required by law), either party may file a petition for writ of mandate of the ruling setting the trial or granting the continuance.

55
Extraordinary Writs

I. INTRODUCTION §55.1

II. USUALLY NOT OBTAINABLE TO CORRECT RULINGS ON EVIDENCE §55.2

III. WHEN OBTAINABLE
    A. To Enforce Privilege §55.3
    B. To Protect Right to Privacy §55.4
    C. To Stay Contempt Order §55.5
    D. To Overcome Shield Law Order §55.6

IV. OTHER EXCEPTIONS §55.7

§55.1 I. INTRODUCTION

A writ is an order by a reviewing court ordering the lower tribunal to do something or refrain from doing something. Writ review is an appellate procedure for reviewing nonappealable trial court rulings. In exceptional circumstances, writ review may be allowed from an appealable order. Typical writs of mandate, prohibition, and certiorari are considered to be extraordinary because they are equitable, completely discretionary, and rarely granted.

Most orders and rulings made during trial are appealable only at the conclusion of the case. CCP §904.1(a)(1). Code of Civil Procedure §904.1 specifies when an appeal may be taken from a judgment or ruling other than in a limited case. When read together with CCP §577, which specifies that a judgment is a final determination, §904.1 is interpreted to mean appeal from a final judgment. Appellate practice is not within the scope of this book. For discussion, see California Civil Appellate Practice (3d ed Cal CEB 1996).

If a piecemeal approach to appeals were allowed, it would be contrary to judicial policy and cause judicial gridlock, confusion, delay, and expense. *Guntert v City of Stockton* (1974) 43 CA3d 203, 117 CR 601, disapproved on other grounds in 82 CA4th at 634. Certain trial court rulings, orders, and judgments, however, may be reviewed by extraordinary writ.

This chapter focuses on trial court rulings that have been successfully challenged by writ. To obtain writ review, the petitioner must plead the following:

- That there is no other adequate remedy at law;
- Irreparable injury;

- Standing;
- That a proper record was made in the trial court;
- Abuse of discretion; and
- Unusual urgency.

See also CCP §1068.

A detailed discussion of writ review is beyond the scope of this book. For a thorough discussion, see California Civil Writ Practice, chap 3 (3d ed Cal CEB 1996); Eisenberg, Horvitz, & Wiener, California Practice Guide: Civil Appeals and Writs, chap 15 (1989).

§55.2 II. USUALLY NOT OBTAINABLE TO CORRECT RULINGS ON EVIDENCE

A party usually cannot obtain an extraordinary writ to correct an erroneous ruling by the trial judge on an evidentiary point. See *Ballard v Superior Court* (1966) 64 C2d 159, 164, 49 CR 302. The rationale for this limitation was expressed in *People v Superior Court* (1955) 137 CA2d 194, 195, 289 P2d 813.

> While a writ of mandate may, in a proper case, be used to correct an abuse of judicial discretion, it cannot be used to control a discretionary act of a superior judge. In particular, the writ may not be used to compel a judge to admit or exclude evidence during a trial, even if such ruling is an erroneous one. It is elementary that a trial judge has the jurisdiction to decide matters before him erroneously as well as correctly. That is one reason why we have appellate courts. A ruling on the admissibility of evidence, even if wrong, is not an abuse of discretion but simply an erroneous ruling.

See also *People v Municipal Court* (Ahnemann) (1974) 12 C3d 658, 660, 117 CR 20; *Cash v Superior Court* (1973) 35 CA3d 226, 229, 110 CR 612.

The reasoning in *People v Superior Court, supra,* also applies to writs of prohibition and certiorari, which by definition are available only to restrain or review acts taken in excess of jurisdiction. CCP §§1102 (prohibition), 1068 (certiorari). When there is no right to an appeal, the prosecution may not circumvent this rule by seeking a writ to review an evidentiary question. See, e.g., *People v Superior Court* (Howard) (1968) 69 C2d 491, 499, 72 CR 330 (writ relief not available to prosecutor when judge dismisses case under Pen C §1385 following adverse jury verdict).

III. WHEN OBTAINABLE

§55.3 A. To Enforce Privilege

When a witness claims a privilege and the trial judge rules that the privilege does not apply, the witness usually has the choice either of disclosing the information or of being held in contempt of court. To forestall an adjudication of contempt or enforcement of that adjudication, the witness may be able to obtain an extraordinary writ from an appellate court. See, *e.g., Allen v Superior Court* (1976) 18 C3d 520, 134 CR 774 (writ granted prohibiting trial judge from ordering defense counsel to disclose names of prospective defense witnesses to jurors during voir dire examination).

Case law offers incomplete guidance regarding which writ applies and when a writ is obtainable. See California Civil Writ Practice §§4.65-4.67 (3d ed Cal CEB 1996); California Criminal Law Procedure and Practice, chap 40 (7th ed Cal CEB 2004).

Extraordinary writs may also be available to a nonwitness who unsuccessfully claims a privilege to prevent a witness from disclosing confidential information. See §33.24.

§55.4 B. To Protect Right to Privacy

California Constitution art I, §1, added in 1972, provides a litigant with a presumptive right to privacy, which typically is raised during discovery (see *Moskowitz v Superior Court* (1982) 137 CA3d 313, 187 CR 4; *Richards v Superior Court* (1978) 86 CA3d 265, 150 CR 77) but may also come into play during trial. No case law appears to exist that involves the exercise of the right to privacy during trial.

Writs have been allowed when questions of first impression involving constitutional issues are raised. See, *e.g., Mitchell v Superior Court* (1984) 37 C3d 268, 208 CR 152 (disclosure of identity of confidential news sources).

§55.5 C. To Stay Contempt Order

A judgment of contempt is final. CCP §1222. Although such a judgment is not appealable, it may be reviewed by certorari, habeas corpus, or extraordinary writ. See CCP §904.1(a)(2); *McComb v Superior Court* (1977) 68 CA3d 89, 137 CR 233; *In re Buckley* (1973) 10 C3d 237, 259, 110 CR 121; *In re Charbonneau* (1974) 42 CA3d 505, 507, 116 CR 153. If the petitioner is jailed, or threatened to be jailed, a writ of habeas corpus is proper. *In re Buckley, supra*. If the petitioner is fined, a writ of certiorari is proper. *Mitler v Municipal Court* (1967) 249 CA2d 531, 532, 57 CR 578.

If an order of contempt is made against an attorney or his or her agent, the execution of any sentence must be stayed for three judicial days pending the filing of a petition of extraordinary writ testing the lawfulness of the court's order. CCP §128(b). However, violations of Bus & P C §6068 relating to an attorney's duty to maintain respect due the courts and judicial officers do not come within this stay provision. CCP §§128(b), 1209(c).

§55.6 D. To Overcome Shield Law Order

Shield laws protect journalists against contempt in a number of different circumstances. See chap 48. Their immunity from contempt may be challenged by writ review if the granting of immunity jeopardizes a criminal defendant's right to a fair trial. See *Miller v Superior Court* (1999) 21 C4th 883, 89 CR2d 834; *New York Times Co. v Superior Court* (1990) 51 C3d 453, 273 CR 98; *Delaney v Superior Court* (1990) 50 C3d 785, 268 CR 753.

§55.7   IV. OTHER EXCEPTIONS

Cases in which an extraordinary writ was issued during trial to resolve a dispute concerning evidence are extremely rare. Examples include *Kohn v Superior Court* (1936) 12 CA2d 459, 462, 55 P2d 1186 (trial judge, in replevin action to recover possession of certain personal letters, cards, and telegrams, ruled that these documents could all be read into evidence; writ of prohibition granted because it was trial judge's duty to protect confidential nature of documents as much as issues would permit and not to aid in their wrongful disclosure), and *Kullman, Salz & Co. v Superior Court* (1911) 15 CA 276, 285, 114 P 589 (trial judge held witness in contempt for refusing to produce certain corporate records; writ of prohibition granted to restrain enforcement of contempt order because no showing had been made that requested records were relevant to issues).

Proposition 115 added Pen C §871.6, which allows either the prosecution or the defense to file a petition for writ of mandate or prohibition in the superior court to challenge the granting of a continuance of a preliminary hearing without good cause.

Penal Code §1512 gives the prosecution the right to seek writ review of the grant of either discovery or a continuance to the defense. Proposition 115 also added Pen C §1511, which provides that if in a felony case the superior court sets the trial beyond the period of time specified in Pen C §1049.5, in violation of §1049.5, or continues the hearing of any matter without good cause when good cause is required by law, either party may file a petition for writ of mandate of the ruling setting the trial or granting the continuance.

56
Motion for Mistrial

I. INTRODUCTION §56.1

II. GROUNDS
    A. Irreparable Prejudicial Incident §56.2
    B. Irregularity in Proceedings §56.3

III. TRIAL JUDGE'S DISCRETION §56.4

IV. TACTICAL CONSIDERATIONS §56.5

V. PROCEDURE
    A. Irreparable Prejudicial Incident
        1. Incident Constituting Misconduct §56.6
        2. Incident Not Constituting Misconduct §56.7
    B. Irregularity in Proceedings §56.8

§56.1 I. INTRODUCTION

Certain events that occur during the course of trial may be so improper and prejudicial that they deprive a party of the right to a fair trial, *e.g.*, the prosecutor's allusion to the defendant's withdrawn guilty plea. See Evid C §1153. Although prejudicial misconduct by counsel, the court, or a juror is usually the most common ground for a mistrial, any other irregularity or error that either prevents the trial from proceeding or prevents either party from receiving a fair trial can also result in a mistrial. 7 Witkin, California Procedure, *Trial* §181 (4th ed 1997). Although most prejudicial occurrences can theoretically be cured by prompt admonitions to the jury (see chap 53), some incidents cannot be effectively erased from the jurors' minds. When the harm done is irreparable, counsel for the aggrieved party should consider making a motion for mistrial.

A motion for mistrial is infrequent in a court trial because the judge is presumably less likely to be affected by misconduct or other irregularity than a jury. When the prejudicial error is committed by the judge, however, a motion for mistrial may be appropriate. Because a motion for mistrial may be futile and tactically unwise if it is based on the judge's own misconduct or on procedural irregularities condoned by the judge, the discussion in this chapter focuses exclusively on the motion for mistrial as a possible remedy in a trial by jury. To avoid the need to move for a mistrial, counsel should consider discussing potential problem areas at the chambers conference before trial and moving in limine to exclude any inadmissible evidence or anticipated improper behavior.

There is no specific statutory authority for granting a mistrial based on irreparable prejudicial incidents; the trial judge's power to do so is assumed. Mistrials usually are based on grounds for which a new trial would be authorized under CCP §657(1)-(2); CCP §616 authorizes mistrials inferentially. There is also authority in various statutes for granting a mistrial based on certain irregularities in the proceedings. For a list of some of these grounds, see §56.3.

Direct review of an order granting or denying a mistrial is not available. See *Reimer v Firpo* (1949) 94 CA2d 798, 212 P2d 23. The order may be reviewed, however, on appeal from the judgment. *Warner v O'Connor* (1962) 199 CA2d 770, 774, 18 CR 902 (mistrial requested because judge allegedly ruled improperly on probable cause issue in prosecution case; appellate court upheld trial court's ruling). See also *People v Dominguez* (1981) 121 CA3d 481, 175 CR 445 (no error in refusing mistrial when evidence that prompted mistrial request was cumulative and trial judge gave strong admonition to jury). But compare *People v Brandon* (1995) 40 CA4th 1172, 47 CR2d 383 (no error in granting defense counsel's motion for mistrial over objections of defendant).

An extraordinary writ has been successfully used for review of an order declaring a mistrial. See *Heavy Duty Truck Leasing, Inc. v Superior Court* (1970) 11 CA3d 116, 89 CR 598 (trial court's mistrial order held to be in error; court ordered to enter verdict reached by jury). See generally California Trial Practice: Civil Procedure During Trial §§18.98-18.102, 25.77 (3d ed Cal CEB 1995); 7 Witkin, Procedure, *Trial* §163.

II. GROUNDS

§56.2   A. Irreparable Prejudicial Incident

A variety of prejudicial incidents can occur during a trial that commonly constitute misconduct. For discussion of misconduct of counsel (*e.g.,* making untrue inflammatory statements during argument), the trial judge (*e.g.,* ridiculing or disparaging one of the parties), and the jurors (*e.g.,* receiving evidence out of court), see §§29.2-29.20, 29.21-29.32, and 29.33-29.49, respectively. See also 7 Witkin, California Procedure, *Trial* §181 (4th ed 1997).

To warrant granting a mistrial, the incident must be more than just prejudicial; it must be irreparable. In many situations, the trial judge can dispel the prejudicial effect of an incident by admonishing the jury to disregard what has occurred. A motion for mistrial presupposes that the harm done is so great that even a well-crafted admonition would not effectively remedy the unfair impression made on the jury. *People v Romero* (1977) 68 CA3d 543, 137 CR 675 (motion for mistrial may properly be refused when court is satisfied that no injustice has resulted or will result from alleged misconduct); *People v Ward* (1968) 266 CA2d 241, 72 CR 46 (motion for mistrial is addressed to trial court's sound discretion).

Some irreparable incidents cannot be corrected even by ordering a mistrial. See, *e.g., People v Upshaw* (1974) 13 C3d 29, 117 CR 668 (in criminal proceeding, defendant's waiver of jury trial without concurrence of counsel violates mandatory provisions of Cal Const art I, §16; if witness is called, putting defendant in jeopardy, court cannot grant mistrial and must dismiss case).

§56.3   B. Irregularity in Proceedings

Various statutes require the trial judge to declare a mistrial for specified irregularities in the proceedings. These irregularities include:

- Calling the judge presiding at the trial as a witness, over objection. Evid C §703(c). See §§18.14–18.16 (incompetency).

- Calling a juror in the case as a witness, over objection. Evid C §704(c). See §18.17 (incompetency).

- Absence of a juror in a criminal case at the time the verdict is announced. Pen C §1147.

- Illness of a juror in a civil case if no alternate juror can replace the ill juror and the attorneys do not agree to proceed with fewer jurors. CCP §233.

- Discharge of a juror in a criminal case for good cause when no alternate can take the juror's place. CCP §233. (If there was no legal necessity for discharging the juror and jeopardy had attached, the defendant cannot be retried. *Larios v Superior Court* (1979) 24 C3d 324, 329, 155 CR 374.)

- Inability of the jury in a civil case to render a verdict "by reason of accident or other cause." CCP §616. In a criminal case, jurors can be discharged when there is "no reasonable probability that [they] can agree. Pen C §1140.

Nonstatutory grounds for dismissing the jury presumably would include such irregular occurrences as the illness or death of the judge, a party, or counsel. The trial judge has unlimited discretion to grant a mistrial on the occurrence of these or any other procedural irregularities that the judge considers sufficient to warrant a mistrial. In criminal cases, however, the "legal necessity" test must be met or the defendant cannot be retried. See *Larios v Superior Court, supra.*

§56.4   III. TRIAL JUDGE'S DISCRETION

A trial judge's erroneous ruling on a motion for mistrial may constitute an abuse of discretion and result in reversal of the judgment on appeal. See *People v Slocum* (1975) 52 CA3d 867, 125 CR 442 (criminal); *Heavy Duty Truck Leasing, Inc. v Superior Court* (1970) 11 CA3d 116, 89 CR 598 (civil). In criminal cases, if jeopardy has attached, the defendant cannot be retried. See *Larios v Superior Court* (1979) 24 C3d 324, 155 CR 374. For discussion of the formalities to preserve, on appeal, the right to assert as error the failure to grant the motion for mistrial, see §§56.6–56.8. On when denial of the motion may be appealed, see §56.1.

Although the trial judge has discretion to grant a motion for mistrial, under CCP §657 the new trial order must be accompanied by a written statement of the trial judge's specific reasons for granting the motion. *Thompson v Friendly Hills Regional Med. Ctr.* (1999) 71 CA4th 544, 84 CR2d 51.

§56.5 IV. TACTICAL CONSIDERATIONS

Counsel should answer the following tactical questions when determining whether to move for a mistrial after a prejudicial incident (see §56.2) or a procedural irregularity (see §56.3) has occurred:

- *How much real harm has been caused?* If the prejudicial effect of an incident or a procedural irregularity obviously cannot be overcome by an admonition to the jury or presentation of evidence, the aggrieved party can only be protected by moving for a mistrial. If the extent of harm is speculative, however, counsel must weigh other factors before moving for a mistrial.

- *How well is the case progressing?* If the presentation of counsel's evidence has gone poorly and the opposing side has made an unexpectedly strong showing, a motion for mistrial may provide counsel with an opportunity to make a fresh start despite the cost. This tactic is not recommended, however, because it may result in the imposition of severe sanctions or counsel's being held in contempt.

- *How would a delay affect the client's and the opponent's cases?* If the jury calendar is congested, the first available date for a retrial may be many months away. By that time, essential witnesses may be unavailable because of, *e.g.*, illness, death, moving from the area, changing allegiance, or losing their powers of recollection. The climate of public opinion may also change. For example, a plaintiff's suit against an automobile manufacturer would have far greater jury appeal if tried during the height of a congressional investigation of automobile safety than during retrial a year later.

- *How much expense would a delay entail?* A retrial inevitably means additional costs. Rather than incurring those costs, the client may prefer to gamble on the case as it stands. Promoting a mistrial could lead to severe personal sanctions.

- *How will the defendant spend the interim?* Moving for a mistrial may not be wise in a criminal case if the defendant may spend the interim in jail rather than out on bail.

- *How will the granting of a mistrial affect the defendant's ability to raise the defense of prior jeopardy to preclude a retrial?* In a criminal case, the granting of a mistrial will enable the defendant to raise the defense of prior jeopardy to preclude a retrial if, after the jury has been sworn, the judge declares a mistrial without the defendant's consent and a mistrial is not strictly necessary. See Pen C §1141; *People v Upshaw* (1974) 13 C3d 29, 117 CR 668. This rule is designed to prevent the prosecutor from moving for a mistrial to forestall a probable acquittal, in the hope of subjecting the defendant to a retrial before new jurors who may prove easier to persuade. *Green v U.S.* (1957) 355 US 184, 188, 2 L Ed 2d 199, 204, 78 S Ct 221. See also *U.S. v Jorn* (1971) 400 US 470, 484, 27 L Ed 2d 543, 556, 91 S Ct 547. See generally 1 Witkin & Epstein, California Criminal Law, *Defenses* §§123-127 (3d ed 2000).

In some circumstances, attorneys move for a mistrial for tactical reasons, even though they expect the motion to be denied. If the irreparable nature of a prejudicial incident is unclear, trial judges commonly deny a motion for mistrial in trials that have already progressed for several days. By then, the trial represents a considerable investment of time and money. The judge may reason that this investment will not necessarily be wasted if the motion is denied, because the party moving for the mistrial may still win, in which case the question will be moot. If the verdict goes the other way, the judge will reconsider the matter on a motion for new trial. In such a circumstance, counsel will move for a mistrial primarily to improve the chances of securing a new trial if the jurors return a verdict adverse to the client. By moving for a mistrial immediately after the prejudicial incident, counsel's claim of prejudice will not appear to be an afterthought.

V. PROCEDURE

A. Irreparable Prejudicial Incident

§56.6 1. Incident Constituting Misconduct

If the ground for the motion for mistrial is a prejudicial incident that constitutes misconduct, counsel should object to the misconduct and fully describe the facts for the record. To avoid highlighting the harmful matter and aggravating the prejudicial effect, counsel should first request permission to discuss the matter outside the presence of the jury. The objecting attorney should then state:

> Objection, Your Honor. I object as misconduct to _ _[e.g., counsel's showing a photograph to the jury after it was ruled inadmissible/the judge's remarks about the client]_ _.

If, after considering the tactical factors, counsel decides to move for a mistrial, counsel should add the following:

> I move for a mistrial on the ground that the effect of this misconduct is so prejudicial that a fair trial is now impossible.

If the judge denies this motion, counsel should continue along the following lines:

> I request that the jury be admonished _ _[describe, e.g., to disregard that photograph]_ _.

Unless counsel makes a request for admonition, the attorney for the party aggrieved by the misconduct risks waiving that misconduct as a possible ground for appeal. *Seffert v Los Angeles Transit Lines* (1961) 56 C2d 498, 509, 15 CR 161; *Estate of Hart* (1951) 107 CA2d 60, 70, 236 P2d 884. See also *Sabella v Southern Pac. Co.* (1969) 70 C2d 311, 319, 74 CR 534; *Neumann v Bishop* (1976) 59 CA3d 451, 469 n3, 130 CR 786. See §29.14. This rule is based on the premise that a proper admonition, promptly given, is enough to cure the prejudicial effect of the misconduct. *Jonte v Key Sys.* (1949) 89 CA2d 654, 201 P2d 562. See *Horn v Atchison, T. & S.F. Ry.* (1964) 61 C2d 602, 39 CR 721. See also *Neumann v Bishop* (1976) 59 CA3d 451, 469 n4, 130 CR 786; *Hart v Wielt* (1970) 4 CA3d 224, 234, 84 CR 220.

No waiver occurs if the misconduct is so harmful that even a strongly worded admonition cannot cure the problem. *Tingley v Times Mirror Co.* (1907) 151 C 1, 23, 89 P 1097. See also *Simmons v Southern Pac. Transp. Co.* (1976) 62 CA3d 341, 355, 133 CR 42. Nevertheless, it is advisable to request an admonition to the jury to disregard the matter even in this situation. The jury may heed the admonition and return a verdict against the party that committed the misconduct, making an appeal on that ground unnecessary.

§56.7   2. Incident Not Constituting Misconduct

If the motion for mistrial is based on a prejudicial incident that does not fit into any of the recognized categories of misconduct, the procedure is somewhat simpler. Counsel should describe what happened in full detail for the record and then state:

> Your Honor, I move for a mistrial on the ground that the effect of this incident is so prejudicial that a fair trial is now impossible.

If the judge denies this motion, counsel should continue along the following lines (for reasons analogous to those stated in §56.6):

> I request that the jury be admonished to disregard this incident.

§56.8 B. Irregularity in Proceedings

If the opposing party calls as a witness either the judge presiding at the trial or a juror, it is sufficient merely to object. Such an objection is "deemed a motion for mistrial." Evid C §§703(c), 704(c). The judge must grant that motion, declare a mistrial, and order the action assigned for trial before another judge or jury. Evid C §§703(b), 704(b). See §§18.14-18.15 (judge), 18.17 (juror).

The other procedural irregularities mentioned in §56.3 (*e.g.,* absence of a juror) will ordinarily be obvious to the judge, and a mistrial will be granted on the court's own motion.

57

Contempt

I. INTRODUCTION §57.1

II. DEFINITION §57.2

III. TYPES OF CONTEMPT §57.3

IV. COMMON EXAMPLES OF CONTEMPTUOUS TRIAL CONDUCT §57.4

V. PROCEDURE
   A. Who Can Bring and Punish Contempt §57.5
   B. Procedures Under CCP §1209
      1. Direct Contempt §57.6
      2. Indirect Contempt §57.7
      3. Hybrid Contempt §57.8
      4. Sentence §57.9
   C. Procedures Under Pen C §166 §57.10
   D. Stay of Contempt Sentence §57.11

VI. REVIEW BY APPELLATE COURT §57.12

§57.1 I. INTRODUCTION

Contempt as a remedy and sanction is being used more frequently than ever before in response to improper conduct and actions by any individual or officer of the court. This chapter focuses on contempt by counsel, which may arise from counsel's lack of civility, "Rambo" tactics during discovery and at trial, and willful trial misconduct. See §§29.2-29.20.

For an egregious example of contemptuous conduct during discovery, see *Daigle v City of Portsmouth* (1993) 630 A2d 776, 778. Examples of such conduct during trial include counsel's ignoring warnings, disobeying clear court orders, willfulness, insolent behavior toward the court, and interfering with the orderly conduct of the proceedings.

The court may impose sanctions against contemptuous conduct during discovery (CCP §2033(*l*)) and at trial (Cal Rules of Ct 227; CCP §128.5). Section 128.5 applies to actions or tactics arising from a complaint filed, or a proceeding initiated, on or before December 31, 1994. See CCP §§128, 1209(a). Code of Civil Procedure §128.7 (effective January 1, 1995, and operative until January 1, 2003) imposes sanctions that mirror Fed R Civ P 11 when "bad-faith actions or tactics that are frivolous or solely intended to cause unnecessary delay" occur in pleading practice. Before filing, submitting, or advocating a pleading, petition, written notice of motion, or similar paper, counsel must make reasonable efforts to ensure that:

- It is not being presented primarily for an improper purpose;
- The claims, defenses, and other legal contentions are warranted;
- The allegations and other factual contentions have evidentiary support; and
- The denials of factual contentions are warranted or based on a lack of information or belief.

See CCP §128.6, which becomes operative January 1, 2003.

Except in extreme circumstances, the court will first warn counsel and instruct the jury to disregard the misconduct before imposing the sanction and penalties of contempt.

§57.2 II. DEFINITION

"Contempt" of court is any act committed in or out of the trial judge's presence that tends to impede, embarrass, or obstruct the judge in the discharge of his or her duties. See *Lloyd v Superior Court* (1982) 133 CA3d 896, 900, 184 CR 467. The major types of contempt are classified in CCP §1209 and Pen C §166.

Code of Civil Procedure §1209(a)-(c) states:

> (a) The following acts or omissions in respect to a court of justice, or proceedings therein, are contempt's of the authority of the court:
>
> 1. Disorderly, contemptuous, or insolent behavior toward the judge while holding the court, tending to interrupt the due course of a trial or other judicial proceeding;
>
> 2. A breach of the peace, boisterous conduct, or violent disturbance, tending to interrupt the due course of a trial or other judicial proceeding;
>
> 3. Misbehavior in office, or other willful neglect or violation of duty by an attorney, counsel, clerk, sheriff, coroner, or other person, appointed or elected to perform a judicial or ministerial service;
>
> 4. Abuse of the process or proceedings of the court, or falsely pretending to act under authority of an order or process of the court;
>
> 5. Disobedience of any lawful judgment, order, or process of the court;
>
> 6. Rescuing any person or property in the custody of an officer by virtue of an order or process of such court;
>
> 7. Unlawfully detaining a witness, or party to an action while going to, remaining at, or returning from the court where the action is on the calendar for trial;

8. Any other unlawful interference with the process or proceedings of a court;

9. Disobedience of a subpoena duly served, or refusing to be sworn or answer as a witness;

10. When summoned as a juror in a court, neglecting to attend or serve as such, or improperly conversing with a party to an action, to be tried at such court, or with any other person, in relation to the merits of such action, or receiving a communication from a party or other person in respect to it, without immediately disclosing the same to the court;

11. Disobedience by an inferior tribunal, magistrate, or officer, of the lawful judgment, order, or process of a superior court, or proceeding in an action or special proceeding contrary to law, after such action or special proceeding is removed from the jurisdiction of such inferior tribunal, magistrate, or officer.

(b) No speech or publication reflecting upon or concerning any court or any officer thereof shall be treated or punished as a contempt of such court unless made in the immediate presence of such court while in session and in such a manner as to actually interfere with its proceedings.

(c) Notwithstanding Section 1211 or any other provision of law, if an order of contempt is made affecting an attorney, his agent, investigator, or any person acting under the attorney's direction, in the preparation and conduct of any action or proceeding, the execution of any sentence shall be stayed pending the filing within three judicial days of a petition for extraordinary relief testing the lawfulness of the court's order, the violation of which is the basis of the contempt, except for such conduct as may be proscribed by subdivision (b) of Section 6068 of the Business and Professions Code, relating to an attorney's duty to maintain respect due to the courts and judicial officers.

Penal Code §166(a) states:

Except as provided in subdivisions (b) and (c), and (d), every person guilty of any contempt of court, of any of the following kinds, is guilty of a misdemeanor:

(1) Disorderly, contemptuous, or insolent behavior committed during the sitting of any court of justice, in the immediate view and presence of the court, and directly tending to interrupt its proceedings or to impair the respect due to its authority;

(2) Behavior as specified in paragraph (1) committed in the presence of any referee, while actually engaged in any trial or hearing, pursuant to the order of any court, or in the presence of any jury while actually sitting for the trial of a cause, or upon any inquest or other proceedings authorized by law;

(3) Any breach of the peace, noise, or other disturbance directly tending to interrupt the proceedings of any court;

(4) Willful disobedience of the terms as written of any process or court order or out-of-state court order, lawfully issued by any court, including orders pending trial;

(5) Resistance willfully offered by any person to the lawful order or process of any court;

(6) The contumacious and unlawful refusal of any person to be sworn as a witness; or, when so sworn, the like refusal to answer any material question;

(7) The publication of a false or grossly inaccurate report of the proceedings of any court;

(8) Presenting to any court having power to pass sentence upon any prisoner under conviction, or to any member of the court, any affidavit or testimony or representation of any kind, verbal or written, in aggravation or mitigation of the punishment to be imposed upon the prisoner, except as provided in this code.

With the approval of the California Supreme Court, the Board of Governors of the State Bar may formulate and enforce rules of professional conduct for all members of the State Bar. A breach of these rules subjects a member to disciplinary proceedings, and certain conduct may also constitute contempt. Bus & P C §§6076-6077; CCP §1209. See also Cal Rules of Ct 227 (sanctions for violations of rules of court or local rules).

Other rules and statutes that provide for contempt include:

- Cal Rules of Ct 225(a) (failure to notify court of settlement);
- CCP §482.080 (refusal to comply with writ of attachment);
- CCP §574 (refusal to deposit money or property as ordered by court);
- CCP §1008 (applying to judge for an order without telling him or her that counsel had applied to another judge for the same order and had been refused);
- CCP §1209.5 (failure to pay child support);
- CCP §§1991-1992, 1985.1 (failure to appear in response to subpoena);
- CCP §2023(b)(5) (misuse of discovery process);
- Evid C §914 (failure to disclose alleged privileged information under court order);
- Fam C §7883 (failure to bring child to court for Fam C §7880 proceeding);
- Pen C §136.2 (intimidating or dissuading victim or witness);
- Pen C §1331, 1331.5 (disobeying subpoena or refusing to testify);
- Prob C §§8500(c), 8501, 8505 (executor or administrator's failure to appear or obey order);
- Prob C §§8870-8872 (failure to comply with inventory and appraisement provisions);
- Pen C §11205 (violating injunction concerning unlawful liquor sale); and

- Pen C §11311 (violating injunction concerning gambling ships).

§57.3 III. TYPES OF CONTEMPT

The type of contempt affects the procedures used to remedy it. There are three types of contempt: direct contempt, indirect (constructive) contempt, and hybrid contempt:

- A direct contempt is one committed in the judge's presence. CCP §1211. See *Pounders v Watson* (1997) 521 US 982, 138 L Ed 2d 976, 117 S Ct 2359.

- An indirect contempt is one committed outside the judge's immediate presence. CCP §1211.

- Hybrid contempt occurs in the judge's presence, but it may be excused by matters that did not occur before the judge. See, *e.g., Arthur v Superior Court* (1965) 62 C2d 404, 408, 42 CR 441.

For discussion of the distinction between direct and indirect contempt, see *Reliable Enters. v Superior Court* (1984) 158 CA3d 604, 611, 204 CR 786, disapproved in part by *Mitchell v Superior Court* (1989) 49 C3d 1230, 1248 n 13, 265 CR 144.

There is confusion over the use of the terms "civil" and "criminal" when applied to contempt. Because contempt under CCP §1209 and Pen C §166 may be punished by incarceration (CCP §1218; Pen C §§19.2, 166), they both are sometimes referred to as criminal or quasi-criminal. A distinction is sometimes drawn, however, between a coercive sentence under CCP §1209 and a punitive sentence under CCP §1209. To distinguish the different results, the coercive sentence is sometimes called civil, and the punitive sentence is sometimes called criminal. Yet another distinction is sometimes made between contempt under CCP §1209 and Pen C §166. The former is called civil contempt and the latter criminal contempt.

§57.4 IV. COMMON EXAMPLES OF CONTEMPTUOUS TRIAL CONDUCT

This section focuses on contempt as a possible remedy in the following two situations:

(1) When counsel deliberately introduces improper matter that, because of its prejudicial effect, threatens to deprive the opposing party of a fair trial. In this situation, the key element is counsel's willfulness rather than counsel's manner.

(2) When counsel's insolent behavior in arguing the merits of an objection to evidence threatens to undermine the respect due the court. In this situation, the key element is counsel's contemptuous manner.

Counsel is guilty of contempt if the acts amount to "disorderly, contemptuous, or insolent behavior toward the judge." CCP §1209(a)(1). It is an attorney's duty "to maintain the respect due to the courts of justice and judicial officers" and "to advance no fact prejudicial to the honor or reputation of a party or witness, unless required by the justice of the cause with which he or she is charged." Bus & P C §6068(b), (f). Attorneys are also obligated, however, to protect their clients' interests. *Gallagher v Municipal Court* (1948) 31 C2d 784, 796, 192 P2d 905.

The line between permissible advocacy and contemptuous behavior is a difficult one to draw. An attorney has the dual, sometimes conflicting, responsibility of supporting the client's position while maintaining a respectful attitude toward the court. When does the attorney's conduct exceed the bounds of discharging the duty toward the client and become contemptuous? No simple rule applies. Much depends on the type of litigation, the point in dispute, and the attorney's sincerity, words, tone of voice, and prompt responses to warnings and admonitions. See Note, *Contempt: How Far An Attorney May Go In Support of His Client's Position*, 35 S Cal L Rev 104 (1961). For example, counsel may wish to support an objection to the introduction of evidence with extended argument. Although counsel's duty to the client may oblige counsel to ensure that the judge fully understands the basis for the objection, the extent to which counsel can present supporting argument is largely in the trial judge's discretion.

In *Cooper v Superior Court* (1961) 55 C2d 291, 298, 10 CR 842, an attorney had been adjudged guilty of two counts of contempt and fined $250 on each count for objecting to the trial judge's comments to the jury regarding the comparative credibility of certain witnesses. On certiorari, the supreme court annulled this adjudication in view of the special circumstances of the case. The trial judge had, on his own initiative, recalled the jury from their deliberations for the purpose of reading to them a statement containing his comments, which the attorney had not been given a prior opportunity to examine. Although the trial judge had instructed the attorney to "keep seated and wait until the jury is out to make your objections," the supreme court held that

> it is not contempt for a lawyer to seek respectfully to make and press upon a trial court, even though the court does not desire to hear him at that time, some objection or other contention which he deems it necessary to make in the interests of his client. Such conduct on the lawyer's part is not a contempt because, as this Court and the District Courts of Appeal have held, it is not only the lawyer's right, it is his duty, at all times to protect and advance the interests of his client.

Appellate courts tend to support the attorney if the overall conduct appears from the record to be respectful. In *Platnauer v Superior Court* (1917) 32 CA 463, 475, 163 P 237, as in *Cooper,* a contempt adjudication was annulled on certiorari because it did not appear that the attorney, in arguing the objection, at any time used disrespectful language. In an opinion that has been frequently quoted, the appellate court declared:

If, in discharging his duty, he happens to be persistent or vehement or both in the presentation of his points, he is still, nevertheless, within his legitimate rights as an attorney, so long as his language is not offensive or in contravention of the common rules of decorum and propriety. As well as may be expected in forensic polemics, he cannot always be right, and may wholly be wrong in his position upon the legal question under argument, and to the mind of the court so plainly wrong that the latter may conceive that it requires no enlightenment from the argument of counsel. But, whether right or wrong, he has the right to an opportunity to present his theory of the case on any occasion where the exigency of the pending point in his judgment requires or justifies it.

See also *In re Carrow* (1974) 40 CA3d 924, 929, 115 CR 601; *O'Laughlin v Superior Court* (1957) 155 CA2d 415, 419, 318 P2d 39.

The trial judge must give counsel a reasonable opportunity to state and argue the objection. The judge need not, however, listen to more than the judge considers necessary. As the court stated in *Hallinan v Superior Court* (1925) 74 CA 420, 426, 240 P 788 (dismissing a writ of certiorari):

> When the court reaches the point that it feels that it is fully advised as to the question under discussion and ready to rule upon the same, and, therefore, requires no further enlightenment from counsel, it is surely clothed with adequate power and authority to order the argument at an end, and when necessary, in order to enforce its order, to punish the attorney guilty of its infraction. Under such circumstances, the action of counsel in persisting in arguing the matter to the court, after the court has repeatedly ordered him to desist, amounts to disorderly behavior towards the judge of the court, which directly tends to interrupt the due course of the trial and is also disobedience of the lawful order of the court. Such acts are defined as contempt by the provisions of section 1209 of the Code of Civil Procedure.

Under no circumstances need the trial judge listen to an argument on an objection that is presented in a "disorderly, contemptuous, or insolent" manner. CCP §1209(a)(1). See, *e.g., Rose v Superior Court* (1934) 140 CA 418, 35 P2d 605; *In re Hallinan* (1932) 126 CA 121, 14 P2d 797.

Local rules often limit objections to a statement of the ground for objection unless the judge requests that counsel state the reasons for the objection. Because local rules change often, counsel should consult the most recent version.

V. PROCEDURE

§57.5   A. Who Can Bring and Punish Contempt

Parties to the original civil or criminal proceedings, persons beneficially interested (see *Bank of America v Carr* (1956) 138 CA2d 727, 733, 292 P2d 587), and the judge (*Lyons v Superior Court* (1955) 43 C2d 755, 758, 278 P2d 681) may initiate contempt proceedings. Persons other than judges can only bring indirect contempt charges. See *Rosenstock v Municipal Court* (1976) 61 CA3d 1, 7, 132 CR 59 (contempt proceedings initiated by court commissioner must be treated as indirect contempt in absence of stipulation giving commissioner authority as judge).

Only judges are usually allowed to punish contempt. Non-judges hearing cases must usually present an affidavit to a judge to initiate contempt proceedings. See CCP §1211. See also CCP §259(f); *Rosenstock v Municipal Court, supra*.

When the judge hearing a case brings contempt charges and has become so personally embroiled in the matter that the judge is unfit to hear the contempt charge, then, as a matter of due process, the hearing must be referred to another judge for adjudication of the alleged contempt. *Offutt v U.S.* (1954) 348 US 11, 14, 99 L Ed 11, 16, 75 S Ct 11; *In re Buckley* (1973) 10 C3d 237, 255, 110 CR 121. Similarly, if asserted acts of misconduct are directed to the judge personally, then the judge should recuse himself or herself so that the matter may be heard by another judge. *In re Martin* (1977) 71 CA3d 472, 480, 139 CR 451.

The judicial disqualification provisions of CCP §§170 and 170.6 apply only to indirect contempt under CCP §1209 and to Pen C §166 prosecutions.

B. Procedures Under CCP §1209

§57.6   1. Direct Contempt

If a contempt is committed "in the immediate view and presence of the court, or of the judge at chambers," it is a direct contempt and may be punished summarily. CCP §1211; see *Pounders v Watson* (1997) 521 US 982, 138 L Ed 2d 976, 117 S Ct 2359.

The court must prepare an order reciting the facts, adjudging the person guilty, and prescribing the punishment. CCP §1211. No hearing is required. If the judge states that a hearing will be held on the contempt matter, however, a hearing is required. *DeGeorge v Superior Court* (1974) 40 CA3d 305, 315, 114 CR 860. Further, if the judge defers the entire contempt matter until after the trial is concluded, the alleged contemner is entitled to notice of the charges and an opportunity to respond, with a hearing held before another judge. *In re Karagozian* (1975) 44 CA3d 516, 522, 118 CR 793.

The most effective procedure to curb counsel's conduct and make a record that will support an adjudication of contempt is for the trial judge to resolve the matter as follows:

- The judge should take a brief recess, go into chambers, and reflect on the appropriate action before proceeding.

- If the judge determines that counsel's actions are serious enough to warrant a contempt, the judge should warn counsel outside the jury's presence. The warning should include a detailed statement for the record of the offensive conduct, especially if it must be seen or heard to be properly evaluated, *e.g.,* facial expressions, gestures, and tone of voice. The judge should also caution counsel that further similar behavior will not be tolerated and that counsel will be held in contempt if it occurs again.

- The judge should then allow counsel to explain or justify the action.
- After counsel's explanation, the judge may want to modify the warning or may choose to repeat it.
- If counsel persists in the disrespectful courtroom behavior, the judge should hold counsel in contempt, out of the jury's presence, by (a) reciting for the record the facts committed in the judge's presence that gave rise to the contempt, (b) reviewing the earlier incident and warning, (c) finding the person guilty of contempt, and (d) prescribing punishment. The judge may want to accept counsel's apology at this time and purge the contempt. If there is no apology, punishment should be announced but stayed until the trial concludes except under extraordinary circumstances.
- The judge then must make an order in strict compliance with the requirements of CCP §1211.

When the offensive conduct involves a subjective determination (*i.e.,* offensive tone of voice and facial expressions), the court is required to issue a warning before trial counsel may be cited for contempt. *Boysaw v Superior Court* (2000) 23 C4th 215, 221, 96 CR2d 531 ("When an order of contempt is based on tone of voice ... the order must recite that he was warned his tone of voice was objectionable."); *In re Hallinan* (1969) 71 C2d 1179, 81 CR 1. Although warnings are not required in other circumstances, they are advisable. Regarding the advisability of such a warning, Justice Traynor observed in *Gallagher v Municipal Court* (1948) 31 C2d 784, 797, 192 P2d 905.

> If the words used by counsel are respectful and pertinent to the matter before the court, it is not unnecessarily burdensome to require the judge first to warn the attorney that his tone and facial expressions are offensive and tend to interrupt the due course of the proceeding. Otherwise, attorneys could be subjected to fines and jail sentences because of personal annoyance and pique on the part of trial judges; and these penalties could be rendered unassailable, as is contended here, by lengthy recitals in the orders of contempt respecting the demeanor of the contemner.

Code of Civil Procedure §1211 mandates that "an order must be made, reciting the facts as occurring in such immediate view and presence, adjudging that the person proceeded against is thereby guilty of a contempt, and that he be punished as therein prescribed." The judge must comply with the strict and technical requirements of this statute. *In re Hallinan* (1969) 71 C2d 1179, 1180, 81 CR 1; *Gallagher v Municipal Court* (1948) 31 C2d 784, 795, 192 P2d 905. Compliance with the requirements of CCP §1211 is jurisdictional. The order must recite facts with sufficient particularity to demonstrate on its face that counsel's conduct constituted legal contempt, and it must recite all the other elements of contempt. *In re Buckley* (1973) 10 C3d 237, 247, 110

CR 121. See *Chula v Superior Court* (1962) 57 C2d 199, 203, 18 CR 507; *In re Morelli* (1970) 11 CA3d 819, 850, 91 CR 72.

The order must be made and entered promptly. If the determination of contempt is not made within a reasonable time, the court loses jurisdiction to act. *In re Foote* (1888) 76 C 543, 18 P 678. Until an order of contempt is signed and entered, the contemner has nothing against which to test the commitment. Furthermore, the contempt order and judgment of commitment must be entered in the court's permanent minutes and not just in the file of the case. *In re Jones* (1975) 47 CA3d 879, 120 CR 914 ("too late entry" case). On issuing a judgment of contempt, the court loses jurisdiction. Hence, the court cannot amend the order to correct a deficiency once the contempt order has been reduced to writing and signed by the judge. *County of Lake v Superior Court* (1977) 67 CA3d 815, 136 CR 830.

§57.7 2. Indirect Contempt

The person initiating indirect contempt charges must file an affidavit alleging the facts that support the charge. CCP §1211. Either the person charged with contempt may be served with an order to show cause, the usual procedure, or a warrant of attachment may be issued to bring the offending party directly to court. CCP §1212. The accused may file a counteraffidavit. *Lyon v Superior Court* (1968) 68 C2d 446, 452, 67 CR 265; see also *Cedars-Sinai Imaging Med. Group v Superior Court* (2000) 83 CA4th 1281, 100 CR2d 320 (court's contempt order was void for lack of jurisdiction where it had stated its intent to issue order to show cause for contempt, but never actually did so).

The accused is entitled to the same rights as a criminal defendant, except for the right to a jury trial. See *In re Morelli* (1970) 11 CA3d 819, 850, 91 CR 72. Constitutional due process requires that the affidavit required by CCP §1211 contain adequate notice of the charges, including the date of the alleged offense. *Reliable Enters. v Superior Court* (1984) 158 CA3d 604, 618, 204 CR 786, disapproved in part by *Mitchell v Superior Court* (1989) 49 C3d 1230, 1248 n 13, 265 CR 144. The rules on disqualification of judges (CCP §§170, 170.6) apply in cases of indirect contempt. See *Briggs v Superior Court* (1931) 211 C 619, 297 P 3.

If the accused is found in contempt, the order must show that (a) the court had jurisdiction to make the order that was disobeyed, (b) the accused had knowledge of the order, and (c) the accused was able to comply with the order but refused to do so. *In re Jones* (1975) 47 CA3d 879, 120 CR 914; *Darden v Superior Court* (1965) 235 CA2d 80, 83, 45 CR 44.

For procedure that should be followed by trial court, see CCP §1212.

§57.8 3. Hybrid Contempt

The procedures for hybrid contempt are the same as for direct contempt, except that the attorney must be given a reasonable opportunity to explain.

Cannon v Commission on Judicial Qualifications (1975) 14 C3d 678, 693 n13, 122 CR 778; *Inniss v Municipal Court* (1965) 62 C2d 487, 42 CR 594.

§57.9   4. Sentence

If a contemner is punished punitively, the most severe sentence that can be imposed is five days in jail, a $1000 fine, or both. CCP §1218. If, however, the contemner is being coerced into an action (*e.g.,* testifying during trial), he or she can be imprisoned until the trial is over or until the trial court determines that further imprisonment would not compel compliance. CCP §1219. When the sentence is no longer coercive, it is limited by the five-day, $1000 maximum sentence provided by CCP §1218. *In re Farr* (1974) 36 CA3d 577, 111 CR 649. Separate acts of contempt are separately punishable. *Reliable Enters. v Superior Court* (1984) 158 CA3d 604, 621, 204 CR 786, disapproved in part by *Mitchell v Superior Court* (1989) 49 C3d 1230, 1248 n 13, 265 CR 144.

Notwithstanding the limit of punishment for contempt provided in CCP §1218, the court may impose a jail sentence in lieu of payment of a fine and thereby extend the period of incarceration beyond five days. *In re Ciraolo* (1969) 70 C2d 389, 74 CR 865 (upholding sentence of three days in jail and fine of $200 or additional ten days).

The court may not order punishment of the contemner unless it is authorized by statute. *Bauguess v Paine* (1978) 22 C3d 626, 150 CR 461 (trial court's order requiring plaintiff's attorney to pay defendant's attorney fees as a contempt sanction for misconduct resulting in a mistrial was not within equitable powers of court and thus constituted reversible error).

The victim of a sexual assault may not be imprisoned for contempt for refusing to testify concerning the assault. CCP §1219(b). See also CCP §128(d) (3-day stay of sentence pending filing of petition for extraordinary relief testing court's contempt order for refusal of sexual assault victim to testify).

§57.10   C. Procedures Under Pen C §166

A violation of Pen C §166 is prosecuted in the same manner as any other misdemeanor. See generally California Criminal Law Procedure and Practice §51.12 (7th ed Cal CEB 2004). Usually, the punishment for violation of Pen C §166 is a maximum of six months in jail and a $1000 fine. However, the statute contains many additional sentencing provisions for specific types of contempts.

The court can choose to proceed under CCP §1209 instead of under Pen C §166, even though the violation is specified in §166. *In re San Francisco Chronicle* (1934) 1 C2d 630, 636, 36 P2d 369.

§57.11   D. Stay of Contempt Sentence

A judge should not jail an attorney during a trial except under extraordinary circumstances, because it would interfere with his or her client's rights. See *People v Fusaro* (1971) 18 CA3d 877, 890, 96 CR 368.

A stay of three judicial days is *mandated* during trial for:

- An "attorney, his agent, investigator, or any person acting under the attorney's direction," unless that person violated Bus & P C §6068(b) (CCP §§128(b), 1209(c)); and

- A "public safety employee acting within the scope of employment for reason of the employee's failure to comply with a duly issued subpoena or subpoena duces tecum" (CCP §§128(c), 1209(d)).

§57.12   VI. REVIEW BY APPELLATE COURT

An adjudication of contempt is "final and conclusive" (CCP §1222) and therefore is not appealable. Review must be by extraordinary writ. Contempt orders are carefully reviewed and strictly construed by appellate courts. *Smith v Superior Court* (1968) 68 C2d 547, 560, 68 CR 1; *Uhler v Superior Court* (1953) 117 CA2d 147, 151, 256 P2d 90. See generally 8 Witkin, California Procedure, *Enforcement of Judgment* §354; 9 Witkin, Procedure, *Appeal* §354 (4th ed 1997).

Table of Statutes, Regulations, and Rules

CALIFORNIA

Constitution

Art I
- **§1:** §§33.3, 36.3, 55.4
- **§2(a):** §§48.2, 48.5, 48.17-48.18
- **§2(b):** §§1.7, 48.6-48.8, 48.10-48.11, 48.13, 48.15, 48.17-48.18, 48.20
- **§4:** §6.39
- **§7:** §§6.2, 6.27
- **§13:** §§28.2-28.3, 28.13
- **§14.1:** §§1.5, 1.7
- **§15:** §§19.19, 26.8, 29.45, 46.8, 46.19, 46.21, 47.1, 47.10, 54.16
- **§16:** §§6.2, 6.12, 6.27-6.29, 29.23, 56.2
- **§18:** §27.7
- **§20:** §§1.5, 1.7
- **§24:** §§1.5, 1.7, 17.4
- **§28:** §§1.5-1.6, 18.30
- **§28(d):** §§1.6, 1.11-1.12, 17.4, 18.5, 18.27, 20.7, 20.11, 21.4, 22.9, 23.4, 27.1, 28.11, 29.46, 32.4, 32.7, 33.1, 37.1, 38.1, 39.1, 40.1, 47.1, 48.11, 51.1
- **§28(f):** §§17.5, 21.4, 22.2, 31.4, 47.4
- **§29:** §§1.5, 1.7, 48.11
- **§30:** §§19.29, 19.38
- **§30(b):** §19.38

Art II, §7: §49.2

Art VI
- **§4 (former):** §52.12
- **§10:** §§29.23, 53.1
- **§13:** §§5.4, 6.6, 6.16, 6.50, 6.54, 21.16, 29.17-29.18, 29.31, 29.46, 30.2, 52.12, 54.13

Statutes

BUSINESS AND PROFESSIONS CODE
- **Division 2:** §37.20
  - **Chapter 6:** §37.20
  - **Chapter 6, art 9:** §37.20
  - **Chapter 6.6, art 9:** §37.20
  - **Chapter 13, art 5:** §37.20
  - **Chapter 13, art 9:** §37.20
  - **Chapter 14:** §37.20
  - **Chapter 14, art 5:** §37.20
- **2700:** §37.20
- **2838:** §37.20
- **2900:** §37.20
- **2900-2989:** §37.2
- **2909:** §37.20
- **2909(d):** §37.2
- **2911:** §37.20
- **2913:** §37.20
- **2995:** §37.20
- **4980:** §37.20
- **4980.03:** §37.2
- **4980.03(c):** §37.20
- **4980.40(b):** §§37.2, 37.20
- **4980.44:** §37.20
- **4986:** §37.20
- **4987.5:** §37.20
- **4996:** §37.20
- **4996.20:** §37.20
- **4998:** §37.20
- **6000-6159.2:** §14.1
- **6000-6172:** §29.2
- **6068:** §§14.1, 29.2, 55.5, 57.2
- **6068(b):** §§57.4, 57.11
- **6068(d):** §29.6
- **6068(e):** §§34.1, 34.12
- **6068(e)(1):** §§34.12, 34.20
- **6068(e)(2):** §34.12
- **6068(f):** §§29.7, 57.4
- **6068(i):** §34.16
- **6076-6077:** §§2.17, 57.2
- **6086.7:** §29.2
- **6103:** §29.15
- **6128(a):** §29.2
- **6160-6172:** §34.25

CIVIL CODE
- **1624:** §25.1
- **1632:** §33.31
- **1698:** §25.11
- **3295:** §29.7
- **3333.1:** §32.6
- **3426-3426.11:** §45.2

3426.1(d): §45.2
3426.5: §45.6

CODE OF CIVIL PROCEDURE
33: §32.4
128: §§2.17, 22.7, 57.1
128(a): §2.17
128(a)(3): §2.1
128(a)(5): §29.15
128(b): §§55.5, 57.11
128(c): §57.11
128(d): §57.9
128.5: §57.1
128.6: §57.1
128.7: §§54.11, 57.1
170: §§57.5, 57.7
170.6: §§57.5, 57.7
170.6(3): §29.30
190-237: §29.34
191: §§6.27, 6.52, 6.54
197: §§6.52, 6.54
197(a): §§6.2, 6.27
203: §§6.2, 29.35
203(a)(1): §6.18
203(a)(2): §6.18
203(a)(3): §6.18
203(a)(4): §6.18
203(a)(5): §6.18
203(a)(6): §6.18
203(a)(7): §6.18
203(a)(8): §6.18
204: §§6.27, 6.52, 6.54
204(a): §6.2
204(b): §6.2
205: §§6.18, 6.28, 6.52, 6.54
205(a): §6.4
205(c): §§6.4, 6.10
205(d): §6.10
219(b): §6.2
220: §6.12
222.5: §§6.5, 6.7, 6.10, 6.14-6.15, 6.33, 6.35, 6.37, 6.43, 6.46, 6.52
223: §§1.7, 6.4, 6.6, 6.10, 6.16, 6.41, 6.43, 6.50, 6.54
224: §6.18
225: §§6.2-6.3, 6.18, 6.21, 6.52, 6.54, 29.35
225(a)(1): §6.3
225(a)(1)-(3): §6.2
225(a)(2): §6.3
225(b)(1)(A): §6.18
225(b)(1)(A)-(C): §6.17
225(b)(1)(B): §6.19
225(b)(1)(C): §6.20
226: §§6.52, 6.54
226(b): §§6.23-6.24, 6.27
226(c): §§6.22, 6.24
226(d): §§6.12, 6.22
227: §§6.21, 6.52, 6.54
228: §§6.10, 6.18, 6.52, 6.54, 29.35
228(b): §6.18
229: §§6.19, 6.52, 6.54, 29.35
230: §§6.23, 6.52, 6.54
231: §§6.23, 6.52
231(a): §6.26
231(a)-(b): §§6.52, 6.54
231(b): §6.26
231(c): §§6.5, 6.25, 6.54
231(c)-(e): §6.52
231(d): §6.24
231(d)-(e): §6.54
232(a): §§29.34-29.35
232(b): §29.34
233: §§6.52, 6.54, 29.45, 56.3
233-234: §6.24
234: §§6.52, 6.54, 29.45
259(f): §57.5
372-373: §§34.22, 36.5, 36.20, 37.5, 37.17
375(c): §54.1
376: §§36.23, 37.20
377: §§36.23, 37.20
473: §§54.1, 54.11
482.080: §57.2
568: §29.45
574: §57.2
575.2: §2.17
577: §55.1
592: §3.7
594(a): §54.1
595: §54.1
595.2: §54.2
595.4: §§54.1-54.2, 54.5-54.6, 54.8
596: §54.10
597: §3.7
597.5: §3.7
597.5-598: §3.1
598: §3.7
598 (former): §3.7
607: §§3.2-3.3, 26.2
607a: §53.2
607a-609: §53.2
611: §§29.36, 29.39, 53.1
612: §29.42
612.5: §29.42
616: §§56.1, 56.3
631.3: §54.12
631.7: §§3.2-3.3, 26.2

647: §§4.20, 29.28
657: §56.4
657-658: §18.27
657(1): §§29.17, 29.30, 29.46
657(1)-(2): §56.1
657(2): §§18.27, 29.43, 29.46
657(3): §54.14
658: §29.46
659: §§29.17, 29.30, 29.46
659a: §§29.17, 29.30, 29.46
877.5: §32.2
904.1: §55.1
904.1-904.2: §29.46
904.1(a)(1): §55.1
904.1(a)(2): §55.5
906: §29.46
1005: §43.15
1008: §57.2
1024: §54.11
1068: §§55.1-55.2
1086: §33.22
1102: §55.2
1103: §33.22
1205: §25.2
1209: §§2.17, 57.2-57.5, 57.10
1209(a): §§29.15, 57.1
1209(a)-(c): §57.2
1209(a)(1): §57.4
1209(c): §§55.5, 57.11
1209(d): §57.11
1209.5: §57.2
1211: §§57.2-57.3, 57.5-57.7
1212: §57.7
1218: §§57.3, 57.9
1219: §57.9
1219(b): §57.9
1222: §§55.5, 57.12
1280-1298.8: §1.2
1854 (former): §26.7
1856: §§25.2, 25.4-25.5, 25.7-25.8
1856-1866: §25.1
1856(a): §§25.2-25.3
1856(b): §25.10
1856(d): §§25.1, 25.10
1856(f): §25.6
1856(g): §25.8
1856(h): §25.2
1860: §§25.2, 25.7
1867-1868 (former): §17.8
1880 (former): §4.19
1881 (former), Comment: §§41.3, 41.8
1881(1) (former): §§41.6, 41.8, 41.22
1881(2) (former): §34.14
1881(3) (former): §§50.1, 51.1
1881(6) (former): §48.6
1985.1: §57.2
1985.3: §46.6
1991-1992: §57.2
2015.5: §§29.43, 29.45-29.46, 54.7
2016(d)(3): §46.19
2017(a): §§33.2, 33.25, 42.10
2018: §§35.2, 35.5-35.6, 35.10, 36.9
2018(a): §35.1
2018(b): §§33.31, 34.2, 35.3-35.4, 35.9, 35.11
2018(c): §§6.30, 33.31, 34.2, 35.3-35.4, 35.9-35.11
2018(f): §35.5
2019 (former): §46.16
2019(d): §45.1
2020(h): §41.22
2023: §2.6
2023(a)-(b): §41.22
2023(b): §2.6
2023(b)(5): §57.2
2025(h): §41.22
2025(i): §§42.10, 46.14, 46.16
2025(i)(9): §46.16
2025(j)(2): §41.22
2025(l)(1): §41.22
2025(m)(1): §§33.2, 33.25
2025(m)(2): §52.17
2025(u): §33.9
2028(d)(2): §§33.2, 33.25
2030(a): §36.9
2030(k)-(l): §41.22
2030(n): §36.9
2031(a): §36.9
2032(f): §41.22
2032(h): §41.22
2032(j): §41.22
2033(k): §35.8
2033(l): §57.1
2034: §22.11
2034 (former): §43.13
2034(a)(2): §22.11
2034(e): §2.6
2034(f): §22.11
2034(f)(2): §22.11
2034(g): §22.11
2034(i): §§22.11, 35.6
2034(j): §§2.3, 22.11
2034(m): §22.11
2034(m)(1): §35.6
2042 (former): §3.7

COMMERCIAL CODE
- **1205(1):** §25.7
- **1205(3)-(4):** §25.7
- **1206:** §25.1
- **2102:** §25.2
- **2105(1):** §25.2
- **2106(1):** §25.2
- **2201:** §25.1
- **2202:** §§25.2, 25.4
  - **Official Comment 1(a):** §25.10
  - **Official Comment 1(c):** §25.7
- **2202(a):** §§25.7-25.8
- **2202(b):** §25.10
- **2208:** §25.2
- **8113:** §25.1
- **9203:** §25.1

CORPORATIONS CODE
- **25531(e):** §46.17

EDUCATION CODE
- **72621:** §32.9

EVIDENCE CODE
- **Division 8:** §33.2
- **12(a):** §§1.8-1.9
- **105:** §§1.8-1.9, 41.21
- **110(b):** §31.4
- **115:** §21.15
- **130:** §36.10
- **140:** §§1.3, 31.3
- **150:** §19.2
- **160:** §§19.2, 44.3
- **175:** §§34.4, 48.7
- **190:** §1.3
- **195:** §§19.27, 43.2
- **200:** §§19.27, 34.4, 43.2, 43.6-43.7, 44.3, 44.7
- **210:** §§1.4, 17.1-17.2, 18.27, 23.3
  - **Comment:** §17.2
- **220:** §43.9
- **225:** §19.3
- **230:** §§32.1, 33.3, 43.4, 44.3, 44.6
- **240:** §19.11
- **240(a)(1):** §§33.9, 46.19
- **240(a)(2):** §19.11
- **240(a)(3):** §19.11
- **240(a)(5):** §19.11
- **240(c):** §19.11
- **250:** §§2.3, 21.6, 24.2, 33.12
- **255:** §24.2
- **260:** §24.3
- **300:** §§1.2, 1.8-1.9, 6.23, 33.2
  - **Comment:** §33.2
- **310(a):** §§33.17, 33.26
- **320:** §§3.1, 3.6-3.7, 5.3, 15.6, 21.16, 26.2, 27.11, 52.1, 52.5
  - **Comment:** §3.2
- **350:** §§1.13, 2.1, 17.1-17.2, 19.4, 19.9, 19.26
- **350-351:** §36.9
- **351:** §§17.1, 19.8, 19.16A, 23.3, 31.2, 31.5, 32.1, 33.1, 33.3
  - **Comment:** §§17.1, 32.1, 32.9
- **351.1:** §§1.10, 2.3, 20.14
- **352:** §§1.6, 1.11, 1.13, 2.1, 2.3, 2.14, 4.2, 4.6, 5.11, 11.2, 11.4, 17.4-17.6, 19.9, 19.16A, 19.24, 19.26, 20.7, 20.11-20.12, 20.20, 20.28, 21.4, 22.2-22.3, 22.7-22.10, 23.2-23.4, 26.6, 26.8, 28.7, 28.13, 30.1-30.3, 30.6, 31.1-31.7, 31.9-31.10, 31.12-31.19, 32.2, 32.4-32.5, 32.7, 38.10, 38.13, 47.4
- **352.1:** §§1.10, 31.4
- **353:** §§2.18, 4.6, 4.15, 6.47, 25.12, 29.17-29.18, 29.46, 52.1
  - **Comment:** §§4.11, 4.17, 4.19, 17.8
- **353-354:** §31.12
- **353(a):** §§4.8, 4.16, 4.18-4.20, 31.17, 32.1, 52.1, 52.7, 52.9
- **353(b):** §§21.16, 30.2
- **354:** §§5.4, 31.17, 33.27, 52.12, 54.13
- **354(a):** §§5.4, 5.7-5.8, 5.10-5.12, 31.14, 53.5
- **354(b):** §5.6
- **354(c):** §5.5
- **355:** §§2.4, 5.1, 17.3, 31.4, 32.8, 53.1, 53.5
- **356:** §§2.3, 26.7
  - **Comment:** §26.7
- **400:** §§17.7, 18.5, 18.10, 18.23, 33.17
- **400-401:** §21.1
- **400-402:** §§33.15, 33.26, 36.21, 38.11, 39.11, 40.18, 43.13, 45.6, 51.9
- **400-406:** §§2.3, 33.17
- **401:** §§2.3, 21.1
- **401.6:** §3.6
- **402:** §§18.5, 18.10, 18.23, 19.11, 20.10, 22.10, 37.18, 41.23, 42.17
- **402(a):** §§33.17, 33.26
- **402(b):** §§1.10, 2.1, 2.12, 20.24, 21.9
- **403:** §§5.2, 19.10, 21.1-21.12, 21.14, 21.16, 21.18, 27.6, 32.7, 33.17
  - **Comment:** §§17.7, 18.23, 19.10

403(a): §21.3
   Comment: §§17.7, 21.4, 21.6-21.7
403(a)(1): §§3.6, 5.3, 5.12, 17.7, 19.10, 21.4, 52.5
403(a)(2): §§3.6, 5.3, 18.1, 18.23, 21.5, 21.11
403(a)(3): §§3.6, 21.6, 52.5
403(a)(3)-(4): §5.3
403(a)(4): §§3.6, 21.7, 52.5
403(b): §§3.6, 5.3, 17.7, 21.11, 21.16, 52.1, 52.5
403(c): §52.1
403(c)(1): §§21.12, 52.7
403(c)(1)-(2): §52.5
403(c)(2): §§21.11, 21.13, 52.1, 52.7
404: §§21.8, 21.18, 33.17, 46.2, 46.5, 46.8, 46.20
   Comment: §46.20
404-405: §33.26
405: §§3.6, 5.2, 16.5, 19.10, 20.3, 20.6, 20.10, 20.23, 21.2, 21.8-21.9, 21.15-21.16, 21.18, 25.1, 25.3, 25.10, 27.6, 33.1, 33.15, 33.17, 34.23, 36.21, 37.18, 38.11, 39.11, 40.18, 41.23, 42.17, 43.13, 45.6, 48.12, 49.7, 50.9, 51.9
   Comments: §§18.5, 18.9, 19.12, 21.8, 21.15, 33.18, 34.24, 36.22, 37.19, 38.12, 39.12, 40.19, 41.24, 42.18, 43.14, 45.7, 51.10
405(a): §§18.5, 18.10, 21.15-21.16, 33.26
405(b): §21.17
406: §21.15
411
   Comment: §27.7
412: §§33.29, 46.12
   Comments: §§33.29, 46.12
412-413: §33.29
413: §§33.29, 46.12
452(h): §19.36
452.5(b): §19.27
501: §1.10
520: §1.10
522: §1.10
600(a): §1.3
600(b): §1.3
601: §1.3
606: §1.3
607: §1.10
700: §§18.1, 18.3, 18.14-18.15
700-704: §18.1
701: §§18.5, 21.8
   Comment: §§18.4, 18.9, 18.23
701-702: §18.22
701(a): §§18.4-18.6
701(a)(1): §§18.2, 18.5
701(a)(2): §§18.2, 18.9-18.11, 18.22
702: §§5.3, 9.3, 16.2, 16.4, 16.6, 18.21-18.24, 19.9, 19.26, 20.4, 20.23, 21.5, 21.11, 21.14
   Comment: §§18.21, 18.25
702(a): §§3.6, 18.1-18.2, 18.21, 18.23, 21.5, 21.11, 52.5
703: §18.18
703(b): §§18.2, 18.17, 56.8
703(c): §§56.3, 56.8
703.5: §18.17
704(b): §§18.2, 18.20, 56.8
704(c): §§56.3, 56.8
720: §§20.10, 21.8, 31.2
720(a): §§20.6, 20.23
721: §22.10
   Comment: §§20.25, 22.10
721(a): §26.3
721(b): §§20.25, 22.10
721(b)(1): §22.10
721(b)(3): §22.10
722(b): §§20.25, 26.3
723: §§31.7, 31.9
730: §45.6
730-732: §3.1
730-733: §20.21
731: §1.10
732: §20.21
750-752: §18.5
751(a): §18.5
751(d): §18.5
752-754: §3.1
754: §18.5
754(j): §1.10
760: §3.5
760-763: §3.5
761: §§3.5, 22.4, 26.2, 47.7
762: §3.5
763: §3.5
764: §13.1
765: §§3.1, 3.5, 4.2, 4.7, 7.1, 8.4, 9.4, 10.4-10.5, 11.3-11.4, 12.3-12.4, 13.5, 13.7, 13.10, 14.1, 14.3, 15.8, 22.7, 31.7
765-778: §3.5
765(a): §§1.11, 7.5, 8.4, 11.3
765(b): §13.1
766: §§4.16, 8.5, 52.3, 52.9
767: §§13.4, 13.10, 13.12-13.13, 26.2
   Comment: §§1.11, 13.4-13.8, 13.12, 26.2

767(a): §§1.11, 13.9-13.10, 13.12, 15.3
767(a)(1): §13.1
767(a)(2): §13.1
767(b): §13.7
767(b)(2): §13.1
769: §22.5A
   Comment: §22.5A
770: §§19.19, 19.26, 22.6
770(a): §13.10
770(b): §22.6
771: §§19.21, 19.26, 33.12
771(c): §33.12
772: §3.5
   Comment: §26.9
772(b): §§3.6, 5.3, 21.16
772(c): §§5.17, 26.2, 26.8-26.9
772(d): §§26.8, 47.1, 47.7
773: §§6.30, 26.2, 47.7
   Comment: §§13.12, 47.7
773(a): §§3.5, 22.4, 47.7, 52.2
773(b): §§13.12, 47.7
774: §§3.5, 11.2, 11.4, 12.4, 26.9, 52.2
775: §§3.1, 20.21
776: §§1.11, 5.17, 13.9, 13.12, 26.2-26.3, 41.10, 42.9
   Comment: §§13.9, 13.12, 26.2
776(a): §§13.9, 41.22
776(b): §§13.12, 26.2
776(d): §§13.9, 20.22
776(d)(1): §41.22
776(e): §§13.9, 26.2
776(e)(1): §26.2
776(e)(2): §26.2
777: §3.5
778: §3.5
780: §§22.1, 22.3, 22.8, 22.12, 23.2-23.3, 26.3, 31.5
   Comment: §§22.3, 23.2, 26.3, 31.2, 31.5
780(h): §13.10
782: §§1.6, 1.10, 17.4, 20.11, 22.8, 38.10, 38.13
783: §22.8
785: §§13.9-13.10, 22.1, 22.12, 23.1, 23.5, 26.3
   Comment: §26.3
786: §1.11
786-787: §§22.8, 23.4
787: §§1.11, 2.3
788: §§1.11, 2.3, 21.4, 22.8, 31.4, 47.4, 47.7
788(a): §22.8
788(b): §22.8
788(c)-(d): §22.8

788(d): §22.8
789: §22.9
790: §§1.11, 23.4, 31.17
791: §§19.20, 19.26, 23.4
791(a): §23.4
791(b): §23.4
795: §§1.10, 18.21, 19.11, 20.13-20.14
795(a): §§19.11, 20.7
795(a)(1)-(2): §19.11
795(a)(3): §19.11
795(a)(4): §19.11
800: §§2.3, 16.4, 16.6, 20.1, 20.3, 20.5, 26.8
   Comment: §§16.4, 20.3
800-801: §19.26
800-803: §19.9
800-805
   Comment: §§20.1, 20.8
800(a): §§16.2, 20.1, 20.4
800(a)-(b): §20.2
800(b): §20.4
801: §§16.5-16.6, 18.21, 18.24, 19.26, 20.1, 20.22
   Comment: §§16.5, 20.7-20.9
801-804: §20.22
801(a): §§20.7, 20.9
801(b): §§16.5, 20.1, 20.8-20.9, 20.19
802: §§16.4-16.5, 20.5, 20.8, 20.22-20.23, 26.8
   Comment: §§20.20, 20.23
803: §§20.5, 20.8, 20.22
804: §§20.22, 20.27
804(b): §20.27
805: §§20.7, 20.28
810-824: §20.28
813: §20.3
815: §20.3
817: §20.3
822: §20.3
870: §§20.4, 20.28, 21.8, 34.19
895: §20.7
900: §33.31
900-905: §33.31
900-920: §§33.3, 33.31
900-1070: §§21.8, 33.2, 33.31
901: §§33.2, 33.31, 41.21, 47.2
902: §33.31
903: §§33.31, 36.10
905: §33.31
910: §§33.2, 33.31, 47.2
   Comment: §§33.1-33.2
911: §§33.3, 33.31, 34.22B
911-1070: §§19.9, 19.26

912: §§33.6, 33.31, 34.4, 34.22, 34.25, 36.20, 36.23, 37.17, 37.20, 38.9, 39.9, 40.20, 45.5, 50.11, 51.11
912(a): §§33.9, 33.11, 33.24, 34.22-34.22A, 36.20, 37.17, 38.9, 40.17, 50.8, 51.8
912(a)-(c): §40.17
912(b): §§33.24, 33.28, 34.22, 36.20, 37.17, 38.9, 40.4, 40.17
912(c): §§34.22, 36.20, 37.17, 38.9, 40.17, 50.5, 50.8, 51.8
912(d): §§34.22, 34.22B, 36.20, 37.17, 38.9, 40.17
913: §§22.7, 29.23, 33.9, 33.13, 33.20, 33.25, 33.29, 33.31, 46.8, 46.12, 47.6
   Comment: §§33.20, 33.29, 46.11-46.12
913(a): §53.7
913(b): §53.7
914: §§33.31, 34.23, 57.2
915: §§1.10, 33.31, 40.19, 43.15
   Comment: §33.1
915(a): §§33.17, 34.23-34.24, 36.21, 37.18, 38.11, 39.11, 40.18, 41.23-41.24, 49.7, 51.9
915(b): §§33.1, 33.17, 35.9, 36.21, 37.18, 43.6, 43.13, 45.6, 50.9, 51.9
916: §§33.5, 33.11, 33.14-33.16, 33.21, 33.24, 33.26, 33.28, 33.31, 34.24, 34.29, 36.7, 36.20, 36.22, 36.26, 37.7, 37.17, 37.19, 37.23, 38.7, 38.9, 38.12, 38.16, 39.7, 39.9, 39.12, 39.16, 40.7, 40.17, 40.19, 40.23, 43.7-43.8, 43.12-43.13, 43.18, 44.7, 44.15, 45.4, 45.6, 45.10, 49.4, 50.6, 50.8-50.9, 50.14, 51.6, 51.14
   Comment: §§33.14-33.15, 33.21, 49.4
916(a): §§33.15, 34.13
916(a)(1): §33.15
916(a)(1)-(2): §33.15
916(a)(2): §§33.21, 34.20
916(b): §33.15
916(b)(1): §§33.16, 33.28
916(b)(2): §§33.16, 33.28, 34.20, 36.19, 37.16, 38.8
917: §§21.8, 33.18, 33.31, 34.10, 34.24, 36.4, 36.22, 37.4, 37.19, 38.3, 38.12, 39.3, 39.12, 40.4, 40.19, 50.5, 50.10, 51.5, 51.10

918: §§33.7, 33.21-33.22, 33.31, 36.20, 37.17, 38.9, 39.9, 40.17, 41.8, 41.21, 42.10, 43.7, 44.7, 46.3, 46.7, 50.8
918-919: §41.21
919: §§33.24, 33.26, 33.31, 38.9, 39.9, 41.21, 46.19, 47.7, 50.8
   Comment: §43.12
   Comment: §49.6
919(a): §§33.24, 36.20, 37.17, 40.17
919(a)-(b): §34.22A
919(b): §§33.6, 33.24, 36.20, 43.12, 49.6
   Comment: §§34.22A, 36.20
920: §§33.3, 33.31
   Comments: §33.3
930: §§1.10-1.11, 26.8, 33.3-33.4, 33.13, 41.6, 42.1, 42.9, 47.1, 47.9-47.10
   Comment: §47.1
940: §§26.8, 33.3-33.4, 33.10-33.11, 46.2, 46.8, 46.21, 47.1-47.2, 49.5
950: §§33.17, 34.8, 34.25, 50.2, 51.2
950-962: §§34.1, 34.25
951: §§34.3-34.4, 34.25
952: §§33.3, 34.9-34.10, 34.22B, 34.25, 35.2
   Comments: §§34.9-34.10, 36.1, 36.4, 37.1
953: §§33.4, 34.22A, 34.25
   Comment: §§34.4, 34.22, 36.5, 37.5
953-954: §§34.20, 34.24
953(a)-(b): §§34.11, 34.22, 40.6
953(b): §§34.4, 34.20
953(c): §§34.11, 34.20, 34.22
953(d): §§34.11, 34.21-34.22
954: §§33.5, 33.10, 33.14, 33.31, 34.4, 34.8, 34.10, 34.25, 35.2
   Comments: §§34.10, 34.20, 36.4, 37.4, 38.4
954-955: §33.4
954(a): §§34.11, 40.6
954(b): §34.11
954(c): §§34.12, 34.20, 34.22A
955: §§33.15, 34.12, 34.20, 34.22A, 34.25
956: §§34.15, 34.25, 35.6-35.7, 36.15, 37.11
956.5: §34.25
957: §§34.18, 34.25, 36.17, 37.13
958: §§34.16, 34.25
   Comment: §34.16

959: §§34.19, 34.25
  Comment: §34.19
960: §34.25
960-961: §§34.19, 36.17, 37.13
961: §34.25
962: §§34.17, 34.22A, 34.25
970: §§33.10, 33.21, 33.24, 33.31, 41.1, 41.4-41.6, 41.13, 41.19, 41.25, 42.1-42.2, 42.7
  Comment: §§41.1, 42.1
970-971: §§33.22, 41.22
970-973: §§33.21, 40.1, 40.8, 41.1, 41.15, 41.25, 42.1, 42.19
971: §§33.10, 33.13, 33.21, 33.31, 41.1, 41.5, 41.19, 41.25, 42.1-42.2, 42.4-42.5, 42.9-42.11, 42.14, 42.18
  Comment: §§41.7, 42.1, 42.4, 42.10
972: §§40.10, 41.9, 41.25, 42.12
  Comment: §41.10
972-973: §41.1
972(a): §§41.6, 41.10, 41.22, 42.2, 42.9, 42.12
972(b): §41.11
972(b)-(c): §42.12
972(c): §41.11
972(d): §§41.12, 42.12
972(e): §§33.17, 41.13, 42.12
972(e)(1): §41.13
972(e)(2): §41.13
972(e)(3): §41.13
972(e)(4): §41.13
972(f): §41.14
972(g): §41.15
973: §§33.6, 41.17, 41.25
  Comment: §§41.10, 41.18, 41.21-41.22
973(a): §§33.9, 41.1, 41.5-41.7, 41.17-41.21, 42.2, 42.10, 42.14-42.15
  Comment: §41.19
973(b): §§41.6, 41.10, 41.22, 42.2, 42.9, 42.16
977: §33.4
980: §§33.4, 33.10, 33.14-33.15, 33.24, 33.31, 40.2, 40.4-40.6, 40.17, 40.20, 41.1, 41.3, 41.8, 42.1
  Comment: §§40.4-40.6, 40.16, 41.16, 42.13
980-987: §§40.1, 40.20
981: §§33.10, 36.15, 37.11, 40.3, 40.8, 40.19-40.20
  Comment: §40.8
982: §§40.11, 40.20
  Comment: §§40.11, 41.11
982-986: §§40.10, 41.9
983: §§40.11, 40.20
984: §§40.17, 40.20
984(a): §40.12
984(b): §§33.24, 40.13
985: §§1.10, 33.17, 40.20
985(a): §40.15
985(a)-(b): §40.15
985(b): §40.15
985(c): §40.15
985(d): §40.15
986: §§1.10, 40.14, 40.20
987: §§1.10, 40.9, 40.20, 41.3
990: §§33.17, 36.2, 36.23, 50.2, 51.2
990-1007: §§36.1, 36.23
991: §§36.2, 36.23
992: §§33.3, 36.3-36.4, 36.6, 36.20, 36.23, 36.26
  Comments: §§36.3-36.4
993: §§33.4, 36.20, 36.23
  Comment: §§36.5, 36.19-36.20, 37.5, 37.16-37.17, 38.8
993-994: §§36.19, 36.22
993(a)-(b): §§36.20, 40.6
993(b): §§36.5, 36.19, 37.16
993(c): §§36.5, 36.19-36.20
994: §§33.10, 33.14, 33.31, 36.2-36.3, 36.23
  Comments: §36.4
994-995: §33.4
994(a): §§36.5, 40.6
994(b): §36.5
994(c): §§36.6, 36.19-36.20
995: §§36.6, 36.19-36.20, 36.23
996: §§33.10, 36.1, 36.9, 36.22-36.23, 37.8, 43.1, 43.15
996(b): §§36.9, 36.17
996(b)-(c): §36.9
996(c): §36.9
997: §§34.15, 36.15, 36.23, 37.11
998: §§1.10, 33.10, 36.1, 36.10, 36.23, 37.9
999: §§36.9, 36.11, 36.23-36.24
  Comment: §36.11
1000: §§36.17, 36.23, 37.13
1001: §§36.16, 36.23
1002: §§36.17, 36.23
1002-1003: §37.13
1003: §§36.17, 36.23
1004: §§36.14, 36.23
  Comment: §§40.11, 41.11
1004-1005
  Comments: §36.14
1005: §§36.14, 36.23

1006: §§36.18, 36.23, 37.14
1007: §§36.12, 36.23
  Comment: §36.12
1010: §§33.17, 36.1, 37.2, 37.20, 38.2, 38.13, 39.13
1010-1027: §§37.1, 37.20
1010(a): §§50.2, 51.2
1010(c): §37.20
1010(d): §37.20
1010(e): §37.20
1010.5: §§37.2, 37.20
1011: §§37.2-37.3, 37.20
1012: §§33.3, 37.3-37.4, 37.17, 37.20, 37.23
  Comment: §37.3
1013: §§33.4, 37.5, 37.17, 37.20
1013-1014: §§37.16, 37.19
1013(a)-(b): §§37.5, 37.17, 40.6
1013(c): §§37.5, 37.16-37.17
1014: §§33.14, 33.22, 33.31, 37.2, 37.4, 37.10, 37.20
  Comments: §§37.1, 37.9
1014(a): §§37.5, 40.6
1014(b): §37.5
1014(c): §§37.5-37.6, 37.16-37.17
1015: §§33.4, 37.6, 37.16, 37.20
1016: §§37.8, 37.13, 37.18-37.20, 43.1, 43.15
1016-1017: §37.9
1017: §§37.9, 37.20
  Comments: §37.9
1018: §§34.15, 36.15, 37.11, 37.20
1019: §§36.17, 37.13, 37.20
1020: §§37.12, 37.20
1021: §§37.13, 37.20
1021-1022: §36.17
1022: §§37.13, 37.20
1023: §§37.9, 37.20
1024: §§37.10, 37.18, 37.20
1025: §§36.14, 37.20
1026: §§36.18, 37.14, 37.20
1027: §§37.15, 37.20
1030: §§33.17, 50.2, 50.10-50.11, 51.2, 51.10
1030-1033: §§50.1, 50.11, 51.11
1031: §§50.1, 50.3, 50.11, 51.3
1032: §§50.1-50.2, 50.4-50.5, 50.10-50.11, 51.1-51.2, 51.4-51.6, 51.10
1033: §§33.14-33.15, 33.31, 50.1, 50.5-50.7, 50.11, 51.1, 51.6-51.7
1033-1034: §33.4

1034: §§33.15, 33.31, 50.1, 50.7, 50.11, 51.1, 51.6-51.7, 51.11
  Comment: §§50.8, 51.6, 51.8
1035: §§38.2, 38.13
1035-1036.2: §§38.1, 38.13
1035.2: §§38.2, 38.11, 38.13
1035.4: §§1.10, 38.3-38.4, 38.9-38.13, 39.13
1035.4(1)-(3): §§38.10, 39.10
1035.4(3): §38.10
1035.6: §§33.4, 38.5, 38.9, 38.13
1035.6(a)-(b): §§38.9, 40.6
1035.6(c): §§38.8-38.9
1035.8: §§33.14, 33.31, 38.4, 38.8, 38.13
1035.8(a): §40.6
1035.8(a)-(b): §38.5
1035.8(c): §38.6
1036: §§33.4, 38.6, 38.9, 38.13
1036.2: §38.13
1036.2(a)-(i): §38.2
1036.2(j): §38.2
1036.6: §38.8
1037: §39.13
1037-1037.7: §§33.14, 39.1, 39.9, 39.13
1037.1: §§39.2, 39.11, 39.13
1037.2: §§1.10, 39.4, 39.10-39.13
1037.3: §39.13
1037.4: §§39.5, 39.8-39.9, 39.13
1037.5: §§33.1, 33.31, 39.4, 39.9, 39.13
1037.5(a)-(b): §39.5
1037.5(b): §39.8
1037.5(c): §§39.6, 39.8, 39.13
1037.6: §§39.6, 39.9, 39.13
1037.7: §§39.2, 39.13
1040: §§33.14, 43.1, 43.6, 43.11, 43.15, 44.1, 44.9
  Comments: §§33.3, 43.1, 43.3, 43.6
1040-1041: §33.4
1040-1047: §33.31
1040(a): §§43.1-43.3, 43.7, 43.11-43.12
1040(b): §§43.2, 43.7, 43.12
1040(b)(1): §§43.4, 43.6, 43.13
1040(b)(2): §§33.1, 43.1, 43.3, 43.6, 43.13-43.14
1041: §§33.14, 43.1, 43.8, 43.15, 44.1, 44.12
1041-1042: §44.12
1041(a): §§44.1, 44.3, 44.5, 44.7
1041(a)(1): §44.6
1041(a)(2): §§33.1, 44.6, 44.8, 44.11

1041(b): §§44.5, 44.9
1041(b)(1): §44.4
1041(b)(2): §44.4
1041(b)(3): §44.4
1041(c): §44.5
1042: §§32.9, 43.1, 44.1, 44.12
  Comment: §43.9
1042-1045: §43.15
1042(a): §§43.6, 43.8-43.10, 44.2, 44.9
1042(a)-(b): §43.15
1042(b): §43.11
1042(c): §44.2
1042(c)-(d): §43.15
1042(d): §§44.2, 44.10
1043: §§43.4, 43.13, 43.15
1043-1045: §§43.1, 43.8
1044: §§43.1, 43.15
1045: §43.15
1045(a)-(c): §43.13
1045(b)(1): §43.4
1045(b)(2): §43.4
1045(d)-(e): §43.13
1045(e): §43.4
1046: §§43.13, 43.15
1047: §§43.13, 43.15
1050: §§33.4, 49.1-49.4, 49.6, 49.9, 49.12
1060: §§33.1, 33.3-33.4, 33.14, 33.31, 45.1, 45.3-45.4, 45.6, 45.8
1070: §§33.20, 48.6, 48.17-48.18, 48.20
1070(a): §48.7
1070(a)-(b): §48.7
1070(b): §48.7
1100: §22.8
  Comment: §22.8
1100-1104: §20.28
1101: §§32.7, 47.4
  Comment: §22.8
1101-1102: §26.8
1101(a): §32.7
1101(b): §§17.5, 22.8, 32.7, 46.5, 46.17
1102: §§22.8, 26.8
1103: §§1.6, 1.12, 17.4, 20.11, 22.8, 36.10, 38.10, 38.13
1103(c): §22.8
1103(c)(4): §22.8
1103(c)(5): §22.8
1106: §22.8
1106(c): §23.2
1108: §§17.5, 22.8, 32.7
1108(a): §32.7
1108(b): §17.5
1109: §§22.8, 32.7
1109(a): §32.7
1119: §§33.3A, 34.10A
1119-1128: §34.10A
1121: §§32.9, 34.10A
1122: §§33.3A, 34.10A
1122(a): §34.10A
1126: §§33.3A, 34.10A
1150: §§18.2, 29.46
  Comment: §§18.20, 18.27
1150(a): §§18.20, 18.27, 29.46
1151: §§2.3, 32.5
  Comment: §32.5
1152: §§1.10, 2.3, 21.8, 32.2, 34.10A
  Comment: §32.2
1152(a): §§32.2-32.3
1152.5: §2.3
1153: §§32.4, 56.1
1153-1153.5: §1.12
1153.5: §32.4
1154: §§21.8, 32.3
1155: §§2.3, 6.39, 29.7, 32.6, 32.11
1156: §§36.20, 37.17
1157(a): §20.9
1160: §19.5
1200: §§19.2, 19.43
  Comment: §§19.3, 19.5
1200-1350: §21.8
1200(a): §§19.1, 19.43
1200(b): §§19.2, 19.43
1200(c): §19.43
1201: §§2.3, 19.26
1202: §§19.16A, 19.39, 22.1, 23.1
  Comment: §19.39
1203: §§19.38-19.39
  Comment: §19.39
1203(b)-(c): §19.39
1203.1: §§1.7, 1.10, 19.38-19.39
1204: §§19.9, 19.26, 46.11, 47.7
1220: §§19.13, 19.26, 21.7, 46.11, 47.7
1220-1228: §§19.8, 19.39
1221: §19.14
1221-1222: §21.7
1222: §§19.15, 53.5
1223: §§19.16, 21.7
1224: §19.17
1224-1227: §21.7
1224-1228: §19.8
1225: §19.17
1226: §19.17
1227: §19.17
1228: §§19.5, 19.17
1230: §§19.8, 19.11, 19.13, 19.18, 46.11

1231: §19.16A
1231-1231.4: §19.8
1231(a): §19.16A
1231(b): §19.16A
1231(c): §19.16A
1231(d): §19.16A
1231(e): §19.16A
1231(f): §19.16A
1231.1: §19.16A
1231.2: §19.16A
1231.3: §19.16A
1231.4: §19.16A
1235: §§1.12, 19.19, 19.26, 19.31A, 22.5
1235-1236: §§19.39, 21.7
1235-1238: §§19.8, 19.39
1236: §§19.20, 19.26, 23.4
1237: §§19.21, 19.26
1238: §19.22
1238(a): §19.22
1238(b): §19.22
1238(c): §19.22
1240: §§5.2, 19.23, 19.41, 21.8
1240-1242: §19.8
1240(b): §19.23
1241: §§19.23, 19.41
   Comment: §19.23
1242: §19.23
1250: §19.24
   Comment: §19.24
1250-1252: §§19.8, 19.12
1250(b): §19.24
1251: §§19.11, 19.24, 19.26
   Comment: §19.24
1252: §§19.12, 19.24
   Comment: §19.12
1260: §§19.11-19.12
1260-1261: §19.8
1260(a): §19.25
1260(b): §19.25
1261: §19.12
1261(a): §19.25
1261(b): §19.25
1270: §§19.26, 19.36
1270-1272: §19.8
1271: §§5.2, 5.17, 19.26-19.27, 19.33, 21.8
   Comments: §§19.12, 19.26
1271(c): §19.26
1271(d): §19.12
1272: §19.26
1280: §19.27
   Comment: §19.27
1280-1284: §19.8

1280(c): §§19.12, 19.27
1281: §19.27
1282: §19.27
1283: §19.27
1290: §19.28
1290-1292: §33.24
1290-1293: §19.8
1290(a): §19.28
1290(b): §19.28
1290(c): §19.28
1290(d): §19.28
1291: §§19.11, 19.29, 19.31A, 46.11
1291-1292: §§19.11, 41.21, 46.19
1291(a): §19.11
1291(a)(1): §19.29
1291(a)(2): §§19.29, 46.19
1291(b): §19.29
1291(b)(1): §19.29
1291(b)(2): §§19.29, 33.24
1292: §19.30
1292(a)(1): §19.30
1292(a)(2): §19.30
1292(a)(3): §19.30
1292(b): §§19.30, 33.24
1292(c): §19.31
1293: §19.31
1293(a)(1): §19.31
1293(a)(2): §19.31
1293(b): §19.31
1294: §19.31A
1300: §19.32
   Comment: §19.32
1300-1302: §§19.8, 19.39
1301: §19.32
1302: §19.32
1310: §19.33
1310-1311: §§19.11-19.12
1310-1316: §19.8
1310(b): §19.33
1311: §19.33
1311(b): §19.33
1312: §19.33
1313: §19.33
1314: §19.33
1315: §19.33
1316: §19.33
1320: §19.34
1320-1324: §19.8
1321: §19.34
1322: §19.34
1323: §§19.11-19.12, 19.34
1324: §§19.34, 31.17
1330: §19.35
1330-1331: §19.8

1331: §19.35
1340: §19.36
1340-1341: §19.8
1341: §19.36
1350: §§19.11, 19.29
1400: §21.6
1401: §§21.6, 24.2, 24.6
1401(a): §21.6
1402: §21.6
1410-1421: §21.6
1410.5: §1.10
1411-1413: §34.19
1415: §21.8
1416: §20.28
1418: §20.28
1451: §33.28
1500 (former): §§24.1-24.2
1520: §24.2
1520-1523: §21.8
1521: §§22.5, 24.1, 24.3, 24.6
1521(a): §§2.3, 21.8, 24.2
1521(a)(1): §24.2
1521(a)(2): §24.2
1521(c): §24.2
1521(d): §24.2
1522: §24.3
1522(a)(1): §24.3
1522(a)(2): §24.3
1522(a)(3): §24.3
1522(a)(4): §24.3
1522(b): §24.3
1523: §24.6
1523(a): §24.4
1523(b): §24.4
1523(c): §24.4
1523(d): §24.4
1552-1553: §24.5
1560: §19.26
1561: §19.26

FAMILY CODE
Division 12, pt 3: §39.13
308: §§40.2, 42.3
1818: §32.9
3160-3186: §18.17
6209: §39.13
6211: §§39.2, 39.13
6924: §37.20
6924(b): §§37.2, 37.5-37.6
7550-7557: §20.28
7600: §39.13
7880: §57.2
7883: §57.2
8718: §32.9

FINANCIAL CODE
8754: §32.9

FISH AND GAME CODE
7923: §32.9

GOVERNMENT CODE
3060-3074: §33.31
6250: §43.1
6250-6268: §43.1
6253-6253.1: §43.1
6254-6255: §43.1
6254.7(d): §45.2
6255: §43.1
6260: §43.1
7460-7493: §32.9
9410: §46.17
11500-11530: §1.2
15619: §32.9
18573: §32.9
18676-18677: §46.17
18934: §32.9
18952: §32.9
20134: §32.9
31532: §32.9

HEALTH AND SAFETY CODE
1598-1598.5: §38.2
11367: §1.12
100330: §32.9
103550: §19.27
103990: §32.9

INSURANCE CODE
735: §32.9
790.03: §32.2
855: §32.9
10381.5: §32.9
11582: §32.2
12924: §46.17
12924(b): §46.17

PENAL CODE
Part 2, Title 10, ch 6: §37.20
Part 3, Title 1, ch 7, art 4: §37.20
16: §47.2
19.2: §57.3
25(a): §1.6
25(b): §1.6
109(f): §29.42
132: §29.8
136.2: §57.2
148: §43.8
166: §§2.17, 29.15, 57.2-57.3, 57.5, 57.10

166(a): §57.2
182: §46.13
187(a): §§54.3, 54.15
190.1: §3.8
190.2: §3.8
190.2(a)(17): §27.2
190.41: §27.2
261: §§22.8, 38.13
261.5: §38.13
262: §§22.8, 38.13
264.1: §§22.8, 38.13
270: §§40.20, 41.25
270-270a: §§40.15, 41.13
270a: §§40.20, 41.25
273a: §13.13
273d: §13.13
286: §§22.8, 38.13
288: §§13.13, 22.8, 38.13
288a: §§22.8, 38.13
288.5: §22.8
289: §§22.8, 38.13
290(i): §32.9
499c(a)(3): §45.2
631: §32.9
647(b): §33.11
647a: §38.13
653f: §27.7
683: §36.10
799-803: §46.13
800: §46.13
801: §46.13
830-830.5: §44.4
830.1(b): §44.4
830.6: §44.4
830.7: §44.4
830.8: §44.4
831-831.5: §44.4
831.5: §43.15
832.5: §43.15
832.7-832.8: §§43.1, 43.8
871.6: §§54.17, 55.7
872: §§1.7, 19.38
872(b): §§19.38-19.39
872.5: §24.2
938: §32.9
995: §43.13
1004-1005: §1.10
1009: §54.3
1016: §29.6
1016(3): §19.32
1017: §§1.10, 3.8
1023: §1.10
1025: §§1.10, 17.5
1026(a): §3.8

1027(a): §37.9
1041: §1.10
1043: §1.10
1043(b): §33.15
1043(b)(2): §54.3
1044: §4.7
1045: §1.10
1046: §1.10
1047: §1.10
1048: §54.3
1049: §54.3
1049.5: §§54.17, 55.7
1050: §§54.3, 54.15
1050(b): §§54.3, 54.15
1050(c)-(d): §54.15
1050(e): §§54.3, 54.15
1050(f): §§54.3, 54.15
1050(g): §54.15
1050(g)(1): §54.15
1050(g)(2): §§54.3, 54.15
1050(g)(3): §§54.3, 54.15
1050(h): §54.3
1050(i): §54.15
1050.1: §54.3
1050.5: §54.15
1051: §54.3
1053: §54.3
1054-1054.7: §§1.7, 18.5
1054(e): §18.5
1054.3: §35.4
1054.5(b): §54.3
1054.6: §§6.30, 33.2, 33.25, 35.4, 35.10-35.11
1054.7: §35.9
1061-1063: §1.10
1088 (former): §6.13
1089: §29.45
1093: §§3.4, 3.8, 29.23, 29.42
1093-1094: §§3.1-3.2, 26.2
1093(6): §53.2
1093.5: §53.2
1094: §§3.4, 27.11
1096: §§1.10, 6.35, 27.9
1099: §46.14
1101: §46.14
1101-1103: §1.10
1102: §§1.8-1.9, 37.2
1107: §1.10
1108: §1.10
1112: §18.5
1118: §47.4
1118-1118.1: §27.11
1118.1: §47.4
1120: §29.40

Pen C

1122: §§29.36, 29.39
1127: §§29.23, 53.2
1137: §29.42
1140: §56.3
1141: §56.5
1147: §56.3
1153: §1.10
1156: §1.10
1157: §1.10
1181: §§29.17, 29.30, 29.46
1181(2): §29.46
1181(3): §29.46
1181(4): §§29.43, 29.46
1181(5): §29.17
1182: §§29.17, 29.46
1192.4: §§1.12, 32.4
1192.7: §1.6
1203.4: §22.8
1204: §1.10
1223: §1.10
1228: §1.10
1237: §29.46
1238: §1.10
1293: §1.10
1322 (former): §§41.8, 41.13
1323.5 (former): §47.1
   Comment: §47.1
1324: §§46.9, 46.14-46.15, 46.17-46.18
1324-1324.1: §1.12
1324.1: §§46.9, 46.14-46.15
1331: §57.2
1331.5: §57.2
1335-1336: §54.16
1336: §54.16
1337: §54.16
1350: §1.10
1367: §37.20
1367.1: §37.20
1368: §34.9
1369(a): §37.9
1385: §55.2
1511: §§54.17, 55.7
1512: §§54.17, 55.7
1524(c): §§33.17, 33.31, 36.21, 37.18, 50.9, 51.9
1538.5: §§1.12, 28.12
2600-2601: §40.4
2960: §37.20
3046: §32.9
4001.1: §1.12
4011.6: §37.20
5078: §43.6
11105: §32.9
11164-11174.3: §§36.13, 37.15
11165.1(a): §§54.3, 54.15
11165.6: §§54.3, 54.15
11166: §39.13
11171(b): §37.15
11171.2(b): §§36.13, 37.15
11205: §57.2
11311: §57.2
13700: §§54.3, 54.15
13835.2: §§38.13, 39.13
13835.10: §§38.13, 39.13
13837: §§38.2, 38.13

PROBATE CODE
103: §25.8
1003: §§36.5, 36.20, 37.5, 37.17
1600: §37.16
1600(a): §§34.20, 36.19
1607: §34.22
1860(a): §§34.20, 36.19, 37.16
8481: §§34.20, 36.19, 37.16
8500(c): §57.2
8501: §57.2
8505: §57.2
8524: §§34.20, 36.19, 37.16
8540-8547: §§34.20, 36.19, 37.16
8870-8872: §57.2
12252: §§34.20, 36.19, 37.16

PUBLIC RESOURCES CODE
3234: §32.9

REVENUE AND TAXATION CODE
7056: §43.7
19286.5 (former): §43.7
19542-19566: §43.7
19553: §43.7

UNEMPLOYMENT INSURANCE CODE
1094: §32.9
2111: §§32.9, 43.12
2714: §§32.9, 43.12

VEHICLE CODE
1808: §32.9
1812: §6.52
12800: §6.52
13000: §6.52
13353: §46.6
16005: §32.9
20001: §46.17
20002: §§46.6, 46.17
20012: §§19.26, 43.4
20012-20014: §43.4

20012-20015: §32.9
20013: §19.26
40306: §54.3
40803: §32.9
40804: §§18.2, 32.9
40804(a): §18.30
40805: §18.30
40808: §18.30
40832: §32.9

WATER CODE
1106: §46.17
1251: §32.9

WELFARE AND INSTITUTIONS CODE
Division 2, pt 1: §§40.20, 41.25
200: §§40.20, 41.25
200-987: §§40.14, 41.12
300: §§46.17, 54.3
355.1(f): §46.17
601: §§46.17, 54.3
602: §§46.4, 46.17, 54.3
634: §34.11
827: §32.9
5328: §32.9
6500-6512: §47.2
6601(d): §20.18
10850: §§32.9, 43.4
10950: §34.8
18294: §§39.2, 39.13

ACTS BY POPULAR NAME
Administrative Procedure Act: §1.2
Arnold–Kennick Juvenile Court Law: §§40.14, 40.20, 41.12, 41.25
Child Abuse and Neglect Reporting Act: §§36.13, 37.15
Crime Victims Justice Reform Act (Proposition 115): §§1.5, 1.7, 6.16, 17.4, 19.29, 27.2, 43.4, 43.9, 46.1, 54.17, 55.7
Medical Practice Act: §36.23
Proposition 8 (Victim's Bill of Rights): §§1.5-1.6, 17.4, 18.30, 20.7, 21.4, 22.2, 22.9, 23.4, 28.11, 29.46, 31.4, 32.4, 33.1, 37.1, 38.1, 39.1, 40.1, 47.1, 47.4, 51.1
Proposition 115 (Crime Victims Justice Reform Act): §§1.5, 1.7, 6.16, 17.4, 19.29, 27.2, 43.4, 43.9, 46.1, 54.17, 55.7
Psychology Licensing Law: §37.20

Public Records Act: §§43.1, 46.15
Right to Financial Privacy Act: §32.9
Street Terrorism Enforcement and Prevention Act: §19.16A
Uniform Parentage Act: §39.13
Uniform Trade Secrets Act: §45.2
Victim's Bill of Rights (Proposition 8): §§1.5-1.6, 17.4, 18.30, 20.7, 21.4, 22.2, 22.9, 23.4, 28.11, 29.46, 31.4, 32.4, 33.1, 37.1, 38.1, 39.1, 40.1, 47.1, 47.4, 51.1

SESSION LAWS
Stats 2000, ch 192: §§1.7, 6.16
Stats 1998, ch 100: §24.2
Stats 1998, ch 100, §9: §24.2
Stats 1997, ch 499, §2: §19.16A

ASSEMBLY BILLS
988: §46.15

Rules

CALIFORNIA RULES OF COURT
4.113: §§54.3, 54.15
4.200: §§6.6-6.7, 6.16, 6.53
4.200(a)-(b): §6.6
4.200(b): §6.4
4.201: §§6.10, 6.53
154: §54.2
201: §§2.11, 2.19
225(a): §57.2
227: §§2.17, 22.7, 54.1, 54.11, 57.1-57.2
228: §§6.5, 6.14-6.15, 6.51
312(d): §2.11
313: §§2.11, 2.19
315: §2.11
316: §2.11
375(a): §54.2
375(a) (former): §54.13
375(b): §54.7
375(c): §§54.1-54.2, 54.7
375(c)(1)-(7): §54.2
375(d): §§54.2, 54.9
1421: §46.17
1422(a): §54.3
1422(b): §54.3
1616(c): §22.11A
App Div I: §6.16
  8(a): §6.51
  8(a)(2): §6.7
  8(b): §§6.5, 6.7, 6.51

8(c): §6.51
8(c)-(d): §§6.5, 6.15
8(c)(4): §6.5
8(c)(6): §6.5
8(e): §6.51
8(f): §§6.5, 6.7, 6.14, 6.33, 6.35, 6.37, 6.44, 6.51
8.5: §6.4
8.5(a): §6.53
8.5(a)(2): §6.16
8.5(b): §§6.16, 6.41, 6.53
8.5(c): §§6.7, 6.16
8.5(d): §§6.5, 6.7, 6.14, 6.33, 6.35, 6.37, 6.44
8.5(f): §§6.7
App Div I (former)
9: §54.13
App Div II
Canon 3(B)(1)-(8): §29.21
Canon 3(B)(4): §29.21
Canon 3(B)(8), Commentary: §29.21

CALIFORNIA RULES OF PROFESSIONAL CONDUCT
2-100: §34.6
2-111(A)(4) (former): §§18.14, 34.22
3-700: §47.4
5-120: §29.2
5-200: §§2.17, 22.7, 29.2, 29.5-29.7
5-200(A): §29.2
5-200(B): §§29.2, 29.8
5-200(B)-(C): §12.1
5-200(E): §29.5
5-210: §§18.2, 18.14-18.15
5-210(C): §18.14
5-220: §§29.2, 34.1
5-300: §33.17
5-310: §29.4
5-320: §§29.4, 29.6
5-320(D)-(E): §29.8

LOCAL COURT RULES
Los Angeles Superior Court Rules
7.12(a): §54.1
8.0: §2.17
8.20(a)-(b): §6.5
8.20(f): §6.25
8.32: §6.22
8.33: §6.25
8.34: §6.24
8.37: §29.42
8.66-8.68: §29.42
8.76: §4.13

8.92: §2.11
San Francisco Uniform Local Rules
6.2: §6.5

Jury Instructions

CALIFORNIA JURY INSTRUCTIONS, CIVIL (CACI)
100: §53.1
106: §§21.13, 29.14, 52.1, 52.7, 53.2
206: §§2.4, 32.8, 53.2
207: §2.4
218: §20.9
5000: §29.23
5001: §§29.43, 29.44A
5003: §§21.13, 29.14, 52.1, 52.7, 53.2
5003-5004: §29.23
See also §29.34

CALIFORNIA JURY INSTRUCTIONS, CIVIL (BAJI)
1.00.5 (former): §53.1
1.02 (former): §§29.14, 52.1, 52.7, 53.2
2.05 (former): §§32.8, 53.2
15.21 (former): §29.23
15.30 (former): §29.44A
15.30-15.31 (former): §29.44A
15.33 (former): §29.43
See also §29.34

CALIFORNIA JURY INSTRUCTIONS, CRIMINAL (CALJIC)
1.02: §§52.7, 53.2
2.07-2.08: §53.2
2.09: §52.7
2.50: §52.1
2.52: §19.3
2.60: §47.6
2.61: §§47.4, 47.6
2.62: §47.7
2.72: §§27.7-27.8
4.60: §53.2
17.32: §29.23
17.40: §29.44A
See also §29.34

UNITED STATES

Constitution

Art III, §3: §27.7
Amend I: §§48.2, 48.4-48.5, 48.17-48.18

Amend IV: §§28.2-28.6, 28.11, 28.13, 28.15, 47.3
Amend V: §§6.2, 6.27, 19.9, 19.11, 19.29, 26.8, 46.2-46.4, 46.8, 46.11, 46.19, 46.21, 47.1, 47.6-47.7, 47.10
Amend VI: §§1.12, 6.2-6.3, 19.9, 19.11-19.12, 19.16A, 19.26, 19.31A, 19.38, 23.7, 42.5, 46.19, 48.11
Amend XIV: §§6.2, 6.27-6.29, 28.2-28.5, 28.13, 46.2, 46.8, 46.19, 46.21, 47.1, 47.6, 47.10

Statutes

UNITED STATES CODE
Title 5
 552(b)(5): §43.1
 552a(b)(7): §43.4
 552a(b)(11): §43.4
Title 15
 13(a): §28.6
Title 18
 921-928: §28.11
 3055-3056: §44.4
 6001-6005: §§46.14-46.15
 6002: §46.15
Title 30
 813(a): §28.11
Title 42
 1983: §§22.8, 28.2, 28.4

INTERNAL REVENUE CODE
 5146(b): §28.11
 7606: §28.11

ACTS BY POPULAR NAME
Clayton Act: §28.6
Employees Liability Act: §32.6
Freedom of Information Act: §46.15
Gun Control Act of 1968: §28.11
Mine Safety and Health Act of 1977: §28.11
Privacy Act of 1974: §43.4

Regulations

CODE OF FEDERAL REGULATIONS
Title 28
 50.10: §48.4
 50.10(a)-(c): §48.4
 50.10(e): §48.4
 50.10(f)(1): §48.4
 50.10(f)(1)-(2): §48.4
 50.10(f)(2): §48.4

Court Rules

FEDERAL RULES OF CIVIL PROCEDURE
 11: §57.1
 26(b)(3): §35.6

FEDERAL RULES OF EVIDENCE
 403: §2.3
 702: §§20.10, 20.15
 803(18): §22.10

Ethics

ABA MODEL RULES OF PROFESSIONAL CONDUCT
 3.4(e): §29.5

Table of Cases

A

A&M Records, Inc. v Heilman (1977) 75 CA3d 554, 142 CR 390: §46.11

ACLU v Deukmejian (1982) 32 C3d 440, 186 CR 235: §46.15

Abbett Elec. Corp v Sullwold (1987) 193 CA3d 708, 238 CR 496: §2.7

Abercrombie v Thomsen (1943) 59 CA2d 331, 138 P2d 701: §29.46

Acosta v Southern Cal. Rapid Transit Dist. (1970) 2 C3d 19, 84 CR 184: §31.12

Adams v Young (1967) 255 CA2d 145, 62 CR 877: §19.25

Adams, People v (1960) 182 CA2d 27, 5 CR 795: §29.9

Adcox, People v (1988) 47 C3d 207, 253 CR 55: §29.7

Aetna Cas. & Sur. Co. v Superior Court (1984) 153 CA3d 467, 200 CR 471: §§34.3, 35.7, 35.9

Aguayo v Crompton & Knowles Corp. (1986) 183 CA3d 1032, 228 CR 768: §§31.2, 31.8, 32.5

Aguilar, People v (1984) 35 C3d 785, 200 CR 908: §18.5

Aguilar, People v (1971) 16 CA3d 1001, 94 CR 492: §19.26

Aguimatang v California State Lottery (1991) 234 CA3d 769, 286 CR 57: §19.26

Ah Lee Doon, People v (1893) 97 C 171, 31 P 933: §6.45

Ahnemann (People v Municipal Court) (1974) 12 C3d 658, 117 CR 20: §55.2

Alameda, County of v Superior Court (1987) 194 CA3d 254, 239 CR 400: §37.3

Alatorre, U.S. v (9th Cir 2000) 222 F3d 1098: §20.15

Albert, People v (1960) 182 CA2d 729, 6 CR 473: §31.7

Alberts v Lytle (1934) 1 CA2d 682, 37 P2d 705: §29.7

Albertson v Subversive Activities Control Bd. (1965) 382 US 70, 15 L Ed 2d 165, 86 S Ct 194: §46.6

Albrecht v Broughton (1970) 6 CA3d 173, 85 CR 659: §20.4

Alcala, People v (1992) 4 C4th 742, 15 CR2d 432: §19.11

Alden v Superior Court (1963) 212 CA2d 764, 28 CR 387: §49.2

Alexander v Superior Court (1993) 5 C4th 1218, 23 CR2d 397: §§31.5, 31.12

Alfaro, People v (1976) 61 CA3d 414, 132 CR 356: §5.5

Alhambra, City of v Superior Court (1980) 110 CA3d 513, 168 CR 49: §37.3

Allen v Superior Court (1976) 18 C3d 520, 134 CR 774: §55.3

Allen v Toledo (1980) 109 CA3d 415, 167 CR 270: §53.5

Allen, People v (1986) 42 C3d 1222, 232 CR 849: §30.2

Allen, People v (1999) 72 CA4th 1093, 85 CR2d 655: §20.12

Allen, People v (1976) 65 CA3d 426, 135 CR 276: §20.4

Allen, U.S. v (10th Cir 1977) 554 F2d 398: §43.7

Alpert v Villa Romano Homeowners' Ass'n (2000) 81 CA4th 1320, 96 CR2d 364: §32.5

Alpha Beta Co. v Superior Court (1984) 157 CA3d 818, 203 CR 752: §§34.5, 34.9

Amber B., In re (1987) 191 CA3d 682, 236 CR 623: §§20.13, 20.18

Ambrose, People v (1986) 183 CA3d 136, 227 CR 885: §19.16

American Mut. Liab. Ins. Co. v Superior Court (1974) 38 CA3d 579, 113 CR 561: §§34.2, 35.2

American Nat'l Ins. Co. v Continental Parking Corp. (1974) 42 CA3d 260, 116 CR 801: §25.3

Anderson v Savin Corp. (1988) 206 CA3d 356, 254 CR 627: §25.7

Anderson, People v (1990) 52 C3d 453, 276 CR 356: §30.2

Andrews v City & County of San Francisco (1988) 205 CA3d 938, 252 CR 716: §§31.4–31.5, 31.16, 32.7

Andrews v County of Orange (1982) 130 CA3d 944, 182 CR 176, disapproved on other grounds in 16 C4th at 582 n5: §29.46

Andrews, People v (1989) 49 C3d 200, 260 CR 583: §19.20

Andrews, People v (1972) 23 CA3d Supp 1, 100 CR 276: §20.25

Andrews, People v (1970) 14 CA3d 40, 92 CR 49: §§23.4, 29.11

Andrews v County of Orange (1982) 130 CA3d 944, 182 CR 176, disapproved on other grounds in People v Nesler (1997) 16 C4th 561, 66 CR2d 454: §29.39

Anti-Defamation League of B'nai B'rith v Superior Court (1998) 67 CA4th 1072, 79 CR2d 597: §§48.5, 48.7

Arcega, People v (1982) 32 C3d 504, 186 CR 94: §37.9

Archer, People v (2000) 82 CA4th 1380, 99 CR2d 230: §§19.4, 32.7

Archerd, People v (1970) 3 C3d 615, 91 CR 397: §§29.24, 29.28

Arends, People v (1957) 155 CA2d 496, 318 P2d 532: §52.10

Armendariz, People v (1984) 37 C3d 573, 209 CR 664: §29.45

Arneson v Webster (1964) 226 CA2d 370, 38 CR 88: §52.11

Arthur v Superior Court (1965) 62 C2d 404, 42 CR 441: §57.3

Ascherman v Superior Court (1967) 254 CA2d 506, 62 CR 547: §36.3

Augustin, People v (2003) 112 CA4th 444, 5 CR3d 171: §13.7

Ault v International Harvester Co. (1974) 13 C3d 113, 117 CR 812: §32.5

Austin v Lambert (1938) 11 C2d 73, 77 P2d 849: §6.24

Ayala, People v (2000) 23 C4th 225, 96 CR2d 682: §19.8

B

BMW of N. Am. v New Motor Vehicle Bd. (1984) 162 CA3d 980, 209 CR 50: §25.1

BP Alaska Exploration, Inc. v Superior Court (1988) 199 CA3d 1240, 245 CR 682: §§35.2, 35.5–35.7

Babbitt, People v (1988) 45 C3d 660, 248 CR 69: §§17.2, 17.6

Badgett, People v (1995) 10 C4th 330, 41 CR2d 635: §§40.2, 42.3, 46.15

Bailey v Superior Court (1970) 4 CA3d 513, 84 CR 436: §46.17

Baird v Koerner (9th Cir 1960) 279 F2d 623: §34.9

Baker, People v (1978) 88 CA3d 115, 151 CR 362: §40.8

Balcom v Growers Warehouse Co. (1921) 55 CA 474, 204 P 39: §4.10

Balderas, People v (1985) 41 C3d 144, 222 CR 184: §6.43

Baldwin Contracting Co. v Winston Steel Works (1965) 236 CA2d 565, 46 CR 421: §32.5

Balistreri v Turner (1964) 227 CA2d 236, 38 CR 553: §29.11

Ballard v Superior Court (1966) 64 C2d 159, 49 CR 302: §§33.22, 55.2

Ballard, People v (1980) 104 CA3d 757, 164 CR 81: §29.2

Balsys, U.S. v (1998) 524 US 666, 141 L Ed 2d 575, 118 S Ct 2218: §§46.4, 46.13, 46.15

Banco Do Brazil, S.A. v Latian, Inc. (1991) 234 CA3d 973, 285 CR 870: §25.7

Bank of America v Carr (1956) 138 CA2d 727, 292 P2d 587: §57.5

Bank of America v Lamb Fin. Co. (1960) 179 CA2d 498, 3 CR 877: §25.5

Bank of America v Taliaferro (1956) 144 CA2d 578, 301 P2d 393: §19.6

Barajas v USA Petroleum Corp. (1986) 184 CA3d 974, 229 CR 513: §20.20

Barber v Page (1968) 390 US 719, 20 L Ed 2d 255, 88 S Ct 1318: §19.29

Bardessono v Michels (1970) 3 C3d 780, 91 CR 760: §§29.43, 29.46

Barker (People v Superior Court) (1965) 232 CA2d 178, 42 CR 651: §46.10

Barlin v Barlin (1957) 156 CA2d 143, 319 P2d 87: §29.11

Baroni v Rosenberg (1930) 209 C 4, 284 P 1111: §29.17

Barr v Scott (1955) 134 CA2d 823, 286 P2d 552: §§2.3, 19.26

Barrett (People v Superior Court) (2000) 80 CA4th 1305, 96 CR2d 264: §§43.4, 43.9

Barrick, People v (1982) 33 C3d 115, 187 CR 716: §26.7

Bates v Newman (1953) 121 CA2d 800, 264 P2d 197: §52.3

Batson v Kentucky (1986) 476 US 79, 90 L Ed 2d 69, 106 S Ct 1712: §§6.27-6.28, 6.32

Bauguess v Paine (1978) 22 C3d 626, 150 CR 461: §57.9

Baumann, People v (1985) 176 CA3d 67, 222 CR 32: §46.17

Baxter v Palmigiano (1976) 425 US 308, 47 L Ed 2d 810, 96 S Ct 1551: §46.11

Beagle, People v (1972) 6 C3d 441, 99 CR 313: §27.7

Bean, People v (1988) 46 C3d 919, 251 CR 467: §32.7

Beckett v Kaynar Mfg. Co. (1958) 49 C2d 695, 321 P2d 749: §5.4

Beecher v Stafford (1927) 83 CA 408, 256 P 870: §29.7

Behr v County of Santa Cruz (1959) 172 CA2d 697, 342 P2d 987: §§19.26, 20.8

Belcher, People v (1961) 189 CA2d 404, 11 CR 175: §10.4

Bell v Moloney (1917) 175 C 366, 165 P 917: §4.7

Bell, People v (1989) 49 C3d 502, 262 CR 1: §§6.2, 29.7

Bellah v Greenson (1978) 81 CA3d 614, 146 CR 535: §37.10

Bellis v U.S. (1974) 417 US 85, 40 L Ed 2d 678, 94 S Ct 2179: §§46.2-46.3

Belton, People v (1979) 23 C3d 516, 153 CR 195: §§6.30, 47.4

Beneficial Fire & Cas. Ins. Co. v Kurt Hitke & Co. (1956) 46 C2d 517, 297 P2d 428: §25.8

Benge v Superior Court (1982) 131 CA3d 336, 182 CR 275: §34.10

Bennett v Hoge (1930) 108 CA 180, 291 P 444: §52.14

Bennett, People v (1991) 54 C3d 1032, 2 CR2d 8: §29.7

Berger v U.S. (1935) 295 US 78, 79 L Ed 1314, 55 S Ct 629: §12.2

Berger, People v (1955) 44 C2d 459, 282 P2d 509: §28.12

Bergonzi, U.S. v (ND Cal 2003) 216 FRD 487: §34.22B

Berguin v Pacific Elec. Ry. (1928) 203 C 116, 263 P 220: §29.28

Berry, People v (1968) 260 CA2d 649, 67 CR 312: §18.9

Biaggi, U.S. v (2d Cir 1988) 853 F2d 89: §6.27

Bibeau v Pacific Northwestern Research Found. (9th Cir 1999) 188 F3d 1105: §47.3

Bigboy v County of San Diego (1984) 154 CA3d 397, 201 CR 226: §§15.5, 29.18

Biggs (People v Superior Court) (1971) 19 CA3d 522, 97 CR 118: §§43.8, 43.13

Binder v Superior Court (1987) 196 CA3d 893, 242 CR 231: §36.3

Biswell, U.S. v (1972) 406 US 311, 32 L Ed 2d 87, 92 S Ct 1593: §28.11

Bittaker, People v (1989) 48 C3d 1046, 259 CR 630: §6.23

Black v State Bar (1972) 7 C3d 676, 103 CR 288: §47.2

Blackburn v Superior Court (1993) 21 CA4th 414, 27 CR2d 204: §46.5

Blagg, People v (1970) 10 CA3d 1035, 89 CR 446: §§18.10, 21.5

Blagg, People v (1968) 267 CA2d 598, 73 CR 93: §19.26

Blanco, People v (1992) 10 CA4th 1167, 13 CR2d 176: §1.12

Bledsoe, People v (1984) 36 C3d 236, 203 CR 450: §§20.14, 20.18

Bloyd, People v (1987) 43 C3d 333, 233 CR 368: §20.6

Blue Cross v Superior Court (1976) 61 CA3d 798, 132 CR 635: §§36.3-36.5

Bly-Magee v Budget Rent-A-Car Corp. (1994) 24 CA4th 318, 29 CR2d 330: §§6.7, 6.15, 6.49

Board of Trustees v Porini (1968) 263 CA2d 784, 70 CR 73: §20.8

Bobby B., In re (1985) 172 CA3d 377, 218 CR 253: §28.11

Bobele v Superior Court (1988) 199 CA3d 708, 245 CR 144: §34.6

Boehm, People v (1969) 270 CA2d 13, 75 CR 590: §4.19

Bolden, People v (1979) 99 CA3d 375, 160 CR 268: §34.9

Bole v Bole (1946) 76 CA2d 344, 172 P2d 936: §29.25

Bolton, People v (1979) 23 C3d 208, 152 CR 141: §§29.2, 29.9, 29.14, 29.18

Bonds v Roy (1999) 20 C4th 140, 83 CR2d 289: §22.11

Bonin, People v (1989) 47 C3d 808, 254 CR 298: §§6.23, 20.6-20.7, 31.4

Booth v Bond (1942) 56 CA2d 153, 132 P2d 520: §3.7

Borchers, People v (1958) 50 C2d 321, 325 P2d 97: §27.4

Bormann v Chevron USA, Inc. (1997) 56 CA4th 260, 65 CR2d 321: §29.39

Borunda, People v (1974) 11 C3d 523, 113 CR 825: §§44.9-44.10

Bowens v Superior Court (1991) 1 C4th 36, 2 CR2d 376: §1.7

Box, People v (2000) 23 C4th 1153, 99 CR2d 69: §§30.2, 31.6

Boyd, People v (1990) 222 CA3d 541, 271 CR 738: §29.7

Boyette, People v (1988) 201 CA3d 1527, 247 CR 795: §18.5

Boysaw v Superior Court (2000) 23 C4th 215, 96 CR2d 531: §57.6

Bradford, People v (1997) 15 C4th 1229, 65 CR2d 145: §29.44

Bradford, People v (1969) 70 C2d 333, 74 CR 726: §40.3

Bradley v Brown (7th Cir 1994) 42 F3d 434: §§20.15-20.16

Brandon, People v (1995) 40 CA4th 1172, 47 CR2d 383: §56.1

Branzburg v Hayes (1972) 408 US 665, 33 L Ed 2d 626, 92 S Ct 2646: §48.2

Braswell v U.S. (1988) 487 US 99, 101 L Ed 2d 98, 108 S Ct 2284: §§46.3, 46.7

Brawley, People v (1969) 1 C3d 277, 82 CR 161: §30.4

Brawthen v H & R Block, Inc. (1972) 28 CA3d 131, 104 CR 486: §§25.7, 25.12

Breaux, People v (1991) 1 C4th 281, 3 CR2d 81: §6.2

Brecht v Abrahamson (1993) 507 US 619, 123 L Ed 2d 353, 113 S Ct 1710: §29.9

Brewer v City of Napa (9th Cir 2000) 210 F3d 1093: §22.8

Briggs v Superior Court (1931) 211 C 619, 297 P 3: §57.7

Britt v Superior Court (1978) 20 C3d 844, 143 CR 695: §§36.1, 36.9

Brokopp v Ford Motor Co. (1977) 71 CA3d 841, 139 CR 888: §§29.5, 29.7, 35.6, 35.8

Brown v Pacific Elec. Ry. (1947) 79 CA2d 613, 180 P2d 424: §32.2

Brown v Spencer (1912) 163 C 589, 126 P 493: §17.7

Brown v Superior Court (1977) 71 CA3d 141, 139 CR 327: §§43.7, 43.12

Brown v U.S. (1958) 356 US 148, 2 L Ed 2d 589, 78 S Ct 622: §46.19

Brown, People v (2003) 31 C4th 518, 3 CR3d 145: §2.1

Brown, People v (1988) 46 C3d 432, 250 CR 604: §31.4

Brown, People v (1989) 212 CA3d 1409, 261 CR 262, disapproved on other grounds in People v Hayes (1990) 52 C3d 577, 276 CR 874: §29.7

Brown, People v (1971) 14 CA3d 334, 92 CR 370: §46.9

Brown, People v (1962) 200 CA2d 111, 19 CR 36: §52.9

Browning, People v (1980) 108 CA3d 117, 166 CR 293: §47.3

Brunner v Superior Court (1959) 51 C2d 616, 335 P2d 484: §34.9

Brunner, People v (1973) 32 CA3d 908, 108 CR 501: §46.15

Bruno & Stillman, Inc. v Globe Newspaper Co. (1st Cir 1980) 633 F2d 583: §48.2

Buchanan v Nye (1954) 128 CA2d 582, 275 P2d 767: §26.5

Buchman, Estate of (1954) 123 CA2d 546, 267 P2d 73: §29.31

Buckley, In re (1973) 10 C3d 237, 110 CR 121: §§55.5, 57.5-57.6

Buckwalter v Airline Training Ctr. (1982) 134 CA3d 547, 184 CR 659: §20.9

Buford, People v (1982) 132 CA3d 288, 182 CR 904: §6.2

Bui, People v (2001) 86 CA4th 1187, 103 CR2d 908: §20.12

Bumb v Bennett (1958) 51 C2d 294, 333 P2d 23: §19.6

Bunyard, People v (1988) 45 C3d 1189, 249 CR 71: §§19.20, 19.24

Burdeau v McDowell (1921) 256 US 465, 65 L Ed 1048, 41 S Ct 574: §28.3

Burgener, People v (1986) 41 C3d 505, 224 CR 112, disapproved on other grounds in 19 C4th at 239: §§29.34, 29.44-29.45, 31.8

Burke v Almaden Vineyards, Inc. (1978) 86 CA3d 768, 150 CR 419: §32.5

Burke, U.S. v (2d Cir 1983) 700 F2d 70: §48.2

Burns, People v (1952) 109 CA2d 524, 241 P2d 308: §§29.27, 29.31, 30.2

Burton, People v (1989) 48 C3d 843, 258 CR 184: §47.4

Burton, People v (1961) 55 C2d 328, 11 CR 65: §§5.5, 18.9

Busch, People v (1961) 56 C2d 868, 16 CR 898: §20.25
Butler v Stratton (1949) 95 CA2d 23, 212 P2d 43: §26.2
Buyle, People v (1937) 22 CA2d 143, 70 P2d 955: §6.20
By-Buk Co. v Printed Cellophane Tape Co. (1958) 163 CA2d 157, 329 P2d 147: §45.4
Byers v Justice Court (1969) 71 C2d 1039, 80 CR 553, vacated on other grounds (1971) 402 US 424, 29 L Ed 2d 9, 91 S Ct 1535: §§46.6, 46.17

C

C.S. Smith Metro. Mkt. Co. v Superior Court (1940) 16 C2d 226, 105 P2d 587: §33.22
CBS, Inc. v Superior Court (1978) 85 CA3d 241, 149 CR 421, disapproved on other grounds in Delaney v Superior Court (1990) 50 C3d 785, 268 CR 753: §§48.7, 48.9
Cabral, People v (1993) 12 CA4th 820, 15 CR2d 866: §37.2
Cade v Mid-City Hosp. Corp. (1975) 45 CA3d 589, 119 CR 571: §54.9
Cahill, People v (1993) 5 C4th 478, 20 CR2d 582: §47.3
Caldwell v Caldwell (1962) 204 CA2d 819, 22 CR 854: §29.25
Caldwell, People v (1921) 55 CA 280, 203 P 440: §20.4
California v Green (1970) 399 US 149, 26 L Ed 2d 489, 90 S Ct 1930: §46.19
California Francisco Inv. Corp. v Vrionis (1971) 14 CA3d 318, 92 CR 201: §45.2
Calloway, People v (1954) 127 CA2d 504, 274 P2d 497: §13.3
Camara v Municipal Court (1967) 387 US 523, 18 L Ed 2d 930, 87 S Ct 1727: §28.11
Campbell v General Motors Corp. (1982) 32 C3d 112, 184 CR 891: §20.7
Campbell v Gerrans (9th Cir 1979) 592 F2d 1054: §46.11
Campbell, People v (1982) 137 CA3d 867, 187 CR 340: §46.14
Campbell, People v (1965) 233 CA2d 38, 43 CR 237: §§13.8, 13.11
Campbell, People v (1958) 162 CA2d 776, 329 P2d 82: §§4.7, 29.21
Canard, People v (1967) 257 CA2d 444, 65 CR 15: §46.11
Canfield, People v (1974) 12 C3d 699, 117 CR 81: §34.9
Cannady, People v (1972) 8 C3d 379, 105 CR 129: §19.20
Cannon v Commission on Judicial Qualifications (1975) 14 C3d 678, 122 CR 778: §57.8
Cantrell, People v (1973) 8 C3d 672, 105 CR 792, overruled in part on other grounds in People v Flannel (1979) 25 C3d 668, 160 CR 84, and People v Wetmore (1978) 22 C3d 318, 149 CR 265: §27.2
Cardenas, People v (1982) 31 C3d 897, 184 CR 165: §30.5
Carlson, Collins, Gordon & Bold v Banducci (1967) 257 CA2d 212, 64 CR 915: §34.16
Carlton v Superior Court (1968) 261 CA2d 282, 67 CR 568: §§36.3, 36.9
Carlucci, People v (1979) 23 C3d 249, 152 CR 439: §3.1
Carmen O., In re (1994) 28 CA4th 908, 33 CR2d 848: §§19.8, 19.17
Carney v Santa Cruz Women Against Rape (1990) 221 CA3d 1009, 271 CR 30: §32.2
Carpenter, People v (1997) 15 C4th 312, 63 CR2d 1: §§27.7, 27.11, 29.28, 32.7
Carroll, People v (1970) 4 CA3d 52, 84 CR 60: §21.9
Carrow, In re (1974) 40 CA3d 924, 115 CR 601: §57.4
Carter, People v (1997) 55 CA4th 1376, 64 CR2d 747: §20.9
Cartwright, People v (1980) 107 CA3d 402, 166 CR 37: §26.8
Casey v Ohio Med. Prods. (ND Cal 1995) 877 F Supp 1380: §20.17
Casey v Proctor (1963) 59 C2d 97, 28 CR 307: §25.5
Cash v Superior Court (1973) 35 CA3d 226, 110 CR 612: §55.2
Castaldia, People v (1959) 51 C2d 569, 335 P2d 104: §§29.18, 29.46
Castorena, People v (1996) 47 CA4th 1051, 55 CR2d 151: §29.44A
Castro v Fowler Equip. Co. (1965) 233 CA2d 416, 43 CR 589: §29.35

Castro, People v (1985) 38 C3d 301, 211 CR 719: §§1.6, 21.4, 22.2, 22.8, 31.4, 47.4
Castro, People v (1986) 184 CA3d 849, 229 CR 280: §29.38
Catchpole v Brannon (1995) 36 CA4th 237, 42 CR2d 440: §29.27
Cavanaugh, People v (1955) 44 C2d 252, 282 P2d 53: §30.2
Cedars-Sinai Imaging Med. Group v Superior Court (2000) 83 CA4th 1281, 100 CR2d: §57.7
Cervantes v Time, Inc. (8th Cir 1972) 464 F2d 986: §48.2
Cervantes, People v (1978) 87 CA3d 281, 150 CR 819: §47.5
Chandler, People v (1971) 17 CA3d 798, 95 CR 146: §46.9
Chapman v California (1967) 386 US 18, 17 L Ed 2d 705, 87 S Ct 824: §§29.9, 29.18, 47.1, 47.5–47.6
Chapman, People v (1975) 50 CA3d 872, 123 CR 862: §21.8
Charbonneau, In re (1974) 42 CA3d 505, 116 CR 153: §§2.15, 2.17, 55.5
Chavez, People v (1980) 26 C3d 334, 161 CR 762: §§19.19, 23.7
Chicago Title Ins. Co. v Superior Court (1985) 174 CA3d 1142, 220 CR 507: §§34.3, 34.22A
Chrisman, People v (1967) 256 CA2d 425, 64 CR 733: §16.4
Christine C., In re (1987) 191 CA3d 676, 236 CR 630: §20.13
Christy v Superior Court (1967) 252 CA2d 69, 60 CR 85: §35.7
Chronicle Publishing Co. v Superior Court (1960) 54 C2d 548, 7 CR 109: §43.6
Chula v Superior Court (1962) 57 C2d 199, 18 CR 507: §57.6
Chula v Superior Court (1952) 109 CA2d 24, 240 P2d 398: §13.8
Church v Capital Freight Lines (1956) 141 CA2d 246, 296 P2d 563: §18.27
Cimijotti v Paulsen (ND Iowa 1963) 219 F Supp 621: §§50.3, 51.3
Cindy L., In re (1997) 17 C4th 15, 69 CR2d 803: §§19.8, 19.17
Ciraolo, In re (1969) 70 C2d 389, 74 CR 865: §57.9
Citrino, People v (1956) 46 C2d 284, 294 P2d 32: §26.8
City of _____ (see name of city)

Clair, People v (1992) 2 C4th 629, 7 CR2d 564: §§6.29, 31.12
Clark v Laughlin (1977) 68 CA3d 506, 137 CR 354: §29.23
Clark, People v (1990) 50 C3d 583, 268 CR 399: §§6.16, 37.10
Clark, People v (1980) 109 CA3d 88, 167 CR 51: §20.20
Clark, People v (1970) 6 CA3d 658, 86 CR 106: §19.3
Clarke, In re (1899) 126 C 235, 58 P 546: §33.22
Clemens v Regents of Univ. of Cal. (1970) 8 CA3d 1, 87 CR 108: §§18.27, 29.35
Coast Bank v Holmes (1971) 19 CA3d 581, 97 CR 30: §§25.2–25.3, 25.6
Cobb, People v (1955) 45 C2d 158, 287 P2d 752: §27.1
Coble, People v (1976) 65 CA3d 187, 135 CR 199, disapproved on other grounds in 61 CA4th at 969: §46.11
Coddington, People v (2000) 23 C4th 529, 97 CR2d 528, overruled on other grounds in Price v Superior Court (2001) 25 C4th 1046, 108 CR2d 409: §31.4
Cohen v Cowles Media Co. (1991) 501 U.S. 663, 115 L Ed 2d 586, 111 S Ct 2513: §33.3A
Cohen v Superior Court (1959) 173 CA2d 61, 343 P2d 286: §§33.22, 46.4–46.5
Cohen, In re (1894) 104 C 524, 38 P 364: §46.13
Cohen, People v (1976) 59 CA3d 241, 130 CR 656: §19.26
Cohn v Bugas (1974) 42 CA3d 381, 116 CR 810: §3.7
Cole, People v (1956) 47 C2d 99, 301 P2d 854: §20.7
Coleman v Galinin (1947) 78 CA2d 313, 177 P2d 606: §46.4
Coleman, People v (1988) 46 C3d 749, 251 CR 83: §§20.12, 30.2
Coleman, People v (1985) 38 C3d 69, 211 CR 102: §§2.6, 20.8
Coleman, People v (1975) 13 C3d 867, 120 CR 384: §§46.4, 46.17
Coleman, People v (1969) 71 C2d 1159, 80 CR 920, overruled on other grounds in 14 C4th at 966: §41.3
Coleman, People v (1970) 8 CA3d 722, 87 CR 554: §5.5

Collin, Estate of (1957) 150 CA2d 702, 310 P2d 663: §20.20

Collins, People v (1986) 42 C3d 378, 228 CR 899: §§22.8, 31.4

Collins, People v (1975) 44 CA3d 617, 118 CR 864: §21.3

Colonnade Catering Corp. v U.S. (1970) 397 US 72, 25 L Ed 2d 60, 90 S Ct 774: §28.11

Comden v Superior Court (1978) 20 C3d 906, 145 CR 9: §18.14

Compton, People v (1971) 6 C3d 55, 98 CR 217: §6.20

Conderback, Inc. v Standard Oil Co. (1966) 239 CA2d 664, 48 CR 901: §26.7

Conkling, People v (1896) 111 C 616, 44 P 314: §29.38

Conservatorship of Isaac O. (1987) 190 CA3d 50, 235 CR 133: §20.9

Conservatorship of Susan T. (1994) 8 C4th 1005, 36 CR2d 40: §§28.2, 28.4–28.5, 28.12

Continental Airlines v McDonnell Douglas Corp. (1989) 216 CA3d 388, 264 CR 779: §31.17

Continental Dairy Equip. Co. v Lawrence (1971) 17 CA3d 378, 94 CR 887: §29.6

Coogan Fin. Corp. v Beatcher (1932) 120 CA 278, 7 P2d 695: §20.20

Cook v Superior Court (1971) 19 CA3d 832, 97 CR 189: §3.7

Cook, People v (1983) 33 C3d 400, 189 CR 159, overruled in part by People v Rodriguez (1986) 42 C3d 730, 230 CR 667: §§29.21, 29.23

Cooke v Superior Court (1978) 83 CA3d 582, 147 CR 915: §34.10

Cooke, People v (1993) 16 CA4th 1361, 20 CR2d 506: §§46.17–46.18

Cooper v Superior Court (1961) 55 C2d 291, 10 CR 842: §57.4

Cooper, People v (1991) 53 C3d 771, 281 CR 90: §29.42

Cooper, People v (1979) 95 CA3d 844, 157 CR 348: §29.38

Cooper, People v (1970) 10 CA3d 96, 88 CR 919: §47.6

Cope v Davison (1947) 30 C2d 193, 180 P2d 873: §20.3

Cordova, People v (1979) 97 CA3d 665, 158 CR 852: §1.4

Corey, In re (1964) 230 CA2d 813, 41 CR 379: §20.4

Cornejo, People v (1979) 92 CA3d 637, 155 CR 238: §46.9

Correa, People v (2002) 27 C4th 444, 117 CR2d 27: §19.38

Corrigan, People v (1957) 48 C2d 551, 310 P2d 953: §29.28

County Sanitation Dist. v Watson Land Co. (1993) 17 CA4th 1268, 22 CR2d 117: §2.15

County of _____ (see name of county)

Cox, People v (2003) 30 C4th 916, 135 CR2d 272: §19.24

Cox, People v (1991) 53 C3d 618, 280 CR 692: §§5.4, 18.27

Coy v Superior Court (1962) 58 C2d 210, 23 CR 393: §34.9

Coy v Superior Court (1959) 51 C2d 471, 334 P2d 569: §44.9

Craib v Bulmash (1989) 49 C3d 475, 261 CR 686: §46.6

Crail v Blakely (1973) 8 C3d 744, 106 CR 187: §§20.3, 24.2

Cramer v Morrison (1979) 88 CA3d 873, 153 CR 865: §21.19

Cramer v Tyars (1979) 23 C3d 131, 151 CR 653: §§46.2, 47.2

Crawford v Washington (2004) ___ US ___, 158 L Ed 2d 177, 124 S Ct 1354: §§1.12, 19.9, 19.11–19.12, 19.16A, 19.38, 42.5

Crespo v Cook (1959) 168 CA2d 360, 336 P2d 31: §§29.35, 29.46

Crest Catering Co. v Superior Court (1965) 62 C2d 274, 42 CR 110: §43.12

Critchlow, In re (1938) 11 C2d 751, 81 P2d 966: §46.14

Crittenden, People v (1994) 9 C4th 83, 36 CR2d 474: §6.29

Cromer, People v (2003) 24 C4th 889, 103 CR2d 23: §19.11

Crook (People v Superior Court) (1978) 83 CA3d 335, 147 CR 856: §46.15

Crosby v Martinez (1958) 159 CA2d 534, 324 P2d 26: §§54.4, 54.9, 54.13

Crovedi, People v (1966) 65 C2d 199, 53 CR 284: §54.3

Crow, People v (1994) 28 CA4th 440, 33 CR2d 624: §1.12

Crume, People v (1976) 61 CA3d 803, 132 CR 577, disapproved on other grounds in People v Gaston (1978) 20 C3d 476, 143 CR 205: §26.6

Cubic Corp. v Marty (1986) 185 CA3d 438, 229 CR 828: §31.7

Cucamonga County Water Dist. v Southwest Water Co. (1971) 22 CA3d 245, 99 CR 557: §2.18

Cudjo, People v (1993) 6 C4th 585, 25 CR2d 390: §17.4

Cullen, People v (1951) 37 C2d 614, 234 P2d 1: §27.4

Culpepper v Volkswagen of Am., Inc. (1973) 33 CA3d 510, 109 CR 110: §§2.3, 21.8

Culton, People v (1992) 11 CA4th 363, 14 CR2d 189: §27.1

Curcio v U.S. (1957) 354 US 118, 1 L Ed 2d 1225, 77 S Ct 1145: §46.3

Curtis v McAuliffe (1930) 106 CA 1, 288 P 675: §29.7

Cuthbertson, U.S. v (3d Cir 1980) 630 F2d 139: §48.3

D

D.I. Chadbourne, Inc. v Superior Court (1964) 60 C2d 723, 36 CR 468: §§34.5, 34.9

Dacy, People v (1970) 5 CA3d 216, 85 CR 57: §30.4

Daggett v Atchison, T. & S.F. Ry. (1957) 48 C2d 655, 313 P2d 557: §§26.3, 32.5

Daigle v City of Portsmouth (1993) 630 A2d 776: §57.1

Daly v Superior Court (1977) 19 C3d 132, 137 CR 14: §§46.13-46.16, 46.18

Daniels, People v (1991) 52 C3d 815, 277 CR 122: §32.7

Darden v Superior Court (1965) 235 CA2d 80, 45 CR 44: §57.7

Dastagir v Dastagir (1952) 109 CA2d 809, 241 P2d 656: §§29.6, 29.11

Daubert v Merrell Dow Pharmaceuticals, Inc. (1993) 509 US 579, 125 L Ed 2d 469, 113 S Ct 2786 (Daubert I): §§20.10-20.11, 20.15-20.17

Daubert v Merrell Dow Pharmaceuticals, Inc. (9th Cir 1995) 43 F3d 1311 (Daubert II): §20.16

Davenport v Waite (1959) 175 CA2d 623, 346 P2d 501: §29.42

Davenport, People v (1995) 11 C4th 1171, 47 CR2d 800: §§6.32, 20.6

Davenport, People v (1966) 240 CA2d 341, 49 CR 575: §47.6

Davies v Superior Court (1984) 36 C3d 291, 204 CR 154: §43.4

Davies, U.S. v (7th Cir 1985) 768 F2d 893: §33.1

Davis, People v (1907) 6 CA 229, 91 P 810: §10.4

Dawkins, People v (1992) 10 CA4th 565, 12 CR2d 633: §19.38

De Gross, U.S. v (9th Cir 1992) 960 F2d 1433: §6.27

De Lancie v Superior Court (1982) 31 C3d 865, 183 CR 866, superseded by statute as stated in People v Loyd (2002) 27 C4th 997, 119 CR2d 360: §40.4

De Los Santos v Superior Court (1980) 27 C3d 677, 166 CR 172: §§34.4, 34.9, 34.11, 36.5, 37.5

De la Cruz v Quackenbush (2000) 80 CA4th 775, 96 CR2d 92: §46.6

DeCamp v First Kensington Corp. (1978) 83 CA3d 268, 147 CR 869: §46.3

DeGeorge v Superior Court (1974) 40 CA3d 305, 114 CR 860: §57.6

Dean v Feld (1946) 77 CA2d 327, 175 P2d 278: §20.4

Dean v Superior Court (1951) 103 CA2d 892, 230 P2d 362: §41.6

Decker, People v (1954) 122 CA2d 447, 265 P2d 41: §29.43

Deegan, People v (1891) 88 C 602, 26 P 500: §18.27

Del Ruth v Del Ruth (1946) 75 CA2d 638, 171 P2d 34: §§29.25-29.26

Delaney v Superior Court (1990) 50 C3d 785, 268 CR 753: §§48.7-48.9, 48.11, 48.14-48.16, 55.6

Delaware v Van Arsdall (1986) 475 US 673, 89 L Ed 2d 674, 106 S Ct 1431: §22.7

Dell M. v Superior Court (1977) 70 CA3d 782, 144 CR 418: §43.8

Delph, People v (1979) 94 CA3d 411, 156 CR 422: §§40.2, 42.3

Delta Dynamics, Inc. v Arioto (1968) 69 C2d 525, 72 CR 785: §5.8

Delucchi v County of Santa Cruz (1986) 179 CA3d 814, 225 CR 43: §25.1

Delzell v Day (1950) 36 C2d 349, 223 P2d 625: §§29.28, 29.31

Dennis, People v (1986) 177 CA3d 863, 223 CR 236: §46.17

Dennis, U.S. v (2d Cir 1950) 183 F2d 201, aff'd (1951) 341 US 494: §27.10

Department of Pub. Works, People ex rel v Lillard (1963) 219 CA2d 368, 33 CR 189: §15.5

Department of Transp., State ex rel v Superior Court (Hall) (1985) 37 C3d 847, 210 CR 219: §43.4

Deward v Clough (1966) 245 CA2d 439, 54 CR 68: §29.46

Di Donato v Santini (1991) 232 CA3d 721, 283 CR 751: §§6.2, 6.27–6.29, 6.31

Diamond Springs Lime Co. v American River Constructors (1971) 16 CA3d 581, 94 CR 200: §29.43

Diaz, People v (1992) 3 C4th 495, 11 CR2d 353: §§1.12, 27.1

Diaz, People v (1984) 152 CA3d 926, 200 CR 77: §29.35

Dickerson v Superior Court (1982) 135 CA3d 93, 185 CR 97: §§33.3, 34.15, 34.24

Dickerson v U.S. (2000) 530 US 428, 147 L Ed 2d 405, 120 S Ct 2326: §§19.9, 19.13, 28.10, 46.1, 47.1

Dickinson, People v (1976) 59 CA3d 314, 130 CR 561: §19.26

Dincau v Tamayose (1982) 131 CA3d 780, 182 CR 855: §20.20

Dionisio, U.S. v (1973) 410 US 1, 35 L Ed 2d 67, 93 S Ct 764: §46.6

Doe v Glanzer (9th Cir 2000) 232 F3d 1258: §46.12

Doe, U.S. v (1984) 465 US 605, 79 L Ed 2d 552, 104 S Ct 1237: §46.3

Doebke, People v (1969) 1 CA3d 931, 81 CR 391: §26.8

Dominguez v Pantalone (1989) 212 CA3d 201, 260 CR 431: §15.5

Dominguez v Superior Court (1980) 101 CA3d 6, 161 CR 407: §43.13

Dominguez, People v (1981) 121 CA3d 481, 175 CR 445: §56.1

Donahue v Ziv Television Programs, Inc. (1966) 245 CA2d 593, 54 CR 130: §20.3

Donnelly v DeChristoforo (1974) 416 US 637, 40 L Ed 2d 431, 94 S Ct 1868: §29.7

Donovan v Dewey (1981) 452 US 594, 69 L Ed 2d 262, 101 S Ct 2534: §28.11

Donovan v Security-First Nat'l Bank (1945) 67 CA2d 845, 155 P2d 856, disapproved on other grounds in 57 C2d at 252: §3.7

Dorsey, People v (1975) 46 CA3d 706, 120 CR 508: §§40.2, 40.4, 40.8, 41.1, 42.1

Dorshkind v Harry N. Koff Agency, Inc. (1976) 64 CA3d 302, 134 CR 344: §§6.46, 29.23

Douglas, People v (1990) 50 C3d 468, 268 CR 126: §47.4

Douillard v Woodd (1942) 20 C2d 665, 128 P2d 6: §§5.13–5.14

Dowden v Superior Court (1999) 73 CA4th 126, 86 CR2d 180: §35.5

Downing v Barrett Mobile Home Transp. (1974) 38 CA3d 519, 113 CR 277: §32.7

Dreher v Superior Court (1932) 124 CA 469, 12 P2d 671: §33.22

Du Jardin v City of Oxnard (1995) 38 CA4th 174, 45 CR2d 48: §29.7

Duane, People v (1942) 21 C2d 71, 130 P2d 123: §5.8

Duarte, People v (2000) 24 C4th 603, 101 CR2d 701: §19.18

Dub, People v (1930) 110 CA 631, 294 P 496: §46.11

Dunn, People v (1956) 46 C2d 639, 297 P2d 964: §52.6

Dunn, People v (1995) 40 CA4th 1039, 47 CR2d 638: §6.32

Duran, People v (2002) 97 CA4th 1448, 119 CR2d 272: §19.27

Duren v Missouri (1979) 439 US 357, 58 L Ed 2d 579, 99 S Ct 664: §6.2

Dussault v Condon (1959) 170 CA2d 693, 339 P2d 896: §19.5

Dyson v State Personnel Bd. (1989) 213 CA3d 711, 262 CR 112: §28.6

E

Eaton v Brock (1954) 124 CA2d 10, 268 P2d 58: §5.11
Eaugharn v Chamberlain (1934) 139 CA 601, 34 P2d 756: §52.10
Echeles, U.S. v (7th Cir 1965) 352 F2d 892: §§47.1, 47.5
Edgar v Superior Court (1978) 84 CA3d 430, 148 CR 687: §43.4
Edmonson v Leesville Concrete Co. (1991) 500 US 614, 114 L Ed 2d 660, 111 S Ct 2077: §6.27
Edward D., In re (1976) 61 CA3d 10, 132 CR 100: §37.4
Edwards v Centrex Real Estate Corp. (1997) 53 CA4th 15, 61 CR2d 518: §2.1
Edwards v Comstock Ins. Co. (1988) 205 CA3d 1164, 252 CR 807: §§25.5, 25.7
Edwards, People v (1988) 203 CA3d 1358, 248 CR 53: §§50.4, 50.10
Ehrhardt v Brunswick, Inc. (1986) 186 CA3d 734, 231 CR 60: §31.11
Eichel v New York Cent. R.R. (1963) 375 US 253, 11 L Ed 2d 307, 84 S Ct 316: §32.6
Eisenberg, People v (1968) 266 CA2d 606, 72 CR 390: §23.2
Eisendraft v Superior Court (2003) 109 CA4th 351, 134 CR2d 716: §34.10A
Eisenmayer v Leonardt (1906) 148 C 596, 84 P 43: §16.5
Elder v Board of Med. Examiners (1966) 241 CA2d 246, 50 CR 304: §§28.5-28.6
Elder v Pacific Tel. & Tel. Co. (1977) 66 CA3d 650, 136 CR 203: §20.7
Elizabeth T., In re (1992) 9 CA4th 636, 12 CR2d 10: §19.31
Ellis v International Playtex, Inc. (4th Cir 1984) 745 F2d 292: §22.10
Ellis, People v (1966) 65 C2d 529, 55 CR 385: §§46.6, 47.3
Ellis, People v (1995) 33 CA4th Supp 25, 40 CR2d 111: §18.30
Emslie v State Bar (1974) 11 C3d 210, 113 CR 175: §§28.5-28.6, 28.8-28.10
Enos, People v (1973) 34 CA3d 25, 109 CR 876: §3.1
Enriquez, People v (1977) 19 C3d 221, 137 CR 171: §19.11
Ernst v Municipal Court (1980) 104 CA3d 710, 163 CR 861: §27.4
Erving, People v (1998) 63 CA4th 652, 73 CR2d 815: §32.7
Espinoza, People v (1992) 3 C4th 806, 12 CR2d 682: §29.7
Estelle v Williams (1976) 425 US 501, 48 L Ed 2d 126, 96 S Ct 1691: §2.18
Etzel v Rosenbloom (1948) 83 CA2d 758, 189 P2d 848: §29.31
Evans, People v (1952) 39 C2d 242, 246 P2d 636: §29.9
Ewoldt, People v (1994) 7 C4th 380, 27 CR2d 646: §47.4

F

Fabert, People v (1982) 127 CA3d 604, 179 CR 702: §33.29
Fair, People v (1988) 203 CA3d 1303, 250 CR 486: §19.5
Falsetta, People v (1999) 21 C4th 903, 89 CR2d 847: §32.7
Farmer, People v (1989) 47 C3d 888, 254 CR 508, overruled on other grounds in People v Waidla (2000) 22 C4th 690, 94 CR2d 396: §§19.23, 30.3
Farr v Pitchess (9th Cir 1975) 522 F2d 464: §48.2
Farr v Superior Court (1971) 22 CA3d 60, 99 CR 342: §48.6
Farr, In re (1974) 36 CA3d 577, 111 CR 649: §57.9
Fatone, People v (1985) 165 CA3d 1164, 211 CR 288: §§22.5A, 29.21, 29.27-29.28, 29.31
Fauber, People v (1992) 2 C4th 792, 9 CR2d 24: §§6.2, 6.18, 29.7, 47.7
Federal Sav. & Loan Ins. Corp. v Rodrigues (ND Cal 1988) 717 F Supp 1424: §46.3
Feldman v Allstate Ins. Co. (2003) 322 F3d 660: §40.17
Fellom v Adams (1969) 274 CA2d 855, 79 CR 633: §4.19
Ferguson v Koch (1928) 204 C 342, 268 P 342: §25.3
Ferguson v Williams (NC App 1991) 399 SE2d 389: §22.10
Ferguson, In re (1971) 5 C3d 525, 531 96 CR 594: §29.2
Ferro, People v (1993) 21 CA4th 1, 25 CR2d 747: §6.28

Fibreboard Paper Prods. Corp. v East Bay Union of Machinists (1964) 227 CA2d 675, 39 CR 64: §4.20
Fielder v Berkeley Props. Co. (1972) 23 CA3d 30, 99 CR 791: §§46.2, 47.2
Fierro, People v (1991) 1 C4th 173, 3 CR2d 426: §§20.11-20.13
Fildew v Shattuck & Nimmo Warehouse Co. (1918) 39 CA 42, 177 P 866: §18.22
Finch, People v (1963) 213 CA2d 752, 29 CR 420: §47.7
Finkelstein v State Personnel Bd. (1990) 218 CA3d 264, 267 CR 133: §28.6
Finn v G.D. Searle Co. (1984) 35 C3d 691, 200 CR 870: §32.5
Fish v Guevana (1993) 12 CA4th 142, 15 CR2d 329: §22.11
Fisher v U.S. (1976) 425 US 391, 48 L Ed 2d 39, 96 S Ct 1569: §§46.3, 46.6-46.7
Flanagan v Flanagan (2002) 27 C4th 766, 117 CR2d 574: §21.6
Flannel, People v (1979) 25 C3d 668, 160 CR 84: §27.2
Flannery, People v (1985) 164 CA3d 1112, 210 CR 899: §44.10
Flores, People v (1977) 71 CA3d 559, 139 CR 546: §33.15
Fonts v Southern Pac. Co. (1916) 30 CA 633, 159 P 215: §20.6
Foote, In re (1888) 76 C 543, 18 P 678: §57.6
Ford v Georgia (1991) 498 US 411, 112 L Ed 2d 935, 111 S Ct 850: §6.28
Ford, People v (1988) 45 C3d 431, 247 CR 121: §47.2
Forman v Alexander's Mkts. (1956) 138 CA2d 671, 292 P2d 257: §29.39
Forte v Schiebe (1956) 145 CA2d 296, 302 P2d 336: §§29.21, 29.28
Fortes v Municipal Court (1980) 113 CA3d 704, 170 CR 292: §41.13
Fortner v Bruhn (1963) 217 CA2d 184, 31 CR 503: §§17.9, 26.5
Fosselman, People v (1983) 33 C3d 572, 189 CR 855: §§29.6, 29.11, 29.30
Fost v Superior Court (2000) 80 CA4th 724, 95 CR2d 620: §48.14
Fowler, People v (1918) 178 C 657, 174 P 892: §6.37
Fox v Kramer (2000) 22 C4th 531, 93 CR2d 497: §§20.9, 32.5
Foxgate Homeowners' Ass'n v Bramalea Cal., Inc. (2001) 26 C4th 1, 108 CR2d 642: §§32.9, 34.10A
Frahm, People v (1930) 107 CA 253, 290 P 678: §46.14
Frances W., In re (1974) 42 CA3d 892, 117 CR 277: §27.2
Francis, People v (1957) 156 CA2d 1, 319 P2d 103: §5.9
Francisco, People v (1964) 228 CA2d 355, 39 CR 503: §27.4
Frank, People v (1990) 51 C3d 718, 274 CR 372: §30.2
Franklin v Gibson (1982) 138 CA3d 340, 188 CR 23: §20.7
Freeman, People v (1994) 8 C4th 450, 34 CR2d 558: §17.2
Fremont Indem. Co. v Superior Court (1982) 137 CA3d 554, 187 CR 137: §46.11
Friedman (City of Los Angeles v Superior Court) (1985) 170 CA3d 744, 216 CR 311: §35.8
Friend, People v (1958) 50 C2d 570, 327 P2d 97: §29.23
Frierson, People v (1991) 53 C3d 730, 280 CR 440: §19.18
Frierson, People v (1985) 39 C3d 803, 218 CR 73: §47.4
Fries, Estate of (1963) 221 CA2d 725, 34 CR 749: §5.10
Frohner, People v (1976) 65 CA3d 94, 135 CR 153: §46.9
Fross v Wotton (1935) 3 C2d 384, 44 P2d 350: §33.29
Frye v U.S. (DC Cir 1923) 293 F 1013: §§20.10-20.13, 20.15, 20.17-20.18
Fuentes v Tucker (1947) 31 C2d 1, 187 P2d 752: §17.2
Fuentes, People v (1991) 54 C3d 707, 286 CR 792: §§6.28, 6.31
Fuentes, People v (1985) 40 C3d 629, 221 CR 440: §6.43
Fuentes, People v (1998) 61 CA4th 956, 72 CR2d 237: §19.11
Fusaro, People v (1971) 18 CA3d 877, 96 CR 368: §57.11
Futurecraft Corp. v Clary Corp. (1962) 205 CA2d 279, 23 CR 198: §45.2

G

Gadson, People v (1993) 19 CA4th 1700, 24 CR2d 219: §47.4

Gallagher v Municipal Court (1948) 31 C2d 784, 192 P2d 905: §§29.15, 57.4, 57.6

Gallaher v Superior Court (1980) 103 CA3d 666, 162 CR 389: §§5.5, 52.6

Gallego, People v (1990) 52 C3d 115, 276 CR 679: §19.23

Gambos, People v (1970) 5 CA3d 187, 84 CR 908: §17.9

Gamez, People v (1991) 235 CA3d 957, 286 CR 894: §16.5

Garcia v Hoffman (1963) 212 CA2d 530, 28 CR 98: §26.4

Garcia v Truck Ins. Exch. (1984) 36 C3d 426, 204 CR 435: §§25.4, 25.8

Garcia, People v (2000) 77 CA4th 1269, 92 CR2d 339: §§6.27, 6.31

Garcia, People v (1996) 45 CA4th 1242, 53 CR2d 256: §17.5

Garcia, People v (1972) 27 CA3d 639, 104 CR 69: §20.4

Garcia, People v (1970) 4 CA3d 904, 84 CR 624: §27.4

Garden Grove Sch. Dist. v Hendler (1965) 63 C2d 141, 45 CR 313: §§4.8, 29.6, 29.9, 29.13, 29.39, 29.45

Gardner v Broderick (1968) 392 US 273, 20 L Ed 2d 1082, 88 S Ct 1913: §46.4

Gardner, People v (1954) 128 CA2d 1, 274 P2d 908: §26.4

Garrison, People v (1989) 47 C3d 746, 254 CR 257: §46.15

Garrison, People v (1966) 246 CA2d 343, 54 CR 731: §4.3

Garrity v New Jersey (1967) 385 US 493, 17 L Ed 2d 562, 87 S Ct 616: §§46.4, 46.11

Gaston, People v (1978) 20 C3d 476, 143 CR 205: §26.6

Gates, People v (1987) 43 C3d 1168, 240 CR 666: §29.7

Gates, People v (1979) 97 CA3d Supp 10, 158 CR 759: §29.24

Gault, In re (1967) 387 US 1, 18 L Ed 2d 527, 87 S Ct 1428: §46.4

General Elec. Co. v Joiner (1997) 522 US 136, 139 L Ed 2d 508, 118 S Ct 512: §20.16

Genrich v State (1988) 202 CA3d 221, 248 CR 303: §20.9

Gentry, People v (1968) 257 CA2d 607, 65 CR 235: §27.4

George v City of Los Angeles (1942) 51 CA2d 311, 124 P2d 872: §29.46

Georgia v McCullum (1992) 505 US 42, 120 L Ed 2d 33, 112 S Ct 2348: §6.27

Gerhard v Stephens (1968) 68 C2d 864, 69 CR 612: §13.9

Germ v City & County of San Francisco (1950) 99 CA2d 404, 222 P2d 122: §29.31

Gherman v Colburn (1977) 72 CA3d 544, 140 CR 330: §§3.1, 5.4, 31.17

Gibbs, People v (1967) 255 CA2d 739, 63 CR 471: §19.29

Gibson, People v (1976) 56 CA3d 119, 128 CR 302: §§4.8, 30.5

Gilbert v California (1967) 388 US 263, 18 L Ed 2d 1178, 87 S Ct 1951: §47.3

Gillette v WCAB (1971) 20 CA3d 312, 97 CR 542: §19.24

Gionis, People v (1995) 9 C4th 1196, 40 CR2d 456: §§29.2, 29.7, 29.18, 31.3, 34.3

Glacier Gen. Assur. Co. v Superior Court (1979) 95 CA3d 836, 157 CR 435: §34.17

Glade v Superior Court (1978) 76 CA3d 738, 143 CR 119: §§34.1, 34.15

Glage v Hawes Firearms (1990) 226 CA3d 314, 276 CR 430: §29.38

Glancy, People v (1956) 142 CA2d 669, 299 P2d 18: §16.2

Glendale Fed. Sav. & Loan Ass'n v Marina View Heights Dev. Co. (1977) 66 CA3d 101, 135 CR 802: §25.5

Golden, Estate of (1935) 4 C2d 300, 48 P2d 962: §29.28

Goldstein, People v (1982) 130 CA3d 1024, 182 CR 207: §18.14

Gonzales v Municipal Court (1977) 67 CA3d 111, 136 CR 475: §34.10

Gonzales v Superior Court (1980) 117 CA3d 57, 178 CR 358: §46.16

Gonzalez v Commission on Judicial Performance (1983) 33 C3d 359, 188 CR 880: §29.27

Goodale v Thorn (1926) 199 C 307, 249 P 11: §4.20

Goodale, People v (1939) 33 CA2d 80, 91 P2d 163: §29.39

Goodner, People v (1992) 7 CA4th 1324, 9 CR2d 543: §46.4
Gordon, People v (1990) 50 C3d 1223, 270 CR 451: §32.7
Gordon J. v Santa Ana Unified Sch. Dist. (1984) 162 CA3d 530, 208 CR 657: §28.11
Gore, People v (1993) 18 CA4th 692, 22 CR2d 435: §6.28
Gorgol, People v (1953) 122 CA2d 281, 265 P2d 69: §19.26
Goulet, People v (1992) 13 CA4th Supp 1, 17 CR2d 801: §18.30
Governing Bd. v Metcalf (1974) 36 CA3d 546, 111 CR 724: §28.6
Graham, People v (1978) 83 CA3d 736, 149 CR 6, disapproved on other grounds in 18 C4th at 569: §31.8
Grand Lake Drive In, Inc. v Superior Court (1960) 179 CA2d 122, 3 CR 621: §34.9
Granville v Parsons (1968) 259 CA2d 298, 66 CR 149: §29.5
Graves v Union Oil Co. (1918) 36 CA 766, 173 P 618: §20.20
Gray v Southern Pac. Co. (1944) 23 C2d 632, 145 P2d 561: §52.12
Gray, People v (2001) 87 CA4th 781, 104 CR2d 848: §6.28
Gray, U.S. v (9th Cir 1989) 876 F2d 1411: §34.9
Green v Southern Pac. Co. (1898) 122 C 563, 55 P 577: §4.10
Green v U.S. (1957) 355 US 184, 2 L Ed 2d 199, 78 S Ct 221: §56.5
Green, California v (1970) 399 US 149, 26 L Ed 2d 489, 90 S Ct 1930: §46.19
Green, People v (1980) 27 C3d 1, 164 CR 1: §§4.8, 17.2, 29.11, 29.18, 30.3, 31.7, 31.12, 31.17
Green, People v (1971) 3 C3d 981, 92 CR 494: §§22.5, 23.7
Green & Shinee v Superior Court (2001) 88 CA4th 532, 105 CR2d 886: §34.9
Greenly v Cooper (1978) 77 CA3d 382, 143 CR 514: §45.4
Greer, People v (1947) 30 C2d 589, 184 P2d 512: §3.8
Grey v Superior Court (1976) 62 CA3d 698, 133 CR 318: §§37.8, 37.17
Grey, People v (1972) 23 CA3d 456, 100 CR 245: §13.12

Griffin v California (1965) 380 US 609, 14 L Ed 2d 106, 85 S Ct 1229: §§29.23, 33.29, 46.8, 46.12, 47.1, 47.6-47.7
Grimshaw v Ford Motor Co. (1981) 119 CA3d 757, 174 CR 348: §§2.6, 26.3, 29.9, 29.11, 29.18, 53.1
Grosslight v Superior Court (1977) 72 CA3d 502, 140 CR 278: §§37.3-37.4
Grudt v City of Los Angeles (1970) 2 C3d 575, 86 CR 465: §23.2
Guiterrez, People v (1991) 232 CA3d 1624, 284 CR 230: §19.11
Gulf Islands Leasing, Inc. v Bombardier Capital, Inc. (SD NY 2003) 215 FRD 466: §34.22B
Guntert v City of Stockton (1974) 43 CA3d 203, 117 CR 601, disapproved on other grounds in 82 CA4th at 634: §55.1
Gutierrez, People v (2000) 78 CA4th 170, 92 CR2d 626: §§19.23, 19.41

H

Haeussler, People v (1953) 41 C2d 252, 260 P2d 8: §47.3
Haines v Snedigar (1895) 110 C 18, 42 P 462: §26.2
Haldeen, People v (1968) 267 CA2d 478, 73 CR 102: §47.1
Hall, People v (1986) 41 C3d 826, 226 CR 112: §§1.12, 17.6
Hall, People v (1983) 35 C3d 161, 197 CR 71: §6.32
Hall, People v (1980) 28 C3d 143, 167 CR 844: §§17.2, 17.4
Hall, People v (2000) 78 CA4th 232, 92 CR2d 687: §19.13
Hall, People v (1980) 108 CA3d 373, 166 CR 578: §§18.27, 29.43
Hallendorf v Superior Court (1978) 85 CA3d 553, 149 CR 564: §36.9
Hallinan v Superior Court (1925) 74 CA 420, 240 P 788: §57.4
Hallinan, In re (1969) 71 C2d 1179, 81 CR 1: §57.6
Hallinan, In re (1932) 126 CA 121, 14 P2d 797: §57.4
Hammarley v Superior Court (1979) 89 CA3d 388, 153 CR 608: §48.8
Hammon, People v (1997) 15 C4th 1117, 65 CR2d 1: §18.5

Hand v Scodeletti (1900) 128 C 674, 61 P 373: §15.5
Hankey, U.S. v (9th Cir 2000) 203 F3d 1160: §20.15
Hardeman, People v (1982) 137 CA3d 823, 187 CR 296: §§44.6, 44.9
Hardy, People v (1992) 2 C4th 86, 5 CR2d 796: §§18.27, 47.6
Harlan, People v (1990) 222 CA3d 439, 271 CR 653: §20.18
Harper v French (1938) 29 CA2d 214, 84 P2d 216: §25.6
Harris v New York (1971) 401 US 222, 28 L Ed 2d 1, 91 S Ct 643: §22.2
Harris, People v (1989) 47 C3d 1047, 255 CR 352: §§1.6, 1.11, 20.7, 23.4, 29.7
Harris, People v (1992) 10 CA4th 672, 12 CR2d 758: §§6.16, 6.31
Harris, People v (1992) 8 CA4th 104, 10 CR2d 42: §46.17
Harris, People v (1978) 85 CA3d 954, 149 CR 860: §4.19
Harris, People v (1969) 270 CA2d 863, 76 CR 130: §§16.4, 20.4
Hart v Wielt (1970) 4 CA3d 224, 84 CR 220: §§6.39, 6.47, 32.6, 56.6
Hart, Estate of (1951) 107 CA2d 60, 236 P2d 884: §56.6
Haskett, People v (1982) 30 C3d 841, 180 CR 640: §29.7
Hasson v Ford Motor Co. (1982) 32 C3d 388, 185 CR 654: §§18.27, 20.7, 29.44, 29.46
Hastings v Serleto (1943) 61 CA2d 672, 143 P2d 956: §4.16
Hatfield v Levy Bros. (1941) 18 C2d 798, 117 P2d 841: §32.5
Hatfield, People v (1933) 129 CA 162, 18 P2d 366: §11.3
Hathcock, People v (1973) 8 C3d 599, 105 CR 540: §4.16
Hathcock, People v (1971) 17 CA3d 646, 95 CR 221: §§46.13, 46.15
Hawk v Superior Court (1974) 42 CA3d 108, 116 CR 713: §§2.17, 29.15
Hawthorne, People v (1992) 4 C4th 43, 14 CR2d 133: §29.7
Hayes, People v (1999) 21 C4th 1211, 91 CR2d 211: §18.27
Hayes, People v (1990) 52 C3d 577, 276 CR 874: §29.7
Hayes, People v (1989) 49 C3d 1260, 265 CR 132: §20.13
Hays v Viscome (1953) 122 CA2d 135, 264 P2d 173: §54.4
Heard, People v (2003) 31 C4th 946, 4 CR3d 131: §30.2
Heavy Duty Truck Leasing, Inc. v Superior Court (1970) 11 CA3d 116, 89 CR 598: §§56.1, 56.4
Hecker, People v (1990) 219 CA3d 1238, 268 CR 884: §6.20
Hedgecock, People v (1990) 51 C3d 395, 272 CR 803: §18.27
Hedrington, People v (1985) 171 CA3d 517, 217 CR 754: §19.5
Hefner, People v (1981) 127 CA3d 88, 179 CR 336: §29.28
Heiner v Kmart (2000) 84 CA4th 335, 100 CR2d 854: §4.8
Heldenburg, People v (1990) 219 CA3d 468, 268 CR 255: §§4.8, 29.14
Helfend v Southern Cal. Rapid Transit Dist. (1970) 2 C3d 1, 84 CR 173: §52.11
Helina, U.S. v (9th Cir 1977) 549 F2d 713: §46.3
Hempstead, People v (1983) 148 CA3d 949, 196 CR 412: §26.8
Henderson, People v (1977) 19 C3d 86, 137 CR 1: §37.4
Hendricks, People v (1987) 43 C3d 584, 238 CR 66: §§30.2, 47.4
Hernandez, People v (1997) 55 CA4th 225, 63 CR2d 769: §19.26
Hernandez, People v (1979) 94 CA3d 715, 156 CR 572: §6.46
Hernandez, People v (1976) 63 CA3d 393, 133 CR 745: §23.2
Hernandez (County of Los Angeles v Superior Court) (1990) 222 CA3d 647, 271 CR 698: §35.8
Herrera, People v (2000) 83 CA4th 46, 98 CR2d 911: §19.16
Hertz, People v (1980) 103 CA3d 770, 163 CR 233: §43.13
Hickambottom v Cooper Transp. Co. (1960) 186 CA2d 479, 9 CR 276: §29.27
Hickman v Arons (1960) 187 CA2d 167, 9 CR 379: §19.6
Hickman v Taylor (1947) 329 US 495, 91 L Ed 451, 67 S Ct 385: §35.1
Higgins v Los Angeles Gas & Elec. Co. (1911) 159 C 651, 115 P 313: §29.36

Hill v NCAA (1994) 7 C4th 1, 26 CR2d 834: §33.3
Hill, People v (1998) 17 C4th 800, 72 CR2d 656: §§29.4, 29.7, 29.11
Hill, People v (1992) 3 C4th 959, 13 CR2d 475, overruled on other grounds in Price v Superior Court (2001) 25 C4th 1046, 108 CR2d 409: §§33.13, 46.9
Hill, People v (2001) 89 CA4th 48, 107 CR2d 110: §20.13
Hill, People v (1992) 3 CA4th 16, 4 CR2d 258, disapproved on other grounds in People v Nesler (1997) 16 C4th 561: §§18.27, 29.46
Hill, People v (1976) 64 CA3d 16, 134 CR 443: §54.5
Hilliard v A.H. Robins Co. (1983) 148 CA3d 374, 196 CR 117: §32.5
Hillman v Stults (1968) 263 CA2d 848, 70 CR 295: §54.5
Hinson v Clairemont Community Hosp. (1990) 218 CA3d 1110, 267 CR 503, disapproved in part on other grounds in Alexander v Superior Court (1993) 5 C4th 1218, 23 CR2d 397: §§31.5, 31.12
Hobbs v Municipal Court (1991) 233 CA3d 670, 284 CR 655, disapproved on other grounds in 18 C4th at 295: §35.4
Hoel v City of Los Angeles (1955) 136 CA2d 295, 288 P2d 989: §19.26
Hoffman v Brandt (1966) 65 C2d 549, 55 CR 417: §§29.7, 29.9
Hoffman v U.S. (1951) 341 US 479, 95 L Ed 1118, 71 S Ct 814: §46.4
Hogan, People v (1982) 31 C3d 815, 183 CR 817, disapproved on other grounds in People v Cooper (1991) 53 C3d 771, 281 CR 90: §29.42
Holley v J & S Sweeping Co. (1983) 143 CA3d 588, 192 CR 74: §§6.27–6.29, 6.32
Holloway, Estate of (1925) 195 C 711, 235 P 1012: §20.3
Holm v Superior Court (1954) 42 C2d 500, 267 P2d 1025, disapproved on another ground in Suezaki v Superior Court (1962) 58 C2d 166, 23 CR 368: §34.9
Holmes v Southern Cal. Edison Co. (1947) 78 CA2d 43, 177 P2d 32: §20.3
Honeycutt, People v (1977) 20 C3d 150, 141 CR 698: §29.46
Hood, People v (1969) 1 C3d 444, 82 CR 618: §53.2
Hoover, People v (1986) 187 CA3d 1074, 231 CR 203: §29.34
Hope v Arrowhead & Puritas Waters, Inc. (1959) 174 CA2d 222, 344 P2d 428: §20.25
Hord, People v (1993) 15 CA4th 711, 19 CR2d 55: §18.27
Horman, Estate of (1968) 265 CA2d 796, 71 CR 780: §4.20
Horn v Atchison, T. & S.F. Ry. (1964) 61 C2d 602, 39 CR 721: §§29.7, 29.11, 29.14, 29.45, 56.6
Horn v General Motors Corp. (1976) 17 C3d 359, 131 CR 78: §§31.7, 31.9
Horowitz, People v (1945) 70 CA2d 675, 161 P2d 833: §29.42
Horton, People v (1995) 11 C4th 1068, 47 CR2d 516: §§6.4, 6.28
Houston Gen. Ins. Co. v Superior Court (1980) 108 CA3d 958, 166 CR 904: §34.17
Hovey v Superior Court (1980) 28 C3d 1, 168 CR 128: §6.16
Howard (People v Superior Court) (1968) 69 C2d 491, 72 CR 330: §55.2
Hoze, People v (1987) 195 CA3d 949, 241 CR 14: §31.3
Hrnjak v Graymar, Inc. (1971) 4 C3d 725, 94 CR 623: §§31.12, 31.17, 32.6
Hubbard v Calvin (1978) 83 CA3d 529, 147 CR 905: §33.20
Huber, Hunt & Nichols, Inc. v Moore (1977) 67 CA3d 278, 136 CR 603: §19.26
Huelter v Superior Court (1978) 87 CA3d 544, 151 CR 138: §§37.8, 37.17
Huggins, People v (1986) 182 CA3d 828, 227 CR 547: §§17.6, 21.8
Humphries, People v (1986) 185 CA3d 1315, 230 CR 536: §§19.14, 22.3
Hunter, People v (1989) 49 C3d 957, 264 CR 367: §46.18
Hurd, People v (1970) 5 CA3d 865, 85 CR 718: §26.8
Hurley v Kazantzis (1947) 82 CA2d 378, 186 P2d 434: §54.5
Hurlic, People v (1971) 14 CA3d 122, 92 CR 55: §20.4
Huston, People v (1989) 210 CA3d 192, 258 CR 393: §46.6

Hutchinson, People v (1969) 71 C2d 342, 78 CR 196: §§18.20, 18.27, 29.43, 29.46
Hutton v Brookside Hosp. (1963) 213 CA2d 350, 28 CR 774: §§5.11, 19.26
Hutton, People v (1986) 187 CA3d 934, 232 CR 263: §29.18
Hyatt v Sierra Boat Co. (1978) 79 CA3d 325, 145 CR 47: §§2.2-2.3, 2.8

I

In re _____ (*see* name of party)
INS v Lopez-Mendoza (1984) 468 US 1032, 82 L Ed 2d 778, 104 S Ct 3479: §28.6
Ing, People v (1967) 65 C2d 603, 55 CR 902: §47.7
Ingle, People v (1986) 178 CA3d 505, 223 CR 723: §20.4
Inniss v Municipal Court (1965) 62 C2d 487, 42 CR 594: §57.8
Insurance Co. of N. Am. v Superior Court (1980) 108 CA3d 758, 166 CR 880: §34.10
Inyo Chem. Co. v City of Los Angeles (1936) 5 C2d 525, 55 P2d 850: §32.5
Iocca, People v (1974) 37 CA3d 73, 112 CR 102: §54.3
Irvin v Padelford (1954) 127 CA2d 135, 273 P2d 539: §29.46
Irvin, People v (1996) 46 CA4th 1340, 54 CR2d 450: §6.28
Isaac O., Conservatorship of (1987) 190 CA3d 50, 235 CR 133: §20.9
Isaac Upham Co. v United States Fid. & Guar. Co. (1922) 59 CA 606, 211 P 809: §29.5
Isaacs v Huntington Mem. Hosp. (1985) 38 C3d 112, 211 CR 356: §20.9
Isenor, People v (1971) 17 CA3d 324, 94 CR 746: §47.5
Ivy, People v (1966) 244 CA2d 406, 53 CR 47: §29.23
Izazaga v Superior Court (1991) 54 C3d 356, 285 CR 231: §§1.7, 46.1

J

J.E.B. v Alabama ex rel T.B. (1994) 511 US 127, 128 L Ed 2d 89, 114 S Ct 1419: §6.27
Jackson, People v (1971) 18 CA3d 504, 95 CR 919: §§31.1-31.2
Jackson, People v (1960) 183 CA2d 332, 6 CR 505: §26.3
Jackson, People v (1954) 124 CA2d 787, 269 P2d 17: §13.7
Jacobs, People v (2000) 78 CA4th 1444, 93 CR2d 783: §22.8
Jacobs, People v (1925) 73 CA 334, 238 P 770: §4.19
Jacobson, People v (1965) 63 C2d 319, 46 CR 515: §29.36
Jambazian v Borden (1994) 25 CA4th 836, 30 CR2d 768: §2.3
Janis, U.S. v (1976) 428 US 433, 49 L Ed 2d 1046, 96 S Ct 3021: §§28.2, 28.4
Jasmine Networks, Inc. v Marvell Semiconductor, Inc. (2004) 117 CA4th 794, ___ CR3d ___: §§34.15, 34.22-34.23
Jasper Constr., Inc. v Foothill Jr. College Dist. (1979) 91 CA3d 1, 153 CR 767: §§35.6-35.7
Jeanette H., In re (1990) 225 CA3d 25, 275 CR 9: §§34.2, 35.3
Jenkins v Tuneup Masters (1987) 190 CA3d 1, 235 CR 214: §32.7
Jenkins, In re (1999) 70 CA4th 1162, 83 CR2d 232: §29.30
Jenkins, People v (1974) 40 CA3d 1054, 115 CR 622: §29.2
Jennings, People v (1991) 53 C3d 334, 279 CR 780: §27.1
Jennings, People v (1988) 46 C3d 963, 251 CR 278: §§2.7, 2.18
Jennings, People v (2000) 81 CA4th 1301, 97 CR2d 727: §32.7
Jentry, People v (1977) 69 CA3d 615, 138 CR 250: §30.2
Jessica B., In re (1989) 207 CA3d 504, 254 CR 883: §46.17
Jessup v Superior Court (1957) 151 CA2d 102, 311 P2d 177: §§43.3, 43.6
Jimena v Alesso (1995) 36 CA4th 1028, 43 CR2d 18: §22.11A
Jimenez, People v (1978) 21 C3d 595, 147 CR 172: §21.15
Jiminez, People v (1992) 11 CA4th 1611, 15 CR2d 268: §6.21
John B., People v (1987) 192 CA3d 1073, 237 CR 659: §36.13
John W., People v (1986) 185 CA3d 801, 229 CR 783: §20.14

Johnson v Aetna Life Ins. Co. (1963) 221 CA2d 247, 34 CR 484: §19.26

Johnson v Campbell (9th Cir 1996) 92 F3d 951: §6.31

Johnson, People v (1992) 3 C4th 1183, 14 CR2d 702: §46.6

Johnson, People v (1989) 47 C3d 1194, 255 CR 569: §§6.27, 6.29, 6.32

Johnson, People v (1993) 19 CA4th 778, 23 CR2d 703: §20.7

Johnson, People v (1988) 200 CA3d 1553, 247 CR 767: §29.45

Johnson, People v (1974) 39 CA3d 749, 114 CR 545: §§19.18, 46.9

Johnson, People v (1969) 270 CA2d 204, 75 CR 605: §§50.4, 50.8, 50.10, 51.4

Johnson, People v (1964) 229 CA2d 162, 40 CR 105: §§17.9, 26.5, 52.10

Johnston v Beadle (1907) 6 CA 251, 91 P 1011: §52.3

Joiner v General Elec. Co. (11th Cir 1996) 78 F3d 524: §20.16

Joiner v General Elec. Co. (ND Ga 1994) 864 F Supp 1310: §20.16

Jones v Moore (2000) 80 CA4th 557, 95 CR2d 216: §22.11

Jones v Superior Court (1981) 119 CA3d 534, 174 CR 148: §§36.9, 36.20

Jones v Superior Court (1979) 96 CA3d 390, 157 CR 809: §27.4

Jones, In re (1996) 13 C4th 552, 54 CR2d 52: §4.8

Jones, In re (1971) 5 C3d 390, 96 CR 448: §47.4

Jones, In re (1975) 47 CA3d 879, 120 CR 914: §§57.6–57.7

Jones, People v (1971) 19 CA3d 437, 96 CR 795: §21.5

Jones, People v (1970) 7 CA3d 48, 86 CR 717: §§21.6, 53.1

Jonte v Key Sys. (1949) 89 CA2d 654, 201 P2d 562: §§29.7, 56.6

Jorn, U.S. v (1971) 400 US 470, 27 L Ed 2d 543, 91 S Ct 547: §56.5

Joseph G., In re (1970) 7 CA3d 695, 87 CR 25: §20.4

Jurcoane v Superior Court (2001) 93 CA4th 886, 113 CR2d 483: §41.9

K

Kadelbach v Amaral (1973) 31 CA3d 814, 107 CR 720: §§22.5A, 26.4

Kadison, People v (1966) 243 CA2d 162, 52 CR 114: §47.7

Karagozian, In re (1975) 44 CA3d 516, 118 CR 793: §57.6

Karis, People v (1988) 46 C3d 612, 250 CR 659: §§6.2, 19.24, 29.38, 31.3

Karvoski v Grant (1938) 30 CA2d 171, 85 P2d 944: §§29.24, 29.28

Kasson, Estate of (1900) 127 C 496, 59 P 950: §26.3

Kastigar v U.S. (1972) 406 US 441, 32 L Ed 2d 212, 92 S Ct 1653: §§46.2, 46.13, 46.15

Kauffman v De Matiis (1948) 31 C2d 429, 189 P2d 271: §54.14

Kaufman (People v Superior Court) (1974) 12 C3d 421, 115 CR 812: §§46.16–46.17, 47.2

Kaurish, People v (1990) 52 C3d 648, 276 CR 788: §§6.23, 29.34

Keena v United R.R. (1925) 197 C 148, 239 P 1061: §29.7

Keller, People v (1963) 212 CA2d 210, 27 CR 805: §46.9

Kelley v Bailey (1961) 189 CA2d 728, 11 CR 448: §19.26

Kelley, Estate of (1920) 184 C 448, 194 P 4: §§34.20, 36.19, 37.16

Kelly v New West Fed. Savings (1996) 49 CA4th 659, 56 CR2d 803: §2.1

Kelly v Trans Globe Travel Bureau, Inc. (1976) 60 CA3d 195, 131 CR 488: §§6.35, 6.46

Kelly, People v (1992) 1 C4th 495, 3 CR2d 677: §6.23

Kelly, People v (1990) 51 C3d 931, 275 CR 160: §30.2

Kelly, People v (1976) 17 C3d 24, 130 CR 144: §§4.4, 19.36, 20.7, 20.10–20.12, 20.14–20.15, 20.18

Kelly, People v (1986) 185 CA3d 118, 229 CR 584: §29.35

Kern, County of v Superior Court (1978) 82 CA3d 396, 147 CR 248: §3.7

Kerns Constr. Co. v Superior Court (1968) 266 CA2d 405, 72 CR 74: §§33.12, 35.2, 35.8

Kessler v Gray (1978) 77 CA3d 284, 143 CR 496: §§30.3, 31.12

Killbrew, People v (2002) 103 CA4th 644, 126 CR2d 876: §20.6

Killpatrick v Superior Court (1957) 153 CA2d 146, 314 P2d 164, overruled on other grounds at 29 C4th 1210: §47.2

Kimbley v Kaiser Found. Hosp. (1985) 164 CA3d 1166, 211 CR 148: §6.23

King, People v (1967) 66 C2d 633, 58 CR 571: §46.17

King, U.S. v (ED Va 2000) 194 FRD 569: §48.2

Knights, People v (1985) 166 CA3d 46, 212 CR 307: §§20.6-20.7

Knoll Assocs. v FTC (7th Cir 1968) 397 F2d 530: §§28.5-28.6

Knox, People v (1979) 95 CA3d 420, 157 CR 238: §18.9

Koeberle v Friganza (1924) 66 CA 323, 226 P 35: §42.8

Kohn v Superior Court (1936) 12 CA2d 459, 55 P2d 1186: §55.7

Kolaric v Kaufmann (1968) 261 CA2d 20, 67 CR 729: §§29.6-29.7

Kor, People v (1954) 129 CA2d 436, 277 P2d 94: §34.12

Kraft, People v (2000) 23 C4th 978, 99 CR2d 1: §19.13

Kramer, People v (1968) 259 CA2d 452, 66 CR 638: §26.8

Kramm v Stockton Elec. R.R. Co. (1913) 22 CA 737, 136 P 523: §6.45

Kronemyer, People v (1987) 189 CA3d 314, 234 CR 442: §32.7

Krouse v Graham (1977) 19 C3d 59, 137 CR 863: §§17.3, 29.46

Kullman, Salz & Co. v Superior Court (1911) 15 CA 276, 114 P 589: §55.7

Kumho Tire Co. v Carmichael (1999) 526 US 137, 143 L Ed 2d 238, 119 S Ct 1167: §§20.15-20.16

L

Label, People v (1974) 43 CA3d 766, 119 CR 522: §46.15

Laboa v Calderon (2000) 224 F3d 972: §29.9

Ladas v California State Auto. Ass'n (1993) 19 CA4th 761, 23 CR2d 810: §2.8

Laird v I.W. Mather, Inc. (1958) 51 C2d 210, 331 P2d 617: §26.3

Lake, County of v Superior Court (1977) 67 CA3d 815, 136 CR 830: §57.6

Lam Choi, People v (2000) 80 CA4th 476, 94 CR2d 922: §33.17

Lambright, People v (1964) 61 C2d 482, 39 CR 209: §§29.37, 29.45-29.46

Lancaster, People v (1957) 148 CA2d 187, 306 P2d 626: §5.5

Lang, People v (1989) 49 C3d 991, 264 CR 386: §19.24

Lankford, People v (1989) 210 CA3d 227, 258 CR 322: §§1.6, 1.11, 31.17

Lankford, People v (1976) 55 CA3d 203, 127 CR 408: §§41.19, 41.21, 41.23

Lanphear, People v (1980) 26 C3d 814, 163 CR 601, opinion restated at 28 C3d 463, 171 CR 505: §§26.8, 29.45

Larios v Superior Court (1979) 24 C3d 324, 155 CR 374: §§29.45, 56.3-56.4

Larson v Solbakken (1963) 221 CA2d 410, 34 CR 450: §§20.3, 53.5, 54.13

Lasky, Haas, Cohler & Munter v Superior Court (1985) 172 CA3d 264, 218 CR 205: §35.5

Laursen v Tidewater Assoc. Oil Co. (1954) 123 CA2d 813, 268 P2d 104: §26.4

Laursen, People v (1972) 8 C3d 192, 104 CR 425: §54.5

Lavergne, People v (1971) 4 C3d 735, 94 CR 405: §§22.3, 26.4

Lawlor v Linforth (1887) 72 C 205, 13 P 496: §6.20

Lawrence, People v (1959) 168 CA2d 510, 336 P2d 189: §46.19

LeCyr v Dow (1939) 30 CA2d 457, 86 P2d 900: §3.9

LeMons v Regents of Univ. of Cal. (1978) 21 C3d 869, 148 CR 355: §53.2

Leahy, People v (1994) 8 C4th 587, 34 CR2d 663: §§4.4, 20.7, 20.10-20.13, 20.17

Leainitt, In re (1959) 174 CA2d 535, 345 P2d 75: §§46.4, 47.2

Leary, People v (1946) 28 C2d 740, 172 P2d 41: §27.4

Lee v Gregoriou (1958) 50 C2d 502, 326 P2d 135: §25.12

Lee, People v (1970) 3 CA3d 514, 83 CR 715: §34.15

Leibman v Curtis (1955) 138 CA2d 222, 291 P2d 542: §§6.20, 6.23, 6.47

Lemelle v Superior Court (1978) 77 CA3d 148, 143 CR 450: §34.13

Lemer v Boise Cascade, Inc. (1980) 107 CA3d 1, 165 CR 555: §§2.18, 32.2

Lemley v Doak Gas Engine Co. (1919) 40 CA 146, 180 P 671: §21.19

Lemon, In re (1936) 15 CA2d 82, 59 P2d 213: §§41.7, 42.4, 47.2

Lepe, People v (1997) 57 CA4th 977, 67 CR2d 525: §19.29

Levine v Pollack (1995) 37 CA4th 129, 43 CR2d 491: §54.11

Levy-Zentner Co. v Southern Pac. Transp. Co. (1977) 74 CA3d 762, 142 CR 1: §19.26

Lewis v Robertson & Sons (1984) 162 CA3d 650, 208 CR 699: §29.23

Librach, U.S. v (8th Cir 1976) 536 F2d 1228: §46.15

Liddicoat, People v (1981) 120 CA3d 512, 174 CR 649: §18.9

Lifschutz, In re (1970) 2 C3d 415, 85 CR 829: §§33.17, 36.22, 37.18–37.19, 50.1, 51.1

Lilly v Virginia (1999) 527 US 116, 144 L Ed 2d 117, 119 S Ct 1887: §19.2

Lindemann v San Joaquin Cotton Oil Co. (1936) 5 C2d 480, 55 P2d 870: §29.45

Lindsey, People v (1988) 205 CA3d 112, 252 CR 96: §29.7

Lindsey, People v (1949) 90 CA2d 558, 203 P2d 572: §26.6

Lines, People v (1975) 13 C3d 500, 119 CR 225: §§33.10, 36.1, 37.1

Linhart v Nelson (1976) 18 C3d 641, 134 CR 813: §§18.27, 29.46

Lipman v Ashburn (1951) 106 CA2d 616, 235 P2d 627: §54.9

Lipschutz, In re (1970) 2 C3d 415, 85 CR 829: §37.8

Littlefield v Superior Court (1982) 136 CA3d 477, 186 CR 368: §34.12

Lloyd v Superior Court (1982) 133 CA3d 896, 184 CR 467: §57.2

Lohman v Superior Court (1978) 81 CA3d 90, 146 CR 171: §§34.22A, 35.8

Lombardi v California St. Ry. Co. (1899) 124 C 311, 57 P 66: §6.20

Long Beach, City of v Superior Court (1976) 64 CA3d 65, 134 CR 468: §§34.2, 35.3

Loper v Beto (1972) 405 US 473, 31 L Ed 2d 374, 92 S Ct 1014: §22.8

Lopez, People v (1991) 3 CA4th Supp 11, 5 CR2d 775: §6.27

Lopez, People v (1980) 110 CA3d 1010, 168 CR 378: §§46.13, 47.2

Los Angeles Memorial Coliseum Comm'n v National Football League (CD Cal 1981) 89 FRD 489: §48.17

Los Angeles, City of v Decker (1977) 18 C3d 860, 135 CR 647: §§29.7, 29.9, 29.17–29.18, 29.46

Los Angeles, City of v Lowensohn (1976) 54 CA3d 625, 127 CR 417: §29.39

Los Angeles, City of v Superior Court (Friedman) (1985) 170 CA3d 744, 216 CR 311: §35.8

Los Angeles, County of v Superior Court (1975) 13 C3d 721, 119 CR 631: §43.4

Los Angeles, County of v Superior Court (Hernandez) (1990) 222 CA3d 647, 271 CR 698: §35.8

Loth v Truck-A-Way Corp. (1998) 60 CA4th 757, 70 CR2d 571: §20.7

Louis, People v (1986) 42 C3d 969, 232 CR 110: §19.11

Love v Wolf (1964) 226 CA2d 378, 38 CR 183: §§15.5, 29.5–29.6, 29.18

Love, People v (1960) 53 C2d 843, 3 CR 665: §6.7

Lowery v Anders (2000) 225 F3d 833: §29.9

Loyd, People v (2002) 27 C4th 997, 119 CR2d 360: §40.4

Lucero L., In re (2000) 22 C4th 1227, 96 CR2d 56: §19.17

Luflin v City of Bakersfield (1933) 131 CA 21, 20 P2d 788: §29.7

Lugashi, People v (1988) 205 CA3d 632, 252 CR 434: §19.26

Luhdorff v Superior Court (1985) 166 CA3d 485, 212 CR 516: §§37.3, 37.10

Luis, People v (1910) 158 C 185, 110 P 580, overruled on other grounds in 27 C4th 444: §20.8

Lunghi v Clark Equip. Co. (1984) 153 CA3d 485, 200 CR 387: §35.6

Lust v Merrell Dow Pharmaceuticals, Inc. (9th Cir 1996) 89 F3d 594: §20.15

Lyle v Superior Court (1981) 122 CA3d 470, 175 CR 918: §18.14

Lynch, People v (1971) 14 CA3d 602, 92 CR 411: §54.9

Lynn, People v (1971) 16 CA3d 259, 94 CR 16: §26.8

Lyon v Superior Court (1968) 68 C2d 446, 67 CR 265: §57.7

Lyons v Superior Court (1955) 43 C2d 755, 278 P2d 681: §57.5

Lysick v Walcom (1968) 258 CA2d 136, 65 CR 406: §20.7

M

Mabry, People v (1969) 71 C2d 430, 78 CR 655: §§40.2, 40.17
Macias, People v (1997) 16 C4th 739, 66 CR2d 659: §46.17
Maffeo v Holmes (1941) 47 CA2d 292, 117 P2d 948: §29.37
Magana, People v (1979) 95 CA3d 453, 157 CR 173: §19.7
Magee v Wyeth Labs. (1963) 214 CA2d 340, 29 CR 322: §26.7
Maggipinto v Reichman (ED Penn 1979) 481 F Supp 547: §22.10
Maglaya, People v (2003) 112 CA4th 1604, 6 CR3d 155: §20.4
Magnante v Pettibone-Wood Mfg. Co. (1986) 183 CA3d 764, 228 CR 420: §32.5
Magnolia Square Homeowners Ass'n v Safeco Ins. Co. (1990) 221 CA3d 1049, 271 CR 1: §19.13
Malavasi, Estate of (1929) 96 CA 204, 273 P 1097: §6.39
Malkasian v Irwin (1964) 61 C2d 738, 40 CR 78: §§29.5, 29.7, 29.9, 29.11, 29.17
Malloy v Hogan (1964) 378 US 1, 12 L Ed 2d 653, 84 S Ct 1489: §§46.2, 46.5, 46.8, 46.13, 46.20, 47.1
Malone, People v (2003) 112 CA4th 1241, 5 CR3d 741: §19.29
Manney v Housing Auth. (1947) 79 CA2d 453, 180 P2d 69: §16.4
Manriquez, People v (1999) 72 CA4th 1486, 86 CR2d 69: §20.7
Manson, People v (1977) 71 CA3d 1, 139 CR 275: §§27.1, 27.4, 27.9
Manuel v Flynn (1907) 5 CA 319, 90 P 463: §26.2
Mapp v Ohio (1961) 367 US 643, 6 L Ed 2d 1081, 81 S Ct 1684: §28.3
Marani v Jackson (1986) 183 CA3d 695, 228 CR 518: §25.11
Marcario, In re (1970) 2 C3d 329, 85 CR 135: §46.7
Marchetti v U.S. (1968) 390 US 39, 19 L Ed 2d 889, 88 S Ct 697: §46.6
Marchialette, People v (1975) 45 CA3d 974, 119 CR 816: §19.23

Marcus v Palm Harbor Hosp. (1967) 253 CA2d 1008, 61 CR 702: §§15.5, 29.6
Marcus v Superior Court (1971) 18 CA3d 22, 95 CR 545: §36.3
Mark C., In re (1992) 7 CA4th 433, 8 CR2d 856: §5.4
Marocco v Ford Motor Co. (1970) 7 CA3d 84, 86 CR 526: §31.2
Marriage of Parks (1982) 138 CA3d 346, 188 CR 26: §43.12
Marsh, People v (1985) 175 CA3d 987, 221 CR 311: §23.2
Marshall v Barlow's, Inc. (1978) 436 US 307, 56 L Ed 2d 305, 98 S Ct 1816: §28.11
Martin v Miqueu (1940) 37 CA2d 133, 98 P2d 816: §17.3
Martin, Estate of (1915) 170 C 657, 151 P 138: §29.6
Martin, Estate of (1969) 270 CA2d 506, 75 CR 911: §20.4
Martin, In re (1977) 71 CA3d 472, 139 CR 451: §57.5
Martin, People v (1998) 64 CA4th 378, 75 CR2d 147: §6.27
Martinez, People v (2000) 22 C4th 106, 91 CR2d 687: §§19.26–19.27
Martinez, People v (2003) 113 CA4th 400, 7 CR3d 49: §§4.8, 19.31A
Martinez, People v (1991) 228 CA3d 1456, 279 CR 858: §6.2
Martinez, People v (1987) 191 CA3d 1372, 237 CR 219: §29.18
Martinez, People v (1985) 175 CA3d 881, 221 CR 258: §31.4
Martinez, People v (1978) 82 CA3d 1, 147 CR 208: §29.42
Martinez, People v (1972) 27 CA3d 131, 103 CR 451: §27.4
Martinez, U.S. v (5th Cir 1973) 486 F2d 15: §47.5
Marwell, People v (1979) 94 CA3d 562, 156 CR 630: §47.7
Marx, People v (1975) 54 CA3d 100, 126 CR 350: §20.13
Marylander v Superior Court (2000) 81 CA4th 1119, 97 CR2d 439: §43.6
Massie, People v (1967) 66 C2d 899, 59 CR 733: §47.5
Masterson v Sine (1968) 68 C2d 222, 65 CR 545: §25.3
Matlock, People v (1970) 11 CA3d 453, 89 CR 862: §26.5

Matteson, People v (1964) 61 C2d 466, 39 CR 1: §47.3

Matthews v Superior Court (1988) 201 CA3d 385, 247 CR 226: §22.1

Mattson, People v (1984) 37 C3d 85, 207 CR 278: §27.2

Mavroudis v Superior Court (1980) 102 CA3d 594, 162 CR 724: §§33.17, 37.18

Maxwell, People v (1979) 94 CA3d 562, 156 CR 630: §§46.11, 46.19–46.20

May, People v (1988) 44 C3d 309, 243 CR 369: §§19.13, 46.2

Mayberry, People v (1982) 31 C3d 335, 182 CR 617: §28.2

Mayfield, People v (1972) 23 CA3d 236, 100 CR 104: §§19.3, 22.7, 31.5

Mayorga, People v (1985) 171 CA3d 929, 218 CR 830: §29.30

McAlpin, People v (1991) 53 C3d 1289, 283 CR 382: §20.4

McCabe v Snyder (1999) 75 CA4th 337, 89 CR2d 315: §43.7

McCarthy v City of Manhattan Beach (1953) 41 C2d 879, 264 P2d 932: §31.8

McCarthy, People v (1978) 79 CA3d 547, 144 CR 822: §44.10

McCartney v Commission on Judicial Qualifications (1974) 12 C3d 512, 116 CR 260: §§4.7, 29.24, 29.27

McCaslin, People v (1986) 178 CA3d 1, 223 CR 587: §40.4

McClain v Great Am. Ins. Cos. (1989) 208 CA3d 1476, 256 CR 863: §2.3

McClellan, People v (1969) 71 C2d 793, 80 CR 31: §17.4

McCollum v Barr (1918) 38 CA 411, 176 P 463: §29.6

McComb v Superior Court (1977) 68 CA3d 89, 137 CR 233: §§46.2, 47.2, 55.5

McCoy, People v (1944) 25 C2d 177, 153 P2d 315: §26.7

McDaniel, People v (1976) 16 C3d 156, 127 CR 467: §29.11

McDaniel, People v (1943) 59 CA2d 672, 140 P2d 88: §26.5

McDonald v Price (1947) 80 CA2d 150, 181 P2d 115: §§15.2, 15.5, 29.6

McDonald v Southern Pac. Transp. Co. (1999) 71 CA4th 256, 83 CR2d 734: §29.38

McDonough, In re (1915) 170 C 230, 149 P 566: §34.9

McDowd v Pig n' Whistle Corp. (1945) 26 C2d 696, 160 P2d 797: §19.26

McFaddin v H. S. Crocker Co. (1963) 219 CA2d 585, 33 CR 389: §54.11

McFarland, People v (2000) 78 CA4th 489, 92 CR2d 884: §32.7

McFeely v IAC (1923) 65 CA 45, 223 P 413: §4.16

McGee v Cessna Aircraft Co. (1983) 139 CA3d 179, 188 CR 542: §31.8

McGee, People v (1947) 31 C2d 229, 187 P2d 706: §5.8

McGowan v City of Los Angeles (1950) 100 CA2d 386, 223 P2d 862: §19.26

McJimson, People v (1982) 135 CA3d 873, 185 CR 605: §54.3

McKesson HBOC, Inc. v Superior Court (2004) 115 CA4th 1229, 9 CR3d 812: §§34.22B, 35.8

McMonigle, People v (1947) 29 C2d 730, 177 P2d 745: §27.5

McNeil v Yellow Cab Co. (1978) 85 CA3d 116, 147 CR 733: §§20.4, 20.7

McPeters, People v (1992) 2 C4th 1148, 9 CR2d 834: §6.28

McShann, People v (1958) 50 C2d 802, 330 P2d 33: §§43.8, 44.6

Meacham, People v (1984) 152 CA3d 142, 199 CR 586: §31.12

Medina, People v (1990) 51 C3d 870, 274 CR 849, aff'd on other grounds in 505 US 437, 120 L Ed 2d 353, 112 S Ct 2572: §§19.14, 20.4

Medina, People v (1974) 41 CA3d 438, 116 CR 133: §46.15

Mehaffey, People v (1948) 32 C2d 535, 197 P2d 12: §27.4

Melvin, Estate of (1927) 85 CA 691, 259 P 980: §13.3

Mendieta, People v (1986) 185 CA3d 1032, 230 CR 162: §19.29

Mendoza, People v (2000) 78 CA4th 918, 93 CR2d 216: §22.8

Mendoza, People v (1974) 37 CA3d 717, 112 CR 565: §54.5

Menendez v Superior Court (1992) 3 C4th 435, 11 CR2d 92: §§37.2, 37.4, 37.10

Mercado v Ahmed (7th Cir 1992) 974 F2d 863: §22.10
Mertsching v U.S. (D Colo 1982) 547 F Supp 124, aff'd without published opinion (10th Cir 1983) 716 F2d 907: §46.11
Meschino v North Am. Drager, Inc. (1st Cir 1988) 841 F2d 429: §22.10
Mesner, Estate of (1947) 77 CA2d 667, 176 P2d 70: §29.35
Michigan v Clifford (1984) 464 US 287, 78 L Ed 2d 477, 104 S Ct 641: §28.11
Mickey, People v (1991) 54 C3d 612, 286 CR 801: §§40.4, 54.3
Milan, People v (1973) 9 C3d 185, 107 CR 68: §30.2
Miller v National Am. Life Ins. Co. (1976) 54 CA3d 331, 126 CR 731: §§29.45-29.46
Miller v Superior Court (1999) 21 C4th 883, 89 CR2d 834: §§1.7, 48.8, 48.11, 48.14, 48.19, 55.6
Miller v Superior Court (1980) 111 CA3d 390, 168 CR 589: §34.22A
Miller v Superior Court (1977) 71 CA3d 145, 139 CR 521: §43.7
Miller v Transamerican Press (5th Cir 1980) 621 F2d 721: §48.2
Miller, People v (2000) 81 CA4th 1427, 97 CR2d 684: §§21.6, 32.7
Miller, People v (1996) 46 CA4th 412, 53 CR2d 773, disapproved on other grounds in 18 C4th at 1240: §19.21
Milner, People v (1988) 45 C3d 227, 246 CR 713: §31.11
Minnesota v Murphy (1984) 465 US 420, 79 L Ed 2d 409, 104 S Ct 1136: §46.4
Minnick v Mississippi (1990) 498 US 146, 112 L Ed 2d 489, 111 S Ct 486: §19.9
Miranda v Arizona (1966) 384 US 436, 16 L Ed 2d 694, 86 S Ct 1602: §§19.9, 19.13, 28.10, 46.1, 47.1
Miranda, People v (2000) 23 C4th 340, 96 CR2d 758: §19.38
Miron, People v (1989) 210 CA3d 580, 258 CR 494: §19.23
Mitcham, People v (1992) 1 C4th 1027, 5 CR2d 230: §33.29
Mitchell v Superior Court (1989) 49 C3d 1230, 1248 n 13, 265 CR 144: §§57.3, 57.7, 57.9
Mitchell v Superior Court (1984) 37 C3d 268, 208 CR 152: §§48.5, 55.4
Mitchell, People v (1964) 61 C2d 353, 38 CR 726: §§6.35, 6.45
Mitler v Municipal Court (1967) 249 CA2d 531, 57 CR 578: §55.5
Mize v Atchison, T. & S.F. R.R. (1975) 46 CA3d 436, 120 CR 787: §§21.9, 35.6, 35.8
Mobil Oil Corp. v Handley (1978) 76 CA3d 956, 143 CR 321: §25.10
Modesto, People v (1967) 66 C2d 695, 59 CR 124: §§47.1, 47.6
Modesto, People v (1965) 62 C2d 436, 42 CR 417: §33.29
Molano, People v (1967) 253 CA2d 841, 61 CR 821: §47.6
Monogram Indus. v Sar Indus. (1976) 64 CA3d 692, 134 CR 714: §4.20
Montebello Rose Co. v ALRB (1981) 119 CA3d 1, 173 CR 856: §34.3
Montgomery, People v (1976) 61 CA3d 718, 132 CR 558: §19.6
Montiel, People v (1993) 5 C4th 877, 21 CR2d 705: §§20.9, 29.7
Montiel, People v (1985) 39 C3d 910, 218 CR 572: §31.12
Montoya de Hernandez, U.S. v (1985) 473 US 531, 87 L Ed 2d 381, 105 S Ct 3304: §28.11
Moore v Rogers (1958) 157 CA2d 192, 320 P2d 524: §§5.10, 5.12
Morale v Grigel (D NH 1976) 422 F Supp 988: §28.6
Moran, People v (1970) 1 C3d 755, 83 CR 411: §4.8
Moran, People v (1974) 39 CA3d 398, 114 CR 413: §30.4
Morehouse v Taubman (1970) 5 CA3d 548, 85 CR 308: §32.5
Morelli, In re (1970) 11 CA3d 819, 91 CR 72: §§57.6-57.7
Moreno, People v (1973) 32 CA3d Supp 1, 108 CR 338: §§16.4, 20.4
Morganti, People v (1996) 43 CA4th 643, 50 CR2d 837: §20.13
Morris, People v (1991) 53 C3d 152, 279 CR 720: §§2.1-2.2, 2.11, 4.18, 6.12, 20.11, 20.13
Morris, People v (1988) 46 C3d 1, 249 CR 119: §§3.8, 29.7
Morrison, Estate of (1926) 198 C 1, 242 P 939: §19.25
Morse v Southern Pac. Transp. Co. (1976) 63 CA3d 128, 133 CR 577: §32.6

Morse, People v (1964) 60 C2d 631, 36 CR 201: §29.7
Mortenson, People v (1966) 241 CA2d 137, 50 CR 269: §26.8
Mosesian v Pennwalt Corp. (1987) 191 CA3d 851, 236 CR 778: §20.9
Moskowitz v Superior Court (1982) 137 CA3d 313, 187 CR 4: §55.4
Motton, People v (1985) 39 C3d 596, 217 CR 416: §6.28
Moving Picture Mach. Operators Union v Glasgow Theatres, Inc. (1970) 6 CA3d 395, 86 CR 33: §32.2
Mullanix v Basich (1945) 67 CA2d 675, 155 P2d 130: §52.11
Munchow v Kraszewski (1976) 56 CA3d 831, 128 CR 762: §25.5
Municipal Court, People v (Ahnemann) (1974) 12 C3d 658, 117 CR 20: §55.2
Municipal Court, People v (Runyan) (1978) 20 C3d 523, 143 CR 609: §54.16
Muniz, People v (1989) 213 CA3d 1508, 262 CR 743: §1.11
Munoz, People v (1992) 11 CA4th 1190, 15 CR2d 21: §18.30
Murphy v Waterfront Comm'n (1964) 378 US 52, 12 L Ed 2d 678, 84 S Ct 1594, overruled on other grounds in U.S. v Balsys (1998) 524 US 666, 141 L Ed 2d 575, 118 S Ct 2218: §§46.4, 46.13, 46.15
Murr v Murr (1948) 87 CA2d 511, 197 P2d 369: §29.25
Muszalski, In re (1975) 52 CA3d 475, 125 CR 281: §33.17

N

NLRB v South Bay Daily Breeze (9th Cir 1969) 415 F2d 360: §28.4
Namet v U.S. (1963) 373 US 179, 10 L Ed 2d 278, 83 S Ct 1151: §33.13
Naples Restaurant, Inc. v Coberley Ford (1968) 259 CA2d 881, 66 CR 835: §20.6
Nathaniel C., In re (1991) 228 CA3d 990, 279 CR 236: §20.6
National Auto. Ins. Co. v Fraties (1941) 46 CA2d 431, 115 P2d 997: §29.25
Navarette, People v (2003) 30 C4th 458, 133 CR2d 89: §20.4
Navarez, People v (1985) 169 CA3d 936, 215 CR 519: §31.12
Navarro, In re (1979) 93 CA3d 325, 155 CR 522: §34.9
Navarro, People v (1933) 135 CA 535, 27 P2d 652: §54.15
Neal v Farmers Ins. Exch. (1978) 21 C3d 910, 148 CR 389: §20.7
Neal, People v (2003) 31 C4th 63, 1 CR3d 650: §28.10
Nebraska Press Ass'n v Stuart (1976) 427 US 539, 49 L Ed 2d 683, 96 S Ct 2791: §54.1
Neder v U.S. (1999) 527 US 1, 144 L Ed 2d 35, 119 S Ct 1827: §§29.9, 29.18
Nelson v Gaunt (1981) 125 CA3d 623, 178 CR 167: §29.11
Nelson v Municipal Court (1972) 28 CA3d 889, 105 CR 46: §§46.13, 46.15
Nelson v Southern Pac. Co. (1937) 8 C2d 648, 67 P2d 682: §33.29
Nesler, People v (1997) 16 C4th 561, 66 CR2d 454: §§18.27, 29.39–29.40, 29.46
Neumann v Bishop (1976) 59 CA3d 451, 130 CR 786: §§6.47–6.48, 29.5, 56.6
Neustice, People v (1972) 24 CA3d 178, 100 CR 783: §§52.2, 52.10
Neverkovec v Fredericks (1999) 74 CA4th 337, 87 CR2d 856: §25.4
New v Consolidated Rock Prods. Co. (1985) 171 CA3d 681, 217 CR 522: §20.7
New Jersey v T.L.O. (1985) 469 US 325, 83 L Ed 2d 720, 105 S Ct 733: §28.11
New York Times Co. v Superior Court (1990) 51 C3d 453, 273 CR 98: §§48.10, 48.12, 48.19, 55.6
Newman v Emerson Radio Corp. (1989) 48 C3d 973, 258 CR 592: §2.8
Newman v First Cal. Co. (1975) 47 CA3d 60, 120 CR 494: §29.31
Newson v City of Oakland (1974) 37 CA3d 1050, 112 CR 890: §46.11
Newton v Thomas (1955) 137 CA2d 748, 291 P2d 503: §29.42
Newton, People v (1970) 8 CA3d 359, 87 CR 394: §22.5
Nguyen v Scott (1988) 206 CA3d 725, 253 CR 800: §19.36
Nguyen, People v (1994) 23 CA4th 32, 28 CR2d 140: §6.2

Nielsen v Superior Court (1997) 55 CA4th 1150, 64 CR2d 566: §37.9
Nixon, U.S. v (1974) 418 US 683, 41 L Ed 2d 1039, 94 S Ct 3090: §43.5
Norgart v Upjohn Co. (1999) 21 C4th 383, 87 CR2d 453: §4.8
North v Superior Court (1972) 8 C3d 301, 104 CR 833: §40.4
North, U.S. v (DC Cir 1990) 910 F2d 843: §46.15
North, U.S. v (DC Cir 1990) 910 F2d 843, modified on other grounds (DC Cir 1990) 920 F2d 940: §46.15
Nowell v Superior Court (1963) 223 CA2d 652, 36 CR 21: §34.15
Nugent, People v (1971) 18 CA3d 911, 96 CR 209: §4.18
Nye, People v (1969) 71 C2d 356, 78 CR 467: §§20.25, 30.4

O

Oceanside Union Sch. Dist. v Superior Court (1962) 58 C2d 180, 23 CR 375: §43.6
O'Connell, People v (1984) 152 CA3d 548, 199 CR 542: §46.17
Odom, People v (1980) 108 CA3d 100, 166 CR 283: §26.5
Offutt v U.S. (1954) 348 US 11, 99 L Ed 11, 75 S Ct 11: §57.5
O'Gan v King City Joint Union High Sch. Dist. (1970) 3 CA3d 641, 83 CR 795: §31.3
Ohio v Roberts (1980) 448 US 56, 65 L Ed 2d 597, 100 S Ct 2531: §1.12
Okun v Morton (1988) 203 CA3d 805, 250 CR 220: §25.7
O'Laskey v Sortino (1990) 224 CA3d 241, 273 CR 674, disapproved on other grounds in Flanagan v Flanagan (2002) 27 C4th 766, 117 CR2d 574: §21.6
O'Laughlin v Superior Court (1957) 155 CA2d 415, 318 P2d 39: §57.4
Olinger v Pacific Greyhound Lines (1935) 7 CA2d 484, 46 P2d 774: §29.46
Olson, In re (1974) 37 CA3d 783, 112 CR 579: §43.6
One Ruger.22 Caliber Pistol, People v (2000) 84 CA4th 310, 100 CR2d 780: §37.10
Orange County Flood Control Dist. v Sunny Crest Dairy, Inc. (1978) 77 CA3d 742, 143 CR 803: §52.8
Orange, County of v Superior Court (2000) 79 CA4th 759, 94 CR2d 261: §§43.1, 43.3, 43.6
Orduno, People v (1978) 80 CA3d 738, 145 CR 806: §19.41
Oregon v Kennedy (1982) 456 US 667, 72 L Ed 2d 416, 102 S Ct 2083: §29.45
Orona, People v (1947) 79 CA2d 820, 180 P2d 694: §13.5
Ortiz, People v (1995) 38 CA4th 377, 44 CR2d 914: §19.24
Osborn v Irwin Mem. Blood Bank (1992) 5 CA4th 234, 7 CR2d 101: §20.7
Osborn v Mission Ready Mix (1990) 224 CA3d 104, 273 CR 457: §20.4
Osterhoudt, In re (9th Cir 1983) 722 F2d 591: §34.9
Otte, People v (1989) 214 CA3d 1522, 263 CR 393: §44.2
Oxy Resources California LLC v Superior Court (2004) 115 CA4th 874, 9 CR3d 621: §§34.22B, 34.23, 35.8–35.9

P

PG&E v G.W. Thomas Drayage & Rigging Co. (1968) 69 C2d 33, 69 CR 561: §§19.37, 25.7
Pacchioli, People v (1992) 9 CA4th 1331, 12 CR2d 156: §§1.12, 46.4
Pacific Tel. & Tel. Co. v Superior Court (1970) 2 C3d 161, 84 CR 718: §33.23
Paez v Alcoholic Beverage Control Appeals Bd. (1990) 222 CA3d 1025, 272 CR 272: §20.28
Pagel, People v (1986) 186 CA3d Supp 1, 232 CR 104: §6.27
Palmer, U.S. v (9th Cir 1993) 3 F3d 300: §2.15
Parham, People v (1963) 60 C2d 378, 33 CR 497: §§43.4, 43.9, 44.7
Parker v Otis (1900) 130 C 322, 62 P 571, aff'd in 187 US 606, 47 L Ed 323, 23 S Ct 168: §20.3
Parker v Smith (1854) 4 C 105: §18.25
Parks, Marriage of (1982) 138 CA3d 346, 188 CR 26: §43.12
Parks, People v (1971) 4 C3d 955, 95 CR 193: §22.5

Parlier Fruit Co. v Fireman's Fund Ins. Co. (1957) 151 CA2d 6, 311 P2d 62: §21.19
Parrish v Civil Serv. Comm'n (1967) 66 C2d 260, 57 CR 623: §28.11
Pating v Board of Med. Quality Assur. (1982) 130 CA3d 608, 182 CR 20: §28.6
Patty v Board of Med. Examiners (1973) 9 C3d 356, 107 CR 473: §§28.6, 28.9
Payette v Sterle (1962) 202 CA2d 372, 21 CR 22: §26.4
Peacock v Levy (1931) 114 CA 246, 299 P 790: §§29.7, 29.11
Peat, Marwick, Mitchell & Co. v Superior Court (1988) 200 CA3d 272, 245 CR 873: §§2.1, 2.6, 31.7
Peck's Liquors, Inc. v Superior Court (1963) 221 CA2d 772, 34 CR 735: §§33.22–33.23, 46.13
Peete, People v (1946) 28 C2d 306, 169 P2d 924: §26.8
Pellon, U.S. v (SD NY 1979) 475 F Supp 467: §46.15
People ex rel Dep't of Pub. Works v Lillard (1963) 219 CA2d 368, 33 CR 189: §15.5
People v _____ (see name of defendant)
Perez, People v (1967) 65 C2d 615, 55 CR 909: §47.7
Perez, People v (1996) 48 CA4th 1310, 56 CR2d 299: §6.27
Perkey v DMV (1986) 42 C3d 185, 228 CR 169: §47.3
Perkins v Sunset Tel. & Tel. Co. (1909) 155 C 712, 103 P 190: §20.20
Perry, People v (1972) 7 C3d 756, 103 CR 161: §§4.16, 37.17, 53.3
Perry, People v (1976) 60 CA3d 608, 131 CR 629: §20.4
Peters, People v (1950) 96 CA2d 671, 216 P2d 145: §27.2
Peterson v Peterson (1946) 74 CA2d 312, 168 P2d 474: §3.7
Pfingst v Goetting (1950) 96 CA2d 293, 215 P2d 93: §20.4
Philbrick v Weinberger (1964) 228 CA2d 681, 39 CR 617: §29.35
Phillips, People v (1981) 122 CA3d 69, 175 CR 703: §29.38
Pierce v J.C. Penney Co. (1959) 167 CA2d 3, 334 P2d 117: §§2.2, 2.12, 2.18, 32.5
Pierce, People v (1979) 24 C3d 199, 155 CR 657: §29.39
Pierce, People v (1969) 269 CA2d 193, 75 CR 257: §23.4
Pike, People v (1962) 58 C2d 70, 22 CR 664: §§26.4, 26.8
Pineda, People v (1973) 30 CA3d 860, 106 CR 743: §46.18
Piper, People v (1980) 103 CA3d 102, 162 CR 833: §19.26
Pitchess v Superior Court (1974) 11 C3d 531, 113 CR 897: §§43.1, 43.8
Pitts, People v (1990) 223 CA3d 606, 273 CR 757: §29.7
Pizarro, People v (2003) 110 CA4th 530, 3 C3d 21: §20.13
Pizarro, People v (1992) 10 CA4th 57, 12 CR2d 436: §§20.12, 20.14
Planned Parenthood v Casey (1992) 505 US 833, 120 L Ed 2d 674, 112 S Ct 2791: §47.3
Platnauer v Superior Court (1917) 32 CA 463, 163 P 237: §57.4
Playboy Enters. v Superior Court (1984) 154 CA3d 14, 201 CR 207: §48.17
Pointer v Texas (1965) 380 US 400, 13 L Ed 2d 923, 85 S Ct 1065: §19.29
Pope, People v (1979) 23 C3d 412, 152 CR 732: §4.8
Popelka, Allard, McCowan & Jones v Superior Court (1980) 107 CA3d 496, 165 CR 748: §§35.6, 35.8
Pounders v Watson (1997) 521 US 982, 138 L Ed 2d 976, 117 S Ct 2359: §§57.3, 57.6
Powell v Texas (1989) 492 US 680, 106 L Ed 2d 551, 109 S Ct 3146: §37.9
Powers v Ohio (1991) 499 US 400, 113 L Ed 2d 411, 111 S Ct 1364: §6.27
Pratt, In re (1980) 112 CA3d 795, 170 CR 80: §43.9
Preis v American Indem. Co. (1990) 220 CA3d 752, 269 CR 617: §19.27
Press-Enterprise Co. v Superior Court (1984) 464 US 501, 78 L Ed 2d 629, 104 S Ct 819: §6.16
Price v Northern Elec. Ry. (1914) 168 C 173, 142 P 91: §4.16
Price v Superior Court (2001) 25 C4th 1046, 108 CR2d 409: §§31.4, 33.13, 46.9
Price, People v (1991) 1 C4th 324, 3 CR2d 106: §§6.23, 16.5, 19.29, 20.14

Pride, People v (1992) 3 C4th 195, 10 CR2d 636: §§6.2, 20.12
Prince, People v (1968) 268 CA2d 398, 74 CR 197: §5.3
Procunier v Superior Court (Herth) (1973) 35 CA3d 211, 110 CR 531: §43.12
Procunier v Superior Court (Losoya) (1973) 35 CA3d 207, 110 CR 529: §43.12
Producer's Dairy Delivery Co. v Sentry Ins. Co. (1986) 41 C3d 903, 226 CR 558: §25.7
Provencio, People v (1989) 210 CA3d 290, 258 CR 330: §19.23
Province v Center for Women's Health & Family Birth (1993) 20 CA4th 1673, 25 CR2d 667: §22.11
Prudhomme v Superior Court (1970) 2 C3d 320, 85 CR 129: §46.4
Pugh v See's Candies, Inc. (1988) 203 CA3d 743, 250 CR 195: §§2.7, 5.4, 32.7
Purkett v Elem (1995) 514 US 765, 131 L Ed 2d 834, 115 S Ct 1769: §§6.27–6.31
Purvis, People v (1963) 60 C2d 323, 33 CR 104: §§29.7, 29.18
Putensen v Clay Adams, Inc. (1970) 12 CA3d 1062, 91 CR 319: §20.6

Q

Quintana v Municipal Court (1987) 192 CA3d 361, 237 CR 397: §46.6
Quintas W., In re (1981) 120 CA3d 640, 175 CR 30: §27.4

R

Ramona v Superior Court (1997) 57 CA4th 107, 66 CR2d 766: §20.14
Ramona R. v Superior Court (1985) 37 C3d 802, 210 CR 204: §46.17
Raven v Deukmejian (1990) 52 C3d 336, 276 CR 326: §§1.7, 17.4
Ravey, People v (1954) 122 CA2d 699, 265 P2d 154: §20.4
Raymond v Glover (1898) 122 C 471, 55 P 398: §4.20
Raytheon Co. v Superior Court (1989) 208 CA3d 683, 256 CR 425: §34.22B
Reber, People v (1986) 177 CA3d 523, 223 CR 139, disapproved on other grounds in People v Hammon (1997) 15 C4th 1117, 65 CR2d 1: §18.5
Redmond, People v (1981) 29 C3d 904, 176 CR 780: §47.4
Redner v WCAB (1971) 5 C3d 83, 95 CR 447: §28.8
Reed, People v (1996) 13 C4th 217, 52 CR2d 106: §§19.11, 19.29
Reeder, People v (1978) 82 CA3d 543, 147 CR 275: §31.4
Reeves, People v (1980) 105 CA3d 444, 164 CR 426: §30.4
Regalado, People v (2000) 78 CA4th 1056, 93 CR2d 83: §32.7
Regents of Univ. of Cal. v Superior Court (1962) 200 CA2d 787, 19 CR 568: §46.19
Reich v Club Universe (1981) 125 CA3d 965, 178 CR 473: §18.14
Reilly, People v (1987) 196 CA3d 1127, 242 CR 496: §20.13
Reimer v Firpo (1949) 94 CA2d 798, 212 P2d 23: §56.1
Reisman v Los Angeles City Sch. Dist. (1954) 123 CA2d 493, 267 P2d 36: §19.26
Reliable Enters. v Superior Court (1984) 158 CA3d 604, 204 CR 786, disapproved in part by Mitchell v Superior Court (1989) 49 C3d 1230, 1248 n 13, 265 CR 144: §§57.3, 57.7, 57.9
Resendes, People v (1985) 164 CA3d 812, 210 CR 609: §18.5
Resendez, People v (1993) 12 CA4th 98, 15 CR2d 575: §§41.17, 41.19
Reyes, People v (1974) 12 C3d 486, 116 CR 217: §19.26
Reynaud v Superior Court (1982) 138 CA3d 1, 187 CR 660: §37.6
Reynolds v Natural Gas Equip. (1960) 184 CA2d 724, 7 CR 879: §16.5
Reynolds, U.S. v (1953) 345 US 1, 97 L Ed 727, 73 S Ct 528: §§43.5, 43.7
Rhinehart, People v (1973) 9 C3d 139, 107 CR 34, disapproved by People v Bolton (1979) 23 C3d 208, 152 CR 141: §29.2
Richards v Gemco (1963) 217 CA2d 858, 32 CR 65: §29.46

Richards v Superior Court (1978) 86 CA3d 265, 150 CR 77: §55.4

Richards v Superior Court (1968) 258 CA2d 635, 65 CR 917: §43.12

Richards, People v (1976) 17 C3d 614, 131 CR 537: §53.1

Richardson v Employers Liab. Assur. Corp. (1972) 25 CA3d 232, 102 CR 547: §29.6

Richmond v Moore (1930) 103 CA 173, 284 P 681: §6.49

Riel, People v (2000) 22 C4th 1153, 96 CR2d 1: §§19.14, 20.13, 29.14, 30.2

Rigging Int'l Maintenance Co. v Gwin (1982) 128 CA3d 594, 180 CR 451: §45.2

Rigney, People v (1961) 55 C2d 236, 10 CR 625: §29.24

Riley v City of Chester (3d Cir 1979) 612 F2d 708: §48.2

Rivera, People v (1986) 186 CA3d 251, 230 CR 533: §19.11

Robbins v Wong (1994) 27 CA4th 261, 32 CR2d 337: §22.2

Roberson, People v (1959) 167 CA2d 429, 334 P2d 666: §19.7

Roberts v Reynolds (1963) 212 CA2d 818, 28 CR 261: §25.9

Roberts v Superior Court (1973) 9 C3d 330, 107 CR 309: §§33.22, 36.20, 37.8, 37.17

Roberts, People v (1992) 2 C4th 271, 6 CR2d 276: §20.6

Robinson v Kelly (1949) 95 CA2d 320, 212 P2d 921: §11.3

Robinson v McAbee (1923) 64 CA 709, 222 P 871: §46.7

Robinson, People v (1964) 61 C2d 373, 38 CR 890: §26.8

Robinson, People v (2000) 85 CA4th 434, 102 CR2d 179: §19.13

Robinson, People v (1960) 179 CA2d 624, 4 CR 50: §29.28

Robles, People v (1970) 2 C3d 205, 85 CR 166: §§30.4, 47.4

Rochin v California (1952) 342 US 165, 96 L Ed 183, 72 S Ct 205: §47.3

Rock v Arkansas (1987) 483 US 44, 97 L Ed 2d 37, 107 S Ct 2704: §§17.4, 19.11

Rodgers v Kemper Constr. Co. (1975) 50 CA3d 608, 124 CR 143: §19.37

Rodgers, People v (1976) 54 CA3d 508, 126 CR 719: §§44.2, 44.9

Rodrigues, People v (1994) 8 C4th 1060, 36 CR2d 235: §1.3

Rodriguez v McDonnell Douglas Corp. (1978) 87 CA3d 626, 151 CR 399: §§4.16, 35.6

Rodriguez v North Am. Rockwell Corp. (1972) 28 CA3d 441, 104 CR 678: §34.9

Rodriguez v Superior Court (1993) 14 CA4th 1260, 18 CR2d 120: §33.2

Rodriquez, People v (1969) 274 CA2d 770, 79 CR 240: §5.4

Roe v Superior Court (1991) 229 CA3d 832, 280 CR 380: §37.15

Roemer v Retail Credit Co. (1975) 44 CA3d 926, 119 CR 82: §29.7

Rogers v Foppiano (1937) 23 CA2d 87, 72 P2d 239: §29.7

Rogers v U.S. (1951) 340 US 367, 95 L Ed 344, 71 S Ct 438: §46.19

Rojas, People v (1975) 15 C3d 540, 125 CR 357: §§19.11, 19.29

Romero v Volunteer State Life Ins. Co. (1970) 10 CA3d 571, 88 CR 820: §19.27

Romero, People v (1977) 68 CA3d 543, 137 CR 675: §56.2

Ron Greenspan Volkswagen, Inc. v Ford Motor Land Dev. (1995) 32 CA4th 985, 38 CR2d 783: §25.5

Rosales v City of Los Angeles (2000) 82 CA4th 419, 98 CR2d 144: §§43.4, 43.8

Rosato v Superior Court (1975) 51 CA3d 190, 124 CR 427: §48.6

Roscoe Moss Co. v Jenkins (1942) 55 CA2d 369, 130 P2d 477: §20.8

Rose v State (1942) 19 C2d 713, 123 P2d 505: §52.8

Rose v Superior Court (1934) 140 CA 418, 35 P2d 605: §57.4

Rosenberg v Wittenborn (1960) 178 CA2d 846, 3 CR 459: §26.7

Rosenberg, U.S. v (3d Cir 1986) 806 F2d 1169: §2.3

Rosenfield v Vosper (1941) 45 CA2d 365, 114 P2d 29: §29.26

Rosenstock v Municipal Court (1976) 61 CA3d 1, 132 CR 59: §57.5

Ross v Lighter (1956) 139 CA2d 756, 294 P2d 59: §29.35

Rousseau v West Coast House Movers
(1967) 256 CA2d 878, 64 CR 655:
§§2.5, 6.7, 6.46, 6.49
Rowe v Such (1901) 134 C 573, 66 P
862: §20.20
Rowland, People v (1992) 4 C4th 238, 14
CR2d 377: §29.7
Rubio v Superior Court (1988) 202 CA3d
1343, 249 CR 419: §§18.5, 40.4
Rudnick v Superior Court (1974) 11 C3d
924, 114 CR 603: §§36.3-36.5, 36.20,
37.3
Ruess v Baron (1932) 217 C 83, 17 P2d
119: §25.6
Ruffalo, In re (1968) 390 US 544, 20 L Ed
2d 117, 88 S Ct 1222: §28.5
Rufo v Simpson (2001) 86 CA4th 573,
103 CR2d 492: §§19.23-19.24, 19.30,
31.12
Ruiz, People v (1968) 265 CA2d 766, 71
CR 519: §16.4
Rumac, Inc. v Bottomley (1983) 143 CA3d
810, 192 CR 104: §§35.6-35.7
Runyan (People v Municipal Court) (1978)
20 C3d 523, 143 CR 609: §54.16
Rupp, People v (1953) 41 C2d 371, 260
P2d 1: §27.4
Russell v Geis (1967) 251 CA2d 560, 59
CR 569: §4.8
Russell v Langford (1902) 135 C 356, 67
P 331: §19.35
Ryner, People v (1985) 164 CA3d 1075,
211 CR 140: §29.39
Rysdale v Superior Court (1978) 81 CA3d
280, 146 CR 633: §46.16

S

Sabella v Southern Pac. Co. (1969) 70
C2d 311, 74 CR 534: §§2.17,
6.47-6.48, 56.6
Sacramento & San Joaquin Drainage Dist.
v Goehring (1970) 13 CA3d 58, 91 CR
375: §20.3
Sacramento & San Joaquin Drainage Dist.
v Reed (1963) 215 CA2d 60, 29 CR
847, modified on other grounds at 217
CA2d 611, 31 CR 754: §2.18
Saddler, People v (1979) 24 C3d 671, 156
CR 871: §47.7
Saidi-Tabatabai, People v (1970) 7 CA3d
981, 86 CR 866: §40.3

Sales, In re (1933) 134 CA 54, 24 P2d
916: §46.19
Salgo v Leland Stanford Jr. Univ. Bd. of
Trustees (1957) 154 CA2d 560, 317
P2d 170: §29.7
Salyer Grain & Milling Co. v Henson
(1970) 13 CA3d 493, 91 CR 847: §25.3
Sam, People v (1969) 71 C2d 194, 77 CR
804: §22.5
Sammut v Sammut (1980) 103 CA3d 557,
163 CR 193: §43.7
Samson v Transamerica Ins. Co. (1981)
30 C3d 220, 178 CR 343: §17.8
San Bernardino, County of v Doria Mining
& Eng'g Corp. (1977) 72 CA3d 776,
140 CR 383: §§54.2, 54.13
San Diego Prof. Ass'n v Superior Court
(1962) 58 C2d 194, 23 CR 384: §21.8
San Diego Trolley, Inc. v Superior Court
(2001) 87 CA4th 1083, 105 CR2d 476:
§37.17
San Diego, City of v Sobke (1998) 65
CA4th 379, 76 CR2d 9: §20.8
San Francisco Chronicle, In re (1934) 1
C2d 630, 36 P2d 369: §57.10
San Francisco Unified Sch. Dist. v
Superior Court (1961) 55 C2d 451, 11
CR 373: §34.9
San Francisco, City & County of v
Superior Court (1951) 37 C2d 227, 231
P2d 26: §§34.9, 36.1
San Francisco, City & County of v
Superior Court (1951) 38 C2d 156, 238
P2d 581: §§43.6-43.7
San Luis Obispo, County of v Bailey
(1971) 4 C3d 518, 93 CR 859: §§3.1,
3.6
San Mateo, County of v Christen (1937)
22 CA2d 375, 71 P2d 88: §16.2
Sanchez v Bagues & Sons Mortuaries
(1969) 271 CA2d 188, 76 CR 372:
§32.5
Sanchez, People v (1995) 12 C4th 1, 47
CR2d 843: §48.14
Sanchez, People v (1994) 24 CA4th 1012,
30 CR2d 111: §46.3
Sanders, People v (1990) 51 C3d 471,
273 CR 537: §6.24
Sandoval v Southern Cal. Enters. (1950)
98 CA2d 240, 219 P2d 928: §§19.5,
26.4
Sandoval, People v (1992) 4 C4th 155, 14
CR2d 342: §29.7

Sandoval, People v (2001) 87 CA4th 1425, 105 CR2d 504: §19.29
Santa Cruz, City of v Superior Court (1995) 40 CA4th 1146, 48 CR2d 216: §43.4
Santelli v Otis Elevator Co. (1989) 215 CA3d 210, 263 CR 496: §32.5
Sappenfield v Main St. & Agric. Park R.R. (1891) 91 C 48, 27 P 590: §32.5
Saulter v Municipal Court (1977) 75 CA3d 231, 142 CR 266: §§43.4, 43.9
Sav-On Drugs, Inc. v Superior Court (1975) 15 C3d 1, 123 CR 283: §§33.22, 43.7
Savoy Club v Board of Supervisors (1970) 12 CA3d 1034, 91 CR 198: §28.12
Scally v PG&E (1972) 23 CA3d 806, 100 CR 501: §§6.39, 29.4
Schall v Lockheed Missiles & Space Co. (1995) 37 CA4th 1485, 44 CR2d 191: §§18.21, 19.11, 20.13
Schelbauer v Butler Mfg. Co. (1984) 35 C3d 442, 198 CR 155: §32.5
Schindler, People v (1980) 114 CA3d 178, 170 CR 461: §33.29
Schmerber v California (1966) 384 US 757, 16 L Ed 2d 908, 86 S Ct 1826: §§46.2, 46.6, 47.3
Schreiber v Estate of Kiser (1999) 22 C4th 31, 91 CR2d 293: §22.11
Schroeder v Auto Driveaway Co. (1974) 11 C3d 908, 114 CR 622: §20.3
Schroeder, People v (1991) 227 CA3d 784, 278 CR 237: §§33.11, 46.10
Schuur v Rodenback (1901) 133 C 85, 65 P 298: §9.3
Schwartz v Shapiro (1964) 229 CA2d 238, 40 CR 189: §§25.3, 52.5
Schwartz, Estate of (1945) 67 CA2d 512, 155 P2d 76: §20.3
Scott, In re (2003) 29 C4th 783, 129 CR2d 605: §§46.12, 47.2
Scott, People v (1978) 21 C3d 284, 145 CR 876: §47.3
Scott, People v (1987) 194 CA3d 550, 239 CR 588: §32.7
Scott, People v (1959) 176 CA2d 458, 1 CR 600: §27.4
Scripps Health v Superior Court (2003) 109 CA4th 529, 135 CR2d 126: §34.9
Seastone, People v (1969) 3 CA3d 60, 82 CR 907: §30.4

Seaton v Spence (1963) 215 CA2d 761, 30 CR 510: §20.4
See v City of Seattle (1967) 387 US 541, 18 L Ed 2d 943, 87 S Ct 1737: §28.11
Seering v Department of Social Servs. (1987) 194 CA3d 298, 239 CR 422: §§20.12, 20.18
Seffert v Los Angeles Transit Lines (1961) 56 C2d 498, 15 CR 161: §56.6
Segretti v State Bar (1976) 15 C3d 878, 126 CR 793: §46.2
Seidenberg v George (1946) 76 CA2d 306, 172 P2d 891: §14.1
Seimon v Southern Pac. Transp. Co. (1977) 67 CA3d 600, 136 CR 787: §§29.7, 29.9, 29.11
Selby, People v (1926) 198 C 426, 245 P 426: §27.9
Self v General Motors Corp. (1974) 42 CA3d 1, 116 CR 575, overruled on other grounds in 8 C4th at 580: §§20.7, 29.6
Sena v Turner (1961) 195 CA2d 487, 15 CR 857: §5.14
Sepulveda v Ishimaru (1957) 149 CA2d 543, 308 P2d 809: §29.45
Shade Foods, Inc. v Innovative Products Sales and Mktg. (2000) 78 CA4th 847, 93 CR2d 364: §32.2
Shadow Traffic Network v Superior Court (1994) 24 CA4th 1067, 29 CR2d 693: §35.8
Sharer, People v (1964) 61 C2d 869, 40 CR 851: §47.6
Sharp v Hoffman (1889) 79 C 404, 21 P 846: §26.4
Shaw v Bolduc (Me 1995) 658 A2d 229: §22.10
Sheldon, Estate of (1977) 75 CA3d 364, 142 CR 119: §19.24
Shelton v American Motors Corp. (8th Cir 1986) 805 F2d 1323: §34.5
Shepherd v Superior Court (1976) 17 C3d 107, 130 CR 257: §§33.29, 43.1, 43.6, 46.2, 46.11
Shepherd v Walley (1972) 28 CA3d 1079, 105 CR 387: §32.2
Shipley v Permanente Hosp. (1954) 127 CA2d 417, 274 P2d 53, disapproved on another ground in 50 C2d at 773: §29.35

Shippy v Peninsula Rapid Transit Co. (1925) 197 C 290, 240 P 785: §29.26
Shirley, People v (1982) 31 C3d 18, 181 CR 243: §§18.21, 19.11, 20.12-20.14
Shoen v Shoen (9th Cir 1995) 48 F3d 412: §§48.3, 48.7
Shoen v Shoen (9th Cir 1993) 5 F3d 1289: §48.7
Shooker v Superior Court (2003) 111 CA4th 923, 4 CR3d 334: §34.22
Short v Frink (1907) 151 C 83, 90 P 200: §4.19
Silkwood v Kerr-McGee Corp. (10th Cir 1977) 563 F2d 433: §48.2
Silva v Dias (1941) 46 CA2d 662, 116 P2d 496: §10.4
Silva, People v (2001) 25 C4th 345, 106 CR2d 93: §§6.27, 6.29
Silva, People v (1988) 45 C3d 604, 247 CR 573: §19.14
Simek v Superior Court (1981) 117 CA3d 169, 172 CR 564: §37.8
Simmons v Southern Pac. Transp. Co. (1976) 62 CA3d 341, 133 CR 42: §§2.17, 15.5, 29.5-29.7, 29.11, 53.3, 56.6
Simmons v U.S. (1968) 390 US 377, 19 L Ed 2d 1247, 88 S Ct 967: §46.17
Simon v Steelman (1990) 224 CA3d 1002, 274 CR 218: §19.13
Simon, People v (1989) 208 CA3d 841, 256 CR 373: §§29.17, 29.46
Simon, People v (1986) 184 CA3d 125, 228 CR 855: §32.7
Sims, People v (1958) 165 CA2d 108, 331 P2d 799: §47.7
Sinclair v Aquarius Elec. (1974) 42 CA3d 216, 116 CR 654: §45.2
Singletary v Kelley (1966) 242 CA2d 611, 51 CR 682: §49.5
Sinohui, People v (2002) 28 C4th 205, 120 CR2d 783: §41.13
Siripongs, People v (1988) 45 C3d 548, 247 CR 729: §§29.7, 31.4
Skinner v Railway Labor Executives' Ass'n (1989) 489 US 602, 103 L Ed 2d 639, 109 S Ct 1402: §§28.11, 47.3
Slivinsky v Watkins-Johnson Co. (1990) 221 CA3d 799, 270 CR 585: §25.7
Slocum, People v (1975) 52 CA3d 867, 125 CR 442: §56.4
Slone, People v (1978) 76 CA3d 611, 143 CR 61: §17.2
Smith v Board of Supervisors (2002) 104 CA4th 1104, 128 CR2d 700: §28.11
Smith v Covell (1980) 100 CA3d 947, 161 CR 377: §§2.5, 29.5, 29.35, 29.46
Smith v Laguna Sur Villas Community Ass'n (2000) 79 CA4th 639, 94 CR2d 321: §34.5
Smith v Lewis (1975) 13 C3d 349, 118 CR 621: §26.3
Smith v Lockheed Propulsion Co. (1967) 247 CA2d 774, 56 CR 128: §§20.4, 20.7
Smith v Smith (1935) 7 CA2d 271, 46 P2d 232: §§6.20, 6.39
Smith v Superior Court (1968) 68 C2d 547, 68 CR 1: §57.12
Smith v Superior Court (1981) 118 CA3d 136, 173 CR 145: §37.3
Smith v Superior Court (1980) 110 CA3d 422, 168 CR 24: §46.16
Smith v Thomas (1898) 121 C 533, 54 P 71: §49.6
Smith, People v (2003) 30 C4th 581, 134 CR2d 1: §19.11
Smith, People v (1993) 21 CA4th 342, 25 CR2d 850: §§6.28, 6.31
Smith, People v (1989) 215 CA3d 19, 263 CR 678: §§19.36, 20.12
Smith, People v (1989) 214 CA3d 904, 263 CR 155: §19.23
Smith, People v (1973) 33 CA3d 51, 108 CR 698, overruled on other grounds in 22 C3d at 327 n7: §§2.3, 30.2, 30.5
Smith, People v (1970) 13 CA3d 897, 91 CR 786: §§18.14, 46.6
Smith, People v (1956) 142 CA2d 287, 298 P2d 540: §§20.6, 47.3
Sneed v Marysville Gas & Elec. Co. (1906) 149 C 704, 87 P 376: §18.25
Snow, People v (2003) 30 C4th 43, 132 CR2d 271: §17.2
Snow, People v (1987) 44 C3d 216, 242 CR 477: §6.32
Soldal v Cook County (1992) 506 US 56, 121 L Ed 2d 450, 113 S Ct 538: §§28.2, 28.4
Solin v O'Melveny & Myers (2001) 89 CA4th 451, 107 CR2d 456: §34.1
Solis v Southern Cal. Rapid Transit Dist. (1980) 105 CA3d 382, 164 CR 343: §20.8
Solomos, People v (1978) 83 CA3d 945, 148 CR 248: §47.5

Son, People v (2000) 79 CA4th 224, 93 CR2d 871: §20.7
Sonoma, County of v Grant W. (1986) 187 CA3d 1439, 232 CR 471: §§19.26, 20.7
Soto, People v (1999) 21 C4th 512, 88 CR2d 34: §20.13
South Bay Irr. Dist. v California-American Water Co. (1976) 61 CA3d 944, 133 CR 166: §20.28
Southern Cal. Edison Co., People v (1976) 56 CA3d 593, 128 CR 697: §18.22
Specht v Keitel (1961) 190 CA2d 332, 12 CR 95: §54.4
Spectra-Physics, Inc. v Superior Court (1988) 198 CA3d 1487, 244 CR 258: §34.5
Spencer, In re (1965) 63 C2d 400, 46 CR 753: §37.9
Spencer, People v (1969) 71 C2d 933, 80 CR 99: §19.12
Spencer, People v (1984) 153 CA3d 931, 200 CR 693: §47.5
Spevack v Klein (1967) 385 US 511, 17 L Ed 2d 574, 87 S Ct 625: §§46.4, 46.11
Spurgeon v Buchter (1961) 192 CA2d 198, 13 CR 354: §25.10
St. Andrew, People v (1980) 101 CA3d 450, 161 CR 634: §§18.21–18.22
Stankewitz, In re (1985) 40 C3d 391, 220 CR 382: §§18.27, 29.41
Stanley, People v (1986) 187 CA3d 248, 232 CR 22, disapproved on another ground in People v Bennett (1991) 54 C3d 1032, 2 CR2d 8: §29.7
Stanwood v Carson (1915) 169 C 640, 147 P 562: §4.20
Stanworth, People v (1969) 71 C2d 820, 80 CR 49: §30.4
Staples v Hoefke (1987) 189 CA3d 1397, 235 CR 165: §§19.13, 20.8, 32.6
Starr, People v (1970) 11 CA3d 574, 89 CR 906: §§27.7, 27.10
State Farm Fire & Cas. Co. v Eddy (1990) 218 CA3d 958, 267 CR 379: §32.5
State ex rel Dep't of Transp. v Superior Court (Hall) (1985) 37 C3d 847, 210 CR 219: §43.4
Steccone, People v (1950) 36 C2d 234, 223 P2d 17: §17.7
Steele v Langmuir (1976) 65 CA3d 459, 135 CR 426: §25.8
Steelhammer, U.S. v (4th Cir 1976) 539 F2d 373, rev'd in part on reh'g en banc (4th Cir 1977) 561 F2d 539: §48.2
Stein v Superior Court (1959) 174 CA2d 21, 344 P2d 406: §§41.6, 41.22
Steiny & Co. v California Elect. Supply Co. (2000) 79 CA4th 285, 93 CR2d 920: §45.1
Stephenson v Kaiser Found. Hosps. (1962) 203 CA2d 631, 21 CR 646: §20.7
Stevens v Parke, Davis & Co. (1973) 9 C3d 51, 107 CR 45: §29.18
Stevenson v Link (1954) 128 CA2d 564, 275 P2d 782: §53.3
Stevenson, People v (1970) 4 CA3d 443, 84 CR 349: §29.46
Stewart v Marvin (1956) 139 CA2d 769, 294 P2d 114: §13.7
Stewart, U.S. v (SD NY 2003) 287 F Supp 2d 461: §34.22B
Stickel v San Diego Elec. Ry. (1948) 32 C2d 157, 195 P2d 416: §§5.10, 5.14
Stoll, People v (1989) 49 C3d 1136, 265 CR 111: §§20.12, 20.18
Stone v Foster (1980) 106 CA3d 334, 164 CR 901: §§29.9, 29.18
Stoneking v Briggs (1967) 254 CA2d 563, 62 CR 249: §19.6
Story v Superior Court (2003) 109 CA4th 1007, 135 CR2d 532: §37.2
Stout, People v (1967) 66 C2d 184, 57 CR 152: §47.6
Strickland, People v (1974) 11 C3d 946, 114 CR 632: §§22.6, 29.7
Stritzinger, People v (1983) 34 C3d 505, 194 CR 431: §§19.11, 36.13, 37.15
Stromerson v Averill (1940) 39 CA2d 118, 102 P2d 571: §26.3
Sturm (People v Superior Court) (1992) 9 CA4th 172, 11 CR2d 652: §35.4
Subpoena to Testify Before the Grand Jury, In re (Alexiou) (9th Cir 1994) 39 F3d 973: §34.9
Sudduth, People v (1966) 65 C2d 543, 55 CR 393: §47.3
Suezaki v Superior Court (1962) 58 C2d 166, 23 CR 368: §34.9
Sullivan v Superior Court (1972) 29 CA3d 64, 105 CR 241: §33.12
Sullivan, People v (1922) 59 CA 633, 211 P 467: §6.20

Summers v A.L. Gilbert Co. (1999) 69 CA4th 1155, 82 CR2d 162: §§20.7, 20.28
Sundlee, People v (1977) 70 CA3d 477, 138 CR 834: §19.3
Superior Court, People v (1955) 137 CA2d 194, 289 P2d 813: §55.2
Superior Court, People v (Barker) (1965) 232 CA2d 178, 42 CR 651: §46.10
Superior Court, People v (Barrett) (2000) 80 CA4th 1305, 96 CR2d 264: §§43.4, 43.9
Superior Court, People v (Biggs) (1971) 19 CA3d 522, 97 CR 118: §§43.8, 43.13
Superior Court, People v (Crook) (1978) 83 CA3d 335, 147 CR 856: §46.15
Superior Court, People v (Howard) (1968) 69 C2d 491, 72 CR 330: §55.2
Superior Court, People v (Kaufman) (1974) 12 C3d 421, 115 CR 812: §§46.16-46.17
Superior Court, People v (Sturm) (1992) 9 CA4th 172, 11 CR2d 652: §35.4
Susan T., Conservatorship of (1994) 8 C4th 1005, 36 CR2d 40: §§28.2, 28.4-28.5, 28.12
Sutter, People v (1982) 134 CA3d 806, 184 CR 829: §46.18
Swacker, U.S. v (9th Cir 1980) 628 F2d 1250: §46.19
Swift v Winkler (1957) 148 CA2d 927, 307 P2d 666: §§6.39, 6.50, 29.4
Szeto, People v (1981) 29 C3d 20, 171 CR 652: §§20.8, 31.7, 33.29

T

Tabatha G., In re (1996) 45 CA4th 1159, 53 CR2d 93: §37.2
Taggart v Super Seer Corp. (1995) 33 CA4th 1697, 40 CR2d 56: §19.26
Tahl, People v (1967) 65 C2d 719, 56 CR 318: §19.23
Tahoe Nat'l Bank v Phillips (1971) 4 C3d 11, 92 CR 704, modifying Lee v Gregoriou (1958) 50 C2d 502, 326 P2d 135: §25.12
Takencareof, People v (1981) 119 CA3d 492, 174 CR 112: §19.13
Talle, People v (1952) 111 CA2d 650, 245 P2d 633: §§47.1, 47.5

Tanuvasa v City & County of Honolulu (Haw App 1981) 626 P2d 1175: §28.7
Tarantin v Superior Court (1975) 48 CA3d 465, 122 CR 61: §46.17
Tarasoff v Regents of Univ. of Cal. (1976) 17 C3d 425, 131 CR 14: §37.10
Taylor v Bell (1971) 21 CA3d 1002, 98 CR 855: §§3.8, 10.4
Taylor, People v (1982) 31 C3d 488, 183 CR 64: §54.3
Taylor, People v (1992) 5 CA4th 1299, 7 CR2d 676: §6.16
Taylor, People v (1986) 180 CA3d 622, 225 CR 733: §§1.11, 23.4
Tealer, People v (1975) 48 CA3d 598, 122 CR 144: §47.7
Tedesco, People v (1934) 1 C2d 211, 34 P2d 467: §29.37
Tennessee v Street (1985) 471 US 409, 85 L Ed 2d 425, 105 S Ct 2078: §19.5
Terrell, People v (1955) 138 CA2d 35, 291 P2d 155: §19.26
Terry, People v (1970) 2 C3d 362, 85 CR 409, overruled on another ground in People v Carpenter (1997) 15 C4th 312, 63 CR2d 1: §29.28
Terry W., In re (1976) 59 CA3d 745, 130 CR 913: §33.3
Thiel v Southern Pac. Co. (1946) 328 US 217, 90 L Ed 1181, 66 S Ct 984: §6.2
Thomas v Buttress & McClellan, Inc. (1956) 141 CA2d 812, 297 P2d 768: §53.2
Thomas, People v (1974) 43 CA3d 862, 118 CR 226: §46.10
Thompson v Friendly Hills Regional Med. Ctr. (1999) 71 CA4th 544, 84 CR2d 51: §56.4
Thompson, People v (1980) 27 C3d 303, 165 CR 289: §17.2
Thompson, People v (1982) 133 CA3d 419, 184 CR 72: §§50.4-50.5, 51.4-51.5
Thompson, U.S. v (9th Cir 1987) 827 F2d 1254: §6.30
Thor v Boska (1974) 38 CA3d 558, 113 CR 296: §31.17
Thoroman v David (1926) 199 C 386, 249 P 513: §25.3
Thourwald, People v (1920) 46 CA 261, 189 P 124: §47.7
Tibbetts, People v (1929) 102 CA 787, 283 P 830: §6.35

Times Mirror Co. v Superior Court (1991) 53 C3d 1325, 283 CR 893: §43.1

Tingley v Times Mirror Co. (1907) 151 C 1, 89 P 1097: §§29.14, 56.6

Tolbert, People v (1969) 70 C2d 790, 76 CR 445: §§6.35, 6.43

Toomes v Nunes (1938) 24 CA2d 395, 75 P2d 94: §52.9

Tornay v U.S. (9th Cir 1988) 840 F2d 1424: §34.9

Torres v Municipal Court (1975) 50 CA3d 778, 123 CR 553: §34.9

Torres v Superior Court (2000) 80 CA4th 867, 95 CR2d 686.: §43.6

Torrey v Shea (1916) 29 CA 313, 155 P 820: §25.9

Tossman v Newman (1951) 37 C2d 522, 233 P2d 1: §5.5

Toth, People v (1960) 182 CA2d 819, 6 CR 372: §26.8

Touhy, U.S. ex rel v Ragen (1951) 340 US 462, 95 L Ed 417, 71 S Ct 416: §§43.7, 44.7

Towler, People v (1982) 31 C3d 105, 181 CR 391: §44.9

Tracy L., In re (1992) 10 CA4th 1454, 13 CR2d 593: §46.15

Travis v Southern Pac. Co. (1962) 210 CA2d 410, 26 CR 700: §26.6

Trejo, People v (1990) 217 CA3d 1026, 266 CR 266: §6.12

Trevino, People v (1985) 39 C3d 667, 217 CR 652, disapproved on other grounds in 47 C3d at 1291: §§6.29, 29.44

Triple A Mach. Shop v State (1989) 213 CA3d 131, 261 CR 493: §34.6

Truckenmiller, Estate of (1979) 97 CA3d 326, 158 CR 699: §19.24

Truman v Vargas (1969) 275 CA2d 976, 80 CR 373: §§20.4, 20.7

Trummel v U.S. (1980) 445 US 40, 63 L Ed 2d 186, 100 S Ct 906: §51.1

Turner v Mannon (1965) 236 CA2d 134, 45 CR 831: §52.11

Turner v Marshall (9th Cir 1995) 63 F3d 807, overruled on other grounds in 182 F3d at 677: §6.28

Turner v Safely (1987) 482 US 78, 96 L Ed 2d 64, 107 S Ct 2254: §40.4

Turner, People v (1990) 50 C3d 668, 268 CR 706: §30.2

Twiggs v Superior Court (1983) 34 C3d 360, 194 CR 152: §44.2

U

U.S. Coin & Currency, U.S. v (1971) 401 US 715, 28 L Ed 2d 434, 91 S Ct 1041: §§46.4, 47.2

U.S. ex rel Touhy v Ragen (1951) 340 US 462, 95 L Ed 417, 71 S Ct 416: §§43.7, 44.7

U.S. v _____ (see name of defendant)

Uhler v Superior Court (1953) 117 CA2d 147, 256 P2d 90: §57.12

United Sav. & Loan Ass'n v Reeder Dev. Corp. (1976) 57 CA3d 282, 129 CR 113: §§5.10, 31.14

Upjohn Co. v U.S. (1981) 449 US 383, 66 L Ed 2d 584, 101 S Ct 677: §34.7

Upshaw, People v (1974) 13 C3d 29, 117 CR 668: §§56.2, 56.5

Uram v Abex Corp. (1990) 217 CA3d 1425, 266 CR 695: §19.13

Uribe v Howie (1971) 19 CA3d 194, 96 CR 493: §45.2

V

Valerio v Andrew Youngquist Constr. (2002) 103 CA4th 1264, 127 CR2d 436: §19.13

Valles, People v (1979) 24 C3d 121, 154 CR 543: §29.45

Valley Bank v Superior Court (1975) 15 C3d 652, 125 CR 553: §33.3

Vargas, People v (1975) 53 CA3d 516, 126 CR 88: §§33.15, 34.16

Venegas, People v (1998) 18 C4th 47, 74 CR2d 262: §§20.7, 20.13

Vichroy, People v (1999) 76 CA4th 92, 90 CR2d 105: §32.7

Villarino, People v (1970) 7 CA3d 56, 86 CR 338: §42.5

Vindiola, People v (1979) 96 CA3d 370, 158 CR 6: §30.5

Vinson v Superior Court (1987) 43 C3d 833, 239 CR 292: §37.8

Visciotti, People v (1992) 2 C4th 1, 5 CR2d 495: §6.16

Vogt v McLaughlin (1959) 172 CA2d 498, 342 P2d 481: §§2.18, 29.9

Vomaska v City of San Diego (1997) 55 CA4th 905, 64 CR2d 492: §29.44A

Von Villas, People v (1992) 10 CA4th 201, 13 CR2d 62: §48.7

Vorse v Sarasy (1997) 53 CA4th 998, 62 CR2d 164: §31.3
Vu, People v (1991) 227 CA3d 810, 278 CR 153: §20.18

W

W.C. Cook & Co. v White Truck & Transfer Co. (1932) 124 CA 721, 13 P2d 549: §4.10
Wade v Terhune (9th Cir 2000) 202 F3d 1190: §6.28
Wade, People v (1959) 53 C2d 322, 1 CR 683, overruled on another ground in People v Carpenter (1997) 15 C4th 312, 63 CR2d 1: §§27.11, 32.7
Wade, U.S. v (1967) 388 US 218, 18 L Ed 2d 1149, 87 S Ct 1926: §46.6
Wagner v Benson (1980) 101 CA3d 27, 161 CR 516: §§31.2–31.3, 31.17
Wagner v Doulton (1980) 112 CA3d 945, 169 CR 550: §§29.36, 29.38
Wagner v Glendale Adventist Med. Ctr. (1989) 216 CA3d 1379, 265 CR 412: §25.7
Wagner, People v (1975) 13 C3d 612, 119 CR 457: §§26.8, 29.9
Wahlefeld, Estate of (1930) 105 CA 770, 288 P 870: §4.19
Waidla, People v (2000) 22 C4th 690, 94 CR2d 396: §§19.23, 30.3
Wainwright v Greenfield (1986) 474 US 284, 88 L Ed 2d 623, 106 S Ct 634: §33.29
Waite v Godfrey (1980) 106 CA3d 760, 163 CR 881: §20.3
Walker v Nitzberg (1970) 13 CA3d 359, 91 CR 526: §52.5
Walker, People v (1948) 33 C2d 250, 201 P2d 6: §11.3
Wallace, People v (1993) 14 CA4th 651, 17 CR2d 721: §20.12
Waller v Southern Cal. Gas Co. (1959) 170 CA2d 747, 339 P2d 577: §16.5
Waller v Southern Pac. Co. (1967) 66 C2d 201, 57 CR 353: §20.20
Walter v Ayvazian (1933) 134 CA 360, 25 P2d 526: §29.37
Walter v U.S. (1980) 447 US 649, 65 L Ed 2d 410, 100 S Ct 2395: §28.3
Waples, People v (2000) 79 CA4th 1389, 95 CR2d 45: §32.7

Ward, People v (1999) 71 CA4th 368, 83 CR2d 828: §20.18
Ward, People v (1968) 266 CA2d 241, 72 CR 46: §56.2
Ware, People v (1924) 67 CA 81, 226 P 956: §20.3
Warner v O'Connor (1962) 199 CA2d 770, 18 CR 902: §56.1
Warner, People v (1905) 147 C 546, 82 P 196: §6.37
Warner, People v (1969) 270 CA2d 900, 76 CR 160: §19.5
Warner Constr. Corp. v City of Los Angeles (1970) 2 C3d 285, 85 CR 444: §§4.8, 29.11, 32.2
Warren, People v (1984) 161 CA3d 961, 207 CR 912: §§33.11, 46.7
Wash, People v (1993) 6 C4th 215, 24 CR2d 421: §29.7
Washington, People v (1979) 95 CA3d 488, 157 CR 58: §17.4
Washington, People v (1968) 263 CA2d 814, 70 CR 80: §52.11
Washington, U.S. v (1977) 431 US 181, 52 L Ed 2d 238, 97 S Ct 1814: §47.2
Watenpaugh v State Teachers' Retirement (1959) 51 C2d 675, 336 P2d 165: §52.12
Watson, People v (1956) 46 C2d 818, 299 P2d 243: §§26.3, 29.9
Watson, People v (1989) 213 CA3d 446, 261 CR 635: §19.11
Watt Indus. v Superior Court (1981) 115 CA3d 802, 171 CR 503: §35.7
Watters, People v (1927) 202 C 154, 259 P 442: §27.4
Weathers v Kaiser Found. Hosps. (1971) 5 C3d 98, 95 CR 516: §§19.6, 29.35, 29.45–29.46
Webb v Standard Oil Co. (1957) 49 C2d 509, 319 P2d 621: §43.7
Webber v Webber (1948) 33 C2d 153, 199 P2d 934: §§29.30–29.31
Weber v Leuschner (1966) 240 CA2d 829, 50 CR 86: §19.5
Webster v Board of Dental Examiners (1941) 17 C2d 534, 110 P2d 992: §28.5
Wehling v Columbia Broadcasting Sys. (5th Cir 1979) 608 F2d 1084: §46.11
Weisbart v Flohr (1968) 260 CA2d 281, 67 CR 114: §29.7

Welborn, People v (1966) 242 CA2d 668, 51 CR 644: §29.23

Welfare Rights Org. v Crisan (1983) 33 C3d 766, 190 CR 919: §34.8

Weller v American Broadcasting Co. (1991) 232 CA3d 991, 283 CR 644: §20.4

Weller v Chainarria (1965) 233 CA2d 234, 43 CR 364: §31.7

Wells Fargo Bank v Superior Court (2000) 22 C4th 201, 91 CR2d 716: §§34.22B, 35.3

Wempe, Estate of (1921) 185 C 557, 197 P 949: §52.5

West Coast Home Improvement Co. v Contractor's State License Bd. (1945) 72 CA2d 287, 164 P2d 811: §47.2

Westbrook v Gordon H. Ball, Inc. (1967) 248 CA2d 209, 56 CR 422: §32.5

Weston v Kernan (1995) 50 F3d 633: §29.45

Wetmore, People v (1978) 22 C3d 318, 149 CR 265: §27.2

Whalen v Municipal Court (1969) 274 CA2d 809, 79 CR 523: §46.6

Wharton, People v (1991) 53 C3d 522, 280 CR 631: §37.10

Wheeler v St. Joseph Hosp. (1976) 63 CA3d 345, 133 CR 775: §16.4

Wheeler, People v (1992) 4 C4th 284, 14 CR2d 418: §§1.6, 1.11, 21.4, 22.8, 31.4, 47.4

Wheeler, People v (1978) 22 C3d 258, 148 CR 890: §§6.2, 6.19, 6.27–6.29, 6.31–6.32, 6.50

Wheeler, People v (2003) 105 CA4th 1423, 129 CR2d 916: §19.18

Wheeler, People v (1966) 243 CA2d 340, 52 CR 508: §46.7

Whelchel, People v (1967) 255 CA2d 455, 63 CR 258: §46.2

White, People v (1984) 161 CA3d 246, 207 CR 266: §40.4

White, U.S. v (1944) 322 US 694, 88 L Ed 1542, 64 S Ct 1248: §§46.2, 46.7

Whitfield v Roth (1974) 10 C3d 874, 112 CR 540: §§29.14, 29.45

Whitman v Superior Court (1991) 54 C3d 1063, 2 CR2d 160: §§1.7, 19.38

Wicktor v County of Los Angeles (1960) 177 CA2d 390, 2 CR 352: §53.5

Wiese v Rainville (1959) 173 CA2d 496, 343 P2d 643: §8.3

Willden v Washington Nat'l Ins. Co. (1976) 18 C3d 631, 135 CR 69: §53.2

William G., In re (1985) 40 C3d 550, 221 CR 118: §28.11

Williams v Bridges (1934) 140 CA 537, 35 P2d 407: §29.35

Williams v City of Los Angeles (1988) 47 C3d 195, 252 CR 817: §46.4

Williams v Goodman (1963) 214 CA2d 856, 29 CR 877: §29.5

Williams v Superior Court (1989) 49 C3d 736, 263 CR 503: §6.2

Williams v Superior Court (1974) 38 CA3d 412, 112 CR 485: §44.2

Williams, People v (1997) 16 C4th 153, 66 CR2d 123: §20.7

Williams, People v (1988) 44 C3d 883, 245 CR 336: §20.4

Williams, People v (1981) 29 C3d 392, 174 CR 317: §§2.5, 6.35, 6.45, 29.35

Williams, People v (1976) 16 C3d 663, 128 CR 888, superseded by statute (Evid C 1294) on other grounds as stated in People v Martinez (2003) 113 CA4th 400, 7 CR3d 49: §4.8

Williams, People v (1973) 9 C3d 24, 106 CR 622: §19.11

Williams, People v (1969) 71 C2d 614, 79 CR 65: §47.3

Williams, People v (2000) 79 CA4th 1157, 94 CR2d 727: §22.2

Williams, People v (1994) 26 CA4th Supp 1, 31 CR2d 769: §§6.28, 6.31

Williams, People v (1988) 199 CA3d 469, 245 CR 61: §6.20

Williams, People v (1979) 93 CA3d 40, 155 CR 414: §19.29

Williams, People v (1960) 187 CA2d 355, 9 CR 722: §19.26

Williams, People v (1942) 55 CA2d 696, 131 P2d 851: §§29.21, 29.27

Willis v Superior Court (1980) 112 CA3d 277, 169 CR 301: §34.9

Willis, People v (Apr. 4, 2002; S096349) 2002 Cal LEXIS 2011: §6.31

Willson v Superior Court (1924) 66 CA 275, 225 P 881: §§45.1, 45.3

Wilson v Gilbert (1972) 25 CA3d 607, 102 CR 31: §§32.5, 32.8

Wilson v Phillips (1999) 73 CA4th 250, 86 CR2d 204: §§20.14, 20.18

Wilson v Superior Court (1976) 63 CA3d 825, 134 CR 130: §43.12

Wilson, People v (1944) 25 C2d 341, 153 P2d 720: §20.20
Wilson, People v (1941) 46 CA2d 218, 115 P2d 598: §13.11
Wilson, U.S. v (1975) 421 US 309, 44 L Ed 2d 186, 95 S Ct 1802: §46.15
Winston v Lee (1985) 470 US 753, 84 L Ed 2d 662, 105 S Ct 1611: §47.3
Wong v State Bar (1975) 15 C3d 528, 125 CR 482: §28.6
Wong, People v (1973) 35 CA3d 812, 111 CR 314: §§27.2, 27.4
Woodberry, People v (1970) 10 CA3d 695, 89 CR 330: §52.6
Woolman, People v (1974) 40 CA3d 652, 115 CR 324: §43.13
Worthington, People v (1974) 38 CA3d 359, 113 CR 322: §40.17
Wright v Eastlick (1899) 125 C 517, 58 P 87: §29.39
Wright, People v (1990) 52 C3d 367, 276 CR 731: §§6.13, 6.24, 6.31, 29.45
Wysock v Borchers Bros. (1951) 104 CA2d 571, 232 P2d 531: §4.16

Y

Yorba, People v (1989) 209 CA3d 1017, 257 CR 641: §20.13

Young v Brunicardi (1986) 187 CA3d 1344, 232 CR 588: §29.41
Young v Evans (1944) 62 CA2d 365, 144 P2d 651: §54.5
Yu, People v (1983) 143 CA3d 358, 191 CR 859: §1.4

Z

Zack, People v (1986) 184 CA3d 409, 229 CR 317: §§19.5, 19.13
Zal v Steppe (9th Cir 1992) 968 F2d 924: §2.5
Zarafonitis v Yellow Cab Co. (1932) 127 CA 607, 16 P2d 141: §4.8
Zellerino v Brown (1991) 235 CA3d 1097, 1 CR2d 222: §§2.3, 2.6
Zerilli v Smith (DC Cir 1981) 656 F2d 705: §48.2
Zerillo, People v (1950) 36 C2d 222, 223 P2d 223: §§26.4, 26.8
Zibbell v Southern Pac. Co. (1911) 160 C 237, 116 P 513: §29.45
Zingarelli, People v (1934) 137 CA 61, 29 P2d 905: §42.6

Table of References

Appeals and Writs in Criminal Cases (2d ed Cal CEB 2000): §§4.6, 5.4, 47.1
Bell, Arthur S. Bell's Searches, Seizures and Bugging Compendium. Woodland Hills, CA: Court Compendiums, 1970: §28.1
Bennett, Cathy E., Robert B. Hirschhorn & Jo–Ellan Dimitrius. Bennett's Guide to Jury Selection and Trial Dynamics in Civil and Criminal Litigation. San Francisco: Bancroft–Whitney, 1992: §6.1
California Administrative Hearing Practice (2d ed Cal CEB 1997): §§1.2, 28.6, 28.11
California Civil Appellate Practice (3d ed Cal CEB 1996): §§2.18, 29.31, 55.1
California Civil Discovery Practice. 2 vols (3d ed Cal CEB 1998): §§34.2, 35.5, 35.7
California Civil Litigation Forms Manual. 2 vols (Cal CEB 1980): §§3.7, 54.2
California Civil Procedure Before Trial. 3 vols (3d ed Cal CEB 1990): §§3.7, 54.2
California Civil Writ Practice (3d ed Cal CEB 1996): §§55.1, 55.3
California Criminal Law Forms Manual (Cal CEB Annual): §§6.10, 54.15
California Criminal Law Procedure and Practice (5th ed Cal CEB 2000): §§1.2, 1.7, 1.12, 6.1, 6.4, 6.16, 17.5, 18.5, 19.13, 22.8, 27.1, 28.1, 29.15, 29.17, 29.43, 30.3, 32.7, 33.11, 34.15, 43.8, 44.1, 46.1, 46.13, 47.1, 54.1, 55.3, 57.10
California Decedent Estate Practice. 3 vols (Cal CEB 1986-1987): §§34.20, 36.19, 37.16
California Expert Witness Guide (2d ed Cal CEB 1991): §§15.4, 20.7, 20.19, 20.25-20.26, 21.19, 34.2, 35.1, 35.3, 35.7
California Judicial Council Forms Manual (Cal CEB Annual): §6.10
California Judges Benchbook: Civil Trials (Cal CJER 1981): §§4.16, 6.5, 20.19, 29.2-29.3, 29.14-29.15, 29.22, 29.35-29.36, 29.38-29.39, 29.42-29.43, 29.45-29.46, 53.2, 54.1-54.2, 56.1-56.2, 57.5, 57.12
California Personal Injury Proof (Cal CEB 1970): §36.9
California Trial Practice: Civil Procedure During Trial. 3 vols (3d ed Cal CEB 1995): §§4.20, 5.4, 6.1, 29.3, 29.17, 29.30, 29.46, 34.12, 34.22, 54.1, 56.1
California UCC Sales and Leases. 2 vols (Cal CEB 2002): §§25.2, 25.7, 25.10
Chernow, Eli. Courtroom Evidence. Encino, CA: Rutter Group, 1993: §31.1
Cleary, Edward. McCormick's Handbook of the Law of Evidence. St. Paul, MN: West Publishing, 3d ed 1984: §§13.3, 17.2, 17.8, 19.36, 19.41, 26.2
Competitive Business Practices (2d ed Cal CEB 1991): §§45.2, 45.4
Effective Direct and Cross–Examination (Cal CEB 1986): §26.1
Effective Introduction of Evidence in California (2d ed Cal CEB 2000): §22.8
Eisenberg, Jon B., Ellis J. Howvitz, & Howard B. Wiener. California Practice Guide: Civil Appeals and Writs. 2 vols. Encino, CA: Rutter Group, 1989: §55.1
Federal Judicial Center. Reference Manual of Scientific Evidence, 1995: §20.10
Ginger, Ann Fagan. Jury Selection in Civil and Criminal Trials. Tiburon, CA: Lawpress Corp., 2d ed 1984-1985: §6.1
Hunter, Robert. Federal Trial Handbook. 2 vols. Rochester, NY: Lawyer's Cooperative Publishing, 3d ed 1993: §§2.1, 2.5
Jefferson, Bernard S. Jefferson's California Evidence Benchbook. 2 vols (3d ed CJA–CEB 1997): §§19.14, 19.16-19.17, 19.27, 20.28, 25.3, 34.2, 35.3, 51.4
LaFave, Wayne. Search and Seizure: A Treatise on the Fourth Amendment. St. Paul, MN: West Publishing, 3d ed 1996: §28.1
National Jury Project. Jurywork: Systematic Techniques. New York: Clark Boardman, 2d ed 1983: §6.4

Practicing California Judicial Arbitration (Cal CEB 1983): §1.2
Purver, Jonathan M., Douglas R. Young, & James J. Davis. California Trial Handbook. San Francisco: Bancroft–Whitney, 2d ed 1987: §20.26
Schreiber, Sol, ed. Civil Practice and Litigation in Federal and State Courts. 2 vols. Philadelphia: ALI–ABA, 6th ed 1994: §35.1
Stanbury, Raymond C. California Trial and Appellate Practice. St. Paul, MN: West Publishing, 1958: §29.16
Trade Secrets Practice in California (2d ed Cal CEB 1996): §45.2
Wegner, William E., Robert K. Fairbank, & Norman L. Epstein. California Practice Guide, Civil Trials and Evidence. Encino, CA: Rutter Group, 1993: §6.1
Weil, Robert I., & Ira A. Brown, Jr. California Practice Guide: Civil Procedure Before Trial. 2 vols. Encino, CA: Rutter Group, 1983: §35.1
Wigmore, John H. Evidence in Trials at Common Law. 13 vols. Boston: Little, Brown, 4th ed 1961-1988: §§19.36, 34.1
———. Evidence in Trials at Common Law. 11 vols. Boston: Little, Brown, 3d ed 1940: §§13.12, 25.3
Witkin, Bernard E. California Evidence. 3 vols. San Francisco: Bancroft–Whitney, 4th ed 2000: §§1.3, 3.7, 4.7, 4.10, 4.16, 4.19-4.20, 5.4, 13.3, 17.2, 17.8, 19.11, 19.19, 19.42, 20.18, 25.2, 25.10, 26.2-26.3, 26.6, 26.9, 27.7, 29.7, 29.23, 31.11, 32.2, 32.5, 32.7, 33.1-33.3, 33.9, 33.17, 33.22, 34.2-34.3, 34.9, 34.15-34.18, 35.3, 36.1-36.3, 37.1, 40.2-40.3, 41.2, 41.22, 42.3, 43.4-43.6, 43.8, 43.13, 46.1, 46.15, 46.19, 47.1, 50.1, 52.3, 52.5, 52.8, 52.11, 52.14, 53.5
———. California Procedure. 10 vols. San Francisco: Bancroft–Whitney, 4th ed 1997: §§3.7, 6.1, 29.2-29.3, 29.15, 29.22, 29.35, 29.43, 29.46, 34.12, 54.2, 54.13, 56.1-56.2
———. Summary of California Law. 13 vols. San Francisco: Bancroft–Whitney, 9th ed 1987: §§34.8, 36.2
——— & Norman L. Epstein. California Criminal Law. 6 vols. San Francisco: Bancroft–Whitney, 3d ed 2000: §§27.1-27.2, 27.11, 28.1, 29.17, 46.13, 56.5

Table of Forms

In limine motion, 2.19
Order in limine, 2.20

Index

The symbol "f" after a section number indicates that a form appears in the section.

Abuse of Children. See **Child Abuse**

Accident Reports. See **Motor Vehicles**

Administrative Proceedings
Defendant's privilege not to be called and not to testify, inapplicability in administrative proceeding to suspend or revoke license, 47.2
Exclusion of evidence
  Confessions and admissions illegally obtained, exclusion of, 28.10
  Search and seizure. See **Search and Seizure**
Kelly test for admission of scientific evidence, applicability in administrative hearings, 20.12

Administrators. See **Executors and Administrators**

Admissibility of Evidence
See also **Evidence**; **Exclusion of Evidence**
Character evidence. See **Character Evidence**
Conditional admission of evidence
  Generally, 5.3, 15.6, 17.7, 21.11, 21.16
  Confessions or admissions, 27.11
  Motion to strike. See **Strike, Motion to**
  Testimony, 3.6
Domestic violence, admissibility of similar acts of, 32.7
Expert testimony. See **Experts**
Foundational or preliminary facts supporting. See **Foundational or Preliminary Facts**
Habit or custom, admissibility of evidence to show, 32.7
Hearsay. See **Hearsay**
Inflammatory evidence. See **Inflammatory Evidence**
In limine motion seeking admission of evidence, 2.7
Insufficient foundation for. See **Insufficient Foundation, Objections to**
Jury admonition concerning evidence admitted for limited purpose. See **Jury Admonitions**
Jury instruction on limited admissibility. See **Jury Instructions**
Learned treatise, admissibility of, 22.10
Narrative answers, inadmissible matter contained in, 10.2
Objections to evidence. See **Evidence**
Opinion testimony. See **Opinion Testimony**
Order of proof distinguished from ruling on admissibility of evidence ruling, 3.9
Parol evidence rule. See **Parol Evidence Rule**
Prior convictions, admissibility of, 17.5
Prior inconsistent statement, requirements for admissibility of, 19.31A, 22.5
Privilege. See **Privilege**
Proposition 8, effect of, 1.6, 17.4, 38.1
Relevant evidence. See **Relevant Evidence**
Scientific evidence. See **Scientific Evidence**
Secondary evidence rule. See **Secondary Evidence Rule**
Stipulations. See **Stipulations**
Striking inadmissible evidence. See **Strike, Motion To**
Transcripts. See **Transcripts**
Writs
  Correcting erroneous ruling by trial court on admissibility of evidence, availability of writ for, 55.2, 55.7
  Issue of admissibility resolved by, 33.22

Admissions. See **Confessions and Admissions**

Admonitions
Attorney, admonishment of, 6.47, 29.7
Jury admonitions. See **Jury Admonitions**

Affidavits and Declarations
Business records, sufficiency of custodian's declaration as foundation for, 19.26
Contempt sought by nonjudge, affidavit presented to judge to initiate indirect contempt proceedings, 57.5, 57.7
Continuance, motion for, 54.7
Jurors impeaching verdict. See **Incompetent Witnesses**
Misconduct of attorney, influencing jurors to submit false affidavits, 29.8
Misconduct of juror, affidavits or declarations by jurors to prove, 18.20, 29.46
Voir dire, affidavit to prove juror lied during, 18.27

Age
Competency of witness, effect of age on, 18.1

Agents
Attorney-client privilege, inapplicability to attorney acting as business agent, 34.3
Trade secrets privilege claimed by owner's agent, 45.4

Alcohol
See also **Drugs**
Lay witness opinion regarding intoxication, 20.4
Misconduct of jurors to consume alcohol during trial or deliberations, 29.44

Alternatives to Objecting
Combining series of objections
  Generally, 4.10
  Adoptive objections, 4.12
  Continuing objections, 4.11
  Summary objections, 4.13
Compound question, alternative to objecting to, 8.5
Impeachment of witness, 4.14
Inability of witness to communicate, 18.7
Lack of personal knowledge on part of witness, alternative to objecting to, 18.25
Not objecting, 4.9
Secondary evidence rule, 24.7
Weighing alternatives, importance of, 4.1

Ambiguities
Appellate court's interpretation of ambiguous ruling on objection supporting verdict, 4.20
Parol evidence, admissibility to resolve ambiguities in agreement, 25.8

Ambiguous or Unintelligible Questions
Analysis of problem, 7.3
Dangers presented by, 7.2
Defined, 7.1
Stating objecting, 7.6
Statutory authority for objection, 7.5

Amendments and Modifications
Continuance of trial as result of amended charging instrument, 54.3
Parol evidence, admissibility to show subsequent modifications to agreement, 25.11

Appeals
See also **Writs**
Contempt, appellate review of, 57.4, 57.12
Continuance, appeal of trial judge's ruling on motion for, 54.13
Criminal defendant's privilege not to be called and not to testify
  Codefendants, defendant's refusal to be called by, 47.2
  Denial of privilege as grounds for appeal, 47.1
Cross-examination
  Improperly sustained objection on cross-examination, reversal of, 5.5
  Scope of cross-examination, appeal of judge's determination of, 26.4
Hypothetical question, failure to object resulting in waiver on appeal, 20.20

Appeals—*cont.*
Inability of witness to understand duty to tell truth, appeal of judge's ruling, 18.10
In limine motions. See **In Limine Motions**
Invited error doctrine, effect on appeal, 4.8
Journalist's refusal to disclose information, appellate review of contempt citation, 48.19
Misconduct of counsel, appeal based on, 29.11, 29.18
Misconduct of judge, appeal from ruling as remedy for, 29.31
Mistrial, review of order granting or denying motion for, 56.1
Offer of proof
  Generally, 5.4
  Cross-examination, reversal of improperly sustained objection on, 5.5
Order of proof, appeal of ruling determining, 3.1
Peremptory challenges, appellate review of trial court's ruling on discriminatory use of, 6.32
Privilege, appeal of ruling on claim of, 33.17
Record on appeal
  Exclusion of evidence under Evid C §352, record for appeal on, 31.16
  Objection to preserve record on appeal, 4.2, 4.20
Scientific evidence, standard of review for *Daubert* hearing, 20.16
Voir dire
  Incorrect statement of law during voir dire, appeal on grounds of, 6.35
  Reversal of judgment based on voir dire rulings, 6.50

Arbitration
Impeachment, admissibility of arbitration testimony for, 22.11A
Incompetence of arbitrator to testify as witness. See **Incompetent Witnesses**
Privilege. See **Privilege**

Argument
Argumentative objections, prohibition against, 4.13
Evid C §352, argument on exclusion of evidence under, 31.15
Judge's power to close argument, 57.4
Misconduct of attorney, improper actions during closing argument constituting, 29.7
Speaking objections. See **Speaking Objections**

Argumentative Questions
Defined, 14.1
Examples of argumentative question, 14.2
Stating objection, 14.4
Statutory authority for objection, 14.3

Asked and Answered Objection
Alternatives to objecting. See **Alternatives to Objecting**
Cumulative evidence, ask and answered objection distinguished from objection, 11.1, 31.6
Dangers presented by question, 11.2
Defined, 11.1
Discretion of trial court to allow repetitive questions, 11.3
Stating objection, 11.6
Statutory authority for objection, 11.4

Assuming Facts in Dispute or Not in Evidence
Conditional admission of evidence, 15.6
Cross-examination, question asked on, 15.4
Dangers presented by question, 15.2
Direct examination, question assuming facts in dispute or not in evidence characterized as leading question, 15.3
Examples of questions, 15.5
Miscellaneous remedies, 15.7
Question defined, 15.1
Stating objection, 15.9
Statutory authority for objection, 15.8

Attorney-Client Privilege
Generally, 34.1
Corporation as client
  Generally, 34.5
  Current and former corporate employees, ex parte contact with, 34.6
  Dissolution of corporation, termination of attorney-client privilege on, 34.21

Attorney-Client Privilege—*cont.*
Corporation as client—*cont.*
Dominant purpose rule, determining applicability of privilege to communications transmitted between corporate client's employees and attorneys, 34.9
Upjohn decision, effect on communications between corporate employees and in-house counsel, 34.7
Waiver of privilege by corporation's representative, 34.22
Exceptions to privilege
Generally, 34.14
Breach of attorney-client duty, 34.16
Business agent, attorney acting as, 34.3
Crime or fraud, assistance of attorney sought in committing, 34.15
Deceased client, claim of privilege through, 34.18–34.19
Joint clients, subsequent litigation between, 34.17
Statutory basis for exceptions, 34.25
Guardians or conservators. See **Guardianship and Conservatorship**
Illustrations of privilege, 34.26
Joint clients
Exception to privilege for subsequent litigation between, 34.17
Waiver of privilege by one client, effect on other client, 34.22
Judges
Exclusion of privileged information by judge, 34.13, 34.20
Ruling on claim of privilege (see Ruling on claim of privilege, below)
Persons who can claim privilege
Client or client's representative, 34.11
Duty of attorney to claim privilege on client's behalf, 34.12
Exclusion of privileged information by judge, 34.13, 34.20
Holder of privilege, 33.4, 34.4, 34.20
Psychiatric examination by request of patient's attorney, applicability of attorney-client privilege to, 37.1
Public entity. See **Public Entities and Employees**
Requirements for existence of privilege
Communications protected by privilege, 34.9
Confidentiality of communication, 34.10
Corporation as client (see Corporation as client, above)
Individual as client, 34.4
Persons or entities qualifying as attorney, 34.8
Professional consultation of attorney by client, 34.3
Ruling on claim of privilege
Burden of proof concerning claim of privilege, 34.10, 34.24
Procedure for obtaining ruling on claim of privilege, 34.23
Stating claim of privilege
Attorney-witness, claim of privilege on behalf of client by, 34.28
Client's claim of privilege, 34.27
Trial counsel's claim of privilege on behalf of client, 34.29
Statutory basis for privilege, 34.25
Termination of privilege
Death of client, effect of, 34.20
Dissolution of organization client, termination of privilege on, 34.21
Types of protection, 35.2
Waiver of privilege
Generally, 34.22
Business agent or adviser, privilege waived by attorney acting as, 34.3
Failure to claim privilege as waiver, 34.22A
Joint defense agreements, effect of, 34.22B, 35.8
Mediation, waiver by disclosures made to mediator in course of, 33.3A, 34.10A
Work product doctrine distinguished, 34.2, 35.2

Attorney-General
Subpoena issued to journalist, Attorney General's authorization required for, 48.4

Attorneys
Admonishment of, 6.47, 29.7
Cleric's privilege, attorney's objection to evidence based on, 51.14
Contempt. See **Contempt**

Attorneys—*cont.*
Deposition of opposing counsel, foundation required for, 34.5
Disparagement of counsel, misconduct by judge, 29.27
Domestic violence victim-counselor privilege, attorney's objection to evidence based on, 39.16
Incompetence of counsel, appeal based on, 4.8
Informer, prosecuting attorney's claim of privilege for identity of, 44.15
In limine motions. See **In Limine Motions**
Jury admonitions, request for. See **Jury Admonitions**
Marital communications privilege, attorney's objection to evidence based on, 40.23
Misconduct of attorneys. See **Misconduct of Attorneys**
Official information privilege claimed by attorney, 43.18
Penalties. See **Penalties**
Penitent's privilege, attorney's objection to evidence based on, 50.14
Physician-patient privilege, attorney's objection to question based on, 36.26
Privileges to be exercised at trial, role of counsel in deciding, 33.8
Psychotherapist-patient privilege, attorney's objection to question based on, 37.23
Self-incrimination, attorney stating or supporting claim of privilege against, 46.8
Sexual assault victim-counselor privilege, attorney's objection to evidence based on, 38.16
Speaking objections. See **Speaking Objections**
Spouse, party's attorney asserting privilege not be called as witness against, 42.22
Spouse, trial counsel asserting privilege not to testify against. See **Spouse, Privilege Not To Testify Against**
State Bar. See **State Bar**
Trade secrets privilege, attorney's objection to evidence based on, 45.10
Trial tactics. See **Trial Tactics**
Voir dire. See **Voir Dire Examination of Jurors; Voir Dire Examination of Witnesses**
Voter's privilege, attorney's objection to evidence based on, 49.12
Witness, attorney as
  Informed consent of client required for attorney to testify as witness, 18.2, 18.14
  Question and answer testimony by attorney-witness, 10.4
  Rules of Professional Conduct concerning attorney acting as advocate and testifying, 18.15
  Stating objection, 18.16
  Statutory basis for allowing attorney to testify, 18.15
Work product doctrine. See **Work Product Doctrine**

Attorneys' Fees
Contemnor, payment of fees by, 57.9
In limine motion, fees assessed against party violating, 2.17
Sliding scale recovery agreements, disclosure to jury of, 32.2

Automobiles. See **Motor Vehicles**

Bad Acts. See **Similars**

Bad Faith
Prosecutorial misconduct, establishing bad faith not required, 29.2

Best Evidence Rule. See **Secondary Evidence Rule**

Bias and Prejudice
See also **Discrimination; Inflammatory Evidence**
Argumentative question creating improper bias, 14.1
Business records, exclusion on grounds of undue prejudice, 19.26
Cross-examiner's introduction of inadmissible evidence to offset effect of highly prejudicial evidence, 26.6
Cumulative evidence, court's analysis of prejudicial effect versus probative value of, 31.7

Bias and Prejudice—*cont.*
Evid C §352, exclusion of evidence under
Balancing probative value of offered evidence against potential prejudicial effect and undue consumption of time, 31.12, 31.17
Civil trials, exclusion of unduly prejudicial evidence in, 31.3
Criminal trials, exclusion of unduly prejudicial evidence in, 31.4
Foundational evidence, dangers of undue prejudice if judge fails to rule on, 21.9
In limine motion to exclude prejudicial evidence. See **In Limine Motions**
Misconduct of attorneys. See **Misconduct of Attorneys**
Mistrial, motion on grounds of prejudice. See **Mistrial**
Peremptory challenges, bias in use of. See **Jury Trial**
Sanctions for impropriety and prejudicial effect of introducing inadmissible evidence, 52.11
Selection of jurors. See **Jury Trial**

Bifurcated Proceedings
Time for order bifurcating trial of issue, 3.7

Bigamy
Spouse, exception to privilege not to testify against in bigamy action, 41.13, 41.25

Border Inspections. See **Custom Agents**

Briefs. See **Trial Briefs**

Burden of Proof
See also **Proof**
Generally, 21.3
Attorney-client privilege, burden of proof for claim of, 34.10, 34.24
Cleric's privilege, burden of proof on person claiming, 51.10
Domestic violence victim-counselor privilege, burden of proof, 39.12
Exclusionary rule, burden of proof on party invoking exception to, 5.2
Foundational evidence on existence of preliminary facts, burden of proof, 17.7, 21.15
Holder of privilege authorizing disclosure of information, burden of proof on proponent of evidence, 33.16
Impeachment evidence, burden on proponent to show admissibility of, 32.5
Informer, burden of proof in claiming privilege for identity of, 44.11
Learned treatise, burden of proof on party offering text as, 22.10
Marital communications privilege, burden of proof on person claiming, 40.19
Official information privilege, burden of proof claim of, 43.14
Penitent's privilege, burden of proof on claimant, 50.10
Peremptory challenge of prospective juror, burden of proof to provide race-neutral explanation of, 6.28
Physician-patient privilege, burden of proof for claim of, 36.22
Presumption affecting burden of proof, effect of, 1.3
Privilege, burden of proving exception to, 21.8, 33.18, 33.31
Psychotherapist-patient privilege, burden of proof, 37.4, 37.19
Secondary evidence rule, printed representation of computer information, 24.5
Self-incrimination, burden on person claiming privilege against, 46.20
Sexual assault victim-counselor privilege, burden of proof, 38.12
Similar offense, burden of proof regarding, 32.7
Spouse, burden of proof for privilege not to be called as witness against, 42.18
Spouse, burden of proof for privilege not to testify against, 41.24
Trade secrets privilege, burden of proof regarding claim of, 45.7
Voter's privilege, burden of proof regarding claim of, 49.8

Business Records
Hearsay rule, exception to, 19.12, 19.26

Business Records—*cont.*
Secondary evidence rule. See **Secondary Evidence Rule**

Chambers, Conference in
Cleric's privilege, confidential disclosure of documents in chambers in order to rule on, 51.9
Confidential disclosure of privileged information, court-ordered, 33.17
Evidentiary problems, in chambers discussion of, 21.9
Hypothetical questions for expert witness, request for review and circulation of, 15.4
Informer, in camera hearing on identity of, 44.2, 44.10
Offer of proof in chambers outside presence of jury, 5.9
Official information, disclosure in chambers prior to ruling on privilege against nondisclosure, 43.13
Trade secret, in camera disclosure of, 45.6
Work product protection, court's review of documents in camera to determine applicability of, 35.7, 35.9

Character Evidence
Generally, 22.8, 23.4
Cross-examination of witness concerning criminal defendant's prior misconduct, 26.8
Hearsay rule, exception to, 19.34
Opinion testimony, 20.28
Restrictions on character evidence in criminal cases, 1.11
Similar acts or occurrences, admissibility of, 32.7

Charts, Checklists, Questionnaires, and Tables
Hearsay problems, checklist of, 19.42
Juror questionnaires, 6.4, 6.10, 6.51–6.52
Objections to evidence, checklist of, 1.13
Responses to objections, checklist of, 5.1

Child Abuse
Domestic violence victim-counselor privilege, court compelled disclosure of privileged information despite, 39.10
Hearsay rule, exception for statements of minor children in action for sexual abuse, 19.17
Kelly test for admission of scientific evidence, applicability in child abuse cases, 20.13, 20.18
Physician-patient privilege, exception for reporting suspected child abuse, 36.13
Psychotherapist-patient privilege, child abuse exception, 36.13, 37.15

Child Dependency Proceedings
Hearsay exception, 19.17
Use immunity, 46.17

Children. See **Minors**

Child Support
Spouse, exception to privilege not to testify against, 41.15

Cleric's Privilege
See also **Penitent's Privilege**
Generally, 51.1
Confessions privilege superseded by, 51.1
Illustrations of privilege, 51.12
Judges (see Ruling on privilege, below)
Persons who may claim privilege, 51.6
Requirements for existence of privilege
Communication between penitent and cleric, 51.4
Confidentiality of communication between penitent and cleric, 51.5
Penitent defined, 51.3
Penitential communication received by cleric, 51.2
Ruling on privilege
Burden of proof regarding claim of privilege, 51.10
Procedure for obtaining ruling on privilege, 51.9
Stating claim of privilege
Attorney's objection to evidence based on cleric's privilege, 51.14
Witness's claim of privilege, 51.13

Cleric's Privilege—cont.
  Statutory authority for privilege, 51.11
  Termination of privilege, death of cleric resulting in, 51.7
  Waiver of privilege
    Generally, 51.8
    Burden of proof regarding waiver, 51.10

Coercion
  Attorney-client privilege, effect of coercion on waiver of, 34.22
  Sexual assault victim-counselor privilege, effect of coercion on waiver of, 38.9

Competency
    See also **Incompetent Witnesses**
  Conservatorship. See **Guardianship and Conservatorship**
  Hearsay rule, exception involving incapacitated witness, 19.11
  Juror's competency, hearing on, 29.45
  Marital communications privilege, inapplicability in action involving spouse's competency, 40.11
  Opinion testimony regarding testator's sanity, 20.3, 20.28
  Physician-patient privilege, exception for proceedings concerning patient's competency, 36.14
  Spouse's competency, exception to privilege not to testify against spouse in actions involving, 41.11

Compound Questions
  Alternatives to objecting, 8.5
  Dangers presented by, 8.2
  Defined, 8.1
  Examples of compound questions, 8.3
  Stating objection, 8.6
  Statutory authority for objection, 8.4

Compromise. See **Settlement**

Computers
  Business records, computer printouts as, 19.26
  Secondary evidence rule, application to computer information, 24.5

Conditional Admission of Evidence. See **Admissibility of Evidence**

Conferences
  Bench conference requested to object to question asked by judge, 4.17
  Chambers, conference in. See **Chambers, Conference in**
  Sidebar conference, objections during voir dire decided at, 6.7

Confessional, Privilege of. See **Cleric's Privilege; Penitent's Privilege**

Confessions and Admissions
  Generally, 21.7
  Conditional admission of confessions or admissions, 27.11
  Criminal conduct, admission of, 21.8
  Hearsay rule, exceptions to. See **Hearsay**
  Illegally obtained confessions and admissions
    Exclusion of, 28.10
    Stating objection to, 28.14
  Jury, determining admissibility of confession or admission outside presence of, 21.9
  Settlement negotiations, exclusion of admissions made during, 21.8
  Unverified pleading as party admission, 19.13

Confidentiality
  Conference in chambers, confidential disclosure of privileged information in, 33.17
  Motor vehicle accident reports, confidentiality of, 43.4
  Privilege. See **Privilege**

Conjecture. See **Speculative Answers, Questions Calling for**

Consent
  Attorney testifying as witness, client's informed consent required for, 18.2, 18.14
  Spouse's consent to being called as witness by adverse party resulting in waiver of privilege not to be called as witness against spouse, 42.14

Conservatorships. See **Guardianship and Conservatorship**

Conspiracy
Hearsay rule exception for admission by co-conspirator, 19.16

Constitutional Law
Body examination, constitutional right against, 47.3
Business records, constitutional grounds for exclusion in criminal case, 19.26
Continuance versus right to speedy trial, 54.1
Criminal cases, application of constitutional law to, 1.12
Criminal defendant's privilege not to be called and not to testify, 47.1
Hearsay exception subject to constitutionally protected right to confrontation, 19.2
Journalist's constitutional right not to disclose information. See **Journalist's Immunity From Contempt**
Peremptory challenges, unconstitutionality of discriminatory use of, 6.27
Privacy, constitutional right to, 33.3
Search and seizure, constitutional basis for objecting to, 28.3
Self-incrimination, constitutional basis for privilege against, 46.2
Sex offense case, use of propensity evidence, 32.7

Construction and Interpretation
See also **Definitions**
Ambiguous rulings on objections, construction by appellate courts in support of verdict, 4.20
Fourth amendment, 28.3
Hearsay rule, exception for publications, 19.36
Joint defense privilege, 34.22B, 35.8
Journalist's constitutional privilege not to disclose information, *Mitchell* factors, 48.5
Parol evidence, admissibility to aid agreement's interpretation, 25.7
Prejudice under Evid C, §352, 31.3–31.4

Wheeler rule, 6.27, 6.30

Contempt
Generally, 57.1
Appellate review of contempt order, 57.4, 57.12
CCP §1209, contempt procedures under
  Direct contempt, judge's response to, 57.6
  Hybrid contempt, 57.8
  Indirect contempt, 57.5, 57.7
  Sentence, 57.9
Civil and criminal contempt distinguished, 57.3
Defendant's privilege not to be called and not to testify, applicability in contempt proceedings, 47.2
Defined, 57.2
Examples of contemptuous trial conduct, 57.4
Habeas corpus, review of contempt order by writ of, 33.22
In limine motion, contempt penalty for violation of, 2.17
Journalist's immunity from contempt. See **Journalist's Immunity From Contempt**
Jury trial, no right to, 57.7
Misconduct of attorney, contempt as remedy for, 29.15
Procedures
  CCP §1209 (see CCP §1209, contempt procedures under, above)
  Pen C §166, procedures under, 57.10
  Persons who can initiate contempt proceedings, 57.5
Statutory basis for contempt penalty, 57.2
Stay of contempt
  Generally, 57.11
  Writ to stay contempt order, 55.5, 57.12
Types of contempt, 57.3

Continuance
Generally, 54.1
Civil cases, procedure for obtaining continuance in
  Appeal of trial judge's ruling on motion, 54.13
  Depositions. See **Depositions**
  Expenses, judge's discretion to award as condition of continuance, 54.11

Continuance—*cont.*
   Civil cases, procedure for obtaining continuance in—*cont.*
      Factors considered by judge in deciding motion for continuance, 54.9
      Form of motion, 54.7
      Jury fee deposit, court's retention of, 54.12
      New trial motion, effect of failure to move for continuance on, 54.14
      Stipulations (see Stipulations, below)
   Criminal law, procedure for continuance
      Generally, 54.15
      Conditional examination of material witness, 54.16
      Preliminary hearing, writ review of continuance of, 54.17
   Discretion of court. See **Discretion of Court**
   Good cause for continuance, requirement of
      Civil trials, continuance disfavored in, 54.2
      Criminal trials, 54.3
   Judges. See **Judges**
   Preliminary hearing, writ review of continuance of, 54.17, 55.7
   Sanctions
      Generally, 54.1
      Procedures for obtaining continuance in criminal case, sanction for failure to follow, 54.15
   Stipulations
      Generally, 54.2
      Avoiding continuance by stipulating to testimony, 54.8
   Surprise evidence as grounds for
      Genuineness of surprise, 54.4
      Relevant opposing evidence, requirement that party requesting continuance show availability of, 54.5
      Undisputed evidence, continuance unnecessary for, 54.6

Continuing Objections
   Generally, 4.11
   Request for ruling on record, 4.10

Contracts. See **Parol Evidence Rule**

Corporations
   Attorney-client privilege. See **Attorney-Client Privilege**
   Self-incrimination, inapplicability of privilege to corporations, 46.2, 46.7
   Work product doctrine, applicability to investigations performed within corporation, 35.1

Corpus Delicti Rule
   Generally, 27.1
   Circumstantial evidence, establishing corpus delicti by, 27.4
   Conditional admission of confessions or admissions, 27.11
   Elements of crime, requirements of independent proof of, 27.1–27.2, 27.4
   Examples of situations requiring objection, 27.3
   Judge, determination by
      Generally, 27.6
      Separate determination by judge and jury, 27.5
   Jury, determination by
      Corpus delicti, determination of, 27.8
      Guilt, determination of, 27.9
      Separate determination by judge and jury, 27.5, 27.7
      Separating jury's determinations, difficulty of, 27.10
   Stating objection, 27.12

Costs
   See also **Expenses and Expenditures; Fees**
   Continuance granted on condition of costs award, 54.11
   In limine motion
      Costs of bringing motion, 2.9
      Ruling on motion, costs assessed against party violating, 2.17

Court Reporters
   Asked and answered question, requesting court reporter to read, 11.3
   Conditionally admitted evidence, reporter's notation of beginning and ending of, 52.5
   Transcripts. See **Transcripts**

Credibility of Witnesses. See **Impeachment of Witnesses; Rehabilitation of Witnesses**

Criminal Defendant's Privilege Not To Be Called and Not To Testify
See also **Self-Incrimination, Privilege Against**
Generally, 33.13, 47.1
Appeals. See **Appeals**
Assertion of privilege, 47.5
Comment on or inference from failure to testify, rule against, 47.6
Deciding whether to testify, 47.4
Definition of criminal proceeding, 33.31
Grand jury proceedings, inapplicability of privilege in, 47.2
Judges
   Advising unrepresented defendant of privilege, 47.5
   Commission on Judicial Performance, inapplicability of privilege in proceedings before, 47.2
   Ruling on claim of privilege, 47.8
Prior testimony, effect of privilege on introduction of, 47.7
Requirements for existence of privilege
   Prosecution of defendant, 47.2
   Testimonial or communicative evidence, applicability of privilege to, 47.3
Stating objection based on privilege, 47.10
Statutory basis for privilege, 47.1, 47.9
Waiver of privilege, 47.7

Criminal Law
Attorney-client privilege, exception if attorney's services sought in committing crime, 34.15
Attorney testifying as witness, denial of due process in prohibiting, 18.14
Character evidence. See **Character Evidence**
Constitutional rights. See **Constitutional Law**
Contempt as misdemeanor. See **Contempt**
Continuance. See **Continuance**
Corpus delicti rule. See **Corpus Delicti Rule**
Cross-examination of criminal defendants, constitutional privileges affecting, 26.8
Death penalty, bifurcated trial for, 3.8
Defendant's privilege not to be called. See **Criminal Defendant's Privilege Not To Be Called and Not To Testify**
Discovery restrictions in criminal actions. See **Discovery**
Evidence Code, applicability of
   Generally, 1.9
   Exclusion of evidence under Evid C §352, 31.4
   Provisions inapplicable in criminal trials, 1.11
   Provisions of Code that differ in criminal trials, 1.10
Fingerprinting, 47.3
Guilty plea, inadmissibility of offer to enter, 32.4
Hearsay. See **Hearsay**
Impeachment of witness with criminal convictions, 22.8
Informer, identity of. See **Informer, Privilege for Identity of**
Journalist's immunity from contempt for refusal to disclose information. See **Journalist's Immunity From Contempt**
Marital communications privilege. See **Marital Communications Privilege**
Misdemeanors. See **Misdemeanors**
Official information privilege. See **Official Information Privilege**
Order of proof. See **Order of Proof**
Peremptory challenges in criminal trial, prohibition against discriminatory use of, 6.27
Physician-patient privilege, exception in criminal proceedings. See **Physician-Patient Privilege**
Preliminary hearings. See **Preliminary Hearings**
Prior convictions. See **Prior Convictions**
Prior criminality, exclusion of similar bad acts to prove, 32.7
Proposition 8. See **Proposition 8**
Proposition 115, 1.7
Psychotherapist appointed by judge to examine criminal defendant, 37.9
Psychotherapist-patient privilege. See **Psychotherapist-Patient Privilege**
Rehabilitation of witness. See **Rehabilitation of Witnesses**

Criminal Law—*cont.*
  Relevancy issues
    Generally, 1.5, 17.2, 17.4
    Prior convictions, admissibility of, 17.5
    Proposition 8, 1.6
    Proposition 115, 1.7
    Third party defense, admissibility of evidence to support, 17.6
  Search and seizure. See **Search and Seizure**
  Self-incrimination. See **Self-Incrimination, Privilege Against**
  Similars, 32.7
  Size of jury, waiver regarding, 6.13
  Spouse, privilege not to be called as witness against spouse. See **Spouse, Privilege Not To Be Called as Witness Against**
  Spouse, privilege not to testify against. See **Spouse, Privilege Not To Testify Against**
  Stipulations. See **Stipulations**
  Vicinage, drawing jury panel in criminal case from, 6.4
  Voir dire examination of jurors in criminal case. See **Voir Dire Examination of Jurors**
  Work product doctrine
    Applicability of doctrine in criminal cases, 35.4
    Assistance of attorney in commission of crime or fraud, writings protected by work product doctrine, 35.7
    In camera review of documents to determine applicability of work product protection, 35.9

Cross-Examination
  See also **Direct Examination; Examination of Witnesses**
  Appeals. See **Appeals**
  Assuming facts not in evidence, 15.4
  Defendant's privilege not to testify, effect of cross-examination exceeding scope of direct examination on, 47.7
  Defined, 26.2
  Discretion of trial judge to allow repetitive questions during, 11.3
  Domestic violence victim-counselor privilege, cross-examination of witnesses on issues raised by, 39.11
  Expert witnesses. See **Experts**
  Foundational evidence, cross-examination of witness on, 21.19
  Impeachment of witnesses. See **Impeachment of Witnesses**
  Lack of personal knowledge, cross-examination of witness to show, 18.25
  Leading questions
    Impeachment of witness with leading questions, 13.10
    Improper leading questions during cross-examination, 13.12
    Statutory authority for permitting leading questions on cross-examination, 13.13
  Offer of proof, no requirement of during cross-examination, 5.5
  Opening the door exception
    Limited nature of exception, 26.5
    Offsetting highly prejudicial evidence, 26.6
    Placing evidence in proper context, 26.7
  Scope of cross-examination exceeding direct examination
    Generally, 26.2
    Alternatives to objecting. See **Alternatives to Objecting**
    Criminal defendants, rules on cross-examination of, 26.8
    Determining scope of direct examination, 26.4
    Impeachment of witness, unlimited scope for purposes of, 22.4, 26.3
    Opening the door exception (see Opening the door exception, above)
    Recross-examination, rules affecting, 26.9
  Sexual assault victim-counselor privilege, cross-examination of witnesses on issues raised by, 38.11
  Stating objection, 26.11
  Striking admitted evidence shown to be inadmissible on cross-examination, 52.6
  Types of cross-examination, 26.1

Cumulative Evidence
  Generally, 31.6

Cumulative Evidence—*cont.*
Analysis by court of prejudicial effect and time-consuming nature of evidence versus probative value of evidence, 31.7
Asked and answered objection distinguished, 11.1, 31.6
Illustrations of, 31.8
In limine motion to exclude cumulative evidence, 2.3
Stating objection, 31.10
Statutory basis for objecting to, 31.18
Tactical considerations in objecting to cumulative evidence, 31.9

Custom Agents
Search and seizure of contraband by, 28.11

Custom. See **Habit or Custom**

Damages
Physician-patient privilege, exception in action for damages based on patient's conduct, 36.11

Death
Attorney-client privilege, effect of client's death on, 34.20
Cleric's privilege against disclosure of penitent's confidential communication, cleric's death terminating, 51.7
Decedent's estate. See **Decedent's Estate**
Domestic violence victim-counselor privilege, effect of victim's death on, 39.8
Hearsay rule, exception for statements made by deceased person, 19.17
Marital communications privilege, effect of spouse's death on, 40.16
Penitent's privilege, death of penitent resulting in termination of, 50.7
Physician-patient privilege. See **Physician-Patient Privilege**
Psychotherapist-patient privilege, termination by death. See **Psychotherapist-Patient Privilege**
Sexual assault victim-counselor privilege, effect of victim's death on, 38.8
Ward or conservatee, effect of death on privilege. See **Guardianship and Conservatorship**

Death Penalty
Separate trial for penalty phase, 3.8

Decedent's Estate
Hearsay rule, exception for declarant's statements in action against declarant's estate, 19.25

Declarations Against Interest
Hearsay rule, exception to, 19.8, 19.18

Declarations. See **Affidavits and Declarations**

Defenses
Not guilty by reason of insanity. See **Not Guilty by Reason of Insanity**
Separate trial for certain defenses, 3.7–3.8
Statute of limitations. See **Statutes of Limitations**

Definitions
See also **Construction and Interpretation**
Actual bias, 6.20
Ambiguous or unintelligible questions, 7.1
Argumentative questions, 14.1
Assigning improper statement or conduct as misconduct, 29.12
Assuming facts in dispute or not in evidence, 15.1
Business, 19.26
Challenge method (jury selection), 6.13
Civil contempt, 57.3
Civil proceeding, 33.31
Client, 34.4, 34.25
Collateral matter, 22.3
Compound questions, 8.1
Conditional examination of material witness, 54.16
Confidential communication between attorney and client, 34.25
Confidential communication between domestic assault counselor and victim, 39.13
Confidential communication between patient and physician, 36.3, 36.23

Definitions—*cont.*
  Confidential communication between patient and psychotherapist, 37.3, 37.20
  Confidential communication between sexual assault counselor and victim, 38.13
  Contempt, 57.2
  Corpus delicti, 27.4
  Criminal contempt, 57.3
  Criminal proceeding, 33.31, 36.10
  Cross-examination, 26.2
  Cumulative evidence, 31.6
  Demonstrative evidence, 1.3
  Direct contempt, 29.15, 57.3
  Domestic violence, 39.2
  Domestic violence counselor, 39.13
  Evidence, 1.3
  General acceptance (of scientific evidence), 20.12
  Golden rule argument, 29.5
  Hearsay evidence, 19.1, 19.43
  Holder of (attorney-client) privilege, 34.25
  Holder of (domestic assault victim-counselor) privilege, 39.13
  Holder of (physician-patient) privilege, 36.23
  Holder of (psychotherapist-patient) privilege, 37.20
  Holder of (sexual assault victim-counselor) privilege, 38.13
  Holder of privilege, 33.4
  Hovey voir dire, 6.16
  Hybrid contempt, 29.15, 57.3
  Improper question (on voir dire), 6.52
  Inability of witness to communicate, 18.4
  Inability of witness to understand duty to tell truth, 18.9
  Incompetent witness, 18.1
  Indirect contempt, 29.15, 57.3
  Inference, 1.3
  Inflammatory evidence, 30.1
  In limine motion, 2.2
  Journalist, 48.7
  Jury admonitions, 53.1
  Jury box (method of jury selection), 6.12
  Latent ambiguities, 25.8
  Law, 19.2
  Law enforcement officer, 44.4
  Lawyer, 34.25
  Leading questions, 13.1

  Learned treatise, 22.10
  Marital testimonial privileges, 40.1, 41.1, 42.1
  Matter, 20.8
  Member of the clergy, 50.2, 50.11, 51.2
  Misconduct of counsel, 29.2
  Misquoting witness, 12.1
  Moral turpitude, 31.4
  Narrative answer objection, 10.1
  Offer of proof, 5.4
  Official information, 43.15
  Opinion, 20.1
  Original, 24.2
  Out-of-court statement, 19.3
  Parol evidence rule, 25.1
  Patent ambiguities, 25.8
  Patient, 36.23, 37.20
  Penitent, 50.1, 50.3, 50.11, 51.3
  Penitential communication, 50.11, 51.1
  Perceived by witness, 20.4
  Peremptory challenge, 6.24
  Personal knowledge, 18.21
  Persons, 34.25
  Physical evidence, 1.3
  Physician, 36.23
  Prejudicial evidence, 31.17
  Preliminary fact, 33.17
  Presiding officer, 33.31
  Presumption, 1.3
  Proceeding, 33.31, 41.21
  Proffered evidence, 21.1
  Proof, 1.3
  Proof of criminal agency, 27.2
  Psychiatric personnel, 37.4
  Psychotherapist, 37.2, 37.20
  Public entity, 34.4
  Reiteration requirement, 2.18
  Relevant evidence, 17.1
  Reliable authority (learned treatise), 22.10
  Required records doctrine, 46.6
  Res gestae, 19.41
  Ring-wise expert witness, 52.11
  Search, 28.2
  Self-serving evidence, 19.40
  Sexual assault, 38.13
  Sexual assault victim counselor, 38.13
  Shield law (for journalists), 48.1
  Six pack (method of jury selection), 6.13
  Speaking objections, 7.4
  Speculation, question calling for, 16.1
  Statement, 19.3
  Statute, 32.1, 33.3, 43.4

Definitions—cont.
  Struck juror (method of jury selection), 6.13
  Sua sponte instructions, 53.2
  Sweetheart cross-examination, 13.12
  Too general a question, 9.1
  Trade secret, 45.2
  Transactional immunity, 46.15
  Unavailable witness, 19.11
  Unpublished information, 48.20
  Use and derivative use immunity, 46.15
  Vicinage, 6.4
  Victim (of domestic violence), 39.13
  Victim (of sexual assault), 38.13
  Wheeler rule, 6.27
  Work product, 34.2
  Writ, 55.1
  Writing, 24.2

Delaney Test. See **Journalist's Immunity From Contempt**

Depositions
  Continuance
    Criminal case, deposition of material witness, 54.16
    Opposing party witness's testimony taken by deposition as result of, 54.10
  Foundation required for deposition of opposing counsel, 34.5
  Nonresponsive answer during deposition, effect on motion to strike during trial, 52.17
  Self-incrimination, deponent's claim of privilege against, 46.2
  Spouse, privilege not to be called as witness against. See **Spouse, Privilege Not To Be Called as Witness Against**
  Spouse, privilege not to testify against, 41.8

Direct Examination
  See also **Cross-Examination; Examination of Witnesses**
  Domestic violence victim-counselor privilege, examination of witnesses on issues raised by, 39.11
  Leading questions
    Generally, 4.13, 13.1, 13.4
    Assistance in testifying, witnesses requiring, 13.7

Leading questions—cont.
  Assuming facts in dispute or not in evidence, question characterized as leading question on direct examination, 15.3
  Changed testimony, situations involving, 13.10
  Exhibits, identification of, 13.11
  Expert witnesses, questioning of, 13.8
  Hostile witnesses, questioning of, 13.9
  Preliminary matters, use of leading questions to establish, 13.5
  Refreshing recollection of witness, 13.6
  Stating objection to leading question, 13.15
  Statutory authority for prohibiting leading questions on direct examination, 13.13
Redirect examination
  Leading questions (see Leading questions, above)
  Scope of direct examination, redirect examination limited to, 26.9
Scope of direct examination
  Determination of, 26.4
  Redirect examination, effect on, 26.9
Sexual assault victim-counselor privilege, examination of witnesses on issues raised by, 38.11

Disabled Persons
  Stipulation to presence of disabled juror's assistant in jury room, 6.18

Disclosure
  Journalist's immunity from contempt for nondisclosure of information. See **Journalist's Immunity From Contempt**
  Prior inconsistent statement, disclosure to witness of, 22.6
  Privilege against disclosure of confidential information. See **Privilege**
  Sliding scale recovery agreements, discretion of court concerning disclosure to jury of, 32.2
  Spouse, dissolution of marriage terminating privilege not to be called as witness against, 42.13
  Trade secret, in camera disclosure of, 45.6

Disclosure—cont.
Work product doctrine waived through disclosure of protected material, 33.3A, 34.10A, 35.8

Discovery
Criminal actions
Restrictions on discovery in, 18.5
Writ review of discovery motion granted defendant, 54.17
Depositions. See **Depositions**
Inflammatory evidence, discovery of, 30.3
Medical malpractice case, hospital peer review records immune from discovery in, 20.9
Privilege. See **Privilege**
Sanctions
Contempt penalty for egregious conduct during discovery. See **Contempt**
In limine motion to prohibit use of evidence as sanction for abuse of discovery, 2.6
Self-incrimination privilege in pretrial discovery, court precluding parties in civil action from testifying after invoking, 46.11
Work product doctrine. See **Work Product Doctrine**

Discretion of Court
Collateral matter, discretion of judge to allow or exclude evidence on, 22.3
Continuance motion
Expenses, court's discretion to grant continuance contingent on payment of, 54.11
Grant or denial of motion, judge's discretion concerning, 54.9
Cumulative evidence, discretion of court to exclude, 31.7
Expert, qualifications of, 20.6
Hypothetical questions, court's discretion concerning form of, 20.20
Impeachment of witness with prior inconsistent statement without opportunity to explain, court's discretion to allow, 22.6
Inflammatory evidence, admission of. See **Inflammatory Evidence**
In limine motion, discretion of court in imposing sanctions for violation of, 2.17

Juror challenged for cause, court's discretion on, 6.23
Juror's failure to deliberate, court's discretion regarding investigation of, 29.44A
Lay witness opinion, admissibility of, 20.4
Mistrial, court's discretion in ruling on motion for, 56.4
Narrative testimony, judge's discretion to allow, 10.4
Order of proof, court's discretion to regulate, 3.1, 3.8, 26.2
Peremptory challenges, discretion of court in distinguishing valid reasons for use of, 6.31
Prejudicial evidence, court's discretion to exclude under Evid C §352, 31.2
Prior convictions offered for impeachment of witness, court's discretion to exclude, 21.4
Rehabilitation of witness, admissibility or exclusion of evidence on, 23.2–23.3
Relevancy of evidence, court's discretion in determining, 17.2
Repetitive questions, trial court's discretion to allow, 11.3
Sliding scale recovery agreements, court's discretion on disclosure to jury of, 32.2
Strict liability cases, court's discretion to exclude evidence under Evid C §352, 31.2
Voir dire examination of jurors, court's discretion regarding, 6.16
Witness's ability to understand duty to tell truth, judge's discretion to determine, 18.10
Writ, availability of to correct erroneous ruling by court. See **Writs**

Discrimination
See also **Bias and Prejudice**
Peremptory challenges, discriminatory use of. See **Jury Trial**

Dismissal of Action
Self-incrimination privilege invoked by plaintiff, defendant's motion for dismissal of action based on, 46.11

Disqualification of Jurors. See **Jury Trial**

Dissolution of Marriage
Marital communications privilege, effect of termination of marriage on, 40.2
Spouse, dissolution of marriage terminating privilege not to be called as witness against, 42.13
Spouse, dissolution of marriage terminating privilege not to testify against, 41.16

DNA Testing
Kelly test, applicability to DNA profiling or typing for identification, 20.13

Documentary Evidence
Conditional admission of, 5.3
Self-incrimination, effect of privilege against on production of documents, 46.3

Domestic Violence
Continuance, good cause for, 54.3, 54.15
Similar acts of domestic violence committed by defendant, admissibility of, 32.7

Domestic Violence Victim-Counselor Privilege
Generally, 39.1
Communication or information protected by privilege, 39.3
Illustrations of privilege, 39.14
Judges
 Exclusion of privileged information by, 39.7
 Ruling on privilege (see Ruling on claim of privilege, below)
Persons who may claim privilege
 Counselor's duty to claim privilege on behalf of victim, 39.6
 Holder of privilege, 33.4, 39.5
 Victim or victim's representative, 39.5
Qualifications of counselor, 39.2, 39.13
Relationship between counselor and victim as prerequisite for existence of privilege, 39.2
Ruling on claim of privilege
 Burden of proof for claim of privilege, 39.12
 Court compelled disclosure of privileged information, 39.10, 39.13

Ruling on claim of privilege—*cont.*
 Other issues raised by claim of privilege, resolution of, 39.11
Stating claim of privilege
 Attorney's claim of privilege, 39.16
 Witness's claim of privilege, 39.15
Statutory basis of privilege, 39.13
Termination of privilege
 Death of victim, effect of, 39.8
 Waiver of privilege, 39.9
Third parties, privilege dependent on nondisclosure of confidential information to, 39.4

Drugs
See also **Alcohol**
Sale, admissibility of police officer's opinion on possession of drugs for purposes of, 20.9

Dying Declarations
Hearsay rule, exception to, 19.8, 19.23

Elections. See Voter's Privilege

Employers and Employees
Trade secrets privilege claimed by owner's employee, 45.4

Equitable Issues
Trial of equitable issues before legal issues, 3.7

Error
Admission or exclusion of evidence, availability of writ to correct erroneous ruling by trial court. See **Admissibility of Evidence**
Appeals. See **Appeals**
Impeach witness, analysis of denial of opportunity to, 22.7
Invited error, doctrine of, 4.8
Official information privilege, extraordinary writ as remedy for erroneous denial of, 43.7
Privilege, erroneous denial of. See **Privilege**
Standing to assert claim of error. See **Standing**

Evid C §352. See Exclusion of Evidence

Evid C §403. See Insufficient Foundation, Objections to

Evid C §405. See **Insufficient Foundation, Objections to**

Evidence
See also **Admissibility of Evidence; Exclusion of Evidence**
Assuming facts in dispute or not in evidence. See **Assuming Facts in Dispute or Not in Evidence**
Character evidence. See **Character Evidence**
Checklist of objections, 1.13
Conditional admission of evidence. See **Admissibility of Evidence**
Conference in chambers, discussion of evidentiary problems in, 21.9
Continuance, surprise evidence as grounds for. See **Continuance**
Corpus delicti rule. See **Corpus Delicti Rule**
Cumulative evidence. See **Cumulative Evidence**
Definition of evidence, 1.3
Documentary evidence. See **Documentary Evidence**
Evid C §352, exclusion of evidence under. See **Exclusion of Evidence**
Evidence Code
  Civil cases, applicability of Evidence Code in, 1.8
  Criminal cases. See **Criminal Law**
Foundational or preliminary facts. See **Foundational or Preliminary Facts**
Hearsay. See **Hearsay**
Incompetent evidence, improper objection, 17.8
Inflammatory evidence. See **Inflammatory Evidence**
In limine motions for exclusion of evidence. See **In Limine Motions**
Insufficient foundation for evidence. See **Insufficient Foundation, Objections to**
Invited error, doctrine of, 4.8
Judge's power to comment on evidence. See **Misconduct of Judges**
Objecting to evidence
  Generally, 1.1
  Alternatives to objecting. See **Alternatives to Objecting**

Objecting to evidence—*cont.*
  General objection without stating legal grounds for objection, insufficiency of, 4.8, 4.19
  Invited error, doctrine of, 4.8
  Reasons for not objecting (see Reasons for not objecting to evidence, below)
  Reasons for objecting to evidence, 4.2
  Responding to objections. See **Responses to Objections**
  Ruling on objection, obtaining from trial judge, 4.20
  Specific ground for objection, necessity of stating, 4.18
  Statutory requirements for valid objection, 4.15
  Timeliness of objection, 4.16
  Waiver of error by failure to object, 4.8
  Wording of objection, 4.17
Opinion testimony. See **Opinion Testimony**
Parol evidence rule. See **Parol Evidence Rule**
Peremptory challenges, presenting evidence at hearing on discriminatory use of, 6.28–6.29
Privilege. See **Privilege**
Reasons for not objecting to evidence
  Alienating jury, dangers of, 4.3
  Highlighting harmful evidence, 4.4
  Negligible harm threatened, 4.5
  Reversal on appeal unlikely, 4.6
  Trial judge, objectionable questions asked by, 4.7, 4.17
Relevant evidence. See **Relevant Evidence**
Scientific evidence. See **Scientific Evidence**
Search and seizure. See **Search and Seizure**
Secondary evidence rule. See **Secondary Evidence Rule**
Sexual assault victim-counselor privilege, presentation of evidence on issues raised by claim of, 38.11
Striking evidence. See **Strike, Motion To**

Examination of Witnesses
See also **Cross-Examination; Direct Examination**
Alternatives to objecting. See **Alternatives to Objecting**
Ambiguous or unintelligible questions. See **Ambiguous or Unintelligible Questions**
Argumentative questions. See **Argumentative Questions**
Asked and answered objection. See **Asked and Answered Objection**
Assuming facts in dispute or not in evidence. See **Assuming Facts in Dispute or Not in Evidence**
Compound questions. See **Compound Questions**
Incompetent witness. See **Incompetent Witnesses**
Judges
 Authority of judge to examine witnesses, 3.1
 Misconduct of judge in examination of witnesses or prospective witnesses, 29.24
 Objectionable questions by judge, treatment of, 4.7, 4.17
Leading questions. See **Leading Questions**
Misconduct of attorney during examination of witnesses, 29.6
Misquotation of witness. See **Misquotation of Witness, Objection Based on**
Narrative answer objection. See **Narrative Answer Objection**
Order of examining witnesses
 Generally, 3.5
 Conditional admission of testimony, 3.6
Speculative answers. See **Speculative Answers, Questions Calling for**
Too general a question
 Dangers presented by, 9.2
 Defined, 9.1
 Examples of overly general questions, 9.3
 Stating objection, 9.5
 Statutory authority for objection, 9.4
Unintelligible questions. See **Ambiguous or Unintelligible Questions**

Exclusion of Evidence
See also **Admissibility of Evidence; Evidence**
Generally, 32.1
Administrative proceedings. See **Administrative Proceedings**
Alternatives to objecting. See **Alternatives to Objecting**
Burden of proof on party invoking exception to exclusionary rule, 5.2
Business records, exclusion on grounds of irrelevancy, 19.26
CCP §2034, exclusion of witness for noncompliance with, 22.11
Cleric's privilege. See **Cleric's Privilege**
Defendant's privilege not to be called. See **Criminal Defendant's Privilege Not To Be Called and Not To Testify**
Evid C §352
 Generally, 31.1–31.2
 Appeal, record for, 31.16
 Argument on whether evidence causes undue prejudice, consumption of time, or misleads jury, 31.15
 Confusing issues in case or misleading to jury, grounds for exclusion of evidence, 31.11, 31.15
 Cumulative evidence. See **Cumulative Evidence**
 Inflammatory evidence. See **Inflammatory Evidence**
 Offer of proof by proponent of evidence, 31.14
 Prejudicial evidence. See **Bias and Prejudice**
 Procedure for requesting exclusion of evidence, 31.17
 Search and seizure, Evid C §352 objection used in place of objection to, 28.7
 Stating objection, 31.19
 Striking evidence, motion for, 31.13
 Time-consuming evidence, exclusion of, 31.5
Fraud and deceit, exclusion of evidence obtained by. See **Fraud and Misrepresentation**
Hearsay. See **Hearsay**
Inflammatory evidence. See **Inflammatory Evidence**

Exclusion of Evidence—cont.
In limine motions for exclusion of evidence. See **In Limine Motions**
Liability insurance, exclusion of evidence concerning, 32.6
Offer of proof. See **Offer of Proof**
Penitent's privilege. See **Penitent's Privilege**
Prejudicial evidence. See **Bias and Prejudice**
Prior criminality, exclusion of similars to prove, 32.7
Privilege. See **Privilege**
Rehabilitation of witness, evidence of collateral nature to prove, 23.2
Responding to objections, invoking exceptions to exclusionary rule, 5.2
Scientific evidence. See **Scientific Evidence**
Search and seizure. See **Search and Seizure**
Self-incrimination. See **Self-Incrimination, Privilege Against**
Settlement negotiations. See **Settlement**
Spouse, privilege not to be called as witness against. See **Spouse, Privilege Not To Be Called as Witness Against**
Spouse, privilege not to testify against. See **Spouse, Privilege Not To Testify Against**
Stating objection, 32.11
Statutes authorizing exclusion of evidence, 32.9
Strict liability. See **Strict Liability**
Strike, Motion To. See **Strike, Motion To**
Subsequent safety measures, exclusion of evidence concerning, 32.5

Executors and Administrators
Attorney-client privilege, executor or administrator as holder of, 34.20
Physician-patient privilege
Holder of privilege, executor or administrator as, 36.5
Termination of privilege, 36.19
Psychotherapist-patient privilege, executor or administrator as holder of, 37.5
Sexual assault victim-counselor privilege, decedent's personal representative as holder of, 38.5, 38.9

Exhibits
Jury room, exhibits allowed into, 29.42
Leading questions used to identify exhibit, 13.11
Scientific or technical publications admitted into evidence, prohibition against offering publication as exhibit, 20.25

Expenses and Expenditures
See also **Costs; Fees**
Contemnor, payment of expenses by, 57.9
Continuance granted on condition of paying expenses, 54.11

Experiments
Misconduct of jurors, independent experiments by jurors as, 29.38
Preliminary facts required prior to introduction of evidence of experiments, 21.8

Experts
See also **Opinion Testimony**
Appointment of expert, 20.21
Attorney-client privilege
Communications between client and expert consultant, protection of, 34.9
Party designating himself as expert witness in own case, effect of, 34.22
Basis of expert opinion
Generally, 20.8
Hearsay. See **Hearsay**
Inadmissible matter, expert's reliance on, 20.9
CCP §2034 requirements, 22.11
Court's authority to examine expert witnesses, 3.1
Cross-examination of expert
Court-appointed expert, cross-examination of, 20.21
Learned treatise, cross-examination of expert on, 22.10
Testing expert's opinion testimony through cross-examination, 20.25

Experts—*cont.*
  Cross-examination of third party if expert's opinion based on hearsay, 20.27
  Direct examination of expert witness, use of leading questions on, 13.8
  Examples of expert testimony, 20.7
  Foundational requirements
    Generally, 20.23
    Opinion testimony, foundational requirements for, 21.8
    Qualifications of expert, 20.6
    Speculative testimony by expert witness, laying foundation for, 16.5
    Voir dire of expert regarding qualifications, 21.19
  Hypothetical questions
    Generally, 20.19
    Framing hypothetical question, rules for, 20.20
    Review and circulation of hypothetical questions to judge and counsel before examination of expert witness, 15.4, 20.19
  In limine motions. See **In Limine Motions**
  Mistrial, inappropriate questions asked of expert witness as grounds for, 52.11
  Narrative answer, dangers of questions calling for, 10.2
  Personal knowledge, experts testifying to events not based on, 18.21
  Procedures for testing opinion testimony
    Cross-examination of expert (see Cross-examination of expert, above)
    Foundation examination prior to expert's testimony, 20.23
    Impeachment of expert witness. See **Impeachment of Witnesses**
    Voir dire examination of expert's qualifications, 20.24, 21.19
  Qualifications of expert
    Generally, 20.6
    In limine motion challenging, 4.4
    Voir dire examination of, 20.24, 21.19
  Scientific evidence. See **Scientific Evidence**
  Stating objection to expert witness testimony, 20.31
  Statutory basis for admissibility of expert opinion testimony, 20.22
  Subject matter beyond common experience, rules governing, 20.7
  Treating physician, 22.11
  Work product doctrine
    Opinions of expert, protection for, 35.6
    Report by consulting expert, protection for, 35.8
    Waiver of protection, calling expert as witness resulting in, 35.8

Extraordinary Writs. See **Writs**

Extrinsic Evidence. See **Parol Evidence Rule**

Family Members. See **Relatives**

Fees
  See also **Costs; Expenses and Expenditures**
  Attorneys fees. See **Attorneys' Fees**
  Jury fees, court's retention of after granting motion for continuance, 54.12

Fingerprinting
  Defendant's privilege not to testify, inapplicability to fingerprinting, 47.3

Foreign Countries
  Official information privilege claimed by public entity of foreign country, 43.6

Form of Objection
  Generally, 4.17
  Adoptive objections, 4.12
  Ambiguous or unintelligible objection, 7.6
  Argumentative question, 14.4
  Asked and answered objection, 11.6
  Assuming facts in dispute or not in evidence, 15.9
  Attorney-client privilege. See **Attorney-Client Privilege**
  Attorney testifying as witness, objection to, 18.16
  Cleric's privilege. See **Cleric's Privilege**
  Compound question, 8.6
  Confession or admission illegally obtained, objection to, 28.14
  Continuing objections, 4.11
  Corpus delicti, failure to prove, 27.12

Form of Objection—*cont.*
Criminal defendant's privilege not to be called and not to testify, 47.10
Cross-examination exceeding scope of direct examination, 26.11
Cumulative evidence, objection to, 31.10
Domestic violence victim-counselor privilege. See **Domestic Violence Victim-Counselor Privilege**
Evid C §352, invoking judge's authority to exclude evidence under, 31.19
Exclusion of evidence, statutory basis for, 32.11
Expert testimony, objection to, 20.31
Fraudulently obtained evidence, 28.15
Hearsay evidence, objection to, 19.45
Impeachment of witness improper, objection to, 22.14
Inability of witness to communicate, 18.8
Inability of witness to understand duty to tell truth, 18.13
Inflammatory evidence, objection to, 30.7
Informer's identity. See **Informer, Privilege for Identity of**
Insufficient foundation for admission of evidence, 21.20
Irrelevancy, 17.11
Journalist's privilege against disclosure of information, 48.18
Judge testifying as witness, objection to, 18.19
Juror's incompetence to impeach verdict, 18.29
Lack of personal knowledge on part of witness, 18.26
Leading question, objection to, 13.15
Marital communications privilege. See **Marital Communications Privilege**
Misconduct of counsel, stating objection to, 29.12, 29.29
Misconduct of judge, stating objection to, 29.33
Misconduct of jury. See **Misconduct of Jurors**
Misquotation of witness, 12.5
Mistrial on grounds of irreparable prejudicial incident, 56.6–56.7
Narrative testimony, objection to, 10.6
Official information privilege. See **Official Information Privilege**
Opinion testimony. See **Opinion Testimony**
Parol evidence, objection to, 25.13
Penitent's privilege. See **Penitent's Privilege**
Physician-patient privilege, objection to question on grounds of. See **Physician-Patient Privilege**
Psychotherapist-patient privilege, objection to question on grounds of. See **Psychotherapist-Patient Privilege**
Question asked by trial judge, objection to, 4.17
Rehabilitation of witness, objection to improper evidence, 23.8
Search and seizure. See **Search and Seizure**
Self-incrimination, stating claim of privilege against, 46.8, 46.21
Sexual assault victim-counselor privilege. See **Sexual Assault Victim-Counselor Privilege**
Speculative answer, objection to question calling for, 16.7
Speedtrap, objection to testimony based on use of, 18.32
Spouse, privilege not to be called as witness against. See **Spouse, Privilege Not To Be Called as Witness Against**
Spouse, privilege not to testify against. See **Spouse, Privilege Not To Testify Against**
Summary objections, 4.13
Too general a question, 9.5
Trade secrets privilege. See **Trade Secrets Privilege**
Voir dire examination, stating objection to improper. See **Voir Dire Examination of Jurors**
Voter's privilege. See **Voter's Privilege**
Work product protection, stating claim of, 35.11

Foundational or Preliminary Facts
See also **Incompetent Witnesses**; **Insufficient Foundation, Objections to**
Burden of proof, 17.7, 21.15
Business records, 19.26

Foundational or Preliminary Facts—*cont.*
Confession or admission by criminal defendant, prima facie showing of elements of crime required for introduction of, 27.4
Cross-examination of witness on, 21.19
Definition of preliminary fact, 33.17
Deposition of opposing counsel, preliminary foundation required for, 34.5
Direct examination, use of leading questions to establish preliminary matters on, 13.5
Experiments, preliminary facts required prior to introduction of evidence of, 21.8
Experts. See **Experts**
Hearsay. See **Hearsay**
In limine motion to exclude evidence lacking foundation, 2.3
Interpreter's qualifications, preliminary fact hearing on, 18.5
Liability insurance, foundational showing for admission of, 32.6
Misconduct of attorney occurring outside judge's presence, laying foundation for objection to, 29.13
Motion to strike after opposing party's failure to provide foundation for conditionally admitted evidence. See **Strike, Motion To**
Opinion testimony, establishing foundation for, 20.23
Prejudicial effect of judge's failure to rule on foundational evidence, 21.9
Privilege claimed, preliminary facts establishing applicability of, 21.8
Relevancy of evidence dependent on establishing preliminary facts, 17.7, 21.4
Scientific evidence, foundation hearing to determine admissibility of, 20.10

Fraud and Misrepresentation
Attorney-client privilege, exception if attorney's services sought in committing fraud, 34.15
Exclusion of evidence obtained by fraud and deceit
Generally, 28.8
Stating objection, 28.15
Marital communications privilege, inapplicability to communications aiding fraud, 40.3, 40.8
Parol evidence to prove fraud, admissibility of, 25.5
Work product doctrine, applicability despite attorney's assistance in commission of fraud, 35.7

Gangs
Admissibility of testimony on gang code of silence to impeach testimony of codefendant, 20.15
Hearsay exception in gang-related criminal prosecution for deceased declarant's prior statement made under penalty of perjury, 19.16A

Good Faith
Spouse, effect of good faith ignorance of marital relationship on privilege not to be called to testify against, 42.11

Grand Jury Proceedings
Defendant's privilege not to be called and not to testify, inapplicability in grand jury proceedings, 47.2
Spouse, privilege not to be called as witness against in grand jury proceedings, 42.4
Spouse, privilege not to testify against in grand jury proceedings, 41.7

Guardianship and Conservatorship
Attorney-client privilege
Death of ward or conservatee, effect of, 34.20
Holder of privilege, guardian or conservator as, 34.4
Waiver of privilege by guardian or conservator, 34.22
Domestic violence victim-counselor privilege, guardian as holder of, 39.5
Marital communications privilege claimed by guardian or conservator of spouse, 40.6, 40.16–40.17
Physician-patient privilege
Death of ward or conservatee, termination of privilege as result of, 36.19
Holder of privilege, guardian or conservator as, 36.5

Guardianship and Conservatorship—*cont.*
Physician-patient privilege—*cont.*
Waiver of privilege by guardian or conservator, 36.20
Psychotherapist-patient privilege
Applicability of privilege in guardianship proceedings, 37.1
Death of patient, effect of, 37.16
Holder of privilege, guardian or conservator as, 37.5
Waiver of privilege by guardian or conservator, 37.17
Sexual assault victim-counselor privilege
Holder of privilege, guardian as, 38.5
Waiver of privilege by guardian, 38.9

Habeas Corpus
Contempt order, review of, 33.22

Habit or Custom
Admissibility of evidence to show, 32.7

Handicapped Persons. See **Disabled Persons**

Handwriting Samples
Defendant's privilege not to testify, inapplicability to handwriting samples, 47.3
Opinion testimony, 20.28

Harmless Error
Impeach witness, analysis of denial of opportunity to, 22.7

Hearings
Chambers. See **Chambers, Conference in**
Cleric's privilege, hearing on claim of, 51.9
Competency of juror, hearing on, 29.45
Contempt penalty, hearing on, 57.6
Discharge of juror with personal knowledge of facts of case, hearing on, 29.40
Expert opinion, hearing to determine if hearsay basis for, 20.8
Hypnotized witness's testimony, hearing on admission of, 19.11
Informer, identity of. See **Informer, Privilege for Identity of**
Kelly test for admission of scientific evidence, applicability in administrative hearings, 20.12
Mistrial. See **Mistrial**
New trial. See **New Trial, Motion for**
Peremptory challenges, hearing on discriminatory use of. See **Jury Trial**
Physician-patient privilege, hearing on claim of privilege against search warrant for documentary evidence in physician's possession, 36.21
Preliminary hearings. See **Preliminary Hearings**
Psychotherapist-patient privilege, hearing on privilege claimed against search warrant for documentary evidence held by psychotherapist, 37.18

Hearsay
Admissible hearsay (see Exceptions to hearsay rule, below)
Admissions (see Confessions and admissions, exception to hearsay rule for, below)
Alternatives to objecting. See **Alternatives to Objecting**
Child dependency hearsay exception, 19.17
Confessions and admissions, exception to hearsay rule for
Generally, 19.8
Adoptive admissions, 19.14
Authorized admissions, 19.15
Co-conspirators, admissions of, 19.16
Parties, admissions of, 19.13
Definition of hearsay evidence, 19.1
Elements of hearsay
Checklist of hearsay problems, 19.42
Circumstantial evidence, statement offered as (nonhearsay), 19.5
Knowledge or belief, statement offered to prove, 19.7
Out-of-court statement, 19.3
Out-of-court statement offered to prove truth of matter stated, 19.4
Statement offered to prove that statement was made (nonhearsay), 19.6
Exceptions to hearsay rule
Admissions against interest, 21.7

Hearsay—*cont.*
  Exceptions to hearsay rule—*cont.*
    Bills or invoices offered to corroborate other evidence, 19.37
    Business records exception, 19.12, 19.26
    Confessions and admissions (see Confessions and admissions, exception to hearsay rule for, above)
    Declarant unavailable, 19.11, 19.16A
    Declarations against penal interest, 19.8, 19.18
    Dispositive instruments or ancient writings, 19.35
    Exclusionary rules, applicability of, 19.9
    Family history, declarant's statements concerning, 19.33
    Former testimony, 19.28–19.31A
    Foundation for proving exception to hearsay rule, burden on party offering evidence, 19.10
    Judgments, 19.32
    Major categories of exceptions, 19.8
    Mental or physical state, declarant's statement of, 19.24
    Miscellaneous exceptions under Evid C §§1224-1228, 19.17
    Official records and writings, 19.27
    Preliminary hearing in criminal case, testimony given at, 1.7, 19.29, 19.38
    Prior statements of witnesses (see Prior statements of witnesses, exception to hearsay rule for, below)
    Publications of commercial, scientific, or historical nature, 19.36
    Reputation or statements concerning community history, property interests, or character, 19.34
    Res gestae not exception, 19.41
    Spontaneous, contemporaneous, and dying declarations, 19.8, 19.23
    Trustworthiness of statement, requirement of, 19.12
    Wills or claims against estate, declarant's statements relating to, 19.25
  Experts
    Cross-examination of third party if expert's opinion based on hearsay, 20.27

Experts—*cont.*
  Hearing to determine if hearsay basis for expert opinion, 20.8
  Reliance on hearsay in formulating opinion, 20.9
  Foundational determination
    Exception to hearsay rule, laying foundation for, 19.10
    Identity of hearsay declarant, foundational determination on, 21.8
  Impeachment of hearsay declarant, 19.39
  Prior statements of witnesses, exception to hearsay rule for
    Gang-related criminal prosecution exception for deceased declarant's prior statement made under penalty of perjury, 19.16A
    Identifying person, prior statements, 19.22
    Past recollection recorded, 19.21
    Present testimony, statement inconsistent with, 19.19
    Prior consistent statements, admissibility of, 19.20
  Self-serving evidence, improper objection to, 19.40
  Stating objection, 19.45
  Statutory basis for hearsay rule, 19.2, 19.43
  Strike, Motion To. See **Strike, Motion To**

Hospitals. See **Medical Records**

Husband and Wife. See **Spouses**

Hypnosis
  Competency of hypnotized witness to testify, 18.21
  Hearing on admission of hypnotized witness's testimony, 19.11
  Kelly test for admission of scientific evidence, applicability to hypnosis, 20.13

Hypothetical Questions
  Expert witness. See **Experts**
  Voir dire examination of prospective jurors, use of hypothetical questions, 6.45

Identity
Attorney-client privilege, refusal of attorney to disclose identity of client, 34.9
Informer. See **Informer, Privilege for Identity of**

Illness
Continuance as result of witness's or attorney's incapacity, 54.3

Immunity
Journalist's immunity from contempt. See **Journalist's Immunity From Contempt**
Self-incrimination. See **Self-Incrimination, Privilege Against**
Use immunity
  Generally, 46.17
  Protective orders in civil actions equivalent to use immunity in exchange for testimony, 46.14

Impeachment of Verdict by Jurors. See **Incompetent Witnesses**

Impeachment of Witnesses
Generally, 22.1, 26.1
Alternative to making objection, impeachment of witness as, 4.14
Arbitration testimony, admissibility to impeach, 22.11A
Collateral matter, impeachment of witness on, 22.3
Exceeding scope of direct examination on cross-examination for purposes of impeachment, 22.4, 26.3
Expert witnesses
  Extrinsic evidence, impeachment of expert with, 20.26
  Noncompliance with expert witness list, effect of, 22.11
  Scientific, technical, or professional publications, restrictions on impeachment of expert using, 20.25, 22.10
Hearsay declarant, impeachment of, 19.39
Limits on impeachment
  Applicability of evidentiary objections to evidence offered for impeachment purposes, 22.7

Limits on impeachment—*cont.*
  Character evidence, restrictions on, 22.8
  Criminal convictions, 22.8
  Expert witnesses. See **Expert Witnesses**
  Religious beliefs, absence of, 22.9
Party calling witness, impeachment of witness by, 13.9
Prior convictions offered for impeachment of witness, court's discretion to exclude, 21.4, 22.2, 22.8, 31.4, 47.4
Prior inconsistent statements
  Determining, 22.5
  Hearsay rule, exception to, 19.19, 19.31A
  Judge's discretion to allow impeachment despite witness's lack of opportunity to explain inconsistency, 22.6
  Leading questions on cross-examination, use of, 13.10
  Showing statement to witness, no requirement of, 22.5A
Privilege
  Effect of privilege on impeachment evidence, 22.7
  Previous claim of privilege, prohibition against impeachment of witness with, 33.20
Rehabilitation of witness. See **Rehabilitation of Witnesses**
Stating objection, 22.14
Statutory authority for impeaching witness, 22.12
Statutory changes affecting impeachment of witnesses, 22.2
Subsequent safety measures, admissibility of evidence for impeachment purposes, 32.5
Superseded pleading, impeachment of party with, 19.13

In Camera Proceedings. See **Chambers, Conference in**

Incapacity. See **Competency**

Incompetence of Counsel
Failure of counsel to object to inadmissible evidence, effect on appeal, 4.8

Incompetent, Irrelevant, and Immaterial
General objection, insufficiency of, 17.8

Incompetent Witnesses
See also **Competency; Foundational or Preliminary Facts**
Defined, 18.1
Evid C §700, competency of witnesses under, 18.3
Inability to communicate
   Alternatives to objecting, 18.7
   Defined, 18.4
   Ruling on objection, 18.5
   Stating objection, 18.8
   Statutory basis for objection, 18.6
Inability to understand duty to tell truth
   Defined, 18.9
   Ruling on objection, 18.10
   Stating objection, 18.13
   Statutory authority for objection, 18.11
Judge as witness, objection to
   Generally, 18.17
   Stating objection, 18.19
   Statutory authority for objection, 18.18
Juror's incompetence to impeach verdict
   Generally, 18.27
   Stating objection, 18.29
Mental capacity, proving incompetence of witness due to lack of, 21.8
Oath
   Capacity of witness to understand oath, 18.4
   Duty to tell truth (see Inability to understand duty to tell truth, above)
Personal knowledge, lack of
   Alternatives to objecting, 18.25
   Defined, 18.21
   Examples of witnesses testifying to events outside their personal knowledge, 18.22
   Ruling on objection, 18.23
   Stating objection, 18.26
   Statutory authority for objection, 18.24
Speedtraps, testimony based on use of. See **Speedtraps**
Statutory grounds for incompetence
   Generally, 18.2
   Impeaching verdict (see Juror's incompetence to impeach verdict, above)
   Inability to communicate (see Inability to communicate, above)

Statutory grounds for incompetence—*cont.*
   Inability to understand duty to tell truth (see Inability to understand duty to tell truth, above)
   Judges (see Judge as witness, objection to, above)
   Juror called as witness incompetent to testify, 18.2, 18.20
   Personal knowledge (see Personal knowledge, lack of, above)
   Speedtraps. See **Speedtraps**

Inconsistent Testimony. See **Impeachment of Witnesses**

Inflammatory Evidence
See also **Bias and Prejudice**
Defined, 30.1
Discretion of court
   Examples of court's abuse of discretion in admitting inflammatory evidence, 30.5
   Examples of court's discretion in admitting inflammatory evidence, 30.4
In limine motion to exclude inflammatory evidence, 30.3
Pretrial tactics to discover and exclude inflammatory evidence, 30.3
Probative value of evidence versus danger of undue prejudice, court's analysis of, 30.2
Stating objection, 30.7
Statutory basis for objection to inflammatory evidence, 30.6

Informer, Privilege for Identity of
Generally, 44.1
Grounds for nondisclosure of identity, 44.6
Hearings and rulings on privilege
   Generally, 44.9
   Burden of proof, 44.11
   In camera hearing on motion to discover informer's identity, 44.2, 44.10
Illustrations of privilege, 44.13
Information from informer, requirement of
   Confidentiality, information furnished in, 44.5

Informer, Privilege for Identity of—*cont.*
  Information from informer, requirement of—*cont.*
    Purported disclosure of law violation, 44.3
    Recipient of informer's information, peace officer as, 44.4
  Motion by defense counsel for order or finding adverse to prosecution, 44.16
  Persons who may claim privilege, 44.1, 44.7
  Pretrial procedures concerning privilege, 44.2
  Ruling on claim of privilege (see Hearings and rulings on privilege, above)
  Stating claim of privilege
    Prosecutor's claim of privilege, 44.15
    Witness's claim of privilege, 44.14
  Statutory authority for privilege, 44.12
  Termination of privilege, 44.8
  Waiver of privilege, 44.8

In Limine Motions
  Admission of evidence, in limine motion seeking, 2.7
  Admonishment to jury concerning counsel's violation of in limine motion, 2.17
  Advantages and disadvantages of in limine motion, 2.8–2.9
  Appeals
    Renewing motion during trial to preserve record for appeal, 2.15
    Timely objection, preserving record on appeal through use of, 2.18
  Clothing or symbols worn by counsel, motion to prohibit specific types of, 2.5
  Continuing objection, motion in limine instead of, 4.11
  Costs. See **Costs**
  Definition of in limine motion, 2.2
  Exclusion of evidence
    Generally, 2.3, 32.11
    Evid C §352, motion in limine to exclude evidence under, 31.17
  Experts
    Exclusion of expert testimony, motion for, 2.3
    Qualifications of expert, in limine motion challenging, 4.4
  Form, 2.19*f*
  Historical background of in limine motions, 2.1
  Inability of witness to communicate, motion in limine on competency of witness, 18.7
  Inflammatory evidence, motion in limine to exclude, 30.3
  Judges
    Favorable opinion of in limine motion, 2.10
    Ruling on motion (see Ruling on motion, below)
  Learned treatise, motion in limine for admissibility of, 22.10
  Limiting instruction to jury, motion seeking, 2.4
  Order in limine, 2.20*f*
  Parol evidence, in limine motion to exclude, 25.11
  Penalties (see Sanctions, below)
  Prejudicial words or phrases, in limine motion to prohibit counsel's use of, 2.5
  Procedures for making motion
    Format and notice requirements, 2.11
    Oral motions in limine, 2.2, 2.12
  Record of proceedings. See **Record of Proceedings**
  Reiteration requirement, 2.18
  Rules of court. See **Rules of Court**
  Ruling on motion
    Final or absolute rulings, 2.14
    Making record on degree of damage caused by violation of order, 2.16
    Preliminary or conditional rulings, 2.13
    Reconsideration of ruling, party's request for, 2.15
    Sanctions imposed for violation of in limine order, 2.17
  Sanctions
    Abuse of discovery, motion to prohibit use of evidence as sanction for, 2.6
    Violation of in limine order, sanction for, 2.17
  Self-incrimination, in limine hearing to decide claim of privilege against, 46.9
  Time limits for motions in limine, San Francisco Superior Court rule on, 6.5
  Timing of motion, 2.10A

In Limine Motions—cont.
Voir dire questions, in limine motions during pre-voir dire conference concerning, 6.8, 6.33, 6.39

In Pro Per
Judge's treatment of in pro per litigant, 10.4
Work product privilege claimed by pro per litigant, 35.5

Insanity. See **Not Guilty by Reason of Insanity**

Inspections
Administrative inspections, exclusion of evidence obtained during, 28.11

Instructions to Jury. See **Jury Instructions**

Insufficient Foundation, Objections to
See also **Foundational or Preliminary Facts**
Generally, 21.1
Classification of foundation problem, determining, 21.2
Evid C §403 problem
  Generally, 21.3
  Conditional admission of evidence if no prima facie showing made, 21.11
  Exclusion of evidence on judge's redetermination of admissibility, 21.13
  Identity, preliminary proof of, 21.7
  Jury, hearing on preliminary facts out of presence of, 21.9
  Jury instruction on determining existence of preliminary fact, 21.12
  Personal knowledge of lay witness, 21.5
  Prima facie showing of preliminary facts, judge's determination of, 21.10
  Relevancy of proposed evidence, 21.4
  Statute, text of, 21.14
  Writing, authenticity of, 21.6
Evid C §405 problem
  Generally, 21.8
  Conditional admission of evidence, 21.16

Evid C §405 problem—cont.
  Judge, admission or exclusion of evidence determined by, 21.15
  Jury, hearing on preliminary facts out of presence of, 21.9
  Statute, text of, 21.18
  Ultimate fact to be determined by jury, consequences when preliminary fact same as, 21.17
  Responses to objection, 21.19
  Stating objection, 21.20
  Statutory basis for objection, 21.14, 21.18
  Voir dire of witness on foundational evidence, 21.19

Insurance
Exclusion of evidence on insurance, 32.6
Misconduct of attorney, reference to insurance constituting, 29.4
Voir dire examination on insurance, 6.39

Intent
Integration of agreement, parties' intent concerning, 25.3

Interpretation of Cases and Statutes. See **Construction and Interpretation**

Interpreters
Preliminary fact hearing on interpreter's qualifications, 18.5

Investigations
Misconduct of jurors, independent investigation by jurors constituting, 29.37
State Bar's investigation or proceeding against attorney, duty of attorney to cooperate and participate in, 34.16

Invited Error, Doctrine of, 4.8

Irrelevancy. See **Relevant Evidence**

Jail. See **Prisons and Prisoners**

Journalist's Immunity From Contempt
Generally, 48.1
Appellate review of contempt citation for refusing to answer question, 48.19

Journalist's Immunity From Contempt—*cont.*
Assertion of privilege or claim of immunity
Generally, 48.12
Civil trials, 48.13
Criminal trials (see Criminal trials, asserting privilege in, below)
Time for claiming immunity, 48.9
California's constitutional and statutory basis for immunity
Generally, 48.6
Civil trials, scope of immunity in, 48.10
Claim of immunity by journalist in response to question or demand calling for disclosure of information, 48.9
Criminal trials, scope of immunity in, 48.11
Definition of journalist and journalist purposes, 48.7
Information protected by immunity, 48.8
Text of California constitutional provision establishing basis for journalist's immunity from contempt, 48.20
Constitutional basis for privilege not to disclose information
California's constitution (see California's constitutional and statutory basis for immunity, above)
Historical development of privilege, 48.2
Interpretation of constitutional privilege by California Supreme Court, *Mitchell* factors, 48.5
Subpoenaing journalists, guidelines for, 48.4
Test for compelling testimony by journalist, 48.3
Criminal trials, asserting privilege in
Balancing test under *Delaney*, application of, 48.15
Hypothetical case history, applying *Delaney* to, 48.16
Triggering procedural and substantive protection under *Delaney*, 48.14
Delaney test (see Criminal trials, asserting privilege in, above)
Stating objection, 48.18
Unpublished information defined, 48.20
Waiver of privilege and immunity from contempt, 48.17
Writs
Contempt citation, extraordinary writ to review, 48.19
Shield law for newsmedia, writ review to challenge journalist's immunity under, 55.6

Judges
Argument, judge's authority to close, 57.4
Attorney-client privilege, ruling on. See **Attorney-Client Privilege**
Chambers, conference in. See **Chambers, Conference in**
Cleric's privilege. See **Cleric's Privilege**
Competency of witness to testify, questions asked by judge to determine, 18.5
Compound question, judge asking attorney to rephrase, 8.5
Contempt power. See **Contempt**
Continuance
Absence of judge, continuance based on, 54.3
Factors considered by judge in deciding motion for, 54.9
Corpus delicti rule. See **Corpus Delicti Rule**
Defendant's privilege not to be called, judge's duties concerning. See **Criminal Defendant's Privilege Not To Be Called and Not To Testify**
Discretion of court. See **Discretion of Court**
Disqualification of judge, judgment void, 29.30
Domestic violence victim-counselor privilege. See **Domestic Violence Victim-Counselor Privilege**
Examination of prospective jurors. See **Voir Dire Examination of Jurors**
Examination of witness by trial judge. See **Examination of Witnesses**
Foundational or preliminary facts, determination by judge of, 21.10
Incompetence of judge to testify as witness in trial. See **Incompetent Witnesses**
Informer, identity of. See **Informer, Privilege for Identity of**

Judges—*cont.*
   In limine motions. See **In Limine Motions**
   In pro per litigant, judge's treatment of, 10.4
   Judicial notice of conclusions regarding scientific evidence reached by other courts, 20.12
   Marital communications privilege. See **Marital Communications Privilege**
   Misconduct. See **Misconduct of Judges**
   Mistrial. See **Mistrial**
   Official information privilege. See **Official Information Privilege**
   Penitent's privilege, judge ruling on claim of. See **Penitent's Privilege**
   Peremptory challenges, ruling on discriminatory use of, 6.31
   Physician-patient privilege, ruling on. See **Physician-Patient Privilege**
   Privilege, duty of judge to inform unrepresented witness of right to claim, 33.15
   Psychotherapist-patient privilege. See **Psychotherapist-Patient Privilege**
   Question of law and fact. See **Questions of Law and Fact**
   Self-incrimination, privilege against. See **Self-Incrimination, Privilege Against**
   Sexual assault victim-counselor privilege. See **Sexual Assault Victim-Counselor Privilege**
   Spouse, privilege not to be called as witness against. See **Spouse, Privilege Not To Be Called as Witness Against**
   Spouse, privilege not to testify against spouse. See **Spouse, Privilege Not To Testify Against**
   Stipulation concerning, 29.36
   Trade secrets privilege. See **Trade Secrets Privilege**
   Trustworthiness of statement, trial judge's preliminary determination of, 19.12
   Voir dire. See **Voir Dire Examination of Jurors**
   Voter's privilege, ruling on. See **Voter's Privilege**
   Witnesses. See **Witnesses**

Judgments and Decrees
   See also **Verdicts**
   Disqualification of judge, judgment void, 29.30
   Hearsay rule, exception to, 19.32

Judicial Notice
   Scientific evidence, judicial notice of conclusions reached by other courts, 20.12

Jury Admonitions
   During trial, 53.1
   Exercise of privilege, admonition against drawing inference from, 33.20, 53.7
   Experiments by jury improper, admonition against, 29.38
   In limine motion, admonishment to jury concerning counsel's violation of, 2.17
   Jury instructions, admonitions given as part of, 53.2
   Limited purpose, evidence admitted for
      Request by counsel for limiting admonition or instruction, 53.5
      Sample limiting instructions, 53.6
   Misconduct of attorney, admonitions concerning, 29.14, 53.3
   Misconduct of judge, admonitions to jurors after, 29.23, 29.28
   Misquotation of witness by counsel, admonition to disregard false statement, 12.3
   Mistrial as alternative to admonition, 56.2
   Stricken or excluded evidence, admonition on. See **Strike, Motion To**
   Voir dire, request for jury to disregard prejudicial matter raised on, 6.40
   Waiver of objection to inadmissible evidence, failure to request jury admonition as, 4.8

Jury Instructions
   Admitted evidence, instruction to disregard, 21.13
   Admonitions to jury given as part of instructions, 53.2
   Criminal defendant's failure to testify, jury instruction on, 47.6

Jury Instructions—*cont.*
  Elements of crime, instruction on proof of, 27.7
  In limine motion, instruction to jury concerning violation of, 2.17
  Limited admissibility of evidence, instruction on
    Generally, 20.9, 32.8
    In limine motion for limiting instruction, 2.4
  Preliminary facts or foundation for evidence, instruction on, 21.12
  Stricken evidence, instruction on, 52.7
  Sua sponte. See **Sua Sponte**

Jury Trial
  Admonitions to jury. See **Jury Admonitions**
  Alternate jurors, statutory provisions governing, 6.52
  Argument. See **Argument**
  Challenges
    Cause (see Challenges for cause, below)
    Peremptory challenges (see Peremptory challenges, below)
  Challenges for cause
    Entire panel (see Challenges for cause to panel as a whole, below)
    Exercise of challenge by either court or counsel, 6.21
    Grounds for challenge (see Grounds for challenging prospective juror, below)
    Procedures for exercising challenge, 6.22
    Trial of challenge for cause, 6.23
    Voir dire in criminal case. See **Voir Dire Examination of Jurors**
  Challenges for cause to panel as a whole
    Generally, 6.2
    Civil and criminal cases, differences between, 6.4
    Discriminatory use of peremptory challenge by opposing counsel, challenge to entire jury panel after, 6.28
    Procedure for challenging entire panel, 6.3
  Contempt proceeding, no right to jury trial in, 57.7
  Continuance. See **Continuance**
  Corpus delicti rule. See **Corpus Delicti Rule**
  Cross-examination. See **Cross-Examination**
  Direct examination. See **Direct Examination**
  Discharge of juror
    Incompetence, discharge based on, 29.45
    Personal knowledge of facts of case, hearing on discharge of juror with, 29.40
  Disclosure to jury of sliding scale recovery agreements, court's discretion on, 32.2
  Discretion of court regarding jurors. See **Discretion of Court**
  Discriminatory use of peremptory challenges
    Appellate review of trial court's ruling, 6.32
    Civil and criminal trials, prohibition against discriminatory use of peremptory challenges in, 6.27
    Prima facie case of group bias in exercise of peremptory challenges, proof of, 6.28
    Procedures for objecting to discriminatory use of peremptory challenges, 6.27–6.28
    Proof accepted at *Wheeler* hearings, 6.27, 6.30
    Rebutting prima facie case, 6.29
    Ruling by trial court, 6.31
    Subjective explanations for challenging jurors, 6.29
  Disparagement of jurors, misconduct by judge, 29.27
  Evidence. See **Evidence**
  Examination of witnesses. See **Examination of Witnesses**
  Exclusion of evidence. See **Exclusion of Evidence**
  Exhibits allowed into jury room, 29.42
  Foreperson of jury selected by judge, objection to, 6.46
  Grounds for challenging prospective juror
    Generally, 6.17
    Actual bias, disqualification on grounds of, 6.20
    General disqualification of juror, 6.18

Jury Trial—*cont.*
  Grounds for challenging prospective juror—*cont.*
    Implied bias, disqualification on grounds of, 6.19
    Impeach verdict, incompetence of juror to. See **Incompetent Witnesses**
    Misconduct of attorney, interviewing potential jurors constituting, 29.4
    Misconduct of jurors. See **Misconduct of Jurors**
  Mistrial. See **Mistrial**
  Offer of proof outside jury's presence, 5.9
  Opening statement. See **Opening Statement**
  Peremptory challenges
    Civil action, number of challenges permitted in, 6.25
    Criminal action, number of challenges permitted in, 6.26
    Discriminatory use of peremptory challenges (see Discriminatory use of peremptory challenges, above)
    Procedures for exercising challenge, 6.24
  Privilege. See **Privilege**
  Question of law and fact. See **Questions of Law and Fact**
  Racial discrimination in selection of jurors (see Discriminatory use of peremptory challenges, above)
  Secondary evidence, motion to exclude made outside jury's presence, 24.3
  Selection of jury
    Challenges (see Challenges, above)
    Statutory provisions governing, 6.52
    Vicinage, drawing jury panel in criminal case from, 6.4
    Voir dire. See **Voir Dire Examination of Jurors**
  Statutory provisions governing jury trials, 6.52, 6.54
  Sufficiency of foundation for evidence, jury's determination of. See **Insufficient Foundation, Objections to**
  Wheeler rule (see Discriminatory use of peremptory challenges, above)
  Witness, incompetence of juror to testify as, 18.2, 18.20

Juvenile Court Proceedings
  Continuance in, 54.3
  Marital communications privilege, exception in juvenile court proceedings, 40.14
  Spouse, exception to privilege not to testify against, 41.12

***Kelly* Test for Scientific Evidence.** See **Scientific Evidence**

Labor Unions. See **Unions**

Law Enforcement Personnel
  Hearsay exception for testimony by law enforcement officers, 19.16A, 19.38
  Personnel files or records of citizen complaints, procedures for obtaining, 43.13
  Possession of drugs for sale, admissibility of police officer's opinion on, 20.9
  Speedtraps, testimony by law enforcement officer on, 18.32

Lay Witnesses. See **Opinion Testimony**

Leading Questions
  Alternatives to objecting. See **Alternatives to Objecting**
  Cross-examination. See **Cross-Examination**
  Defined, 13.1
  Direct examination. See **Direct Examination**
  Examples of leading questions, 13.2
  Examples of nonleading questions, 13.3
  Stating objection, 13.15
  Voir dire examination of prospective jurors, use of leading questions, 6.45

Legal Malpractice
  Attorney-client privilege, failure of attorney to claim on behalf of client, 34.12

Legislative Privilege
  Motives of legislators, legislative privilege prohibiting court's inquiry into, 43.4

Legislature
　Continuance of legislative session, 54.3

Licenses and Permits
　Physician-patient privilege, exception in disciplinary proceedings brought by public entity to terminate license, 36.12
　Privilege not to be called and not to testify, inapplicability in administrative proceeding to suspend or revoke license, 47.2

Lie Detector Test. See **Polygraph Test**

Limitation of Actions. See **Statutes of Limitations**

Local Rules of Court. See **Rules of Court**

Malpractice
　Legal malpractice. See **Legal Malpractice**
　Medical malpractice. See **Medical Malpractice**
　Statute of limitations defense, separate trial for, 3.7

Mandate
　Continuance of preliminary hearing, writ review of, 54.17, 55.7

Marital Communications Privilege
　Generally, 40.1
　Communications between spouses, applicability of privilege to, 40.3
　Confidentiality of communication, 40.4
　Exceptions
　　Generally, 40.10
　　Assistance in crime or fraud, 40.3, 40.8
　　Competence of spouse at issue, 40.11
　　Defendant in criminal proceeding, spouse as, 40.9, 40.15
　　Juvenile court proceedings, 40.14
　　Litigation between spouses, 40.12
　　Litigation between surviving spouse and claimant through deceased spouse, 40.13
　　Statutory basis for exceptions, 40.20
　Illustrations of privilege, 40.21

　Judges
　　Exclusion of privileged information by judge, 40.7
　　Ruling on privilege (see Ruling on claim of privilege, below)
　Marital testimonial privileges distinguished, 41.1, 42.1
　Persons who can claim privilege
　　Guardian or conservator, 40.6, 40.16–40.17
　　Spouse, 40.5
　Ruling on claim of privilege
　　Burden of proof regarding claim of privilege, 40.19
　　Procedure for obtaining ruling, 40.18
　Stating claim of privilege
　　Attorney's claim of privilege, 40.23
　　Witness's claim of privilege, 40.22
　Statutory basis for privilege, 40.20
　Termination of marriage, effect on privilege, 40.2
　Termination of privilege
　　Death of spouse, effect of, 40.16
　　Waiver of privilege, 40.17
　Valid marriage as prerequisite to existence of privilege, 40.2

Marital Dissolution. See **Dissolution of Marriage**

Marriage. See **Spouses**

Materiality. See **Relevant Evidence**

Medical Malpractice
　Discovery in medical malpractice case, hospital peer review records immune from, 20.9
　Postevent hospital peer review evidence, 32.5
　Psychotherapist-patient privilege, exception in malpractice cases, 37.12

Medical Records
　Hearsay rule, exception to, 19.26
　Physician-patient privilege. See **Physician-Patient Privilege**
　Psychotherapist-patient privilege. See **Psychotherapist-Patient Privilege**

Memorandum of Points and Authorities
　In limine motion, memorandum of points and authorities for, 2.19

Mental Competency. See **Competency; Incompetent Witnesses**

Mental Examination. See **Psychiatric or Psychological Examination**

Military and State Secrets
  Privilege protecting, 43.5

Minors
  Child abuse. See **Child Abuse**
  Child dependency hearsay exception, 19.17
  Guardianship. See **Guardianship and Conservatorship**
  Hearsay rule, exception to
    Dependent child, proceeding to declare minor, 19.31
    Injuries to children, exception for statements by children offered against parents in action for, 19.17
  Juvenile court proceedings. See **Juvenile Court Proceedings**
  Leading questions asked of minor under age 10, statutory authority permitting, 13.13
  Undue harassment or embarrassment, court's duty to protect minors under age 14 from, 7.5

Misconduct of Attorneys
  Alternatives to objecting to misconduct. See **Alternatives to Objecting**
  Bias (see Prejudice, below)
  Definition of attorney misconduct, 29.2
  Examples of misconduct
    Generally, 29.3
    After trial, 29.8
    Argument, misconduct during, 29.7
    Before trial, 29.4
    Examination of witnesses, misconduct during, 29.6
    Opening statement, actions constituting misconduct during, 29.5
    Voir dire examination, misconduct during, 29.4
  In limine motion, misconduct of attorney in violating, 2.17
  Misquoting witness characterized as misconduct, 12.3
  Mistrial. See **Mistrial**
  Objections
    Laying foundation for misconduct occurring outside presence of judge, 29.13
    Purpose of objecting to misconduct, 29.10
    Stating objection, 29.12, 29.20
    Timeliness of objection, importance of, 29.11
  Penalties. See **Penalties**
  Prejudice
    Appealing to jurors' prejudice as misconduct, 29.6
    Determining prejudicial effect of attorney's misconduct, 29.9
  Privilege claimed by witness, misconduct in asking similar questions after, 33.13
  Prosecutor calling criminal defendant to testify, 47.5
  Remedies for misconduct
    Admonishment of counsel, 6.47, 29.7, 29.12
    Appeal of judgment, 29.18
    Contempt, 29.15
    Curative admonition to jury, request for, 29.14, 53.3
    Mistrial. See **Mistrial**
    New trial, 29.11, 29.17
    Objection (see Objections, above)
  Waiver of objection to misconduct, failure to object promptly as, 29.11

Misconduct of Judges
  Admonitions to jurors after, 29.23, 29.28
  Alternatives to objecting. See **Alternatives to Objecting**
  Commenting on evidence
    Abuse of power, 29.23
    Automatic objection to, 29.28
  Examples of misconduct
    Coercive actions, 29.26
    Commenting on evidence (see Commenting on evidence, above)
    Disparagement of counsel, witness, or party, 29.27
    Examination of witnesses or prospective witnesses, abuse of power, 29.24
    Proof, interference with production of, 29.25
  Remedies for misconduct
    Appeal from judgment, 29.31

Misconduct of Judges—*cont.*
Remedies for misconduct—*cont.*
Mistrial, motion for, 29.29
New trial. See **New Trial, Motion for**
Objection to judicial misconduct, 29.28
Standards of judicial conduct, 29.21
Stating objection, 29.33

Misconduct of Jurors
Affidavits or declarations by jurors to prove misconduct of juror, 18.20, 29.46
Alternatives to objecting. See **Alternatives to Objecting**
Deliberations, failure of juror to take part in, 29.44A
Examples of misconduct
Receiving evidence out of court (see Receiving evidence out of court, below)
Voir dire examination, concealment of information during, 29.35, 29.46
Inattentiveness or sleeping during trial, 29.44
New trial. See **New Trial, Motion for**
Polling jurors regarding misconduct of juror, 29.45
Reading prepared statement to other jurors in deliberations room, no juror misconduct in, 29.39
Receiving evidence out of court
Generally, 29.36
Discussion of case prior to deliberations, 29.39
Independent experiments, 29.38
Independent investigations by jurors, 29.37
Personal knowledge of facts, duty of juror to reveal, 29.40
Personal knowledge of law, 29.41
Unauthorized matter in jury room, 29.42
Remedies for misconduct
After verdict returned, 29.31, 29.46
Before verdict rendered, 29.45
Standards of conduct, 29.34
Stating objection
After verdict returned, 29.49
Before verdict rendered, 29.48
Verdicts
Chance or quotient verdict, prohibition against, 29.43

Verdicts—*cont.*
Remedies for misconduct (see Remedies for misconduct, above)
Stating objection before or after verdict (see Stating objection, above)

Misdemeanors
Contempt of court. See **Contempt**
Past criminal conduct amounting to misdemeanor, admissibility of, 21.4

Misquotation of Witness, Objection Based on
Defined, 12.1
Examples of misquotations, 12.2
Remedies for misquoting witness, 12.3
Stating objection, 12.5
Statutory authority for objection, 12.4

Misrepresentations. See **Fraud and Misrepresentation**

Mistakes
Parol evidence to prove mistake, admissibility of, 25.5

Mistrial
Generally, 56.1
Discretion of court in ruling on motion for mistrial, 56.4
Grounds for
Assuming facts in dispute or not in evidence, undue prejudicial effect caused by question, 15.7
Conditionally admitted confession or admission, motion for mistrial after prosecution's failure to establish corpus delicti for, 27.11
Expert witness, inappropriate questions asked of, 52.11
In limine motion, mistrial ordered for violation of, 2.17
Irregularity in proceedings (see Irregularity in proceedings as grounds for mistrial, below)
Irreparable prejudicial incident (see Irreparable prejudicial incident as grounds for mistrial, below)
Judges (see Judges, below)
Misconduct of attorneys (see Misconduct of attorneys as grounds for mistrial, below)

Mistrial—*cont.*
  Grounds for—*cont.*
    Misconduct of jury, 29.45
    Misquoting witness, 12.3
    Voir dire, improper questioning as grounds for mistrial, 6.48
  Irregularity in proceedings as grounds for mistrial
    Generally, 56.3
    Procedure for requesting mistrial, 56.8
  Irreparable prejudicial incident as grounds for mistrial
    Generally, 56.2
    Misconduct, incident constituting, 56.6
    Misconduct, incident not constituting, 56.7
  Judges
    Misconduct of judge, 29.29
    Testifying as witness in action, 18.18, 56.8
  Misconduct of attorneys as grounds for mistrial
    Generally, 29.16
    Irreparable prejudicial incident (see Irreparable prejudicial incident as grounds for mistrial, above)
    Objection to misconduct and request for curative admonition as prerequisite to motion for mistrial, 29.10
  Prejudice (see Irreparable prejudicial incident as grounds for mistrial, above)
  Procedures for requesting mistrial
    Irregularity in proceedings, 56.8
    Irreparable prejudicial incident (see Irreparable prejudicial incident as grounds for mistrial, above)
  Trial tactics in requesting mistrial, 56.5

Modifications. See **Amendments and Modifications**

Motions
  Continuance, motion for. See **Continuance**
  Informer's identity, motion by defense counsel for order or finding adverse to prosecution, 44.16
  In limine motions. See **In Limine Motions**
  Mistrial. See **Mistrial**
  New trial. See **New Trial, Motion for**
  Order or finding adverse to prosecution, motion for, 43.19
  Search and seizure, motion to exclude evidence obtained during. See **Search and Seizure**
  Strike. See **Strike, Motion To**

Motor Vehicles
  Confidentiality of accident reports, 43.4
  Speedtraps. See **Speedtraps**
  Use immunity for accident reports, 46.17

Multiple Parties
  Peremptory challenges in civil action involving multiple parties, number of, 6.25
  Spouse, privilege not to be called as witness against, 42.2
  Spouse, privilege not to testify against in action involving multiple parties, 41.5, 42.2
  Work product doctrine, applicability in cases involving multiple parties, 35.1

Murder
  Continuance, good cause for, 54.3, 54.15

Narcotics. See **Drugs**

Narrative Answer Objection
  Dangers presented by, 10.2
  Defined, 10.1
  Discretion of court to allow narrative testimony, 10.4
  Examples of questions calling for narrative answers, 10.3
  Stating objection, 10.6
  Statutory authority for objection, 10.5

Negotiations. See **Settlement**

Newsmedia
  Journalist's immunity. See **Journalist's Immunity From Contempt**
  Voir dire, exclusion of newsmedia during, 6.16

New Trial, Motion for
  Continuance, effect on motion for new trial of failure to move for, 54.14

New Trial, Motion for—*cont.*
  Disqualification of judge, judgment void, 29.30
  Misconduct of attorney as grounds for new trial, 29.11, 29.17
  Misconduct of judge as grounds for
    Generally, 29.30
    Affidavits or declarations, evidence in hearing on motion for new trial limited to, 29.46
  Misconduct of jury as grounds for new trial
    Affidavits, evidence at hearing for new trial limited to, 18.27
    Voir dire, concealment of information during, 29.35
  Time limits for filing motion, 29.46
  Voir dire, new trial motion based on incorrect statement of law during, 6.35

Not Guilty by Reason of Insanity
  Psychotherapist-patient privilege, exception to, 37.9
  Separate trial for defense of, 3.8

Notice and Notification
  Contempt hearing, notice to contemnor of charges, 57.6
  In limine motions, notice requirements, 2.11
  Judicial notice. See **Judicial Notice**
  Peace or custodial officer's personnel files, notice to officer on disclosure of, 43.13

Oaths
  Competency of witness to understand oath. See **Incompetent Witnesses**
  Juror's oath prior to voir dire, 29.34

Offer of Proof
  Generally, 5.4
  Appeals. See **Appeals**
  Competency of witness to testify, offer of proof on, 5.4, 18.1
  Conditional admission of evidence, opposing party's request for specific offer of proof of necessary preliminary fact, 52.5
  Evid C §352, offer of proof by proponent of evidence after objection under, 31.14
  Objections to offer of proof, 5.14
  Privilege. See **Privilege**
  Procedures for offer of proof
    Availability of offered evidence, 5.13
    Jury, making offer of proof outside presence of, 5.9
    Purpose of offered evidence, 5.11
    Relevancy of offered evidence, 5.12
    Substance of offered evidence, 5.10
  Responses to objections
    Alternate methods of proving facts, 5.17
    Duty of counsel to seek other methods of proof, 5.15
    Rephrasing question, 5.16
  Reversal of exclusionary ruling, offer of proof in motion for, 2.15
  Situations not requiring offer of proof
    Alternatives to offer of proof, 5.8
    Broad exclusionary ruling, offer of proof not required after, 5.6
    Cross-examination, 5.5
    Question containing necessary elements, 5.7

Official Information Privilege
  Generally, 43.1
  Confidence, information acquired in, 43.3
  Criminal proceedings
    Generally, 43.1
    Adverse finding, motion for, 43.19
    Adverse finding rule, 43.8
    Federal statute forbidding disclosure, exception to adverse finding rule, 43.10
    Information to support search warrant, exception to adverse finding rule, 43.11
    Privilege invoked by non-California public entity, exception to adverse finding rule, 43.9
  Examples of information protected by state statute, 43.4
  Exceptions (see Criminal proceedings, above)
  Foreign state or country, privilege claimed by, 43.6
  Grounds for nondisclosure
    Consequences of disclosure versus nondisclosure, balancing of, 43.6
    Federal or California statute, 43.4
    Military and state secrets, 43.5

Official Information Privilege—cont.
  Holder of privilege, public entity as, 43.2, 43.7
  Illustrations of privilege, 43.16
  Information acquired by public employee acting in official capacity as prerequisite to existence of privilege, 43.2
  Judges (see Ruling on claim of privilege, below)
  Person or entity who may claim privilege, 43.2, 43.7
  Ruling on claim of privilege
    Burden of proof regarding claim of privilege, 43.14
    Procedure for obtaining ruling, 43.13
  Stating claim of privilege
    Attorney's claim of privilege, 43.18
    Witness's claim of privilege, 43.17
  Statutory basis for privilege, 43.15
  Termination and waiver of privilege, 43.12

Opening Statement
  Evid C §352, exclusion of references to evidence during opening statement, 31.17
  Misconduct of attorney, improper actions during opening statement constituting, 29.5

Opening the Door Exception. See **Cross-Examination**

Opinion Testimony
  See also **Experts**
  Admissible opinion by lay witnesses
    Generally, 16.4, 20.2
    Essential elements for admission of lay opinion, 20.4
    Statutory basis for admission of lay witness opinion, 20.5
    Subject matter for lay opinion, evidentiary rules affecting, 20.3
    Testator's sanity, opinion testimony on, 20.3, 20.8
  Alternatives to objecting. See **Alternatives to Objecting**
  Definition of opinion, 20.1
  In limine motion to exclude lay witness's opinion testimony, 2.3
  Lay witnesses (see Admissible opinion by lay witnesses, above)
  Motion to strike opinion testimony, 20.32
  Procedures for testing opinion testimony
    Cross-examination of witness, 20.25
    Expert's opinion. See **Experts**
    Foundational examination prior to witness's opinion testimony, 20.23
  Speculation. See **Speculative Answers, Questions Calling for**
  Stating objection
    Expert witness testimony, objection to, 20.31
    Lay witness testimony, objection to, 20.30
  Ultimate issue of case, witness's opinion on, 20.28

Order of Proof
  Admissibility of evidence ruling, distinguishing ruling on order of proof from, 3.9
  Discretion of court to regulate, 3.1, 3.8, 26.2
  Examination of witnesses. See **Examination of Witnesses**
  Issues, determining order of
    Civil cases, 3.7
    Criminal cases, 3.8
  Usual order of proceedings
    Generally, 3.2
    Civil trials, 3.3
    Criminal trials, 3.4

Other States
  Official information privilege claimed by sister state, 43.6

Parol Evidence Rule
  Defined, 25.1
  Exceptions to rule
    Additional terms consistent with original agreement, admissibility of extrinsic evidence to prove, 25.10
    Ambiguities in document, resolution of, 25.8
    Invalidity of agreement, admissibility of evidence to show, 25.6
    Mistake, illegality, or fraud, admissibility of extrinsic evidence to prove, 25.5
    Multiple writings constituting single agreement, 25.9
    Subsequent modifications, evidence of, 25.11

Parol Evidence Rule—*cont.*
　Exceptions to rule—*cont.*
　　Terms of agreement, admissibility of evidence to explain, 25.7
　　Integration of agreement, determination of, 25.3
　　Objection, promptness requirements, 25.12
　　Parties who may invoke rule, 25.4
　　Stating objection, 25.13
　　Statutory basis for objection based on parol evidence rule, 25.2

Past Recollection Recorded
　Hearsay rule, exception to, 19.21

Patents
　Trade secrets protection, inapplicability to patented ideas, 45.2

Paternity
　Opinion testimony on, 20.28

Peace Officers. See **Law Enforcement Personnel**

Penalties
　Contempt. See **Contempt**
　Continuance. See **Continuance**
　Discovery sanctions. See **Discovery**
　Inadmissible evidence, sanctions for impropriety and prejudicial effect of introducing, 52.11
　In limine motions. See **In Limine Motions**
　Misquoting witness characterized as misconduct, penalties for, 12.3
　Question assuming facts in dispute or not in evidence, penalties for, 15.7

Penitent's Privilege
　See also **Cleric's Privilege**
　Generally, 50.1
　Confessions privilege replaced by, 50.1
　Illustrations of privilege, 50.12
　Judges (see Ruling on claim of privilege, below)
　Persons who can claim privilege, 50.6
　Requirements for existence of privilege
　　Cleric, 50.2
　　Communication between penitent and cleric, 50.4

Requirements for existence of privilege—*cont.*
　Confidentiality of communication between penitent and cleric, 50.5
　Penitent, 50.3
Ruling on claim of privilege
　Burden of proof on claimant, 50.10
　Procedure for obtaining ruling, 50.9
Stating claim of privilege
　Attorney's objection to evidence based on penitent's privilege, 50.14
　Witness's claim of privilege, 50.13
Statutory authority for privilege, 50.11
Termination of privilege, death of penitent resulting in, 50.7
Waiver of privilege, 50.8

Peremptory Challenges. See **Jury Trial**

Perjury
　Gang-related criminal prosecution hearsay exception for deceased declarant's prior statement made under penalty of perjury, 19.16A

Permits. See **Licenses and Permits**

Personal Injuries
　Physician-patient privilege, patient-litigant exception to, 36.9

Personal Property
　Hearsay exception for recitals in writing affecting property, 19.35

Personal Representative. See **Executors and Administrators**

Photographs
　Defendant's privilege not to testify, inapplicability to being photographed, 47.3
　Inflammatory evidence, admission of photographs characterized as. See **Inflammatory Evidence**
　In limine motion for exclusion of photographs. See **In Limine Motions**
　Physician-patient privilege, applicability to photographs of patient's ailments, 36.3

Physician-Patient Privilege
See also **Psychotherapist-Patient Privilege**
Generally, 36.1
Criminal and quasi-criminal exceptions
  Child abuse, reporting of, 36.13
  Civil damages for patient's conduct, 36.11
  Disciplinary proceedings brought by public entity, 36.12
  General rule affecting criminal proceedings, 36.10
  Physician's assistance sought in commission of crime or tort, 36.15
Death of patient
  Exception to privilege for claims through deceased patient, 36.17
  Termination of privilege on, 36.19
Exceptions to privilege
  Generally, 36.8
  Breach of physician-patient duty, 36.16
  Competency of patient, proceedings concerning, 36.14
  Criminal and quasi-criminal exceptions (see Criminal and quasi-criminal exceptions, above)
  Deceased patient, claims through, 36.17
  Patient-litigant exception, 36.9
  Public record, exception for information placed in, 36.18
  Statutory authority for exceptions, 36.23
Executors. See **Executors and Administrators**
Guardians. See **Guardianship and Conservatorship**
Illustrations of privilege, 36.24
Judges (see Ruling on claim of privilege, below)
Names of patients, disclosure of, 36.3
Persons who can claim privilege
  Duty of physician to claim privilege on behalf of patient, 36.6
  Holder of privilege, 33.4
  Judge's motion to exclude privileged information, 36.7
  Patient or patient's representative, 36.5
Requirements for existence of privilege
  Communication between patient and physician, 36.3
Requirements for existence of privilege—*cont.*
  Confidentiality of communication between patient and physician, 36.4
  Relationship between patient and physician, 36.2
Ruling on claim of privilege
  Burden of proof concerning claim of privilege, 36.22
  Procedure for obtaining ruling, 36.21
Stating claim of privilege
  Attorney's claim of privilege, 36.26
  Witness's claim of privilege, 36.25
Statutory authority for claim of privilege, 36.23
Waiver of privilege, 36.20

Plea Bargaining
Proposition 8, effect on plea bargaining, 1.6

Pleadings
Admission of party, unverified pleading as, 19.13
Voir dire examination on pleadings, objection to, 6.33

Points and Authorities. See **Memorandum of Points and Authorities**

Police. See **Law Enforcement Personnel**

Polygraph Test
Stipulation to admissibility of polygraph test, 20.14

Prejudice. See **Bias and Prejudice**

Preliminary Hearings
Continuance of preliminary hearing, writ review of, 54.17, 55.7
Hearsay exception for testimony at, 1.7, 19.11, 19.29, 19.38

Preliminary Matters. See **Foundational or Preliminary Facts**

Presumptions
Attorney-client communications, presumption of confidentiality, 34.10
Burden of proof, effect of presumption on, 1.3

Presumptions—*cont.*
Competency of witness, presumption concerning, 18.5
Definition of presumption, 1.3
New trial motion, presumption of prejudice on appeal from juror misconduct after denial of, 29.46
Penitent-cleric communication, presumption of confidentiality, 51.5
Peremptory challenges, presumption concerning exercise of, 6.27
Privileged communications, presumption concerning, 33.31
Psychotherapist-patient privilege, presumption of confidentiality for information protected by, 37.4
Secondary evidence rule, printed representation of computer information, 24.5
Self-incrimination, no presumption from witness's claim of privilege against, 46.12

Prior Convictions
Admissibility of, 17.5
Discretion of court to exclude prior convictions offered for impeachment of witness, 21.4
Evid C §352, exclusion of prior felony convictions under, 31.4
Impeachment of witness with, 21.4, 22.2, 22.8, 31.4, 47.4

Prior Statements
Defendant's privilege not to be called and not to testify, effect of introducing prior testimony on, 47.7
Hearsay. See **Hearsay**
Impeachment of witnesses. See **Impeachment of Witnesses**

Prisons and Prisoners
Board of Prison Terms, qualified privilege for official information, 43.6
Communications between prisoner and spouse, effect of marital communications privilege on, 40.4
Contemnor, imprisonment of, 57.9

Privacy
Constitutional right to privacy, 33.3
Privilege. See **Privilege**

Work product doctrine. See **Work Product Doctrine**
Writ to protect right of privacy, 55.4

Privilege
Generally, 33.1
Admonition to jury against drawing inference from exercise of privilege, 33.20, 53.7
Applicability of privileges to all testimonial proceedings, 33.2
Attorney-client privilege. See **Attorney-Client Privilege**
Claim or assertion of privilege
  Generally, 33.5
  Claiming privilege at trial, 33.11
  Comment and inference on exercise of privilege, prohibition against, 33.20, 53.7
  Discovery as means of testing claim of privilege, 33.25
  Erroneous denial of privilege (see Erroneous denial of privilege, remedies for, below)
  Exclusion of privileged information (see Exclusion of privileged information, below)
  Opposition to claim of privilege (see Opposition to privilege, below)
  Outside presence of jury, claim of privilege made, 33.13
  Refreshing memory, witness's use of privileged writing for, 33.12
  Upholding privilege contested at trial (see Upholding privilege contested at trial, below)
Cleric's privilege. See **Cleric's Privilege**
Confidential disclosure of privileged information, court-ordered, 33.17
Defendant's privilege not to be called. See **Criminal Defendant's Privilege Not To Be Called and Not To Testify**
Discovery
  Application of privileges to discovery proceedings, 33.9
  Claims of privilege, discovery as means of testing, 33.25
Domestic violence victim-counselor privilege. See **Domestic Violence Victim-Counselor Privilege**
Erroneous allowance of privilege, remedy for, 33.30

Privilege—*cont.*
Erroneous denial of privilege, remedies for
Generally, 33.7, 55.3
Party's assertion of error, 33.21
Person other than witness, extraordinary writ to review denial of privilege, 33.23
Subsequent use of erroneously compelled disclosure, objection to, 33.24
Witness's claim of privilege, extraordinary writ to review denial of, 33.22
Exclusion of privileged information
Generally, 33.14
Exceptions to exclusion of privileged information, 33.16
Requirements for exclusion of privileged information subject to claim, 33.15
Holder of privilege defined, 33.4
Impeachment of witnesses. See **Impeachment of Witnesses**
Incompetence of witness distinguished from privilege against testifying, 18.1
Informer. See **Informer, Privilege for Identity of**
Journalist's immunity from contempt. See **Journalist's Immunity From Contempt**
Judge's duty to inform unrepresented witness of right to claim privilege, 33.15
Legislative privilege, 43.4
Marital communications privilege. See **Marital Communications Privilege**
Offer of proof
Party claiming privilege, offer of proof by, 33.19
Proponent of evidence, offer of proof by, 33.27
Official information. See **Official Information Privilege**
Opposition to privilege
Absence of claimant of privilege, subsequent admission of evidence previously excluded as privileged, 33.28
Before trial, 33.25

Opposition to privilege—*cont.*
Commenting on opponent's failure to explain or deny evidence or produce stronger favorable evidence, 33.29
Controverting claim of privilege at trial, 33.26
Offer of proof concerning excluded information by proponent of evidence, 33.27
Penitent's privilege. See **Penitent's Privilege**
Physician-patient privilege. See **Physician-Patient Privilege**
Preliminary facts establishing applicability of claimed privilege, 21.8
Presumption concerning confidentiality of privileged communication, 33.31
Psychotherapist-patient privilege. See **Psychotherapist-Patient Privilege**
Response to claim of privilege (see Opposition to privilege, above)
Selection of privilege to invoke, 33.10
Self-incrimination. See **Self-Incrimination, Privilege Against**
Sexual assault victim-counselor privilege. See **Sexual Assault Victim-Counselor Privilege**
Spouse, privilege not to be called as witness against. See **Spouse, Privilege Not To Be Called as Witness Against**
Spouse, privilege not to testify against. See **Spouse, Privilege Not To Testify Against**
Statutory authority for privileges, 33.3, 33.31
Tax returns. See **Tax Returns**
Trade secrets. See **Trade Secrets Privilege**
Trial, attorney's preparation for, 33.8
Upholding privilege contested at trial
Burden of proof, 21.8, 33.18, 33.31
Offer of proof, 33.19
Procedure for ruling on privilege, 33.17
Voter's privilege. See **Voter's Privilege**
Waiver of privilege
Generally, 33.6

Privilege—*cont.*
  Waiver of privilege—*cont.*
    Attorney-client privilege. See **Attorney-Client Privilege**
    Cleric's privilege. See **Cleric's Privilege**
    Criminal defendant's privilege not to be called and not to testify, waiver of, 47.7
    Domestic violence victim-counselor privilege, waiver of, 39.9
    Informer, waiver of privilege for identity of, 44.8
    Journalist's privilege against disclosure of information, waiver of, 48.17
    Marital communications privilege, waiver of, 40.17
    Official information privilege, 43.12
    Penitent's privilege, waiver of, 50.8
    Physician-patient privilege, waiver of, 36.20
    Psychotherapist-patient privilege, waiver of, 37.17
    Self-incrimination, waiver of privilege against, 33.9, 46.19
    Sexual assault victim-counselor privilege, waiver of, 38.9
    Spouse, privilege not to be called as witness against. See **Spouse, Privilege Not To Be Called as Witness Against**
    Spouse, privilege not to testify against. See **Spouse, Privilege Not To Testify Against**
    Subsequent admission of previously excluded evidence, waiver of privilege resulting in, 33.28
    Trade secrets privilege, waiver of, 45.5
    Voter's privilege, waiver of, 49.6
    Work product doctrine, 33.3A, 34.10A, 35.8
  Work product doctrine. See **Work Product Doctrine**
  Writ for review of denial of privilege (see Erroneous denial of privilege, remedies for, above)

Probation
  Psychotherapy as condition of probation, applicability of psychotherapist-patient privilege when, 37.2
  Self-incrimination, probationer's right to claim privilege against, 46.4

Professional Rules of Conduct
  Contempt, violation of rules punishable as, 57.2
  State Bar. See **State Bar**

Prohibition, Writ of
  Continuance of preliminary hearing, writ review of, 54.17, 55.7

Proof
  See also **Burden of Proof**
  Definition of proof, 1.3
  Elements of crime, requirements of independent proof of, 27.1–27.2, 27.4
  Misconduct of judge in interfering with production of proof, 29.25
  Offer of proof. See **Offer of Proof**
  Order of proof. See **Order of Proof**

Proposition 8
  Exclusion of relevant evidence, effect of Proposition 8 on, 31.4
  Expert opinion, effect of Proposition 8 on admissibility of, 20.7
  Truth-in-evidence provisions in, 1.6, 17.4, 38.1

Proposition 115
  Generally, 1.7
  Writ review of continuance of preliminary hearing, 54.17, 55.7

Protective Orders
  Use immunity in exchange for testimony, protective orders in civil actions equivalent to, 46.14

Psychiatric or Psychological Examination
  Attorney-client privilege, applicability to psychiatric examination requested by patient's attorney, 37.1
  Judge's appointment of psychotherapists to examine criminal defendant, 37.9
  Scientific evidence, admissibility of psychological opinion as, 20.18
  Sexual assault action, prohibition against ordering examination of witness, 18.5

Psychotherapist-Patient Privilege
See also **Physician-Patient Privilege**
Generally, 37.1
Confidential communication between patient and psychotherapist, applicability of privilege to, 37.3
Death of patient
  Exception to privilege for claims through deceased patient, 37.13
  Termination of privilege by patient's death, 37.16
Exceptions to privilege
  Generally, 37.1
  Breach of psychotherapist-patient privilege, 37.12
  Child abuse, 36.13, 37.15
  Dangerous patient, 37.10
  Deceased patient, claims through, 37.13
  Patient-litigant exception (see Patient-litigant exception, below)
  Psychotherapist's assistance in commission of crime or tort sought by patient, 37.11
  Public record, information placed in, 37.14
  Statutory authority for exceptions, 37.20
Guardianship, effect on privilege. See **Guardianship and Conservatorship**
Illustrations of privilege, 37.21
Judges
  Appointment of psychotherapist by judge to examine criminal defendant, 37.9
  Disclosure of confidential information required by judge prior to ruling on claim of privilege, 37.18
  Exclusion of privileged information by judge, 37.7
  Ruling on claim of privilege (see Ruling on claim of privilege, below)
Patient-litigant exception
  Civil cases, 37.8
  Criminal cases, 37.9
Persons who may claim privilege
  Holder of privilege, 33.4, 37.5
  Patient or patient's representative, 37.5
  Psychotherapist's duty to claim privilege on behalf of patient, 37.6, 37.16
Qualifications of therapist, 37.2, 37.20
Relationship between psychotherapist and patient, prerequisites for, 37.2
Ruling on claim of privilege
  Burden of proof regarding claim of privilege, 37.4, 37.19
  Procedure for obtaining ruling on claim of privilege, 37.18
Stating claim of privilege
  Attorney's claim of privilege, 37.23
  Witness's claim of privilege, 37.22
  Statutory authority for claim of privilege, 37.20
Termination of privilege
  Death of patient, effect of, 37.16
  Waiver of privilege, 37.17
Third parties, privilege dependent on nondisclosure of confidential communications to, 37.4

Public Entities and Employees
Attorney-client privilege
  Information held by public entity, applicability of privilege to, 34.4, 43.6
  Successor or assignee of public entity, privilege held by, 34.21
Definition of public entity, 34.4
Informer, public entity as holder of privilege for identity of, 44.7
Official information privilege. See **Official Information Privilege**
Physician-patient privilege, exception in disciplinary proceedings brought by public entity to terminate license, 36.12

Public Records
Physician-patient privilege, exception for information placed in public records, 36.18
Psychotherapist-patient privilege, exception for information placed in public records, 37.14

Qualifications of Expert. See **Experts**

Questions of Law and Fact
Expert opinion, 20.7
Integrated instrument, determination as question of law reserved for judge, 25.1
Prior conviction, determination if moral turpitude involved, 31.4

Questions of Law and Fact—*cont.*
Trial of questions of law before questions of fact, 3.7

Racial Discrimination in Selection of Jurors. See **Jury Trial**

Radar Speedtraps, Testimony on. See **Speedtraps**

Real Property
Hearsay exception for recitals in writing affecting real property, 19.35

Reasons for Objecting or Not Objecting to Evidence. See **Evidence**

Recess. See **Continuance**

Recollection of Witness, Refreshing
Direct examination, use of leading questions to refresh witness's recollection on, 13.6
Privileged writing used to refresh recollection, production of, 33.12
Work product doctrine, waiver if protected material used to refresh witness's recollection, 35.8

Record of Proceedings
Appeals. See **Appeals**
Continuing objection, request for ruling on record, 4.10
Cumulative evidence, court's analysis of, 31.7
Exclusion of evidence under Evid C §352, record of court's weighing of risk of undue prejudice against probative value of evidence, 31.12, 31.17
In limine motions
  Placing oral motion on record, 2.2
  Renewing motion during trial to preserve record for appeal, 2.15

Records and Reports
Accident reports. See **Motor Vehicles**
Business records. See **Business Records**
Discovery. See **Discovery**
Medical records. See **Medical Records**
Privilege against disclosure of records. See **Privilege**

Public records. See **Public Records**
Secondary evidence rule. See **Secondary Evidence Rule**
Self-incrimination, inapplicability of privilege to records and reports required by regulatory statutes, 46.6
Trial record, effect of striking evidence on, 52.12
Work product doctrine. See **Work Product Doctrine**

Redirect Examination. See **Direct Examination**

Refreshing Recollection of Witness. See **Recollection of Witness, Refreshing**

Rehabilitation of Witnesses
Generally, 23.1
Alternatives to objecting. See **Alternatives to Objecting**
Failure to rehabilitate witness, effect of, 23.7
Limits on rehabilitation evidence, 23.3–23.4
Party calling witness, rehabilitation of witness by, 13.9
Relevant evidence of collateral nature, admissibility or exclusion of, 23.2
Stating objection to improper rehabilitation evidence, 23.8
Statutory authority for, 23.5

Relatives
Psychotherapist-patient privilege, applicability to statements made by patient's family, 37.3

Release
Parol evidence to show inconclusive effect of boilerplate language in release, admissibility of, 25.5

Relevant Evidence
Civil cases, relevant evidence in, 1.4
Continuance based on surprise evidence, requirement that party requesting continuance show availability of relevant opposing evidence, 54.5
Criminal actions, relevancy in. See **Criminal Law**

Relevant Evidence—*cont.*
Elements required for evidence to be classified as relevant under Evidence Code, 17.2
Evid C §403, relevancy of proposed evidence under, 21.4
Exclusion of evidence. See **Exclusion of Evidence**
Failure to object to irrelevant evidence, effect of, 17.9
Foundational or preliminary facts, relevancy of evidence dependent on establishing, 17.7, 21.4
Hearsay evidence, determining relevance of, 19.10
Impeachment evidence, effect of irrelevancy objection on, 22.7
Incompetent, irrelevant, and immaterial objection, insufficiency of general objection, 17.8
Inflammatory or gruesome photograph, admission of, 30.2
Offered evidence, demonstration of relevancy of, 5.12
Physician-patient privilege, relevant information as prerequisite for patient-litigant exception to, 36.9
Prior convictions, admissibility of, 17.5
Privilege. See **Privilege**
Proposition 115, effect of, 1.7
Rehabilitation of witness, evidence of collateral nature to prove, 23.2
Specific grounds for objection based on irrelevancy, statement of, 4.19
Stating irrelevancy objection, 17.11
Statutory authority for objection on basis of irrelevancy, 17.1
Stipulation by opposing counsel to facts, effect on introduction of evidence, 17.3

Religion
Cleric's privilege. See **Cleric's Privilege**
Closing argument, prosecutor's reliance on biblical doctrine as misconduct, 29.7
Hearsay exception for church records concerning family history, 19.33
Impeachment of witness on grounds of lack of religious beliefs, prohibition against, 22.9
Penitent's privilege. See **Penitent's Privilege**

Peremptory challenge, prohibition against discriminatory use of. See **Jury Trial**
Voir dire examination on prospective juror's religious beliefs, 6.39

Reporters. See **Court Reporters**

Repressed Memories
Sexual abuse memories refreshed by drugs, *Kelly* test, 20.14, 20.18

Reputation. See **Character Evidence**

Responses to Objections
Checklist of responses, 5.1
Conditional admission of evidence in response to objection, 5.3
Exclusionary rule, invoking exceptions to, 5.2
Insufficient foundation for admission of evidence, response to objection based on, 21.19
Offer of proof. See **Offer of Proof**
Voir dire examination of jury, connecting question to basis for challenge, 6.43

Rules of Court
Argumentative objections, prohibition against, 4.13
Attorney testifying as witness, client's informed consent to, 18.14
Contempt penalty for failure to notify court of settlement, 57.2
In limine motions
 San Francisco Superior Court rule setting time limits for, 6.5
 Written motion, requirements of, 2.11
Peremptory challenge of juror, local rules of court affecting, 6.24
Sanctions for violating rules of court, 2.17
Voir dire examination of prospective jurors. See **Voir Dire Examination of Jurors**

Rules of Professional Conduct
Attorney acting as advocate and testifying as witness, 18.15

Safety
Exclusion of evidence concerning subsequent safety measures, 32.5

Sanctions. See **Penalties**

Sanity. See **Competency; Not Guilty by Reason of Insanity**

Schools
Illegal search and seizure by school authorities, student's objection to, 28.11

Scientific Evidence
Generally, 20.10
Balancing test (see *Daubert* test in federal courts, below)
California's *Kelly* test
  Forensic techniques, applying *Kelly* test to, 20.13–20.14
  New scientific technique or theory, establishing general acceptance of, 20.12
Daubert test in federal courts
  Appeal of *Daubert* decision, standard of review for, 20.16
  California, impact of *Daubert* test in, 20.17
  Daubert I, balancing test for admission of scientific evidence, 20.15
  Daubert II, test for admitting scientific evidence under, 20.16
  Effect of *Kumho,* 20.15
DNA evidence, applicability of *Kelly* test to, 20.13
Impeachment of expert about scientific, technical, or professional publications, restrictions on, 20.25, 22.10
Kelly-Frye standard, 20.11
Psychological opinion, admissibility of, 20.18

Search and Seizure
Generally, 28.1
Administrative inspections, exclusion of evidence obtained during, 28.11
Administrative proceedings
  Exclusionary rule in, 28.6
  Procedure for objecting to illegally seized evidence, 28.12
Cleric, procedures for determining claims of privilege for documents seized under search warrant issued against, 50.9
Evid C §352 objection used in place of search and seizure objection, 28.7
Exclusionary rule for illegally seized evidence
  Administrative proceedings, 28.6
  Civil cases, 28.4
  Constitutional provisions, 28.3
  Quasi-criminal cases, 28.5
Fraud and deceit, excluding evidence obtained by. See **Fraud and Misrepresentation**
Outrageous or shocking methods
  Excluding evidence obtained by, 28.9
  Stating objection, 28.15
Procedure for objecting to illegal search and seizure, 28.12
Stating objection
  Illegally obtained confessions and admissions, 28.14
  Illegally obtained evidence, 28.15
  Illegal search and seizure, 28.13
Statutory basis for objection to illegal search and seizure, 28.2
Warrantless searches, reasonableness of, 28.11

Search Warrants
Official information privilege, rules affecting, 43.11
Physician-patient privilege, hearing on claim of privilege against search warrant for documentary evidence in physician's possession, 36.21
Psychotherapist-patient privilege, hearing on claim of privilege against search warrant for documentary evidence held by psychotherapist, 37.18
Warrantless searches, reasonableness of, 28.11

Secondary Evidence Rule
Generally, 24.2, 24.6
Alternatives to objecting, 24.7
Best evidence rule repealed, 24.1
Criminal proceedings, 24.3
Exclusion of, 24.3
Oral testimony, 24.4
Repeal of best evidence rule, 24.1
Wording of objection, 24.8

Self-Incrimination, Privilege Against
See also **Criminal Defendant's Privilege Not To Be Called and Not To Testify**
Generally, 46.1
Burden of proof on person claiming privilege, 46.20
Claim of privilege
  Manner of claiming privilege, 46.9
  Outside presence of jury, raising claim of privilege, 33.13, 46.9
  Persons who may claim privilege, 46.7
  Stating claim of privilege, 46.8, 46.21
  Unrepresented witness, court's duty to advise, 46.10
Comment on or inference from exercise of privilege, rule against, 46.11–46.12
Constitutional basis for privilege, 46.2
Corporations, inapplicability of privilege to, 46.2, 46.7
Cross-examination of criminal defendants, effect of constitutional privilege on, 26.8
Hearsay rule, exception for extrajudicial declarations made against penal interest, 19.18
Immunity
  Termination of privilege (see Immunity, privilege terminated by grant of, below)
  Waiver of immunity, 33.9, 46.19
Immunity, privilege terminated by grant of
  Generally, 46.14
  Civil cases, immunity in, 46.16
  Criminal defense witness, immunity for, 46.18
  Individual questions, claiming privilege for, 46.9
  Miscellaneous statutory immunity provisions, 46.17
  Transactional or use immunity in criminal proceedings, 46.15
Judges
  Procedure for ruling on claim of privilege, 46.20
  Unrepresented witness, court's duty to advise, 46.10
Regulatory statutes, inapplicability of privilege to records and reports required by, 46.6
Requirements for existence of privilege
  Connection between evidence and punishable act, 46.5
  Criminal penalties, testimony or evidence resulting in, 46.4
  Demand for testimony or communication belonging to witness, 46.3
Responses of party opposing privilege in civil case, 46.11
Statutory authority for claim of privilege, 46.2
Termination of privilege
  Immunity (see Immunity, privilege terminated by grant of, above)
  Prosecution of witness barred, 46.13
Third person, inapplicability of privilege to testimony incriminating, 46.4
Unavailability, declarant asserting Fifth Amendment privilege not to testify, 19.11
Unions, inapplicability of privilege to, 46.7
Use immunity for records relating to accident, 46.6
Writings qualifying for privilege, 46.6

Setting Aside. See **Vacating and Setting Aside**

Settlement
Admissions made during settlement negotiations, exclusion of, 21.8
Contempt penalty for failure to notify court of settlement, 57.2
Exclusion of evidence concerning settlement negotiations
  Acceptance of compromise payment in civil cases, 32.3
  Offer of compromise payment in civil cases, 32.2
  Offer to plead guilty, 32.4

Sex Offenses
Contempt penalty for refusing to testify about sexual assault, prohibition against imprisonment, 57.9
Exclusion of evidence under Evid C §352, 31.4
Hearsay rule, exception for statements of minor children in action for sexual abuse of child, 19.17

Sex Offenses—cont.
   Prior sexual offense evidence, admissibility in sexual offense trial, 17.5
   Psychiatric or psychological examination of witness in sexual assault action, prohibition against, 18.5
   Psychological opinion, 20.18
   Repressed sexual abuse memories refreshed by drugs, *Kelly* test, 20.14, 20.18

Sexual Assault Victim-Counselor Privilege
   Generally, 38.1
   Communication or information protected by privilege, 38.3
   Court compelling disclosure of confidential information, 38.3, 38.13
   Guardianship, effect on privilege. See **Guardianship and Conservatorship**
   Illustrations of privilege, 38.14
   Judges
      Exclusion of privileged information by, 38.7
      Ruling on privilege (see Ruling on claim of privilege, below)
   Persons who may claim privilege
      Counselor's duty to claim privilege on behalf of victim, 38.6
      Holder of privilege, 33.4, 38.5, 38.9
      Victim or victim's representative, 38.5
   Qualifications of counselor, 38.2, 38.13
   Relationship between counselor and victim as prerequisite for existence of privilege, 38.2
   Ruling on claim of privilege
      Burden of proof, 38.12
      Other issues raised by claim of privilege, resolution of, 38.11
      Procedure for resolving privilege disputes, 38.10
   Stating claim of privilege
      Attorney's claim of privilege, 38.16
      Witness's claim of privilege, 38.15
   Statutory authority for claim of privilege, 38.13
   Termination of privilege
      Death of victim, effect of, 38.8
      Waiver of privilege, 38.9

   Third parties, privilege dependent on nondisclosure of confidential communications to, 38.4

Shield Law. See Journalist's Immunity From Contempt

Sidebar Conferences
   Objections during voir dire decided at, 6.7

Similars, 31.4, 32.7

Sister States. See Other States

Speaking Objections
   Ambiguous or unintelligible questions, 7.3–7.4
   Voir dire examination of prospective jurors by counsel, local rules of court prohibiting speaking objections, 6.47

Speculative Answers, Questions Calling for
   Analysis of question, 16.3
   Defined, 16.1
   Examples of objectionable questions, 16.2
   Expert witnesses, laying foundation for speculative testimony by, 16.5
   Lay witnesses, opinion testimony versus speculation, 16.4
   Stating objection, 16.7
   Statutory authority for objection, 16.6

Speedtraps
   Testimony based on use of
      Generally, 18.30
      Alternatives to objecting. See **Alternatives to Objecting**
      Law enforcement officer, testimony by, 18.32
      Stating objection, 18.32

Spouse, Privilege Not To Be Called as Witness Against
   See also **Spouse, Privilege Not To Testify Against**
   Generally, 33.13, 42.1
   Adverse party in civil action, witness called by
      Both spouses as parties in proceedings, exception to privilege, 42.9

Spouse, Privilege Not To Be Called as Witness Against—*cont.*
Adverse party in civil action, witness called by—*cont.*
Multiple parties including one spouse, 42.8
Two-party action, 42.7
Waiver of privilege, consent to being called by adverse party resulting in, 42.14
Adverse party in criminal action, witness called by
Codefendant, witness called by, 42.6
Prosecutor, witness called by, 42.5
Waiver of privilege, consent to being called by adverse party resulting in, 42.14
Criminal action (see Adverse party in criminal action, witness called by, above)
Depositions
Noticing spouse's deposition as violation of privilege, 42.10
Waiver of privilege, 33.9
Exceptions to privilege
Both spouses as parties on opposite sides in proceedings, 42.9
Good faith ignorance of marital relationship, witness called in, 42.11
Proceedings in which privilege not available, 42.12
Voluntary testimony by spouse, no privilege against, 42.1, 42.10
Exercise of privilege, 42.10
Illustrations of privilege, 42.20
Judges (see Ruling on claim of privilege, below)
Marital communications privilege distinguished, 42.1
Multiple parties, effect of, 42.2
Ruling on claim of privilege
Burden of proof, 42.18
Procedure for obtaining ruling, 42.17
Spouse of witness as party to proceedings, 42.4
Stating objection based on privilege
Attorney's claim of privilege, 42.22
Witness's claim of privilege, 42.21
Statutory authority for privilege, 42.19
Termination of privilege
Dissolution of marriage, termination of privilege as result of, 42.13
Waiver (see Waiver of privilege, below)
Valid marriage as prerequisite to privilege, 42.3
Waiver of privilege
Action or defense for immediate benefit of spouse, 42.16
Both spouses parties in proceedings, 42.9
Consent to being called by adverse party, 42.14
Deposition testimony, 33.9
Multiple parties in action, effect on privilege, 42.2
Statutory provisions governing waiver, 33.6
Testimony by spouse, waiver of privilege as result of, 42.10, 42.15

Spouse, Privilege Not To Testify Against
See also **Spouse, Privilege Not To Be Called as Witness Against**
Generally, 41.1
Demand for testimony against spouse
Both spouses parties to action, 41.6
Multiple parties including one spouse, 41.5
Nonparty spouse, testimony against, 41.7
Refusal of spouse to testify on behalf of other spouse, no privilege for, 41.3
Exceptions to privilege
Generally, 41.9
Before marriage, criminal acts occurring, 41.14
Child support obligations, action by one spouse against former spouse to enforce, 41.15
Competence of spouse at issue, 41.11
Harm to defendant's spouse or child, exception to privilege in criminal actions involving, 41.13
Juvenile court proceedings, 41.12
Litigation between spouses, 41.10
Statutory basis for exceptions, 41.25
Illustrations of privilege, 41.26
Judges (see Ruling on claim of privilege, below)
Marital communications privilege distinguished, 41.1
Multiple parties, effect of, 41.5, 42.2

Spouse, Privilege Not To Testify Against—*cont.*
Ruling on claim of privilege
Burden of proof, 41.24
Procedure for obtaining ruling on claim of privilege, 41.23
Stating claim of privilege when spouse not party to action
Attorney's claim of privilege, 41.30
Witness's claim of privilege, 41.29
Stating claim of privilege when spouse party to action
Attorney's claim of privilege, 41.28
Witness's claim of privilege, 41.27
Statutory basis for privilege, 41.25
Termination of privilege
Dissolution of marriage, termination by, 41.16
Waiver of privilege (see Waiver of privilege, below)
Two-party action, 41.4
Valid marriage as prerequisite to privilege, 41.2
Waiver of privilege
Generally, 41.17
Action or defense for immediate benefit of spouse, 41.22
Extent of waiver, 41.21
Statutory provisions governing waiver, 33.6
Testimony against nonparty spouse, 41.20
Testimony against party spouse, 41.19
Testimony for spouse, 41.18
Witness spouse, limitation of privilege to, 41.8

Spouses
Dissolution of marriage. See **Dissolution of Marriage**
Domestic violence. See **Domestic Violence Victim-Counselor Privilege**
Marital communications privilege. See **Marital Communications Privilege**
Privilege not to be called as witness against spouse. See **Spouse, Privilege Not To Be Called as Witness Against**
Privilege not to testify against spouse. See **Spouse, Privilege Not To Testify Against**

Surviving spouse. See **Surviving Spouse**

Standing
Informer's identity, standing to claim error if privilege erroneously disallowed, 44.7
Official information privilege, standing of public entity to claim, 43.7
Physician-patient privilege, standing to claim, 36.21
Privilege, standing to assert erroneous denial of claim of, 33.21

State Bar
Discovery of attorney's work product in disciplinary actions, 35.10
Investigation or proceeding against attorney, duty of attorney to cooperate and participate in, 34.16

State Secrets. See **Military and State Secrets**

Stating Objection. See **Form of Objection**

Statutes of Limitations
See also **Time**
Malpractice action, separate trial on statute of limitations defense, 3.7

Statutory Authority for Objections
Ambiguous or unintelligible question, 7.5
Argumentative question, 14.3
Asked and answered objection, 11.4
Assuming facts in dispute or not in evidence, 15.8
Attorney-client privilege, statutory authority for claiming, 34.25
Cleric's privilege, 51.11
Compound question, 8.4
Criminal defendant's privilege not to be called and not to testify, 47.1, 47.9
Cumulative evidence, statutory authority for objection to, 31.18
Domestic assault victim-counselor privilege, statutory authority for claiming, 39.13
Hearsay rule, 19.2, 19.43
Inability of witness to communicate, 18.6
Inability of witness to understand duty to tell truth, 18.11

Statutory Authority for Objections—*cont.*

Inflammatory evidence, objection to, 30.6
Informer, statutory authority for privilege for identity of, 44.12
Insufficient foundation for evidence, 21.14, 21.18
Irrelevancy, 17.1
Judge testifying as witness, objection to, 18.18
Marital communications privilege, statutory authority for claiming, 40.20
Misquoting witness, 12.4
Narrative answers, objections to, 10.5
Official information privilege, 43.15
Overly general question, 9.4
Parol evidence rule, 25.2
Penitent's privilege, statutory authority for objection based on, 50.11
Personal knowledge, witness's lack of, 18.24
Physician-patient privilege, statutory authority for claiming, 36.23
Privilege, objection based on, 33.3, 33.31
Psychotherapist-patient privilege, statutory authority for claiming, 37.20
Search and seizure, objection to illegal, 28.2
Self-incrimination, privilege against, 46.2
Sexual assault victim-counselor privilege, statutory authority for claiming, 38.13
Speculative answer, question calling for, 16.6
Spouse, statutory authority for privilege not to be called as witness against, 42.19
Spouse, statutory authority for privilege not to testify against, 41.25
Trade secrets privilege, statutory basis for, 45.8
Valid objection, statutory requirements for, 4.15
Voter's privilege, statutory basis of, 49.9
Work product protection, statutory basis for, 35.10

Stay of Sentence. See Contempt

Stipulations

Admonitions to jurors, stipulation concerning, 29.36
Continuance. See **Continuance**
Criminal actions
Issue in case, effect of defendant's offer to stipulate to, 17.4
Prior convictions, effect on prosecution of defendant's stipulation to, 17.5
Disabled juror's assistant, stipulation to presence in jury room, 6.18
Polygraph test, stipulation to admissibility of, 20.14
Relevancy of evidence, effect of opposing counsel's stipulation to facts, 17.3
Voir dire examination
Juror questionnaires, stipulation concerning, 6.10
Outside judge's presence, stipulation for examination of prospective jurors, 6.52

Strict Liability

Admission or exclusion of evidence on subsequent safety measures, 32.5
Court's discretion to exclude evidence under Evid C §352, 31.2

Strike, Motion To

Generally, 52.1
Admonition to jury to disregard stricken evidence
Generally, 9.2, 43.19, 52.7, 52.11, 53.4
Stating request for admonition, 52.18
Alternatives to motion to strike, 52.16
Conditionally admitted evidence
Answer to question, motion to strike, 5.3, 15.6
Confession or admission conditionally admitted, motion to strike after prosecution's failure to establish corpus delicti, 27.11
Foundation for conditionally admitted evidence, motion to strike after opposing party's failure to show, 52.5
Cross-examination, motion to strike evidence shown to be inadmissible on, 52.6

Strike, Motion To—*cont.*
　Deposition, effect of failure to object to nonresponsive answer given during, 52.17
　Evid C §352, motion to strike evidence properly excluded under, 31.13
　Examination of witnesses by judge, motion to strike evidence, 4.7
　Form of motion, 52.18
　Improper question answered too quickly for objection, motion to strike, 52.4
　Judge's motion to strike evidence, 52.2, 52.10
　Nonresponsive answers, motion to strike, 52.2–52.3
　Opinion testimony, motion to strike, 20.32
　Personal knowledge of witness, motion to strike testimony not based on, 18.25
　Persons who can make motion to strike, 52.2
　Procedures for making motion
　　Grounds for motion, specification of, 52.9
　　Specification of particular evidence to be stricken, 52.8
　　Timeliness of motion, 4.16, 52.7, 52.13
　Self-incrimination, motion to strike witness's testimony after invoking privilege against, 46.11
　Tactical advantages and disadvantages of motion to strike, 52.15
　Trial record, effect of striking evidence on, 52.12
　Waiver
　　Obtain ruling on motion to strike, effect of failure to, 52.14
　　Timely motion to strike, effect of failure to make, 52.13

Sua Sponte
　Attorney-client privilege, judge's exclusion of privileged information, 34.13, 34.20
　Court orders, enforcement of, 2.17
　Evid C §352, sua sponte exclusion of evidence under, 31.17
　Excusing prospective juror sua sponte, 6.21
　Jury instructions
　　Civil actions, no duty on court to give instructions in, 53.2
　　Limiting or cautionary instructions during trial, no sua sponte duty on court to give, 53.1
　Peremptory challenges, sua sponte objection to discriminatory use of, 6.27
　Physician-patient privilege, judge's motion to exclude evidence protected by, 36.7
　Striking evidence, judge's powers regarding, 52.2, 52.10

Subpoenas
　Journalists, guidelines for issuing subpoenas to, 48.4

Support Obligations. See **Child Support**

Surviving Spouse
　Marital communications privilege, exception for litigation between surviving spouse and deceased spouse's claimant, 40.13

Tax Returns
　Nondisclosure of tax returns, privilege for, 43.7
　Taxpayer's waiver of privilege, 43.12

Testimony. See **Witnesses**

Third Parties
　Attorney-client privilege dependent on nondisclosure of confidential information to third parties, 34.10
　Criminal action, admissibility of evidence to support third party defense, 17.6
　Cross-examination of third party if expert witness's testimony based on hearsay, 20.27
　Domestic violence victim-counselor privilege dependent on nondisclosure of confidential information to third parties, 39.4
　Marital communications privilege dependent on nondisclosure of confidential communications to third parties, 40.4
　Penitent's communication to cleric, effect of third party's presence on confidentiality of, 50.5

Third Parties—*cont.*
  Physician-patient privilege, effect of third party's knowledge of confidential communication on, 36.4
  Psychotherapist-patient privilege dependent on nondisclosure of confidential communications to third parties, 37.4
  Self-incrimination privilege, inapplicability to testimony incriminating third person, 46.4
  Sexual assault victim-counselor privilege dependent on nondisclosure of confidential communications to third parties, 38.4

Time
  See also **Statutes of Limitations**
  Bifurcating trial of issue, time limit for order, 3.7
  Contempt order, entry of, 57.6
  Exclusion of time-consuming evidence under Evid C §352, 31.5
  Misconduct of attorney, timeliness of objection to, 29.11
  Motion in limine, timing of, 2.10A
  New trial motion, time limit for filing, 29.46
  Objection, timeliness of, 4.16
  Peremptory challenge, timely objection to discriminatory use of, 6.28
  Strike evidence, timeliness of motion to, 4.16, 52.7, 52.13
  Voir dire examination by judge, timely objection to, 6.46
  Work product protection, duration of, 35.6

Trade Secrets Privilege
  Generally, 45.1
  Definition of trade secret, 45.2
  Existence of trade secret, applicability of privilege dependent on, 45.2
  Judges (see Ruling on privilege, below)
  Persons who may claim privilege, 45.4
  Restrictions on allowing privilege, 45.3
  Ruling on privilege
    Burden of proof regarding claim of privilege, 45.7
    Procedure for obtaining ruling on claim of privilege, 45.6
  Stating claim of privilege
    Attorney's claim of privilege, 45.10
    Witness's claim of privilege, 45.9
  Statutory basis for privilege, 45.8
  Termination of privilege, 45.5
  Waiver of privilege, 45.5

Transcripts
  Misconduct of attorney, tampering with reporter's transcript constituting, 29.8
  New trial motion on grounds of jury misconduct during voir dire examination, transcript of voir dire examination attached to, 29.46
  Preliminary hearing transcript containing hearsay, admissibility under unavailable witness exception to hearsay rule, 19.11

Translators. See **Interpreters**

Trial Briefs
  Pre-voir dire conference, use of trial brief at, 6.9

Trial Record
  Striking evidence, effect on trial record, 52.12

Trial Tactics
  Advantages of not objecting, 4.3
  Criminal defendant's decision to testify, 47.4
  Cumulative evidence, considerations in objecting to, 31.9
  Inflammatory evidence, pre-trial tactics to discover and exclude, 30.3
  In limine motions. See **In Limine Motions**
  Mistrial, motion for, 56.5
  Strike evidence, tactical advantages and disadvantages of motion to, 52.15

Uniform Commercial Code
  Parol evidence rule in, 25.2, 25.8

Unintelligible Questions. See **Ambiguous or Unintelligible Questions**

Unions
  Self-incrimination privilege, inapplicability to unions, 46.7

Use Immunity. See **Immunity**

Vacating and Setting Aside
Inflammatory evidence, test for reversing judgment based on admission of, 30.2

Valuation
Opinion testimony about valuation of property or services, 20.3, 20.28

Venue
Corpus delicti, venue not element of, 27.4

Verdicts
See also **Judgments and Decrees**
Juror impeaching verdict. See **Incompetent Witnesses**
Misconduct of jury. See **Misconduct of Jurors**

Voice Identification
Defendant's privilege not to testify, inapplicability to voice identification, 47.3

Voir Dire Examination of Jurors
Generally, 6.1
Affidavit to prove that juror lied during voir dire, 18.27
Appeals. See **Appeals**
Challenge for cause in criminal case, question unrelated to
  Nature of objection, 6.41
  Response to objection, connecting question to basis for challenge, 6.43
  Stating objection, 6.42
Code of Civil Procedure
  Civil cases, provisions effecting, 6.52
  Criminal cases, provisions affecting, 6.54
Criminal cases, 6.16
Evid C §352, exclusion of evidence under, 31.17
Exclusion of press and public during voir dire, 6.16
Grounds for objecting to improper voir dire
  Challenge for cause in criminal case (see Challenge for cause in criminal case, question unrelated to, above)
  Form of question, objection to, 6.45

Grounds for objecting to improper voir dire—*cont.*
  Incorrect statement of law (see Incorrect statement of law, question based on, below)
  Indoctrinating jurors on law (see Indoctrinating jurors on law, below)
  Prejudging evidence (see Prejudge evidence, jurors asked to, below)
  Prejudicial matter (see Prejudicial matter, introduction of, below)
  Standards of Judicial Administration, question prohibited by, 6.44
Groups permissibly excluded from voir dire panel, 6.2
Incorrect statement of law, question based on
  Nature of objection, 6.35
  Stating objection, 6.36
Indoctrinating jurors on law
  Nature of objection, 6.33
  Stating objection, 6.34
Judges
  Improper voir dire by judge, objection to, 6.46
  Limits imposed on voir dire by judge, 6.5
Leading questions, use of, 6.45
Methods of seating jurors for questioning and challenging
  Generally, 6.11
  Jury box method, 6.12
  Six pack or struck juror method, 6.13
Misconduct of attorney during, 29.4
Misconduct of prospective juror in concealing information during voir dire, 29.35, 29.46
Mistrial motion on grounds of improper voir dire, 6.48
Oath required of jurors prior to voir dire, 29.34
Objections at pre-voir dire conference
  Generally, 6.7
  In limine motions concerning voir dire questions, 6.8
  Juror questionnaires, 6.10
  Trial brief, 6.9
Prejudge evidence, jurors asked to
  Nature of objection, 6.37
  Stating objection, 6.38
Prejudicial matter, introduction of
  Nature of objection, 6.39
  Stating objection, 6.40

Voir Dire Examination of Jurors—*cont.*
  Pre-voir dire conference
    BAJI or CALJIC instruction, request for judge to read, 6.35
    Challenging juror for cause, inquiry at pre-voir dire conference on procedures for, 6.22
    Civil cases, 6.5
    Criminal cases, 6.6
    In limine motion to exclude questions relating to law, 6.33
    Objections (see Objections at pre-voir dire conference, above)
  Procedures for objecting to improper voir dire
    Examination by counsel, local rules of court prohibiting speaking objections, 6.47
    Judge's examination of prospective jurors, objection to, 6.46
  Questioning by trial judge and counsel
    Generally, 6.14
    Civil cases, judge's initial examination of jurors in, 6.15
    Criminal cases, 6.16
    Improper voir dire questions by counsel, 6.15–6.16
  Questionnaires, use of, 6.4, 6.10, 6.51–6.52
  Rules of court
    Civil actions, examination of prospective jurors in, 6.51
    Criminal actions, examination of prospective jurors in, 6.53
    Examination by counsel, local rules of court prohibiting speaking objections, 6.47
    Sidebar conferences, objections during voir dire decided at, 6.7
  Stipulations. See **Stipulations**
  Waiver of objection to unreasonable limits placed on voir dire, 6.49

Voir Dire Examination of Witnesses
  Expert witness's qualifications, voir dire examination of, 20.24, 21.19

Voter's Privilege
  Generally, 49.1
  Illegal vote, exception to privilege regarding, 49.5
  Illustrations of privilege, 49.10
  Judges (see Ruling on privilege, below)
  Persons who can claim privilege, 49.4
  Public election by secret ballot as prerequisite to existence of privilege, 49.2
  Ruling on privilege
    Burden of proof, 49.8
    Procedure for obtaining ruling on privilege, 49.7
  Stating claim of privilege
    Attorney's claim of privilege, 49.12
    Witness's claim of privilege, 49.11
  Statutory basis for privilege, 49.9
  Tenor of vote, disclosure of, 49.3
  Waiver of privilege through disclosure of vote, 49.6

Waiver
  Hypothetical question, effect of failure to object to, 20.20
  Lay witness's opinion testimony, effect of failure to object to, 20.4
  Misconduct of attorney, failure to object resulting in waiver of, 29.11
  Privilege. See **Privilege**
  Striking evidence, waiver of rights regarding. See **Strike, Motion To**
  Voir dire, waiver of objection to unreasonable limits placed on, 6.49

Warrants. See **Search Warrants**

Wills
  Executors and administrators. See **Executors and Administrators**
  Hearsay rule, exception for declarant's statements about will, 19.25

Witnesses
  Attorney testifying as witness. See **Attorneys**
  Court's authority to call and examine witnesses, 3.1
  Cross-examination. See **Cross-Examination**
  Direct examination. See **Direct Examination**
  Domestic violence victim-counselor privilege, witness's claim of, 39.15
  Evid C §352, exclusion of testimonial evidence under, 31.2
  Examination of witnesses. See **Examination of Witnesses**
  Expert witnesses. See **Experts**

Witnesses—*cont.*
  Impeachment. See **Impeachment of Witnesses**
  Incompetent witnesses. See **Incompetent Witnesses**
  Informer, witness's claim of privilege regarding identity of, 44.14
  Intimidation of witnesses by prosecutor as misconduct, 29.4
  Journalists. See **Journalist's Immunity From Contempt**
  Judges
    Mistrial granted on grounds judge or juror called as witness, 56.8
    Power of judge to comment on witness's credibility. See **Misconduct of Judges**
  Marital communications privilege, witness's claim of, 40.22
  Misconduct of attorney, encouraging false testimony constituting, 29.4
  Narrative answers. See **Narrative Answer Objection**
  Official information privilege, witness's claim of, 43.17
  Opinion testimony. See **Opinion Testimony**
  Past recollection recorded, exception to hearsay rule for, 19.21
  Penitent's privilege, witness's claim of, 50.13
  Physician-patient privilege, witness's claim of, 36.25
  Prior inconsistent testimony. See **Impeachment of Witnesses**
  Prior statements. See **Prior Statements**
  Privilege. See **Privilege**
  Psychotherapist-patient privilege, witness's claim of, 37.22
  Recollection of witness. See **Recollection of Witness, Refreshing**
  Rehabilitation of witnesses. See **Rehabilitation of Witnesses**
  Sexual assault victim-counselor privilege, witness's claim of, 38.15
  Spouse, privilege not to be called as witness against. See **Spouse, Privilege Not To Be Called as Witness Against**
  Spouse, privilege not to testify against. See **Spouse, Privilege Not To Testify Against**
  Surprise witness or unavailable witness, continuance as result of, 54.3
  Trade secrets privilege, witness's claim of, 45.9
  Voter's privilege, witness's claim of, 49.11
  Work product protection for witness statements and interviews, 35.4, 35.7

Words and Phrases. See **Definitions**

Work Product Doctrine
  Generally, 35.1
  Attorney-client privilege distinguished, 34.2, 35.2
  Criminal actions, applicability of work product protection in. See **Criminal Law**
  Definition of work product, 34.2
  Duration of work product protection, 35.6
  Exceptions to doctrine
    Generally, 35.7
    Action between attorney and client, no work product protection in, 35.5
    Statutory basis for exceptions, 35.10
  Experts. See **Experts**
  Federal and state work product rules distinguished, 35.6
  In camera review of documents to determine applicability of work product protection, 35.7, 35.9
  Joint defense agreements, effect of, 34.22B, 35.8
  Peremptory challenge of jurors, inquiry into discriminatory use of, 6.30
  Persons who can claim protection, 35.5
  Restrictions on availability of work product protection during trial, 35.6
  Stating claim of protection, 35.11
  Statutory basis for work product protection, 35.10
  Types of work product
    Civil cases, qualified versus absolute protection for work product in, 35.3
    Criminal cases, absolute protection for work product in, 35.4
  Waiver of protection, 33.3A, 34.10A, 35.8

Writings
    Admission of party, handwritten document listing murder victims as, 19.13
    Authenticity of, 21.6
    Continuance motion, writing requirement for, 54.7, 54.15
    Defined, 21.6
    Exclusion of writings under Evid C §352, 31.3
    In limine motion in writing, rules of court requiring, 2.11
    Multiple writings constituting single agreement, 25.9
    Privileged writing used to refresh recollection of witness, production of, 33.12
    Secondary evidence rule. See **Secondary Evidence Rule**
    Self-incrimination, writings qualifying for privilege against, 46.6
    Work product doctrine. See **Work Product Doctrine**

Writs
    See also **Appeals**
    Generally, 55.1
    Admissibility of evidence. See **Admissibility of Evidence**
    Contempt order, review of, 55.5, 57.12
    Continuance of preliminary hearing, writ review of, 54.17, 55.7
    Habeas corpus. See **Habeas Corpus**
    Journalist's refusal to disclose information. See **Journalist's Immunity From Contempt**
    Official information privilege, extraordinary writ as remedy for erroneous denial of, 43.7
    Pleading in the alternative, 33.22
    Privacy, petition for writ to protect right of, 55.4
    Privilege, denial of. See **Privilege**
    Self-incrimination, extraordinary writ review after denial of claim of privilege against, 46.20

Wrongful Death
    Hearsay rule, exception for statements made by deceased person, 19.17

Make sure you are using the latest update

For your convenience, the following list identifies the most recent publication date of each CEB update (as of July 2004).

Update Title	Product Number	Publication Date
Advising and Defending Corporate Directors and Officers	BU-32726	11/03
Advising California Common Interest Communities, 2d Ed	RE-33431	3/04
Advising California Employers, 2d Edition	BU-32039	1/04
Advising California Nonprofit Corporations, 2d Edition	BU-32956	4/04
Advising California Partnerships	BU-32885	5/04
Appeals and Writs in Criminal Cases, 2d Edition	CR-33194	12/03
Bernhardt's California Real Estate Cases	RE-33202	4/02
Business Buy-Sell Agreements	BU-31493	10/03
California Administrative Hearing Practice, 2d Edition	CP-32677	1/04
California Administrative Mandamus, 3d Edition	CP-32891	5/04
California Attorney Fee Awards, 2d Edition	CP-32169	11/03
California Automobile Insurance Law Guide	TO-30756	10/03
California Breach of Contract Remedies	CP-34466	7/04
California Business Litigation	BU-33571	12/03
California Civil Appellate Practice, 3d Edition	CP-32438	5/04
California Civil Discovery Practice, 3d Edition	CP-32876	5/04
California Civil Litigation Forms Manual	CP-34474	9/03
California Civil Writ Practice, 3d Edition	CP-32788	5/04

Update Title	Product Number	Publication Date
California Conservatorships and Guardianships	ES-31504	6/04
California Construction Contracts and Disputes, 3d Edition	RE-33165	11/03
California Criminal Law Forms Manual	CR-32154	4/03
California Criminal Procedure and Practice, 6th Edition	CR-32115	4/04
California Decedent Estate Practice 1, 2	ES-35667	5/04
California Decedent Estate Practice 3	ES-30867	5/04
California Durable Powers of Attorney	ES-32668	3/04
California Elder Law Litigation: An Advocate's Guide	ES-33621	5/04
California Elder Law Resources, Benefits, and Planning: An Advocate's Guide	ES-33631	5/04
California Estate Planning	ES-33462	6/04
California Eviction Defense Manual, 2d Edition	RE-32082	4/04
California Expert Witness Guide, 2d Edition	CP-31684	1/04
California Government Tort Liability Practice	TO-33135	1/04
California Juvenile Dependency Practice	CR-33531	2/04
California Landlord-Tenant Practice, 2d Edition	RE-32697	1/04
California Liability Insurance Practice 1, 2	CP-39264	7/04
California Local Probate Rules, 24th Edition	ES-39666	1/04
California Marital Settlement and Other Family Law Agreements	FA-32967	3/04
California Mechanics' Liens and Related Construction Remedies	RE-32686	11/03
California Mortgage and Deed of Trust Practice, 3d Edition	RE-33114	2/04
California Personal Injury Proof	TO-30568	12/03
California Probate Code Annotated to CEB Publications	ES-31196	1/04
California Probate Workflow Manual	ES-31565	6/04
California Real Estate Finance Practice: Strategies and Forms	RE-33184	11/03
California Real Property Practice Forms Manual	RE-30925	8/03

Update Title	Product Number	Publication Date
California Real Property Remedies and Damages, 2d Edition	RE-33442	9/03
California Real Property Sales Transactions, 3d Edition	RE-32996	12/03
California Subdivision Map Act, 2d Edition	RE-33253	2/04
California Title Insurance Practice, 2d Edition	RE-32625	7/04
California Tort Damages, 2d Edition	TO-33512	3/04
California Tort Guide, 3d Edition	TO-32548	12/03
California Trial Objections, 10th Edition	CP-32557	6/04
California Trial Practice: Civil Procedure During Trial, 3d Edition	CP-32199	4/04
California Trust Administration, 2d Edition	ES-33303	1/04
California Trust and Probate Litigation	ES-32855	3/04
California UCC Sales and Leases	BU-33472	5/04
California Uninsured Motorist Practice, 2d Edition	TO-33282	8/03
California Will Drafting, 3d Edition	ES-30323	12/03
California Workers' Compensation Practice, 4th Edition	WC-31534	6/04
California Workers' Damages Practice, 2d Edition	WC-33293	1/04
California Zoning Practice	RE-30516	11/03
Capitalizing & Protecting New Businesses	BU-32947	10/03
Condemnation Practice in California	RE-32419	11/03
Counseling California Corporations, 2d Edition	BU-33174	3/04
Debt Collection Practice in California, 2d Edition	BU-32985	2/04
Debt Collection Tort Practice	TO-30105	8/97
Drafting Business Contracts: Principles, Techniques and Forms	BU-30805	7/04
Drafting California Irrevocable Trusts, 3d Edition	ES-32718	7/04
Effective Direct & Cross Examination	CP-32339	11/03
Effective Introduction of Evidence, 2d Edition	CR-33234	10/03
Employment Law Compliance for New Businesses	BU-32917	7/04
Fee Agreement Forms Manual	MI-30442	9/03
Financing California Businesses, 2d Edition	BU-32428	4/04

Update Title	Product Number	Publication Date
Forming & Operating California Limited Liability Companies	BU-32519	3/04
Ground Lease Practice	RE-30527	8/03
Jefferson's California Evidence Benchbook, 3d Edition	CP-32636	3/04
Landslide and Subsidence Liability	RE-31039	8/01
Lis Pendens, 2d Edition	RE-32176	9/01
Office Leasing: Drafting and Negotiating the Lease	RE-30898	12/03
Organizing Corporations in California, 3d Edition	BU-33423	4/04
Personal and Small Business Bankruptcy Practice in California	BU-33521	1/04
Persuasive Opening Statements and Closing Arguments	CP-39653	10/03
Practice Under the California Environmental Quality Act	RE-30268	12/03
Practice Under the California Family Code: Dissolution, Legal Separation, Nullity	FA-31954	2/04
Practicing California Judicial Arbitration	CP-30668	7/03
Real Property Exchanges, 3d Edition	RE-33562	3/04
Sales and Merges of California Businesses	BU-33452	4/04
Secured Transactions in California Commercial Law Practice, 2d Edition	BU-33392	4/04
Selecting & Forming Business Entities	BU-32578	6/04
Trade Secrets Practice in California, 2d Edition	BU-32597	11/03
Trial Attorney's Evidence Code Notebook, 3d Edition	CP-30292	2/04
The Internet Guide for California Lawyers	MI-33212	11/01
Wrongful Employment Termination Practice, 2d Edition	CP-32657	5/04

Not Yet Updated	Product Number
California Attorney's Guide to Damages, 2d Edition	CP-3355*
California Civil Procedure Before Trial, 4th Edition	CP-3170*
California Judges Benchbook: Search and Seizure, 2d Edition	CR-3359*

Not Yet Updated	**Product Number**
California Judges Benchbook: Domestic Violence in Criminal Cases, 3d Edition	CR-3327*
Drafting California Revocable Trusts, 4th Edition	ES-3361*
Forming California Common Interest Developments	RE-3361*
Internet Law & Practice in California	BU-3358*
Jefferson's Synopsis of California Evidence Law	CP-3079*

Ensure That Your Legal Know-How Is Always Up To Date.

We recommend that you keep your practice materials current by purchasing regular updates. CEB updates provide the latest developments, rulings, and case law to guarantee that you will be working with the most timely information possible. Our Automatic Update customers also receive reduced pricing on new editions and other discounts.

If you bought this book from a book store, you may not be registered as an Automatic Update Customer. Please take a moment to photocopy, fill out, and send us this form—or call CEB Customer Service at 1-800-232-3444—to ensure the accuracy of your CEB legal materials.

Title of Publication _____

Product Number _____
(CEB product numbers can be found stamped or printed on the back cover of all CEB books and Action Guides.)

Date Purchased _____

Name _____

State Bar # _____

Firm Name _____

Address _____

Telephone (   ) _____

E-mail Address _____

Authorized Signature _____

As an Automatic Update Customer, updates, revisions, and new editions will be sent to you automatically as they are released with an invoice (including sales tax and $5.95 for shipping). Full 30-day return privileges apply. You may cancel this service at any time.

Add This Title To Your Legal Arsenal

You can order this book and ensure that you always have the legal background and practical guidance of this CEB publication at hand. To order, fax or mail a photocopy of this order form, call CEB Customer Service at 1-800-232-3444, or visit our website at ceb.com

TITLE	Product Number	Price	No. of Copies	Price Paid

RISK-FREE 30-DAY APPROVAL

Full return privileges apply on all purchases except forms disks, electronic products, *Reporters* and sale items. Defective disks may be returned for replacement. Return undamaged products to CEB, postage paid, within 30 days of the invoice date and the bill will be canceled. No questions asked.

Subtotal	
State and local sales tax	
Shipping*	
TOTAL REMITTANCE	

Add $7.95 for the first item and $2.00 for each additional item.*

ALL PRICES ARE SUBJECT TO CHANGE. THANK YOU FOR YOUR ORDER!

SHIP TO:

Name _____

Firm _____

E-Mail Address _____

Address _____
(street address required for UPS delivery)

City _____

State _____ Zip _____

Telephone ( ) _____

☐ This is a new address

METHOD OF PAYMENT: (please check one)

☐ Check enclosed *(Make all checks payable to The Regents of the University of California)*

☐ Credit Card

|_|_|_|_|_|_|_|_|_|_|_|_|_|_|_|_|
(VISA, MasterCard, American Express)

|_|_|_|_|
(Expiration Date)

Signature: _____
(required for credit card approval)

☐ Charge to my CEB Account _____

AUTOMATIC UPDATE SERVICE.

Ownership of a CEB book makes you a CEB Automatic Update customer. Updates, revisions, and new editions of CEB books, Action Guides, and software will be sent to you automatically as they are released with an invoice (including sales tax and $5.95 for shipping of the first item and $2.00 for each additional item). Full 30-day return privileges (postage paid) apply. You may cancel this service at any time.

Priority Source Code: 5454

Book Order 6x9